The Routledge Handbook of White-Collar and Corporate Crime in Europe

The study of white-collar crime remains a central concern for criminologists around the world and research concentrates on its nature, prevalence, causes and responses. However, most books on white-collar crime tend to focus on Anglo-American examples, which is surprising given the amount of rich data and research taking place in mainland Europe. This new Handbook seeks to redress the balance and, for the first time, presents an overview of state-of-the-art research on white-collar crime in Europe.

Adding to the existing Anglo-American body of knowledge, the Handbook will discuss specific European topics and typical European features of white-collar crime. The *Routledge Handbook of White-Collar and Corporate Crime in Europe* consists of more than 30 chapters on topics ranging from the Icelandic Banking Crisis, to the origins of the study of white-collar crime, to contemporary topics, such as white-collar crime in countries post-transition from communist regimes; the illegal e-waste trade and white-collar crime in professional football. Furthermore, the book contains extensive case study analyses of landmark European cases of white-collar crime.

The editors have gathered together the leading voices in the field and a final section offers commentaries on white-collar crime in Europe from eminent criminologists David Friedrichs and Hazel Croall. This Handbook will thus serve as a work of reference for all scholars and students engaged in the study of corporate and white-collar crime and will also set out directions for new research in the future.

Judith van Erp is Professor of Public Institutions at Utrecht University.

Wim Huisman is Professor of Criminology at VU University Amsterdam.

Gudrun Vande Walle is Visiting Professor in Ethics at Ghent University and works at Brussels public prosecutor's office.

'This superb handbook brings together leading European scholars of white-collar and corporate crime. In light of the increasing globalization of manufacturing, markets, finance, and governance, its expansive coverage of landmark cases throughout Europe and European responses to them could not have appeared at a more opportune time. The editors and contributors are to be commended for enlarging our vision of white-collar and corporate crime as a problem of worldwide significance.'

Michael L. Benson, *Professor, School of Criminal Justice, University of Cincinnati, USA*

'The concept of white-collar crime originated in the United States, and much of the subsequent research in the field has been conducted in English-speaking nations. So it is indeed exciting to see this welcome collection of European scholarship. With its rich case studies, and its interpretive essays on generic crime types, this book is indispensable reading for scholars of white-collar and corporate crime across the globe.'

Peter Grabosky, *Professor Emeritus, RegNet, Australian National University, Australia*

'This well-crafted volume breaks new intellectual ground with its European-focused scholarship on white-collar and corporate crime. An excellent resource to stimulate new thinking and research topics for a new generation of scholars.'

Sally Simpson, *Professor of Criminology and Criminal Justice and Director, Center for the Study of Business Ethics, Regulation, and Crime, University of Maryland, USA*

'This book is a stellar contribution to the evolving global understanding of white-collar and corporate crime. As the editors note in the introduction, the field has been dominated by American, Australian and British scholars for an array of reasons and with resulting limited applications and relevance to different economies and political systems. The *Handbook of White Collar and Corporate Crime in Europe* successfully changes the existing intellectual landscape by broadening our understanding of what most experts agree are the most costly forms of crime in regard to measurement, definitions, types of offenses, human rights issues, state crime, victimization, and matters of prevention and control. It will be a major resource for scholars and students for years to come.'

Henry N. Pontell, *Presidential Scholar, John Jay College of Criminal Justice and Research Professor and Professor Emeritus, University of California, Irvine, USA*

The Routledge Handbook of White-Collar and Corporate Crime in Europe

Edited by Judith van Erp, Wim Huisman and Gudrun Vande Walle, with the assistance of Joep Beckers

Routledge
Taylor & Francis Group
LONDON AND NEW YORK

First published 2015
by Routledge
2 Park Square, Milton Park, Abingdon, Oxon, OX14 4RN

and by Routledge
52 Vanderbilt Avenue, New York, NY 10017, USA

First issued in paperback 2020

Routledge is an imprint of the Taylor & Francis Group, an informa business

British Library Cataloguing in Publication Data
A catalogue record for this book is available from the British Library

Library of Congress Cataloging-in-Publication Data
The Routledge handbook of white-collar and corporate crime in Europe / edited by Judith van Erp, Wim Huisman and Gudrun Vande Walle, with the assistance of Joep Beckers.
pages cm
1. White collar crimes—Europe. 2. Commercial crimes—Europe. I. Erp, Judith Gabriel van.
HV6771.E855R68 2015
364.16′8094—dc23
2014036525

ISBN 13: 978-0-367-58179-4 (pbk)
ISBN 13: 978-0-415-72214-8 (hbk)

Typeset in Bembo
by Apex CoVantage, LLC

Contents

Figures

Tables

Notes on contributors

Editors

Judith van Erp is Professor of Public Institutions at Utrecht University, the Netherlands. Her research addresses corporate compliance and corporate crime. She has published on various public and private modes of regulation and governance of corporate behavior and their intersection, and in particular, on the role of the media and 'naming and shaming' in governing corporate crime. Together with Gudrun Vande Walle and Wim Huisman, she founded and co-chairs the European Working Group on Organizational Crime, a subdivision of the European Society of Criminology. She also co-chairs the Collaborative Research Network on Regulatory Governance of the Law and Society Association.

Wim Huisman is Professor of Criminology at the VU University Amsterdam. He specializes in prevalence and causes of corporate and white-collar crime. Recently he published on corporate crime and economic crisis, corporate involvement in gross human rights violations, environmental crime, food fraud and corporate crime theory. He teaches courses on white-collar crime in the Criminology programmes of the VU School of Criminology and is the co-chair of the European Society of Criminology's Working Group on Organizational Crime.

Gudrun Vande Walle recently exchanged academic research for the practice of investigation and prosecution of economic and financial crime for the Belgian public prosecutor. Gudrun teaches a course on Governance and Ethics in the Master's programme in Public Administration and Public Management at Ghent University and is member of the research unit 'Government and Law' at University of Antwerp. She is co-chair of the European Society of Criminology's Working Group on Organizational Crime.

Contributors

Tage Alalehto is Associate Professor at the department of Sociology at Umeå University in Sweden. His research interest is white-collar crime and he recently co-authored *The Roots of Modern White-Collar Crime: Does the Modern Form of White-Collar Crime Have its Foundation in the Transition from a Society Dominated by Agriculture to One Dominated by Industry?* and *The Reaction Towards White Collar Crime: When White Collar Crime Matters.*

Paul Almond is a professor of Law at the University of Reading, UK. His research interests include regulatory law and criminal enforcement, and occupational health and safety regulation. He has published widely on these issues, including *Corporate Manslaughter and Regulatory Reform*, published in 2013.

Rosalba Altopiedi holds a PhD in Comparative Social Research and currently works as a research fellow and adjunct professor of Sociology of Deviance at the University of Turin. As a researcher she is predominantly interested in corporate crimes, environmental and health activism, and legislation and social policies regarding drug abuse.

Anthony Amicelle is currently Assistant Professor at the École de criminologie, Université de Montréal. His previous posting was with the Peace Research Institute Oslo (PRIO) and he received a PhD in political science and international relations from Sciences Po, Paris. He is particularly interested in examining anti-money laundering and counter-terrorist financing practices. He is the author of *Towards a 'New' Political Anatomy of Financial Surveillance* and *Financial Surveillance: Who Cares?*.

Annika van Baar is a PhD candidate at the Criminology department of VU University Faculty of Law. She holds an MA in Holocaust and Genocide Studies and an MSc (*cum laude*) in International Crimes and Criminology. Her research focuses on (historical and contemporary) corporate involvement in international crimes.

Joep Beckers, MSc (*cum laude*), LLB, is a PhD candidate at the Erasmus School of Law in Rotterdam, the Netherlands. His criminological doctoral dissertation focuses on the criminal sanctioning of corporate crime in the Netherlands. He has written about media representations of white-collar crime, whistleblowing and prosecutorial decision-making. Since its foundation in 2010 he has been the Secretary of the European Working Group on Organizational Crime (EUROC).

Barbara Bischoff, attorney at law, specializes in criminal law. Her current research interests are internal investigations, economic crime, and the privatization of East German corporations. She recently published *Formelle und informelle soziale Kontrolle im Zusammenhang mit der Privatisierung von DDR-Betrieben*.

Lieselot Bisschop is Assistant Professor at John Jay College of Criminal Justice (USA). She is also a part-time post-doctoral researcher at Ghent University (Belgium). Her areas of interest and expertise include environmental crime, organizational crime, environmental governance and policing. She is an assistant editor of the *European Journal of Policing Studies*. An important publication is *Governance of the Illegal Trade in E-waste and Tropical Timber: Case Studies on Transnational Environmental Crime*.

Klaus Boers studied Law and Criminology. He is Professor of Criminology at the Universitaet Münster, Rechtswissenschaftliche Fakultaet. Current research areas include life-course criminology, economic crime, theory and model construction, juvenile delinquency, and penal crime control. He recently published *Explaining the Development of Adolescent Violent Delinquency*.

Henk van de Bunt is Professor of Criminology at the Erasmus University of Rotterdam. He has written extensively on the subjects of corporate crime, organized crime and the administration of criminal justice. Major publications are *Walls of Secrecy and Silence* and *Prosecutors and Politics* (with Jean-Louis van Gelder).

Kai Bussmann has been Professor of Penal Law and Criminology at the Martin Luther University in Halle-Wittenberg, Germany, since 1999. His main research interests include economic crime, family violence as well as evaluation of crime-prevention measures. He co-edited *Social Dynamics of Crime and Control: New Theories for a World in Transition.*

Marc Cools is Professor of Criminology at the Free University of Brussels and at Ghent University. His research interests are private security, corporate security and intelligence services. He has written several publications on these subjects, such as the Dutch monographs *Employee Crime* and *175 Years of State Security in Belgium.*

Hazel Croall is Professor Emeritus at Glasgow Caledonian University. In Glasgow she set up and managed the Criminology degree. Her current research interests include crime and inequality (especially in Scotland), corporate and state corporate crime, criminal justice and the corporate offender. She has published extensively in the area of white-collar and corporate crime. Her most recent publications include chapters on race, ethnicity and crime, crime and social inequality and corporate crime, all with a Scottish focus, in *Criminal Justice in Scotland*, which she also co-edited (with Gerry Mooney and Mary Munro).

José N. Cruz is Associate Professor of Law and Economics at the University of Porto. He is affiliated with the Centre for Law and Economics Research and with the School of Criminology, of the Faculty of Law of University of Porto. His research interests are white-collar crime, entrepreneurship and public economics. Recent publications include *Is the White Collar Offender an Entrepreneur?* and he co-authored *Economic and Financial Criminality in Portugal.*

Rita Faria is a lecturer and researcher at the School of Criminology, of the Faculty of Law of the University of Porto. Her main research topics are deviancy in science, economic and financial offences, and the history of criminology. She recently published *Intransparency: Deviance and Crime in Science* and co-authored *Economic and Financial Criminality in Portugal.*

David O. Friedrichs is Distinguished Professor of Sociology, Criminal Justice and Criminology at the University of Scranton (Pennsylvania, USA). He is author of *Trusted Criminals: White Collar Crime in Contemporary Society* (4th edn) and co-author of *Crimes of Globalization.* His current research interests focus on white-collar crime and crimes of states.

Stratos Georgoulas is Assistant Professor and Director of the Laboratory EKNEXA at University of the Aegean in Greece. His working experience concerns amongst others several legislative committees and special advising (Greek Ombudsman, Ministry of Justice, etc.). He has been Visiting Professor at Florida State University, the University of Toronto, the University of Damascus, the Slovak Academy of Science and the University of Amman. He has published several books, chapters in edited volumes and journal articles in Greek and English. He is the editor of the journal *Youth, Crime and Society.*

Csaba Győry is a researcher at the Max Planck Institute for Foreign and International Criminal Law in Freiburg, Germany, and research fellow at the Institute of Legal Studies of the Hungarian Academy of Sciences in Budapest, Hungary. His main research interests are the political economy of corporate and financial crimes, cross-border corporate crime, and qualitative research on law enforcement.

Patrick Hebberecht (1951–2015) was Professor of Criminology and Sociology of Law at Ghent University. His research interests included crime prevention, ethnic minorities and the sociology of criminal law. He recently co-edited *Social Crime Prevention in Late Modern Europe: A Comparative Perspective* (with Evelyne Baillergeau).

Éva Inzelt is an assistant professor at the Department of Criminology, Faculty of Law, Eötvös Loránd University, Budapest, Hungary. Her current research interests are white-collar crime, corruption and economic crime. She recently published *White-collar Crime during the Political and Economic Transition in Hungary* and *Corruption in Hungary from the Viewpoint of Finnish Investors: An Empirical Study*.

Kari-Maria Karliczek is a criminologist. She worked on economic crime from 1999 to 2005 at Westfaelische Wilhelms University, Münster. In 2007 she published the book *Strukturelle Bedingungen von Wirtschaftskriminalität* (Structural Conditions for Economic Crime). Today she heads the Research Centre on Youth Violence Prevention on behalf of the federal state of Berlin.

Susanne Karstedt is a Professor in the School of Criminology and Criminal Justice at Griffith University, Australia. Her current research and writing encompasses cross-national and cross-cultural comparative perspectives in criminology, mass atrocity crimes, state crime, and international and transitional justice. She recently co-edited *Emotions, Crime and Justice*.

Julian Klinkhammer works as a research associate at Heidelberg University's Max-Weber Institute of Sociology. His research interests cover many areas of organizational sociology, especially those that relate to the sociology of labour markets, economic sociology and organizational criminology. In 2013, he published a peer-reviewed article in the interdisciplinary journal *Crime, Law and Social Change*, addressing the organizational challenges to an effective anti-corruption strategy.

Marieke Kluin is a lecturer in Criminology at the Institute for Criminal Law and Criminology at Leiden University, the Netherlands. Her doctoral research focuses on the possible relationship between rule violation, compliance, corporate crime and safety in the Dutch chemical industry. She has published a book chapter in *Emerging Issues in Green Criminology: Exploring Power, Justice and Harm* and co-authored a book chapter in *Environmental Crime and its Victims*.

Ralf Kölbel is Professor and heads the Chair of Criminal Law and Criminology at the Faculty of Law, Ludwig Maximilian University, Munich. His main research aims are in the fields of white-collar crime, law of criminal procedure, basic issues of criminal law, and sociology of criminal law. Recently he published *Hostile Intent – the Terrorist's Achilles Heel? Observations on Pre-Crime Surveillance by Means of Thought Recognition*.

Lars Korsell, BA, LLD, lawyer and criminologist is the head of the Economic and Organised Crime Research Division at the Swedish National Council for Crime Prevention in Stockholm. His main research interest is economic and organized crime, i.e. regulation and crime control, but also organizational pattern, interaction with legal economy and crime strategies. He has published several articles, reports and books. A recent publication is *Organized Crime the Nordic Way* (with Paul Larsson).

Daniel Larsson is a lecturer at the Department of Sociology at Umeå University in Sweden. His research interests are white-collar crime and welfare policy and recent publications include *The Roots of Modern White-Collar Crime: Does the Modern Form of White-Collar Crime have its*

Foundation in the Transition from a Society Dominated by Agriculture to One Dominated by Industry? and *The Reaction Towards White Collar Crime: When White Collar Crime Matters* (both with Tage Alalehto).

André Lamas Leite is Assistant Professor at the Faculty of Law of the University of Porto (Portugal), where he teaches both Criminal Law and Criminology. His major research interests are penology, corporate offences and criminal procedure law. He has published several books and articles on these topics, both in Portugal and abroad.

Michael Levi has been Professor of Criminology at Cardiff University School of Social Sciences since 1991. His major research interests are the organization and control of white-collar and organized crime, corruption, cybercrime and money laundering/financing of terrorism. His books include *The Phantom Capitalists*, *Regulating Fraud*, and *Drugs and Money*. In 2013 he was given the Distinguished Scholar Award by the International Association for the Study of Organised Crime and in 2014 the Sellin-Glueck Award by the American Society of Criminology.

Nicholas Lord holds a PhD in Criminology and is a lecturer in Criminology in the School of Law at the University of Manchester and has research interests in white-collar and corporate crimes of a financial and economic nature such as fraud, corruption and bribery. A recent notable publication is *Regulating Corporate Bribery in International Business.*

Aleksandar Maršavelski, LLM (Yale), is Assistant Lecturer at the Department of Criminal Law of Faculty of Law, University of Zagreb. He is enrolled in a PhD programme in cooperation with the Max Planck Institute for Foreign and International Criminal Law, University of Freiburg. The topic of his PhD research is the responsibility of political parties for criminal offences.

Joe McGrath is a lecturer in law at University College Dublin, specializing in corporate and financial regulation. He has published in books, journals and the national newspapers in these areas. He is also the author of the monograph *Corporate and White-Collar Crime: A New Architecture of Regulatory Enforcement.*

Hans Nelen is Professor of Criminology at the Department of Criminal Law and Criminology of the Faculty of Law of Maastricht University. He has conducted research and published extensively on a variety of criminological subjects, including police, drugs, corruption, fraud, organized crime, corporate and occupational crime. He is also an expert in the field of evaluation studies.

Petar Novoselec is Professor of Criminal Law (in retirement) at the Faculty of Law, University of Zagreb. He is head of the Law Commission for Monitoring the Application of the Croatian Criminal Code (Ministry of Justice of Croatia) and a former judge of the Supreme Court of Croatia (1991–1995).

Veerle Pashley is an assistant in Ghent University. Her PhD focuses on the role of accountability of private military companies in military combat (joint degree Ghent University – Vrije Universiteit Brussel – Royal Military Academy). Veerle Pashley is a member of the Belgian Intelligence Studies Centre (BISC). She is also a member of the *Journal of Intelligence* editorial board.

Paul Ponsaers is Emeritus Professor at Ghent University, Department of Penal Law and Criminology. His main domain of research is policing, other formal/informal forms of social control, and financial and economic crime. He recently published *Social Analysis of Security: Financial, Economic and Ecological Crime – Crime, (In)security and (Dis)trust – Public and Private Policing.*

Brendan Quirke is currently a senior lecturer in Accounting and Financial Management at Manchester Metropolitan University. His major research interests include EU fraud and corruption and he recently published *EU Fraud: Institutional and Legal Competence* and *Croatia and the Fight against EU Fraud: A Case of Work in Progress?*

Sunčana Roksandić Vidlička is Assistant Lecturer at the Department of Criminal Law, Faculty of Law, University of Zagreb. She is a PhD candidate at the University of Zagreb and University of Freiburg in cooperation with the Max Planck Institute for Foreign and International Criminal Law, University of Freiburg. The topic of her research is criminal responsibility for severe economic crimes committed in a transitional period.

Pedro Sousa is Assistant Professor of Statistics, Economics and Criminology at the University of Porto. He is affiliated with the Centre for Law and Economics Research and with the School of Criminology, of the Faculty of Law of University of Porto. His research interests are white-collar crime, costs of crime, and deterrence theory. He recently co-authored *Economic and Financial Criminality in Portugal* and *Explicit Social Costs of Crime in a Time of Crisis: Costs of Law Enforcement in the Drivers' Crimes.*

Hans Theile, LLM, holds the chair of Criminal Law, Criminal Procedural Law, Economic Criminal Law and Criminology at the University of Constance. He is Director of the Institute for Empirical Legal Research of the University of Constance. A recent major publication is *Economic Crime and Criminal Procedural Law.*

Gudrun Vande Walle, co-chair of the European Society of Criminology's Working Group on Organizational Crime, started to work as a researcher in Criminology in 1997. Since then she has done research at Ghent University, University College Ghent and University of Antwerp on the topics of victimization and conflict resolution in relation to corporate crime; integrity and anti-corruption policy in the private and public sectors; and whistleblowing and has given many courses on these topics. Her PhD (2003) concerned conflict resolution between pharmaceutical companies and victims of corporate misconduct. She recently exchanged academic research for the practice of investigation and prosecution of economic and financial crime for the Belgian public prosecutor. She is still Visiting Professor for the course Governance and Ethics in the Master's programme Public Administration and Public Management at Ghent University and is member of the research unit Government and Law at the University of Antwerp.

Antoinette Verhage holds a PhD in Criminology (Ghent, 2009), and has worked at Ghent University since 2001. She is the joint director of the Institute of Urban Security and Policing Studies together with Professor Dr. Pauwels. Her dissertation 'The anti-money laundering complex and its interactions with the compliance industry' highlighted private financial institutions' role in the (sometimes paradoxical) anti-money laundering system. Currently, Antoinette is working on a post-doctoral research project consisting of a systematic review of research in policing. Research interests are policing, financial-economic crime and radicalization. She has an extensive interest in qualitative research methods. Aside from research, tutoring and supervising (PhD) students,

Antoinette is an active member of editorial boards (e.g. the *Cahiers Politiestudies, het Tijdschrift voor Criminologie, Panopticon*). Since 2012 she has been the chief editor of a new journal, the *European Journal of Policing Studies* (EJPS).

Aimilia Voulvouli is Assistant Professor at Abdullah Gül University in Turkey. She has done extensive ethnographic fieldwork in Turkey and Greece focusing on environmental activism, criminality and LGBT issues. She is the author of the book *From Environmentalism to Transenvironmentalism: The Ethnography of an Urban Protest in Modern Istanbul.*

Christian Walburg serves as a lecturer at the Institute of Criminal Sciences, Department of Criminology at the University of Münster (Germany). He has received his PhD with a thesis on migration and juvenile delinquency. His main research interests include juvenile delinquency and juvenile justice, migration research, economic crime and criminal procedure. His current focus is on a research project on corporate crime.

Susan Will is an assistant professor of Sociology at John Jay College of Criminal Justice, City University of New York where she teaches courses on white-collar and corporate crime and sociology of law. She has written about the American Ponzi culture, bankruptcy and is a co-editor of *How They Got Away With It: White-Collar Criminals and the Financial Meltdown.*

Karin van Wingerde (PhD) is an assistant professor of Criminology at Erasmus School of Law, Erasmus University, Rotterdam, the Netherlands. Karin's research interests include the regulation of corporate behaviour, and corporate, financial and environmental crimes. Particularly, she is interested in the relationship between various legal and extralegal mechanisms of social control, and the behaviour of business firms.

Acknowledgements

The Siemens corruption case, the *Probo Koala* toxic waste scandal, the Icelandic banking crisis, Jerome Kerviel's illegal trading behaviour at the French Bank Société Générale, the Ahold and Parmalat accounting frauds ... Corporate crime and white-collar crime are abundant in European countries. They are also the topic of a large body of criminological scholarship in various European countries. Only a small part of this work reaches an international academic audience, due to language differences and differences in local publication cultures. This led to the situation in which we teach courses in white-collar crime to European students using textbooks about US cases of white-collar crime, while criminological analysis of European cases remains unknown to them. This also raises the question of whether characteristics and explanations for white-collar crime that may be 'typically European', as well as similarities and differences between European countries, are perhaps understudied.

The establishment of the European Working Group on Organisational Crime, as a subdivision of the European Society for Criminology in 2011, has brought together a vibrant community of European white-collar crime criminologists. Seeing their research presented in a growing number of panel sessions each year at the annual meetings of the ESC, we took up the idea of bringing together some of this research to enrich the academic literature on white-collar and corporate crime and of contributing to the question of whether there is something 'typically European' about white-collar crime.

Originally intended as a modest edited volume primarily intended as teaching material in our own courses, our idea soon got out of hand and eventually resulted in this handbook. With 33 chapters, it is beyond what we ever imagined. We thank our editor at Routledge, Tom Sutton, for stimulating us to take this project a step further. We also thank Heidi Lee for her pleasant editorial assistance.

The annual meetings of the European Society for Criminology have provided an invaluable platform for the development of an academic network, and dialogue and discussion about this handbook. We are grateful to the ESC, and the local organizations of the ESC conferences in Vilnius, Bilbao and Budapest for giving us the opportunity to organize a 'white-collar crime stream' of panels, thus enabling a community of researchers to develop. Also, this handbook benefitted from several roundtable sessions with authors and external participants at the ESC conferences as well as at the conference of the American Society for Criminology in Atlanta in 2013. We thank all participants in these sessions for their stimulating comments and support for this project.

The editors would like to thank the Westfries Museum in Hoorn, Netherlands for allowing us to use a painting from their collection on the front cover of this handbook. The image shown on the cover is only part of the whole painting, which was painted by Jan de Baen in 1682. More information about the image is available at https://rkd.nl/nl/explore/images/15386.

Thanks also to Ashgate, Gower & Lund Humphries Publishing, Springer and Professor Dr. Brigitte Unger for their kind permission to reproduce previously published material in this handbook.

Without the editorial assistance by Joep Beckers, this project would certainly have grown over our heads. Joep's organizational skills and practical assistance have been an indispensable support to the project in general and its timely finish in particular. We are very grateful for his assistance and also thank him for his contribution to the introduction chapter of this handbook. By the time this handbook is published, Joep will have finished his dissertation, which will beyond doubt also make a valuable contribution to white-collar crime scholarship.

We hope that this handbook may help to stimulate criminological research into white-collar and corporate crime in Europe.

Judith van Erp, Wim Huisman, Gudrun Vande Walle
Rotterdam, Amsterdam, Gent
15 August 2014

1

Criminology and white-collar crime in Europe

Wim Huisman, Judith van Erp, Gudrun Vande Walle and Joep Beckers

Introduction

Although most hand- and textbooks on white-collar crime and corporate crime begin with the statement that the topic is neglected in criminology, white-collar crime research is a well-established discipline in criminology. That is: in Anglo-American criminology. American, British and Australian white-collar crime research prevails in the criminological journals and major publishers. This might lead to the impression that the topic is understudied in other parts of the world, such as continental Europe. This is far from true. The European Working Group on Organizational Crime of the European Society of Criminology has brought together more than 60 scholars from across Europe, all studying white-collar crime. Most publish, however, in their own language. This means that there is a substantial body of knowledge on the nature, prevalence, causes and responses to white-collar crime in many European countries, but it is hardly accessible to the international academic community. Because of this, many European criminologists use American textbooks in academic courses of white-collar crime. As a result, German, Italian or Hungarian students know all about the Saving and Loans debacle in the US, the accounting fraud at ENRON, the Ponzi scheme of Bernhard Madoff and the operations of US regulatory agencies such as the Securities and Exchange Commission. But they will hardly know about the corruption at Siemens, the accounting fraud at Parmalat and the securities fraud at Postabank, nor will they know about the operations of the regulatory agencies in their home countries, let alone in other European countries.

In some European countries (e.g. the Netherlands, Belgium, the Scandinavian countries and of course the United Kingdom) the study of white-collar crime is well established. In other countries (such as Hungary and Croatia) criminological as well as governmental interest in white-collar crime is fairly new. Some countries have statistics that show that white-collar crime is widespread. Most countries have witnessed serious cases of white-collar crime, which have raised a lot of media coverage and political concern. Only when the offenders were top politicians or (executives of) multinational corporations are these cases known to a wider, international audience. In many European countries, tackling white-collar or financial-economic crime is a priority of law enforcement agencies, as it is at the level of the European Union and the Council of Europe.

This *Handbook of White-Collar and Corporate Crime in Europe* aims to provide an overview of academic knowledge of white-collar and corporate crime in Europe and aims to contribute to a broader and more balanced account of white-collar crime.[1] As such, the book also aims to add to the existing body of work on white-collar and corporate crime.

Being the first handbook on the topic, this book takes a traditional and, for criminologists, familiar approach. Common aspects of the criminological study of crime are used to explore this fairly new topic of study: white-collar and corporate crime in Europe. The first part of this handbook focuses on the issues of defining white-collar and corporate crime and measuring the prevalence of white-collar crime. The authors in these chapters look at the way white-collar crime is conceptionalized and defined in the various European countries. As the term 'white-collar crime' was coined by the American criminologist Sutherland in his presidential address to the American Sociological Association in 1939, most Europeans take his work as the starting point of criminological interest in white-collar crime. However, both the work of Sutherland and the study of white-collar crime have earlier roots in European criminology and sociology. Also, the many differences in legal and administrative systems between European countries generate various problems in terms of measurement and comparison. An inventory of the various definitions, registration systems, and measurement problems in various countries, is a necessary first step for comparative research in the future.

The second and third parts of this handbook address historical and contemporary manifestations of corporate and white-collar crime. By doing so, the various chapters in this handbook will also touch upon typical European features of white-collar crime. Among these are: fraud with funds of the European Union, EU policies regarding economic crime, and white-collar crime in countries of transition from communist to capitalist economies, as well as European case studies. This raises the question of what is 'European' about white-collar crime in European countries. And therefore, is there a (need for a) 'European' criminology of white-collar crime?

The fourth part of the handbook discusses a variety of developments in the regulation, governance and enforcement of white-collar and corporate crime in Europe. Regulatory and law enforcement responses might be as plural as the number of countries in Europe, as this involves many nation states. A large proportion of these states however are members of the European Union. The European Union sets standards for legislation and law enforcement in the member states and has law enforcement agencies on its own. This multi-level framework of regulation and enforcement invokes many questions about combatting white-collar crime in Europe.

The handbook ends with the view of two well-experienced Anglo-American criminologists on this first overview of white-collar crime scholarship in Europe. This introductory chapter will offer a first exploration of the topics covered in this handbook.

White-collar crime in Europe

Historical accounts of 'white-collar crime'

The rich history of Europe holds many accounts of white-collar crime. One must be aware, however, of presenting anachronisms in discussing historical accounts of crime – for a start using a term that refers to the early-twentieth-century dress of the corporate (male) elite to define situations that occurred in times when this specific context did not yet exist. Yet a historical account might offer interesting insights and analogies, as is shown for example by Hanawalt's use of the concept of 'fur-collar crime' to label medieval nobles (robber barons) who used their castles to extort money from peasants (Hanawalt 1975).

Also, as the historical accounts below illustrate, regulation of trade and of occupations did exist in most eras and places of European history. As with modern-day law making, these regulations were responses to unfair or harmful trading practices. And as with modern-day law breaking, once put in place, these laws could be broken. The accounts can therefore fulfil Sutherland's definition of 'crime', which he defined as violations of 'the regular penal code or special trade regulations' and 'the laws designed to regulate [...] occupational activities' (Geis 2007).

Economic crimes in ancient times

As Friedrichs observes in his award-winning textbook on white-collar crime (Friedrichs 2010: 3), records from ancient times include cases of fraud and sanctions against fraud carried out in the context of various types of commercial transactions. According to Geis, 'the records show that there has been a long-standing ancient tradition, passed on to the Judeo-Christian world, that associated commerce with fraud and avarice and that held such endeavors were a potential source of moral corruption and decay' (Geis 2007: 51). In publications on white-collar crime, not seldom examples of fraudulent behavior in business transaction from as long ago as ancient Greece are given to illustrate that white-collar crime is as old as mankind, or at least as old as trade (Clarke 1990: 13; Croall 2001; Johnstone 1999: 107).

For early civilizations access to food, essential for human survival, was not certain and therefore a concern for rulers responsible for safeguarding production and regulating trade. Evidence has been found of counterfeit Roman seals on amphorae containing fraudulent olive oil and wine (Spink and Moyer 2011). Contemporary legal systems of most European countries are still based on the laws that evolved in the Roman Empire and that were codified in AD 529 by emperor Justinian in the Codex Justinianus. Being basically a system of civil law, it did contain trade regulations and provisions for unfair trading practices.

Economic crime in the Middle Ages

After the fall of the Western Roman empire, Roman law continued to be used and further evaluated throughout the Middle Ages in the larger part of Europe. The modern-day concept of fraud developed from Roman law.

With the growth of urban economies in late medieval Europe, the power balance gradually shifted away from the aristocracy to the cities. In these cities, crucial trades for the local economy organized themselves into associations, the so-called 'guilds'. While the practices of guilds to limit competition closely resemble to what nowadays would be anti-trust offences, **Ponsaers** in this handbook portrays guilds as predecessors of contemporary regulatory authorities, regulating and monitoring production and trade. The guilds became more and more autonomous in controlling industrial regulation. This regulation was aimed at standardizing the quality of production and the goods produced.

Overseas trading companies

Trading companies set up by the Dutch and the British are claimed to be the first modern corporations: funded by private capital, in tradable shares, aimed at profit. The two most prominent examples are the British East India Company (1600) and the Dutch Vereenigde Oost-Indische Compagnie (VOC, 1602). Both companies started as speculative companies importing spices from South-East Asia and gradually obtained tremendous wealth and power. In the Netherlands, the VOC is synonymous with both the 'Dutch Golden Age', as well as with widespread fraud and corruption. In popular belief, the company's abbreviation also stands for *Vergaan Onder Corruptie* meaning 'Perished By Corruption'. Illicit trade on the side on the part of the company's agents, breaching the company's monopoly, contributed to its downfall (Nierstrasz 2007). The British company suffered a similar fate (Robins 2002).

The introduction of tradable securities soon also brought the drawbacks that still plague today's financial markets: speculation, bubbles, crashes and securities fraud (Garper 2000), such as the notorious South Sea Company bubble in which outrageous and often fraudulent claims were made to raise capital and to boost stock prices. When the bubble burst, thousands were financially ruined (Carruthers 2005).

The crimes of colonial states

Besides these economic crimes, the VOC and the British trading companies were also engaged in actions that would today be labelled as state crime, because these companies also exercised state authorities, such as waging war. Many of their actions would nowadays constitute breaches of international criminal law, such as crimes against humanity and war crimes. For example, in 1621 the VOC eradicated most of the indigenous population of the Banda Islands to install a more profitable system of plantation.

Dutch and British states took over the assets of the trading companies after their bankruptcy respectively in 1795 and 1858. In contemporary (anachronistic?) terminology this would mean a shift from corporate crime to state crime. In recent times, the colonization itself and many of the practices executed in the name of colonization have been deemed as wrong and even criminal. An extreme example of economic exploitation for private gain that has been the topic of criminological study is the Congo Free State (Ward 2005). From 1885 to 1908 this country mainly served for the enrichment of the Belgian King Leopold II and the exploitation of the Congo's natural resources (then mainly ivory and rubber) was mainly left in the hands of commercial enterprises. In furthering this goal, massacres, hostage taking, rape, death by starvation and extremes of physical cruelty were common occurrences. Particularly for employees of the companies, terror and atrocities became standard business practices (Ward 2005).

The excrescences of industrial revolution

The industrial revolution that dramatically transformed civil society and the economy in many European countries in the nineteenth century came with the rise of labour-related crimes, such as child labour, slavery-like working conditions and unsafe working conditions resulting in injury and death. Excrescences of labour exploitation brought the first social regulations for businesses (Tombs and Whyte 2007). Besides the exploitation of labour and the crimes related to this exploitation, the industrial revolution also had an impact on the structure of the economy and the opportunities for fraud. Industrialization required considerable investment and as corporate business proliferated, businesses became larger, and this placed ever greater distance between investors providing capital and those managing business decision making (Wilson 2006). Monitoring directors became increasingly difficult, while reduced opportunity for detecting derelictions of duties allowed incompetence to flourish and, in some cases, actually provided an incentive to partake in fraud (Robb 1992).

In Victorian England the excitement of the intense stock market activity because of the railway boom promoted empty and asset-less 'bubble' companies alongside legitimate rail schemes (Wilson 2006: 1076). A panic over the widespread fraudulent schemes made the railway bubble burst and led to a crash in the market. The crash and the outrage at the financial dishonesty that created it generated a number of landmark criminal trials against company directors.

As in the case of the trading companies already discussed, the case of fraud in the financial markets in Victorian England shows a pattern that would reappear in modern European and American history: inflated, 'bull' markets tempt established, bona fide actors to take excessive risks while they also attract *mala fide* actors drawn to the lure, both resulting in fraud schemes that contribute to implosion of these inflated markets. A further pattern is that the public outrage about the excessive behavior in the build-up to the burst of economic bubbles, and the economic crisis as a result of that, have led to cycles of criminalization of harmful and fraudulent business conduct. The financial crisis of 1720 in England led to the introduction of white-collar crime as an offence, although at this time it was referred to as a 'scandal' (Johnstone 1999). The Victorian cases constituted the discovery of 'financial crime' and led to the redefinition of certain kinds of business activity as being criminal activity in England (Wilson 2006). In France, business crime as a specific criminal offence was established in 1935 in response to the economic crisis of 1929 and a feeling from within the financial community that commerce needed protection from price depreciation and growing overseas competition. During this period a series of financial scandals in France further prompted a move to bring moral order to business life and government efforts to clean up the image of the financial institutions (Johnstone 1999).

War profiteering and war crime

The twentieth century is defined by the two world wars that raged through Europe. Besides the atrocities later being outlawed by international treaties and labelled as war crimes and even genocide (for the similarities between this 'gold-collar crime' and white-collar crime see Brants 2007), the wars also encouraged 'ordinary' economically motivated white-collar crimes. It is not widely known that in his landmark book on white-collar crime, Sutherland devoted considerable attention to corporate crimes in the context of World Wars I and II (Galliher and Guess 2009). Major American and European corporations profited from the rapid and increased demand because of the war, for instance by providing inferior products and overcharging for products. Some companies even engaged in price-fixing schemes and trading with the enemy. Controlling production in this manner was profitable for business on both sides of the military divide.

Corporate complicity went further than profiteering from the war effort. Both German and foreign companies contributed to the gross human rights violations committed by the Nazi regime (Matthews 2006; Van Baar and Huisman 2012). Only German captains of industry have been prosecuted in the post-war Nuremburg trials, such as the directors of Krupp and IG Farben. The corporate involvement in the Holocaust will be further analysed by **Van Baar** in this handbook.

Post-communism looting

The aftermath of the World War II brought the division of Europe into two opposing political and economical systems: democracy and a free-market-based economy in the West and communism and a state-controlled economy in the East. In Western criminology, white-collar crime has been strongly related to capitalism and the culture of competition that is central to capitalism (Coleman 1987), a view that has long been held in Marxist criminology as well (Bonger 1916; Friedrichs 2010). Although the prevalence of corruption and the economical exploitation of power in communist systems are widely known, hardly any criminological research has been done on white-collar crime in communist Europe or in post-soviet transition economies. The rapid and radical political and economical transformation in former communist countries brought both a state of anomie and many opportunities for fraud, often related to the privatization of former governmentally owned companies and assets. Due to widespread looting, a class of a new kind of 'robber barons' emerged. In this book, three chapters will focus on this important chapter in the history of Europe and discuss white-collar crime in countries of transition: **Boers, Theile, Bischoff and Karliczek** on former Eastern Germany; **Novoselec, Roksandić Vidlička and Maršavelski** on Croatia and **Inzelt** on Hungary.

Contemporary white-collar crime in Europe

While there are of course many historical, political, economical and cultural differences between countries in Europe, because of the fall of the iron curtain and the expansion of the European Union, similarities seem to prevail over differences when looking at the contemporary manifestation of white-collar crime in Europe. And to a large extent, manifestations of white-collar crime in Europe seem to be of the same sorts and have the same characteristics as the ones described in Anglo-American literature. Typologies such as suggested by Clinard and Yeager (1980) and Friedrichs (2010) seem to be largely applicable in a European context. For instance, European corporate crimes are also violations of laws regarding environmental pollution, occupational safety and health, consumer safety and health, economic competition, financial administration, taxation and so on. Similarities are also found on a case level, such as cases of accounting fraud: there are several 'European ENRONs' involving major European companies, such as Italian Parmalat and Dutch Ahold.[2] Likewise, the foreign bribery cases against major US companies Halliburton and Wal-Mart resemble high-level bribery cases against European corporations such as Philips, Elf and BAE. In this book **Klinkhammer** discusses the Siemens cases, one of the biggest corruption cases in European history. Further, the predatory lending practices of mortgage companies that triggered the global financial crisis after 2007 were not unique to the US (Huisman 2011). In this volume, **Will** elaborates on the banking crisis in Iceland.

Globalization and the integration of economies and markets can be an explanation for the similarities in white-collar crime. White-collar crime on global markets surpasses regional boundaries. Sutherland (1949) already gave examples of transatlantic price-fixing schemes. In modern times, the auction houses Christies (UK) and Sotheby's (US) were found to have formed a cartel, inflating prices by dominating the global auction market (Aschenfelter and Graddy 2005). A very recent case of fraud on the global financial market is the LIBOR scandal. The London Interbank Offered Rate (LIBOR) is the world's most widely used benchmark for short-term interest rates. It underpins approximately $350 trillion in derivates. The LIBOR is derived from a filtered average of the interbank interest rates banks are paying, or would expect to pay, for borrowing from other banks. The LIBOR panel consists of 18 banks, including Asian banks, but most of these are European and American banks. Some of these banks were found to be falsely inflating or deflating their rates so as to profit from trades, or to give the impression that they were more creditworthy than they were. Up to ten banks, including Royal Bank of Scotland, Deutsche Bank and Société Générale, expected to settle the LIBOR and EURIBOR (a European version of LIBOR) rigging allegations against them. Barclays was fined $452.5 million by US and UK regulators for the LIBOR manipulation. The European Union fined a group of European and American banks for a total of 1.7 billion euros. Too recent to be included in this handbook, the LIBOR case certainly deserves a criminological analysis.

Another example of crime on global markets is the transnational shipment of waste from Western industrialized economies – like Europe – to developing nations. The analysis of the role of the international port of Antwerp by **Bisschop** and the Trafigura case study by **Van Wingerde** illustrate that European companies and locations can just be local nodes in transnational flows of waste.

Notwithstanding similarities and 'global' forms of white-collar crime, there are also differences in European and American manifestations of white-collar crime. These can be partly related to different economies (Esping-Anderson 1990). As **Korsell** observes in this book, in a market-liberal country like the United States, the functioning of the market is of supreme significance. Consequently, anti-trust offences such as insider trading, price fixing and market manipulation are emphasized, as they eliminate free competition. European countries have market economies as well, but a number of them are also advanced social welfare states. In social welfare states, taxes are of strategic importance as they are an instrument for redistribution – to be sure, with a varying level of ambition depending on the current political situation. Consequently, it is primarily tax offences and the closely related accounting violations that have high priority in these countries and this typifies the nature of many white-collar crime cases. In this handbook **Karstedt** further explores the differences in the distribution of wealth in the various national economies across Europe, leading to regional differences in the nature and manifestations of white-collar crimes.

Further, the creation and the expansion of the European Union and the introduction of many regulations and subsidy schemes by the European Union have created the problem of crimes targeted against the European Union. These might take the form of organized crime when criminal groups specialize in, for instance, VAT fraud schemes, but also take the form of white-collar crime when regular European businesses are involved. The anti-fraud bureau OLAF investigates fraud against the EU budget, corruption and serious misconduct within the European institutions. The Structural Fund money is given out by the European Commission in Brussels. The EU-wide budget for Structural Funds is 350bn euros for the latest seven-year period (2007–2013), distributed across 650,000 programmes in 27 countries. Fraud against these funds seems to be widespread. The Commission itself estimates that across the EU's 27 member states, in 2009 alone, 1.22bn euros' worth of Structural Funds involved irregularities and fraud, which represents a 100 per cent rise on the previous year.[3] In this handbook, **Quirke** considers the difficulties new EU member states encounter to be in compliance with EU regulations and the opportunities for EU fraud that come out of these difficulties.

European criminology and white-collar crime

The historical and contemporary manifestations as well as the European particularities of white-collar crime justify the study of white-collar crime in European criminology. Criminological interest in white-collar crime issues is (almost) as old as European criminology itself. Beccaria (1764) recognised that 'the great and rich' committed acts that caused immense public injury, and that had to be kept in check by law (Forti and Visconti 2007). Although Edwin Sutherland, and sometimes also Edward Ross before him, are often considered the founding fathers of white-collar crime scholarship, the Dutch criminologist Willem Bonger (1876–1940) is among the early criminologists who paid considerable attention to white-collar crime or 'crimes of the bourgeoisie'. Bonger's life and work and his work's relevance for criminology are discussed by **Hebberecht** in this handbook. Following his Marxist convictions, Bonger saw the capitalist economic system and economic conditions as a major cause of crime. A capitalist society teaches people to become rich as the principal end in life; and therefore teaches bourgeois business people to make profit even to the detriment of those with whom they do business (Bonger 1916). Bonger regarded position, rather than individual characteristics, as the major explanation of white-collar crime. In other words, he considered crime not a consequence of innate human qualities, but of social and economic conditions. Financial crimes, such as stock market frauds, even are 'the consequence of the economic environment exclusively'. In 1916, Bonger wrote, 'such crimes can be committed only in a time like ours, with its insatiable thirst for gold, with the unlimited opportunity to deceive the public, greedy for great profits' (Bonger 1916: 140). One hundred years later, these words have not lost their relevance for contemporary analyses of stock fraud. In the same vein, for example, is Jock Young's portrait of Bernie Madoff not as a deviant outsider but as a perfectly normal representation of the narcissistic culture and moral emptiness of modern finance capitalism (Young 2012). Hebberecht justly credits Bonger as one of the founding fathers of white-collar crime scholarship. Unfortunately, Patrick Hebberecht passed away in January 2015.

Norwegian sociologist Aubert (1952) has been another major contributor to white-collar crime scholarship. Whereas scholars in the Sutherland tradition seem driven by the agenda to demonstrate that white-collar is genuine crime (Sutherland 1949: 132–139), Aubert placed the ambiguity of white-collar crime at the centre of his research:

> For purposes of theoretical analysis it is of prime importance to develop and apply concepts which preserve and emphasize the ambiguous nature of the white-collar crimes and not to 'solve' the problem by classifying them either as 'crimes' or 'not crimes'. Their controversial nature is exactly what [...] gives us a clue to important norm conflicts, clashing group interests, and maybe incipient social change.
>
> *(Aubert 1952: 266)*

He regards the ambivalence associated with white-collar crimes as 'a barometer of structural conflicts and change'. Criminalization of white-collar crime, for example, performs a social function by symbolically fulfilling workers' demand for suppression of economic power while at the same time safeguarding the interests of those who execute this power, because the criminalized offences are not actually prosecuted. Aubert's study of the legislation protecting working conditions of domestic help is illustrative. This new law introduced penal sanctions for employers who violate the law, but since violations occur within the household, the law is practically unenforceable. Aubert interprets the function of this law as a form of societal pacification: it satisfies the demands of those ideological groups in society (the left) who wish to take action against misuse of housemaids, but at the same time protects employers by a lack of enforcement. It thus limits social conflict and contributes to the social peace.

Aubert's perspective of white-collar crime as an indicator of social hierarchies, power balances and social structure in a particular society continues to inspire research regarding criminalization of white-collar crime, and the interpretation of rules by those subject to it as well as those enforcing it. Nelken for example has identified seven sources of ambiguity, around the conceptualization, the causes and the responses to white-collar crime, as a framework to a better understanding of white-collar crime (Nelken 2012). In various publications, Nelken has explored the relation between ambiguity and various forms of corruption, such as corruption in relation to university appointments in Italy (2009). Because this behavior is normalized in Italian culture but would be considered inappropriate in many other cultures, his work also indicates that an analysis of the different perceptions towards white-collar crime in different cultures or periods of time is a fruitful approach for comparative research. Criminological accounts of differences in reactions to white-collar crime between countries are not only relevant for academics, but may also contribute to public debates about stringency of enforcement.

While Bonger and Aubert belong to the founding fathers of the criminological interest for white-collar crime, it is the perception of the authors of this introduction that further interest in white-collar crime by European criminologists – mostly from the 1980s on – should be seen as a response to the body of Anglo-American research that followed and built upon the work of Sutherland. This is at least true for the Netherlands (Van de Bunt and Huisman 2007). Since then, particularly British scholars left their mark on the criminology of white-collar crime in Europe (e.g. Croall 2001; 2008; Nelken 1997; Punch 1996; Tombs and Whyte 2007). As mentioned in the introduction of this chapter, only recently the initiative was taken to bring together white-collar crime scholars from other – non-English-speaking – European countries by setting up a special working group of the European Society of Criminology (EUROC). And as also mentioned in the introduction as well, this handbook aims to further contribute to the development of the criminological study of white-collar crime in Europe.

Defining white-collar crime in Europe

Although its roots can be traced back to Europe, it was the American criminologist Sutherland who publicly and academically introduced the term 'white-collar crime'. Sutherland's 'approximate' definition caused much conceptual and linguistic confusion (Friedrichs 2010). Various authors deemed it to be rather vague, imprecise and ideologically charged (Aubert 1952; Croall 2001; Green 2006; 2007; Nelken 1997; Punch 1996; Slapper and Tombs 1999). Notwithstanding these criticisms, due to globalization, white-collar crime has now become a worldwide and discipline-transcending umbrella term (Green 2004). In Europe, many countries adopted it and several of them translated it literally into their own language (although some European countries seem to prefer using the English word or a derived term). Examples of literal translations can be found in German (*Weiße-Kragen-Kriminalität*) (Binder 1962), French (*criminalité en col blanc*) (Normandeau 1965), Italian (*criminalità dei colletti bianchi*) (Loschiavo 1952), Spanish (*delito de cuello blanco*), Portuguese (*crime branco de colarinho*) (Cruz Santos 2001), Dutch (*witteboordencriminaliteit*) (Van de Weringh 1969) and Norwegian (*hvit krageforbrytelse*) (see Green 2004).

Nevertheless, in Europe, the term 'white-collar crime' has been relied upon mainly by journalists and social scientists (Croall 2001). Due to its broadness, European legal scholars have been reluctant to use the concept as an umbrella term. In fact, few European law schools offer a course on 'white-collar crime'. Academic lawyers in Europe seem to prefer using separate crime categories like 'corporate', 'economic', 'business' and 'administrative' crime, instead of a unified category of white-collar crime (Green 2004). But also the fairly common use of the term 'white-collar crime' by social scientists can be misleading. As Nelken (2012: 734–735) points out: 'Despite the similarities of modern industrialized economies there are important differences in general and legal culture, which affect the meaning of and response to white-collar crime'. According to various authors, these contrasts have not yet been sufficiently explored (Levi and Nelken 1996; Nelken 1994; 2000; 2012).

Several chapters in this volume (most notably **Lord and Levi**, **Korsell**, **Walburg**, **Alalehto and Larsson**), however, do explore the definitional differences within Europe. Both **Korsell** and **Walburg**, for example, point out that these definitional differences are partly due to differences in economic systems. In Sweden, the most commonly used term for white-collar offences is 'economic crimes'. Central to this category are acts of tax evasion. This may have something to do with the Swedish welfare state. In other European countries, just like in the United States, crimes against free-market competition are more in the spotlight (**Korsell** 2002: 9; this volume). **Karstedt**, in this volume, extends the concept of white-collar crime to crimes of the middle classes, and thereby presents a European answer to Weisburd et al.'s (1991) overview of these crimes, and places these middle-class fraudsters in the context of the increasingly liberalized European economies.

Another topic that deserves further exploration is the analogy between corporate crime and organized crime. In his book *Organized and Corporate Crime in Europe*, Ruggiero (1996) points out that corporate and organized criminals use the same techniques, such as corruption, embezzlement and falsification. His analysis of the trade of stolen art, weapon manufacturing and trade, illegal processing of chemical and toxic waste, and money laundering reveals that corporations and organized crime groups often commit crimes jointly and form mutually beneficial partnerships. Similar examples are provided by Van Duyne (1993), who identified organized crime enterprises in the Dutch meat market and waste processing industry. Ruggiero (1996: 21) argues that the focus on the respectable status and social background of white-collar offenders hinders our understanding of the deviant acts and of the techniques utilized to perform these acts. Research into the similarities, differences and relations between organized and corporate crime may help to understand criminal opportunities. In this volume, the chapters on crime and sports by **Nelen**, the chapter on real estate fraud by **Van de Bunt and Van Wingerde**, the chapter on illegal export by **Bisschop**, and the chapter on the Belgian Agusta affair by **Cools and Pashley** reveal that organized and corporate crime have parallel characteristics and sometimes close relations.

Measuring white-collar crime in Europe

Measuring white-collar crime is notoriously difficult. Various aspects of white-collar crime can be measured: its prevalence (Clinard and Yeager 1980; **Korsell** this volume; Sutherland 1949; **Walburg** this volume), its costs (Kane and Wall 2006; Rosoff et al. 2002), its victimization (Bussmann and Werle 2006; Kellens et al. 2007), but also public perceptions on white-collar crime and its punishment (**Alalehto and Larsson** this volume; Almond 2008; Holtfreter et al. 2008) and the adequate level of enforcement (**Lord and Levi** this volume). To aptly measure these aspects of white-collar crime requires quantitative data to be collected. Diverse data sources and research methods have been used: analysis of official (secondary) statistics (Clinard and Yeager 1980; Levi 2007; Weisburd and Waring 2001; Wheeler et al. 1988), (victim) surveys (Burns et al. 2004; **Bussmann** 2007; this volume; Bussmann and Werle 2006; Wells 2004), self-report studies (Long and Swingen 1991), but also perception studies (Grabosky et al. 1987; Schoepfer et al. 2007) and, where accessible, private-sector data (Levi 2011). All these data sources and research methods have their own problems, however, and, as is commonly accepted, these problems are magnified when it comes to white-collar crimes (Friedrichs 2010).

Measurement problems are magnified in case of white-collar crime as a result of its relative invisibility (relatively low levels of detection and prosecution, ambiguous legal and criminal status, unaware/unreporting victims – Croall 2001; Levi 1992; Tombs and Whyte 2003), lack of identifiable consequences (diffuse nature of the harm caused by white-collar victimization – Friedrichs 2010), knowledge and power problems in attempts to understand corporate (sub)systems (Croall 2001), and the complexities of ascertaining legal responsibility (complex nature of offences, diffusion of responsibility, apparent lack of intent – Geis 2007; Gobert and Pascal 2011; Gobert and Punch 2003; Laufer 2008). Gaining access to valuable secondary data can also be very difficult, especially in Europe, due to its comparatively strict data protection laws (**Walburg** this volume).

Measurement problems are even further magnified when it comes to comparing white-collar crime rates across Europe. As noted earlier, the equivalent term for 'white-collar crime' is widely found in Europe. There are also interesting contributions, often in non-English languages, which could be a useful starting point for comparative research (e.g. Clarke 1990; Cosson 1978; Delmas-Marty 1990; Magnusson 1985; Passas and Nelken 1993; Savelsberg 1994; Tiedemann 1974; Van Duyne 1993; Ziegler 1990; see Nelken 2012: 734). Nevertheless, European social scientists tend to write about their own society (and in their own language). The few comparative studies that have been conducted reveal wide national and cultural variations in business–government relations, in regulatory regimes, in implementing legislation, and in notions of risk, blame culpability, responsibility and morality (Nelken 2012; Punch 1996).

So, although we live in an increasingly 'Europeanized society', in which cross-national comparative studies become ever more important, and although some comparative European white-collar crime research has already been conducted, comparing crime rates from country to country remains notoriously difficult and therefore sparsely done (Friedrichs 2010). Von Hofer (2000) systematizes the difficulties inherent to crime rate comparisons by identifying three types of factors that determine the outcome of crime statistics: substantive, legal and statistical factors. These factors affect national crime statistics in different ways, consequently complicating cross-national comparisons (Aebi 2008; 2010; Van Dijk et al. 2012). Substantive factors refer to the tendency of victims, bystanders, witnesses and offenders to report offences, to the proclivity of the police and other authorities to record offences, and to the actual crime levels. Legal factors refer to the influence of legal definitions and the characteristics of the legal process. These include the statutes of limitations and the prosecuting authorities' powers to conclude agreements with the parties in the legal process, but also the application of the legality (e.g. Czech Republic, Germany and Sweden) or the opportunity (or expediency) principle (e.g. Austria, Belgium, Denmark, Estonia, Finland, France, Ireland, Italy, Lithuania, Luxembourg, Netherlands, Poland, Portugal, Romania, Slovenia, Spain and the United Kingdom). Statistical factors, finally, refer to the way in which crime statistics are elaborated. Each country applies its own rules to count the offences that will be included in crime statistics. Since these rules vary from country to country, they introduce differences in recorded crime rates that do not reflect actual differences in the levels of crime (Aebi 2010).

But although quantitative comparative research is seriously hindered by these magnified measurement problems, the differences in substantive and legal factors across Europe can also make European comparisons all the more worthwhile. This is demonstrated by **Lord and Levi** in this volume. Their comparative analysis focuses on responses to transnational bribery in Germany and the United Kingdom. Because of several key intellectual similarities (both are important economic players and members of the G8, and both have the largest share of world exports in the EU) and differences (with regard to enforcement rates, anti-corruption systems and corporate liability), **Lord and Levi** stress that a comparative analysis of Germany and the United Kingdom is 'particularly suitable' for understanding the impact of international frameworks for enforcement and the limits and strengths of national enforcement frameworks. So, comparative European white-collar crime research is perhaps very challenging, but it can also be hugely rewarding. The fact that on the European level several projects to stimulate meaningful cross-national research have been initiated (**Walburg** this volume) is therefore a positive sign.

Assessing harm and victimization of white-collar crime in Europe

Victims have long been a forgotten category in the study of white-collar and corporate crime (Snell and Tombs 2011). In their overview of the attention for victimization of white-collar crime in the US, Cullen, Hartman and Jonson see a slow evolution from a total ignorance of white-collar crime victimization to a kind of awareness in the twenty-first century. Ross (1907) and Sutherland (1949) attributed this limited awareness to an insensible public opinion towards white-collar crime. The 'criminaloid' succeeds in getting away with law violations because the public accepts the new sins, harmful activities by powerful men and organizations. This passivity is often due to unconsciousness of the public about the true impact of the specific cases of white-collar crime (Cullen et al. 2009). In Europe we see a same kind of evolution from total ignorance to some recognition of victimization and the needs of victims of corporate crime. Expert knowledge and scientific support are often the turning point for consciousness and recognition. **Altopiedi** explains in this handbook the asbestos case and how knowledge and scientization made the public aware of their victimization and enabled victims to translate their suffering into a legal question about the responsibility of the producers. Scientific knowledge about the causes of victimization often means a turning point from disbelief to general recognition. This was also the case for the victims of pharmaceutical products who first thought their heart failure was the consequence of their physical weakness until details of the fatal effects of the diet pills were publicized (Vande Walle 2003). This scientization also plays an important role for environmental victimization (Bisschop and Vande Walle 2013).

Besides the scientific support, the level of recognition also depends on the more or less democratic character of victimization. The more social levels in society are affected by white-collar crime, the stronger the reaction. The effect of the democratization of victimization was obvious in cases related to the financial markets. At the end of the 1990s some European companies were accused of fraud on the stock exchange market. Well-known European cases were the fraud case of the Italian milk producer Parmalat and the case of the Belgian producer of the innovative speech technology Lernout and Hauspie (L&H). Both were charged with accounting fraud. The case of L&H certainly stimulated the consciousness of victimization of the sometimes small stockholders who invested all their money in this new promising company. The group of known victims would have been larger if the number of small investors who invested their black savings in the company had not been that large. In 2010 three managers of L&H were given prison sentences. Other important players involved in the fraud were acquitted for lack of proof. Consumer organizations succeeded for the first time in Belgium in uniting victims in order to sue for compensation. The democratic character of victimization and the collective reaction were even more obvious during the latest financial crisis. The collapse of financial institutions caused a general anger throughout the whole of society. First there were the small depositors who lost all their savings because of the irresponsible investments of financial institutions. At the same time a lot of companies and wealthy people became victims. However, Croall warned that this democratic character is true only to a certain degree. Even if the poor, the middle class and the wealthy have an equal chance of becoming victims of consumer products, there still remains a difference in victim-proneness based on gender, age and socio-economic conditions (Croall 2008).

The recognition of victims also differs between European countries. This could be explained by cultural differences. In the comparative study of the victimization by the defective pharmaceutical product Diethylstibestrol (DES) in France, the Netherlands and Belgium, the differences in the numbers of known victims were striking. While the main producer of DES-containing medicines was a Belgian company and the pharmaceutical product was largely commercialized in Belgium, almost no victims came to light there after a public call. In the Netherlands, where production was lower, 4710 people submitted a request for the prohibition of the drug after a damages fund was founded. In France, about 150 to 170 people submitted individual claims in court. Eternit produced asbestos in Italy as well as in Belgium (see **Altopiedi** in this handbook). In Italy, the victims succeeded in creating a powerful collectivity. In Belgium people remained quite silent. These differences in cultural reactions can partially be explained by differences of legal cultures: the Netherlands is more oriented towards the Anglo-Saxon system of collective settlement while Belgium and France favour individual court action. Other explanatory factors may be related to the economic and political situations, as well as political and cultural heritages (Larsson and Alalehto 2013). It is important for a better understanding of this awareness of victimization to further explore why people in some countries react publicly while other people accept the damage done in silence.

Another reason why people remain silent about their victimization might be their economic dependency. This would be the case for the victimization of employees due to the violation of occupational safety and health standards. Tombs and Whyte (2007) studied the large number of employees that become victim of unsafe and unhealthy working conditions and the vulnerability of some groups of employees to this kind of victimization. The main reason for the vulnerability of employees is their financial dependence on their employers. Also employee mobility resulting from the opening of the borders within the European Union, combined with bad economic conditions in some European countries, created new risks for exploitation, as is illustrated by recent criminal investigations into slavery-like working conditions of migrant workers from Eastern European countries in Western Europe.

Lots of questions about victimization of white-collar crime are still unanswered in European criminology and victimology. At the same time new challenges are waiting. Hall (2013) has invoked criminologists and victimologists to study environmental pollution. For corporate crime researchers it can be a challenge to find a way to deal with environmental victimization where the responsible actor cannot be found. Closely related to white-collar criminology, the *green criminology* movement has answered this call (South 1998; Spapens et al. 2014). Another challenge is gaining knowledge about cross-border victimization in the different regions of Europe because the impact of food fraud or ecological disasters doesn't stop at the borders.

Explaining European white-collar crime

Defining white-collar crime, measuring its prevalence and assessing its harm, would be the most obvious first steps in a criminological exploration in any country in Europe. Nevertheless such explorations have not been carried out in every European country, making it troublesome to say anything on the European level about prevalence and victimization. Yet, the next step in any study of white-collar crime would be to search for explanations. As in Anglo-American theory making on white-collar crime, in European criminology a division between traditions of positivist criminology and that of critical criminology can be made. In the final chapter, **Friedrichs** elaborates on this distinction.

From a critical criminology perspective white-collar crime – and especially corporate crime – can be explained as the detrimental effect of capitalist economy and the result of unequal distributions of wealth in Western industrialized societies and the concentration of power with big corporations. As socialist movements have been stronger in Europe, critical criminology has also been more influential in Europe than in the United States. A classic book in this tradition is *Power, Crime and Mystification* by Steven Box (1983), a prominent scholar in the 'left realism' movement in British criminology. As mentioned above, prominent contemporary critical scholars like Tombs, Whyte and **Croall** (see her epilogue in this handbook) mainly focus on the harms of corporate crime. A critical analysis of the corporatization of academia as an explanation for corporate crime in Greek universities is offered in this book by **Georgoulas and Voulvouli**.

While in critical criminology the central question in explaining white-collar crime would be why corporations and elite offenders are able to escape the criminalization of their harmful conduct, the central question in more positivist approaches is why people (or corporations) commit the acts that have been criminalized by law. In Anglo-American literature, criminological studies on the causes of white-collar crime are usually applications of general theories of crime or they are tests of the applicability of these general theories with the use of white-collar crime data (Friedrichs 2010). While it may be too farfetched to label these as 'Anglo-American' theories, it is true that many of the original authors were Americans, using American empirical findings to develop their theories. Examples of such popular theories to explain white-collar crime are Agnew's strain theory (Agnew et al. 2009), Sutherland's differential association theory (Piquero et al. 2005), Gottfredson and Hirschi's self-control theory (Piquero et al. 2010) and Felson's routine activities theory (Benson et al. 2009). Again, it might be wrong to label these theories as Anglo-American because European scholars such as Durkheim and Bonger were sometimes the initiators of the theories that were further developed by Americans. The point here is that many European studies on the causes of white-collar crime use the same theories and apply them to European data (Boers et al. 2010; Huisman and Van Erp 2013; Van Onna et al. 2014). Most studies seem to assume universal validity of these theoretical frameworks (or at least the application in the context of a European state). Hardly any studies explicitly question validity and test applicability.

But is there such a thing as 'European' explanations? Certain political and economical conditions might be so unique for certain countries, that they really test the applicability of common explanations for white-collar crime. **Korsell** typifies a number of European countries as social welfare states, in which taxes are of strategic importance as they are an instrument for redistribution. This could lead to a stronger motivation for tax fraud and more opportunities for the misuse of public provisions, compared with market-liberal countries. Van de Bunt and Huisman showed how the Dutch form of public governance ('poldermodel') of organised cooperation between government, employers and labour unions also has its criminogenic effects (Van de Bunt and Huisman 2007). Another national peculiarity is the focus on agriculture (and agricultural values) that typified the Irish economy for a long time, as **McGrath** explains in this book. And of course the huge budgets and funds of the European Union, in combination with countless subsidy schemes, ambiguous regulation and a lack of control are in themselves important sources of opportunity for fraud (Passas and Nelken 1993; Quirke 1999; **Quirke** this volume).

Another obvious example is the case of white-collar crime in countries in the transition from communism to free-market-based democracy. As mentioned, various chapters in this book analyse the forms of white-collar crime that occurred in these situations of transition and the factors that contributed to these crimes. Elements of both anomie theory and opportunity theory can be recognized: rapid and even chaotic social changes, opportunities to loot former public assets as attractive and suitable targets, and a total breakdown of social control as governments had no experience in regulating markets, conditions for regulation were missing and the prevention of white-collar crime had low priority.

While after these transitions, all European countries have (more or less) free-market-based economies, research shows that corporate cultures differ between countries and between (continental) Europe and the United States and to a lesser extent Britain. In criminology, strong explanatory value is attributed to corporate cultures (Shover and Hochstetler 2002). Corporate culture is also widely seen as one of the contributing factors to the economic crisis; that is, Anglo-American corporate culture that puts a strong emphasis on maximizing shareholder value and that is related to excessive risk taking. In the aftermath of the financial crisis, various committees of inquiry, seeking the root causes of the crisis and options for prevention of such crisis, have rediscovered the so-called continental 'Rhineland model' for corporate governance suggested as a less criminogenic alternative. Compared with the competitive 'casino capitalism' of the Anglo-American culture, the Rhineland culture (referring to continental Western Europe's heartland) is more oriented towards compromise, stakeholder interest and corporate social responsibility, and is therefore seen as less criminogenic (Albert 1993).

Responding to white-collar crime in Europe

The intensity, character and priorities in regulating and enforcing corporate crime vary immensely throughout Europe. This variation stems from huge differences in legal systems and legal cultures; from political differences between European countries; from differences in structural and institutional features of the economy and from sociocultural differences. A major recent development is the introduction of corporate criminal liability in a growing number of European states (Beale and Safwat 2004). Whereas corporate criminal liability has existed in the United Kingdom and the Netherlands for several decades, most other European states have introduced corporate criminal liability between 1994 (France) to as recently as 2012 (Czech Republic). Germany and Sweden (**Korsell** this volume; Weigend 2008), however, have eschewed criminal liability in favour of an administrative approach to liability.

An important consequence of variations in legal systems is that large differences exist between countries in the balance between criminal or administrative enforcement. Legislation often creates an ambiguity, as a certain action can qualify both as a regulatory violation as well as a criminal offence: for the enforcement of tax transgressions in France see **Amicelle** in this handbook. In many European countries, however, a relatively small part of business misconduct is enforced through criminal law: the majority of business conduct is supervised by specialized regulatory market authorities such as financial services authorities, competition authorities and consumer protection authorities, and inspectorates such as environmental inspectorates or health and safety inspectorates. Businesses are subject to regulatory enforcement such as administrative fines, penalties, and licence suspension; and criminal enforcement is considered a last resort and reserved for only the most serious cases. But although criminal enforcement may appear more severe than administrative enforcement on paper, this may not be true in reality. Actual prison sentences are an exception, and administrative fines are often higher than the fines imposed in criminal courts. Also, specialized administrative authorities generally have more capacity and expertise to supervise particular areas of business conduct than criminal prosecutors. Last, administrative enforcement authorities often have more proactive media strategies than prosecution agencies; sometimes resulting in more press coverage of administrative fines than of criminal sentences (Wagner-von Papp 2011). Countries such as Italy and Ireland, which have few special enforcement agencies but instead rely on normal police forces to investigate and prosecute white-collar crime, are therefore not necessarily more stringent. The chapter by **McGrath** in this handbook demonstrates how police prosecution of corporate crime has resulted in very limited enforcement in Ireland. In comparison with continental Europe and Ireland, the United Kingdom can be considered more active in criminal enforcement against white-collar crime. Its tradition of corporate criminal liability is expanding to new domains, as is illustrated in the chapter on criminalization of corporate manslaughter in this handbook by **Almond**. A British Parliamentary Commission on Banking Standards has recently proposed individual criminal sanctions against 'reckless misconduct' by incompetent bankers.[4] In general, western and northern European countries are considered more sophisticated regulators and more stringent enforcers, but a closer analysis may reveal that levels of enforcement against, for example, environmental crime, are still less than deterrent (Huisman and Van Erp 2013). Differences in enforcement between countries also create opportunities for calculating criminals, as is illustrated by the active information exchange among exporters of illegal waste about chances of detection in various ports (see **Bisschop** in this volume).

As a result of the large differences between countries, it is very difficult to speak about a 'European way of law' in the context of white-collar crime (Gessner and Nelken 2007; cf. Kagan 2003). Nevertheless, despite the differences between countries, business regulation generally seems to be more compliance oriented than sanctioning in Europe when compared with the United States. A history of corporatism in a number of European countries, the widespread Rhineland model of stakeholder responsibility, and a less adversarial legal culture in European countries in general when compared with the United States have contributed to a relatively strong tradition of self-regulation of business sectors and professions. Rather than pure market-based economies or capitalist laissez faire, a wide variety of forms of collaborative governance, smart regulation and public private regulation exists in European countries. European case studies of various forms of co-regulation can make an important contribution to the literature on effective business regulation.

Despite the differences between European countries, several trends towards harmonization can be discerned. First, the regulation of businesses by the European Union is intensifying. Particularly in areas such as environmental regulation (SEVESO regulation), telecommunication regulation and financial regulation (BASEL frameworks), uniform rules are imposed that may spur a harmonization between countries. In competition law, the European Commission can even impose huge sanctions independent of national governments. European Union regulation also tends to promote more stringent enforcement: member states have for example been obliged to install criminal sanctions for environmental offences.[5] But despite the increased level of international and EU regulation, the implementation of EU law in national legislation and enforcement practice differs, as is illustrated in the chapter on anti-bribery regulations by **Verhage** and the chapter on the implementation of SEVESO regulations by **Kluin**. Comparative research between European countries can contribute to more effective enforcement across EU law and a reduction of opportunities for offenders to find the weakest link.

Another harmonizing tendency stems from the globalization of business. International governing bodies such as the FATF oblige European governments to implement and enforce anti-money-laundering rules (see **Amicelle** in this handbook). European multinationals operating in the US have to comply with Sarbanes-Oxley legislation, accounting rules and anti-bribery laws. European multinationals will be prosecuted by the American government when offending US rules. This can place European prosecutors in an awkward position, such as in the recent LIBOR rate fraud, where Rabobank was prosecuted by the American and British governments but not by the Dutch prosecutor. Such international developments can put pressure on local enforcement bodies and might give rise to a global compliance culture. The chapter by **Bussmann** in this handbook explains how compliance and corporate governance rules are transferred from the United States to European businesses, and asks whether this results in real change or mere 'going by the book'. **Győry** explains how Germany – as a model for continental European economies – adopted the Anglo-American approach against insider trading, despite this not being regarded as a 'real' problem in the German political economy.

This raises the question of whether we can speak to a certain extent of an 'Americanization' of European law. However, major differences between the United States and Europe exist, both in legal culture, socio-economic policy and cultural attitudes. An important difference between the United States and Europe in the reactions to corporate crime is the lesser or even largely absent role of class action suits. Civil law countries, as most European countries are, have no tradition of class action, although examples of collective action by victims exist. Particularly in northern European countries, the tort landscape may also be influenced by the strong social security system, which may have the perverse effect of taking away victims' motivation to take civil action against corporate harm. While providing a strong safety net on the one hand, on the other hand, social security transforms the physical or mental damage of corporate or white-collar crime into an illness that needs medical treatment. The social security system is a welcome safety net, but is paid for by employees and taxpayers as well as businesses, and thus transfers financial risks from corporate offenders to the community and prevents corporations from taking responsibility and recognizing their guilt. This can change in Europe now that citizens feel the deterioration of the social security systems and the conditions for insuring damages become stricter. A turning point in thinking about conflict resolution of corporate crime may dawn now that consumer and investor associations increasingly stand up for victims. The Dutch law on Collective Settlement of Mass Damage and recently accepted comparable legislations in other countries are examples of a reinforcement of tort-related instruments in the regulatory landscape, although they are not comparable to American class action suits.

Concluding remarks

The *Routledge Handbook of White-Collar Crime in Europe* is the first of its kind. This chapter serves as an introduction to the handbook and as such, it shows that the handbook is timely. In this chapter, the main topics of this handbook and their authors were introduced. The length of this introduction and the diversity of the issues covered illustrates that the nature, the harms and the causes of and the responses to white-collar crime in Europe are multi-faceted, and that this real and complex phenomenon needs to be further explored by criminological study. Some of the authors made their debut to international criminology with their chapter in this handbook. And by doing so, they present knowledge about white-collar crime in their country to an international audience. Other authors in this handbook are internationally well-established scholars in the field of criminology and the study of white-collar crime. This is particularly true for the authors that provide the epilogue of this handbook. Instead of drawing conclusions at the end of this introduction chapter on the criminology of white-collar crime in Europe, we would like to join their call for comparative research on white-collar crime. The many legal, political, cultural and language differences across Europe do not only bring challenges to such study, but also provide opportunities for groundbreaking research and producing universal knowledge on white-collar crime. We would like to express the need for comparative research and the ambition to take the criminological study of white-collar crime in Europe further. Building on a rich history, this handbook is only the beginning.

Notes

1 Due to the explorative nature of this first handbook, 'Europe' can have different meanings in different chapters and contexts. Europe can have a geographical meaning, when the word is used to refer to the countries that are situated on the European continent. Europe can have an institutional meaning, when it is used to refer to European international institutions – especially in the field of regulation and law enforcement – such the European Union and the Council of Europe. And Europe can have a cultural meaning, when it is used to refer to commonalities such as business practices or characteristics of civil society that differ from non-European countries.
2 The Ahold case was dubbed by *The Economist* as 'Europe's Enron' (*The Economist*, 27 February 2003).
3 European Commission (2010) IP/10/937, 14 July 2010.
4 Report of the Parliamentary Commission on Banking Standards, Changing Banking for Good, HL paper 27–1, June 2013.
5 Guideline COM (2007) 51, 2007/0022 (COD).

References

Aebi, M.F. (2008) 'Measuring the influence of statistical counting rules on cross-national differences in recorded crime', in K. Aromaa and M. Heiskanen (eds) *Crime and Criminal Justice Systems in Europe and North America*, Helsinki: Heuni, pp. 196–214.
Aebi, M.F. (2010) 'Methodological issues in the comparison of police-recorded crime rates', in S.G. Shoham, P. Knepper and M. Kett (eds) *International Handbook of Criminology*, London: CRC Press, pp. 211–227.
Agnew, R., Piquero, N.L. and Cullen, F.T. (2009) 'General strain theory and white-collar crime', in D. Weisburd and S. Simpson (eds) *The Criminology of White-Collar Crime*, New York: Springer, pp. 35–62.
Albert, M. (1993) *Capitalism Against Capitalism*, London: Whurr.
Almond, P. (2008) 'Public perceptions of work-related fatality cases: Reaching the outer limits of "populist punitiveness"?', *British Journal of Criminology*, 48: 448–467.
Aschenfelter, O. and Graddy, K. (2005) 'Anatomy of the rise and fall of a price-fixing conspiracy: Auctions at Sotheby's and Christie's', *Journal of Competition Law and Economics*, 1(1): 3–20.
Aubert, V. (1952) 'White-collar crime and social structure', *American Journal of Sociology*, 58: 263–271.

Baar, A. van, and Huisman, W. (2012) 'The over builders of the Holocaust: A case study of corporate complicity in international crimes', *British Journal of Criminology*, 52: 1033–1050.
Beale, S. and Safwat, A. (2004) 'What developments in Western Europe tell us about American critiques of corporate criminal liability', *Buffalo Criminal Law Review*, 8: 89–163.
Beccaria, C. (1994 [1764]) *Dei delitti e delle pene*, Turin: Einaudi.
Benson, M.L, Madensen, T. and Eck, J. (2009) 'White-collar crime from an opportunity perspective', in S. Simpson and D. Weisburd, *The Criminology of White-Collar Crime*, New York: Springer, pp. 175–193.
Binder, M. (1962)'Weisse-Kragen-Kriminalität', *Kriminalistik*, 16: 251.
Bisschop L. and Vande Walle, G. (2013) 'Environmental victimization and conflict resolution. A case study of e-waste', in T. Wyatt, R. Walters and D. Westerhuis, *Debates in Green Criminology: Power, Justice and Environmental Harm*, Basingstoke: Palgrave Macmillan, pp. 34–54.
Boers, K., Nelles, U. and Theile, H. (2010) *Wirtschaftskriminalität und die Privatisierung der DDR-Betriebe*, Baden-Baden: Nomos Verlag.
Bonger, W.A. (1916) *Criminality and Economic Conditions*, Boston: Little, Brown.
Box, S., (1983) *Power, Crime and Mystification*, London: Tavistock.
Brants, C.H. (2007) 'Gold collar crime', in G. Geis and H. Pontell (eds) *International Handbook of White-Collar Crime*, New York: Springer, pp. 309–326.
Bunt, H.G. van de and Huisman, W. (2007) 'Organizational crime in the Netherlands', *Crime & Justice. A Review of Research*, 35: 217–260.
Burns, R.G., Whitworth, K. and Thompson, C. (2004) 'Addressing law enforcement preparedness to address Internet fraud', *Journal of Criminal Justice*, 32: 477–493.
Bussmann, K. (2007) 'The control paradox and the impact of business ethics: A comparison of US and German companies', *Monatsschrift für Kriminologie und Strafrechtsreform*, 90: 260–276.
Bussmann, K. and Werle, M.M. (2006) 'Addressing crime in companies: First findings from a global survey on economic crime', *British Journal of Criminology*, 46: 1128–1144.
Carruthers, B. (2005) 'The first crash: Lessons from the South Sea Bubble' *The American Historical Review*, 110: 1244–1245.
Clarke, M. (1990) *Business Crime: Its Nature and Control*, Oxford: Polity Press.
Clinard, M.B. and Yeager, P.C. (1980) *Corporate Crime*, New York: Free Press.
Coleman, J.W. (1987) 'Toward an integrated theory of white-collar crime', *Americal Journal of Sociology*, 93: 406–439.
Cosson, J. (1978) *Les industriels de la fraude fiscale*, Paris: Editions du Seuil.
Croall, H. (2001) *Understanding White Collar Crime*, Buckingham: Open University Press.
Croall H. (2008) 'White-collar crime, consumers and victimisation', *Crime, Law and Social Change*, 51: 127–146.
Cruz Santos, C.M. (2001) *O crime de colarinho branco: Da origem do conceito e sua relevância criminológica à questão da desigualdade na administração da justiça penal*, Coimbra: Coimbra Editora.
Cullen, F.T., Hartman, J.L. and Jonson, C.L. (2009) 'Bad guys: Why the public supports punishing white collar-offenders', *Crime, Law and Social Change*, 51: 31–44.
Delmas-Marty, M. (1990) *Droit pénal des affaires*, Paris: Presses Universitaires de France.
Dijk, J. van, Tseloni, A. and Farrell, G. (eds) (2012) *The International Crime Drop: New Directions in Research*, Basingstoke: Palgrave Macmillan.
Duyne, P. van (1993) 'Organized crime and business crime-enterprises in the Netherlands', *Crime, Law and Social Change*, 19: 103–142.
Esping-Anderson, G. (1990) *The Three Worlds of Welfare Capitalism*, Princeton: Princeton University Press.
Forti, F. and Visconti, A. (2007) 'Cesare Beccaria and white collar crimes' public harm', in H.N. Pontell and G. Geis (eds) *International Handbook of White-Collar and Corporate Crime*, New York: Springer, pp. 490–510.
Friedrichs, D.O. (2010) *Trusted Criminals: White Collar Crime in Contemporary Society*, 4th edn, Belmont, CA: Wadsworth Cengage Learning.
Galliher, J.F. and Guess, J.F. (2009) 'Two generations of Sutherland's white-collar war crime data and beyond', *Crime, Law and Social Change*, 51(1): 163–174.
Garber, Peter M. (2000) *Famous First Bubbles: The Fundamentals of Early Manias*, Cambridge: MIT Press.
Geis, G. (2007) *White-Collar and Corporate Crime*, Upper Saddle River, NJ: Pearson.
Gessner, V. and D. Nelken (2007) *European Ways of Law: Towards a European Sociology of Law*, Oxford: Hart.
Gobert, J. and Pascal, A.-M. (eds) (2011) *European Developments in Corporate Criminal Liability*, New York: Routledge.
Gobert, J. and Punch, M (2003) *Rethinking Corporate Crime*, Cambridge: Cambridge University Press.

Grabosky, P.N., Braithwaite, J. and Wilson, P.R. (1987) 'The myth of community tolerance toward white collar crime', *Australian and New Zealand Journal of Criminology*, 20: 33–44.
Green, S.P. (2004) 'The concept of white collar crime in law and legal theory', *Buffalo Law Review*, 8: 101–134.
Green, S.P. (2006) *Lying, Cheating, and Stealing: A Moral Theory of White-Collar Crime*, New York: Oxford University Press.
Green, S.P. (2007) 'White-collar crime', in D.S. Clark (ed.) *Encyclopedia of Law & Society*, Los Angeles: Sage, pp. 1580–1582.
Hall, M. (2013) 'Environmental victims: Challenges for criminology and victimology in the 21st century', *Journal for Criminal Justice and Security*, 4: 371–391.
Hanawalt, B.A. (1975) 'Fur-collar crime: The pattern of crime among the fourteenth-century English nobility', *Journal of Social History*, 8: 1–17.
Hofer, H. von (2000) 'Crime statistics as constructs: The case of Swedish rape statistics', *European Journal on Criminal Policy and Research*, 8: 77–89.
Holtfreter, K., Van Slyke, S., Bratton, J. and Gertz, M. (2008) 'Public perceptions of white-collar crime and its punishment', *Journal of Criminal Justice*, 36: 50–60.
Huisman, W. (2011) 'Corporate crime and crisis: Causation scenarios', in M. Deflem (ed.) *Economic Crisis and Crime: Sociology of Crime, Law and Deviance, Volume 16*, Bingley: Emerald Publishing, pp. 107–125.
Huisman, W. and van Erp, J. (2013) 'Opportunities for environmental crime: A test of Situational Crime Prevention Theory', *British Journal of Criminology*, 53(6): 1178–1200.
Johnstone, P. (1999) 'Serious white collar fraud: Historical and contemporary perspectives', *Crime, Law & Social Change*, 30: 107–130.
Kagan, B. (2003) *Adversarial Legalism: The American Way of Law*, Harvard: Harvard University Press.
Kane, J. and Wall, A.D. (2006) *The 2005 National Public Survey on White Collar Crime*, Freemont, WV: National White Collar Crime Center.
Kellens, G., Dantinne, M. and Demonceau, B. (2007) 'Enron, Lemont & Hauspie, and Parmalat: Comparative case studies', in H.N. Pontell and G. Geis (eds) *International Handbook of White-Collar and Corporate Crime*, New York: Springer, pp. 540–551.
Korsell, L.E. (2002) *Ekobrott: Utvecklingen av Några Centrala Brottstyper*, Stockholm: National Council for Crime Prevention (BRÅ).
Larsson, D. and Alalehto, T. (2013) 'The reaction towards white collar crime: When white collar crime matters', *The Open Criminology Journal*, 6: 1–9.
Laufer, W.S. (2008) *Corporate Bodies and Guilty Minds: The Failure of Corporate Criminal Liability*, Chicago: University of Chicago Press.
Levi, M. (1992) 'White-collar crime victimization', in K. Schlegel and D. Weisburd (eds) *White Collar Crime Reconsidered*, Boston: Northeastern University Press, pp. 169–194.
Levi, M. (2007) 'Policing financial crimes', in H.N. Pontell and G. Geis (eds) *International Handbook of White-Collar and Corporate Crime*, New York: Springer.
Levi, M. (2011) 'Assessing the costs of frauds', in D. Gadd, S. Karstedt and S. Messner (eds) *The SAGE Handbook of Criminological Research Methods*, London: Sage, pp. 461–474.
Levi, M. and Nelken, D. (1996) 'The corruption of politics and the politics of corruption: An overview', *Journal of Law and Society*, 23: 1–17.
Long, S.B. and Swingen, J.A. (1991) 'Taxpayer compliance: Setting new agendas for research', *Law & Society Review*, 25: 637–689.
Loschiavo, G.G. (1952) 'La Mafia della Lupara e quella dei "colletti bianchi"', *La Giustizia Penale*, 68: 336.
Magnusson, D. (ed.) (1985) *Economic Crime: Programs for Future Research*, Report no. 18, Stockholm: National Council for Crime Prevention (BRÅ).
Matthews, R.A. (2006) 'Ordinary business: State corporate crime – Nazi Germany', in R. Michaelowski and R. Kramer (eds) *State-Corporate Crime: Wrongdoing at the Intersection of Business and Government*, New Brunswick, NJ: Rutgers University Press, pp. 116–133.
Nelken, D. (1994) 'Whom you can trust? The future of comparative criminology', in D. Nelken (ed.) *The Futures of Criminology*, London: Sage, pp. 220–244.
Nelken, D. (1997) 'White collar crime', in M. Maguire, R. Morgan and R. Reiner (eds) *The Oxford Handbook of Criminology*, 2nd edn, Oxford: Clarendon Press, pp. 891–924.
Nelken, D. (2000) 'Telling difference', in D. Nelken (ed.) *Contrasting Criminal Justice*, Aldershot: Dartmouth, pp. 233–264.

Nelken, D. (2012) 'White-collar and corporate crime', in M. Maguire, R. Morgan and R. Reiner (eds) *The Oxford Handbook of Criminology*, 5th edn, Oxford: Oxford University Press, pp. 623–659.
Nierstrasz, J.C. (2007) *In the Shadow of the Company: The VOC (Dutch East India Company) and its Servants in the Period of its Decline (1740–1796)*, Leiden: Research School.
Normandeau, A. (1965) 'Les déviations en affaires et la "crime en col blanc"', *Rev. Intl. Crime & Police Tech.*, 19: 247.
Passas, N., and Nelken, D. (1993) 'The thin line between legitimate and criminal enterprises: Subsidy frauds in the European Community', *Crime, Law and Social Change*, 19: 223–243.
Piquero, N.L., Schoepfer, A. and Langton, L. (2010) 'Completely out of control or the desire to be in complete control? An examination of how low self-control and the desire for control relate to corporate offending', *Crime and Delinquency*, 56(4): 627–647.
Piquero, N.L., Tibbetts, S.G. and Blankenship, M.B. (2005) 'Examining the role of differential association and techniques of neutralization in explaining corporate crime', *Deviant Behavior*, 26(2): 159–188.
Punch, M. (1996) *Dirty Business: Exploring Corporate Misconduct*, London: Sage.
Quirke, B. (1999) 'Fraud against European public funds', *Crime, Law and Social Change*, 31(3): 171–191.
Robb, G. (1992) *White-Collar Crime in Modern England: Financial Fraud and Business Morality, 1845–1929*, Cambridge: Cambridge University Press.
Robins, N. (2002) Loot: In search of the East India Company, the world's first transnational corporation', *Environment & Urbanization*, 14: 79–88.
Rosoff, S.M., Pontell, H.N. and Tilman, R. (2002) *Profit without Honor: White-Collar Crime and the Looting of America*, Upper Saddle River, NJ: Prentice Hall.
Ross E.A. (1907) *Sin and Society: An Analysis of Latter-Day Iniquity*, Boston: Houghton Mifflin Company.
Ruggiero, V. (1996) *Organized and Corporate Crime in Europe: Offers that Can't be Refused*, Aldershot: Dartmouth.
Savelsberg, J. (1994) *Constructing White-Collar Crime: Rationalities, Communication, Power*, Philadelphia, PA: University of Pennsylvania Press.
Schoepfer, A., Carmichael, S. and Piquero, N.L. (2007) 'Do perceptions of punishment vary between white-collar and street crimes?', *Journal of Criminal Justice*, 35: 151–163.
Shover, N. and Hochstetler, A. (2002) 'Cultural explanation and organizational crime', *Crime, Law, and Social Change*, 37: 1–18.
Slapper, G. and Tombs, S. (1999) *Corporate Crime*, London: Addison Wesley Longman.
Snell K. and Tombs, S. (2011) '"How do you get your voice heard when no-one will let you?" Victimisation at work', *Criminology & Criminal Justice*, 11(3): 207–223.
South, N. (1998) 'Corporate and state crimes against the environment: Foundations for a green perspective in Europe', in V. Ruggiero, N. South and I. Taylor (eds) *The New European Criminology: Crime and Social Order in Europe*, London: Routledge, pp. 443–461.
Spapens, A.C.M., White, R.D. and Kluin, M. (eds) (2014) *Environmental Crime and its Victims: Perspectives within Green Criminology*, Farnham: Ashgate.
Spink, J. and Moyer, D.C. (2011) 'Defining the public health threat of food fraud', *Journal of Food Science*, 76: R157–R163.
Sutherland, E.H. (1949) *White Collar Crime*, New York: Dryden Press.
Tiedemann, K. (1974) 'Kriminologische und Kriminalistische Aspekte der Subventionse-schteigung', in H. Schafer (ed.) *Grundlagen der Kriminalistik (Wirtschaftskriminalität, Weissen-Kragen Kriminalität)*, Hamburg: Steinton.
Tombs, S. and Whyte, D. (eds) (2003) *Unmasking the Crimes of the Powerful and Scrutinizing States and Corporations*, New York: Peter Lang.
Tombs, S. and Whyte, D. (2007) *Safety Crimes*, Portland, OR: Willan.
Van Onna, J., van der Geest, V. Huisman, W. and Denkers, A. (2014) 'Divergent trajectories: Criminal careers of white collar crime offenders in the Netherlands', *Journal of Research in Crime and Delinquency* (OnlineFirst).
Vande Walle, G. (2003) *Conflictafhandeling of Risicomanagement? Een Studie van Conflicten Tussen Slachtoffers en Ondernemingen in de Farmaceutische Sector*, Brussels: VUB-Press.
Wagner-von Papp, F. (2011) 'What if all bid riggers went to prison and nobody noticed?', in Beaton Wells, C. and A. Ezrachi (eds) *Criminalising Cartels, Critical Studies of an International Regulatory Movement*, Oxford: Hart publishing, pp. 157–182.
Ward, T. (2005) 'State crime in the heart of darkness', *British Journal of Criminology*, 45: 434–445.
Weigend, T (2008) 'Societas delinquere non potest? A German perspective', *Journal of International Criminal Justice*, 6(5): 927–945.

Weisburd, D., Waring E., with Chayet, E. (2001) *White-Collar Crime and Criminal Careers*, Cambridge: Cambridge University Press.
Weisburd, D., Wheeler, S., Waring, E. and Bode, N. (1991) *Crimes of the Middle Classes: White-Collar Offenders in the Federal Courts*, New Haven, CT and London: Yale University Press.
Wells, J.T. (2004) *Corporate Fraud Handbook: Prevention and Detection*, New York: John Wiley & Sons.
Weringh, J. van de (1969) 'White collar crime: Een terreinverkenning', *Tijdschrift voor Criminologie*, 11(3): 133–144.
Wheeler, S., Mann, K. and Sarat, A. (1988) *Sitting in Judgment: The Sentencing of White-Collar Criminals*, New Haven, CT: Yale University Press.
Wilson, S. (2006) 'Law, morality and regulation: Victorian experiences of financial crime', *British Journal of Criminology,* 4: 1073–1090.
Young, Jock (2012) 'Bernie Madoff, finance capital and the anomic society', in D. Brotherton, S. Handelman and S. Will (eds) *How They Got Away With It: White Collar Crime and the Financial Meltdown.* New York: Columbia University Press, pp. 68–82.
Ziegler, J. (1990) *La Suisse lave plus blanc*, Amsterdam: Uitgeverij Balans.

Part I

Defining and measuring white-collar and corporate crime in Europe

2

The measurement of corporate crime

An exercise in futility?

Christian Walburg

Introduction

Although corporate crime has been on the research agenda for some decades now, many criminologists throughout Europe share the impression that this type of crime still constitutes a blind spot (see, for example, Boers 2001 and Verhage 2009, both taking up this metaphor). However, this view might have to be elaborated. While important insights into crime-promoting and crime-preventing factors in business organizations have been gained especially from in-depth case studies and studies of specific industries or types of corporate crime, there is a significant lack of *quantitative* information on the extent, development, structures, and control of corporate crime and its varieties. While in criminology in general the value of statistics is widely acknowledged, measuring corporate crime is sometimes suspected to be ideology-driven, and quite often the lack of data is stated with a shrug of resignation. After a brief discussion of the necessity of measuring corporate crime, this chapter will address the specific difficulties that occur when examining the official registration and dealing with unofficial measures of corporate crime. Since prior research and literature on these issues predominantly refer to US-American experiences, the analysis will focus on specific European observations and difficulties. In order to explore possible ways to obtain a more complete and meaningful picture, the particular advantages and shortcomings of both classical and unconventional sources of information will be considered.

Why measure corporate crime?

Corporate crime, defined as offences committed by corporate officers and employees on behalf of and for the benefit of a legitimate business organization, lies at the core of broader concepts such as white-collar or economic crime (see Boers et al., this volume). It draws the attention to the organizational context of many business-related crimes, from which both a high potential for damages and resources for prevention emerge. Indisputably, there is corporate crime in all types of industry and business organization (Slapper and Tombs 1999: 50), and corporate crime exists in various forms (Hagan 2010: 226–247): from tax evasion and accounting fraud to violations of environmental and safety regulations, antitrust violations, bribery and even complicity in gross human rights violations (Huisman and van Sliedregt 2010). Yet, as will be shown, little is known about the extent, structures and control of such crimes.[1]

Poor data can result from a limited accessibility of certain crime phenomena. Moreover, this can indicate that public and political concern about a certain social problem is low (Levi and Burrows 2008: 293). As to corporate crime, arguably both aspects come into play. The lack of quantitative data might in turn lead to a lower visibility of corporate crime, since crime debates largely refer to 'numbers' (Slapper and Tombs 1999: 55–56). Thus some authors suggest that improved data on corporate crime would help make it a more pressing issue (Friedrichs 2009: 48–49; Nader 2013).

In fact, conventional approaches to measure crime are still one-sided: focusing on street crimes, most official crime statistics as well as self-report offending and victimization surveys give a distorted picture of how and by whom criminal law is getting violated. Business organizations as such rarely appear as crime scenes and origins of crime. On the other hand, business scandals regularly hit the headlines these days (Levi 2006). The newspapers' business sections sometimes resemble the crime news sections, and even business magazines see ubiquitous breaches of law and ethics and proclaim 'the end of the reputable businessman'.[2] Unlike in Sutherland's time, it seems to be widely acknowledged that illegal business practices should be taken seriously (as to reasons for growing concern in the 1960s and 1970s, see Clinard and Yeager 1980: 12–16). And despite significant deregulation in certain sectors, business-related criminal law as a whole has rather been tightened throughout the last decades (Simpson 2002: 10–16; Theile 2010: 149–150). Moreover, and perhaps most important, non-governmental organizations, unions and other stakeholders these days quite frequently succeed in initiating broad debates on issues such as the denial of basic social rights of (especially migrant and low-qualified) workers in Western countries, child labour or dangerous and exploitative working conditions in developing-world factories, environmental harms, corruption, or tax evasion or avoidance by multinational corporations. However, such initiatives do not always have a sustainable impact and usually disappear from the public agenda rather quickly. Improved and regularly collected quantitative data would probably make it somewhat harder for policy-makers and the media to ignore such problems.

Moreover, our basic knowledge about corporate crime and its control is incomplete as long as we do not have at least a rough idea about the amount, distribution, patterns and development of corporate crime as well as about the quantitative dimensions of its detection and regulation. Just like for any other type of crime, quantitative descriptive information forms a basis for criminological theories, which then can be tested and further developed with at best both qualitative and quantitative research methods. Such knowledge is crucial to an evaluation of different enforcement strategies, too (see Lord and Levi, this volume).

Officially recorded corporate crime

Two main features of official crime data make them interesting for criminologists: they are periodically collected and generally cover all kinds of crime. The problems begin when it comes to the question of whether official data reflect the 'true' amount, trends and structures of crime. For certain types of ordinary crimes, for instance burglary or car theft, the dark figure of hidden crime is presumed to be comparably low, and official counts reflect the 'real' incidence of these offences rather adequately. Such crimes have in common that there is a direct individual victim, who typically detects his victimization, defines it as a crime, and is motivated to report it to the police. When it comes to corporate crime, these conditions are typically not met, be it that there is no direct individual victim (as is the case with environmental crimes, tax fraud, antitrust violations, and many others), the victim does not (immediately) discover the offence (e.g. deceived consumers, trading partners or authorities), the definition as a crime is ambiguous (for instance with regard to broad offences like breach of trust or cases of negligence), or the victim is reluctant to contact the police (including affected corporations who fear reputational damage, or victimized employees who fear to lose their jobs).

For these reasons, the official registration of corporate crime heavily depends on the resources, priorities and expertise of the law enforcement agencies (Albrecht 2003: 46; van de Bunt and Huisman 2007: 223). Their activities are further influenced by the (sometimes) complex nature of business-related crimes as well as by the power of the perpetrators (Braithwaite 1985: 5). All in all, it is fair to assume that officially recorded corporate crime represents only the tip of a large iceberg (Gobert and Punch 2003: 12). Moreover, official data are not only inadequate to draw conclusions about the actual scope and trends of corporate crime, but also on its structures. Being an unrepresentative selection of rule-breaking by corporations, such data are of limited use as dependent variables in causal analysis as well. In the absence of more appropriate alternatives, they can serve as a starting point, but should be interpreted cautiously.[3]

The value of police, prosecution and sentencing statistics is further limited by the fact that a systematic and all-embracing collection of official data on corporate wrongdoing usually does not exist (Simpson 2011: 483–485). As a result, it is difficult to draw overall conclusions not only on the 'true' scope and structures of corporate crime, but even on its formal control: it is scarcely possible to overview how often what kind of corporate crime comes to the attention of what kind of law enforcement or regulatory agency, and how these agencies react to them. In 1981, reflecting growing concerns about economic crimes in a time of increasing cross-border business activities, the Council of Europe recommended that the member states should keep detailed statistics on such crimes[4] to facilitate criminological research. Almost two decades later, in 1998, the German government, responding to an interpellation, still professed itself unable to deliver any statistics on the control of corporate crime.[5] The situation has not changed since then, and similar observations (to varying degrees) can be made in other European countries (Albrecht 1999: 108; Fuchs et al. 2011: 21; Slapper and Tombs 1999: 54–56; van de Bunt and Huisman 2007: 223).

Corporate crime is not a legal category, but a heterogeneous analytical concept. This is why official statistics generally do not include a separate category of corporate crime. Regarding single types of offences (e.g. fraud), it has to be considered that these are not necessarily cases of corporate crime as defined by criminologists, but can just as well constitute occupational crimes or conventional property offences (Slapper and Tombs 1999: 55). The same applies to categories like 'economic crime' or 'white-collar crime' which can be found in some official statistics. What is more, such categories are often restricted to financial losses caused by economic activities, thus not including corporate offences involving physical injuries or environmental damage. Moreover, the terms and their definitions vary from country to country, making cross-country comparisons of such counts futile.

Definitional differences within Europe may in part have to do with what is considered as most problematic in different types of society. In Sweden, crimes like tax evasion are central to the category of 'economic crimes' as it is used in official statistics and reports, while in other countries crimes against free-market competition are more in the spotlight (Korsell 2002: 9; this volume). In German police statistics and official reports on economic crime (see, e.g. Bundeskriminalamt 2012), tax evasion remains completely unmentioned, which is why this quantitatively important offence is sometimes overlooked in discussions on business-related crime.

What is additionally lying behind here is the very nature of police statistics. Besides other general shortcomings partly mentioned above, these do not include all those cases that are dealt with by prosecutors or other agencies (such as the tax administration) alone. And, more generally, official statistics are often guided by considerations of law enforcement rather than by research interests. For instance, in the case of German police data, certain offences are counted as 'economic crimes' when the police estimate that specific economic expertise is necessary to handle these cases.

Political support for more comprehensive and meaningful approaches of data collection is often limited. In Germany, a more systematic registration of severe business-related crimes had been started in the 1970s, but was stopped after only a few years (Albrecht 2003: 45). From these efforts it is known that a vast majority of cases that have been registered as 'economic crime' by prosecutors actually have an organizational background (Liebl 1984: 136). The financial loss caused by business-related crimes clearly exceeded the officially recorded total damage caused by ordinary property offences (Liebl 1984: 155). These findings support the widespread impression that business-related crimes make up only a small fraction of all officially recorded crimes, but are responsible for huge parts of the crime-related financial losses (Clinard and Yeager 1980: 7–8; Slapper and Tombs 1999: 67).

At the other end of the criminal justice process, the few statistics which are available on the punishment of corporate crimes are similarly non-uniform and have to be interpreted with caution. Here, the situation is complicated by the fact that corporate crimes can result in criminal and non-criminal sanctions against the corporation itself,[6] in criminal charges against the individuals acting on behalf of it, or both. Thus the same illegal activity can not only entail the punishment of different individuals (in quite many cases of corporate crime, more than one person is involved), but, additionally or alternatively, lead to sanctions against the corporation. The respective sanctioning and enforcement rules and their application vary quite largely across Europe, which complicates attempts to analyse and compare the enforcement of corporate offences. When examining the prosecution of particular types of corporate crime, additional problems can occur since these are not always clearly distinguishable in official statistics. For instance, while shoplifting is rather consistently classified as theft by the police and the courts, criminal actions in the context of corruptive business practices can result in convictions for breach of trust,[7] tax evasion or similarly broad offences. General statistics based on such legal categories therefore do not necessarily give a clear picture of social phenomena like foreign bribery.

All national data have in common that, considering proceedings against individuals, it is usually not possible to identify cases with an organizational background in prosecution and sentencing statistics (see, e.g. Fuchs et al. 2011: 24). Therefore, a classification of criminal proceedings against individuals as cases of corporate crime is only possible by file analysis (as to an examination of convicted 'white-collar' offenders, see Weisburd et al. 1991; on offenders convicted of corruption, see Bannenberg 2002).

However, even actions directed against corporations themselves are not always centrally documented. In the case of Austria, this is even true for *criminal* charges against judicial persons under the jurisdiction of the criminal justice system, which are not statistically collected and published on a yearly basis. Anyhow, in order to analyse the (according to the study rather reluctant) application of the new Austrian rules on corporate criminal liability, it was possible to search for charges against corporations in an electronic database of criminal proceedings (Fuchs et al. 2011). In this context, Dutch data point to the fact that most actions and decisions taken against legal persons concern relatively minor offences (van de Bunt and Huisman 2007: 226) – contrary to the impression one might gain from media coverage, but perfectly in line with the well-known distribution of minor and more serious offences among natural persons.

With regard to *non-criminal* proceedings against corporations, a comprehensive source of information is often lacking due to the fact that these proceedings are usually conducted by a huge variety of regulatory agencies, often located on different levels of government (e.g. national, state/district, municipal). Sometimes there is a central agency to which local or state agencies have to report their data (see, e.g. Gibbs and Simpson 2009, concerning the regulation of pollution in the United States). Otherwise, the respective information needs to be collected directly at the often numerous authorities. When analysing their statistical reports, it has to be taken into account that regulatory agencies as 'responsive regulators' usually have considerable discretionary power in defining and responding to rule breakings (Friedrichs 2009: 47). Thus regulatory statistics restricted to sanctioning decisions cover only a small part of the picture and are substantially biased. File analysis can help to address this problem, enabling researchers to gather information on the whole regulation process (at least as far as documented in the files), including possible negotiations and informal settlements. Anyhow, the collection and analysis of statistical reports and case files from many different authorities require a lot of resources. In their seminal studies, Sutherland (1949) and Clinard and Yeager (1980) made huge efforts to collect information on administrative, civil, and criminal actions against a sample of the then largest US-American corporations, but had to restrict their analysis to a limited range of violations and selected agencies in charge of conducting the proceedings (as to data sources on environmental offences, see Burns and Lynch 2004). Nevertheless, similarly broad attempts to gather data on the formal control of corporations have not been made in Europe so far. European data protection laws, considered to be comparatively strict, can set limits to such research.

In some jurisdictions, the sanctioning of corporate wrongdoing is centrally registered in order to provide information for future administrative decisions – an institution roughly comparable with criminal records for individuals. The German 'Central Register of Companies' (*Gewerbezentralegister*) can serve as an example. In this register, every fining decision against a business organization taken by any prosecuting or regulatory authority has to be registered, usually for five years. Although only the fining decision as such is registered – negotiations and informal settlements are not (directly) covered – such a register can be a valuable source of information on the use of certain sanctions (here: fines).[8]

According to these data, the annual total number of fining decisions against German companies was about 3000 in 2012 (Table 2.1).[9] Compared with overall 1.3 million business organizations[10] (sole traders excluded), this number may seem surprisingly low: there were 230 registrations of

Table 2.1 Fines against business entities (except sole traders): annual number of registrations (total and by amount), Germany 2000–2012

	Number of registered fining decisions												
Year	*2000*	*2001*	*2002*	*2003*	*2004*	*2005*	*2006*	*2007*	*2008*	*2009*	*2010*	*2011*	*2012*
Total	3295	4067	2286	4745	2804	1911	2222	2487	2483	2617	2871	2273	3035
By amount													
200 to 300 euros	486	669	608	817	562	491	410	514	456	405	412	396	418
> 300 to 1000 euros	1357	1610	914	2488	1356	661	884	929	1147	1143	1297	1066	1604
> 1000 to 5000 euros	962	1343	547	922	708	561	791	884	727	850	893	641	830
> 5000 to 20,000 euros	339	364	162	375	137	115	92	106	95	136	164	125	132
> 20,000 to 50,000 euros	90	0	24	91	28	39	29	30	36	42	30	21	16
> 50,000 euros	61	81	31	52	13	44	16	24	22	41	75	24	35

Source: Annual report 'Übersicht über die Eintragungen im Gewerbezentralregister. Teilregister für juristische Personen und Personenvereinigungen'. Online. Available HTTP: <http://www.bundesjustizamt.de/> (accessed 8 July 2014); Engelhart 2010: 493

fining decisions on 100,000 business organizations (own calculation). The rather small numbers indicate that the imposition of fines, in line with the enforcement pyramid model (Fisse and Braithwaite 1993), is used as a last resort by regulatory agencies. All in all, about 30 per cent of all fining decisions were directed against companies involved in the transportation of goods (not reported in the table). It can only be assumed that many of these fines are related to traffic code violations. Unfortunately, information on the type of offence and the characteristics of the corporations is not published. A more detailed analysis remains to be done, which will also have to take into account possible flaws in the accuracy of this register.

A clear trend in the use of this most important penalty for corporations cannot be observed over the last decade. But it is worth noting that there has not been an increase in the number of fines. This is not only true for the total number of fining decisions, but also applies to the generally small number of high amounts imposed on corporations. Impressive fines against companies that usually attract much public attention are clearly exceptional, with fines exceeding 20,000 euros being rather rare. About two-thirds of the fines do not exceed 1000 euros.

Huge fines are permissible and in fact quite common under both national and European competition law. The amounts often exceed one million euros (Engelhart 2010: 491). Antitrust authorities make rather few fining decisions, which are usually well documented and easily accessible. This is why the control of antitrust offences is comparatively easy to assess. The German federal competition authority reports that during the last years, the number of cases has increased, in part due to a rise of whistleblowing.[11] The antitrust decisions concern smaller as well as larger companies and different types of industry (Feld et al. 2012: 6–8).

Aiming at ensuring an effective and consistent application of the EU competition rules, the European Commission is entitled to initiate proceedings in antitrust cases with a cross-border dimension.[12] The Commission still deals with a rather small annual number of cartel cases (4) and involved companies (19, both numbers referring to 2013; see Table 2.2). Here, immunity applicants[13] seem to be of growing importance. The total amounts imposed have increased over the last years and added up to 1.9 billion euros in 2013, with single companies sometimes being fined hundreds of millions of euros. The highest total cartel fines imposed in a single case so far concerned TV and computer monitor tubes (approx. 1.5 billion euros), car glass (1.2 billion euros), automotive bearings (0.95 billion euros), elevators and escalators, and air cargo (both approx. 0.8 billion euros).[14] Recently major European banks have been fined 1.7 billion euros on the whole for participating in cartels in the interest rate derivatives industry.

Table 2.2 European Commission cartel statistics 1990–2014.* Cases, number of decisions, amount of fines imposed

	1990–1994	*1995–1999*	*2000–2004*	*2005–2009*	*2010–2014*
Cartel cases decided	10	10	30	33	25
Number of decisions (business entities involved)	185	45	157	205	167
Fines imposed (total amount in million €, adjusted for court judgments)	344	271	3157	8182	8417

* Cases and decisions covered until 2 April 2014

Source: European Commission, Cartel Statistics, http://ec.europa.eu/competition/cartels/statistics/statistics.pdf (last change: 2 April 2014)

The imposition of such staggering fines is based on deterrence theory. It can serve as an example of a generally optimistic view of EU institutions on deterrence. Anyhow, some multinational companies or investment banks might still pretty easily get over these financial damages, while others might be hit hard. Based on insights from deterrence research, it seems doubtful whether a strategy of ever higher penalties will have the intended effect; all the more so when we assume that cartel infringements rather are committed by employees without the knowledge (and careful cost–benefit analysis) of the top management (Forrester 2009: 826). From a legal perspective, such high penalties can be characterized as criminal when substantive (rather than formalistic) criteria are adopted. This raises concerns about the adequacy of the existing procedural safeguards in the European Commission proceedings, which arguably have to be measured against the requirements laid out in Article 6 ECHR.[15] Moreover, it seems somewhat questionable that competition fines to such a great extent exceed penalties imposed for other kinds of corporate offences, e.g. breaches of health and safety rules or environmental legislation with sometimes fatal consequences (see, with several British examples, Forrester 2009: 824).

As to the prevalence of cartel infringements, an analysis of detected cases reveals that being faced with cartel proceedings is the rule rather than the exception at least for major companies. For as many as 16 of the 30 largest German corporations, one or more fining decisions (during a period of 10 years and taken by the EU Commission or any national competition authority) could be tracked down from publicly accessible sources for (sometimes long-term) involvement in price fixing or market allocation.[16] Such numbers at first glance may shock us with the apparent widespread readiness of 'big business' to illegally reduce the uncertainties inherent in free-market competition, all the more when taking into account the dark figure of such phenomena and the fact that certain corporations have repeatedly been charged with antitrust violations. Yet the assessment becomes more complex when taking into account that each of these corporations represents a broad scope of business areas, often with more or less independently operating subsidiaries, hundreds of thousands of employees, and corresponding motivations and opportunities to break competition laws. Standards for meaningful corporate crime rates have yet to be developed (as to environmental crime rates, see Gibbs and Simpson 2009).

Regarding most other types of corporate crime, proceedings and final decisions are much less readily accessible. Since certain business-related crimes attract a lot of public attention when they are detected, media coverage can be a useful additional source of information for research. Here, the selectivity of reporting has to be taken into account (and can also be an interesting object of investigation in itself). Annual reports of publicly traded companies, where prosecution risks have to be disclosed, can be helpful, too. Moreover, national governments under certain international treaties are obliged to collect and report information on certain types of crime. To give an example, the OECD Working Group on Bribery in International Business Transactions regularly collects information on detected cases of transnational bribery, based on information by the national governments. According to these data and in line with earlier assumptions and findings, the most important industries involved in bribery of foreign officials include oil, energy, mining, military, civil aviation, procurement of trucks, vessels and trains, IT, and the pharmaceutical industry. More than 50 per cent of the cases took place in developing countries, and criminal proceedings generally seem to play a minor role (Pieth 2010). All in all, in 38 States Parties to the Anti-Bribery Convention,[17] 221 individuals and 90 legal persons have been criminally punished for foreign bribery between 1999 and 2012 (OECD 2013: 9). The Working Group has counted at least 83 prison sentences for individuals. While such reporting systems can be seen as a step forward in analysing certain structures and trends in an international perspective, a closer look will be necessary to assess the reliability and comparability of such numbers based on government reports. Moreover, mere numbers of criminal and other proceedings do not permit us to draw comparative conclusions on the level of transnational corporate corruption and the adequacy of its control in different countries (see Lord and Levi, this volume).

Cases of transnational bribery illustrate another important fact. Especially multi- and transnational corporations are subject to regulatory bodies in more than one country. They are not only faced with European law and institutions on top of national authorities, but also with foreign legislation with sometimes extraterritorial applicability (e.g. the US Foreign Corrupt Practices Act or the UK Bribery Act). This raises questions on the growing interdependency of national legal systems, with stricter systems possibly influencing the legislation, its enforcement, and the level of compliance in more lenient systems. But such developments make it necessary to take a transnational perspective for quantitative research on corporate crime, too. Already posing a problem on the national level, international attempts to gather data on business-related crimes are rather rare (Albrecht 2003: 44). The greatest obstacle seems to be the big variation in the legal definition, prosecution and statistical collection of such crimes (see, e.g. Aebi et al. 2010: 34; van Dijk 2010: 132).

At the European level, a uniform crime reporting system does not yet exist. Anyhow, there are several approaches to develop statistics on the structure, levels and trends of crime and official reactions to crime in European countries. The European Sourcebook, originally developed under the umbrella of the Council of Europe, provides police and conviction data on various offences, including (partially) business-related crimes like fraud, offences against computer data and systems, money laundering and corruption (Aebi et al. 2010). However, the reported registration rates for crimes like fraud still vary extremely between European countries.[18] Therefore it is unclear to what extent these data, beyond reflecting certain trends within a country, already permit reliable country-level comparisons for such crimes.

The EU also promotes the collection of European crime data. In the Action Plan on Measuring Crime and Criminal Justice,[19] adopted by the Commission in 2006, both the measurement of environmental crimes and of victimization in the business sector have been mentioned. Moreover, the Commission highlighted the importance of regular data collection on certain types of serious and cross-border crime, including corruption and fraud. In the subsequent Statistics Action Plan 2011–2015, the Commission once more committed itself to these objectives, while at the same time recognizing that data on such crimes are less comparable and of lower quality than information on traditional forms of crime (which are usually outside EU competence).[20] So far, business-related crimes have not been included in Eurostat's database and annual reports on recorded crime trends.[21]

Unofficial measures of corporate crime

Not being restricted to crimes reported to the police, self-report offending and victimization surveys have become important tools to obtain a more complete and accurate picture of the extent, structures and trends of crime (see Cantor and Lynch 2000; Thornberry and Krohn 2000). However, as with official statistics, these techniques are of limited use when it comes to corporate crime. Gaining access to the corporate world (for a general discussion, see Verhage 2009) seems unrealistic when researchers request self-reports on publicly unknown illegal acts committed on behalf of the company; unlike adolescents in school, 'company directors do not respond to questionnaires about their criminal activities' (Braithwaite 1985: 5). And even if it should be possible to get one's foot in the door, it is rather unlikely that deviant managers or employees will honestly disclose their offences without rationalizing their behaviour (Punch 1996: 43). Moreover, since corporate offences are typically committed secretly, without being written down in a memo and talked about openly in internal meetings or in the company canteen, it is highly questionable whether it is feasible to interview the 'right' persons in large and complex organizations like transnational corporations. And in some cases of organizational crime, such a 'right' person individually responsible for the crime does not exist at all (Reiss and Biderman 1980: 93).

Regarding victimization surveys among corporations, many of these aspects pose a challenge, too. Such studies can only measure the offences that have come to the attention of the executive answering the survey, and the results are highly dependent on the intensity of the companies' own control efforts. Moreover, victimization is a sensitive topic, too, potentially damaging the public image of a company or 'business' in general, and answering surveys is time-consuming and has no direct benefit for the company. As a result, response rates tend to be rather low in business victimization surveys. A Norwegian study with response rates exceeding 90 per cent is clearly exceptional, probably having to do with the Central Bureau of Statistics conducting the research with support of the Ministry of Justice (Ellingsen 2010: 11–12).[22] The recent British Commercial Victimization Survey, which predominantly covered ordinary crimes against businesses (e.g. burglary, theft), had a response rate of 54 per cent (Home Office 2013: 82). In other studies, the rates were even (sometimes substantially) lower (see Boers 2010: 42).

Over the past decade, crime surveys among corporations were repeatedly conducted by accountancy, consulting and law firms (e.g. KPMG 2013; PricewaterhouseCoopers 2011). While this is arguably helpful to open doors, it has to be taken into account that these private firms pursue their own marketing goals. Methodological information, e.g. on response rates, is not always published (Boers 2010: 42). Moreover, some studies do not systematically differentiate between corporate and occupational crime. With regard to both the motives of the perpetrators as well as to possible reactions of the company, these types of crime are so different in nature that it makes little sense to summarize them in one single dependent variable. Thus bivariate analysis based on the broad and heterogeneous category 'economic crime' is of limited value. In these studies, this variable mainly reflects asset misappropriation, a typical occupational crime that constitutes a minor problem for society at large.[23] It is not surprising that, according to these studies, the offenders often belong to the companies' own staff and management (see, e.g. Bussmann and Werle 2006: 1135).

By definition, business victimization surveys give a somewhat distorted picture of what is at the core of business-related crimes. Corporations are not the only and definitively not the most vulnerable victims of such crimes. Harms inflicted on employees, consumers, the environment and the public are not covered at all or only marginally. When the media, often uncritically repeating the press handouts of private firms (Levi and Burrows 2008: 295), report that 'economic crimes' as a whole are not being taken seriously enough and have gone up,[24] or are effectively tackled by internal compliance measures and have gone down,[25] these statements are not based on a comprehensive understanding and measurement of business-related crimes.

Rather than accurately reflecting the incidence and structures of such crimes, business surveys can bring valuable insights into the way crime is perceived by managers, and into the coping strategies of corporations (see, e.g. Bussmann and Werle 2006: 1139–1141). One important finding from a recent survey conducted among German major enterprises is that internal compliance measures have increased notably during the last decade. On the other hand, the existing anti-corruption programmes quite often do not meet the requirements, e.g. of the UK Bribery Act (Bussmann et al. 2013). Whether the observed increase of internal compliance measures, established to reduce liability risks, has contributed to a real reduction of corruption and other corporate crimes, is an interesting question which as yet has not been answered convincingly.

As to the perception of crime, its causes and development, corporate executives serve as experts. Since their answers are not always based on personal experiences, they can be influenced by prejudices, particular incidents and public debates. Nevertheless (and in the absence of reliable self-report offending and victimization data), expert surveys seem to be comparatively appropriate to reflect certain trends. The studies on bribery in the private sector conducted by Transparency International belong to this category, too. According to these surveys, corporate executives did not perceive significant changes in the likelihood of European corporations committing bribery abroad between 2008 and 2011 (Hardoon and Heinrich 2011: 28). In line with findings based on prosecution data reported above, foreign bribery is perceived to occur in all business sectors, while the public works contracts and construction sector is seen to be most bribery-prone (Hardoon and Heinrich 2011: 14–15).

A recent special Eurobarometer survey revealed public perceptions of the prevalence of corruption (European Commission 2014). One finding is that among all EU citizens, two-thirds believed that corruption was part of the business culture in their country. In the newer member countries, the rate tended to be above average, while a majority of the respondents in the Nordic countries and the Netherlands disagreed (European Commission 2014: T67). Somewhat contradictory, Dutch and Swedish respondents most frequently thought that corruption (including both giving and taking of bribes) was widespread in private companies in their country (European Commission 2014: T19) – which might reflect a high public awareness in these countries. Nevertheless, according to the above mentioned Transparency International's Bribe Payers Index (with a sample of worldwide business executives), Dutch companies (along with other European companies, e.g. from Switzerland, Belgium and Germany) were perceived to be least engaged in bribery (Hardoon and Heinrich 2011: 5).

Household victimization surveys can cover additional aspects of corporate crime. Consumer fraud was included in the International Crime Victims Survey (van Dijk et al. 2007: 85–88), and a more detailed household survey on experiences with various kinds of fraud was conducted in the United States (Huff et al. 2010). These studies reveal that the overall victimization rate for consumer fraud is (much) higher than for conventional crimes. At the same time, these offences (which do not always originate from legitimate business organizations) are rarely reported to the authorities. Admittedly more difficult to accomplish than consumer surveys, additional important insights might be expected from victimization studies among other specific groups (e.g. employees) exposed to often more serious risks of corporate wrongdoing.

Conclusion

Quantitative description can be only a starting point for research on corporate crime (Slapper and Tombs 1999: 41). Nevertheless, some more empirical basis is needed, and it is indeed possible to accomplish. Although measuring corporate crime poses big challenges – in general, but even more on the European level with heterogeneous legal systems, law enforcement practices, and different systems of data collection – there is no reason to throw in the towel. There are numerous approaches and data sources, of which only some could be discussed here, and which all show specific strengths and weaknesses. In many cases, their potential has not been exhausted so far. Some shortcomings, e.g. the often incomplete and unsystematic documentation of proceedings against judicial persons, at least in principle seem to be possible to remedy – provided that there is sufficient political will. The introduction of more meaningful and comparable national statistics will probably be stimulated by initiatives already in progress on the European level. Ideally, quantitative research on corporate wrongdoing and its regulation will contribute to a rational and evidence-based European corporate crime control policy in an increasingly integrated economy.

The ambiguity and complexity of certain offences, many of them always remaining undetected, and similar problems are much more difficult to overcome, and it is highly questionable whether it will be possible to summarize the numerous and diverse varieties of corporate crime in one measure. And when it comes to the calculation of meaningful crime rates, which would allow comparisons of the level of corporate crime between different national economies or between business organizations with different sizes and opportunity structures, many open questions remain unanswered, too.

Beyond naïve empiricism, a triangulation of different measurement strategies, each of them conveying different perspectives on certain segments of corporate crime, can further improve the understanding of its amount, trends, structures, and control. The different approaches of measuring bribery described above can serve as a promising example, and more systematic steps have been taken, e.g. for environmental offences. The collection and analysis of information from various data sources in sourcebooks, as has been suggested by several authors (see, e.g. Friedrichs 2009: 48), might be a useful framework and an important step forward.

Notes

1 In line with prior research, the term 'corporate crime' as used in this paper is not restricted to violations of legal requirements that can result in criminal sanctions. The object of investigation should not be dependent on the legislator's decision to provide for criminal or non-criminal sanctions, which might be affected by the influence of powerful actors such as corporations. In order to assess the prevalence and effects of both criminal and non-criminal responses to law violations, it is indispensable to include legal regulations that provide for non-criminal actions.

2 See the editorial and the cover story of the German business periodical *Manager Magazin* 1/2013.

3 Clinard and Yeager (1980: 112) expressed the 'hope' that their data were not biased, without being able to further examine this question.

4 As can be concluded from the economic offences listed in the recommendation, the Council of Europe essentially referred to corporate crimes; see Council of Europe Recommendation no. R (81) 12.

5 See Bundestag Printed Paper 13/11425: 3.

6 Meanwhile, many European jurisdictions not only provide for administrative sanctions against corporations, but also allow for criminal charges, following the concept of corporate criminal liability originally developed in common law countries (Engelhart 2010: 618).

7 This happened in the Siemens corruption case where managers were convicted of breach of trust for creating and maintaining slush funds (see Klinkhammer, this volume).

8 Under German law, administrative fines are the most important sanction against judicial persons. While they are not formally referred to as penal sanctions, they are in many respects comparable with criminal sanctions and can be imposed both by prosecutors and administrative authorities.

9 Fines below 200 euros are not registered.

10 By May 2012 (source: Federal Statistical Office. Online. Available HTTP: <http://www.destatis.de/>. Accessed 8 July 2014).

11 See Bundestag Printed Paper 17/13675: 28–32.

12 See Article 101 TFEU and Council Regulation (EC) No 1/2003.

13 By leniency programmes, competition authorities provide an incentive (immunity from fines) to disclose an alleged cartel. Total immunity is granted to the corporation that first conveys the necessary information.

14 Source: European Commission, Cartel Statistics. Online. Available HTTP: <http://ec.europa.eu/competition/cartels/statistics/statistics.pdf> (accessed 8 July 2014).

15 As to the criteria adopted by the European Court of Human Rights to define a 'criminal charge' in the sense of Article 6 ECHR (the so-called *Engel criteria*), see the Court's judgment of 11 June 2009, Dubus SA v France, App no. 5242/04.

16 Own inquiry; the numbers refer to the 30 companies currently listed on the German stock index DAX during the period from 2004 to 2013. Ten of these companies have been fined by the EU Commission (or have avoided fining as immunity applicants; see footnote 13). In some cases, court decisions are pending.

17 Including most European as well as North and South American countries, Japan, Korea and South Africa.

18 To give an example: for 2007, the offender rate (per 100,000 population) for fraud was reported to be 39 in the Netherlands, and 345 in Germany (Aebi et al. 2010: 80). The respective conviction rate was 7 (the Netherlands) and 135 (Germany) (Aebi et al. 2010: 187).

19 Communication from the Commission to the European Parliament, the Council and the European Economic and Social Committee. Developing a comprehensive and coherent EU strategy to measure crime and criminal justice: An EU Action Plan 2006–2010. 7 August 2006, COM (2006) 437 final.
20 Communication from the Commission to the European Parliament and the Council. Measuring Crime in the EU: Statistics Action Plan 2011–2015. 18 January 2012, COM (2011) 713 final.
21 Online. Available HTTP: <http://epp.eurostat.ec.europa.eu/portal/page/portal/crime/introduction> (accessed 8 July 2014).
22 Unlike in this particular survey, companies generally have an obligation to report certain data to the Bureau of Statistics, and some might have felt obliged to participate.
23 In the most recent global survey conducted by PricewaterhouseCoopers, 24 per cent of the corporations reported that they had experienced at least one case of asset misappropriation. Accounting fraud, bribery and corruption, and cybercrime were each reported by 8 per cent of the corporations, whereas the victimization rates for all other types of economic crime were 3 per cent or lower (PricewaterhouseCoopers 2011; own calculations).
24 See *Zeit Online*, 12 January 2010, 'Economic crime increases notably'. Online. Available HTTP: <http://www.zeit.de/wirtschaft/unternehmen/2010-01/wirtschaftskriminalitaet-kpmg-studie> (accessed 8 July 2014).
25 See *Focus Online*, 7 November 2013, 'Economic crime decreases'. Online. Available HTTP: <http://www.focus.de/finanzen/diverses/kartellfragen-wirtschaftskriminalitaet-sinkt-nsa-affaere-verunsichert-unternehmen_aid_1151387.html> (accessed 8 July 2014).

References

Aebi, M.F., Aubusson de Cavarlay, B., Barclay, G., Gruszczyńska, B., Harrendorf, S., Heiskanen, M., Hysi, V., Jaquier, V., Jehle, J.-M., Killias, M., Shostko, O., Smit, P. and Þórisdóttir, R. (2010) *European Sourcebook of Crime and Criminal Justice Statistics – 2010*, 4th edn, Onderzoek en beleid 285, The Hague: Boom Juridische Uitgevers.

Albrecht, H.-J. (1999) 'Forschungen zur Wirtschaftskriminalität in Europa. Konzepte und empirische Befunde', in S. Bauhofer, N. Queloz and E. Wyss (eds) *Wirtschaftskriminalität: Criminalité économique*, Chur/Zürich: Rüegger.

Albrecht, H.-J. (2003) 'Forschungen zur Wirtschaftskriminalität in Europa: Konzepte und empirische Befunde', in H.-J. Albrecht and H. Entorf (eds) *Kriminalität, Ökonomie und Europäischer Sozialstaat*, Heidelberg: Physica Verlag.

Bannenberg, B. (2002) *Korruption in Deutschland und ihre strafrechtliche Kontrolle: Eine kriminologisch-strafrechtliche Analyse*, Neuwied: Luchterhand.

Boers, K. (2001) 'Wirtschaftskriminologie: Vom Versuch, mit einem blinden Fleck umzugehen', *Monatsschrift für Kriminologie und Strafrechtsreform*, 84(5): 335–356.

Boers, K. (2010) 'Wirtschaftskriminalität: Begriffe, Methoden, empirische Erkenntnisse, Theorien und Forschungsziele. Einführung in die Untersuchung', in K. Boers, U. Nelles and H. Theile (eds) *Wirtschaftskriminalität und die Privatisierung der DDR-Betriebe*, Baden-Baden: Nomos.

Braithwaite, J. (1985) 'White collar crime', *Annual Review of Sociology*, 11: 1–25.

Bundeskriminalamt (2012) *Wirtschaftskriminalität. Bundeslagebild 2012*, Wiesbaden: Federal Criminal Police Office.

Bunt, H.G. van de and Huisman, W. (2007) 'Organizational crime in the Netherlands', in M. Tonry and C. Bijleveld (eds) *Crime and Justice in the Netherlands*, Crime and Justice: A Review of Research, vol. XXXV, Chicago: University of Chicago Press.

Burns, R.G. and Lynch, M.J. (2004) *Environmental Crime: A Sourcebook*, New York: LFB Scholarly Publishing.

Bussmann, K.-D., Nestler, C. and Salvenmoser, S. (2013) *Wirtschaftskriminalität und Unternehmenskultur 2013*, PricewaterhouseCoopers AG Wirtschaftsprüfungsgesellschaft and Martin-Luther-Universität Halle-Wittenberg.

Bussmann, K.-D. and Werle, M.M. (2006) 'Addressing crimes in companies: First findings from a global survey of economic crime', *British Journal of Criminology*, 46(6): 1128–1144.

Cantor, D. and Lynch, J.P. (2000) 'Self-report surveys as measures of crime and criminal victimization', in D. Duffee (ed.) *Measurement and Analysis of Crime and Justice*, Criminal Justice 2000, vol. IV, Washington, D.C.: National Institute of Justice.

Clinard, M.B., and Yeager, P.C. (1980) *Corporate Crime*, New York: The Free Press.

Dijk, J. van (2010) 'The International Crime Victims Survey and complementary measures of corruption and organised crime', in M. Hough and M. Maxfield (eds) *Surveying Crime in the 21st Century*, Boulder, London: Lynne Rienner Publishers.
Dijk, J. van, Kesteren, J. van and Smit, P. (2007) *Criminal Victimisation in International Perspective: Key Findings from the 2004–2005 ICVS and EU ICS*, The Hague: Boom Juridische Uitgevers.
Ellingsen, D. (2010) *Virksomheter som Ofre for økonomisk Kriminalitet – 2008-undersøkelsen*, Oslo-Kongsvinger: Statistics Norway.
Engelhart, M. (2010) *Sanktionierung von Unternehmen und Compliance: Eine rechtsvergleichende Analyse des Straf- und Ordnungswidrigkeitenrechts in Deutschland und den USA*, Berlin: Duncker & Humblot.
European Commission (2014) *Special Eurobarometer 397: Corruption. Report*, Brussels. Online. Available HTTP: <http://ec.europa.eu/public_opinion/archives/ebs/ebs_397_en.pdf> (accessed 8 July 2014).
Feld, L.P., Möschel, W., Wieland, V. and Wigger, B.U. (2012) *Reform der Geldbußen im Kartellrecht Uberfällig*, Berlin: Stiftung Marktwirtschaft.
Fisse, B. and Braithwaite, J. (1993) *Corporations, Crime and Accountability*, Cambridge: Cambridge University Press.
Forrester, I.S. (2009) 'Due process in EC Competition Cases: A distinguished institution with flawed procedures', *European Law Review*, 34(6): 817–843.
Friedrichs, D.O. (2009) *Trusted Criminals: White Collar Crime in Contemporary Society*, 4th edn, Belmont: Wadsworth.
Fuchs, W., Kreissl, R., Pilgram, A. and Stangl, W. (2011) *Generalpräventive Wirksamkeit, Praxis und Anwendungsprobleme des Verbandsverantwortlichkeitsgesetzes (VbVG)*, Wien: Institut für Rechts- und Kriminalsoziologie.
Gibbs, C. and Simpson, S.S. (2009) 'Measuring corporate environmental crime rates: Progress and problems', *Crime, Law and Social Change*, 51(1): 87–107.
Gobert, J. and Punch, M. (2003) *Rethinking Corporate Crime*, London: Butterworths.
Hagan, F.E. (2010) *Crime Types and Criminals*, Thousand Oaks: Sage.
Hardoon, D. and Heinrich, F. (2011) *Bribe Payers Index 2011*, Berlin: Transparency International.
Home Office (2013) *Crime against Businesses: Detailed Findings from the 2012 Commercial Victimisation Survey*, London: Home Office.
Huff, R., Desilets, C. and Kane, J. (2010) *The 2010 National Public Survey on White Collar Crime*, Fairmont: National White Collar Crime Center.
Huisman, W. and Sliedregt, E. van (2010) 'Rogue traders: Dutch businessmen, international crimes and corporate complicity', *Journal of International Criminal Justice*, 8(3): 803–828.
Korsell, L.E. (2002) *Ekobrott: Utvecklingen av Några Centrala Brottstyper*, BRÅ-rapport 2002:1, Stockholm: National Council for Crime Prevention (BRÅ).
KPMG (2013) *Wirtschaftskriminalität: Deutschland, Österreich, Schweiz im Vergleich*, KPMG.
Levi, M. (2006) 'The media construction of financial white-collar crimes', *British Journal of Criminology*, 46(6): 1037–1057.
Levi, M. and Burrows, J. (2008) 'Measuring the impact of fraud in the UK: A conceptual and empirical journey', *British Journal of Criminology*, 48(3): 293–318.
Liebl, K. (1984) *Die Bundesweite Erfassung von Wirtschaftsstraftaten nach einheitlichen Gesichtspunkten: Ergebnisse und Analysen für die Jahre 1974 bis 1981*, Freiburg: Max-Planck-Institut für ausländisches und internationales Strafrecht.
Nader, R. (2013) 'Getting tough on devastating corporate crime', *The Huffington Post*, blog entry. Online. Available HTTP: <http://www.huffingtonpost.com/ralph-nader/corporate-crime_b_2934600.html> (accessed 8 July 2014).
OECD (2013) *Working Group on Bribery: Annual Report 2013*. Online. Available HTTP: <http://www.oecd.org/daf/anti-bribery/AntiBriberyAnnRep2012.pdf> (accessed 8 July 2014).
Pieth, M. (2010) 'Bestechung ausländischer Amtsträger im Geschäftsverkehr', in B. Bannenberg and J.-M. Jehle (eds) *Wirtschaftskriminalität*, Neue Kriminologische Schriftenreihe, Band 112, Mönchengladbach: Forum Verlag Godesberg.
PricewaterhouseCoopers (2011) *Cybercrime: Protecting Against the Growing Threat. Global Economic Crime Survey*, PricewaterhouseCoopers.
Punch, M. (1996) *Dirty Business. Exploring Corporate Misconduct: Analysis and Cases*, London, Thousand Oaks, New Delhi: Sage.
Reiss, A.J. Jr. and Biderman, A.D. (1980) *Data Sources on White-Collar Law-Breaking*, Washington, D.C.: U.S. Department of Justice.
Simpson, S.S. (2002) *Corporate Crime, Law, and Social Control*, Cambridge: Cambridge University Press.

Simpson, S.S. (2011) 'Making sense of white-collar crime: Theory and research', *Ohio State Journal of Criminal Law*, 8(2): 481–502.
Slapper, G. and Tombs, S. (1999) *Corporate Crime*, Harlow: Pearson Education.
Sutherland, E.H. (1949) *White Collar Crime*, New York: Holt.
Theile, H. (2010) 'Strafrechtliche Hypertrophie und ihre Folgen: Das Beispiel der verfahrenserledigenden Urteilsabsprachen in Wirtschaftsstrafverfahren', *Monatsschrift für Kriminologie und Strafrechtsreform*, 93(2): 147–163.
Thornberry, T.P. and Krohn, M.D. (2000) 'The self-report method for measuring delinquency and crime', in D. Duffee (ed.) *Measurement and Analysis of Crime and Justice*, Criminal Justice 2000, vol. IV, Washington, D.C.: National Institute of Justice.
Verhage, A. (2009) 'Corporations as a blind spot in research: Explanations for a criminological tunnel vision', in M. Cools, S. De Kimpe, B. De Ruyver, M. Easton, L. Pauwels, P. Ponsaers, T. Vander Beken, F. Vander Laenen, G. Vande Walle and G. Vermeulen (eds) *Contemporary Issues in the Empirical Study of Crime*, Governance of Security Research Paper Series, vol. I, Antwerpen, Apeldoorn: Maklu.
Weisburd, D., Wheeler, S., Waring, E. and Bode, N. (1991) *Crimes of the Middle Classes: White-Collar Offenders in the Federal Courts*, New Haven: Yale University Press.

3

Determining the adequate enforcement of white-collar and corporate crimes in Europe

Nicholas Lord and Michael Levi

Introduction

European nation-states face domestic, regional and international pressures to respond to *some* white-collar and corporate *crimes* and scandals. For example, (1) (inter)national, non-governmental organizations such as Transparency International (TI), Global Witness and Global Financial Integrity in addition to nation-state-specific campaign groups, (2) supra-national regional organizations such as the European Union (EU) and the Council of Europe (CoE) and (3) international intergovernmental organizations such as the United Nations (UN), Organisation for Economic Cooperation and Development (OECD) and the (officially informal) Financial Action Task Force (FATF) develop standards, rules and conventions that nation-states are morally and politically compelled to sign up to and implement in order to respond to those white-collar and corporate crimes that fall within their remit. Increasingly, to ensure that such agreements are not merely symbolic, they are accompanied by periodic evaluations (Halliday et al. 2014; Levi and Gilmore 2002).

These concerned parties often focus on *law* enforcement and other control mechanisms as appropriate policy responses which reflects the symbolic and moral nature of criminal justice in tackling national and transnational impunity. However, this creates tensions with national governments where there has traditionally been a preference for regulation (particularly self-regulation), persuasion, negotiation and non-criminal responses to white-collar and corporate offenders (Slapper and Tombs 1999; Lord 2014c; Nelken 2012; Wells 2011). Both self-regulation and the aversion to criminal prosecution combine ideology with pragmatism, given the huge per-case costs and evidential difficulties in high-profile transnational cases.

But how do we determine when particular sorts of enforcement or regulatory responses are sufficient and adequate, or how active responsible regulators are, both in the immediate case and taking all enforcement responses together? We can properly assess levels of state and non-state activity against crimes and their adequacy only in relation to levels and organization of crime and/or public bads (whether or not the latter can be evidenced as crimes). Existing methodologies for reviewing the latter are under-developed. In light of this, relative to what variables are levels of enforcement and (self-)regulation understood? How can we develop an appropriate 'threshold', against which levels of enforcement and (self-)regulation can be compared? If this is a serious problem at the national level, it is a far more difficult problem transnationally, where consistent data on both the levels of harms and enforcement practices are unobtainable.

This chapter explores these questions and discusses the implications of the difficulties of establishing *adequate enforcement* for methodological approaches to researching white-collar and corporate crimes throughout Europe and the subsequent implications for policing strategies. We begin by considering what is and ought to be understood by *adequate enforcement/ regulatory performance*, followed by a brief analysis of the need to understand extent and scope for performance measures to have value. Given the diversity of white-collar and corporate crimes, it would be over-ambitious in a work of this length to attempt to address all such crimes. Instead, in this chapter we explore these general themes in relation to two concrete issues: transnational corruption in the context of international commerce; and, more briefly, insider dealing. Here, we explore available data to inform extent and consider current performance measures, arguing that as we can only ever understand *some* level of the problem, current performance measures cannot provide valid indicators of levels of enforcement. Instead, research and policing strategies that aim to understand the organization and processes of white-collar and corporate crimes and the corresponding impact of intervention, disruption and prevention strategies provide a more useful indicator of *regulatory performance*. There is the further complication of fairness in the treatment of different sorts of crimes and social status offenders that makes this unbearably difficult, creating the sorts of tensions between retributive and restorative justice that first exercised the critiques by Braithwaite and collaborators in the 1980s and after. We do not claim to resolve these tensions here; rather we hope to illuminate the underlying problems more clearly.

Understanding 'enforcement/regulatory' performance

To determine 'adequate enforcement', we need to understand the available mixture of control responses. Competing (if often merely implicit) ideologies are significant given that in the area of white-collar and corporate crimes there have been conflicting approaches to the most appropriate model of criminal justice and law enforcement. For example, in the 1980s and 1990s we saw debates around the purported role of criminal prosecution as being a tool of last resort or a fundamental part of the enforcement response (Reiss 1984), and often characterised by the contrast between the *compliance* (Clarke 1990; Hawkins 1998) and *deterrence* (Pearce and Tombs 1998; Slapper and Tombs 1999) approaches. Such binary distinctions around whether to criminally prosecute or not were supplanted by innovative regulatory models based on responsive and reflexive regulators that could draw upon a mixture of enforcement responses when determining whether to punish or persuade (Ayres and Braithwaite 1992). The model remains of importance (see Grabosky 2013; Mascini 2013; Parker 2013) but critique does exist, in particular in relation to assumptions of graduated sanctioning models and their lack of credibility when prosecutions are so rare (Lord 2014c) and the relevance and robustness of the concept in relation to deregulation and neoliberalism (see Tombs and Whyte 2013).

Such thinking influenced current regulatory models where it has been argued that we have seen a shift from Old Governance (i.e. state-centric, centralized, bureaucratic expertise, mandatory rules) to New Governance (i.e. state orchestration, decentralized, dispersed expertise, soft law) (Abbot and Snidal 2009) and notions of the regulatory state (Moran 2001) or regulatory capitalism (though the state retains a primary role) (Braithwaite 2008). Such conceptions of regulation have also been developed at the trans-national level (see Abbott and Snidal 2013; Braithwaite and Drahos 2000; Djelic and Sahlin-Andersson 2006) where the roles of intergovernmental and nongovernmental organizations and their interactions with public and private actors become increasingly significant – in this sense, the assumption that the nation-state is the primary unit of analysis when determining the adequacy of enforcement responses might benefit from a re-think.

So policy responses to white-collar and corporate crimes in most European jurisdictions can be located within a spectrum of regulatory mechanisms. At one end of the spectrum, there are a variety of enforcement practices such as criminal prosecution, debarment, civil sanctioning, disruption/reduction/intervention strategies and licensing mechanisms where the state retains a primary role in both the strategic and operational response. But at the other end policy responses also incorporate various levels of self-regulation within business and industry. These include compliance mechanisms and industry/sector regulation that cover a wide range of institutional arrangements and can differ according to the degree of monopolistic power, the degree of formality, their legal status, and the extent to which outsiders participate in rule formulation and enforcement (see for example Ogus 1994: 108–109). The level of state intervention in such practices is often reduced, although such practices may be manufactured/stimulated by the state (e.g. as part of criminal/civil sanctioning or enforced self-regulation) or may be more organic in their creation (e.g. business initiatives, market responses embodying mutual self-interest). Such responses may be targeted at specific offenders or at the markets within which such offenders operate. Also, a variety of regulatory actors is evident that includes both state (e.g. law enforcement, industry regulators) and non-state (e.g. commercial enterprises, voluntary organizations, business communities) organizations and actors. Thus, 'the lines between regulatory and criminal procedures are becoming more tangled and blurred' and in the area of corporate crime, the 'enforcement of criminal law [...] increasingly uses classic regulatory techniques of negotiation and settlement' (Wells 2011: 15, 13), although increased political will, proactive inspectorial strategies and increased resources can enable prosecution (Slapper and Tombs 1999: 186; see also Almond 2013; Pearce and Tombs 1998; Tombs and Whyte 2007).

But if we take enforcement to include traditional policing responses, mechanisms of (enforced) self-regulation and the corresponding multiplicity of regulators, we need to understand the extent and impacts of all such practices, not to mention states or conditions of non-enforcement that may take the form of accommodation, collusion and/or regulatory capture where the state has no desire or ability to provide a formal response (for analysis of these concepts see Edwards and Gill 2002; Gill 2002). But even if an understanding of both enforcement and non-enforcement is obtained, understanding regulatory performance, as above, is part ideological. In the absence of clear evidence for most white-collar offences about what works under what circumstances, it is difficult to adjudicate between preferences for enforcement and regulation, just as there remain tensions between equal punishment for all and a purer effectiveness with minimal punishment perspective.

With this in mind, there is a clear problem with current attempts to understand adequate regulatory performance, as crude indicators of levels of enforcement (in its narrow sense) such as prosecution numbers (see below) are often used to determine how active any given jurisdiction may be in dealing with these problems. An intended or unintended consequence of this is to neglect the performance of broader regulatory practices of negotiation, compliance and self-regulation. If we accept we need to understand performance in relation to this broader notion of regulation, a second problem arises in the realization that determining how adequate and effective such enforcement and self-regulation practices are requires an understanding of the extent and scope of the problem. In short, effective at what, and against which numerator?

Understanding the *extent* and *scope* of white-collar and corporate crimes

> Reports that say that something hasn't happened are always interesting to me, because as we know, there are 'known knowns'; there are things we know we know. We also know there are 'known unknowns'; that is to say we know there are some things we do not know. But there are also 'unknown unknowns' – the ones we don't know we don't know.
>
> *(Donald Rumsfeld, former US Defence Secretary, 2002*[1]*)*

When Donald Rumsfeld spoke of 'known knowns', 'known unknowns' and 'unknown unknowns' in relation to weapons of mass destruction in 2002, he took a phrase from business vocabulary to distinguish between things we know that we know, things we know we do not know, but can anticipate their existence, and things we do not know that we do not know, and therefore cannot anticipate their existence. While these phrases may have several indirect and direct meanings and therefore can be used for rhetorical purposes (e.g. to refute accountability), they do point to a significant criminological limitation – the *dark figure* of crime – that is of significant relevance in relation to white-collar and corporate crimes. There are two components of the dark figure. The first comprises acts that if we knew about them we would unhesitatingly classify as crimes; the second comprises acts that we (and/or lawyers) might argue about whether they were crimes at all and who if anyone was legally culpable for them.

The extent and scope of white-collar and corporate crimes remain difficult to estimate for the following reasons: (1) the complexities of ascertaining who if anyone is *legally* responsible for the conduct; (2) the relative invisibility of white-collar and corporate crimes, the range of actors, their relations and transactions (i.e. insufficient knowledge, statistics, theory, research, control, politics and panic (see Davies et al. 1999: 5–23; Davies et al. 2014, for more extensive analysis of the characteristics of invisible crimes); (3) the lack of identifiable consequences and the long-tailed impact of some of them (e.g. direct victims or harms often obscured); and (4) the knowledge and power problems faced by the state in attempts to understand corporate subsystems (see Mayntz 1993). A more detailed analysis of how we might measure the extent and scope of white-collar crimes is provided elsewhere in this handbook. Generally, however, attempts have been made to infer extent and scope from diverse data sources such as official statistics (limited to enforcement responses), perception studies, victim surveys (individuals and organizational), self-report studies and, where accessible, private-sector data (Levi 2011). These are explored in relation to the two case studies of transnational corruption and insider dealing.

Case study 1: transnational corporate corruption

The EU's Anti-Corruption Report 2014 indicated that while corruption 'varies in nature and extent from one country to another, [...] it affects all Member States', and in doing so 'impinges on good governance, sound management of public money, and competitive markets' (European Commission 2014: 2). According to the report, 76 per cent of Europeans think that corruption (in general terms) is widespread in their country. In terms of business, 81 per cent of Europeans think that too-close links between business and politics in their country lead to corruption and 67 per cent that corruption is part of the business culture in their country, while 75 per cent of European companies say that corruption is widespread in their country and 43 per cent see corruption as a problem when doing business. (The report did not analyse the nature or extent of corruption within EU institutions themselves.) One particular example of the relationship between corruption and business is that of European corporations using bribery (both monetary, e.g. commissions, kickbacks, and non-monetary, e.g. gifts, hospitalities, favours) in international commerce to win or maintain contracts and interests in foreign (European and non-European) jurisdictions. Huge cases involving Siemens in Germany and BAE Systems in the UK provide recent examples. But accepting that there might be judgements based on morality and symbolism as much as more administrative concepts of rationality, how might we go about measuring the extent and scope of this problem in order to determine the adequacy of enforcement responses by European states?

In the TI *Global Corruption Report 2007*, Kaufmann et al. (2007) identified six myths in relation to corruption measurement. Myth one, 'corruption cannot be measured', is from the authors' perspective not the reality. They suggest corruption can be measured (1) by gathering informed views of relevant stakeholders (e.g. firms, public officials, NGOs, experts, etc.), (2) by tracking countries' institutional features (e.g. to determine opportunities of incentives for corruption and therefore provide useful indications of the possibility of corruption), and (3) by careful audits of specific projects (e.g. financial audits and comparisons of spending with the physical output of projects in order to provide project-specific corruption). Myths two and three relate to the vague, generic and unreliable subjective data that is obtained from perception studies. The authors argue that perceptions of corruption are sometimes the best and only information available, suggesting that perceptions matter directly in that they influence individuals' behaviour towards institutions, etc. This may be the case but it does not inform an understanding of measurement or extent. Kaufmann et al. also suggest specific survey questions that enable more specific and focused findings (although such questions remain distanced from the social context); and that any kind of data measurement involves an irreducible element of uncertainty. Myths four and five suggest that though the nature of corruption makes it virtually impossible to satisfy policymakers' desires for objective measures, specific, focused surveys can aid in identifying priority areas for action. Myth six, the notion that countries perceived to have high levels of corruption also have fast economic growth, is also challenged by the authors who argue that in the medium to long term adverse effects can be seen. In short, available empirical data is weak, and no strategy will yield a perfect measure of corruption.

Where collected by the state, data may also be inaccessible, although recording practices vary by jurisdiction. In the UK, for example, the Serious Fraud Office (SFO) maintains an anti-corruption register of all suspicions, allegations and cases of corporate corruption, but these figures are private, although other enforcement agencies are granted access. SFO data are available only in its annual reports and prosecutions are included in Ministry of Justice statistics, but not in recorded crime data. Likewise, neither general victimization and self-report studies (e.g. Crime Survey for England and Wales) nor business victimization surveys (Home Office 2012) have ever included crimes by corporations against consumers, workers or taxpayers in the UK or elsewhere.

Beyond official statistics, attempts to measure corruption have been made in numerous ways – some focus on the number of corrupt transactions that take place in a country, others analyse the amount of money that changes hands as part of corrupt transactions (Bardhan 2006: 342). Theoretical models have measured corruption as a percentage of government officials that are willing to accept a bribe (Çule and Fulton 2005) and by the size of the bribe (Cadot 1987; Choi and Thum 2005). Other methodologies include the use of public expenditure tracking surveys, service provider surveys and enterprise surveys to collect quantitative micro-level data (Reinikka and Svensson 2006). In addition, there have been approaches involving axiomatic measurements that entail formal definition of potentially important properties of a measure and then classification of measures according to such properties (Foster et al. 2009) and approaches involving corruption-victimization measures based on survey research (Seligson 2006). International organizations, such as the World Bank and the World Economic Forum, have conducted large-scale surveys, but the main source of data more broadly comes from studies of perception, such as TI's Corruption Perceptions Index and Bribe Payers Index, but such studies are methodologically limited by their focus on perceptions only. The key question is whether the trend data produced provides valid indicators of corruption, even if numbers might not be accurate. In this sense, some measures may be more convincing than others, e.g. self-report surveys and victimization studies may offer more reliable data than perception studies, while the collation of empirical datasets may increase understanding of levels of transnational corruption.

How do we determine the adequate enforcement of transnational corruption?

The limitations in measuring and understanding the extent and scope of corruption – especially transnational corruption – raise the question as to how an appropriate threshold, against which enforcement and self-regulatory efforts can be compared, can ever be determined. Given this flaw, against which variables should adequate enforcement be measured and more specifically, can adequate enforcement ever be determined?

Current approaches to determining adequacy

According to TI's 2013 progress report on the enforcement of the OECD Anti-Bribery Convention 1997, only three European countries (Germany, the UK, Switzerland) are considered to be active enforcers. The remaining European countries included in the report are located within the categories of 'moderate', 'limited' or 'little or no' enforcement. Levels of enforcement are assessed using arbitrary thresholds that aim to consider a combination of the share of world exports of a country along with the number of investigations, cases and sanctions for foreign bribery in the most recent four-year period. For example, thresholds for enforcement are based on a country's actual percentage of world exports together with a points system that weights different enforcement actions: 1 point for commencing investigations (pre-trial phase), 2 points for commencing cases (trial phase of a legal procedure), 4 points each for commencing major cases or concluding cases with sanctions, and 10 points for concluding major cases with substantial sanctions. (It is unclear on what basis these points thresholds have been allocated.)

Substantial is defined by TI as sanctions that include 'deterring prison sentences, large fines, appointment of a compliance monitor, and/or disqualification from future business'. In previous reports TI failed to define what was meant by substantial and in this instance defines it ambiguously. For example, there is no clarification of what length or form of prison sentence begins to act as a deterrent (should suspended sentences be included?), or whether 'large fines' are considered in relation to an individual's or company's overall turnover and profits, or whether a monitor ought to be appointed by the enforcement authorities rather than the corporation – these are key issues. The blanket application to multiple jurisdictions of this methodology also fails to consider local contexts, e.g. understanding in which jurisdictions corporations conduct their foreign business and in which sectors are they involved is necessary for meaningful comparison. In the report, the three active European enforcers, Germany, the UK, and Switzerland, required scores of 344, 152 and 63 to be categorized as 'active' and scored 464, 251 and 93 respectively, in addition to meeting the requirement of commencing or concluding at least one major case in the last four-year period. In contrast, the only other 'active enforcer' globally was the US which received a score of 1117 to easily reach its target of 407. The general trend appears to be that the larger the share of world exports, the more 'active' a country is at enforcing the OECD Convention, though the most active European states remain substantially behind the US. However, this superficial methodology reinforces the need to understand enforcement responses in the context of the proportion of all bribery cases, otherwise such analyses are meaningless beyond raising awareness of corruption and bribery.

In previous reports, the methodology employed by TI used cumulative raw numbers (e.g. number of prosecutions, investigations and cases since the OECD Convention came into force) combined with a country's share of world exports. The use of raw numbers rather than the proportion of estimated cases dealt with again presented problems for understanding levels of enforcement as well as for comparative understandings between jurisdictions. In TI's 2012 report, 'active enforcers' referred to those countries with a share of world exports over 2 per cent and with at least ten major cases on a cumulative basis, at least three of which were initiated in the last three years and resulted in 'substantial sanctions' (see above). The category 'active enforcer' could also be given to those countries with less than 2 per cent world export shares but these countries had to have brought at least three major cases, at least one of which resulted in substantial sanctions and at least one case pending that was initiated in the last three years. Again, these thresholds were arbitrary and were not premised on any logical foundation (e.g. it is unclear why the threshold was ten major cases – it is possible that this was set as a number that allows a 'reasonable number' of countries to meet the target). Under this methodology, seven countries, the US plus Germany, the UK, Italy, Switzerland, Norway and Denmark, were identified as 'active' enforcers.

In both approaches, enforcement is considered more active and acceptable once a certain number of investigations and prosecutions are being regularly concluded or when prosecution numbers satisfy the informed perspectives of those moral entrepreneurs that played such a significant role in the generation of rules. But how such measures reflect a reduction in prosecution numbers due to effective prevention strategies through, for example, corporate compliance and/or situational measures that remove the opportunities for corruption is uncertain. Prosecution numbers without an understanding of proportion are an insufficient measure of enforcement/regulatory performance.

Although the TI statistics incorporate economic variables such as share of world exports as comparison points, meaningful comparisons cannot be made, given the lack of recognition they give to other key variables, not to mention the social context of regulation and bribery. For example, against what denominator are these enforcement statistics being measured for them to represent active enforcement? While world export shares may be used as markers for the categorization of these jurisdictions within 'active enforcement', this gives a false picture of active enforcement in terms of the broader regulatory landscape, e.g. prevention, disruption and reduction strategies, and therefore may fail to explain how local regulatory regimes and cultures might better explain these (apparent) differences.

For example, European jurisdictions are culturally diverse and represent geo-historical contexts that have developed over time – such diversity represents a distinctive opportunity for cross-European research in this area. Different legal cultures (e.g. adversarial/inquisitorial, opportunity/legality principles), different policy responses (e.g. criminal justice – social justice – risk management – restorative justice) and different political-economic priorities and imperatives (e.g. social/corporate welfare) are fundamental to understanding levels of corruption. However, the same jurisdictions face similar obstacles – the particular nature of transnational corruption (e.g. organized across jurisdictions; clandestine; few direct victims; consensual between transacting parties), as characterized by the necessary and contingent relations and processes of foreign bribery, is common across European jurisdictions. Additionally, normative and legal constructions of the problem are now shared following the harmonization of international standards at the domestic level (see Lord 2014a). In the light of these issues, it is unreasonable to consider that superficial indicators such as prosecution and investigation numbers provide sufficient comparison points.

This can be seen when considering the enforcement numbers of the US with those of Germany and the UK, as above. The legal framework for responding to foreign bribery in the US was enacted in 1977 (Foreign Corrupt Practices Act). However, it was only in 2001 in the UK (following the inclusion of a foreign element to domestic corruption laws in the Anti-Terrorism Crime and Security Act 2001) and in 1998 in Germany (following the enactment of the Act on Combating Bribery of Foreign Public Officials in International Business Transactions) that appropriate legal frameworks were created. This has procedural impacts given the US now has a well-developed structure for entering into deferred prosecution agreements with corporations (the primary enforcement tool for foreign bribery in the US) while similar provisions were only introduced in the UK in 2014 and while Germany continues to have no formal corporate criminal liability – corporations can only be sanctioned through administrative law. Thus, comparing such jurisdictions at different stages of development is problematic.

Furthermore, hypothetically it may be the case that a jurisdiction, such as Germany, has high levels of undetected corruption but retains the 'active enforcer' category for prosecuting a small percentage of this corruption; while other jurisdictions such as Finland or Sweden have lower perceived levels of corruption than Germany but may be prosecuting a higher proportion of these – the percentage of all corruption offences being prosecuted is currently unknowable in any country. Likewise, the Netherlands are considered to have 'little or no enforcement' but, according to TI's Bribe Payers Index 2011, corporations from the Netherlands are least likely to bribe abroad. This may reflect a more effective set of self-regulatory mechanisms but receives no recognition in enforcement rates. Neither do the statistics distinguish between different cases as can be seen with the Siemens case which accounts for over 20 of the prosecutions in Germany, which distorts the picture. International studies such as TI's Bribe Payers Index and Corruption Perceptions Index inform understandings of the extent of transnational bribery, perhaps more so than estimations of the problem by enforcement authorities (whose estimations are based on those cases that come to their attention). In addition, other variables such as the number of companies registered; the size of the corporation and its importance in the economy; the type of products traded; the Gross Domestic Product; and the available enforcement resources along with many significant legal, procedural, evidential and financial processes are not acknowledged. These variables would provide different measures against which prosecution numbers could be considered. Thus, 'active enforcement' in current terms does not necessarily reflect effective anti-corruption systems or measures, and does not inform any understanding of the extent of the corruption problem.

Potential data sources

An understanding of extent requires the collation and analysis of multiple data sources. Such data sources do exist to some extent and emanate from the private, public and third sectors and are located at the local, national and supranational level (see Table 3.1). In this sense, such sources provide proxies for the missing data outlined above and provide data on both traditional enforcement mechanisms of state investigation and prosecution but also mechanisms of a self-regulatory nature.

To determine 'adequate' or 'active' enforcement, consideration needs to be given to the variety of enforcement *and* self-regulatory mechanisms, along with aspects of repression *and* prevention/reduction. Determining an appropriate 'threshold' against which enforcement and self-regulatory mechanisms should be compared is problematic for a number of the reasons outlined above. However, a useful place to start would be within the social contexts where such bribery and corruption occur and where the necessary and contingent relations of corporate bribery can be fully explored and understood. For example, in addition to the methodologies outlined above (e.g. victim surveys and self-report studies, etc.), data collected by and on corporations' anti-bribery

Table 3.1 Potential data sources at the micro, meso and macro levels

Level	*Key organizations*	*Data*
Micro	Individual corporations and business enterprises operating transnationally	Data on contextual factors such as how often bribes are requested from corporations and in which areas (geographical and business), etc. (see points 1–6 below)
	Media outlets	Accounts of investigative journalism as developed through sustained and focused investigations Exposés on multi-national corporations, e.g. the *Guardian* and BAE Systems
	Activist groups	Case construction and analysis to support lobbying and moral entrepreneurship Exposés
Meso	Industry and trade associations of transnational sectors and markets	Industry/trade data generated through member surveys and monitoring of financial transactions and market performance
	Whistleblowing organizations external to corporations	Data on reported cases from multiple sectors/ industries, internal/external reporting and responses and outcomes
Macro	National/regional-level enforcement and regulatory agencies	Data collated on number of cases detected (via myriad sources), on number of cases investigated (or not) and of number of cases concluded (whether (non-)prosecution or closure)
	International organizations, e.g. NGOs such as TI	Large-scale survey data based on self-report studies, victimization surveys and studies of perceptions, etc.
	Intergovernmental organizations, e.g. OECD, UN	Country monitoring to establish enforcement activity whereby investigation and prosecution numbers are collated for jurisdictions
	Transnational business initiatives, e.g. World Economic Forum	Market/sector data generated through disclosure of financial transactions by member corporations and data collected through member surveys

Source: Table 3.1 reprinted by permission of the Publishers from 'Understanding "regulatory" performance and determining "adequate" enforcement', in *Regulating Corporate Bribery in International Business* by Nicholas Lord (Farnham: Ashgate, 2014), pp. 163–178. Copyright © 2014

and corruption compliance departments with regard to the following processes would aid understandings of the impacts of self-regulatory mechanisms:

1 The number of corporations implementing 'certified' anti-bribery and corruption compliance systems and the extent to which these are regularly monitored and adapted, e.g. as compelled by formal or informal self-regulatory mechanisms.
2 The frequency (e.g. how often are bribe requests made to the company), intensity (e.g. how insistent are bribe requests), intention (e.g. facilitation of otherwise legitimate service, to win or maintain business contracts, to be accepted in the tendering process, etc.) and type (e.g. cash bribes, services, hospitality, etc.) of bribery and the extent to which these factors change over time and correlate to different localities.
3 The risk assessments of foreign jurisdictions that are conducted by corporations or third-party experts (e.g. how is the risk of corruption determined?), and the extent to which these risk assessments change over time and why, e.g. have corporate compliance mechanisms reduced bribe frequency in country A and in what ways?

4 The identification and recruitment of potential bribers within the corporation by external solicitors/demanders of bribes, e.g. at which organizational level are employees approached (e.g. executives, middle managers, low-level employees), do these represent particularly 'at risk' positions (e.g. high contact with foreign officials, independent positions, etc.), are certain corporate departments consistently approached (e.g. telecommunications, construction, etc.)?
5 Public disclosure and increased transparency of payments made to foreign public officials and governments for public contracts (in line with the Publish What You Pay (PWYP) initiative in the extractive industries: http://www.publishwhatyoupay.org/ (accessed 7 July 2014)).
6 Public disclosure of country-by-country reporting of financial performance broken down into production, profits, sales and costs to enable transparency of contracts and transactions and discrepancies to be identified.

These processes represent only some of those involved in bribery but an understanding of these would inform an understanding of transnational corporate bribery and more specifically, an understanding of effective prevention and control. The impact of corporations' compliance mechanisms on the regulation of transnational corporate bribery could therefore be measured over time. For example, to what extent are companies operating in high-risk country A receiving fewer bribe demands/requests over time, and how has this been influenced by company policies? Of course, such an approach assumes both that the majority of corporations are good, ethical organizations willing to collect such data accurately and honestly. (There may be many legitimate reasons why they would not wish to, e.g. too much transparency on their legitimate business transactions that may influence competition and the market.) It also focuses only on the demand side of bribery, or passive bribery. Those corporations actively committing bribery would unlikely be reached without some form of mandatory, regulatory intervention (albeit compulsory self-reporting is arguably a violation of the privilege against self-incrimination). If corporations can be encouraged or compelled to collect such data, an understanding of the impacts of self-regulatory mechanisms on bribery reduction could be explored (although gaining access to this data without formal regulatory coercion would prove difficult). Thus, the problem of transnational corporate bribery could be made more tangible through methodological innovations in researching the organization of serious crimes such as corporate victim surveys; but also by altering the research question to ask how known incidents of bribery were organized and what such 'known knowns' do for criminological understanding. The latter would assist corporations' own efforts as well as criminological thinking.

As things stand, however, how 'adequate' or 'active' enforcement may be cannot be determined without some inference about the volume of crime from victim surveys and self-report studies along with official records and other sources of data (e.g. corporations). Given the difficulties of detection and accessing corporate subsystems, while the above proposal may begin to bridge this gap, this knowledge is currently not available, nor is it plausible that it would be in the near future. This in addition to the less tangible nature of transnational corruption reinforces the location of transnational corporate bribery amongst the 'known unknowns'.

Moving beyond estimations of extent and scope towards understanding 'organization'

Two problems are evident. First, determining adequate levels of enforcement only makes sense in relation to accurate judgements about extent and scope but this latter endeavour is methodologically idealistic. Second, the only attempt to address adequate enforcement across Europe comes in the form of the above comparison of prosecution numbers by TI. However, these adopt a narrow view of enforcement that is limited to the investigation, prosecution and sanctioning of transnational corruption – this gives us no insight into those enforcement practices characterized by prevention and self-regulation and which incorporate the widely accepted role of non-state actors and organizations.

With this in mind, in addition to developing estimations of the incidence, prevalence and concentration of transnational bribery and corruption, the analytical focus could be shifted onto the *modus operandi* of *how* transnational bribery and corruption is organized (see Edwards and Levi 2008). For example, white-collar crime reduction has been analysed through an opportunity perspective approach, the tools of which are predominantly situational crime prevention, routine activities theory and crime pattern theory (see Benson and Simpson 2009; Benson et al. 2009). Based on the *crime triangle* (i.e. motivated offender, opportunity and capable guardians), the propensity to commit offences is assumed and analytical focus is placed on opportunity structures. By identifying the features of the immediate situations within which white-collar crimes take place and the processes involved, it is possible to intervene and reduce (or perhaps displace) such crimes. Understanding the technical dimensions of corporate bribery is clearly important for enforcement authorities. However, such approaches must be supplemented with an understanding of the social dimensions (i.e. the necessary and contingent relations (see Edwards and Hughes 2005) of corporate bribery and the nature of these relations in different geo-historical contexts).

In other words, it is important to understand the processes, relations and routine activities of white-collar and corporate crimes in the context of political, cultural and economic structures (see Levi 2008). For example, analysis of the necessary involvement of particular actors (e.g. executives, corporations) in particular economic sectors (e.g. construction, finance, defence, etc.) and in contingent legal or cultural contexts (e.g. UK, Germany) informs an understanding of why such crimes are organized in specific societies. Understanding the organization of transnational corruption over time and in different places informs enforcement practices of intervention – to render social problems such as transnational corruption sufficiently 'tangible', there must be some 'known knowns' from which the impact of self-regulatory and non-repressive mechanisms can be understood. Additionally, analysing context informs an understanding of the impact of mechanisms designed to respond to or reduce corrupt activities. For example, in an enforcement culture of non-prosecution and negotiated civil sanctioning, the ripple effect of one or two notable criminal prosecutions is likely to have a greater impact within business and the market in terms of shifts towards improved compliance and internal oversight. To understand context and the social processes, relations and practices of transnational corruption then, research might aim to understand the following issues (adapted from Lord (2014c), drawing on Levi's (2007: 781) process model of transnational serious crimes):

Table 3.2 Necessary and contingent relations of transnational corporate bribery

Necessary	• How are the finances for bribes obtained? For example, how do legitimate corporations channel funds for the creation of slush funds and what are the concealment practices involved (e.g. use of front companies; fake conferences to generate funds; inflated prices)? • How are bribe payers and receivers recruited (e.g. internal/external, domestic/foreign to the corporation) and how do they develop the expertise/technical ability to develop bribery schemes? Which criteria identify potential intermediaries and bribe receivers (e.g. politicians, state officials)? • Which corporate mechanisms and tools are utilized and necessary to be able to bribe (e.g. bank accounts in difficult-to-reach jurisdictions)? How are the proceeds of bribes concealed and converted (i.e. money laundering) from the various domestic and foreign authorities (e.g. law enforcement, tax authorities) and what are the particular legal/structural contexts that enable this?

	• Which external and internal actors are required to be complicit for bribery to remain undetected and how are these relations developed over time (e.g. external accountants, high-level management)? • How might bribe givers neutralize law enforcement responses and/or 'capable guardians'?
Contingent	• Which jurisdictions, which industries/sectors (e.g. construction, pharmaceutical, manufacturing) and which corporate employees (e.g. sales agents, middle-level managers) are at highest risk of bribery and how can this risk be located within specific geo-historical contexts? • Which antecedent factors exist to facilitate corruption in the offending contexts? E.g. organizational cultures, levels of transparency and accountability, etc. • To what extent do macro social, economic and political structures shape local commerce and thus the contexts within which bribe givers and receivers can operate?

Source: Table 3.2 reprinted by permission of the Publishers from 'Understanding "regulatory" performance and determining "adequate" enforcement', in *Regulating Corporate Bribery in International Business* by Nicholas Lord (Farnham: Ashgate, 2014), pp. 163–178. Copyright © 2014

Understanding the necessary and contingent relations of bribery enables key vulnerabilities in the above processes to be determined for strategic interventions, even if it may not be possible in the short term politically to close off those loopholes. Law enforcement agencies, however, are under pressure to produce results, usually in the form of prosecutions, in order to ensure they maintain their existence and function. Shifts towards prevention and disruption reduce the number of measureable results but may also contradict statutory remits.

A variety of methodologies and data sources would be useful for understanding these issues. For example, primary data may be generated through script analysis of those cases that come to the attention of the authorities, victimization surveys, self-report studies, perceptions studies, interviews with offenders while secondary data collected by corporations, enforcement agencies, business and sector-specific trade associations and bodies, international organizations and development banks as well as court records and police notification schemes could also inform understandings of the bribery problem.

Understanding the non-enforcement of transnational corruption

There is an assumption that if we can understand the abovementioned enforcement and self-regulatory practices in relation to the organization of transnational corruption and white-collar and corporate crimes, then regulatory performance can be determined. In reality, this will not be enough as non-enforcement may emerge. In the case of transnational corruption, even where the will to enforce the law is high and where political support may be evident, the particular nature of transnational corporate bribery can render criminal enforcement implausible while the impact of emerging self-regulatory practices is currently unknown (Lord 2014c). It might seem sensible to think of current enforcement numbers provided by international and intergovernmental organizations in proportion to the corruption problem within and caused by businesses from each jurisdiction: but given our inadequate appreciation of these, it is hard to work out how we might justify the proportionality of these sanctioning efforts. Prosecution numbers may reflect all corrupt activity but this is unlikely, due to legal, evidential, procedural, structural and financial limitations of law enforcement (Lord 2014a). More likely is that much corporate bribery currently goes undetected and is therefore unknown. What is more, of the bribery that is known, limitations in enforcement create difficulties for the criminal prosecution of such crime, highlighting accommodation of the problem by prosecutorial agencies and departments as the default position (Lord 2013, 2014c).

In the UK, for example, the SFO's acceptance criteria make clear that only large, complex cases will be investigated, meaning smaller corruption cases may be accommodated – formal and informal discretion is applied throughout detection and investigation in the (de)prioritization of cases (Lord 2014b). The same can be said of facilitation payments, which although prohibited in UK law, are unlikely to be investigated. Similar accommodation exists in other European jurisdictions, such as Germany, where unevenly distributed funding and expertise results in some *Bundesländer* being less enthusiastic than others in relation to bribery enforcement. Consequently, regulatory agencies, restricted by their powers of enforcement, accommodate a certain level of transnational corruption either through their inability to do otherwise or their conscious or unconscious decisions to prioritize or focus on other issues.

Accommodation occurs not only due to practical limitations but also in respect of political and economic ideologies. The BAE Systems case that involved a government-to-government arms contract between the UK and Saudi Arabia but enlisted BAE Systems as the arms producer and provider in this deal is a prime example of this. In 1985, the UK and Saudi Arabian governments signed the contract for the initial al-Yamamah I arms deal (al-Yamamah II followed in 1988) where it was agreed that the UK would provide 72 Tornado and 30 Hawk aircraft, amongst other defence equipment, in return for oil (up to 600,000 barrels a day) – BAE was appointed to be the prime contractor to deliver the deal and it is estimated to have been worth around 43 billion pounds. However, to facilitate the deal, BAE was alleged to have paid more than 6 billion pounds in bribes and inducements. A Serious Fraud Office (SFO) investigation into the alleged bribery was halted in 2006 following government pressure where the UK Prime Minister at the time, Tony Blair, alluded to national security fears. It was asserted that Saudi Arabia had threatened to withdraw counter-terrorism assistance and intelligence should the investigation continue. Economic interests were also endangered as Saudi Arabia threatened to withdraw from a 10 billion pound deal to buy Eurofighter Typhoons. However, this was an impermissible rationale, since halting an investigation for economic reasons would contravene international conventions – however, governments understand the importance of large corporations to a country's economic and national security interests that are shaped by transnational business agreements (e.g. UK–Saudi Arabia). Simultaneously, however, they must manage criticism from moral entrepreneurs and from international performance evaluations which appears only possible through increasing enforcement successes.

Antecedent influences to non-enforcement are the risk of regulatory capture and the revolving door phenomenon. Where the relationship between the regulator and the regulated becomes too intertwined due to shared ideologies and/or personnel, rewards and/or threats, the regulator may be captured and subsequently ensure non-enforcement. Where the movement of key actors from the public to the private sector, or vice versa, is frequent, conflicts of interest may also emerge which can result in attempts at regulation being undermined. However, accommodation, even where the will to enforce the law is high, may be a significant part of all control responses. In this case, it is more important to understand how resources are allocated and how intelligence is used (e.g. prioritization and disruption) to address certain aspects of any given form of criminality.

Case study 2: insider dealing

Whereas the victim status of corruption, especially transnational bribery, is now culturally assured – at least to the extent that few dare to defend publicly on more than a purely pragmatic basis the giving and acceptance of bribes – this is not true for all white-collar crimes. Insider dealing is a particularly intriguing example since symbolically, profiting from trading on inside non-public information strikes at the heart of the claim that capitalist markets are free and honest. Yet it has no obvious victims, nor is it clear what impact the misconduct itself (or even its exposure) has on investor behaviour or sentiment, at least below the level that everyone assumes that many prices are fixed. An insider dealer who buys shares offers people already in the market to sell at a perhaps higher price than they would have obtained otherwise; though one who sells on the basis of inside information may depress the market slightly for other sellers, which benefits buyers. This is to be distinguished from the real harms caused by boiler rooms scams, market manipulation of share values by false information and/or undisclosed rings of conspirators; and the selling off of state companies using valuations that insiders know to be false, common in the former Soviet bloc in transition to capitalism, but also elsewhere under neoliberal pressures to privatize public assets.

There has been ongoing controversy as to whether criminal or civil measures are the most effective method of reducing insider dealing (Rider 2000; Rider et al. 2009) but as in the corruption case, there are symbolic issues also. In some elite cases, since the mid-1980s, American and to a far lesser extent British prosecutors have sometimes adapted the strategy used in organized crime cases of rolling up white-collar offending networks via plea bargaining: this saw its apotheosis to date in the Michael Milken, Dennis Levine, Martin Siegel and Ivan Boesky insider trading web of the mid–late 1980s, and the US Galleon insider trading case in 2012. These cases offer absorbing examples of how insider dealing is accomplished (see Raghavan 2013 for an absorbing cultural account). But this enforcement strategy applies only where (1) there are such networks of offenders, rather than individuals and small groups acting alone to defraud, and (2) expected probability of conviction and expected sentences are high enough to incentivize betrayal rather than loyalty/self-interest in silence. It is assumed that respectable offenders will fear prison more than organized criminals would, and therefore will need a lower threshold to inform against others.

The direct results of this model are visible. In the Galleon insider dealing case, Raj Rajaratnam, CEO of Galleon, was sentenced to 11 years (plus 156 million dollars in financial penalties); though this was 100 months below the minimum in the sentencing guidelines for an offence of this gravity. Despite support from Bill Gates, Kofi Annan and others for his charitable work carried out prior to the criminal investigation, former Goldman Sachs partner and McKinsey's director Rajat Gupta was jailed for two years for leaking confidential information to Rajaratnam. Under Manhattan US attorney Preet Bharara, 13 out of 72 persons charged with insider dealing cooperated with the government, all but one of whom got probation. Since 2010, the 26 insider-trading defendants who did not cooperate with prosecutors have received an average sentence of two years and ten months: a third under their average federal guideline range (Rothfeld and Strumpf 2012), but significantly (to them) longer than what they would have got had they cooperated. In the UK, sentences have been much smaller, but from zero prosecutions before 2008, the Financial Services (now Conduct) Authority has obtained 23 convictions to May 2013. These cases involved illicit profits totalling less than 9 million dollars, according to a *Wall Street Journal* analysis of public disclosures. Five people charged with insider trading have been acquitted, and seven others were awaiting trial at the beginning of 2014, at which point the Financial Conduct Authority had 480 staff in its intelligence and financial crime section. By not entirely equivalent comparison, the US Securities and Exchange Commission had filed more than 50 insider-trading civil cases in each of the past three years. One recent hedge-fund case featured hundreds of millions of dollars of alleged illicit profits and avoided losses: see Enrich and Agnew (2014).

There are several effects about which one might hypothesize. One relates to deterrence (see generally, Nagin 2013): little is known about what traders and directors know about the law, but it seems reasonable to assert that they are vaguely aware of what is prohibited. However, where enforcement is at or close to zero, both rational choice theorists and neo-Durkheimians looking for evidence that this is viewed as a serious wrong might see little reason to obey the law. When they hear/read about high status and lowly persons prosecuted (and perhaps jailed), however, the risks become more salient. The question then is how much or little prosecutions create this effect, and for how long it persists? This is linked to broader issues of how we can measure credible deterrence among elites. The other approach relates to measures of market cleanliness, which provides insights into the general level of insider trading in markets (Monteiro et al. 2007; Del Guercio et al. 2013). This looks at how many pre-announcement spikes in trading there are, which picks up egregious or heavily networked examples of insider trading, which can be used to guide more detailed investigations into who bought and sold these shares, and whether or not they are (and can be proven to be) linked to insiders as defined variously in national legislation. Developments in software do this relatively more easily today than in earlier times. In some cases, despite anti-money laundering legislation requiring the identification of beneficial owners, it may be too hard to penetrate who controls accounts and to link the perpetrators to insiders: but shareholdings and funds can be frozen depending on the powers available, even without being able to prove a case against anyone. However, given the relatively low actual compared with symbolic harm involved, there is room for argument about how much enforcement against insider dealing is adequate, and how resources should be allocated to this relative to other harmful features of financial crime. This can be intermingled with issues of agency mission and legal mandate: many more harmful financial crimes lie outside the FCA's powers, and it cannot transfer its funds (which come from levies on the financial sector) to police and prosecute them. So we should not see these individual issues in isolation: looking at the adequacy of enforcement across the board – difficult though it is – may hide issues of 'who pays for what' that can be central to the operational component of the analytical task.

Concluding thoughts

White-collar and corporate crimes are not a homogeneous group and vary significantly in terms of their nature and organisation, their intent and purpose, and the harms that they cause. This chapter has used the examples of transnational corporate corruption and insider dealing to instigate a debate over how we might go about determining how adequate white-collar/corporate crime enforcement is, or how active responsible regulatory and enforcement agencies are. The key issue to recognize is that adequacy is dependent upon what we know or could plausibly know about levels of offending behaviour: without a valid indication of the levels and organization of such crimes or public bads, our understanding of the relative impact of enforcement is partial and subjective. Various sources produce data on narrow indices such as prosecution or investigation numbers but without contextual understanding of how important these cases are or without 'good enough' measurement of the scale of the offending, these data are rendered largely meaningless. This is a problem at the national and even more so at the transnational level where available data on enforcement practices and harms are difficult to obtain.

To address this problem, we outlined data sources that have the potential to fill the gaps and provide more valid understandings of prevalence, extent and scope. Collating and analysing data emanating from public, private and third-sector sources across local, national and supranational levels provides proxies for these missing data. But better informing our quantitative understandings of the extent of the problem has much more meaning when supplemented by qualitative understandings of how such crimes are organized domestically and transnationally. Once we know more about the size and distribution of the criminal markets, a major challenge remains in linking different models of enforcement to changes in those actual as well as formal enforcement changes. We see no reason to suppose that 'what works' is independent of cultural context and expectations, including but not restricted to the independence of regulators, prosecutors and the courts. It seems plausible that where compliance is linked to expectations of how others are complying, more can be achieved with a lighter nudge than where offending is or is believed to be commonplace.

In the light of this, the key argument is that understandings of the *organization* of white-collar and corporate crimes offer an alternative means by which enforcement levels can be measured and policing strategies informed. To this end, we identified some key questions to explore the necessary and contingent relations of such activities and the contexts within which they occur. Such thought processes and research questions are transferable to all white-collar and corporate crimes, and provide empirical research frameworks that we consider useful to reasoned assessments that go beyond the normal claims of advocacy organizations.

Beyond this, however, is the more philosophical problem of what we want from the enforcement of white-collar and corporate crimes. Do we want displays of how unfair and unequal enforcement is across the range of crimes and/or of the evils brought about by contemporary capitalism in order to unveil class justice? Do we want fairer treatment of different forms of offending so that enforcement is less the product of social stereotypes and more a reflection of harms (and – a different issue – intentional wrongs) done? Do we want a form of reassurance policing and sanctioning that reduces levels of social anxiety about different harms (e.g. food security, identity theft/fraud)? Or do we mainly want to reduce future harms by negotiating reductions in harmful behaviour, perhaps supplemented by restorative justice mechanisms that incorporate victims personally or at least collective and individual victim interests? These are simply examples within a range of objectives which we may want to satisfice unless we are willing to choose just one primary underlying principle. It seems plain to us that unless we resolve both evidence about effectiveness and the aims of control, we can never properly determine how inadequate the enforcement of white-collar and corporate crime is going to be.

Note

1 Quoted in BBC 'Rum remark wins Rumsfeld an award', 2 December 2003. Online. Available HTTP: <http://news.bbc.co.uk/1/hi/3254852.stm> (accessed 8 July 2014).

References

Abbott, K. and Snidal, D. (2009) 'Strengthening international regulation through transnational new governance: Overcoming the orchestration deficit', *Vanderbilt Journal of Transnational Law*, 42: 501–578.

Abbott, K. and Snidal, D. (2013) 'Taking responsive regulation transnational: Strategies for international organizations', *Regulation and Governance*, 7(1): 95–113.

Almond, P. (2013) *Corporate Manslaughter and Regulatory Reform: Crime Prevention and Security Management*, Basingstoke: Palgrave Macmillan.

Ayres, I. and Braithwaite, J. (1992) *Responsive Regulation: Transcending the Deregulation Debate*, New York: Oxford University Press.

Bardhan, P. (2006) 'The Economist's Approach to the Problem of Corruption', *World Development*, 34(2): 341–348.

Benson, M.L. and Simpson, S.S. (2009) *White-Collar Crime: An Opportunity Perspective*, Abingdon, Oxfordshire: Routledge.

Benson, M.L., Madensen, T.D. and Eck, J.E. (2009) 'White-collar crime from an opportunity perspective', in S.S. Simpson and D. Weisburd (eds) *The Criminology of White-Collar Crime*, New York: Springer.

Braithwaite, J. (2008) *Regulatory Capitalism: How It Works, Ideas for Making It Work Better*, Cheltenham: Edward Elgar.

Braithwaite, J. and Drahos, P. (2000) *Global Business Regulation*, Cambridge: Cambridge University Press.

Cadot, O. (1987) 'Corruption as a gamble', *Journal of Public Economics*, 33: 233–244.

Choi, J.P. and Thum, M. (2005) 'Corruption and the shadow economy', *International Economic Review*, 46(3): 817–836.
Clarke, M. (1990) *Business Crime: Its Nature and Control*, Oxford: Polity Press.
Çule, M. and Fulton, M. (2005) 'Some implications of the unofficial economy-bureaucratic corruption relationship in transition countries', *Economic Letters*, 89: 207–211.
Davies, P., Francis, P. and Jupp, V. (1999) 'The features of invisible crimes', in P. Davies, P. Francis and V. Jupp (eds) *Invisible Crimes: Their Victims and their Regulation*, Basingstoke: Palgrave Macmillan.
Davies, P., Francis, P. and Wyatt, T. (2014) *Invisible Crimes*, 2nd edn, Basingstoke: Palgrave Macmillan.
Del Guercio, D., Odders-White, E., and Ready, M. (2013) *The Effect of SEC Enforcement Intensity on Illegal Insider Trading*. Online. Available HTTP: <http://web.business.queensu.ca/Faculty/fmoneta/Seminar/2012_2013/ddg-eow-mjr_20130329.pdf> (accessed 8 July 2014).
Djelic, M.-L. and Sahlin-Andersson, K. (2006) *Transnational Governance: Institutional Dynamics of Regulation*, Cambridge: Cambridge University Press.
Edwards, A. and Gill, P. (2002) 'Crime as enterprise? The case of "transnational organised crime"', *Crime, Law and Social Change*, 37: 203–223.
Edwards, A. and Hughes, G. (2005) 'Comparing the governance of safety in Europe: A geo-historical approach', *Theoretical Criminology*, 9(3): 345–363.
Edwards, A. and Levi, M. (2008) 'Researching the organisation of serious crimes', *Criminology and Criminal Justice*, 8(4): 363–388.
Enrich, D. and Agnew, H. (2014) *UK Agency Struggles in Fight Against Insider Trading*. Online. Available HTTP: <http://online.wsj.com/news/articles/SB10001424052702303640604579296520563211360> (accessed 8 July 2014).
European Commission (2014) *EU Anti-Corruption Report*, COM (2014) 8, European Commission.
Foster, J.E., Horowitz, A.W. and Méndez, F. (2009) 'An axiomatic approach to the measurement of corruption: Theory and applications', OPHI Working Paper no. 29. Online. Available HTTP: <http://www.ophi.org.uk/wp-content/uploads/OPHI-wp29.pdf> (accessed 8 July 2014).
Gill, P. (2002) 'Policing and regulation: What is the difference?', *Social and Legal Studies*, 11: 523–546.
Grabosky, P. (2013) 'Beyond *Responsive Regulation*: The expanding role of non-state actors in the regulatory process', *Regulation and Governance*, 7: 114–123.
Halliday, T., Levi, M. and Reuter, P. (2014) *Global Surveillance of Dirty Money: Assessing Assessments of Regimes to Control Money Laundering and Combat the Financing of Terrorism*, Chicago: Center on Law and Globalization, American Bar Foundation and University of Illinois College of Law. Online. Available HTTP: <http://www.lexglobal.org/files/Report_Global%20Surveillance%20of%20Dirty%20Money%201.30.2014.pdf> (accessed 8 July 2014).
Hawkins, K. (1998) *Law as Last Resort: Prosecution Decision-Making in a Regulatory Agency*, Oxford: Oxford University Press.
Home Office (2012) *Crime against Businesses: Headline Findings from the 2012 Commercial Victimisation Survey*, London: Home Office.
Kaufmann, D., Kraay, A. and Mastruzzi, M. (2007) 'Measuring corruption: Myths and realities', in Transparency International (TI) *Global Corruption Report 2007*. Online. Available HTTP: <http://www.transparency.org/whatwedo/pub/global_corruption_report_2007_corruption_and_judicial_systems> (accessed 8 July 2014).
Levi, M. (2007) 'The organization of serious crimes', in M. Maguire, R. Morgan and R. Reiner (eds) *The Oxford Handbook of Criminology*, 4th edn, Oxford: Oxford University Press.
Levi, M. (2008) 'Organized fraud and organizing frauds: Unpacking research on networks and organization', *Criminology and Criminal Justice*, 8(4): 389–419.
Levi, M. (2011) 'Assessing the costs of frauds', in D. Gadd, S. Karstedt and S. Messner (eds) *The SAGE Handbook of Criminological Research Methods*, London: Sage.
Levi, M. and Gilmore, W. (2002) 'Terrorist finance, money laundering and the rise and rise of mutual evaluation: A new paradigm for crime control?', *European Journal of Law Reform*, 4(2): 337–364.
Lord, N. (2013) 'Regulating transnational corporate bribery in the UK and Germany', *Crime, Law and Social Change*, 60(2): 127–145.
Lord, N. (2014a) 'Responding to transnational corporate bribery using international frameworks for enforcement', *Criminology and Criminal Justice*, 14(1): 100–120.
Lord, N. (2014b) 'Detecting and investigating transnational corporate bribery in centralised and decentralised enforcement systems: discretion and (de-)prioritisation in the UK and Germany', *Policing and Society:*

An International Journal of Research and Policy. Online. Available HTTP: <http://www.tandfonline.com/doi/abs/10.1080/10439463.2014.895350#.U7ulLfl_tng> (accessed 8 July 2014).
Lord, N. (2014c) *Regulating Corporate Bribery in International Business*, Farnham, Surrey: Ashgate Publishing.
Mascini, P. (2013) 'Why was the enforcement pyramid so influential? And what price was paid?', *Regulation and Governance*, 7: 48–60.
Mayntz, R. (1993) 'Governing failures and the problem of governability', in J. Kooiman (ed.) *Modern Governance: New Government–Society Interactions*, London: Sage.
Monteiro, N., Zaman, Q. and Leitterstorf, S. (2007) *Updated Measurement of Market Cleanliness*, London: Financial Services Authority.
Moran, M. (2001) 'The rise of the regulatory state in Britain', *Parliamentary Affairs*, 54: 19–34.
Nagin, D. (2013) 'Deterrence in the twenty-first century', *Crime and Justice*, 42(1): 199–263.
Nelken, D. (2012) 'White-collar and corporate crime', in M. Maguire, R. Morgan and R. Reiner (eds) *The Oxford Handbook of Criminology*, 5th edn, Oxford: Oxford University Press.
Ogus, A.I. (1994) *Regulation: Legal Form and Economic Theory*, Oxford: Clarendon Press.
Parker, C. (2013) 'Twenty years of responsive regulation: An appreciation and appraisal', *Regulation and Governance*, 7: 2–13.
Pearce, F. and Tombs, S. (1998) *Toxic Capitalism: Corporate Crime and the Chemical Industry*, Aldershot: Ashgate.
Raghavan, A. (2013) *The Billionaire's Apprentice: The Rise of The Indian-American Elite and The Fall of The Galleon Hedge Fund*, New York: BusinessPlusUS.
Reinikka, R. and Svensson, J. (2006) 'Using micro-surveys to measure and explain corruption', *World Development*, 34(2): 359–370.
Reiss, A. (1984) 'Consequences of compliance and deterrence models of law enforcement for the exercise of police discretion', *Law and Contemporary Problems*, 47(4): 83–122.
Rider, B. (2000) 'The control of insider trading: Smoke and mirrors!', *Journal of Financial Crime*, 7(3): 227–250.
Rider, B., Alexander, K. and Linklater, L. (2009) *Market Abuse and Insider Dealing*, London: Tottel.
Rothfeld, M. and Strumpf, D. (2012) *Gupta Gets Two Years for Leaking Inside Tips*. Online. Available HTTP: <http://online.wsj.com/article/SB10001424052970203897404578077050403577468.html> (accessed 8 July 2014).
Seligson, M.A. (2006) 'The measurement and impact of corruption victimization: Survey evidence from Latin America', *World Development*, 34(2): 381–404.
Slapper, G. and Tombs, S. (1999) *Corporate Crime*, London: Longman.
Tombs, S. and Whyte, D. (2007) *Safety Crimes*, Cullompton: Willan Publishing.
Tombs, S. and Whyte, D. (2013) 'Transcending the deregulation debate? Regulation, risk, and the enforcement of health and safety law in the UK', *Regulation and Governance*, 7: 61–79.
Wells, C. (2011) 'Containing corporate crime. Civil or criminal controls?', in J. Gobert and A.-M. Pascal (eds) *European Developments in Corporate Criminal Liability*, London: Routledge.

4

Charting Europe's moral economies

Citizens, consumers and the crimes of everyday life[1]

Susanne Karstedt

From white-collar crime to the crimes of everyday life

From its inauguration by Edwin Sutherland the concept of white-collar crime has posed difficult questions for criminologists. It questioned their focus and perspective, their honed instruments of analysis (Braithwaite 1992), and not the least, their role as observers and analysts of lower-class crime. Two decades after Sutherland first presented the concept in 1939 (Sutherland 1940), Donald Newman (1958: 753) noted: 'No longer is the criminologist a middle-class observer studying lower-class behaviour. He now looks upward at the most powerful and prestigious strata'. The fact that the term is now vernacular in most languages, whether translated or not, speaks to its impact on public imagination and its appeal to criminologists. It evokes images of the rich and powerful who commit serious crimes with impunity, and escape from prosecution and punishment due to their social status and the power they can wield. This has led to the proliferation of concepts and analysis that focus on these groups: 'crimes of the powerful', 'elite criminality', 'criminal elites' and 'corporate crime' are exemplary for the shift towards the 'higher end' of these types of crimes, where damage is normally huge, and victims are numerous. The general public and ordinary citizens thus can feel comfortable with placing themselves between the criminality of the rich and the criminality of the poor (Weisburd et al. 1991: 3), and with seeing themselves in the way as politicians like to address them: as the law-abiding majority (Karstedt and Farrall 2007).

Weisburd and his colleagues (1991) were the first to challenge these common and widely shared assumptions of white-collar crime being mostly perpetrated by men (and women) in positions of power, and mostly crimes of those who are more powerful than the rest. From their research they developed a far 'broader portrait of white collar crime' (Weisburd et al. 1991: 171), and their results challenged widely held assumptions about the role of power and greed in the commission of white-collar crimes (see, e.g., Braithwaite 1992). The white-collar crimes that were committed by their sample of convicted offenders were of a 'mundane, common, everyday character' (Weisburd et al. 1991: 171) rather than highly sophisticated schemes of tax evasion (Braithwaite 2005) and fraudulent accounting (McBarnett and Whelan 1999), or complex Ponzi schemes. The basic ingredients are 'lying, cheating and stealing' (McBarnett and Whelan 1999; see also Green 2006), and the truly complicated offences are drowned out by the bulk of simple ones, which can be carried out by almost everyone. While the offences clearly differed from underclass offences, they were highly variegated, and included securities fraud, antitrust violations, bribery and bank embezzlement, false claims and statements, and credit- and lending-institution fraud (Weisburd et al. 1991: 11). All these offences offered opportunities ranging from highly sophisticated schemes open to high-ranking offenders to the simplest schemes. Consequently the offenders were not drawn from the highest ranks of status and class in American society, nor did they have an underclass background. With only few exceptions they represented 'the broad middle of the society, much above the poverty line, but for most part far from elite social position and status' (Weisburd et al. 1991:171).

This does not seem to be the result of powerful white-collar offenders being shielded from prosecution (Weisburd et al. 1991), as other studies and observations corroborate. Contemporary elites and the powerful are much scrutinized, and their illegal as well as barely legal behaviours become scandals (Levi 2006; 2009), like, for example, in the expenses scandal that involved numerous politicians and members of parliament in Britain over the past years (Winnett and Rayner 2009). Even the most prominent cases of white-collar crime that produced huge losses for banks and even led to their demise, were committed by young middle-class men, who stood out – if in anything – by their normal behaviour and inconspicuous ways. White-collar offenders like accountants, physicians (Jesilow et al. 1993) and lawyers are of solid middle-class background rather than of high status. Given the peculiarity of the term white-collar crime as it is defined both by the type of crime and the type of offender, Weisburd and his colleagues (1991: 172) found 'virtually every possible combination of offence and offender', from professionals committing the most simple forms of crime to persons at the lower ranks of organizations who committed the most sophisticated schemes.

Weisburd and his colleagues thus draw our attention to what they termed 'crimes of the middle classes', coining a term and presenting a new and useful concept. Indeed, Sutherland's focus on the upper classes and their crimes needs to be understood from the perspective of stratification of American society at the time of his writing, with a powerful and small upper class and a large (immigrant) working class, and only a small category of white-collar class in the middle. This middle category has hugely increased since Sutherland's days, and it presently represents the majority in all western industrialized societies. In addition, the income and the share of income of the middle classes have grown during the second half of the past century (Offer 2006), though not in equal measure. The rise of the middle classes has contributed to higher levels of equality in income distribution, even as this process has levelled off during the last decades of the past, and the first decade of the twenty-first century (Wilkinson and Pickett 2009); they are still better off than Sutherland's contemporaries. They represent the 'middle' or centre of contemporary societies, both in the sense of income and lifestyle, and as the normative centre of gravity; they represent the core of shared beliefs and norms. Weisburd and his colleagues restore the 'middle "class" of crime', and with it the middle classes as a population of potential offenders; they thus created an important new category in the study of white-collar crime.

Between the well-established notions of crimes in the suites and crimes in the streets an under-explored terrain opens up at the core of contemporary societies, where we find varying degrees of 'white collarness' of offenders and a range of different offences. 'Ordinary people' are believed to commit white-collar crimes in increasing numbers, due to changes in consumption, finances and banking, and foremost the revolution in technology that came with the internet. These technologies have thoroughly changed the ways in which people work, consume and own property. In addition to consumption and services, welfare programmes have been expanded far into the middle classes, who mainly profit from student loans, and other subsidies (for a comparison between Britain and Germany: Mau 2003). The middle classes are under high pressure to perform and succeed, giving rise to a range of crimes from cheating in exams to research fraud in universities. A survey in the United Kingdom in April 2004 found that more than a quarter of mostly middle-class parents would consider faking a religious commitment or using other dishonest tactics (including bribing the head teacher) to secure their child a place at the school of their choice (Karstedt and Farrall 2006: 1013). These are crimes and unfair practices that are committed at the kitchen table, on the settee and from home computers and laptops, from office desks and call centres, at cash points in restaurants and in face-to-face interactions with builders and other tradespeople, as well as with fellow citizens (Karstedt and Farrall 2006: 1011). These are the 'crimes of everyday life' (Karstedt and Farrall 2006: 1011), often falling into a grey zone of legality and morality, and committed by the middle classes.

Weisburd and his colleagues were the first to use the term 'middle-class crimes', and to establish the link with white-collar crime. Accordingly, they incorporated into their definition both a type and category of offender, and a type of crime. This differs from a delineation merely by the definition of offenders, as we find, for example, in Thomas Gabor's (1994) 'crime by the public'. He predominantly targets all crimes committed by otherwise 'law-abiding citizens' (see also Karstedt and Farrall 2007), and includes traffic offences, domestic violence, sex offences and others. There can be no doubt that usually law-abiding citizens commit all types of crimes including the most heinous ones of mass atrocities and genocide (Karstedt 2013). Weisburd and his colleagues, and likewise Karstedt and Farrall however have a much narrower list of crimes that are essentially white-collar crimes, as they include cheating and lying: making false insurance claims; claiming for refunds one is not entitled to; all types of tax evasion, with the most common forms of requesting and paying 'cash in hand' in order to avoid taxes; cheating on benefits; and deceiving their fellow citizens in second-hand sales. This is 'white-collar crime writ small' (Levitt 2006), and at the lowest end of the scale of white-collar crime that makes it into the public sphere (Levi 2006).

Nonetheless these crimes and those who commit it share most of the characteristics that Sutherland (1940; 1949; see Weisburd et al. 1991: 5–8) identified for white-collar crime and criminals. His observation that these crimes result in a multiplicity of monetary losses in comparison to more common crimes equally applies to the crimes of the middle classes; even if they are individually small, they cause considerable damage and losses (Karstedt and Farrall 2006: 1013). Given his moral concern, Sutherland defined white-collar crime as serious moral transgressions independent of the illegal nature of the act itself. Thus a contemporary 'moral theory' of white-collar crime is based on the analysis of 'lying, cheating and stealing' (Green 2006), which applies in particular to the lower end of white-collar crime, where the crimes of everyday life are situated. There is a 'wide array of peripheral cases in which the line between criminal and noncriminal conduct is unfathomable' (Henning 2008: 325), and of actions that teeter on the boundaries of normative acceptability. This applies both to the legal and moral boundaries, and there is a fine line between bribes and gifts, or between 'aggressive tax planning', still legal, and illegal tax evasion (J. Braithwaite 2005; V. Braithwaite 2009; Tetlock and McGraw 2005). As Karstedt and Farrall (2006: 1011) point out, these types of behaviours 'fall into a grey zone of legality and morality'. As Sutherland focused more on the characteristics of individuals or organizations committing such crimes, for him 'respectability and high status' (1983: 9) of offenders were defining characteristics. The middle classes indeed represent the 'respectable' in society, and consequently they nearly always deny the criminality of their own acts (Karstedt and Farrall 2007; Stadler and Benson 2012; Tunley 2011).

However, the crimes of everyday life and those who commit them also differ from definitions of white-collar crimes and criminals with regard to decisive dimensions. Importantly, even though many of these crimes are committed in professional capacities, for example by doctors and nurses (Jesilow et al. 1993 for the US; Levi and Burrows 2008; Levi et al. 2007), the vast majority of these crimes are committed by individuals in their capacity as consumers and citizens, and in interactions and exchanges with retailers, banks, insurers and other financial services, their fellow citizens when they participate in auctions on the internet, and with the government as taxpayers and claimants of benefits. Thus it is not their status that shields them from prosecution, but simply the sheer amount of often negligible transgressions that would if prosecuted bring the criminal justice system to a creaking halt, and make punishment seemingly senseless. Further, the legal and moral ambiguity of white-collar crime results from the contradiction between often widely shared 'moral intuitions' (Henning 2008; Mikhail 2007) and lacunae in the law itself, or a lack of prosecution, and application of existing laws, thus causing moral outrage among the population (Levi 2009). For middle-class crimes in contrast, shared moral intuitions among the public allow for widely held justifications of such actions, for an array of techniques of neutralization, and in particular for uninhibited discussions of such actions among relatives and friends, amounting to requests for collusion in shady practices and outright illegal acts (Karstedt and Farrall 2006; 2007; for white-collar criminals, Stadler and Benson 2012). Widespread is in particular the belief that 'everybody does it', whether it is insurance fraud (Karstedt and Farrall 2006) or benefit fraud (Dean and Melrose 1997). Finally, and this certainly did not apply to the group that Sutherland targeted, the middle classes are equally victimized by unfair and illegal practices by banks and insurers, or other large companies, at the hands of small retailers and tradespeople, and even by fellow citizens. The majority do not seem to be the powerless and helpless victims as in a bankruptcy case in the United Kingdom (Spalek and King 2007). Thus, victimization and offending are closely related in this group, and the former might give justification and reason to the latter.

Both shared and unique characteristics define a particular type of white-collar crime, which Karstedt and Farrall (2006) have called 'crimes of everyday life', as well as a particular group of offenders, the 'respectable middle classes' at the centre of contemporary societies. As Weisburd and his colleagues have pointed out, this is also the social space of most white-collar offenders. The range of illegal, immoral and illegitimate practices mostly at the lower end of damage, sophistication and complexity, as well as the type of offenders make these crimes just the *everyday crimes of normal people*, who would be filled with indignation if the label of 'criminal' was ever applied to them. What does this position between the upper echelons of society and their crimes in the suites, and the lower strata of society, and their crimes on the street, imply? Where are the middle classes situated between the 'greed' that motivates powerful offenders, and the need that drives offending of the lower classes (Braithwaite 1992)? The middle classes comprise a range of income, financial security and living standards; they include those who live comfortably as well as those who struggle financially (Karstedt and Farrall 2007). Given the hugely different circumstances of living and offending among this group, some crimes like benefit fraud might be caused by need, whilst others like tax evasion by greed, and vice versa (for need: Katungi et al. 2006; Tunley 2011; for tax: Braithwaite 2009).

In this chapter these questions will be addressed, based on data from European countries that were collected in 2004. Even if these might have changed since then, there is no reason to assume that basic processes outlined here are different in substance from what they were then. Importantly, this article contextualizes these crimes within the moral economies of Europe; therefore, it presents an analysis on the macro-level and throughout uses data aggregated on the country level.[2] After a brief overview over contemporary choice theories of white-collar crime, the role of moral commitment, fairness and confidence in market institutions will be explored within the framework of 'moral economies' (Karstedt and Farrall 2006; Thompson 1971). Finally, the European landscape of 'moral economies' will be charted, including offending and victimization, moral commitment, fairness and trust as well as power and powerlessness in markets.

'A cornucopia of new criminal opportunities': from theft to fraud

Theft seems to be the crime of the past. In 2005, Albanese noted that theft had defined the crime scene of the twentieth century, and he predicted for the twenty-first century that fraud would take this position. He corroborated his assumption with data for fraud in the US, which showed a growth of nearly 200 per cent between 1970 and 2003. In 2006, fraud had overtaken theft as the most common crime in Germany, and most western European countries have followed suit since then, including the United Kingdom (Karstedt and Farrall 2006). For the US, evidence suggests that at the beginning of the 2000s, the number of fraud victims exceeded those of victimized by serious street crime (Holtfreter et al. 2008; Labaton 2002; Titus 2001). Albanese named three processes that would make fraud the crime of choice of the future. Both ownership and storage of goods and money have decisively changed over the past decades, with credit cards, online transactions and online retailing; rather than goods being stored in small shops and warehouses, they are now concentrated within a few; banks are not any more 'where the money is'. Finally, and concomitantly, movements of goods, moneys and services have changed. It is a characteristic of internet- and cybercrime that huge numbers of potential victims can be addressed at large distances and in foreign countries. These processes as a result and in conjunction with internet technologies generate the 'cornucopia of new criminal opportunities' that Shover et al. (2003: 490) identify, which lead to widespread victimization as well as rampant offending.

These developments in itself made many of the established interpersonal relationships in banking, consumption and retailing obsolete and changed them beyond belief. They were, however, accompanied by a drive towards deregulation of markets that took up momentum at the same time. The movement of neo-liberalism started in the US and the UK in the 1980s, and has swept through European countries since then. Three processes were decisive in these tectonic shifts in the economies of the Western world, and later in transitional and post-communist societies. Offer (2006: 365) declared the movement from 'social democracy to market liberalism' the 'largest historical shift of the last fifty years'. It came with new technologies and new opportunities and rewards, and transformed economic citizenship into the direction of active self-advancement, and 'entrepreneurial comportment' of the individual (Rose 1996: 340). Consumers were urged to take responsibility and risks. As markets were deregulated, a new 'risk environment' with little oversight or regulation was thus created, with ample opportunities for fraudulent transactions and sharp practices (Ericson et al. 1999). Finally, citizens were urged to become 'consumers' in their relations with government agencies, and they were forced into markets of welfare services, security and other government services. These policies re-shaped the relation between risk and blame, responsibility and conformity for consumers and business alike (Karstedt and Farrall 2006).

For more than two decades, complaints from insurers and representatives from health services about the increase in fraud committed by their customers and clients have been mounting in the United Kingdom, as well as in other European countries (Insurance Europe 2013). Large and small retailers see themselves as victims of those customers who take unfair and often illegal advantage of generous terms and offers. Small tradesmen report that their customers try fraudulently to make them responsible for damages. Citizens do not hesitate to take illegal and unfair advantages, conversely, however, they feel victimized by the practices of insurance companies and financial services. They are sold allegedly useless insurance and financial packages, they are not properly informed about the products, and they feel that they are being defrauded by small-print clauses (Karstedt and Farrall 2004; 2006; 2007). They find themselves charged for undelivered services, bogus repairs and used parts sold as new. 'Consumer revolts' against overcharging banks gained momentum in 2007, and British banks have been forced since then on numerous occasions to compensate consumers for high-risk products, overcharging bouncing cheques and other malpractice.

Fraud and similar crimes are in the course of surpassing ordinary property crimes, in terms of costs and numbers: in the early 2000s, the costs of fraud outstripped the costs of more common crimes like burglary. The 2001 British Crime Survey estimated that there were slightly over 1 million burglaries in the year 2000 and estimated that the costs of burglaries were £2.7 billion (3.4 billion euros, using 1999 prices, Brand and Price 2000: 32–33). The Brand and Price Report however, puts the costs of fraud and forgery at £13.8 billion (17.4 billion euros), roughly four times as much as the costs of one type of common crime.

The following estimations are from the United Kingdom, but other European countries with similar economies and welfare systems should not substantively differ. Karstedt and Farrall (2006) report that the Department of Work and Pensions estimated that 5 per cent of their claims were fraudulent in 2003, resulting in losses of £573 million or 4 per cent of social security payments. The Association of British Insurers claims that 4 per cent of household insurance claims made in 2000 were fraudulent (ABI 2000). The Association for Payments and Clearing Services set the cost of losses due to counterfeit credit card fraud at £108 million in 2000, with a steep increase in the previous years (APACS n.d.). Levi and his colleagues (Levi and Burrows 2008; Levi et al. 2007) estimated losses separately for the private and public sectors in 2005. Financial services suffered losses from fraud at about £1 billion, while for other businesses this figure was estimated at about £2.75 billion, the same as for private individuals. However, these figures are dwarfed by losses in the public sector, both on national and local levels. Tax evasion and fraud, in particular VAT, amount to £5.5 billion, a figure that does not include income tax fraud, which, presumably, is the most common type (Levi et al. 2007: 4); benefit fraud creates losses up to £0.5 billion. These figures are mirrored by cross-country estimates of the shadow or informal economy in a number of European countries; these estimates include lost VAT and undeclared income tax (Schneider et al. 2008). Levi and his colleagues (2007: 87) report a range for benefit fraud between 1 per cent and 4 per cent of payments for different types of benefits and allowances. According to the Committee of Public Accounts, in 2008 the largest losses were accrued from undeclared earnings, fraudulent claims of household size and from clients living abroad (all at about £70 million; Tunley 2011). Charities are vulnerable victims to fraud by their own members and others; a survey revealed that £147 million were lost, about one-third to internal fraud (National Fraud Authority 2013). In 2013, the National Fraud Authority claimed that the British economy had lost £52 billion from fraud.

Opportunity, choice, and moral economies: contextualizing the crimes of everyday life

Given the cornucopia of opportunities as well as mounting risks of victimization, and accounting for the social space where the crimes of everyday life take place, namely markets, it seems reasonable to follow Shover and Grabosky (2010: 430) and other criminologists (Simpson 2011) by employing the concepts of 'crime-as-choice theory' as a starting point. 'Opportunities become crimes only because of decisions made by volitional actors' (Shover and Grabosky 2010: 430). Given the fact that those who transgress legal and moral norms are coming from the centre of society, and do not suffer from the many problems that have been associated with those committing street crimes, it makes sense to see them as actors who make informed even if not always rational decisions. Choice theory is not 'coextensive' with *rational choice theory*. As this approach provides a basic mechanism that links individuals to their environment, choice theories easily are aligned with the aggregate level, and are as suitable for explaining rates of offending as they are for individual behaviour. The logic of choice theories highlights the importance of five causal factors in the exploration of rates of white-collar crime, both the most complex and committed by a few, and the least complex committed by the many. These are, according to Shover and Grabosky (2010: 430): (1) the size of a pool of tempted individuals and organizations; (2) the supply of 'lure', i.e. something 'attractive and covetable' (431); (3) prevailing beliefs about the credibility of external oversight over the alluring offer; (4) 'how extensively and effectively internal oversight and self-restraint are deployed' (430), including conscience, regard for others and a general moral commitment (Granovetter 1985; Henning 2008; Holtfreter et al. 2008); and finally (5) the supply of criminal opportunities.

Though originally conceived as casting a wide net over all types of white-collar crimes and types of offenders, ranging from simple tax evasion to complex financial fraud, and from consumers and citizens to large-scale organizations, the model is particularly pertinent for the analysis of middle-class crime. Shover and Grabosky (2010: 431) point to the 'enormous supply of lure' created by states in policies and programmes that target middle-class and middle-income households. Insurers create 'moral hazards' that tempt citizens not only into reckless but also illegal behaviour (Ericson et al. 1999). They see the 'weakening of external oversight' (432) over economic actors across the past decades as a major cause for the increase in white-collar crime, corroborated by the data presented above. Karstedt and Farrall (2006) argue that moral commitment has widely changed and given way to 'legal cynicism' (Sampson and Bartusch 1998) among consumers and citizens making them more inclined to exploit illegal opportunities when they present themselves. Thus, in order to understand middle-class crime, it is the behaviour of consumers that needs to be understood rather than the behaviour of fraudsters (Holtfreter et al. 2008: 207).

Given the cornucopia of criminal opportunities that markets and governments alike present to consumers, external oversight and internal constraints are decisive conditions for the pool of tempted offenders to increase. External oversight and internal constraints however coalesce in what Granovetter (1985) has called the 'generalized morality' of markets and the economy, referring to the non-contractual basis of economic contracts, as Durkheim had done nearly a century ago. Generalized moralities are external, fairly fixed systems of norms and values; however, they inform individual moral choices and thus act as internal constraints. Generalized morality thus provides the 'communal norms that guide everyday life as a means of evaluating the propriety of conduct' (Henning 2008: 328). These are shared norms and values, and their observance by others provides vital information on their actual 'generalizability'. If others do not comply with legal or moral norms, this has an impact on both external oversight and internal constraints (Dean and Melrose 1997; Kotzian 2011). Restrictions imply regard for others or considerations of fairness, and acknowledgement of the moral values that imbue the economy and economic behaviour. Incentives for criminal choices might not only emerge from opportunities, but equally from perceptions of unfair treatment (Sondak and Tyler 2007; Tyler 1990/2006), from information about high-level and elite white-collar crime (Levi 2006; 2009), and about what others do. Thus, criminal choices in markets are like any economic action embedded in wider structures, of which the fabric of moral values is one component. Middle-class crime thus illuminates the relationship between markets and moral order in contemporary societies.

Markets are increasingly seen as 'moral projects in their own right' (Fourcade and Healy 2007: 285). Shamir observes a 'moralization of economic action' (2008: 1) in the context of neo-liberal policies that took hold in many European countries. Processes of economization are linked to processes of moralization in markets, with socio-moral obligations of market actors coming to the fore. Consumers are increasingly presupposed to be socially and morally responsible actors in markets, implying the 'un-coerced' application of values as a root motivation (Shamir 2008: 7). However, this equally applies to powerful actors in markets whose actions are measured according to moral values and obligations. In the United Kingdom, the public discussion about the morality of bankers or CEOs' bonuses signifies the moralization of markets. In the wake of high-profile cases like Enron, business morality and ethics became a necessary complement to shareholder values.

As markets are seen as not devoid of moral content, a 'moral economy' should shape habits and norms in the economic sphere, and lend legitimacy to the institutions of the economy and markets. The concept was pioneered by the historian E.P. Thompson (1971), who originally developed it as an explanation for the riotous transition from pre-modern to liberal corn markets in seventeenth- and eighteenth-century Britain (and more encompassing of class relations). More recently, the concept has been used in a wider sense to describe the particular set of justice perceptions and the 'moral order' of the economy (Arnold 2001; Booth 1994; Sayer 2007) and the welfare state (Mau 2003). Thompson posited two basic 'laws' of markets: first, that they are grounded in a morality of fairness, justice, roles and rules, and shared notions of acceptable behaviours, profits and entitlements; second, that economic changes inevitably shift and change the moral economy, and, in particular, relations of power and the moral constraints imposed on the powerful. He sought to describe the process of thorough deregulation of the most important consumer market of those times, where deregulation impacted in particular on the poor. It was a process whereby the traditional cultural practices operating in eighteenth-century market places were removed by the new 'market economy'. This considerably shifted the moral order of markets: deeply ingrained beliefs about justice and fairness, about who could be trusted and who not, beliefs about the morality of trading in basic commodities, and beliefs about what set fair and acceptable profits apart from unacceptable and excessive ones, a number of these being enshrined in a set of legal rules and regulations. He also drew attention to the intricate relationship between the regulation of markets and welfare laws, which jointly shaped the moral economy of the time. Contemporary moral economies can be defined as an ensemble of institutional patterns, generalized morality and moral commitment; as such it presents the structural and moral constraints in which individual choices are embedded.

Thompson focused on the contentious nature of such changes; however, he did not expect consumer riots in contemporary society but assumed that 'today we shrug off the extortionate mechanisms of an unregulated market economy because it causes most of us only inconvenience, unostentatious hardships' (Thompson 1971: 134). Whilst British peasants once raised up against millers selling corn or flour at inflated prices, consumers are now exercised by 'value for money', mis-selling, hidden charges and inaccurate product descriptions. According to Karstedt and Farrall (2006), they resist and hit back by inflating insurance claims as a reaction towards small-print rules or overpriced premiums; they retreat into a shadow economy in which they pay cash in hand to circumvent tax and social security laws (Schneider and Enste 2000; Schneider et al. 2008).[3] Recent consumer campaigns against overcharging banks, or tax-evading businesses in Britain show that Thompson underrated the strength of contemporary moral economies, or could not anticipate the recent shifts towards a (re)moralization of markets.

Following Thompson's conceptualization, we can complement the original choice model by Shover and Grabosky (2010) with three factors that capture essential characteristics in particular relevant for middle-class crime. The resulting model of the crimes of everyday life therefore includes besides the original five factors: individual norm commitment as an additional dimension to the original factor internal oversight and constraint. Two factors are added as independent determinants: first, the level of overall commitment to moral and legal norms, the 'generalized morality' in a population and the economy (Granovetter 1985); and second, the (perceived) fairness and legitimacy of market rules and actors (Sondak and Tyler 2007). All three factors restrict the pool of potential offenders as they restrain individual choices.

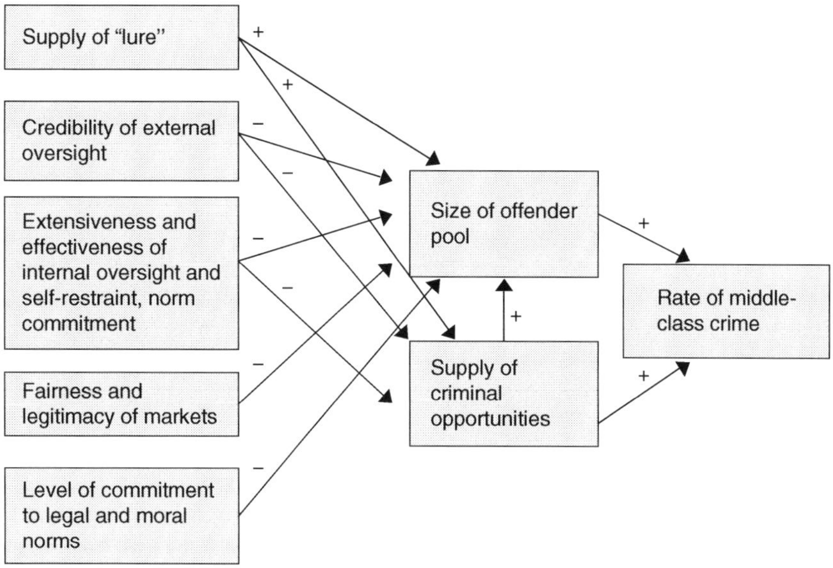

Figure 4.1 A model of variation in middle-class crime

Source: Adapted from Shover and Grabosky (2010)

The contours of European moral economies

Notwithstanding their common market and a host of regulations, European economies, markets and welfare states differ widely (see Mau 2003). The deepest divide existed between the market societies of Western Europe and the state-controlled economies of Central and Eastern Europe until the end of the Cold War. Since then, most of these countries have adopted a market economy with various levels and types of regulation, and Europe's economic institutions have started to converge. However, little is known about the 'moral economies' that were created in the wake of the economic transformation in Central and Eastern Europe, and those that were changing under pressures from deregulation in the other regions of Europe (Karstedt and Farrall 2006). We cannot conclude from changes in the institutional framework in which ways moral economies might be affected, and further, if at all, these changes are related to changes in the amount of middle-class crime. According to the choice model in Figure 4.1, these affect mainly the pool of offenders, whilst criminal opportunities and 'lure' are mainly driven by new technologies, new products and changes in the way that transactions are done. However, European countries still differ widely with regard to regulation of banking and insurers, retail and consumption, types of financial and insurance products available, provision of health care, access to online retail and services, and oversight in general.[4] An assessment of opportunities would require in-depth analyses for all European countries for a range of markets and institutions, which is not available with the exception of analyses and estimates of the informal and 'shadow economy' (Enste 2010; Tafenau et al. 2010; Williams 2012; 2013; for insurance fraud see Insurance Europe 2013). The following analyses are based on data from the European Social Survey 2004, which included questions that probed into the moral economies of 25 European societies, including Turkey (a list of countries is given in the Appendix). Given the collective nature of the moral economy, all data are aggregated on country level, and analyses conducted with country-level data.[5] The role of variegated criminal opportunities for transgressions, moral or legal, can only be concluded from this material.

Victimization and transgressions

In contrast to street crime and common notions of fraud and white-collar crime, victims of the crimes of everyday life are neither from different social backgrounds nor life circumstances than offenders; rather they share the same social space with offenders. In addition, the factors that drive victimization might be the same as those for offending: little restraint and self-control, and a high temptation by 'lure'. Such individuals are easy prey if targeted, and they are also more inclined to offend (Holtfreter et al. 2008). Offending might also constitute a kind of self-help justice for those who feel victimized or treated unfairly in the market place (Karstedt and Farrall 2006), or be an act of defiance in the face of government authorities (Braithwaite 2009).

Table 4.1 gives an overview over different types of consumer victimization in the past five years. Nearly two-thirds (62.8 per cent) of European consumers felt they had been victimized at least

Table 4.1 Consumer victimization in the last five years (% once)

Country	*Overcharged by tradespeople %*	*Been sold bad pieces of food %*	*Bank/insurer did not offer best deal %*	*Cheated upon in second-hand sale %*	*Victimization %*
Austria	****41.3**	****57.0**	****37.5**	19.3	****73.5**
Belgium	35.0	34.1	27.5	19.5	61.9
Czech Republic	****45.8**	52.4	28.6	****34.9**	68.0
Denmark	32.7	50.4	35.2	19.2	69.9
Estonia	****41.0**	****56.3**	21.4	****43.3**	71.6
Finland	***22.3**	29.6	21.9	26.0	***57.9**
France	37.9	***26.0**	31.0	***16.6**	64.8
Germany	38.6	52.9	****35.8**	20.8	72.2
Greece	33.1	***15.8**	***10.7**	***9.8**	***42.0**
Hungary	37.6	****62.8**	33.5	33.3	****76.6**
Iceland	***27.3**	52.4	****40.0**	28.6	71.4
Ireland	***27.9**	29.1	31.8	18.4	***55.7**
Luxembourg	****47.1**	54.3	31.3	22.9	****75.7**
Netherlands	36.8	44.3	28.1	21.0	67.9
Norway	32.8	51.9	****41.8**	24.2	****74.7**
Poland	36.8	52.8	***20.4**	30.4	64.1
Portugal	***18.2**	***21.4**	***14.9**	***12.3**	***35.9**
Slovakia	****40.3**	****64.3**	24.1	****52.3**	****76.2**
Slovenia	35.0	49.4	26.6	****34.2**	69.5
Spain	37.0	***27.6**	31.4	***11.9**	58.9
Sweden	28.0	54.8	31.8	24.5	72.5
Switzerland	29.2	31.7	25.5	***14.3**	58.1
Turkey	***24.2**	***23.9**	***7.6**	16.8	***42.2**
Ukraine	36.3	****58.6**	***19.3**	****36.4**	67.9
United Kingdom	34.4	34.9	****37.0**	23.8	65.9
Europe	**34.6**	**39.9**	**27.3**	**21.7**	**62.8**

Key: Bold, **: five countries with highest levels. Bold, *: five countries with lowest levels

Source: European Social Survey 2004; How often, if ever, have each of these things happened to you in the last five years? a) A plumber, builder, car mechanic or other repair person overcharged you or did unnecessary work. b) You were sold food that was packed to conceal the worse bits. c) A bank or insurance company failed to offer you the best deal you were entitled to. d) You were sold something second-hand that quickly proved to be faulty

once in various ways: being overcharged by tradespeople (plumbers, car mechanics); being sold bad pieces of food in supermarkets and markets; not been offered the best deal by banks and insurers, which mainly amounts to mis-selling; and been sold faulty goods in second-hand sales, thus suffering fraud at the hands of their fellow citizens. Most of the five countries with the highest level of victimization of at about 75 per cent are established market economies in West European countries, Slovakia being the exception. In contrast the countries with the lowest level of victimization are South European countries, including Turkey. These are market economies where personal relationships still are important and with a substantive rural sector, as, for example, in Greece, Portugal and Turkey. Consequently, they also have lowest levels of being mis-sold bad food in supermarkets and by grocers, which is the most common type of victimization of consumers (39.9 per cent), as well as of being overcharged by tradespeople. Consumers in the transition countries are mostly hit by being overcharged for repair services, being sold bad pieces of food, and also been taken for a ride by their fellow citizens in second-hand sales, while those in Switzerland, Spain and Greece can trust others more. Consumers in West European countries mostly suffer from mis-selling by banks and insurers in highly developed financial markets with complex products on offer.[6] Three types of market settings emerge where different types of consumer victimization are prevalent: post-communist economies with comparably high levels of victimization across different types, economies with comparably larger rural populations and personal exchanges with lower levels, and advanced markets with complex products in West European countries.

Offending and transgressions of all types are mostly prevalent in West European countries and established market economies, where at about one-third of the population has engaged in such practices, ranging from minor incidents like keeping too much change to more serious ones like fraudulent insurance claims (Table 4.2). Countries with lowest levels are transitional countries and those where personal exchanges and relationships still play a major role. Highest levels of avoiding paying VAT and other taxes are found in West European countries with high taxes and labour costs, where shadow economies therefore thrive (Schneider et al. 2008; Tafenau et al. 2010). Consumers also take to insurance fraud mostly in established market economies where they are offered complex products, thus mirroring victimization (see for different opportunities and products note 4). Misuse of cards and cheating in second-hand sales is most prevalent in transitional economies reflecting presumably less control and oversight, and quite ruthless practices with fellow citizens.

As Table 4.3 shows, European consumers feel victimized nearly three times more often than they themselves take to immoral and illegal practices (62.8 per cent and 22.9 per cent). Nearly half of them (45 per cent) have only been victimized in the course of the past five years, and at about one-fifth (18 per cent) were both victims and offenders, while one-third neither suffered from fraud nor took to similar practices (31.8 per cent). Consumers who were only victimized, but did not offend, lived mostly in post-communist countries, but also in the North (Norway, Iceland), whilst those who only engaged in transgressions without being victimized were mainly found in the established market economies of Western Europe. It is in these countries where we also find the highest coincidence of victimization and offending, now including Sweden. Established market societies at the beginning of the century obviously offered the 'lure' and the opportunities, combined with new technologies, complex products and inbuilt moral hazards that are conducive to both victimization and offending.

The normative fabric of the moral economy: commitment to moral and legal norms

The lynchpin in the fabric of moral economies is the collective commitment to moral and legal norms, and the strength of 'generalized morality' (Granovetter 1985) in the economy, on which

Table 4.2 Morally dubious and illegal consumer behaviour in the last five years (% at least once)

Country	*Kept change %*	*Avoid VAT/ tax %*	*Cheated in second-hand sale %*	*Misused card/ document %*	*Fraudulent insurance claim %*	*Fraudulent benefit claim %*	*Offending %*
Austria	24.4	29.7	4.4	**6.9	**6.7	**3.5	**29.8
Belgium	**31.6	**33.7	3.5	2.4	1.7	*0.7	**34.2
Czech Republic	22.6	24.7	**4.9	**5.8	**4.3	**3.6	24.8
Denmark	26.0	**38.4	4.1	2.3	**5.2	1.3	28.6
Estonia	17.8	25.0	**5.6	**4.0	1.4	1.3	19.1
Finland	23.7	28.4	**5.6	2.2	2.9	2.2	26.8
France	21.6	31.2	*1.5	*2.0	3.1	1.1	24.2
Germany	23.3	**32.8	3.9	3.8	**4.4	1.6	25.8
Greece	*5.0	22.4	*0.6	*0.5	*0.2	*0.5	*5.6
Hungary	*11.0	31.6	*1.0	*0.6	2.0	*0.3	*12.1
Iceland	18.2	**45.5	4.5	**4.5	**4.8	**4.5	22.7
Ireland	18.8	*15.6	2.0	2.3	*0.7	1.0	19.8
Luxembourg	**31.4	31.4	2.9	2.9	2.9		**33.3
Netherlands	**26.7	27.1	4.1	2.6	1.9	*0.1	**29.7
Norway	23.5	27.5	2.2	2.2	*1.4	1.9	25.0
Poland	*14.3	19.6	**4.6	2.7	1.9	1.8	*16.8
Portugal	*6.9	*15.1	1.9	2.1	2.1	1.5	*8.5
Slovakia	20.2	25.7	4.3	2.4	2.0	**3.2	21.5
Slovenia	17.7	26.4	3.1	3.0	*1.2	1.2	20.7
Spain	20.9	30.3	3.1	3.8	3.5	1.3	24.0
Sweden	**26.4	30.9	3.9	*1.7	2.8	1.0	28.9
Switzerland	20.6	*12.8	*1.2	3.2	2.2	*0.7	22.9
Turkey	*4.1	**32.6	*1.7	*1.0	*0.4	1.0	*5.1
Ukraine	20.6	*13.7	**7.7	**3.8	2.9	**5.4	24.0
United Kingdom	**34.4	*19.1	4.1	3.5	1.8	1.7	**37.4
Europe	20.6	26.7	3.5	2.9	2.7	1.7	22.9

Key: Bold, **: five countries with highest levels. Bold, *: five countries with lowest levels

Source: European Social Survey 2004. How often, if ever, have you done each of these things in the last five years? a) Kept the change from a shop assistant or waiter knowing they had given you too much? b) Paid cash with no receipt so as to avoid paying VAT or other taxes? c) Sold something second-hand and concealed some or all of its faults? d) Mis-used or altered a card or document to pretend you were eligible for something you were not? e) Made an exaggerated or false insurance claim? f) Over-claimed or falsely claimed government benefits such as social security or other benefits?

consumers and businesses can rely. Severe deficits in such moral commitments should not only lead to higher levels of offending and victimization, but also increase distrust as well as the fear of being treated dishonestly. Commitment to moral norms can be expressed in the moral censure of behaviours, as citizens when avoiding paying VAT, as consumers when cheating on insurance claims,

Table 4.3 Crimes of everyday life: victims and offenders

Country	*Victimization %*	*Offending %*	*Victim only %*	*Offender only %*	*Victim and offender %*	*Neither victim nor offender %*
Austria	****73.5**	****29.8**	48.8	4.7	****24.8**	***21.7**
Belgium	61.9	****34.2**	***36.6**	****9.0**	****25.3**	29.2
Czech Republic	68.0	24.8	47.1	4.3	20.8	27.8
Denmark	69.9	28.6	46.8	5.3	23.1	24.8
Estonia	71.6	19.1	****55.3**	2.4	16.5	25.9
Finland	***57.9**	26.8	39.0	****7.6**	19.4	34.0
France	64.8	24.2	47.0	6.5	17.7	28.8
Germany	72.2	25.8	51.0	4.5	21.3	23.2
Greece	***42.0**	***5.6**	***38.6**	***1.9**	***3.8**	****55.7**
Hungary	****76.6**	***12.1**	****66.0**	***1.0**	***11.1**	***21.8**
Iceland	71.4	22.7	****54.5**	4.5	18.2	22.7
Ireland	***55.7**	19.8	42.1	5.5	***13.9**	****38.5**
Luxembourg	****75.7**	****33.3**	48.6	5.7	****28.6**	***17.1**
Netherlands	67.9	****29.7**	45.1	****6.7**	22.9	25.3
Norway	****74.7**	25.0	****53.7**	3.9	21.2	***21.2**
Poland	64.1	***16.8**	51.5	2.5	14.3	31.6
Portugal	***35.9**	***8.5**	***29.1**	***1.9**	***6.4**	****62.5**
Slovakia	****76.2**	21.5	****57.1**	***2.2**	19.1	***21.5**
Slovenia	69.5	20.7	52.7	3.0	17.4	26.9
Spain	58.9	24.0	41.7	****7.0**	17.0	34.3
Sweden	72.5	28.9	49.1	5.2	****23.5**	22.1
Switzerland	58.1	22.9	41.9	6.5	16.6	****35.1**
Turkey	***42.2**	***5.1**	***38.6**	***1.1**	***4.1**	****56.2**
Ukraine	67.9	24.0	46.3	3.9	21.1	28.7
United Kingdom	65.9	****37.4**	***38.3**	****9.6**	****27.7**	24.4
Europe	**62.8**	**22.9**	**45.1**	**5.0**	**18.0**	**31.8**

Key: Bold, **: five countries with highest levels. Bold, *: five countries with lowest levels

Source: European Social Survey 2004; own computations; see Tables 4.1 and 4.2

or generally when cheating in second-hand sales. Table 4.4 demonstrates that the vast majority of Europeans find in particular the latter two of these behaviours morally wrong (88.5 per cent and 91.8 per cent). In contrast only half of them (53 per cent) find tax avoidance morally wrong. There is a clear hierarchy of victims, which indicates highest moral restraint when dealing with fellow citizens, or with insurers, but much less so when the government is the victim, reflecting also levels of offending (Table 4.2). Germany, Austria and France, as well as Slovenia and Ukraine, stand out with comparably low levels of moral condemnation of such behaviours, whilst Nordic countries show a high level of commitment. Consequently, only a minority of European citizens would dare to ask others if they were willing to assist in a fraudulent use of cards (10 per cent).

Commitment to legal norms is generally at lower levels (Table 4.5). Not even the majority (44.7 per cent) of Europeans disagree with the statement: 'If you want to make money, you can't

Table 4.4 Moral commitment (% wrong)

Country	*Avoid VAT, tax %*	*Cheat in second-hand sale %*	*Insurance fraud %*
Austria	***35.2**	***88.2**	***75.3**
Belgium	***40.1**	93.2	90.9
Czech Republic	64.3	95.0	90.4
Denmark	58.2	95.6	93.1
Estonia	****67.6**	94.6	94.4
Finland	64.2	96.2	92.3
France	***32.1**	***88.6**	***81.3**
Germany	***38.3**	***90.2**	***84.1**
Greece	****78.5**	****97.1**	****97.6**
Hungary	60.4	95.8	89.3
Iceland	****68.2**	****100.0**	****95.5**
Ireland	57.6	94.9	****97.5**
Luxembourg	***37.1**	94.6	91.7
Netherlands	41.0	94.0	94.5
Norway	60.7	****97.0**	****97.0**
Poland	54.0	91.8	88.1
Portugal	****75.4**	93.4	90.8
Slovakia	65.5	90.3	88.0
Slovenia	51.2	***88.0**	***85.5**
Spain	55.9	91.1	86.2
Sweden	62.3	****96.6**	95.5
Switzerland	59.7	90.8	93.0
Turkey	****85.0**	****97.8**	****98.4**
Ukraine	59.2	***83.9**	***84.2**
United Kingdom	54.9	93.3	91.1
Europe	**54.0**	**91.8**	**88.5**

Key: Bold, **: five countries with highest levels. Bold, *: five countries with lowest levels

Source: European Social Survey 2004; How wrong, if at all, do you consider the following ways of behaving to be? a) Paying cash with no receipt as to avoid paying VAT or other taxes? b) selling something second-hand and concealing some or all its faults? c) making an exaggerated or false insurance claim. % wrong/seriously wrong

always act honestly'. Slightly contradictorily, when asked whether one 'should always strictly obey the law even if it means missing good opportunities' two-thirds (66.8 per cent) are in agreement. Such discrepancies are observed in particular for Greece or the Netherlands, while in Slovenia, Portugal or Norway commitment to legal norms seems to be more equalized.

However, collective moral commitment hardly translates into actual rates of offending, and neither do experiences of victimization lead to higher moral censure. This applies to general offending as well as to particular transgressions, with one exception. Moral censure of insurance fraud reduces rates of offending, as Figure 4.2 shows. It seems that collective moral commitment acts as little restraint when opportunities and lure are abundant, and has little impact on the pool of potentially motivated offenders.[7]

Table 4.5 Commitment to legal norms

Country	*Cannot always act honestly (% disagree)*	*Strictly obey law (% agree)*
Austria	46.4	***50.7**
Belgium	40.9	***47.5**
Czech Republic	44.0	65.6
Denmark	****63.3**	69.4
Estonia	39.0	65.7
Finland	47.4	69.6
France	50.2	69.7
Germany	43.6	65.3
Greece	***25.7**	****74.2**
Hungary	***35.2**	66.7
Iceland	54.5	63.6
Ireland	48.4	****74.9**
Luxembourg	38.9	66.7
Netherlands	****64.7**	***43.8**
Norway	****65.7**	****74.9**
Poland	***35.4**	67.5
Portugal	****67.0**	****71.1**
Slovakia	41.8	***57.3**
Slovenia	***38.7**	***52.4**
Spain	55.3	65.3
Sweden	****56.5**	63.5
Switzerland	42.1	63.5
Turkey	42.5	****83.2**
Ukraine	***25.8**	57.8
United Kingdom	47.5	67.4
Europe	**44.7**	**66.8**

Key: Bold, **: five countries with highest levels. Bold, *: five countries with lowest levels

Source: European Social Survey 2004; a) If you want to make money, you can't always act honestly (% disagree/strongly); b) You should always strictly obey the law even if it means missing good opportunities (% agree/strongly)

The correlates of moral economies: webs of fear and distrust

Given the high levels of victimization at the hands of supermarkets and grocers, insurers and banks, tradespeople and fellow citizens, fear of being treated unfairly or distrust of these groups and their services should be widespread. Slightly more than a quarter (27.2 per cent) of European citizens are generally worried that they might become a victim of fraud at the hands of these groups. As Table 4.6 shows, countries with high levels of fear are transitional economies as well as in the South of Europe; countries with extremely low levels of fear are the Nordic countries and Switzerland.

Distrust of tradespeople like car mechanics, plumbers and building companies, and of financial services, is generally highest in established market economies, as Table 4.7 demonstrates. Consumers in Germany, Greece, Spain and the United Kingdom distrust either both types of companies and services or only one. The Nordic countries have lowest levels of distrust, including Iceland with little distrust of their banks and insurers, which might have considerably changed after 2008. However,

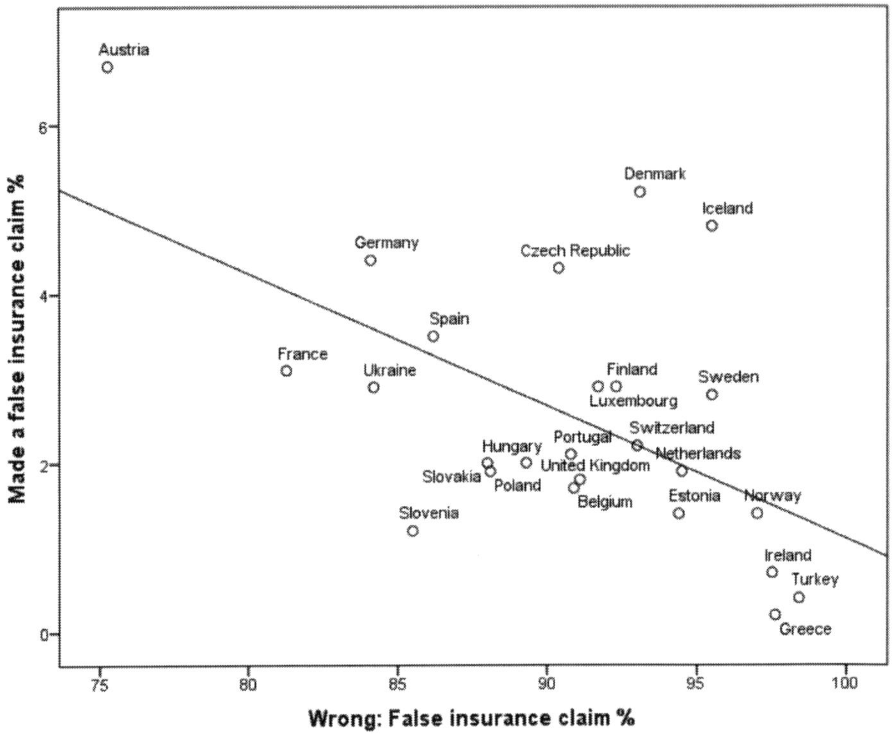

Figure 4.2 Moral commitment and offending: fraudulent insurance claim

R-square: .32; F(1, 23) = 10.75**; p < .01

Source: European Social Survey 2004; see Tables 4.2 and 4.4

Table 4.6 Fear of being treated dishonestly (% worried)

Country	*%*	*Country*	*%*
Austria	15.3	**Netherlands**	12.4
Belgium	19.0	**Norway**	***6.0**
Czech Republic	****50.8**	**Poland**	****58.4**
Denmark	***7.9**	**Portugal**	****33.9**
Estonia	14.8	**Slovakia**	23.6
Finland	13.6	**Slovenia**	16.2
France	16.3	**Spain**	****40.9**
Germany	20.6	**Sweden**	***6.1**
Greece	25.9	**Switzerland**	***7.9**
Hungary	20.9	**Turkey**	28.5
Iceland	***4.8**	**Ukraine**	****46.0**
Ireland	11.7	**United Kingdom**	17.6
Luxembourg	19.4	**Europe**	**27.2**

Key: Bold, **: five countries with highest levels. Bold, *: five countries with lowest levels

Source: European Social Survey 2004; We have just asked you about experiences of being treated dishonestly over the past five years. How worried are you that things like this will happen to you? (% fairly/very worried)

Table 4.7 Distrust: tradespeople and financial services (% distrust)

Country	*Tradespeople %*	*Financial services %*
Austria	19.7	24.9
Belgium	26.2	27.9
Czech Republic	28.2	29.7
Denmark	22.1	***19.2**
Estonia	22.0	***18.9**
Finland	***10.4**	***12.4**
France	28.7	****45.3**
Germany	****30.4**	****39.1**
Greece	****30.3**	****40.4**
Hungary	17.3	31.0
Iceland	***9.5**	***13.6**
Ireland	26.0	36.2
Luxembourg	****31.4**	20.0
Netherlands	24.6	26.2
Norway	***14.9**	***15.9**
Poland	23.0	24.9
Portugal	22.9	27.0
Slovakia	18.0	24.4
Slovenia	***15.7**	19.6
Spain	****32.1**	****40.3**
Sweden	***15.8**	30.1
Switzerland	17.2	30.3
Turkey	23.9	26.5
Ukraine	28.3	****47.1**
United Kingdom	****37.2**	27.3
Europe	**27.7**	**34.0**

Key: Bold, **: five countries with highest levels. Bold, *: five countries with lowest levels

Source: European Social Survey 2004; How much would you trust the following groups to deal honestly with people like you? a) Plumbers, builders, car mechanics and other repair people; b) financial companies such as banks or insurers

worries about being treated dishonestly are only partially related to distrust of particular businesses. It is mainly distrust of the financial sector that drives overall fear ($r = .39; p < .05$), reflecting markets with information that is difficult to understand, and products that are highly complex generating thus more insecurity for consumers (see e.g. Karstedt and Farrall 2006/2007: 53).

Distrust in the market place is not related to rates of general and particular victimization, with the exception of victimization at the hands of tradespeople. Figure 4.3 shows that across Europe, victimization in such common and everyday exchanges, which is perhaps more frequent and palpable, increases distrust of these businesses.

Rather than being linked through actual experience of victimization or offending in markets, fear and distrust are anchored in social trust and moral commitment more generally. Figure 4.4 shows a strong relationship between fear of markets and generalized distrust among citizens: little trust among citizens generally creates increasing levels of fear of victimization in the market.[8] Where citizens more widely disagree that making money implies dishonesty, i.e. where commitment to legal norms is higher, they are also less fearful of being treated dishonestly as shown in

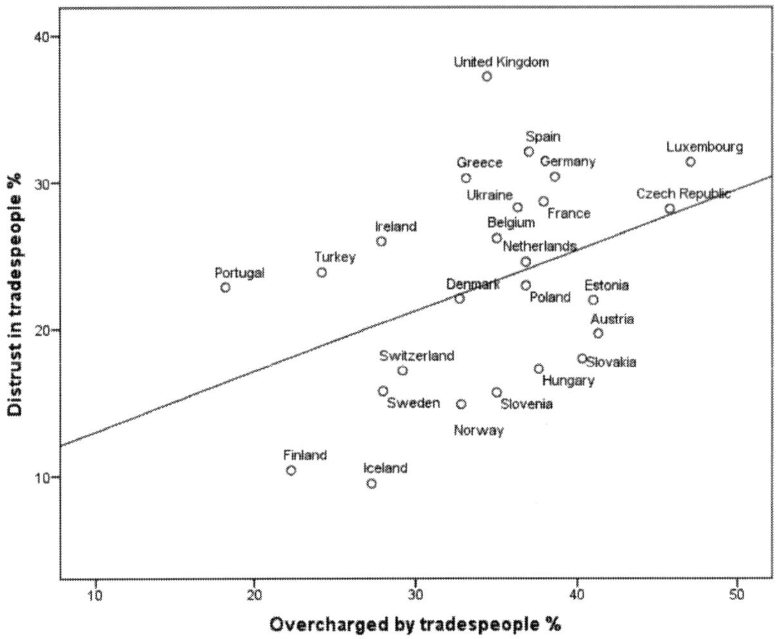

Figure 4.3 Victimization and distrust: tradespeople

R-square: .17; F(1, 23) = 4.56*; $p < .05$

Source: European Social Survey 2004; see Tables 4.1 and 4.7

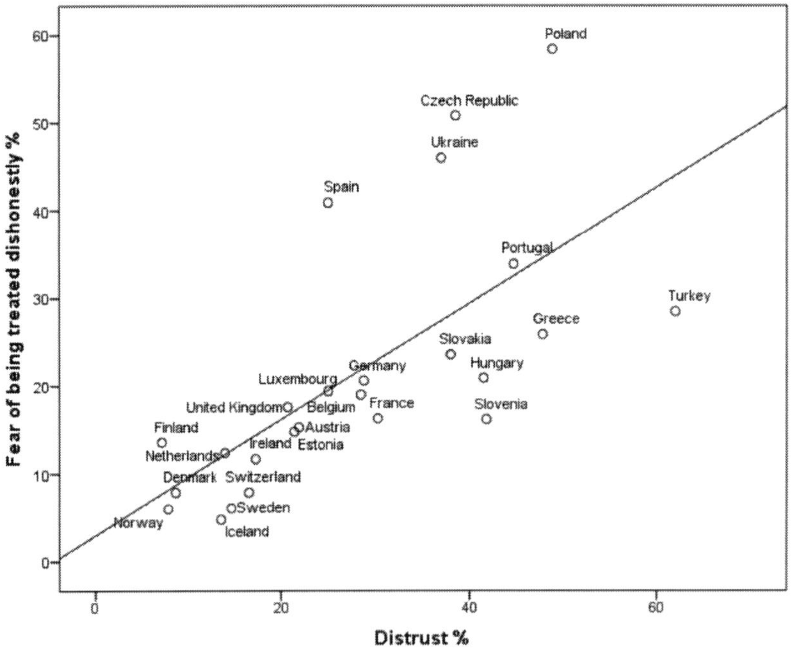

Figure 4.4 Consumer fear and generalized distrust

R-square: .45; F(1, 23) = 18.93***; $p < .001$

Source: European Social Survey 2004; see Table 4.6; Distrust: Generally speaking, would you say that most people can be trusted, or that you can't be too careful in dealing with people? Please tell me on a score of 0 to 10, where 0 means you can't be too careful and 10 means that most people can be trusted; % 0–3

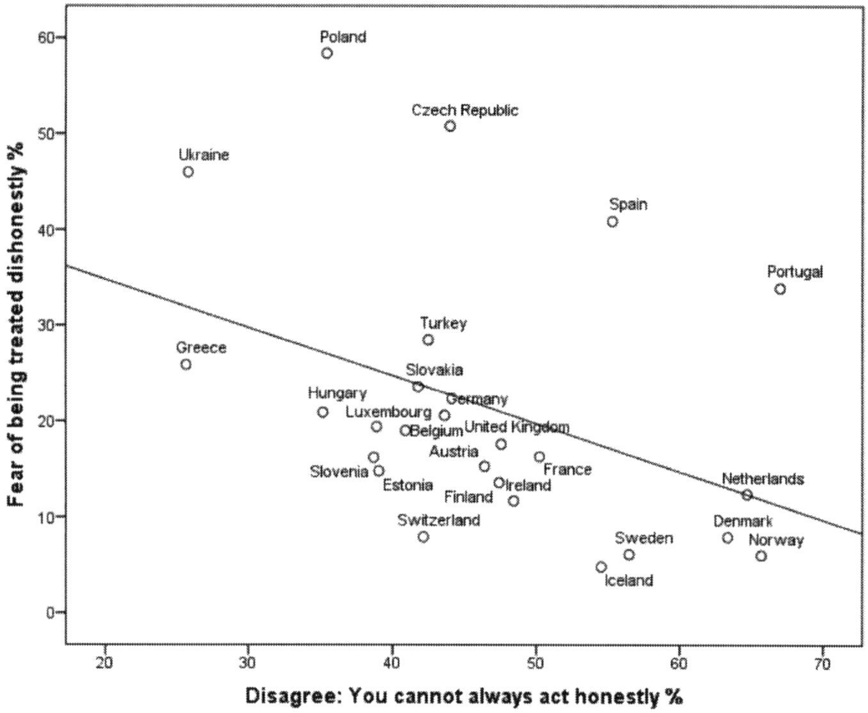

Figure 4.5 Commitment to legal norms and consumer fear

R-square: .16; F(1, 23) = 4.22°; p < .1

Source: European Social Survey 2004; see Tables 4.5 and 4.6

Figure 4.5. However, countries with high levels of distrust generally have a surplus of fear, even when their levels of commitment to legal norms is high, as for example in Spain and Portugal. Fear in markets thus is linked to generalized morality and trust, on which exchanges between strangers and in non-personal relationships are based, in markets as well as in other realms of society.

Justice in the moral economy: power and fairness, commitment and fear

Thompson's (1971) original conceptualization of the moral economy focuses on the acceptance and legitimacy of power relations in market exchanges, and foremost on the perceptions of fairness of prices and profits. Besides being judged by distributive fairness or just outcomes, markets and moral economies are also defined by 'procedural justice', i.e. that vendors and buyers act according to rules and regulations that can guarantee 'fair deals' for all. In particular the powerful – big businesses – have to play by the rules of markets, and this involves transparency, avoidance of bias and honest communication (Sondak and Tyler 2007). The legitimacy of markets and the 'pricing' mechanism (Fiske 1992; McGraw and Tetlock 2005) is based on perceptions of fairness of market procedures, and it is endangered when powerful actors are capable of violating these procedures. Fair treatment at the hands of authorities and their trustworthiness have been identified as important factors in securing compliance with traffic rules (Tyler 1990/2006) and enhancing 'tax integrity' (Braithwaite 2009). Breaches of traffic rules and tax evasion are both typical transgressions of everyday life, and committed by otherwise law-abiding middle classes.

In contemporary European moral economies, fairness and the balance of power relations emerge as one of their most important features. Unfair procedures in consumer markets include little concern for consumers and preoccupation with profits as well as price fixing, both leading to unfair deals for consumers. They also imply that businesses are powerful enough to engage in such practices, and as such they are indicative of an imbalance of power in markets, where consumers have little chance of being properly informed and receiving fair deals. Karstedt and Farrall (2007) report a number of incidents where people felt in particular powerless in dealing with banks, insurers and retailers, and recent regulation of banks has particularly focused on full information for consumers as a necessary counterbalance against their powerful positions.

Table 4.8 shows that the majority of European citizens deem unfair practices widespread in contemporary consumer markets: two-thirds (67.9 per cent) see businesses ignoring the interest

Table 4.8 Power and fairness in markets

Country	*Businesses only profit-oriented %*	*Businesses fix prices %*	*Consumers in better position %*
Austria	58.6	65.6	57.7
Belgium	64.5	67.7	****70.8**
Czech Republic	67.9	70.4	***47.3**
Denmark	***40.0**	68.1	62.3
Estonia	***54.4**	67.7	***43.4**
Finland	***54.4**	***56.6**	61.6
France	****71.6**	****76.8**	65.6
Germany	60.4	72.8	50.2
Greece	****82.0**	****85.8**	61.8
Hungary	69.6	66.4	***20.8**
Iceland	***50.0**	72.7	52.4
Ireland	67.0	73.0	****71.3**
Luxembourg	60.0	70.6	61.8
Netherlands	54.6	***62.1**	****80.4**
Norway	***53.6**	***52.1**	65.6
Poland	****71.4**	74.2	49.1
Portugal	****83.4**	****75.6**	57.4
Slovakia	66.9	66.7	***40.7**
Slovenia	61.3	***62.8**	58.0
Spain	71.3	****78.2**	****70.3**
Sweden	55.7	65.5	59.2
Switzerland	63.5	71.7	66.6
Turkey	****78.4**	****77.6**	****69.8**
Ukraine	70.2	73.9	***31.7**
United Kingdom	66.1	***63.5**	64.5
Europe	**67.9**	**72.3**	**57.9**

Key: Bold, **: five countries with highest levels. Bold, *: five countries with lowest levels

Source: European Social Survey 2004; How much do you agree or disagree with each of the statements about the way the economy works these days? Nowadays ... a) businesses are only interested in making profits and not improving service or quality for consumers; b) large firms work together in order to keep their prices unnecessarily high; c) customers and consumers are in a better position to protect their interests; % agree/strongly

of consumers, and even slightly more (72.3 per cent) fixing prices. On the other hand, more than half (57.9 per cent) agree that consumers are in a better position to protect their interests. Mostly in the established market economies of West and South Europe, business practices are seen as unfair; however, in a number of West European countries consumers feel that they have gained in power, and in Spain and Turkey such perceptions coincide with equal levels of perceptions of unfair business practices. Surprisingly, and in contrast to what would be expected, all five countries with lowest levels of consumer empowerment are post-communist new market economies: Czech Republic, Estonia, Hungary, Slovakia and Ukraine. This might be the result of rising consumer prices for staple goods and energy, which did not keep pace with incomes. Such perceptions of power (or powerlessness) in markets are related to actual and structural power differentials in society: The higher the level of income inequality, the more businesses are perceived as unfair actors in markets.[9] Figure 4.6 demonstrates these structural underpinnings for one of the core components of the moral economy, the unfair disregard of consumer interests by businesses.

Perceived unfairness by businesses is a predictor of distrust of banks and insurers (businesses only interested in profit: $r = .59$; $p < .01$; businesses fix prices: $r = .63$; $p < .01$). It also reduces moral commitment and causes dis-allegiance with norms and rules. The more citizens perceive businesses as unfair in their country, the less they disagree that in order to make money one cannot always act honestly; this applies to businesses disregarding the interests of consumers, as

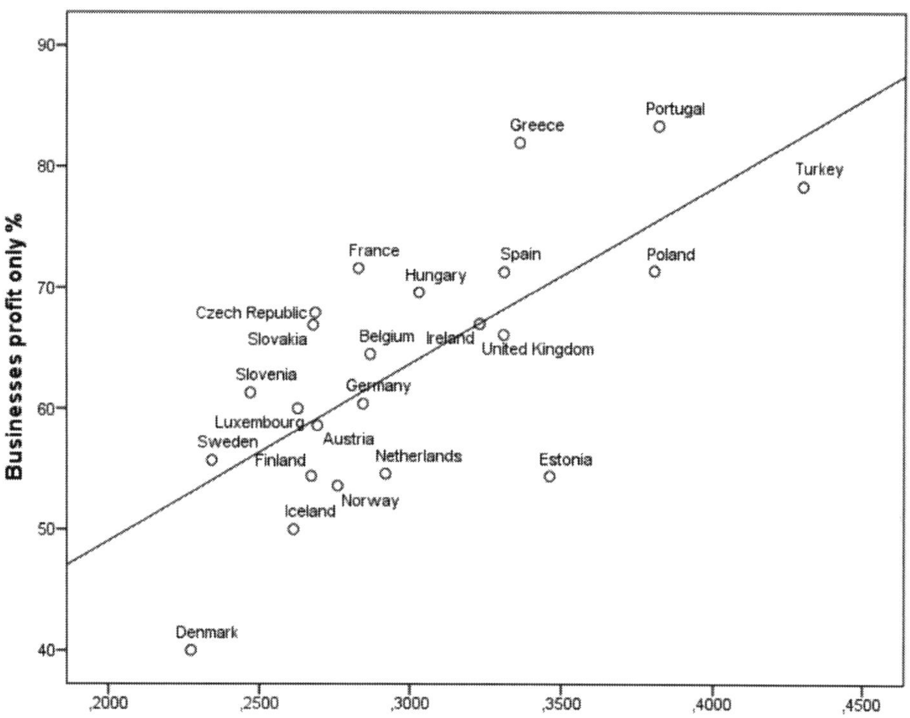

Figure 4.6 Inequality and unfairness: businesses only interested in profit (% agree)

R-square: .50; $F(1, 21) = 20.85^{***}$; $p < .001$

Source: European Social Survey 2004; see Table 4.8. For the Gini Index, see note 9

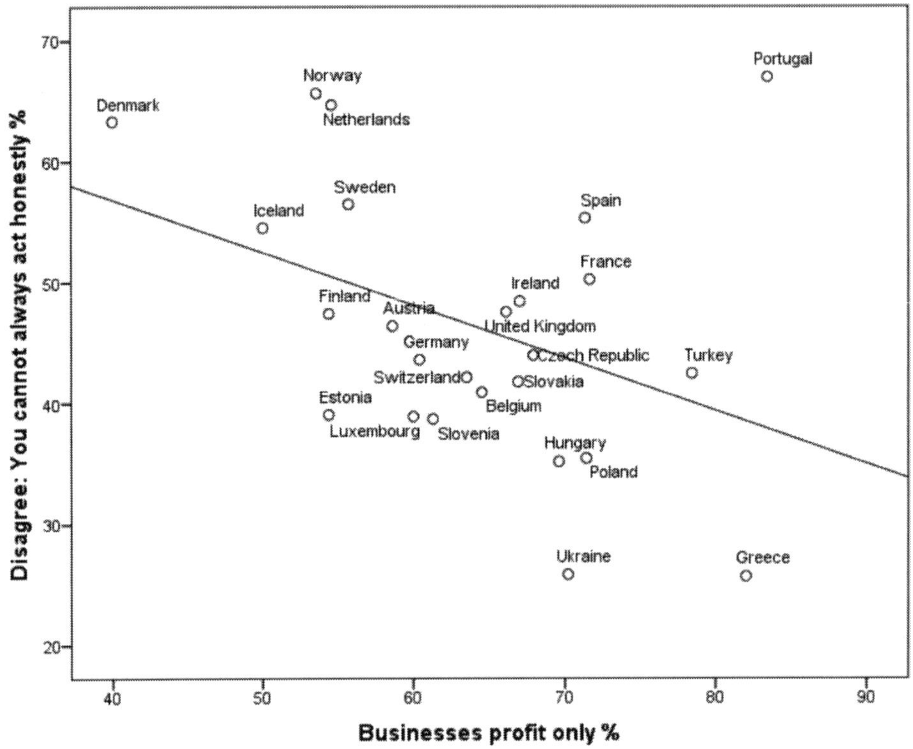

Figure 4.7 Unfairness in markets and commitment to legal norms: businesses only interested in profit

R-square: .15; F(1, 23) = 4.19°; p < .1

Source: European Social Survey 2004; see Tables 4.5 and 4.8

Figure 4.7 shows, as well as to unfair (and illegal) price fixing (r = –.36; p < .05). Perceptions of unfairness of businesses seem to have a similar impact on citizens as for instance in encounters with authorities like the police and judiciary (Tyler 1990/2006). If, however, consumers feel empowered to protect their interests, commitment to legal norms increases substantially, corroborating the effect on potential compliance with norms in markets that has been found for procedural justice in other realms. Figure 4.8 shows that the more consumers feel empowered, the more they disagree that one cannot act honestly when making money. However, the lack of commitment to legal norms does not seamlessly translate into higher rates of actual offending in the market place.

It is important to note that besides the increase of distrust and the decrease of norm commitment, which is to be found in all societal settings, there is a strong impact of perceptions of unfair procedures on the general fear of being treated dishonestly, which seems specific to the setting of markets. Such fears of victimization increase strongly with widespread perceptions of unfair practices, as Figure 4.9 demonstrates for businesses disregarding the interests of consumers and acting exclusively in a self-interested manner (for price fixing: r = .46; p < .05). In contrast, consumers are less fearful if they feel that they can protect their own interests (r = –.34; p < .1).

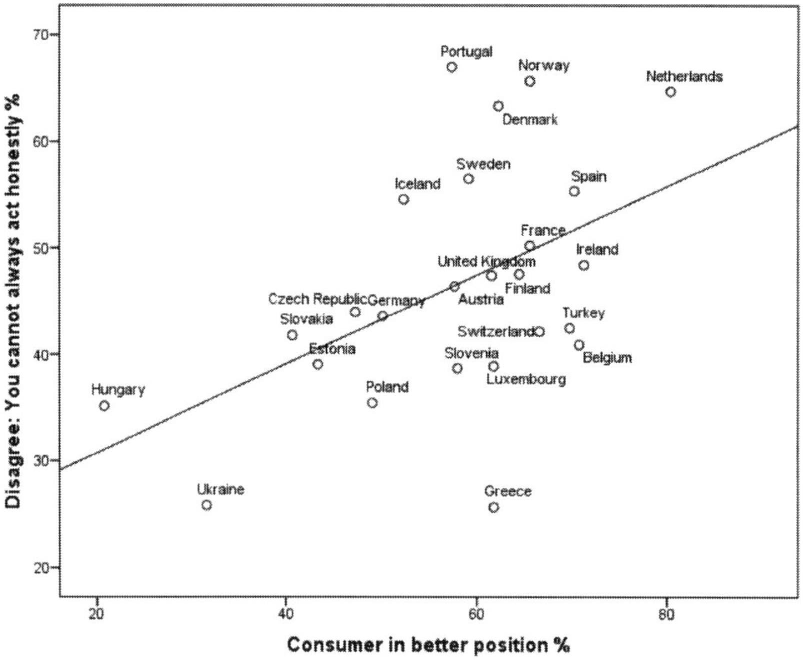

Figure 4.8 Consumer empowerment and commitment to legal norms

R-square: .24; F(1, 23) = 7.44*; p < .05

Source: European Social Survey 2004; see Tables 4.5 and 4.8

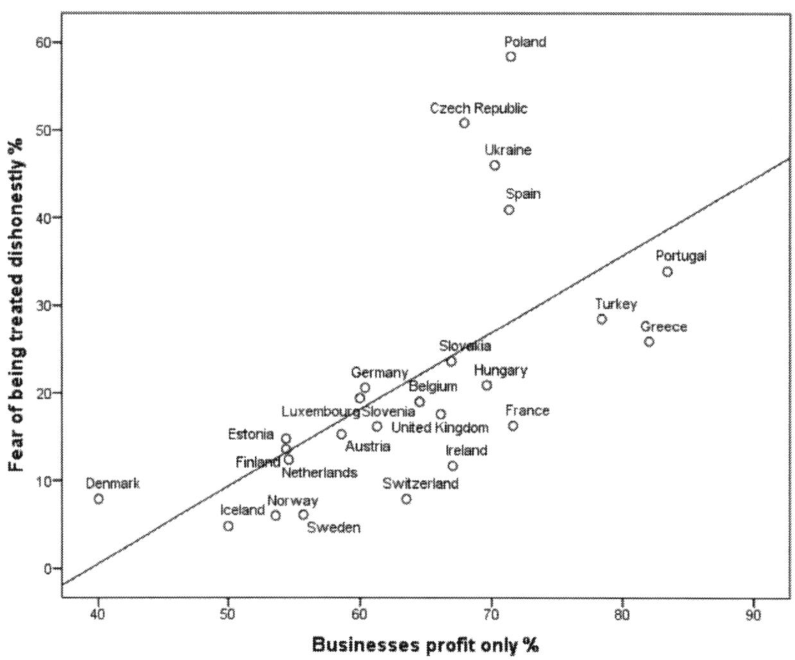

Figure 4.9 Unfairness and consumer fear

R-square: .38; F(1, 23) = 14.34**; p < .01

Source: European Social Survey 2004; see Tables 4.6 and 4.8

Inequality and power: need, greed or opportunities?

Average income earners in the very centre of society have access to a number of illegitimate means that are not available to the less well-to-do strata in society, and not alluring for the well-off upper classes. These include products like insurance (Ericson et al. 1999), services in the banking sector, usage of shops and services with generous policies for replacements and refunds (Karstedt and Farrall 2004), access to specific tax refunds and entitlements (J. Braithwaite 2005; V. Braithwaite 2009) or to government benefits and services, but also to opportunities that arise in their capacity as professionals. These opportunities tend to increase with increasing wealth and income for the average income earner. They constitute opportunities for offending and engaging in illegal and morally dubious practices, but they also make the average income earner susceptible to fraud victimization. According to Braithwaite (1992: 81), inequality increases 'crimes of poverty motivated by *need* for goods to *use*' and 'crimes of *wealth* motivated by greed'; there is a 'social structuring of feelings of need and greed' (Braithwaite 1992: 101), resulting in both high levels of typical crimes of need at the lower end of the social pyramid and high levels of typical crimes of greed at its peak.

This structuring of crimes and their different motivations has recently been corroborated for the peak of the social pyramid by financial crises in European countries, by scandals involving respectable members of parliament in Britain, who exploited tax and refund schemes (Winnett and Rayner 2009), by failures of financial markets caused by 'infectious greed' (Partnoy 2004), and cases of corporate failure caused by greed like Enron (Hamilton and Micklethwait 2006). If 'greed was good' for Wall Street, the average earner, citizen and consumer should also have been affected. Greed rather than need makes this group not only more motivated to engage in illegal practices, but it makes them also easy targets for lure, for investment schemes with incredibly high returns, or for the not-to be-missed deal on the internet and in second-hand sales; they are both predators and prey. Greed loosens the internal constraints that play a decisive role in our choice model of middle-class crime. Accordingly, Holtfreter et al. (2008) found that low self-control was related to significantly higher levels of fraud victimization on the individual level. However, the group of average income earners comprise a range of households from those who live comfortably to those who find themselves in financially difficult situations; accordingly greed as well as need might drive the crimes of everyday life. Average income earners are particularly hit by economic and financial crises, and the 'fear of falling' (Wheeler 1992: 118) might tempt them to take to illegal practices, like fraudulently claiming benefits (Tunley 2011), or reverting into the shadow economy.

According to Braithwaite (1992), inequality increases both crimes in the suites and crimes in the streets, i.e. at the top and bottom strata of society. Does it also increase the crimes and unfair practices that are committed at the kitchen table and from home computers, or in interactions with builders and other tradespeople that are committed by the average income earner and middle-class citizens? As Figures 4.10 and 4.11 show, such crimes are at their highest levels in the most egalitarian societies where income inequality is lowest. Egalitarian countries like the Nordic countries, Germany, Austria or the Netherlands have the highest rates of offenders, and also of victim-offenders; countries with high levels of income inequality like Turkey, Portugal or Poland have lowest levels. Societies with more equal distributions of income have large middle classes. These are not only coveted consumers who are offered and have access to the higher range of consumer goods and services with an array of criminal opportunities; they are also voters, and therefore targeted by state policies with tax breaks, or benefit programmes (J. Braithwaite 2005; V. Braithwaite 2009). More equal societies have a larger pool of offenders of whom many are simultaneously victims. They seem to offer more 'lure' to average earners than societies with less

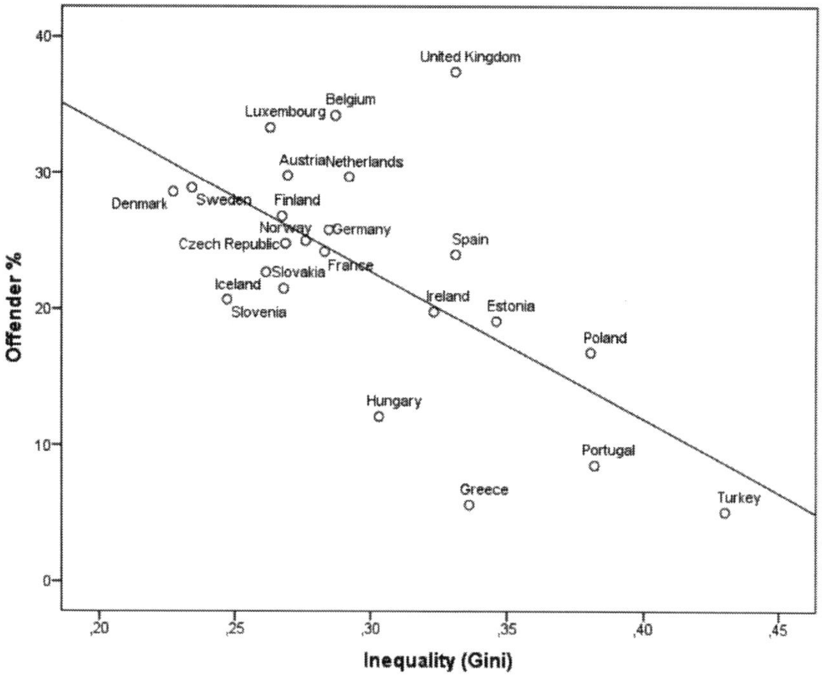

Figure 4.10 Inequality and offending in the market place (% at least once)

R-square: .42; F(1,21) = 14.28**; p < .01

Source: European Social Survey 2004; see Table 4.3, own computations, and Figure 4.6

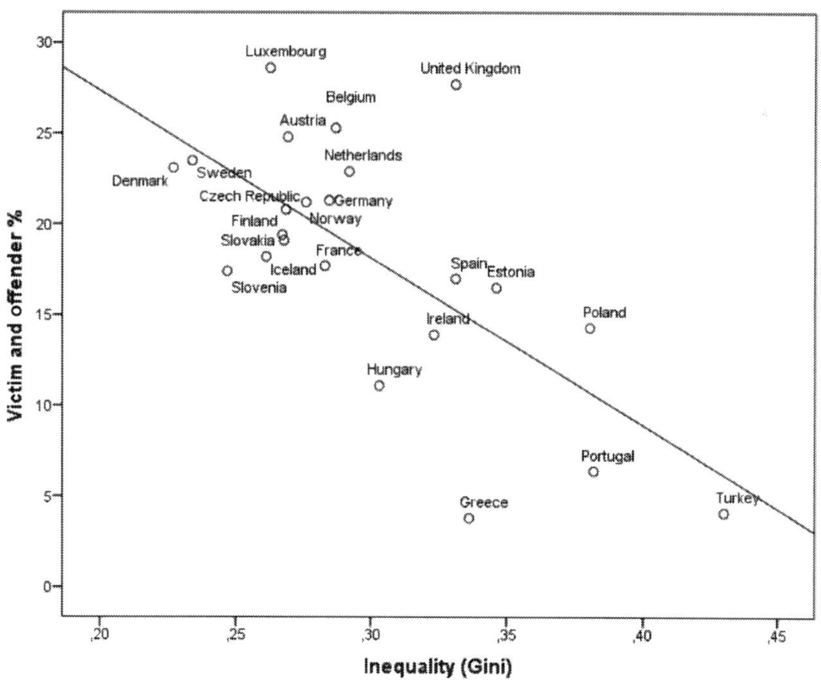

Figure 4.11 Income inequality and victimization/offending

R-square: .47; F(1,21) = 18.45***; p < .001

Source: European Social Survey 2004; see Table 4.3, own computations, and note 10

equal distributions of income, and more equality does not encourage higher levels of commitment to moral and legal norms that might restrain middle-class consumers (see also Offer 2006).

Karstedt and Farrall (2006, 2007) report for the United Kingdom that the crimes of everyday life are more often committed by offenders with average to high incomes, and victim-and-offenders are significantly more often found in this group. This result indicates that greed rather than need motivates these types of illegal and morally dubious practices. When comparing European moral economies according to their median level of household income, i.e. the income that half of the population achieve,[10] the rates of crimes of everyday life are significantly higher in countries where average consumers and earners are better off, as for example in Norway and Luxembourg, and are lower where incomes are at much lower levels as in transition countries or South Europe. This applies to offenders generally as well as to those who are victims and offenders, as Figures 4.12 and 4.13 show. This indicates that greed slightly crowds out need as motivation for the crimes of everyday life; the fact that the relationship is strong for victims and offenders indeed corroborates the strength of greed over need in the middle of society. If taken together both equality and higher incomes provide average consumers, citizens and income earners with opportunities and lure, and also make them targets for others. Thus, rather than need or greed, opportunities seem to shape the moral economies of Europe and the rate of illegal and morally dubious actions of its consumers and citizens.

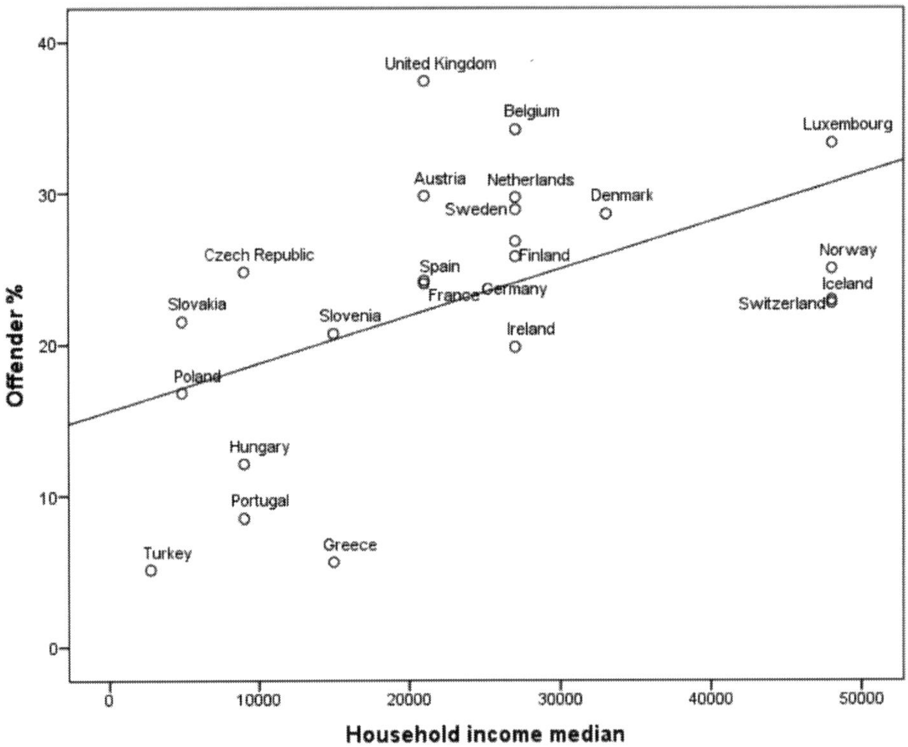

Figure 4.12 Household income and offending in the market place

R-square: .27; F(1, 21) = 7.73*; p < .05

Source: European Social Survey 2004; Table 4.3, own computations; for median household income, see note 10

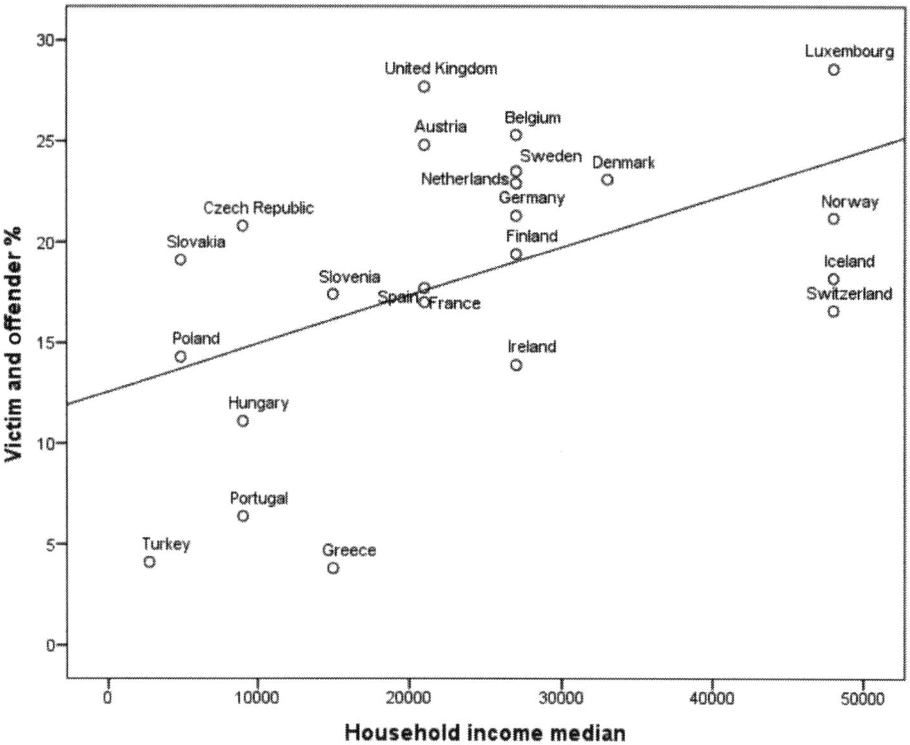

Figure 4.13 Household income and victimization/offending

R-square: 25; F(1, 21) = 6.98*; p < .05

Source: European Social Survey 2004; see Table 4.3, own computations and note 9

The European landscape of moral economies

Compared with other global regions, European societies on average are mostly rich, and combined are more equal than countries in other regions. These characteristics of structuring coincide with generally large middle classes, only equalled by the United States and Canada, Australia and New Zealand. Taken together these characteristics are decisive in shaping the rate of the crimes of everyday life that are committed by members of the otherwise law-abiding classes at the centre of contemporary European societies. This suggests a larger role for greed rather than need as motivation to engage in these crimes and morally dubious practices. Like other contemporary white-collar crimes the crimes of everyday life are a product 'in many ways of an advanced economy with high-speed communications', large government apparatus (Henning 2008: 330) and comparably affluent middle classes. From a perspective of 'choice', European middle classes are confronted with an 'enormous supply of lure' as Shover and Grabosky (2010: 431) note, both by businesses and the state. Lure and opportunities seem to emerge as the most important factors shaping the rates of such crimes and actual engagement in such practices by many citizens.

European countries and their moral economies also typically differ according to the type of relationships that define different markets for consumer goods and services, and according to the ways in which citizens relate to government institutions and agencies when paying taxes and claiming benefits. Roughly three regions emerge. There is still a divide between the transitional economies of the post-communist countries in East and Central Europe and the established market economies in other parts of Europe, which shapes rates of offending and victimization, as well as the prevalence of different types. This coincides with differences in terms of moral and legal commitment, perceptions of power and fairness in markets, as well as distrust of businesses and fear of being treated dishonestly, often related to specific types of markets, products and services, as well as to dealings with the government. The two other regions comprise, first, the most advanced and urbanized economies of West and North Europe and, second, the more rural economies of Southern Europe, where personal relationships still might matter in dealing with tradespeople, banks and insurers. When white-collar crime is 'writ small' (Levitt 2006) personal relations, reciprocity and concern matter.

From the perspective of moral economies collectively shared within each country, experiences of victimization hardly shape distrust, fear or moral commitment; given the considerable overlap between victims and offenders, actual offending itself is mostly immune to commitment to moral and legal norms. 'Generalized morality' and implicit agreements and concern for others (Granovetter 1985: 489) seem to be less important in shaping moral economies, as they do not collectively act as restraints on the pool of potentially motivated offenders. However, and in line with the original concept by Thompson (1971), power relations, and linked to these, collective perceptions of procedural fairness in markets of goods and services are the lynchpin of contemporary moral economies as they were in eighteenth-century Britain. If businesses are seen as being involved in unfair practices that disadvantage consumers, this coincides with dis-allegiance to legal norms, distrust of businesses, and fear of being treated dishonestly. Collectively shared perceptions of fair treatment and fair exchanges are cornerstones of 'generalized morality' in the economies of Europe. Regulating and prosecuting unfair and semi-legal practices of businesses, tightly monitoring abuse of their power, as well as empowering consumers to protect their interests seem to be reasonable routes to reduce losses from widespread fraud. Rather than deploring ever increasing fraud by consumers and citizens, European businesses need to realize that turning 'markets of vice' into 'markets of virtue' – to use Braithwaite's (2005) terms – is also their business.

Appendix

Table 4.A List of countries

Austria	**Netherlands**
Belgium	**Norway**
Czech Republic	**Poland**
Denmark	**Portugal**
Estonia	**Slovakia**
Finland	**Slovenia**
France	**Spain**
Germany	**Sweden**
Greece	**Switzerland**
Hungary	**Turkey**
Iceland	**Ukraine**
Ireland	**United Kingdom**
Luxembourg	

Notes

1 I am grateful to Stephen Farrall, University of Sheffield, and Kai Bussmann, Martin-Luther University Halle, with whom I conducted the original research between 2001 and 2003. I thank Stephen and the European team, with whom I designed the module for the Round Two of the European Social Survey in 2004. Most of all, I thank Michael Koch, University of Bielefeld, for his invaluable contributions and data collection, analyses and graphics.

2 For individual-level analyses of these data from the European Social Survey 2004 see Hirtenlehner et al. 2013; Kotzian 2011; other comparative analyses at the individual level include Karstedt and Farrall (2006).

3 German citizens almost collectively took to insurance fraud when expensive glasses frames were excluded from cover by state health insurance in the early 1990s. Household insurers suddenly were inundated with claims for broken spectacles mainly in the upper range of the price scale, of which about 90 per cent were fraudulent (as the expert hired by the insurance industry estimated; information from interviews in Germany). Consumers reacted with illegal methods on a large scale to the withdrawal of what they felt an entitlement (Karstedt and Farrall 2004: 70).

4 In Germany, personal liability insurance beyond car insurance is available, but not in the United Kingdom. This offers rich opportunities for committing insurance fraud, of which Germans amply take advantage, as the threefold level of insurance fraud compared with the United Kingdom demonstrates (Karstedt and Farrall 2006: 1033). This is mirrored by twice as high intentions to commit such a crime (Karstedt and Farrall 2006: 1023).

5 European Social Survey 2004 available at www.europeansocialsurvey.org. The module 'Economic morality' on which this research is based, is one of the rotating modules and only available for 2004 (see http://www.europeansocialsurvey.org/data/module-index.html). However, there is no reason to assume that opportunities for middle-class crime have changed dramatically since then. In addition, there is no reason to assume that the theorized relationships have changed following, for example, the economic crisis in 2008, which hit European countries quite differently. It can be firmly posited that even if some of the data might change, the ranks of countries will be mainly unchanged and correlations will be robust, and stand the test of time. Weighted data were used in order to account for differences in sampling design and population size. The Design weight corrects for slightly different probabilities of selection, thereby making the sample more representative of a 'true' sample of individuals aged 15+ in each country. The Population Size weight is used when examining data for two or more countries combined. This weight corrects for the fact that most countries taking part in the ESS have very similar sample sizes, no matter how large or small their population. The Population Size weight makes an adjustment to ensure that each country is represented in proportion to its population size. For more information, see the ESS Documentation Report at www.europeansocialsurvey.org.

6 It needs to be noted that the survey in 2004 preceded the banking crisis. In particular consumers in Iceland might have had second thoughts about the deals they had got from their banks after the banking crisis four years later.

7 However, if instead of actual offending rates intentions to offend are used, moral commitment has an impact in a comparative individual-level analysis of Germany (West and East) and England and Wales (Karstedt and Farrall 2006). This result indicates that actual offending, i.e. the realization of offending, to a large extent depends on the availability of opportunities rather than the pool of potential offenders.

8 The measure of generalized (dis)trust is based on the relevant question in the European Social Survey Round 2, 2004. Respondents could use a scale from 0 (no trust at all) to 10 (complete trust). For each country the percentages of categories 0–3 (high distrust) were calculated; for data and questionnaire see www.europeansocialsurvey.org.

9 The Gini Index is a measure of inequality; here inequality of household income is used, based on disposable income, after taxes and transfers have been discounted. The Gini Index of 2004 was used as provided by the OECD in 2014, available at http://stats.oecd.org/Index.aspx?DataSetCode=IDD. For some countries data from previous years were used: Denmark and Netherlands (2000), Hungary (2003).

10 The median household income is a particularly suitable measure for the income of average consumers and the 'middle classes'. It is based on data for annual household income, in euros, from the European Survey 2004; the value is the middle of the category of income that 50 per cent of the population achieve; e.g. for the category of €12,000 to under €18,000 the value of €15,000 was used. Data for Estonia and Ukraine were not included.

References

ABI (Association of British Insurers) (2000) *Update 2000*, London: Association of British Insurers.
Albanese, J.S. (2005) 'Fraud: The characteristic crime of the twenty-first century', *Trends in Organized Crime*, 8(4): 6–14.
APACS (Association for Payment and Clearance Services) (n.d.) *Fraud in Focus 2001*, London: Association for Payment and Clearance Services.
Arnold T.C. (2001) 'Rethinking moral economy', *American Political Science Review*, 95(1): 85–95.
Booth, W. (1994) 'On the idea of the moral economy', *American Political Science Review*, 88(3): 653–667.
Braithwaite, J. (1992) 'Poverty, power and white-collar crime: Sutherland and the paradoxes of criminological theory', in K. Schlegel and D. Weisburd (eds) *White Collar Crime Reconsidered*, Boston: North-Eastern University Press, pp. 78–107.
Braithwaite, J. (2005) *Markets in Vice, Markets in Virtue*, Sydney: Federation Press.
Braithwaite, V. (2009) *Defiance in Taxation and Governance: Resisting and Dismissing Authority in a Democracy*, Cheltenham: Edward Elgar.
Brand, S. and Price, R. (2000) *The Economic and Social Costs of Crime*, Home Office Research Study 217, London: Home Office
Dean, H. and Melrose, M. (1997) 'Manageable discord: Fraud and resistance in the social security system', *Social Policy and Administration*, 31(2): 103–118.
Enste, D. (2010) 'Shadow economy: The impact of regulation in OECD-countries', *International Economic Journal*, 24(4): 551–571.
Ericson, R.V., Barry, D. and Doyle, A. (1999) 'The moral hazards of neo-liberalism: Lessons from the private insurance industry', *Economy and Society*, 29: 532–558.
Fiske, A.P. (1992) 'The four elementary forms of sociality: Framework for a unified theory of social relations', *Psychological Review*, 99(4): 689–723.
Fourcade, M. and Healy, K. (2007) 'Moral views of market society', *Annual Review of Sociology*, 33: 285–311.
Gabor, T. (1994) *Everybody Does It! Crime by the Public*, Toronto: University of Toronto Press.
Granovetter, M. (1985) 'Economic action and social structure: The problem of embeddedness', *American Journal of Sociology*, 91(3): 481–510.
Green, S.P. (2006) *Lying, Cheating and Stealing. A Moral Theory of White-Collar Crime*, Oxford: Oxford University Press.
Hamilton, S. and Micklethwait, A. (2006) *Greed and Corporate Failure*, Basingstoke, New York: Palgrave Macmillan.
Henning, P.J. (2008) 'The DNA of white-collar crime', *New Criminal Law Review*, 11(2): 323–354.
Hirtenlehner, H., Farrall S. and Bacher, J. (2013) 'Culture, institutions and morally dubious behaviours: Testing some core propositions of the institutional anomie theory', *Deviant Behaviour*, 34(4): 291–320.
Holtfreter, K., Reisig, M. and Pratt, T. (2008) 'Low self-control, routine activities, and fraud victimization', *Criminology*, 46(1): 189–220.
Insurance Europe (2013) *The Impact of Insurance Fraud*, Brussels: Insurance Europe.
Jesilow, P. Pontell, H. and Geis, G. (1993) *Prescription for Profit: How Doctors Defraud Medicaid*, Berkeley: University of California Press.
Karstedt, S. (2013) 'Contextualizing mass atrocity crimes: Moving towards a relational approach', *Annual Review of Law and Social Sciences*, 9: 383–404
Karstedt, S. and Farrall, S. (2004) 'The moral maze of the middle class: The predatory society and its emerging regulatory order', in H.-J. Albrecht, T. Serassis and H. Kania (eds) *Images of Crime II*, Freiburg: Edition Iuscrim, pp. 65–94.
Karstedt, S. and Farrall, S. (2006) 'The moral economy of everyday crime: Markets, consumers and citizens', *British Journal of Criminology*, 46(6): 1011–1036.
Karstedt, S. and Farrall, S. (2006/7) 'Crimes of everyday life. Business practices and consumer compliance', *Compliance and Regulatory Journal*, 1(1): 49–59.
Karstedt, S. and Farrall S. (2007) *Law Abiding Majority? The Everyday Crimes of the Middle Classes*, Briefing 3, July 2007, Centre for Crime and Justice Studies, London. http://www.crimeandjustice.org.uk/
Katungi, D., Neale, E. and Barbour, A. (2006) *People in Low-paid Work: Need not Greed*, London: Joseph Rowntree Foundation.
Kotzian, P. (2011) 'Cosi fan tutte: Information, beliefs and compliance with norms', *Zeitschrift für Soziologie*, 40(4): 158–173.

Labaton, S. (2002) 'Downturn and shift in population feed boom in white collar crime', *New York Times*, 2 June.

Levi, M. (2006) 'The media construction of financial white-collar crimes', *British Journal of Criminology*, 46(6): 1037–1057.

Levi, M. (2009) 'Suite revenge? The shaping of folk devils and moral panics about white-collar crimes', *British Journal of Criminology*, 49(1): 48–67.

Levi, M. and Burrows, J. (2008) 'Measuring the impact of fraud in the UK', *British Journal of Criminology*, 48(2): 48–67.

Levi, M, Burrows, J., Fleming, M.H. and Hopkins, M. (2007) *The Nature, Extent and Economic Impact of Fraud in the UK*, London: Association of Chief Police Officers (ACPO).

Levitt, S.D. (2006) 'White-collar crime writ small: A case study of bagels, donuts, and the honor system', *American Economic Association Papers and Proceedings*, May 2006: 290–294.

Mau, S. (2003) *The Moral Economy of Welfare States: Britain and Germany Compared*, London: Routledge.

McBarnett, D. and Whelan, C. (1999) *Creative Accounting and the Cross-eyed Javelin Thrower*, Chichester: Wiley.

McGraw, A.P. and Tetlock, P.E. (2005) 'Taboo trade-offs, relational framing and the acceptability of exchange', *Journal of Consumer Psychology*, 15(1): 2–15.

Mikhail, J. (2007) 'Universal moral grammar: Theory, evidence and future', *Trends in Cognitive Science*, 11(4): 143–152

National Fraud Authority (2013) *Annual Fraud Indicator*, London: National Fraud Authority.

Newman, D. (1958) 'White-collar crime', *Law and Contemporary Problems*, 23(4): 735–753.

Offer, A. (2006) *The Challenge of Affluence. Self-control and Well-being in the United States and Britain since 1950*, Oxford: Oxford University Press

Partnoy, F. (2004) *Infectious Greed. How Deceit and Risk Corrupted the Financial Markets*, London: Profile Books.

Rose, N. (1996) 'The death of the social? Re-figuring the territory', *Economy and Society*, 25: 327–356.

Sampson, R.J. and Bartusch, D.J. (1998) 'Legal cynicism and (subcultural?) tolerance of deviance: The neighbourhood context of racial differences', *Law and Society Review*, 32(4): 777–804.

Sayer, A. (2007) 'Moral economy as critique', *New Political Economy*, 12(2): 261–270.

Schneider, F. and Enste, D. (2000) *Schattenwirtschaft und Schwarzarbeit*, Munich and Vienna: Oldenbourg.

Schneider, F., Torgler, B and Schaltegger, C.A. (2008) *Schattenwirschaft und Steuermoral*, Zürich: Rüegger.

Shamir, R. (2008) 'The age of responsibilization: On market-embedded morality', *Economy and Society*, 27(1): 1–19.

Shover, N., Coffey, G.S. and Hobbs, D. (2003) 'Crime on the line: Telemarketing and the changing nature of professional crime', *British Journal of Criminology*, 43(4): 489–505.

Shover, N. and Grabosky, P. (2010) 'White-collar crime and the Great Recession', *Criminology and Public Policy*, 9(3): 429–433.

Simpson, S. (2011) 'Making sense of white-collar crime: Theory and research', *Ohio State Journal of Criminal Law*, 8(4): 481–502.

Sondak, H. and Tyler, T.R. (2007) 'How does procedural justice shape the desirability of markets?', *Journal of Economic Psychology*, 28(1): 79–92.

Spalek, B. and King, S. (2007) *Farepak Victims Speak Out: An Exploration of the Harms Caused by the Collapse of Farepak*, November 2007, Centre for Crime and Justice Studies, London. http://www.crimeandjustice.org.uk/.

Stadler, W.A. and Benson, M.L. (2012) 'Revisiting the guilty mind: The neutralization of white-collar crime', *Criminal Justice Review*, 37(4): 494–511.

Sutherland, E. (1940) 'White collar criminality. Presidential address to the American Society of Sociology', *American Sociological Review*, 5(1): 1–12.

Sutherland, E. (1949) *White Collar Crime*, New York: Holt, Rinehart and Winston.

Sutherland, E. (1983) *White Collar Crime. The Uncut Version.* New Haven: Yale University Press.

Tafenau, E., Herwartz, H. and Scheider, F. (2010) 'Regional estimates of the shadow economy in Europe', *International Economic Journal*, 24(4): 629–636.

Tetlock, P.E. and McGraw, A.P. (2005) 'Theoretically framing relational framing', *Journal of Consumer Psychology*, 15(1): 35–37.

Thompson, E.P. (1971) 'The moral economy of the English crowd in the eighteenth century', *Past and Present*, 50(1): 76–136.

Titus, R. (2001) 'Personal fraud and its victims', in N. Shover and J.P. Wright (eds) *Crimes of Privilege: Readings in White-Collar Crime*, Oxford: Oxford University Press, pp. 57–66.

Tunley, M. (2011) 'Need, greed or opportunity? An examination of who commits benefit fraud and why they do it', *Security Journal*, 24(4): 302–319.
Tyler, T.R. (1990/2006) *Why People Obey the Law*, 2nd edn, New Haven: Yale University Press.
Weisburd, D., Wheeler, S., Waring, E. and Bode, N. (1991) *Crimes of the Middle Classes: White Collar Offenders in the Federal Courts*, New Haven and London: Yale University Press.
Wheeler, S. (1992) 'The problem of white-collar crime motivation', in K. Schlegel and D. Weisburd (eds) *White Collar Crime Reconsidered*, Boston: North-Eastern University Press, pp. 108–123.
Wilkinson, R.G. and K.E. Pickett (2009) 'Income inequality and social dysfunction', *Annual Review of Sociology*, 35: 493–511.
Williams, C.C. (2012) 'Explaining undeclared wage payments by employers in Central and Eastern Europe: A critique of neo-liberal de-regulatory theory', *Journal of Contemporary Central and Eastern Europe*, 20(1); 3–20.
Williams, C.C. (2013) 'Explaining employers' illicit envelope wage payments in the EU-27: A product of over-regulation or under-regulation?', *Business Ethics: A European Review*, 22(3): 325–340.
Winnett, R. and Rayner, G. (2009) *No Expenses Spared*, London: Transworld Publishers.

5

On the difficulty of measuring economic crime[1]

Lars Korsell

> [T]he value of criminal statistics as a basis for measurement of criminality … decreases as the procedures take us farther away from the offence itself.
>
> Thorsten Sellin (1951: 490)

The magic of figures

The visible part of criminality is made up of the offences that are detected, reported, investigated and prosecuted. As the above quote from Sellin expresses, crime does not actually *exist* until the offences come to the attention of the agencies and get reported in official criminal statistics. This makes criminal statistics central to our understanding of the extent and nature of criminality, or – if you will – the construction of criminality (Coleman and Moynihan 1996). Indeed, statistical data often also makes for a decisive factor in drawing the attention of politicians and the media to a specific area of crime.

In this secular day and age, it is often jokingly said that statistics has become somewhat of a Swedish state religion. It is true that Sweden can boast of possessing some particularly well-developed statistical sources – the longest uninterrupted series of daytime temperature measurements in the world, for example. However, the statistical data on economic crime still has a long way to go in comparison (Bergqvist 2007). Of course, this is not a problem typical of Sweden only. Should someone ask about the extent of economic crime, the short answer reads like this: nobody really knows. In a modern society, where statistics are considered all-important, this of course represents something of a problem. The purpose of this chapter is to address the question of statistics and economic crime, not least the inherent difficulty of trying to quantify this elusive kind of criminality.

In spite of these difficulties, what kind of issues might government authorities, agencies and other stakeholders want to see answered by statistics on economic crime? Such institutions can be expected to want to use statistics for:

1 tracking the evolution of crime over time
2 describing the structure of criminality
3 addressing the problem of economic crime – also in comparison to other areas of crime

4 assessing the impact of law enforcement as well as the performance of agencies in general
5 assessing the impact of criminal justice reforms
6 describing the sanctions brought against those violating the law.

These questions will be summarized and answered in the concluding part of the chapter. In order to address the inherent difficulty of statistically measuring economic crime more concretely, the following section will make use of examples primarily gathered from Sweden. These should however be considered as descriptions of generalizable problems that should apply to most Western countries, minor differences aside.

However, it should already from the outset be stressed that Sweden differs from other Western countries in two important respects when talking about economic crime. First, in Sweden, great emphasis is given to crimes against the public (such as tax offences) and minor crimes against companies and markets (such as acts of fraud and embezzlement). Second, even though the fight against economic crime in the 1970s and 1980s was more explicitly oriented towards offenders of higher social status (similar to white-collar crime), today economic crime is no longer as laden with values and is used as a neutral, descriptive concept.

Economic crime: the big criminal policy issue of the 1970s in Sweden

The magic of figures is well illustrated by the fact that it was precisely figures that caused economic crime to be introduced as a concept as well as a political issue in 1970s Sweden. A calculation of the extent of tax evasion in the country was published (AMOB 1977), with the sum total amounting to a supposed 2 billion euros a year, had the euro existed as a currency (Svensson 1982). Back then this astounding figure became the starting shot of a criminal policy debate on a type of crime that had not been prioritized until then. A favourable climate for highlighting economic crime had also been created in the wake of a number of media revelations about economic irregularities (Heckscher 1979). A shift in criminal policy followed, and as the 1970s turned into 1980s, police authorities started to form a number of special divisions focusing on economic crime, and a row of other initiatives saw the light of day (Korsell 2000; Lindgren 2000).

Looking back on all this 35 years later, we could do well to question how these figures were arrived at. In any event, these should only be considered very rough estimates, and probably more as arithmetical exercises than proper calculations.

The transformation of white-collar crime into economic crime

Before economic crime showed up as a criminal policy issue in the 1970s, Swedes tended to talk about these activities in terms of white-collar crime, a wording which today would evoke images of embezzling accountants in starched collars – this in contrast to the more down-to-earth crime of blue-collar workers. Thus, the concept of white-collar crime both has an archaic ring to it as well as strong associations of influential people in social positions of power. In those days, economic crime had been defined as offences committed within the framework of business operations but in which the business activity itself was considered legal (this in contrast to the illegal activities of organized crime). This definition was also used by the Committee on Justice of the Swedish Parliament, and built on the previously mentioned AMOB inquiry (JuU 1980–1981: 21). After the 1970s, economic crime became an established concept in Sweden, and even though more neutral-sounding than white-collar crime, the wording still evokes vague pictures of high-society criminality (often involving large sums of money) for the general public. Nevertheless, the concept of economic crime has grown less and less politically charged as the years have passed by.

Ironically enough, a number of studies indicate that the majority of those convicted of economic crime are more likely to belong to a class of small businessmen dressed in overalls than that of managing directors (Korsell 2003). This partly has to do with the fact that, in absolute numbers, there are more small businessmen than managing directors in society, but detecting and substantiating offences committed by small businessmen is easier than those carried out higher up the corporate ladder. From a purely fiscal viewpoint, the international business group also plays in a different league than the street corner pizzeria when it comes to using legal manoeuvres to set their own level of taxation. The importance of this selective filtering for statistical outcomes is discussed further on in the chapter.

Despite the fact that economic crime occasionally has come to be considered an important issue in criminal policy matters, the concept never gained a conclusive definition during these last decades. This same is true for organized crime – with the exception of the impractical EU definition and its long list of factors to be considered. Nor does anyone refer to the definition arrived at by the Committee of Justice in the 1970s any longer. As will be expounded upon later in the chapter, the trend is however for Swedish authorities to put an equals sign between economic crime and the types of crimes handled by the Economic Crime Agency.

Organizational crime – that is, crimes committed within the framework of organizational structures – is more or less a foreign concept in the Swedish debate. This is lamentable, as organizational crime also stresses offences that are committed within the public sector, such as corruption – problems which have received a great deal of attention during these last few years.

The question of definition is of course key to deciding what type of crimes are to be included in statistical data on economic crime, an issue which will be discussed later on in the chapter.

The mobilization of the 1990s and the necessity of conducting reviews

A couple of years into the 1990s, the need for quantifying economic crime grew urgent once again. However, this time around the issue did not need to rely on estimates on the extent of economic crime in order for the media and politicians to become interested; the roaring 1980s had set the stage for a new renaissance of economic crime. Speculation, financial yuppies and nouveau wealth came to a bad end with banking crisis and mass bankruptcy (Alalehto 2003).

In the early 1990s, the parliamentary auditors started reviewing the efforts against economic crime (1993/94:6, 1994/95:RR4). The numbers they came up with were indicative of irregularities in the working methods and commitment of the agencies; some investigations dragged on for too long, while other cases went uninvestigated, never reaching court. Merciless criticism followed, and demands were raised for measures like continuous review and control – which of course would be impossible without quantitative data. This was also the dawn of a new era of order and precision: everything had to be measured and tracked (Power 1997). In these modern times marked by revision and auditing, the demand for figures is now greater than ever before. Compared with earlier times, the awareness of risks in society had grown; risks that preferably should be averted through proactive measures (Beck 1992; Larsson 2012). Thus, there was also a parallel increase in need for continuous situational awareness. This reformation of the Swedish efforts against economic crime was also characterized by a focus on situational analysis, management and review (Communication 1994–1995: 217). There clearly was a central bureaucratic element to this process, possibly motivated by concerns that agencies were not handling their assignments as well as they should, thus necessitating a centrally managed process.

Every county had to produce an annual situation analysis of the state of economic crime, and these were then to be merged into an annual national report (Communication 1994–1995: 217). The Swedish Government was supposed to direct the fight against economic crime by means of annually updated guidelines. Or this was the idea, at least.

However, the result of such zeal was not very impressive. When it came to the situation analysis, the picture of the activities of the agencies that emerged was acceptable at best. The statistical data based itself on the country's criminal statistics, with all the associated pitfalls (which really is the main issue of this chapter). Nor were there any appreciable differences in the reports made from year to year. Contrary to commonly held beliefs, economic criminals are not quite so dynamic that they constantly develop or turn to ever more sophisticated methods; in reality, these offenders tend to adhere to the law of least resistance (Brå 2011: 7).

As the years went by, the intervals between the reports became longer and longer. The review system ground to a halt. In the view of the author, the main problem was that the engineers who designed these systems never recognized the inherent difficulty of using statistical measures to paint a somewhat realistic portrait of economic crime. The agencies neither had the capacity nor the competency for conducting such surveys. The problem is essentially the same as when using statistical methods for charting a type of criminality characterized by large numbers of unreported offences. Conducting annual surveys of economic crime successfully would require large-scale research efforts. It might be speculated that the agencies grew increasingly tired of writing more or less the same report year after year. Today, the Economic Crime Agency issues a threat assessment every third year.

The definition problem

As mentioned earlier, the primary responsibility for defining economic crime in Sweden lies on the Swedish Parliament, the government, as well as its agencies (JuU 1980–1981: 21; SOU 1984: 15). Here, the core idea is that the offences must take place as a component of legal activities and carried out for direct or indirect financial gain. The emphasis on legal activities in this definition of economic crime serves to differentiate it from organized crime; here, businesses are indeed used for criminal purposes, but offences are rarely committed within the framework of legal business activities.

However, recent years have seen a shift in what is considered economic crime, so that offences now no longer must occur as a part of ongoing activities and the company may be exploited exclusively for committing economic crimes (Communication 1994–1995: 217; Riksdag's auditors 1993–1994: 6). When it comes to excise and value-added tax evasion schemes, it is extremely common that businesses are exploited as nothing short of criminal instruments in order to perpetrate these offences (Brå 2011: 7).

Individuals who commit offences against welfare or benefit systems may also be considered economic criminals, despite businesses being absent from the picture. Klaus Tiedemann particularly stresses the perspective of economic crime as that which threatens or disturbs economic life in ways that do not exclusively affect the interest of the single individual (Magnusson 1987). As will be developed further on, in the Swedish context, crimes against the welfare or benefit systems do not however count as economic crime.

One problem is that certain types of offences involve a lot of different actors and acts. Acts of fraud – here used in the narrow legal sense according to criminal law – might occur as a part of regular business activities, and should therefore be regarded as economic crime, according to most definitions. However, if the act of fraud instead gets carried out by an individual without business or organizational ties, then most would agree that this is not a case of economic crime. However, things become more complex when people commit fraud against (for example) welfare system functions in order to gain access to things like sickness benefits, early retirement pension or unemployment benefits, all in collusion with an employer who provides them with appropriate certificates as well as illicit employment opportunities. In such cases, the offence committed by the private individual becomes a part of a larger scheme also benefitting the company involved (ISF 2011:12). Therefore, coming up with a definitive answer to what type of fraud should be considered economic crime is not so easily done.

Such acts of fraud exemplify the problem of using types of crime as a starting point. Furthermore, the data which is the basis for criminal statistics frequently suffers from a lack of detail, making it hard to determine which frauds should be classified as economic offences and which should not. This makes it hard to answer any of the six questions about the purpose of statistics formulated in the introduction.

Criminalization as expression of social values

The problematic nature of coming up with a definition of economic crime everyone can agree on reflects the fact that specific societies exhibit certain values and priorities. That this is the case becomes obvious when studying different social systems and countries, such as the United States and Sweden, and whether they have classified different types of offences as economic crime or not. Furthermore, this classificatory process is often influenced by the organizational structures of the law enforcement agencies in question.

In a liberal market society like the United States, market mechanisms are crucial to the functioning of the system. Cartels are therefore consequently regarded as a central type of criminality in the US because of their disruptive effects on free competition (Geis 1967). The same reasons apply for the emphasis on financial crimes such as insider trading and market manipulation.

One reasonable explanation for this is the detrimental effect fraud has on public trust in agreements (Shapiro 1990). Once it becomes impossible to trust a handshake or a promise from a company, there is a risk that the economy will start descending into a negative, downward spiral. When every actor is forced into becoming increasingly cautious about whom they issue credit to or otherwise engage with, this also means increased transaction costs.

Sweden, by contrast – although also a market liberal society – is also a marked welfare state. In such a society, taxes assume such a strategic importance because of their instrumental role for the redistribution of wealth – although the ambition to do so certainly fluctuates with the day-to-day political situation (Korsell 2005). Accordingly, the top priorities in Sweden are first and foremost tax offences and the closely related crime of false accounting, with the addition of bankruptcy-related criminality – including false accounting and tax offences, too – as well as crime against creditors.

Strangely enough, insider trading and market manipulation have recently come to be considered important crimes in the welfare state of Sweden. One possible explanation for this trend might be the prevalence of mutual fund savings schemes, which have turned equity investment into an everyman's activity (Korsell 2012). In addition, an element of the revised pension system (which was introduced 20 years ago) means that every employee must invest a certain share of their accumulated premium pension in mutual funds. Thus, the Swedish people have been transformed into shareholders whose earnings later in life are determined by stock market prices. Therefore it could be said that crimes against financial markets – even if limited to short-term market manipulation – to some extent get interpreted as an attack on collectively held values of an increasingly capitalist society, in a way reminiscent of how tax and welfare fraud are still viewed in a now weakened Swedish welfare state.

As already hinted at, in addition to normative convictions, several Swedish policy choices have resulted in the country taking a quite different approach to certain instances of crime that might otherwise have been considered economic crimes in other countries, but that in Sweden are placed outside the realm of economic crime. For example, the concept of occupational crime – crimes committed by individuals against employers and contractors – expressed in the form of embezzlement, breach of trust and various types of fraud never received any greater attention in the welfare state society (Lindgren 1999). Because these are all offences threatening individual interests, they never sat well in the category of economic crimes, as understood in the Swedish context (Lindgren 1999; Korsell 2006; 2012).

In Sweden, crimes of corruption and against the environment (understood as both workplace and ecological environment) were to be handled by separate organizations, employing specialized prosecutors and sorting under the Public Prosecution Service: the National Anti-Corruption Unit and the National Unit for Environmental and Workplace Safety Crimes. Police specialized within these areas then work alongside the prosecutors at the national units. The fact that these offences are handled in a specific organizational setting means that they are not considered instances of economic crime.

While offences against consumer protection laws are considered typical examples of economic crime in other parts of the world, Sweden long ago adopted a system based on local municipal consumer advisors to guide consumers in the process of making a complaint. There is also a joint body – the National Board for Consumer Disputes – tasked with dealing with consumer grievances, while a state agency – the Swedish Consumer Agency – is tasked with safeguarding consumer interests. The historic background to this cooperation with the retail trade is the fact that efforts to protect consumer interests to a large degree developed under the auspices of the workers' movement. All in all, these developments led to offences against consumer protection laws being taken care of at an early stage, and therefore never discussed in terms of economic criminality at all.

When the Swedish Economic Crime Agency – a prosecuting authority consisting of prosecutors, police officers, and experts such as economists – was established in 1998, the aim of this new spearhead against economic crime was limited to a rather narrow target area; essentially tax and false accounting, crime against creditors, insider trading and market manipulation. All remaining offences that could be regarded as economic crime are left to the regular police and prosecution authorities. In practice, this restriction of the type of crimes handled by the Economic Crime Agency has presumably resulted in a narrower definition of economic crime: 'Economic crime is identical to that which is handled by the Economic Crime Agency' – to all intents and purposes an ironic outcome of a major effort against economic crime (Korsell 2012).

This section has illustrated how the definition of economic crime is influenced by social values and policy choices in a certain state. The Swedish transition from a strongly redistributive welfare state to one less so has caused the focus in the definition of economic crime to change from tax to investment fraud. Also, policy choices regarding the organization of enforcement influence the definition of what counts as economic crime. What is included under the heading of economic crime thus varies from country to country – especially when it comes to criminality that is considered especially significant. The ways in which society chooses to organize its agencies and other bodies also affect the categorization of different types of offences. However, this process is not limited to definitions, but also includes which acts are criminalized by the state as well as where it chooses to deploy its inspectionary resources.

Quantifying offences

A fundamental question becomes whether only offences that lead to conviction should be included in the statistical data. This was once a heavily debated issue. But if the difficulties of investigating and substantiating economic crime are to be taken into account, it seems as if focusing on *reported* offences would produce a truer picture, at least if seen from a purely statistical vantage point. A convenient aspect of economic crime, however, is that the suspect is often readily identified once the offence has been discovered. This might be compared with an ordinary crime like burglary, where a crime obviously has been committed, but there is no offender to be found at the site of the crime; we are left with a case of 'who dunnit?' In economic criminality, the names of companies and managers involved are often easily established – something which explains the high clearance rates in many types of economic crimes. There is, on the other hand, also the problem of the legal ambiguities in many economic regulations – did someone really break the law, and is it possible to prove that all the relevant circumstances have been fulfilled?

Without being able to count the number of offences, keeping any sort of statistics becomes impossible. Should someone want to look at cases of something other than just offences, this reveals something of an Achilles heel in criminal statistics. It is illustrative to consider that many types of economic offences are serial – or even continuous – in nature. Consider the case of tax offences, for example, where a crime is committed every time a tax return is filed. While private citizens only have to file their return once annually, business owners have to submit these monthly, thereby declaring value-added tax, employer's contributions and preliminary taxes withheld. Thus, a large number of offences may have been accumulated if a person has engaged in multiple years of tax evasion.

Fraud especially is characterized by large numbers of offences involving numerous victims; each victim and every case of fraud constitutes an offence. The serial criminality of a limited number of individuals may thus be disproportionately reflected in the statistics.

It is obvious that the methodology used in measuring criminality has a serious impact on statistical results. A somewhat simplified explanation to this is that because all figures in a statistical table assume the same weight, this means that serial crimes will have a significant impact compared with others, which might seem insignificant despite being serious enough in terms of consequences. Therefore, there is an over-arching risk that statistical data ends up reflecting the technical design of crime rather than its abundance.

The nature of crime

It is only natural to begin a discussion on statistics and economic crime at the point when it has been determined that an offence has been committed, or when this is suspected to be the case. As a rule, the process of selection is initiated by legislative decisions that determine which acts should be considered criminal and the legal construction of the offence. Penal regulations may have emerged out of serendipity as well as historical circumstances; in some cases, pure happenstance might have given rise to a regulation (Sigler and Murphy 1988). A new legislation may, for instance, include certain instructions concerning disposal of offal. As the law is being prepared, someone realises that violations of the legislation should prompt some kind of sanction. It would then be logical to solve this by introducing a section determining that those who violate a number of enumerated regulations, with criminal intent or gross negligence, are to be fined (SOU 2013: 38). Aside from the Criminal Code, in Sweden there are 350 laws with criminal law provisions (SOU 2013: 38), many of which are never or rarely used, and which are more or less informal in nature.

At times, legislators have instead chosen to deal with undesirable behaviour outside of the penal code (Zila 1992), giving rise to the question of whether a non-criminal violation should be considered an economic crime. There may also be variations across countries in how they have chosen to regulate different circumstances. For example, the violation of a number of administrative laws is criminalized in the Ordnungswiedrichkeiten in Germany and in the Economic Crime Act in the Netherlands.

A good example of this is the cartel, which, as mentioned previously, is considered a quintessential expression of economic crime in free-market countries (Geis 1967). In Sweden, however, cartel agreements are no longer formally considered criminal offences and are instead handled as market regulation violations. Thus, cartels are not subject to criminal sanctions; these have instead been replaced with administrative sanctions (sanctions that can amount to substantial sums of money).

When it comes to taxation, a large proportion of the violations – for example, the submission of incorrect information by the taxpayer – will result in administrative sanctions, that is, tax penalties. Despite the fact that a considerable proportion of these violations actually are intentional offences, they get handled through administrative channels instead, not least because of practical reasons. This is beneficial to the authorities because it allows the agency in question to enforce the administrative sanctioning directly, therefore eliminating the need for police, prosecuting and court involvement. In 2010, legal proceedings were initiated against 405 individuals suspected of having committed tax offences in Sweden – a figure which can be compared with the 154,000 instances of administrative sanctions related to taxation imposed the same year (Skatteverket 2011). The sum total of these penalties was in excess of 100 million euros; the fines for those who received penal sentences probably amount to some thousand euros, all taken together. These figures clearly show that administrative sanctions are very important in the area of taxation.

A recent ruling by the Supreme Court of Sweden (23 May 2013, case no. B 4946-12) established that tax penalties can be considered penal in character and that they concern identical crimes or identical offences as those prompting penal sanctions as formulated in the European Convention on Human Rights and the EU Charter of Fundamental Rights. This means that if the Swedish Tax Agency already has levied an administrative sanction, it is impossible to sentence the person for the same act in a criminal court at a later point in time.

Administrative sanctions are used in the field of environmental issues as well, and the same is true for financial markets, where sanctions might be imposed on institutions such as banks, perhaps because of inadequate controls against suspected money laundering. This might be illustrated by the fact that Forex Bank was forced to pay fees amounting to no less than 5 million euros because of such failings (Fi 2013).

There is in fact a tendency within legislative bodies to introduce administrative sanctions, prompted by the fact these can be set to enormous sums of money (SOU 2013: 38). When it comes to punishing legal entities such as corporations, administrative sanctions may be regarded as more punishing for a CEO guilty of a given violation than a sentence of means-related day fine. It is evident from these examples that excluding administrative sanctions from the statistical data would result in a false image of the economic criminality that is identified, reported, investigated and sanctioned against in Sweden. These sanctions are, on the other hand, prompted by acts which can be placed on a sliding scale, ranging from premeditated offence to careless negligence. When considering data on administrative sanctions we must therefore account for the fact that an unknown proportion of the reported instances often may be a result of negligence rather than of criminal intent, even if a broad definition is applied.

Edwin Sutherland (1949) addressed this problematic issue in his landmark *White-Collar Crime*. He assumed a broad view of economic crime in his work, choosing to include offences not formally subject to penal sanctions – and was subsequently also criticized for straying from criminal law (Tappan 1947). There is much to support Sutherland's view that limiting economic crime to formal offences would represent all too narrow an outlook.

To sum up, statistics on economic crime cannot be limited to tackling formal offences only, and administrative sanctions should naturally be included in this wider scope.

There are, however, researchers who would go even further than this. Friedrichs (2004) describes *legal bribes*, a concept which denotes the fact that financing of elections and legislative lobbying both cause the transfer of undue benefits, thereby promoting corruption. There are scholars who argue that offences emerge not only from illegal actions related to violations of penal or civil administrative regulations, but also from actions cloaked in legality (McBarnet 2006; Mackenzie and Green 2008). When a scholar asserts that even acts that do not violate any rules should be included in economic crime, this of course represents an especially hard nut to crack when trying to accurately measure the extent of criminality.

The selection process[2]

While we are ignorant of the true extent of unrecorded economic criminality, it should be assumed to be significant (cf. Kivivuori 2011),[3] especially since many types of economic crimes only can be detected by setting up specialized inspections systems. Such criminality is usually termed *investigative crime*.

The case of tax avoidance is illustrative in this regard, since these offences would probably never even be included in criminal statistical data but for the audits and other inspectionary efforts carried out by Swedish Tax Agency (RRV 1998). In the 1980s, when the tax office decided to perform a large number of audits on the local level, many less serious offences were discovered, with subsequent spikes for fines in the statistical data (Korsell 2001a). Today, the tax office takes great care to first sound the waters before proceeding with selective audits, audits which are then allocated major resources. This results in the detection of offences which are fewer, but more serious in nature. Yet another striking example can be found in the curve tracing the supervisory activities of the Swedish Chemicals Agency: as more inspections are carried out, more reports of environmental crime are submitted to prosecutors (Korsell 2001b). An illustrative deviation occurred in the year 1992, when a concerted effort was made to scrutinize companies dealing in preservative-treated wood. The industry was apparently rife with irregularities, and the number of reports skyrocketed, reaching levels significantly higher than seen before or since – and this despite the fact that the number of inspections remained unchanged.

As evidenced by examples of the Tax Agency and Chemicals Agency, a significant proportion of statistically reported economic criminality can be traced back to the methodologies and resources available to the agencies (Korsell 2003; Levi 1993). This is why economic crime statistics actually say more about the inspection methods used by the agencies than the criminality itself. Statistics, then, to a certain extent are somewhat reflective of the efficiency of the agencies as well as the sentences that are meted out for economic crimes.

Statistical data may also mirror the consequences of criminal policy reform. Following the appointment of receivers (lawyers) in all bankruptcy cases in connection with the bankruptcy reform of 1980, there was a sharp increase in the number of reported cases of false accounting (Korsell 2003). This rise was caused by a mandatory review of the book keeping of all companies that went bankrupt, and this new inspection system of course led to an increase in numbers of discovered crimes. The number of reported bankruptcy offences has steadily tracked the business cycles ever since. As times grow harder, bankruptcies increase, and subsequently also the number of identified and reported accounting violations. In 2007, the reported accounting violations amounted to

4713 in Sweden. During the global economic crisis of 2007–2008, these figures doubled, to 8942 in 2008 and then 11,044 in 2009. In the aftermath of the global financial crisis, the number of crimes reported in 2013 remained at roughly 12,000. Thus, criminal statistics make for a flawed method for measuring the structure and development of economic crime, put mildly. Blumberg (1967) expresses a similar sentiment when he, somewhat pointedly, claims that *Wall Street Journal* actually makes for a better source of data than figures taken from criminal statistics.

However, following the line of Black (1970), the statistical outcome may also be regarded as a social fact rather than as an investigative tool; an empirical phenomenon to be studied. Criminal statistics reveal a great deal about the process of selecting crimes; they can both be used to describe the crimes that are brought to the surface as well as hint at those who remain out of sight on the murky bottom. The concept of selection is thus particularly suited for discussing where the economic crimes end up within the framework of statistics. A starting point for such a discussion is to establish that economic crime actually exists, even if this criminality mainly exists as an abstract concept. This actually existing criminality then gets submitted to a gradual process of selection as it moves further up the inspection and legal chain; selected in terms of crime type, frequency, as well as additional factors such as character and inspection system design (Weisburd and Waring 2001). Some offences go undiscovered, others are never reported, and a portion of reported crimes get written off and never reach the court.

This process of selection is not random (see Hawkins 2002); it adheres to a pattern which is obscured by a complex system of agencies, monitoring functions, legislative practices, economic crime strategies and other factors (Korsell 2003). Goldstock (1994: 432) takes on a pessimistic perspective, arguing that the offences that are brought to light and investigated by authorities can 'thus be seen in a Darwinian sense, as creating a hostile environment in which natural selection removes the lame and weak, allowing the more corrupt and powerful to gain control'. The research of the author of this paper instead suggests that the cases that do get caught up in the inspection and legal chain are both the simpler and more easily discovered offences as well as the very serious cases of economic crime (Korsell 2003).[4] The blind spot is, if anything, located in the middle – obscuring relatively serious offences that are never seriously attended to.

To the government authorities, the cases that do attract a lot of attention are charged with symbolic meaning. Prestige therefore becomes a strong force, motivating the deployment of vast resources in order to solve the cases (Levi 1987). Less serious offences are easily discovered and reported, and may also help agencies to show off their success through other means than the less common high-profile cases – simpler cases also mean higher clearance rates (Korsell 2003). At the same time, investigators taking on serious yet complicated and time-consuming cases that do not interest the media or the politicians may hardly expect to be rewarded by their higher-ups.

In conclusion, the process of selection functions in a way which means that statistics tell us more about this selective process than about the structure and scale of criminality.

The characteristics of economic crime

In order for an act to be considered criminal, it must first be detected as well as recognized as an offence (Black 1970; Pontell and Calavita 1992). The nature of the criminal act is a central factor when it comes to trying to explain why certain types of crimes come to the attention of the authorities, and it is also a major factor in the previously addressed problem of selection (Black 1970, 1971). You can never know for sure if a violation will be recognized as criminal by victims, monitoring authorities or anyone else otherwise affected or involved. Consider the case of a company that has fallen victim to fraud in the form of substandard products. A reasonable expectation is for the company to frame the whole thing as a business problem – substandard inputs have caused serious disturbances in the production chain – and not as a crime. Rather than treating this as a judicial matter, the company will direct all its efforts towards finding a new supplier and severing relations with the current one as quickly as possible. The company could conceivably claim damages at a later stage, possibly without ever having entertained the thought of having been made victim of fraud.

Unlike with most traditional offences, victims of economic crime might live on never knowing that they have been preyed upon (Friedrichs 1996). Restaurant guests might suffer food poisoning caused by violations of food hygiene regulations without them realizing the true reason for their stomach pains (Croall 2004). In the case of cartels, there may be agreements to fix the prices for customers who never really reflect on the mechanisms behind the pricing. Thus, the harmful effects of these criminal activities are also distributed over a large population of victims (Slapper and Tombs 1999).

These types of offences can also be quite diffuse and hard to grasp. When it comes to economic crime, the perpetrator generally has control over the situation in which the offence is committed. The company in question is responsible for the activity within which the offences are carried out. The fact that an offence can be *surrounded by normal social life* makes it harder to distinguish from legal business behaviour (Mann 1985: 235). These crimes get committed by the *right* person, who is in the *right* place in the *right* context. The offences are thus concealed by the functional normality of the organization and the legitimacy of the offending party (Clark 1990).

These offences are often committed in environments to which authorities rarely have access (Katz 1979; Persson 1980; Stinchcombe 1963). This is a major difference compared with many traditional types of crime. A case in point is the fact that the Swedish police academies make sure there are training environments that resemble apartments (intimate partner violence), convenience stores (shoplifting) and pubs (violent crime) for the purpose of training police cadets how to act in different situations, but there is nothing similar when it comes to locations that are typical to economic crime, such as banks and business offices. It is true that comparing everyday police life (characterized as it is by constant interventions against volume crime) to the very different world of economic crime might be unfair, but the analogy still says something about the crime type priorities of the Swedish police.

The shortcomings of the inspection systems leads to an almost non-existent risk of being discovered (Coleman 2001). Furthermore, the offences are often complex and are thus quite difficult to investigate for authorities overburdened with work. This means that regulation, inspection, and law enforcement agencies are not well-suited for handling the particularities of this type of criminality – for example the problem of differentiating between criminal and legal acts. Economic crimes are undeniably characterized by certain features that make them difficult to address. Shapiro (1984: 8) almost waxes poetic in the description of economic crime below:

> [W]hite-collar ... criminals ... have perfected the modus operandi of pedestrian property crime. They have learned to rob without force or violence, to steal without break-in or trespass. They need not beat their victims senseless or threaten them. Rather, they convince their victims that, if entrusted with money and property, they can protect, enhance, or increase their victims' assets. They replace force with fraud, robbery with deception. Instead of refining mechanical technology to break into a secured building, they develop social technology to become insiders in the organization. They replace trespass with trust, burglary with self-dealing.

The perpetrators of economic crimes are capable of acting with great determination, and make major efforts to avoid detection and prosecution. With legal advisors engaged at an early stage, these may influence authorities long before any reports of suspicious activities are filed (Mann 1985). This is miles apart from the kind of counter-efforts available to the broader group of victims of economic crime. There is far less at stake for the individual victim – in his or her role as taxpayer, employer, consumer and so on – than for the offending party (Braithwaite 1997; Coleman 2001).

The significance of selection for statistical outcomes has already been addressed in this chapter. The characteristic features of economic crime reviewed above introduce further distortions in the process of selection, which in turn has consequences for the statistical data.

Methods for reporting and handling offences

Reiss (1971, 1974) characterizes the various instances that make up the judiciary as loosely interconnected. Once an offence is discovered, the process of selection gets transferred to the law enforcement authorities. The crime must now be reported to the relevant investigative authorities, and such a decision is always preceded by various rational deliberations (Gottfredson and Gottfredson 1988; Shapiro 1985). The obligation to report stipulated in law may be dispensed with in cases where there is no reason to believe that police and prosecutor would proceed in opening an investigation. In addition, authorities tasked with inspection and supervisory duties may forbear reporting if the matter is eventually seen to, or when it is deemed that reporting would jeopardize future cooperation with the company, and therefore also its future regulatory compliance (Hawkins 1984). These authorities rarely think of offenders as criminals, being more oriented towards solving problems than penalizing people (Benson and Cullen 1998).

The authorities responsible for control functions also have the option of adjusting the level of efforts expended in preparing reports or directly influencing law enforcement agencies through direct contacts. The reporting party might possess knowledge about what attracts the attention of prosecutors and what makes for a good case considered worth pursuing (Emerson and Paley 1992; Wesser 2001). Those carrying out inspection functions may apply pressure in order to get police and prosecutors to take on cases they consider important (Benson and Cullen 1998).

When confronting traditional criminality, police behaviour is influenced by what the person reporting the crime and the witnesses to it want to see happen (Smith and Visher 1981), the available evidence (Myers and Hagan 1979), the extent of the resources available to the authority (Eisenstein and Jacob 1977), as well as the seriousness of the crime (Brown 1988). When there are no victims or others to make demands of the authorities, these are spared the pressure and become free to handle economic crime investigations as they see fit (Korsell 2003). However, a spectacular case attracting a lot of attention might force the judicial system into pouring disproportionate resources into trying to uphold the legitimacy of the authority (Korsell 2003).

Once the offence has been reported, the case is handled by the investigative authorities, where it continues on through *organizational filtering* (Hawkins 1984: 177).[5] MacConville et al. (1991) characterize this selection process as a private trial, which precedes the formal trial. Scarcity of resources too is a major factor in preventing the law enforcement agencies from investigating all reported offences (Brown 1988). In 2002, the Swedish police dismissed 75 per cent of all reported cases (RR 2002–2003: 19). The fact that the different authorities are tasked with incompatible goals in their activities forces them into making divergent priorities (Cox and Wade 2002). There is often a lack of competence for investigating certain types of crimes in the field of economic crime (Friedrichs 1996; Larsson 2003). Sometimes the authorities are under continuous pressure from the media; something more commonly seen in cases of serious violent crime than economic ones (Friedrichs 1996). When cases do lead to prosecution, the process of selection continues in court. Here, the determining factors become those that decide whether an offence leads to conviction or acquittal, as well as the severity of the sanctions. In other words, there is a wide range of different factors that influence whether an offence leads to criminal prosecution or not (Shapland et al. 1985; Zatz and Hagan 1985). The population that subsequently is prosecuted will be highly dissimilar to *the actual criminal population* – in all probability thanks to this process of selection (MacConville et al. 1991: 35). This is why we can conclude that economic crime statistics offer us a distorted view of reality.

Conclusions

The introduction of this chapter posed a few questions, which the uninitiated might have thought to be issues that possibly were relevant to address in a statistical report on economic crime. The first two addressed the question of whether statistics could help us track criminal trends over time and whether they could provide us with a description of the structure of economic crime. As the criminality on record to a large extent reflects the type of crimes targeted, economic crime statistics first and foremost inform us about the initiatives of agencies working in this area. It is only the less serious cases of false accounting that statistics can track with reasonable reliability.

As mentioned previously, this is due to the fact that official receivers (lawyers) are appointed in all cases of company bankruptcies nowadays. These official receivers review the company's book keeping as a part of the administration and liquidation of the bankruptcy estate, which means that they will uncover all cases of false accounting stemming from inadequate book keeping (Korsell 2003). Detecting more sophisticated instances of false accounting is harder, particularly as the receivers are remunerated according to a rate which rewards swiftness. In sharp contrast with the other areas, this system of official receivers makes the control measures against bankrupt companies consistent over time; during economic slumps, there is an increase in bankruptcies, and subsequently also in the cases of false accounting. This makes the curve describing cases of false accounting well-suited as an indicator of the current economic climate, with only a slight lag. In other words, the specificities of less serious false accounting clearly illustrate the important role inspection systems have for guaranteeing that economic crime is included in the statistical data.

The third question concerned the feasibility of using statistics to compare economic crime with other kinds of criminality. Considering the weak initial values we have for economic crime, it is not even worth bothering to try this. Besides, the statistical reporting for other crime areas is ridden with problems that are significant enough all in themselves.

The question could also be extended into one about the feasibility of making cross-country comparisons of local data on economic crime. Here, differences in legislation and statistical processing constitute a fundamental problem for all types of comparative criminal statistics (Brå 2001: 18). This problem is aggravated by the fact that countries are not uniform in how they deploy inspection functions. Should we start producing cross-country comparative statistical data, the best that can be expected is for it to serve as a general indication as to what type of economic crimes are to be prioritized.

The fourth question dealt with the suitability of using statistics in order to assess the effects of various reforms, such as in the area of legislation. When joint-stock company auditors were tasked with reporting crime suspicions arising from the auditing process 15 years ago, this had a marginal effect on the reported crime rates (Brå 2004: 4) This represented the launch of a new control system. The role of the official receivers – yet another example of controls – has already been mentioned. If the rules governing the criminal justice system are revised, this naturally also means a potential change in the influx of reported offences. Therefore, assessing changes in the behavioural patterns of supervisory bodies is to some extent possible, but this is not at all the same thing as gaining a crystal clear picture of the resultant effects – the large amount of offences that go unrecorded makes this a significantly tougher nut to crack.

The penultimate question concerned sanctions against economic crime. Sanctions are instituted because of decisions, and because decisions can always be recorded, this makes this the simplest of our statistical exercises. However, we have at the same time returned to where we started: to the question of how economic crime should be defined, and whether it is realistic to constantly track all the different factors which, according to our definition, turn the individual offence into a case of economic crime. Maybe administrative sanctions could provide us with a feasible way forward?

Even though there certainly is room for improvement in the statistical reporting of economic crime, we should never expect it to provide us with a true picture of the extent and structure of economic crime, nor of how serious the problem of economic crime is. As demonstrated in this paper, the obstacles are insurmountable – and this is true for the question of selection especially (Korsell 2003). What we can say about statistically derived data on economic crime is that it reflects the operation and evolution of the various inspection systems to a considerable degree. In other words, there are not many questions that can be answered by turning to the statistical reporting on economic crime. It is certainly true that there are other, alternative methods we could use, such as economic estimates of the magnitude of tax evasion and surveys designed for potential victims. However, economic estimates tend towards the very general, and are often limited to nothing but mathematical exercises, and while it is true that interviews and surveys bring us closer to the crimes, these methods are, of course, unsuitable for detecting unrecorded offences or incidents that no one has interpreted as criminal.

One improvement which would be simple to implement would be to include administrative sanctions in criminal statistics reports too, or to have them published in conjunction with them. Currently no such statistical reports are compiled. According to the Supreme Court ruling referred to previously, sanctions can, in certain contexts, be considered on par with penalties – perhaps we should start talking about *sanctions statistics* rather than *crime statistics*.

The never-articulated question hovering in the background of this contribution concerns what the remaining alternatives are, given that the statistical methods are as flawed as claimed here. One possible way forward would be to carry out studies focusing on selection processes. This means gearing research efforts towards trying to explore which crimes are discovered and why; which crimes are reported and why; how the receiving authorities deal with reports, tip-offs and discoveries of their own, and why this is. Studies on selection would also open up for making cross-country comparisons of differences in the handling of economic crime. Such studies possibly represent an excellent, if resource-intensive, method for carrying comparative studies, and are certain to yield highly interesting results.

Such research reveals what is lost on the way, with the further advantage of shedding at least some light on that which is never discovered. If combined with the offences that survived the selection process, such a study would allow us to construct a reasonably comprehensive overview of the criminality in question. Even though this overview would deal with structures mainly, extent would be covered to some degree as well. What is more, a study on selection will also highlight the strengths and weaknesses of inspection system, allowing for an improvement of crime prevention and law enforcement (Korsell 2003) – which, after all, is the main issue.

Notes

1 Translation by Mikael Altemark.
2 See Korsell's (2007) article 'A theory of selection in the response to economic crime'.
3 The percentage of unrecorded cases is the ratio between actual crime and registered crime.
4 Sellin (1951) argues that crimes that seriously damage societal values often come to the attention of the authorities.
5 For traditional crime, there is extensive literature addressing the question of when police choose to act or not. Among other things, this is due to whether the police officer thinks it is worth the trouble, the characteristics of the offender, time and place of the offence, whether there is a plaintiff to push the issue or lodge a complaint, and so on (Cox and Wade 2002).

References

Alalehto, T. (2003) *Fiffelstrategier vid ekonomisk brottslighet*, Kågeröd: Barr.
AMOB (1977) *Organiserad och ekonomisk brottslighet i Sverige: Ett åtgärdsförslag*, Stockholm: Arbetsgruppen mot organiserad brottslighet (AMOB): Rikspolisstyrelsen.
Beck, U. (1992) *Risk Society: Towards a New Modernity*, London: Sage.
Benson, M.L. and Cullen, F.T. (1998) *Combating Corporate Crime: Local Prosecutors at Work*, Boston: Northeastern University Press.
Bergqvist, M. (2007) *Räkna med den ekonomiska brottsligheten: Om det kvantitativa studiet av ekonomisk brottslighet*, Stockholm: Kriminologiska institutionen vid Stockholms universitet.
Black, D.J. (1970) 'The production of crime rates', *American Sociological Review*, 35: 733–748.
Black, D.J. (1971) 'The social organization of arrest', *Stanford Law Review*, 23: 1087–1111.
Blumberg, A.S. (1967) *Criminal Justice*, New York: New Viewpoints.
Brå (2001) *Brottsligheten i olika länder*, report 18. Stockholm: Brottsförebyggande rådet.
Brå (2004) *Revisorers anmälningsskyldighet*, report 4. Stockholm: Brottsförebyggande rådet.
Brå (2011) *Storskaliga skattebrott. En kartläggning av skattebrottslingens kostnader*, report 7. Stockholm: Brottsförebyggande rådet.
Braithwaite, J. (1997) 'On speaking softly and carrying big sticks: Neglected dimensions of a Republican separation of powers', in J. Braithwaite, *Regulation, Crime, Freedom*, Aldershot: Ashgate Dartmouth.
Brown, M.K. (1988), *Working the Street. Police Discretion and the Dilemmas of Reform*, New York: Russel Sage.
Clark, M. (1990) *Business Crime. Its Nature and Control*, Oxford: Polity Press.
Coleman, C. and Moynihan, J. (1996) *Understanding Crime Data: Haunted by the Dark Figure*, Buckingham: Open University Press.
Coleman, J.W. (2001) *The Criminal Elite: Understanding White-Collar Crime*, New York: St Martin's Press.
Communication (1994–1995) *Samlade åtgärder mot den ekonomiska brottsligheten*, Stockholm: Regeringens skrivelse.
Cox, S.M. and Wade, J.E. (2002) *The Criminal Justice Network: An Introduction*, Boston: McGraw-Hill.
Croall, H. (2004) *Lurad och förgiftad: Att avslöja utsatthet för ekobrott*, Stockholm: Brottsförebyggande rådet.
Eisenstein, J. and Jacob, H. (1977) *Felony Justice: An Organizational Analysis of Criminal Courts*, Boston: Little, Brown and Company.
Emerson, R.M. and Paley, B. (1992) 'Organizational horizons and complaint-filing', in K. Hawkins (ed.) *The Uses of Discretion*, Oxford: Clarendon Press.
Fi (2013) *Pressmeddelande om Forex från Finansinspektionen 22/05/2013*. Online. Available HTTP: <http://fi.se/Press/Pressmeddelanden/Listan/Forex-varnas-och-ska-betala-50-miljoner/> (accessed 7 July 2014).
Friedrichs, D.O. (1996) *Trusted Criminals: White-Collar Crime in Contemporary Society*, Belmont: Wadsworth.
Friedrichs, D.O. (2004) *Trusted Criminal in Contemporary Society*, Belmont: Wadsworth.
Geis, G. (1967) 'The heavy electrical equipment anti-trust cases of 1961', in M. Clinard and R. Quinney (eds) *Criminal Behavior Systems*, New York: Holt, Rinehart and Winston.
Goldstock, R. (1994) 'The prosecutor as problem solver', in R.J. Kelly et al. (eds) *Handbook of Organized Crime in the Unites States*, Westport: Greenwood Press.
Gottfredson, M.R. and Gottfredson, D.M. (1988) *Decision Making in Criminal Justice: Toward the Rational Exercise of Discretion*, New York: Plenum Press.

Hawkins, K. (1984) *Environment and Enforcement: Regulation and the Social Definition of Pollution*, New York: Oxford University Press.
Hawkins, K. (2002) *Law as Last Resort: Prosecution Decision-Making in a Regulatory Agency*, Oxford: Oxford University Press.
Heckscher, S. (1979) 'Modern ekonomisk brottslighet', *Nordisk Tidskrift for Kriminalvidenskab*. 1979-80 (1).
Heckscher, S. (1980) 'Modern ekonomisk brottslighet', *Nordisk Tidskrift for Kriminalvidenskab*, 1979–1990: 1.
ISF (2011) *Bidragsbrott och skattekriminalitet: Välfärdens dubbla kriminalitet*, report 12, Stockholm: Inspektionen för socialförsäkringen.
JuU (1980–1981) *Justitieutskottets betänkande om den ekonomiska brottsligheten*, 1980/81:21. Online. Available HTTP: <http://www.riksdagen.se/sv/Dokument-Lagar/Utskottens-dokument/Betankanden/198081 om-den-ekonomiska-brott_G401JuU21/?html=true> (accessed 7 July 2014).
Katz, J. (1979) 'Legality and equality: Plea bargaining in the prosecution of white-collar and common crime', *Law & Society Review*, 13(2): 431–459.
Kivivuori, J. (2011) *Discovery of Hidden Crime: Self-Report Delinquency Surveys in Criminal Policy Context*, Oxford: Oxford University Press.
Korsell, L. (2000) 'Ekobrott, liksom!', *Svensk Juristtidning*, 933–965.
Korsell, L. (2001a) 'Ekonomisk brottslighet', in B. Ulriksson (ed.) *Brottsutvecklingen i Sverige 1998–2000*, Stockholm: Brottsförebyggande rådet.
Korsell, L. (2001b) 'Miljöbrott', in B. Ulriksson (ed.) *Brottsutvecklingen i Sverige 1998–2000*, Stockholm: Brottsförebyggande rådet.
Korsell, L. (2003) *Bokföringsbrott – en studie i selektion*, Stockholm: Kriminologiska institutionen vid Stockholms universitet.
Korsell, L. (2005) 'Fiffel och fusk i slott och koja', in G. Sjöstrand (ed.) *Fiffel-Sverige. Sociologiska perspektiv på skandaler och fusk*, Malmö: Liber.
Korsell, L. (2006) 'Ekonomisk och organiserad brottslighet – ett kriminalpolitiskt drama i sju akter', *Nordisk Tidskrift for Kriminalvidenskab*, 93(3): 249–273.
Korsell, L. (2007) 'A theory of selection in the response to economic crime', *Monatsschrift für Kriminologie und Strafrechtsreform*, 07(2/3):140–157.
Korsell, L. (2012) 'Ekonomisk brottslighet; tur och retur', *Nordisk Tidskrift for Kriminalvidenskab*, 99(3): 293–315.
Larsson, P. (2003) *Straffe, veilede eller overtale? En studie av fire tilsynsmyndigheters reguleringsstrategier*, Oslo: Det Kriminalitetsforebyggende Råd.
Larsson, P. (2012) 'Regulering – en inledning', *Nordisk Tidskrift for Kriminalvidenskab*, 99(3): 287–293.
Levi, M. (1987) *Regulating Fraud: White-Collar Crime and the Criminal Process*, London: Tavistock.
Levi, M. (1993) 'White-collar crime: The British scene', *The Annals of The American Academy of Political and Social Science*, 525: 71–82.
Lindgren, S.-Å. (1999) 'Prioriterade och negligerade offer: Reflektioner över den ekonomiska brottslighetens viktimologi', *Nordisk Tidskrift for Kriminalvidenskab*, 86(2): 81.
Lindgren, S.-Å. (2000) *Ekonomisk brottslighet: Ett samhällsproblem med förhinder*, Lund: Studentlitteratur.
McBarnet, D. (2006) 'After Enron will "whiter than white collar crime" still wash?', *British Journal of Criminology*, 46(6): 1091–1109.
MacConville, M., Sanders, A. and Leng, R. (1991) *The Case for the Prosecution*, London: Routledge.
Mackenzie, S. and Green, P. (2008) 'Performative regulation: A case study in how powerful people avoid criminal labels', *British Journal of Criminology*, 48(2): 138–153.
Magnusson, D. (1987) *Fel och oegentligheter i tulldeklarationer: Om ekonomisk brottslighet vid import till Sverige*, Stockholm: Brottsförebyggande rådet.
Mann, K. (1985) *Defending White-Collar Crime. A Portrait of Attorneys at Work*, New Haven: Yale University Press.
Myers, M.A. and Hagan, J. (1979) 'Private and public trouble: Prosecutors and the allocation of court resources', *Social Problems*, 26: 439–451.
Persson, L.G.W. (1980) *Hidden Criminality: Theorethical and Methodological Problems, Empirical Results*, Stockholm: University of Stockholm.
Pontell, H.N. and Calavita, K. (1992) 'Bilking bankers and bad debts: White-collar crime and the savings and loan crisis', in K. Schlegel and D. Weisburd (eds) *White-Collar Crime Reconsidered*, Boston: Northeastern University Press.
Power, M. (1997) *The Audit Society: Rituals of Verification*, Oxford: Oxford University Press.
Reiss, A.J. Jr. (1971) *The Police and the Public*, New Haven: Yale University Press.
Reiss, A.J. Jr. (1974) 'Discretionary justice', in D. Glaser (ed.) *Handbook of Criminology*, Chicago: Rand McNally College Publishing Company.

Riksdag's auditors (1993–1994) *Den ekonomiska brottsligheten och rättssamhället*, Stockholm: Riksdagens revisorer.
RR (2002–2003) *Polisens avskrivningar av brott*, Stockholm: Riksdagens revisorer.
RRV (1998) *Svart arbete, del 2, Omfattning*, Stockholm: Riksrevisionsverket.
Sellin, T. (1951) 'The significance of records of crime', *The Law Quarterly Review*, 67: 489–504.
Shapiro, S. (1984) *Wayward Capitalists: Target of the Securities and Exchange Commission*, New Haven: Yale University Press.
Shapiro, S. (1985) 'The road not taken: The elusive path to criminal prosecution for white-collar offenders', *Law & Society Review*, 19: 179–217.
Shapiro, S. (1990) 'Collaring the crime, not the criminal: Reconsidering the concept of white-collar crime', *American Sociological Review*, 55: 346–365.
Shapland, J., Willmore, J. and Duff, P. (1985) *Victims in the Criminal Justice System*, Aldershot: Gower Publishing Company.
Sigler, S.A. and Murphy, J.E. (1988) *Interactive Corporate Compliance: An Alternative to Regulatory Compulsion*, New York: Quorum Books.
Skatteverket (2011) *Skatter i Sverige. Skattestatistisk årsbok 2011*, Solna: Skatteverket.
Slapper, G. and Tombs, S. (1999) *Corporate Crime*, London: Addison Wesley Longman.
Smith, D.A. and Visher, C.A. (1981) 'Street-level justice: Situational determinants of police arrest decisions', *Social Problems*, 29: 167–177.
SOU (1984) *Ekonomisk brottslighet i Sverige*, 15, Stockholm: Liber.
SOU (2013) *Vad bör straffas?*, 38, Stockholm: Fritzes.
Stinchcombe, A.L. (1963) 'Institutions of privacy in the determination of police administrative practice', *American Journal of Sociology*, 69: 150–160.
Sutherland, E.H. (1949) *White-Collar Crime*, New York: Holt, Rinehart and Winston.
Svensson, B. (1982) 'De ekonomiska brotten', *Apropå*, 3: 25.
Swedish National Council for Crime Prevention (2011) *Storskaliga skattebrott – en kartläggning av skattebrottslingens kostnader*, Stockholm: Brottsförebyggande rådet.
Tappan, P.W. (1947) 'Who is the criminal?', *American Sociological Review*, 12(1): 96–102.
Weisburd, D. and Waring, E.J. (2001) *White-Collar Crime and Criminal Careers*, Cambridge: Cambridge University Press.
Wesser, E. (2001) *'Har du varit ute och shoppat, Jacob?': En studie av Finansinspektionens utredning av insiderbrott under 1990-talet*, Lund: Sociologiska institutionen vid Lunds universitet.
Zatz, M.S. and Hagan, J. (1985) 'Crime, time, and punishment: An exploration of selection bias in sentencing research', *Journal of Quantitative Criminology*, 1: 103–126.
Zila, J. (1992) *I stället för straff: sanktionsavgifter som kriminalpolitiskt medel mot bagatellbrottslighet*, Stockholm: Juristförlaget.

6

Measuring white-collar crime perceptions among public and white-collar offenders

A comparative investigation of four European countries

Tage Alalehto and Daniel Larsson

Introduction

E.H. Sutherland was outraged that the public did not see white-collar crime as a crime. It was incorrectly believed to be victimless, whereas in his opinion white-collar criminality breeds distrust, lowers social morale and constitutes an attack on societal institutions (Sutherland 1940). Subsequent research on the public's perception of white-collar crime seemed to confirm his estimate of the public reaction to it (Aubert 1952; Braithwaite 1985; Evans 1995; Schrager and Short 1978).

More recent research, however, has shown that Sutherland's assumption was wrong; people are as opposed to white-collar crime as to street crime in general (Cullen et al. 2009; Holtfreter et al. 2008; Schoepfer et al. 2007; Stylianou 2003; Unnever et al. 2008). Several subcategories of the public were found to be more condemning of white-collar crime than others. These categories included elderly people (Levi and Jones 1985; O'Connell and Whelan 1996), religious and conservative people (Serajzadeh 2008; Stack and Kposowa 2006) and women with little knowledge of computers and the Internet (Kane and Wall 2006). People in these groups rated white-collar crime as very harmful, and considered it as among the most serious or most wrongful criminal acts.

These results give a much more nuanced picture of the public's reaction to white-collar crime. But there is still a gap in the research in that most of these studies were done in North America or outside Europe. We thus set out to investigate how Europeans react to white-collar crime by asking whether people in different European countries perceive different types of crime as harmful. We will further investigate if differences in sociodemographic distribution share different perceptions of the harmfulness of white-collar crime. That is, do females, the elderly, less educated, etc. consider white-collar criminality as more harmful than the opposite categories? We also set out to investigate whether similar attitudes prevail across Europe despite differences in sociodemographic distribution. That is, do Swedes, Germans, the British and Spaniards have similar attitudes to white-collar crime?

In a previous study limited to Sweden, Larsson and Alalehto (2013) compared those who were most condemning of white-collar crime with those with the most liberal attitudes towards it. Latent class analysis (LCA) was used to identify clusters (or latent classes). The clusters group people who share common characteristics regarding the input variables based on the probability of their belonging to different clusters (Hagenaars and McCutcheon 2002; Magidson and Vermunt 2001).

The analyses examined three categories of white-collar crime, namely insurance fraud, bribery and VAT fraud.[1] Four clusters of attitudes to white-collar crime were identified. The largest cluster, containing 42.7 per cent, represents restricted attitudes. Those in this cluster regarded insurance fraud and bribery as *wrong* but not *seriously wrong*. They were split 50/50 as to whether VAT fraud was *not wrong* or *wrong*. The second largest cluster, containing 35.2 per cent, was the most condemning of white-collar crime in general, regarding all three types of white-collar crime as *seriously wrong*. The third largest cluster, containing 17.5 per cent, displayed a mix of restriction and tolerance. Those in this group were significantly restrictive when it came to insurance fraud and bribery, which they regarded as *seriously wrong*, but were very liberal in their attitudes towards VAT fraud, treating it as *not wrong at all*. The most liberal group of all was cluster 4 (the smallest, containing 4.4 per cent), who considered insurance fraud and VAT fraud *not wrong at all*. However, they were split in regard to bribery, with half rating it as *wrong* and the other half rating it *seriously wrong* (Larsson and Alalehto 2013).

Analysis of the sociodemographic profiles of the condemning group and the liberal group revealed some similarities but also distinct differences. There was no difference between the condemners and the liberals as regards education (mid-level education) and ethnicity. But there were marked differences when it came to age, sex and Internet use. The condemners were mainly elderly people (over 50) and nearly half of them were women who did not regularly use the Internet (once a week or less). The liberals, on the other hand, were predominantly younger males who used the Internet regularly (every day or several times a week) (Larsson and Alalehto 2013).

In this chapter, we extend the earlier study by comparing attitudes to white-collar crime in four different European countries (Germany, Spain, Sweden and the United Kingdom [UK]). We investigate the sociodemographic profile of people with liberal and condemning attitudes to white-collar crime, and compare attitudes to white-collar crime with the prevalence of criminality. In other words, we will also be investigating whether people with a negative attitude to white-collar crime also commit less crime. This question will be answered on the basis of self-reported data, comparing different clusters of people both within countries and across countries. Investigation of the sociodemographic profile of the people in an identified cluster gives information on how the potential offender structure is distributed in each country and between countries. The correlation between attitudes and self-reported criminality gives information on how important an identified attitude is in relation to performing a criminal act. This issue is investigated for each country and across countries.

Previous research using cluster analysis

Only limited use has been made of cluster analysis in investigating profiles of attitudes to white-collar crime (Babakus et al. 2004; Brinkmann and Lentz 2006; Dean 2004). Those investigations that have been done deal only with insurance fraud as the crime category and rely on small and highly local samples. They are thus not representative. The previous research has also worked with a very limited measurement of criminality and limited discussion of the correlation between attitudes and self-reported or actual criminality.

Attitudes to white-collar crime

Dean (2004) collected data using vignettes (questions related to a fictitious fraud scenario) from 296 responding university students (3.2 per cent drop-out). The model contained four factors (tolerance, morality, fairness and award), based on 7 items. The questions concerned attitudes towards aspects of immoral and criminal behaviour in general. Dean found four distinct clusters: those with *strict* perceptions of all forms of insurance crime as a violation of morality (49 per cent of the respondents); those with *sympathetic* perceptions of insurance fraud as a moral violation that was to some degree understandable (32.4 per cent of the respondents); those with *tolerant* perceptions of insurance fraud as neither morally wrong nor right (10.8 per cent of the respondents); and those with *liberal* perceptions of insurance fraud as morally correct, fair and just towards the insurance companies or their agents (7.8 per cent of the respondents). Similar results were found by Jay (1997, cited in Dean 2004). The moralist cluster (30.7 per cent of the respondents) had the least tolerance of insurance fraud, allowing no excuses. They were willing to punish fraudsters severely. The realist cluster (21.6 per cent) had low tolerance for fraud but realised that it happened and could be justified in certain conditions. The conformists (26.4 per cent) were fairly tolerant of fraud, mostly because they believed it was widespread and therefore accepted. Finally, the critics (21.2 per cent) had the highest tolerance of insurance fraud and tended to blame the industry for causing consumer fraud because companies did not conduct business fairly (see also Tennyson 2008).

Similar results were reported by Babakus et al. (2004). But unlike the studies reported above, their study had a comparative approach, comparing attitudes to insurance fraud in different countries. They compared attitudes to a specific form of insurance fraud (reporting a lost item as stolen in order to collect insurance money) in six countries (Austria, Brunei, France, Hong Kong, the UK and the USA). In all, the sample contained 1147 respondents, but the sample in each of the six countries was small and local in character (metropolitan areas arranged by neighbourhoods and shopping districts). The highest number of respondents was in the UK (220) and the lowest in Brunei (176).

In the survey insurance fraud was generally rated as the fourth most serious of eleven wrongful acts, but there were rather large contextual divergences in how the different crime categories were ranked. The contextual divergences were measured using a five-point Likert scale on which 1 represented *completely wrong* and 5 represented *not wrong at all*. Mean values were obtained for each country. The mean value for insurance fraud was 1.3 in the USA compared with 3.9 in Austria. The possibility that this difference was caused by the small, selective samples cannot be excluded (samples were collected more or less in one place in one town in each country).

Babukas et al. identified five clusters based on the eleven wrongful acts: *puritans* (15 per cent), *realists* (36 per cent), *indifferents* (28 per cent), *tolerants* (15 per cent) and *cynicals* (6 per cent). The overall ethical estimation was based mainly on the consumer ethics scale of Muncy and Vitells (cited by Babukas et al.). Twenty-seven ethical statements rated on the five-point Likert scale referred to above showed a continuous increase of acceptance through the clusters from 1.3 among the puritans to 3.3 for the tolerants to 4.1 for the cynicals (i.e. from the attitude that the behaviour was completely wrong in principle to the attitude that it was more or less completely right).

The content of the clusters was practically identical to the clusters that Dean (2004) reported. The demographic profile in the Babakus et al. clusters showed that women were overrepresented in the puritan and realist clusters and underrepresented in the cynical cluster. The proportion of youngsters (up to 35 years old) was significantly overrepresented in the cynical cluster (89 per cent compared with the puritans 57 per cent). Religious affiliation was relatively evenly spread across the five clusters, meaning no variation at all. All demographic values were significant at the one per cent level.

The investigation by Brinkmann and Lentz (2006) is similar to that of Babukas et al. They used the same consumer ethics scale developed by Muncy and Vitell (cited by Brinkmann and Lentz). They listed 16 to 20 ethically questionable consumer activities of which at least four could be classified as white-collar criminality, mainly insurance fraud. The ethics scale contained a reverse six-point Likert scale where 6 stood for *unacceptable* and 1 for *acceptable*. The researchers compared the attitudes of 156 responding Norwegians (70 per cent response rate) and 165 responding Germans (33 per cent response rate) collected by a survey in two business schools in Norway and a web-based questionnaire in Germany. Overall the results showed that the respondents rated the insurance fraud as either unacceptable or indifferent (4.2 for Norwegians and 3.5 for Germans), but regarded illegal copying of computer software and illegal downloading of music as (significantly) acceptable (1.9 for Norwegians and 2.5 for Germans).

Brinkmann and Lentz identified four clusters. The first were *moralists* (Norway, 32 per cent; Germany, 13 per cent) who scored highest on their rejection of fraud (non-acceptability of the act), apology (non-acceptability of forgiveness) and reaction (hardest punishment). Next came *realists* (Norway, 19 per cent; Germany, 27 per cent) and *conformists* (Norway, 21 per cent; Germany, 29 per cent), who had similar scores as regards their acceptance of fraud and reaction to it. However, when it came to accepting an apology, the realists had a harsher attitude than the conformists. Finally *critics* (Norway, 28 per cent; Germany, 31 per cent) were accepting of the fraud, accepting of forgiveness and accepting of the idea that there should be no punishment at all. Two questions were asked about the respondent's experience of insurance fraud, either at first- or second-hand (not self-reported). The *critics* in both Norway and Germany had more experience of insurance fraud while the *moralists* had least experience. In Germany only 16 per cent of the moralist group (non-significant) had experience of insurance fraud, whereas in Norway the corresponding figure was 21 per cent (significant).

Attitudes towards white-collar crime among offenders

Given our goal of investigating the prevalence of criminality as well as attitudes to it, studies that investigated the attitude of offenders were also consulted. Wärneryd and Walerud (1982) investigated tax evasion and tax avoidance in Sweden. Their sample was collected by telephone questionnaires containing 22 items put to 426 respondents (21.2 per cent drop-out). The survey asked about attitudes to tax crimes and self-reported tax criminality. In general 18.6 per cent of the respondents admitted they had evaded taxes sometimes or several times; 12 per cent admitted they had received black money several times or one or two times; 41.6 per cent admitted they had paid black money sometimes or several times. The remainder for each item had not evaded taxes or received or paid any black money. The attitudinal scale of the two groups was measured by three items: *propensity to gambling* (if they had a chance to reduce the tax illegally, would they take it?), *proprietary instincts* (does tax money belong to them, and should it not be taken away from them?) and *feeling of inequity* (is the Swedish taxation system unjust?).

The attitudes were rather as expected. Those who admitted tax evasion were also more into gambling (they would take the chance) and feelings of inequity (the taxation system was unjust), compared with those who did not admit to tax evasion (significant at the 5 per cent level). But proprietary instincts went in the contrary direction: those who did not admit tax evasion considered that the taxed money should belong to them rather than to society, in contrast to those who admitted tax evasion (insignificant). The cluster analysis showed three clusters. *Tax evaders* consisted of younger people (mean 38 years), self-employed, who were mostly satisfied with their economic status and had the greatest opportunity to evade tax. They displayed the most negative attitude to the tax system and sympathized with the Liberal Party of Sweden and the Centre Party (the former Peasant Party). *Regular taxpayers* consisted of older people (mean 58.5 years) with the lowest annual income and the lowest education. They showed the most positive attitude to the tax system and had the harshest attitude to punishing tax crimes. They were inclined to sympathize with socialist parties. *Tax planners* consisted of middle-aged people (mean 43 years), had the highest annual income, the highest proportion of home ownership, the highest education and the smallest opportunity to evade tax and pay black money. They were the most knowledgeable about taxes and sympathized with the Moderaterna Party (a conservative party).

The countries under investigation

For background information on the countries under investigation, we relied on empirical data deduced from the European Social Survey (ESS) (Round 2, collected in 2004).[2] The data is valid only for Germany, the UK, Spain and Sweden,[3] countries that in Esping-Andersen's (1990) and Ferrera's (1996) categorization represent different welfare regimes (Germany – conservative, UK – liberal, Spain – Mediterranean, and Sweden – social democratic).

In the conservative countries, Christian democratic movements laid the basis for the developing welfare state. Their approach is based on the subsidiarity principle, implying that problems should be solved as close to the individual as possible. This primarily means that the state or the market should not be the first to solve the consequences of unemployment, sick leave, childcare etc. The compensation principle in the social insurance system is based on occupational status, implying that the status hierarchy produced by the market is to a large extent sustained in the social insurance system.

In social democratic welfare regimes, social democratic movements rather than Christian democratic movements laid the basis for the development of the welfare state. In these states the important principles are redistribution and de-commodification. Thus the social insurance system to a greater extent equalizes the differences produced by the market and people are supposed to be compensated by the state during periods of unemployment, sick leave etc. to such an extent that they can live relatively normal lives, without being dependent on the labour market. A characteristic of social democratic welfare regimes is that the social insurance system is to a great extent universal: it is a right related to citizenship, and almost every citizen receives social transfers.

In liberal regimes, social movements played a substantially lesser role. The consequence is that the market plays a greater role, and the social insurance system is supposed to deal only with individual market failures. Thus the social insurance system is valid only for the disadvantaged in the society and is means-tested.

Esping-Andersen regards the Mediterranean countries as having a conservative welfare regime. However, Ferrera (1996) identified substantial differences between the description of the conservative welfare regimes and those in Mediterranean countries. These differences included the Mediterranean countries' ground having a highly fragmented income maintenance system, national health services based on universal principles, welfare delivered by a mix of public and non-public actors and a high degree of clientelism in general. The historical background is a weak state and ideological polarization.

An understanding of different welfare regimes is important for this study because the principles of the welfare state have been shown to reflect general trust in society and in the institutions of the state. According to Rothstein and Uslander (2005: 43), 'social trust is a measure of how people evaluate the moral fabric in their society'. Given that attitudes towards white-collar crime reflect the morality of the society, general trust should be related to general attitudes towards white-collar crime. Social trust is further understood to be a product of economic equality and equality of opportunity. Thus, in countries with welfare regimes that are producing economic equality and equality of opportunity, the level of trust should be high, and as a result more people should condemn white-collar crime than in regimes under which there is greater economy inequality and more disparities in access to opportunities.

Trust is related to reciprocity. Individuals who interpret their citizenship solely in terms of contributing without receiving anything back, while they see some others as only receivers of social benefits, will have a substantially lower trust in the state. Trust can also be related to the corporate sphere. A society in which relations between employers and employed are governed by bonds and agreements between unions and corporations will breed trust and solidarity with the industry in the society (Standing 2011). Union density and central bargaining are more common in social democratic welfare regimes than in conservative and Mediterranean regimes, which in turn have higher union density than liberal welfare regimes (European Commission 2009).

Therefore, the more universal the social insurance system, the greater the equality (both economic and regarding opportunity). Thus it can be expected that people in countries with social democratic welfare regimes should in general condemn white-collar crime more than people living in countries with liberal welfare regimes, since the social insurance system in these countries is largely means-tested. The attitude to white-collar crime for those living in countries with conservative welfare regimes should fall between the attitudes in social democratic and liberal welfare regimes, as these countries have more elements of universalism than countries with liberal welfare regimes, but less than countries with social democratic welfare regimes.

Besides belonging to different welfare regimes, the countries studied also represent different parts of Europe (continental countries, the British Isles, Southern Europe and Scandinavia/Northern Europe).

Measuring attitudes to white-collar crime

To investigate whether there are clusters of attitudes to white-collar crime, three crime categories were used: tax fraud, insurance fraud and bribery. The reason why we use only these categories is that the data set is unfortunately limited to these types of crime. The question asked was 'How wrong, if wrong at all, do you consider the following crimes to be?' The following options were available for answers: *Not wrong at all*, *A bit wrong* and *Seriously wrong*. Because very few respondents answered *Not wrong at all*, we have merged the categories *Not wrong at all* and *A bit wrong*.

To investigate whether it is possible to discern divergent categories of attitudes regarding these three crime categories, we used a method that clusters cases based on the probability of being linked to the input variables.[4] This method produced five stable clusters, that is, five different combinations of attitudes regarding the three crime categories (See Table 6.A in the Appendix). Table 6.1 presents the outcome of the cluster model. Cluster 1 (conformists) is the largest cluster. It represents respondents who condemn insurance fraud and bribery but not tax fraud. Cluster 2 (pragmatists) represents respondents who condemn bribery but not tax and insurance fraud. Cluster 3 (partly intolerants) represents respondents who are similar to the conformists except that they condemn these types of crime to a substantially greater extent than the conformists. Cluster 4 (condemners) represents respondents with high probability of giving the answer *Seriously wrong* to all crime categories. Cluster 5 (liberals) represents respondents with high probability of answering *not wrong/a bit wrong* to all crime categories.

Table 6.1 Probability indicator for attitudes towards white-collar crime

	1. Conformists	*2. Pragmatists*	*3. Partly intolerants*	*4. Condemners*	*5. Liberals*
Cluster size	32.89	28.35	23.74	10.62	4.39
Insurance fraud					
Not wrong/a bit wrong	2.18	21.77	0	0	86.27
Wrong	71.91	75.38	0.32	2.93	13.71
Seriously wrong	25.91	2.85	99.68	97.07	0.02
Bribery					
Not wrong/a bit wrong	4.47	0.57	0	0	44.98
Wrong	48.98	22.42	0.06	1.54	50.17
Seriously wrong	46.55	77.02	99.94	98.46	4.85
Tax fraud					
Not wrong/a bit wrong	35.36	75.56	45.86	0	93.57
Wrong	57.01	23.82	49.67	2.36	6.40
Seriously wrong	7.63	0.62	4.47	97.63	0.04

Source: ESS Round 2 – own calculations

The most interesting clusters are the condemners and the liberals. The other three clusters have either a much lower or a much higher probability of having an alternative to one of the extreme attitudes. In the analyses we will focus on those who condemn white-collar crime and those who take a liberal view of white-collar crime. To avoid the risk of having only a small number of responders, we will use continuous variables to measure every respondent's probability of belonging to these two clusters.

Who are the liberals and the condemners in each country?

Table 6.2 shows the size of the clusters in each country. The highest proportion of condemning respondents is found in Sweden, which accords with the earlier reasoning regarding differences between countries. Sweden has a social democratic welfare regime, and would thus be expected to have more people who condemn white-collar crime than the other countries. On the other hand, the lowest proportion is found in Germany, although it is a conservative continental country and might be expected to have a higher proportion of condemners than the liberal UK and the Mediterranean Spain. The proportion of liberal respondents is somewhat higher in Germany (8 per cent) and Spain (7 per cent) than in the UK (3 per cent) and Sweden (2 per cent). This result is also hard to explain in terms of the reasoning about differences between countries. Sweden has a low proportion of liberals, which matches expectations, but there are no differences between the UK and Sweden, even though the UK, belonging to a liberal welfare regime, should have high levels of liberals. It is also problematic that Germany and Spain have a higher proportion of liberals than the UK.

The results from Table 6.3 show some interesting differences between the countries. The results are based on an ordinary least squares fit (OLS) for a linear regression model. In general, the liberals tend to be young, between 15 and 30 years of age. The exception is Spain and to some extent the UK. In Spain the only statistically significant difference is between the age spans 15–30 and 51–64. Thus, even though the results show the same trend as in Germany and

Table 6.2 Cluster distribution by country, in %

	Germany	*Spain*	*United Kingdom*	*Sweden*
Cluster				
1. Conformists	11	40	35	40
2. Pragmatists	58	15	19	2
3. Partly intolerants	19	23	33	37
4. Condemners	5	14	10	20
5. Liberals	8	7	3	2

Source: ESS Round 2 – own calculation

Table 6.3 OLS dependent variables: cluster 5 and cluster 4. Unstandardized regression coefficients

	Sweden		*Germany*		*Spain*		*UK*	
	Liberals	*Condemners*	*Liberals*	*Condemners*	*Liberals*	*Condemners*	*Liberals*	*Condemners*
(Intercept)	**0.050**	**0.415**	**0.140**	**0.062**	0.068	**0.159**	**0.133**	**0.202**
Age								
15–30		**–0.185**		–0.029		–0.063		–0.050
31–50	**–0.030**	**–0.165**	**–0.039**	–0.016	–0.028	–0.049	**–0.027**	–0.042
51–64	**–0.044**		**–0.055**		**–0.052**		**–0.037**	
65–	**–0.046**	–0.102	**–0.064**	–0.013	–0.054	–0.010	–0.031	–0.010
Education								
Low								
Middle	0.002	–0.011	**–0.037**	–0.002	–0.027	0.000	–0.007	–0.012
High	–0.008	0.019	**–0.066**	0.001	–0.024	**0.046**	**–0.024**	–0.003
Other							–0.011	–0.021
Minority								
Yes								
No	–0.001	–0.086	–0.012	–0.006	0.036	–0.009	**–0.062**	**–0.093**
Labour market status								
Employee								
Self-employed	0.005	–0.031	–0.010	0.007	–0.003	0.037	0.002	–0.004
Unemployed	–0.023	**0.088**	–0.006	**0.028**	0.006	0.028	–0.011	–0.031
Retired	0.001	–0.053	–0.009	0.008	0.012	–0.004	–0.024	0.009
Other	–0.013	0.017	–0.007	0.006	0.029	0.005	–0.011	0.019
Partner/spouse								
Yes								
No	**0.019**	–0.024	**0.026**	–0.009	0.012	0.011	–0.002	0.000

Note: Bold = $p < 0.05$

Source: ESS Round 2 – own calculations. Blank indicates that the category is a reference category

Sweden, we cannot say with certainty that people aged 15–30 years are more likely to have liberal attitudes towards white-collar crime than people aged 31–50 years or 65 or older. In the UK the youngest age group tend to be more liberal than those aged 31–50 years and 51–64 years, but there is no significant difference between respondents aged 15–30 years and those aged 65 or older.

The respondents who have a condemning attitude tend to be older in Sweden (older than 51 years) but there are no age differences in the other countries. In Germany and the UK, respondents with liberal attitudes towards white-collar crime tend to have lower education, but education showed no statistical effect in the two other countries. Respondents who condemn white-collar crime tend to have higher education in Spain, but education is not an important variable in the other countries. In the UK both liberal and condemning attitudes are more common among minorities than among respondents who belong to the majority. In the other countries there are no differences between the majority and the minority populations.

In Sweden and Germany condemning attitudes are more common among the unemployed, but labour market status does not have any effect in the other countries. Furthermore, labour market status does not have any impact with regard to liberal attitudes in any of the countries under investigation. It is more common for liberals in Sweden and Germany to have no partner, whereas cohabiting status has no effect with regard to condemning attitudes. In the other countries cohabiting status has no effect with regard to liberal attitudes.

The crime risk

Thus far, this study has shown that although liberal and condemning respondents can be found in all the countries studied, there are differences in their sociodemographic profile between countries. We then moved on to investigate the effect of attitudes on criminal behaviour by investigating self-reported tax fraud and insurance fraud. We are aware that the causality can go in both directions. For one part of the sample the attitudes can cause criminality, and for another the criminal conduct can cause the attitudes.[5] With the data at hand the causal direction cannot be determined.

We used the same sociodemographic indicators mentioned above to investigate whether the impact of attitudes is greater than that of sociodemographic indicators, and whether attitudes are of importance independent of the sociodemographic indicators. The hypothesis is that liberal attitudes are a motivationally driven risk factor for white-collar crime, while condemning attitudes are a motivationally driven protection factor.

In Table 6.4 linear probability model results are presented, with tax fraud as the dependent variable. The results indicate that motivational factors affect tax fraud, and in the expected direction. Having a liberal attitude to white-collar crime is a risk factor for tax fraud in all countries under investigation except Spain, while having a condemning attitude to white-collar crime is a protection factor in all countries. Moreover, these attitudes constitute risk factors/protection factors independent of the sociodemographic indicators used in the model.

When it comes to sociodemographic factors, there are some differences between the countries. In Sweden, age, labour market status and cohabiting status affect self-reported tax fraud, with those between 30 and 64 years old who are self-employed and have a partner/spouse being most likely to commit tax fraud. In Germany it is the respondents who are between 31 and 50 years old, have higher education, are self-employed and have a partner who are more likely to commit tax fraud. In Spain it is only age that matters, while in the UK the respondents who

Table 6.4 Linear probability model: dependent variable = VAT crime. Unstandardized regression coefficients

	Sweden		*Germany*		*Spain*		*UK*	
(Intercept)	0.153	**0.277**	0.080	0.089	**0.208**	**0.201**	0.090	**0.117**
Liberals	**0.239**		0.161		0.082		**0.182**	
Condemners		**–0.260**		**–0.391**		**–0.214**		**–0.179**
Age								
15–30		–0.053		0.026		0.034		0.024
31–50	**0.080**	0.026	**0.085**	**0.110**	**0.083**	**0.118**	**0.063**	0.084
51–64	**0.078**	0.037	0.019	0.043	0.043	0.084	0.049	0.074
65–	0.015		–0.027		–0.044		–0.028	
Education								
Low								
Middle	0.050	0.048	**0.124**	**0.117**	0.017	0.015	0.042	0.039
High	0.063	0.067	**0.165**	**0.155**	0.045	0.054	**0.099**	**0.094**
Other							**0.088**	**0.082**
Ethnic majority/ minority								
Yes								
No	0.095	0.073	0.077	0.072	0.089	0.089	0.054	0.026
Labour market status								
Employee								
Self-employed	**0.168**	**0.160**	**0.123**	**0.125**	0.033	0.042	**0.150**	**0.150**
Unemployed	–0.048	–0.031	**–0.091**	**–0.081**	–0.060	–0.053	–0.005	–0.012
Retired	–0.063	–0.078	–0.028	–0.025	–0.018	–0.019	0.008	0.005
Other	**–0.085**	**–0.084**	–0.003	–0.002	**–0.121**	**–0.118**	–0.048	–0.047
Partner/spouse								
Yes								
No	**–0.062**	**–0.063**	**–0.063**	**–0.063**	–0.035	–0.032	**–0.051**	**–0.052**

Key: Bold = $p < 0.05$

Source: ESS Round 2 – own calculations. Blank indicates that the category is a reference category

tend to commit white-collar crime are between 31 and 50 years old, have higher education, are self-employed and have a partner/spouse.

Table 6.5 presents results from a linear probability model with insurance fraud as the dependent variable. In all countries under investigation, a liberal attitude is a risk factor for insurance fraud. In Sweden, Germany and Spain, a condemning attitude is a protective factor, but this shows no statistically significant effect in the UK. It can also be seen that insurance fraud offenders are in general younger in Sweden and Germany, while no age effect can be observed in Spain and the UK. Educational level, minority status and cohabiting status have no effect in any of the countries. Regarding labour market status, the self-employed in Germany are more likely to commit insurance fraud, but there is no similar effect of labour market status in the other countries surveyed, at least not independent of attitudes.

It appears that liberal attitudes are thus a relevant risk factor, whereas condemning attitudes are a protective factor. The question thus arises, are those with liberal attitudes also the most

Table 6.5 Linear probability model: dependent variable = insurance fraud. Unstandardized regression coefficients

	Sweden		*Germany*		*Spain*		*UK*	
(Intercept)	0.047	–0.003	–0.024	–0.040	–0.009	0.003	0.004	0.023
Liberals	**0.281**		**0.151**		**0.071**		**0.056**	
Condemners		**–0.021**		**–0.047**		**–0.041**		–0.026
Age								
15–30		**0.069**		**0.039**		–0.003		–0.007
31–50	**–0.038**	0.022	0.003	**0.037**	0.009	0.005	0.015	0.007
51–64	**–0.053**	0.005	**–0.028**	0.003	–0.007	–0.012	0.013	0.005
65–	**–0.060**		–0.031		0.004		0.008	
Education								
Low								
Middle	0.003	0.004	0.029	0.023	0.005	0.003	0.007	0.006
High	0.010	0.008	0.026	0.017	0.010	0.011	0.011	0.010
Other							0.004	0.003
Ethnic majority/ minority								
Yes								
No	0.013	0.011	0.038	0.036	0.040	0.042	0.005	–0.001
Labour market status								
Employee								
Self-employed	0.025	0.026	**0.071**	**0.069**	0.005	0.006	–0.006	–0.006
Unemployed	–0.003	–0.007	–0.005	–0.005	0.010	0.012	0.019	0.017
Retired	–0.002	–0.003	0.003	0.002	–0.028	–0.028	–0.016	–0.017
Other	–0.018	–0.021	–0.003	–0.004	**–0.033**	**–0.031**	–0.003	–0.003
Partner/spouse								
Yes								
No	–0.009	–0.004	0.002	0.006	0.014	0.016	–0.001	–0.001

Key: Bold = $p < 0.05$

Source: ESS Round 2 – own calculations. Blank indicates that the category is a reference category

likely to be career criminals[6] in contrast to those in any other cluster, but especially to those in the condemning cluster?

As we can see from Table 6.6, the general answer is yes. Liberal attitudes are significantly more associated with career criminality than condemning attitudes. But the picture presented in Table 6.6 is rather complex. Liberal respondents are not career criminals in such a rigorous way as we intuitively thought, yet this group does clearly show the highest frequency of career criminals. However, career criminality is almost as common among respondents who are pragmatists. An interpretation of this result is that the pragmatist group contains individuals who do not generally

Table 6.6 Career criminals by cluster and country, in %

	Sweden	*Germany*	*Spain*	*UK*
1. Conformists	7	2.1	5.5	3.1
2. Pragmatists	12.5	7.9	11.1	7.8
3. Partly intolerants	9.7	4.9	6.7	1.9
4. Condemners	1.9	0	1.5	0.6
5. Liberals	29.4	11.6	5.1	7.1
Total	**7.5**	**6.5**	**5.8**	**3.5**

Source: ESS Round 2 – own calculations

break the law, but given the right conditions these individuals may assume that breaking the law is the rational thing to do (especially when it comes to tax fraud).

Discussion

The aim of this chapter was to investigate four European countries to see whether there were differences in the sociodemographic profiles of those who had condemning or liberal attitudes towards white-collar crime. A secondary aim was to investigate the correlation between attitudes (liberals and condemners) and self-reported white-collar criminality for the different countries. The latter aim involved comparing context-related phenomena with the correlation between attitude and self-reported criminality.

In our investigation we found five clusters of attitudes related to white-collar crime. The differences between clusters 1 (the conformists), 2 (the pragmatists) and 3 (the partly intolerants) were relatively small. The conformists (who formed the largest cluster) had a relatively restricted attitude to all of the three white-collar crimes (they were all wrong, but not seriously wrong). Of those in the second largest group (pragmatists), one in five could accept insurance fraud and three in four could accept tax fraud; none would find bribery acceptable. The partly intolerants (the third largest group) did not accept insurance fraud and bribery, but differed substantially in their attitudes to tax fraud; half of them did not perceive it as wrong, but the other half did.

The largest difference in attitudes to white-collar crime was between clusters 4 (the condemners) and 5 (the liberals). This was expected, based on a previous investigation (Larsson and Alalehto 2013) and on previous cluster analytical investigation of insurance and tax fraud (Babakus et al. 2004; Dean 2004; Brinkmann and Lentz 2006). The condemners (the second smallest cluster) had a categorical moralistic attitude toward white-collar crime. They showed no acceptance of any of the three crime categories; instead they regarded it as seriously wrong to break the law in any of these categories. By contrast, the liberals (the smallest cluster) had rather extreme liberal attitudes. They appeared to accept insurance fraud and tax fraud without any objections. However, they did find it somewhat difficult to accept bribery (a propensity of 50 per cent), even though nearly half of them (a propensity of 45 per cent) did not consider bribery wrong.

A closer look at Table 6.3 reveals that, even if we can identify five distinct clusters for each of the four countries, there is a large variation in the distribution of all five clusters. This indicates that the respondents in the four countries perceived white-collar crime differently. In addition, the variation is unsystematic, with the conformists making up just 11 per cent of the sample in Germany, compared with 35–40 per cent for the other three countries. The pragmatists made up just 2 per cent in the Swedish sample, whereas their share in Germany was 58 per cent. This large difference may be explained by the partly intolerants in Sweden holding 37 per cent of the sample, compared with only 19 per cent in Germany. The same skewed distribution applies to the condemners (Sweden, 20 per cent; Germany, 5 per cent) and the liberals (Sweden, 2 per cent; UK, 3 per cent in contrast to Germany, 8 per cent; Spain, 7 per cent). It is obvious that contextual factors matter.

It is also clear that this contextual factor is not based on the nature of the welfare-state regime. According to our hypothesis, Sweden should have the highest rate of condemners and the lowest rate of liberals, and the UK should have the lowest rate of condemners and the highest rate of liberals. The results found do not support our hypothesis. Thus, we most probably have to seek for some other explanation for these differences between countries.[7]

However, from a criminological approach our results of the complexity of crime patterns as aggregated processes could also be explained from another level of abstraction, namely communication and social learning (imitation and socialization). This approach implies that individuals learn and confirm criminal strategies from others by context-related cultural strategies (Cohen and Machalek 1988). This is an old and well-known idea in criminology. Social learning of pro-criminality includes learning techniques, definitions and values as justification for crime, irrespective of whether the processes are perceived as reinforcement (Akers 2009) or modelling (Sutherland 1985). In other words, cultural strategies have been extensively studied in the theory of social disorganization, which examines crime patterns in certain communities in contrast to other communities (Shaw and McKay 1969).

This idea can be connected to institutionalized strategies. Institutionalized strategies mean that the culture itself is governed and regulated by some overall norms which steer the forms and content of the individual's capacity to communicate and socially learn *the rules of the game* in wider social contexts. Depending on how the institutional regulation develops over time, it will affect cultural strategies. If institutional regulation is weak, then there is no confidence in the *rules of the game*, and regulation will bring more disorganization. This affects community values and societal norms. On the other hand, if the institutional regulation is strong, it will help individuals organize their lives. When the institutional organization is weak, criminal decision-making may be the first option for individuals seeking to make sense of their lives. This causes the crime rate to increase. Thus, the way an institution regulates itself over time affects the number of individuals who choose crime (Rosenfeld and Messner 2013).

From this perspective it is logical to focus on the sociodemographic profile of the condemners and the liberals, as has been done in the chapter. The only sociodemographic category we found to be of some statistical importance was age, even if it was rather unsystematic across countries. The liberals tended to be younger in Sweden and Germany (significant) and Spain (non-significant), while this was not the case in the UK. When it came to condemners, age was not a statistically significant factor in any of the four countries. The sociodemographic categories of ethnicity and labour market status showed no variation at all with regard to attitudes towards white-collar crime. The other two sociodemographic categories, education and marriage, showed some mixed significant correlation, but on the whole showed a skewed distribution for the liberals and the condemners in the four countries. There is thus no unitary sociodemographic profile for the condemners or the liberals independent of country. The sociodemographic profiles depend ultimately on the national context. However, the mechanism behind the contextual effect is unfortunately still unknown. These results fundamentally contradict those of Babakus et al. (2004), which we believe are biased due to their highly selective method of data collection, in contrast to our data set.

Our investigation of the correlation between attitudes towards tax fraud and insurance fraud and self-reported criminality among condemners and liberals produced the expected results (Larsson and Alalehto 2013; Wärneryd and Walerud 1982). The cluster of condemners contains significantly fewer individuals who break the laws on tax fraud and insurance fraud (except in Spain, although the correlation went in the right direction). The opposite is true for liberals, who are substantially more likely to report having committed tax and insurance fraud in all countries (except in the UK, although the correlation went in the right direction). These results indicate an important non-contextual factor: independent of national context, there seems to be a strong correlation between an individual's attitude towards white-collar crime and his or her decision-making regarding white-collar crime.

When investigating whether the correlations obtained are dependent on any of the sociodemographic categories, we did not find any systematic co-variation, except some age-related effect for the liberals (in all four countries), showing significance for the age span 30–51 years. This result is not surprising given that investigations of sociodemographic profiles over the years show that the mean age for convicted and self-reported white-collar criminals is around 35–45 years (Alalehto and Larsson 2008, 2012; Soothill et al. 2012; Weisburd 1991; Weisburd et al. 2001).

We can conclude that motivation is a crucial factor in creating a crime scene. Based on our empirical findings, we identified a group of individuals (the liberals) with largely accepting attitudes towards crime and criminal decision-making who could serve as a pool of potential predisposed/tempted offenders independent of the society's specific context (Shover et al. 2012). A pool of predisposed/tempted offenders should, according to the theory of crime-as-choice, have a high potential to be attracted by lures (through their pro-criminal definitions and justifications of values) and should have the ability to choose opportunities where external oversight (techniques) is unlikely when suitable objects are available. In this they differ from individuals in any of the other clusters we investigated, but especially from the condemners. When we compared the liberals with the condemners, we also found a distinct difference in criminal decision-making corresponding to pro-criminal attitudes among the liberals and the anti-criminal attitudes among the condemners. This is confirmed in Table 6.6. The liberal cluster had a distribution of 9.6 per cent being career criminals and 29.1 per cent occasional criminals, whereas among the condemners the distribution was 0.8 per cent career criminals and 6.2 per cent occasional criminals. We interpret this result as showing substantial support for the significance of sharing non-criminal attitudes as a protection factor. Such attitudes really serve as a protection factor against crime.

Nevertheless, we have to remember that we also found substantial variations in the size of the liberal cluster between countries, probably indicating the effect of short-term variations (such as temporal business cycles) or long-term variations (such as inflation levels, technological changes or political reforms) in each specific context. The theory of crime-as-choice deems that the aggregated variation of white-collar crime can be predicted if we could estimate: (1) the supply of lure, (2) the size of the pool of predisposed/tempted offenders, and (3) the credibility of external oversight and its link to the supply of white-collar criminal opportunities (Shover et al. 2012: 478). We hypothesize that the liberals with their pro-criminal definitions and justifying values would be the primary group who would decide to act criminally when material conditions (such as recession, high inflation levels, high unemployment rates, and so forth – see Rosenfeld and Messner 2013) in general push individuals to choose crime. Thus the liberals should be the first to be attracted by the supply of lure and the lack of credible external oversight to increase white-collar crime considerably (Shover et al. 2012).

Appendix

Table 6.A Attitudes towards white-collar crime: model fit for latent class analyses

	L^2	$BIC(L^2)$	*df*
1-Cluster	3936.2962	3055.3429	98
2-Cluster	1475.3017	639.2950	93
3-Cluster	1076.3873	285.3272	88
4-Cluster	818.7199	72.6064	83
5-Cluster	522.5375	–178.6294	78

Note: In Table 6.A the model fit for the LCA is presented. The best possible complexity in the model in relation to the reduction of the degree of freedom can be found at six clusters (i.e. when the BIC(L^2) stops decreasing). However, a six-cluster model produces another cluster similar to cluster 1 (see Table 6.2), which is not a cluster we will use in the analyses, while the smallest cluster is somewhat smaller in the six-cluster model (3% compared with 4.4%)

Source: ESS Round 2 – own calculations.

Notes

1 Bribery and tax-related fraud such as VAT fraud are typical of the kinds of fraud that have been discussed in the literature on white-collar crime (see Clinard 1983; Sutherland 1985; Weisburd 1991). Insurance fraud is an atypical kind of white-collar crime, but counts as white-collar crime in reference works (see Croall 1992; Friedrichs 1995; Rosoff et al. 2010). Insurance fraud has been discussed as a white-collar crime in at least three forms: a crime committed by a person against a general insurance system (Geis et al. 1995); crime committed by a person against an insurance company (Clarke and Wheeler 1990); or crime committed by an insurance company against insurance holders (Shapiro 1987).

2 The ESS is an academically driven social survey established in 2001 and conducted every second year since then. It is widely used to investigate such things as attitudes to and trust in different kinds of institutions in society. In Round 2 of ESS one of the rotating modules contains questions about the moral economy inspired by a proposal put forward by a team led by Susanne Karstedt of the Department of Criminology at Keele University in the UK. The questions regarding attitudes towards white-collar crime are derived from this module. For more information, see europeansocialsurvey.org.

3 The response rate was 51 per cent in Germany, 50.5 per cent in the UK, 54.9 per cent in Spain and 65.5 per cent in Sweden.

4 To be sure that the empirical assessments of the theoretical constructs were the same for each country (i.e. whichever country the respondent comes from), country as a variable was used as a covariate. To conduct the LCA we used Latent Gold, version 4.5.

5 We thank the EUROC working group, and especially Judith van Erp for this insightful comment.

6 We use the criteria of four-plus frequencies instead of the traditional five-plus frequencies model, based on the results of Piquero et al. (2007: 132–135). They show that a four-plus offender model differs rather markedly from a three-plus offender, but not from a five-plus offender in recidivism probability. The measurement we use is a proxy for career criminality since we only have information relating to types of crime: tax fraud, insurance fraud, bribery, social insurance fraud, and false claims and concealing some faults in second-hand selling. Consequently some of the respondents who are not identified as career criminals may in reality be criminals, while those we identify as career criminals are most likely career criminals in reality.

7 Differences in white-collar crime between countries can also be a matter of political economy. These differences may cause differences in response because of the public's concern to report white-collar crime and/or the agencies' interest in regulating certain types of white-collar crime (see Győry, this volume).

References

Akers, R. (2009) *Social Learning and Social Structure: A General Theory of Crime and Deviance*, New Brunswick/New Jersey: Transaction Publishers.

Alalehto, T. and Larsson, D. (2008) 'Vem är den ekonomiske brottslingen? En sociodemografisk profilstudie av 23 länder', in I.T. Alalehto and D. Larsson (eds) *Den ljusskygga ekonomin: organiserad och ekonomisk brottslighet*, Umeå: Umeå Universitet.
Alalehto, T. and Larsson, D. (2012) 'Who is the economic criminal? A comparison between countries and types of crime', *Sociologisk forskning*, 49(1): 25–44.
Aubert, V. (1952) 'White-collar crime and social structure', *American Journal of Sociology*, 58(3): 263–271.
Babakus, E., Cornwell, T.B., Mitchell, V. and Schlegelmilch, B. (2004) 'Reactions to unethical consumer behavior across six countries', *Journal of Consumer Marketing*, 21(4): 254–263.
Braithwaite, J. (1985) 'White collar crime', *Annual Review of Sociology*, 11: 1–25.
Brinkmann, J. and Lentz, P. (2006) 'Understanding insurance customer dishonesty: Outline of a moral-sociological approach', *Journal of Business Ethics*, 66(2–3): 177–195.
Clarke, M. and Wheeler, S. (1990) *Business Crime: Its Nature and Control*, London: Polity.
Clinard, M.B. (1983) *Corporate Crime*, New York: Free Press.
Cohen, L. E. and Machalek, R. (1988) 'A general theory of expropriative crime: An evolutionary ecological approach', *American Journal of Sociology*, 94(3): 465–501.
Croall, H. (1992) *White Collar Crime*, Buckingham: Open University Press.
Cullen, F., Hartman, J. and Jonson, C. (2009) 'Bad guys: Why the public supports punishing white-collar offenders', *Crime Law and Social Change*, 51(1): 31–44.
Dean, D.H. (2004) 'Perceptions of the ethicality of consumer insurance claim fraud', *Journal of Business Ethics*, 54(1): 67–79.
Esping-Andersen, G. (1990) *The Three Worlds of Welfare Capitalism*, Cambridge: Polity.
European Commission (2009) *Industrial Relations in Europe 2008*, Luxembourg: Office for Official Publications of the European Communities.
Evans, D.T. (1995) 'Public perceptions of corporate crime', in M.B. Blankenship (ed.) *Understanding Corporate Criminology*, New York: Garland.
Ferrera, M. (1996) 'The "Southern Model" of welfare in Social Europe', *Journal of European Social Policy*, 6(1): 17–37.
Friedrichs, D.O. (1995) *Trusted Criminals: White Collar Crime in Contemporary Society*, Belmont, CA: Wadsworth Publishing.
Geis, G., Pontell, H.N. and Jesilow, P.D. (1995) 'Medicaid fraud', in G. Geis, R.F. Meier and L.M. Salinger (eds) *White-Collar Crime: Classic and Contemporary Views*, New York: The Free Press.
Hagenaars, J. A. and McCutcheon, A.L. (2002) *Applied Latent Class Analysis*, Cambridge: University Press.
Holtfreter, K., Van Slyke, S., Bratton, J. and Gertz, M. (2008) 'Public perceptions of white-collar crime and punishment', *Journal of Criminal Justice*, 36(1): 50–60.
Kane, J. and Wall, A.D. (2006) *The 2005 National Public Survey on White Collar Crime*, Fairmont, WV: National White Collar Crime Center.
Larsson, D. and Alalehto, T. (2013) 'The reaction towards white collar crime: When white collar crime matters', *The Open Criminology Journal*, 6(1): 1–9.
Levi, M. and Jones, S. (1985) 'Public and police perceptions of crime seriousness in England and Wales', *British Journal of Criminology*, 25(3): 234–250.
Magidson, J. and Vermunt, J.K. (2001) 'Latent class factor and cluster models, bi-plots, and related graphical displays', *Sociological Methodology*, 31: 223–264.
O'Connell, M. and Whelan, A. (1996) 'Taking wrongs seriously: Public perceptions of crime seriousness', *British Journal of Criminology*, 36(2): 299–318.
Piquero, A.R., Farrington, D.P. and Blumstein, A. (2007) *Key Issues in Criminal Career Research: New Analyses of the Cambridge Study in Delinquent Development*, New York: Cambridge University Press.
Rosenfeld, R. and Messner, S.F. (2013) *Crime and the Economy*, London: SAGE.
Rosoff, S.M., Pontell, H.N. and Tillman, R. (2010) *Profit Without Honor: White-Collar Crime and the Looting of America*, Upper Saddle River, NJ: Prentice Hall.
Rothstein, B. and Uslaner, E.M. (2005) 'All for one: Equality, corruption, and social trust', *World Politics*, 58(1): 41–72.
Schoepfer, A., Carmichael, S. and Piquero, N.L. (2007) 'Do perceptions of punishment vary between white-collar and street crimes?', *Journal of Criminal Justice*, 35(2): 151–163.
Schrager, L.S. and Short, J.F. (1978) 'Toward a sociology of organizational crime', *Social Problems*, 25(4): 407–419.
Serajzadeh, S.H. (2008) 'Social determinants of the seriousness of crime: An examination of a Muslim sample', *Social Compass*, 55(4): 541–560.

Shapiro, S.P. (1987) *Wayward Capitalists: Targets of the Securities and Exchange Commission*, London: Yale University Press.
Shaw, C.R. and McKay, H.D. (1969) *Juvenile Delinquency and Urban Areas*, 2nd revised edn, Chicago: University of Chicago Press.
Shover, N., Hochstetler, A. and Alalehto, T. (2012) 'Choosing white-collar crime', in F.T. Cullen and P. Wilcox (eds) *The Oxford Handbook of Criminological Theory*, New York: Oxford University Press.
Soothill, K., Humphreys, L. and Francis, B. (2012) 'Middle-class offenders: A 35-year follow-up', *British Journal of Criminology*, 52(4): 765–785.
Stack, S. and Kposowa, A. (2006) 'The effect of religiosity on tax fraud acceptability: A cross-national analysis', *Journal for the Scientific Study of Religion*, 45(3): 325–351.
Standing, G. (2011) *The Precariat: The New Dangerous Class*, London: Bloomsbury Academic.
Stylianou, S. (2003) 'Measuring crime seriousness perceptions: What have we learned and what else do we want to know?', *Journal of Criminal Justice*, 31(1): 37–56.
Sutherland, E.H. (1940) 'White-collar criminality', *American Sociological Review*, 5(1): 1–12.
Sutherland, E.H. (1985) *White Collar Crime: The Uncut Version*, New Haven: Yale University Press.
Tennyson, S. (2008) 'Moral, social, and economic dimensions of insurance claims fraud', *Social Research: An International Quarterly*, 75(4): 1181–1204.
Unnever, J., Benson, M. and Cullen, F. (2008) 'Public support for getting tough on corporate crime: Racial and political divides', *Journal of Research in Crime and Delinquency*, 45(2): 163–190.
Wärneryd, K.-E. and Walerud, B. (1982) 'Taxes and economic behavior: Some interview data on tax evasion in Sweden', *Journal of Economic Psychology*, 2(3): 187–211.
Weisburd, D. (1991) *Crimes of the Middle Classes: White-Collar Offenders in the Federal Courts*, New Haven: Yale University Press.
Weisburd, D., Waring, E.J. and Chayet, E. (2001) *White-Collar Crime and Criminal Careers*, Cambridge: Cambridge University Press.

Part II

Historical perspectives on white-collar and corporate crime in Europe

7

Willem Bonger

The unrecognized European pioneer of the study of white-collar crime

Patrick Hebberecht

Introduction

The dominant belief in criminology is that Edwin Sutherland played a pioneering role in the study of criminality of high executives of companies. In a historical overview of the first criminologists with an interest in white-collar crime, some authors such as Slapper and Tombs (1999) also mentioned Edward A. Ross and Albert Morris. Edward A. Ross (1907, as cited in Geis and Meier 1977: 27) identified as 'criminaloid'

> [T]he director who speculates in the securities of his corporation, the director who lends his depositors' money to himself under diverse corporate aliases, the railroad official who grants a secret rebate for his private graft, the builder who hires walking delegates to harass his rivals with causeless strikes, the labour leader who instigates a strike in order to be paid for calling it off, the publisher who bribes his textbooks into the schools.

In 1935, six years after the great crash, Albert Morris elaborated a long list of 'criminals of the upperworld' who are engaging in 'financial fraud, fraudulent jingoistic propaganda and violations of international law' (Geis 1967, in Slapper and Tombs 1999: 34–39).

In many publications about white-collar crime of the past decades, even in Dutch publications, the name of Willem Bonger remains unmentioned. In the book published on the occasion of the congress on white-collar crime organized in 1984 by the Dutch Society of Criminology no reference was made to the pioneering role of Willem Bonger (Berghuis et al. 1984).

Only some authors refer to the pioneering contribution of the Dutch criminologist and sociologist Willem Bonger to the study of criminality committed by economically powerful people. In his article on 'White collar crime', John Braithwaite (1985: 2) wrote:

> There were great scholars on whose shoulders Sutherland could stand. The Dutch Marxist Willem Bonger, in his *Criminality and Economic Conditions* (1916), was the first to develop a theory of crime that incorporated both 'crime in the streets' and 'crimes in the suites'.

In a review of two books on white-collar crime, Ian Taylor (1988) mentioned that '"white-collar-crime" and "economic crime" were central topics in the work of the great Marxist criminologist Willem Bonger, whose *Criminality and Economic Conditions* was published in 1916'.

In an article on the 'definitional quagmire' of the concept of white-collar crime, David Friedrichs (1992: 6) notes:

> Although Sutherland is generally given credit for having introduced 'white collar crime' into the literature, the recognition of this type of crime extends quite far back in history. There is a long European history (evident in the work of Marx and Engels, and Bonger) recognising that the powerful and the privileged commit 'crimes', loosely defined, as a consequence of the character of the economic system, and their special status in it.

Slapper and Tombs (1999: 2) too mention the pioneering contribution of Willem Bonger in their introduction to the study of corporate crime.

In this contribution, we dwell on the pioneering role of Bonger's PhD 'Criminalité et conditions économiques' (1905) in the study of white-collar crime. First, we situate the PhD in his academic career. We pay attention to the definition of crime elaborated by Willem Bonger. Individuals, also those of high status, who commit crimes are studied by Willem Bonger according to their position in the 'social organization', determined by the 'capitalist economic production regime'. Furthermore, we outline his analysis of the relations between 'capitalist production regime', 'social organization' and crime. In the next section we pay attention to the economic crimes committed by the economically powerful people, who are defined as the 'capitalist bourgeoisie' in the social class analysis of Willem Bonger. Finally, we indicate the differences between Willem Bonger and the other pioneer, Edwin Sutherland, in the study of white-collar crime.

Willem Bonger

Willem Adriaan Bonger (1876–1940) was born on 6 September 1876 in Amsterdam as the youngest of ten children in a rather liberal middle-class family (Bonger 1950; Valkhoff 1950; Van Heerikhuizen 1987). As a law student at the University of Amsterdam he became a socialist and a member of the Sociaal-Democratische Arbeiderspartij (SDAP) (the Social Democratic Workers' Party). Through his political commitment he developed an interest for the pressing social problems at the time, such as alcoholism.

After finishing his law studies in 1900, he worked on a doctoral thesis in law, titled 'Criminalité et conditions économiques' (Criminality and economic conditions), which he defended in 1905 at the University of Amsterdam.

In the same year, Willem Bonger started to work at an insurance company in Amsterdam. He stayed there until 1920. In the meanwhile Willem Bonger continued to do scientific work. His later scientific activities consisted for a large part of the deepening of the analyses he started in his doctoral thesis.

In 1913 he published *Geloof en misdaad: Een criminologische studie* (Religion and Crime: A Criminological Study). For the first time in the Netherlands Willem Bonger analysed the relation between religious denomination and crime. Willem Bonger challenged the thesis that unbelief caused crime. He came to the conclusion that primarily economic and social causes determined the crime level of a religious group.

In 1922, at the age of 46, Willem Bonger became the first professor of sociology and criminology in the Netherlands at the University of Amsterdam. In 1932 Bonger published *Inleiding tot de criminologie*, oriented to a large public and conceived as a historical overview of different criminological schools and theories. An English translation titled *An Introduction to Criminology* was published in 1936.

In 1936 he was one of the founders of the Dutch Sociological Association. He became its first president for the next four years.

In 1939 he published the book *Ras en misdaad*, translated into English in 1943 after his death, titled *Race and Crime* (Hebberecht 2008: 49–53). Because of the growing popularity of racial theories, also in criminology, Willem Bonger felt the need to scientifically challenge the thesis that race had an influence on the committing of crime.

As a criminologist Willem Bonger published many articles in Dutch as well as in foreign journals. As a sociologist he drafted scientific contributions on suicide, prostitution, morality, disability, demography, war, democracy and religion. He has written important statistical studies about property and income and about belief and disbelief in the Netherlands.

Willem Bonger was an academic sociologist and criminologist on the one hand and a theoretician and intellectual of the Social Democratic Workers' Party on the other. The more objective empirical scientific activities during his life were always accompanied by his emotional political stance taking. Willem Bonger defended many courageous viewpoints on different public issues. He was against the discrimination of homosexuals, he opposed the criminalization of abortion and he pleaded for a faster divorce procedure.

Willem Bonger wrote in different Dutch socialist publications about various subjects such as the First World War, democracy and dictatorship, extremism in the left movement and intellectuals and socialism. He presented himself as a democratic and internationalist socialist. He called himself a Marxist but was opposed to any kind of political left extremism (anarchism and Leninism) and to dogmatism in the Marxist movement. He resisted against fascism and national socialism. In the end of the thirties he became a member of the anti-fascist Comité van Waakzaamheid (Committee of Watchfulness) where Christians, social democrats, liberals and communists joined against fascism.

Five days after the German army crossed the Dutch–German border on 15 May 1940, Willem Bonger and his wife committed suicide. It was a well-considered act as could be deduced from his farewell letter: 'I don't see any future for myself and I cannot bow to this scum which will now overmaster us' (Bonger 1950).

'Criminalité et conditions économiques' (Criminality and economic conditions)

After finishing his law studies in 1900, Bonger participated in an academic prize contest organized by the Law Faculty of the University of Amsterdam concerning the influence of economic conditions on criminality. His participation in this contest oriented his scientific interest more specifically towards the problem of crime. Though only honourably mentioned, his paper became the basis for his doctoral thesis in law, titled 'Criminalité et conditions économiques' (Criminality and economic conditions) in 1905. His promoter was the well-known professor of penal law, Van Hamel.

His doctoral thesis consists of two main parts (Hebberecht 2010). In the first part he critically discussed the nineteenth-century authors who had written about the influence of economic conditions on criminality. According to Willem Bonger, most of these authors attached little significance to economic conditions in the sense of poverty or wealth and did not explain these phenomena. They did not look at the broader 'economic production regime'. They neglected to demonstrate how economic conditions indirectly influence the committing of crime through their effects on the 'social organization'.

In this first part Willem Bonger also sharply criticizes the individualist positivist criminology of the second half of the nineteenth century. In a general sense, biological and psychological deficits are not the aetiological factors of crime, according to Bonger. This is only true for a small minority of (pathological) criminals. Economic and social circumstances determine whether individual characteristics lead to criminal involvement.

In the second part of his doctoral thesis Willem Bonger analyses the historically determined and dynamic relation between the 'capitalist production regime', the 'social organization' and crime.

Under the auspices of the American Institute of Criminal Law and Criminology, the doctoral thesis of Willem Bonger was published in English in Boston in 1916 under the title 'Criminality and economic conditions'. The most recent literature was incorporated in this edition. At the same time some extracts of the French edition were deleted, for example his critique of the criminalization of homosexuality (Van Heerikhuizen 1987). Due to this publication Willem Bonger was not only well known in continental Europe but also in the Anglo-Saxon countries.

In this contribution we will discuss the relation between the 'capitalist production regime', 'the social organization' and crime and his focus on the crimes committed by the capitalist class in more detail.

Capitalist production regime and social organization

According to Willem Bonger, crime as a social phenomenon must be studied departing from historically determined and dynamic relations between the 'economic production regime' and the 'social organization'. The 'economic production regime' is very important amongst the economic factors that influence crime. The 'economic production regime' intersects with the whole 'social organization', the living and working conditions, the education system, the marriage, the raising of children, etc. The influence of the 'production regime' on crime is in most cases mediated by its effects on the 'social organization'.

Especially influenced by the interpretation of Karl Marx's work by Friedrich Engels and Karl Kautsky (the theoretician and political leader of the German Social Democrats), Willem Bonger (1905: 311–324; 1916: 247–268) analyses the 'capitalist production regime' and its effects on the 'social organization'. The 'capitalist production regime' is presumed to be characterized by unequal exchange ratios, the quest for maximum profit and competition. The owner of capital tries to realize a maximum added value by paying a minimal price for labour. Workers on the contrary struggle for a fraction of this added value, delivered by means of their labour, in the form of the largest possible wage. The expansion of the 'capitalist production regime' is accompanied by an increasing proletarianization of the population and by the introduction of children's and women's labour. A concentration of capital is occurring. A minority of people enrich themselves and a majority of the population becomes poorer.

Based on the position in the 'capitalist production regime', Willem Bonger (1905: 325–350; 1916: 269–290) distinguishes four social classes: the bourgeoisie, the petty bourgeoisie, the working class and the lumpen.

The bourgeoisie consists of three groups: the capitalists, the rentiers and the liberal professionals. The capitalists own and control the economic means of production. The capitalist production regime creates an added value, which becomes the property of the capitalists and forms the basis of their power. The rentiers use a part of the added value to increase their capital. The other part is consumed for their luxurious lifestyle. They do not work and live from what others produce. The share of this group within the bourgeoisie became greater through the concentration of capital and the growth of limited liability companies. The liberal professionals live from their intellectual work and are not capitalists in the strict sense. However, they originate from the bourgeoisie and share the same way of living. This group became more important due to the expansion of the 'capitalist production regime' and of the state bureaucracy.

The power of the petty bourgeoisie is weakened by the development of the 'capitalist production regime'. The competitive position of the small business owners came under heavy pressure. This social class is numerically strengthened by the economically failed part of the bourgeoisie and by successful members of the working class. This social class has the oldest traditions. They envy the capitalist class for their power and possessions and do not stand in solidarity with the working class.

The working class does not possess economic means of production and can only exchange their labour force for a wage that lets them satisfy their needs. The workers are often confronted with forced unemployment. Factory labour is harmful for their physical, intellectual and moral condition. The interests of the working class are contrary to those of the capitalist bourgeoisie.

The lumpen is situated at the bottom of the social class structure. These classes neither possess economic means of production, nor do they exchange their labour force for a wage. They do not have a position in the economic organization. The already wretched living conditions of the working class are worse for the lumpen.

According to Willem Bonger, these differences of social class in the 'social organization' do not reflect individual differences in predispositions and capacities.

Willem Bonger (1905: 351–378; 1916: 321–356) also analyses the sexual and family relationships in the 'social organization', which, similarly to the social class relationships are determined by the 'economic production regime'. He claims for instance that the role of the family has changed under the conditions of the 'capitalist production regime'.

The relation between the 'capitalist production regime' and the 'social organization' is more concretely demonstrated in his analysis of the effects of the 'capitalist production regime' on 'pathological' social phenomena such as alcoholism, prostitution and militarism, which existed before capitalism (Bonger 1905: 378–414; 1916: 321–380).

Capitalist production regime, social organization and crime

Willem Bonger's sociological concept of crime in 'Criminalité et conditions économiques' is very innovative for his time (Bonger 1905: 432–436; 1916: 377–380). The 'social organization' and consequently also the 'economic production regime' determine which acts are deemed immoral and anti-social and which of them are criminal acts. In a society divided by a dominant and dominated class, the penal law is dictated by the interests of the dominant class.

In 1905 Willem Bonger stated that practices that can harm the interests of the bourgeoisie are always defined as crimes. It does not matter whether these practices are also harmful for the dominated social classes. In fact, many criminalizations (for example rape, murder, etc.) also protect them. But for Willem Bonger it is striking that practices that only harm members of the dominated classes are not defined as crimes. The rare exceptions demonstrate that the lower classes are not entirely powerless.

'Altruism' and 'egoism' are two important social categories in Willem Bonger's analysis of the relation between the 'capitalist economic production regime' and its effects on the 'social organization' on one hand and crime on the other (Bonger 1905: 437–590; 1916: 381–535). In contrast to the social Darwinists who defined 'egoism' as a fundamental characteristic of mankind, Willem Bonger, influenced by Karl Kautsky, claims that human beings have strong social instincts and sentiments, which lie at the basis of 'altruism' in society. The 'capitalist production regime' weakens this 'altruism' and with it also the moral strength of people against the conversion of 'criminal ideas' into criminal acts.

Through the effects on 'social organization', created by the 'capitalist production regime', 'egoism' is directly or indirectly being rewarded. Depending on the economic and social circumstances of the different social classes, the increased 'egoistic ideas' lead to a 'criminal idea'. Being less confronted with unfavourable economic and social circumstances, 'egoism' amongst the bourgeoisie gives fewer tendencies to a 'criminal idea'. When your 'egoistic ideas' can be satisfied in legal ways given your socioeconomic position, why would you commit property crimes? Willem Bonger arrived at the conclusion that the more unfavourable the economic and social circumstances of a social class, the more the increased 'egoism' leads to a 'criminal idea'. Subsequently, due to a weakened 'altruism' it is realized in the committing of a criminal act.

Crimes of the bourgeoisie

Furthermore, Willem Bonger (1905: 592–721; 1916: 536–666) analyses in detail how the 'capitalist production regime' and its effects on the 'social organization', differentiated by social class and sex, form the basis for the five categories of crimes distinguished by the motives of the offenders (namely: economic crimes, sexual crimes, crimes out of revenge and other motives, political crimes and pathological crimes). In this contribution we focus on the economic crimes committed by members of the capitalist bourgeoisie (Bonger 1905: 652–659; 1916: 599–607).

Concerning the first category of crimes, namely economic crimes, the direct relation with economic conditions can easily be demonstrated. For members of the non-owner class, economic conditions may lead to begging and vagrancy, different types of theft, robbery and economically motivated murders. In case of the owner class, economic conditions may lead to fraudulent bankruptcy, adulteration of food and analogous crimes. Some of these economic practices (such as bankruptcy) are criminalized because they are harmful to the regular progress of capitalism. Other economic practices (such as the adulteration of food) are sanctionable as a consequence of the opposition of the consumers to one of the harmful effects of this capitalist system (Bonger 1905: 659; 1916: 607).

These economic crimes of the owner class can be committed as a result of a sudden economic impoverishment, greed or pronounced criminal intent (Bonger 1905: 652; 1916: 599).

Not because of absolute poverty but because of the awareness that due to a sudden economic impoverishment a comfortable life and esteem will come to an end, an opportunity to commit an economic crime can be seized (Bonger 1905: 652–655; 1916: 599–602). In such a case the member of the owner class does not have the moral strength that can prevent her/him from committing this economic crime. According to Willem Bonger, many children of the capitalist bourgeoisie are taught to be honest, when possible, but also to make money. This honesty for the sake of one's own interest has limited preventive effects. Economic and social conditions are the cause of the committing of these crimes, not the individual characteristics of the perpetrators. Individual differences partially explain who are the ones who commit these crimes – in general those whose moral qualities are weaker than average.

Contrary to the first category, bourgeois economic crimes motivated by greed are not committed by those whose business is declining, but by those whose affairs are more or less flourishing (Bonger 1905: 655–657; 1916: 602–604). What they get from their honest business is not enough for them, they wish to become richer. Greed is a strong motive amongst all social classes. It is especially so amongst the bourgeoisie, as a consequence of their economic position, which is the first and most important cause of these crimes. Secondly, the opportunity to commit these crimes undetected is enormous, especially as far as the adulteration of food is concerned. Thirdly, their weakened social sentiments do not have a preventive effect.

The 'great criminals' form the last category of this group of bourgeois criminals (Bonger 1905: 658–660; 1916: 605–607). The 'great criminals' are 'those who throw themselves in gigantic enterprises while knowing beforehand that these will certainly or probably fail, or those who make great purchases of stock, and afterward cause a rise in price through the dissemination of false news, etc.' (Bonger 1905: 658; 1916: 605). These crimes can only be committed under a 'capitalist economic system'. Persons who commit these crimes are in the first place characterized by excessive greed. Furthermore, more than common intelligence and talent, they need 'to cover up malversations for a long time, to organize clever swindles, outrageous frauds and bankruptcies, exploitations of the credulous public' (Bonger 1905: 659; 1916: 606). The intensity of the moral sentiments of these criminals is particularly low.

Willem Bonger, the unrecognized pioneer of the study of white-collar crime, compared with Edwin Sutherland

In 1905 Willem Bonger was strongly influenced by the Dutch Social Democratic Working Party, at that time Marxist and oriented to the replacement of the capitalist economic system by a socialist economic production system. Edwin Sutherland was influenced by the progressive populist movement in the United States, which was concerned with corporate crime (Slapper and Tombs 1999: 2). This movement was not oriented to the collapse of the capitalist economic system but to the elimination of the excesses of individual capitalists.

For Bonger, perpetrators belong to a social class. According to his Marxist social class analysis, they are members of the lumpen, the working class, the middle classes or the capitalist bourgeoisie. For Sutherland, perpetrators have either a low or a high social status. High social status, respectability and occupation are for Sutherland the central characteristics of the white-collar criminal (Berghuis et al. 1984).

Willem Bonger's understanding of the criminality of the capitalist bourgeoisie was limited to the transgression of penal laws. According to Edwin Sutherland a transgression of legal norm and not only of penal norms could be defined as white-collar crime. Both criminologists applied a sociological definition of crime. Practices defined as crime are the result of a social construction, in the first place by an intervention of the (penal) legislator.

For Edwin Sutherland (1947) the principle of 'differential association', an excess of definitions that favour law violation over definitions that are unfavourable for law violations, can explain the committing of a white-collar crime. In the view of Willem Bonger (1905; 1916), the crimes of the capitalist bourgeoisie can be explained by the 'capitalist production system' and by their effects on the 'social organization'.

Conclusion

The PhD 'Criminality and economic conditions' (1905) of the Dutch criminologist Willem Bonger (1876–1940) is still relevant for a structural-historical analysis of late modern developments in crime and crime control.

His sociological concept of crime sometimes (rather implicitly) recognizes the different dimensions of the social construction of crime. In his view, the criminologist must not only study crime but also the patterns in criminalization of certain behaviour by penal law and throughout criminal law enforcement. To a certain extent, in his analysis of the economic and social factors that determine what acts are criminalized by penal law, Bonger elaborated the consequences of his critical concept of crime. The class character of criminal law did not exclude the criminalization of practices of the capitalist establishment that are harmful for the general interest of this dominant class. Bonger was one of the first criminologists to study the economic crimes committed by some members of the capitalist establishment. In the very innovative parts of his PhD about the criminalization of behaviour patterns by penal law, Bonger uses an unelaborated concept of the state (reflecting the unequal power relations between social classes) and the more elaborated concepts of 'capitalist production system' and 'social organization'.

Bonger did not get round to a systematic analysis of penal law enforcement by the police, the public prosecutor, the judges and the instances responsible for the execution of criminal sanctions. His thoughts about the selectivity in the criminal justice system were more elaborated in his critical analysis of the selectivity that plays a role in the construction of criminal statistics. Concerning the study of the enforcement of penal law Bonger, due to his unelaborated concept of the state, fails to provide a detailed analysis of the different instances of the criminal justice system conceptualized as state apparatuses.

Bonger's theory about the economic and social causes of criminalized behaviour is, on the contrary, elaborated on in great detail. His analysis of the relation between the 'capitalist production process', the 'social organization' and crime based on the writings of Karl Marx, Friedrich Engels and Karl Kautsky forms a valuable innovation in critical criminology. Bonger analysed in detail how the capitalist production process and its effects on the social organization are determining the economic crimes committed by the bourgeoisie.

Due to globalization, the effects of the restructuring of the 'capitalist production regime' and the related fundamental social, political and cultural transformations on crime and crime control are becoming increasingly significant. The way Bonger analysed the influence of the development of the 'capitalist production regime' and the related social transformations on crime in the second half of the nineteenth and in the first decades of the twentieth century can help us in our critical understanding of late modern developments in crime and crime control.

References

Berghuis, A., Brants, C., and Willemse, H. (1984) 'Witteboordencriminaliteit, schets van een probleemveld', in A. Berghuis, C. Brants, and H. Willemse (eds) *Witteboordencriminaliteit*, Nijmegen: Ars Aequi Libri, pp. 3–15.

Bonger, H. (1950) 'Korte levensschets van Prof. Mr. W.A. Bonger', in J. Valkhoff (ed.) *Prof. Mr. W.A. Bonger: Verspreide geschriften. Deel I. Criminologie en criminele statistiek*, Amsterdam: Arbeiderspers, pp. ix–xxv.

Bonger, W.A. (1905) *Criminalité et conditions économiques*, Amsterdam: G.P. Tierie.

Bonger, W.A. (1916) *Criminality and Economic Conditions*, Boston: Little, Brown and Company.

Braithwaite, J. (1985) 'White collar crime', *Annual Review of Sociology*, 11: 1–25.

Friedrichs, D.O. (1992) 'White-collar crime and the definitional quagmire: a provisional solution', *Journal of Human Justice*, 3(2): 5–21.

Geis, G. and Meier, R.F. (eds) (1977) *White-collar Crime: Offenses in Business, Politics, and the Professions*, New York: The Free Press.

Hebberecht, P. (2008) 'Willem Adriaan Bonger (1876–1940): Een kritisch criminoloog van de moderniteit', in P. Hebberecht (ed.) *De 'verpaarsing' van de criminaliteitsbestrijding in België: Kritische opstellen over misdaad en misdaadbestrijding in de laatmoderniteit*, Brussel: VUBPress, pp. 21–56.

Hebberecht, P. (2010) 'Willem Bonger', in K. Hayward, S. Maruna and J. Mooney (eds) *Fifty Key Thinkers in Criminology*, Oxon: Routledge, pp. 58–61.

Slapper, G. and Tombs, S. (1999) *Corporate Crime*, Harlow: Longman.

Sutherland, E.H. (1947) *Principles of Criminology*, 4th edn, Philadelphia: Lippincott.

Taylor, I. (1988) 'Loadsa serious money', *London Review of Books*, 10(9): 7–9.

Valkhoff, J. (1950) 'Bongers werken', in J. Valkhoff (ed.) *Prof. Mr. W.A. Bonger: Verspreide geschriften. Deel I. Criminologie en criminele statistiek*, Amsterdam: Arbeiderspers, pp. xxvi–lxxxviii.

Van Heerikhuizen, B. (1987) *W.A. Bonger: Socioloog en socialist*, Groningen: Wolters-Noordhoff/Forsten.

8

Corporate involvement in the Holocaust and other Nazi crimes

Annika van Baar[1]

Introduction

The Holocaust carried out by the Nazi regime during the Second World War is seen by many as *the* crime of the twentieth century (Friedrichs 2012) and is one of the most serious examples of state crime in modern times, at the very least in Europe. During the Nazi regime (1933–1945) European Jews were systematically persecuted and exterminated in what is now called the Holocaust: the genocide of almost six million Jews. The Holocaust was preceded and accompanied by various war crimes, crimes against humanity and other gross human rights violations. In addition to Jews, several other groups such as Poles, Sinti, Roma, Slavs and others deemed 'inferior' by the Nazis were persecuted, used as slave labourers, tortured, looted and murdered.

To carry out its genocidal and expansionist policies, the Nazi regime mobilized large parts of German society, including the business sector. At the Nuremberg trials prosecutors emphasized the importance of the role of German industrialists during the Second World War. During subsequent Nuremberg trials, 46 businessmen were prosecuted and a number of them sentenced for their role in mass murder, plunder and spoliation, financial support to the SS and labour exploitation of both prisoners of war and civilians (Bush 2009; Taylor 1949).

Like criminologists in general, white-collar crime scholars generally do not see the crimes committed during the Nazi-era as phenomena for criminological analysis. Meanwhile, historians, social psychologists and philosophers have produced the largest literature any criminal event has ever generated (Friedrichs 2012). Recently, there has been increasing criminological attention on international crimes and other gross human rights violations (Brannigan 2013; Brants 2007; Cohen 2001; Olusanya 2013; Rothe and Mullins 2009; Smeulers and Grunfeld 2011). Within the field of corporate crime, studies of the connections between corporations or corporate actors and the Holocaust and the Second World War are rare (van Baar and Huisman 2012; Matthews 2006).

The study of corporate involvement in international crimes,[2] including the Holocaust, can be seen as existing in the overlap of the criminological study of international crimes and the study of corporate crime (van Baar and Huisman 2012). Corporations are, in most cases, not the primary perpetrators of such crimes (Huisman 2010). Instead, they are usually accomplices to the primary perpetrators, in this case the Nazi regime and its institutions such as the SS, the SA and the *Reichswirtschaftsministerium* (Ministry of Economic Affairs). For this chapter, corporate involvement in international crimes is defined as corporate conduct that enabled, exacerbated or facilitated international crimes committed by the Nazi regime and its representatives. Involvement is defined as a corporation contributing to the commission of these crimes by the principal perpetrator(s) while knowing (or while it should have known) that its conduct contributed to the commission of these crimes.[3]

Corporations were involved in several stages of the Holocaust. Commercial enterprises were involved in the persecution of Jews in Germany – and later also in the occupied territories – and contributed to their economic marginalization mainly through involvement in policies of aryanization.[4] Corporations were involved in the Nazi crimes of slave labour, looting, mass murder in the gas chambers and the burning of the bodies after the victims were murdered or had died. In addition, corporations were involved in crimes against other victim groups targeted by the Nazi regime, as well as in the use of forced labourers from occupied territories such as France, Italy and the Netherlands.[5]

This chapter aims to provide an overview of some of the best-documented cases of different kinds of corporate involvement in the Holocaust and other Nazi crimes. The majority of this chapter will lean on historical work on the Nazi (war) economy and the role of business in the war effort and the Holocaust.[6] When studying such involvement, the broader economic, social and political context of the Nazi regime as well as the business sector have to be taken into account. Therefore, this chapter will start with a brief description of the state of the German economy shortly before and during the first years of the Nazi Regime. What follows is a description of corporate involvement in different aspects of the Holocaust on the basis of a number of case studies. After considering the way business conduct was dealt with after 1945 the conclusion will present three categories of involvement, namely (1) direct perpetration or cooperation with the principal perpetrator; (2) delivering goods and/or services directly used by the principal perpetrator for the commission of the crime; and (3) increasing the general capacity of the principal perpetrator. The conclusion will consider the relevance of corporate involvement during the Second World War for the study of corporate crime.

This chapter is primarily based on secondary historical literature on business and the Third Reich. The work of business historians has yielded a number of impressive monographs, usually singling out one or a few businesses, limited by the archival data that survived to date, and focusing on various aspects of this business's positions in the Nazi economy and society. While these studies are very valuable, they are for the most part more descriptive than criminologists are accustomed to. While this chapter will cite some very interesting conclusions about how corporate involvement in the Holocaust can be explained, it is difficult to generalize findings from these studies and the selected cases cannot be considered a representative sample. Another methodological point involves the threat of historical anachronism. Looking at historical events taking place in a context that is very different from today, we have to keep in mind that we are applying contemporary concepts with a contemporary view to past events. The legal framework that we know today was largely developed after the end of World War II. Moreover, businesses were operating in a context very different from today. Yet at the same time we should avoid historical or moral relativism. It will become clear that existing moral norms, and sometimes also legal norms, were crossed by corporate leaders and executives, qualifying their behaviour as morally and by and large also legally deviant.

The Nazi regime and German business before 1939: self-sufficiency and rearmament

The behaviour and role of the German business sector during World War II cannot be seen as detached from its behaviour and position in the decades before. In 1918, Germany had lost the First World War and was sanctioned by the Allies to pay 18 billion marks in reparations. This put an enormous strain on the German economy, resulting in an overall drop in living standards. In the early 1920s, the worldwide economic crisis further deteriorated the German situation, causing very high numbers of unemployment: when Hitler came to power there were six million registered unemployed, with an additional two million 'hidden' unemployed who had even given up registering for a job. Combined, 40 per cent of Germans were without a job and many more were underemployed (Gellately 2001: 11). The depression caused profits, imports and exports to plummet. The Great Depression had a deep impact on all Germans, as well as the business community: the pre-existing support for liberal economic practice, for example, had dramatically decreased (Feldman 2004).

Nazi ideology affected the German economy in various ways. First, Nazi economic policy was strongly marked by economic nationalism. Protective tariffs, controlled trade, domestic substitution of import goods, foreign debt reduction and other measures were taken to make the German economy increasingly self-sufficient (Overy 2002: 4). Second, virtually all aspects of economic misfortune were blamed on 'the international conspiracy of world Jewry' and the Bolsheviks (Tooze 2006). Third, there was a general emphasis on technological modernization that was present in all sectors. Motorization received special (and Hitler's personal) attention, for example via the Volkswagen project aimed at increasing the German living standard by making cheap assembly-line produced cars for 'the people' (Overy 2002: 6).

During the first years of the Nazi regime, the German economy recovered rapidly. This was not solely the result of work-creation programmes, but also due to world-wide economic recovery and normal conjuncture fluctuation, debt reduction and default as well as increased controls over import (Overy 2002). According to Tooze (2006), the German economy would have recovered similarly under any type of regime. In spite of the constrictions set by the treaty of Versailles, the first steps towards rearmament were set already in June 1933. At first, this was only by means of indirect rearmament: creating the infrastructure, equipment and structures to sustain military output and capability. Recovery, re-employment and increasing the living standard of the people were politically expedient: providing 'bread and work' was an essential part of the propaganda machinery. The first purely military projects were disguised as civilian ones; only when recovery was sufficiently accomplished and the regime felt politically secure, rearmament accelerated and was carried out more openly. From the summer of 1936 onwards, the balance started to change 'from butter to guns': rearmament was increasingly considered to be more important than further recovery (Overy 2002). Expanding the Reich was aimed at conquering not only living space for the German population, but also markets and raw materials for the German economy – the only way Nazi Germany would ever be able to withstand the economic power of the United States. According to Tooze (2006) and Overy (2002) economic nationalism was one of the essential motives for increasing German *Lebensraum* and economic considerations were central to Nazi expansionism.

Some economic policies, such as the abolition of labour unions, were generally welcomed by German big business. In 1933, the unions were replaced by the *Deutsche Arbeitsfront* (DAF) and regional trustees of labour, which were now to set wages and resolve conflicts (Tooze 2006). Furthermore, increased domestic demand, reduced international competition, increasing prices and frozen wages led to substantial increase of profits, recovery and a general positive outlook for many businesses. However, there was also quite some mutual animosity between the Nazi government and the business sector. Increasing protectionism and obstruction of international trade, as well as the increasing bureaucratic government control over all aspects of the economy were not welcomed by many businessmen, out of fear of being overly constrained. Large corporations initially rejected many economic measures by the Nazi regime, and the expansion of the Reich was often perceived as a risk rather than a commercial interest (Hayes 1987: 209).

The Nazi regime, in turn, mistrusted the power of the business sector. The attitude towards the financial world – with its presumed 'Jewish financial capitalism' – was overtly hostile. Already during the Weimar republic, the German economy had been one of the most controlled and cartelized economies of Europe (Tooze 2006: 29). From the first months of Nazi rule, the German economy quickly became a steered economy or *gelenkte Wirtschaft*. Business opportunities were increasingly determined by the regime and its policies (Feldman 2004). Although the Nazi regime was eventually quite successful in mobilizing the business sector for the Nazis' long-term imperial and racial goals, non-compliance – or 'economical egoism', as Hitler called it – was widespread, also in sectors that were vital to rearmament. The 1937 establishment of the Hermann Göring Reichswerke, to which virtually the entire steel sector was coerced to integrate, is exemplary of the intention of Göring and Hitler to make the economy serve political ends. The establishment of numerous SS businesses, such as publishing houses and construction companies, was another way of streamlining the economy for political goals (Allen 2002b). Hitler saw business as a means, not an end. There was 'no such thing as a commercial balance of expenditures and profits [...] only a national balance of being and not being' Hitler declared (Hayes 2004: 70). As a result, in many branches competition in the market was replaced by competition within the political structure (Overy 2002).

Corporate involvement in Nazi crimes

Since the Nazi regime had come to power,[7] corporations played important roles in their racial policies, crimes and warfare in multiple ways. This section will describe the roles of some key corporations in different phases of exclusion, persecution and extermination. In the first section, the focus will be on the economic marginalization of Jews in the years before the war, looking predominantly at the two largest banks of Germany at the time – Deutsche Bank and Dresdner Bank – and Germany's largest insurance company Allianz. Then, we will look at the widespread use of slave labour in the camps from the start of the war onwards. As the concentration camp system grew, corporations such as Degussa and Hoechst became involved in the dispossession of Jews and illegal medical experiments on concentration camp inmates. In the last phase of the genocide, corporations were involved in the development of the killing facilities by delivery of Zyklon B and the construction of the gas chambers and ovens.

Economic marginalization

The economic marginalization of German Jews started right after the Nazis came to power in 1933, with a thorough purge of Jews from civil service and academic, financial, and economic positions. This purge developed over the subsequent six years, in a rather ad hoc and reactive manner (Hayes 1998). A decree in November 1938 directed all German enterprises to dismiss all their Jewish managers before the end of the year. Although some corporations demonstrated loyalty to their Jewish employees, most Jews were dismissed without much discussion or protest, as an unpleasant necessity. Aryanization by dismissing Jewish board members intensified from

1937 onwards because of new decrees that denied government contracts and allocation of raw materials to businesses with Jewish board members (Hayes 1998). Because of these measures, most corporations came to see Jewish board members, managers or employees as a danger to their corporation and letting them go, however painful because of long-lasting bonds, came to be the only sensible business decision.

The majority of Jews, however, earned their living through independent Jewish firms. Following government policy, these firms were to be transferred into German hands by aryanization. This state policy of dispossession and plunder was aimed at, on the one hand, economic marginalization of Jews and, on the other, maximizing profits from the persecution of these perceived enemies. Large-scale, state-driven aryanization commenced in 1936, when the state needed more funds to finance the rearmament. The state started to actively encourage the takeover of 'non-Aryan' businesses. After initial hesitation by the business sector, some businesses took the opportunity to buy Jewish-owned businesses that could give them new technologies, more raw materials (allocated sparingly by the regime), a larger production power and other advantages. Competition for market share among large firms, as well as banks, sped up the process (Hayes 1998; Stallbaumer 1999). It is hard to say to what extent Nazi policies deliberately induced such competition to make the business sector comply with their policy goals, but it is clear that many companies were willing to go along.

The two largest banks of Germany at the time, the Dresdner Bank and the Deutsche Bank, as well as the insurance sector including Allianz, were involved in several aspects of this policy of economic marginalization – and general persecution – of Jews in Germany and, later, other parts of Europe.

The Banks: Deutsche Bank and Dresdner Bank

German banks were involved in the economic marginalization of German Jews by their handling of many mergers and takeovers of Jewish businesses which, towards the end of the 1930s, had an increasingly state-coerced character. Banks received commission on sale prices, interest on loans and broadened their clientele base (James 2001). Interestingly, many of the transactions carried out by the banks were not very profitable and in some cases they even incurred losses. From the regime's point of view this was as it should be: Hitler and Goebbels repeatedly made clear that all aryanization should 'benefit the Reich and the Reich only' (James 2001: 54).

The relationship between the banks and the Nazi government was often problematic. Many Nazi leaders held a deep, ideological suspicion of the banking sector, individual liberalism and financial capitalism considered to be part of a Jewish world conspiracy (Overy 2002). In fact, Jews were overrepresented in the private banking sector, especially higher up in the hierarchy (Ziegler 2005). At the same time, because of the 1930s banking crisis and depression both Deutsche Bank and Dresdner Bank had become more dependent on – and controlled by – the state than they had ever been before that point (James 2001). At the banks the Nazi government and its policies were generally seen as intrusive, taking over the majority of activities traditionally carried out by banks. The German economy was increasingly less driven by market mechanisms, making the traditional transmission systems for market signals – banks – increasingly redundant. In addition, the Nazi control of foreign trade to control the balance of payments had dramatically reduced Deutsche Bank's business abroad (James 2001).

The German banking sector in the 1930s consisted of a dense network of personal and professional contacts and friendships. Personal contacts between Jewish and non-Jewish bankers and businessmen in many cases resulted in board members and bank managers helping colleagues and friends to keep some of their assets when fleeing abroad, or staying on as long as possible. In fact, many bankers brokered aryanization deals that can be seen as 'reasonable' under the circumstances of the time. Nevertheless, similarly to other sectors, politics and banking became more and more intertwined (James 2004). While only a small number of the active members of the board and the supervisory board of Deutsche Bank were avid National Socialists,[8] early concerns about the anti-Semitic policy of the new regime seem to have been abandoned quite easily. According to James (2001), most of the bankers' activity seems to be motivated by a 'narrowly conceived professionalism'. Ziegler (2005) sees an 'anti-Semitic attitudinal climate', combined with such professional logic, as a robust explanation for the large German banks' conduct. Arguably, the possibility of individuals to withdraw into their professional roles as bankers allowed a degree of compartmentalization or denial of the effects of their conduct and the regime they were contributing to, seen also among other professionals involved in Nazi crimes (Cohen 2001: 86–87; Lifton 1986).

After the *Anschluss* of Austria and the annexation of Czechoslovakia in 1938, aryanization was taken outside the borders of the 'old' Germany and Dutch,[9] French and Polish non-Aryan corporations awaited a similar fate. Deutsche Bank, as well as Dresdner Bank and other large banks, were active participants in the German policy of *Eindeutschung* and (economic) reorganization of the annexed territories.[10] While within the old borders Deutsche Bank personal contacts and concerns about the local economy had precluded very aggressive aryanization, the banks' conduct abroad was much more destructive. Furthermore, it created a dynamic of its own because young bankers, generally more positive towards Nazism and more anti-Semitic, saw a chance to make a career (James 2001: 142).

Working closely with the Gestapo and other Nazi government agencies many of these young bankers came up with their own initiatives to secure take-overs and make a name for themselves (James 2001). Although the board of Deutsche Bank in Berlin certainly received information about these operations abroad, these young bankers had considerable autonomy and their ambitious personal character seems to have been of importance too. To give an example, Walter Pohle was the initiator in one of the more profitable aryanizations of a Czech bank, the Bohmische Union Bank (BUB), and an illustration of the much more relentless bankers that came forward to further develop business for the banks in the expanded Reich. Upon arriving at the BUB, Pohle immediately dismissed all of the Jewish board members of the bank, who were subsequently taken prisoner by the regime and sent to concentration camps.

In 1942, however, Pohle got in trouble with the Nazi authorities after trying to gain indirect control of a part of the Reichswerke Hermann Göring, which cost Pohle a couple of influential positions. This example illustrates how, even when the regime arguably needed zealous bankers like Pohle, one *faux pas* could be enough to be marginalized, showing the tight grip of the regime on bankers even when working towards the regime's goals. It is also interesting how, reacting to this affair, a Deutsche Bank board member criticized Pohle as being 'very much inclined to see things only from the standpoint of commercial success, never mind how that success have been achieved' (James 2001: 187). Clearly, individual aggressive profit-seeking was not appreciated by the regime, nor by Deutsche Bank.

The insurance sector: Allianz

The private insurance industry accommodated the Nazi regime by assisting the regime's anti-Semitic measures and policies, especially with regards to the aftermath of the *Reichskristallnacht*[11] pogrom of November 1938 and Jewish life insurance policies. Further, insurance companies cooperated in aryanization practices, in close association with banks, as a way of getting new policy holders. Feldman (2004) points out that the conduct of the insurance sector helped to legitimize the regime. In Germany's largest insurance company, Allianz, National Socialism was present in all aspects of corporate life and there were many ties between the regime and business. Kurt Schmitt, the general director of Allianz became the Reich economics minister under Hitler in 1933–1934 while director Eduard Hilgard headed the Reich Group for Insurance, one of the seven groups into which Germany's economy was divided.

Following the *Reichskristallnacht* pogroms, the Reich Group for Insurance was instructed by Göring to pay out all Jewish claims directly to the state. The regime maintained that the Jews had brought these 'public disturbances' on themselves. On top of the 'atonement tax' that was issued to all German Jews, they would not receive any compensation for the damage that had resulted from the state-organized pogrom. Instead, the compensation would be paid out to the Reich. The minutes of a meeting between Hilgard and Göring show how Hilgard used 'the language of the Third Reich' to prevent the insurance industry from incurring large losses: Hilgard argued that by making the insurance companies pay up for (part of) the damages of anti-Jewish violence, Aryans would be victimized through decreasing dividends for shareholders and increasing insurance premiums for all Germans (Feldman 2001: 201–205; 2005).

In November 1941 the state issued a decree ordering banks and insurance companies to report all Jewish assets of those who had 'taken up residence abroad' (a definition which in practice included those deported to concentration camps) as of 27 November 1941 and transfer them to the state (Feldman 2004). This decree is a clear example of how the regime used banks and insurance companies to carry out its anti-Semitic policies, giving them the responsibility of locating and identifying the accounts, threatened by fines and even imprisonment if they did not comply within six months (Feldman 2004). There were some complaints by insurance companies but this was only because it would require extra manpower to carry out these transfers (Hilberg 1961). There is no evidence of any actual resistance.

According to Feldman, Allianz's leaders were not rabid anti-Semites and it is quite likely that anti-Semitic language was used out of self-interest instead of ideological agreement. However, they were sufficiently anti-Semitic to approve of early National Socialism measures and then to put up relatively little resistance as the regime intensified its persecution of the Jews (Feldman 2001: 537). It seems that latent anti-Semitism and the gradual radicalization of persecution as well as protective business strategies are particularly meaningful in understanding the transformation of Allianz into a contributor to Nazi policies.

The conduct of most corporations, also in these first phases of the Holocaust, cannot be explained purely by amoral profit seeking. Business efforts were aimed at survival and upholding competitiveness under increasingly difficult circumstances. Moreover, profits were often skimmed by the regime. The defensive posture of the majority of the business sector in many cases led, over time, to initiatives aimed at legitimizing their existence to the regime and competing with Nazi alternatives (Feldman 2004). This could take the forms of electing moderate Nazis to managing boards (to avoid appointment of fanatical Nazis) and using National Socialist rhetoric and language. Such 'anticipatory obedience' awaiting future opportunities, or in some cases to keep control of the company, was surely not always a result of anti-Semitic and National Socialist convictions. Nevertheless, this defensive strategy inevitably led to complicity and increasing adaptation to the opportunity structures created by the regime, making the abnormal business opportunities seem to be normal and acceptable business (Feldman 2004).

Essentially, the behaviour of the employees, managers and board members of German companies was similar to that of German society in general which was characterized by (moral) indifference (Kershaw 2002). While only a small number proved to be aggressive anti-Semitists, a large number accepted the anti-Jewish measures which gradually became more and more brutal over the years leading up to the war. Still, many managers and business leaders were willing to make decisions that resulted in contributions to economic marginalization, thereby helping to pave the road for deportation, concentration and destruction.

Slave labour

Slave labour was an integral feature of both the war economy and the destruction the Jews (Allen 2002a; 2004). In the late 1930s, SS businesses started using slave labour, but the first requests by private businesses for slave labour (i.e. by IG Farben and Volkswagen) were not made until 1941. The satellite camps of Auschwitz are among the most notorious sites where slave labourers were used (Piper 1994). Towards the last year of the war all significant German corporations used slave labourers: nearly half a million camp or ghetto inmates were working under forced or slave labour conditions by 1944 (Hayes 1998). It is estimated that in total ten million deportees or prisoners of war were coerced into forced or slave labour (Chiari 2002).[12] The 'wages' (three to eight marks per 11- to 12-hour workday) went directly to the Reich Finance Ministry or regional agencies and the company had to pay for food, shelter and fences for the workers (Hayes 1998).

Together with the Reichswerke Hermann Göring and munition and arms manufacturers, IG Farben was one of the largest procurers of slave labour (Hayes 1998). Farben had been of crucial importance to Nazi Germany from the early 1930s onwards. As Germany's largest chemical company, it developed and produced synthetic alternatives to nitrate (used in the manufacture of explosives), oil, gasoline and natural rubber crucial to Nazi Germany's self-sufficiency, rearmament and war effort. Carl Krauch, executive and chairman of the supervisory Board of Farben, was one of Göring's most intimate technical and scientific advisors. The most infamous slave labour camp was Monowitz,[13] situated at Auschwitz, where Farben had built a large synthetic rubber plant also known as the Buna Werke (Hayes 1987).

It is estimated that around 35,000 slave workers worked for IG Farben at Auschwitz of whom 25,000 died there (Friedman 1999). Because of the horrifying living conditions, the productivity of forced (but especially slave) labourers was generally very low. A manager of Farben wrote in a letter that 'Our new friendship with the SS is proving very profitable' (Borkin 1978: 118). Nevertheless, Hayes concludes that, to the company itself, the use of slave labourers was not very profitable at all (Hayes 1998).

The Krupp enterprise led by Alfried, and later Gustav Krupp, was Nazi Germany's chief arms provider and also one of the largest users of slave labour. The Flick concern, led by Friedrich Flick, was Germany's largest iron, steel and coal provider and known for its 'highly politicised style of rhetoric' (Priemel 2012). After initial hesitation to use slave labour, because of the quite burdensome maze of relevant government regulations, labour shortages led the concern to actively seek slave labour for many of its factories (Stallbaumer 1999). Flick used a larger share of forced labourers than any other steel corporation, with an estimated 40,000 forced and slave labourers at any given time since the start of the war.

Hayes concludes that corporations became convinced that there was no alternative to using forced or slave labour (1998). The Nazi regime had succeeded in restructuring business opportunities and the labour market as a whole so that resisting employment of slave labour would have been self-destructive and thus not an option for a competitive capitalist. Moreover, not requesting slave labour and thereby reducing maximum capacity, could also lead to accusations of obstruction or 'defeatism'. Especially towards the end of the war, utilizing economic opportunities was closely linked to being deemed 'politically reliable'.

Subsidiaries of US companies such as Ford and Daimler Benz also used slave labourers (Billstein et al. 2004; Matthews 2006). Because they were foreign, these companies were mistrusted and threatened by privatization, depending on how 'German' they were considered to be.[14] At the same time, they were essential for providing technology, vehicles and other products for the war effort. Likewise, IBM provided Hollerith cards and card systems that were used for administration in various sectors of the economy as well as part of the Holocaust (Allen 2002c; Black 2012).

Medical experiments and looting in the camps

The infamous medical experiments carried out on concentration camp inmates also involved corporate activity. To give one example, the pharmaceutical department of Hoechst, part of IG Farben, contacted the SS in the summer of 1942 to carry out tests on concentration camp inmates at Buchenwald, Auschwitz and Gusen/Mauthausen. In these experiments, SS doctors deliberately infected inmates with typhus, after which half of the inmates received a drug while the other half, a control group, received a placebo. The drug caused severe side-effects and did not have a significant effect: in both groups around 50 per cent died (Lindner 2008). Interestingly, one of the employees chiefly responsible for the medical tests within Hoechst, Julius Weber, was also with the Roman Catholic resistance. Lindner concludes that 'naked professionalism', instead of ideological consent, was the main explanation for the corporation's involvement in these gruesome medical experiments (2008).

Banks and insurance companies, that had had such a significant part in the preparation of genocidal mass murder, were also involved in the systematic looting of property of deportees to the concentration and extermination camps. Allianz and a consortium of other insurance companies, for example, insured the transport of looted gold and other valuables. Deutsche Bank and Dresdner Bank were involved in dealing with at least 744 kilograms of 'victim gold' (Steinberg 1999), taken from Jews who were murdered in what became known as the 'Holocaust by bullets' as well as from victims in the extermination camps. This gold was processed into internationally recognized gold bars by Degussa (*Deutsche Gold- und Silber Scheideanstalt*). Subsequently the banks sold the gold in Turkey, so that the *Reichsbank* could receive much needed foreign currency (James 2001). The transportations of gold were carefully disguised and it has never been established to what extent bank directors and others involved in the transactions knew about the origins of the gold (Steinberg 1999).

Mass murder

In eastern Europe the majority of Jews were murdered by German *Einsatzgruppen* and police battalions, complemented by ancillary (also local) groups that followed the army's conquest to the east (Browning 1992). In one of the largest of such mass murders in Babi Yar in Ukraine on 29 and 30 September 1941, 33,771 Jews were murdered. The majority of the Jews of west, middle and south-east Europe died in concentration and extermination camps, either because of illness or starvation or because they were murdered. While in camps such as Belzec, Treblinka and Sobibor mass murder, although part of a larger plan, was of a more ad hoc and improvised nature, at Auschwitz the killing operation of around one million Jews by gas chamber was meticulously planned and designed by SS engineers (Allen 2002b). The technology provided by corporations had a distinct impact on the camp's efficiency.

The murder method that has become one of the hallmarks of the Holocaust was by hydrogen cyanide gas. This gas, Zyklon B, was produced by Degesh, a small subsidiary of IG Farben and

Degussa, and sold to the SS by retailer Tesch & Stabenau.[15] The substance was widely used as a fumigant against lice and diseases such as typhus and tuberculosis in military barracks. From 1938 onwards, the sale of Zyklon B was boosted by the continuously increasing concentration camp system, including Auschwitz I, where Zyklon B was used to disinfect the clothes of inmates upon arrival (Hayes 2007). Fumigation chambers, also developed by Degesh, were advertised as a system for 'processing' in the style of a modern factory and thereby conform to the existing appeal of mass production and efficiency of the time (Allen 2002b: 194).

For Tesch & Stabenau the lift of official regulations on the use of Zyklon B in April 1941 limited their prospective profits drastically, as the SS could now carry out fumigations themselves. Still, the ongoing problem of diseases in the camps – but also in military quarters and labour camps – safeguarded substantive profits for both Tesch and Degesch. In September 1941 a series of experiments carried out by the SS had shown that Zyklon B could also be used as a means of murder, after which the existing crematoria in Auschwitz I were expanded to include the first gas chambers modelled after the existing fumigation chambers (Pressac and van Pelt 1994). When the persecution of the European Jews radicalized into a genocidal policy during the spring and summer of 1942, Auschwitz-Birkenau (initially built to house prisoners of war) was repurposed to an extermination camp with larger gas chambers and crematoria specifically designed for mass murder. This is where, from a moral point of view, the deliveries of Zyklon B (and other corporate contributions to the camp's facilities) cross a boundary: from this point onwards they directly contributed to mass murder and genocide as opposed to facilitating a concentration camp system.

Hayes (2007) estimates that in the end just over 3 per cent of Zyklon B sales were used at sites where it was used to kill. Therefore, the quantities of delivery in itself probably did not give away its purpose. Eyewitness testimony, however, indicates that the director of Tesch & Stabenau, Bruno Tesch, as well as the director of Degesh, Gerhard Peters, were consulted by the SS on using Zyklon B to kill and were fully aware of what was going on in Auschwitz.

The Erfurt-based corporation Topf & Sohne developed and provided the technology for the next stage: the burning of the bodies (van Baar and Huisman 2012; Schüle 2010). After receiving several blueprints from multiple sources, SS engineers designed the crematoria, apparently with great enthusiasm for developing and using modern 'assembly-line' technology. There seems to have been a match between this culture among the SS engineers and within Topf. Topf started working with the SS when the death toll of nearby concentration camp Buchenwald became so high it was no longer feasible to cremate the bodies in the city crematorium of Erfurt. Violating the 1934 Cremation Act, Topf designed and delivered ovens based on animal cadavers incineration ovens to burn (instead of cremate) the inmates that died in the camps. In the autumn of 1941, Topf started producing for Auschwitz-Birkenau and in subsequent years it delivered ovens to several other concentration and extermination camps, now also burning the bodies of victims of the gas chambers. In addition, the corporation developed ventilation systems for the gas chambers in order to increase their capacity (Pressac and van Pelt 1994).

Interestingly, contrary to popular conception of the Holocaust, the 'death factories' model proved to be largely a failure: *ad hoc* solutions often functioned better than the slowly developed and often malfunctioning 'mechanized' installations (Allen 2002b). Here it is important to distinguish between design and actual effectiveness. It is clear that both corporations such as Degesh and Topf, as well as the SS corporations, operated with an ambition to design technologically advanced and 'assembly-line' modern 'production methods', of which the Auschwitz crematoria are the most notorious examples. Their actual effectiveness, however, was often much lower than envisaged. The crematoria in the extermination camps, for example, never reached their 'goal production' – which was set unreasonably high – and the Auschwitz IG Farben plant never produced one drop of Buna rubber.[16] Although remarkable, this is no consolation, nor does it disqualify a *Moral der Effizienz* (Budraß and Grieger 1993) as a promising concept to understand the development of these plans. Some 1.1 million people lost their lives at Auschwitz and it is clear that businesses did increase the capacity of mass murder at the extermination camps.

The aftermath

During the famous Nuremberg trial at the Allied International Military Tribunal (IMT), where 22 high-ranking Nazis – including Hermann Goering and Albert Speer – were tried, no industrialists were indicted. However, at subsequent Nuremberg trials under Control Council Law no. 10 of 1945, 46 owners, employees and managers of five corporations were indicted by the British, French and US military tribunals.[17] A number of them were sentenced for their role in war crimes, crimes against peace and crimes against humanity.

The British Military Tribunal indicted Bruno Tesch and Karl Weinbacher, owner and general manager of Tesch & Stabenau. In 1946 they both received the death penalty because they either 'knew' or 'must have known' that their Zyklon B was used for mass killings by the SS. In 1948 two directors of the Roechling Company were convicted for crimes against peace and war crimes by the French Military Tribunal for actively obtaining slave labour from the regime and using it under atrocious conditions (Stoichkova 2010: 53).

The United States Military Tribunal indicted Friedrich Flick and five managers of Flick for their deployment of slave labour, the spoliation of public and private property in France and the Soviet Union, pre-war aryanization in Germany and participating in persecution and other atrocities by the SS by financial support and consultation in the Freundeskreis Himmler (Taylor 1949). Like other important businessmen (from Deutsche Bank, Dresdner Bank, Allianz, Vereinigte Stahlwerke and others), Flick was a member of a group that became known as Freundeskreis Himmler (the circle of friends of Reichsführer SS Himmler) since the mid-1930s. This was brought forward by the prosecution as proof of influence and close cooperation with the Nazi regime. Nevertheless, the court recognized the 'reign of terror' exercised by the regime and was generally lenient in accepting the defence of necessity, except in those cases where managers had actively sought to obtain free slave labour, as in the case of Friedrich Flick himself. Flick, Steinbrick and Weiss were convicted to seven, five and two-and-a-half years' imprisonment respectively but not for expropriation. Steinbrick was convicted for membership to the SS only; three others were acquitted (Taylor 1949).

Alfred Krupp and 11 other Krupp officials were indicted for providing arms and planning and waging aggressive war, plunder, spoliation and labour exploitation under inhumane conditions. Six were convicted for spoliation and all but one were found guilty under the forced labour count. All defendants were sentenced to six- to 12-year sentences, except one who received a three-year sentence, which he had already served at that time (Taylor 1949).

Twenty-four of the 46 indicted were managers of IG Farben. They were indicted for planning and waging aggressive war, spoliation, and enslavement and mistreatment of slave labourers. Only in the charges connected to Farben's activities at Monowitz did the court establish initiative on the part of the company. Five defendants were found guilty for employing slave labour at this plant. Nine defendants were found guilty for spoliation in Poland, Norway and France, while 14 were acquitted on this count. In the end, 13 IG Farben executives received sentences ranging from 18 months to three years for spoliation and four to eight years for those involved in the Auschwitz project (Taylor 1949).

The prosecution of a part of the German business elite was a result of awareness of some importance of the German business sector in the crimes that were committed (Bush 2009).

At the same time, holding businessmen accountable was at odds with the aims of recovery of German industry and securing political and economic stability of post-war West-Germany, which was soon considered to be an essential ally against the Soviet Union. Baars (2013) argues that geo-political and capitalist (or anti-communist) pressures led to lenient sentences in the industrialist cases compared with other cases at Nuremberg, and that the defence of necessity was granted more easily. In 1951, the US High Commissioner for Germany, John J. McCloy, issued a declaration of clemency by which all those businessmen still imprisoned were released. Most of their assets were returned to them (Wiesen 1999). Friedrich Flick and Krupp both established new corporations and most IG Farben officials were elected on the boards of new businesses (Hilberg 1961: 703), including IG's unofficial successors BASF and Bayer.

In addition to the Nuremberg trials, denazification processes initiated by the Allied powers and carried out throughout Germany over several years led to the investigation of more businessmen. Later, in the 1990s, a series of restitution cases were initiated under US civil law aimed at receiving financial compensation for the surviving victims by corporations that had been implicated in Nazi crimes. There were cases against Swiss banks, Deutsche Bank and Dresdner Bank, Ford Motors, General Motors and several other corporations (see Bazyler 2000). The majority of these cases ended in settlements providing heirs of victims and survivors with some reparations.

Conclusion: corporate crime and the Holocaust

The ways in which corporations contributed to the Holocaust and other Nazi crimes are varied, as were the types of harms that were caused and the number of victims. Looking at the nature of the involvement, it is possible to deduce three different categories of involvement. First, in the most extreme cases, corporations acted in direct cooperation with the principal perpetrator, usually the SS. Examples of this type of involvement are the use of slave labour under inhumane conditions (especially when initiated by the corporation), the development of efficient ovens for use in the crematoria, and requesting unethical medical experiments. In some cases, for example when a slave labour camp was primarily run by corporate officials, such corporate conduct came very close to direct perpetration. However, it is important to keep in mind that the role of slave labour in the persecution and extermination of Jews, as well as the camp system and widespread use of slave labour, were set up by the Nazi regime. Although corporations played important and extremely harmful roles, often helping to keep the system in place or broadening its reach, the system itself was not of corporate design.

In a second category of involvement, corporations supplied goods and services that were used directly by the principal perpetrator, yet without the direct cooperation seen in the first category. An example of this type of involvement could be the delivery of Zyklon B to the sites where it was used for killing. The discernible difference between delivery of gas in this category and the delivery of ovens in the first category is that the ovens were manufactured to suit the demand for efficiency by the SS while Zyklon B was 'only' delivered, not modified, and also had a legitimate use.

Third, corporations at times increased the general capacity of the principal perpetrator more indirectly, by supplying or buying goods and services. In many cases this meant adding to the reach and (perceived) legitimacy of the Nazi regime, thereby broadening its power. Examples of this category would be insurance companies that complied with the Nazi requests to report Jewish assets and banks that bought (regular) gold bars through middlemen. Finally, there were corporations that profited from crimes committed by the SS, such as those trading in looted gold, art and other goods and assets and some cases of aryanization. It is hard to draw the line where corporate involvement in Nazi crimes stops, because the Germany economy was part of a regime that can be considered criminal. The closeness of the causal link between the company's conduct and the crimes, as well as the level of knowledge about the crimes available to the company, may be the most useful tools in determining this demarcation.

Knowledge on the part of the corporation of the goals of the principal perpetrator and the crimes to which it contributes is indeed a very important aspect of the evaluation of the corporation's involvement. In theory, it is possible that a corporation contributes to crimes and has no awareness of this contribution, but this must be evaluated on a case-by-case basis. Nonetheless, it is safe to say that anyone doing business in or around the concentration and extermination camps over time came to know about what was going on (Allen 2002b). The proximity to the crimes is most likely related to the level of knowledge about them, as well as the company's contribution. Finally, the level of coercion by the regime is also important in the analysis of corporate involvement in international crimes: it clearly diminishes the culpability of the corporation.[18]

Hayes (1998), describing German business as a whole, concludes that the ideologically determined Nazi state policy was largely successful in shaping and channelling private commercial interests and that this structure largely predetermined corporate involvement in the Holocaust. He characterizes the state strategy towards the German business sector as the carrot-and-stick approach: the opportunity of (future) profits and benefits was alternated with the threat of taking away business opportunities or even taking over control over business decisions. Feldman concludes that banks and insurance companies were 'at times reluctant and at times willing collaborators with the National Socialist regime' and willingness or reluctance differed over time, place and the relevant interests and issues (Feldman 2004). Most other studies are limited to one corporation or branch, and stay away from such all-embracing conclusions or even focus predominantly on describing how – rather than explaining why – businesses, parts of businesses, or corporate managers or employees, contributed to Nazi crimes.

Providing overarching or definite explanations and conclusions about corporate involvement in Nazi crimes is thus explicitly beyond the scope of this chapter. Nevertheless, the studies mentioned in this chapter do provide a number of possible explanations that are convincing on a smaller scale and that could trigger more research by criminologists. Because of the control of the Nazi regime over the economy, economic competition was largely replaced by political competition, making adhering to and anticipating the regime's economic and social policies a business case. In some cases (prospective) profits and personal benefits seem to have motivated individuals and businesses, such as the young banker Pohle. In other cases loss prevention, continuation of business operations and maintaining a competitive position overall seem to provide better-fitting explanations, for instance at IG Farben. Psychological processes resulting from role specialization, including psychological compartmentalization and an aim for technological perfection seem recurrent explanatory variables that could be further explored. In this respect, neutralization techniques (Alvarez 1997; Neubacher 2006) may well benefit understanding of individuals aiding these crimes. Moreover, anticipatory obedience and latent anti-Semitism could be relevant in explaining the behaviour of individual businessmen. The apparent general lack of discussion of the moral aspects of business, at least until the defeat of Germany became manifest, seems to fall under the general tendency to deny, in one way or another, mass suffering (Cohen 2001) but may also signal the amoral character of business. More research is necessary to gain a clearer understanding of the usefulness and generalizability of such explanations.

In the 1990s, Kramer and Michalowski developed the concept of state–corporate crime to capture the 'illegal or socially injurious actions that result from a mutually reinforcing interaction' between business and state (Michalowski and Kramer 2006), a concept that seems very applicable here. Kramer and Michalowski distinguish between state-initiated corporate crime (at the direction of or with tacit approval of the state) and state-facilitated corporate crime (where the state fails to enforce the law). For a totalitarian state like Nazi Germany, the framework is in a way reversed: the state is not a traditionally controlling actor but an initiator of the crimes. Matthews (2006) therefore advocates a third category of corporate-facilitated state crimes when corporations knowingly facilitate such actions in pursuit of shared goals of itself and the state.[19] Further study of corporate involvement in Nazi crimes could help advance the evolution of the concept of state–corporate crime.

Although the specific contexts of the cases discussed in this chapter clearly pose a limit to the generalizability of any findings, they are relevant for criminologists as an understudied form of corporate crime. The cases mentioned in this chapter are a rarely well-documented category of corporate involvement in international crimes and provide various interesting points of departure for criminologists. Also, these cases could be seen as extreme forms of corporate deviance, at least in terms of the harms that are done, making them particularly interesting as case studies (Yin 2009: 47).

Furthermore, the cases show the variety of ways corporations can contribute to international crimes. For many of them we can find contemporary equivalents. The Dutch businessman van Anraat, for example, provided the precursors for Saddam Hussein's chemical weapons (Huisman and van Sliedregt 2010). Unocal has been accused of using slave labour during construction of an oil pipeline in Burma (Van der Wilt 2013) and the Swiss government have recently announced an investigation of Argor Heraeus, a Swiss gold refinery, for its alleged processing of Congo conflict gold (BBC 2013). Private military/security companies (PMSCs), sometimes taking over public activities, have been accused of direct perpetration of war crimes and crimes against humanity: roughly one-third of the abuses at Abu Ghraib was estimated to have involved private contractors carrying out intelligence functions (Schooner 2005).

In many of the cases – both contemporary and historical – corporations provide the technology that aids the harms committed by state agencies. A shared culture of striving for technological advancement and perfection seems typical for the 1930s and 1940s but may be still relevant today. When technology become the end instead of a means, moral considerations very easily become obsolete. This brings to mind recent accusations that European IT provided the dictatorial regime of Bashar Al-Assad in Syria and other authoritarian regimes with advanced technology that is used to oppress the civilian population (Fuchs 2013; Gupta 2013).

Finally, another reason why historical cases of corporate involvement in mass atrocities are relevant is because they could help us with the difficult task of defining the moral obligations of corporations, help us recognize the pitfalls of over-simplification and appreciate the complexity of the topic. It is very easy to draw superficial, damning conclusions about corporations involved in wrongdoing but this will not aid finding the causes of such involvement or the ways to diminish its harmful outcomes.

Notes

1 The author would like to thank Wim Huisman and Alexandra Popova for their useful comments and suggestions.
2 International crimes entail mass atrocities criminalized by the Rome Statute (2002; genocide, crimes against humanity and war crimes) or other sources of international law (e.g. apartheid, slavery and torture) and in their social reality may also entail gross human rights violations.
3 This definition of involvement is based on the synthesis of relevant legal norms and case law developed for corporate complicity in international crimes as developed by the International Commission of Jurists (International Commission of Jurists 2008) developed for corporate involvement in international crimes: genocide, crimes against humanity and war crimes as defined in the Rome Statute of the International Criminal Court.

4 Aryanization is the overarching term for the process of legalized theft and economic marginalization by transferring Jewish properties and assets to German (or Aryan) ownership and removing non-Aryan persons from positions of commercial or other influence.
5 It is important to take into account that corporate contribution to the German war effort – by manufacturing vehicles, airplane engines and other equipment – helped prolong the Second World War and thereby the continuation of the Holocaust and other Nazi crimes (Matthews 2006).
6 For a description and overview of the historiography of business and the Nazi regime see Berghahn (2004).
7 In the USSR (including the German Democratic Republic, GDR) the 'official view' of the Holocaust portrayed the industrialists as main powers that put Hitler to power (Wiesen 1999). In this anti-capitalist narrative, the link between fascist national socialism and big business was heavily emphasized, without much regard, however, for the Holocaust. Also in the west some historians argued that businessmen were responsible for Hitler's rise but since the mid-80s they generally agree that it was not the big industrialists that brought the Nazis to power (Barkai 1991; Turner 1985).
8 Ziegler gives some examples of anti-Semitic prejudice at including a manager's decision to keep employing 'avaricious Jews [...] predestined for the stock exchange business' to remain competitive with other banks who did the same (2005: 61).
9 In the Netherlands, for example, Dresdner Bank and Allianz were jointly involved in the aryanization of the Jewish bank Lippmann Rosenthal, which was then used to transfer assets of deported Dutch Jews. Allianz also insured the transportation of looted securities and other valuables to Germany 1943–1944 (Feldman 2004: 33).
10 This is exemplified by an apparently popular rhyme at the time: *Wer marschiert hinter dem ersten Tank? Das ist Dr. Rasche von der Dresdner Bank!* (Who marches behind the first tank? It's Dr. Rasche of Dresdner Bank!; James 2001).
11 During the *Reichskristallnacht* ('the night of the broken glass') paramilitary groups throughout Germany attempted, with considerable success, to organize public violence against Jews. The *Kristallnacht* can be seen as a turning point in the persecution of the German Jews as anti-Jewish policies and violence increased sharply after November 1938. Hundreds of synagogues and around 7500 shops were damaged, at least 91 Jews were murdered and around 30,000 Jews were arrested and detained in local concentration camps where they were often tortured (Feldman 2001).
12 Although the differences between forced labourers and slave labourers are not always clear and can change over time, it is useful to make a distinction between (1) forced labourers (mostly from occupied territories in the west), (2) slave labourers (camp inmates from various groups who were forced to work as punishment) and (3) less-than-slaves (mostly Jews but also Slavs and Soviets who no longer had economic value and were destined to work themselves to death).
13 The works of two camp inmates of Monowitz, including Elie Wiesel (e.g. *Night*) and Primo Levi (e.g. *If This is a Man*) illustrate the heinous circumstances at this camp.
14 Silverstein (2000) sees this as the motivation for Ford to change the name of its Cologne plant to Ford Werke.
15 During the Nuremberg trial against IG Farben, Degesh was erroneously depicted as part of IG Farben while the company was an integral part of Degussa, and not IG Farben (Hayes 2007).
16 Another example of a failed, overly ambitious plan is the Volkswagen 'mass mobilization' project, see Konig (2004).
17 The roles of Deutsche and Dresdner Banks were investigated by the Office of the Military Government of the United States (OMGUS), but they were never prosecuted. The 1946 report was only recently published (Simpson 2001).
18 Coercion and knowledge have not been included in the classification above because they do not impact the nature of the involvement per se, they mainly impact the blameworthiness of this involvement.
19 When looking at corporate involvement in international crimes it seems a division can be made between corporations operating within more or less closed authoritarian or totalitarian society on the one hand, and multinational companies becoming involved in international crimes as an outsider to a conflict situation, acting under a traditionally controlling state on the other.

References

Allen, M.T. (2002a) *The Business of Genocide: The SS, Slave Labour and the Concentration Camps*, Chapel Hill: North Carolina Press.

Allen, M.T. (2002b) 'The devil in the details: The gas chambers of Birkenau, October 1941', *Holocaust and Genocide Studies*, 16(2): 189–216.

Allen, M.T. (2002c) 'Stranger than science fiction: Edwin Black, IBM and the Holocaust', *Tehnology and Culture*, 43(1): 151–154.

Allen, M.T. (2004) *Hitler's Slave Lords: The Business of Forced Labour in Occupied Europe*, Stroud: Tempus.

Alvarez, A. (1997) 'Adjusting genocide: The techniques of neutralization and the Holocaust', *Social Science History*, 21(2): 139–178.

Baars, G. (2013) 'Capitalism's victors' stories? The hidden stories behind the prosecution of industrialists post-WWII', in K.J. Heller and G. Simpson (eds) *The Hidden Histories of War Crimes Trials*, Oxford: Oxford University Press, pp. 163–192.

Barkai, A. (1991) 'German entrepreneurs and Jewish policy in the Third Reich', *Yad Vashem Studies*, 21: 125–153.

Bazyler, M.J. (2000) 'Nuremberg in America: Litigating the Holocaust in United States courts', *University of Richmond Law Review*, 34(1): 1–283.

BBC (2013, 4 November) 'Swiss refiner Argor accused of laundering DRC gold'. Online. Available HTTP: <http://www.bbc.com/news/world-europe-24811420> (accessed 8 July 2014).

Berghahn, V.R. (2004) 'Writing the history of business in the Third Reich', in J. Huener and F.R. Nicosia (eds) *Business and Industry in Nazi Germany*, New York/Oxford: Berghahn Books, pp. 129–148.

Billstein, R., Fings, K., Kugler, A. and Nicholas, L. (2004) *Working for the Enemy: Ford, General Motors and Forced Labor in Germany during the Second World War*, New York/Oxford: Berghahn Books.

Black, E. (2012) *IBM and the Holocaust: The Strategic Alliance between Nazi Germany and America's Most Powerful Corporation*, New York: Dialog Press.

Borkin, J. (1978) *The Crime and Punishment of IG Farben*, New York: Free Press.

Brannigan, A. (2013) *Beyond the Banality of Evil: Criminology and Genocide*, New York: Oxford University Press.

Brants, C.H. (2007) 'Gold collar crime', in G. Geis and H. Pontell (eds) *International Handbook of White Collar Crime*, New York: Springer, pp. 309–326.

Browning, C. (1992) *Ordinary Men: Reserve Battalion 101 and the Final Solution in Poland*, London: Penguin.

Budraß, L. and Grieger, M. (1993) 'Die Moral der Effizienz: Die Beschäftigung von KZ-Häftlinge am Beispiel des Volkswagenwerks und der Henschel Flugzeug Werke', *Jahrbuch für Wirtschaftsgeschichte*, 34(2): 89–136.

Bush, J.A. (2009) 'The prehistory of corporations and conspiracy in international criminal law: What Nuremberg really said', *Columbia Law Review*, 109: 1094–2081.

Chiari, B. (2002) 'Forced labourers and POWs in the German war economy', Special issue, *Annali dell'Instituto storico italo-germanico in Trento*, 23.

Cohen, S. (2001) *States of Denial. Knowing about Atrocities and Suffering*, Cambridge: Polity Press.

Feldman, G.D. (2001) *Allianz and the German Insurance Business, 1933–1945*, Cambridge: Cambridge University Press.

Feldman, G.D. (2004) 'Financial institutions in Nazi Germany: Reluctant or willing collaborators?', in F.R. Nicosia and J. Huener (eds) *Business and Industry in Nazi Germany*, New York/Oxford: Berhahn Books, pp. 15–42.

Feldman, G.D. (2005) 'The Reichskristallnacht and the insurance industry: The politics of damage control', in G.D. Feldman (ed.) *Networks of Nazi Prosecution. Bureaucracy, Business and the Organization of the Holocaust*, New York/Oxford: Berghahn Books, pp. 295–320.

Friedman, K. (1999) 'Big business and the Holocaust', *Dimensions: A Journal of Holocaust Studies*, 13(2): 37–38.

Friedrichs, D.O. (2012) 'Crime of the last century – and of this century', in D.L. Rothe and C.W. Mullins (eds) *State Crime*, New Brunswick: Rutgers University, pp. 49–67.

Fuchs, C. (2013) 'Societal and ideological impacts of deep packet inspection internet surveillance', *Information, Communication & Society*, 16(8): 1328–1359.

Gellately, R. (2001) *Backing Hitler, Consent and Coercion in Nazi Germany*, New York: Oxford University Press.

Gupta, R.R. (2013) 'Germany's support of Assad: Corporate complicity in the creation of the Syrian surveillance state under the European Convention on Human Rights', *American University International Law Review*, 28(5): 1357–1391.

Hayes, P. (1987) *Industry and Ideology: I.G. Farben in the Nazi Era*, New York: Cambridge University Press.

Hayes, P. (1998) 'State policy and corporate involvement in the Holocaust', in M. Berenbaum and A.J. Peck (eds) *The Holocaust and History. The Known, the Unknown, the Disputed and the Reexamined*, Bloomington/Indianapolis: Indiana University Press, pp. 197–218.

Hayes, P. (2004) 'Degesh and Zyklon B', in P. Hayes (ed.) *From Cooperation to Complicity: Degussa in the Third Reich*, Cambridge: Cambridge University Press, pp. 272–300.

Hayes, P. (2007) *From Cooperation to Complicity: Degussa in the Third Reich*, Cambridge: Cambridge University Press.

Hilberg, R. (1961) *The Destruction of the European Jews*, Chicago: Quadrangle Books.

Huisman, W. (2010) *Business as Usual? Corporate Involvement in International Crimes*, The Hague: Eleven International Publishing.

Huisman, W. and van Sliedregt, E. (2010) 'Rogue traders: Dutch businessmen, international crimes and corporate complicity', *Journal of International Criminal Justice*, 8(3): 803–828.

International Commission of Jurists (2008) *Report on Corporate Complicity in International Crimes. Part I, II & III*, Geneva: International Commission of Jurists.

James, H. (2001) *The Deutsche Bank and the Nazi Economic War against the Jews: The Expropriation of Jewish Owned Property*, New York: Cambridge University Press.

James, H. (2004) *The Nazi Dictatorship and the Deutsche Bank*, New York: Cambridge University Press.

Kershaw, I. (2002) *Popular Opinion and Political Dissent in the Third Reich. Bavaria 1933–1945*, New York: Oxford University Press.

Konig, W. (2004) 'Adolf Hitler vs. Henry Ford: The Volkswagen, the role of America as a model and the failure of a Nazi consumer society', *German Studies Reveiw*, 27(2): 249–268.

Lifton, R.J. (1986) *The Nazi Doctors: Medical Killing and the Psychology of Genocide*, New York: Basic Books.

Lindner, S.H. (2008) *Inside I.G. Farben: Hoechst During the Third Reich*, New York: Cambridge University Press.

Matthews, R.A. (2006) 'Ordinary business in Nazi Germany', in R.J. Michalowski and R.C. Kramer (eds) *State–Corporate Crime: Wrongdoing at the Intersection of Business and Government*, New Brunswick: Rutgers University Press, pp. 116–133.

Michalowski, R. and Kramer, R.C. (eds) (2006) *State–Corporate Crime: Wrongdoing at the Intersection of Business and Government*, New Brunswick: Rutgers University Press.

Neubacher, F. (2006) 'How can it happen that horrendous state crimes are perpetrated?: An overview of criminological theories', *Journal of International Criminal Justice*, 4(4): 787–799.

Olusanya, O. (2013) 'A macro-micro integrated theoretical model of mass participation in genocide', *British Journal of Criminology*, 53(5): 843–863.

Overy, R.J. (2002) *War and Economy in the Third Reich*, New York: Oxford University Press.

Piper, F. (1994) 'The system of prisoner exploitation', in Y. Gutman and M. Berenbaum (eds) *Anatomy of the Auschwitz Death Camp*, Bloomington: Indiana University Press, pp. 34–49.

Pressac, J. and van Pelt, R. (1994) 'The machinery of mass murder at Auschwitz', in Y. Gutman and M. Berenbaum (eds) *The Anatomy of the Auschwitz Death Camp*, Bloomington: Indiana University Press, pp. 183–247.

Priemel, K.C. (2012) 'Twentieth century Flick: Business history in the age of extremes', *Journal of Contemporary History*, 47(4): 754–772.

Rothe, D.L. and Mullins, C.W. (2009) 'Toward a criminology of international criminal law: An integrated theory of international criminal violations', *International Journal of Comparative and Applied Criminal Justice*, 33(1): 97–118.

Schooner, S.L. (2005) 'Contractor atrocities at Abu Ghraib: Compromised accountability in a streamlined, outsourced government', *Stanford Law and Policy Review*, 16(2): 1–24.

Schüle, A. (2010) *Industrie und Holocaust: Topf & Söhne – die Ofenbauer von Auschwitz*, Göttingen: Wallstein Verlag.

Silverstein, K. (2000) 'Ford and the Fuhrer: New documents reveal the close ties between Dearborn and the Nazis', *The Nation*, 24 January: 10–16.

Simpson, C. (2001) *War Crimes of the Deutsche Bank and the Dresdner Bank*, Office of Military Government (US) Reports: Holmes & Meier.

Smeulers, A. and Grunfeld, F. (2011) *International Crimes and other Gross Human Rights Violations*, Leiden: Martinus Nijhoff Publishers.

Stallbaumer, L.M. (1999) 'Big business and the persecution of the Jews: The Flick concern and the "Aryanization" of Jewish property before the war', *Holocaust and Genocide Studies*, 13(1): 1–27.

Steinberg, J. (1999) 'Investigating Deutsche Bank', *Dimensions: A Journal of Holocaust Studies*, 13(2): 9–14.

Stoichkova, D. (2010) *Towards Corporate Liability in International Criminal Law*, Utrecht: Intersentia.

Taylor, T. (1949) *Final Report to the Secretary of the Army on the Nuernberg War Crimes Trials under Control Council Law No. 10*, Washington DC: Chief Council for War Crimes.

Tooze, A. (2006) *The Wages of Destruction: The Making and Breaking of the Nazi Economy*, London: Allen Lane.

Turner, H.A. (1985) *German Business and the Rise of Hitler*, New York: Oxford University Press.
Van Baar, A. and Huisman, W. (2012) 'The oven builders of the Holocaust: A case study of corporate complicity in international crimes', *British Journal of Criminology*, 52(6): 1033–1050.
Van der Wilt, H. (2013) 'Corporate criminal responsibility for international crimes: Exploring the possibilities', *Chinese Journal of International Law*, 12(1): 43–77.
Wiesen, S.J. (1999) 'German industry in the Third Reich: Fifty years of forgetting and remembering', *Dimensions: A Journal of Holocaust Studies*, 13(2): 3–8.
Yin, R.K. (2009) *Case Study Research: Design and Methods*, Thousand Oaks: Sage.
Ziegler, D. (2005) '"Arianization" and the role of the German great Banks 1933–1938', in G.D. Feldman and W. Seibel (eds) *Networks of Nazi Persecution*, New York/Oxford: Berghahn Books, pp. 44–68.

9

Regulation, governance and enforcement of white-collar crime in Europe

Special criminal law and inspectorates in Europe

Paul Ponsaers

Introduction

In 1994 Bob Hoogenboom published his eloquent doctoral dissertation, entitled 'The policing complex' (Hoogenboom 1994). In this work he observed that in our western late modern societies a differentiated police complex has become increasingly visible. Around a fragmented landscape of regular police forces, a variable network of public inspectorates and private agencies can be observed, according to Hoogenboom. The complexity of contemporary social problems is the general cause of this widespread reality. According to Hoogenboom, different types of crime require different types of responses, and thus mobilize each time different sets of agencies present in this policing complex. A multitude of forms of formal, informal and relational collaborations between the different participants in this complex can be perceived, moving back and forth to each other, depending on the social problem under study. Hoogenboom insists on certain dominances: regular police forces are dominant in tackling the crimes of the *underworld* (organized crime, but also petty crime); inspectorates are mostly active in crimes of the *upperworld* (corporate and economic crime) and private agencies are dominantly engaged in crime in the *private domain* (crime committed by employers, ICT crime). But he also points to the fact that this division of labour is not exclusive and there is a lot of *blurring of boundaries* between the different actors within this complex.

Hoogenboom was well versed in the theoretical and empirical literature on regular policing. In different respects, the work of Hoogenboom was strongly influenced by the work of Clifford Shearing and Philip Stenning on *Private Policing* (Shearing and Stenning 1987). Both authors developed the point of view that the increased use of private policing led to a growing awareness that policing could no longer be thought of as just being about crime, but as the enforcement of order and the way it can be both established and maintained. In their work, Shearing and Stenning chart the development of social control mechanisms – both public and private – from a historical, legal, ethical and managerial perspective. An impressive number of publications on this subject by other authors followed this analysis (see e.g. Crawford 2008), mostly indicating the reality of so-called 'plural policing'.

It is remarkable that minor attention was paid in the years to follow to the domain of public inspectorates. There was some growing attention, but this was not as conclusive as in the other domains of the policing complex of Hoogenboom. It is only with the growing attention on the problem of corporate crime that this subject emerged within the criminological domain in a more prominent way (Van Erp et al. 2008). An impressive stock of research followed, concentrating on the characteristics of corporate crime and the formal and informal, public and private controls which resulted from this phenomenon. Despite the importance of this research interest, an integration of the knowledge within the framework of the global policing complex stayed rather limited and the study of inspectorates became more and more an isolated domain within the study of corporate crime, no longer attached to a broad approach to policing.

In this chapter we develop in a first section the most striking differences between public inspectorates and public police agencies. This part has the aim of delineating better these rather unknown agencies and of circumscribing better the scope of this chapter.

In spite of the fact that a broad range of different agencies are active in this domain today, which have very different competences, the chapter is limited to those agencies that have at least the legal competence to bring a criminal file to the attention of the public prosecutor's office, because the (special criminal) law permits them to do so, when they observe behaviour that is defined as contradictory to (special) criminal law. The chapter leaves out of scope those numerous supervising agencies which dispose only of competences in the framework of administrative law. This chapter considers those inspectorates which intervene on the basis of a penalty clause in a criminal sense, notwithstanding that some of them dispose of *both* criminal *and* administrative competencies at the same time.

In a second section we go into the historical origins of this patchwork of inspection. Without being exhaustive in this attempt, this part tries to give a better understanding of the underlying assumptions of the existence of public inspectorates.

An exhaustive historical overview for Europe seems to be problematic. The chapter goes into the evolution in Central European countries, without aiming to be complete. The fact that the map of Europe has changed several times over time and geographical country borders with it makes it impossible to limit the chapter to national history. The chapter describes to a large extent the evolution of the territory of the United Provinces of the Netherlands, taking into account the imposition of important pieces of foreign law during occupation.

In the conclusion we try to formulate briefly why public inspectorates differ from public police agencies, based on historical insight.

What do we mean by public inspectorates?

What do we mean when we use the notion of *public inspectorates*? In a general sense we use this term to point to a range of different public agencies which have essential tasks in law enforcement in very different and essential domains of social activity. Public inspectorates are active within the domains of labour, trade, social insurance, the environment, and many more social spheres of everyday life (Ponsaers 2009).

The labour inspectorate, for instance, is part of the public administration and responsible for the inspection of the circumstances and conditions labourers are working in. This means more precisely the inspection of health and hygiene and the prevention and control of disease in the workplace; technical requirements in relation to health and safety in production and the prevention of workplace accidents; and the social conditions in relation to working hours, social insurance, unemployment, etc. The domain of labour is to a large extent regulated by labour and social laws, in which these requirements and conditions are stipulated. Most of these regulations include penal sanctions. It is the task of the labour inspectorate to control to what extent enterprises comply with these regulations.

Inspectorates engaged in these kinds of activities have the power to report violations to the public prosecutor's office. In this sense, inspectors are similar to public police officers and are acting similarly to regular public police agencies (Ponsaers et al. 2012). Besides that, they have a lot of other powers that are less common for regular police agencies. In contrast with public police agencies, public inspectorates often dispose of the legal competence not only to draw up a criminal report, with eventually the consequence of penal sanctioning, but their reports can also be settled through administrative procedures and sanctioning (administrative fines). Mostly they can make a choice between a penal or administrative settlement.

Furthermore, inspectorates largely are entitled to use legal discretion, which enables them to give warnings, to fix a time period wherein the problem should be solved (without reporting to public prosecution), to give advice, and so on. They have free access to the workfloor, to inspect production entities, to take samples, to examine the book keeping of the enterprise (without a mandate of a magistrate), etc.

Inspectorates regulate the relations between private interest groups (e.g. employer–employee, producer–consumer, etc.). These relations are often not considered to be part of the so-called 'general interest' or 'public order' that is believed to be the primary domain of public police agencies. Therefore regular police act mostly within the framework of the penal code, and this code is considered to be the servant of this public and general interest. Inspectorates do not function within this framework, but function in relation to specific and special penal laws, which can be situated outside the penal code. These specific and special penal rules are not considered to regulate 'general interest' or 'public order', but regulate relations between private interest groups.

Inspectorates do not have the right to execute legal violence or pressure and do not carry weapons. In case of necessity and resistance, inspectorates can appeal to regular police, who are supposed to support their activities and facilitate inspection. From this point of view, public inspectorates are different from regular public police and rely upon them. Inspectors are law enforcers who are less intrusive than regular police officers, more directed to persuasion of the offender than to immediate prosecution and sanctioning. They tend to use the 'carrot' instead of the 'stick' (Ponsaers and Hoogenboom 2004). In some European countries, e.g. in the Netherlands, certain public inspectorates are more differentiated in their functioning. Some can be more harsh, while they are directed towards investigative tasks in the domain of fiscal, environmental and social fraud, for example, and have more 'police-like' powers than most of the other 'softer' agencies (Ponsaers et al. 2003).

The ultimate goal of regular police intervention is deterrence and ultimately the general preventative effect sanctioning has (or is believed to have) on future 'criminal' behaviour. The police start with an attitude of distrust towards 'suspects'. The activities of inspectorates are much more directed initially towards collaboration and trust. A sanction ultimately given, after a period of trying to settle and solve a problem, is considered to be a failure, while regular police forces would consider this to be a success.

In essence the difference between regular public police services and public inspectorates lies in the pro-activeness of the latter. While the public police are more reactive, directed to the investigation of crime that has already been committed, public inspectorates normally routinely carry out visits to non-suspect enterprises and firms, to investigate to what degree they *comply* with the actual, specific regulation in the economic sector.

Furthermore, inspectorates do get not many complaints from victims, while regular police forces function to a large extent reactively towards these kind of responses. Mostly, inspectorates function simply towards the application of the rule of law, while often employees or customers are not aware whether or not they have been victimized. Victimization is in these domains of inspection mostly a collective problem, not characterized by individual victim responsiveness, while most of the cases investigated by regular police agencies are characterized by recognized individual victimization. Specific and special penal laws are less easy to mobilize by victims than the penal code itself, while they often have a very technical content and need explicit interpretation and knowledge. Special penal laws often determine technical norms, which should be measured or established by experts. Individual employees or consumers often don't have the knowledge nor the tools to determine whether or not they are dealing with an infraction. Because of this characteristic, special penal laws are considered difficult to mobilize.

This kind of functioning has as a consequence that, where inspectorates conclude that illegal behaviour is committed, the 'offender' is known most of the time, while regular public police agencies have to elucidate the question of the identity of the suspect and to look for proof that he/she is really the offender. 'Offenders' of violations against special penal laws commit violations in the environment in which they are routinely functioning, more precisely within the enterprise or the corporation. 'Offenders' are present on the crime scene. This is in sharp contrast with the reality of public police agencies, which often have to look for offenders, who commit their crimes in environments other than those where they work.

It is precisely in these domains wherein inspectorates are functioning that the enterprise itself can become 'offender' (penal responsibility of a legal person) and no longer the individual person, who is the traditional 'suspect' of regular police agencies. In Table 9.1 I summarize the characteristics of the public inspectorates this chapter is dealing with.

Table 9.1 Comparison between public inspectorates and public police agencies

	Public inspectorates	*Public police agencies*
Legal basis	Specific and special penal laws	The Penal Code
	Technical	Non-technical
	Difficult to mobilize	Easy to mobilize
Competencies	Lot of discretion and broad competencies	Less discretion and specific competences
	No use of legal violence and pressure	Use of legal violence and pressure
	Penal and administrative sanctions	Penal sanctions
	Warnings in advance for sanctioning	Warnings afterwards for new sanctioning
Target	Private interest groups	General interest, public order
	Offender is known: inspection, control	Offender is unknown: elucidation, investigation
	Legal persons, corporations and enterprises	Individuals and groups of individuals
Victimization	Collective victimization	Individual victimization
	Often after routine control	Often after complaint of victim
Philosophy	Prevention, pro-active (risk and harm reduction)	Repression, reactive (retribution)
	Collaboration, trust	Deterrence, distrust
	Sanction is a failure	Sanction is a success
	Important effectiveness, problem solving	Limited effectiveness, bureaucratic

In the first part of this chapter we described more precisely what we mean by *public inspectorates*. We compared these agencies with public police agencies and observed rather important differences. These particularities are to a great extent the consequence of the historical development of these inspectorates. In the second part of this chapter, we explore this historical evolution.

The origins of public inspectorates in Europe

On feudalism and the control of handicraft

The first origins of inspectorates can be traced back to the period of feudalism (Ponsaers 2003). During this period political power was distributed through a hierarchical chain of dependencies. At the top of the political-military system was the monarch. The ultimate consequence of this feudal system was that political dominance and power could not be localized in one centre. The functions of what we call today 'a state' were divided through a vertical system of allocation of power and dependencies. The monarch's power was to a large extent determined by his military power and this power was limited by the collaboration of his vassals. The feudal state was an exploding state, a compact web of private jurisdictions, without a real executive power. In other words, an administrative apparatus of the state that was responsible for law enforcement was absent (Anderson 1974: 147–153).

In the countryside, production was in the hands of peasants, slaves, working for the *seigneur*. In autonomous cities and municipalities this relation was completely different. Production was in the hands of the townsmen themselves. Medieval cities were self-governing entities, which exercised political and military autonomy (Hindess and Hirst 1975: 233–242). Feudalism was characterized by a dynamic opposition between the city and the countryside. An opposition existed between the urban economy (where exchange relations became increasingly important), controlled by the townsmen and the rural economy (based on ground rent), controlled by the aristocracy.

Political dominance in the cities was originally exercised by the magistrate during the tenth and the eleventh centuries. In the course of time, industrial regulation came into the hands of the municipality (Laenens 1953; Pirenne 1928; Van Rompaey 1971). From the fourteenth century onwards, municipal magistrates were obliged to include the guilds themselves in this regulatory activity. The crafts became more and more autonomous in controlling industrial regulation. The resistance of the municipal authorities could not stop guilds becoming immune from their intervention from the fifteenth and sixteenth centuries onwards.

Medieval guilds functioned on a basis of mutual exchange relations on the market, based on a uniform standard of trade, which was the duration of labour involved. Industrial regulation was only possible through quantifiable standards, which fixed the exchange value of products. For this reason the necessary production time of a specific good became more and more regulated and controlled. Education and qualification in a profession became a necessary condition to determine the average amount of labour time required. The guild structure was build on the maintenance of this standard. Wastage of labour time was sanctioned because of this reason. The consequence was that labour time had to be *inspected* (Landes 1999).

In the course of time the trade and the market became more complex and anonymous, because of the increasing division of labour. When the guilds wanted to lower production costs, all members had to cooperate to lower the wages of the pupils and when they wanted to keep their reputation high, the guilds could not allow certain members to sell products of bad quality. Under this pressure, industrial regulation became harsher. Because labour conditions had no direct influence on exchange relations, they were not mentioned in these regulations. It was the quality of the goods that was regulated. The number of pupils and the tools became more and more limited, the raw materials codified, the market price and the wage per piece fixed, the duration and the speed of labour strictly determined. Surveillance on these matters was exercised by 'wardens', 'jurors' and 'conservators'. These special officers were partially appointed by the city council, partially by the guilds themselves. They were chosen amongst the 'masters' (Pirenne 1928: 177–182). Especially in the textile industry they had a prominent function. No piece of cloth was permitted to be folded or stored without their approval and seal. Breaching the regulation led to sanctions, e.g. exclusion from the guild; in other words, being obliged to leave the profession. As one of the precursors of the police in the cities, the guild held weapons to enforce such a sanction (Van Overberg 1893: 3–9).

'Jurors' made visits to workshops regularly. They could ask for assistance from the public force of the municipal authority, mostly by members of the civic guards (Espinas and Pirenne 1920: 689–90). Not only could they control the members of the guilds, but they could also confiscate goods of foreign traders, of corporations and even consumers (Nayer 1980: 19–29). 'Wardens' were appointed to certain districts in the city (*ommegancken*). Production was organized in the private houses of the 'masters'. The 'wardens' were permitted to enter the workshop at any time (Demey 1957: 231–237). Pupils were obliged to do their work in the windows. In this way the public and customers could observe whether or not the industrial regulations were being followed.

The officers had a great deal of discretionary power; sometimes they commanded the liquidation of the confiscated goods, issued a prohibition to execute a profession, or issued a fine or a compensation. In certain cases the offender was brought before the dean and his court. The first municipal magistrate could act as a judge, but mostly the 'masters' or 'jurors' acted on their own behalf (Van Overberg 1893: 3).

Absolutism and the first inspectorates of the king

During the sixteenth century, absolute monarchies came into existence in western Europe. In France, England and Spain we see strong central monarchies, representing a rupture with the medieval systems. The crown gained unlimited power over the whole territory. These monarchies were characterized by a growing bureaucracy, a codification of regulations and the existence of regular armies. This trend was the strongest in France. French monarchs considered themselves no longer as referees in feudal conflicts but as owners of the national economy. This economy needed to be increasingly governed as a successful enterprise (Gerstenberger 1976: 488–510). The economical development of the country became a central issue. Industrial regulation was considered to be a tool of the crown for realizing this goal.

Objectively there was a growing collusion of interest between the monarch and the citizens. This did not lead to a partnership between them. Industrial citizens did not have enough political power at that point (Anderson 1977: 15–42). The absolutist monarchs still protected the privileges of the aristocrats. Nevertheless, they started to realize that their political power could only be enforced by gaining economical power (Pernaud 1960: 314). Absolutism implied the introduction of a harsh tax system for the rural population. Farmers became more and more dependent on brutal taxation collectors, who took significant proportions of the collected capital for themselves. A large percentage of the royal incomes was spent on wars.

The birth of absolutism was followed by a mercantile policy. Tax barriers appeared at country borders, with the aim of hindering import and facilitating export. Monarchs tried to get rid of internal borders as much as possible within the country, which were considered relicts of the feudal period. A national market was the ultimate goal (Demey 1957: 283). To facilitate the growth of a national market, absolute monarchs introduced the factory system. Entrepreneurs were encouraged to find skilled workers, which meant that the traditional guilds had to hand in their workforce for the benefit of the new economy. Absolutist rulers tried to dismantle the industrial regulations of the handicrafts in favour of the introduction of new regulation, this time under the supervision of the absolutist state. Strict rules were introduced with the objective of controlling the activities of labourers from morning till evening. The intervention of the absolutist rules was directed to discipline the workers of the guilds (Neuville 1976: 74–80).

Sometimes the absolutist monarchs went so far as to put labourers at the disposal of entrepreneurs (Foucault 1975; Rusche and Kirchheimer 1968). During the sixteenth century, intervention by central government was directed to keep salaries at the same level, while prices increased. Unions were forbidden, striking was sanctioned. Labourers were included in the army during long periods and were forced to work in the developing factory system. Parents who did not allow their children to work in the new industry were severely fined. A French decree of 1669 declared the arrest of emigrants and the confiscation of their goods. In 1682 even the death penalty was introduced for emigration. The conditions for immigration were, on the other hand, very attractive. The state took different initiatives to set up factories by rendering privileges, monopoly rights, the limitation of the guild system, the handing over of premiums, etc.

In France, for instance, the rise of the factory system was to a large extent the consequence of state intervention. Colbert, minister to Louis XIV, advocated important forms of state intervention. He imported an important number of skilled Swedish mining workers with their families to France (Clement 1892: 150–164). Colbert reduced the taxes of those families who married early and had a significant number of children (Rusche and Kirchheimer 1968: 28). He banned vagabonds and criminals and condemned them to work as slaves on the galleys (Gerstenberger 1976: 490).

It was the same Colbert who appointed in 1671 the former 'jurors' of the guilds as agents of the royal crown (Marini 1936: 40–44). They were named 'factory inspectors'. Their function seemed superficially the same as before, but they now had specific tasks. They got an important role in the regulation of trade. It was under their supervision that Flemish textile merchants went to markets abroad. They functioned as a 'trade police' during this mercantile period. While in medieval times the surveillance of the guilds was centred on the introduction of fixed exchange standards, these royal inspectors were focusing on the change of these standards, trying to realize surplus value. They acted as advisors for entrepreneurs (Van Overberg 1893: 10–11). The central government sent them to the provinces to examine the conditions of trade and industry, to find out why development was slow, and to find out what could be done to develop the national economy faster. They prepared from this standpoint new regulations and informed the central administration about the importance of each industrial branch. They searched for new locations for new factories.[1]

State control of the mining industry was introduced early in France.[2] But it was again Colbert who organized a solid administration of mining engineers. The job of these engineers was strongly comparable to that of the factory inspectors. They had an economic function from a mercantile point of view: making mining more profitable (Clement 1892: 150–164). For the time being charcoal mines were not delivering energy for the industry, while steam engines did not yet exist and the development of industry was not dependent on them.

The Austrian Habsburger, Josef II, delivered important concessions to the new industrial entrepreneurs in 1784, detrimental to the guilds (Dotrimont 1980: 59–65). They were permitted to engage as many labourers as they wanted (Godechot 1971: 56–63). In 1736 'ambulant and technical inspectors' were attached to the general factory inspectors. They were asked to improve industrial techniques. In addition to them, there were also 'special inspectors'. They were assigned to verify the quality and the quantity of products, to control the workers' registers, and to pay the wages of the labourers. They intervened also in cases of strikes and social conflicts. Under-inspectors controlled the raw materials that were used during production. All these inspectors were royal agents. In fact we can talk of an 'industrial police'. Day and night they were visiting state and private enterprises. They were permitted to force the doors in the case of resistance. They had the legal competence to make an official report (Marini 1936: 43).

Until 1744 the owner of land was also owner of the mineral substrate underneath. From that year on, the French state declared itself the owner of all substrates. The 'mining engineers' became the supervisors of this new state property. The mining exploitations developed under strict regulation and control. An exploiter needed a permit from the 'general controller of finances'. It was forbidden to stop exploitation before exhaustion of the vein. Even the technical details became regulated: the shanks had to have a minimal diameter, the length of the shanks was regulated, also the supports, etc. These changes went hand in hand with the fact that charcoal was beginning to push aside wood as a fuel. From this moment on, day and night shifts were introduced in the mining industry and women and children involved in the exploitation of the soil.

The French Revolution and the organization of civil inspectorates

In 1789 the aristocratic resistance against the French government weakens and a civil revolution takes place. The *Ancien Régime* is torn down and a declaration of 'immortal principles' is drafted in which liberty, equality and brotherhood are the central themes. Property rights are also enscribed as an inviolable right (Godechot 1968: 789). The privileges of the aristocracy are discharged and the guild system is now completely abandoned. The civil state becomes a fact. It is Napoleon Bonaparte who consolidates this form of state under the first empire.

Napoleon rules firmly and makes the most important economical centres of development (agriculture, industry and trade) domains of important state intervention. The Ministry of the Interior is the primary centre of power, followed by the Ministry of Factories and Trade. Both ministries develop a centrally steered industrial and trade policy. The focus is on markets and fairs, inland navigation, provision of food, recovery of debts, etc. The mechanical arts in particular receive attention. The abolition of the guild system, of the coalition of labourers and of the old industrial regulation becomes the subject of policymaking. The former royal factory inspectors are replaced by a range of consultative and advisory councils for the benefit of industry. The former inspectors become the subject of criticism because they are often corrupted by entrepreneurs and they were considered to be the symbol of the ancient absolutist system (Van Overberg 1893: 10–11). The law of 27 September and 16 October 1791 abolished all functions of directors, inspectors and administrators of factories (Godechot 1968: 218–219). Strict industrial regulation did not exist any more, and was replaced by an active and direct form of support and advice from the central administration (Godechot 1968: 656–658).

Also in the mining industry a similar evolution could be observed. In 1791 the government decided to return possession of the underground substrate to land owners. The state maintained only a right to deliver permits for the exploitation of mines. All the regulation concerning labour was abolished (Godechot 1968: 204–205). It is remarkable that in this context the mining inspectorate was maintained. The inspiration for the law of 1791 was the physiocrat Mirabeau, scholar of Condorcet. Physiocrats were convinced that land owners (small aristocrats, members of royal families) were important economical actors. The growing need for a workforce in the factory system could only be compensated, according to them, by a growth in agriculture. As a consequence of this logic, land owners were obliged to make optimal use of the soil. They received high ground rent, but were obliged to invest this in the exploitation of their land. When prices increased, the ground rent increased also, and the profit was no longer exclusively invested in agriculture, but also in trade and industry. The heavy metal and mining industry could develop to an important degree as a consequence of these high ground rents (Craeybeckx 1963: 419–426). The ideas of the physiocrats were thus completely in line with the interests of the ground owners. All wealth, food, but also metal and charcoal, came from the soil.

It was a combination of the ideas of the physiocrats and the interests of the exploiters that made it possible for Mirabeau to convince the legislator of his proposal. We can deduce the physiocratic character of the law of 1791 from the 'general interest' the mining industry was given. Mining concessions were seen as important instruments in the development of a 'national economy', through an optimal use of the ground. It was the mining administration, including the mining inspectors and engineers, that had to realize this 'general interest'. It is in the same context that we should understand the first occurrence of security measures in the law. The acquisition of a concession was indeed made dependent on a number of security measures taken in favour of the owners of the surface (Velge 1927: 259). In short, it was not an environmental nor a labour problem that inspired these first measures, but rather a need to mediate between owners of the underground, the exploiters and the owners of the surface. It was a matter of property. Complaints came often from the owners of the surface. The law should ensure a maximal and continuous exploitation of the mine, without endangering the use of agricultural land.

Mining engineers should assure themselves of the fact that the holder of a concession made optimal use of the underground. The general principle of the law was maintenance of the continuity of production. The means of production had to be approved by mining engineers. It was not permitted to remove these means when an exploiter stopped his activity in a mine. These regulations were very demanding and required important investments. Only entrepreneurs with significant financial means could invest in this kind of activity and a tendency towards monopolies developed in the mining industry. Fewer entrepreneurs became owners of an increasing number of means of production.

While the napoleonic regime adhered to the general principle of strict non-intervention in industry, this was less the case in the mining industry, where the emperor executed strong control, supported by the ideas of the physiocrats. By decree of 1810, the mining engineers were hosted in the Imperial Mining Corps. Inspector-generals gave advice concerning the delivery of concessions. They had to examine if the would-be mine exploiters were well equipped for optimal exploitation. Once a concession was obtained, the exploiter had to pay a fixed tax (based on the surface area) and a proportional tax (based on production figures). This proportional tax was raised or diminished according to the increase or decrease in production and functioned as a means of motivation or demotivation. The state invested the taxes again in the mining industry. Mining engineers were spread all over the territory of the empire. They had to supervise the application of the mining regulations. The supply of charcoal became increasingly important for the provision of energy, and ultimately for the development of the national economy.

The mines became deeper and the importance of technical means became prominent. The exploitation of mines became an increasingly dangerous enterprise (Pezeril 1978: 68–73). The number of accidents increased (Neuville 1976: 27). Various mining disasters occurred, with a dramatic number of fatalities (Verhaegen 1929: 521). These accidents caused growing awareness of the problem of safety in the mining industry and in 1813 a new decree was passed. The legislator declared the exploiter responsible for informing the local authorities in case of an accident and the mining engineer had to make a report for the prefect. The problem of safety on the job was considered the joint responsibility of employers and employees, but control was concentrated on the miners. Each miner had the duty to function in a loyal way under the guidance of his hierarchical master. A strict and daily control was executed. The result of the controls was noted in a register, kept by the mayor. Any labourer who endangered the safety of persons or goods because of insubordination or disobedience to the master was sanctioned in relation to the seriousness of the accident. In short: when safety at work was at stake, it was the miners who had to be controlled.

It is striking that in this new regulation the municipality and the mayor got an important position. This was no accident. With the disappearance of the guild regulation and the active support for the factory system, functions in the sphere of general public hygiene and health became obsolete. The competence to intervene in these domains was already settled in 1790, where the municipality gained general competence on the 'general and specific police regulations according to the state of decency in the municipality' (Godechot 1968: 91–112). The position of the municipality should be seen in this context as a prolongation of the civil central state. Municipal officers became responsible for traffic regulation, the safety of passers-by in relation to dangerous and annoying emanations, the maintenance of the peace (primarily at public markets), the control of the instruments of measurement used during transactions in the public domain, the quality of food sold on the market, the prevention of accidents and disasters (such as fire and contagious illness of humans and animals) and the provision of aid in these circumstances, and the prevention of damage caused by 'crazy persons' who were not incarcerated or by 'madmen'.

The Industrial Revolution and the responsibility of labourers

While the absolutist states had paved the way for the Industrial Revolution by creating a disciplined labour force, the French Revolution gave birth to another important condition for the Industrial Revolution, specifically a small group of rich entrepreneurs that were solidly anchored in heavy industry. Both conditions for the Industrial Revolution were created by means of state intervention, and more precisely by means of a range of centrally steered national inspectorates.

During the eighteenth century, industry saw the systematic introduction of the steam engine in important industrial branches and centres. The basis for this technological innovation lay in the early English Industrial Revolution. A lot of other European countries were influenced by the events in England (Lebrun et al. 1979: 64–65). While the construction of machinery was in earlier days a matter for wood workers, new industrial techniques permitted production of metal machines. At the same time metal enterprises got involved in the exploitation of charcoal mines, the most important source of the necessary energy of the engines. More and more entrepreneurs in the heavy metal industry controlled mines. The social consequences of this tendency to vertical economical monopolies were dramatic: low wages, extremely bad working conditions, strong density of the labour force and a strong devaluation of labour skills.

More than ever, the state started to interfere in this process by new disciplinary measures towards the new industrial workforce: for instance, the prohibition of coalition into unions and the use of the so-called worker's leaflet, a document that included a multitude of information concerning the person of the worker, his zeal, accommodation and eventual shortages. The leaflet was kept by the employer, who could hinder the worker in searching for another job or make this impossible. A negative note could condemn the worker to unemployment. Problems of labour conditions and circumstances were considered to be problems of the workers themselves on the work floor. Child labour was organized under the supervision of parents. While the state did not interfere in the sphere of the work place, each industrial entrepreneur developed his own disciplinary rules and system of sanctions. These rules determined labour conditions to a large extent, which were the responsibility of the workers themselves (Samyn 1923: 16).

In the meanwhile, English industrialization developed. A Factory Act of 1833 introduced regulations concerning child labour and limited working times. The introduction of this regulation went hand in hand with the introduction of a system of inspection, mostly under social pressure of the labour movement which became stronger. Inspectors were competent to prosecute and acted as magistrates during their activities (Bartrip and Fenn 1980: 88). A range of new Factory Acts followed. It is striking that from the beginning the introduction of these Acts immediately raised the question of the possibility of enforcing them (Reeve-Stearns 1979).

Most European countries followed this tendency in the years to come. For the first time in history inspectors were no longer the sole defenders of the interests of owners of factories or of the state. Different national European states developed from this point in history on an impressive patchwork of inspectorates to mediate between different interest groups in society. Modern states, which were originally constructed around a few authoritarian ministries (of Defence, of the Interior, of Justice and of Finance) embodied to a growing extent other policy domains (of Education, of Agriculture, of Labour, of Social Security, of Public Health, of the Environment, etc.). State intervention became more and more important also in these social domains. Within these new departments new inspectorates were set up, mediating between different interests and logics.

Conclusion

Today, most European countries dispose of a multitude of different inspectorates. The specific organization of each of them is to a large extent nationally conceived. Nevertheless some characteristics seem to be common to all. In this chapter these characteristics were defined and summarized in a comparative table with public police agencies. It is clear that these inspectorates function according to other mechanisms than regular public police forces.

To understand the reasons for these specific characteristics, this chapter discussed the historical logic of these inspectorates in Western Continental Europe. The chapter observed that the first industrial inspectorates stemmed originally from the guilds. These corporations were interested in developing standards for exchange on the market, essentially based on the duration of labour. The consequence was that labour time had to be *inspected*. Surveillance was executed by 'wardens', 'jurors' and 'conservators'. Breaching the regulation led to sanctions. The ultimate goal was the protection of the reputation of the profession.

During the period of absolutism, monarchs considered themselves as owners of the national economy. It was in the interest of these monarchs to sustain the development of the factory system, dismantling the guild system and favouring a new workforce under the supervision of the absolutist state. In this respect, important policy tools were the royal 'factory inspectors' and 'special inspectors' who got an essential role in the regulation of the trade and to speed up the development of the national economy. Also the creation of a royal administration of mining engineers followed the same logic. A real 'industrial police' was created, entirely at the disposal of the crown.

The French Revolution discharges the privileges of the aristocracy and creates the civil state, adhering to the general principle of non-intervention in industry and preparing for the Industrial Revolution. Napoleon replaces the former royal factory inspectors and mining engineers by a range of consultative and advisory councils for the benefit of the industry. Strict industrial regulation and sanctioning are replaced by support and advice from the central administration. He nationalizes to a large extent the mining industry and the ideas of the physiocrats are instrumental in the pacification of different interest groups. Inspectors regulate the ownership of the means of production and ensure the maintenance of the continuity of production.

It was only after a harsh period of brutal economic liberalism at the beginning of the Industrial Revolution that it became clear that a pure 'laissez-faire' policy led to massive social unrest, protest and claims. It became more and more clear that national states had to intervene in a multitude of domains to mediate between different interest and lobby groups, balancing these different logics in a labyrinth of countless inspectorates. New social and labour legislation was introduced and inspected, which gave birth to the new interventionist state.

To summarize this historical development, we observe that inspectorates have served different masters over time. Going from an instrument of power of the corporations and guilds, to the support rendered to the crown and the monarch, at last they became instruments of pacification for the new civil states, culminating in the birth of state interventionism. It is striking that these inspecting bodies developed over time in relative autonomy compared with regular police forces.

Some wonder if these public inspectorates actually have still the same social relevance in a late-modern era, where safety has become a social fetish. Should they be replaced by public police agencies, rendering more guarantees to victims and citizens and facilitating civil claims? This question is steered normatively. This chapter has documented that inspectorates have a very different essential function from public police agencies. They are in essence instruments of social pacification and should be considered as policing agents of social order. That is the reason why they have other –'softer'– powers than public police agencies. This argument gives new content to the image of 'The Iron Fist and the Velvet Glove': to enforce each new law, the government uses persuasion first, and only then force.

Bob Hoogenboom (1994) was right to consider both forms of policing within one integrated *policing complex*, but with different functions.

Notes

1 Indirectly this mercantile policy had also consequences for labour conditions in the factories. In France and England the governments became more and more convinced that the improvement of production could only come about when labourers were healthy. The idea of a 'medical police' started to develop.

2 It was Louis XI who appointed a first 'Maître Général Gouverneur des Mines'. In 1520 this was changed to 'Contrôleur Général de Mines'.

References

Anderson, P. (1974) *Passages from Antiquity to Feudalism*, London: NLB.

Anderson, P. (1977) *Lineages of the Absolutist State*, London: Verso World History Series.

Bartrip, P. and Fenn, P. (1980) 'The administration of safety: The enforcement policy of the early factory inspectorate', *Public Administration*, 58: 84–102.

Clement, P. (1892) *Histoire de Colbert et de son administration*, Paris: Didier.

Craeybeckx, J. (1963) 'De agrarische wortels van de industriële omwenteling', *Belgisch Tijdschrift voor Phylologie en Geschiedenis*, 41: 397–448.

Crawford, A. (2008) 'Plural policing in the UK: Policing beyond the police', in T. Newburn (ed.) *Handbook of Policing*, Cullompton: Willan Publishing.

Demey, J. (1957) 'De Handarbeiders – De Middeleeuwen', in J.L. Broeckx, C. de Clercq, J. Dhondt and M.A. Nauwelaerts (eds) *Flandria Nostra, Ons Land en Ons Volk, Zijn Standen en Beroepen door de Tijden Heen*, Antwerpen: Standaard.

Dotrimont, T. (1980) 'Note sur les mouvements révolutionnaires de 1789–1790', *Contradictions*, 23–24: 59–65.

Espinas, G. and Pirenne, H. (1920) *Recueil de documents relatifs à l'histoire de l'industrie drapière en Flandre*, Volume 3, Bruxelles: CRH.

Foucault, M. (1975) *Surveiller et Punir*, Paris: Éditions Gallimard.

Gerstenberger, H. (1976) 'De wording van de burgerlijke staat', *Te Elfder Ure*, 23(22): 486–503.

Godechot, J. (1968) *Les institutions de la France sous la révolution et l'empire*, Paris: Presses universitaires de France.

Godechot, J. (1971) *France and the Atlantic Revolution of the Eighteenth Century – 1770–1799*, London: Free Press.

Hindess, B. and Hirst, P.Q. (1975) *Pre-capitalist Modes of Production*, London: Routledge.

Hoogenboom, B. (1994) *Het politiecomplex: Over de samenwerking tussen politie, bijzondere opsporingsdiensten en particuliere recherche*, Arnhem: Gouda Quint.

Laenens, C. (1953) *De geschiedenis van het Antwerpse gerecht*, Antwerpen: Van de Velde.

Landes, D. (1999) *The Wealth and Poverty of Nations*, New York: W.W. Norton.

Lebrun, P., Bruwier, M., D'Hondt, J. and Hansotte, G. (1979) *Essai sur la Révolution Industrielle en Belgique (1770–1847)*, Bruxelles: Académie Royale de Belgique.

Marini, L. (1936) 'L'inspection du travail', unpublished PhD thesis, Paris: Université de Paris, Faculté de Droit.

Nayer, A. (1980) *Les inspections sociales en Belgique*, Bruxelles: Vie Ouvrière.

Neuville, J. (1976) *La condition ouvrière du XIXième siècle*, Bruxelles: Vie Ouvrière.

Pernaud, R. (1960) *L'histoire de la bourgeoisie en France*, Paris: Vie Ouvrière.

Pezeril, C. (1978) *Ces mineurs de Littry: Pionniers de l'ouest*, Bayeux: Imprimerie Bayeusaine.

Pirenne, H. (1928) *Histoire de Belgique*, Volume I, Bruxelles: Henri Lamertin.

Ponsaers, P. (2003) 'Oorsprong en ontwikkeling van de inspectie op de nijverheid in België: Stalen vuisten of helpende handen?', in Ph. De Baets, S. De Keulenaer and P. Ponsaers (eds) *Het Belgisch Inspectiewezen: Een niet ingeloste belofte*, Antwerpen-Apeldoorn: Maklu.

Ponsaers, P. (2009) 'Services spéciaux d'inspection: Etude sur leurs habitudes en matière de verbalisation', in C. Nagels and S. Smeets (eds) *La fraude sociale: Une priorité de politique criminelle*, Bruxelles: Bruylant.

Ponsaers, P. and Hoogenboom, B. (2004) 'Het moeilijke spel van wortel en stok: Organisatiecriminaliteit en handhaving-strategieën van bijzondere inspectie- en opsporingsdiensten', *Tijdschrift voor Criminologie*, 46(2): 165–181.

Ponsaers, P., De Keulenaer, S. and Vanhaverbeke, W. (2003) *Bijzondere inspectiediensten: Empirisch onderzoek naar hun verbaliseringsgedrag*, Gent: Academia Press.

Ponsaers, P., Vande Walle, G. and De Pauw, E. (2012) 'De bijzondere inspectiediensten', in F. Goossens (ed.) *Dragers van de politiefunctie: Een dwarsdoorsnede van de reguliere politie, de Veiligheid van de Staat, de bijzondere inspectiediensten en de private politie*, Kluwer: Mechelen.

Reeve-Stearns, L. (1979) 'Fact and fiction of a model enforcement bureaucracy', *British Journal of Law and Society*, 6(2): 1–23.

Rusche, G. and Kirchheimer, O. (1968) *Punishment and Social Structure*, New York: Columbia University Press.

Samyn, J. (1923) *De geschiedenis der socialistische vakvereniging van de vlasbewerkers en –bewerksters*, Gent: Volks-drukkerij.

Shearing, C. and Stenning, P.C. (1987) *Private Policing*, Newbury Park: Sage Publications.

Van Erp, J., Huisman, W., Van de Bunt, H. and Ponsaers, P. (2008) 'Toezicht en compliance', *Tijdschrift voor Criminologie*, 50(2): 83–95.

Van Overberg, C. (1893) *Les inspecteurs du travail dans les fabriques et les ateliers*, Louvain: Uystpruyst-Dieudonné.

Van Rompaey, J. (1971) 'Middeleeuws recht en onrecht in Vlaanderen', *Spiegel Historiael*, 6(1): 4–16.

Velge, H. (1927) *Eléments de droit industriel belge, Volume 2: Les services d'inspection*, Bruxelles: Dewit et Édition Universelle.

Verhaegen, P. (1929) *La Belgique sous la domination française (1792–1814), Volume 4: L'empire*, Bruxelles/Paris: Goemaere.

Part III

Contemporary white-collar and corporate crime in Europe

10

Economic crime and the privatization of East German corporations

Klaus Boers, Hans Theile, Barbara Bischoff and Kari-Maria Karliczek

Introduction

In the German Democratic Republic (GDR), the former East German socialist state, all enterprises were public property. The privatization or liquidation of these public corporations was the most significant economic consequence of the German reunification process. Beginning in 1990, approximately 12,000 enterprises had to be privatized or liquidated as quickly as possible by the Treuhandanstalt, a semi-official agency responsible to the federal government and parliament, but organized and acting like a corporation. There were no script-books and no prior experiences of how to privatize the economy of an entire country. The huge number of enterprises to be privatized along with – in particular in the beginning – almost non-existent privatization rules, business controls and law enforcement agencies specialized in economic crime provided extraordinary opportunities for criminal activities. Although economic crime incidents occurring in connection with the privatization process were part of the overall picture of criminal activities during the reunification period, we did not focus on this unique historical situation. From a criminological perspective, it was just as important that one could study relatively many cases of economic crime within a short time period, and that almost all of the participating actors (on whichever side) came from West Germany or Western countries. Hence, the German reunification provided also a unique opportunity to study several cases of economic crime which were by and large typical for Western economies.

As is not unusual in economic criminology, it was impossible to investigate the prevalence of unreported economic crime events; it was not even possible to gain a reliable picture of reported and investigated cases. Following the definitional distinction between occupational and corporate crime, our research rather focuses on the structural conditions as well as the penal and informal control of these two kinds of economic crime. This could be analysed in qualitative case studies and by carrying out expert interviews. All in all, 76 qualitative interviews were conducted. The analysis followed conceptional frameworks developed from rational choice theory (mostly for occupational crime) and systems theory (for corporate crime).

After briefly clarifying the definitional understanding of economic crime, the establishment and tasks of the Treuhandanstalt will be addressed. The next section gives information about the data collection and empirical methods and, in the following section, one case each of occupational and corporate crime will be described. Afterwards, empirical findings about the structural conditions of each type of economic crime as well as about the penal control by law enforcement agencies and by a corporate compliance unit established within the Treuhandanstalt will be presented.

Economic crime

Under the general notion of economic crime scholars nowadays distinguish between corporate crime and occupational crime. Even though the boundary between these two types of economic crime sometimes becomes blurry, this is an adequate differentiation from a phenomenological and conceptual point of view. The criterion of differentiation is the interest behind the crime. The term *corporate crime* thus refers to those offences that employees commit while acting in the interest of their company. *Occupational crime*, on the other hand, refers to offences that employees conduct in their own interest but to the detriment of their company (Boers 2001: 338–339; 2010: 18–24; Braithwaite 1984: 6; Clinard and Quinney 1973: 17–21; Friedrichs 2010: 6–7). Corporate crime is increasingly understood as the more important type of economic crime. In this study, the focus was also on those offences that benefit a particular company. This conceptual approach allows us to take a closer look at the central organizational units and thus at the most important core areas of the economy. This is of particular significance since the economic power of a company expresses itself both in the economic and societal damages it can incur as well as in the necessary use of resources to prevent and remove them (see Clinard 2006; Friedrichs 2010: 60–94; Minkes and Minkes 2008; Simpson 2002: 4–9; Slapper and Tombs 1999: 14–15).

Treuhandanstalt

Responsible for the privatization of the state-owned GDR corporations was the Treuhandanstalt. The Treuhandanstalt was originally created in March 1990 by the last GDR government and became the owner of all East German corporations. Following the *Einigungsvertrag* (reunification treaty), signed between the governments of East and West Germany in August 1990, the Treuhandanstalt was restructured to a semi-official federal authority. It was internally organized like a private corporation, but legally, politically and financially under the control of and responsible to the federal government and parliament.

The goal of the privatization programme was to privatize or, if unavoidable, close down all former 8,500 GDR corporations as quickly as possible, at the latest by the end of 1994 – an objective that could be achieved to a large extent. Mainly due to spin-offs the number of companies increased to around 12,000 after the reunification. The politically and economically intended privatization programme was executed by selling the East German companies and businesses to individual or corporate private investors, to the current management or to communities (e.g. public transport, waste management, etc.), or by retransferring the property to the original owners. Companies and businesses or parts of them that could not be sold by the end of 1994 were mostly liquidated. By and large, one-third of the 12,000 companies and businesses were sold to private investors and communities, one quarter to management, one-eighth given back to original owners, and one-third were liquidated. Of the 4 million employees who were employed in 1990 in a former GDR corporation 2.5 million had lost their jobs by 1994. The Treuhandanstalt was closed down by the end of 1994. The remaining unsettled cases were handed over to a successor institution, the Bundesanstalt für vereinigungsbedingte Sonderaufgaben, which finished its operations de facto by the end of 2000 (Bundesanstalt 2003: 31, 230, 398–399; Gellert 2003; Grosser 2003: 628–629; Karliczek and Theile 2010).[1]

Aside from these general macro-economic conditions, the ability to act autonomously, which was granted by the federal government, was of significance for the Treuhandanstalt in the privatization process. The government had set merely a vague objective: the rapid privatization of state-owned GDR corporations (Breuel 1993: 149; Grosser 1998: 349–351; see Raab 2002: 84). The autonomy of the Treuhandanstalt was only slightly limited in 1992 when the federal ministries and the parliament were allowed to partly intervene in the privatization process. It was only after the Treuhandanstalt was closed down and its successor institution was founded that political committees took over direct control functions (Lüken 1998). Until then, there were only few publicly debated cases of privatization that became subjected to parliamentary committees of investigation.

Internal guidelines, which were further developed and specified in the course of the privatization activity, existed in the Treuhandanstalt since October 1990 (Treuhandanstalt 1994a: 313–392). In practice, however, they were only of little significance as most of the employees of the Treuhandanstalt paid little attention to them at least at the beginning of the sale process. The 1992 handbook of privatization (Treuhandanstalt 1994b: 44–418) issued by the administration was also considered rather non-binding. One likely reason for this was the insufficient control of the privatization processes within the Treuhandanstalt itself. It was only at the beginning of 1991 that efforts were undertaken to create units which would be in charge of control functions. The newly developed areas Revision and Financial Control, which were created following the model of large corporations, were, however, not able to conduct a systematic control due to the large number of privatization processes. A department for contract management was created as late as 1993 even though the contracts made by the Treuhandanstalt often contained agreements such as job security and investment obligations, compliance to which required a regular evaluation (Bundesanstalt 2003: 114–115, 118–139; Küpper 1993: 334–336; Treuhandanstalt 1994d: 1020–1049).

Data and methods

This study is based empirically on media analyses, file analyses and overall 76 qualitative in-depth interviews (Karliczek and Boers 2010). The procedure was as follows: evaluation of media reports, material from the Treuhandanstalt-Investigation Committee of the Bundestag (German Parliament), as well as initial conversations with people working for the Treuhandanstalt allowed us to pre-select cases that seemed appropriate for our study. A more precise selection of cases was achieved by an analysis of the respective files of the administrative judicial department of the Treuhandanstalt as well as of the departments of public prosecution.

This analysis provided a number of potential respondents, defendants and experts, who were to be interviewed via guideline-oriented interviews. All those people were considered experts who had specific experience and knowledge regarding the cases and the field of study as a result of their institutional and organizational involvement (see Meuser and Nagel 2002). Interviewing defendants and officials from the areas of penal prosecution, penal defence, the Treuhandanstalt, the companies as well as other experts made it possible to view the individual cases from different perspectives. With such a multicontextual case study, the important aspects for the respective cases were elaborated and compared with each other (Boers et al. 2004: 473).

All in all, 11 case studies were conducted through 53 guideline-oriented interviews (case-specific interviews). Eight cases were selected because they involved delinquent activities, and three cases because delinquent activities did not come to the knowledge of anybody. The latter allowed us to compare penally relevant with penally irrelevant privatization cases (not reported in this paper, see Techmeier 2012: 186–191). The remaining 23 interviews were conducted with decision makers from economic (above all managers of the Treuhandanstalt), criminal justice (leading prosecutors, police chiefs) and political institutions (e.g. head of a Justice Department) in order to understand the institutional and structural background of the privatization process and of its social control (institution specific interviews).

Following the grounded theory developed by Glaser and Strauss, the initial assumptions guiding our research could be specified, developed further or dismissed in the course of the empirical study (Glaser and Strauss 1967). The multicontextual case studies, the institutional background information as well as the use of already existing theoretical knowledge allowed us to view the field of study from different empirical and theoretical perspectives.

Cases

Out of the investigated cases two are presented here in more detail. These cases were (in our study) the most typical examples for either occupational crime or corporate crime.

Occupational crime in the Treuhandanstalt district branch of Halle

The Treuhandanstalt district branch of Halle had already completed all its privatizations by September 1992, strongly applauded by the board of the Treuhandanstalt and in the media. Most of these privatizations were about criminal personal enrichments to the detriment of the Treuhandanstalt. They had been committed by the district branch's director of privatization, his collaborators as well as freelance lawyers who were working for the Treuhandanstalt as liquidators. The district branch's director had the authority to decide about the prices of the companies that were to be privatized and to check and approve the privatization contracts. He engaged a lawyer whom he knew to sell the companies for the Treuhandanstalt as a liquidator. This liquidator sold the companies to adequate buyers at too low a price and demanded provisions from the buyers for the approval of the contracts. After the director had approved the contracts, he received half of the bribery money. A little while later, the liquidator arranged a contract with an entrepreneur and investor whose company was in great financial trouble. The investor wanted to move his production to East Germany because the level of wages was significantly lower there and because he could then expect public subsidies from the Treuhandanstalt for the rehabilitation of East German enterprises. This investor as well as several others bought numerous East German enterprises, which often still had liquid financial resources or valuable properties, at very low prices. These sale contracts were not checked by the district branch's director, competitive offers were overlooked, commitments on investments and securing jobs were not adhered to, and existing rules of the Treuhand on contractual design were ignored. Significant amounts of bribery money were paid to the district branch's director and other employees of the district branch Halle for the procurement of sale contracts and their approval. The bribery money was often taken from the liquid funds of the purchased enterprises. The properties as well as lucrative enterprise units were sold at much higher prices.

The district attorney's office began investigating 30 suspects. Some of them had already been in pre-trial detention for a long period of time. In the course of pre-trial detention, some of the suspects made confessions which, in turn, incriminated some of the other defendants. The penal investigations ended with sentences of four to five years in prison for bribery (§ 331–335 StGB[2]), breach of trust (§ 266 StGB), fraud (§ 263 StGB) and tax evasion (§ 370 AO[3]) At least in some of the investigations there were plea agreements between the district attorney's office, the court, the defendants and defence lawyers, because, due to the complexity and extent of the events, a result-oriented investigation and trial seemed to be possible in this way only.

Corporate crime: Metallurgiehandel–Thyssen Handelsunion

Already in spring 1990 – six months before the reunification was formally enacted on October 3 – the West German Thyssen Group and the East German VEB Metallurgiehandel (MH) – a world renowned steel enterprise – started a cooperation. Chiefly agreed upon was a trainee programme for MH employees, for which MH paid 40 million DM (Deutsch marks, 20 million euros) to the Thyssen Handelsunion (THU), a subsidiary Thyssen company in charge of the cooperation with MH. However, after becoming the owner of MH in July 1990, the Treuhandanstalt mandated THU to liquidate MH. In the view of the Treuhandanstalt, MH would not have been able to survive in the (Central and Eastern) European market. The contract with the Treuhandanstalt allowed THU an honorarium of 25 per cent of the liquidation profit gained by the Treuhandanstalt, at least 5 million DM per year. In 1992 the Treuhandanstalt complained that THU had designed their accounts quite arbitrarily in a way that led to an increased liquidation benefit and, hence, to an unjustifiedly large honorarium.

There was also an argument about the payment for the trainee programme for those MH employees who were taken over by the THU but whose training was still paid out of the Treuhandanstalt supported budget of MH. As an outcome of a non-penal mediation agreement THU paid a compensation of 240 million DM to the Treuhandanstalt. Yet, this did not finally settle the case. Based on the facts described in the mediation agreement the public prosecution launched a preliminary investigation and charged ten managers of THU at the district court with suspicion of breach of trust (§ 266 StGB). Paid by the Thyssen Group, defence lawyers set up a very costly and time-consuming defence strategy. The court, eventually, dismissed the case under monetary condition (§ 153a subsection 2 StPO[4]). Each defendant had to pay one million DM to the Treasury, which was also paid by Thyssen.

Structural conditions of economic crime

The structural conditions of economic crime were analysed against this political and institutional background.[5] It turned out to be reasonable to make use of different theoretical approaches. The structural conditions of occupational crime could best be specified using the framework of rational choice approaches while considerations gained from systems theory were most suitable for those of corporate crime. Here, it was also possible that both occupational as well as corporate crime occurred in one and the same case.

Structural conditions of occupational crime

From a rational choice perspective, violating the law follows a cost-benefit calculus. In cases of occupational crime, illegal business strategies appear as a behavioural option when individually defined goals cannot be achieved in a legal manner or when pursuing the legal pathway entails higher costs. As long as the illegal actions do not endanger other, more important goals of the actor, the legal limits are transgressed when the accompanying risks are viewed as low. In view of an insufficient formal control system, only individual values and personal attitudes could prevent actors from pursuing personal goals with illegal means.

Control deficits accompanying the privatization process were the result of the political decision of a rapid privatization in which the employees of the Treuhandanstalt were given great leeway regarding their actions. Thus, the internal guidelines for privatizations remained very vague at the beginning and implementing them was not obligatory. Instead, the employees were given three rough objectives: (1) the investor was to keep the corporation operating and secure as many jobs as possible, (2) the corporation was not be sold under value, and (3) the corporations were to be sold as quickly as possible. Since these objectives contradicted each other (e.g. estimating the value of a corporation was often difficult and thus a long-term procedure), priority was given to a rapid sales process. For instance, the Treuhandanstalt's branch in Halle was also oriented towards high sales numbers and thus corresponded to the Treuhandanstalt's internal guidelines. The fact that less attention was paid to the other two objectives (for their own personal benefit) was considered to be without risk by the actors as long as the main objective was achieved. Thus, through their own work they knew that the internal control structures hardly allowed for the inspection of single privatizations. Furthermore, as a result of the political change, the capacities of the legal supervisory bodies were limited in the East German states.

Independent of the specific historical context, the following five general statements can be made about the structural conditions of occupational crime (Karliczek 2010: 233–234). The probability that individual actors break legal norms for personal profit maximization within an economic context increases when:

- a business deal has to be concluded under time pressure
- business regulations are insufficient
- there is too much leeway regarding actions and a simultaneous lack of precise setting of goals
- the making and fulfilling of contracts is not controlled
- the likelihood of a legal investigation is minimal.

Findings gained from the perspective of rational choice theory (Becker 1976; Diekmann 1999: 140; Simpson 2002; Wittig 1993: 331) cannot, however, be easily applied to decision-making processes within a corporation. The reason is that this approach, because of its individualistic orientation, may not allow for the specific complexity necessary for an analysis of corporate crime: one cannot follow the calculation of the individual actors within the company. Nor can one follow the calculation of a decision-making centre within the company with reference to the figure of a corporate actor. The former is not complex enough because of the diversity of internal corporate decision-making processes. The latter, on the other hand, is not complex enough because of the assumption of a corporate actor by which the company is attributed the characteristics of a real person (anthropomorphism).[6]

Structural conditions of corporate crime

To analyse the complexity of corporate operations and decision making it appeared adequate to choose considerations developed in systems theory as an analytical framework. Systems theory allows the observation of corporate operations not only as the sum of individual actions but as a phenomenon *sui generis* in its specific and unique organizational quality (Boers 2001: 350–353; 2010: 53–59; 2012: 257–271).[7]

Consequently, in a newer, autopoietic version of systems theory developed by Niklas Luhmann, communication, and not an individual's action, is regarded as the basic element of a social system (Luhmann 1995: 137–175). All decisions made by organizations are determined by their internal structures and dependent on past experiences. They are also based on external structures which are formed by a system's environment. Yet, external structures can be taken into account only if they can be modified into an organization's internal structures. In this way, organizations – like all social systems – operate in a dual modus: operatively closed (otherwise they would not form a unique social entity) while at the same time cognitively open (otherwise they could not survive in a social environment). They, thus, perceive their environment as contingency and restriction of their decision-making processes (Luhmann 1995: 282–287). If such processes are repeated and become more robust over time, a structural coupling between an organization and its environment may occur so that an organization can take certain environmental presuppositions for granted and can rely on them (Luhmann 1990: 38–44; 1997: 92–120).[8]

Since the environment constantly changes, a company continuously needs to adapt to these changes and has to redefine its internal structures and operations. If, how and when such processes of adapting or not adapting led to violations of penal law were the central questions of the empirical study. By comparing penally relevant with penally non-relevant privatizations, it should be possible to identify those internal structures of a company that promote or prevent penal conflicts. Here, the focus is on the relevant areas of the structural coupling: the interfaces between the companies examined and the respective political, legal or economic system.

With regard to the political system our research focused on the legislation issued especially for the Treuhandanstalt as well as on certain political programmes, e.g. to support a rapid privatization process through granting public subsidies.

In non-penal privatization cases, the political programmes were perceived as support measures but solvency was not dependent on subsidies or other political programmes.

On the contrary, in a penal privatization case, the Thyssen Handelsunion (THU) experienced disappointment regarding the reliability of the political programmes. As a reaction to an initial change of the structural conditions in the wake of the monetary, economic and social union, the corporation adequately reorganized its decisions. There had already been business relations at the time of the GDR between the THU and Metallurgiehandel (MH) which became property of the Treuhandanstalt in the course of the restructuring of state combines, companies and institutions into corporate entities.

The then existing joint venture with MH was thereupon terminated by the THU. Instead, lucrative business divisions of MH were taken over and the remaining units were liquidated by order of the Treuhandanstalt. In doing so, THU achieved a system internal adaptation to the changed environmental conditions without coming into conflict with the political privatization programmes. Since the political authorities were especially interested in a rapid and unbureaucratic privatization of the East German corporations, the THU was not likely to become subject to in-depth investigations. It seemed to be without particular risk to enter the grey area between legality and illegality in the preparation of the balance sheet for the liquidated business divisions. In fact, the Treuhandanstalt strengthened its control practices as a result of an increasing number of publicly scandalized cases of privatizations. Subsequently, the THU was requested to change its accounting practices as well as to return excessive fees. This, however, did not lead to a change of the company's internal practices. The prevailing view was that the changed control regime of the Treuhandanstalt could not really be enforced. One reason, among others, was that in East Germany an enforcement of penal law was at that time almost non-existent in corporate crime cases.

Also in the realm of the free market, business people became disappointed as they had expected a profitable development in the acquisition of East German companies. Since this did not happen, corporations had to change their strategies. While in the penally non-relevant privatizations lucrative fields of production were transferred from the West to the newly acquired East German corporations, the THU was not subject to a comparable adaptation. As a consequence of the new control regime of the Treuhandanstalt, the THU redefined its internal structure but by doing so neared the penal risk area since the expected profits had now been realized through a (to put it mildly) creative design of the balance sheets.

In general, the following *internal structures* that promote corporate crime became apparent (Karliczek 2010: 238):

- The coincidence of a problematic internal situation with external pressure on the company, e.g. through a liquidity crisis or a strong orientation towards the shareholder value without being able to fulfil the expectations of the shareholder.

- Penally relevant decisions become more likely the less a company's perceived external (political, legal, regulatory, social) conditions correspond with its past experiences. It is then less possible to further rely on well tested decision-making patterns.
- Things become even more problematic if a company's economic performance is mainly based on non-economic external programmes, in particular political subsidy programmes. Such a dependence on political decision-making may lead to a serious financial threat if these political programmes are changed in a direction that is unfortunate for the company.

Penal control

With regard to the question of penal control of corporate crime, the interviews provided insights into the possibilities, limitations and problems of penal regulation. Here, considerations from systems theory were again used as a theoretical framework. On the other hand, the activities and functions of the Treuhandanstalt's special task force Stabsstelle Besondere Aufgaben, in charge of internal penal investigations, could be examined more closely – in Germany the first example of corporate criminal compliance.

Regulating economic crime by penal law

Regarding the question of possibilities of penal control of corporate crime from the perspective of systems theory, it can be noted that under the conditions of a functionally differentiated society, an impact of penal law enforcement on economic processes cannot be modelled as a causal deterministic control process, but only in the sense of non-causal regulation. Such a regulation presupposes a structural coupling between the penal system and the economic system whereby, on the level of substantive criminal law, the economically relevant criminal offences and, on the level of procedural criminal law, the criminal procedural measures represent the decisive media of structural coupling (Theile 2009: 88–162; 2010: 333–337).

The concept of structural coupling implies that penal law enforcement can only have an influence on *whether* a corporation will be disturbed by penal investigations, but not on *how* a corporation will cope with such a perturbation internally.[9] In the context of regulation, cases of corporate crime are particularly difficult. Penal law is, in principle, oriented towards individual responsibility. It is, thus, problematic to make an organization responsible under the jurisdiction of penal law (and also, to attribute an organizational operation to an individual's responsibility). These problems are apparent on the levels of both substantive and procedural penal law where this structural problem is accompanied by power asymmetries between law enforcement agencies and corporations under investigation. It could be observed empirically that, due to their financial power, corporations are able to mobilize substantive judicial expertise (law firms) if they perceive their interests as being threatened by penal investigations. As a consequence, the procedural practice is based more and more on informal normative programmes which are often contrary to the formal law. In the long run, this may undermine the general social function of penal law, i.e. to stabilize normative social expectations since one can no longer rely on the validity of penal law regulations (Theile 2009: 225–315).

Regarding procedural penal law, it becomes apparent that the regulation of economic crime by penal law is based on the paradigms of selectivity and consensus. In view of the impossibility of an extensive penal control, the selectivity of criminal prosecution becomes the central concept, which may be observed in the widespread mechanisms of consensual case settlements, in particular (conditional) dismissals (following the principle of discretionary prosecution – *Opportunitätsprinzip*, §§ 153, 153a StPO[10]) and case terminating plea agreements (§ 257c StPO). These consensual mechanisms may be viewed as particular examples of a dialogue-oriented procedural style that is prevalent in economic crime cases and aims at reconciling opposing systemic interests. The considerable practical relevance of these consensual settlements illustrates that at least in corporate crime cases penal law, to be efficient, operates mainly in a relationship of equality instead of performing in a subordinating manner.

In corporate crime procedures, the classic authoritative character of penal law can, if at all, only be observed in coercive measures like searches (§§ 102 ff. StPO) and pre-trial detention arrests (§§ 112 ff. StPO). They create, however, a tremendous threat to a corporation's public reputation and profit interests, and may subsequently foster a corporation's readiness to participate in a consensual settlement strategy. In this way, coercive measures and consensual settlement may even functionally correspond to each other (Theile 2009: 235–280). Overall, it appears not absolutely necessary that an effective penal regulation needs to take place on the basis of a subordinating penal law enforcement and must always lead to a conviction. It can also result from consensual mechanisms. This holds true even more so, as the criminal investigation as such already has significant effects on an enterprise.

Internal penal control by the Treuhandanstalt

In 1991 the Treuhandanstalt created the special task force Stabsstelle Besondere Aufgaben to follow up on all internal and external suspicions against business partners and employees which appeared along with the privatizations. The Stabsstelle was a new phenomenon in the economic field, since this internal investigation unit's control activities were (and should be) directed solely from the perspective of penal law. In Germany it was the first institution of corporate criminal compliance. All heads of the Stabsstelle were experienced former public prosecutors who had dealt with cases of economic crime before. During an unpaid leave from their prosecution office they were employed by the Treuhandanstalt as regular employees on the basis of a civil law contract. They formally did not act as public prosecutors and therefore did not underlie the duty of mandatory prosecution implemented in the German Code of Criminal Procedure (*Legalitätsprinzip*, § 152 subsection 2 StPO).

Its creation occurred at a time when public critique regarding the work of the Treuhandanstalt increased. The management of the Treuhandanstalt became more and more aware of the negative effects that resulted especially from the penally questionable privatizations. Thus, with the creation of the Stabsstelle it was intended to improve its image among the public and also to compensate the scarce resources of the criminal justice institutions (Bischoff and Wiepen 2010: 548–636).

In particular in the beginning a lack of formal working rules or structures provided the head of the Stabsstelle with a significant independence in organizing the department's work. However, the Stabsstelle was not entirely independent from the interests of the Treuhandanstalt. Its efficiency was determined especially through the resources of personnel as well as its embeddedness in the organizational structure of the Treuhandanstalt. Until the end of 1994, there was only one lawyer, the Stabsstelle's head, even though the work load was the highest during this period. A strategic planning of the activities of the Stabsstelle was therefore almost impossible and the actual risk of criminal prosecution thus remained significantly limited. It was only in 1995, after the former GDR corporations had already been privatized or closed down, that additional lawyers were employed. At that time they mainly had to deal with the completion of remaining cases which were often complicated and extensive (see Erbe 1999: 26–27; Treuhandanstalt 1994e: 933–1008).

Since the Stabsstelle was also created with regard to its public impact, its large independence from other areas of the Treuhandanstalt was the precondition for its credibility (Erbe 1999: 28). This, however, entailed the risk that the Stabsstelle had the possibility of investigating to the detriment of the Treuhandanstalt. Therefore, its head had to regularly report to a member of the board or to the chief representative of the Treuhandanstalt; the relationship was consistently described as one of trust. The heads of the Stabsstelle felt free in making their decisions but had, in some highly controversial cases, violated their obligation to report in order to preserve their independence. The decision whether to close a case internally or whether to hand it over to the public prosecutor's office lay solely with the Stabsstelle. Since due to the obligation to report, subtle possibilities of influence could be used, one may speak of an 'orchestrated' independence. A real stress test of the Stabsstelle's independence would have been whether it could take up investigations in case of suspicion regarding a member of the board of the Treuhandanstalt. Interviewees from the Stabsstelle reported, however, that substantive suspicion was never brought up against board members.

One argument for the special efficiency of internal penal investigation units is that they would receive many more anonymous tip-offs than the formal control units. Anonymous tips were, in fact, only of secondary relevance for the activities of the Stabsstelle. Until its closure in July 2000, all in all 3,661 suspicious cases were registered from different sources (e.g. media reports, tip-offs, complaints by competitors or employees of privatized or closed corporations). At the same time, the public prosecutor's office opened 1,426 preliminary investigations of which only 30 per cent were based on penal complaints issued by the Stabsstelle (Treuhandanstalt 1994e: 904–953, unpublished statistics, own calculation). Due to the insufficient statistics, the Treuhandanstalt relevant quota of charges or convictions could not be determined. The same goes for the number of conditional dismissals (§§ 153, 153a StPO) or dismissals because of insufficient evidence (§ 170 subs. 2 StPO). Quota of charges are only available for individual areas of prosecution: quota of charges between 21 per cent and 28 per cent correspond to the overall quotas that have been observed in economic crime cases since the 1990s (Boers 2010: 38–41). Therefore it cannot be said that the Stabsstelle has contributed to an intensification of criminal prosecution as a result of its better access to inside information.

The success of the Stabsstelle can, however, only be measured in terms of a successful penal prosecution. It additionally fulfilled other, non-penal functions that were of significant importance for the work of the Treuhandanstalt. For the Treuhandanstalt, it was less about enforcing penal law but more about pursuing organizational goals. First of all, the Stabsstelle fulfilled a control function. In particular in the beginning, there was a huge lack of enforced regular business rules and control within the Treuhandanstalt. Penal law-directed investigations were supposed to compensate this gap by increasing the detection risk for potential law breakers and thus marking the borderline between allowed and illicit business activities (Bischoff and Wiepen 2010: 635; Erbe 2003: 367). In addition, the interviews revealed that there were further manifest as well as latent functions of the Stabsstelle for the Treuhandanstalt (Bischoff and Wiepen 2010: 635–636; Erbe 2003: 369–371; see Treuhandanstalt 1994c: 897–962, 1002–1008):

- A *manifest support and counselling function* both internally for all units of the Treuhandanstalt regarding penal issues as well as externally for the law enforcement authorities regarding investigations against the Treuhandanstalt. By collaborating with the law enforcement authorities, coercive measures (such as conducting searches within the Treuhandanstalt) could be prevented.
- A *manifest protection function* against public and political criticism. In view of the public scandalization of delinquent privatization activities, the Stabsstelle could be referred to as an internal agency of penal self-control since the 'prosecutor was in the house'. This was of significant importance for the necessary public acceptance of the privatization process.

- In addition, a *latent moderating and filtering function* in that it attempted to influence prosecutors' investigations in a certain direction. Thus, the Stabsstelle actively supported the prosecution process of the Thyssen Handelsunion only until a significant compensation of loss could be achieved through a solution based on civil law. In another case (Bremer Vulkan Verbund, not reported here), however, the Stabsstelle tried to promote the likelihood of a conviction through a very detailed, so-called qualified penal complaint.

Yet, the heads of the Stabsstelle felt themselves, in the first place, to be obliged to the principle of mandatory prosecution. It was, however, acknowledged that several cases had not been dealt with due to the enormous work load. The reported selectivity criteria were, first of all, the quantum of financial damage and the personal enrichment of individual suspects. Even though it was impossible to deal with all cases, representatives of the Treuhandanstalt emphasized that the Stabsstelle was not serving as a fig leaf for the Treuhandanstalt. Interviewees from the police and the department of public prosecution had a different view. They emphasized a latent alibi function of the Stabsstelle which, in their opinion, rather served as obscuring efficient law enforcement.

In the end, most important for the success of such an internal penal investigation agency is that it can operate independently at all important stages of a penally relevant decision-making process, in particular in cases of corporate crime, and also even if a top manager is involved. It is, however, unlikely that a company will make internal criminal activities public if this would contradict the company's interests by harming its public image. Decisions concerning a company are, in the end, made according to corporate, not penal, criteria. And this will especially be so in corporate crime cases.

Summary and discussion

After the German reunification the privatization of former state-owned East German corporations by the semi-official agency Treuhandanstalt provided a rare opportunity to investigate a remarkable number of economic crime cases within a short time period. Since almost all people who were involved in the privatization process in a leading position were West Germans, one could expect to find typical structures of economic crime as well as typical problems of its (penal) control. Exceptional due to the unique historical situation was above all the stimulating delinquent opportunity structure with (1) 12,000 enterprises to be privatized or liquidated within a short time period, (2) generous grants of public subsidies, (3) in particular in the beginning, no elaborated rules about how to execute and to control a privatization process of an industrial economy of an entire country, and (4) neither effective nor experienced institutions of business or penal control existent. By conducting qualitative multi-contextual case studies, typical cases of occupational as well as corporate crime could be investigated.

It turned out that no or only vague and, above all, uncontrolled business rules appeared to provide the major structural conditions for both types of economic crime. It is, furthermore, very unlikely that under severe time pressure to achieve business goals, an effective control of reasonable business rules will be carried out. For corporate crime, in addition, public subsidies as a major source of profit accumulation as well as a business orientation towards share-holders in lieu of stake-holders were of equal importance.

To understand the causes of economic crime as well as the impact of penal law enforcement, different explanatory concepts were applied. Rational choice theory, i.e. a cost-benefit calculus, may explain the behavioural decision making of an occupational offender. It may also explain the economic decision-making process of a corporation's executives. However, the more complex process of how a corporation during the privatization process adapted to changes of the

Treuhandanstalt's regimes of regulatory control as well as of subsidy granting could be understood more comprehensively by self-referential dynamics elaborated in systems theory.

As regards the penal control of delinquent privatization processes, there was in the beginning neither an effective internal control regime established within the Treuhandanstalt (not to mention any nowadays common compliance institution) nor a mentionable penal law enforcement in effect towards economic crime. Thus, for occupational offenders as well as for corporations, a detection risk (or sentencing certainty) was almost nonexistent. In cases of occupational crime, some of the individual offenders received severe prison sentences without probation. From a rational choice perspective this should have had – and was supposed to have by prosecutors and courts – a specific as well as general deterrent effect through increasing the cost factor in an offender's cost-benefit calculus. Whether this was the case here could not be analysed sufficiently in this qualitative case study. The large body of deterrence research on conventional crime shows that there may be a deterrent effect of penal sanctioning (1) only for those who are less committed to conventional beliefs and, hence, may perceive crime as a behavioural option, (2) mainly through the subjectively perceived certainty, not the type or severity of a sanction, and could (3) be observed only in the context of less severe offences like shoplifting, traffic offences or tax evasion (for a meta-analysis, Pratt et al. 2006). Although an economic offender might appear as a paradigm rational choice actor, research in the field of economic crime suggests that the evidence for deterrence may not be different from these findings for conventional crime. However, deterrence research here is less elaborated than it is within the field of conventional crime (see Simpson 2002: 35–60).

Research on corporate crime found that informal corporate sanctions, a corporate compliance system and administrative regulation appear to be more successful in preventing corporate crime than formal penal sanctions (Simpson 2002: 80–97, 116–152). Hence, cooperative models of corporate compliance (Simpson 2002: 98–115) or a model of enforced self-regulation (Braithwaite 1982; Braithwaite and Fisse 1987) are proposed, which include in a *pyramid of enforcement* corporate compliance measures, cooperative administrative regulation and penal prosecution as a complementary strategy with formal penal control intervention as a last resort. This is in line with our findings concerning the penal control of corporate crime cases. The prosecution of these cases did not even lead to convictions (not to mention prison sentences). On the contrary, the penal procedure was dominated by a consensual, dialogue-oriented procedure between penal law enforcement agencies and corporations' defence lawyers. This usually resulted in conditional case dismissals although financial damages in corporate crime cases are mostly very much higher than in occupational crime cases. That in cases of corporate crime the criminal justice system is apparently not able to enforce a traditional subordinating criminal procedure that ends in a penal sentence could fruitfully be analysed with the concept of structural coupling developed in systems theory.

The observed relationship of equality between penal law enforcement and delinquent corporations raises questions regarding the applicability of penal law. Although our empirical findings do not suggest a total abolition of penal law in cases of corporate crime, one may, however, consider how far civil and administrative law could be a more adequate means to regulate these cases. At least civil law is based on the idea of a relationship of equality between conflicting parties, and this would also be in line with the last resort (*ultima ratio*) principle. Even if the crime-policy discourse points in the opposite direction at the moment and those areas, in which a recourse to non-penal regulation is possible, can so far hardly be identified, the possibilities of a decriminalization are far from being exhausted. On the contrary, an expansion of economic penal law will not lead to a more efficient regulation of corporate crime. A consensual case settlement is also not unique to economic crime cases but – as 'diversion' – also well known in the area of everyday crime and, in particular, in cases of juvenile delinquency. In the latter cases, however, the amount of damage is on average much smaller and diversion does not serve here to cope with complex cases but to cope with large case loads and to avoid stigmatizing effects caused by formal sanctions. Cooperative, consensual settlement strategies appear to follow a general trend of mediative conflict resolution and may be less difficult to justify than insisting on punitive reactions (Theile 2009: 217–283).

The Stabsstelle Besondere Aufgaben was one of the first attempts to institutionalize criminal compliance within an economic organization. It was established in 1991 when the Treuhandanstalt came under public pressure because of criminal suspicions about several privatization cases. Although directed – surprisingly and innovative in itself – by former public prosecutors experienced in economic crime cases, the organizational structure of the Stabsstelle provides evidence that a corporation may take the risk of internal penal investigations only if such a unit can also provide an advantage for the corporation itself.

Hence, original penal investigations covered only but one of the Stabsstelle's activities. It fulfilled also several other functions that were of advantage for the implementing organization: support and counselling in penal issues, also through cooperation with prosecution offices to avoid coercive enforcement measures; protection against public and political criticism; and a moderating and filtering function by focusing investigative activities on those cases that were of greater interest for the Treuhandanstalt. Such a corporate unit of penal compliance will work quite well with economic offences directed against their own enterprise: occupational crime by their own employees, and other persons' or corporations' delinquent activities. Of major importance is the independence of such a unit: both in its organization and in its decision making (how and against whom to set up investigations). The Stabsstelle was broadly independent in cases directed against the Treuhandanstalt. It is crucial, however, whether such a unit will also be able to file in investigations against delinquent activities of its own company, in particular against members of the board. In the case of the Treuhandanstalt's Stabsstelle, this did not – as far as we could observe – undergo a rigid test.

Notes

1 This privatization process was accompanied by a tremendous structural change of political, economic, infrastructure and social conditions which cannot be discussed here (see Techmeier 2012: 57–129). The structural change in East Germany cost a total of 1.6 trillion euros net transfer from West to East Germany between 1991 and 2009 (Schroeder 2009: 87–88).

2 StGB: German Criminal Code (*Strafgesetzbuch*).

3 AO: German tax law (*Abgabenordnung*).

4 StPO: German Code of Criminal Procedure (*Strafprozessordnung*).

5 For details, see Karliczek 2007; 2010.

6 Boers 2001: 347–352; 2010: 49–53; Karliczek 2007: 113–118; see Powell and DiMaggio 1991; Kappelhoff 2000: 233. Critical about Sutherland's (1983 [1949]: 13–14, 62) 'anthropomorphism' also Braithwaite and Fisse 1990; Cressey 1989: 37; Geis 1982: 9.

7 This argument is different from that of Braithwaite and Fisse 1990: 26–35.

8 For the limitations of a political control of the economic system, see Luhmann 1988: 324.

9 An intervening system can hence exert an initializing causal effect (*Auslösekausalität*), but not a sustained causal effect (*Durchgriffskausalität*, Luhmann 2000: 401).

10 StPO: German Code of Criminal Procedure (*Strafprozessordnung*). The alternative to discretionary prosecution (*Opportunitätsprinzip*) is the principle of mandatory prosecution (*Legalitätsprinzip*). It states in Germany that a public prosecutor (as well as a police officer) is obliged to take action in relation to all prosecutable criminal offences, provided there are sufficient factual indications (§ 152 subsection 2 StPO). In German criminal procedural law, the *Legalitätsprinzip* is viewed as the rule while the *Opportunitätsprinzip* is viewed as an exception in how to deal with a criminal suspicion. However, in reality, over half of adult and more than two-thirds of juvenile crime cases, which could be brought to court, are dismissed by public prosecutors on the basis of the *Opportunitätsprinzip*. And in economic crime cases, the dismissal rate based on discretionary prosecution is not much different from that in ordinary adult crime cases (see Boers 2010: 38–41).

References

Becker, G. (1976) *The Economic Approach to Human Behavior*, Chicaco: University of Chicago Press.

Bischoff, B. and Wiepen, T. (2010) 'Formelle und informelle soziale Kontrolle im Zusammenhang mit der Privatisierung von DDR-Betrieben', in K. Boers, U. Nelles and H. Theile (eds) *Wirtschaftskriminalität und die Privatisierung der DDR-Betriebe*, Baden-Baden: Nomos.

Boers, K. (2001) 'Wirtschaftskriminologie – Vom Versuch, mit einem blinden Fleck umzugehen', *Monatsschrift für Kriminologie und Strafrechtsreform*, 84: 335–356.

Boers, K. (2010) 'Wirtschaftskriminalität: Begriffe, Methoden, empirische Erkenntnisse, Theorien und Forschungsziele. Einführung in die Untersuchung', in K. Boers, U. Nelles and H. Theile (eds) *Wirtschaftskriminalität und die Privatisierung der DDR-Betriebe*, Münster: Waxmann, pp. 17–66.

Boers, K. (2012) 'Kriminologische Forschung und Systemtheorie', in K. Boers (ed.) *Kriminologische Perspektiven. Wissenschaftliches Symposium zum 70. Geburtstag von Klaus Sessar*, Münster, New York: Waxmann.

Boers, K., Theile, H. and Karliczek, K.-M. (2004) 'Wirtschaft und Strafrecht – Wer reguliert wen?' in D. Oberwittler and S. Karstedt (eds) *Soziologie der Kriminalität: Kölner Zeitschrift für Soziologie und Sozialpsychologie, Sonderheft 43/2003*, Wiesbaden: VS Verlag für Sozialwissenschaften.

Braithwaite, J. (1982) 'Enforced self-regulation: A new strategy for corporate crime control', *Michigan Law Review*, 80: 1466–1507.

Braithwaite, J. (1984) *Corporate Crime in the Pharmaceutical Industry*, London: Routledge.

Braithwaite, J. and Fisse, B. (1987) 'Self-regulation and the control of corporate crime', in C.D. Shearing and P.C. Stenning (eds) *Private Policing*, Newbury Park: Sage.

Braithwaite, J. and Fisse, B. (1990) 'On the plausibility of corporate crime theory', in W.S. Laufer and F. Adler (eds) *Advances in Criminological Theory*, vol. II, New Brunswick: Transaction Publishers.

Breuel, B. (ed.) (1993) *Treuhand intern. Tagebuch*, Frankfurt a.M.: Ullstein.

Bundesanstalt für vereinigungsbedingte Sonderaufgaben (2003) *Schnell privatisieren, entschlossen sanieren, behutsam stilllegen*, Berlin: Wegweiser.

Clinard, M.B. (2006) 'Corporate crime: Yesterday and today – a comparison', in M.B. Clinard and P.C. Yeager, *Corporate Crime*, New Brunswick: Transaction Publishers, pp. ix–xliii.

Clinard, M.B. and Quinney, R. (1973) *Criminal Behavior Systems: A Typology*, 2nd edn, New York: Holt, Rinehart and Winston.

Cressey, D.R. (1989) 'The poverty of theory in corporate crime research', in W.S. Laufer and F. Adler (eds) *Advances in Criminological Theory*, New Brunswick: Transaction Publishers.

Diekmann, A. (1999) 'Homo ÖKOnomicus: Anwendungen und Probleme der Theorie rationalen Handelns im Umweltbereich', in J. Straub and H. Werbik (eds) *Handlungstheorie*, Frankfurt a.M.: Campus.

Erbe, J. (1999) 'Die Stabsstelle Recht der Treuhandanstalt', *Neue Kriminalpolitik*, 11(3): 26–30.

Erbe, J. (2003) 'Die Sonderstabsstelle Recht', in Bundesanstalt für vereinigungsbedingte Sonderaufgaben (ed.) *Schnell privatisieren, entschlossen sanieren, behutsam stilllegen*, Berlin: Wegweiser Verlag.

Friedrichs, D.O. (2010) *Trusted Criminals: White Collar Crime in Contemporary Society*, 4th edn, Belmont: Wadsworth.

Geis, G. (1982) [1962] *On White-Collar Crime*, Lexington: Lexington Books.

Gellert, O. (2003) 'Der Übergang von der Treuhandanstalt zur BvS', in Bundesanstalt für vereinigungsbedingte Sonderaufgaben (ed.) *Schnell privatisieren, entschlossen sanieren, behutsam stilllegen*, Berlin: Wegweiser Verlag.

Glaser, B.G. and Strauss, A.L. (1967) *The Discovery of Grounded Theory: Strategies for Qualitative Research*, Chicago: Aldine.

Grosser, D. (1998) *Das Wagnis der Währungs- Wirtschafts- und Sozialunion: Politische Zwänge im Konflikt mit ökonomischen Regeln*, Stuttgart: Deutsche Verlags-Anstalt.

Grosser, D. (2003) 'Treuhandanstalt', in U. Andersen and W. Woyke (eds) *Handwörterbuch des politischen Systems der Bundesrepublik Deutschland*, 5th edn, Opladen: Leske + Budrich.

Kappelhoff, P. (2000) 'Rational Choice, Macht und die korporative Organisation der Gesellschaft', in G. Ortmann, J. Sydow and K. Türk (eds) *Theorien der Organisation: Die Rückkehr der Gesellschaft*, 2nd edn, Wiesbaden: Westdeutscher Verlag.

Karliczek, K.-M. (2007) *Strukturelle Bedingungen von Wirtschaftskriminalität: Eine empirische Untersuchung am Beispiel der Privatisierungen ausgewählter Betriebe der ehemaligen DDR*, Münster: Waxmann.

Karliczek, K.-M. (2010) 'Strukturelle Bedingungen der Wirtschaftskriminalität', in K. Boers, U. Nelles and H. Theile (eds) *Wirtschaftskriminalität und die Privatisierung der DDR-Betriebe*, Baden-Baden: Nomos.

Karliczek, K.-M. and Boers, K. (2010) 'Qualitative Methoden zur Erhebung der Wirtschaftskriminalität', in K. Boers, U. Nelles and H. Theile (eds) *Wirtschaftskriminalität und die Privatisierung der DDR-Betriebe*, Baden-Baden: Nomos.
Karliczek, K.-M. and Theile, H. (2010) 'Rahmenbedingungen der Arbeit der Treuhand', in K. Boers, U. Nelles and H. Theile (eds) *Wirtschaftskriminalität und die Privatisierung der DDR-Betriebe*, Baden-Baden: Nomos.
Küpper, H.U. (1993) 'Vertragsgestaltung und Vertragsmanagement der Treuhandanstalt', in W. Fischer, H. Hax and H.K. Schneider (eds) *Treuhandanstalt: Das Unmögliche Wagen*, Berlin: Akademie Verlag.
Luhmann, N. (1988) *Die Wirtschaft der Gesellschaft*, Frankfurt a.M.: Suhrkamp.
Luhmann, N. (1990) *Die Wissenschaft der Gesellschaft*, Frankfurt a.M.: Suhrkamp.
Luhmann, N. (1995) *Social Systems*, Stanford: Stanford University Press.
Luhmann, N. (1997) *Die Gesellschaft der Gesellschaft*, Frankfurt a.M.: Suhrkamp.
Luhmann, N. (2000) *Organisation und Entscheidung*, Opladen: Westdeutscher Verlag.
Lüken, N. (1998) *Treuhand: BvS. Unternehmenspolitik und Organisationsentwicklung in der Transformation*, Münster: Eigenverlag.
Meuser, M. and Nagel, U. (2002) 'ExpertInneninterviews – vielfach erprobt, wenig bedacht: Ein Beitrag zur qualitativen Methodendiskussion', in A. Bogner, B. Littig and W. Menz (eds) *Das Experteninterview: Theorie, Methode, Anwendung*, Opladen: Leske + Budrich.
Minkes, J. and Minkes, L. (2008) 'Introduction', in J. Minkes and L. Minkes (eds) *Corporate and White Collar Crime*, London: Sage.
Powell, W.W. and DiMaggio, P.J. (eds) (1991) *The New Institutionalism in Organizational Analysis*, Chicago: University of Chicago Press.
Pratt, T.C., Cullen, F.T., Blevins, K.R., Daigle, L.E. and Madensen, T.D. (2006) 'The empirical status of deterrence theory: A meta-analysis', in F.T. Cullen, J.P. Weight and K.R. Blevins (eds) *Taking Stock: The Status of Criminological Theory*, New Brunswick: Transaction.
Raab, J. (2002) *Steuerung von Privatisierung: Eine Analyse der Steuerungsstrukturen der Privatisierung der Ostdeutschen Werft- und Stahlindustrie 1990–1994*, Wiesbaden: Westdeutscher Verlag.
Schroeder, K. (2009) *Ostdeutschland 20 Jahre nach dem Mauerfall: Eine Wohlstandsbilanz*, Berlin: Freie Universität Berlin.
Simpson, S.S. (2002) *Corporate Crime, Law, and Social Control*, Cambridge: Cambridge University Press.
Slapper, G. and Tombs, S. (1999) *Corporate Crime*, Harlow: Pearson Longman.
Sutherland, E.H. (1983) [1949] *White Collar Crime. The Uncut Version*, New Haven: Yale University Press.
Techmeier, I. (2012) *Das Verhältnis von Kriminalität und Ökonomie*, Wiesbaden: Springer VS.
Theile, H. (2009) *Wirtschaftskriminalität und Strafverfahren: Systemtheoretische Überlegungen zum Regulierungspotential des Strafrechts*, Tübingen: Mohr Siebeck.
Theile, H. (2010) 'Die Regulierung der Wirtschaftskriminalität durch Strafrecht', in K. Boers, U. Nelles and H. Theile (eds) *Wirtschaftskriminalität und die Privatisierung der DDR-Betriebe*, Baden-Baden: Nomos.
Treuhandanstalt (1994a) *Dokumentation 1990–1994 Band 2*, Berlin: JOVIS.
Treuhandanstalt (1994b) *Dokumentation 1990–1994 Band 7*, Berlin: JOVIS.
Treuhandanstalt (1994c) *Dokumentation 1990–1994 Band 10*, Berlin: JOVIS.
Treuhandanstalt (1994d) *Dokumentation 1990–1994 Band 11*, Berlin: JOVIS.
Treuhandanstalt (1994e) *Dokumentation 1990–1994 Band 13*, Berlin: JOVIS.
Wittig, P. (1993) 'Der Ökonomische Ansatz zur Erklärung kriminellen Verhaltens', *Monatsschrift für Kriminologie und Strafrechtsreform*, 76: 328–335.

11

White-collar crime in countries of transition

The lesson of Hungary

Éva Inzelt

Introduction

Although the term 'white-collar crime' was introduced by Edwin H. Sutherland in 1939 as 'a crime committed by a person of respectability and high social status in the course of his occupation' (Sutherland 1949: 9), we can state that this type of crime existed since the establishment of the first societies. As Horace wrote: 'There's never enough, you're only what you own'.[1] The nature of white-collar crime depends on the actual state (health) of the society which is related to the culture and the political system of a given country, as well as to the international environment via effects of political and economic relations (Goel and Nelson 2010: 433–447; World Bank 2000: 1–101).

It is evident that traditions, e.g. opinions about accepting any kind of bribe, vary in different countries. In Hungary the misuse of power for illegitimate private gain has always been present. During the Turkish occupation from the beginning of the fifteenth until the end of the seventeenth century, the baksheesh system was common. The ruling class, the nobility, was engaged in corruption in the course of the industrial development of the country at the second half of the nineteenth century. Nepotism and cronyism flourished. The shortage economy during the socialist period between 1948 and 1989 made (mostly minor) bribery an everyday practice. When the first redistributive system is good, in other words, if the primary income is properly distributed, corruption (as a secondary redistributive system) practically does not exist. In this respect the situation in Hungary has always been far from the ideal, and it remained so after the change in the system. However, instead of minor bribes, white-collar crime became more sophisticated and the money involved became orders of magnitude higher (Kránitz 1999: 35–54). It should be mentioned that despite all the problems, according to the World Bank report, the situation in Hungary was one of the best regarding the administrative corruption index and the state capture index, respectively, in 2000 among the countries of the former Soviet Bloc (World Bank 2000: 7–17).

The notion of white-collar crime rather quickly appeared in the literature of Hungarian criminology. In 1948 István Schäfer in his book entitled *The White Collar Criminal* (*Fehérgalléros bűntettes*) gives a detailed analysis of this category of crime. First, he emphasizes the moral harm in society: 'The financial loss caused by a white collar crime is usually substantial but in many cases harm in the morals of society or the organization is even higher'. Second, he also tries to explain the curious fact that rich and powerful people commit such crimes as follows: 'desire for more wealth is practically infinite'. Third, he also recognizes the importance of latency in white-collar crime: 'The high position and prestige help to hide the substantial part of white collar crimes' (Schäfer 1948). The research on white-collar crime then stopped because the ruling party denied its existence in socialism.

Only a few publications that appeared after 1980 touched upon this problem. However, during the last 24 years several important works on white-collar crime have appeared in Hungary. Unfortunately, most of these papers were published in Hungarian and therefore their impact outside Hungary was negligible.

In this chapter I focus on a special situation, namely on the changing forms of white-collar crime with the emphases on different types of corruption during the political and economic transitions in Hungary, which show several similarities to events in other countries but also possess particular features. First, we summarize the essential features concerning the nature of the transition in Hungary after 1989, when the so-called socialist system was replaced by a multiparty democracy and market economy. Second, some forms of the white-collar crimes are illustrated by showing typical cases. The case studies that will be described in this chapter are from the twenty-first century because the characteristic cases belonging to the period of 1989–2000 have already been reviewed in a previous paper (Inzelt 2011: 359–379). Third, we try to answer the question of why white-collar crime, corporate crime including state–corporate crime, flourishes during the transition period. Due to the overlap between different terms, it is difficult to separate the categories. In the majority of cases corporate crime belongs to the concept of white-collar crime. We may distinguish whether the crime benefits the company and its top officers, shareholders, etc. or benefits an individual (insider trading, fraud, etc.). However, there are corporate crime cases when the company is established for the purpose of committing criminal activities, e.g. see later: illegal reclaim of VAT. Herein the stress will be laid on financial-economic violations; however, in almost all cases corruption, abuse of authority, forgery of private documents, etc. played a role. Although environmental crime committed by corporates or individuals is also present, I do not deal with it in detail. In fact, it is among one of the few areas where the situation has improved. In some cases this was spontaneous because closing the factories of heavy industry – after the change of the system – decreased air pollution. New waste water plants were built; the water pollution also decreased. There was only one large-scale accident, the alumina sludge spill in 2010, when the alkaline red mud devastated Kolontár and Devecser, killed eight people and injured 122. Although the managing director of Hungarian Aluminum was arrested after the catastrophe, responsibility has not yet been ascertained; however, a corporate or state–corporate crime cannot be excluded.

Political and economic transitions in Hungary

At the end of the 1980s the general easing of geopolitical tensions between the Soviet Union and the United States, the so-called *détente*, resulted in an agreement which effected the liberation of the countries that used to belong to the sphere of interest of the former Soviet Union. In 1989 in these countries not only was the Soviet-type political system replaced by a multiparty democratic one, but the so-called planned economy was intended to be transformed into a market-oriented, capitalistic one as fast as possible. The political transition was peaceful; however, a fight started for the state-owned wealth of the country and economic power.

The free parliamentary elections in spring 1990 brought an end to 40 years of socialist dominance in Hungary, and opened up new vistas concerning the development of Hungary towards a capitalist society based upon parliamentary democracy, a market economy, social, cultural and political pluralism, the protection of human rights, and membership in the political, economic and military organizations of the Western countries (Lévay 2012: 103–104).

During the socialist period, the market existed in principle but market competition was strongly limited. Bankruptcy was unknown; central actions were taken to ensure profits. The 'no risk, the state will help attitude' has been deeply fixed in the thinking of economic actors (Lévay and Inzelt forthcoming).

A period of wild capitalism started with so-called spontaneous privatization. In the course of this a substantial portion of national wealth passed into private hands practically without any control. Legislation could only follow the changing forms of economic and white-collar crime; the transition period posed a practically insolvable problem in the former socialist countries for legislators and the judicial system. For a long time legislators were occupied with the adjustment of the constitution and the most important laws of democracy to the principles of human rights, freedom of media, financing the members of parliament and parties, distribution of the wealth (e.g. buildings) of the former ruling party among the new parties, the establishment of new self-governments and also with symbolic issues, e.g. whether the Hungarian coronation crown be a part of the new coat of arms of Hungary or not. Much less effort was spent on the regulation of economic aspects like the privatization of factories, banks, etc. This situation has been exploited by several groups in different areas of the economy and banking for their own goals (Inzelt 2011: 360). Because Hungary was a moderately developed country there was not enough capital. The newly formed banks and enterprises were often operated by businesspeople who were just starting out, and the newly formed political parties also needed financial resources.

Since the change of the political and economic systems, new forms of white-collar crimes have appeared in Hungary. Although different forms of white-collar crimes have always existed in all previous political and economic systems, the transition periods produced special opportunities for white-collar criminal activities, mostly for the people who were close to the political parties and/or had good connections with the establishment (Inzelt 2011: 360).

Collusion of the political élite and the entrepreneurs, i.e. certain forms of state–corporate crime (as defined by Kramer et al. 2002: 263–282), has a long history in Hungary. The state orders were always the best businesses, e.g. 100 years earlier the building of railways provided outstanding opportunities to make fantastic sums of money; at the end of the twentieth century and the beginning of the twenty-first century, highway construction played a similar role, i.e. an extra income for the politicians as well as the source of the party financing in the last two decades. Ibolya Dávid, then the president of the MDF (Hungarian Democratic Forum), said in 2004 that the governing parties and the opposition parties shared the money originating from overcharging of state-financed projects in such a way that the governing party got 70 per cent, the opposition 30 per cent (Spirk 2004). She probably knew well since she was the Minister of Justice between 1998 and 2002. Although there was some outcry on the part of the parties, nobody sued her.

Typical white-collar crime cases occurring after 2000

The cases that occurred between 1989 and 2000 such as the bank scandals (e.g. Ybl Bank, Lupis brokerage, Agrobank, Postabank), abuse of the development fund, privatization, criminal bankruptcy and phantomization of firms,[2] illegal reclaiming of VAT, the receipt factories,[3] the oil affair,[4] the healthcare insurance fraud, cartels and corruption of politicians have already been analysed in detail (Inzelt 2011: 359–379).

Herein we mention characteristic cases that happened after 2000. Unfortunately, due to the slowness of the criminal justice system, in several cases the criminal proceedings have not finished yet, which is partly connected with the complexity of the cases. Because of that fact, in this study I can explain mostly judgments of the court of first and second instances which are not legally binding and ongoing cases where impeachment has occurred and the first instance trial is taking place at the moment. I also write about white-collar criminal activities that were not treated by the criminal justice system at all.

Finance crime

Fraud and embezzlement: 'The broker scandal' *(Cseri 2003; Féderer 2003; Fekete 2006; Mester 2005; Trencséni 2005)*

The so-called broker scandal, one of the biggest, broke out in May 2003. A huge amount of money (several billion forints, i.e. tens of millions of euros) was at stake. However, what made the case even more remarkable was the fact that prominent public people (politicians, businessmen or leading figures of cultural life) were also involved. The key actor was Attila Kulcsár, the executive director of K&H Bank and the investment adviser of K&H Equities, which was a brokerage firm of K&H Bank. There were many curious elements, including the promotion of Kulcsár to this position since he had no higher education, having finished grammar school only, and had a criminal record after a Ponzi scheme case including bribery and forgery. In fact, he had a falsified broker licence. Nevertheless, he was employed by the CEO of K&H Bank, Tibor E.R., and they had a strong working relationship. Formally, Kulcsár was an employee of the brokerage firm, and he had no direct duty to the CEO. Kulcsár could offer his VIP clients promising high interest rates. His clients certainly were aware that these high interest rates originated from wrongful sources, because they received the money via offshore firms or in a plastic bag delivered by a taxi driver. Later on in the case the victims of this white-collar crime participated actively in the criminal activity.

The case started in the Metropolitan Court on 3 May 2005. The accusations (against Kulcsár and 24 others) were embezzlement, money laundering and forgery of private documents. Twenty-three billion forints were embezzled. The damage to the K&H Bank was 8.3 billion forints. The court of the first instance (in this case the Metropolitan Court) sentenced Kulcsár to eight years in prison and ordered the confiscation of 230 million forints, and ordered the pre-trial detention in July 2008. The court sentenced seven out of the 24 accused to prison and confiscations; and a dozen perpetrators were given suspended prison sentences and fines. However, strangely enough, the CEO of K&H bank (T.E.R.) was acquitted due to lack of evidence. The prosecutor's indictment contained only the persons whom Kulcsár mentioned in his testimony. As Kulcsár modified his testimony the prosecutor modified the indictment and the accused persons. Much of the evidence has been ignored. The file consists of 150,000 pages including 600 pages of Kulcsár's confession (György and Mong 2003; Kende 2009; Mong and Vajda 2009). On 27 May 2010 the Court of Second Instance (the Metropolitan Court of Appeal) repealed the judgment of the Court of First Instance on the ground of unfounded and serious procedural errors, and ordered a new first instance procedure. The case started again in the Metropolitan Court on 1 December 2010. There were several hearings during 2011 and 2013 to clarify several points of this case. The case is still pending in 2014.

White-collar crime cases involving politicians

Party financing and the harsh sentence of a young socialist

Politicians – both from right and left parties – were also involved in the Kulcsár case but none of them were convicted. There were only a few cases where legal actions were initiated against politicians.

One of the first and most publicized cases was that of János Z., the former representative and one of the leading persons of the youth organization of the Hungarian Socialist Party (MSZP), who applied for and got around 100,000 million HUF for different youth organizations. However, it was used for different purposes, most likely for party financing. He was kept for more than two years (from 19 September 2007) in remand, and eventually he was sentenced to eight-and-a-half years in prison on 31 March 2010 (just before the national election) because, according to the judge of Bács-Kiskun County, it was a professional white-collar fraud committed in an organized way. In so doing, the judge applied a relatively new law, which was intended to punish criminals of organized crime. The sentences were rather harsh, not only because János Z. paid back the money at a very early phase of the procedure (it is still a question from which source) but also because what he and his accomplices did had been a general practice for years. Party financing has been maintained by the flow of money from different sources provided by the government for civil organizations, industrial promotion or after a tender including a big amount of money. The other members of the youth organization, altogether 16 accused, were sentenced to between two and five-and-a-half years and their property confiscated. Four of them were fined (Rajnai 2010). After the appeal, this case continued; the next trial started in Szeged in January 2011 where the sentence of János Z. was reduced to six years (Origo (31 January 2011); K-monitor (2011–2014)). He was released in September 2013 after six years.

Although the sentence of János Z. was very harsh, it was certainly rightful. The problem remains, though, that all governing parties and even those in opposition have been involved in some kind of manipulation of reports, fraud and bribery from 1990, and there are several signs that this practice continues.[5]

The real estate swindle in downtown Budapest

According to the charge the local municipality of the VII District of Budapest sold several municipality-owned real estates in 2003 and in 2004 under unclear and suspicious circumstances. Twenty-one persons were charged in the case, *inter alia* György H., the mayor of VII District of Budapest and György G., the chairman of the Economic Council of the Municipality.

In February 2012 the Metropolitan Court – as a Court of First Instance – found György H. guilty of asset misappropriation, abuse of authority and forgery of private documents and sentenced him to one-and-a-half years in prison, two years' deprivation of civil rights and 21 million HUF in fines.

György G. was found guilty of fraud, bribery, asset misappropriation, abuse of authority, forgery of private documents and sentenced to eight-and-a-half months' imprisonment and 366 million HUF confiscation of property (because it was proved that he obtained that sum in bribes).

According to the judgment the former mayor had concluded fictitious consulting contracts, and allocated maisonettes – which were owned by the municipality – for his friends and acquaintances for discounted rents. As far as the chairman of the Economic Council of the Municipality was concerned, he sold 16 municipality-owned properties below the market price (albeit it was disputed by the experts) for acquaintances' companies and via these offshore companies resold the real estates for much higher prices. He got in each case a bribe of around 20–30 million HUF. The Court of Second Instance approved the previous judgment in October 2013 in Szeged (Index (24 February 2012); HírTV (2 March 2013); Hungarian News Agency (MTI) (15 April 2013); K-monitor (1999–2014); Mandiner (19 June 2013)).

Bribery

The case of the generals

Another widely publicized legal proceeding was started against generals and other military officers as well as the former Minister and Secretary of the Ministry of Defence in 2010 because of corruption in an organized form between 2001 and 2009. They pressed the companies that supplied different materials or provided service to the army to bribe them for the business opportunity. At the end of February 2013 all defendants have been acquitted in their absence at the first instance. In his summing up, the judge said that accusations of the public prosecutor were based entirely on the confession of one of the generals (Hungarian News Agency (MTI) (28 February 2013)).

Another scandal in the military circle was the case of J. Szabó, the rector of the Zrinyi Miklós National Defence University, who was sentenced to four years in prison for abuse of authority in 2012 (Hungarian News Agency (MTI) (13 January 2012 and 14 January 2012)).

Relationship between business and politics after 2010

There are several cases that have been brought to light by the media. These are not criminal cases (at least for the time being) but they are relevant to the present discussion. The characteristic feature is the preference for people who have been close to the present governing party. In public procurement processes involving all areas of business from motorway constructions to media, these entrepreneurs got the projects. Recently, there were even cases without any public procurement by using the argument of outstanding interest of the state, or accelerating the procedure. Several scandals erupted also in the course of the distribution of state-owned agricultural lands and licensing of tobacco shops. The commission of advisory firms (e.g. lawyers' offices) by ministries and municipalities follows a similar practice as during the previous governments, i.e. friendly firms get the money. Albeit, nowadays this is one of the charges against several functionaries of ministries, municipalities and state-owned firms that were in charge between 2006 and 2010 in the ongoing lawsuits (Keserű and Vincze 2011; Mong 2012).

The study of concrete cases always sheds light on the complex nature of white-collar criminality. The affairs discussed above are typical white-collar cases. Those include financial crime with the involvement of top managers of a bank in partnership with leading persons of the economy, media and politics. It is also evident that high-ranking politicians, office holders and military officers have more opportunities and less risk in all countries; however, newly born democracies are more vulnerable due to shortcomings of the law and the inadequate activity of law enforcement. This will be discussed in the next section in detail.

Exploration of white-collar crime

In this section I deal mostly with corruption, economic crime, corporate crime and state–corporate crime, which are the most harmful types of white-collar crime in Hungary, making use of the analyses of Hungarian experts.

Interrelation of politics and economy and its changing face

The fundamental element of the economic and political transition in Hungary was to separate the closely intertwined economic and political spheres. In the socialist period both the economy and politics were parts of the state: the direction of the planned economy was both an economic and political process; directors of the largest corporations were found in the Central Committee of the Hungarian Socialist Workers' Party. Both the political and economic élite careers were easily interchanged at that time (Vedres 2006: 1339). The aim of the transition was to establish a democracy where parties compete for votes and to create a market economy with free competition.

The existence of the grey and black economy, tax evasion, lack of business morals, are traceable to the socialist period. It can be stated that the basis of the present day's economic and organized crimes has been developed from the socialist period under the previous mentioned factors and features (Barabás and Irk 2001: 60–66). A former prosecutor, Mihály Tóth, analysed the problem of the black and grey economy, i.e. why a substantial number of firms continue with their illegal activities, do not pay taxes and other duties or pay much less than they should. It is partly due to overtaxation, i.e. paying all the duties would ruin the company, but the entrepreneurs also exploit the opportunities offered by the shortcomings of the law and the inadequate activity of law enforcement. The inconsistent and fast variations of the laws and uncontrolled state support system have also contributed to the expansion of different forms of white-collar crimes such as corruption including bribery, cronyism, embezzlement, fraud and insider trading. In addition to adequate legislation, he emphasizes the importance of the development of written and unwritten business ethics and the moral development of the Hungarian economy (Tóth 2009: 5–23).

Economic and white-collar crimes appear to be contagious, i.e. if market players have started to use unfair tools in order to strengthen their positions in the market, sooner or later others will behave in a similar way, especially if it is not followed by rapid detection and appropriate punishment (Korinek 2009: 39–57).

It should, however, be mentioned that getting round the law and tax fraud became almost a national pastime during the previous centuries. There are many examples in the history of Hungary of the people's tricks aimed at evading taxation (in many cases overtaxation) by Hungarian kings and noblemen, by the pashas during the Turkish occupation, or of the bribery of officials to achieve their goals. The experience of ordinary people was that there was no connection between the law and justice; powerful people were never punished.

The relationship between politics and corruption during the last 24 years in Hungary can be divided into three periods (Lengyel 2010: 11). The first period was between 1989 and 1994. It was the *Wild East* or *Gold-digger* era. Features of this period are spontaneous privatization, the uncontrolled political system, the change in the direction of corruption from the shortage economy of socialism when the corruption was directed from buyer to seller to the opposite direction, i.e. from seller to buyer (Kránitz 2006: 10–11), which implied that the invisible power of information became more important. During privatization a huge amount of money went from public ownership to private ownership. Sufficient private capital was not available, because the socialist system did not allow for the accumulation of private capital (see also Korinek 2009: 48). Therefore, the so-called *capital of connections* which survived the change of the regime became very important. Unfortunately, the misuse of insider information – e.g. in public procurements – is still observed in Hungary.

The second period spanned from 1994 to 2004 can be called the *consensual corruption era.* The market of corruption was regulated by agreements between the main political parties in Hungary. The parties concluded three agreements: the first one occurred in 1993 in which the treasurers of the parties agreed on the utilization of the parties' headquarters and on the methods of party and campaign finance. The second contract was in 1994 after the change of government. The heads of the governments made an informal pact that they would not unveil each other's former corrupt transactions and the ruling party would not make it impossible for the opposition to have access to the current state economic resources. They were permitted to carry out negative smear campaigns in the media, but could not bring criminal proceedings.

The third agreement dealt with the regulation of public media, the distribution of commercial television and radio frequencies and sharing the infrastructure investment funds, e.g. building, highways, roads, bridges or investments in education, culture and the healthcare system. In order to achieve this type of funding method, the parties needed to establish their own business network via networks of offshore companies and other enterprises. In this way both the parties and the entrepreneurs involved used illegal money with no real control.

The third period, named the *Cold War period*, started in 2004 and still exists. In October 2004 the new prime minister wanted to eliminate the corrupt consensual system.

The common and secret corruption circle was terminated among the political parties. The internal development resources ran out, and so the direct sharing of large investment projects has finished. As a consequence the main economic actors directly make approaches to the members of parliament for a favourable regulatory change (Lengyel 2010: 11–20).

Several authors have raised the question of 'who guards the guardians'. If civil society cannot control the actual power/government, the elite's self-punishment and self-cleaning policy is just make-believe (Horváth 2010: 47).

The crucial cause of Hungarian political corruption (or white-collar criminality) is the malfunctioning of the Hungarian economic system. During the socialist regime the main reason was the shortage of goods and services; in present days it is overproduction. The problem with impeachment of white-collar criminals is that these persons are part of the same political network as their possible accusers (Kőhalmi 2010: 301).

While whitening, i.e. the elimination of the grey economy, has been the topic of political discourse during the last decades, the whitening of government not of the economy would be the absolute priority (Sebestyén 2008). It is of primary importance since the proper utilization of public funds depends on state and political decision-makers. The relationship between white-collar and economic crime during the transition from planned economy to market economy was discussed by Tóth. According to him, despite the development in this field of criminal law, there are still gaps and shortcomings in the law that have been misused by persons in business, banking, as well as in politics (Tóth 2006: 409–11).

Analysis of recent events can be found in the National Integrity Study (NIS) 2011 (Burai and Hack 2011: 1–279). It was pointed out that there is a close relationship between the political and business élites, and the institutions of control are not independent, either. The best expression to describe the situation is *state capture*: a situation where powerful individuals, institutions, companies or groups within or outside a country use their power to dominate and define a nation's policy, legal environment and economy for their private interests. This can be observed in Hungary. The whole situation is partly connected with the inadequate regulation of party and campaign financing.

The new feature for Hungary since 2007 – when the previous NIS study was published – is the high risk of political influence on the control institutions. While state audit institutions, ombudspersons, constitutional courts, prosecution services and the judiciary are strong pillars of the integrity system in most European countries, in Hungary these institutions are at significantly higher risk of conflicts of interest of political and control functions. Control agents used to be politicians before. Constitutional court judges are selected because of their political background, judges were appointed by the governing party without consensus while earlier new judges were always elected on the basis of a multiparty agreement. As a consequence of the weakened control system in Hungary, business and political interest groups are able to influence the operation of the state.

The National Integrity Study 2011 also emphasized that the regulations on party and campaign financing are inadequate because the spending limit is very low. Parties still submit their reports with unrealistic figures to comply with the law. According to the calculations 90 per cent in 2006 and 75 per cent in 2010 was financed from illegal sources. Research showed that 65 per cent of public procurement procedures were somehow related to corruption, and a substantial amount of public funds is illegally diverted to finance political campaigns through transactions of the business community. The weakening of the control institutions helps state–corporate crime (Aulette and Michalowski 1993: 171–206) even in a more intense form. We witness several state actions (laws, regulations, distributions of goods) where the government gave preference to companies and individuals (mostly close to the ruling party), which caused serious harm to enterprises, free competition, and also taxpayers in general. There were cases when a cartel was initiated by the Ministry of Agriculture. A typical example was the so-called watermelon case (Index (21 July 2012)), when the ministry forced companies to sell watermelon at a fixed prize. The government's purpose was to oust a huge shipment of imported watermelon from the market. The otherwise rather strict Hungarian Competition Authority (HCA) did nothing. A similar event was the new regulation of taxi companies in Budapest which introduced a uniform price without any possibility of discounts, which means the total elimination of competition between companies (Kurunczi and Székely 2013). In this case the HCA expressed its concern but no fine was imposed. Another strange case was when gambling was banned on the basis of moral arguments (Hungarian News Agency (MTI) (2 October 2012); Index (25 June 2013)). It happened overnight with no compensation nor opportunity to appeal against the decision. Consequently, several owners lost their businesses, and employees their work; however, later new casinos were permitted, of course, with new players in the market. The redistribution of tobacco shops (Hungarian News Agency (MTI) (11 September 2012)) happened in the same way. In order to protect the health of young people, the government regulated the number and location of tobacco shops. It might have been an action with good intentions; however, strangely not the experienced shop managers and companies got permission but instead new ones from the circle close to the governing party. We can consider these and several other actions not mentioned herein as the redistribution of the market by state regulations for private gain.

Noémi Alexa, the head of the Hungarian branch of Transparency International, emphasized that despite the new and increased number of regulations, corruption has not disappeared; instead, it has become more organized. The initiation of any legal procedure also depends on the political parties which are actually in power (Plankó and Tamás 2012).

The Visegrad Integrity System Study (Jancsics 2012: 1–74) on the Corruption Risks in the Visegrad Countries (Czech Republic, Hungary, Poland and Slovakia) made a comparison concerning integrity issues. It established that there are common and special features in the four post-socialist countries. Based on the research results, business is the weakest sector in Poland and Hungary and prosecution is especially weak and vulnerable to direct political influence in the Czech Republic and Slovakia. This study claims that the state capture mechanism is working in a different way in Hungary where corrupt interest groups are able to capture the state and in Poland where the state captures business. However, since about 2012 the situation became more complicated in Hungary. While state capture still prevails, the state's intervention in the business and banking sphere has become strongly enhanced. The latter helps the private enrichment of politicians, their relatives and cronies.

One of the most important findings of the Visegrad research is that

> an adequate legal framework cannot provide sufficient protection against doubtful individual or organizational behavior in these post-communist countries. Too much political influence over institutions and over-politicized public administration also seem to be a common and serious deficiency among V4 countries. Party financing is another critical issue in the region that has a significant negative impact on the integrity system.
>
> *(Jancsics 2012: 8)*

It seems to be that the transition countries are facing similar problems whose origins are the historical, legal, political, economic and cultural heritage of the countries.

Attempts to measure the extent of white-collar crime

There are several reasons why white-collar crime is practically immeasurable. First is its latency. Second, there are no such statistics of the law enforcement agencies. Statistics on economic crime, corruption, etc. can give us the basis for estimation; however, those are unreliable, too. Third, another problem is the definition; in some cases it covers too many kinds of crime or it is reduced only to certain sorts of criminal activity.

According to the Unified Criminal Statistics of the Police and Prosecution Services[6] in Hungary in the last 22 years the number of the reported corruption cases was between 300 and 1000 (see Figure 11.1). In this analysis we use the legal approach of corruption according to the criminal law valid in Hungary, involving the offences of bribery and trading in influence.

The number of offenders was between 190 and 500, and the number of convictions was between 110 and 350.[7] The number of registered corruption offences shows a fluctuation due to the nature of

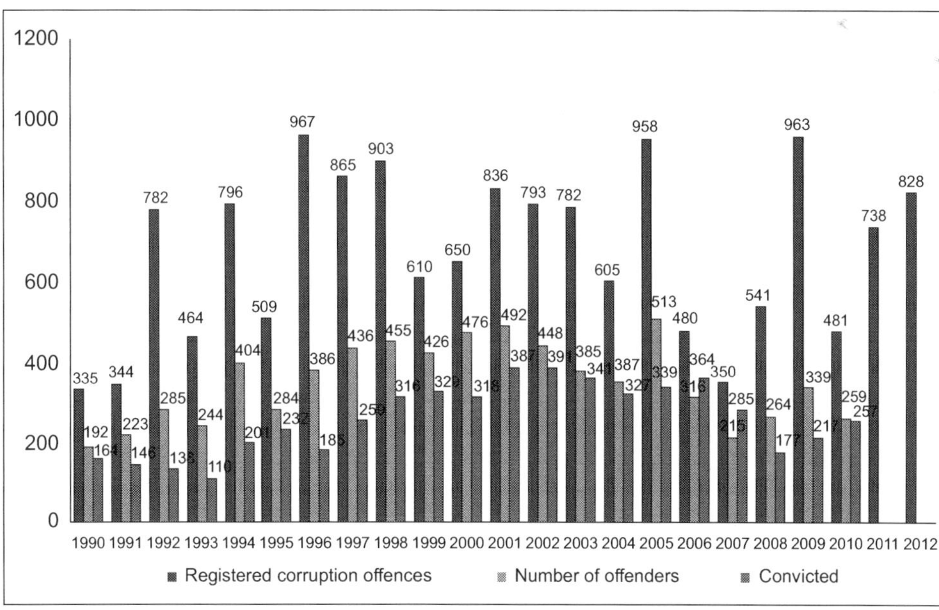

Figure 11.1 Number of registered corruption offences, offenders and convictions in the criminal statistics in Hungary

the statistics based on relatively small samples. The ratio of corruption within the total registered crime rate is around one thousandth due to its latency. It should be mentioned that among the registered corruption cases we could only find *petty corruption* cases. Unfortunately, only a few high-profile perpetrators (e.g. politicians or businessmen) have been prosecuted.

However, the real extent of briberies could not be revealed from the statistical data. These data were able to show the minimum number of corruption cases in Hungary. Because of that we need empirical research to figure out the approximate volume of these crimes.

The Transparency International Corruption Perception Index (CPI) scores countries on a scale from 0 (highly corrupted) to 10 (very clean) which is a result of different sources (poll of polls). According to it the score of Hungary is 4.8 ± 0.3 with a slightly declining trend. The rank of the country deteriorates: 31–33 (1991– 2004), 39–43 (2005–2007), 46–54 (2008–2012). From this data it follows that Hungary is perceived as a moderately corrupt country.

According to the criminal statistics from the last 22 years, registered economic crimes continuously increased (see Figure 11.2.).

The number of economic crimes has increased after the transition, but their proportion (3 per cent of the total registered crime) has not changed significantly (in 2009 4.3 per cent, in 2010 4.7 per cent), except for the year 2011 when it was 7.2 per cent.

Sentencing practices for economic crimes show that the typical punishment is the fine. The rate of fines among all the conventional convicted was near to 50 per cent a year, while it was around 60 per cent for economic crime offenders. The rate of immediate imprisonment has increased in recent years, but the rate of 4 per cent is far from the 10 per cent of the total conviction rate. Studies of those convicted of economic crimes show that the proportion of university or college graduates and women is much higher than in the average population of convicts (Tóth 2006: 407). The punishment is still not proportional to the amount of money involved and to the moral harm for society; i.e. 'it is worth a go'. Tóth also published several data. For instance, in the 2000s the damage caused from the point of view of criminal law was about 30 billion HUF

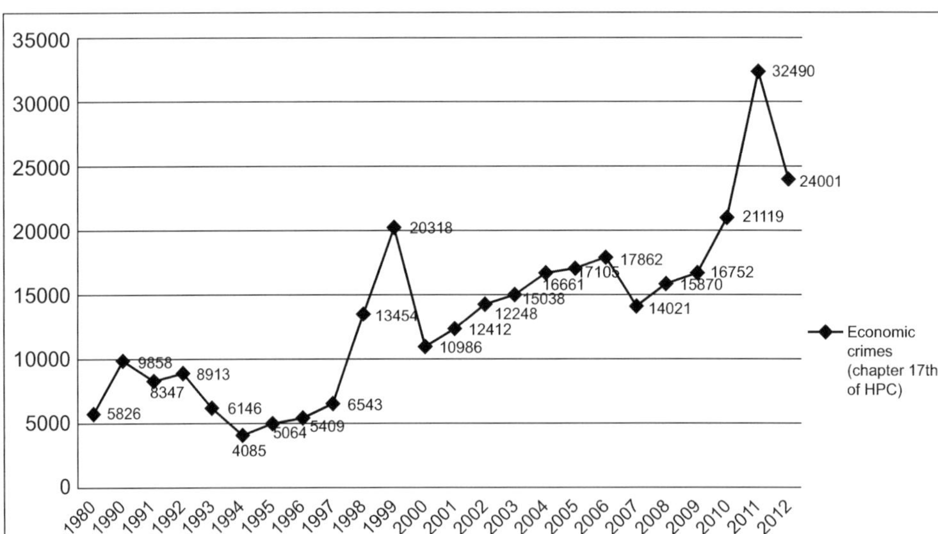

Figure 11.2 Number of registered economic crimes in Hungary in 1980 and between 1990 and 2012

a year, which is equal to about 120 million euros. Rate of return of damages was approximately 20 per cent a year (Tóth 2006: 406–408).

Research conducted by Vedres and others analysed the linkages between politicians and large companies in Hungary between 1987 and 2001. The main research question was how stable and exclusive the political parties' corporate relations are. The sample was 1696 companies, the biggest in the country at that time. The results show that most companies (45 per cent) maintain a stable political relationship (Vedres 2006: 1339–1344). It could mean that the parties have their own 'network' among the important economic actors.

We have to mention some recent empirical research on organizational corruption in Hungary (Jávor and Jancsics 2011: 181–197). Based on 42 in-depth interviews the authors drew the conclusion that corruption is closely related to the power system of the organizations. The illegal acts occur with the participation of all players from the top management down to the people in lower positions. For the execution of corrupt businesses, networks are formed by the managements of companies, lawyers, political actors, decision-makers at different state offices, e.g. responsible for the public procurement processes, etc. The connection among the participants is established by corruption brokers.

Any statistics, surveys and research based on interviews with representatives of the authorities and business and analysis of the available data are certainly useful; however, usually they do not reveal the true dimensions of white-collar crime, especially corruption and state capture which have been studied extensively. The criminal statistics rather show the effectiveness of the law enforcement agencies, and in many cases the methodology is questionable (e.g. 100 cases involving 100 euros committed by a single person counts 100 times more than one case where a million euros was involved).

Conclusion

White-collar crime is present even in societies that have long democratic traditions and stable economic systems. In the states where the political and economic systems have been changing, special problems arise. Similar events have occurred in all former socialist countries. Because the changes started in Hungary, the other countries might have been able to avoid at least some of the mistakes by looking to the experiences of Hungary. States where these changes will take place in the future may also profit from these experiences. It would be useful if they could be prepared for the inevitably arising problems occurring during such a transition, and prevent opportunities for white-collar crime.

The problems during the transition in Hungary can be summarized as follows:

1 The unprepared legislative and the justice system; law enforcement was unable to follow such fast changes. Private interests prevailed; in some cases – due to the mutual interest of the players in economic and political spheres – could even prevent effective jurisdiction. Party financing was not regulated properly, or the regulations were broken with no consequences because every party was involved.
2 In Hungary the situation of white-collar criminality was not different from that in other states at a similar level of economic development and social structure (constitutional democracy, market economy, etc.). At the dawn of the change of regime spontaneous privatization and later the state-run privatization opened up opportunities for rapid and sometimes large-scale enrichment. Due to the uncertainty of the law, the loopholes in the law and deregulation, not all suspected cases were unlawful. The judiciary has also been confused, a situation which, unfortunately, still prevails. There were and still are

very unfortunate consequences with legal proceedings lasting for many years, sometimes more than ten years, and the sentences were rather erratic. Contradictory judgments were made, e.g. the accused was convicted at the first instance, and acquitted at the Court of Appeal or vice versa. One of the reasons for this was the underdeveloped conceptual and legal framework for economic crimes. In many cases, the prosecutor refused to prosecute on the basis of police investigative material. Many behaviours were unethical but were legal. Corruption occurred not only in the economic sphere but also in politics even at high levels. Practically all types of white-collar crime have been committed in Hungary in the last 24 years such as securities fraud, deceit of consumers, tax evasion, bribery, economic and political corruption, insider trading, larceny, forgery of private documents, asset misappropriation, capital investment fraud, negligent administration/defalcation, money laundering and embezzlement.

3 In the fight against white-collar crime, improvement of legislation and the activity of law enforcement is inevitable; the wicket gates should be closed; punishment should be proportional to the amount of money involved and the moral harm to society. However, the moral state of the society is also crucial. The latter is connected with the history, moral and political cultural heritage of the country and standards of life. The latest developments have made the situation even worse. Although several regulations and campaigns against corruption have been initiated, their impact has been negligible. According to several experts, white-collar crimes including corruption have not diminished but became organized. In the immediate future or in the long term several measures should be taken. Among these are the liberation of the independent institutions from political influence, the regulation of party funding, long-term anti-corruption education and programmes, transparency concerning state spending, projects and players, as well as transparent and accountable state decisions. Unfortunately, improvements seem to take a long time. There are several reasons for this. One of the evident points is that as the governing parties and leading persons change, they again want to take part in the redistribution of national wealth. They continue the same practice as their predecessors. The hostility between the parties increases as less state wealth remains and politically initiated legal proceedings are taken against members of the opposition to regain possessions of state.

Notes

1 See in Horace (Quintus Horatius Flaccus) *Satires*, Book I, 'The miseries of the wealthy', 1–91.

2 The expression 'phantomization of the firms' means: after the bankruptcy of a firm with a substantial debt the firm was sold legally with the participation of a lawyer's office; however, the consumer used a false identification (sometimes they used stolen passports).

3 VAT fraud became widespread in the 1990s in Hungary. Fictitious – without completion – invoices were issued and the respective amounts of VAT were reclaimed. Companies specialized in this kind of activity. For example the so-called 'receipt factory of Vecsés', in which more than 70 companies were involved, caused damage of 5 billion forints (approximately 2 million euros). It was important that the legislation observed the loopholes and introduced – albeit rather late – more detailed and effective regulations in this field.

4 The state – for reasons connected to social policy – had subsidized for a long time oil used as fuel in burners for heating by selling it at a lower price. They coloured it by adding a dye; however, it was very easy to remove by a treatment with sulphuric acid. There was a 'great' chance for abuse. One of the biggest oil scandals was the so-called 'Energol case'. The Energol firm dealt with oil imports. They paid taxes on the cheap oil; however, later they removed the dye and sold it as fuel for vehicles at a much higher price. The case was reported to the police by the Bureau of Consumer Protection in 1996 for 'marketing of product of bad quality'. The damage was approximately 2.5 billion forints (another estimation was 6.7 billion forints).

5 The Freedom House (FH) Europe and Transparency International (TI) Hungary have a joint initiative to bring more transparency and accountability to party and campaign financing in Hungary. They named their project 'képmutatás' which means 'hypocrisy'. According to the Electoral Procedure Act, parties can spend around 400 million HUF on their election campaigns. According to the estimation of FH and TI, the parties currently in parliament spent ca. 15 billion HUF on their parliamentary election campaigns during the last election 2010. The main problem with the Hungarian regulation of the party and campaign financing is that it allows many opportunities for clientalism. http://kepmutatas.hu/english/ (accessed 19 May 2014).
6 http://crimestat.b-m.hu/Default.aspx (accessed 19 May 2014).
7 Unfortunately no data are available for the number of offenders and convicted persons in 2011 and 2012.

References

Aulette, J.R. and Michalowski, R. (1993) 'Fire in Hamlet: A case study of state–corporate crime', in K.D. Tunnell (ed.) *Political Crime in Contemporary America: A Critical Approach*, New York: Garland, pp. 171–206.

Barabás, A. and Irk, F. (2001) 'Gazdaság, bűnözés, gazdasági bűnözés, szervezett bűnözés, szervezett gazdasági bűnözés I. rész', *Kriminológiai Tanulmányok*, OKRI 38: 60–66.

Goel, R.K. and Nelson, M.A. (2010) 'Causes of corruption: History, geography, and government', *Journal of Policy Modeling*, 32: 433–447.

György, B. and Mong, A. (2003) *Milliárdok mágusai: A brókerbotrány titkai*, Budapest: Watergate Könyvek. Vízkapu Kiadó.

Horváth, Cs. (2010) 'A politikai korrupció közvetett eszközei és formái', in F. Csefkó and and Cs. Horváth (eds) *Politika és korrupció: A törvényesség és törvénytelenség határai*, Pécs: Konferencia kötet, p. 47.

Inzelt, É. (2011) 'White-collar crime during the political and economic transition in Hungary', *US-China Law Review*, 8: 359–379.

Jancsics, D. (ed.) (2012) *Corruption Risks in the Visegrad Countries: Visegrad Integrity System Study*, Budapest: Transparency International Hungary, 1–74.

Jávor, I. and Jancsics, D. (2011) 'Szervezeti korrupció: Empirikus vizsgálat és modell', *Kriminológiai Közlemények*, 70: 181–197.

Kende, P. (2009) *Nesze neked, igazság!/A Kulcsár-ügy*, Budapest: Hibiszkusz Könyvkiadó Kft.

Kőhalmi, L. (2010) 'Büntetőjogi eszközök a politikai korrupció elleni küzdelemben', in F. Csefkó and Cs. Horváth (eds) *Politika és korrupció: A törvényesség és törvénytelenség határai*, Pécs: Konferencia kötet, pp. 299–301.

Korinek, L. (2009) 'A gazdasági bűnözés kriminológiai szempontú megközelítése', *Rendészeti Szemle*, 57(7/8): 39–57.

Kramer, R.C., Michalowski, R.J. and Kauzlarich, D. (2002) 'The origins and development of the concept and theory of state-corporate crime', *Crime & Delinquency*, 48(2): 263–282.

Kránitz, M. (1999) 'A fehérgalléros bűnözés Magyarországon az ezredfordulón', *Kriminológiai és kriminalisztikai Tanulmányok*, 36: 35–54.

Kránitz, M. (2006) 'On corruption', in *Fight Against Corruption*, Budapest: IM, pp. 10–11.

Lengyel, L. (2010) 'Korrupció és politika', in F. Csefkó and Cs. Horváth (eds) *Politika és korrupció: A törvényesség és törvénytelenség határai*, Pécs: Konferencia kötet, pp. 11–20.

Lévay, M. (2012) 'A gazdasági bűnözés jogi kontrollja Magyarországon a rendszerváltozás óta', in *Bűnügyi Tudományi Közlemények 9. Tanulmányok*, Bíbor Kiadó Miskolc, pp. 103–104.

Lévay, M. and Inzelt, É. (forthcoming) 'Relationships between the financial crisis and the economic crime in Hungary: Legislative responses to the financial crisis', in *Conference Book on International Conference of the Max Planck Institute for Foreign and International Criminal Law on the 'Let's Prevent the Last One! Regulation, Law Enforcement and the Financial Crisis'.*

Mong, A. and Vajda, É. (2009) *Az ártatlanok kora*, Budapest: Elektromédia Kft.

Schäfer, I. (1948) *A 'fehérgalléros' bűntettes*, Budapest: Pázmány Péter Tudományegyetem.

Sutherland, E.H. (1949) *White-Collar Crime*, New York: Dryden Press.

Tóth, M. (2006) 'A fehérgalléros bűnözés; a gazdasági bűnözés', in K. Gönczöl, K. Kerezsi, L. Korinek and M. Lévay (eds) *Kriminológia-Szakkriminológia*, Budapest: Complex, pp. 406–411.

Tóth, M. (2009) 'Húsz év mérlege, Gazdasági bűneink és következményeink egy szép új világban', *Rendészeti Szemle*, 57(7/8): 5–23.

Vedres, B. (2006) 'Politikusok a magyar nagyvállalatok hálózatában 1987–2001 között', *Magyar Tudomány*, 11: 1339–1344.

Newspapers and Internet sources

Burai, P. and Hack, P. (eds) (2011) *Corruption Risks in Hungary 2011 – National Integrity Study*, Transparency International. Online. Available HTTP: <http://www.transparency.hu/uploads/docs/Corruption_Risks_in_Hungary_NIS_2011.pdf> (accessed 19 May 2014); and <http://www.transparency.hu/uploads/docs/Attacking_public_interest.74.pdf> (accessed 19 May 2014).

Cseri, P. (2003, 13 July) 'A bróker merész karrierje', *Népszabadság*.

Féderer, Á. (2003, 17 July) 'Kulcsár milliárdokkal sakkozott', *Népszabadság*.

Fekete, G.Á. (2006, 24 August) 'Függőben lévő brókerügyek újabb vádemelés Kulcsár Attila ellen', *Népszabadság*.

HírTV (2013, March 2) *Ítélőtáblán a Hunvald-ügy anyaga*. Online. Available HTTP: <http://mno.hu/ahirtvhirei/itelotablan-a-hunvald-ugy-anyaga-1142275> (accessed 19 May 2014).

Homepage of the Unified Criminal Statistics of the Police and Prosecution Services. Online. Available HTTP: <http://crimestat.b-m.hu/Default.aspx> (accessed 19 May 2014).

Horace (Quintus Horatius Flaccus) *Satires*. Book I 'The miseries of the wealthy', 1–91.

Hungarian News Agency (MTI) (2012, 13 January) *Hír Tv: Négy évet kapott a Zrínyi volt rektora másodfokon is*. Online. Available HTTP: <http://hvg.hu/itthon.bunugy/20120113_zrinyi_volt_rektora> (accessed 19 May 2014).

Hungarian News Agency (MTI) (2012, 14 January) *Jogerős: Négy évet kapott a Zrínyi volt rektora*. Online. Available HTTP: <http://mandiner.hu/cikk/20120114_jogeros_negy_evet_kapott_a_zrinyi_volt_rektora> (accessed 19 May 2014).

Hungarian News Agency (MTI) (2012, 11 September) *Cigarettabevételek: A Nemzet Dohánya*. Online. Available HTTP: <http://www.piacesprofit.hu/kkv_cegblog/cigarettabevetelek_a_nemzet_dohanya/> (accessed 19 May 2014).

Hungarian News Agency (MTI) (2012, 2 October) *Betiltották a nyerőgépeket*. Online. Available HTTP: <http://index.hu/gazdasag/magyar/2012/10/02/megszavaztak_a_nyerogepek_betiltasat/> (accessed 19 May 2014).

Hungarian News Agency (MTI) (2013, 28 February) *Tábornokok pere: Mindenkit felmentettek*. Online. Available HTTP: <http://index.hu/belfold/2013/02/28/tabornokok_pere_mindenkit_felmentettek/> (accessed 19 May 2014).

Hungarian News Agency (MTI) (2013, 15 April) *Nagyobbacska kavarás a Hunvald-ügy másodfokú tárgyalása körül*. Online. Available HTTP: <http://mno.hu/belfold/nagyobbacska-kavaras-a-hunvald-ugy-masodfoku-targyalasa-korul-1152118> (accessed 19 May 2014).

Index (2012, 24 February) *Másfél év börtönt kapott Hunvald György*. Online. Available HTTP: <http://index.hu/belfold/2012/02/24/iteletet_hirdetnek_a_hunvald-perben/> (accessed 19 May 2014).

Index (2012, 21 July) *Dagad a dinnyebotrány*. Online. Available HTTP: <http://index.hu/gazdasag/magyar/2012/07/21/dinnye/#> (accessed 19 May 2014).

Index (2013, 25 June) *Strasbourgban védik a nyerőgépeket*. Online. Available HTTP: <http://index.hu/gazdasag/2013/06/25/strasbourgban_vedik_a_nyerogepeket/> (accessed 19 May 2014).

K-monitor (1999–2014) *Belvárosi ingatlanpanama*. Online. Available HTTP: <http://www.k-monitor.hu/adatbazis/aktak/belvarosi-ingatlanpanama> (accessed 19 May 2014).

K-monitor (2011–2014) *Zuschlag János*. Online. Available HTTP: <http://www.k-monitor.hu/adatbazis/cimkek/zuschlag-janos> (accessed 19 May 2014).

Kepmutatas. Online. Available HTTP: <http://kepmutatas.hu/english/> (accessed 19 May 2014).

Keserű, J. and Vincze, O. (2011, 14 December) 'Furcsa közpénzügyek, torz elszámoltatás – ez volt 2011 a K-Monitor szerint', *HVG*. Online. Available HTTP: <http://hvg.hu/velemeny/20111214_k_monitor_2011> (accessed 19 May 2014).

Kurunczi, G. and Székely, L. (2013) *Az alapvető jogok biztosának Jelentése*. Online. Available HTTP: <http://www.ajbh.hu/documents/10180/111959/201303268.pdf> (accessed 19 May 2014).

Mandiner (2013, 19 June) *Kiengedték a börtönből a Hunvald-ügy fő vádlottját*. Online. Available HTTP: <http://mandiner.hu/cikk/20130619_kiengedtek_a_bortonbol_a_hunvald_ugy_fo_vadlottjat> (accessed 19 May 2014).

Mester, Á. (2005, 18 August) 'Kulcsár kihallgatása: Videojáték', *Magyar Narancs*.

Mong, A. (2012, 17 July) *Nyergesék első milliárdjai I*. Online. Available HTTP: <http://atlatszo.hu/2012/07/11/nyergesek-elso-milliardja-i-tuntesd-el-az-adossagot/> (accessed 19 May 2014).

Origo (2011, 31 January) *Enyhítették Zuschlag büntetését: Tudósítás percről percre*. Online. Available HTTP: <http://www.origo.hu/itthon/percrolpercre/20110131-zuschlagper-masodfoku-itelet-kihirdetese-percrol-percre.html> (accessed 19 May 2014).

Plankó, G. and Tamás, G.B. (2012, 28 March) 'Már lefizetni sem kell', *Index*. Online. Available HTTP: <http://index.hu/belfold/2012/03/28/transparency/> (accessed 19 May 2014).

Rajnai, A. (2010) 'Zuschlag mosatlan milliói', *Élet és Irodalom*, 55(39).

Sebestyén, T. (2008) 'A politikai korrupció piramisa és kármultiplikátora', *Polgári Szemle*. Online. Available HTTP: <http://www.polgariszemle.hu/index.php?view=v_article&ID=277> (accessed 7 July 2014).

Spirk, J. (2004, 6 May) '70-30-as kampányba kezdett az MDF', *Index*. Online. Available HTTP: <http://index.hu/belfold/mdf0506/> (accessed 19 May 2014).

Trencséni, D. (2005, 27 September) 'Az ügyészség álmennyezete', *Élet és Irodalom*.

World Bank (2000) *Anticorruption in Transition: A Contribution to the Policy Debate*, Washington, DC. Online. Available HTTP: <http://siteresources.worldbank.org/INTWBIGOVANTCOR/Resources/AnticorruptioninTransition.pdf> (accessed 7 July 2014).

12

Retroactive prosecution of transitional economic crimes in Croatia

Testing the legal principles and human rights

Petar Novoselec, Sunčana Roksandić Vidlička and Aleksandar Maršavelski

Introduction to the historical, political and economic background

After the fall of the Berlin Wall in 1989, a political crisis began in former Yugoslavia that led to its dissolution. Although in this period Yugoslavia chaired the Non-Aligned Movement, a severe recession was at its peak, reaching an annual inflation rate of 2665 per cent and an unemployment rate of 15 per cent at the turn of the 1980s and 1990s (Engelberg 1991). In the new decade, most countries of former Yugoslavia, including Croatia, went through one of the most difficult transitions of all European countries. Apart from the recession, the difficulties were related to two major factors that impacted this transition simultaneously: (1) Yugoslav wars, and (2) the process of privatization and ownership transformation. These two contexts have determined two categories of transitional economic crimes committed in this period: (1) *war profiteering*, and (2) *crimes in the process of privatization and ownership transformation*. However, in many cases the transitional economic crimes[1] amounted to both categories as the circumstances often intertwined.

During and after the Croatian War of Independence (1991–1995), Croatia had suffered major financial losses due to the severe armed conflict that took place. According to the findings of State Audit Report the direct war damage in the period 1990–1999 was DEM 65 billion, i.e. 32 billion euros (Perković and Puljiz 2001: 235). An important part of the war damage was a result of war crimes and collateral damage. In addition to this, every war brings the war profiteers along with it: 'People who are harmed and killed in war often die unnecessarily gruesome deaths, often the hands of those in uniforms. [...] No matter who shoots whom, certain power elites make a profit' (Nordstrom 2004: 33). Although Croatian war profiteers abused the state of war for personal financial gain (e.g. setting disproportionately high prices of basic products, sale of state property substantially below its value, etc.), the profiteering was not included in the overall amount of war damage. And not only that, how much war profiteers gained was never officially revealed.

On the other hand, the process of privatization and ownership transformation, which began in 1988, was far from transparent and fully legal. The initial concept was to transfer a substantial part of the state-owned corporations' shares to the workers for a privileged price, but a substantial number of shares were purchased by hawkers and peddlers, while corruption was omnipresent (see Derenčinović 2001: 7–33; Grozdanić and Martinović 2012; Luburić et al. 2010: 13–20; OECD 2000). Therefore, this chapter will provide an analysis of the problems of combatting transitional economic offences, primarily from the process of privatization and ownership transformation in Croatia from the beginning of the privatization process in 1988. We shall reveal the impact that was given to the findings of the State Audit Report that carried out revisions of the privatization processes in 2004. Although auditing bodies are different from truth commissions, their controlling tasks include truth-finding activities which make applicable what Laplante (2008) said for truth commissions, as they 'could contribute to post-conflict recovery first by diagnosing the socioeconomic causes of conflict and then by issuing recommendations that would orient national political agendas toward addressing poverty and structural inequalities, namely through the promotion of sustainable development' (331). Following the publication of the report in 2004, a new approach has been searched for in order to bring those cases to justice. Ultimately this resulted in passing the Constitutional amendments allowing retroactive prosecution of all transitional economic crimes in 2010. Although the public took with great acclamation the proposed legislation and the prosecutions created great expectations, so far only eight criminal proceedings have reached first instance judgments. The most interesting case for the general public and with a high impact for the development of morality and justice in society is the case against the former prime minister of Croatia, Ivo Sanader. As the first instance judgment, based partially on the Law on Exemption from Statute of Limitations for War Profiteering and Crimes Committed in the Process of Ownership Transformation and Privatization (2011, hereinafter: Law on Exemption), was just recently rendered, we will devote part of this chapter to elaborate this case in more detail.

Impunity for perpetrators of serious transitional economic crimes that occurred in Croatia prior, during and immediately after the Croatian War of Independence is an example of ill treatment and neglect of committed economic offences in conflict and post-conflict society. The new legal tools to prosecute these crimes, however, opened many questions from criminological, sociological, political and legal perspectives: 'It is necessary to examine why economic, social and cultural rights have not traditionally been a central part of transitional justice initiatives and whether there are real impediments to the pursuit of such a comprehensive ideal of justice in societies in transition' (Arbour 2007: 4). The Constitutional amendments and subsequent legislation, while trying to provide a solution toward combatting transitional economic crimes, also created some ambiguities. This is particularly related to the definition of the crimes that are exempted from the statute of limitations, the prescribed time-frame of perpetration of those crimes, and the legal continuity and retroactive application of the exemption from the statute of limitations. There is no doubt that the European Court of Human Rights will address the latter issue in the following years.

Finally, it is important to discuss whether the introduction of new legal tools, like the ones that were adopted in Croatia after 25 years since privatization began, will fulfil the quest for justice. If we see these long-needed transitional justice mechanisms applied to strengthen economic rights and the principle of justice, then the Constitutional amendments should be welcomed with acclamation in those societies that have long neglected prosecution of economic crimes committed in the transitional period. Welcomed but with an important remark – the new legal tools must be enforced with reason and in accordance with the rule of law – if not, an additional circle of injustice would be created.

Reflection of an age – treatment of (transitional) economic offences in Croatia from 1988 until 2011

In the last two decades Croatia has been through at least four political transitions[2] while shifting from an economy based on 'social' state-ownership (*društveno vlasništvo*) and socialist self-management (*socijalističko samoupravljanje*) to the capitalist market economy. These political transitions include: (1) gaining independence from being a constituent republic within Yugoslavia, (2) shifting from a single-party communist governance to a semi-presidential democratic system, (3) transformation from a conflict to a post-conflict state, and ultimately (4) shifting from a semi-presidential system to a parliamentary democratic system (see Dolezal 2010: 60–61). The dynamics of these political transitions substantially impacted the privatization process itself.

The process of privatization and ownership transformation, which began in 1988, was far from transparent and fully legal, especially during the rule of President Franjo Tuđman (1990–1999). The initially established concept was to transfer a substantial part of the state-owned corporations' shares to the workers for a privileged price, but hawkers and peddlers managed, sometimes illegally, to purchase the shares from the workers and obtain managing control of these corporations for an excessively low price. In addition to this, corruption was omnipresent, with the realization of President Tuđman's plan to create a wealthy class of '200 families' that would control major companies in Croatia (see Gall 2000). Therefore, in Croatian history, the 1990s shall be remembered not only for the War of Independence, but also as the period of 'privatization robbery' (*privatizacijska pljačka*). The economic consequences of that period are obvious: low production, high unemployment, high national debt, poverty in the devastated parts of the country, etc.

The process of transformation of social enterprises already started in the former Yugoslavia by adopting the Enterprise Act 1988 which enabled a transformation of social enterprises into corporate enterprises. The Law on Transactions with Disposal of Social Capital 1989 enabled the acquisition of the social capital of enterprises. The transformation and the privatization process continued in Croatia on the basis of these laws also after dissolution of Yugoslavia up to and until the adoption of the Social Enterprises Transformation Act 1991 replacing the Law on Transactions with Disposal of Social Capital 1989. The Social Enterprises Transformation Act 1991 remained in force in Croatia until January 2011, when the new Law on Management of State-Owned Property 2010 replaced it. Parallel to the laws that were passed and in order to ease privatization and ownership transformation processes, Croatia adopted a new up-to-date Company Act 1993, which was mainly a reception of the German company law (Novoselec and Roksandić Vidlička 2010: 699). Privatization is defined, pursuant to Art. 1 para. 2 of the Privatization Act 1996, as the sale of shares, assets and rights and transfer of shares of the transformed state-owned enterprises without payment to natural persons or legal entities in a manner defined by the Privatization Act 1996 itself.

Moreover, the privatization law was very complex, because the legislator endeavoured to transform the former enterprise capital, but also wanted to enable particular groups (employees, disabled persons and similar) to acquire shares on favourable terms. Various exceptions led to ambiguities, which in some cases made it more difficult to estimate if there was a wrong interpretation of the Law, wrong practice or abuse that would justify criminal prosecution.

Furthermore, legal pluralism was present throughout the phases of Croatian transition and, particularly, a dichotomy existed between company law and criminal law and between provisions of criminal law itself. In Croatia there is a lack of in-depth analysis in addressing the critical questions that countries in transition are faced with, such as: 'what kind of changes does post-communist transition imply for criminal law'? (Solomon 2013: 95) or 'how does the law react, to state-supported crime committed before a political system change'? (Eser et al.

2002: 1). That ultimately hindered the full application of the Company Act 1993 (and all the laws that were regulating privatization and ownership transformation), which most certainly contributed to numerous illegalities in business dealings and processes of ownership transformation and privatization.

The causes of such an unsound legal system are twofold. On the one hand, the Croatian government was focused primarily on finding adequate solutions to the ongoing armed conflict, leaving all other problems aside. On the other hand, within the Croatian government certain politicians, while being aware of the loopholes, did not demonstrate the political will to change the chaotic legal system because some of them personally benefitted from it (directly or indirectly).

Furthermore, the changes in the political and economic system during this period make Croatia comparable with other countries in the region (e.g. Hungary: see Inzelt 2011: 352–378) that have shifted to a market economy and undergone a privatization process (a common denominator with other countries of central, eastern and southeastern Europe). However, Croatia had at the same time experienced war and peaceful reintegration (a differentiating factor). This differentiating factor, or *local context* (Teitel 2003: 93), has proven to be of a dominant nature for the Croatian transitional society, at least for prioritizing protection of civil and political rights over economic ones. According to Teitel (2003: 93), two political dimensions determine what signifies rule of law in periods of transition: the transitional context, specifically the circumstances relating to political and legal conditions associated with periods of political change, and other political factors, such as local context. Neglecting economic rights in Croatia led to a number of social, economic, political and legal problems in the years that followed and created conditions for what Durkheim calls the state of anomie, as Cejp and Scheinost stated for Czech Republic: 'as a result of the social disintegration and disorientation brought by fundamental and ongoing changes in values and behavioral patterns' (Cejp and Scheinost 2012: 158–159). Although the mentioned circumstances make Croatia's transition somewhat specific, political weakness in addressing economic crimes in conflict and post-conflict societies was not typical only for Croatia (see Bassiouni 2010: 18). The countries in transition share some common characteristics: increase in volume of crime, growing anomie, growing weakness of control mechanisms, emergence of new types of crime, decrease in the efficiency of law enforcement, limited economic sources, perception of an erosion of the state monopoly of legitimate violence, omnipresent fear of crime and preoccupation with safety concerns, etc. (Albrecht 1990: 448–450).

One of the most common side-effects of transition is the 'state of de-regulation' or anomie, i.e. a 'condition in which society provides little moral guidance to individuals' (Macionis and Gerber 2010: 97) because of the breakdown of social bonds between the individual and society.

Durkheim's anomie theory demonstrates the repercussion of such a situation to crime: 'Every abnormal relaxation of the system of repression results in stimulating criminality' (Durkheim 1897/2005: 330). Although more empirical research is needed to confirm this statement for Croatia, the *State Audit Office Report on Revision of Ownership Transformation and Privatisation* (2004) is a good indicator of unachieved results of privatization, at least for its first phase that lasted until 1994, as we will see in the following section.

The growing anomie in Croatia caused two parallel stages of mass delinquent behaviour that Merton calls 'rebellion' and 'innovation'. While the 'rebellion' was linked to the War of Independence, the 'innovation' was linked to unjust enrichment. The war and transition profiteers wanted financial power – the main 'culturally induced success-goal' in the new capitalist society:

> The extreme emphasis upon the accumulation of wealth as a symbol of success in our own society militates against the completely effective control of institutionally regulated modes

> of acquiring a fortune. Fraud, corruption, vice, crime, in short, the entire catalogue of proscribed behavior, becomes increasingly common when the emphasis on the culturally induced success-goal becomes divorced from a coordinated institutional emphasis.
>
> *(Merton 1939: 678)*

Since the institutionalized legitimate means for accumulating wealth was limited, the *nouveau riche* used 'innovative' means to achieve their goals: corruption, tax evasion, fraud, etc.

The economic transformations that took place required an adequate criminal law response; however, the legal order did not manage to keep up with the new economic order. The descriptions of most economic crimes in the Yugoslav criminal legislation were completely obsolete and were adverse for the new constitutional order in Croatia. At the beginning of 1990s, after abolishing a broad but very state-protective criminal offence of 'robbery of public finances' (*pljačka*), for which there was a prescribed punishment of up to 20 years of imprisonment (Criminal Code of the Socialist Republic of Croatia 1977, Art. 143), the state budget and state-owned companies remained only partially protected with the remaining prescribed criminal offences. In addition to this, the criminal legislation was inadequate to deal with the challenges of the free market economy, where state officials do not play a crucial role any more, but corporate managers instead. Unfortunately, it took too long to pass the new legislation and once it was passed, it was not completely sound. With the enactment of the Criminal Code 1997, the Croatian government attempted to introduce criminal offences that would address rising economic crime; however, it also wanted to preserve continuity with the old legislation, thereby creating 'hybrid' economic criminal offences. Still the new economic crimes lagged behind their time and the vast majority of them originated in the legal system based on social ownership. For example, the key economic criminal offence of 'abuse of office and authority' (Art. 337 of the Criminal Code 1997) was originally designed in former Yugoslavia with the purpose of criminalizing financial abuses by public officials and managers of (public) companies. This worked well in socialism, where there was practically no difference between the public and private economic sectors as everything was practically owned by the state. However, this offence was proven to be inadequate when privatization began and private companies were introduced; namely, responsible persons in private enterprises were not comparable to public officials any more, which means that they ought to bear different types of responsibility.

On the other hand, in order to preserve continuity with the old legislation and avoid loopholes at the same time, some economic crimes amended or introduced in Criminal Code 1997 were vaguely broad. For example, the crime of 'abuse of authority in business dealings' (Art. 292 of Criminal Code 1997), originally designed in Yugoslavia for criminalizing the so-called *beneficial malversations* (i.e. for the benefit of the state-owned companies), remained still in force with an expanded definition that had the purpose of addressing new types of economic crime. Both criminal offences remained in the Criminal Code until 2011 although they significantly overlapped, causing unequal application in practice (Novoselec and Roksandić Vidlička 2010: 700). In addition to this, there were loopholes as some criminal offences were missing in the legislation (e.g. subsidy fraud, bankruptcy, etc.).

An example can be used to illustrate the overlapping nature of the aforementioned criminal offences 'abuse of office and authority' and 'abuse of authority in business dealings'. Before the Croatian Supreme Court there was a case of a defendant, a legal representative of several corporations, whose shares he sold to individuals at a low price. Afterwards, he bought the same shares on the behalf of the corporations at a high price, while splitting the price difference (approximately 2 million euros) with those individuals. According to the Croatian Supreme Court Decision (2002), the defendant was convicted for abuse of office and authority (Art. 337 Criminal Code 1997) and sentenced to seven years of imprisonment. However, a better solution would have been to convict the defendant for 'abuse of authority in business dealings' (Art. 292 Criminal Code 1997), because he did not act as state official but as a corporate manager. This example is one of the typical *modus operandi* that occurred in the privatization process.

The Law on Amendments to Criminal Code 2003 made substantial interventions in the field of economic crimes, but unfortunately the Constitutional Court repealed the amendments for procedural reasons and they were never enforced (the law was not passed with qualified majority). Therefore, the first comprehensive reform with the purpose to adequately address contemporary economic crimes failed. The Criminal Code amendments of 2004 only partially accepted the solutions that were unsuccessfully proposed by failed reform in 2003. Hence, those obsolete economic offences, based on so-called administrative socialism, survived in somewhat changed forms until the extensive reform of economic crimes took place with passing the new Criminal Code 2011. This reform of economic crimes, its definitions and conceptualization was also, as the Company Law in Croatia, under significant influence of German law. The new reform of the Croatian criminal law of 2011, including the reform of economic offences, was associated with the accession of Croatia to the European Union in 2013 (the same year that Criminal Code 2011 entered into force), which requires, to a certain extent, the harmonization of national criminal law systems. The harmonization requirements included, for example, legal protection of market competition from prohibited cartels, suppression of frauds damaging the EU budget, combatting active and passive bribery in business dealings, insider trading, etc. In the meantime, the Law on Responsibility of Legal Entities for Crimes was passed already in 2003 enabling criminal prosecution of legal entities, but since the substantive criminal legislation was inadequate, the new Law was not able to address contemporary economic crimes committed by corporations.

There are several social and political reasons for these flaws in criminal law legislation. We have already mentioned some: related to the state of war that had been taking most of the political attention, and political unwillingness to pass new legislation because of the personal benefits of the status quo by certain high-ranking officials. In addition to these, the problem was with certain law commissions that drafted the proposals of new legislation, which were sometimes appointed according to the political preferences, which means that they lacked enough power to introduce much needed changes. Furthermore, the opinion of experts was not always given much attention by the ruling officials. However, even when the law commissions were appointed independently from politics, some Croatian legal experts lacked knowledge about the rules of a free market economy, and how they work in practice. In addition, this contributed to flaws and frequent legislative amendments that created legal uncertainty. Frequent legal amendments are also typical for other countries in transition: e.g. Russia has already amended Chapter 22 of its Criminal Code, regulating economic crimes, two dozen times and, in the process, introduced ten new additional business-related crimes (Solomon 2013: 99).

The shift in paradigms: new legal responses to combat transitional economic crimes and initial concerns about the applicability of introduced responses

After a long period of neglecting criminal prosecutions of transitional economic crimes (see e.g. Rajkovic 2011), a turning point occurred in 2010 when the general public finally demanded a reaction from politicians and justice authorities. The public perception of the impact of the transitional economic crimes became more obvious when the State Audit Office (2004) published the Transformation and Privatization Revision Report. However, from the criminal law point of view, the report seemed in most cases irrelevant because the statute of limitations for economic crimes committed in the process of transformation and privatization was soon to expire, or had already expired. Even the Transformation and Privatization Revision Report decisively stated the same (Final State Audit Office Report on Revision of Ownership Transformation and Privatisation 2004: 41). The formal legal obstacle did not prevent a necessary criminal policy reaction because the constitutional quest of social justice prevailed, and new solutions had to be found as a reaction to irregularities found in the report.

The State Audit Office found irregularities in 1936 audited cases, of which 1215 irregularities did not qualify as criminal acts, but merely contained inconsistencies in financial reports (without evidence of deliberate financial misrepresentation). From the remaining 721 irregularities, for 271 there was a reasonable doubt that they could qualify as criminal offences and 247 as misdemeanours, while 203 irregularities were no longer punishable after enactment of the new Law on Issuance of and Trade with Securities 1995. For 71 irregularities, crime reports were filed to the prosecution's office. Where there was insufficient evidence, State Audit Office filed 107 notifications with all elements normally included in the offence reports; criminal charges were not brought in cases in which the charges had been brought earlier and where the facts and the legal basis were the same, and if upon enactment of the new laws the irregularity would no longer qualify as a crime. When the report was published, 93 criminal proceedings were pending (State Audit Office Report on Revision of Ownership Transformation and Privatisation 2004: 43). The main cases concerned were related to the auditing findings that: (1) payment claims of other corporations to the enterprise had been unlawfully transformed into investing assets, or when (2) a property, which was not included in the estimated value of the enterprise, had been unlawfully sold (State Audit Office Report on Revision of Ownership Transformation and Privatisation 2004: 17–18). Although aware of the fact that the statute of limitations had expired or would soon expire, reports and notifications were filed from the State Audit Office regardless of the time of perpetration of the act due to the Constitutional amendments.

The Constitution was amended in June 2010 in order to prescribe exemption from the statute of limitations for criminal offences committed in the course of economic transformation and privatization and for the war profiteering crimes perpetrated during the period of the Croatian War of Independence and peaceful reintegration, wartime and during times of clear and present danger to the independence and territorial integrity of the state. It also prescribed that any profit obtained by such criminal acts or in connection therewith would be confiscated.

Ivo Josipović, president of Croatia, not only eagerly supported the Constitutional amendments, but he was one of its initiators. President Josipović proposed amendments to the Constitution in order to enable prosecution of transitional crimes already in 2007, stating that this new regulation was necessary for 'the restoration of justice and the return of the moral principles in the economic development of the society'. When the Law on Exemption was passed in 2011, Mrs Jadranka Kosor, then prime minister, gave the statement: 'From this day on it will not be the same for those who thought about their benefit while young people were dying in the war'.

The Decision Proposal to Amend the Constitution of Croatia (2009) explicitly stated that the amendment adopted an exemption from the statute of limitations for transitional economic crimes, because such crimes are regarded, both by the public and expert groups, as extremely grave crimes for which it is necessary and just to rule out the application of statute of limitations, particularly having in mind the time, circumstances and consequences of such crimes. Moreover, the Decision Proposal to Amend the Constitution of Croatia (2009: 8) specified that transformation and privatization did not have the expected economic outcomes, hence transformation and privatization had no significant positive impact on the economic development of the state:

> Quite contrary, the implementation of transformation and privatization resulted in the increase of domestic and foreign debt, caused a significant increase in unemployment, disproportionate and fast enrichment of individuals, and unjust impoverishment of many. Also, on the other hand, this implementation caused the fall of wages and pensions in real terms in comparison to costs of living and a number of other consequences. It is just and in spirit of international law to deny the perpetrators of such grave crimes the possibility to avoid criminal liability by application of the institute of statute of limitations. The basis for the institute of statute of limitations is the guarantee of legal certainty to citizens, but it is certain that this institute should not be the benefit for the perpetrators enabling them to practically legalize the effects of such acts through statute of limitations.
>
> *(Decision Proposal to Amend the Constitution of Croatia 2009: 8)*

In other words, it is clearly apparent that without the Constitutional amendments most of the reported criminal acts could not be prosecuted today because of the expiration of the limitation period. Therefore, the publication of this Report was of great importance as Laplante (2008) stated for the role of truth commissions in general. Although it was not a report from an independent body such as a truth commission, it contributes to post-privatization recovery by diagnosing privatization's failures and by issuing recommendations that would orient policy makers toward addressing breaches from the privatization processes. Hence, the public mood in Croatia changed, demanding responsibility from politicians and privatization profiteers, and this shift in paradigms demanded a criminal law reaction as other forms of responsibility seemed inadequate to respond to grave breaches committed in privatization.

However, no matter how luminous the idea of passing such Constitutional amendment was, its effective application is not an easy task for prosecutors. According to the European Commission on Democracy Through Law [Venice Commission] Report on the Rule of Law (2011: para 48), legal certainty also means that actions or promises given by the state to individuals should in general be honoured (the notion of the 'legitimate expectation'). Moreover, 'legal certainty – and supremacy of the law – imply that the law is implemented in practice. This means also that it is implementable' ([Venice Commission] Report on the Rule of Law 2011, para 51). However, the crimes were committed long ago; many perpetrators and witnesses have already passed away (or their testimony lacks credibility due to the time elapsed); a lot of concerned companies do not exist any more; financial documentation is destroyed or non-existent; there are difficulties in collecting evidence; and such *ex post facto* amendments again create legal uncertainty. According to financial accounting regulations, accounting documents and financial reports must be kept between seven and 11 years from the year to which documents relate.

Furthermore, the problems that are emerging in prosecution of transitional economic offences committed more than 20 years ago are not only legal in nature. There is also fierce opposition by parties with financial interests, as well as the risk of political manipulation. Therefore, 'legitimate expectation' given by the state to individuals by amending the Constitution and banning the statute of limitation for transitional economic crimes will be hard to justify. As mentioned, so far only eight cases reached first instance judgments. However, according to the press releases of the State Office for Administrating State Property, in the process of privatization and ownership transformation 7700 stock holders of 3270 corporations have abused the statutory privileges in stocks transactions, directly damaging the state's budget for at least DEM

200 million (100 million euros, Jutarnji list 2013). In addition to this, many major state-owned corporations of the socialist period had been ruined by dubious investors who not only purchased them below their value, but also drained out all the money and shut them down after bankruptcy. Therefore, we can conclude that Croatia introduced legal mechanisms to address crimes committed in privatization and ownership transformation and is determined to put an end to impunity of profiteers. However, the success of the reform will depend on the realization of those mechanisms by the enforcement bodies.

New approach to transitional justice: the Law on Exemption from Statute of Limitations

General introduction

An approach toward (re)building transitional and post-conflict societies based solely on the improvement of civil and political rights[3] was proven to be counterproductive (Carranza 2008: 329). It is more and more argued among scholars that neglecting the prosecution of transitional economic crimes only enhances an impunity gap and social conflict by focusing almost exclusively on civil and political human rights violations while leaving accountability for economic crimes behind: 'literature, institutions and international enterprises of transitional justice historically have failed to recognize the full importance of structural violence, inequality and economic (re)distribution to conflict, its resolution, transition itself and processes of truth or justice-seeking and reconciliation' (Miller 2008: 266; see also Parmientier and Weitekamp 2007: 110–111). As Carranza (2008:310) argues, while transitional justice promotes accountability by what it chooses to confront, it may reinforce impunity by what it chooses to ignore. In our opinion, the strengthening of the protection of economic and social rights in transitional states, including adequately regulating economic crimes, is a *conditio sine qua non*, especially in states that shifted from a socialist economic system to a free market economy. As Sutherland (1940: 6) points out, the financial loss from white-collar crime, great as it is, is less important than the damage to social relations: 'White-collar crimes violate trust and therefore create distrust, which lowers social morale and produces social disorganization on a large scale.' Therefore, the retroactive approach to introducing non-application of the statute of limitations for transitional economic crimes seems to be the major legal solution in overcoming anomie in Croatian society.

It is interesting to note that Sutherland's initial study was also about war profiteering. In his famous book on white-collar crime, Sutherland (1949: 164–175) dealt with various unlawful acts by 70 large corporations (e.g. DuPont) in the US during the two world wars: (1) violations of special war regulations against profiteering, (2) tax evasion, (3) restraint of trade on war materials, (4) interference with war policies in order to maintain competitive positions, (5) violations of embargoes and neutrality, and (6) treason. The documentary evidence he analysed indicated that many corporations abused the national emergency as an opportunity for extraordinary enrichment (Sutherland 1949: 175). However, the names of all corporations have become public only in the 1983 uncut version of the book as they were left out in the initial publication because of fear of legal action: most of the corporations have never formally been convicted of crimes related to war (see Sutherland 1983; see also Galliher and Guess 2009). The list is most stunning as it includes the great names of American corporate capitalism: 'Its effect on the reader is similar to the listing of atrocities or of crimes of violence without the psychological relief provided by legal terms' (Monkonnen 1984: 293). However, as Galliher and Guess (2009: 173) pointed out: 'Had Sutherland known about the wartime behavior of Kodak, ITT, and IBM it is likely that he would have created a new and more extreme category beyond the "treason" of DuPont. Genocide is one likely candidate'. These arguments bring us to the conclusion that such crimes are not just regular white-collar crimes, but should be treated similarly to international crimes for which statutory limitations do not apply (see UN Convention on the Non-Applicability of Statutory Limitation to War Crimes and Crimes Against Humanity 1968).

As noted earlier, in order to bring back trust in the legal system and enhance social morale, Croatia passed the mentioned Constitutional amendments in order to enable prosecutions for transitional crimes. However, these amendments raised further legal questions that needed to be regulated more accurately: e.g. which crimes should be exempted from the statute of limitations?; what is the temporal applicability of the exemption?; is the retroactivity of this exemption legally acceptable?, etc.

Subsequently, the Law on Exemption was passed in 2011. Article 1 of this Law defines that war-profiteering crimes and transformation and privatization crimes include crimes committed during the Homeland War, peaceful reintegration, wartime and time of clear and present danger to the independence and territorial integrity of the state. We may say that the Constitutional change and the Law on Exemption thereby address the question of change of focus of transitional justice, by giving an affirmative answer to the third question that Mani posed:

> Should transitional justice concern itself directly with the war economies and corruption, particularly the exploitation of natural and mineral resources, as these are often perpetrated by the same war criminals – and with the same abusive, violent and exploitative means and devastating effects on victims – as the war crimes that historically fall within the purview of transitional justice?
>
> *(Mani 1940: 253)*

The Law on Exemption gives the answer to the question by stating that the removal of the statute of limitations addresses equally war profiteering and transitional economic crimes of privatization and ownership transformation. They should be treated equally as they are both equally relevant for the transitional society's development.

The Law on Exemption requires weighing legal principles. A key question that is arising from the application of this Law is how to respect the principles of non-retroactivity, legal certainty and/or principle of justice and fight transitional economic crimes that were unprosecuted for 15 to 25 years. Croatia obviously decided to put an end to the widespread and systematic economic abuses from the time of ownership transformation and privatization that caused enormous loss of profit and workplaces that led to gross social inequality. On the other hand, this new legal tool could bring even more legal ambiguities to the already unjust situation, because some will be prosecuted, while others will manage to escape prosecution due to a lack of evidence. Furthermore, the attempt to impose accountability with retroactive effect through criminal law, as the law of last resort (*ultima ratio*), often raises rule-of-law dilemmas especially in the 'transitional justice' cases and could lead to a high degree of prosecutorial selectivity (Teitel 2003: 76–77). It is especially arguable when a law aims to restore confidence between citizens and the state and among citizens themselves.

Economic crimes to which the Law on Exemption applies

In every armed conflict, there are always unscrupulous individuals called *war profiteers*, sometimes willing even to support the conflict in order to turn a profit from it. Their actions are usually referred to as 'profiteering', which can be defined as 'taking advantage of unusual or exceptional circumstances to make excessive profits as in the selling of scarce goods at inflated prices during war' (Garner and Black 2009: 1330). However, the vulnerable process of ownership transformation and privatization also amounts to 'exceptional circumstances' that make *transition profiteers* (see e.g. Karklins 2005: 89; Perquel 1998: 11). In a situation of war and transition, it is difficult to draw a line between war profiteers and transition profiteers, which is the reason why the two categories were addressed together in the Constitutional amendments.

However, the Law of Exemption differentiates war profiteering crimes from other transitional crimes that occurred in the process of ownership transformation and privatization. The Law defines war profiteering crimes as criminal acts aimed at achieving disproportionate property gains by raising prices for goods in scarcity, by sale of state-owned property far below its value or otherwise taking advantage of wartime and clear and present danger to the independence and territorial integrity of the state. Such a definition leaves many ambiguities and requires interpretation, especially in order to understand what 'excessive property gain' means (Novoselec and Novosel 2011: 615).

On the other hand, regarding other transitional economic crimes, the condition for the applicability of the Law on Exemption *ratione temporis* is that the crimes took place in the transformation and privatization process during: (1) the Homeland War, (2) peaceful reintegration, (3) warfare, and (4) during a direct threat to the independence and territorial integrity of the state. This means that there must be a link between the process of transformation and privatization and the commission of a crime, i.e. that the perpetrator used that process as an opportunity to commit the crime. In addition to this, there are certain temporal requirements related to the time-frame of the application of the Law, but they are not so clear.

First, there is a problem of determining the beginning and the end of the Homeland War. Ultimately, the courts will have to make this determination by taking into account deferring provisions of certain laws. The Law on Liability of the Republic of Croatia for Damage Caused by Members of Armed and Police Forces during the Homeland War (2003) determines the period of the Homeland War from 17 August 1990 until 30 June 1996; while the Homeland War Declaration 2000 of the Croatian Parliament defines the duration of the war as a period from 1991 to 1995.

The next time-frame of the Law on Exemption is 'peaceful reintegration', which refers to the restoration of Eastern Croatian territories (Danube region) that ended on 15 January 1998.

The Law on Exemption is not only applicable to periods of war, but also to times of clear and present danger to the independence and integrity of the state, which primarily refers to the period when it was already certain that there would be war in Croatia. Some Croatian scholars argue that, since the transformation started even before the independence of Croatia – in 1988 – the same year can be taken as the start for the applicability of the Law on Exemption; and the end for the applicability may be taken as 15 January 1998 when a peaceful reintegration occurred (Novoselec and Novosel 2011: 612). Hence, this is also not precisely defined, which means that the courts will have to rule on this.

Finally, the Law prescribes a catalogue of war and transition profiteering crimes, including typical white-collar crimes: fraud, embezzlement, money laundering, bankruptcy, illegal trade, forgery, bribery, abuse of office and official authority, etc.

Many amendments of criminal statutes in the past raise the question of legal continuity, i.e. whether the 'old' crimes correspond to the 'new' crimes while the principle of *lex mitior* is applicable in Croatia. If, namely, there is no such continuity between the Criminal Code applicable at the time of ownership transformation and privatization process and the current Criminal Code 2011, there will be no justification for the punishment under the Law on Exemption from Statute of Limitations. Since the new Criminal Code entered into force, the courts are obliged to examine if there is a legal continuity between repealed and new criminal offences. If the answer is affirmative, the courts are obliged to apply the law in force at the time of commission of the crime, or the new law if it is more lenient for the perpetrator (retroactively *in mitius*). On the other hand, where there is no continuity, the defendant is exonerated. Namely, if the courts would find that for certain economic crimes the chain of legal continuity was at some point 'broken', this may lead to public disappointment with respect to the application of the Law on Exemption from Statute of Limitations. This puts a lot of pressure on prosecutors and judges to interpret the law in a more flexible way and may even lead to violations of defendants' rights.

A further problem of countries in transition is that in fields where civil or administrative instruments have not yet developed, criminal law sometimes gains the position of *prima ratio* means in combatting illegal activities (Albrecht 1990: 452). Thus, there is a danger of 'overcriminalization' (Husak 2008: 3–4) as a way of abusing criminal law to minimize the risk of crime or to achieve other criminal policy goals. Given that law covers a number of crimes, the courts could broadly interpret the correlation of criminal acts and the ownership transformation and the privatization process. Such practice should not be opposed if the main determinant will be the gravity of the damaging consequences, i.e. the amount of obtained property gain and damage that occurred. If that condition is not fulfilled, it is doubtful if the institution of criminal proceedings especially after considerable elapse of time from the perpetration of the offence would serve the principle of justice. Some perceive the *ex post facto* laws as a sign of an overcriminalization tendency because it is theoretically possible to prosecute a perpetrator who committed a $500 fraud in the privatization process 15 years ago. Therefore, in each case the prosecution needs to consider criminal policy issues and the quest for justice before initiating proceedings.

Retroactivity of exemption from statute of limitations as a precondition for transitional justice

As stated earlier, the Constitutional provision and the new Law on Exemption regarding non-applicability of the statute of limitations of transitional economic crimes attracted a lot of public attention. The public expected a significant increase in the number of prosecuted cases (see Novoselec and Novosel 2011: 603), while ownership transformation and privatization with all the implications that followed became a synonym for anomie and unjust enrichment. At the same time, the new provisions raised many legal questions which are not easy to answer. The main one is the retroactive effect of non-applicability of statute of limitations. The question is whether the retroactive application refers to the crimes for which the limitation period has already expired or only to those where the period of limitation still runs (for general arguments for both solutions see Posner and Vermeule 2003/2004: 795–800). As discussed in the previous part of this chapter, for most of these crimes the limitation period has already expired. Therefore, the answer to the question of whether it is legally permissible and tenable to exempt from the statute of limitations crimes for which the limitation period has already expired directly affects the issue of whether the Law on Exemption will stay solely a political proclamation or will be applied in practice (the notion of the 'legitimate expectation'). We refer here to the conclusion of the Venice Commission's Report on the Rule of Law (2011), which says that respecting the principle of legal certainty implies that laws are *implemented* in practice. As Sweeney points out:

> Successor trials have a complex relationship with international human rights law because the conduct of the individual on trial is subjected to a set of standards that is applied with some degree of hindsight and is, therefore, potentially tainted with retroactivity – which runs counter to institutions founded on the rule of law [...] The new democratic regime must attempt to sidestep or eliminate the rule of law dilemma that retroactivity presents through the deployment of legal techniques of varying degrees of ingenuity.
>
> *(Sweeney 2013: 48)*

Chief among these is the appeal to a higher pre-existing law, such as international humanitarian law, which can 'mediate' the rule of law dilemma (Teitel 2000: 21). Other options include strictly applying the law of prior totalitarian regime under which certain actions carried out by that regime should have been criminal at the time (Sweeney 2013: 48–49). Again, we agree with the Venice Commission's Report on the Rule of Law (2011), which says that 'the need for certainty does not mean that rules should be applied so inflexibly as to make it impossible to take into account the dictates of humanity and fairness'.

However, the European Court of Human Rights will ultimately decide to what extent the retroactive application of exemption from the statute of limitations is permissible. As Lamont (2011: 100) argues, it is the ability of regional human rights systems to ensure adherence to human rights norms during processes of political transition and violent conflict that present a key test for supra-national judicial oversight of states:

> In the context of transitional jurisprudence, Yugoslavia's violent collapse and the creation of new states during the 1990s constituted a fundamental test of not just European Union's ability to respond to humanitarian crisis, but of the ECtHR's ability to ensure the protection of human rights norms in the aftermath of violent conflicts and during transitions from authoritarianism.
>
> *(Lamont 2011: 100)*

The question of retroactive prosecution of transitional economic crimes is one of those questions that challenge the protection of human rights norms.

The case against former Croatian prime minister Ivo Sanader

In spite of strong political proclamations, only a few cases have been prosecuted under the Law on Exemption, and only one has reached a final judgment. That is the case against the former Croatian prime minister Ivo Sanader. In August 2011, the prosecution indicted Mr. Sanader because he, during the negotiations of the terms of the loan to be granted by the Austrian bank Hypo-Alpe-Adria International AG to the government of the Republic of Croatia, in position of a Croatian deputy minister of foreign affairs, made a deal that the bank should pay to him in return for that bank's entry into the Croatian market as consideration a commission in cash in the amount of 7 million Austrian schillings, which the bank indeed paid in the course of 1995. The crime was classified as a war profiteering crime and the abuse of office and authority. The contextual link necessary for the application of the Law on Exemption existed as he abused office to

> obtain for himself an unlawful property gain in the amount of HRK 3,610,528.18 [approx. €500,000] in a difficult situation the country was going through [...] during the Homeland War due to a high inflation and extremely high interest rates on loans which made it difficult to find banks ready to grant favorable loans.

In September 2011, the County Court of Zagreb confirmed the indictment, while holding that

> it was beyond doubt that the incriminated period was during the Homeland War, while the objection of the defendant's legal counsel was based on the analysis of facts imputing that the criminal act in question had not been connected to the wartime in the Republic of Croatia in which part of the objection represents an analysis of facts to be deliberated in the course of main hearing.
>
> *(Zagreb County Court Decision 2011)*

In addition to this, in September 2011 the prosecution charged Sanader for receiving a 10 million euro bribe, while serving as the prime minister of Croatia, from Zsolt Hernadi, the chairman of the management board of the Hungarian oil company MOL, in return for transferring the controlling rights in the Croatian oil company INA to MOL. The indictment charged Mr. Sanader with making a deal at the beginning of 2008 with a representative from MOL that he would receive 10,000,000 euros to take action for amending the shareholders' agreement, whereby Croatia would hand the control over INA to MOL. They also agreed that the said amount would include the arrangement of conclusion of an agreement on spin-off of the gas business, which generated losses, from the company INA and the takeover of it by Croatia:

> With the aim of realizing the deal Ivo Sanader, by using his authority as prime minister of the Government of the Republic of Croatia, knowing that the conclusion of such agreements was not in the interest of the Republic of Croatia, communicated and imposed his conclusions prepared in advance about essential elements of the agreements so that the agreements indeed were concluded on 30 January 2009 and all requests of MOL fully accepted, whereupon Ivo Sanader was fully paid the agreed amount in several instalments.
>
> *(Zagreb County Court Decision 2011)*

These two indictments merged into one trial and the trial judgment was rendered on 20 November 2012. Sanader was found guilty on both charges (Zagreb County Court Judgment 2012).

In the judgment, the judges pointed out that Sanader abused his position for its own enrichment and not for the common good. According to the judges, 'this judgment sends a message to people in power, current and future, that holding a public office must be performed for the common good and in the interest of society!' Furthermore, according to the judges, Sanader's behaviour harmed

> not only vital strategic interests but also damaged the reputation of Croatia in the world [...] contributed to apathy and disillusionment of people in the system, created a belief among young people that the honest labour does not pay, but the violation of the law and the morality of the society does.

The judgment emphasized that Sanader was 'the architect of the system [...] that was an illusion of democracy' (Zagreb County Court Judgment 2012).

Sanader was sentenced to, altogether, ten years' imprisonment (three-and-a-half years for war profiteering and the abuse of office and seven-and-a-half years for passive bribery). The prosecution appealed to the Supreme Court because of the duration of punishment, which the prosecutor's office held was too lenient:

> Considering that Ivo Sanader committed the crimes by using the office he held as an official of the highest rank, specifically deputy foreign minister in the wartime in Croatia and later prime minister of the Republic of Croatia, and that he used the office, instead of for the protection of the interests of the Republic of Croatia, for his own interests, the prosecutor's office is of the opinion that the defendant should have been sentenced to imprisonment of the maximum duration. It therefore requested in the appeal from the Supreme Court of the Republic of Croatia to change the judgment of the first instance regarding the penalty and to sentence the defendant Ivo Sanader to a maximum imprisonment of the duration of 15 years.

The defence also appealed and requested reversal of the judgment and a retrial arguing gross violation of criminal procedural rules, wrongly and incompletely established facts, and the sentencing decision:'The most contentious fact is that the court refused a number of witnesses whilst believing false testimonies'. In the Supreme Court Judgment and Decision 2014, the judges of the Supreme Court upheld the first instance judgment, altering only the sentence for Sanader: altogether, eight-and-a-half years' imprisonment (three years for war profiteering and the abuse of office and six-and-a-half years for passive bribery). Since this case represents the first application of the Law on Exemption, it is of great importance for future case law.

This case is not the only criminal case brought against Sanader. In March 2014, he was also convicted of abuses of position and authority, while in office as a prime minister of Croatia, of receiving illegal donations for his political party – the Croatian Democratic Union (one of the two major political parties in Croatia). In the trial judgment of this case he was additionally sentenced to nine years of imprisonment, but due to the concurrence statutory norms, in any case, he will serve no longer than 15 years of imprisonment. Furthermore, there are three more pending criminal trials against him.

The case of Ivo Sanader demonstrates the anomie of Croatian society, in which a profiteer has become a prime minister and subsequently convicted and imprisoned. The Sanader case will very likely have its epilogue before the European Court of Human Rights and in the forthcoming paragraphs a short analysis of similar relevant cases will be given.

Human rights, criminal and political concerns in high-profile transitional economic crime trials

In such high-profile trials dealing with transitional economic crime, one of the most controversial issues is ensuring fair trials and respecting the principle of legality (Articles 6 and 7 of the ECHR). For instance, in the case of Khodorkovskiy and Lebedev v. Russia (2013), the ECtHR found, *inter alia*, a violation of Art. 6 of the Convention on account of the breach of lawyer–client confidentiality, and unfair taking and examination of evidence by the trial court. The case of Geir H. Haarde, who was tried for negligence and mismanagement (abuse of office) during the prelude to the 2008 recession, is also relevant. Haarde was convicted in April 2012 for one of the four charges, based on not holding cabinet meetings when 'things turned critical' (for not discussing the financial situation in the markets frequently enough at cabinet meetings in the period leading up to the crisis in 2008), contrary to obligation of Article 17 of Icelandic Constitution. However, the court did not impose a punishment on Haarde. This case influenced the initiation for drafting the Venice Commission Report on the relationship between political and criminal ministerial responsibility (2013):

> it is clear that criminal procedures against government ministers have to respect Art. 6 of the ECHR on the right to a fair trial, including the minimum rights set out in Art. 6 (3) for persons charged with a criminal offence. The same goes for the principle of 'no punishment without law' in Art. 7. These rules apply regardless of whether the person accused is an ordinary citizen or a government minister, and regardless of whether the minister is charged before the ordinary criminal courts or before a special court of impeachment.

The case of the former prime minister of Ukraine, Yulia Tymoshenko (Tymoshenko v. Ukraine (2013)), is also relevant for answering what constitutes political and criminal responsibility of governmental officials for economic crimes. In 2011, Tymoshenko was charged under Article 365(3) of the Criminal Code of Ukraine (abuse of power) for exceeding her authority and abusing her office in ordering the head of a state-owned enterprise Naftogaz to sign an agreement with the Russian company Gazprom providing for the importation of natural gas at a price of $450 per 1000 cubic meters, which had caused the state to suffer considerable financial losses. She was sentenced in 2011 to seven years in prison for 'misuse of powers' concerning the gas deal and got a three-year prohibition on exercising public functions and the judgment became final in November 2012. In the Tymoshenko case the ECtHR found violation of Articles 5 and 18 of the Convention.

Finally, the ECtHR's reasoning on conformity of the retroactive application of criminal legislation with the principle of legality cases such as Streletz, Kessler and Krenz v. Germany (2001) is also relevant for the Sanader case. In the mentioned case, the ECtHR adopted the Radbruch's Formula of 'statutory injustice' (*das gesetzliche Unrecht*) following the reasoning of the German Constitutional Court. Furthermore, in the landmark case of C.R. v. United Kingdom (1995) dealing with principle of legality, the ECtHR specified that Art. 7 'cannot be read as outlawing the gradual clarification of the rules of criminal liability through judicial interpretation from case to case, provided that the resultant development is consistent with the essence of the offence and could reasonably be foreseen'. The 'foreseeability' of proscribing statute of limitations to transitional cases is one of the issues that will be addressed by the ECtHR in the Sanader case in order to justify or deny the legality of retroactive implementation of the Law on Exemption.

Final remarks: *Realpolitik* vs. restoration of justice and return of moral principles

When gross violations of economic rights take place in transitional settings, the society and the state must find a proper way to respond to such violations. Croatia chose to amend its Constitution, its Criminal Code and to adopt the Law on Exemption from Statute of Limitations. At present, there are only eight first instance judgments in Croatia based on the Law on Exemption of the Statute of Limitations. So far the most important case was the trial against the former prime minister Ivo Sanader. According to the data of the State Attorney's Office, the application of the Law on Exemption from Statute of Limitations is highly probable in 116 cases in which investigations or criminal proceedings are under way (Novoselec and Novosel 2011: 618). Moreover, if the Law on Exemption were not applied retroactively, the aim of its adoption would be missed and this new legal tool would end up as a mere political proclamation. There is a growing dissatisfaction of the Croatian public with the processes of ownership transformation and privatization. If transitional economic crimes are not prosecuted and 'lost property' is not returned to the state, it will probably always haunt society as an unresolved matter. In today's globalized society it is becoming harder to argue that only violent crimes represent a threat to the well-being of humanity and that only they shock the conscience of mankind and justify non-applicability of statutory limitations internationally (see UN Convention on the Non-Applicability of Statutory Limitation to War Crimes and Crimes Against Humanity 1968).

One of the most important questions related to abolishing the application of the statute of limitations for transitional economic crimes is whether such *ex post facto* laws are in conformity with the principle of legality. The sensitivity of the matter is even more visible when we acknowledge the fact that these transitional economic crimes mainly took place during the 'Homeland War' and in the post-conflict period. As Teitel stated, in regional case law, and in transitional jurisprudence, the conception of law is partial, contextual and situated between at least two legal and political orders. Legal norms are necessarily multiple (legal pluralism), while the idea of justice is always a compromise. The transitional cases present a double legal legacy: (1) they are read into domestic judicial reasoning and thereby inform and shape political and legal agendas at the national level, and (2) they can fundamentally strengthen the jurisprudence of the ECtHR (Hamilton and Buyse 2011: 20–21). In our opinion, these legal solutions and tools introduced to fight against transitional economic crimes could serve as a valuable contribution to European and worldwide jurisprudence in (re)building new transitional societies and their economies, either by legally justifying Croatian solutions or by questioning reasoning for its rendering and avoiding the same mistakes.

To answer the question from the title of this chapter, whether *Realpolitik* or *restoration of justice and return of moral principles* would win, after examining recent literature and Reports of the Venice Commission on the Rule of Law (2011) and on the Relationship between Political and Criminal Ministerial Responsibility (2013), we can conclude that both could win, at least in the 'clear-cut' cases when we apply Law on Exemption to cases where statute of limitations did not yet expire at the moment of its entry into force. In cases where it has already expired, a more progressive approach should be taken, in order to achieve social justice and overcome anomie, by allowing retroactivity in those cases as well. As stated in the Venice Report:

> An area of criminal law that may be of particular relevance for ministers is that of corruption, embezzlement and other forms of economic crime. It is of particular importance that such rules be strictly and effectively enforced against ministers and other publically appointed officials, since such offences are not only to be seen as criminal, but may also easily undermine public trust and the legitimacy and authority of the democratic system.
>
> *(Venice Commission Report on the Relationship between Political and Criminal Ministerial Responsibility 2013: para 97)*

The challenge for a democracy is how to reduce opportunities of wartime and/or transition periods for white-collar crime, i.e. how to make the costs of such behaviour so high that it will provide deterrence for profiteers.

We could conclude by expressing moderate satisfaction with the Croatian attempt to put to an end systematic, widespread transitional economic crime that was occurring for more than two decades. On the other hand, selective and non-systematic prosecution, or no prosecution at all, is not something that should occur as a result of the adoption of the Law on Exemption from Statute of Limitations. It is also of the utmost importance to respect human rights standards and guarantee fair trial to all possible defendants. Otherwise, the rule of law and principles of justice will not prevail again.

Notes

1 For the empirical and normative approach to research of economic crimes see e.g. Albrecht 2003.
2 For the 'deeds of fallen dictatorship' see Arnold and Silverman 1998: 140–158.
3 For the overview of truth comissions, see e.g. Wiebelhaus-Brahm 2010.

References

Albrecht, H.-J. (1990) 'Countries in transition: Effects of political, social and economic change on crime and criminal justice – sanctions and their implementation', *European Journal of Crime, Criminal Law and Criminal Justice*, 7(4): 353–485.

Albrecht, H.-J. (2003) 'Forschungen zur Wirtschaftskriminalität in Europa: Konzepte und empirische Befunde', in H.-J. Albrecht and H. Entorf (eds) *Kriminalität, Ökonomie und Europäischer Sozialstaat*, Heidelberg: Physica-Verlag.

Arbour, L. (2007) 'Economic and social justice for societies in transition', *International Law and Politics*, 40(1): 1–27.
Arnold, J. and Silverman, E. (1998) 'Regime change, state crime and transitional justice: A criminal law retrospective concentrating on former Eastern bloc countries in European Journal of Crime', *Criminal Law and Criminal Justice*, 6(2): 140–158.
Bassiouni, M.C. (2010) 'Assessing conflict outcomes: Accountability and impunity in the pursuit of international criminal justice, a world study on conflicts, victimization and post-conflict justice', in M.C. Bassiouni (ed.) *The Pursuit of International Criminal Justice: A World Study on Conflicts, Victimization, and Post-Conflict Justice*, Antwerp: Intersentia.
Carranza, R. (2008) 'Plunder and pain: Should transitional justice engage with corruption and economic crimes?', *International Journal of Transitional Justice*, 2: 310–330.
Cejp, M. and Scheinost, M. (2012) 'Organized and economic crime: A common problem', in A. Selih and A. Zavrsnik (eds) *Crime and Transition in Central and East Europe*, New York: Springer.
CROATIA (1977, 1978, 1984, 1987, 1989, 1990, 1991) *Criminal Code of the Socialist Republic of Croatia*, Zagreb: Narodne novine.
CROATIA (1990, 1997, 1998, 2000, 2001, 2010 and 2014) *Constitution*, Zagreb: Narodne novine.
CROATIA (1991, 1992, 1993, 1994 and 1995) *Social Enterprises Transformation Act*, Zagreb: Narodne novine.
CROATIA (1993, 1999, 2000, 2003, 2007, 2008, 2009, 2011, 2012 and 2013) *Company Act*, Zagreb: Narodne novine.
CROATIA (1995) *Law on Issuance of and Trade With Securities*, Zagreb: Narodne novine.
CROATIA (1996, 1997, 1998 and 2000) *Privatization Act*, Zagreb: Narodne novine.
CROATIA (1997, 1998, 2000, 2001, 2003, 2004, 2005, 2006, 2007, 2008, 2011) *Criminal Code*, Zagreb: Narodne novine.
CROATIA (2000) *Homeland War Declaration*, Zagreb: Narodne novine.
CROATIA (2003) *Amendments to Criminal Code*, Zagreb: Narodne novine.
CROATIA (2003) *Law on Liability of the Republic of Croatia for Damage Caused by Members of Armed and Police Forces during the Homeland War*, Zagreb: Narodne novine.
CROATIA (2004) *Amendments to Criminal Code*, Zagreb: Narodne novine.
CROATIA (2004) *State Audit Office Report on Revision of Ownership Transformation and Privatisation*, Republika Hrvatska: Državni ured za reviziju. Online. Available HTTP: <http://www.revizija.hr/izvjesca/2007/revizije-pretvorbe-i-privatizacije/000-izvjesce_o_radu.pdf> (accessed 8 July 2014).
CROATIA (2009) *Decision Proposal to Amend the Constitution of Croatia*, Zagreb: Vlada RH.
CROATIA (2010) *Amendments to Constitution*, Zagreb: Narodne novine.
CROATIA (2010 and 2012) *Law on Management of State-Owned Property*, Zagreb: Narodne novine.
CROATIA (2011) *Law on Exemption from Statute of Limitations for War Profiteering and Crimes Committed in the Process of Ownership Transformation and Privatization*, Zagreb: Narodne novine.
CROATIA (2011) Zagreb County Court Decision, 6-KOV-US-27/11.
CROATIA (2011 and 2012) *Criminal Code*, Zagreb: Narodne novine.
CROATIA (2012) Zagreb County Court Judgment, K-Us-26/11.
CROATIA (2014) Supreme Court Judgment and Decision, I Kž-Us 94/13-10.
C.R. v. United Kingdom (1995) App no 20190/92, ECtHR, 22 November 1995.
Derenčinović , D. (2001) *Mit(o) korupciji*, Zagreb: NOCCI d.o.o.
Dolezal, D. (2010) 'Organized crime and corruption in Croatia: A criminological view', in S.P. Stoychev (ed.) *Organized Crime and the Balkan Political Context*, Sofia: Risk Monitor Foundation.
Durkheim, E. (1897/2005) *Suicide: A Study in Sociology*, trans. J.A. Spaulding and G. Simpson, London: Routledge.
Engelberg, K. (1991, 20 April) 'Feuds Crippling Yugoslav Economy', *New York Times*. Online. Available HTTP: <http://www.nytimes.com/1991/04/20/business/feuds-crippling-yugoslav-economy.html> (Accessed 8 July 2014).
Eser, A., Arnold, A. and Kreicker, H. (2002) *Criminal Law in Reaction to State Crime, Comparative Insights into Transitional Processes*, Freiburg i.B.: Max-Planck-Institut für ausländisches und internationales Strafrecht.
European Commission on Democracy Through Law [Venice Commission] (2011) *Report on the Rule of Law*, 86th Plenary session, study no. 512/2009, CDL-AD(2011)000rev.
European Commission on Democracy Through Law [Venice Commission] (2013) *Report on the Relationship between Political and Criminal Ministerial Responsiblity*, 94th Plenary Session, study no. 682/2012, CDL-AD(2013)001.

Gall, C. (2000, 3 September) 'A feeble Croatia is battling its ex-leaders', *NY Times*. Online. Available HTTP: <http://www.nytimes.com/2000/09/03/world/a-feeble-croatia-is-battling-its-ex-leaders.html> (accessed 8 July 2014).

Galliher, J.F. and Guess, T.J. (2009) 'Two generations of Sutherland's white-collar war crime data and beyond', *Crime, Law and Social Change*, 51: 163–174.

Garner, B.A. and Black, H.C. (2009) *Black's Law Dictionary*, 9th edn, St. Paul: Thomson West.

Grozdanić, V. and Martinović, I. (2012) 'Corruption as a metaphor for societies in transition?', in A. Selih and A. Zavrsnik (eds) *Crime and Transition in Central and East Europe*, New York: Springer.

Hamilton, M. and Buyse, A. (2011) 'Introduction', in M. Hamilton and A. Buyse (eds) *Transitional Jurisprudence and the ECHR: Justice, Politics and Rights*, Cambridge: Cambridge University Press.

Husak, D. (2008) *Overcriminalization: The Limits of the Criminal Law*, Oxford: Oxford University Press.

Inzelt, E. (2011) 'White-collar crime during the political and economic transition in Hungary', *US-China Law Review*, 8(4): 352–379.

Jutarnji list (2013, 25 June) 'Počinje sudski progon 7700 sudionika pretvorbe i privatizacije: Sporno je 100 milijuna eura u dionicama', *Jutarnji list*. Online. Available HTTP: <http://www.jutarnji.hr/drzava-pokrece-sudski-progon-7700-sudionika-pretvorbe-i-privatizacije-sporno-100-milijuna-eura-u-dionicama/1110965/> (accessed 8 July 2014).

Karklins, R. (2005) *The System Made Me Do It: Corruption in Post-communist Societies*, Armonk, London: M.E. Sharpe.

Khodorkovskiy and Lebedev v. Russia (2013) App no 11082/06 and 13772/05 (ECtHR, 25 July 2013).

Lamont, C.K. (2011) 'Confronting the consequences of authoritarianism and conflict: The ECHR and transition', in A. Buyse and M. Hamilton (eds) *Transitional Jurisprudence and the ECHR: Justice, Politics and Rights*, Cambridge: Cambridge University Press.

Laplante, L.J. (2008) 'Transitional justice and peace building: Diagnosing and addressing the socioeconomic roots of violence through a human rights framework', *The International Journal of Transitional Justice*, 2(3): 331–355.

Luburić, A., Matić, R. and Quien, M. (2010) *Mito i korupcija u hrvatskom društvu*, Split: Redam.

Macionis, J.J. and Gerber, L.M. (2010) *Sociology*, 7th edn, Toronto: Pearson Canada.

Mani, R. (2008) 'Dilemmas of expanding transitional justice, or forging the nexus between transitional justice and development', *The Journal of Transitional Justice*, 2(3): 253–265.

Merton, R. (1939) 'Social structure and anomie', *American Sociological Review*, 3(5): 672–682.

Miller, Z. (2008) 'Effects of invisibility: In search of the "economic" in transitional justice', *The International Journal of Transitional Justice*, 2(3): 266–291.

Monkkonen, E.H. (1984) 'Review of Sutherland, E.H. "White Collar Crime: The Uncut Version"', *Business History Review*, 58(2): 293–294.

Nordstrom, C. (2004) *Shadows of War: Violence, Power, and International Profiteering in the Twenty-First Century*, Berkeley: University of California Press.

Novoselec, P. and Novosel, D. (2011) 'Nezastarijevanje kaznenih djela ratnog profiterstva i kaznenih djela iz procesa pretvorbe i privatizacije', *Croatian Annual for Criminal Law and Practice*, 18(2): 603–620.

Novoselec, P. and Roksandić Vidlička, S. (2010) 'Gospodarska kaznena djela u novom kaznenom zakonu', *Croatian Annual for Criminal Law and Practice*, 17(2): 699–728.

OECD (2000) *No Longer Business as Usual: Fighting Bribery and Corruption*, Paris: OECD.

Parmientier, S. and Weitekamp, E.G.M. (2007) 'Political crimes and serious violations of human rights: Toward a criminology of international crimes', in S. Parmentier and E.G.M. Weitekamp (eds) *Crime and Human Rights*, Bingley: Emerald.

Perković, M. and Puljiz, V. (2001) 'Ratne štete, izdaci za branitelje, žrtve i stradalnike rata u Republici Hrvatskoj', *Revija za socijalnu politiku*, 8(2). Online. Available HTTP: <http://www.rsp.hr/ojs2/index.php/rsp/article/viewFile/225/996> (accessed 8 July 2014).

Perquel, F.-E. (1998) *Financial Markets of Eastern Europe and the Former Soviet Union*, Cambridge: Gresham Books.

Posner, E. and Vermeule, A. (2003/2004) 'Transitional justice as ordinary justice', *Harvard Law Review*, 117: 762–825.

Rajkovic, D. (2011) *How Ivo Sanader Stole Croatia* (in Croatian), Zagreb: Jesenski&Turk.

Solomon, P.H. Jr. (2013) 'Criminalisation, decriminalization and post-communist transition, The case of the Russian Federation', in K. Goodall, M. Malloch and B. Munro (eds) *Building Justice in Post-Transitional Europe? Processes of Criminalization within Central and Eastern European societies*, New York: Routledge.

Streletz, Kessler and Krenz v. Germany (2001) App nos 34044/96, 35532/97 and 44801/98 (ECtHR, 22 March 2001).
Sutherland, E.H. (1940) 'White-collar criminality', *American Sociological Review*, 5(1): 1–12.
Sutherland, E.H. (1949) *White Collar Crime*, New York: Dryden Press.
Sutherland, E.H. (1983) *White Collar Crime: The Uncut Version*, New Haven and London: Yale University Press.
Sweeney, J.A. (2013) *The European Court of Human Rights in the Post-Cold War Era*, London and New York: Routledge.
Teitel, R.G. (2000) *Transitional Justice*, New York: Oxford University Press.
Teitel, R.G. (2003) 'Transitional justice genealogy', *Harvard Human Rights Journal*, 16: 69–94.
Tymoshenko v. Ukraine (2013) App no 49872/11. (ECtHR, 30 April 2013).
UN Convention on the Non-Applicability of Statutory Limitation to War Crimes and Crimes Against Humanity (1968), 754 U.N.T.S. 73.
Wiebelhaus-Brahm, E. (2010) 'Truth commissions and other investigative bodies', in M.C. Bassiouni (ed.) *The Pursuit of International Criminal Justice: A World Study on Conflicts, Victimization, and Post-Conflict Justice*, Antwerp: Intersentia.
YUGOSLAVIA (1988, 1989 and 1990) *Enterprise Act*, Beograd: Službeni list: SFRJ.
YUGOSLAVIA (1989 and 1990) *Law on Transactions with Disposal of Social Capital*, Beograd: Službeni list: SFRJ.

13

Within our walls

White-collar crime in Greek academia

Stratos Georgoulas and Aimilia Voulvouli

Introduction

During the end of the 1990s, Greek academia was shaken to the core by the burst of a huge economic scandal known as the 'Panteion University Scandal' concerning the embezzlement of 8 million euros by high-ranking executives and members of the Rectorate of the University. The scandal was highly publicized by the press for various reasons. First, because of the amount of the embezzlement. Second, because part of the embezzled amount was donated to the University on a regular basis by then prime minister of Greece, Kostas Simitis. Third, because Panteion University is a publicly funded institution, which means that the embezzled sum was public money. Finally, because of the profile of the offenders, who were high-ranking employees, respected academics and public figures. But then, doesn't this last point constitute the archetype of the white-collar offenders? What's more, is the Panteion Scandal the only scandal in Greek academia? If not, why did it shake the Greek academic community so? As Professor Demetris Demeroulis stated, 'It is clear that there was a scandal in Panteion. But in Panteion, an investigation has been conducted about it. The question brought to the fore here is whether other universities have also done the same. They might have … I wish they have. I just don't know that they have' (Kelly 2012). Indeed, Panteion is not the only university in Greece in which white-collar offences have taken place. In the following pages, we will discuss other cases concerning illegalities committed by the state itself and cases concerning not only financial crimes but also cases of illegal hiring of staff, illegal selection of postgraduate students, human rights violations, disciplinary methods against union participation and intellectual theft.

Our main goal is to map an existing, distinctive phenomenon that causes social damage, which is discussed in studies of other disciplines, and is in dialectical relationship with social reality but has not been adequately analysed as a white-collar type of crime. It is our firm belief that using white-collar crime as an analytical tool in order to examine criminality in academia can prove quite fruitful, as far as social research about academia is concerned as well as its correlation with criminal and educational policy.

In doing this, our aim is to answer the following questions: What constitutes the criminogenic character of academia? Is it the social status of the agents, the power they have, and their general social characteristics? Is it the structural and organizational culture that exists in higher education?

A macrosociological approach focusing on the current economic and social crisis as well as on policy making in general and policy making within Greek higher education in particular is also in order to examine how they produce and protect phenomena of white-collar criminality. Who are the victims and what are the social damages caused by such offences? Which criminal policy is applied (if so) and what is the outcome? How does public opinion view this policy? At the same time, the question that arises here is: What are the predicaments that such a research faces given the limited literature on the subject; the limited access of the field; the seemingly all-too-powerful gatekeepers; the virtually non-existent statistics; the fact that cases that have gone to the court are exceptionally few; and the ethics that one should follow? Finally, understanding and approaching the phenomenon of white-collar crime within academia holds a degree of difficulty which lies in the predicament of defining white-collar crime as an analytical tool in all its complexity.

Methodological issues

How can such an issue be approached when there is very limited access to data, as other studies have pointed out? The answer is that these researches rely on materials of the public domain such as official inquiries, newspaper reports (Coleman 1985; Punch 1996), agency records (Clinard and Yeager 1980), interviews (Braithwaite 1984; Carson 1970; Hawkins 1984; Nelken 1991) and participant observation in order to obtain access to data from multiple sources. This is the methodological path that we too have followed. Our research was multi-sited among newspaper archives covering the period from 1992 until today, parliamentary documents, internet websites, interviews with individuals implicated in some of the cases mentioned in this chapter and participant observation. In total we have gone through 89 newspaper articles and interviews, 12 parliamentary documents concerning questions regarding the issues discussed below and six interviews conducted by us. Access to the documents was relatively easy; however getting the interviews was the most difficult task due to the reluctance of the informants to disclose information. It has to be noted here that the anonymity of the people who talked to us is fully protected not only because qualitative methodology entails strict ethical protocols but also because all of our informants are directly involved in the cases that will be discussed below, most of which are still in court.

State of the art

According to Thompson (2002), crime and deviance by academics have not been studied in much detail to date, and definitional or conceptual disputes persist on the specific parameters of such crime and deviance. Friedrichs (2010) stated that the principal types of academic professors and research scientists include plagiarism – although charges are relatively rare – (Green 2002), misuse or embezzlement of university discretionary funds or research grants, forgery or fraudulent claims about credentials, unresolved conflicts of interest in connection with grants (administrators and employees often have better opportunities than professors to embezzle or obtain improper payments), peer reviews or evaluations of students, cheating and unauthorized photocopying, gross negligence in the fulfilment of teaching responsibilities, exposing students or research subjects to unsafe or harmful conditions or procedures, and fabrication of scholarship or the use of fraudulent data in research studies (when research is industry-sponsored, it is significantly more likely to reach conclusions favourable to the industry than when the research funding comes from some other source) (Washburn 2005: 84). The above types of academic crimes help to constitute a theoretical framework for academic crimes to be analysed as white-collar crimes.

For Sutherland the concept of white-collar crime (Nelken 2002: 855) aims at reforming criminological theory against the tendency to explain crime in terms of individual or social pathology. The genealogy of the concept reveals its dual character: on the one hand it indicates the offender as an individual of respectability and high social status in the context of his occupation (Sutherland 1940) and on the other hand it refers to the organizations that are the scenes of white-collar crime (Sutherland 1949). The labels used, when such actions are revealed beyond the nutshell of the organism in which they are protected, by mass media or institutions of official social control are 'violations', 'misconduct', 'wrong-doing', 'harm', 'liability', 'malpractice', 'accident', 'mistake' and rarely 'deviance', 'violence' and 'crime'.

Furthermore, white-collar crime in academia is action clearly committed for the 'New University'[1] and not against it. Therefore, acts of omission as well as acts of commission should be included in the definition of the concept. First, we have to document the organizational goals of the 'New University' which are deeply implicated in the cause of this type of crime. Organizational goals are what they are perceived to be by officials who have been socialized into the organizational 'way of life' and who strive in a highly co-ordinated fashion collectively to bring about their realization (Box 1983: 21) and not the manifestation of personal motives cast adrift from organizational moorings. In that case, we have to examine the possibility of overlap between white-collar crime in academia and more clear-cut kind of crime, such as organized crime (Nelken 2002: 862). As Ruggiero (1996) has mentioned in relation to organized crime, once we get away from ethnic stereotypes, it involves the same flexible consumer-oriented behaviour. He argues that both white-collar and organized criminals use similar techniques, share the same illegal know-how and the same values even if perpetrators come from different backgrounds. Their crimes are performed in or by organized structures and normally enjoy the connivance of administrators and legislators.

What's more, analysing white-collar crime in academia demands a concrete analysis of the particular type of organization, in which the phenomenon is produced as well as of the relations that are developed between this structure and the agent. For 'the root causes of this criminality lie more fully in a political economy that places the accumulation of advantage by the rich and powerful above the needs of the average citizen. The press for profits and power is the criminogenic force at the heart of upper-world lawlessness' (Balkan et al. 1980: 174–175; Barnett 1981; Conklin 1977: 34–71). Therefore, it is necessary to look at class, political and organizational interests (Cullen et al. 1983: 489).

Box (1983: 35) has developed some theoretical insights helpful for such a case; for example, anomie analysis applied to corporate crime, assuming that all organizations are orientated towards the achievement of a particular goal-profit. 'This defining characteristic – a goal-seeking entity – makes a corporation inherently criminogenic as it necessarily operates in an uncertain and unpredictable environment such that it is a purely legitimate alternative'. From the above, a hypothesis can be inferred: when these contextual uncertainties increase so the strain towards corporate criminal activity will increase. In that sense, is Greek academia orientated towards the achievement of a particular goal-profit? Is contemporary Greece characterized by uncertainty and unpredictability such that purely legitimate opportunities for goal achievement are limited and constrained? Do university managements make their decisions based on that? Is Greek academia characterized by a 'metaphysical pathos of Godfatherism' (Needleman and Needleman 1979: 518)? That is, a context in which higher-placed administrative employees achieve power on a frequent basis and therefore feel less limited, which in turn renders them immune to many of the sanctions that constrain and punish the less successful, while their subordinates find it hard to refuse co-operation in illegal activities?

In addition, research on white-collar crime in Greek academia should pose the following questions:

a) *Concerning organizational characteristics*

According to the literature, the size of organizations (namely large organizations) (Baucus 1989; Dalton and Kesner 1988; Gricar 1983; Kesner et al. 1988; Staw and Swajkoski 1975), as well as the size and level of bureaucracy of the organizations (Smigel and Ross 1970), plays a key role. The larger the size and level of bureaucracy, the greater the possibility for white-collar crime to develop. Do Greek universities possess those characteristics?

b) *Concerning the profile of the offenders*

According to the literature the perpetrator is a highly educated male in the upper ranks of his organization (Holtfreter 2005: 354), aged 40 or more (Wheeler et al. 1988), with higher level of education (Benson and Moore 1992). Does this apply to our case study?

c) *Concerning the relationship between structure and offender through the viewpoint of individual motives*

The literature mentions greed and power (Nelken 1994; 1997) but also the desire to secure career advancement or at least non-prejudice career chances (Stotland 1977), flexibility to meet shifting organizational demands and therefore identification with the goals of the organization. Based on the above, the question brought to mind is whether potential white-collar criminals in Greek academia are those who will be placed in high posts in the 'New Academia'?

d) *Concerning the relationship between structure and offender through the viewpoint of structural opportunities*

According to Shapiro (1989), the study of white-collar crime belongs to the wider study of the maintenance and abuse of trust. To understand causation, therefore, we need to link a systematic understanding of the distribution of structural opportunities for trust abuse with an understanding of the conditions under which individual or organizational fiduciaries seize or ignore these illicit opportunities (Nelken 2002: 855; Shapiro 1989: 353). These officials – perpetrators – are able to transform motives into actual behaviour because they operate in a subculture of structural immoralities (Mills 1956: 183).

Specifically, the system should be protected from any intervention of mechanisms of social control and if possible, the system should be self-regulated and in such a case of self-monitoring, the 'autonomy of Greek university' leads to self-regulation of the phenomenon of white-collar crime within academia; self-regulation is open to abuse particularly amongst those who have the power, the organizational position and a clear but perhaps not clean motive for doing so. This is hardly surprising considering that white-collar crime offenders are, in most cases, due to profile and position, committed to conventional values and have a respectable self-identity. Furthermore, their academic-corporate environment provides a library of verbal techniques for neutralizing the moral bind of laws against this kind of behaviour. They could deny responsibility, plead 'ignorance', 'accident', deny intent, shifting the blame to even higher officials or even the government or the capitalist mode of production. They can deny the victim ('there is no real criminal victim here'), they can condemn the condemners, claiming that the 'academic ethos' is morally superior to formal legalism (Box 1983: 54–57).

e) *Concerning the victim of white-collar crime in Greek academia, the state and the wider public*

An interesting volume issued by the USA's Federal Bureau of Investigation (Barnett 2000), under the framework of the National Incident-Based Reporting System (NIBRS), identifies victims of white-collar crime not just as individuals but especially government institutions and society as a whole. Could we also speak about concrete physical effects of academic white-collar crime in cases of discrimination as far as equal opportunities in hiring is concerned, promotions, infringement of duties, oversights etc. with specific victims and offenders and similarly with economic costs? The attempt to estimate the economic cost of this kind of crime and to compare it with the total number of white-collar crimes results in the conclusion that it is much higher than ordinary economic crime (robbery, theft, larceny) (Conklin 1977: 4; Johnson and Douglas 1978: 151). Is this the case for white-collar crime in Greek academia? How are public funds of millions of euros distributed through the research units of the universities that even though they are public, function like private corporations considering the fact that the state does not control them?[2] But even beyond the economic costs, what are the social costs, from the part of the students and their parents who have to pay for accommodation and food even though funds are allocated every year both by the Ministry and the EU that could accommodate such needs? And if these can be denounced and become the subject of scientific research, can we speak about a social cost that victimizes society? Is there collective ignorance?

According to Box the root cause of this ignorance could be explained by the fact that this kind of crime is rendered invisible by its complex and sophisticated planning and execution, by non-existent or weak law enforcement and prosecution, and by lenient legal and social sanctions which fail to reaffirm or reinforce sentiments in moral boundaries (Box 1983: 16). And, as Nelken wonders (2002: 847), do even we, the social scientists, find it difficult to see 'the criminal' and 'the respectable person' in one and the same figure, and even more so when the respectable person is our colleague in academia? Or, does this reflect an inclination of social scientists to 'protect their own kind' (Johnson and Douglas 1978: 227; Little 1989: 298)? Cullen et al. (1983), in their research, put emphasis on the roots of this issue rather than attempting to blame tolerant public attitudes for the problem of white-collar crime, this latter idea being based more on impressionistic instead of empirical evidence, as was also the case with the research of Ross (1907) and Sutherland (1940). As Conklin (1977: 27) mentions, there is in reality a greater degree of public condemnation of business violations than is thought to exist by those who claim that the public is apathetic. Similarly, Braithwaite (1982: 732–734) claims that there is considerable evidence to support the view that ordinary people subjectively perceive many types of white-collar crime as more serious than most traditional crime. According to Cullen et al. (1983), the root cause is the failure of state political elites and criminal justice officials to do away with such criminality. The ideology shared by government and business elites is often sufficient to restrict state intervention, legitimizing white-collar crime. Does this apply to the white-collar crime within Greek academia?

In this sense, our questions should not be limited only to academia but also to the attitude that the Greek state has towards white-collar crime within academia. In addition to acknowledging the gravity of the phenomenon and the destructive effects that has on Greek society and hence requiring solutions, we will attempt to propose certain policies. Could the control of white-collar crime play a part in its causation? In this case, is it plausible to assume that the Ministry of Education and the mechanisms of control actually produce and reproduce white-collar crime in Greek academia? Does the very function of criminal justice dealing with this phenomenon play a vital part in the history of corporate legislation enforcement, a history of penalizing the small fish whilst letting the big ones escape (Box 1983: 74; Croall 1989; Levi 1991; Nelken 1983; Shapiro 1984, 1989)?

Greek academia in the new world order

'We are attempting to alter the DNA of Greek universities' was the expression used by former Minister of Education, Anna Diamantopoulou, in one of her declarations regarding the intentions of the Ministry to introduce the new law (4009/2011 later replaced by 4076/2012) governing higher education. Even though the new law rendered deregulation and neo-liberalization of Greek academia official, such practices had already taken place during the 1990s as they were introduced by the Bologna Agreement in 1999[3] and some of these changes took place even earlier than that. The creation of research units, for example, which took place in the first half of the 1990s, was a first and fundamental step towards neo-liberalization and deregulation as they function like private bodies that manage public money with minimum control by the state, as mentioned above.[4] Needless to say, most of the economic scandals that have come to light over the years are related to these bodies. Before that, Greek higher education had followed a path of liberalization with the law of 1982 which put an end to the 'aristocratic slavery' in which a few agreeable to the power of the political elite as well as certain members of the elite held seats until their retirement, while the students and the research staff could be released only if their 'master' decided, in order later on to assume the latter's post. The sociopolitical change of the 1980s resulted in the 1268/1982 law of higher education based on the 'democratization' of academia that brought about a new structure in Greek universities. Its main characteristic was democratic participation in administration by all groups (academic, research, administrative staff as well as students) although the small feudalisms characterized by the respect given to age, years of work and ranking, remained.

During the following years, especially during the 1990s and the 2000s, Greek academia was influenced by the capitalist domination of the markets. The government policies of higher education have promoted 'greater market responsiveness' and an 'increasing openness to alternative financing mechanisms' (Rikowski 2001:8). The aim was to enhance the corporate role in a determined effort to harness knowledge to wealth creation (Beckmann and Cooper 2004). In this framework market terminology was rendered a guiding principle for the function of Greek university. One of the terms often used was, and still is, 'performativity'. According to Ball, performativity (in schools) works in at least three ways: First, it works as a disciplinary system of judgments, classifications and targets towards which schools and teachers must strive and through which they are evaluated. Second, as a part of the transformation of education and schooling and the expansion of the power of capital. Performativity provides sign systems which 'represent' education in a self-referential and reified form for consumption. Both of these aspects of educational performativity are linked to and 'valorized' within the market form in education. Third, performativity also resides in the pragmatics of language (Ball 1998: 150–151).

In this performance culture, deprofessionalization enters the discourse as well as the loss of critical thought (Boxley 2003; Hill 2007; Mahoney and Hextall 2000), while at the same time high-ranking academic staff who carry out managerial work have simulations of control over statutory performance management systems as well as an increasingly variegated pay structure. Another popular term is 'outsourcing'. Private sector involvement in education services in Greek academia includes selling services to educational institutions (e.g. cleaning, catering, security, etc.). In this way, 'public' money for public Greek academia undergoes transformation into private capital, once the contract is signed to deliver services.

Another guiding principle is the need for all members of the academic community to go through a 'normalization' process evident from the homogenized processes of evaluation of both students and academic staff. In reality, it is a process that adapts people's subjectivities to the shifting shapes of the mantra of 'market demands' (Beckmann et al. 2009: 320) and the generation of a 'consumerist ethos' in university campuses (Furedi 2009: 32). Arguably, genuine creativity has been the greatest victim of new regulation, as more rule-bound and quota-driven forms of competitiveness are superimposed on an already competitive profession. It would appear that universities have become 'enterprises' to be managed by business principles, not by collegiality (Fisher 2007: 508). The bottom line of all the above is summed up in the concepts of managerialism and managerial ethics that have gained ground in Greek academia, concepts that describe the anti-professional, anti-intellectual values that have all destroyed Humboldt's[5] vision for the university (Taylor 2002). This is a project that pressures the university sector to train future employees (White 2013) with minimum professional rights, easily exploitable in the labour market rather than generally creative and well-rounded citizens. A very nice example is given by Pechar (2012: 627) who claims that

> the refusal of structural curricula and the replacement of them by a single module (modularization) is regarded as a destruction of a holistic and integrated form of the cultivation of mind. It is viewed as disintegrating the content of higher learning into unrelated little bits and bytes that prevent a deeper understanding of the knowledge base. An implication of this is that only a small elite can achieve a truly cultivated mind. This elitist concept is not compatible with the idea of incremental steps (= accumulation of credits), it is based on that assumption that one can have either a full education or no education at all (either the whole or nothing). In this way, it significantly raises the risk of an investment in higher education and thus protects the educated upper middle class against upward mobility from the lower social strata.

The irony is that this managerial activity becomes self-validating and legitimizing (Power 1997) since it is grounded on the fact that it has no substantive outputs beyond its own frame of reference. This inability to provide demonstrable evidence of its own success leads to an attempt to make everything part of its frame. The newly introduced legislation along with the governmental management of the huge economic crisis are forming a strategy of 'tiding up' and saving of funds.

Greek academia and white-collar crime

According to Pickett and Pickett (2002) white-collar crime contains several clear components. It is deceitful, it is intentional, it breaches trust, it involves losses, it may be concealed, and there may be an appearance of outward respectability. How are the above data along with the theoretical viewpoints concretized in actions and behaviours produced and protected in the context of Greek academia as described in the previous part of this chapter? While the managerial imperative came to dominate the educational agenda, government policies of higher education focused on the production of 'docile bodies' members of Greek academia. The creation of such conditions of domination within the 'life-worlds' of higher education results in micro-physics of power (Foucault 1976) aiming at academic staff and reducing them to 'puppets' within the emerging realm of 'academic capitalism'. If you don't accept or you cannot become a puppet, then you become the subject of exclusion for any alternative perspective, practices, possibilities, research design, teaching, etc., as well as the subject of human rights violations.

At one university of the periphery, for example, Associate Professor D.P. is being persecuted and called before the Hellenic Council of State (HCS) with the accusation that in articles he authored in newspapers as well as on internet sites he referred to 'the Rector and the vice-Rectors of the University where he works in a disrespectful manner not worthy of their status'. It is the first time since 1943 that an academic is being persecuted due to his political persuasions which were in opposition to the opinions of the Rectorate.[6] The fact of his persecution can be regarded as unconstitutional as it is opposing article 14 of the Constitution of the Hellenic Republic, concerning the freedom of the press and the freedom of expression through it. Recently another case was completed in court. The case has been widely known in Greece as the 'Stelios Alexandropoulos Case'. Stelios Alexandropoulos was Associate Professor at the Department of Political Sciences at the University of Crete. In 2006, he was accused of spreading lies regarding the University of Crete, by the Rectorate of the institution, due to his claims of non-meritocratic processes of selection of candidates for the postgraduate course of the department. After he heard about this, he asked to defend himself during the general assembly of his department but the Head did not allow him to do so. After the end of the assembly, frustrated and disappointed, he went to his office, where a few hours later he was found dead. The cause of his death was a heart attack (Voulvouli 2013b).

A couple of years ago another case shook Greek academia. It was the case of A.I. who after being accused by LAOS, an extreme-right wing party, of engaging in 'nationally suspicious' research activities, lost her job because the General Secretary of the Ministry of Education, J. Panaretos, had accepted the petition of her co-candidate.[7] The case was again highly publicized amongst academics and there have been reactions both within the Greek and the international academia. A.I. applied to the Ministry asking for the annulment of her discharge, which was accepted by the then Minister of Education, Anna Diamantopoulou (Voulvouli 2013b).

The latest case is the case of S.G., Assistant Professor at another university of the Greek periphery and president of the local association of the teaching and research staff of the university who was up for promotion to the position of Associate Professor, having fulfilled all the criteria required by the law governing Greek higher education. His application was turned down (the committee was constituted by ten individuals, five of whom voted in favour and five voted against his promotion). Amongst the reasons expressed by those who voted against S.G. – according to the minutes of the session – was the fact that 'he is very young' and that part of his work has been published by 'a publishing house of leftist orientation' and thus 'non-academic' (the specific publishing house has translated and published books by Marx, Feurbach, Hobson, Harvey, etc.). After the results were announced a massive campaign was organized by student unions demanding the annulment of the electoral process, which not only was offensive in terms of academic criteria but also illegitimate as far as procedural criteria were concerned. An international campaign from academics from all over the world was organized and an e-petition was launched. Many of his international colleagues wrote to the Rector of the university, asking him to examine his case in a manner that secures the legitimacy of the process. In addition, they asked the Rector to condemn this attempt at politicization of the electoral process. The Rector replied that the 'intervention' of the international academic community was 'somewhere between paternalism and racism'. The issue has been picked up by the local and national press as well as by blogs and social media (ibid.).

Two things have to be noted here: first, S.G. has repeatedly been in conflict with the university's authorities regarding the consequences of austerity measures in the Greek public university sector. Also, in January 2011, he, as a representative of his department in the research committee of the university, had exposed the issue of the huge bonuses that a few high-ranking employees of the university receive, whilst teaching staff are being underpaid and laid off. Moreover students drop out of the school because their parents are unable to afford the expenses of a higher degree education and the university has a very poor scholarship scheme. Second, one of the members of the electoral committee that turned down S.G.'s application for promotion is currently Vice-Rector of the university, supporter of the new law with ties to the government and is a close associate of the Rector of the University. Also, as it has been reported and criticized in the local and national press, he, along with the rest of the members of the Rectorate, is also a recipient of the bonuses that S.G. has exposed in the general assembly of his department. A few months later the Greek Ombudsman issued a decision, sent to the Ministry of Education, the university, as well as to the members of S.G's electoral committee, claiming that there are strong indications that there has been both political bias (even though at a later stage of the electoral process the member of the electoral body who had expressed that bias asked the secretary to erase the comments) and age discrimination. In light of the above, the Ombudsman asked the Rector to further investigate the issue (ibid.).[8]

In addition to the above, all educational services are made more unequal and selective, intensifying 'racial', 'gendered' and class-based hierarchies as a consequence (Whitty et al. 1998). These are the seeds that partly give rise to white-collar crime in Greek academia which is being de-democratized as education workers' rights and securities erode. In addition public service morale and standards of provision have declined. This creates a framework in which if one wishes to assume administrative positions on top of academic responsibilities he/she should become a 'market prostituting and authority opportunistic personality' (Beckmann et al. 2009: 321). High-ranking academic staff who decide to execute faithfully the principles of the neo-liberal development of Greek university replace the concept of 'common good' and the state's responsibility for public welfare with the monadic vision of an 'entrepreneurial individual' whose sole mission and determination is to aim to 'succeed' within increasingly competitive markets (Leitner et al. 2007). In the name of personal benefit the so-called autonomy of Greek university is interpreted as immune from committing financial crimes. This kind of property offence may take the form of misappropriating intellectual property as well, such as plagiarism, which according to Heeren and Shicher (1993: 53) and Shils (1983: 43) is equivalent to theft. An example from one of the biggest universities of southern Greece, concerning the intellectual theft of a PhD student's work by her supervisor, supports this claim. The case went to court in 2004 and is still going on since intellectual theft was only one aspect of the dispute. The other aspect was money embezzlement, as according to the court, individuals from the family environment of the above-mentioned professor embezzled the salaries from the scholarship of the PhD student.[9] Furthermore, we have an anti-educational behaviour by high-ranking academics generated by bureaucratic/managerial structures that create a distance from ethical concepts (Taylor 2002: 3). This is evident in the evaluation forms of students, administrative assistants and other academics, in hiring protocols and promotion procedures, in which negative evaluation, dismissal and promotion refusal are the alternative to forced prostitution of 'hearts and minds' for external funding of administrative obedience. In addition, ethnic, gender, age, class and ideology prejudice is also part of such processes.

Alexandropoulos' case illustrates just that. According to his claims, the students that were selected for the postgraduate programme of his department were either students with 'friends in high places' or students who were members of the two largest student political factions (DAP and PASP) which are controlled by the right-wing New Democracy and the so-called socialist PASOK political parties, both part of the previous[10] government.[11] Apart from the aforementioned examples that support this assumption, another case from one of the universities already mentioned above can also be used in this context. It concerns the declaration of the Union of Adjunct Administrative Staff, regarding the sacking of members of the union and the vague hiring procedures followed by the institutions.[12] Several of these cases were trialled in court, the decisions of which were still not issued before the publication of the present volume.

Moreover, the amount of money that circulates in such a publicly funded, private body as the research units is quite large. The administrative staff, acting under a managerial ethos that embodies a fragmented vision of social being, seem empty of ethical dimensions and informed by materialist and reductionist opportunism that pays for those who 'play the game' (Taylor 2002: 1).

The above case of Panteion University, as well as the case discussed below, are only two of many other cases that substantiate this claim. In the context of the economic crisis the above practices result in continuing and intensifying pressure to find their own resources. Institutions of higher education frequently engage in highly problematic and often unethical partnerships with businesses, thereby transforming themselves into and being run like businesses (Fairweather 1988). Similar practices are pertinent as far as the administration of the universities is concerned to the extent that they have the possibility of implicating themselves in financial scandals. The rest of the academic community either does not know about it or, if it does, keeps silent due to fear or due to the fact that managerialism produces manipulative communication, a form of communication in which no communication is possible.

For example, at the time of writing there is an investigation which started in February 2013, from the local district attorney regarding the allocation of public funds and the hiring procedures of a small university of the periphery. Those who know about it, a minority, keep silent and the rest have only now begun to hear about it due to the fact that the press is focusing on the institution because of another scandal that implicates the Rector, who according to a wide-circulation national newspaper, illegally occupies a position in the Greek Open University. The illegality of this lies in the fact that according to the Law 4009/2011, it is strictly prohibited to rectors, vice-rectors and deans of universities to occupy any other paid and/or unpaid position outside the university in which they are elected to serve in the above mentioned positions. This scandal brought media attention and older media pieces re-surfaced. One of them, entitled 'Do it like Panteion', related the case of the Panteion scandal on the grounds that both cases involved the research units, the nature and function of which as institutions, as discussed above, are the very heart of this problem.

The Greek state 'reforms' academia

During the summer of 2011, Greek academia was informed about the new legislative framework for higher education. In 2012, a few minor changes occurred but the main philosophy of the law remained intact. This philosophy intensifies the authoritarianism of the administration and the disappearance of any remains of democratic participation and accountability from below (Voulvouli 2013a) as well as the corporate character of the Greek university. As for the first aspect, a very small minority of academic members are eligible for election for administrative posts from an electoral body constituted only by academic staff and not the other groups of the academic community as was established by the previous law. Furthermore, the elected members act in a non-transparent and non-accountable board constituted by them and external members (preferably from the corporate world) which are non-elected but selected behind closed doors by the internal members. The corporate ethos is witnessed also in the student loans provided by private banks, guaranteed by the state. 'Academic freedom is guaranteed' in a much smaller Senate in which not all academic departments are represented and that has only a consultative and not a decision-making role, which means the reduction of freedom in academic issues. 'High quality of studies' (according to the Law 4009/2011) is ensured with the reduction or complete abandonment of the policy of free academic texts distributed to students and the reduction of years of study. The programmes of study will be built 'according to the needs of economic growth' but the most interesting element is the transformation of the legal status of the research units from public to private bodies of anonymous companies which will manage all the research funds, the student welfare funds as well as the money of life-long training programmes. The violation of the Constitution is more than obvious since according to article 16, higher education in Greece should be public and provided only by public bodies (article 16, Constitution of the Hellenic

Republic). The Board of the Institute is also another case of constitution violation since it opposes article 16, paragraph 5 of the Constitution of the Hellenic Republic, according to which public institutions of higher education should be completely self-governed. What's more, the very process of election of this board which occurred through e-voting due to the large demonstrations that occurred in every university of the country when conventional elections were to be held, is also challenged as unconstitutional and appeals in the constitutional court have been made by several members of Greek academia. On the altar of rapid and effective integration of academia in the market and banking system, democracy is sacrificed; institutions are cancelled and freedom is limited. In this sense, legislation is part of the problem rather than a source of solution to white-collar crime in Greek academia.

Conclusions

How do we explain a phenomenon, considerably damaging both for individuals and society, not easily identifiable, whose official confrontation is part of the problem rather than its solution? First, by starting a dialogue illustrating the reality. The case studies discussed above illustrate that white-collar crime in Greek academia is directly related to the current structural and organizational culture that exists in higher education, namely neo-liberalization, deregulation, the creation of research units (private bodies that manage public money with minimum control by the state), deprofessionalization, a consumerist ethos and managerialism. It is conducted by individuals of respectability and high social status in the upper ranks of academic administration. Victims of this type of white-collar crime are public education and society as a whole (allocation of public funds), and individuals – in the case of discrimination – who do not execute the principles of neo-liberal development and are not docile bodies in this 'New University'. Governmental policies, public ignorance and the autonomy of the university are obstacles in the way of every effort to tackle the phenomenon. But, it is this reality that presses us to view it as a serious social problem, one that generates an anger and an outrage necessary for the oppressed to forge a plan of action for social change.

Key to such change is the self-awareness of the structural determinants of oppression and social injustice, and the formation of a cohesive political strategy (Beckmann et al. 2009: 336). We may agree that white-collar crimes are embedded and endemic within the capitalist system, but also believe that something good can be achieved and realized in practice (Box 1983: 63–65).

First of all, following Box's recommendations, intense and widespread publicization of this kind of crime (and offenders) could produce a greater public sensitivity (as within academia) and this in turn could become the catalyst out of which stronger and tougher enforcement programmes blossom. Moreover, in order to be effective, the level of intervention required to regulate white-collar crime within academia has to be organizational, aiming at the asymmetric power relationship within academia, as well as New University's operating procedure. This intervention should be proactive, monitoring operating procedures, research strategies, communication networks, command structures, etc., focusing on recommendations that should be implemented in order to avoid this kind of white-collar crime. As it is generally accepted a self-monitoring system risks being the subject of abuse, and the same risk exists also for self-regulating institutions like Greek universities to the extent that this characteristic can be used as an excuse for the implementation of authoritarian policies, the perpetration of economic scandals as well as the institutional (ministerial, party political and parliamentary) 'oversight' of such crimes. A solution could be the creation of monitoring councils concerning the funds of Greek universities, consisting of public officials (and not by individuals from the market arena as is the case now) who will be accountable to wider society. At the end of the day, however, the solution should be structural aiming at the creation of another university far from the current criminogenic university-corporation. A university that accepts diversity, protects human rights, treats students as citizens and not as customers, in a wider social framework of democracy with means of production and distribution that are socialized.

Notes

1 'New University' is a phrase used both by its advocates and its opponents. In the context of the present chapter it is used to describe the process by which the new legislation regarding Greek academia deregulates and opens universities to the market arena.
2 In a statement issued by the Minister of Education in December 2012, it was said that the Ministry has no control whatsoever over the function of research units (http://www.hellenicparliament.gr/UserFiles/67715b2c-ec81-4f0c-ad6a-476a34d732bd/7904048.pdf).
3 The Bologna Agreement (named after the city in which it was signed) was the outcome of the Bologna Process which was a series of meetings amongst ministers of European states regarding the integration of higher education in the context of EU and other partner countries. It currently involves 47 countries, including Greece, whose universities did not welcome the signing of the Agreement, even though the country joined the Bologna Process from the very beginning. One of the main reasons that the Greek higher education institutes resisted the reforms that were attempted to be introduced for the first time during 2006–2007 was the idea of competition by cutting down costs and the erosion of all effective forms of democratic control within higher education that runs through the Bologna Agreement. Although those changes were interrupted by massive student reactions, they were eventually put in effect by the new law of higher education in 2011.
4 As mentioned in an official reply issued by the Ministry of Education in 2013 addressed to a group of MPs of the Communist Party who have submitted a question to Minister K. Arvanitopoulos: The Ministry does not have any control over the management of funding of the research units of the universities.
5 Wilhelm von Humboldt, the founder of Berlin University which was later named Humboldt University, envisaged the concept of *Universitas litterarum*, which means the unity of research and teaching that provides a comprehensive education for its students without research restrictions under the principle of humanism. His ideas were very influential and the principles of the Humboldtian university became general practice in university education throughout the world.
6 http://tsak-giorgis.blogspot.gr/2012/10/blog-post_6310.html (accessed 31 May 2013).
7 http://www.enet.gr/?i=news.el.article&id=293932 (accessed 31 May 2013).
8 In March 2013 the court decision was issued, according to which the electoral process was found to be characterized by irregularities and oversights, and the university was ordered to repeat it.
9 sys.glotta.ntua.gr/announcements/2007-10-31_Uni-Business.doc (accessed 31 May 2013).
10 During the writing of this chapter Greece went through general elections which resulted in government change. The new government is the first Left-wing government in the history of the country and has a completely different vision of education than that of the neo-liberal model. In this framework, the new minister of education Tasos Kourakis (an academic himself) has declared his intentions to replace the Law 4076/2012 with a new law which would 'ensure the public character of higher education, and bring back the democratic function of it' (www.left.gr, accessed 3 February 2015).
11 http://protovoulia-alexandropoulou.blogspot.gr (accessed 31 May 2013).
12 https://forum.aegean.gr/viewtopic.php?f=130&t=11200 (accessed 31 May 2013).

References

Balkan, S., Berger, R.J. and Schmidt, J. (1980) *Crime and Deviance in America: A Critical Approach*, Belmont, CA: Wadsworth.

Ball, S.J. (1998) 'Performativity and fragmentation in postmodern schooling', in J. Carter, (ed.) *Postmodernity and the Fragmentation of Welfare*, London: Routledge, pp. 187–203.

Barnett, C. (2000) *The Measurement of White Collar Crime Using Uniform Crime Reporting (UCR) Data*, US Department of Justice, FBI, Criminal Justice Information Services Division. Available at: http://www.fbi.gov/about-us/cjis/ucr/nibrs/nibrs_wcc.pdf.

Barnett, H.C. (1981) 'Corporate capitalism, corporate crime', *Crime and Delinquency*, 27: 4–23.

Baucus, M.S. (1989) 'Why organizations do it and what happens to them: A reexamination of the theory of illegal corporate behavior', *Research in Corporate Social Performance and Policy*, 11: 93–118.

Beckmann, A. and Cooper, C. (2004) 'Globalisation, the new managerialism and education: Rethinking the purpose of education in Britain', *Journal of Critical Education Policy Studies*, 2/2. Available at: http: // www.jceps.com/print. php?articleID=31.
Beckmann, A., Cooper, C. and Hill, D. (2009) 'Neoliberalization and managerialization of education in England and Wales: A case for reconstructing education', *Journal for Critical Education Policy Studies*, 7(2): 310–345.
Benson, M.L. and Moore, E. (1992) 'Are white-collar and common offenders the same? An empirical and theoretical critique of a recently proposed general theory of crime', *Journal of Research in Crime and Delinquency*, 29: 251–272.
Box, S. (1983) *Power Crime and Mystification*, London: Tavistock.
Boxley, S. (2003) 'Performativity and capital in schools', *Journal for Critical Education Policy Studies*, 1. Available at: http://www.jceps.com/index.php?pageID=articleandarticleID=3.
Braithwaite, J. (1982) 'Challenging just deserts: Punishing white-collar criminals', *Journal of Crime, Law and Criminology*, 73: 723–763.
Braithwaite, J. (1984) *Corporate Crime in the Pharmaceutical Industry*, London: Routledge and Kegan Paul.
Carson, W.G. (1970) 'White-collar crime and the enforcement of factory legislation', *British Journal of Criminology*, 10: 383–398.
Clinard, M. and Yeager, P. (1980) *Corporate Crime*, New York: Free Press.
Coleman, J.W. (1985) *The Criminal Elite: The Sociology of White-collar Crime*, New York: Martins Press.
Conklin, J.E. (1977) *Illegal But Not Criminal*, New Jersey: Spectrum.
Croall, H. (1989) 'Who is the white-collar criminal?' *British Journal of Criminology*, 29: 157–174.
Cullen, F., Mathers, R.A., Clark, G.A. and Cullen, F.T. (1983) 'Public support for punishing white collar criminals', *Journal of Criminal Justice*, 11: 481–493.
Dalton, D.R. and Kesner, I. (1988) 'On the dynamics of the corporate size and illegal activity: An empirical assessment', *Journal of Business Ethics*, 7: 861–870.
Fairweather, J. (1988) *Entrepreneurship and Higher Education: Lessons for Colleges, Universities, and Industry*, College Station: Association for the Study of Higher Education.
Fisher, G. (2007) 'You need tits to get on round here: Gender and sexuality in the entrepreneurial university of the 21st century', *Ethnography*, 8: 503–517.
Foucault, M. (1976) *Discipline and Punish*, London: Allen Lane.
Friedrichs, D.O. (2010) *Trusted Criminals: White Collar Crime in Contemporary Society*, Belmont: Wadsworth.
Furedi, F. (2009) 'Now is the age of the discontented', *Times Higher Education*, 1/899: 30–35. Available at: http://www.timeshighereducation.co.uk/406780.article.
Green, S.P. (2002) 'Plagiarism, norms, and the limits of theft law: Some observations on the use of criminal sanctions on enforcing intellectual property rights', *Hastings Law Journal*, 54: 167–242.
Gricar, B. (1983) 'A preliminary theory of compliance with OSHA regulation', *Research in Corporate Social Performance and Policy*, 5: 121–141.
Hawkins, K. (1984) *Environment and Enforcement: Regulation and the Social Definition of Pollution*, Oxford: Clarendon Press.
Heeren, J.W. and Shicher, D. (1993) 'Faculty malfeasance: Understanding academic deviance', *Sociological Inquiry*, 63(1): 49–63.
Hill, D. (2007) 'Critical teacher education. New Labour in Britain, and the Global Project of Neoliberal', *Policy Futures*, 5(2): 204–225. Available at: http/www.wwwords.co.uk/pfie/content/pdfs/issue5 2.asp.
Holtfreter, K. (2005) 'Is occupational fraud "typical" white collar crime? A comparison of individual and organizational characteristics', *Journal of Criminal Justice*, 33: 353–365.
Johnson, J.M. and Douglas, J.D. (1978) *Crime at the Top*, New York: Lippincott.
Kelly, K. (2012) 'Tí ègine sto Pánteio (What happened to Panteion)?' Available at: http://www.tovima.gr/vimagazino/views/article/?aid=468080
Kesner, I.F., Victor, B. and Lamont, B.T. (1988) 'Board compensation and the commission of illegal acts: An investigation of Fortune 500 companies', *Academy of Management Journal*, 29: 789–799.
Law 4009/2011. Available at: http://www.et.gr/images/stories/eidika_themata/n4009_2011.pdf.
Leitner, H., Sheppard, E.S., Sziarto, K. and Maringanti, A. (2007) 'Contesting urban futures: Decentering neoliberalism', in H. Leitner, E.S. Sheppard and J. Peck (eds) *Contesting Neoliberalism: Urban Frontiers*, New York: Guilford Press, pp. 1–25.
Levi, M. (1991) 'Fraudulent justice? Sentencing the business criminal', in P. Carlen and D. Cook (eds) *Paying for Crime*, Milton Keynes: Open University Press, pp. 86–108.
Little, C.B. (1989) *Deviance and Control*, Itasca, IL: Peacock.
Mahoney, P. and Hextall, I. (2000) *Reconstructing Teaching: Standards, Performance and Accountability*, London: Routledge Falmer.

Mills, C.W. (1956) *The Power of Elite*, Oxford: Oxford University Press.
Needleman, M.L. and Needleman, C. (1979) 'Organizational crime: Two models of criminogenesis', *Sociological Quarterly*, 20: 517–528.
Nelken, D. (1983) *The Limits of the Legal Process: A Study of Landlords, Law and Crime*, London: Academic Press.
Nelken, D. (1991) 'Why punish?', *Modern Law Review*, 53: 829–834.
Nelken, D. (1994) 'White-collar crime', in M. Maguire, B. Morgan and R. Reiner (eds) *Oxford Handbook of Criminology*, Oxford: Oxford University Press, pp. 355–393.
Nelken, D. (1997) 'White-collar crime', in M. Maguire, B. Morgan and R. Reiner (eds) *Oxford Handbook of Criminology*, 2nd edn, Oxford: Oxford University Press, pp. 891–924.
Nelken, D. (2002) 'White-collar crime', in M. Maguire, B. Morgan and R. Reiner (eds) *Oxford Handbook of Criminology*, 3rd edn, Oxford: Oxford University Press, pp. 844–877.
Pechar, H. (2011) 'The decline of an academic oligarchy: The Bologna process and "Humboldt's Last Warriors"', paper presented at the Conference on Future of High Education, Bucharest, 17–19 October.
Pechar, H. (2012) 'The decline of an academic oligarchy: The Bologna Process and "Humboldt's last warriors"', in A. Curaj, P. Scott and L. Vlasceanu (eds) *European Higher Education at the Crossroads: Between the Bologna Process and National Reforms*, Dordrecht: Springer.
Pickett, K.H.S. and Pickett, J.M. (2002) *Financial Crime Investigation and Control*, New York: John Wiley & Sons.
Power, M. (1997) *The Audit Society: Rituals of Verification*, Oxford: Oxford University Press.
Punch, M. (1996) *Dirty Business: Exploring Corporate Misconduct*, London: Sage.
Rikowski, G. (2001) *The Battle in Seattle: Its Significance for Education*, London: The Tufnell Press.
Ross, E.A. (1907) *Sin and Society: An Analysis of Latter-day Inquity*, Boston: Mifflin Company.
Ruggiero, V. (1996) *Organised Crime and Corporate Crime in Europe*, Aldershot: Dartmouth.
Shapiro, S. (1984) *Wayward Capitalist*, New Haven: Yale University Press.
Shapiro, S. (1989) 'Collaring the crime not the criminal: Reconsidering "white-collar crime"', *American Sociological Review*, 55: 346–365.
Shils, E. (1983) *The Academic Ethic*, Chicago: University of Chicago Press.
Smigel, E.O. and Ross, H.L. (1970) *Crimes against Bureaucracy*, New York: Van Norstraand Reinhold.
Staw, B.M. and Swajkoski, E. (1975) 'The scarcity munificence component of organizational environments and the commission of illegal acts', *Administrative Science Quarterly*, 20: 345–354.
Stotland, E. (1977) 'White-collar criminals', *Journal of Social Issues*, 33: 179–196.
Sutherland, E.H. (1940) 'White collar criminality', *American Sociology Review*, 5: 1–12.
Sutherland, E.H. (1949) *White-collar Crime*, New York: Holt, Rinehart and Winston.
Taylor, P. (2002) 'The Project meets The Office: Managerialism in UK Plc', *Variant*, 16: 31–33. Available at: http://variant.org.uk/pdfs/issue16.managerial.phf.
Thompson, B. (2002) 'Toward an understanding of academic deviance', in G.W. Potter (ed.) *Controversies in White-collar Crime*, Cincinnati: Anderson.
Voulvouli, A. (2013a) 'H apporýthmisi os aitía anádysis enós aftónomou akadimaikoù syndikalistikoù kinímatos' (Deregulation as a cause of instigation of an autonomous academic union movement). Available at: http://www.rednotebook.gr/details.php?id=8873.
Voulvouli, A. (2013b) 'Greek Academia and the violations of human rights', *Newsletter of the European Group for the Study of Deviance and Social Control*.
Washburn, J. (2005) *University, Inc.: The Corporate Corruption of Higher Education*, New York: Basic Books.
Wheeler, S., Weisburd, D., Waring, E. and Bode, N. (1988) 'White-collar crimes and criminals', *American Criminal Law Review*, 25: 331–357.
White, J. (2013) 'Rich colleges, poor professors'. Available at: http://www.huffingtonpost.com/jane-white/college-professor-salaries_b_3271404.html?utm_hp_ref=tw
Whitty, G., Power, S. and Halpin, D. (1998) *Devolution and Choice in Education. The School, the State and the Market*, Buckingham: Open University Press.

Websites (all accessed 31 May 2013)

http://www.enet.gr/?i=news.el.article&id=293932
https://forum.aegean.gr/viewtopic.php?f=130&t=11200
sys.glotta.ntua.gr/announcements/2007-10-31_Uni-Business.doc
http://www.hellenicparliament.gr/UserFiles/67715b2c-ec81-4f0c-ad6a-476a34d732bd/7904048.pdf
http://protovoulia-alexandropoulou.blogspot.gr
http://tsak-giorgis.blogspot.gr/2012/10/blog-post_6310.html

14

EU fraud and new member states – a success story?

The case of Bulgaria

Brendan Quirke

Introduction

The purpose of this paper is to consider the experience of a member state in seeking to establish and strengthen anti-EU fraud structures and measures. It will consider the problems Bulgaria encountered and how the country sought to overcome them as well as the wider lessons that can be drawn for other new member states and for those countries that wish to join the European Union.

The methodology employed was a review of secondary materials such as European Commission reports, academic articles, government documents and semi-structured interviews with government officials of Bulgaria.

This chapter on EU fraud is a necessary addition to a handbook on white-collar crime as the issue of the fraudulent misuse of European funds and the seeming inability to control such misuse say much about regulatory fragmentation and inadequate fraud-proofing of legislation and these are highly relevant issues in the conversation between academics and practitioners regarding the control of white-collar crime.

Background

Bulgaria joined the European Union in January 2007, along with its neighbour Romania. As with any club or society, whether it is the European Union, the Freemasons or the local tennis club, every new member has to abide by the rules of the club, but in order to be able to abide by the rules and also to make a positive contribution, the new member needs help and support from both existing members as well as from the senior officials of the club or society. What kind of support did Bulgaria receive? This chapter will attempt to make an assessment.

Membership of the EU created opportunities for development for Bulgaria, but also opened up possibilities to engage in fraudulent activities for criminal entrepreneurs. The problems that Bulgaria faced in combatting EU fraud, and the support it received from the EU in attempting to professionalize its anti-fraud and anti-corruption measures, exemplify the experiences of other East European applicants and also the issues facing future applicants from the Balkan region for example. Bulgaria therefore forms a suitable case study which should enable a deeper understanding of the problems facing candidate countries for EU membership as they seek to play their part in the fight against EU fraud.

It is not appropriate to study the phenomenon of EU fraud in isolation, but also to consider the broader context within which it operates such as the political, economic, social and historical circumstances (Scheinost 2006). Bulgaria has had a quite positive attitude towards the European Union, both before and after accession, yet by 2008 she was the subject of a highly critical report from the European Commission regarding the progress she had made to address corruption which reflected continuing concern as to how she would address potential abuse of EU funds.

Bulgaria: the developmental context

As Krastev (2002) outlines, corruption in Bulgaria is not a new phenomenon. He explains how Bulgaria's political history over the last 100 years or so demonstrates that there have been many attempts to pursue anti-corruption policies, but these have invariably led to more state regulation and these have in his view been anti-market and anti-liberal. He quotes the example of the Zveno political circle which was a political organization that established a dictatorial regime in Bulgaria in 1934–1935. This regime attempted to respond to widespread public disgust and disillusionment with a political and economic environment which was described by the press of the time as: 'totally corrupt'. It implemented a crackdown that was based on total state interference in public and political life. Krastev (2002) believes that this demonstrates that the tradition in Bulgaria is to fight corruption with more state regulation and more administration.

Under the communist regime of Todor Zhivkov from 1954 to 1989, nepotism was widely practised. He promoted his daughter to a senior position in the Communist Party and membership of the *politburo*. His son also rose to a senior position in the party. His son-in-law became head of the state airline and chairman of the Olympic Committee. Party members received access to luxury goods through the state shops as well as holidays on the Black Sea and privileged accommodation. For those who were not members of the political elite or did not have strong connections to it, the harshness and privations of daily life meant having to engage in the bribery of state officials in order to make life a little more tolerable and comfortable (Chavdarova 2001). Giatzidis (2004) comments that corruption under the communist regime concentrated mainly at the individual level, being the result of the individual citizen's dependence on officials. The rigidity of the communist system and the functioning of state bureaucracy gave officials the opportunity to exploit their position for private gain. According to a 1991 national survey quoted by Chavdarova (2001), the giving and taking of bribes was spread among 30 per cent of the population under the communist regime. Chavdarova (2001: 11) believes that bribery was fostered mainly by 'omnipresent deficits, nepotism and the privileges enjoyed by virtue of party membership. Corruption was an outgrowth of the individual citizen's dependence on officials and offices'.

Barnes (2007) considers that the Bulgarian Communist Party and its leader Todor Zhivkov were unashamedly opposed to Mikhail Gorbachev's reforms in the Soviet Union in the late 1980s. This opposition precipitated the fall of his regime and the decision to rename the Communist Party as the Bulgarian Socialist Party. Barnes (2007), however, also points out that behind the appearance of inertia (or a desired adherence to the status quo by those who were the beneficiaries), changes had been under way for several years that would undermine any post-communist Bulgarian government's ability to shape the political economy. These changes also sowed the seeds for the 'smash and grab' capitalism of the post-communist transition in the 1990s. Barnes (2007) provides a representative example of how the growth of an economic conglomerate – Multigroup – was aided by its patron Andrei Lukanov who served in the foreign trade ministry in the Zhivkov era. Lukanov helped prepare Bulgaria's regulations governing economic liberalization in the late 1980s and these rules had sufficient loopholes for Multigroup to exploit and amass great wealth through 'arbitrage, smuggling and money laundering' (Barnes 2007: 76).

At the same time from a position of a command economy which was totally controlled by the state, state control of the banking sector also began to weaken and in Barnes' (2007) view, this enabled well connected actors to siphon resources from the state. From a position of a single bank controlling the regulation of the money supply and acting as a creditor for industrial and commercial enterprises, the banking sector became a collection of poorly monitored banks which were owned by former ministries which often had 80 per cent of their assets tied up in one firm and could blackmail the central bank for refinancing aid, since they could claim that allowing them to fail would cause irreparable damage to an entire sector of a local economy (Barnes 2007). So as communism started to fade and fail there were emerging conglomerates developing methods to transfer state assets to their own control. Elites had a nose for a good business opportunity in order to prepare themselves for the free-for-all of the post-communist era.

From the commentary provided by both Barnes (2007) and Chavdarova (2001), one can see that although corruption did not start with Bulgaria's transition from a communist to a democratic state, the change to a democratic system did create new permutations of and opportunities for corruption. Ghitescu and Banciu's (2001: 44) observations about Romania could equally apply to Bulgaria after the Communist Party was pushed from power: 'it did not take long until a number of people identified the lack of legal regulations in certain areas – such as banking, commerce, foreign trade and so on – and started to exploit this vacuum for their own benefit'. An environment in Bulgaria was created which was similar to that of its neighbour Romania, where institutionalized theft became the norm rather than the exception (Quirke and Doig 2011).

An area where the potential for corruption or at least inside influence became apparent, after the transition to democracy, was the privatization of state-owned enterprises. Privatization was regarded as essential to transform the country from a communist centralized command economy to a market economy. As Gheorge (2006) comments, there are standard and non-standard means of privatization: the standard means would include public auction, public tender and direct sell. The non-standard means are employed in general mass privatization schemes like the manager employee buyout scheme applied to some extent in Romania.

In Bulgaria in the early 1990s, there was no consensus about which model of privatization should be applied. The former Communist Party which had rebranded itself into the Bulgarian Socialist Party (BSP) was openly against large scale privatization. As Bojicic-Dzelilovic and Bojkov (2005) observe, the BSP favoured attempting to recover as much as possible from every state enterprise before selling it and preferred selling to Bulgarian citizens and employees rather than outright to foreign buyers. In such circumstances, the emergence of economic counterparts of the state was encouraged by the state itself – manager–employee associations, banks operating with money borrowed from the state and having loan policies that favoured certain state-owned enterprises, joint venture enterprises involving an investing partner, holdings composed of state-owned enterprises. In such conditions, as Bojicic-Dzelilovic and Bojkov (2005) comment, the creation of informal networks with influence over the process had to have the approval of at least part of the governing elite, and strategically placed individuals who possessed power themselves or who had access to those in power were able to enter into transactions with large state-owned companies and commercial banks and thereby exclude less powerful and influential sections of society. There is a tradition in South East Europe of a system of networks which are based on personal relationships and the communist state acknowledged the existence of such networks, was never challenged by them and did not discourage them. This was because they were seen to have a positive function of creating a safety net for people – they helped them gain better and faster access to health services, scarce goods and preferred employment.

The other main party, the Union of Democratic Forces (UDF), was concerned to gain control over the privatization process and withdraw it from its political opponent. As Bojicic-Dzelilovic and Bojkov (2005) comment, the UDF favoured restitution to previous owners and sale to foreign investors. However, once they gained power in 1992, they adopted the Privatization Act and then began to adopt the same mechanisms as their opponents – such as manager and employee buyouts (MEBOs) – once a critical number of friendly managers were appointed. This helped to speed up the existing privatization process that favoured insiders to the processes and operated on the basis of the existing informal networks.

Despite political power changing hands in the 1990s between the BSP and UDF and changes to the methods adopted for the privatization process, the widespread allegations of corruption persisted. Economic groups or 'networks' like Multigroup – mentioned above and which grew to prominence in the dying days of communism – had the advantage of its patron, Lukanov, sitting in the prime minister's seat, and who, in the view of Barnes (2007), pursued policies which weakened the state's ability to uncover and punish economic crimes. As Ganev (2001) outlines, he hindered the investigation of crimes such as embezzlement in state-owned organizations and also allowed several ministries such as Economics, Internal Affairs, Defence and Transport to sell off state assets such as oil and metal reserves, trucks and property. Barnes (2007) observes that even after Lukanov was removed from the premiership, Multigroup's directors continued to build on the ties they had developed in the Zhivkov era and moved without hindrance between commercial boardrooms and policy offices.

Other economic networks such as Orion which had close connections to the then prime minister Zhan Videnov in the mid-1990s sought to gain control of a number of banks in the deregulated banking sector to help facilitate its programme to acquire state assets. Orion fared well under the Videnov regime. Barnes (2007) observes how, when the civil courts declared invalid the registration of one of Orion's banks, the government amended the law on banks to enable it to keep operating. Interior ministry documents showed that Orion firms channelled loans out of state banks and failed to repay them; no action was taken by the government to force repayment.

As noted above, this process was facilitated by the failure to ensure a matching legal and regulatory system. The Privatization Agency which had been established by the Privatization Act of 1992 did not have the independence, power or will to effectively regulate the privatization process. It quickly developed in the view of Bojicic-Dzelilovic and Bojkov (2005) an inborn state of denial against any blame for misconduct. Its regulatory role was also hampered by the degree of fragmentation which existed, as it was not the only privatizing body. Below a certain asset value threshold, the principal ministries (who effectively owned the enterprises) were also responsible for implementing privatization deals. Relevant ministers were the only ones in charge of administering and approving deals. In theory they were responsible to parliament and the relevant parliamentary committee, but it is reasonable to ask the question of how effective this was, given there was no specific privatization committee (Bojicic-Dzelilovic and Bojkov 2005). Indeed, as also noted above, the informal networks could bypass what formal procedures were in place because influential buyers connected to the networks, which politicians were close to or perhaps even part of, enabled the former to determine which body would privatize the enterprise they were bidding for and the processes to be followed.

Overall, there was therefore a situation of no consistent policy on the privatization process and there was a pervasive influence of powerful economic networks with access to and indeed membership by political elites and competition between such networks. The situation was made worse by a weak regulatory structure hampered by fragmentation and the ability of government ministers to privatize parts of the state asset portfolio without any political or democratic oversight. In addition, there was a consequent climate of allegations of corruption in the privatization process with officials and politicians accused of being offered bribes to favour certain economic actors and networks or indeed having economic or financial interests which depended upon and could well prosper with the success of such favoured bidders (Chavdarova 2001).

All these incidences of corrupt behaviour together with the numerous incidents of low-grade corruption involving ordinary citizens and officialdom have had unfortunate consequences for Bulgaria's reputation abroad. Engelbrekt (2007) cites a study by PricewaterhouseCoopers that suggested that in 2005, as many as 39 per cent of all large foreign companies operating in Bulgaria reported instances of bribery and corruption, a figure that is amongst the highest in Central and Eastern Europe. It would, in terms of risk, be clear that bringing Bulgaria into the club could, given the manipulation and exploitation of in-country resources, the informal networks and the weak legal and regulatory framework, provide significant opportunity to exploit access to EU funds.

Now that this 'swashbuckling' period of transition is over, economic crime has become established as a feature of criminal activity and given the entry of the country into the European Union, then a 'honeypot' of EU funds must be an attractive opportunity for fraudsters. Criminals want to make money and they do undertake their own form of risk analysis – if the risks of detection appear to be low and the rewards are attractive, then it appears inevitable that they will direct their attention towards EU funds. In the late 1990s as the process of preparing for enlargement gained pace, officials of the then anti-fraud unit of the European Commission – UCLAF – were very worried about organized economic criminals in Central and Eastern Europe getting their hands on EU funds: 'Officials here are worried sick about EU money disappearing into a black hole' (interview with UCLAF officials 1998). How 'organized' these criminals are, is a matter of some debate both within and without the academic community. Van Duyne (2003) and Spencer (2007) have both noted that organization can be very loose and local and consist of entrepreneurs looking for opportunities in a very enterprising way. There may well not be a 'Dr Evil' directing hierarchical criminal networks which are hell-bent on swindling the European Budget and taxpayer. This does not mean that EU funds are not under threat. Even locally based fraudsters can still swindle the EU out of thousands of euros and even more. In order to counter this threat, a system of financial aid and technical support to candidate countries was introduced.

Impact of the expansion of the EU on the fight against fraud

Prior to the expansion of the EU in 2004, fraud has been a major issue. Academic commentators such as Tutt (1989), Sherlock and Harding (1991), Passas and Nelken (1993), Sieber (1998), Quirke (2006), amongst others, have all highlighted the issue and problem of fraud. When there were just 15 member states, the fight against fraud was dogged by the fragmented response from a multiplicity of member state agencies operating within 15 separate legal systems, all of which defined fraud differently, investigated it differently and reported it differently. The true extent of fraud has never been quantified; given that fraudsters like to keep their activities secret, this is not surprising. Estimates have ranged from 2 per cent to 10 per cent and above (Ruimschotel 1994). Now that EU membership has increased, first to 25, and then to 27 and now to 28, this problem of fragmentation can only be exacerbated. For example, Community institutions have now to cope with 13 new legal systems – this is unlikely to improve the existing situation.

Fraudsters exploit differences in legal systems and procedures; they operate in 'real time'; they do not have to comply with legal protocols and agreements. There were attractive sums for the fraudsters to consider focussing their attention upon, as Murawska (2004) outlines, the candidate countries received on average about 3 billion euros per year and from 2004 to 2006, the new member states received about 16 billion euros. In order to minimise the risk of fraud, the European Fraud Prevention Office (OLAF), which administratively is part of the European Commission, made checks and investigations in the candidate states and sought to ensure good cooperation between itself and the administrations of the new member states (Murawska 2004). The role of OLAF is to protect the finances of the European Community and to support and liaise with national investigative bodies particularly where investigations have a cross-border dimension (Illett 2004).

Prospective member states made efforts to adopt the *acquis communitaire* in the protection of the communities' financial interests and the candidate countries were required to: 'create an efficient anti-fraud protection system with respect to funds provided in the framework of the Accession Partnership such as the programmes PHARE, ISPA or SAPARD[1]' (Murawska 2004: 3).

Efforts of Bulgaria to prepare for accession

Bulgaria was obliged to make its legal system comply with the *acquis communitaire*, under the first pillar of the European Union, as part of its preparation for accession. As Murawska (2004), comments, the Community measures about protection of the Community's finances are fairly modest. These consist of three EC Regulations:

- Council Regulation (EC Euratom) No. 2988/95 of 18 December 1995 on the protection of the European Communities' financial interests[2]
- Council Regulation (EC Euratom) No. 2185/96 of 11 November 1996 concerning on-the-spot checks and inspections carried out by the Commission in order to protect the European Communities' financial interests against fraud and other irregularities[3]
- Regulation (EC) No. 1073/99 of the European Parliament and of the Council of 25 May 1999 concerning investigations conducted by the European Fraud Prevention Office (OLAF)[4].

Also, the Bulgarian government was expected to incorporate into its legal system, the Convention on the Protection of the European Communities' Financial Interests (the PFI Convention) together with its associated protocols. The PFI Convention is intergovernmental and lies within the third pillar of the European Union.[5] The convention as Fenyk (2007) details, requires that member states shall incorporate frauds against the European Communities' financial interests into their criminal code and should take the necessary steps to ensure that fraudulent behaviour and conduct is punishable by criminal penalties that are effective and reasonable and also that heads of businesses and other senior executives that have the power to take decisions or exercise control 'to be declared criminally liable in accordance with the principles defined by national law in cases of fraud affecting the European Community's financial interests' (Fenyk 2007: 2).

The First Protocol to the PFI Convention requires that definitions on what is termed corruption, both active and passive (Articles 2–3) be assimilated into the criminal law and the Second Protocol to the PFI Convention requires national law to provide that legal persons can be held liable in cases of fraud or active corruption and money laundering committed that damage or are likely to damage the European Communities' financial interests (Fenyk 2007).

Bulgaria did institute amendments to its criminal code to bring it into line with the PFI Convention and also ratified the Council of Europe's Criminal Law Convention on Corruption, and in February 2005, amended the National Strategy for Combatting Corruption to include a number of measures designed to combat high-level corruption.

In order to ensure effective co-operation between OLAF and the national administrations in the candidate countries as well as seeking to have in place organizational arrangements which would be capable of preventing and detecting frauds and irregularities as Murawska (2004) outlines, OLAF supported the creation of independent anti-fraud structures at a national level in then candidate countries. The rationale behind such structures was to ensure effective coordination between legislative and administrative measures dealing with EU fraud policy (Murawska 2004). OLAF provided training and support although it has been acknowledged by academic commentators such as Murawska (2004) and by national officials that such support was not sufficient and in some cases was regarded as being fairly minimal (interview with Czech officials 2006). This is an important consideration; given the complexity of EU programmes and fraud investigation, there was an obvious need for substantial and substantive support both from OLAF and from the Commission as a whole. For such support to be found wanting can have major consequences in terms of present and indeed future fraud investigation capacity and effectiveness.

The Bulgarian AFCOS structure

In order to ensure effective co-operation between OLAF and the national administrations in the candidate countries as well as seeking to have in place organizational arrangements which would be capable of preventing and detecting frauds and irregularities, OLAF supported the creation of an independent anti-fraud service at a national level in the then candidate countries (Murawska 2004). These structures were known as AFCOS – Anti-Fraud Coordination Service. The rationale behind the decision to create such networks was to ensure effective co-ordination between legislative and administrative measures dealing with EU fraud policy (Murawska 2004). It is interesting to note that established member states in Western Europe had no such AFCOS (see below) structures – 'Where are the British, French and German AFCOS?' (interview with Bulgarian Officials 2010). It did appear, to new countries, at that time, that the EU was asking new members to meet requirements that existing members did not have to meet, an appearance that suggested to them dual, if not double, standards (interview with Bulgarian Officials 2010). The EU has now decided that every member state should have an AFCOS network (interview with Maltese officials 2012). It will be interesting to see how established member states put this provision into practice.

OLAF has provided training and support to anti-fraud bodies and officials in candidate states and although some national officials regarded such support as not being sufficient (interview with Czech Officials 2006) and some as fairly minimal (interview with Maltese Officials 2007), the Bulgarians seem to be fairly satisfied with the support and training they have received (interview with Bulgarian Officials 2010). A country like Bulgaria which is one of the poorest in the EU, with a nascent anti-fraud service with officials who did not have the experience of dealing with the complexities of EU policy regimes, with a bureaucracy which did not have the capacity to absorb billions of euros of EU funds (Center for the Study of Democracy 2007), as well as perhaps not having the experience of investigating transnational frauds, obviously was in need of support and nurturing.

In the case of Bulgaria, in 2002, unlike its neighbour Romania which had established an AFCOS structure (Quirke 2009), no designated AFCOS body had been established. The anti-fraud co-ordination structure – the council coordinating the fight against the infringements affecting the financial interests of the European Communities (the Council) – was set up by Council of Ministers Decree no. 18 of 4 February 2003 (interview with Bulgarian Officials

2010). The objectives behind establishing such a structure were to co-ordinate and combine the efforts of the competent authorities, including the bodies of the independent judiciary, rather than duplicating their activities (interview with Bulgarian Officials 2010). The Council was entrusted with the following functions: to propose to the Council of Ministers draft anti-fraud legislation, to develop strategies to combat infringements affecting the financial interests of the European Communities, and respective action plans to implement the strategies, to report annually on its activity to the Council of Ministers and to discuss issues related to the fight against fraud and irregularities and to interact as appropriate with the judicial authorities (interview with Bulgarian Officials 2010). The Council was chaired by the Minister of the Interior.

Sigma, the consulting arm of the OECD in Paris, was commissioned by the European Commission to undertake an assessment of the anti-fraud structure in Bulgaria and it reported in 2004. The objectives of Sigma's assessment in Bulgaria were to: 'evaluate the operational and administrative capacities of AFCOS and its partner institutions in the protection of the European Community's financial interests and, where needed, to put forward proposals and recommendations for strengthening their capacities' (Sigma 2004: 7). Sigma's evaluation of the operational and administrative capacities of AFCOS and its partner institutions was made on the basis of an AFCOS' basic functions: co-ordination, co-operation and communication (the 3 Cs) which signify the ability:

- to co-ordinate, within Bulgaria, all legislative, administrative and operational obligations and activities related to the protection of the community's financial interests
- to co-operate with OLAF and its partner institutions whenever OLAF requires investigative assistance or, on the other hand, whenever OLAF assistance is required
- to communicate with OLAF and its partner institutions with regard to mandatory reporting and information exchange (Sigma 2004).

The main findings of the Sigma report were as follows:

- In 2002, no AFCOS existed in Bulgaria. Valuable time had already been lost as AFCOS was only established in 2003. There needed to be an urgent recruitment drive with regards to staff and AFCOS needed to be firmly embedded with respect to its legal position and also with respect to its interaction with relevant investigative bodies in Bulgaria and with OLAF.
- The Council had not carried out a risk analysis and had not developed a national anti-fraud strategy. A strategy for fighting fraud would be useful in harmonizing the various efforts undertaken by different ministries and bodies to protect both national and international financial interests, including the EU budget and own resources. Such a strategy would have signalled Bulgaria's willingness to take action in this respect.
- The Council had not forwarded reporting guidelines on irregularities to partner institutions, accompanied by additional guidance and/or training.
- The Anti-Fraud Information System (AFIS) was not yet operational and no terminals were linked to the National Customs Agency, which had a gateway link to OLAF.

A major problem with the Council was that it was not a body that could take care of daily operations. Sigma acknowledged that it had a useful role in directing and controlling operations, but in 2003, it met only three times and there was a need, therefore, for an active support unit to drive forward the implementation of anti-fraud policy. There was a need for an active secretariat staffed by people with technical expertise and language skills who could provide the link between national institutions and OLAF and also act as a help desk in order to bridge the gap between national institutions and OLAF (Sigma 2004). OLAF had already made the point that unless the Council had such a secretariat, it could not act as an AFCOS.

In summary, the genesis of the AFCOS regime in Bulgaria was beset by problems. It was not established when it should have been in 2002, and when a body had been constructed, it had too many problems – lack of resources, lack of administrative capacity, lack of will – to meet the requirements and strictures of OLAF and the demands of the fight against fraud. This was not a promising start, requiring a quick response in anticipation of EU membership.

In order to respond effectively to the weaknesses and issues identified by the Sigma assessment (2004), the Bulgarian authorities adopted and implemented a national anti-fraud strategy against fraud affecting the financial interests of the European Communities. The strategic aims set by the Bulgarian government were as follows:

- 'To ensure the efficient prevention and fight against fraud, misuse, inefficient management or utilisation of EU funds
- To detect and suppress fraud, misuse, ineffective management or utilisation of financial assets and property belonging to the European Union or provided to the Bulgarian state [...]
- To develop a common approach towards the prevention and fight against corruption within the state institutions [...] to achieve as an ultimate goal, high level protection of the EC's financial interests' (AFCOS 2007: 2).

The provisions of the Convention on the Protection of the European Communities' Financial Interests were transposed into Bulgarian law with, however, some delay and omissions as identified above.

In order to meet the demands of OLAF for a properly resourced AFCOS structure, a Central Co-ordination Unit was established within the Ministry of the Interior, yet this was only in 2006 – two years after the Sigma Report (2004) was published and evidence of yet another delay and lost time (interview with Bulgarian officials 2010). In the first two years of its existence, there were ten officials working in the Central Co-ordination Unit (now been increased to 12 since 2008 (interview with Bulgarian Officials 2010)). The directorate should ensure operational co-ordination between OLAF and the competent agencies and bodies which are members of the AFCOS network in terms of carrying out investigations in Bulgaria, it maintains a database with information about suspected irregularities and frauds, communicates alerts about suspected irregularities to relevant organizations and bodies in the AFCOS network and communicates irregularity reports on a quarterly basis to OLAF (AFCOS 2007).

Efforts to support the Bulgarian authorities were enhanced by the decision to base an OLAF official in Sofia in order to be a source of on-the-spot support and advice. This official stayed in Sofia from 2004 until 2008, but was then recalled (interview with Bulgarian officials 2010). This was premature and indeed a mistake. The early years of membership of the EU are a time of transition and challenge. There is inevitably a steep learning curve for national officials and to have an experienced OLAF official in such close proximity was a very valuable resource. This should be borne in mind for future enlargements.

As has been identified in previous studies in Romania (Quirke 2009) and the Czech Republic (Quirke 2008), Bulgaria had a number of different agencies/bodies working within the AFCOS network which have a role in the reporting, investigation and prosecution of fraud cases. There are directorates from the Ministry of the Interior such as the Combatting Organized Crime Unit, the Border Police and a very powerful new agency, SANS – the State Agency for National Security – which has responsibility for investigating economic crime as well as other national security duties. There is also Department VIII of the Supreme Prosecution Authority of Cassation which oversees all cases regarding abuse of EU funds. From the Ministry of Finance there is the Customs Agency, the Financial Intelligence Agency, the Public Financial Inspection Agency, the Audit of European Funds Directorate, the Management of European Funds Directorate. There is also the Ministry of Agriculture, Regional Development, Transport and so on. Some of these bodies such as the police units from the Interior Ministry and Customs are investigative bodies, whilst others manage funds such as CAP[6] and structural and cohesion funds and have their own units (internal audit and inspection) for carrying out investigations of irregularities.

Within the many agencies involved in detecting/investigating EU frauds and irregularities in Bulgaria, it is possible to identify two sub-groups in these arrangements. In one which could be called criminal investigation groups, there are well established arrangements for contact and co-ordination between the Ministry of the Interior police directorates dealing with organized crime and the protection of the borders and Customs, SANS and the Supreme Prosecution Authority of Cassation. In the other sub-group, there are organizations which tend to undertake non-criminal investigations such as the Audit of European Funds Directorate, internal audit units of the Agriculture Ministry, etc. and these have no or very little experience of liaising with criminal investigative bodies. Just as Quirke (2008; 2009) identified in the cases of the Czech Republic and Romania, here in Bulgaria, there is the potential for confusion, inefficiencies, duplication and misunderstanding.

Another difficulty has been the fact that the position of AFCOS has been the subject of both uncertainty and political infighting. In 2008 after the elections, a political decision was taken to create a deputy prime minister post in charge of EU funds and AFCOS was moved away from the Ministry of the Interior to become part of the administration of the Council of Ministers (interview with Bulgarian officials 2010). Yet in 2009, after new elections, the decision was taken to switch AFCOS back to the Interior Ministry. Such instability is not good for an organization in its formative years, when it needs stability in order to become embedded in the anti-fraud process and to become accepted. This instability was damaging to staff morale and to say the least was highly unfortunate (interview with Bulgarian officials 2010). All this was happening at a time when Bulgaria and its management of EU funds and attitudes to fraud and irregularity with respect to them were under severe scrutiny.

Post-accession experience

In terms of the Bulgarian post-accession experience, the country still appears to have retained its enthusiasm for membership of the European Union, if public opinion surveys are anything to go by. In 2010, a survey by Eurobarometer quoted in a Europa Press Release noted that 61 per cent of Bulgarians favoured Bulgaria's membership of the EU.[7]

On the other hand, the reform process has not gone smoothly. The efforts to amend the criminal code to incorporate aspects of the Convention have not yet been completely implemented and proposals to reform part of the Criminal Procedure Code to allow OLAF reports to be submitted in pre-trial proceedings and for OLAF reports and related documents to be submissible as evidence were only contained in a draft law submitted to parliament in November 2009, nearly three years after Bulgaria acceded (interview with Bulgarian Officials 2010). This is unacceptable. Bulgaria may have indeed ratified the Convention on the Protection of the EU's financial interests, but this is not just a 'box-ticking' exercise. What really matters is how the provisions of the Convention are implemented. In order to have a level playing field across the EU, it is imperative that all member states not just ratify – and indeed some, like the Czech Republic, have not even achieved that yet (Quirke 2008) – but also fully implement the Convention. Ratification and implementation are important steps towards reducing the fragmentary nature of the legal approaches to fighting fraud against the EU. Given that such serious concerns had been expressed about the general level of corruption and economic crime – as well as the demands made by the EU for Bulgaria to 'clean up its act' – it is very surprising that implementation of the Convention – or at least evidence of substantive progress – was not made a pre-condition for entry.

The management of EU funds

In 2008, the European Commission published a damning report on the management of EU funds in Bulgaria. The Commission was very concerned that administrative capacity was weak and that there had been serious allegations of irregularities as well as suspicions of fraud and conflicts of interest in the award of contracts. This led to a temporary suspension of pre-accession funds and the freezing of payments under various other financial instruments. There were many areas of concern but those relating to the PHARE and Transition Facility programmes which supported Bulgaria to complete institutional reforms and to prepare for the absorption of much larger amounts of assistance under the Structural Funds are worth noting.

The total amount allocated under PHARE and Transition Facility programmes was around 650 million euros (European Commission 2008). Monitoring and audit work had shown that there were serious weaknesses in the management and control systems and there were a number of irregularities, suspected fraud cases and conflicts of interest between the programme administration and contractors. Two of the implementing agencies – the Central Financing and Contracting Unit (CFCU) and the Implementing Agency at the Ministry of Regional Development and Public Work (MRDPW) had their right to manage aid withdrawn. Also, at the SAPARD agency which would oversee the implementation of 445 million euros of funding to modernize agriculture and the countryside, there were a number of serious problems. First, there were OLAF investigations relating to projects worth 26 million euros regarding fraud and corruption. Second, the former executive director of the SAPARD Agency was accused of the wrongful approval of projects and criminal proceedings had been initiated against him. Third, 105 million euros had still to be paid to beneficiaries and there were serious control weaknesses in the investment aid system. OLAF commented about there being a lack of haste in the investigation of the SAPARD irregularities (European Commission 2008). There were also concerns expressed by OLAF about breaches in confidentiality, improper transmission and leaks of sensitive information, possibly involving organized crime. This has been strongly disputed by Bulgarian officials who argue that one such major leak involved journalists and not organized criminals – (interview with Bulgarian Officials 2010).

The report caused immense damage to Bulgaria's reputation and, as Gawthorpe (2010) observes, it severely damaged confidence in Bulgaria's capacity to function as a full member of the EU. Owing to the pressure she was under, Bulgaria did attempt to respond quickly to these concerns to try to strengthen administrative capacity, control systems and to guard against potential conflicts of interest. The Commission recognized in its 2010 Report on Progress in Bulgaria under the Co-operation and Verification Mechanism, that progress had been made but Bulgaria still needed to substantially strengthen its capacity to correctly manage EU funding and that OLAF was concerned about leaks of confidential information as well as the slow progress of cases through the Bulgarian legal system (European Commission 2010a).

Working with OLAF

Despite the difficulties discussed above and the concerns expressed by OLAF, the Bulgarian AFCOS officials believe that there is a very good and co-operative relationship (interview with Bulgarian officials 2010). They cite the investigations into the SAPARD frauds and irregularities, which although damaging to Bulgaria's reputation did illustrate the close co-operation that exists between AFCOS and OLAF. One of the frauds investigated concerned a scam involving 50 Bulgarian enterprises defrauding SAPARD of 4 million pounds involving grants to replace old meat-processing equipment. Old East-German-built meat processors were shipped from Germany and bought as 'new' for 24 times the original price. From a distance the machines which had been painted white looked very new; up close and investigators having scraped some of the paint away, the unmistakable mark of quality 'Made in the GDR' was revealed (interview with Bulgarian officials 2010). The investigations and co-operation were greatly facilitated by OLAF in the opinion of Bulgarian officials – 'They put us in touch with the right people in Germany' (interview with Bulgarian officials 2010). OLAF agents were able to ascertain that invoices had been overpriced for purchases by SAPARD for meat-processing plants in Bulgaria (European Commission 2010b). The former head of the State Agriculture Fund, Assen Droumov, and a political associate and a businessman and fund-raiser of the Socialist Party with ties to then prime minister Stanishev were indicted for fraud and received substantial prison sentences in 2010 (interview with Bulgarian officials 2010).

In the area of cigarette smuggling and counterfeiting and the avoidance of duty, there has also been a good level of co-operation between AFCOS and OLAF. In 2008, OLAF requested assistance from the Bulgarian authorities with respect to contraband Chinese cigarettes – Jin Ling – which had been found in several EU member states. There was suspected involvement of Bulgarian companies in the counterfeiting and smuggling of these contraband cigarettes and there was co-operation between OLAF officials, the AFCOS Directorate, Customs Agency and the Border Police. Customs offences and illegal production of cigarettes were discovered and the Bulgarian authorities received a commendation from OLAF for their co-operation in this case (interview with Bulgarian officials 2010). Despite the difficulties and problems that have been discovered and pointed out above, on the ground, there are instances of effective and valuable co-operation. AFCOS officials do stress that when they require assistance from other member state agencies, they always approach them through OLAF as they know that they will be put in touch with the most appropriate people and they greatly value this (interview with Bulgarian officials 2010).

Conclusions

Bulgaria has had a rocky path to accession and since accession. There have been serious concerns expressed about her ability to adequately manage EU funds and also to effectively fight fraud and corruption. She has made genuine attempts to create and install an effective anti-fraud structure but, given the high levels of fraud and corruption in the country, EU funds will be vulnerable from corrupt officials and the activities of organized criminals. Not all the blame for this situation can be laid at the door of Bulgaria. She was not adequately prepared for accession and there had been a failure to adequately strengthen administrative capacity. There is obviously much work that needs to be done. However, to be fair to Bulgaria, she is one of the poorest countries in Europe; it was inevitable therefore that she would find it difficult to absorb hundreds of millions of euros of pre-accession aid. She did not have sufficient administrative or bureaucratic capacity; therefore in the absence of such a legitimate and administrative network, it was inevitable that informal networks which have long existed in this part of Europe would become involved. The Bulgarian bureaucracy had not been prepared to handle such vast amounts of funds and the authorities in Brussels as well as more established member states should bear some of the responsibility for a failure to tackle such a crucial structural weakness.

There are examples of effective co-operation with OLAF and there is a genuine appreciation on the part of AFCOS officials for the help and support which OLAF has offered to Bulgaria over the years. The question will remain: was and is Bulgaria being asked to reach – and reach quickly – a standard that few of the established member states reach, or which took them many years and a significant investment to achieve? Is this a case of stable doors slamming as consequence of a hasty accession process or is it a case of political necessity with the desire and even need to reassure domestic audiences in Western Europe that a tough line is being taken with so-called 'corrupt' member countries in relation to EU funds? And how long will the EU support Bulgaria until and when both the standard and the reassurance are achieved?

Notes

1 PHARE: Poland and Hungary Assistance for Restructuring their Economies programme; ISPA: Instrument for Structural Policies for Pre-Accession; SAPARD: Special Accession Programme for Agriculture and Rural Development.
2 OJL 312, 23/12/1995, pp. 1–4.
3 OJL 292 15/11/1996, pp. 2–5.
4 OJL 136 31/05/1999, pp. 1–7.
5 OJ C316, 27/11/1995, p. 49.
6 The Common Agricultural Policy.
7 Online. Available HTTP: <http://ec.europa.eu/public_opinion/index_en.htm> (accessed 8 July 2014).

References

AFCOS Bulgaria (2007) *Strategy for the Protection of the Financial Interests of the European Community.*

Barnes, A. (2007) 'Extricating the state: The move to competitive capture in post-Communist Bulgaria', *Europe-Asia Studies*, 59(1): 71–95.

Bojicic-Dzelilovic, V. and Bojkov, V.D. (2005) 'Informality in post-communist transition: Determinants and consequences of the privatization process in Bulgaria', *Southeast European and Black Sea Studies*, 5(1): 69–88.

Center for the Study of Democracy (2007) *Anti-Corruption Reforms in Bulgaria Key Results and Risks*, Sofia: Centre for the Study of Democracy.

Chavdarova, T. (2001) 'Corruption in the Bulgarian post-Communist transformation', *South-East Europe Review for Labour and Social Affairs*, 3: 9–18.

Duyne, P.C. van (2003) 'Greasing the organisation of crime markets in Europe', in P.C. van Duyne, K. von Lampe and J.L. Newell (eds) *Criminal Finances and Organising Crime in Europe*, Nijmegen: Wolf Legal Publishers.

Engelbrekt, K. (2007) 'Bulgaria's EU accession and the issue of accountability: An end to buck passing?', *Problems of Post Communism*, 54(4): 3–14.

European Commission (2008) *Report on the Management of EU Funds in Bulgaria*, Luxembourg: Office of Official Publications of the European Communities.

European Commission (2010a) *Report of the European Anti-Fraud Office*, Tenth Activity Report for the period 1 January 2009 to 31 December 2009, Luxembourg: Office of Official Publications of the European Communities.

European Commission (2010b) *Report on Progress in Bulgaria under the Co-operation and Verification Mechanism*, Luxembourg: Office of Official Publications of the European Communities.

Fenyk, J. (2007) 'The level of implementation of the Convention on the protection of the EC's financial interests and of the follow-up protocols in the Czech Republic', *European Law and National Criminal Legislation*, 1: 116–121.

Ganev, V.I. (2001) 'Winners as state breakers in post communism', *Communist and Post Communist Studies*, 34(1): 1–25.

Gawthorpe, S. (2010) 'Unstable membership: Bulgaria, corruption and policy of the European Union', *New Voices in Public Policy*, 4(2): 1–14.

Gheorge, L. (2006) *Privatisation, Institutional Culture and Corruption in Romania*. Online. Available HTTP: < http://www.10iacc.org/content-ns.phtml?documents=300&art=11 > (accessed 8 July 2014).

Ghitescu, F. and Banciu, M. (2001) 'Economic crime in Romania', *The Journal of Social, Political & Economic Studies*, 26(4): 643–669.

Giatzidis, E. (2004) 'Bulgaria on the road to European Union', *Southeast European and Black Sea Studies*, 4(3): 434–457.
Illett, N. (2004) 'The European Anti-Fraud Office (OLAF)', *Journal of Financial Crime*, 12(2): 120–122.
Krastev, I. (2002) 'How to control corruption in South Eastern Europe: The case of Bulgaria', *Southeast European and Black Sea Studies*, 2(1): 119–125.
Murawska, A. (2004) 'Impact of the enlargement on the protection of the financial interests of the European community against fraud', Second Pan-European Conference Standing Group on EU Politics, Bologna, 24–26 June 2004.
Passas, N. and Nelken, D. (1993) 'The thin line between legitimate and criminal enterprises: Subsidy frauds in the European Community', *Crime, Law and Social Change*, 19: 223–243.
Quirke, B. (2006) 'Economic crime and legal competence in the EU', in P.C. van Duyne, A. Maljevic, M. van Dijck, K. von Lampe and J.L. Newell (eds) *The Organisation of Crime for Profit*, Nijmegen: Wolf Legal Publishers.
Quirke, B. (2008) 'EU Fraud and new member states: The case of the Czech Republic', in P.C. van Duyne, J. Harvey, A. Maljevic, K. von Lampe and M. Scheinost (eds) *European Crime Markets at Cross-roads*, Nijmegen: Wolf Legal Publishers.
Quirke, B. (2009) 'Romania and the fight against EU fraud: A Balkan success story?', in P.C. van Duyne, S. Donati, J. Harvey, A. Maljevic and K.von Lampe (eds) *Crime, Money and Criminal Mobility in Europe*, Nijmegen: Wolf Legal Publishers.
Quirke, B. and Doig, A. (2011) 'Bulgaria and EU fraud: A case of better late than never', in G. Antonopoulos, M. Groenhuijsen, J. Harvey, T. Kooijmans, A. Maljevic and K. von Lampe (eds) *Usual and Unusual Organizing Criminals in Europe and Beyond*, Apeldoorn: MAKLU, 190.
Ruimschotel, D. (1994) 'The EC budget: Ten per cent fraud? A policy analysis approach', *Journal of Common Market Studies*, 32(3): 319–342.
Scheinost, M. (2006) 'Some reflections on researching financial and economic crime', in P.C. van Duyne, A. Maljevic, M. van Dijck, K. von Lampe and J.L. Newell (eds) *The Organisation of Crime for Profit*, Nijmegen: Wolf Legal Publishers.
Sherlock, A. and Harding, M. (1991) 'Controlling fraud within the European Community', *European Law Review*, 16(1): 20–36.
Sieber, U. (1998) 'Eurofraud: Organised fraud against the financial interests of the EU', *Crime, Law and Social Change*, 30(1): 1–42.
Sigma (2004) *Draft Report of the Assessment of the Anti-Fraud System in Bulgaria*, Paris: OECD.
Spencer, J. (2007) 'The illicit movement of people across borders', in P.C. van Duyne, A. Maljevic, M. van Dijck, K von Lampe and J. Harvey (eds) *Crime Business and Crime Money in Europe*, Nijmegen: Wolf Legal Publishers.
Tutt, N. (1989) *Europe on the Fiddle: The Common Market Scandal*, London: Croom Helm.

15

Facilitators of environmental crime

Corporations and governments in the port of Antwerp

Lieselot Bisschop

Introduction

The focus of this chapter is on environmental crime, a topic that challenges our criminological thinking. First, it requires us to consider harm that might not be readily observable and might only manifest itself over time (Hillyard et al. 2004; White 2011). In considering the potential causes of transnational environmental crime, it boils down to everyday practices in contemporary society (Croall 2005; Long et al. 2012; Snider 2008). The emergence can be explained by the actions and omissions of corporations, state actors and individuals. It is difficult and maybe even confrontational to pinpoint the causes. Second, environmental crime and harm also easily transcend national borders, requiring us to think outside of traditional state-based frames of reference. Today's globalized world is contributing to the occurrence of harms and crimes due to its 'criminogenic asymmetries'. These are 'structural discrepancies, mismatches and inequalities in the realms of economy, law, politics and culture [...] fuelling the demand for illegal goods and services; generating incentives for people and organisations to engage in illegal practices; and reducing the ability of authorities to control crime' (Passas 1999: 3). In environmental matters, regulation or enforcement can be asymmetrical and cause corporations to look for the most profitable (illegal) arrangement to trade waste (legal asymmetry). In other words, global trade flows create the opportunity of 'using the space between the laws' (Passas 1999). Awareness about environmental issues can also be different between regions and countries (cultural asymmetries). Communities affected by the environmental crimes of pollution are often unaware of harm causes (knowledge asymmetry) or do not have the economic means or political rights to oppose to the polluter (economic/political asymmetry) (Andreas 2002). Legal, cultural, knowledge and economic asymmetries can create an extra incentive for the illegal trade in waste (Passas 2000). In this way, social, political and economic power asymmetries between and within nations affect the occurrence of environmental crime.

The aetiology of transnational environmental crime is thus inherently connected to the broader context of today's globalized asymmetric society (Ruggiero 2009; Van Erp and Huisman 2010). The environmental harm is then externalized through the global supply chains which allow harm and risk to be far removed from the consumers of the products (Lynch and Stretesky 2003; White 2008). Thinking about environmental crime from a supply chain perspective implies paying attention to the transferences of harm, the departure locations, followed routes and final destinations of illicit commodities. This chapter provides insights on environmental crime in one location on the global flows of waste: the port of Antwerp (Belgium). Attention will be paid to the broader European (and global) context that shapes both the emergence and the governance of the illegal trade in (e)waste.

The focus of this analysis is on the role of corporate and government actors in environmental crime. Corporations might see opportunities for profit through criminal activities because the risk of detection is low. Other companies might see criminality as a sole option in order to survive. The former is what Gobert and Punch (2003) referred to as crime-facilitative industries whereas the latter are crime-coercive. Crime-coercive and crime-facilitative are extremes on a continuum rather than strict categories. Further in this chapter, the characteristics of the waste sector are discussed, providing insights about to what extent it is crime-prone. Individual and organized criminals could also merely be using the ports as means for their illegal trade. Companies working in the port might be unknowingly infiltrated by criminals. As for the role of government actors, Michalowski and Kramer (2007) referred to state-facilitated crime when governments fail to regulate illegal behaviour. When state actors initiate harmful activities, this is state-initiated crime. Governmental actors have for instance been found to facilitate illegal trade in clothes manufacturing through weak legislative frameworks, a lack of implementation of regulation and some state actors have been found to be complicit in crime (Connor and Haines 2013). Both corporations and governments can thus be involved in criminality through actions and inactions. The goal of this chapter is to examine whether and how corporate and government actors in the port of Antwerp facilitate environmental crime.

The findings are based on a multi-method approach of document analyses, interviews and field visits. Both the document analyses and the interviews triangulate government, corporate and civil society perspectives. The document analyses studied the existing international, European and national (Belgian and Ghanaian) regulation and litigation as well as available corporate and NGO documents. This study was further based on 56 semi-structured interviews with law enforcement (customs, police, environmental inspectorates, port authority, and judiciary), corporate actors (shipping lines and agents, e-waste collectors and recyclers) and civil society actors (informal e-waste workers, NGOs, local communities). The findings from the document analyses and the interviews were triangulated with data from the field visits in the port of Antwerp (Belgium) and Tema (Ghana). This research is based in a local research setting: the port of Antwerp. The analysis is thus tailored to that specific empirical reality. By analysing the cases within their broader context – looking at the global trade flows – dimensions that reach beyond the local research setting of Antwerp were accounted for. The flows between Antwerp and Ghana were the particular focus. This chapter makes no claims for generalization of the findings to other regions and trade flows, but does provide insights that help understand the social organization, emergence and governance of illegal trade in (e-)waste in other locations.

In answering this research question, this chapter starts out by discussing the general context of ports, crime and security. It continues by summarizing the characteristics of the (European) waste sector and its connection to environmental crime. Then the emergence of the illegal trade in e-waste is explained. Building on this general context, the role of corporate and government actors in the illegal trade in e-waste in the port of Antwerp is discussed. The discussion relates these findings back to frameworks on organizational, state–corporate and environmental crime.

Ports, crime and security

Containerized transport has become the norm, ever increasing since the first container ship crossed the Atlantic 60 years ago. This allows for easy transport throughout the world, changing between sea, road and rail, and significantly reduced vessel turnaround times and costs of shipping (Coulter 2002). Containerized transport has enabled the rapid growth of international trade in recent decades (Levinson 2006). Within this context of increased speed and quantity of trade, the transport sector has a difficult task of finding a balance between the conflicting demands of flexibility and security. The transport system is deemed vulnerable to diverse crimes against property and persons such as terrorism, smuggling of weapons and various kinds of contraband (Vander Beken and Van Daele 2008). There are a number of general criminogenic characteristics of trade and port activities. First, the anonymity of containers offers opportunities for transporting illicit commodities (Griffiths and Jenks 2012; UNODC 2011). Second, the sector of international maritime transports and trade through ports is known for its somewhat in-transparent way of communication (Denoiseux 2010). Third, the massive amount of goods traded, the short time frame, the diversity of people and activities and the scale of the area make controls difficult. Fourth, there is a diversity of actors that might be involved. A twenty-first-century ship may be owned by a transnational corporation, operated by a specialist international ship management company, crewed by an international crewing company with employees from throughout the world and licensed in an offshore commercial registry (Bloor et al. 2013).

Seaports are at the intersection of trade management, security and crime prevention (Eski 2011). In port governance different stakeholders need to be taken into account. A port is much more than simply a place where ships dock. It is a crossroad of different trade flows and harbours diverse activities from transport and handling over storage to production. This goes hand in hand with the presence of many actors in different sectors. This concerns port employees, corporations located in the port, auxiliary services, governments, communities and the general public. Balancing the interests of these different stakeholders can be difficult. The main concern used to be with safety and efficiency of transportation, which changed to a focus on port security and the prevention of terrorism in the 9/11 aftermath (Helmick 2008). Besides avoiding accidents and other safety issues, the main concern in securing harbours ever since 9/11 has been with terrorism. Environmental security in ports largely boils down to port pollution, in reference to the pollution of nearby ecosystems by ballast water and port emissions. The maximization of port through-put may not be in the same line as concerns for security or to protect the environment (Talley 2009). This case study aims to illustrate how corporate and government port actors potentially play a role in environmental crime in the broader sense of the externalization of harm through supply chains. Before this article turns to the particular case study, this chapter discusses the characteristics of the (European) waste sector and its connection to environmental crime.

Waste and environmental crime

Waste is one of the most prominent environmental issues in contemporary society and at the same time one of the most normalized. The proportions of the waste problem are significant and have increased with the pace of world population and consumption. As a consequence of more stringent regulations on releasing waste in water, air or land, waste management prices increased in the industrialized countries. This caused waste to become a true article of trade. Waste is not just something a society wants to get rid of; it is an important commodity.

As a forerunner in environmental policy-making (Vig and Faure 2004) and a major consumption region, responsible waste management is an important goal for the EU, especially in view of using the secondary resources that lie within Europe's urban mine. Europe has a thriving recycling sector with several of the world's highest-standards recycling facilities located on the continent (e.g. Belgium and Germany). Waste transports for instance make up a share of about 15 per cent of all transports within the EU (IMPEL-TFS 2006; 2012). As for the transnational dimension of the waste trade, most stays within the EU or takes place between OECD countries. Problematic flows are mostly from the EU, North America, Australia to (West) Africa, Southeast Asia and South America, so basically from the global North to the global South. Together with the Netherlands, Germany and Switzerland, Belgium is among the top four exporters of hazardous waste according to the data of the Basel Convention Secretariat. Both Belgium and the Netherlands are however mainly waste trade countries since their populations do not produce the massive quantities of waste exported from their countries. An estimated 80 per cent of waste in the port of Antwerp is in transit. Belgium trades about 1.3 million tonnes of hazardous waste per year. One in five containers exported from the EU contains waste and an estimated 20 per cent of those are in violation of export bans or administrative requirements for waste trading (Baird et al. 2014). Belgium is also an important country for e-waste trade, together with Germany, the Netherlands and the United Kingdom. These four also register the most illegal transports. Rotterdam and Antwerp have both been labelled hubs for (illegal) waste shipments (De Rijck 2011; IMPEL-TFS 2005). In part, this is a mere consequence of the economic and geographic reality for Belgium and the Netherlands, which means they have important seaports and function as transit countries for inland Europe.[1] As ports that serve shipping routes to Africa and China, the high number of waste transports to non-OECD countries could partially be a mere economic given. In contrast, ports in Southern Europe hardly ever control for illegal e-waste transports, thereby reducing their likelihood of having high statistics (Van Erp and Huisman 2010).

The waste sector is part of the legal economy, but meanwhile prompts different kinds of illegalities. It has several vulnerabilities to crime in both the characteristics of the sector and the product (Vander Beken 2007). As for the sector, its rapid growth and international character allowed a diversity of actors to work in the waste industry, with brokers involved at different stages. In collection, transport and treatment, multiple smaller companies try to compete with the few big ones. There are also a number of tensions inherent to waste as a commodity. It has been linked to price fixing, racketeering and a black market in waste (Van Daele et al. 2007). It has an inverse incentive structure due to its negative value. It is a product of low integrity since it can be easily mixed up or sold as second-hand commodities (Gibbs et al. 2010; Vander Beken 2007). Waste crimes, whether in transport or disposal, answer to several characteristics of corporate crime (Huisman 2001). Because the crimes often remain hidden, the transition from legal to illegal can occur at several stages of the waste process. This can happen in national and cross-border transport but also in collection or disposal. Waste can be more cheaply dealt with by illegal enterprises who disregard environmental regulations or by legal companies in Europe who treat waste they are not licensed for with potential partnerships between the two (Ruggiero and South 2010).

Illegal transports of waste have been identified as a major form of environmental crime by the international law enforcement community (e.g. Interpol, IMPEL) and led to the adoption of international and European legislative frameworks that regulate waste transports (e.g. Basel Convention on the control of transboundary movements of hazardous wastes and their disposal, European Waste Shipment Regulation, etc.). Waste crimes are considered an important type of environmental crime and make up an important share of the cases reported by enforcement agencies. However, the legislation itself holds several vulnerabilities to crime (Vander Beken 2007). The Basel Convention and EU legal framework for waste are not always interpreted and implemented with the same commitment amongst the parties. Moreover, the Basel Convention is primarily intended to regulate trade and not to control for illegal trade. National differences in policy and particularly implementation still exist, even within the EU. Waste is a topic just like other environmental issues that can be about administrative as well as criminal proceedings and both do not necessarily have the same objectives in mind. Against this background, this chapter turns to a discussion of the illegal trade in e-waste within the research setting of the port of Antwerp.

Explaining the illegal trade in e-waste

The intent of this chapter is to pinpoint the activities within one location on the global flows of e-waste. Before turning to the role of corporate and government actors within the port of Antwerp, this chapter summarizes the findings of a previous study into the illegal trade of e-waste between Belgium and Ghana (Bisschop 2012). This will help understand the global dimensions that influence the local setting in its connection to environmental crime. Supply and demand provide motivations and opportunities for illegal e-waste transports (Gibbs et al. 2010; Van Erp and Huisman 2010). Explanations for the illegal trade can be found in individuals, corporations as well as societal structures (Clinard and Yeager 1980; Huisman 2001; Slapper and Tombs 1999). To understand the illegal trade in e-waste, this study looked at the supply chain from producers and consumers through collection and transport to destinations of e-waste. At the start of the e-waste flow, consumers discard their no longer functioning television sets, refrigerators or computers. Next in line are e-waste collectors, recyclers and refurbishers in developed as well as developing countries (Schluep et al. 2008; 2011). The following summarizes push factors in countries of origin and pull factors in countries of destination.

The push factors in countries of origin refer to production, consumption and collection of e-waste. Virtually every day a new electronic device is released, one that we cannot seem to live without. By 2017, an estimated annual volume of 65.4 million tonnes of electronics will be end-of-life (Duan et al. 2013). With regular new releases and sometimes even planned obsolescence, producers influence the quantity of electronics consumers perceive as waste (Pellow 2007). By (not) choosing to phase out toxic components they impact the quality and toxicity. Consumers obviously play an important role in pushing the illegal trade in e-waste. Because of a choice for cheaper disposal or because of limited awareness about proper recycling, consumers influence the illegal trade in e-waste. Corporate, government and individual consumers sometimes sell their e-waste to actors who offer to treat it for (too) low prices. Generally, the collection of e-waste is a concern for government and corporate consumers, but the necessary due diligence about where the e-waste ends up afterwards is not always present. Legal and environmentally sound treatment of e-waste is only possible in a handful of companies whose prices are often high. This makes it attractive to look for cheaper – less environmentally sound – alternatives. E-waste includes devices with waste treatment costs for which the exportation as second-hand products saves the cost of treatment. Other products hold enough valuable components (e.g. precious metals) to make recycling or treatment profitable, creating a motivation to dismantle the goods as cheaply as possible (Sander and Schilling 2010).

The collection phase of e-waste is another push factor for illegal transports of e-waste, with various interconnections between legal and illegal actors. The collection takes places through metal scrap dealers, urban recycling centres, refurbishers, official take-back systems (e.g. Recupel), registered metal collectors (e.g. picking up disposal skips from electronic hardware stores) and informal actors (e.g. waste tourists, internet or charities). These collectors are located throughout Belgium as well as other European countries. Several of the companies involved in e-waste collection work legally and see traffickers as competitors. Others engage in export – often through brokers – to developing countries. Other legal actors in e-waste collection are scrap metal dealers and refurbishers. However, some of those also feed into illegal transports (un)intentionally. More individual shippers of e-waste are so-called 'waste tourists', who often have family connections in the countries of destination and sometimes use false passports to travel to the EU.

The pull factors are located at the end of the e-waste flows, in countries of destination. The institutional framework in countries of destination – or lack thereof – is a first pull factor, although this should not be overstated (Schluep et al. 2008). Second, the precarious socio-economic situation of many of these countries makes the import of e-waste financially attractive (Basel Action Network and Silicon Valley Toxics Coalition 2002). Imports of e-waste are a way to increase revenue (through taxes), so-called garbage imperialism (Pellow 2007). Informal repair, refurbishment, collection and dismantling of discarded and second-hand electronics is estimated to be the sole source of livelihood for almost 1 per cent of the Ghanaian population. In countries like Ghana, the import, sale, fixing and dismantling of UEEE (used electronic and electrical equipment) employs many in the informal economy (Amoyaw-Osei et al. 2011; Prakash and Manhart 2010). Regardless of whether this concerns illegally traded e-waste or legally traded second-hand electronics, both are likely to end up on the dumpsites, because there are no adequate recycling facilities in the region. This results in harm to environmental and human health. A little under 1 per cent of Ghanaians have informal WEEE (waste electronic and electrical equipment) repairs or refurbishing as their sole means of livelihood (Prakash and Manhart 2010). This is a third pull factor. Fourth, electronics imports into Ghana help people to be part of the digital world. Bridging this digital divide is not entirely positive. Inadequate handling and disposal of e-waste harms environmental and human health as well as the economy and politics. Developing countries are left with old technologies and e-waste. Fifth and finally, the informal e-waste collectors and dismantlers feed into the legal e-waste industry through the increased demand for secondary raw materials on the global market.

In between those push factors in countries of origin and those pull factors in countries of destination lie facilitating factors in the transport phase. These corporate and government actors in transport set the structural context for illegal flows and may even actively facilitate smuggling. The following case study of the port of Antwerp – one crossroad on the global supply chain of e-waste – sheds light on this.

Case study of the port of Antwerp

Despite being influenced by global trade and asymmetries, the port of Antwerp has particular characteristics. Antwerp developed into an international trade market in the fifteenth century. Despite some setbacks throughout the centuries, Antwerp developed into the well-known and flourishing international port it is today (Blondé and Deceulaer 2002). It is ranked amongst the top three ports in Europe with Rotterdam and Hamburg. About 185 million tonnes of commodities are traded in Antwerp each year. Given its inland location, the port has multiple connections to Europe's hinterland. Antwerp is a transit port, a stopover on global trade routes where cargo is unloaded and redirected within limited time frames. Of all the freight, 37 per cent is loaded back onto sea-going vessels and 35 per cent goes to neighbouring countries by inland shipping and rail. Only 12 per cent is destined for companies located in the port and 16 per cent is for Belgian distribution. Singapore is the typical example of a transit port, with a reputation of high efficiency (40,000 containers per day) and low corruption,[2] but it is at the same time known as a hub for environmental contraband because transit inspections are limited (Schmidt 2004). When compared with the port of Rotterdam, Antwerp does not have the best reputation for environmental crime control (Huisman and Van Erp 2013). Antwerp has been labelled a hub for environmental crime.[3]

Antwerp is a so-called a landlord port, where the land is owned by government and managed by a port authority who gives up its control over port operations by leasing the infrastructure to private terminal operators (Talley 2009). In fact, the territory of the port of Antwerp is governed by two jurisdictions (Dendermonde and Antwerp) and three municipalities (Antwerp, Beveren and Zwijndrecht) and falls under the responsibility of two provincial governments (East Flanders and Antwerp). The Antwerp port is a complex area for prevention and control. It covers 130km^2, has 180km of quay, 400km of roads, 1000km of railway and about 900 companies work in the port area. The following sections focus on the role of corporate and government actors in the port of Antwerp in the illegal trade in e-waste.

Corporate actors in the port

Often located in the vicinity of ports, storage and transhipment facilities can be involved in illegal waste shipments. This refers to facilities that receive e-waste or used goods of different quality by rail or road transport from other countries. In the storage facilities this is mixed up for the overseas shipments. Often, these facilities for storage and handling buy and sell the waste and as brokers they organize the transport. Government respondent 27 explained that these businesses create invoices with little information about the origin of the waste or second-hand commodities with the intent of hampering controls. Some of the brokers and traders in e-waste are thus deliberately participating in the illegal trade. Several of the respondents believed the traders, brokers and intermediaries to be the 'biggest crooks'. E-waste is considered especially prone to fraud, because many actors can buy and sell, often as their sole means of income.

The role of other corporate actors in the illegal trade in e-waste is of a more facilitative nature, often unknowingly aiding the illegal trade, resulting from a lack of due diligence and/or awareness. First, there is the role played by shipping agents. A shipping agent is paid by the buyer or seller to organize the transport over road or inland waterways to the nearest port and handles the goods in the port. They take care of the bill of lading and other transport documentation and arrange the payments and deposits. Shipping agents usually do not engage themselves with the content of the transports. As they explained in the interviews, the shipping agents base their business on trusting the shippers. They shift the responsibility for the content of the transports to actors earlier in the chain: the shippers. 'The papers are faxed and I don't know what's truly inside the containers or vehicles. I'm not there when they are loaded' (corporate respondent 23). Shipping agents, and especially those that do the handling and storage as well, however, have a possibility to know both the content and the shipper. Some shipping agents acknowledged there had been problems with second-hand vehicles being used as vessels for illegal trade. They therefore took initiative to know their clients, refusing the problematic ones or informing them about what is allowed, warning them about possible fines. Others, however, work with whatever clients they can get and expressed that these shipments should not be prohibited because they are useful for the countries of destination. They allow their clients to deliberately withhold information about final destinations of shipments of waste, despite this being a requirement in the European Waste Shipment Regulation. Several actors thus shift the responsibility to someone else in the supply chain. This denial of responsibility is a way to reason away their role in the harm that might have occurred, a typical neutralization technique for white-collar crime (Coleman 1987). Similar neutralization techniques have been found in other studies on environmental crime in Europe

(Huisman and Van Erp 2013). This illustrates how difficult it is to pinpoint who is responsible for corporate environmental crime.

Shipping lines are generally not concerned with the contents of the containers (Sander and Schilling 2010). Environmental issues are not a major concern. As an NGO respondent (20) phrased it: 'Many shipping lines are not intrinsically motivated to know what is inside containers'. Through their services, however, they facilitate illegal transports. Only few take the initiative to refuse certain shipments, informed by economic, ethical and political considerations (Bartley 2007). They also face the financial risk of fines and of costs of transports not being refunded after seizures. Although shipping lines do not strictly have a legal responsibility in illegal e-waste, fear for criticism by their stakeholders can play a role (reputational damage). Shipping lines have started to cooperate with European government agencies to see how they can help in prevention and control. However, as witnessed during the field visits and interviews, many port actors continue to be unaware of the illegal trade and its potential harms. 'Although environmental issues could be part of the broader denominator of security, it is still not a major concern' (corporate respondent 5).

Shipping lines, agents and terminal operators thus have e-waste smugglers as clients. Therefore they engage in the transport, whether knowingly or unknowingly. Some of these transit actors lack due diligence and/or awareness and deny being responsible.

Government actors in the port

Due to their massive quantities, flows of commodities are difficult to govern. To a certain extent however, law enforcement is inherently limited in their focus on this topic. We argue that this lack of control can facilitate illegal trade. A detailed account of each of the governance challenges would take us too far, but has been elaborated elsewhere (Bisschop 2013). The following nevertheless illustrates the core issues.

The regulatory framework for waste is very complex. It requires knowledge and technical expertise which is not often available with front-line governance actors. Many actors that are on crossroads of these trade flows (in harbours) do not have enough time or expertise to deal with the issue. Customs and the Harbourmaster's Office (HMO) in Antwerp, due to a lack of sufficient training on these issues, for instance, depend on the environmental inspectorates to judge the suspicious shipments. The low priority and limited resources invested in preventing and controlling the illegal trade in e-waste go against one of the requirements of effective environmental governance as identified by Holley et al. (2012). On a global level, the (inter)governmental initiatives have not addressed the emerging transnational environmental problems or are at least characterized by doubtful enforceability (Meidinger 2002).

Waste fraud is a priority in policy-making and different government actors focus on it. Environmental inspectorates, environmental administrations, customs, maritime and environmental police and public prosecutors are crucial for definitional guidance, for inducing corporate actors to participate through both positive and negative incentives and for using their enforcement capacity (Holley et al. 2012). Despite waste fraud being a priority in Belgian policy, law enforcement efforts are often beset by practical limitations. For example, despite the best efforts of many individual government officials, much of the implementation currently remains local and fragmented. Environmental law enforcement agencies suffer from a lack of funding which negatively affects the available personnel and training resources. In the port of Antwerp, less than 1 per cent of containers are scanned, despite the scanning capacity being much higher. Even if containers were scanned more frequently, the follow-up of cases further in the law enforcement chain is impossible to guarantee. Also inspectorates are limited in staff and the same inspectors often need to check the waste company's premises for licence purposes as well as inspect waste transports in the harbour. This obviously has an impact on the potential for follow-up of detected illegal transports to their source, in view of preventing future illegal trade. There is prosecution of waste cases, but this is difficult to get through court successfully because laws are very complex. Fines that are imposed for illegal e-waste transports are perceived as too low to be effective, although every now and then high fines are imposed. 'A fine is hardly ever imposed. If you're in the waste business, you make that part of your business plan' (corporate respondent C22). For waste in general, 1200 illegal waste shipments were intercepted in the last five years. The Belgian federal police discovered 500 waste companies who worked without the proper licence for the work they were doing and 100 companies even worked completely under the radar.[4] A major flaw in enforcement is that the implementation of the EU conventions in view of determining sanctions is lacking which leaves member states a great margin of interpretation (Billiet and Meeus 2010). It is generally light-handed and inadequate in dealing with environmental crime despite being in the hands of passionate but very few individuals (Fyfe and Reeves 2010; White 2009). They are not always backed up hierarchically let alone politically. 'The problem is not that we don't know where the illicit traffic is, know where to find it or know how to check it. The problem is that we don't have the means to guarantee the follow-up' (government respondent 14).

Port authorities are responsible for port safety, but at the same time they are concerned with the economic prosperity of the harbour (Coulter 2002). As part of the Antwerp Port Authority (APA) the HMO is the department responsible for the safety, peace, public order, integrity and environment of the port area. They most often deal with dangerous goods regulation, the vessel traffic system and violations of environmental legislation. The HMO, together with the waterway police and the inspectorates drafted a regulation[5] on the transport of additional cargo in second-hand vehicles, imposing stricter controls. This occurred because e-waste smugglers increasingly started using cars, trucks and vans to transport waste. Based on the interviews, it indeed seemed that Antwerp had a particular reputation for allowing the extra load. 'There are currently vehicles that are driven from Greece or Italy to be shipped in Antwerp, so there has to be a reason for making this trip worthwhile' (government respondent 15). The regulation requires a bill of lading for the extra load in vehicles and imposes stricter loading instructions. This regulation was difficult in drafting because of fear for economic consequences. This is understandable given that end-of-life vehicles are a major commodity for the port, which might be relocated to lower control ports. The following quote illustrates this tension between environmental and economic issues: 'We have enough traffic now, but it would be bad to see that disappear. Illegal and legal traffic tends to go down and shifts to ports where one feels less targeted. It is better to increase controls in the EU hinterland by means of harmonized legislation and enforcement' (government respondent 9).

Another element in reference to Antwerp's flexible port policy is the possibility of having a 'late bill of lading'. Several respondents stated that it was possible for shippers to deliver the cargo in the port and provide the necessary documentation afterwards, often after the unit had been loaded on the ship. Other respondents said this might have been possible in the past, but was no longer the case. They did say that Antwerp had a more fragmented policy at the terminals, whereas for instance Rotterdam was deemed to be a more 'closed' port, with a more integrated policy. In any case, it is hard to assess to what extent this flexibility of the port of Antwerp is criminogenic. The flexibility can be Antwerp's strengths in competing with Rotterdam and Hamburg which largely have the same hinterland. Antwerp is a harbour that is fairly open, allowing people and goods to get to and out of the port guaranteeing quick shipping. This flexibility is not necessarily a bad thing. It can however provide opportunities for smuggling and make controls difficult. The port policy might simply be shaping the structural context for these trade flows, but could be interpreted as facilitating illegal activities (Kramer et al. 2002).

Discussion: facilitating or governing environmental crime?

Already in 1987, Michalowski and Kramer argued that the transport of hazardous waste to countries with fewer or no legal controls should be studied under the heading of corporate wrongdoing, because it requires active circumventing of laws in home countries. Environmental crimes like the illegal trade in e-waste are inevitably influenced by the global market. Indeed, 'only by moving beyond national laws can we begin to study transgressions that arise in the space between national legal systems' (Michalowski and Kramer 1987: 397). The global supply chains, containerization and the increasing quantity and flexibility of shipments provide a fertile context for economic trade, but at the same time harbour opportunities for those looking to smuggle illicit commodities. In environmental matters these opportunities generally go hand in hand with a small risk of control. This is partially motivated by profit-seeking, but the emergence of these flows is much more complex. The motivations for the smuggling of e-waste are to be understood as part of a broader context, relating to elements throughout the supply chain and within the broader socio-economic context of trade.

Environmental crime has been labelled a crime of the powerful (Lynch and Stretesky 2003; Pearce and Tombs 1998). Indeed, it is a crime of the powerful in the sense that corporate actors from the waste sector are involved in the illegal flows. There is, therefore, undoubtedly a link with white collar crime and corporate crime. Throughout the flows, there is however a diversity of actors, legal, illegal and even more informal (e.g. in Ghana) that contribute to their emergence. Because e-waste and especially second-hand electronics are an accessible trade, individual shippers can get involved in collection and transport of waste and second-hand electronics towards for instance Ghana. Therefore, the social organization of these illegal flows is not only shaped by the involvement of corporate actors, but also by governments and by more informal actors. Actors and organizations in countries of origin, transit and destination each shape the illegal trade flows. The involvement of actors throughout the supply chain varies from crime-facilitating to crime-initiating.

Environmental crime is one of the topics where the realms of politics and economy interrelate. This chapter intended to explore how that applied to the port of Antwerp. This case study illustrated how actors in the port may facilitate illegal transports of e-waste. Some corporations indeed see opportunities for profit through illegal transports of e-waste because the risk of detection is low. For others illegal trade is necessary to survive. It seems like the trade in waste in its different forms is spread out across the continuum from crime-facilitative to crime-coercive (Gobert and Punch 2003). Shipping lines, terminal operators, expeditors and shipping agents – and by extension banks and insurance firms – each have e-waste smugglers as their clients. They do not have a strict legal responsibility for shipping the illegal goods. As a consequence, many shipping actors are not concerned about these issues, shifting the responsibility to other actors involved in the trade flows, thereby facilitating the illegal trade. Few shipping actors feel they have a moral responsibility. Some participate deliberately and actively, which implies their activities facilitate the illegal trade. Others can at least be perceived as lacking due diligence (Kramer et al. 2002).

This case study also illustrated that the lack of governmental control shapes the smuggling of e-waste. Theoretically, the role of governmental actors can be seen on a continuum from a weakness causing the law not to be implemented to the state being complicit to crime (Connor and Haines 2013). In examining the role of actors in the port of Antwerp, the findings do not show an active involvement of governmental actors in crime. The lack of control on the part of the governmental actors could however be labelled as state-facilitated environmental crime (Michalowski and Kramer 2007). Government actors have not failed to develop policy on waste, since there is ample legislation. That policy is however not always met with equal prioritization in enforcement, especially when economic interests are at stake. Future research could continue this inquiry into the variety of social harms that potentially lie at the intersection of business and government. Indeed, 'a full understanding of environmental crime requires an analysis of the illegal behavior of conventional criminal organizations but also of the illicit practices pursued by legitimate economic actors and political representatives' (Ruggiero and South 2013: 370).

At the same time however, this case illustrates that these same actors hold potential for prevention and control. Governing social phenomena requires an understanding about the complexity of elements and actors that explains its emergence. Starting at one location on those flows can help to identify this governance potential. It is crucial to invest in prevention throughout the supply chain to account for the complexity of actors involved. This is especially so given the large amount of goods that enters and leaves a port each day. One way to come across any of these actors transporting e-waste illegally is through the controls of shipments in harbours. To a certain extent this is looking for a needle in a haystack. The port of Antwerp is thus a location of great potential for smugglers of environmental commodities, but at the same time, it is a crucial site for governance.

Notes

1 Geographically, Switzerland, a land without seaports, relies on exports to neighbouring EU countries. It is known to ship waste directly to Belgium, Bulgaria, France, Germany, Poland, Italy, Romania, Serbia, Spain and the Netherlands, but indirectly transports to Africa, Gabon, Nigeria, Brazil and Togo. Germany has an own seaport (Hamburg), but given the size of the country and the distance to Hamburg it is often economically more feasible to ship goods through the ports of Rotterdam and Antwerp from the nearby *Länder* (e.g. Northrein-Westfalen).

2 Singapore has low corruption rates, ranking fifth on the Corruption Perception Index (http://cpi.transparency.org/cpi2013/results/). Possible reasons are that it tries all cases of white- or blue-collar crime stringently (e.g. Corrupt Practices Investigation Bureau) and because public officials and civil servants have high wages (Quah 2003).

3 See for example Belgian news reports: Blokland, H. (27/06/2010) 'Afvallozers glippen te vaak door de mazen van het net' (Waste dumpers too often slip through meshes of the net), *De Morgen*; Holderbeke, J. (2009) *Ons vuil in Afrika* (Our dirt in Africa), Vranckx, Belgium: Canvas; Vanacker, B. (17/2/2010) 'Verdacht hout in Antwerpen' (Suspicious timber in Antwerp), MO*; Debruyne, A. (31/10/2013) 'Dossier E-waste', MO*.

4 As reported by Lars Bove in the newspaper *De Tijd* on 8 February 2014: 'België telt honderden criminele afvalbedrijven' (Belgium has hundreds of criminal waste companies) and 'Georganiseerde criminaliteit springt op afvalkar' (Organized crime jumps on waste trucks).

5 Regulation of 24 November 2011 for handling of second-hand vehicles in the Port of Antwerp (Reglement voor het behandelen van tweedehands voertuigen in de haven van Antwerpen) – entered into force 1 January 2012.

References

Amoyaw-Osei, Y., Opoku Agyekum, O., Pwamang, J.A., Mueller, E., Fasko, R. and Schluep, M. (2011) *Ghana e-Waste Country Assessment. SBC e-Waste Africa Project*. Online. Available HTTP: <http://ewasteguide.info/files/Amoyaw-Osei_2011_GreenAd-Empa.pdf> (accessed 1 July 2014).

Andreas, P. (2002) 'Transnational crime and economic globalization', in M. Berdal and M. Serrano (eds) *Transnational Organized Crime and International Security*, Boulder: Lynne Riener.

Baird, J., Curry, R. and Cruz, P. (2014) 'An overview of waste crime, its characteristics, and the vulnerability of the EU waste sector', *Waste Management and Research*, 32(2): 97–105.

Bartley, T. (2007) 'Institutional emergence in an era of globalization: The rise of transnational private regulation of labor and environmental conditions', *American Journal of Sociology*, 113(2): 297–351. Online. Available HTTP: <http://www.jstor.org/stable/10.1086/518871> (accessed 30 June 2014).

Basel Action Network and Silicon Valley Toxics Coalition (2002) *Exporting Harm: The High-tech Trashing of Asia*, Seattle; San Jose: The Basel Action Network (BAN); Silicon Valley Toxics Coalition (SVTC). Online. Available HTTP: <http://www.ban.org/E-waste/technotrashfinalcomp.pdf> (accessed 1 July 2014).

Billiet, C. and Meeus, R. (2010) 'Europese verordeningen en de handhaver: De sanctieregelingen van milieuverordeningen in het licht van de handhavingspraktijk', *Tijdschrift Voor Milieurecht*, 19(2): 164–202.

Bisschop, L. (2012) 'Is it all going to waste? Illegal transports of e-waste in a European trade hub', *Crime, Law and Social Change*, 58(3): 221–249.

Bisschop, L. (2013) 'Go with the e-waste flows: The governance reality of illegal transports of e-waste in a European trade hub,' in Petrus van Duyne, Jacki Harvey, Georgios Antonopoulos, Klaus von Lampe, Almir Maljević and Jon Spencer (eds) *Human Dimensions in Organised Crime, Money Laundering and Corruption*, Nijmegen: Wolf Legal Publishers, 393–424.

Blondé, B. and Deceulaer, H. (2002) 'The port of Antwerp and its hinterland: Port traffic, urban economies and government policies in the 17th and 18th centuries', in R. Ertesvag, D. Starkey and A. Anne (eds) *Maritime Industries and Public Intervention: The Fourth North Sea History Conference*, Stavanger: Maritime Museum.

Bloor, M., Sampson, H., Baker, S., Walters, D., Dahlgren, K. and Wadsworth, E. (2013) 'Room for manoeuvre? Regulatory compliance in the global shipping industry', *Social and Legal Studies*, 22(2): 171–189.

Clinard, M. and Yeager, P. (1980) *Corporate Crime*, New York: Free Press.

Coleman, J. (1987) 'Towards an integrated theory of white-collar crime', *American Journal of Sociology*, 93(2): 406–439.

Connor, T. and Haines, F. (2013) 'Networked regulation as a solution to human rights abuse in global supply chains? The case of trade union rights violations by Indonesian sports shoe manufacturers', *Theoretical Criminology*, 17(2): 1–18.

Coulter, D. (2002) 'Globalization of maritime commerce: The rise of hub ports', in S. Tangredi (ed.) *Globalization and Maritime Power*, Washington: Institute for National Strategic Studies and National Defense University.

Croall, H. (2005) 'Transnational white collar crime', in J. Sheptycki and A. Wardak (eds) *Transnational and Comparative Criminology*, London: Greenhouse Press.

De Rijck, R. (2011) 'A flaw in the criminal approach of international waste transport in Europe': INECE 9th International Conference. Online. Available HTTP: <http://inece.org/conference/9/papers/de_Rijck_Europe_Final.pdf> (accessed 30 June 2014).

Denoiseux, D. (2010) 'L'exportation de déchets dangereux vers l'Afrique: de las du Probo Koala', *Courrier Hebdomadaire*, 2071: 47.

Duan, H., Miller, T.R., Gregory, J. and Kirchain, R. (2013) *Quantitative Characterization of Domestic and Transboundary Flows of Used Electronics*, Massachusetts: Institute of Technology. Online. Available HTTP: <http://www.step-initiative.org/tl_files/step/_documents/MIT-NCER%20US%20Used%20Electronics%20Flows%20Report%20-%20December%202013.pdf> (accessed 30 June 2014).

Eski, Y. (2011) '"Port of call": Towards a criminology of port security', *Criminology and Criminal Justice*, 11(5): 415–431.

Fyfe, N. and Reeves, A. (2010) 'The thin green line? Police perceptions of the challenges of tackling wildlife crime in Scotland', in R. Yarwood and R. Mawby (eds) *Policing, Rurality and Governance*, London: Ashgate.

Gibbs, C., McGarrell, E.F. and Axelrod, M. (2010) 'Transnational white-collar crime and risk: Lessons from the global trade in electronic waste', *Criminology and Public Policy*, 9(3): 543–560.

Gobert, J. and Punch, M. (2003) *Rethinking Corporate Crime*, London: Reed Elsevier.

Griffiths, H. and Jenks, M. (2012) 'Maritime transport and destabilizing commodity flows', SIPRI Policy Paper, Solna: Stockholm International Peace Research Institute.

Helmick, J. (2008) 'Port and maritime security: A research perspective', *Journal of Transportation Security*, 1(1): 15–28.

Hillyard, P., Pantazis, C., Tombs, S. and Gordon, D. (2004) *Beyond Criminology: Taking Harm Seriously*, Manitoba: Fernwood Publishing.

Holley, C., Gunningham, N. and Shearing, C. (2012) *The New Environmental Governance: Earthscan*, Abingdon: Routledge.

Huisman, W. (2001) *Tussen winst en moraal: Achtergronden van regelnaleving en regelovertreding door ondernemingen*, Den Haag: Boom Juridische Uitgevers.
Huisman, W. and van Erp, J. (2013) 'Opportunities for environmental crime: A test of situational crime prevention theory', *British Journal of Criminology*, 53(6): 1178–1200.
IMPEL-TFS (2005) *IMPEL-TSF Threat Assessment Project, The Illegal Shipments of Waste among IMPEL Member States*. Online. Available HTTP: <http://impel.eu/wp-content/uploads/2010/02/2006-x-Threat-Assessment-Final-Report.pdf> (accessed 1 July 2014).
IMPEL-TFS (2006) *IMPEL-TFS Verification – 2 Project Report. Is What you See What You Get?* Online. Available HTTP: <http://impel.eu/wp-content/uploads/2010/02/2004-16-Verifications-II-Final-Report.pdf> (accessed 1 July 2014).
IMPEL-TFS (2012) *IMPEL – TFS Enforcement Actions III Project Report Enforcement of the European Waste Shipment Regulation. Document Control Sheet Project: Client: Document title: IMPEL Enforcement Actions III IMPEL / SEPA Project No: Originated Document status*, Brussels. Online. Available HTTP: <http://impel.eu/wp-content/uploads/2013/07/IMPEL-Enforcement-Actions-III-Year-1-FINAL-Report-amended-MN-080713.pdf> (accessed 1 July 2014).
Kramer, R., Michalowski, R. and Kauzlarich, D. (2002) 'The origins and development of the concept and theory of state-corporate crime', *Crime and Delinquency*, 48(2): 263–282.
Levinson, M. (2006) *The Box: How the Shipping Container Made the World Smaller and the World Economy Bigger*, Princeton: Princeton University Press.
Long, M.A., Stretesky, P.B., Lynch, M.J. and Fenwick, E. (2012) 'Crime in the coal industry: Implications for green criminology and treadmill of production', *Organization and Environment*, 25(3): 328–346.
Lynch, M. and Stretesky, P. (2003) 'The meaning of green: Contrasting criminological perspectives', *Theoretical Criminology*, 7(2): 217–238.
Meidinger, E. (2002) 'Forest certification as environmental law making by global civil society', in E. Meidinger, C. Elliot and G. Oesten (eds) *Social and Political Dimensions of Forest Certification*, Remagen-Oberwinter: Forstbuch.
Michalowski, R. and Kramer, M. (1987) 'The space between laws: The problem of corporate crime in a transnational context', *Social Problems*, 34(1): 34–53.
Michalowski, R. and Kramer, R. (2007) 'State-corporate crime and criminological inquiry', in H. Pontell and G. Geis (eds) *International Handbook of White-Collar and Corporate Crime*, New York: Springer US.
Passas, N. (1999) 'Globalization, criminogenic asymmetries and economic crime', *European Journal of Law Reform*, 1(4): 399–423.
Passas, N. (2000) 'Global anomie, dysnomie, and economic crime: Hidden consequences of neoliberalism and globalization in Russia and around the world', *Social Justice*, 27(2): 16–44.
Pearce, F. and Tombs, S. (1998) *Toxic Capitalism: Corporate Crime and the Chemical Industry*, Aldershot: Dartmouth Publishing Company.
Pellow, D. (2007) *Resisting Global Toxics: Transnational Movements for Environmental Justice*, Cambridge: MIT Press.
Prakash, S. and Manhart, A. (2010) *Socio-economic Assessment and Feasibility Study on Sustainable E-waste Management in Ghana*, Freiburg: Öko-Instutut e.V.; Inspectorate of the Ministry of Housing, Spatial Planning and the Environment of the Netherlands (VROM-Inspectorate) and the Dutch Association for the Disposal of Metal and Electrical Products (NVMP).
Quah, J. (2003) *Curbing Corruption in Asian: A Comparative Study of Six Countries*, Singapore: Eastern Universities Press.
Ruggiero, V. (2009) 'Transnational crime and global illicit economies', in E. Wilson and T. Lindsey (eds) *Government of the Shadows: Parapolitics and Criminal Sovereignty*, New York: Pluto Books.
Ruggiero, V. and South, N. (2010) 'Green criminology and dirty collar crime', *Critical Criminology*, 18: 251–262.
Ruggiero, V. and South, N. (2013) 'Green criminology and crimes of the economy: Theory, research and praxis', *Critical Criminology*, 21: 359–373.
Sander, K. and Schilling, S. (2010) *Transboundary Shipment of Waste Electrical and Electronic Equipment/Electronic Scrap: Optimization of Material Flows and Control*, The Federal Environment Agency (Germany) – Ökopol GmbH. Online. Available HTTP: <http://www.umweltbundesamt.de/sites/default/files/medien/461/publikationen/k3933.pdf> (accessed 1 July 2014).
Schluep, M., Manhart, A., Osibanjo, O., Rochat, D., Isarin, N. and Mueller, E. (2011) *Where Are WEEE in Africa? Findings from the Basel Convention E-waste Africa Programme*, Berlin: Secretariat of the Basel Convention, UNEP, EU, EMPA, Öko-Institut, IMPEL.

Schluep, M., Rochat, D., Wanjira, A.M., Laissaoui, S.E., Wone, S., Kane, C. and Hieronymi, K. (2008) 'Assessing the e-waste situation in Africa', *Electronics Goes Green 2008+*. Online. Available HTTP: <http://www.academia.edu/1531912/Assessing_the_e-waste_situation_in_Africa> (accessed 1 July 2014).

Schmidt, C. (2004) 'Environmental crimes: Profiting at the Earth's expense', *Environmental Health Perspectives*, 112(2): 96–103.

Slapper, G. and Tombs, S. (1999) *Corporate Crime*, Harlow: Pearson Education Limited.

Snider, L. (2008) 'Corporate economic crimes', in J. Minkes and L. Minkes (eds) *Corporate and White-Collar Crime*, London: Sage.

Talley, W. (2009) *Port Economics*, Florence: Routledge.

UNODC (2011) *Countering the World of Smuggling through Container Control*, UN Office on Drugs and Crime. Online. Available HTTP: <http://www.unodc.org/unodc/en/frontpage/2011/May/countering-the-world-of-smuggling-through-container-control.html> (accessed 30 June 2014).

Van Daele, S., Vander Beken, T. and Dorn, N. (2007) 'Waste management and crime: Regulatory, business and product vulnerabilities', *Environmental Policy and Law*, 37(1): 34–38.

Van Erp, J. and Huisman, W. (2010) 'Smart regulation and enforcement of illegal disposal of electronic waste', *Criminology and Public Policy*, 9(3): 579–590.

Vander Beken, T. (2007) *The European Waste Industry and Crime Vulnerabilities*, Antwerpen: Maklu.

Vander Beken, T. and Van Daele, S. (2008) 'Legitimate business and crime vulnerabilities', *International Journal of Social Economics*, 35(10): 739–750.

Vig, N.J. and Faure, M.G. (2004) *Green Giants? Environmental Policies of the United States and the European Union*, Massachussets: Institute of Technology.

White, R. (2008) *Crimes against Nature: Environmental Criminology and Ecological Justice*, Cullompton: Willan Publishing.

White, R. (2009) *Environmental Crime: A Reader*, Cullompton: Willan Publishing.

White, R. (2011) *Transnational Environmental Crime: Towards an Eco-global Criminology*, New York: Routledge.

16

The limits of environmental regulation in a globalized economy

Lessons from the *Probo Koala* case

Karin van Wingerde

Introduction

Since the 1970s business firms have increasingly been operating across national borders (Braithwaite and Drahos 2000; Gibbs et al. 2010). They exchange products, information, services and personnel all around the globe, thereby increasing the complexity of businesses and creating more complex trade and financial relationships amongst them. The ways in which modern business firms are organized, structured and governed have fundamentally changed (Biermann and Pattberg 2012; DiMaggio 2001; Forsgren 2008; Powell 2001): the traditional firm operating from a fixed location has given way to international dynamic networks of products and services.

While these developments created new opportunities for business firms, they also created greater opportunities for white-collar crime and the transferences of social and environmental risks (Gibbs et al. 2010; Passas 1999; Van Erp and Huisman 2010). The relationship between globalization and white-collar crime has traditionally been explained by the emergence of structural inequalities between different parts of the globe and an uneven distribution of demand and supply (Gibbs et al. 2010; Passas 1999; Van Erp and Huisman 2010). This is what Passas (1999: 400) referred to as 'criminogenic asymmetries' or 'structural disjunctions, mismatches, and inequalities in the spheres of politics, culture, the economy, and the law' that are fostered and intensified by the process of globalization. These asymmetries can cause crime by creating the opportunities to commit crimes, by offering the rationale to engage in these offences, and by making it more difficult for authorities to effectively control these crimes (Passas 1999: 400). For example, globalization has also created the opportunity to transport illegal goods and services across borders. Moreover, differences in regulatory frameworks and low-cost solutions to dispose of and process waste provide growing opportunities for companies to relocate environmentally unfriendly operations to developing countries where environmental regulations are less strict or even absent. In addition, as developing countries often depend on foreign investments to best foster their search for money and job opportunities, they often welcome these firms while at the same time accepting the illegal or harmful activities that come with them (Van Erp and Huisman 2010: 582). These asymmetries between countries thus influence the opportunities for white-collar crime and create serious problems for the regulation and enforcement of business behaviour.

This chapter discusses the problematic nature of regulation and enforcement of these types of crimes based on a single case study of corporate environmental crime in Europe: the *Probo Koala* case. In the summer of 2006, the *Probo Koala*, a Korean-built, Greek-owned, Panamanian-flagged oil tanker chartered by the Dutch-based company Trafigura, arrived in the port of Amsterdam to discharge 554 tonnes of hazardous waste. During the discharge of the waste it appeared that the slops were heavily contaminated. Therefore, the company that was supposed to process the waste could not process it for the fee that both parties had agreed upon and increased its price. Trafigura however declined the renewed offer and, subsequently, the *Probo Koala* left Amsterdam. About a month later the waste was dumped throughout Abidjan, the capital of Ivory Coast, causing health problems amongst local residents as well as worldwide consternation.

The *Probo Koala* case is one of the largest European environmental scandals to date. The case offers an illustrative example of the transference of environmental harms from European to developing countries and of the enforcement problems regarding corporate environmental crime. This chapter offers a detailed analysis of the *Probo Koala* case. In doing so, I will only briefly touch upon the facilitating circumstances that cause these types of crimes, as those are discussed by Lieselot Bisschop in this volume (Chapter 15). The focus of this chapter lies on the ambiguities regarding these types of offences, the problematic nature of legal enforcement against corporate environmental crime, and the possibilities of non-state types of enforcement, particularly the effect that can be expected from social pressures.

Methodology

The *Probo Koala* case is well documented. In the description and analysis of this case I used several investigative reports, parliamentary proceedings, court cases in the Netherlands and the United Kingdom, as well as journal articles, book chapters, books and media reports. Despite the amount of information, there was little consistent reporting about the facts of the case (also White 2008: 108). For instance, the various reports demonstrated significant differences in important details of the case, such as dates, amounts of waste materials involved, and amounts of money paid for the treatment of the waste. Furthermore, findings presented as facts in one report were contradicted by another. As will be discussed in the following sections, this is in part due to the many legal complexities and ambiguities that characterize cases of corporate environmental crime. At the same time, however, we should also consider the potential bias that may be present in many of the sources about this case. As is common for corporate or white-collar crime, there are many different actors involved in the *Probo Koala* case. These include governments, inspection authorities, firms, victims, lawyers, experts and NGOs. Consequently, there are many different interests at play. As these actors look after their own interests, their reports may be designed to support their own positions (also Gibbs and Simpson 2009). On the one hand, this collection of materials offers a rich description of the case, enabling an increased understanding of the complexities involved and of the problematic nature of the regulation and enforcement of corporate environmental crimes. On the other hand, we should keep the conflicting interests of the involved parties in mind when evaluating the information from the different sources.

This chapter begins by providing a chronology of the incident in Abidjan. The three sections that follow discuss the legal ambiguities regarding these types of offences, the problematic nature of legal enforcement against corporate environmental crime, and the possibilities of non-state types of enforcement, particularly the effect that can be expected from social pressures. The analysis in these sections identifies two conditions under which regulation may result in better compliance with environmental regulations. These conditions will be discussed in the final section of this chapter.

The *Probo Koala* case: chronology of events

Although many of the details of the *Probo Koala* case are still debated, according to the reports of several investigation committees instituted after the incident,[1] the story began in October 2004 when Trafigura first chartered the *Probo Koala* (Lord Fraser 2010: 5; United Nations 2009: 7). Trafigura is one of the world's largest independent commodity trading companies. The firm is privately owned and its operations include the trading of oil, petroleum, gasoline, metals, coal and naphtha (Trafigura n.d.b: 10–11; Trafigura 2009: 22). Between September 2005 and June 2006, Trafigura bought approximately 28,000 tonnes of coker naphtha, originating from Mexico, in Brownsville, United States (District Court of Amsterdam 2010a: par. 5.2; Minton, Treharne and Davies Ltd. 2006: 1). Trafigura intended to resell the naphtha as a blendstock for fuels (Amnesty International and Greenpeace Netherlands 2012: 25). However, this naphtha contained high levels of sulphur (mercaptans) that produce a terrible smell (Minton, Treharne and Davies Ltd. 2006: 3; Trafigura n.d.a: 6). In order to reduce the level of sulphur and make the naphtha available for sale as a tradable commodity, Trafigura needed to find a way of refining the naphtha. One way of doing this is to 'wash' the naphtha with caustic soda. Trafigura subsequently looked for suitable locations to carry out this process (District Court of Amsterdam 2010a: par. 5.2; High Court of Justice 2011: par. 3). However, according to internal emails that were disclosed during criminal proceedings in the Netherlands, this search also revealed that 'caustic washings are banned by most countries due to the hazardous nature of the waste [...] and suppliers of caustic are unwilling to dispose of the waste since there are not many facilities remaining in the market' (Amnesty International and Greenpeace Netherlands 2012: 26; District Court of Amsterdam 2010a: par. 5.2; High Court of Justice 2011: par. 3). Nevertheless, Trafigura found the company Tankmed, a refinery in La Skhirra, Tunisia, willing to carry out two washing operations (Amnesty International and Greenpeace Netherlands 2012: 26; District Court of Amsterdam 2010a: par. 5.3; High Court of Justice 2011: par. 3). During the second washing operation, however, the presence of a terrible smell raised concerns among Tunisian authorities. As a result, the refinery became unwilling to perform any further washings (Amnesty International and Greenpeace Netherlands 2012: 26; District Court of Amsterdam 2010a: par. 5.3; High Court of Justice 2011: par. 4).

After running out of options to carry out the caustic washings on land at a specialized refinery, Trafigura decided to perform the washings at sea, on board the *Probo Koala* (Amnesty International and Greenpeace Netherlands 2012: 28; District Court of Amsterdam 2010a: par. 5.3; High Court of Justice 2011: par. 4; Lord Fraser 2010: 5; Trafigura n.d.a: 6). The Dutch District Court later concluded that caustic washings on board of a ship constituted a new industrial process that had never taken place before (District Court of Amsterdam 2010a: par. 5.4; par. 8.3.2.8; par. 13.3.4). After the washings, approximately 554 tonnes of slops, a hazardous waste comprising a mixture of coker naphtha, water and caustic soda, remained (Hulshof Committee 2006: 9–12). These were stored in the two slops tanks of the *Probo Koala*.

During the operations at sea, Trafigura had already contacted several companies in Malta, Italy and Gibraltar to process the slops. However, 'due to the chemical content of the waste' these parties did not accept the slops (District Court of Amsterdam 2010a: par. 5.8; High Court of Justice 2011: par. 8). At the end of June 2006, the *Probo Koala* received instructions to set sail to Paldiski (Estonia) to discharge a petrol cargo and to load a gasoline cargo for the Nigerian market. Because Amsterdam was on the way to this port, Trafigura decided to enter the port to refuel the ship, to change crew and to discharge the slops (District Court of Amsterdam 2010a: par. 5.9; High Court of Justice 2011: par. 8; Trafigura n.d.a: 6).

On 20 June 2006, Trafigura contacted the Dutch-based company Amsterdam Port Services (APS) to handle the discharge and disposal of the slops. APS specializes in the collection and processing of ship-generated waste and is licensed by the Dutch authorities to process waste from ships in line with the MARPOL convention: the International Convention for the Prevention of Pollution from ships. Trafigura intended to discharge approximately 554 cubic metres of slops and requested the disposal of slops described as 'gasoline slops (majority is water, gasoline, and caustic soda)' (ibid.). APS accepted the contract and provided an estimated cost of €27 per cubic metre, which was accepted by Trafigura six days later (District Court of Amsterdam 2010a: par. 5.12; Trafigura n.d.a: 7).

In the Dutch criminal proceedings it became apparent that if APS had known the origin of the slops, e.g. by means of caustic washings on board of the *Probo Koala*, they would have offered a different price and disposal procedure. Trafigura subsequently claimed that one of its employees had described the origin and composition of the waste to APS in a telephone conversation. This was denied by APS. The District Court of Amsterdam later concluded that it did not find Trafigura's statement, that they had fully informed APS regarding the nature and origin of the slops, credible (Amnesty International and Greenpeace Netherlands 2012: 35; District Court of Amsterdam 2010a: par. 8.3.3.2; par. 8.3.3.3).

July 2006, the Probo Koala *in Amsterdam, the Netherlands*

On 2 July 2006, the *Probo Koala* arrived at the port of Amsterdam. During the discharge of the waste, the presence of an abnormal smell urged APS to take samples of the waste. The analysis showed a significantly higher chemical oxygen demand and higher levels of mercaptans than normal slops. Due to this, APS could not process the waste (District Court of Amsterdam 2010a: par. 5.16; Hulshof Committee 2006: 26). Treatment of the waste required the use of a more specialized facility of another company close to Rotterdam and would cost approximately €1000 per cubic metre (District Court of Amsterdam 2010a: par. 5.16; Hulshof Committee 2006: 26; Trafigura n.d.a: 7). According to Trafigura, APS had no justification for the increased price. Trafigura rejected the offer and requested that the slops be pumped back into the *Probo Koala* (District Court of Amsterdam 2010a: par. 5.17; Hulshof Committee 2006: 26; Trafigura n.d.a: 7).

Meanwhile, municipal environmental authorities were alerted by local complaints about the odours emanating from APS. APS requested the authorities to allow the firm to return the waste to the *Probo Koala*. The municipal environmental authorities were uncertain about returning the waste to the *Probo Koala* and they contacted the national environmental inspectorate. In the following days, a discussion emerged between local environmental authorities, port state control, the national environmental inspectorate, and the criminal authorities about whether or not national and international environmental regulations prohibit the return of the slops to the *Probo Koala* and whether or not the ship could be detained for further investigations (District Court of Amsterdam 2010a: par. 5.18–5.28; Hulshof Committee 2006: 26–36). The key issue at stake here was whether or not APS had already accepted the waste and, if so, had legal authority over it. The Dutch Environmental Management Act expressly prohibits the transfer of industrial or hazardous waste to anyone who is not authorized to receive such waste. If APS had acquired legal authority over the waste, reloading the waste to the *Probo Koala* would constitute a violation of the aforementioned act because as a ship the *Probo Koala* was not authorized to receive the waste (Hulshof Committee 2006: 29–31; Spapens et al. 2013: 155).

The authorities were hesitant about allowing APS to return the waste to the *Probo Koala* because they suspected that the waste would be illegally dumped somewhere along the route of the vessel.[2] However, under pressure to find a solution, they decided that APS had not yet accepted the slops and that the waste could be reloaded to the *Probo Koala* (Amnesty International and Greenpeace Netherlands 2012: 40; District Court of Amsterdam 2010a: par. 5.26–5.28; Hulshof Committee 2006: 29–31). The committee that investigated the events in Amsterdam later stated that much of the discussion and the sense of urgency were probably dictated by financial considerations (Hulshof Committee 2006: 33). After all, there were many additional costs (port fees; demurrage) involved in keeping the *Probo Koala* in Amsterdam longer than expected. Also, APS was concerned about being left with the waste and threatened to hold the municipality liable for the additional costs involved (Hulshof Committee 2006: 33).

Eventually, on 5 July 2006, the authorities allowed APS to return the slops to the *Probo Koala*. Immediately thereafter, the *Probo Koala* set sail for Paldiski, Estonia. Port officials in the Netherlands sent a message to their counterparts in Estonia urging them to check whether the suspicious cargo was still on board. This proved to be the case (District Court of Amsterdam 2010a: par. 5.29).

The Hulshof Committee later concluded that even though environmental regulations prohibited the return of the slops to the ship and the ship could have been detained in Amsterdam, the situation at the time of decision-making was unclear and unprecedented (2006: 27).

From Amsterdam to Abidjan, Ivory Coast

Between 9 and 13 July 2006, the *Probo Koala* docked at the port of Paldiski, Estonia where it loaded a cargo of gasoline for the African market (Lord Fraser 2010: 5). The vessel left Estonia on July 13 for Lagos, Nigeria, where between 30 July and 16 August 2006 the gasoline was discharged to the state-owned oil company. According to Trafigura (n.d.a: 7), while in Nigeria, the captain of the *Probo Koala* sought a suitable solution to process the waste since Nigeria also ratified the MARPOL convention. Nonetheless, no agreement was reached and the *Probo Koala* left for Abidjan, Ivory Coast with the slops still on board.

August 2006, the Probo Koala *in Abidjan, Ivory Coast*

On 19 August 2006, the *Probo Koala* arrived at the port of Abidjan, Ivory Coast. A local company, called Compagnie Tommy, was contracted to handle the waste. This company had only been in the possession of a licence to treat this type of waste for one month (Amnesty International and Greenpeace Netherlands 2012: 46; Verschuuren 2012: 633). Compagnie Tommy agreed to process the waste for roughly the initial price that APS had offered Trafigura before being aware of the hazardous nature of the waste (United Nations 2009: 8).

According to the United Nations report, Compagnie Tommy rented 12 trucks that dumped the total amount of 554 tonnes of waste at multiple sites across the city between the evening of 19 August and the morning of 20 August 2006 (United Nations 2009: 8).

On the morning of 20 August 2006, residents near the dump sites complained of nose bleeds, diarrhea, nausea, irritated eyes and respiratory problems (ibid.). Early news reports indicated that 16 people died as a result of the toxic materials and over 100,000 people sought medical attention.[3] In the weeks thereafter, the incident not only led to worldwide consternation, but it also emerged into a crisis with social, economic and sanitary consequences (Amnesty International and Greenpeace Netherlands 2012: 52–67; Eze 2008: 353; United Nations 2009: 9; Verschuuren 2012: 633–634). Widespread public demonstrations were held, there was a displacement of residents leaving near the dump sites, schools closed down, many farms near the dump sites had to be closed down which resulted in job losses, and the city's household waste treatment centre was closed down for several months causing sanitary problems on top of the problems caused by the dumped waste. Within a matter of weeks after the incident, the government of Ivory Coast resigned, although some officials were reinstated later (Amnesty International and Greenpeace Netherlands 2012: 12).

Aftermath

In the aftermath of the disaster, court cases were initiated in Ivory Coast, the United Kingdom and the Netherlands. In Ivory Coast, shortly after the incident, the authorities arrested the director of Compagnie Tommy, and a local shipping agent. In October of 2008 the director of Compagnie Tommy was sentenced to 20 years' imprisonment and the shipping agent to five years of imprisonment (Verschuuren 2012: 634).

On 18 September 2006, Claude Dauphin, the chief executive officer (CEO) of Trafigura, Trafigura's regional director for West Africa, and a local manager of a Trafigura subsidiary, were arrested by the Ivorian government and subsequently imprisoned by way of pre-trial detention for a period of five months (Trafigura n.d.a: 9). They were released on 15 February 2007 after Trafigura agreed to pay €152 million to the government of Ivory Coast. The agreement included a guarantee by the Ivorian government that Trafigura would not be criminally prosecuted in the future. Moreover, Trafigura made this deal without accepting liability (Trafigura n.d.a: 13).

In the United Kingdom a class action lawsuit on behalf of 30,000 claimants was brought before the London High Court in May 2009.[4] In September 2009 a settlement was reached. Trafigura agreed to pay 950 pounds to each of the claimants. Part of the settlement was a joint statement by Trafigura and Leigh Day & Co., the British law firm representing the claimants, declaring that independent experts thus far were unable to identify a link between the exposure to the waste and the health problems of the claimants and that the slops 'could at worst have caused a range of short term low-level flu like symptoms and anxiety' (Trafigura n.d.a: 17).[5]

In the Netherlands, criminal investigations were started against Trafigura, one of its employees who was leading the blending operations, as well as against APS and various authorities involved. Moreover, in May 2007, the criminal authorities in the Netherlands decided to prosecute Claude Dauphin as well.

The employee of Trafigura was sentenced to a conditional sentence of six months' imprisonment and a fine of €25,000 for leading the operations and for concealing the hazardous nature of the waste (District Court of Amsterdam 2010d). Both APS and its director were found guilty of the violation of Dutch environmental regulations by having reloaded the waste to the *Probo Koala*. However, they were not sentenced because the decision to reload the waste was based on the permission of the municipal environmental authorities (District Court of Amsterdam 2010b; 2010c).

Trafigura was sentenced to pay a fine of €1 million for the transportation of the waste in violation of the EU regulation on the shipment of waste, and for concealing the hazardous nature of the waste (District Court of Amsterdam 2010a). Both Trafigura and the prosecution office lodged an appeal against the rulings of the District Court. In December 2011 the Court of Appeal reaffirmed the decision of the District Court (Court of Appeal Amsterdam 2011). In the fall of 2012, the Dutch prosecution office and Trafigura reached a settlement that entailed the payment of the aforementioned fine of one million dollars by Trafigura, the payment of €67,000 by Claude Dauphin, and the payment of the aforementioned fine of €25,000 by the employee of Trafigura. In exchange, the prosecution office was not to further prosecute the case against Claude Dauphin.

The above description of this case shows that legal and economic complexities can make it difficult to effectively enforce and prosecute corporate environmental crime. In the next section, various sources of ambiguity will be discussed that are often said to explain how and why responding to these types of offences is challenging (Nelken 2002). Drawing on this analysis, the problematic nature of legal enforcement against this type of crime will be discussed and, subsequently, the possibilities for non-state types of enforcement are explored.

Ambiguities in corporate environmental crime

On the face of it, the *Probo Koala* case seemed fairly straightforward. In an effort to make a lot of money out of reselling dirty naphta as a blendstock for fuels, the multinational business firm Trafigura employed a new industrial process that they knew would result in hazardous waste. In order to get the best deal in waste disposal, Trafigura subsequently transported the waste to Ivory Coast where it was dumped by a newly established firm at several locations in Abidjan which has led to extremely serious social and environmental consequences. However, in the weeks following the incident it soon became apparent that the case was everything but straightforward. There was a lot of discussion about the nature and composition of the waste, the ascertainment of responsibility, and the most effective way of responding to it. As a result it took more than six years before this case resulted in final criminal sentences. The *Probo Koala* case therefore exhibits many of the legal complexities and ambiguities that often characterize cases of white-collar crime (Nelken 2002).

One of the biggest issues in this case was the ambiguous nature of the product waste. Waste is a product that is often very difficult to define. Historically, waste has always been associated with a negative value: it is a product that we want to get rid of. However, due to changes in treatment and disposal techniques and growing opportunities to recycle and reuse waste, waste can be transformed into something useful, into a tradable commodity (White 2008: 115). A key issue in relation to waste is how to distinguish between waste and reusable products (Spapens et al. 2013; Van Daele et al. 2007; Van Erp and Huisman 2010; White 2008). This is often very difficult to assess because in different parts of the world there are different values attached to products. For instance, electronics that people in Europe do not consider useful any more can be perfectly useful in developing countries where there is a growing market for second-hand goods (Van Erp and Huisman 2010: 579).

In the *Probo Koala* case this issue became apparent with regard to the naphtha bought by Trafigura. Amnesty International and Greenpeace (2012) argued that state parties should ensure that naphtha is defined as a hazardous waste under the Basel Convention.[6] The Dutch government however stated that it is very difficult to define it as a hazardous waste, because it can also be used as a fuel.[7] As a result, the origin of the waste no longer determines its definition, but its use in practice. However, it is often very difficult to assess whether or not a product can and will be used in a different country across the globe, leaving aside the difficulties of proving it in a court case. In many court cases, the defence uses this line of reasoning to limit or exclude liability, often with success (De Rijck 2011).

Another problem with waste is that it is extremely difficult to assess the composition of the waste. During the court cases and in the media, there was intense debate about the exact composition of the waste and whether or not the reported health effects and deaths could be attributed to the waste from the *Probo Koala*. Various experts appointed to determine the nature of the waste came to different conclusions about its toxicity and the causality between the waste and the health effects in Abidjan (Amnesty International and Greenpeace Netherlands 2012; Dutch Forensic Institute 2007; Minton, Treharne and Davies Ltd. 2006; WSP Environmental 2009). For example, Special Rapporteur for the United Nations, Professor Ibeanu, came to the conclusion that there was 'strong *prima facie* evidence that the reported deaths and adverse health consequences are related to the dumping of the waste' (United Nations 2009: 10). At the same time, however, he also suggested that a causal link between the deaths and health problems and the waste from the *Probo Koala* had not yet been fully established (United Nations 2009: 10). As previously discussed, part of the class action suit in the United Kingdom in 2009 was a joint statement by Trafigura and the claimants saying that at best the waste could have caused flu-like symptoms. In 2011, Dutch journalist Jaffe Vink published a book about the case claiming that the waste was not toxic and that the media in the Netherlands and abroad hyped up the negative effects of the waste. To date, the exact composition of the waste still has not been made public (Amnesty International and Greenpeace Netherlands 2012).

As the composition of the waste and the causality were cause for so much discussion, Trafigura fought tooth and nail to contest any allegations regarding the toxicity of the waste or its link to the problems in Abidjan. In its reaction to the United Nations report about the events in Abidjan, Trafigura contested the use of the word 'toxic' by claiming that 'any substance can be toxic in a given set of circumstances'.[8] In an interview with BBC journalist Jeremy Paxman in August 2007, Eric de Turckheim, founding partner of Trafigura, claimed that the waste was 'absolutely not dangerous to human beings, smelly but not dangerous'.[9]

Since the facts of the case are already subject to very different interpretations, it is often also difficult to distinguish who is responsible, which is a next source of ambiguity. In cases of corporate environmental crime there are often many actors involved in different countries which makes it difficult to decide who is ultimately culpable and which country and authority has jurisdiction for enforcement. In the *Probo Koala* case, for instance, the ship was owned by a Greek firm; it was registered in Panama; it was chartered by a Dutch-based firm with its operating headquarters in London; and the ship sailed from Amsterdam to Estonia, Nigeria and Ivory Coast where the waste was eventually dumped by a local firm. Trafigura has always denied responsibility based on the fact that they were given permission by the Dutch authorities to leave Amsterdam. Moreover, they blamed Compagnie Tommy claiming that 'Abidjan has one of the largest and most sophisticated ports in West Africa, and contains one of the region's most important refineries' (Trafigura n.d.a: 8); and 'Compagnie Tommy was fully informed of the nature of the slops and the fact that they were to be handled correctly to avoid any environmental concerns. [...]. Compagnie Tommy was licensed to receive slops discharged from vessels at the Port of Abidjan' (Lord Fraser 2010: 6–7).

A final source of ambiguity derives from the ambivalent response to these types of crime. There are many different ways to respond to corporate environmental crimes in criminal law, administrative law, and in civil law. In the *Probo Koala* case there were criminal cases in Ivory Coast and the Netherlands, and there was a class-action lawsuit in London. However, most cases of corporate environmental crime are either dealt with by administrative sanctions or by out-of-court settlements. Especially the Dutch approach to regulating corporations has been characterized as being rather pragmatic in this regard (Van de Bunt and Huisman 2007). In the Netherlands, enforcement authorities have a great deal of discretionary authority to decide whether or not a case should be prosecuted, and to settle cases out of court. As mentioned previously, it is often very difficult to find sufficient evidence to bring the case before the criminal court due to the nature of the products involved and the problems with ascertaining responsibility. An out-of-court settlement thus offers a solution to make sure that these types of offences are dealt with and to punish the offenders for their wrongdoings without the time, energy and money it would take to bring the case before the courts. For this reason, the Public Prosecution Service in the Netherlands eventually decided to settle the case against Trafigura's CEO. Under the Dutch criminal procedure an admission of guilt by the perpetrator is however not required in settlements. The most widespread means of dealing with corporate environmental crime, therefore, do not carry the same stigma or send the same moral message as a criminal sanction and they might not be as effective in terms of deterrence.

As these ambiguities are mutually reinforcing, they create serious problems for deterrence and enforcement.

'Weak signal, weak threat': limitations to the deterrence model of corporate compliance

Disasters such as the *Probo Koala* case tend to call forth a strong public demand for increasing supervision and harsher, more deterrent sanctions. In the aftermath of the *Probo Koala* disaster the European Commission issued a new directive that compelled the Member States of the European Union to enforce environmental violations by means of criminal law.[10] The underlying assumption posited was that imposing severe penalties is crucial to ensure corporate compliance with environmental regulations. Even more so: 'only criminal penalties will provide a sufficiently dissuasive effect'.[11]

The deterrence literature however indicates that the deterrent effect of formal legal sanctions is not as strong as often expected (Kagan et al. 2011; Thornton et al. 2005; Van Wingerde 2012). First and foremost, this derives from the fact that instead of a threat message, sanctions only provide a very weak signal and therefore impose only a weak threat on business firms (Thornton et al. 2005). Especially for large multinational business firms penalties for environmental violations may be considered insignificant compared with the profits of most of those firms. In the *Probo Koala* case, Trafigura was sentenced to pay a fine of €1 million in 2011. However, in the same year, the company had its best year ever, with a turnover of US$121.6 billion and a net profit close to US$1 billion.[12] Even if the financial penalty had been much higher than it was, such a firm could easily overcome the financial damages.

Another problem lies in the character of most environmental regulations. Most environmental regulations and many socio-economic regulations in general are either administrative or quite technical in nature. The problem with those types of regulations is that violation of these rules often does not have the same moral meaning, as actually dumping toxic chemicals in Africa and being punished for it might not result in the same loss of face. In the *Probo Koala* case, for example, both the criminal investigations and the court cases in the Netherlands essentially revolved around the question of which regulation was applicable to the discharging and reloading of the slops in Amsterdam. The Dutch court case itself did not concern the dumping of the waste in Ivory Coast (District Court of Amsterdam 2010a). Trafigura used this in its representation of the facts by stating that its prosecution and conviction in the Netherlands concerned a highly technical question but had nothing to do with the events in Ivory Coast (District Court of Amsterdam 2010a).[13] As such, Trafigura dismissed the blameworthiness of transporting the waste to a developing country where – at best – environmental regulations are less stringent.

The limited impact of sanction threats on the behaviour of multinational business firms has traditionally been explained as a result of information and power asymmetries between these large firms on the one hand and governments and regulatory bodies on the other (Hertz 2003; Snider 2010; Stone 1975; Sutherland 1980). In her book *The Silent Takeover*, economist Noreena Hertz reveals that of the world's 100 largest economies, 51 are now corporations; only 49 are nation-states. The sales and profits of some of these firms are greater than the gross national product of many countries in Africa and Asia. Established in 1993, Trafigura is one of the world's largest independent oil trading companies. The firm is privately owned and it has 167 offices in 58 countries all around the globe.[14] By way of comparison, in 2006, Trafigura's turnover was US$45 billion, while Ivory Coast had a gross national product of approximately US$18 billion (Amnesty International and Greenpeace Netherlands 2012: 14). As this example demonstrates, most of these corporations are more powerful than nation-states. And while most of these firms operate on a global level, the enforcement and prosecution of environmental violations have been organized almost exclusively at a national level (Braithwaite and Drahos 2000; Gibbs et al. 2010; Verschuuren 2012). Therefore, it should not be surprising that the impact of formal legal sanction threats is often very limited.

Social licence pressures

Socio-legal researchers have often suggested that a much stronger effect can be expected from social pressures, as for example from nongovernmental organizations (NGOs), neighbours, employees, the local community, environmental interest groups, and the media (Gunningham et al. 2003; 2004; Hutter and O'Mahony 2004; Kagan et al. 2011; Van Rooij 2006; Van Erp 2011; Van Wingerde 2012). These groups are able to produce negative publicity about a firm's environmental performance that may affect its reputation. This could make it more difficult to recruit well-trained employees, to renew the firm's environmental licence, it could make it more difficult to attract investors, getting long-term loans, or finding affordable insurances (Gunningham et al. 1999; Lynch-Wood and Williamson 2007; Minoli and Bell 2003). These consequences are often reported far more threatening than the risk of legal sanctions (Gunningham et al. 2003; 2004; Kagan et al. 2011; Van Wingerde 2012).

In the literature on organizational responses to regulation, this has been conceptualized as the regulated firm's 'social licence', meaning the demands and expectations from the local community and environmental interest groups (Gunningham et al. 2003; 2004; Joyce and Thomson 2000; Lynch-Wood and Williamson 2007). The social licence seems especially effective as a regulatory mechanism with larger firms that have a reputation to uphold (Gunningham et al. 2003; 2004; Joyce and Thomson 2000; Lynch-Wood and Williamson 2007). These firms are generally more visible to the public and therefore an easier target for environmental interest groups and NGOs. In order to maintain their reputation and the support of the public, these firms are often strongly motivated to comply with the demands of their social licence. Another advantage of the social licence lies in the fact that NGOs as opposed to national regulatory bodies are often not bounded by national borders and therefore better suited to steer multinational corporations towards better environmental performances (Verschuuren 2012: 623).

There are, however, limitations to the effectiveness of the social licence. In order to be able to pressure firms, the social environment first needs to be equipped with information about the environmental performances of firms as well as their environmental offences. However, especially with multinational business firms, information generated in one country may not always reach the social environment in others thereby reducing the potential strength of the social licence. For example, although Trafigura is a multinational global firm with ties all around the world, as White (2008: 108) shows, there was a lack of reporting about the *Probo Koala* incident in Australian as well as North American media.

Second, the social environment needs to be able to recognize potential harms. It is clear that while odours, noise and dust are quite easily detected, other more serious environmental problems remain undetected by the social environment. As described previously, in the *Probo Koala* case, experts still debate about the composition of the waste and whether or not a link exists between the exposure to the waste and the health problems of the people near the dump sites. If experts are already debating the actual harm the waste may have caused, how can we expect that environmental interest groups or the media can recognize the potential risks, much less the people living near the dump sites?

Third, the social environment should also be able and willing to enforce the demands of the social licence. It is clear that not all social environments have the means and the knowledge to address complex environmental and legal issues. There appears to be a growing body of evidence suggesting that especially the poor and minorities worldwide suffer the negative side effects of this unequal distribution of waste disposal on the one hand and the knowledge and means to fight against it on the other (Bandyopadhyay and Horowitz 2006; White 2008). This is also referred to as 'environmental racism' (White 2008: 114).

Last, social licence pressures do not always lead to meaningful compliance. Business firms respond in different ways to the pressures of the local community. Some firms have been able to effectively neutralize the pressure from their local community by manipulating information about their environmental performances, or by relocating their activities to jurisdictions where the local community is expected to be less powerful. As Van Erp (2011: 330) shows, large and powerful corporations are often well equipped to defend themselves against negative publicity. They are able to hire the best lawyers and firms specialized in reputation management. By doing that, they are often able to reframe the image of the incidents in which they are involved. In the *Probo Koala* case, Trafigura employed the legal firm Carter-Ruck, specialized in reputation management. In 2009, the British newspaper the *Guardian* obtained a confidential document – later known as the Minton report – that contained information on the nature of the waste as well as the relationship between the waste and the health problems of people living near the dump sites (Trafigura n.d.a: 18–19).[15] Subsequently, Carter-Ruck issued an injunction against the paper that prevented the paper from publishing the report. Moreover, the *Guardian* was issued a so-called super-injunction preventing it from mentioning the injunction as well (Trafigura n.d.a: 18–19). About a month later, however, a member of parliament scheduled a parliamentary question revealing the existence of the injunction. The *Guardian* informed Trafigura's lawyers that it intended to report about this question. Immediately thereafter, Carter-Ruck warned the newspaper that if they reported about the parliamentary proceedings, they would breach the injunction and would be held liable (Trafigura n.d.a: 18–19). The *Guardian* therefore decided to publish a front-page story saying that – a first in British history – a newspaper was prevented from reporting about parliamentary proceedings. Trafigura stated this has been 'a complete distortion of the facts' since neither Trafigura nor its lawyers could possibly have known a question on the subject would have been tabled in Parliament a month after the injunction was issued (Trafigura n.d.a: 19). Nevertheless, the story was picked up by the internet community and within a matter of hours details about the injunction and the Minton report were spread around the internet, urging Trafigura to lift the injunction. Although the information was eventually publicized, this example shows how powerful a firm such as Trafigura is in neutralizing pressure from the media.

Another example is the way in which Trafigura used the website Wikipedia to reframe the image of what had happened in the *Probo Koala* case. In May 2007, Dutch media reported that editors of Wikipedia were forced to change the editing settings to *non-editable*, because someone from Trafigura kept changing the entry for the incident saying that Trafigura had done nothing wrong.[16] Until today, the Dutch Wikipedia page on the *Probo Koala* case contains the warning that the information on the page may not be neutral.[17]

In summary, because large multinational business firms are often concerned about acquiring and maintaining a good reputation for environmental performance, they are often motivated to comply with the demands of their social licence. At the same time, however, social licence pressures do not always result in better compliance as the example of the *Probo Koala* case shows.

Conclusions

This chapter described one of the largest European environmental scandals to date: the *Probo Koala* case. This case study highlighted several legal complexities and ambiguities that occur when multinational business firms move their operations across national borders. Furthermore, this chapter uncovered the challenges for the regulation and enforcement of corporate environmental crimes that result from the globalization of business behaviour. Given the theme of this handbook – European white-collar crime – the question remains whether or not the *Probo Koala* case is a typically European example of white-collar crime. Of course, Trafigura is a

European-based firm, authorities in the Netherlands could have detained the ship, and criminal proceedings against Trafigura largely took place in the Netherlands. In terms of its scale and complexity, however, the *Probo Koala* case is in no way simply an example of European white-collar crime. Rather this case is symptomatic of what can happen when multinational business firms cross jurisdictions and exploit differences in enforcement regimes across the globe. As such, the *Probo Koala* case offers an example of a type of crime that transcends the distinction in the criminological literature between European and Anglo-American white-collar crime. Its international scale and complexity nevertheless offer important lessons for the regulation and enforcement of business behaviour and for the study of white-collar crime in Europe.

Sanctions as moral messages

Although a significant formal legal sanction threat is certainly necessary to ensure compliance with environmental regulations, the *Probo Koala* case has shown that especially with large multinational business firms, legal sanctions may simply not be deterrent enough. In reaction, politicians, the public, and the media often call for increased supervision and harsher, more deterrent sanctions. However, considering the profits of most of those firms this would mean that sanctions need to be multiplied several times in order to be deterrent enough. This is often neither possible nor desirable. Moreover, as White (2008: 116) shows, tightening monitoring and enforcement may 'feed the spiral of rising waste management costs' and this increases the risks of illegal waste shipments by corporations looking for cheaper ways to dispose of their waste. Instead of a race to the top, this may lead to a race to the bottom in which firms are trying to get the best deal in waste disposal.

At the same time, the case study of the *Probo Koala* shows us that a key issue with environmental regulations is that these types of regulations are either administrative or quite technical in nature. This is problematic because violations of these rules often do not have the same moral meaning, as actually dumping toxic chemicals in Africa and being punished for it might not result in the same loss of face. When a sanction is imposed, however, other firms in the regulated community expect it to be about something blameworthy. Sanctions that only communicate a threat message and focus on the technical interpretation of the violation, therefore, are not very effective in terms of the awareness they create. In order to create a more meaningful message, the sanction has to communicate a moral message instead, that emphasizes that the penalized behaviour is condemned and that creates consensus about the blameworthiness of the penalized offence. As such the sanction may create discussion amongst the regulated community about the offence, it may change perceptions about right and wrong and, as Thornton et al. (2005) suggest, to firms that are already in compliance the sanction may then serve as a 'reminder' to check whether they still operate in accordance to their previous commitment to comply with the law; or as a 'reassurance' by sending the message that 'bad apples' are caught and punished, reaffirming their commitment to invest in costly compliance measures.

Empowering third parties

This chapter also showed that the demands and expectations from third parties, such as non-governmental organizations, the media and the local community may be more effective in pressurizing firms to comply with environmental regulations. To most multinational business firms negative publicity and reputational concerns are far more threatening than formal legal sanction threats. At the same time, the *Probo Koala* case shows that multinational business firms, such as Trafigura, can sometimes easily overpower their social environment and effectively neutralize or overcome negative publicity. The research presented in this chapter, therefore, advocates an active role for governments to empower third parties to pressurize firms into compliance and even beyond compliance behaviour, for example by making information about the environmental performance of firms more easily accessible and providing the social environment with the procedural tools to effectively articulate their demands and making firms respond.

Lastly, from a methodological viewpoint this case study showed how valuable the use of open sources such as investigative reports, criminal proceedings and parliamentary proceedings can be for the study of white-collar crime. At the same time, however, this case study pointed out how difficult it can be to assess the value of the materials collected. Especially in white-collar crime cases, there are often many different actors involved that all have their own interests at play. In describing their side of the story it might be convenient to try to fit facts and figures into their own objectives. Nevertheless, in their study of corporate and white-collar crime criminologists should take advantage of the wealth of information that is filed in criminal cases, investigative reports, parliamentary proceedings, media reports, etc. These sources offer ample opportunities for empirical research into the rather secluded world of business firms. Using these sources may enrich our understanding of white-collar crime and may broaden our criminological thinking.

Notes

1 This description of the case is largely based on the report of the Dutch committee on the state of affairs in Amsterdam (Hulshof Committee 2006), the verdict of the District Court of Amsterdam (2010a), the judgment of the England and Wales High Court of Justice (2011), the United Nations report on the adverse effects of the incident (2009), and the joint report of Amnesty International and Greenpeace Netherlands (2012). These sources were complemented with media reports, journal articles as well as reports on the incident conditioned or conducted by Trafigura itself (Lord Fraser of Carmyllie PC QC 2010; Minton, Treharne and Davies Ltd. 2006; Trafigura n.d.a).
2 This was reinforced by an anonymous fax that port state control received saying that the waste on board of the Probo Koala was heavily contaminated. The sender of the fax feared that the waste would 'disappear' at open sea and strongly urged the port authorities to notify the next port of call to check whether the slops were still on board (District Court of Amsterdam 2010a: par. 5.2.1).
3 Later reports, however, contested the hazardous nature of the waste as well as its adverse health effects (Vink 2011).
4 The class action suit was initiated in the UK because the firm's operating headquarters, Trafigura Ltd., is based in London. Trafigura Beheer B.V., the group's holding company, is legally based in the Netherlands.
5 http://news.bbc.co.uk/2/shared/bsp/hi/pdfs/20_09_09_trafigura_statement.pdf.
6 The Basel Convention on the Control of the Transboundary Movements of Hazardous Wastes and their Disposal is the main instrument regulating the transboundary movements of hazardous wastes around the world.
7 Dutch minister for environmental affairs, letter to parliament, 25 February 2013, IenM/BSK-2012/257141.
8 Trafigura (2009). Trafigura detailed response to Professor Ibeanu 13 August 2009, pp. 11-13.
9 http://www.youtube.com/watch?v=tQBS82kFQjE&app=desktop (accessed 30 June 2014).
10 Directive 2008/99/EC of 19 November 2008, official journal L328/28 of 6 December 2008.
11 Ibid.
12 Trafigura (n.d.b). *Corporate Brochure*, http://www.trafigura.com/useful_links/corporate_brochure.aspx (accessed 24 May 2013); also http://www.ft.com/cms/s/0/99241c2c-2998-11e1-8b1a-00144feabdc0.html#axzz2UClTHeoY (accessed 24 May 2013).
13 http://www.trafigura.com/media-centre/probo-koala/timeline/2008/april/12592/?lang=NL (accessed 24 May 2013).
14 Trafigura (n.d.b) *Advancing Trade. Trafigura Group Corporate Brochure.* Amsterdam: Trafigura Beheer B.V., http://www.trafigura.com/site-information/corporate-brochure/trafigura/corporate-brochure-en/ (accessed 26 June 2014).

15 http://www.guardian.co.uk/world/2009/oct/16/trafigura-carter-ruck-the-guardian (accessed 2 June 2013); http://news.bbc.co.uk/2/hi/uk_politics/8311885.stm (accessed 2 June 2013).
16 http://web.archive.org/web/20070520062852/http://www.fembusiness.nl/fembusiness/content/nieuws/57110/article.html (accessed 2 June 2013).
17 http://nl.wikipedia.org/wiki/Probo_Koala (accessed 24 May 2013).

References

Amnesty International and Greenpeace Netherlands (2012) *The Toxic Truth: About a Company Called Trafigura, a Ship Called the Probo Koala, and the Dumping of Toxic Waste in Côte d'Ivoire*, London/Amsterdam: Amnesty International and Greenpeace Netherlands.

Bandyopadhyay, S. and Horowitz, J. (2006) 'Do plants overcomply with water pollution regulations? The role of discharge variability', *Topics in Economic Analysis and Policy*, 6(1), 1–30.

Biermann, F. and Pattberg, P. (eds) (2012) *Global Environmental Governance Reconsidered*, Cambridge, MA: MIT Press.

Braithwaite, J. and Drahos, P. (2000) *Global Business Regulation*, Cambridge: Cambridge University Press.

Bunt, H.G. van de and Huisman, W. (2007) 'Organizational crime in the Netherlands', in M. Tonry and C. Bijleveld (eds) *Crime and Justice in the Netherlands. Series Crime and Justice: A Review of Research*, Chicago: University of Chicago Press, pp. 217–260.

Court of Appeal Amsterdam (2011) 'Case number LJN: BU9239', 23 December 2011, http://jure.nl/bu9239.

Daele, S. van, Vander Beken, T. and Dorn, N. (2007) 'Waste management and crime: Regulatory, business, and product vulnerabilities', *Environmental Policy and Law*, 37(1): 34–38.

DiMaggio, P.J. (2001) 'Introduction: Making sense of the contemporary firm and prefiguring its future', in P.J. DiMaggio (ed.) *The Twenty-First-Century Firm: Changing Economic Organization in International Perspective*, Princeton: Princeton University Press, pp. 3–30.

District Court of Amsterdam (2010a) 'Case number LJN: BN2149 (Trafigura)', 23 July 2010, http://jure.nl/bn2149.

District Court of Amsterdam (2010b) 'Case number LJN: BN2106 (Amsterdam Port Services)', 23 July 2010, http://jure.nl/bn2106.

District Court of Amsterdam (2010c) 'Case number LJN: BN2185 (Director Amsterdam Port Services)', 23 July 2010, http://jure.nl/bn2185.

District Court of Amsterdam (2010d) 'Case number LJN: BN2068 (Employee Trafigura)', 23 July 2010, http://jure.nl/bn2068.

Dutch Forensic Institute (2007) *Expert Report Odour Nuisance Incident APS Amsterdam. Report*, 29 January 2007, retrieved from http://www.trafigura.com/pdfs/16951/16957/NFI_Report_29_January_2007.pdf.

Erp, J.G. van (2011) 'Naming and shaming in regulatory enforcement', in C. Parker and V. Lehmann Nielsen (eds) *Explaining Regulatory Compliance: Business Responses to Regulation*, Cheltenham: Edward Elgar, pp. 322–342.

Erp, J.G. van and Huisman, W. (2010) 'Smart regulation and enforcement of illegal disposal of electronic waste', *Criminology & Public Policy*, 9(3): 579–590.

Eze, C.N. (2008) 'The Probo Koala incident in Abidjan Cote D'Ivoire: A critique of the Basel Convention compliance mechanism', *8th International Conference on Environmental Compliance and Enforcement. Conference Proceedings*, London: Cameron May Ltd.

Forsgren, M. (2008) *Theories of the Multinational Firm: A Multidimensional Creature in the Global Economy*, Cheltenham: Edward Elgar.

Gibbs, C. and Simpson, S.S. (2009) 'Measuring corporate environmental crime rates: Progress and problems', *Crime, Law & Social Change*, 51(1): 87–107.

Gibbs, C., McGarrell, E.F. and Axelrod, M. (2010) 'Transnational white-collar crime and risk: Lessons from the global trade in electronic waste', *Criminology & Public Policy*, 9(3): 543–560.

Gunningham, N., Kagan, R. and Thornton, D. (2003) *Shades of Green: Business, Regulation, and Environment*, Stanford: Stanford University Press.

Gunningham, N., Kagan, R. and Thornton, D. (2004) 'Social license and environmental protection: Why businesses go beyond compliance', *Law & Social Inquiry*, 29: 307–341.

Gunningham, N., Philipson, M. and Grabosky, P. (1999) 'Harnessing third parties as surrogate regulators: Achieving environmental outcomes by alternative means', *Business, Strategy and the Environment*, 8(4): 211–224.

Hertz, N. (2003) *The Silent Takeover: Global Capitalism and the Death of Democracy*, Amsterdam: Pandora Pockets.
High Court of Justice [Queen's Bench Division, Senior Courts Costs Office] (2011) *Motto & Ors vs Trafigura Ltd. & Trafigura Beheer B.V. EWHC 90201 (Costs). Case No: HQ06X03370 (15 February 2011)*, http://www.bailii.org/ew/cases/EWHC/Costs/2011/90201.html (accessed 26 June 2014).
Hulshof Committee (2006) 'Rapport van bevindingen naar aanleiding van het onderzoek van de gang van zaken rond aankomst, verblijf en vertrek van de Probo Koala in juli 2006 te Amsterdam' (Report on the State of Affairs Surrounding the Arrival, Stay, and Departure of the Probo Koala in Amsterdam in July 2006), Amsterdam: Municipality of Amsterdam.
Hutter, B.M. and O'Mahony, J. (2004) 'The role of civil society organizations in regulating business', Center for Analysis of Risk and Regulation. Discussion paper no. 26, London: London School of Economics and Political Science.
Joyce, S.A. and Thomson, I. (2000) 'Earning a social license to operate: Social acceptability and resource development in Latin America', *The Canadian Mining and Metallurgical Bulletin*, 93(1037): 49–52.
Kagan, R.A., Gunningham, N. and Thornton, D. (2011) 'Fear, duty and regulatory compliance: Lessons from three research projects', in C. Parker and V. Lehmann Nielsen (eds) *Explaining Regulatory Compliance: Business Responses to Regulation*, Cheltenham: Edward Elgar, pp. 37–58.
Lord Fraser of Carmyllie PC QC (2010) *The Probo Koala Inquiry: Second Interim Report*, http://www.probokoalainquiry.com/interim%20report.htm (accessed 26 March 2013).
Lynch-Wood, G. and Williamson, D. (2007) 'The social license as a form of regulation for small and medium enterprises', *Journal of Law & Society*, 34(3): 321–341.
Minoli, D.M. and Bell, J.N.B. (2003) 'Insurance as an alternative environmental regulator: Findings from a retrospective pollution claims survey', *Business Strategy and the Environment*, 12(2): 107–117.
Minton, Treharne and Davies Ltd. (2006) *Draft Report*, http://www.trafigura.com/1524/16951/16957/Draft_Minton_Report_14_September_2006.pdf (accessed 1 June 2013).
Nelken, D. (2002) 'White-collar crime', in M. Maguire, R. Morgan and R. Reiner (eds) *The Oxford Handbook of Criminology*, Oxford: Oxford University Press, pp. 844–877.
Passas, N. (1999) 'Globalization, criminogenic asymmetries and economic crime', *European Journal of Law Reform*, 1(4): 399–423.
Powell, W.W. (2001) 'The capitalist firm in the twenty-first century: Emerging patterns in Western enterprise', in P.J. DiMaggio (ed.) *The Twenty-First-Century Firm: Changing Economic Organization in International Perspective*, Princeton: Princeton University Press, pp. 33–68.
Rijck, R. de (2011) 'A flaw in the criminal approach of international waste transport in Europe', *9th International Conference on Environmental Compliance and Enforcement, Conference Proceedings*, Whistler, British Columbia, Canada, http://inece.org/conference/9/papers/de_Rijck_Europe_Final.pdf (accessed 25 March 2013).
Rooij, B. van (2006) *Regulating Land and Pollution in China: Lawmaking, Compliance, and Enforcement; Theory and Cases*, Leiden: Leiden University Press.
Snider, L. (2010) 'Framing e-waste regulation: The obfuscating role of power', *Criminology & Public Policy*, 9(3): 569–577.
Spapens, T., Bruinsma, M., Hout, L. van and Jong, J. de (2013) *Vuile olie: Onrechtmatig verwerken en mengen van olieproducten als vormen van milieucriminaliteit (Dirty Oil: Blending of Dirty Oil Products as a Form of Environmental Crime)*, The Hague: Boom Lemma Publishers.
Stone, C.D. (1975) *Where the Law Ends: The Social Control of Corporate Behavior*, New York: Harper & Row.
Sutherland, E.H. (1980) *White-Collar Crime: The Uncut Version*, New Haven: Yale University Press.
Thornton, D., Gunningham, N.A. and Kagan, R.A. (2005) 'General deterrence and corporate environmental behavior', *Law & Policy*, 27(2): 262–287.
Trafigura (n.d.a) *Trafigura & the Probo Koala*, http://www.trafigura.com/media-centre/probo-koala/trafigura-and-probo-koala/?view=Standard (accessed 26 March 2013).
Trafigura (n.d.b) *Advancing Trade: Trafigura Group Corporate Brochure*, Amsterdam: Trafigura Beheer B.V., http://www.trafigura.com/site-information/corporate-brochure/trafigura/corporate-brochure-en/ (accessed 26 June 2014).
Trafigura (2009) *Response to Professor Ibeanu Concerning the Report of the Special Rapporteur on the Adverse Effects of the Movement and Dumping of Toxic and Dangerous Products and Wastes on the Enjoyment of Human Rights (dated 10 July 2009)*, 13 August 2009, http://www.trafigura.com/pdfs/16951/16957/Trafigura_Detailed_Response_to_Professor_Ibeanu_13_August_2009.pdf?lang=NL (accessed 26 June 2014).

United Nations (2009) *Report of the Special Rapporteur on the Adverse Effects of the Movement and Dumping of Toxic and Dangerous Products and Wastes on the Enjoyment of Human Rights, Okechukwu Ibeanu*, General Assembly, Human Rights Council, 3 September 2009, A/HRC/12/26/Add2.

Verschuuren, J. (2012) 'Overcoming the limitations of environmental law in a globalised world', in F. Wijen, K. Zoeteman, J. Pieters and P. van Seters (eds) *A Handbook of Globalisation and Environmental Policy: National Government Interventions in a Global Arena*, Cheltenham, Northampton: Edward Elgar, pp. 616–640.

Vink, J. (2011) *Het gifschip: Verslag van een journalistiek schandaal (The Toxic Ship: Report of a Media Scandal)*, Amsterdam: Prometheus.

White, R. (2008) 'Toxic cities: Globalizing the problem of waste', *Social Justice*, 35(3): 107–119.

Wingerde, C.G. van (2012) *De afschrikking voorbij: Een empirische studie naar afschrikking, generale preventie en regelnaleving in de Nederlandse afvalbranche (Beyond Deterrence: Deterrence, Prevention, and Compliance in the Dutch Waste Industry)*, Nijmegen: Wolf Legal Publishers.

WSP Environmental (2009) *Works in Abidjan, Ivory Coast. Summary Report*, London: WSP Environmental.

17

The Icelandic approach to the 2008 banking crisis

Susan Will

Introduction

Iceland is often cited as a country that took a different approach to the economic crisis of 2008 because it refused to rescue its banks (which infuriated its foreign investors) and it prosecuted its prime minister and many bankers. Although it received threats from its creditors, the truth is that Iceland had little choice in how it reacted to the crisis for several reasons. First, its banks were too large for the country to bail out as their assets were nine to ten times the country's GDP when the 2008 crisis occurred – an amount far beyond the central bank's capacity to intervene. Second, '[b]y global standards, the banks weren't so large that the world couldn't afford to let them fail. Although the Icelandic economy is closely tied to Europe, the country is not a member of the euro zone or the European Union, and so neither Brussels nor Berlin was compelled or interested to intervene' (Faris 2013). Third, its citizens, facing decreased personal wealth and unemployment, protested against bailing out the banks when they acted irresponsibly. When questioned about Iceland's novel approach, its president Olafur Ragnar Grimsson echoed his citizens' sentiment in asking

> Why are the banks considered to be the holy churches of the modern economy? Why are private banks not like airlines and telecommunication companies and allowed to go bankrupt if they have been run in an irresponsible way? The notion that countries have to bail out failing banks allows bankers to enjoy the profits of their successes, while ordinary people will be left to bear their failures through taxes and austerity. People in enlightened democracies are not going to accept that in the long run.
>
> *(Greenstein 2013)*

Several criminologists have questioned why the state feels compelled to rescue financial institutions from the consequences of their folly and thereby violate a basic principle of capitalism that bad businesses should fail (Black 2013; Calavita et al. 1997; Friedrichs 2013). The answer, according to instrumentalists, is that law reflects the interests of the economic elite (Domhoff 1978). For structuralists that answer is too simple. They believe the state enacts laws that favor the economic elite, not because the economic elite directed it to do so, but because the state and the economic elite have a symbiotic relationship (O'Connor 1973; Poulantzas 1969). By advancing the interest of the economic elite, the state is advancing its own interests. The state is particularly reticent to act when it comes to regulation that can be viewed as anti-capitalist (Calavita and Pontell 1994). Dialectical structuralists, such as William Chambliss, recognize that the interests of the elite and other citizens are often in conflict in democracies. Therefore, the state cannot be seen as working only for the economic elite. As a result, political leaders constantly search for ways to contain and diffuse conflicts (Zatz 1993).

This chapter adapts Michalowski and Kramer's (2006) concept of state–corporate crime to the area of state–financial crime. It contends that owners or managers of financial institutions who commit crimes against their institutions and customers usually face few or no repercussions because of their deliberate collaboration or structural relationship with the state. This intersection of political and economic interests that characterizes state–financial crime jeopardizes societal well-being. As will be demonstrated in this chapter, the financial crimes that occurred in Iceland can easily be classified as state-facilitated crimes because the Icelandic government failed to maintain regulatory institutions 'capable of restraining deviant business activities either because of direct collusion between business and government or because they adhere to shared goals whose attainment would be hampered by aggressive regulation' (Kramer and Michalowski 2006: 21). Although finance crime 'threatens the integrity of the economic system', it is among the most difficult forms of white-collar crime to regulate, contain and adjudicate precisely because of the relationship between the state and economic elite (Friedrichs 2013: 10).

Iceland provides an interesting landscape to examine several concepts. It offers clear examples of normalization of deviance, state financial crime, control fraud, concerted ignorance, differential association, techniques of neutralization and gambling for resurrection. At the heart of the Icelandic banking meltdown is crony capitalism.

Information included in this essay is drawn from English language secondary sources including online newspapers and blogs. Readers may not be familiar with a couple of the sources. The blog *Icelog* is written by London-based journalist, Sigrún Davíðsdóttir, who covers the Icelandic economy and European issues for Icelandic and foreign media. *IceNews* is an Icelandic-based online publication focusing on news from the Nordic Region – Iceland, Denmark, the Faroe Islands, Finland, Greenland, Norway and Sweden.

This chapter is organized in the following manner. After providing a brief description of Iceland and the years leading up to the 2008 crisis, it will provide examples of crimes committed by bankers, control fraud, looting (collective embezzlement), market manipulation and the reactions of government officials. Then it will present concluding comments.

Background

Under Prime Minister David Oddsson's government (1991–2004), Iceland, a nation of 320,000 people, transformed from a country that tightly regulated its economy and owned its banks to one that embraced the Reagan–Thatcher model of deregulation and privatization in the late 1990s and early 2000s. Oddsson wanted Iceland to develop into a tax haven and one of the richest countries in the world. To accomplish this, his government began the process of liberalizing the economy. In 1994, as a member of the European Free Trade Association, it joined the European Economic Area (EEA), which freed it from cross-border restrictions in Europe (Wade and Sigurgeirsdottir 2010). It lowered income and VAT taxes. Then the government deregulated and sold state-owned assets. The banks were generally sold to individuals connected to the ruling political parties. The new owners, like the individuals who bought newly deregulated banks in the United States during the 1980s,[1] deemphasized retail banking and used the banks' retail deposits to enter the world of leverage and speculation associated with the casino economy (Wade 2009). Thanks to the banks' political connections, the free flow of capital (courtesy of the EEA), the government's banking guarantees, the state-owned banks' reputation as reliable and conservative, and Iceland's low sovereign debt which helped provide a high credit rating, created a criminogenic environment that set the stage for disaster (Hilmarsson 2013). The new bankers quickly took advantage of these conditions to: invest in companies that they knew little or nothing about, finance many questionable leveraged buyouts, create fake capital by trading assets with inflated values amongst themselves, and take out billions of dollars in foreign short term-loans and then loan the money to themselves and their friends (Lewis 2009). These conditions should have forewarned observers of possible accounting control fraud (Black 2005).

In the early years following privatization and deregulation, Iceland appeared to be the economic equivalent of 'the little engine that could'. Between 2003 and 2007, its three largest banks – Glitnir, Kaupthing, and Landsbanki – grew at unprecedented rates. This growth, for the most part, was funded by international capital markets (Baldursson and Portes 2013: 34). By the end of 2007, the banks' reported combined assets were almost nine times Iceland's GPD, situating all three banks within the ranks of the 300 largest banks in the world – quite a feat for banks from such a small country and economy (Wade 2009).

Icelandic citizens, experiencing a dramatically increased standard of living, quickly embraced the idea that rapid 'economic growth with a large trade deficit and ballooning foreign debt was a sign of success' (Wade 2009). As they accepted and normalized a Ponzi culture (Will 2013)[2], they adopted a 'concerted ignorance' or a willingness to turn a blind eye to signs of potential problems (Katz 1979). After all, they benefited from the newly relaxed mortgage rules that allowed loans for 90 per cent of the property's value. These inexpensive domestic loans fuelled a property bubble and 'high interest rates that were supposed to help control inflation instead just heralded the arrival of the "carry trade" – the process of borrowing money in a low-interest rate economy and then lending it out somewhere you can earn a healthy return' (Bland 2013). Politicians and regulators, not wanting to jeopardize their close relationships with bankers and recognizing their success was tied to Iceland's new-found prosperity, also embraced concerted ignorance as their *modus operandi*.

During this period of rapid growth, government agencies failed to regulate, in part because of deregulatory policies and partly from a lack of knowledge and experience. Instead of raising critical voices, they seemed to listen to bankers (Davíðsdóttir 2013c). For example, the central bank lowered reserve requirements for banks during the 2000s and then left the rates unchanged when it should have raised them in order to have significant reserves to cover deposits and debt. The central bank defended its actions by first saying that reserve requirements were not a preferred monetary policy in neighboring countries, which was true. Later, however, it admitted that it was responding to pressure from the banks, which did not want the rates to be raised (Wade 2009: 19).

A mini-economic crisis, which revealed fundamental problems with the banks, was evident by July 2006. Several entities including the International Monetary Fund (IMF), several economists from Iceland and other countries, the Ministry of Finance, the Central Bank of Iceland, and Iceland's Financial Supervisory Authority (FSA) all expressed concern about the growth of Iceland's banks' balance sheets (Wade 2009). The three largest banks were dependent upon short-term borrowing for two-thirds of their funding (Wade and Sigurgeirsdottir 2010). In addition, Fitch Credit Rating Agency downgraded Iceland from stable to negative, the krona and the stock market fell, and the Bank of England, the European Central Bank, and the United States Federal Reserve refused to increase the Icelandic Central Bank's foreign exchange reserves (Hilmarsson 2013; Wade and Sigurgeirsdottir 2010).

The negative reports and lowered credit rating angered Icelanders, who believed the criticism was unfair, unsubstantiated and the result of envy over what the country was able to achieve. Regulators failed to take meaningful corrective action. Instead of reassessing their position, the business community and cabinet ministers engaged in a public relations campaign to paint a positive picture. For example, Prime Minister Haarde assured Wall Street that Iceland's banks were sound and government officials stressed that the country was virtually debt free (Hilmarsson 2013). Kaupthing used a significant individual who purchased bank shares to endorse its financial health.

No one faulted the banks' reaction to the problems uncovered during the mini-crisis. According to publicly available materials, all three banks seemed to have responded properly. They appeared to have reduced large exposures and acted to diminish the effects of concentrated ownership (Baldursson and Portes 2013: 7). The government formed an ad hoc group to share information and to develop contingency plans in the event of a crisis, but the group lacked a mandate and did little (Wade and Sigurgeirsdottir 2010).

The banks faced unsustainable debts that required an ever-increasing revenue stream. In moves typical of a Ponzi, the banks sought to attract foreign depositors' funds by offering Icesave (Landsbanki) and Kaupthing Edge internet accounts at higher interest rates than depositors could receive elsewhere (Wade 2009: 18). However, the banks' reliance on short-term financing put them in a no-win situation. By 2008, it was clearly beyond the Central Bank of Iceland's capacity to support the banks (Wade 2009). Iceland's deficit, close to the world's largest, reached 24 per cent of the country's GDP. After Lehman Brothers collapsed in the fall of 2008, the three Icelandic banks followed suit. Iceland's stock market plunged by about 98 per cent, the exchange rate to euro went from around 70 to 190 to one, and senior bank bonds were traded at less than 10 per cent of their face value (Wade and Sigurgeirsdottir 2010). Foreign bond holders and investors demanded that the Icelandic government protect them from loss. When the government said it would, at the cost of 135 dollars per month per citizen for eight years, enraged Icelanders took to the streets. This triggering event, as Chambliss's dialectical structuralist model suggests, forced the government to address the needs of its citizens.

Parliament responded to citizens' outrage by appointing a three-member Special Investigation Commission (SIC) to study the causes of the crash and by creating the Office of the Special Prosecutor (OSP) to investigate suspicious activities, fraud related to the banks' collapse, and all serious cases of financial crime in Iceland (ACFE 2012).[3] Parliament provided OSP not only prosecutorial powers, but also police powers (Faris 2013).[4]

The 2010 SIC's 3,000 page report on the nation's financial meltdown declared a 'moral void' was at the heart of Icelandic finances (Higgins 2013). The banking system was compromised by close relations with large borrowers and was riddled with corruption (Bowers 2013). Furthermore, the banks, which were supposed to be in competition, often worked together (Wade and Sigurgeirsdottir 2010). The report described several forms of criminal behaviour in which the banks, their owners and managers engaged including: market manipulations, refinancing owners' and large borrowers' loans in violation of the FSA rules, money laundering, corporate misconduct, and violations of bookkeeping rules.

Control fraud

Iceland's three major banks were operated by control frauds who used their firms as weapons. As defined by American criminologist and former financial regulator William K. Black (2005, 2013), control frauds are individuals in top management who create a fraud-friendly – criminogenic – corporate culture that enables them to reward themselves by looting their business and to avoid detection. They accomplish this by: hiring yes-men, attracting political support through political contributions and by granting large loans (Wade and Sigurgeirsdottir 2010), using investments with no readily ascertainable value, employing accounting tricks and fictitious income to make their businesses appear to grow rapidly (because many of them are Ponzis, they need new money to pay off old investments), and providing ways for CEOs to convert the company's assets into personal assets through collective embezzlement[5] (Black 2005; Calavita and Pontell 1991; Calavita et al. 1997). Control frauds can defeat and suborn both internal and external controls because they create the company's policies. They victimize customers, investors, taxpayers and the company. As will be clear, control frauds were at the heart of Iceland's financial crisis.

Collective embezzlement: refinancing owners' and large borrowers' investments

Icelandic banks' CEOs and their largest shareholders understood that the best way to rob a bank is to own one (Black 2005). Their pillaging of Icelandic banks replicated the looting in United States savings and loans so aptly described by Black (2005) and Calavita et al. (1997). They paid themselves more than their institutions were worth and borrowed extensively with little or no collateral and then defaulted because of poor accounting, lax regulation, and/or low penalties for abuse or criminal activities (Barak 2012; Wade and Sigurgeirsdottir 2010).

All three banks engaged in extensive refinancing of their owners' and other favored borrowers' investments despite FSA rules that 'large exposure due to a group of financially related (connected) parties cannot exceed 25% of regulatory capital. A large exposure due to the parent company of a bank or due to a subsidiary cannot exceed 20% of capital' (Baldursson and Portes 2013: 75). In the months before it collapsed, Landsbanki loaned 36 per cent of its capital to a few of its main owners. The amount at Glitnir was 17 per cent. Kaupthing took the practice to extremes. The bank's credit committee approved loans equal to more than 100 per cent of the bank's equity on 24 September 2008, primarily to a few of its owners and closely connected parties (Wade and Sigurgeirsdottir 2011). Its practice of lending to linked companies and high-profile major shareholders with partial or no collateral was documented in internal bank records, including a 205-page document from a 25 September 2008 bank meeting that subsequently found its way onto Wikileaks. The behaviour of all three banks was consistent with control fraud and crony capitalism.

Glitnir and Jón Ásgeir Johannesson

Jón Ásgeir Johannesson[6] and his Baugur Group[7] provide clear examples of violations of FSA rules. Baugur borrowed heavily from all three banks,[8] but its relationship with Glitnir was excessive. The bank's loans to Baugur Group and related parties rapidly rose from about 40 per cent of Glitnir's capital base at the beginning of September 2007 – a few months after Baugur Group became the bank's controlling shareholder of Glitnir – to a high of 85 per cent in March 2008 (Baldursson and Portes 2013). Just three months prior to failing, Glitnir lent 29 million pounds to Baugur – a sum contrary to the bank's best interest and which led to a large loss (Steiner 2012). It was not surprising, therefore, that the OSP charged Glitnir's managers with causing the bank's collapse by depleting its cash reserves through heavy and improper lending to entities linked to Glitnir.

In one instance, Baugur used Aurum Holdings shares as collateral for a loan (Bowers 2013).[9] However, according to statements made by Glitnir administrators during UK civil proceedings, the shares were effectively worthless by the time they were offered as collateral (Bowers 2013).

In other related legal actions, Glitnir's bankruptcy management sued Johannesson and eight others – Glitnir managers and board members – for a fraudulent lending of ISK 15 billion to companies related to Johannesson shortly before the crash. Glitnir's board also filed suit against Johannesson in London, New York, and Reykjavik, alleging he and other members of a cabal conspired to siphon 2 billion dollars (1.4 billion pounds) out of Glitnir in order to enrich themselves and prop up their failing companies (Mason 2010). It charged that Johannesson and his co-defendants,[10] in typical control fraud fashion, staffed the bank with 'willing accomplices' and ignored the risk committee. The lawsuit also alleged that bondholders, primarily from New York, were misled by Johannesson and his associates concerning a 1 billion dollar issue in September 2007 (Mason 2010). Both suits contend that although Johannesson was not a legal director of the bank, he was a shadow director who pressured managers and the board to loan large sums to companies related to him and his business associates, which resulted in substantial losses for the bank (Davíðsdóttir 2013a).

Despite protesting his innocence, emails between Jón Ásgeir Johannesson and Larus Welding[11] indicate that his position as a major stockholder created a conflict for the bank (Steiner 2012). The presiding judge claimed these emails make 'The prospect of establishing that he had no control over the bank and/or that the loan was a bona fide commercial transaction looks somewhat forlorn' (Bowers 2013).

In another case involving improper loans, Larus Welding and Glitnir's former Chief of Corporate Banking were convicted of fraud for lending ISK 10 billion (around 60 million euros) in February 2008 to the Milestone Investment Company – a company that owned shares in Glitnir (News of Iceland 2012). The two bankers left several indications that they knew what they were doing was illegal: they circumvented the regular decision-making process for issuance of loans, insufficient collateral was provided, and they used two other companies to hide the loan (News of Iceland 2012). In the end, both men were sentenced to nine months (six of which are probational for two years) of jail time for the banking fraud that caused a 53 million euro (71 million dollar) loss for the bank (Valdimarsson 2012).

Collusion

At times the banks worked together. Landsbanki's Chief Executive Officer, along with the bank's former director of corporate accounts (who became the head of the bank from October 2008 to January 2009) were indicted for allowing Landsbanki to guarantee Kaupthing loans totalling 6.8 billion ISK to two companies with Panamanian registry without collateral (Valdimarsson 2014). It is apparent that the banks colluded and learned from one another.

Collective embezzlement: market manipulations

The SIC report described a pattern of Icelandic bank officials using a 'complex series of financial transactions – including loans to shareholders and close business associates – to prop up their institution's share prices and mask weaknesses' that is consistent with control frauds (Faris 2013). The banks sold shares by lending money to a linked private equity company, which, in turn, pledged the shares as collateral. Often the shares themselves were the only collateral for the loans, which made the banks the ultimate owners of the stock. Then, investment companies could buy assets at deliberately inflated values with high leverage from their linked banks. These related-party transactions created fake 'new capital', that appeared to strengthen the balance sheets of both the companies and the banks (Wade 2009: 19). However, this practice actually made the banks more vulnerable to collapse.

While bankers such as Sigurjón Árnason and his joint CEO, Halldór Kristjánsson, at Landsbanki and four other former employees of the bank were indicted for alleged manipulation of share price in 2013, the practice by bankers at Kaupthing rose to the level of an art form. Kaupthing repeatedly lent large sums of money to individuals and holding companies with the intent that these entities would buy shares in Kaupthing in order to prop up the bank's share price. As a result, virtually all of the bank's stated profits were from marking up assets it had bought at inflated prices (Lewis 2009). According to the OSP, on 31 August 2008, a little over a month before its collapse, Kaupthing owned 32.1 per cent of its own stock – a sum far beyond what was permitted by Icelandic law. The bank's profits derived from actual banking at the time were less than ten per cent (Lewis 2009).

On average, Kaupthing was purchasing a third of its own shares each month. From June through September of 2008, the last four months of its existence, the bank was 'the buyer in over 60% of all purchases of its own stock' (Baldursson and Portes 2013). By the end of September 2008, almost 42 per cent of Kaupthing shares were retained by the bank as loan collateral, much of which was without the knowledge of the bank's other stakeholders. Regulators should have been alerted to investigate when the bank approached the ownership limit of its own shares as a percentage of shares issued, which it frequently did between July 2007 and its collapse in October 2008. Whenever the bank approached the 5 per cent limit, it found buyers for excess shares (Baldursson and Portes 2013).

One of the companies Kaupthing worked closely with to manipulate share prices was Exista. Its loans to Exista gave that company a 22 per cent stake in the bank, which made it the bank's largest shareholder (Mason 2009). The manipulation went beyond simply lending Exista the money to purchase its shares. Daniel Thordarsson, Kaupthing's former asset manager, and Stefnir Ingi Agnarsson, former stock broker, were found guilty of submitting false purchase inquiries and share price manipulation for placing offers to buy Exista shortly before the close of business with the purpose of affecting the end-of-day value of Exista shares (IceNews 2009).

Other entities that Kaupthing allegedly worked with included:

1 Lydur Gudmundsson, who founded the Bakkavör food empire and who sat on the boards of both Kaupthing and Exista. He received loans worth 1.86 billion euros for companies connected to him and his brother, Agust. A 791.2 million euro loan to Exista indicated that most of the loans were unsecured (Mason 2009). In the end, Agust and Lydur Gudmundsson owned a 25 per cent stake in Kaupthing (Baldursson and Portes 2013: 31).
2 British retail entrepreneur Kevin Stanford, director of House of Fraser and Kaupthing's fourth largest shareholder, with a 4.2 per cent stake in the bank, 'was given a €519m loan to buy shares' (Mason 2009) of which 181 million euros were to purchase Kaupthing shares. Although Stanford has not been accused of any wrongdoing, the loan appears to be made for 'the express purpose of artificially maintaining its share price' (*Guardian* 2013).
3 Kaupthing's annual reports indicated that the bank lent board members money to buy shares in Kaupthing and provided them the option to sell those shares back to the bank at a guaranteed profit (Lewis 2009).
4 Kaupthing covertly lent Sheikh Mohammed Bin Khalifa al Thani of Qatar's royal family millions to buy Kaupthing shares in 2008 (*Guardian* 2013). At the time of the purchase, Kaupthing's Chair of the Board of Governors, Sigurður Einarsson and its former CEO, Hreiðar Már Sigurðsson, and the bank's second largest shareholder, Ólafur Ólafsson, appeared in the media heralding al Thani's investment as evidence of the bank's strong position and promising outlook. Al Thani personally proclaimed his confidence in the bank by stating, 'Kaupthing's position is strong and we believe in the bank's strategy and management team,

> as Kaupthing has performed well in the current market turbulence and has proven it can change and adapt to a new reality in banking' (as quoted in Faris 2013). What everyone neglected to mention was that the bank provided the funds for the sheikh's purchase.

In 2009, the Special Prosecutor investigating the case focused attention on Einarsson, who had fled the country. Only after an international arrest warrant was issued and he appeared on Interpol's wanted list accused of counterfeiting, forgery and fraud did he agree to return to Iceland and was arrested (*Guardian* 2013; Veal 2010).[12]

The investigation expanded to include Sigurðsson; the former director of the bank in Luxembourg, Magnus Gudmundsson; and shareholder, Ólafur Ólafsson. OSP charged the four and other former senior bank staff members with conspiring to orchestrate five large-scale market manipulations in the al Thani case. Although OSP did not accuse al Thani of wrongdoing, the banks sued the sheikh and later settled with no claim of liability by any party (Faris 2013; Ice-News 2013). The terms of the settlement remain confidential.

The scheme in which al Thani acquired a 5.1 per cent stake in Kaupthing – just days before the bank's collapse – was planned in Kaupthing's subsidiary in Luxembourg, where Guðmundsson played a key role in granting the loan (Davíðsdóttir 2013b).[13] The plan operated in the following manner. On 19 September 2008, Sigurðsson arranged for a 50 million dollar loan to be paid into a Kaupthing account belonging to Brooks Trading, a British Virgin Island (BVI) company owned by another BVI company, Mink Trading, of which al Thani was the beneficial owner (Davíðsdóttir 2013b). Despite Kaupthing teetering on the verge of collapse at the time, the loans were issued with little or no requirements for collateral or guarantees. Since Sigurðsson did not have the authority to authorize a loan of this size, he needed to bypass the bank's credit committee. On 29 September 2008, he initiated two ISK 12.8 billion loans to two BVI companies with Kaupthing accounts: Serval Trading,[14] which belonged to al Thani, and Gerland Assets, which belonged to Ólafsson. These loans were then channeled into the account of a Cyprus company, Choice Stay, which had Ólafsson, al Thani and another al Thani, Sheikh Sultan al Thani, as beneficial owners. From Choice Stay, the money went into Q Iceland Finance's Kaupthing account, owned by Q Iceland Holding, of which al Thani was the beneficial owner. Q Iceland Finance then bought the Kaupthing shares (Davíðsdóttir 2013b).

Sigurðsson, Einarsson, Guðmundsson, and Ólafsson were convicted and sentenced in 2013 for violating their ethical obligations, stock market manipulation, and fraud related to al Thani's purchase. Sigurðsson received a five-and-a-half-year sentence; Einarsson five years; and Guðmundsson, who played a key role in granting the loan, negotiated and organized payment to Brooks Trading and should have known that Sigurðsson did not have the authority to generate the loan, was sentenced to three years. Ólafsson, who approved the loan, was sentenced to three-and-a-half years. He faces additional charges of money laundering for accepting loans to his companies without providing adequate guarantees (Davíðsdóttir 2013b). The arrests and convictions would have been unlikely had it not been for SIC's thorough and hard-hitting report on the causes of the 2008 collapse of the Icelandic banks that OPS used as guidance in questioning Sigurðsson and Gudmundsson (Veal 2010).

Inflating the Ponzi Bubble

Icesave and Edge

While the banks were not officially labeled as insolvent in 2006 or 2007, all three were in need of constant new revenue sources. They had grown rapidly since 2003 – their loan portfolios increased[15] and they were buying assets including other banks. In search of funds, the banks entered the European debt market and then the American debt securities market. When access to the international financial markets that was responsible for much of their growth closed to them in late 2007, they became dependent on short-term financing to refinance their debt.

As borrowing became increasingly difficult for all three banks, they needed to obtain new sources of revenue. In typical Ponzi fashion, Landsbanki, to lure new customers, developed Icesave internet accounts that offered higher yields than could be earned by bricks-and-mortar bank customers in Great Britain (October 2006) and the Netherlands (May 2008). By offering these accounts through its overseas branches instead of through subsidiaries, the accounts fell into a regulatory black hole. They were outside of the purview of the host country's regulators and – by residing outside Iceland – out of Icelandic regulators' sight. Icesave accounts temporarily allowed Landsbanki to repay its loans and buy more assets (Wade and Sigurgeirsdottir 2011).

Kaupthing followed suit by offering Edge accounts, their version of the Icesave accounts, to customers in ten countries between 2007 and 2008. In six countries – Belgium, the Isle of Man, Luxembourg, Sweden, Switzerland, and the United Kingdom – the accounts were offered through bank branches, but in Finland, Norway, Germany, and Austria, Edge accounts were offered in subsidiaries.

Individuals, companies, and even government entities outside of Iceland, lured by the promise of up to 14 per cent interest, invested heavily in Icelandic banks.[16] Investors believed they were safe because, as a member of the EEA, Iceland's citizens would be responsible to compensate depositors if the bank failed (Wade and Sigurgeirsdottir 2010). Furthermore, many customers did not realize that their country's regulations did not protect their deposits in Icelandic bank branches in their own countries. United Kingdom investors gave the banks over 30 billion dollars, German banks provided 21 billion dollars, the Netherlands gave the banks 305 million dollars, and Sweden 400 million dollars (Lewis 2009). By the middle of 2007, the problematic imbalance should have been recognized. Deposits in Landsbanki's UK branch, including Icesave accounts, amounted to 5.5 billion pounds, but the foreign currency reserves of the Central Bank of Iceland were only 1.2 billion pounds (Peel 2010).

In March 2008, as increasing evidence of a crisis loomed, the Icelandic government launched a PR campaign. Prime Minister Haarde assured Wall Street that contrary to rumours, Icelandic banks were sound. The foreign minister, joined by Professor Richard Portes from London Business School, provided similar assurances in Copenhagen. Prior to the May 2008 opening of the Icesave branch in the Netherlands, Landsbanki published a prospectus containing an interview with the chairman of Iceland's FSA in which he asserted all was well with Iceland's banks (Wade and Sigurgeirsdottir 2010). Despite the public relations campaign, by August 2008, the United Kingdom, the Netherlands, and Sweden all asked how Iceland planned to stand behind the accounts if the banks collapsed. To which, the government responded that it would take out loans (Farrer 2012).[17]

Alchemy of love letters

This section addresses how the banks were able to receive funds when they had nothing to offer but debt. Needing liquidity, but having exhausted their borrowing capacity from the Central Bank, Glitnir, Kaupthing, and Landsbanki developed a novel way to generate revenue that skirted regulations, but did not violate the law because of how it was staged. This method became known as 'love letters' because it was based on little more than trust and promises. The banks sold debt securities to smaller regional banks in the country, which in turn took the bonds to the Central Bank and borrowed against them without having to provide collateral. Then, the regional banks lent the money to the originating bank. With apparently improved balance sheets, the big three sold the 'love letters' overseas first to subsidiaries in Luxembourg and then to either the Central Bank of Luxembourg or the European Central Bank. The cash received from the transactions found its way back to parent banks in Iceland (Wade and Sigurgeirsdottir 2010). Interestingly, a US credit rating agency rewarded Glitnir bonds a AAA rating (Wade and Sigurgeirsdottir 2010).

Courts outside of Iceland

Legal actions against Icelandic banks and individuals connected to them were initiated in several countries outside of Iceland. One example of this is a trial involving Landsbanki in a Paris court. The court initially indicted the Luxembourg subsidiary of the bank for fraud and 'lack of approval'. Then, in January 2014, it indicted three former executives of Landsbanki's Luxembourg subsidiary for fraud (Equity Release Victims Association 2014). According to the charges, between 2006 and 2008 Landsbanki, through its Luxembourg subsidiary, offered mortgages with favorable 'equity release loans' in the south of France, Portugal, and Spain. Borrowers there would 'receive a portion of the sum, while the bank reinvested the rest in markets. The value of this portfolio would grow to the point of covering all aspects of the loan, which was repayable upon its conclusion' (Equity Release Victims Association 2014). As with the subprime mortgage scandal in the United States, the bank offered the mortgages without checking the borrowers' capacity to repay their debt.

Government negligence

By spring 2008, the IMF and the European Central Bank were well aware of Iceland's precarious economic position. The IMF provided Prime Minister Haarde with a confidential report that expressed the need to 'rein in' the banks and even offered how to go about it. But the Central Bank of Iceland concluded that scaling back was impossible and desired to borrow more foreign-exchange reserves.

The co-dependence of the international banking system was demonstrated when the Central Banks of Denmark, Sweden and Norway, fearing the impact on their finances if Iceland's banks collapsed, extended lines of credit to Iceland. Of course, because Iceland's financial institutions were Ponzis, their actions only delayed the inevitable.

One of the SIC's main conclusions was that Prime Minister Geir Haarde; the Finance Minister; the Minister of Business Affairs and the Chief of the Central Bank, David Oddsson, were negligent 'by omitting to respond in an appropriate fashion to the impending danger for the Icelandic economy that was caused by the deteriorating situation of the banks'[18] (*Daily Mail Reporter* 2012; Hilmarsson 2013). The SIC also found that the Director General of the Icelandic Supervisory Authority and two governors of the CBI were negligent (Hilmarsson 2013). In the end, parliament referred only Geir Haarde for prosecution, making him the first world leader charged criminally for his role in a financial crisis (*Daily Mail Reporter* 2012).

Parliament charged that Haarde neglected to cut the size of the banking system and failed to transfer British depositors' accounts in one bank to a separate subsidiary (Higgins 2013). Furthermore, Haarde failed to implement recommendations of a 2006 government committee report on how to strengthen Iceland's economy. Haarde responded that 'neither he nor financial regulators knew the real state of Icelandic banks' precarious finances until they collapsed in October 2008' (Huffington Post 2012), yet he sought to assure Wall Street that the Icelandic banks were sound a mere six months prior to their collapse (Wade and Sigurgeirsdottir 2011). He stated, 'We knew about the crisis, but not the banks' lack of accountability and their illegal activities, which not even the Financial Supervisory Authority seems to have realized' (Huffington Post 2012).

Haarde was cleared of all the charges, except for not holding cabinet meetings when things turned critical. He believes the only reason he was convicted on that one count was because the judges 'found themselves pressed to come up with a guilty verdict [...] to save the neck of the parliamentarians who instigated this' (Brown 2012).

While Haarde bore some responsibility as the leader of the country, Iceland's financial ministers – the Finance Minister, Minister of Business Affairs, and the chief of the Central Bank – and regulators all failed to protect citizens and depositors. The government's structural reliance on the financial sector caused it to be lax with its oversight. In fact, the government increasingly relied on the banks to provide information about the economy (Wade and Sigurgeirsdottir 2010). Government regulators did not look for fraud or indications of problems, so they were unlikely to find fraud or problems (Black 2013). On the international front, there was a lack of serious cross-border regulation (Wade and Sigurgeirsdottir 2010).

The CBI should have known prior to the crisis that its deposit insurance fund was underfunded, its foreign reserves were low, and that it was incapable of acting as a credible lender of last resort. Although members of the CBI's Board of Governors shared some concerns with the Prime Minister and a small group of ministers, there was no evidence that they suggested a course of action (Hilmarsson 2013). Instead, a half a year prior to the Icelandic banking collapse, Central Bank chairman Oddsson dismissed criticism of the country's banks and those who were shorting the banks as attempts 'to harm the Icelandic financial system' (Lewis 2009).

Icelandic regulators also failed to spot the danger posed by the banks' heavy dependence on foreign deposits for funding as they lured British and Dutch depositors into high-interest accounts. Even after concerned United Kingdom regulators met with Icelandic officials to urge Landsbanki to transfer the Icesave accounts to a UK subsidiary so that accounts would fall under British deposit guarantee fund, Landsbanki continued to drag its feet.

The deregulatory atmosphere left regulatory agencies understaffed. They had a limited capacity to look for fraud and generate criminal referrals and lacked the will to do so. The understaffed and inexperienced FSA's primary responsibility was to monitor the activities of the banks and to know the health of the banks' balance sheets; but it was incapable of doing its job. Its regulators failed to ask proper questions and lacked the firmness and assertiveness needed to conduct and resolve cases (Hilmarsson 2013: 44). The best qualified individuals worked for the banks, which paid much better than the government. The agency that may have warned about the dangerous banking practices, the independent-thinking National Economic Institute, was abolished in 2002 after taking stands that were contrary to the government's official position (Wade and Sigurgeirsdottir 2010).

The truth is, politicians and regulatory agencies had no incentive to question the 'success' of the banks. No one wanted do to anything that would challenge the country's new-found prosperity that seemed to benefit everyone or to cause the bubble to burst. Instead of pointing out that the emperor had no clothes, they adopted 'concerted ignorance'. Challenged with uncomfortable questions, individuals neutralized them by claiming critics were jealous at what this small country was able to achieve. Furthermore, when conditions became critical, individuals who could have done something did not act for fear of triggering a run on the banks (Wade and Sigurgeirsdottir 2010). Only after citizens took to the streets questioning the state's behavior did the state consider reregulating and investigating the crisis. The SIC took its job seriously and OSP was funded to conduct meaningful investigations.

Conclusion

The crime-facilitative environment created by deregulation and the failure to regulate combined with the active promotion of questionable financial products by government officials, indicates that the banking crisis was a state–financial crime which makes it infinitely more difficult to control and punish. As is apparent in the preceding paragraphs, government officials should have known of growing problems within the country's financial institutions prior to the meltdown.

Instead, they ignored the warning signs, failed to act, put the country and its citizens at risk, and helped obscure or cover up problems. While regulators and politicians benefited from the status quo and their close relationships with bankers, there are indications that structural factors also played an important role in their actions or lack of action.

State officials know that the public needs to believe in the integrity of the banking system. To reveal the existence of a problem could undermine a bank's already precarious health, create a run and cause the economy to collapse (Calavita and Pontell 1991). Furthermore, the three banks were so interconnected that the collapse of one would surely bring down the others. Along the same lines, Wade and Sigurgeirsdottir (2010) describes an irony. The worse the economic situation appeared to be, the less regulators should say. They saw, both within Iceland and on the global stage, bankers and politicains softened their position or refrained from acting when 'the situation had become so fragile that to speak might trigger a run on the banks which might otherwise be averted' (Wade and Sigurgeirsdottir 2010: 28). Within Iceland this situation played out when officials engaged in a public relations campaign instead of taking their actions against the banks once they realized that the CBI did not have the resources to bail out the banks. Within the global economy, the IMF consciously toned down its concerns from 2006 on. Several central banks actively worked with Icelandic banks out of fear that if they did not, they may lose their capital. The problem was, without regulators taking action, bad behavior escalated as the banks engaged in questionable and criminal behavior as they gambled for ressurection seeking ways out of their financial difficulties. The banks learned from one another; they normalized their deviance.

Financial regulators face a conundrum or regulator's dilemma – to deter bad behavior by financial institutions, regulators must act at the first indications of wrongdoing. If they pass a tipping-point, as Wade and Sigurgeirsdottir (2010: 28) indicated, the economic consequences not only for that institution, but other related institutions and customers may seem too great if they discipline the banks or allow them to fail. While Iceland may be an example for other countries on how to investigate and prosecute crimes related to the financial meltdown, the jury is still out on how successful the OSP has been. Although the office has had successful convictions, as of early 2013, OSP still had 17 or 18 cases related to the banking crisis that have yet to be tried (Finkle 2013). The cases, as with all white-collar crimes, are difficult to develop. Law is often unclear on what constitutes a criminal offence in high finance. According to Special Prosecutor Hauksson, 'It was often easy to show that bankers violated their own internal rules for lending and other activities,' but 'as in all cases involving theft or fraud, the most difficult thing is proving intent' (Higgins 2013). Bankers may 'not [be] aware of when they crossed the line' (as quoted in Higgins 2013). As Hauksson's statements suggests, the banking culture normalized, justified, and reinforced bankers' actions. Bankers neutralize their action with the belief that everyone is doing it.

Iceland seemingly has weathered the collapse of its major banks and its economy is recovering. The banks that have replaced Glitnir, Kaupthing, and Landsbanki are smaller and much more conservative. Investors who have been victimized are leery, which may force them to question promised higher returns. Perhaps knowing Iceland will not bail out its banks if they act irresponsibly or criminally will have a deterrent effect. But, the deterrent effect may be very limited for a couple of reasons. First, as demonstrated in the preceding paragraphs, the fear of a financial crisis lead several central banks and the IMF to become enablers instead of entities that disciplined the Icelandic banks. Second, the cycle of regulation, deregulation, and reregulation is the result of the state attempting to balance the interests of citizens with business interest. As a rule, the regulation stage lasts just long enough to assure citizens that the state will work on their behalf. Then the state will once again deregulate in response to pressure from the business community (Calavita and Pontell 1994; Snider 2013). By late 2014, there have been signs that Iceland is backing away from a strong regulatory stance. The government has decreased OSP's 2015 budget from ISK 900 million to ISK 295 million.

Notes

1 See Calavita et al. (1997) for a detailed description of the savings and loan crisis in the United States. Deregulation in both countries allowed individuals with no banking experience to purchase and operate financial institutions. It also permitted these institutions to expand services and engage in risky business with little oversight.

2 Ponzi schemes are named after Charles Ponzi, who enticed people to give him money with promises of high returns. The problem was that he paid early participants with moneys collected from newer investors. Once the number of new contributors ceased to increase, the scheme collapsed. Ponzi schemes are unsustainable because they rely on ever increasing number of participants.

In a Ponzi culture, a population believes everything will increase in value and normalizes Ponzi schemes despite warnings signs. A symbiotic relation between government and financial institutions facilitates this by providing a hospitable environment for speculation, unsustainable debt, and bubbles.

3 The OSP began early 2009 with just five employees, but grew into an organization with approximately 110 employees.

4 The office used several strategies to pursue cases against financial institutions and their principles that were generally reserved for investigations into a 'drug ring or smuggling operation – house and office raids, phone taps, eavesdropping with shotgun microphones, property seizure, and stints in solitary confinement' (Faris 2013).

5 Collective embezzlement – 'the siphoning off of company funds for personal use by top management' – ranged from 'outright looting of an institution's cash or other resources to business practices where the sole purpose is the generation of personal profit for management' (Calavita and Pontell 1991: 94, 99).

6 Troubles began in 2002 for Jón Ásgeir Johannesson and Johannes Jonsson, his father and business partner, when tax authorities raided their offices. In 2005, the two were charged with 40 counts including: violations of the Accounting Act, Annual Accounts Act and Firms Act, failing to report large payments, failing to pay tax on sale shares, fraud and embezzlement (Holland 2013). Jón Ásgeir was convicted and received a three-month suspended sentence for corporate misconduct in 2007 – breach of bookkeeping rules (Bowers 2013; Steiner 2012). He attempted to neutralize the investigation and subsequent conviction as the work of those wanting to destroy Baugur and his reputation out of jealousy (Bowers 2013).

In February 2013, Jón Ásgeir Johannesson, his sister, and Baugur's former finance director were convicted of operating a 2.4 million dollar (1.5 million pound) tax evasion scheme from 1998 to 2003. This time Jón Ásgeir received a one year suspended sentence and a 62 million kronur fine (312,000 pounds or 371,445 euros) on nine tax evasion charges including not declaring all his capital gains income, profit from shares he sold, and violating accounting laws while running Baugur (Valdimarsson 2013). His sister received a three-month suspended sentence. Baugur's former finance director received an 18-month suspended sentence and a fine of 32 million kronur.

7 Baugur Group began as the Bonus Supermarket. The rapidly growing supermarket chain eventually was restructured into three independent units: Baugur-Iceland; Bonus Stores, Inc.; and Baugur ID. Baugur Group is the holding company.

8 The banks' exposure to Baugur Group was well above the regulatory maximum of 25 per cent. In December 2007, the three banks loaned Baugur Group and related parties over 5.5 billion euros. By that time, the capital base of the three banks, as well as the 2007 GDP of Iceland, was approximately 14 billion euros (Baldursson and Portes 2013).

9 Aurum's pretax profit for the year ending in February 2008 was just 800,000 pounds but by year-end it had more than 170 million pounds in liabilities. Johannesson, however, insisted the valuation of the Aurum shares for the loan was fair at the time the loan was made (Bowers 2013).

10 Co-defendants included his wife, Ingibjorg Palmadottir (owner of a major Icelandic newspaper); investor Palmi Haraldsson; Glitnir's former chairman Thorsteinn Jonsson; its former chief executive Larus Welding; and two former directors, Jon Sigurdsson and Hannes Smarason (Mason 2010).

11 Larus Welding was appointed Chief Executive Officer of Glitnir in April 2007, shortly after Jón Ásgeir became a major shareholder in the bank (Bowers 2013).

12 The Financial Services Authority struck a deal with Einarsson in 2012 which barred him from the City of London for five years (Bowers 2013).

13 Davíðsdóttir (2013c) asserts that it was well-known in Iceland that many of the country's banks' most questionable deals were carried out in Luxembourg.

14 This loan had al Thani's personal guarantee. On 8 October 2008, after Kaupthing collapsed, US dollars were sent express to Iceland where it was converted into kronur, at twice the going rate in Iceland that day, to repay Serval's loan to Kaupthing. This freed the Sheik from his personal guarantee (Davíðsdóttir 2013b).

15 The greatest increase was in loans to related companies and individuals, and to foreign parties (SIC 2010, Ch. 21: 2). Unfortunately, many of the loans were of questionable quality.

16 Account holders included Cambridge University, the London Metropolitan Police Authority, and probably to its embarrassment, the UK Audit Commission (Wade and Sigurgeirsdottir 2010).

17 After Icelandic citizens voted three times to reject agreements (in 2010, less than two per cent voted in favor of the agreement (Wade and Sigurgeirsdottir 2010)) that would make them liable for the banks' debts, the case went to the European Free Trade Association (EFTA), *Court EFTA Surveillance Authority v. Iceland*, which cleared Iceland of all claims.

18 The report also identifies a key error made by the staff at the Icelandic central bank – they forgot to extend a 316 million pound loan agreement with the Bank of International Settlements in Basel, Switzerland (*Daily Mail Reporter* 2012).

References

Association of Certified Fraud Examiners (ACFE) (2012, December) *Fighting Fraud in Iceland: The Fraud Examiner.* Online. Available HTTP: <http://www.acfe.com/fraud-examiner.aspx?id=4294976262&terms=%28fraud+prevention%29+> (accessed 11 July 2014).

Baldursson, F.M. and Portes, R. (2013) *Gambling for Resurrection in Iceland: The Rise and Fall of the Banks*, Centre for Economic Policy Research. Online. Available HTTP: <http://www.sedlabanki.is/library/Skr%C3%A1arsafn/M%C3%A1lstofur/Gambling%20for%20resurrection%20in%20Iceland-the%20rise%20and%20fall%20of%20the%20banks%20%28Baldursson,%20Portes%29%20-%20Copy%20%281%29.pdf> (accessed 8 July 2014).

Barak, G. (2012) *Theft of a Nation: Wall Street Looting and Federal Regulatory Colluding*, Lanham, MD: Rowman & Littlefield Publishers, Inc.

Black, W.K. (2005) *The Best Way to Rob a Bank is to Own One: How Corporate Executives and Politicians Looted the S & L Industry*, Austin: University of Texas.

Black, W.K. (2013) 'Why CEOs are able to loot with impunity', in S. Will, S. Handelman and D.C. Brotherton (eds) *How They Got Away With It: White-Collar Criminals and the Financial Meltdown*, New York: Columbia University Press, pp. 171–177.

Bland, A. (2013, 7 September) 'After the storm: Has Iceland learned its lesson from its financial meltdown?', *The Independent.* Online. Available HTTP: <http://www.independent.co.uk/news/world/europe/after-the-storm-has-iceland-learned-its-lesson-from-its-financial-meltdown-8798365.html> (accessed 11 July 2014).

Bowers, S. (2013, 13 January) 'Ex-Baugur boss Jon Asgeir Johannesson lashes out at "persecution"', *Guardian.* Online. Available HTTP: <http://www.theguardian.com/business/2013/jan/13/baugur-jon-asgeir-johannesson> (accessed 11 July 2014).

Brown, R. (2012, 24 April) 'Iceland's former prime minister faces criminal charges over financial crisis', *PM with Mark Colvin.* Online. Available HTTP: <http://www.abc.net.au/pm/content/2012/s3488180.htm> (accessed 11 July 2014).

Calavita, K. and Pontell, H.N. (1991) '"Other people's money" revisited: Collective embezzlement in the savings and loan and insurance industries', *Social Problems*, 38(1): 94–112.

Calavita, K. and Pontell, H.N. (1994) 'The state and white-collar crime: Saving the savings and loans', *Law & Society Review*, 28(2): 297–324.

Calavita, K., Pontell, H.N. and Tillman, R.H. (1997) *Big Money Crime: Fraud and Politics in the Savings and Loan Crisis*, Berkeley: University of California Press.

Daily Mail Reporter (2012, 5 March) 'Former Iceland PM could become first leader to face criminal charges over global financial meltdown.' Online. Available HTTP: <http://www.dailymail.co.uk/news/article-1316132/Ex-Iceland-PM-Geir-Haarde-face-criminal-charges-global-financial-meldown.html#ixzz2jhp2Z5Z7> (accessed 11 July 2014).

Davíðsdóttir, S. (2013a, 8 February) 'Jon Asgeir Johannesson yet again on the FT front page – this time for tax fraud', *Sigrún Davíðsdóttir's Icelog.* Online. Available HTTP: <http://uti.is/2013/02/jon-asgeir-johannesson-yet-again-on-the-ft-front-page-this-time-for-tax-fraud/> (accessed 11 July 2014).

Davíðsdóttir, S. (2013b, 23 February) 'The al Thani story behind the Kaupthing indictment (updated)', *Sigrún Davíðsdóttir's Icelog.* Online. Available HTTP: <http://uti.is/2012/02/the-al-thani-story-behind-the-kaupthing-indictment/> (accessed 11 July 2014).

Davíðsdóttir, S. (2013c, 31 March) 'Truth and investigations: What Cyprus can learn from Iceland', *Sigrún Davíðsdóttir's Icelog.* Online. Available HTTP: <http:// uti.is/2013/03/truth-and-investigations-what-cyprus-can-learn-from-iceland/> (accessed 11 January 2014).

Domhoff, G.W. (1978) *The Powers That Be*, New York: Random House.

Equity Release Victims Association (2014, 31 January) '3 Landsbanki former executives indicted in a fraud criminal investigation.' Online. Available HTTP: <http://erva.es/2014/01/31/3-landsbanki-former-executives-indicted-in-a-fraud-criminal-investigation/> (accessed 11 July 2014).

Faris, S. (2013, 12 September) 'The financial crisis: Five years later: Iceland prosecutor investigates, convicts bankers for financial crimes', *Business Week*. Online. Available HTTP: <http://www.businessweek.com/articles/2013-09-12/iceland-prosecutor-investigates-convicts-bankers-for-financial-crimes> (accessed 11 July 2014).

Farrer, M. (2012, 26 June) 'Timeline: Kaupthing Edge and Icesave', *Guardian*. Online. Available HTTP: <http://www.theguardian.com/business/2012/jun/26/timeline-kaupthing-edge-icesave> (accessed 24 March 2014).

Finkle, V. (2013, 28 March) 'Iceland indicts bankers over financial crisis', *American Banker*. Online. Available HTTP: <http://www.americanbanker.com/people/iceland-indicts-bankers-over-financial-crisis-1057928-1.html> (accessed 12 October 2013).

Friedrichs, D.O. (2013) 'Wall Street: Crime never sleeps', in S. Will, S. Handelman and D.C. Brotherton (eds) *How They Got Away With It: White-Collar Criminals and the Financial Meltdown*, New York: Columbia University Press, pp. 3–25.

Greenstein, T. (2013, 20 February) 'Iceland's stabilized economy is a surprising success story', *Forbes*. Online. Available HTTP: <http://www.forbes.com/sites/traceygreenstein/2013/02/20/icelands-stabilized-economy-is-a-surprising-success-story/> (accessed 11 July 2014).

Guardian (2013, 21 March) 'Nine former top Kaupthing Bank staffers indicted', *Tapei Times*. Online. Available HTTP: <http://www.taipeitimes.com/News/biz/archives/2013/03/21/2003557582> (accessed 6 November 2013).

Higgins, A. (2013, 2 February) 'Iceland, fervant prosecutor of bankers, sees meager return', *New York Times*. Online. Available HTTP: <http://www.nytimes.com/2013/02/03/world/europe/iceland-prosecutor-of-bankers-sees-meager-returns.html?pagewanted=all> (accessed 8 September 2013).

Hilmarsson, H.Þ (2013) 'Small states and big banks – the case of Iceland', *Baltic Journal of Economics*, 13(1): 31–48.

Holland, T. (2013, 1 July) 'Former Baugur boss Jon Asegir [sic] Johannesson goes to European Court to fight tax conviction', *RetailWeek*. Online. Available HTTP: <http://www.retail-week.com/people/former-baugur-boss-goes-to-european-court-to-fight-tax-conviction/5050604.article> (accessed 11 November 2013).

Huffington Post (2012, 5 March) 'Geir Haarde, Iceland's ex-PM, the first world leader to face criminal charges over financial crisis.' Online. Available HTTP: <http://www.huffingtonpost.com/2012/03/05/geir-haarde-trial_n_1320682.html> (accessed 29 August 2013).

IceNews (2009, 9 December) 'Kaupthing men sentenced.' Online. Available HTTP: <http://www.icenews.is/2009/12/09/former-kaupthing-men-sentenced/> (accessed 11 July 2014).

IceNews (2013, 16 February) 'Iceland's Kaupthing resolves Qatari dispute.' Online. Available HTTP: <http://www.icenews.is/2013/02/16/icelands-kaupthing-resolves-qatari-dispute/> (accessed 29 August 2013).

Katz, J. (1979) 'Concerted ignorance: The social construction of cover-up', *Journal of Contemporary Ethnography*, 8(3): 295–316.

Kramer, R.C. and Michalowski, R.J. (2006) 'The original formulation', in R.J. Michalowski and R.C. Kramer (eds) *State-Corporate Crime: Wrongdoing at the Intersection of Government and Business*, New Brunswick, NJ: Rutgers University Press, pp. 18–26.

Lewis, M. (2009, April) 'Wall Street on the tundra', *Vanity Fair*. Online. Available HTTP: <http://www.vanityfair.com/politics/features/2009/04/iceland200904> (accessed 7 November 2013).

Mason, R. (2009, 4 August) 'Kaupthing leak exposes loans', *Telegraph*. Online. Available HTTP: <http://www.telegraph.co.uk/finance/newsbysector/banksandfinance/5968231/Kaupthing-leak-exposes-loans.html> (accessed 17 November 2013).

Mason, R. (2010, 13 May) 'Former Baugur boss Jon Asgeir Johannesson accused of $2bn fraud', *Telegraph*. Online. Available HTTP: <http://www.telegraph.co.uk/finance/newsbysector/retailandconsumer/7716599/Former-Baugur-boss-Jon-Asgeir-Johannesson-accused-of-2bn-fraud.html> (accessed 7 November 2013).

Michalowski, R.J. and Kramer, R.C. (2006) 'The critique of power', in R.J. Michalowski and R.C. Kramer (eds) *State-Corporate Crime: Wrongdoing at the Intersection of Government and Business*, New Brunswick, NJ: Rutgers University Press.

News of Iceland (2012, 28 December) 'Bankers from Glitnir bank sentenced to jail', *News of Iceland*. Online. Available HTTP: <http://www.newsoficeland.com/home/business-economics/private-sector/item/410-bankers-from-glitnir-bank-sentenced-to-jail> (accessed 23 November 2013).

O'Connor, J. (1973) *The Fiscal Crisis of the State*, New York: St. Martin's Press.

Peel, M. (2010, 13 April) 'Bribery curbs spawn specialist firm', *Financial Times*. Online. Available HTTP: <http://www.ft.com/intl/cms/s/0/ce32681a-4696-11df-9713-00144feab49a.html#axzz2xTNyhIC9> (accessed 6 December 2013).

Poulantzas, N. (1969) 'The problem of the capitalist state', *New Left Review*, 58: 67–78.

Report of the Special Investigative Commission (SIC) (2010, 12 April) 'Chapter 21: Causes of the collapse of the Icelandic Banks: Responsibilities, mistakes and negligence', *Althingi*. Online. Available HTTP: <http://www.rna.is/media/skjol/RNAvefurKafli21Enska.pdf> (accessed 28 February 2014).

Snider, L. (2013) 'The technological advantages of stock market traders', in S. Will, S. Handelman and D. Brotherton (eds) *How They Got Away With It: White-Collar Criminals and the Financial Meltdown*, New York: Columbia University Press, pp. 151–170.

Steiner, R. (2012, 19 December) 'Jon Asgeir Johannesson charged with criminal offences linked to collapse of Iceland banks', *Mail*. Online. Available HTTP: <http://www.thisismoney.co.uk/money/news/article-2250406/Jon-Asgeir-Johannesson-charged-criminal-offences-linked-collapse-Iceland-banks.html> (accesssed 8 November 2013).

Valdimarsson, O. (2012, 28 December) 'Executives at collapsed Iceland bank jailed for fraud', *Chicago Tribune*. Online. Available HTTP: <http://articles.chicagotribune.com/2012-12-28/news/sns-rt-iceland-crisisl5e8ns4tn-20121228_1_glitnir-omar-valdimarsson-special-prosecutor> (accessed 11 July 2014).

Valdimarsson, O. (2013, 7 February) 'Iceland top court hands prison term to Johannesson on taxes', *Bloomberg*. Online. Available HTTP: <http://www.bloomberg.com/news/2013-02-07/iceland-top-court-hands-prison-term-to-johannesson-on-taxes-1-.html> (accessed 11 July 2014).

Valdimarsson, O. (2014, 31 January) 'Iceland prosecutor indicts two former Landsbanki bosses on fraud', *Bloomberg*. Online. Available HTTP: <http://www.bloomberg.com/news/2014-01-31/iceland-prosecutor-indicts-two-former-landsbanki-bosses-on-fraud.html> (accessed 11 July 2014).

Veal, L. (2010, 12 May) 'ICELAND: Int'l arrest warrant against top bank official', *Inter Press Service News Agency*. Online. Available HTTP: <http://www.ipsnews.net/2010/05/iceland-intl-arrest-warrant-against-top-bank-official/> (accessed 16 November 2013).

Wade, R. (2009) 'The crisis: Iceland as Icarus', *Challenge*, 52. Online. Available HTTP: <http://www.challengemagazine.com/extra/005_033.pdf> (accessed 11 July 2014).

Wade, R. and Sigurgeirsdottir, S. (2010) 'Lessons from Iceland', *New Left Review*, 65: 5–29.

Wade, R. and Sigurgeirsdottir, S. (2011) 'Iceland's meltdown: The rise and fall of international banking in the North Atlantic', *Brazilian Journal of Political Economy*, 31(5): 684–698.

Will, S. (2013) 'America's Ponzi Culture', in S. Will, S. Handelman and D. Brotherton (eds) *How They Got Away With It: White-Collar Criminals and the Financial Meltdown*, New York: Columbia University Press, pp. 45–67.

Zatz, M.S. (1993) 'Preface', in W.J. Chambliss and M.S. Zatz (eds) *Making Law: The State, The Law, and Structural Contradictions*, Indianapolis: Indiana University Press, pp. ix–xi.

18

Professional football and crime

Exploring *terra incognita* in studies on white-collar crime

Hans Nelen[1]

Introduction

In 2012, much media attention was paid to (various) irregularities in professional sports. A first wave of media reports focused on the manipulation of match results by means of bribing referees and/or players, i.e. *match fixing* in football. An interesting example can be found in a report, circulated by South American news agencies, that the Fédération Internationale de Football Association (FIFA) had launched an investigation into irregularities concerning the match Argentina vs Peru during the 1978 World Cup in Argentina. The homeland won that game with 6–0 and consequently made the finals in which they proved too strong for the Dutch national team. According to a statement made under oath by a former Peruvian senator, the then president of the country, Francisco Bermudez, apparently made a deal with the Argentinean military dictator of those years, Jorge Videla: in exchange for a large victory, the Argentinian secret service would 'take care of' 13 Peruvian dissidents. In the Netherlands, it was not so much the degrading agreement that led to consternation, but rather the possibility that the Netherlands could still be crowned world champion after 34 years!

A second wave of media attention was triggered by the report of the United States Anti-Doping Agency (USADA) in October 2012 on doping and manipulation by sevenfold Tour de France-winner Lance Armstrong (USADA 2012). This report revealed that the US Postal Service Pro Cycling Team ran the most sophisticated, professionalized and successful doping programme that sport has ever seen. Until recently, Armstrong seemed to have built up enough goodwill to counteract allegations of doping, but the aftermath of the USADA report shows that even the 'Boss' – Armstrong's former nickname in professional cycling – is not untouchable, despite the fact that, officially, he never tested positively during his professional career.

Although these two waves relate to different irregularities and disciplines and involve different *modi operandi*, the essence of both phenomena is that the results of the competitions were presumably not achieved in a fair manner. Both match fixing and the use of doping can therefore be considered as fraud. A second similarity resides in the fact that these issues were hidden from view for a long time. The rumours about all kinds of criminal activities in sports – varying from fraud, corruption, money laundering, the use of doping, and so on – are widespread but in most cases it is hard to confirm or falsify these rumours, partly as a result of the fact that the sport bastions concerned are inward-bound communities and difficult to get access to as outsiders.

So far, the relationship between sports and crime has hardly been addressed by criminologists. In a sector where financial interests and performance pressure have been forced up to staggering heights, different forms of white-collar crime are likely to occur. Considering the wide range of manifestations and the (presumed) scale of crime, as well as the ambivalent social response towards all kinds of regularities (varying from denial and looking the other way to downplaying the extent and seriousness of the problem), this lack of interest is surprising.

This chapter can be considered as a modest attempt to fill the knowledge gap. Its main goal is to raise questions in relation to sports-related criminal activities that cry out for a profound criminological analysis in the future. Based upon a review of the relevant – sparsely available – literature, the chapter aims to shed some light on the nature of two types of sports-related criminal activities in the world of professional football: the financing of professional football clubs, and corruption of players, referees and high-ranking officials. Next to a criminological *Verstehen* of these phenomena, the ambivalent societal reaction towards criminal activities in the world of sports will be addressed.

The focus on professional football does not imply that the crime-related problems in this subsector are more serious than in other sports disciplines. There is ample evidence of the prevalence of criminal activities in sectors like boxing, car racing, basketball, baseball, the aforementioned cycling and many others.[2] However, as a start of criminological exploration of the sports sector, it makes perfect sense – especially in a European handbook on white-collar and corporate crime – to take professional football as a first case study. After all, football is the most popular sport in Europe, and continues to attract many spectators worldwide. To illustrate: the 2010 World Cup was shown in every country of the world and viewed by an estimated 2.2 billion people.[3] This development has added a dimension to the operation of organizations like the Union of European Football Associations (UEFA) and FIFA, as the practice of football has become an act of consumption in itself (Andreff 2000).

The first section of this chapter deals with the financing of professional European football clubs. It is widely accepted that top clubs increasingly are purchased by investment groups and fabulously rich tycoons, but whether the investments in these clubs have a legitimate or illegitimate background seems to be of little public concern. This section is based upon the premise that it is likely that parts of the funds invested in contemporary football can be linked to fraud, money laundering and other forms of white-collar crime.

The second section deals with the manipulation of match results and major decisions by means of bribing relevant participants. What do we know about these forms of corruption? And how do sport associations and law enforcement agencies respond to it? Under what conditions are they inclined to begin an investigation as a result of allegations of corruption?

Building castles in the air

The essence of the problem

Since the outbreak of the financial crisis in 2008, the banking sector has been under fire. Banks have been criticized for taking irresponsible risks concerning mortgage packages and the short-term strategies that led to the bursting of the financial bubble. With the help of a significant amount of government funding, a number of financial institutions were bailed out. Since 2008, public opinion has become considerably more critical towards the conduct of the financial sector.

In the light of this social indignation, it is most striking that no one seems to be really bothered by the financial state that professional football is in today. As nearly all European countries are forced to make drastic cutbacks to put their government finances back in order, many football clubs continue to build their castles in the air without abatement. Two of the absolute top clubs of today, Real Madrid and Barcelona, owe a debt of hundreds of millions of euros, but no one in Spain hits the streets to raise their voice in protest. In a different country that is going through rough economic times and where its citizens are asked to make great sacrifices, Italy, clubs from Serie A recorded a loss of 428 million euros during 2011, but the *Tifosi* are unlikely to turn their backs on their favourite team for that reason (they undoubtedly will if their team loses a bit too often).

The last sentence already captures an important part of the explanation for why the chance for social protest against financial mismanagement of sport clubs is so marginal. The strong identification and solidarity of supporters with their club reflect a number of functions that sport fulfils in contemporary society. Apart from the diversion that sport offers, club loyalty also contributes to the construction of identity, something that is desired more than ever in this fragmented and individualized society (Boutellier 2002). It is with good reason that far more people visit the matches of the Dutch team Ajax today than they did in the seventies, when the club belonged to the absolute elite and won the Champions League three times in a row. Sport also delivers much-needed distraction from day-to-day worries. The Greeks and Romans knew they could keep their people calm with bread and games, and it is that variant that is still embroidered on. The fact that Manchester City has a team of purchased foreign top stars does not bother the fans in the least, as long as the team meets their expectations. The *Tifosi* in South Italy are prepared to live on water and bread, as long as Napoli wins.

A second aspect relating to the financing of football clubs that requires criminological attention has to do with money laundering. In criminological literature, many definitions of money laundering can be found. Most of them concentrate on the concealment of the origins of the proceeds of crime.[4] In the fight against this phenomenon, the spotlight has been put on various social sectors for the past decades – such as banking, legal services, notaries and real estate agencies – but the surprising thing is that, in the area of laundering illegally obtained capital, there has never been in-depth criminological research into the way football clubs are financed. The above-mentioned Manchester City, Chelsea, Paris St. Germain, Monaco, and the Russian FC Anzhi Makhachkala are only a few examples of clubs that have been formed by purchase by fabulously rich tycoons.[5] The question of where the money invested in these clubs comes from and just how the players are paid, however, does not seem to interest us a whole lot. Of course, this does not imply that the money is illegally obtained in all cases, but as long as there is no willingness to cast a critical eye on the source, the rumours about dubious practices will not be refuted.

Let us take a look at Manchester City football club. In 2007, former Thai business tycoon and prime minister Thaksin Shinawatra took control of the club. Thaksin had fled his home country as he was prosecuted – and later convicted and sentenced to two years' imprisonment – by the Supreme Court's Criminal Division for Holders of Political Positions of abusing his power to help his wife buy public land at an auction.[6] Various other criminal charges – mostly in relation to corruption – await him if he returns to Thailand. However, the fact that Thaksin Shinawatra was associated with fraud and corruption did not prevent Manchester City from allowing him to have a major financial and executive role in the organization. However, when the assets of Shinawatra had been frozen due to the aforementioned criminal charges, Manchester City had to be sold again. The club was purchased in 2008 by Abu Dhabi United Group and became even wealthier than before.[7]

Another interesting example – at a lower level – is the Dutch football club Vitesse Arnhem. In 2010, this club became the first Dutch football association to be acquired by a foreign investor.

The Georgian investor and former football player Merab Zjordania bought all the shares of the club. With this take-over Vitesse Arnhem was saved from bankruptcy, as the club had been in financial difficulties for several seasons. In his home country Zjordania was arrested twice. The first case relating to tax fraud was dismissed in 2003 after he had paid 340,000 euros. The second criminal case concerned allegations on embezzlement and deception. Again, the charges were dropped after Zjordania paid a substantial sum of money.[8] He popped up for the first time in western professional football as the alleged ringleader of a group of Georgian entrepreneurs that invested large sums of money into the Belgian club Racing Mechelen.[9] The Belgian police suspected the group of money-laundering activities and started a criminal investigation at the end of 1998. The criminal investigation focused on the Georgian businessmen who actually stayed in Belgium. Zjordania was not one of them, although he was believed to be in control of the investments out of Georgia.[10] The investigation did not result in a criminal charge on money laundering, but the Georgian group left Belgium when they could not convince the authorities that the money they had invested into Racing Mechelen had a legitimate source.[11] In 2010, the Dutch football association KNVB – with the help of a private investigator – tried to gather some background information on the investments of Zjordania in Vitesse, but they did not find any evidence of irregularities.[12] On 22 October 2013 it was announced that Zjordania had sold his shares to Russian billionaire Aleksandr Tsjigirinski, who is now the new owner of Vitesse Arnhem.

Risk assessments

The aforementioned cases illustrate that the way top clubs are financed gives rise to some concern. Criminological research in this field is of added value as it may reveal in what manner and to what extent irregularities are detected, dealt with or suppressed. With regard to the latter, it is interesting to pay some attention to the Financial Fair Play (FFP) plan. This plan was designed by the European Football Association UEFA to stop the reckless spending by clubs and to stop rich benefactors from injecting large amounts of cash as this distorts the transfer market. The principal objectives of the FFP concept are:

- to introduce more discipline and rationality in club football finances
- to decrease pressure on salaries and transfer fees and limit inflationary effect
- to encourage clubs to compete with(in) their revenues
- to encourage long-term investments in the youth sector and infrastructure
- to protect the long-term viability of European club football
- to ensure clubs settle their liabilities on a timely basis.[13]

UEFA has introduced a number of measures to achieve these goals. They include an obligation for clubs, over a period of time, to balance their books or break even. Under this concept, clubs cannot repeatedly spend more than their generated revenues and clubs will be obliged to meet all their transfer and employee payment commitments at all times. Higher-risk clubs that fail certain indicators will also be required to provide budgets detailing their strategic plans.[14]

These objectives and measures reveal that the efforts of UEFA are primarily directed at the assessment of the level of corporate *stability*, rather than corporate *integrity*. The containment of financial risks predominates, but UEFA seems to have little, if any, interest in the origins of the investments in European professional football. The latter is surprising, especially in light of the fact that the Financial Action Task Force already in 2009 published the results of a risk assessment in relation to money laundering through the football sector (FATF 2009). This report identified vulnerabilities for money-laundering activities at three different levels, i.e. structure, financing and culture.

The main issues that are addressed in the FATF report in relation to the structure of professional football concern the high levels of accessibility, the diversity of legal structures and the complicated networks. Many parties are involved in the complex financial structures of professional football, including clubs, players, corporate sponsors, media,[15] private investors (*tycoons* or *barons*), institutional investors, football agents (intermediaries on the transfer market), real estate proprietors and local governments.[16]

The vulnerabilities in relation to finance that are mentioned in the risk analysis of FATF are threefold. First, the sector deals with considerable cash flows and large financial interests. Many of the transactions within the sector involve large amounts of money, for instance on the transfer market. Transfers are carried out all over the world, providing ample opportunities to launder money. Financial circuits are multiple and global, and the international money flows that are involved risk falling outside the control of national and football organizations. Often these money flows move in and out of tax havens or involve many countries (FATF 2009). Second, the intangibleness of player values is emphasized. To a large extent, prices for players are irrational and hard to control. The value is dependent on a number of factors that can be manipulated quite easily. Nobody can tell whether the official price that CF Barcelona had to pay to Santos in the summer of 2013 to contract Brazilian striker Neymar (58 million euros) is a good bargain.[17] The value of this player may well be over- or underrated. What is more, we do not exactly know how much Barcelona actually paid for contracting Neymar, as parts of the deal may have been well concealed.[18] A third vulnerability in relation to finance is related to the financial needs of football clubs. Despite the tremendous growth of the industry as a whole, many professional football clubs are financially in bad shape and their financial trouble could urge football clubs to accept funds from dubious parties. The inherent financial fragility could be exaggerated by the recent global financial crisis, which has made it harder to find sponsors. There is a risk that clubs that are in debt will not ask many questions when a new investor appears (FATF 2009). The aforementioned case of the Belgian club Racing Mechelen is a good example of this risk.

The FATF (2009) also distinguishes two key elements in the analysis of the vulnerabilities in relation to culture. The first element that is highlighted concerns the societal role of football. People are reluctant to shatter sports' illusion of innocence. Therefore, illegal activities may not often be reported. Furthermore, the image of sports is very important, particularly to the sponsors. Sponsors try to buy a good image by supporting a particular sport. A rumour about money laundering will likely result in the withdrawal of the sponsor and his funds and loss of fans and the revenue they bring. This makes it less likely that money laundering or other crimes are reported by the management of football clubs. Secondly, football has a status with which many people would like to be associated. Criminal entrepreneurs often seek status and respect in the legitimate industry and football can offer the opportunity to acquire such a patron status (*sugar daddy*), thanks to supporting a club no matter where the money comes from. Additionally, by investing in football, criminal organizations might also gain control of associated activities such as betting, real estate businesses and contracts with the local government (FATF 2009).

The FATF report (2009) does not pay any attention to the world of written and unwritten codes of conduct to which the participants in the football market have to comply. The fact that many financial aspects of professional football are kept in the dark is linked to the main features of this market: a closed circuit, hard to access for outsiders, strong internal ties, old boys' networks, and an unofficial code of silence. The key to a successful conspiracy of silence is that no one has an interest in asking what is going on, and the violators have no interest in telling. Very likely the situation in the football sector can be labelled with what Van de Bunt (2010) identifies as 'inaction in the face of knowing' – participants and bystanders know something is wrong but have no interest in doing anything about it. According to Van de Bunt (2010), people in this position need to manage their ignorance. This can be done by making sure that a story is ready to explain this ignorance, a type of reasoning Katz (1979) defined as *concerted ignorance*. One way of realizing such concerted ignorance is to look the other way in the face of a misdemeanour and to censor (official) information.

The challenges for organizational criminology

The FATF report (2009) is based upon various methods, including a literature review, questionnaires, a typology workshop and interviews. The study is a risk assessment by nature. As a result, the report is not very informative with regard to actual manifestations, *modi operandi*, dynamics and the environmental conditions of money-laundering schemes within professional football. In order to shed some light on these aspects, tailor-made criminological studies are necessary. Some of the questions that could be addressed in these studies are:

- In what ways does economic crime, and money laundering in particular, manifest itself within professional football?
- What does the relationship between the financing of professional football and economic crime look like?
- To what extent and in what ways does the management of professional football clubs – and the sector as a whole – put effort into preventing clubs' being infected by various forms of economic crime?
- What external regulation and control mechanisms do exist, how are they applied and what is their added value?

These questions can be approached from different theoretical perspectives. One of the criminological theories that might be of added value in studying forms of economic crime in professional football is the crime pattern theory as developed by Brantingham and Brantingham (1995). Like routine activity frameworks, crime pattern frameworks – developed within the school of environmental criminology – assume that a crime must be viewed as an event which takes place at a specific spatio-temporal location in a specific environmental context (Brantingham and Brantingham 1995). Environmental criminologists study patterns of crime in relation to patterns of environmental characteristics. Within this particular form of criminology a significant amount of research has been documented to conclude that generally most (exploitative) crime is highly patterned by regular legitimate activities. These activities are clustered in terms of high activity nodes (i.e. highly concentrated hot spots of crime) and interconnecting pathways. Understanding changing crime-potential contexts involves understanding criminal opportunities as processes, influenced by factors such as friendship networks and socio-economic conditions (Brantingham et al. 2005). It is well worth trying to analyse the patterns and high activity nodes in relation to the financing of professional football, although it would be naive to expect that the wheat can easily be separated from the chaff. Legitimate and illegitimate activities are strongly intertwined, so it will be hard to identify and detect clear-cut examples of financial crime.[19]

Besides studying patterns of legitimate and illegitimate behaviour, it may be of added value to include insights from cultural criminology in future research designs in order to grasp the complexity of the reality in professional football. In order to understand why certain behaviours emerge and persist we must understand the socio-cultural contexts in which these behaviours occur, and the socio-cultural meanings that these contexts and processes have for those who practise them. Cultural criminologists switch the focus from background factors to the foreground factors and try to grasp what crime means, feels or tastes like by studying crime from within (Ferrell et al. 2009). Doing ethnographic research in the business environment of a professional football club may well contribute to a better *Verstehen* of the ways professional football is being financed, managed and controlled and how the key players perceive (and neutralize and rationalize) their involvement in sometimes dubious financial transactions. Attention has to be paid to their behaviour, as well as their attitude, language and the interactive patterns within the setting of a professional football organization.

Greasing the wheels

Corruption in football

Similar to money laundering, corruption is a contested concept in criminological literature. The term has been used to describe many different activities: bribery, embezzlement, nepotism, conflict of interests, exploitation of national resources, etc. The most common definition of corruption is any action – or the lack thereof – that can be characterized as 'the abuse of public office for private gain' (Transparency International 2011). This definition is also at the basis of the 2003 United Nations Convention on Anti-Corruption (UNCAC). The central element of this definition is that, due to a decay in the process of decision taking, the resources of an organization or the state are abused for private gain. The definition has met criticism, because many scholars consider it to be too broad, too vague and too moralistic (Van de Bunt and Nelen 2012). Some scholars tend to focus on a three-party relationship. They claim that in order to understand the mechanisms and logic of corruption, it is necessary to analyse the relationship between the *agent*, e.g. the person delegated to take decisions, the *principal*, on whose behalf that agent acts, and the *corrupter*, e.g. the third party in the scheme from which the agent receives a reward (Della Porta and Vannucci 1999; Huberts and Nelen 2005).

Corruption in sports is generally divided into two categories. These relate to the exertion of a delinquent influence over:

1 competition results, whereby the parties can be athletes and/or sporting officials
2 non-competition-focused decisions by sporting bodies and sporting officials, in particular concerning host venues for important competitions, allocation of rights, nomination for positions and commissioning construction works for sports arenas and other venues (Maennig 2005).

Lately, there has been a lot of media attention focused on the first category, i.e. the manipulation of match results by means of bribing referees and/or players. There is not much criminological research available on *match fixing*.[20] This means that, again, we will have to do with the contributions by investigative journalists. Although these are of varying quality, they in any case suggest that Asian – mostly Chinese – and Eastern European key players are overrepresented in *match fixing* in European football. In this context, corruption is generally not used to put an unexpected score on the board – underdog winning over the favourite – but to ensure that the favourite does not need to make every effort to achieve victory. It works in multiple ways: the favourite rakes in the expected and much-needed points for the championship, the underdog receives his bribe without raising suspicions and several Asian gamblers make serious money betting on a certain result, goal difference or goal total (Hill 2008).

In addition to corruption being part of the *modus operandi* of criminal networks as outlined above, it can also be used for the purpose of criminal implantation in legal industries and, in line with that, unwanted manipulation of the decision making. Based on criminological research, we also know next to nothing about these last forms of strategic corruption. And yet the gossip mill is working overtime and interesting reports cry out for in-depth criminological research. For instance, doubts have been openly expressed regarding the integrity of the decision making within FIFA that led to the 2018 Football World Championship being awarded to Qatar. Also, court documents have revealed that FIFA board members took bribes from a marketing company, which, in exchange, would have acquired the exclusive marketing rights from FIFA for two World Cups. As a result of this scandal, two Brazilians – former FIFA president Joao Havelange and the former head of the Brazilian football federation, Ricardo Teixeira – stood down from their senior positions in the organization. The two were accused of disloyal management towards FIFA, more specifically the unlawful use of assets entrusted to them for personal enrichment.[21] FIFA was blamed of having deficient organization in its enterprise.[22] It was evident that other board members of FIFA knew about the bribes. This was never questioned during the criminal investigation, which was conducted in 2010 by the Swiss judicial authorities.[23] At the time, the Swiss Penal Code had no provision on commercial bribery.[24] Criminal proceedings were eventually dismissed on the basis of Article 53 of the Swiss Penal Code after reparation had been made in the form of payments to a non-profit organization.[25]

The challenges for criminology

The FIFA corruption case is an interesting example of white-collar crime that can be studied from different angles. First, the case can be analysed from the perspective of the legal and organizational structure of FIFA. With its headquarters in Zurich, FIFA is registered as a person with corporate existence under Article 60 of the Swiss Civil Code. Article 60 of the Civil Code serves as a legal base for associations that have a political, religious, scientific, artistic, charitable, social or any object other than an industrial object. Its actions are accordingly governed by Swiss law. Although FIFA is officially a non-profit organization, the analogy with a corporate entity is hard to overlook.[26] Of the total revenues of 1166 million USD in 2012, 561 million USD came from the sale of television rights.[27] The sale of marketing rights was worth 307 million USD, and income from brand licensing amounted to another 34 million USD.[28] Though FIFA's objectives are mainly concerned with improving, controlling and promoting football and the prevention of practices jeopardizing its integrity,[29] in reality, and looking at the revenues, a large part of FIFA's executive activities cannot but be concerned with market-based practices. According to Swiss law, however, FIFA can remain registered as a non-profit organization regardless of its economic significance as long as it invests its surplus in the objectives of the organization.[30] It is questionable whether FIFA could have acquired its powerful monopoly under EU competition law if it were not registered as a non-profit organization.[31]

Not only the organizational and legal structure of FIFA are of influence on the occurrence of corruption, so is the larger cultural setting in which FIFA operates. The cultural environment in any business or social environment has a major influence on common practice within an organization and the way internal and external relations are maintained (Van de Bunt and Nelen 2012). The dynamics that take place between internal organizational capacity and external pressure are the key elements of Moore's theoretical concept of *semi-autonomous social fields* (Moore 1973). According to this theory, the mode of compliance to state-made legal rules is effectively determined by the self-regulating capacity of an organization. Given the specific combination of being registered as a non-profit organization while operating as a commercial party with a unilateral monopoly, FIFA has much freedom in determining its internal rules. It can operate autonomously to a large extent. A few officials in the top layer, the president in particular, have high discretionary powers. Mechanisms to ensure accountability have turned out to be insufficient.[32]

Moore (1973) presupposes that every semi-autonomous field is inclined to resist norms and rules imposed by the outside world. The degree to which a field (be it a branch of industry, or an association such as FIFA) is able to prevent or hinder the penetration of external rules depends on two important factors: its own organizational abilities and capacity on the one hand, and the nature and intensity of the efforts by the external fields to impose new norms and rules on the other.

One of the most usual forms in which the self-regulatory capacity of a semi-autonomous social field is limited is by boundaries formed by legislation set up by centralized governments (Moore 1973). As mentioned before, FIFA is a non-governmental organization, meaning that national governments of the members have no direct control.[33] Switzerland is the only country that governs FIFA based on its statutory registration.[34] Hence the boundaries could be formed by criminal law penalizing bribery or, in absence of penalizing, the misuse of assets for private gains. In addition, possibilities of controls offered by private and administrative law could pressure internal regulations. So far, a profound scientific analysis of the nature and extent to which these controls are used has not been conducted. At first sight, it seems debatable whether external pressure can outweigh the strong self-regulated internal organization of FIFA. Switzerland does not seem to be very keen on bringing legal proceedings to fight and contain corruption within FIFA. This impression is in line with the research finding that, in general, only in a limited number of (grand) corruption cases is a criminal investigation started (Huberts and Nelen 2005). The reluctance to start a criminal investigation is inextricably linked with the complexity of this type of crime. Corrupt practices may not leave a paper trail. Often it remains unclear whether something was exchanged between parties in a corrupt transaction and, if so, what was exchanged. None of the parties has an interest in disclosing the specificities, and therefore the investigating authorities have to rely on the presence of witnesses and their willingness to testify. Yet, these witnesses may be reluctant to do so because of their loyalty towards persons in their social environment, fear of expulsion from society as well as repercussions, including threats, harassment and physical violence (Huberts and Nelen 2005).

Conclusion

In this chapter, parts of the professional football market have been scrutinized from the angle of crime-inducing conditions and circumstances. A central premise of the routine activity theory (Felson 1987) is that opportunities to commit crime exist when motivated offenders and suitable targets are present and capable guardians are absent. Despite the exploratory character of the analysis, the conclusion can be drawn that these pre-conditions are definitely met in the world of professional football. The market of professional football lends itself very well to an entwining of regular and irregular activities, as market conditions are attractive both for legitimate and illegitimate entrepreneurs. Football has become a booming business and attracts large sums of (domestic and foreign) investments. The market is global, consists of networks of various key players, and offers many possibilities to conceal irregularities. Regulations, law enforcement and (informal) control seem to be inadequate. In contrast to many other sectors that are strongly regulated and supervised, the market of professional football lacks sufficient transparency and adequate (informal and formal) control.

Considering the wide range of manifestations and the (presumed) scale of crime, as well as the ambivalent social response, criminologists who are interested in white-collar and corporate crime should be licking their lips at the prospect of descrying so many interesting research subjects.

Not only is there an urgent need for more insight into the nature and extent of crime-related activities within football and other sports disciplines, but the social and cultural context in which these activities flourish also deserves more criminological attention. Tentatively, I raised a number of relevant questions that may be addressed in studying money laundering, corruption and other forms of white-collar and corporate crime in professional football and the societal reactions to these forms of crime. A number of theoretical perspectives were suggested as well – including crime-pattern theory, cultural criminology and Moore's theory of semi-autonomous social fields – but, of course, these suggestions are not exhaustive and reflect primarily the personal interest of the author. There is much more to explore in the field of sports and crime, and it is up to criminologists to rise to that challenge in the upcoming years.

Notes

1 The author wishes to thank Carol Ni Ghiollarnath for the language review and Violette Mols for her literature search. Section 2.2 on corruption within FIFA is partly based on the information Violette collected.

2 Even a decent sports discipline like cricket with its exquisite manners has recently been confronted with corruption scandals. These scandals concern so-called *spot-fixing*. This term refers to illegal activity in a sport where a specific part of the game is fixed. Examples include something as minor as timing a no ball or wide delivery in cricket. In India, allegations of spot-fixing are widespread since the arrest of three top players in May 2013. In the neighbouring country Bangladesh, former captain Mohammad Ashraful admitted to spot-fixing, both in the Bangladesh Premier League and in three international matches. After issuing a tearful public apology, Ashraful was suspended indefinitely by the Bangladesh Cricket Board. Online. Available HTTP: <http://online.wsj.com/article/SB10001424127887323734304578543113514823852.html> (accessed 8 July 2014).

3 Official FIFA media release. Online. Available HTTP: <http://www.fifa.com/mm/document/affederation/tv/01/47/32/73/2010fifaworldcupsouthafricatvaudiencereport.pdf> (accessed 8 July 2014).

4 There are two perspectives on the construct of money laundering. In the criminological literature, the phenomenon is mostly confined to the activities of 'sanitizing' criminal proceeds, so that criminals can keep up the appearance that their funds have been obtained legitimately. This approach treats money laundering as a separate activity from predicate crimes generating illicit funds to launder (Levi 2002; Van Duyne 2003). The legal construct includes not only legitimizing criminal proceeds, but also any form of hiding or disguising the identity of criminal proceeds. From the perspective of the legal construct, money laundering is thought of as an integral part of certain criminal acts (Levi and Reuter 2006). This broad interpretation can also be found in the Third Money Laundering Directive of the European Union (2005/60/EC). According to Article 1 of this Directive the term includes:

a the conversion or transfer of property, knowing that such property is derived from criminal activity or from an act of participation in such activity, for the purpose of concealing or disguising the illicit origin of the property or of assisting any person who is involved in the commission of such activity to evade the legal consequences of his action;

b the concealment or disguise of the true nature, source, location, disposition, movement, rights with respect to, or ownership of property, knowing that such property is derived from criminal activity or from an act of participation in such activity;

c the acquisition, possession or use of property, knowing, at the time of receipt, that such property was derived from criminal activity or from an act of participation in such activity;

d participation in, association to commit, attempts to commit and aiding, abetting, facilitating and counseling the commission of any of the actions mentioned in the foregoing points.

5 The case of Anzi Makhachkala underlines the vulnerability of becoming too dependent on one 'sugar daddy'. On 18 January 2011, the club was purchased by Dagestani billionaire Suleyman Kerimov, who planned to invest more than 200 million dollars in infrastructure and players. Kerimov did invest substantial amounts of money in the purchase of players and the establishment of a youth academy, but decided suddenly, in August 2013, to drastically cut the teams' budget. Most of the top players were sold to other clubs and manager Guus Hiddink resigned. The budget cut has resulted in Anzhi performing

badly in the 2013–2014 Russian Premier League. (Online. Available HTTP: <http://en.wikipedia.org/wiki/FC_Anzhi_Makhachkala> (accessed 8 July 2014)).

6 Online. Available HTTP: <https://en.wikipedia.org/wiki/Thaksin_Shinawatra> (accessed 8 July 2014).

7 Ibid.

8 Online. Available HTTP: <http://nl.wikipedia.org/wiki/Merab_Zjordania> (accessed 8 July 2014).

9 Online. Available HTTP: <http://www.voetbalbelgie.be/nl/article.php?id=35059> (accessed 8 July 2014).

10 Ibid.

11 Ibid.

12 Algemeen Dagblad, 28/8/2010. KNVB-onderzoek geldstroom Vitesse.

13 Online. Available HTTP: <http://www.uefa.org/protecting-the-game/club-licensing-and-financial-fair-play/index.html> (accessed 8 July 2014).

14 Ibid.

15 According to the FATF report (2009), the relevance of television money is especially big for top-division clubs in the big five European leagues, depending on the size of the television market (35 to over 60 per cent of total revenues). Clubs in countries with less developed economies rely for the biggest part on financial support from owners and in some cases also local or national government.

16 Many examples can be found of local governments (municipalities) that have supported clubs financially. Until recently, one of the common financial constructions in this respect was the purchase of the stadium complex by a local government; the clubs could rent the stadium in return on the basis of very attractive financial conditions. The European Commission recently has decided to study these kinds of 'bail-outs' profoundly, in order to assess whether they have to be considered as illegitimate state aid.

17 Online. Available HTTP: <http://www.bbc.co.uk/sport/0/football/22760770> (accessed 8 July 2014).

18 Strikingly, at the beginning of 2014 it became clear that FC Barcelona has paid more than 95 million euros to contract Neymar. Forty million euros supposedly have flowed to a company which is close to the Neymar family (*Die Welt*, 10 January 2014).

19 Benson et al. (2009) have introduced a similar application of crime-pattern theory to white-collar crime. Their analysis reveals that routine activity theory, crime-pattern theory and situational crime prevention theory can be used to uncover how specific forms of white-collar crime are committed and help structure the underlying opportunity structures associated with these offences.

20 In 2013, at the request of the Dutch Ministry of Health, Welfare and Sports and the Ministry of Safety and Justice, research was conducted in the Netherlands to find out more about match-fixing in five sports: football, boxing, horse racing, basketball and tennis (Spapens et al. 2013). This research indicates that the extent of the problem of match-fixing in the Netherlands is rather limited, although it is stressed in the report that probably a minority of cases have been detected and investigated. One of the methods used in the research was a survey amongst athletes. The main results of this survey were that 8 per cent of the respondents knew someone in their environment who had been approached for corruption purposes; 4 per cent of the athletes had been approached themselves (Spapens et al. 2013).

21 Translation of the Order on the Dismissal of the Criminal Proceedings of 11 May 2010, paras 4.1, 4.2 and 6.3.

22 Ibid, para 4.3.

23 Ibid, para 6.6.

24 Ibid, para 6.3.2.

25 Ibid, para 8.1 ff.

26 M. Pieth, 'Governing FIFA', concept paper and report 19 September 2011. Online. Available HTTP: <http://www.baselgovernance.org/fileadmin/FIFA/governing_fifa_mark_pieth.pdf> (accessed 8 July 2014).

27 FIFA Financial Statement 2012.

28 Ibid.

29 Art. 2 of the FIFA Statutes 2012.

30 M. Pieth, 'Governing FIFA', concept paper and report 19 September 2011. Online. Available HTTP: <http://www.baselgovernance.org/fileadmin/FIFA/governing_fifa_mark_pieth.pdf> (accessed 8 July 2014).

31 For more information see EU Competition Law; Rules Applicable to Merger Control, European Commission 2010.

32 M. Pieth, 'Governing FIFA', concept paper and report 19 September 2011. Online. Available HTTP: <http://www.baselgovernance.org/fileadmin/FIFA/governing_fifa_mark_pieth.pdf> (accessed 8 July 2014).
33 R. Pielke Jr. (2012) 'How can FIFA be held accountable?', *Sport Management Review*. Online. Available HTTP: <http://sciencepolicy.colorado.edu/admin/publication_files/2013.01.pdf> (accessed 8 July 2014).
34 Art. 1 of the FIFA Statutes 2012.

References

Andreff, W. (2000) 'Financing modern sport in the face of a sporting ethic', *European Journal for Sport Management*, 7(1): 5–30.

Benson, M.L., Madensen T.D. and Eck, J.E. (2009) 'White-collar crime from an opportunity perspective', in S. Simpson and D. Weisburd (eds) *The Criminology of White-Collar Crime*, New York: Springer.

Boutellier, H. (2002) *Crime and Morality: The Significance of Criminal Justice in Post-modern Culture*, Dordrecht: Kluwer Academic Publishers.

Brantingham, P.L. and Brantingham, P.J. (1995) 'Criminality of place: Crime generators and crime attractors', *European Journal of Criminal Policy and Research*, 3: 5–26.

Brantingham, P.L., Brantingham, P.J. and Taylor, W. (2005) 'Situational crime prevention as a key component in embedded crime', *Canadian Journal of Criminology and Criminal Justice*, 47(2): 271–292.

Bunt, H.G. van de (2010) 'Walls of secrecy and silence: The Madoff case and cartels in the construction industry', *Criminology & Public Policy*, (9)3: 435–453.

Bunt, H.G. van de and Nelen, H. (2012) 'Corruption in various shapes and sizes: Some criminological reflections', in Mededelingen van de Koninklijke Nederlandse Vereniging voor Internationaal Recht, *International Law and the Fight against Corruption*, The Hague: Asser Press.

Duyne, P.C. van (2003) 'Money laundering policy: Fears and facts', in P.C. van Duyne, A. Maljevic, M. van Dijck, K. von Lampe and J. Harvey (eds) *Criminal Finances and Organizing Crime in Europe*, Nijmegen: Wolf Legal Publishers.

Felson, M. (1987) 'Routine activities, social controls, rational decisions, and criminal outcomes', *Criminology*, 25: 911–931.

Ferrell, J., Hayward, K.J. and Young, J. (2009) *Cultural Criminology: An Invitation*, London: Sage.

Financial Action Task Force (FATF) (2009) *Money Laundering through the Football Sector*, Paris: FATF/OECD.

Hill, D. (2008) *The Fix*, Toronto: McClelland & Stewart Ltd.

Huberts, L.W.J.C. and Nelen, J.M. (2005) *Corruptie in het Nederlandse openbaar bestuur; omvang, aard en afdoening*, Utrecht: Lemma.

Katz, J. (1979) 'Concerted ignorance: The social construction of a cover-up', *Journal of Contemporary Ethnography*, 8(3): 295–316.

Levi, M. (2002) 'Money laundering and its regulation', *The Annals of the American Academy of Political and Social Science*, 582(1): 181–194.

Levi, M. and Reuter, P. (2006) 'Money laundering', in M. Tonry (ed.) *Crime and Justice, Volume 34: A Review of Research*, Chicago: University of Chicago Press.

Maennig, W. (2005) 'Corruption in international sports and sport management: Forms, tendencies, extent and countermeasures', *European Sport Management Quarterly*, 5(2): 187–225.

Moore, S. (1973) 'Law and social change: The semi-autonomous social field as an appropriate subject of study', *Law & Society Review*, 7(4): 719–746.

Porta, D. della and Vannucci, A. (1999) *Corrupt Exchanges. Actors, Resources, and Mechanisms of Political Corruption*, New York: Aldine de Gruyter.

Spapens, T., Olffers, M. and Ernst and Young (2013) *Matchfixing in Nederland: De aard en reikwijdte van het probleem, de risico's en de aanpak*, Tilburg/Amsterdam: Tilburg University, VU Amsterdam.

Transparency International (2011) *Corruption Perceptions Index 2011*. Online. Available HTTP: <http://www.transparency.org/research/cpi/overview> (accessed 8 July 2014).

United States Anti-Doping Agency (USADA) (2012) *Report on Proceedings under the World Anti-Doping Code and the USADA-protocol: United States Anti-Doping Agency versus L. Armstrong. Reasoned decision of the United States Anti-Doping Agency on disqualification and ineligibility*, Colorado Springs: USADA. Online. Available HTTP: <http://d3epuodzu3wuis.cloudfront.net/ReasonedDecision.pdf> (accessed 8 July 2014).

19

'We are all going to be rich'

A case study of the Dutch real estate fraud case

Henk van de Bunt and Karin van Wingerde

Introduction

On 27 January 2012, the District Court of Haarlem, the Netherlands, convicted 11 defendants and four companies for their involvement in a case that became known as the biggest fraud trial in Dutch history. This case concerned a large and long-running fraud with offshoots that extended throughout the world of commercial real estate in the Netherlands. Because of these offshoots, the criminal investigation quickly became known as the 'Klimop' case (Ivy case). The fraud was committed by a group of employees who held leading positions in semi-public bodies and commercial enterprises in the real estate sector in the Netherlands.

The heart of the fraud consisted of these officials committing fraud during the execution of major construction projects by artificially increasing the invoices and by sending invoices for work which was never actually carried out. In addition, development projects and buildings were traded to investors at a price that was either too high or too low. The profits derived by the perpetrators in this way ended up in the private bank accounts of the perpetrators via intermediaries. As a consequence, the public investment funds Bouwfonds Real Estate Development (Bouwfonds Vastgoedontwikkeling) and Philips Pension Fund (Stichting Philips Pensioenfonds) in particular were defrauded of tens of millions of euros.

The District Court of Haarlem sentenced the perpetrators for a range of serious criminal offences, including forgery, bribery, embezzlement, money laundering, and membership of a criminal organization. They were given prison sentences ranging from one to four years and community service orders ranging from 40 hours to 240 hours. Furthermore, several legal entities were sentenced to pay fines ranging between €10,000 and €200,000. The prime perpetrator, Mr. Van V. (director of Bouwfonds Real Estate Development), was sentenced to four years of imprisonment.[1] Furthermore, he agreed to a settlement of €70 million in order to dismiss cases against several of his companies.[2]

The real estate fraud case received a great deal of media attention. This led to considerable consternation amongst media commentators, politicians, and society in general, as well as within the commercial real estate sector itself, all of whom were incredulous about the size of the case. What amazed people the most was that such a widespread fraud, involving so many perpetrators, could be conducted over a period of almost ten years without anybody finding out about it. The real estate fraud had remained a very well-kept secret for a very long time.

This chapter first describes the nature of this extensive fraud, and the way in which the perpetrators worked together. Secondly, it discusses the circumstances under which the fraud could have continued over a period of almost ten years. In doing so we will attempt to explain how the real estate fraud was undoubtedly a product of its time and place. In Western Europe, this era – the 1980s and 1990s – was characterized by rapid economic growth, a fervent belief in the blessings of privatization and the power of market forces, and (too) high optimism about the future of the economy. As has subsequently become apparent, the coincidence of these factors was the root cause of the numerous aberrations in international trade and industry that precipitated the credit crunch of 2008. However, the seeds of this crisis were sown during the lengthy period of prosperity that preceded this downturn. During this period, businessmen in many industries became much more risk tolerant: 'we became greedy and this greed was spurred on by the profit motive, the intoxicating and anesthetic effects of success' (Reavis 2009: 5).

Methodology

In the description and analysis of this case, we have used an investigative report that was written about the Klimop case together with several colleagues (Van de Bunt et al. 2011) at the request of the Dutch Public Prosecution Service. We were given access to the complete investigation file. This file contains reports of eight large-scale investigations into fraud in the development and trade of commercial real estate. Due to the large size of this file, we decided to select three of the eight investigations that together provide a good illustration of the real estate fraud case as a whole. The police files were analysed and summarized using a checklist that was previously used in the Dutch *Organized Crime Monitor* (Kleemans and Van de Bunt 1999: 20–24). In addition, interviews were conducted with investigative authorities, such as the Public Prosecution Service, the Dutch Fiscal Information and Investigation Service (Fiscale Inlichtingen- en Opsporingsdienst – FIOD), the Dutch Tax and Customs Administration (Belastingdienst), and with regulatory authorities, such as the Dutch Central Bank (De Nederlandsche Bank), the Netherlands Authority for the Financial Markets (Autoriteit Financiële Markten), and the Dutch Financial Supervision Office (Bureau Financieel Toezicht). Furthermore, we interviewed several real estate experts, property developers, and other commercial services providers, such as civil-law notaries and valuers. In total 26 respondents were interviewed.[3]

The Dutch real estate fraud case in a nutshell

This real estate fraud case extended to numerous property development projects and involved a whole range of individuals and organizations. The total criminal investigation file comprised eight different commercial real estate projects and 125 natural persons and legal entities were identified as suspects.

The criminal offences were committed in two different criminal alliances, one related to Bouwfonds Real Estate Development and the other one to Philips Pension Fund. Both were led by Mr. Van V. and in both of the alliances his uncle by marriage, who by no means fulfilled any formal position within the companies involved, but who played a key facilitating role in the fraud. The participants in the fraud made use of third parties, such as civil-law notaries and valuers, to channel money to private bank accounts or to act as front men.

In the three projects we analysed, the modus operandi was as follows: on each occasion Bouwfonds Real Estate Development, in the person of Mr. Van V., concluded contracts with the same property developer to build one or more buildings, or to sell an option right on such. A private arrangement was then made with the property developer about the price for which the project would be carried out. The official price that was agreed upon – and thus that was shown in the administration – however, was much higher than the price that had been agreed upon privately. The surplus difference between the two prices was then eventually diverted, via manipulated invoices and an anonymous account of a civil-law notary, to the bank accounts of privately owned companies of the perpetrators involved. These privately owned companies existed in name only, and were simply shell corporations used to conceal the origin of the money and the name of the person who was the ultimate beneficiary of the money.

In several cases, the development of a real estate project was purely fictitious and existed only on paper. For example, Bouwfonds Real Estate Development developed a plan for the construction of an office building with a theatre, an underground car park and residential units in the centre of Rotterdam. Bouwfonds, in the person of Mr. Van V., hired a property developer to realize the project and paid the development costs upfront. The plan was ultimately never realized, but the amount of money that was set aside for developing the project was still paid out via an intermediary to the fraudsters. They defrauded Bouwfonds, their employer, for roughly €4.5 million.

In other cases, the perpetrators colluded with each other to either sell existing commercial property at a price that was too low or to purchase it for a price that was too high. These property bundles were then sold on or purchased at their real market value. By way of so-called 'A-B-C-D transactions' the 'surplus profit' eventually became part of the equity of the privately owned businesses of the perpetrators. For instance, in one case, Philips Pension Fund wanted to sell an entire property bundle consisting of several office buildings, residential properties and commercial buildings (shops, leisure). The perpetrators colluded to sell this property bundle for a price unfavourable to Philips, because it was too low. Subsequently, the property bundle was sold on several times in a single day first to legal entities owned by the perpetrators and eventually to a third party. On each occasion the price of the property was increased dramatically, while the size of the property bundle got gradually smaller. Although it is not unusual – and not even illegal – for property to change hands several times in such a short period of time, these transactions were solely and purely conducted by the perpetrators in order to drive up the price of the properties and to sell them for an enormous profit. These transactions enabled the fraudsters to make a profit of around €68 million at the expense of Philips Pension Fund.

Defining the Dutch real estate fraud case

How should the Dutch real estate fraud case be characterized? The perpetrators in the real estate fraud case match the definition formulated by Edwin Sutherland for white-collar criminals perfectly. According to Sutherland, white-collar criminals are people of high social standing who commit crimes 'in the course of their occupations' (1983: 7). The perpetrators had been operating within the commercial real estate sector for many years in a perfectly legal and successful way. The perpetrators then used their position of trust to enrich themselves at the cost of the organizations they worked for.

Nonetheless, there are also certain similarities with the definition of organized crime: the criminal affiliations between the perpetrators were primarily aimed at achieving illegal profits, their 'conspiracy' resulted in serious social harm, and – as will become clear – they were relatively successful in concealing their illegal activities from the outside world by making use of corruption and by misusing legal entities. There is however a significant difference from the traditional forms of organized crime. Traditional organized crime is primarily aimed at illegal markets. The property fraudsters in this case, on the other hand, were active in a legal sector, and almost all of them also had normal, legal occupations. Furthermore, traditional organized crime often has 'symbiotic' relationships with legal sectors and markets (Kleemans et al. 1998: 61 et seq.). Yet, in the real estate fraud case, there was a closely interwoven relationship between their legal and illegal activities. In fact, the perpetrators were highly respected legal actors in the world of commercial real estate. They committed their crimes by making use of the powers, expertise and contacts they had acquired during the performance of their occupations. Their illegal activities were embedded in the social world of commercial real estate in the Netherlands (Kleemans and Van de Bunt 1999; Van de Bunt et al. 2014).

In summary, the Dutch real estate fraud case comprised various projects, in connection with which several actors from different organizations worked together to siphon off money from commercial transactions. Because of their positions within these organizations, they had the power to take decisions, set prices, and misuse the money of the companies they worked for, for their own private gain. On the face of it, they were working in a professional capacity in the interests of their respective organizations, but in reality they were participating in manipulated transactions with the aim of deriving personal profits for themselves or others.

In this chapter, we will discuss the three most notable circumstances that played a role in the inception and evolution of the real estate fraud case. In the following section we will first look at the rapid economic growth that many West European countries experienced in the 1980s and 1990s. This development created a fertile breeding ground so to speak for the fraud. Thereafter, we will look at the internal organization and the internal and external regulation of the two key businesses where the fraud took place: Bouwfonds Real Estate Development and Philips Pension Fund. Finally, we will look at the culture within the commercial real estate sector and the social relationships between the perpetrators, and the way in which these relationships created an opportunity for the fraud to be committed.

Unrestrained pursuit of profit and belief in the power of market forces

According to Hansen and Mohavedi (2010: 367), one of the most popular explanations of the contemporary financial crisis is personal greed: 'a "selfish" pursuit of "self-interest" that has no recognition of others at its boundaries or limits and involves no connection between satisfaction and further pursuit of attainment'. We are doubtful that this pursuit of personal greed provides the key to understanding the full nature of the real estate fraud case. The perpetrators of the real estate fraud were undoubtedly greedy, but that alone is not sufficient for a complete understanding of how the real estate fraud could have become so extensive and lasted so long. Greed is nothing new, and normally it is counterbalanced by social norms, such as criminal codes, professional disciplinary codes and codes of conduct.

The French sociologist Emile Durkheim, on the other hand, would probably characterize the real estate fraud case as an example of anomie. Anomie (literally: normlessness) occurs when existing, traditional ethics and legal standards lose their authority because they do not keep pace with major, rapid changes taking place in society. The traditional standards therefore no longer effectively regulate the behaviour of people and organizations. According to Durkheim, people and organizations then engage in an unrestrained pursuit of their ambitions or personal gain (Durkheim 1997 [1893]). Their greed becomes excessive because there are no longer any rules that set boundaries for the insatiable human desires. Durkheim therefore attaches a great deal of value to the reinforcement of ethical standards (professional disciplinary codes, codes of conduct, etc.) as a way of regulating deviant behaviour (Bernburg 2002; Hendry 2001).

The world of commercial real estate in the Netherlands was going through a major transformation when the real estate fraud took place. The developments in this sector can only be understood against the background of the major international economic developments of the preceding decades. The rapid economic growth of the 1980s and 1990s strengthened the belief in the positive influence of privatization and the power of market forces. It was at this time that in the Netherlands public utilities, such as energy companies, postal services and water companies, were privatized based on the assumption that competition was the best way to guarantee high quality and low prices. There was great optimism about the future of the economy and economic prosperity in the European Union. Banks were eager to lend money to private individuals and businesses and to provide mortgages for property acquisitions (Kuiper 2014).

The commercial property sector in the Netherlands was right at the heart of these developments. Enormous sums of money were involved in the transactions between property developers, construction companies, contracting authorities, and investors. Nelen and Ritzen (2012: 225) show that the amount of money invested in the Dutch real estate market had more than doubled from €27 billion in 1994 to €58.3 billion in 2009. These numbers correspond to the increase in real estate investments on a global level, as Brounen indicates (2008: 11–12). Furthermore, the return on investment was also enormous. Basically, everyone seemed to make a profit, and the sky was the limit. And then came the credit crunch, first in the USA and later in the EU, with all the associated negative consequences for trade and industry and for ordinary citizens.

Bouwfonds Real Estate Development had been able to ride on the waves of privatization, and had evolved from a public service into a privately owned and market orientated enterprise. Bouwfonds was set up, namely, as a public service to help Dutch municipalities develop and build homes for 'ordinary people'. The organization was founded in 1946 specifically for the purpose of increasing the level of home ownership amongst the Dutch population. Bouwfonds built family homes, which were then rented or sold at affordable prices. At the end of the 1980s, the executive board of Bouwfonds decided it was time for a radical change of direction. It decided to transform Bouwfonds from a public service into a commercial enterprise (Linker 2006: 88). As part of this process, Bouwfonds started buying and selling commercial property, such as office buildings and shopping malls. Bouwfonds shifted its focus away from low-cost residential housing towards the more lucrative sector of commercial real estate. The number of municipalities involved in Bouwfonds gradually declined, and the company formed an alliance with banks (De Wit 2001; Van Enk and Hentenaar 2000).

In an interview with the former CEO of Bouwfonds in a popular real estate trade magazine in 2001, he provides a very succinct explanation for how the emphasis had come to be placed on making profit instead of the fulfilment of the original social function:

> All that nonsense about social commitment we had in the past ... I am not saying social commitment is nonsense in itself, but the way in which this concept was applied for our business definitely was. [...]. That is not the aim of any business. The aim of a business is to make money.
>
> *(Crone and Mulder 2001)*

The people at the top were convinced that the commercialization of Bouwfonds would have a positive effect. Numerous articles appeared in various national newspapers which provide a clear picture of the ambitions of the Bouwfonds: Bouwfonds needed to make a profit, become the market leader in real estate in the Netherlands, and become a leading real estate developer in Europe (De Volkskrant 1999; *Het Financieel Dagblad* 1999; Rooijakkers 2003: 35). Because Bouwfonds thought it would not be possible for it to achieve this transformation with its existing personnel, an expert was brought in from outside: in September 1995 Bouwfonds took over the business of Mr. Van V., who would later become the central figure in the real estate fraud case. Mr. Van V. was appointed as the director of Bouwfonds' newly founded Real Estate Development department, and was assigned the task of developing commercial real estate. There were very high expectations for this new department, and Van V. was given a mandate to achieve the commercial ambitions of Bouwfonds.

The tone of the advertisements of Bouwfonds provides a good characterization of the prevailing *Zeitgeist*. These advertisements contained very few words, but they were very evocative. For example, one advertisement has a photograph of a tall building with the logo and the name of Bouwfonds on it, followed by just three words: *room for pioneers*. Ironically, this particular building was never actually built, but the message was clear nonetheless: Bouwfonds was aiming to put itself on the map in the commercial real estate market in a big way. In another advertisement placed by Bouwfonds in newspapers and magazines, there was a subtle abandonment of the traditional, social principles of the company:

> New philosophies. New theories. New standards. New values. This calls for vision. For an understanding of those changes. And room for success.

Although these words are very vague, it was a clear statement of intent by Bouwfonds that it was planning to seize the opportunities that were there for the taking in this 'new' age. No effort or expense was spared when it came to announcing this new mentality to the outside world. For example, Bouwfonds invested considerably in customer relationship management, which involved amongst other things the acquisition of a pleasure cruiser and a hot air balloon for the entertainment of business partners (Van der Boon and Van der Marel 2009: 181).

Deficient oversight and internal control: room for the pursuit of (personal) ambition

In order to achieve these lofty ambitions, the executive management felt it was necessary to dispense with the numerous, outdated rules and traditional forms of oversight and control. This was just another feature of the prevailing *Zeitgeist*. A lack of internal control gradually became to be seen as 'normal' in the 1980s and 1990s. The discussion about corporate governance was mainly centred around the question of what type of relationship should exist between organizations and businesses on the one side, and the regulatory authorities on the other. The question of how integrity had to be monitored and how regulatory supervision had to be carried out *within* an organization was overshadowed by the predominantly ideological nature of the discussion concerning the regulatory supervision of commercial enterprises by the government. During this economic boom, wherever possible, regulation was placed in the hands of the private sector. 'Deregulation' and 'self-regulation' were supposed to take the place of 'command and control' by the government (Shover 2008; Shover and Cullen 2008). Consequently, people working for real estate companies and investment funds often had a great deal of discretionary freedom. The infamous cases of so-called 'rogue traders', such as Nick Leeson (Barings Bank) and Jérôme Kerviel (Société Générale), show just how much independence and autonomy individual employees had and just how inadequate the internal, organizational supervision was of such individuals (Canac and Dykman 2011; Gilligan 2011; Grener 2006; Krawiec 2009; Wexler 2010). Despite the fact such practices put the continued existence of the companies they worked for in jeopardy, these traders were hardly bound by any instructions and rules in relation to accountability.

There was also very little regulation and control of the practices of the fraudsters in the real estate fraud case. Our analysis showed that the former business of Van V. was never actually integrated within Bouwfonds after it was taken over by Bouwfonds. Instead it continued to function as a separate business unit. This unit had an autonomous role within Bouwfonds, and in practice Van V. behaved as if he was still running an independent enterprise. A forensic investigation carried out by PricewaterhouseCoopers after the full extent of the real estate fraud became known revealed the following:

> The impression that is formed now, afterwards, is that nothing changed for the business of Van V. The integration of this type of external organization [...] requires a robust executive board that wants to integrate that organization, and an organization that will allow itself to be integrated. There was no convincing evidence of either in this case.
>
> *(PricewaterhouseCoopers 2008, cited in Van de Bunt et al. 2011: 35)*[4]

For all intents and purposes, the business of Van V. remained intact, and in practice Bouwfonds' Executive Board had very little influence over its new business unit.

The new Real Estate Development department also had a mysterious reputation within Bouwfonds. The department was jokingly referred to by insiders as the 'Villa Van V'. When Van V. joined Bouwfonds, he took several of his former employees with him, who were installed in key positions. The other employees of the Real Estate Development department were then recruited by the Van V. clique. This created a closed circle within the department itself. For example, Van V. generally discussed matters one-on-one, instead of with the whole department, so he was able to control which information was disclosed to whom.

In addition, there were insufficient checks and balances within both Bouwfonds and Philips Pension Fund to control and regulate the behaviour of the people involved. As an executive director, Van V. had considerable discretionary powers. For example, for a long time he was able to, more or less independently, sell real estate via obscure, private procedures. Only in 2006 was a limit set for private sales and tendering procedures made compulsory for transactions that exceeded €50 million. The principal perpetrators in the real estate fraud case held executive positions within Bouwfonds and Philips Pension Fund. This gave them a decisive vote when it came to making decisions about the purchase or sale of (bundles of) real estate. In practice, they generally conducted the crucial discussions and negotiations with business partners on their own.

The influence and control of the Executive Board of Bouwfonds were also relatively weak in practice. The CEO of Bouwfonds, who was responsible for the supervision within Bouwfonds Real Estate Development, had personally appointed Mr. Van V. and consequently gave him a great deal of operational freedom. A witness testified, for example, that the executive board had never refused a proposal made by Van V. There were also dual positions within the organization, so that some directors – such as the aforementioned CEO – were also members of the supervisory board, which in effect meant that they were charged with the supervision of their own conduct. The members of the executive board were moreover found to have insufficient expertise in the field of commercial real estate to be able to offer adequate resistance. Consequently, the CEO of Bouwfonds, who was eventually sentenced to serve 240 hours of community service, had a free hand when it came to taking decisions about real estate transactions.

Furthermore, Van V. and his staff were known within Bouwfonds as the experts in the field of commercial real estate, and they thus had considerable freedom in the planning and execution of their work. At the end of the day, Van V. had been given the task of elevating the status of the entire organization. Other employees who had to sign documents and contracts, such as the other directors and controllers, relied heavily on the judgement and expertise of the aforementioned key figures. The situation was exactly the same within Philips Pension Fund. The people who were given responsibility for investments in real estate were trusted implicitly by the other Philips employees:

> 'I trusted the knowledge and expertise of those people, and I had no reason whatsoever to doubt their reliability and integrity.'
>
> *(Van de Bunt et al. 2011: 38)*

It is precisely this trust that was placed in these new arrivals that illustrates the incompetency of the 'old' guard. The investigation of PricewaterhouseCoopers cited above found that Bouwfonds had very little executive control over the new department of Van V. due to its limited knowledge of commercial real estate business practices:

> 'Looking back, the organization of Bouwfonds that existed at that time didn't know what hit them. When they took over Van V. Vastgoed BV, they took on board an organization that developed projects of an enormous size, that operated extremely autonomously, and which moreover appeared at face value to be very profitable. [...] The sums of money, the scale of the operations, the markets, and the business practices were totally alien to the existing Bouwfonds setup.'
>
> *(PricewaterhouseCoopers 2008, cited in Van de Bunt et al. 2011: 35)*

The above report describes a situation where the traditional Bouwfonds organization lost oversight and control over the new department. The people involved in the fraud were therefore able to operate in an informal and unorthodox way in relative freedom. This was possible because there were either very few or only vague guidelines for their work, and because there were only very general parameters set for the approval of real estate transactions, the limits for buying and selling, the delineation of tasks and responsibilities, and the requirement of accountability.

At the same time, there was a lack of any effective internal platform for criticism by employees within these organizations. In some cases, when employees expressed a critical viewpoint about the state of affairs surrounding the development and trading of commercial real estate, this criticism was either ignored or they were manoeuvred out of the way. This situation was allowed to continue because one of the perpetrators actually held the position of compliance officer for a long period of time. No critical questions were asked, which would have gone against the prevailing *Zeitgeist* and the ambition of achieving growth. As a result of this freedom, Van V. and his clique thought they were untouchable: 'anything goes' (Van de Bunt et al. 2011: 36).

Sometimes the perpetrators used bribes to silence any criticism or to circumvent control. For example, the criminal investigation discovered that the CEO of Bouwfonds readily accepted the expensive gifts that were offered by Van V. This effectively placed the CEO in the hands of Van V. Several other executive directors turned a blind eye in exchange for a share in the 'surplus profits' or for expensive gifts.

In conclusion, although Bouwfonds had set itself very high ambitions, it paid very little attention to the question of how these ambitions were to be achieved in practice, or the ethical standards and practices that needed to be introduced to replace the old ones. The CEO of Bouwfonds played a significant role in the creation of a situation of anomie because he failed to explicitly define the ethical standards and practices that Van V. and his staff had to comply with during the realization of their ambitions. In other words, he allowed the organization to accelerate to top speed without bothering to check if the brakes worked first.

Big ambitions, but very little transparency and accountability

The performance of effective regulation in the commercial real estate sector is impeded by the fact that the valuation of property and the reporting of financial transactions are relatively poorly developed. The business practices in some areas of the real estate sector appear to be very informal and are difficult to reconstruct. For example, it is evident that crucial decisions concerning the purchase or sale of real estate were only set out on paper or accounted for in a very summary way. Reference was made several times in our interviews to the proverbial 'beer mat' in order to illustrate how decisions and agreements were put down on paper or accounted for in a very sketchy way. Systems have naturally been developed in order to measure the value of commercial property and to measure the return on investment in real estate. For example, one of our respondents formulated an international benchmark for institutional investors. This enabled these investors to make quarterly comparisons between the return on investment for different projects, and to make sure that market-conform prices were being applied when property objects were being bought or sold (IVBN 2008). Nonetheless, the valuers and property developers we interviewed made it clear in a variety of ways that any attempt to make property valuations more transparent had very little chance of success. One property developer made the following point:

> 'An inherent characteristic of the property market is that prices are so difficult to quantify. It's not an objective process: it's not something you can work out with a calculator; the price depends on so many different variables.'
>
> *(Van de Bunt et al. 2011: 54)*

The value of property can therefore change from one moment to the next depending on a range of different factors and circumstances. In the literature (Unger et al. 2010) and in the interviews, constant reference was made to the 'heterogeneity', and even the 'unicity', of commercial real estate and thus the value of such. One respondent put it this way:

> 'Every single building or piece of land is different, which makes a meaningful price comparison very difficult. You never really know exactly what factors have influenced the setting of the different prices.'
>
> *(Van de Bunt et al. 2011: 54)*

This process becomes even less transparent when several unique buildings are clustered together in large property portfolios. However, within the world of commercial real estate in the Netherlands this type of complication is not seen as much of a problem. It is this lack of hard criteria for the setting of property prices that allows the parties involved to negotiate 'a good price'. And it is precisely this lack of transparency about the calculation of 'the right price' that enables insiders to make a profit on property transactions. One valuer who was interviewed acknowledged that the valuation of commercial property is not based on mathematical formulas alone:

> 'Every firm of valuers has its own calculation model, but the fact is that these do not determine the ultimate price; you set the price yourself.'
>
> *(Van de Bunt et al. 2011: 55)*

The real estate fraud case has shown that the lack of transparency in property valuation also creates opportunities for fraudulent practices: how can you prove, namely, that Philips Pension Fund sold real estate at a price that was too low?

The role of facilitators

In addition to the deficient organization of internal supervision within Bouwfonds and Philips Pension Fund, business services providers also played a facilitating role in the real estate fraud, in particular civil-law notaries. Civil-law notaries are closely involved in real estate transactions on account of their statutory task, and they form an essential link in the chain of property sales and transactions. They consequently play both an important supporting and controlling role (Nelen and Lankhorst 2008).

In the real estate fraud case, one civil-law notary in particular played a major facilitating role in the perpetration of the fraud. He made a numbered account available for the holding and concealment of the 'surplus profits', and participated in A-B-C-D transactions to significantly manipulate the value of the property. This civil-law notary was eventually sentenced to five months' imprisonment for his part in the real estate fraud case. He was also struck off the register of civil-law notaries by the disciplinary court. Another civil-law notary, who was acting on behalf of the party acquiring the property, failed to exercise the necessary diligence when executing the highly unusual A-B-C-D transaction.

Although the valuers were not found guilty of complicity with the criminal activities, the control possibilities offered by them, such as an annual property price benchmark, were insufficiently utilized by Bouwfonds and Philips Pension Fund. This made it possible for fraudulent real estate transactions to take place based on relatively low internal valuations. Furthermore, the prices were calculated based on outdated valuations in a market where the prices were shooting up all the time. This meant, for example, that a price that had been fixed in 2004 was used as a benchmark to set the price for a transaction that took place in 2006. If external valuers had been consulted on a more regular basis, this manipulation could probably have been prevented (Hordijk 2008).

In summary, none of the facilitators acted as a barrier to prevent the fraud taking place, for example by adopting a critical and challenging approach. The real estate fraud was ultimately uncovered by the alertness of a tax inspector who was carrying out a tax audit.

Culture within the commercial real estate sector: little competition, lots of trust, and a great deal of reciprocity

When the real estate fraud took place, there was a firm belief in the Netherlands in the power of market forces. Market competition was believed to exert a much greater regulatory effect than government regulation via command and control. This belief in the power of market forces was accompanied by a call for less government intervention. However, the slimming down of government regulation was not compensated for by self-regulation and disciplinary procedures within the market itself.

Generally speaking, the commercial real estate market is not an arena where property traders are engaged in fierce competition and negotiations with each other. The commercial real estate market is more like a collaborative network than a market with competing enterprises. There (still) seems to be a relative lack of competition between the various actors within the property market: there are relatively few conflicts and very few legal disputes. On the contrary, the different players rely heavily on each other in order to achieve the realization of projects, often in partnership with each other. An extensive network is therefore essential in order to be successful in the real estate business. A central characteristic of this sector is that all the parties are continuously looking for relevant information that influences the setting of prices (Nelen 2009: 78). It is therefore only possible to do business in the commercial real estate world if you have a network of close contacts to help identify the opportunities and developments within the market. The commercial real estate world is very much an 'old boys' network (Berkhout and Jeurissen 2009). This does not have to be a problem in itself, but a closed network in which tips are exchanged and everybody does everyone else a favour is susceptible to abuse.

It is normal for information to be shared and parties to be put in touch with each other in such networks; and this is often accompanied by inducements and incentives. These types of inducements and incentives are sometimes referred to as 'gentlemen's agreements', and are frequently non-specific and not put down on paper. It is also common for the activities associated with such agreements to be described very generally in invoices, with such words as 'consultancy' or 'for services rendered'. These types of business transactions are therefore largely based on trust: 'a man's word is his bond'. The mutual relationships therefore appear to be based on reciprocity: 'you scratch my back, and I'll scratch yours', and are not characterized by rivalry and competition. In this sense, the commercial real estate sector as a whole exhibits many similarities to the property development companies that were at the centre of the Dutch construction fraud case. The construction industry is also characterized by a sophisticated system of mutual price and work agreements (Van de Bunt 2010). In such a culture of mutual interdependency and reciprocity, there is always a risk that the boundaries between mutual favours and bribery and corruption will become blurred.

The commercial real estate sector is a separate niche within the property market. This sector therefore consists of a relatively small group of property developers, construction companies, architects, valuers, and civil-law notaries who regularly come into contact with each other during business transactions. Everyone knows everyone else in this social world. The real estate fraudsters were able to exploit these characteristics for their own purposes.

A major factor that made this fraud possible was the network that Van V. had managed to build up in order to perpetrate the fraud. He was very adept at developing relationships based on trust and he had known most of the people in his network for many years. This network was made of people he knew both privately, for example at the hockey club, and old business acquaintances he had kept in touch with years after deals had taken place.

Every person in the network had their own specific role, based on their expertise, capabilities, tasks, and responsibilities. Van V. was able to gain their affiliation by letting them share in the 'surplus profits' or by persuading them with gifts, business favours or inducements. One witness put it this way:

> 'He [Van V.] always used to say: "We've got a great project here, and there is enough to go round for everyone. Bouwfonds will make a good profit and we are going to get a share of that profit."'
>
> *(Van de Bunt et al. 2011: 27)*

During the trial, Van V. explained that his approach was centred around making sure that everyone was always happy; he often used to say 'We are all going to be rich.' In this way he managed to gain the complicity of other people and persuaded them to play an active role in the fraudulent transactions.

These business associates were not only motivated by the immediate financial gain, but also by the promise of more lucrative business in the future. One of these business associates said during police questioning:

> 'I thought to myself, this is your first time, so you've got no choice. I wanted to have a successful business. They [Van V. and his uncle] gave me the impression that there would be many more and much larger projects for us in the future.'
>
> *(Van de Bunt et al. 2011: 46)*

Once they had fallen into the trap, there was no way out. But why did the business associates of Van V. allow themselves to be corrupted so easily? Our analysis has found that being part of a good network was very important for many of the people involved in the fraud: 'to keep friends with everyone in order to get business. And also in order not to lose any business' (Van de Bunt et al. 2011: 44). By helping to facilitate a shady deal in one project, this would increase the likelihood of getting business in another project.

Several of the defendants answered questions about the allegations made against them both inside and outside the courtroom. Their statements provide an insight into the motives and neutralization techniques adopted by them in order to justify their behaviour (Sykes and Matza 1957). A frequently used justification for the corruption and bribery and illicit earnings was that it was normal practice within the commercial real estate sector to entice prospective business partners with expensive watches and all-expenses-paid business trips. In an interview with a Dutch national newspaper, *NRC Handelsblad*, Van V. said (Kreling 2011: 4): 'I became so steeped in the culture of the property sector that I lost my sense of perspective'. He knew in the back of his mind that offering bribes was a criminal offence, but it was just an everyday part of doing business in the commercial real estate world. It was necessary in order to 'win people for your cause'. This example makes it clear that in a period of anomie, people are quick to justify their behaviour with clichés, precisely because there is so little clarity about the acceptable ethical standards (Passas 1990: 166). In the opinion of Van V. this is why it would be totally wrong to depict him as an ordinary criminal. In an interview with a popular Dutch magazine, *Elsevier*, Mr. Van V. described how devastated he was when the Dutch Fiscal Information and Investigation Service raided his home, his personal possessions were seized, and how unpleasant his time in detention was (De Winter and Van Rijckevorsel 2011: 70 et seq.). He was locked up 'in total confinement, just like a dangerous terrorist, even though he always paid his taxes on time'. This was completely unjustified according to him because: 'the Treasury had made tens of millions out of him from income tax and corporation tax.'

As a consequence of these mutual interdependencies it is very difficult for outsiders to get an insight into the workings of the sector. Regulatory bodies, both internal and external, are still finding it difficult to get the sector and its practices under control even today. On the other hand, once they had got involved in the fraudulent practices and shared in the 'surplus profits', the people that took part in the fraud did not make any attempt to break free from the network or to break the silence. This was another contributory factor that enabled the real estate fraud to continue for such a prolonged period.

Conclusion

The initial response to the real estate fraud case was amazement: how could this happen, on such a big scale, and for such a long time? Was it a case of a proverbial 'rotten apple', or was the whole orchard infected? The unique character of this case makes it ideal for a case study into the factors and circumstances that contributed to the perpetration of the fraud.

Our analysis has shown that the real estate fraud was undoubtedly a product of its time. Briefly summarized, the fraud can be attributed to the major developments that took place in the 1980s and 1990s, which were characterized by a belief in economic growth, unbridled ambition and a move towards self-regulation by the private sector. During this period, Bouwfonds went through a radical transformation and was vulnerable in the face of the sophisticated approach of Van V. and the other key figures in his network combined with the lack of adequate internal supervision within Bouwfonds and Philips Pension Fund. All of these developments should be seen against the background of the relatively non-transparent business practices within the sector, and the closed culture that was normal at that time within certain segments of the property sector. Furthermore, facilitators, such as the civil-law notary, played an important role in maintaining silence. At the same time, the external regulatory authorities also failed to detect the fraud. The convergence and interrelationship between these factors makes it very difficult to argue that there were only one or two 'rotten apples'.

The analysis in this chapter shows that any belief in the self-regulating capacity of the market becomes meaningless if there are no preconditions within the sector itself for competition to have a beneficial effect. This applies all the more in this case since there was virtually no market competition whatsoever in the world of commercial real estate. Instead of competition acting as a corrective mechanism, there was a network that brought together people who supposedly represented different interests, but who in practice engaged in mutually beneficial transactions. The nature of this network opened up the possibility for the pursuit of personal wealth to become an important factor in the decision-making process. This ultimately led to the pursuit of personal profit becoming more important for the people involved than serving the interests of the organizations they were working for. Furthermore, because all the participants received a share of the enormous profits, this motivated the network to continue with the highly lucrative fraudulent practices over an extended period of time.

Notes

1 District Court of Haarlem (2012). 'Case numbers LJN: BV2194; LJN: BV2196; LJN BV2197; LJN BV2198; LJN BV2199; LJN BV2200, BV2202; LJN BV 2204', 27 January 2012, http://jure.nl/[case-number].
2 These companies were mostly shell corporations that existed only on paper.
3 Due to the fact that criminal investigations were still ongoing during the time of our research, we were not able to interview any of the perpetrators in this case or any representatives of the companies involved. Therefore, the interviewees in this case study are by no means involved in the fraud. Nonetheless, these respondents have a lot of expertise in the real estate sector in the Netherlands and were therefore the most knowledgeable persons to reflect on this fraud case.
4 This report was the result of an internal investigation carried out by PricewaterhouseCoopers at the request of Bouwfonds. This report was part of the investigation file and was never made public.

References

Berkhout, T.M. and Jeurissen, R. (2009) *Net werken en netwerken: Onderzoek naar de percepties van integriteit in de Nederlandse vastgoedsector*, Breukelen: Nyenrode Business University.
Bernburg, J.G. (2002) 'Anomie, social change and crime: A theoretical examination of institutional-anomie theory', *British Journal of Criminology*, 42: 729–742.
Boon, V. van der and Marel, G. van der (2009) *Real Estate Fraud: Fraud at the Top of the Dutch Economy (De Vastgoedfraude; miljoenenzwendel aan de top van het Nederlandse bedrijfsleven)*, Amsterdam: Uitgeverij Nieuw Amsterdam.
Brounen, D. (2008) 'The boom and gloom of real estate markets' (inaugural lecture), Rotterdam: Erasmus Research Institute of Management.
Bunt, H.G. van de (2010) 'Walls of secrecy and silence: The Madoff case and cartels in the construction industry', *Criminology & Public Policy*, 9(3): 435–453.
Bunt, H.G. van de, Holvast, N.L., Huisman, K., Meerts, C., Mein A.G. and Wingerde, C.G. van (2011) *Final Report Real Estate Fraud Case 'Ivy' (Bestuurlijke rapportage vastgoedfraudezaak 'Klimop'. Eindrapportage)*, Utrecht/Rotterdam: Verwey-Jonker Instituut/Erasmus Universiteit Rotterdam.
Bunt, H.G. van de, Siegel, D. and Zaitch, D. (2014) 'The social embeddedness of organized crime', in L. Paoli. (ed.) *The Oxford Handbook of Organized Crime*, New York/Oxford: Oxford University Press, pp. 321–339.
Canac, P. and Dykman, C. (2011) 'The tale of two banks: Société Générale and Barings', *Journal of the International Academy for Case Studies*, 17(7): 11–32.
Crone, J. and Mulder, H. (2001) 'Relatief het meest maatschappelijk betrokken', *BouwWereld*, 2 July.
De Volkskrant (1999) 'Overheid schuld aan slecht werkende woningmarkt', *De Volkskrant*, 21 April.
District Court of Haarlem (2012a) 'Case number LJN: BV2194', 27 January, http://jure.nl/bv2194.
District Court of Haarlem (2012b) 'Case number LJN: BV2196', 27 January, http://jure.nl/bv2196.
District Court of Haarlem (2012c) 'Case number LJN BV2197', 27 January, http://jure.nl/bv2197.
District Court of Haarlem (2012d) 'Case number LJN BV2198', 27 January, http://jure.nl/bv2198.
District Court of Haarlem (2012e) 'Case number LJN BV2199', 27 January, http://jure.nl/bv2199.

District Court of Haarlem (2012f) 'Case number LJN BV2200', 27 January, http://jure.nl/bv2200.
District Court of Haarlem (2012g) 'Case number LJN BV2202', 27 January, http://jure.nl/bv2202.
District Court of Haarlem (2012h) 'Case number LJN BV 2204', 27 January, http://jure.nl/bv2204.
Durkheim, E.D. (1997 [1893]) *The Division of Labor in Society* (translation by W.D. Halls from the original), New York: Free Press.
Enk, W. van and Hentenaar, R. (2000) 'Bouwfonds wacht op dubbel A-status', *Vastgoedmarkt*, February, pp. 55–57.
Gilligan, G. (2011) 'Jérôme Kerviel the "Rogue Trader" of Société Générale: Bad luck, bad apple, bad tree or bad orchard?', *The Company Lawyer*, 32(12): 355–362.
Greener, I. (2006) 'Nick Leeson and the collapse of Barings Bank: Socio-technical networks and the "Rogue Trader"', *Organization*, 13(3): 421–441.
Hansen, L.L. and Movahedi, S. (2010) 'Wall Street scandals: The myth of individual greed', *Sociological Forum*, 25(2): 367–374.
Hendry, J. (2001) 'After Durkheim: An agenda for the sociology of business ethics', *Journal of Business Ethics*, 34: 209–218.
Het Financieel Dagblad (1999) 'Bouwfonds richt vizier op Europa', *Het Financieel Dagblad*, 21 April.
Hordijk, A.C. (2008) *Marktwaarde van Vastgoed: De maatschappelijke en taxatietechnische impact van internationale standaarden* (Inaugural lecture), Breukelen: Nyenrode Business University.
IVBN [Vereniging van Institutionele Beleggers in Vastgoed Nederland] (2008) *Beheersing van frauderisico's in de institutionele vastgoedsector*, Voorburg: IVBN.
Kleemans, E.R., Berg, E.A.I.M. van den and Bunt, H.G. van de (1998) *Georganiseerde criminaliteit in Nederland: Rapportage op basis van de WODC-monitor*, Den Haag: Wetenschappelijk Onderzoek- en Documentatiecentrum.
Kleemans, E.R. and Bunt, H.G. van de (1999) 'Social embeddedness of organized crime', *Transnational Organized Crime*, 5(1): 19–36.
Krawiec, K.D. (2009) 'The return of the Rogue', *Arizona Law Review*, 51: 127–174.
Kreling, T. (2011) 'Jan van V. spreekt', *NRC Handelsblad*, 11 May, p. 4.
Kuiper, R. (2014) *De terugkeer van het algemeen belang*, Amsterdam: Van Gennep.
Linker, P. (2006) *Sturing in de rijksdienst: Nieuwe en bestaande inzichten verenigd in het sturingsmodel*, Assen: Van Gorkum.
Nelen, H. (2009) 'Tussen de stenen: Een criminologische blik in de keuken van het commerciële vastgoed', in G. Van de Walle and P. Van Calster (eds) *De criminologische kant van het ondernemen*, Den Haag: Boom Juridische uitgevers, pp. 81–96.
Nelen, H. and Lankhorst, F. (2008) 'Facilitating organized crime: The role of lawyers and notaries', in D. Siegel and H. Nelen (eds) *Organized Crime: Culture, Markets and Policies*, New York: Springer, pp. 127–144.
Nelen, H. and Ritzen, L. (2012) 'How they still try to get away with it: Crime in the Dutch real estate sector before and after the crisis', in S. Will, S. Handelman and D.C. Brotherton (eds) *How They Got Away With It: White Collar Criminals and the Financial Meltdown*, New York: Columbia University Press, pp. 223–245.
Passas, N. (1990) 'Anomie and corporate deviance', *Contemporary Crises*, 14: 157–178.
Reavis, C. (2009) *The Global Financial Crisis of 2008: The Role of Greed, Fear, and Oligarchs*, Massachusetts Institute of Technology, MIT Sloan Management, https://mitsloan.mit.edu/LearningEdge/CaseDocs/09-093%20 The%20Financial%20Crisis%20of%202008.Rev.pdf.
Rooijakkers, P. (2003) 'Grootste ontwikkelaar van Nederland richt zich op eerste plaats in Europa', *Vastgoedmarkt*, March, p. 35.
Shover, N. (2008) 'Zelfregulering door ondernemingen: Ontwikkeling, beoordeling, en bange voorgevoelens', *Tijdschrift voor Criminologie*, 50(2): 169–181.
Shover, N. and Cullen, F.T. (2008) 'Studying and teaching white-collar crime: Populist and patrician perspectives', *Journal of Criminal Justice Education*, 19(2): 155–174.
Sutherland, E.H. (1983) *White Collar Crime: The Uncut Version*, New Haven: Yale University Press.
Sykes, G.M. and Matza, D. (1957) Techniques of neutralization: A theory of delinquency', *American Sociological Review*, 22(6): 664–670.
Unger, B., Ferwerda, J., Nelen, H. and Ritzen, L. (2010) *Detecting Criminal Investments in the Dutch Real Estate Sector*, The Hague: Ministry of Finance.
Wexler, M.N. (2010) 'Financial edgework and the persistence of rogue traders', *Business and Society Review*, 115(1): 1–25.
Winter, L. de and Rijckevorsel, R. van (2011) 'De halfgod die de regels van het spel negeerde', *Elsevier*, 21 May, p. 70.
Wit, R. de (2001) 'Boegbeeld Bouwfonds Cees Hakstege stapt aan wal', *Vastgoedmarkt*, May, pp. 26–27.

20

Varieties of corruption in the shadow of Siemens

A modus operandi study of corporate crime on the supply side of corrupt transactions

Julian Klinkhammer

Introduction

Company officials of the industrial conglomerate Siemens Aktiengesellschaft (Siemens AG) – Europe's biggest private employer at the time as well as an economic 'flagship firm' (Börsch 2004) – apparently embezzled more than 1.3 billion euros, between 2001 and 2007, as part of the biggest corruption case in German corporate history (Wolf 2009a). Subsequent investigations revealed structural corruption[1] across most divisions, a range of offences that the prosecution labelled as the Siemens complex. Forensic analyses by the law firm Debevoise & Plimpton LLP in cooperation with the accountancy firm Deloitte Touche Tohmatsu were able to trace illicit payments back to their corporate sources. After two years of private investigation,[2] they established that Siemens had lost the most money in those divisions responsible for telecommunication (449 million euros) and power generation (301 million euros), and in regional offices or subsidiaries abroad (258 million euros). The investigation also revealed that these funds were used to a large extent to bribe foreign officials. In 2008, the group and three subsidiaries pled guilty to charges of having violated the US Foreign Corrupt Practices Act (FCPA) and settled with authorities in the United States as well as in Germany, by paying fines and penalties that amounted to 1.6 billion US dollars (United States Department of Justice 2008), roughly one billion euros at the time.

What are the stories behind these large numbers? How could such a blatant case of corporate corruption take place at a renowned company like Siemens? Despite the fact that regulators as well as corporations have been fighting certain forms of corruption for decades, the 'business of bribery' emerged as one of the most persistent and challenging global crime problems from the discourse on corruption during the 1990s (Williams and Beare 1999). Corrupt practices proved to be highly resilient against tough domestic anti-corruption laws as well as against compliance efforts at the firm level (Weismann 2009). The criminological paradox, as Edwin Sutherland (1940) pinpointed more than 70 years ago, is to explain 'the persistence of commercial bribery in spite of the strenuous efforts of business organizations to eliminate it' (Sutherland 1940: 11). While there is a vast literature on demand patterns (e.g. political corruption), the supply side of corrupt transactions has since received considerably less attention. However, the social science literature on bribery and other crimes against competition provides very different explanations for corporate corruption with respect to their disciplinary origins:

1 From an economics/rational-choice perspective, the persistence of the challenge is bound to raise suspicions that corporations are reluctant to control corruption effectively, especially in cases of 'active corruption' which is supposed to benefit the firm (Rose-Ackerman 1978/1999: 191 ff.). Criminologists (Braithwaite 1985) likewise, stress the general theoretical distinction between crimes which are attributable to the business organization (i.e. corporate crime) and those crimes which have to be regarded as non-organizational (i.e. occupational crime).[3] Interestingly, it seems that many offenders from the Siemens complex *allegedly acted on behalf of the company*, which is why Dombois (2009) assumes that decentralization and an indirect (financial) control of Siemens divisions enabled the 'strategic ignorance' of its top management.
2 Management scientists (Daboub et al. 1995) and criminologists (Simpson and Koper 1997) have further examined the influence of firm and top management team characteristics with regard to crimes against competition. Simpson and Koper (1997) find that company structure (i.e. decentralized management structures) increases the likelihood of corporate illegality only in interaction with declining firm performance, which produces organizational strain (see Simpson and Koper 1997: 394 f.). Thus pressure to perform, on behalf of influential administrative or financial officers, on the subunit level – especially in view of *divisional losses* – might not only increase the likelihood of antitrust offences but of active corruption (i.e. corporate crimes against competition) as well.
3 Business ethicists usually argue – in line with a rational-choice perspective – for the strict condemnation of corrupt practices by management and a consistent 'tone at the top' (Ziegleder 2007). Wieland (2005) even calls for a new sort of values management to provide wayward employees with 'moral incentives' that are supposed to prevent corruption. In this view, even structural corruption is first and foremost a matter of unethical choices – caused by rogue agents who immorally maximize their *personal gain*, and by principals that either fail in terms of control (i.e. compliance management) or do not sufficiently incentivize 'good' employee behaviour (Wieland 2008).
4 Business economists have pointed at cognitive 'normalization' processes rooted in organizational cultures. These processes might lead morally upright employees down a slippery slope to the point where corrupt practices become a *mindlessly* performed aspect of organizational behaviour. Ashforth and Anand (2003) provide a theoretical framework, by explicating the organizational processes and social psychological mechanisms that supposedly underpin structural corruption – a popular model that has since informed many studies on corruption (Ashforth et al. 2008), including research on the Siemens case (Graeff et al. 2009). Dombois' (2009) assessment concluded that all three pillars necessary for the normalization of corruption (i.e. the institutionalization of corrupt practices, the socialization of new members and ideological rationalizations) were present within the corporate culture of Siemens. Grieger (2009) even made the case for a Siemens-specific 'culture of corruption'.
5 Sociologists view corrupt practices historically in relation to institutional changes, especially with regard to differentiation processes that constitute structurally different 'value spheres' (Max Weber) or 'functional systems' (Niklas Luhmann). Hiller (2005) and Baecker (2000) have argued accordingly that corruption surfaces on the organizational level, but that it undermines modern institutions empirically on the level of social networks. Network features have indeed been used to categorically distinguish structural from situational corruption (Bannenberg 2002; Höffling 2002). Yet sociological systems theory would rather question empirically whether the

illegal actions of employees systematically draw on a network-specific trust that requires long-term acquaintance and personalized norms of reciprocity (Luhmann 2000). From a different theoretical vantage point, Graeff's (2009) principal-agent analysis of the Siemens case reached the conclusion that close social networks, based on familiarity, *interpersonal trust* and group control, were necessary to circumvent the company's formal structure.

6 Another line of thought developed within organizational theory and drawn from Niklas Luhmann's works points instead to the functional requirement that every organization depends on certain forms of 'illegal' behaviour – i.e. *behaviour that violates formal organizational expectations* – in order to survive (Luhmann 1964). A consistent formal structure will then only increase the dilemma for employees of how to adapt to contrary expectations in the environment, when they are threatened with the loss of their membership (e.g. loss of employment). Persistent adaptation problems (e.g. 'passive corruption') thus increase the likelihood for corporate deviance only if those deviant acts gain informal legitimacy as 'useful' actions. This old sociological idea of 'useful illegality' interpenetrates criminological accounts of corporate crime (Klinkhammer 2013) and is in line with an organizational strain perspective (Simpson and Koper 1997; Vaughan 1982). But it emphasizes that cultural factors – especially traditional values (which have been shown to operate in the Siemens case as well; see Klinkhammer 2011) – are able to undermine ordinary modes of corruption control in cases of active corruption (Pohlmann 2008).

Each of these different perspectives arguably features one distinctive indicator for the empirical analysis, which should be observed in cases of structural corruption. Table 20.1 illustrates the operationalization on which the following analyses draw.

The goal of the following analyses is to explain the perpetuation of corrupt practices in a formal legal corporate setting – such as Siemens. To this end, I report on the results of a modus operandi study of corrupt practices at Siemens, based on data that were systematically gathered in 2009 from various publicly available sources. In particular, document analyses of court decisions revealed ample evidence on the modus operandi of corrupt practices, though only a fraction of all employees involved in the encompassing Siemens complex were tried in German courts.[4] However, these few criminal trials highlighted the social mechanisms that explain the scale and scope of the crime problem at Siemens. Employees who were held criminally responsible for sustaining corruption on the organizational 'dark side' had worked at three Siemens divisions – *Power Generation* (PG), *Communications* (COM), and *Automation and Drives* (A&D). Court decisions were available in full text for the PG (Bundesgerichtshof 2008; Landgericht Darmstadt 2007) and A&D cases (Landgericht Nürnberg-Fürth 2008), and published through press releases for the COM case (Oberlandesgericht München 2008a; 2008b; 2010). Furthermore, media coverage of the scandal and of the trials, as well as journalistic interviews with convicts Reinhard S. and

Table 20.1 Operationalization of theoretical explanations for structural corruption

Hypothesis number	*Theoretical construct*	*Empirical indicator*
H1	Corporate crime	Useful action (in pursuit of the organization's primary purpose)
H2	Organizational strain	Divisional losses
H3	Occupational crime	Personal gain (in pursuit of immoral values)
H4	Normalization	Mindlessness
H5	Social networks	Interpersonal trust
H6	Illegality	Behaviour violates formal organizational expectations

Wilhelm S., proved valuable to corroborate the reconstruction of individual action orientations. Thus, the collected material allows for an organizational analysis of decision-making processes within Siemens and their dynamic relation to institutions, individuals, networks and cultures – by focusing on those offenders whose responsibility was symbolically reaffirmed by a conviction.[5]

This chapter combs through the findings of the modus operandi study, asking (1) whether Siemens had a consistent anti-corruption policy before the crimes occurred, (2) what the social structure of offenders reveals about the individuals who carried out corrupt practices (3), whether these individuals acted for personal gain, on behalf of social networks or the company, and (4) whether their actions were indicative of organizational cultures or strain. The final synopsis (5) shows which conditions can be assumed to explain the perpetuation of corrupt activities within Siemens, and questions whether the company used an adequate anti-corruption strategy in the aftermath of the scandal.

Institutions and organizations: how management implemented anti-corruption policies into Siemens' formal front side

Prior to the discovery of structural corruption, Siemens' image generally commanded public admiration. The company's 475,000 employees generated revenues totaling 87 billion euros in 2006. With operations in almost 190 countries and strong subsidiaries abroad as a competitive edge, only half of its revenues came from European markets (Löscher 2012; Siemens AG 2007). Restructuring throughout the 1990s apparently yielded an investor-friendly and transparent information policy as well as an adjusted governance style that was characterized as 'rejecting short-term profit maximization and stressing a long-term orientation' (Börsch 2004). Siemens even became a corporate member of Transparency International's German chapter in 1998 – a non-governmental organization devoted to the fight against corruption. Thus, police raids of company headquarters in Munich and other Siemens sites in Germany on 15 November 2006 came as a surprise to the public, stirred up the media and thus produced a major scandal. Top management clarified only a week after the police raids that the so-called 'ostrich defence' was not an option, by stating in a letter to all employees: 'No member, no manager can plead ignorant to the ethical conduct that is expected within our house'. In fact, it was then-CEO Heinrich von Pierer himself who had signed a circular letter to all employees in 1999, urging them to 'strictly mind legislation'. An analysis of the company's code of conduct revealed that its formal normative structure was consistent with management's tone at the top.

According to Siemens, anti-corruption norms on the group level were established in 1991. The same year also saw the exposure of a corruption scandal in Munich, where Siemens officials had apparently bribed local civil servants to foster bid rigging in the public procurement of electrical equipment for the supply of construction projects (Leyendecker 2007). Corporate anti-corruption norms were updated in 1998. This change in Siemens' formal structure coincided with the passing of a bill that regulated Germany's adoption of a convention by the Organisation for Economic Co-operation and Development (OECD) on combatting bribery of foreign public officials in international business transactions. In particular, this 'Act Against International Corruption' finally outlawed some corrupt foreign practices, which had long been tax-deductible as 'useful expenditures' in Germany.[6] The update of Siemens' formal anti-corruption policy also came in the wake of another corruption scandal in East Asia.[7]

Though the specific content of these older policies is unknown, Siemens acknowledged that its provisions were analogous to those in the code of conduct, a document that was published in 2001. The same year also marked the company's initial public offering at the New York Stock Exchange, a crucial event in Siemens' recent corporate history. This event made the company subject to American jurisdiction – especially to the US Foreign Corrupt Practices Act. And Siemens came within reach of powerful state authorities, such as the United States Department of Justice as well as the Securities and Exchange Commission. As a consequence, Siemens' code of conduct complied with FCPA standards since July of 2001. The company's policy concerning competition and anti-corruption in the document named 'Business conduct guidelines' read as follows:

> Every employee is obligated to abide by the rules of fair competition. [...] No employee may directly or indirectly offer or grant unjustified advantages to others in connection with business dealings, neither in monetary form nor as some other advantage.

In view of Siemens' very rigid, consistent formal structure and the subsequent personal risk (e.g. legal accountability) associated with deviation (Dombois 2009), we have to turn our attention to the perpetrators and ask to what extent their actions relate to individual characteristics or informal organizational structures, in search of an explanation for their crimes.

Individuals and organizations: who were the offenders that carried out the corrupt practices at Siemens?

A social structure analysis (documented in Table 20.2) illustrates that the convicts from the Siemens case featured typical characteristics in line with previous research on offenders who were tried for corruption in Germany (Bannenberg 2002; 2003).

Convicts were middle-aged or elderly males of German nationality; most had 'remarkably unremarkable' (Bannenberg) personalities. On average, they were more than 50 years old at the beginning of their criminal activities and equipped with some organizational power and authority, but without relevant previous conviction or immoral values.[8] However, three of them were divisional directors and thus held positions just below top management. Two convicts had reached retirement age. Occupational mobility after the onset of criminal offences was low. Only one individual was promoted within this timeframe and advanced from middle to top management shortly after the crime, thus becoming a member of the group's board of directors (*Zentralvorstand*).

Although exact information on the duration was sometimes missing, all convicts had long tenures – most of more than 20 years – with the same company. This has traditionally been characteristic of the large internal labour markets at Siemens, where internal recruitment had long been the predominant career pattern (Dombois 2009). Such a career pattern is typically associated with a strong identification of employees with organizational values and above-average loyalty towards their employer (Kotthoff and Wagner 2008; Simon 1991). This hypothesis was reaffirmed by three different judges who independently characterized convicts from divisions PG, COM and A&D as old-school *Siemensianer*[9] – a term that is also commonly used by Siemens employees as a self-description of their social identity, symbolizing the strong integration of a person with the organization. New members would become part of the Siemens 'family', would undergo a process of professional socialization (usually right after completing their formal education), and thus learn to value seniority and loyalty towards superiors and the firm (Dombois 2009).

In conclusion, offenders rather represent respectable individuals with high social status, not least due to their occupational prestige and the fact that none had previously experienced a relevant conviction. Due to mitigating circumstances, all prison sentences were eventually suspended, except for one which exceeded the legal limit of 24 months. The one person who served a prison term (Wilhelm S.) was also the only convict described as equipped with a colourful personality, who displayed some characteristics of a fraudster – e.g. since he embezzled money from Siemens for his personal gain (see section below). The following sections will place these findings in the context of the offenders' individual part in the modus operandi of criminal offences.

Table 20.2 The social structure of individual offenders from the Siemens corruption cases

Convict	*Business unit*	*Sex*	*Year of birth*	*Hierarchical position*	*Age at time of offence (start)*	*Age at time of offence (end)*	*Year of recruitment*	*Tenure at time of offence (start)*	*Prison sentence (months)*
Horst V.	PG	M	1934	Freelancer & Consultant(*)	65	68	—	—	9
Andreas K.	PG	M	1944	Divisional Director	55	58	1968	31	24
Reinhard S.	COM	M	1950	Commercial Director	52	54	1966	33	24
Heinz K.	COM	M	1949	Accountant	53	55	—	—	24
Wolfgang R.	COM	M	1940	—	62	64	—	—	9
Hans-Werner H.	COM	M	1955	Comptroller	47	49	1978	24	18
Michael K.	COM	M	1955	Divisional Director	47	49	1974	28	24
Wilhelm S.	A&D	M	1948	Union Chairman(*)	42	58	1973	17	54
Johannes F.	A&D	M	1956	Divisional Director	45	50	1977	24	24

Key: Horizontal lines represent separate criminal cases; (*) position outside the corporate hierarchy at the time of offence

Networks and organizations: did offenders sustain structural corruption on the dark side of the code to benefit the company, social networks or rather themselves?

While the analysis of individual offenders from the Siemens case revealed a very homogeneous social structure, the criminal cases featured striking differences with regard to the modus operandi. Short vignettes establish, in the following, why employees deviated from organizational norms, whether they acted on behalf of social networks and whether evidence allows making the case for occupational or corporate crime.

Siemens Power Generation: commercial bribery in Europe

The PG case is an example par excellence of corporate crime; due to the notable absence of occupational crime, and the fact that the divisional management's decision to deviate from corporate provisions was guided by the usefulness of corrupt practices – in terms of market entry and return on investment. Manager Alexander K. learned in 1998 that his division had obtained a slush fund from a 1970s merger. Instead of whitening the black money, he ordered its transfer to a new foundation created in Liechtenstein[10] and advised a subordinate commercial director, and later the retired senior executive Horst V., to manage assets of about 12 million Swiss francs. The whole amount was used to acquire contracts, and thus absorbed the uncertainty associated with free competition. For instance, the goal of Siemens' divisional management was to enter the Italian market for large-scale power generators. Some of the illicit funds from the foundation were used to acquire two major contracts for the supply of heavy duty gas turbines to the Italian energy company ENEL S.p.A. (formerly a state-owned enterprise) at costs that ran into triple-digit millions. Two ENEL managers offered to prefer Siemens in return for a bribe of about 2.56 million euros and 3 million euros plus 500,000 US dollars per contract. Horst V., who spent most of his time as a retiree and Siemens consultant in charge of organizing illicit financial flows, channelled the money from Liechtenstein via accounts in Dubai or Abu Dhabi (United Arab Emirates) into the accounts of these ENEL managers.

Personal acquaintance – as a basis for interpersonal trust – between both agents of active and passive corruption was observed in the PG case and could thus account for the opportunity structure of corruption,[11] but not for the means to bribe ENEL executives (i.e. the availability of slush funds). The presiding judge acknowledged that both convicts had not acted for personal gain. Instead they had supposedly misread which actions were in the best interest of Siemens. Furthermore, both convicts had violated formalized expectations: freelancer Horst V. violated the provisions regulating the employment of external advisors, while his supervisor Alexander K. acted contrary to his duties as the officer responsible for compliance in that division. Both contracts combined yielded a gross profit of approximately 100 million euros for Siemens PG – yet the proceeds of the crime were recovered in an out-of-court settlement by the ENEL Corporation.

Siemens Communications: systematic bribery via international networks of slush funds

The COM case is also emblematic of corporate crime due to the notable absence of occupational crime. Three related criminal trials led to five guilty verdicts against individuals involved in the major case on the divisional level in terms of scale. This case was triggered by allegations of corruption that had surfaced in Nigeria, in 2001. Siemens' compliance managers subsequently advised divisional management at Siemens COM to change its ways of dealing with commercial bribery abroad. Michael K., then senior executive at COM's fixed-line branch Information and Communication Networks (ICN), had to learn from his subordinate, Reinhard S., that ICN accounts in Austria had long been used as slush funds, siphoning amounts that ran into triple-digit millions. This 'old system' had used a pretty straightforward method to illicitly transfer funds from Siemens headquarters to sales agents abroad. They simply had to request kickbacks by filling out a special form called a 'policy paper', which required authorization according to the four-eye principle. The necessary signatures were usually attached to the form via sticky notes.

Instead of closing the corrupt activities down, Michael K. gathered three heads of department at the tavern 'Alter Wirt' (English:'Old Landlord'), early in 2002. They decided on a more sophisticated 'new system' that should successfully disguise the origin of illegal payments. The round included representatives from internal audit, accounting and sales who agreed to establish a new method for arranging the payments. According to Reinhard S., the attendees lapsed into silence and all eyes turned to him when it was time to decide on the responsibility for the architecture of the necessary structures. He received the authorization to create accounts on behalf of Siemens by the end of 2002. The document was signed by Michael K. and another ICN executive. The former supervised Reinhard S. in his subsequent activities for creating a web of financial accounts and transactions in order to conceal the continuous use of slush funds. Together with experienced colleagues Heinz K. and Wolfgang R., they developed a new method to transfer the necessitated funds to sales agents and bribe recipients abroad. Via fiduciaries in Liechtenstein and Switzerland, they built up a global network of dummy companies, which allowed for diverting funds from official ICN accounts, by pretending to fulfil sham contracts with these dummies (e.g. in payment of advisory services). The result was a vast pool of money (more than 48 million euros in only two slush funds) that Reinhard S. could access and use at his own discretion. In fact, he was authorized to initiate payments without a value limit. Though he enjoyed almost entrepreneurial liberties and even executed manual cash transfers with fiduciaries, Reinhard S. was eager to point out that there was 'never any money lost' under his aegis. His view, that he had always used the funds for the organization's purposes, was eventually confirmed by the court's assessment that the formally illegal system was geared entirely towards bribery and that the convicts had not acted for personal gain. Interpersonal trust was remarkably dubious in the COM case, where actors' cooperation was mainly based on hierarchical position and organizational trust. Although personal characteristics such as 'trustworthiness' apparently played a role in the recruitment of Reinhard S., there was no indication of personalized trust among participants of the conspiracy. Even more importantly, the court established that the round at the 'Old Landlord' did not meet the legal requirements of a 'gang'.

Siemens Automation and Drives: the corruption of industrial relations in Germany

The A&D case featured elements of both corporate and occupational crime. Related criminal trials centred on a management decision in 2001, sustaining the support of the company union AUB e.V. – officially an independent union that had been infiltrated by former Siemens officials since 1990. Johannes F., then board member at the automation engineering division, authorized the diversion of funds from his division at the request of a superior at the group's board level. According to court documents, he violated Siemens' policy of representation by signing a contract with AUB chairman and former Siemens sales agent Wilhelm S., who, likewise, violated formal (accounting) rules laid down in the registered association's statute. The court acknowledged that the agreement had proven vastly beneficial for Siemens, if regarded merely in economic terms. The court's decision provides ample evidence of AUB activities in great detail, showing that Wilhelm S. served as an agent of Siemens who successfully orchestrated many subverted elections of employee representatives, thus corrupting Germany's strict legislation with regard to the co-determination of industrial relations. As a consequence, managers were frequently enabled to determine loyal staff as potential employee representatives and had them appointed to works councils all across Siemens AG. Although the court did not always find an evident service in return for Siemens investments in AUB activities, which amounted to approximately 30 million euros, it stressed that divisional director Johannes F. had not acted for personal gain, but in the belief that he acted on behalf of Siemens AG. On the other hand, there is evidence of embezzlement on the part of Wilhelm S., who lied to Siemens officials about the usage of at least three million euros that he channelled to sports sponsoring (≈2.5 million euros), to private ends (≈350,000 euros) and to other enterprises (≈190,000 euros). Although this fact could be regarded as evidence for business economists' normalization hypothesis, it is an unlikely assumption that the occupational crime of Wilhelm S. represents more than an adjunct to his actions on behalf of Siemens AG; for occupational crime occurred in the last two years of his tenure as omnipotent head of the AUB, while the corporate crimes lasted for at least 16 years.

In the A&D case, interpersonal trust among organizational actors initially played a part in the decision to dispatch Wilhelm S.; however, in the criminally relevant period, network structures were notably absent from the decision to sustain Siemens' funding of the company union. Wilhelm S. retrospectively wondered at how many people within Siemens knew at least in part about the financing of the AUB (see Ritzer 2008), but refrained from blowing the whistle, which would have confirmed suspicions of IG Metall and other observers (Zugehör 2003).

While the modus operandi of corruption on the divisional level thus showed considerable variation, an in-depth analysis of the criminal cases revealed how deeply corrupt practices were entrenched in the corporate culture at Siemens.

Cultures and organizations: did organizational cultures or strain sustain structural corruption on the dark side of the code?

This section links analyses of the previously identified varieties of corruption to individual action orientations or 'rationalizations'. These orientations were interpreted as individually acquired reflections of collective semantics that root in organizational cultures – i.e. the informal dark side of different business divisions. Although previous studies on Siemens corporate culture represent ambitious attempts to consider the difference between the formal and the informal organization, they either lack in scope (Gebhardt and Müller-Seitz 2011; Lässig 1999; Stadler and Hinterhuber 2005) or their scientific validity is uncertain (Decurtins 2002). However, we have to assume that Siemens featured a rather strong and rigid corporate culture during the relevant period (Decurtins 2002: 46; Stadler and Hinterhuber 2005). Available evidence serves as a backdrop to explore issues of organizational strain (e.g. divisional losses) and the cultural dimension of corporate crime with respect to ongoing historical research.[12]

Siemens Power Generation: commercial bribery was a heritage of the 1970s/80s

Siemens' former joint venture with competitor Allgemeine Elektricitäts-Gesellschaft (AEG), the power generation company Kraftwerk Union (KWU), was wholly acquired by Siemens at the end of the 1970s. Although it later became fully integrated as business unit 'Power Generation', the division apparently continued the legacy of its bribe-paying predecessor, despite periods of restructuring during the 1990s. Commercial bribery in Italy was triggered by the bribe request of ENEL managers, one of them acquainted with then-Siemens consultant Horst V. (a former

AEG employee (Leyendecker 2007)), and initially enabled by slush funds from the former KWU. This is typical for structural corruption, which is based on long-term relationships (Bannenberg 2002) and inherently linked to money laundering (Levi et al. 2007; Satzger 2009). Organizational strain was not an issue in the court's decision, although the division reported losses of more than 200 million euros for fiscal year 1999 (Siemens AG 2002). Some intra-organizational strain existed since 1998 as a result of top management's introduction of quarterly goal-oriented performance reviews in meetings with divisional managers (Decurtins 2002). Yet the relevant decisions were both taken in 2000, when the division returned to profitability (Decurtins 2002), which implies that performance increased during that period. Instead of complaining about pressure from the top, Horst V. claimed that bribery had been common practice at Siemens, which led him to believe that top management tacitly approved of his actions. Bribe payments were informally referred to as 'useful expenditures' within the division – semantics that mirror the dominance of economic values in the old era of tax-deductible corrupt foreign practices. However, Alexander K. was well aware of possible legal ramifications, since he was the officer responsible for compliance in the PG division. He warned his companions in crime accordingly; they should not expect any support by Siemens, in case their covert actions were to be revealed. K. confessed to the court that according to his calculus, ENEL managers did not fall within the category of public officials as defined by the OECD convention, and that offering advantages to private officials would represent lawful behaviour, at least in Germany. The district court considered as mitigating circumstance that the crimes occurred amidst radical legal changes – a fact reflected in the revision by Germany's federal court, which overturned the conviction for commercial bribery based on the principle of non-retroactivity. Instead, lead action (the so-called Siemens decision) by the federal court established that Alexander K. had deliberately jeopardized the (black) money in his trust and sanctioned his handling of slush funds as embezzlement – to the detriment of his employer.[13] This legal proceeding points to a cultural lag with respect to the effectiveness of institutional changes, such as Germany's adoption of the said OECD convention.

Siemens Communications: slush funds point to management failures of the 1990s

Siemens AG underwent major restructuring during the 1990s, which resulted in a more decentralized corporate structure, giving more autonomy to the separate divisions. Restructuring was legitimized by a dominant financial ('shareholder value') ideology that focused on economic challenges, such as undervalued stocks (due to a significant 'conglomerate discount'), fundamental changes in the shareholder structure of Siemens,[14] and competitive pressures of 'globalization' to which this multinational company would seem especially exposed since it generated 80 per cent of its revenues abroad.

Siemens COM employed about 60,000 employees and had a turnover of roughly 17 billion euros per annum. Whereas previous decades had seen considerable cross-subsidization of costly business units, the top management introduced performance reviews by the corporate head office in the middle of the 1990s, and thus increased pressure on the divisional management (see Dombois 2009: 144 ff.). From this time on, divisions would compete with one another under the new regime of financial measurement and benchmarking (Decurtins 2002). At the beginning of the new millennium, COM was divided into the fixed-line branch ICN and another branch for mobile networks. ICN recorded heavy losses (i.e. negative earnings before interest and taxes) for the years 2001, 2002 and 2003, and only returned to profitability in 2004 thanks to a massive reduction in force by a third. This development is reflected by the statements of Reinhard S. who revealed that managers used to talk about corruption 'with a twinkle in their eyes', suggesting that ICN's revenues were dependent on corrupt foreign practices. Managers used to refer to corruption only as 'the issue' and apparently framed the illegal behaviour as 'business conduct necessary for survival':

> We calculated that we would lose a billion Euro in revenues, when not doing business in countries where one has to pay bribes. That was every fourth Euro in revenues in this branch. The entire fixed-networks-business with its 56.000 employees was doomed to die, it would have gone down.
>
> *(Freiberger et al. 2008)*

Available evidence thus indicates that the offenders did not mindlessly engage in corrupt practices.[15] Instead, the findings are in line with Dombois' (2009) hypothesis that the indirect (financial) control of Siemens divisions enabled a 'strategic ignorance' of its top management – a factor that would facilitate corrupt practices on the supply side. Top managers were thus able to maintain control of the corporation's commercial success, without assuming (criminal) responsibility for how the performance goals were achieved. However, the court argued with regard to the evidentiary hearing that other divisional directors and members of Siemens' board of directors were informed about the fact that Reinhard S. organized 'discrete payments' to set up slush funds. They could remain ignorant of the details and obviously refrained from taking action against the corrupt practices.[16] In conclusion, the slush funds of the COM division point to management failures during the 1990s, when decentralization and an output-centred 'performance culture' – at odds with the traditions of the company – were promoted as catch-all solutions to the economic challenges of globalization.

Siemens Automation and Drives: the company union was forged from management ideologies of the Cold War era

Although the company union was established during the 1990s, the modus operandi study revealed that it was essentially an ideological offspring of the Cold War era. The reasons for the decision to foster a 'democratic' opposition against the 'leftist' union Industriegewerkschaft Metall (IG Metall[17]) echoed the socio-economic situation of the 1980s. In the elections of 1988, IG Metall won nine out of ten seats designated for employee representatives within Siemens' supervisory board – the only exception being the representative of senior executives. From this time on, some senior executives and members of Siemens' top management developed a strategy to push IG Metall's influence back to the degree of employee organization (25 per cent at that time). This strategy centred on the covert control of a company union. A draft budget was developed, which calculated costs for indirect funding and foresaw the dispatch of Siemens employee Wilhelm S., who had served as chairman of a works council since 1984 and was appointed head of the small union AUB a year later. Wilhelm S. asked Hermann F., then-Siemens' informal CEO (who would later become chairman of the supervisory board), for his permission. He received F.'s authorization to give the concept a 'sound footing' (i.e. money) and to expand its scope to other companies. A written agreement provided Wilhelm S. – who was supposed to take his leave by mutual consent to found a consulting firm – with guarantees of reemployment, pension claims and administrative support by Siemens. Siemens even provided the AUB with office personnel, which it kept on its payroll until 2001. During the following years, the 'indirect' mode of transferring Siemens funds to Wilhelm S.'s consulting firm was subject to technical changes, due to employee turnover and the necessity of concealing dubious payments. Although it was not part of any written agreement, Wilhelm S., Johannes F. and Hermann F. acknowledged in court that they knew they had to keep Siemens' support of the AUB confidential – apparently for 'political' reasons. While Wilhelm S. and Johannes F. both referred to the threat of a scandal and possible legal action on behalf of IG Metall, Hermann F. testified that a company should use all available means to protect itself against 'communist infiltration' – semantics which had also been cultivated within the AUB since the 1970s with reference to IG Metall. Again, these findings point to a cultural lag in the corporation's adaptation to social change in its environment (e.g. the decline of communism).[18] Intra-organizational strain was minimal – confined to a rather general obedience to authority of superiors – and notably missing in financial terms, since the division A&D was the high performance star of the new millennium within Siemens (Decurtins 2002).

Synopsis of corporate corruption: did Siemens overcome the organizational challenges associated with commercial bribery, slush funds and a company union?

Corrupt practices at Siemens ranged from subtle influence on the selection of employee representatives to the straightforward bribery of private and public officials. The social structure analysis revealed a strong commitment of offenders towards their employer or 'principal'. This is a relevant finding, even from a systems theory perspective (Luhmann 1964), which locates individuals by definition in the environment of social systems. As a consequence, careers move to the centre of the explanation (Luhmann 2000), suggesting that the long tenures of offenders put them at a higher risk of getting involved in corporate illegality (Pohlmann et al. 2011). Their strong personal integration into the firm as company men (social identity: 'Siemensianer') provided them with motive for crimes that promised neither personal gain nor career advancement. Illegal practices were instead performed with a sense of duty, with knowledge of the danger involved and in light of the narrative assumption of their collective usefulness. Analyses on the level of specific divisions and business units thus highlighted the semantic variety underpinning the corrupt practices at Siemens:

a Siemens Power Generation: Commercial bribery is useful for Siemens, as a traditional strategic means to enter new markets and to generate excess profit.
b Siemens Communications: Slush funds are useful for Siemens, because they help to bolster revenues, and thus guarantee the survival of the division.
c Siemens Automation and Drives: Maintaining a company union is useful for Siemens, as a tool that favours management in labour conflicts (and keeps leftist political ideas at bay).

At the heart of these very different cognitive expectations thus runs a common normative thread, which explains the perpetuation of corrupt practices in a formal legal corporate setting: a 'good' Siemensianer *should* do what is best for the company, even if the behaviour violates formalized expectations – as was the case with active corruption. The violation of occupational duties to perpetrate corporate crime and the nearly complete absence of occupational crime are thus striking indications of 'useful illegality'; corruption in its various forms served as a convenient informal remedy to enduring adaptation problems regarding the organizational environment. Whether it was the conquest of new markets, losses in sales or the threatened industrial peace – some of the most effective means to organizationally useful ends became formally blocked. Top management certainly raised the stakes for deviant personnel by introducing a formal anti-corruption policy, but it was not nearly as effective in changing organizational cultures as it was in increasing the pressure (strain) or the dilemmas (illegality) on lower management levels. Thus informal semantics continued to legitimize illegal adjustments to problems that were *located* in the environment, but *caused* by the strict and consistent formal structure of the organization.[19] Notwithstanding the

Table 20.3 Explaining the Siemens corruption cases: a qualitative analysis

Explanations		PG: Horst V.	PG: Andreas K.	COM: Reinhard S.	COM: Heinz K.	COM: Wolfgang R.	COM: Hans-Werner H.	COM: Michael K.	A&D: Wilhelm S.	A&D: Johannes F.
H1	**Corporate crime** (useful action)	1	1	1	1	1	1	1	1	1
H2	**Organizational strain** (divisional losses)	.5	.5	1	1	1	1	1	0	0
H3	**Occupational crime** (personal gain)	0	0	0	0	0	0	0	.5	0
H4	**Normalization** (mindlessness)	.5	0	0	0	0	0	0	.5	0
H5	**Social networks** (interpersonal trust)	.5	0	0	0	0	0	0	.5	0
H6	**Illegality** (behaviour violates formal organizational expectations)	.5	1	1	1	1	1	1	.5	1

Key: Within-case comparison of different explanations (indicators in parentheses) for corruption on the individual (convict) and sub-system (business division) level, presented in a three-value qualitative coding scheme. Observations are coded as either 1 (true proposition) or 0 (false proposition) or .5 (fuzzy proposition)

radical institutional change towards anti-corruption since the 1990s, organizational cultures sufficiently sustained certain corrupt practices in the shadow of Siemens' formal structure – in order to ensure the economic success of the company. Table 20.3 summarizes the findings of the modus operandi study with regard to theoretically relevant indicators.

Only hypotheses H1 and H6 were verified for all three cases on the divisional level, and thus could be assumed to operate as necessary conditions for an explanation of structural corruption within Siemens. The results regarding H2 are mixed; the role of organizational strain is thus difficult to assess, but it might have served as a mediating factor that facilitates corrupt activities on the supply side of business transactions. Other hypotheses, in particular H3 to H5, fall short of expectations and only explain some variance in the vertical dimension (i.e. individual behaviour). It is apparently misleading to assume that individuals either immorally maximize their personal gain (H3), or are led to believe that corruption is the right thing to do (H4). The collective normalcy and good of the company may neither be normal nor beneficial to the individual. In contrast to Graeff's (2009) findings, not even close social networks (H5) were necessary to sustain active corruption on the dark side of Siemens or to circumvent formal controls and procedures – arguably, organizational trust among the loyal 'Siemensianer' served as a functional equivalent. These negative findings further corroborate an explanation build on the concept of useful illegality.

A double limitation of this research is associated with the case study approach, which is further confined to criminal trials in Germany. One implication is that the interpretation as 'useful illegality' runs the risk of selection bias. Selection bias might limit the validity of the finding that occupational crime was not the driving motive of agents – to the centre of organizational structures and to upper levels of the hierarchy. On lower management levels, in other divisions, or in the periphery of Siemens, considerably more amalgamation of occupational and corporate crime might have occurred. Occupational crime in the periphery of Siemens is indeed likely, given the inherently limited bureaucratic control over illicit transactions (see Klinkhammer 2013) – but it would not diminish the explanatory power of H1 and H6. A more significant limitation concerns the degree to which case study findings generally apply to other cases of corporate corruption. Despite the global scale of structural corruption at Siemens, some of its normative and organizational foundations were linked to national institutions (e.g. the tax deductibility of bribes paid abroad) and national cultures (e.g. West German anti-communism of the Cold War era) as well as to problems rooted in the transnational regulation of multinational corporations (see Braithwaite 1993; Lord 2013). Future research has to investigate whether the Siemens complex might represent a typically German or typically European case of corporate corruption; in comparison with other cases of structural corruption on behalf of large industries, corporations from different nations and regions of the world economy.

Despite those limitations, the above analyses lead to the conclusion that organizational cultures played a dominant role in the perpetuation of corrupt practices at Siemens. If this is true, it is of the essence to assess whether the consequences of the public scandal might have triggered cultural changes within Siemens. Though I can only touch on the most salient aspects here, the organizational response in the aftermath of the scandal aimed at signalling the company's capacity to fight corruption by the centralization of resources and employee turnover (Gebhardt and Müller-Seitz 2011). Measures included an increase in personnel from 80 part-time (2006) to 600 full-time (2009) compliance officers (Pohlmann 2009). The more radical reaction was a significant managerial turnover – which is known to decrease offending levels for other crimes against competition (Simpson and Koper 1997) – that affected most board members (except for three), including then-CEO Klaus Kleinfeld. He took his leave in 2007, as well as then-chairman Heinrich von Pierer ('Mr. Siemens') who had served as CEO for most of the criminally relevant period.

Although company officials are eager to stress that the new top management – headed by Peter Löscher, a former top manager of Siemens' main competitor General Electric – initiated a cultural change in the aftermath of the scandal (Löscher 2012; Pohlmann 2009), vacant positions were mostly filled 'from below in the organization' (Löscher 2012), which is unlikely to induce cultural change. After only six years in office, Löscher was replaced in 2013 by his chief financial officer, Joe Kaeser – who has been with Siemens since 1980. Also in 2013, a former compliance officer turned whistleblower, and brought new charges of corruption against the Siemens healthcare subsidiary in China. The alleged 'systematic evasion' of due diligence practices in the subsidiary (Scannell 2013) gives rise to scepticism about the validity of the managerial mantra 'Only clean business is Siemens business' and whether it will eventually prove to be the epitaph of corporate corruption in this company. After all, cultural changes typically require the scarcest resource in a corporate setting more than anything else, and that is: time.

Notes

1 This article uses a narrow, formal understanding of corruption, describing the phenomenon as a specific type of transaction that is defined by the granting ('active corruption') or acceptance ('passive corruption') of undue advantages and third-party damage (Pohlmann et al. 2011). 'Structural corruption' is then further defined by planning and long-term orientation – in marked contrast to 'situational corruption', which takes advantage of a convenient opportunity (Dölling 2007).

2 The leading private law firm reported (Debevoise & Plimpton LLP 2008) on its methods that '[t]he Siemens investigation [...] included 1,750 interviews; over 1,000 informational briefings; 82 million documents electronically searched and 14 million documents reviewed; 38 million financial transactions analysed; and 10 million bank records reviewed.'

3 Corporate crime encompasses 'offences committed by corporate officials for the corporation and the offences of the corporation itself' (Clinard and Quinney 1973: 188), whereas occupational crime (Green

1990) relates to organizations only in terms of an opportunity structure that serves as the trigger for individual offences committed for private gain.

4 A lot of offences were already barred at the time of the investigation, which led to some open-hearted testimonies during court trials. Many employees who were compromised by the disclosures confessed to their involvement in so called 'interviews' with private investigators, especially when the company granted them amnesty for blowing the whistle – which did not necessarily spare them from criminal prosecution (Wastl et al. 2009).

5 Although new data might prove the courts' assessment wrong, or the judges' perception might be biased, a crucial goal of each criminal trial is to establish the facts of the case, with the hearing of evidence at the heart of this process (Löffelmann 2008). Thus I side with Palmer (2012: 31) who argues that 'there is a good chance that we can record and interpret observations of social control agent actions with reasonable unanimity'.

6 See Wolf (2009b) for the foreign economic policy parameters of the Siemens case, Wolf and Schmidt-Pfister (2010) on the comparative state of German anti-corruption law, and again Wolf (2006; 2007) on its development in the wake of international political change.

7 Subsidiary Siemens General Medical had allegedly diverted eight million Deutschmarks, e.g. to bribe South Korean hospital officials, in the attempt to acquire business (Knop 2006).

8 Instead, the previous lives of two convicts were described by the judge as 'completely flawless' (one of them had previously received the 'Order of Merit of the Federal Republic of Germany'), and another had been awarded an honorary professorship.

9 The literal meaning is 'inhabitants/natives of Siemens'.

10 According to findings of the private investigation, Siemens-PG had previously transferred about 190 million euros to slush funds in Liechtenstein – only between 1997 and 1999.

11 However, this acquaintance was a result of Horst V.'s professional career, and did not qualify as close network ties either, since they had lost touch for years (see Landgericht Darmstadt 2007: Rn. 90).

12 Historians Hartmut Berghoff and Cornelia Rauh were commissioned to reappraise Siemens' recent development till 2011, covering 30 years of corporate history. They were granted unconditional access to corporate archives, which might even lead to new insights into the Siemens corruption complex.

13 See Satzger (2009) for a juridical critique of the so-called Siemens decision, and Niehaus (2009) for related criminal proceedings.

14 At the beginning of the 1990s, foreign capital held 45 per cent of Siemens stocks. The proportion of institutional investors rapidly increased from 24 per cent in 1990, to 35 per cent in 1991, to 45 per cent in 1997 (Decurtins 2002: 100).

15 See Klinkhammer (2013) for a lengthy discussion of the COM case.

16 The director heading the COM-division – appointed as 'hatchet man' in 2001, when the dot-com bubble collapsed, and promoted to the corporate board of directors in 2004 – was indicted for an intentional breach of his supervisory duties; yet the proceedings were closed against a fine of 175,000 euros (Oberlandesgericht München 2011). Thomas G. apparently argued successfully (Busse 2011) that he had tried to fight corruption in his division (to little avail), while having to choose 'between the devil and the deep blue sea' (i.e. closing his eyes to corruption vs. losing orders and jobs).

17 IG Metall has long been the largest single union in Germany, and worldwide, with more than 2 million members.

18 The findings also illustrate the dire consequences if senior executives act in opposition to employee participation (Jirjahn and Smith 2006), and they reflect the deinstitutionalization processes during the 1990s that were undermining the German variety of 'organized capitalism', as indicated by shifts of power from unions to work councils (Beyer and Höpner 2003).

19 From a functionalist perspective, useful illegality is indeed necessary to keep the system running. Yet, it remains an empirical question which forms of illegality become selected, whether these are criminally relevant, and to what extent or in which situations illegal behaviour is informally legitimized.

References

Ashforth, B.E., and Anand, V. (2003) 'The normalization of corruption in organizations', *Research in Organizational Behavior*, 25: 1–52.

Ashforth, B.E., Gioia, D.A., Robinson, S.L. and Trevino, L.K. (2008) 'Re-viewing organizational corruption', *Academy of Management Review*, 33: 670–684.

Baecker, D. (2000) 'Korruption, empirisch', *Die Tageszeitung/taz Nr. 6049 vom 24.1.2000*: 14.

Bannenberg, B. (2002) *Korruption in Deutschland und ihre strafrechtliche Kontrolle: Eine kriminologisch-strafrechtliche Analyse*, Neuwied/Kriftel: Luchterhand.

Bannenberg, B. (2003) 'Korruption in Deutschland: Befunde und Konsequenzen', in V. v. Nell, G. Schwitzgebel and M. Vollet (eds) *Korruption: Interdisziplinäre Zugänge zu einem komplexen Phänomen*, Wiesbaden: DUV, pp. 119–135.

Beyer, J. and Höpner, M. (2003) 'The disintegration of organised capitalism: German corporate governance in the 1990s', *West European Politics*, 26(4): 179–198.

Börsch, A. (2004) 'Globalisation, shareholder value, restructuring: The (non)-transformation of Siemens', *New Political Economy*, 9: 365–387.

Braithwaite, J. (1985) 'White collar crime', *Annual Review of Sociology*, 11: 1–25.

Braithwaite, J. (1993) 'Transnational regulation of the pharmaceutical industry', *The Annals of the American Academy of Political and Social Science*, 525: 12–30.

Bundesgerichtshof (2008) 'Federal Court of Justice Decision of August 29', *juris.de database, Az. 2 StR 587/07*.

Busse, C. (2011) 'Schmiergeldskandal bei Siemens: Mister Perfect vor Gericht', *Süddeutsche Zeitung/April 6*: 17.

Clinard, M.B. and Quinney, R. (1973) *Criminal Behavior Systems: A Typology*, 2nd edn, New York: Holt, Rinehart and Winston.

Daboub, A.J., Rasheed, A.M., Priem, R.L. and Gray, D. (1995) 'Top management team characteristics and corporate illegal activity', *Academy of Management Review*, 20: 138–170.

Debevoise & Plimpton LLP (2008) 'Debevoise conducted Siemens internal investigation', *Press Release/December 15*.

Decurtins, D. (2002) *Siemens: Anatomie Eines Unternehmens*, Frankfurt/Wien: Redline.

Dölling, D. (2007) 'Grundlagen der Korruptionsprävention', in D. Dölling (ed.) *Handbuch Der Korruptionsprävention: Für Wirtschaftsunternehmen und öffentliche Verwaltung*, München: C.H.Beck, pp. 1–43.

Dombois, R. (2009) 'Von Organisierter Korruption zu individuellem Korruptionsdruck? Soziologische Einblicke in die Siemens-Korruptionsaffäre', in P. Graeff, K. Schröder and S. Wolf (eds) *Der Korruptionsfall Siemens: Analysen und praxisnahe Folgerungen des wissenschaftlichen Arbeitskreises von Transparency International Deutschland*, Baden-Baden: Nomos, pp. 131–150.

Freiberger, H., Hagelüken, A. and Ott, K. (2008) 'Eine Million Euro Passen Bequem in Diese Aktentasche', *Süddeutsche Zeitung/August 1*: 28.

Gebhardt, C. and Müller-Seitz, G. (2011) 'Phoenix arising from the ashes: An event-oriented analysis of the Siemens' corruption scandal as nexus between organization and society' (German language), *Managementforschung*, 21: 41–90.

Graeff, P. (2009) 'Im Sinne Des Unternehmens? Soziale Aspekte Der Korrupten Transaktionen Im Hause Siemens', in P. Graeff, K. Schröder and S. Wolf (eds) *Der Korruptionsfall Siemens: Analysen und praxisnahe Folgerungen des wissenschaftlichen Arbeitskreises von Transparency International Deutschland*, Baden-Baden: Nomos, pp. 151–171.

Graeff, P., Schröder, K. and Wolf, S. (2009) *Der Korruptionsfall Siemens: Analysen und praxisnahe Folgerungen des wissenschaftlichen Arbeitskreises von Transparency International Deutschland*, Baden-Baden: Nomos.

Green, G.S. (1990) *Occupational Crime* (Nelson Hall Series in Law, Crime and Justice), Chicago: Burnham Inc Pub.

Grieger, J. (2009) 'Korruption und Kultur bei der Siemens AG: Eine Handlungs-Struktur-Analyse', in P. Graeff, K. Schröder and S. Wolf (eds) *Der Korruptionsfall Siemens: Analysen und praxisnahe Folgerungen des wissenschaftlichen Arbeitskreises von Transparency International Deutschland*, Baden-Baden: Nomos, pp. 103–130.

Hiller, P. (2005) 'Korruption und Netzwerke: Konfusionen im Schema von Organisation und Gesellschaft', *Zeitschrift fur Rechtssoziologie*, 26: 57–77.

Höffling, C. (2002) *Korruption als soziale Beziehung*, Opladen: Leske + Budrich.

Jirjahn, U. and Smith, S.C. (2006) 'What factors lead management to support or oppose employee participation – with and without works councils? Hypotheses and evidence from Germany', *Industrial Relations: A Journal of Economy and Society*, 45(4): 650–680.

Klinkhammer, J. (2011) 'Korruption Powered by Siemens: Alte, korruptionsaffine Wertorientierungen in den Führungsetagen des Geschäftsbereichs Power Generation', in M. Pohlmann, and G. Lämmlin (eds) *Neue Werte in den Führungsetagen? Kontinuität und Wandel in der Wirtschaftselite* (Herrenalber Forum, 64 ed.), Karlsruhe: Evangelische Akademie Baden, pp. 136–168.

Klinkhammer, J. (2013) 'On the dark side of the code: Organizational challenges to an effective anti-corruption strategy', *Crime, Law and Social Change*, 60: 191–208.

Knop, C. (2006) 'In schlechter Gesellschaft', *Frankfurter Allgemeine Zeitung, 293/December 16*: 14.

Kotthoff, H., and Wagner, A. (2008) *Die Leistungsträger: Führungskräfte im Wandel der Firmenkultur – Eine Follow-up-Studie*, Berlin: Edition Sigma.

Landgericht Darmstadt (2007) 'Regional Court Decision of May 14', *juris.de database, Az. 712 Js 5213/04-9 KLs.*

Landgericht Nürnberg-Fürth (2008) 'Regional Court Decision of November 24', *juris.de database, Az. 3KLs 501 Js 1777/2008.*

Lässig, A. (1999) *Gestaltung der Organisationskultur: Evaluation kultureller Veränderungsprozesse in der Zentralabteilung Technik der Siemens AG*, München: Ludwig-Maximilians-Universität.

Levi, M., Dakolias, M., and Greenberg, T.S. (2007) 'Money laundering and corruption', in J.E. Campos (ed.) *The Many Faces of Corruption: Tracking Vulnerabilities at the Sector Level*, Washington, DC: World Bank, pp. 389–426.

Leyendecker, H. (2007) *Die große Gier: Korruption, Kartelle, Lustreisen: Warum unsere Wirtschaft eine neue Moral braucht*, Berlin: Rowohlt.

Löffelmann, M. (2008) *Die normativen Grenzen der Wahrheitserforschung im Strafverfahren: Ideen zu einer Kritik der Funktionsfähigkeit der Strafrechtspflege*, Berlin: De Gruyter.

Lord, N. (2013) 'Regulating transnational corporate bribery: Anti-bribery and corruption in the UK and Germany', *Crime, Law and Social Change*, 60: 127–145.

Löscher, P. (2012) 'The CEO of Siemens on using a scandal to drive change', *Harvard Business Review*, 90(11): 39–42.

Luhmann, N. (1964) *Funktionen und Folgen formaler Organisation*, Berlin: Duncker & Humblot.

Luhmann, N. (2000) *Organisation und Entscheidung*, Wiesbaden: WDV.

Niehaus, H. (2009) 'Strafrechtliche Folgen der Bestechung im vermeintlichen Unternehmensinteresse', in P. Graeff, K. Schröder and S. Wolf (eds) *Der Korruptionsfall Siemens: Analysen und praxisnahe Folgerungen des wissenschaftlichen Arbeitskreises von Transparency International Deutschland*, Baden-Baden: Nomos, pp. 21–46.

Oberlandesgericht München (2008a) 'Strafverfahren gegen Reinhard S. (57) wegen Untreue (Siemens-Komplex)', *Press Release, Criminal Cases of July 28.*

Oberlandesgericht München (2008b) 'Strafverfahren gegen Wolfgang Ru. und Heinz Wolfgang Ernst K. – Von J. wegen Beihilfe zur Untreue U. A. (Siemens-Komplex)', *Press Release, Criminal Cases of November 19.*

Oberlandesgericht München (2010) 'Strafverfahren gegen Hans-Werner H. und Jörg Michael K. wegen Untreue U.A. (Siemens-Komplex)', *Press Release, Criminal Cases of April 20.*

Oberlandesgericht München (2011) 'Strafverfahren gegen Dr. H.C. Thomas G. (50) wegen vorsätzlicher Verletzung der Aufsichtspflicht in Betrieben und Unternehmen U.A. (Siemens-Komplex)', *Press Release, Criminal Cases of May 19.*

Palmer, D. (2012) *Normal Organizational Wrongdoing: A Critical Analysis of Theories of Misconduct in and by Organizations*, Oxford: Oxford University Press.

Pohlmann, A. (2009) 'Über die Aufarbeitung des Bestechungsskandals bei Siemens: Prävention, Aufdeckung und Kampf für saubere Geschäfte', *Betriebswirtschaftliche Blaetter*, 58(12): 679–682.

Pohlmann, M. (2008) 'Management und Moral', in T. Blank, T. Münch, S. Schanne and C. Staffhorst (eds) *Integrierte Soziologie: Perspektiven zwischen Ökonomie und Soziologie, Praxis und Wissenschaft*, München und Mering: Rainer Hampp Verlag, pp. 161–176.

Pohlmann, M., Markova, H. and Klinkhammer, J. (2011) 'Moral und Korruption', in M. Pohlmann, and H. Markova *Soziologie der Organisation: Eine Einführung*, Stuttgart: UTB, pp. 155–180.

Ritzer, U. (2008) 'Haft für Ex-Siemens-Vorstand gefordert', *süddeutsche.de/November 17.*

Rose-Ackerman, S. (1978/1999) 'Corruption and the private sector', in A.J. Heidenheimer, M. Johnston and V. Levine (eds) *Political Corruption: A Handbook*, 5th edn, New Brunswick: Transaction.

Satzger, H. (2009) '"Schwarze Kassen" Zwischen Untreue und Korruption – Eine Besprechung des Urteils BGH-2 Str 587/07 (Siemens-Entscheidung)', *Neue Zeitschrift für Strafrecht*, 29(6): 297–306.

Scannell, K. (2013) 'Siemens case involves China healthcare unit', *Financial Times, ft.com/January 15.*

Siemens AG (2002) *SEC Annual Report for the Fiscal Year 2001 (Form 20-F).*

Siemens AG (2007) *Annual Report 2006*, Munich.

Simon, H.A. (1991) 'Organizations and markets', *The Journal of Economic Perspectives*, 5(2): 25–44.

Simpson, S.S. and Koper, C.S. (1997) 'The changing of the guard: Top management characteristics, organizational strain, and antitrust offending', *Journal of Quantitative Criminology*, 13(4): 373–404.

Stadler, C. and Hinterhuber, H.H. (2005) 'Shell, Siemens and Daimlerchrysler: Leading change in companies with strong values', *Long Range Planning*, 38(5): 467–484.

Sutherland, E.H. (1940) 'White-collar criminality', *American Sociological Review*, 5(1): 1–12.

United States Department of Justice (2008) 'Siemens AG and three subsidiaries plead guilty to Foreign Corrupt Practices Act violations and agree to pay $450 million in combined criminal fines', *Press Release 08-1105/December 15*.

Vaughan, D. (1982) 'Toward understanding unlawful organizational behavior', *Michigan Law Review*, 80(7): 1377–1402.

Wastl, U., Litzka, P. and Pusch, M. (2009) 'SEC-Ermittlungen in Deutschland: Eine Umgehung rechtsstaatlicher Mindeststandards!', *Neue Zeitschrift für Strafrecht*, 29(2): 68–74.

Weismann, M. (2009) 'The Foreign Corrupt Practices Act: The failure of the self-regulatory model of corporate governance in the global business environment', *Journal of Business Ethics*, 88(4): 615–661.

Wieland, J. (2005) 'Die Governance der Korruption', in S.A. Jansen and B.P. Priddat (eds) *Korruption: Unaufgeklärter Kapitalismus – Multidisziplinäre Perspektiven zu Funktionen und Folgen der Korruption*, Wiesbaden: VS, pp. 43–62.

Wieland, J. (2008) 'Die Kunst der Compliance', in A. Löhr and E. Burkatzki (eds) *Wirtschaftskriminalität und Ethik*, München: Hampp, pp. 155–169.

Williams, J. and Beare, M. (1999) 'The business of bribery: Globalization, economic liberalization, and the "problem" of corruption', *Crime, Law and Social Change*, 32(2): 115–146.

Wolf, S. (2006) 'Modernization of the German anti-corruption criminal law by international legal provisions', *German Law Journal*, 7(9): 785–192.

Wolf, S. (2007) *Der Beitrag internationaler und supranationaler Organisationen zur Korruptionsbekämpfung in den Mitgliedstaaten*, Speyer: Dt. Forschungsinst. für Öffentliche Verwaltung.

Wolf, S. (2009a) 'Die Siemens-Korruptionsaffäre – Ein Überblick', in P. Graeff, K. Schröder and S. Wolf (eds) *Der Korruptionsfall Siemens: Analysen und praxisnahe Folgerungen des wissenschaftlichen Arbeitskreises von Transparency International Deutschland*, Baden-Baden: Nomos, pp. 9–17.

Wolf, S. (2009b) 'Korruption und Außenwirtschaftspolitik: Zu den politischen Rahmenbedingungen des Siemens-Falls', in P. Graeff, K. Schröder and S. Wolf (eds) *Der Korruptionsfall Siemens: Analysen und praxisnahe Folgerungen des wissenschaftlichen Arbeitskreises von Transparency International Deutschland*, Baden-Baden: Nomos, pp. 63–76.

Wolf, S. and Schmidt-Pfister, D. (2010) 'Between corruption, integration, and culture: The politics of international anti-corruption', in S. Wolf, and D. Schmidt-Pfister (eds) *International Anti-Corruption Regimes in Europe: Between Corruption, Integration, and Culture*, Baden-Baden: Nomos, pp. 13–21.

Ziegleder, D. (2007) 'Business and self-regulation: Results from a comparative study on the prevention of economic crime', *Zeitschrift fur Rechtssoziologie*, 28(2): 203–213.

Zugehör, R. (2003) 'Kapitalmarktorientierung und Mitbestimmung: Veba und Siemens', in W. Streeck and M. Höpner (eds) *Alle Macht dem Markt? Fallstudien zur Abwicklung der Deutschland AG*, Frankfurt am Main: Campus.

21

Shadows of power

Agusta, a Belgian affair

Marc Cools and Veerle Pashley[1]

The contextualization of white-collar crime, the Agusta affair and the homicide of André Cools

In 1991, the Belgian Minister of State André Cools was murdered. He was famous for his political achievements, but he was also a successful businessman with a large network of holdings. During the judicial investigation of his murder, the Agusta affair came to light. The Italian helicopter company Agusta paid bribe money to the Belgian Socialist Party in exchange for a contract to provide helicopters to the Belgian army.

'Crimes of the powerful' (Sheptycki 2010: 68–71) are an essential criminological area of research. This key concept refers to crimes that are difficult to track and committed by people having a high function in society (Pearce 1976). White-collar crimes are an example of this categorization. The Agusta case is an illustration of what Kramer and colleagues called state–corporate crime: the mutual beneficial relation between political actors and businesses. Thus, this case sheds light on the political-economic interests and power relations that can induce white-collar crime, interpreted here as work-related misdemeanours committed by politicians, public authorities and business people which have a high social status and commit crime to obtain political or financial profit (Hoefnagels 1981: 4–5).

So how is our chapter constructed? First, this chapter focuses on the homicide of André Cools and his political power. Second, we will discuss the Agusta affair in Wallonia. Third, the extension of the Agusta affair will be described. Since this event was originally a matter of interest in Wallonia which soon extended to Flanders as well, it is necessary to reflect on the developments that led to this expansion. Fourth, we will focus on the judicial completion of this Belgian case of white-collar crime and the homicide of André Cools. Last, we will present some criminological reflections.

Belgium has a remarkable index of white-collar crime. There are numerous scandals which had a long-lasting impact on citizens. Social and Christian Democratic mandatories, having access to the public market, are often protagonists of these cases (Cools 1999: 15). The former prime minister of Belgium, Guy Verhofstadt, called this 'the Belgian disease' (Verhofstadt 1997: 44). This 'disease' refers to a combination of the strong culture of clientelism that is inherent to the culture of some political parties and the collusion of political and economic interests.

The following examples illustrate this assertion: the fraud of RTT,[2] the Ibramco affair,[3] the de Beaulieu case,[4] the Decaux affair[5] and the illegal tender of parking meters in Liège by the local government. However, it was the Agusta affair and the homicide of André Cools that truly shocked society. In this affair, citizens witnessed a 'political thriller' featuring white-collar crime (Cools 2001: 66–68).

We have chosen it for a case study because it highlights several characteristics of this culture. Before we describe the essential structures of the homicide of André Cools and the Agusta affair, it is useful to reflect on the 'typical Belgian context'. In the end, white-collar crime is often intertwined with the political, economic and social texture of a nation (Green and Ward 2004; Kramer et al. 2002).

Belgium is divided into three cultural communities: the Flemish community, the German community and the French-speaking community. More important for the governance of the Belgian state are the regions: the Flemish region, the Walloon region and the capital of Brussels. Matters that are supposed to have a general impact like the police and justice are centralized at the federal government. Belgium has in total five governments: a federal government, three regional governments and the Walloon region that has kept its community and the regional matters separate in two governments. Ever since its independence and existence as a nation state in 1830, Belgium is an artificial country. We can only understand its functioning if we consider its fracture lines. The first fracture line is a linguistic and cultural one. After the intense political, economic and social dominance of the French language, Dutch and German have been recognized as official Belgian languages. This problem can also be found in the state-centred and communal debate which is driven by the Dutch-, French- and German-speaking communities. The second fracture line is an ideological and philosophical one. Flanders has a strong and secularized Catholic substructure with a minority of atheistic humanists. Wallonia, on the other hand, has an atheistic humanist majority. The third fracture line can be found in the administrative communities and has a social-economic nature. On an economic scale, Flanders prefers entrepreneurship and free-market initiatives. Wallonia tends to a state-centred structure. In short, the reader should take these three fracture lines into account in reflecting on the Agusta affair and the homicide of André Cools. The description of the intertwined case in the next part is chronological.

André Cools or the 'master of Flémalle'

Socialist Minister of State André Cools, originating from Wallonia, was shot on 18 July 1991 at 7.25 a.m. He was killed in front of his house called 'La Coline', at the Avenue de l'Observatoire in Liège. A man with dark hair, approximately 40 years old, dressed in jeans and boots, shot André Cools and his girlfriend Marie-Hélène Joiret. Afterwards, he fled. André Cools was fatally shot in the throat (Vansevenant 1993: 8). His partner, Marie-Hélène Joiret, was severely wounded. However, she survived the attack. The whole scene looked like a professional murder (Carrozzo et al. 1996: 16).

André Cools was the grandson of labourers, who used to live in a poor community near Antwerp. Later, his grandparents moved to Liège. Marcel Cools (the father) was a council member in Flémalle and he was killed by national socialists in a concentration camp. André Cools grew up at his 'Maison du Peuple' (People Mansions, Maraite 2012: 23). These mansions always had an important purpose in the socialist movement, since they were used as formal and informal venues between mandatories, politicians and electors. Cools was a well-known politician, since he had experience as a mayor, a member of parliament, Minister of Budgets, President of his Socialist Party, First President of the Council of the Walloon Region, Deputy Prime Minister, Minister of Economics, Minister of the Walloon Region authorized for public work, water supply and secondary policies, and Minister of State (Collette and Halleux 1996). In addition to his political successes, he also controlled a network of 'holdings' where he centred his trustees, better known as 'Coolsiens'. They were very powerful and had the ability to 'get things done'. His consortium consisted of several organizations: the private organization Compagnie Générale des Eaux (a water supplier), the insurance company OMOP/SMAP, Network Research Belgium and Groupement d'Intérêt Economique (financial investors), Neos holding, Meusinvest (an investment company), Société de Gestion de l'Aéroport de Bierset and the Société de Leasing (a leasing company) and Financement et Economie d'Energie (an energy company) (Vansevenant 1993: 10–13).

He abused this combination of connections and powers in order to favour the Walloon Region, and called himself 'a gangster of the public sector'. However, although collusion of interests was considered normal by Cools, he never enriched himself personally.

Important for his political power was the membership of l'Incorruptible, a section of the Belgian freemasonry (Collette and Halleux 1996: 36–38; Maraite 2012: 39). It has been alleged that the freemasonry obstructed the judicial investigation of Cools' murder and the Agusta case, but evidence to support this has never been found (Collette and Halleux 1996: 273).

First, the helicopters flew over Wallonia

Magistrate Véronique Ancia led the judicial investigation into the homicide of André Cools. She came from a Walloon family with relations with the Belgian French-speaking party Parti Social Chrétien[6] (Christian Social Democratic Party). As a result, Ancia raised the suspicions of the members of the Socialist Party as she investigated the homicide of the Minister of State André Cools. She succeeded in revealing several corruption scandals in which Walloon socialists were involved (Carrozzo et al. 1996: 27–30). The aforementioned ideological fracture lines entered the judicial investigation, which affected a thorough examination of the case.

In the course of the murder investigation, former Minister of Justice and Deputy Prime Minister Philippe Moureaux and the leader of the trade union for metals in Liège Carol Gluza, who are both members of the French-speaking Socialist Party, revealed that Guy Spitaels, the former president of the French-speaking Socialist Party, had been bribed by the Italian helicopter producer Agusta, in order to ascertain a helicopter contract with the Belgian army. They also revealed briberies from the Minister of Defence, Guy Coëme, and the Walloon Minister, Guy Mathot. As a result, the parliamentary invulnerability of these 'three Guys' was ended (Vansevenant 1994: 9) and their political careers were, temporarily, over (Coeck and Willems 1994: 187). Also several colonels of the Belgian army with a socialist background (also called *socquettes rouges*) accepted bribes from the Italian company Agusta in exchange for the political and economic approval of Agusta's A109 helicopter. These bribes were intended for the Parti Socialiste and the economic benefit of Wallonia, and approved of by André Cools and, as it turned out, the revelation of these bribes was an essential clue for the investigators in solving his murder.

This contract was worth 300 million former Belgian francs (now 7.5 million euros). This deal was at the expense of the helicopter BK117 made by the German aerospace company Messerschmitt-Bolkow-Blohm and the helicopter Ecureuil of the French company Aérospatiale.

The Socialist Party received 50 million Belgian francs (1.25 million euros) in bribes which were transferred to a Swiss bank account.

On 8 December 1988, Socialist Minister of Defence Guy Coëme decided in favour of Agusta, despite Agusta neither offering the best price nor having many references, since their helicopters were only active in Switzerland and Italy. Furthermore, this initiative was supported with a note praising Agusta. This praise was, however, not in accordance with reality. The former Minister of Economy and Dutch-speaking socialist Willy Claes approved the order of the Agusta helicopters.[7]

André Cools thought bribe money was an important investment for his political party and for economic compensations in Liège as well as a financial opportunity for his computer company Trident that was almost bankrupt (Carrozzo et al. 1996: 81). These compensations were mainly seen as an opportunity for state intervention in the economy. But in secret new negotiations with Agusta, Guy Coëme and the Walloon Minister Alain Van der Biest managed to obtain the bribe money and compensations. André Cools and his confidents or 'Coolsiens' were excluded from these secret negotiations (Vansevenant 1994: 33). André Cools felt deceived and he threatened to expose this corruption.

Second, the helicopters of Agusta flew over Flanders

In the beginning, the Agusta affair and the homicide of André Cools were interpreted as a business of Walloon socialists. Nevertheless, Flemish socialists eventually came under the spotlight. The former chamberlain of the Dutch-speaking Socialist Party Etienne Mangé, assistant secretary Luc Wallyn and a co-worker of the former chief of cabinet of Willy Claes, Johan Delanghe, were arrested during the judicial investigation. It did not take long before they confessed their involvement. The former president of the Flemish Socialist Party, Frank Vandenbroucke, had provided instructions to the chamberlain of the Socialist Party to burn the bribe money from Agusta (Bats 1995: 72). However, the money was invested (Collette and Halleux 1996: 276–286) and used to pay off debts of the Socialist Party (Bats 1995: 64). The Belgian delegate of Agusta, George Cywie, frequently tried to discredit the former chief of cabinet Willy Claes. He referred to the suggested compensations or economic investments made by Agusta in and for Flanders. Evidently, if Wallonia was to be the only beneficiary, it was possible that Flanders would block the Agusta deal and alter the army equipment. It is worth noticing that Willy Claes always denied his role in the Agusta affair (Vansevenant 1994: 23–27).

A closer look: co-workers of the cabinet and the homicide of André Cools

The magistrate Véronique Ancia investigated several leads and hypotheses regarding the true circumstances of the homicide of André Cools. In the end, the ministerial cabinet of the Walloon Minister Alain Van der Biest would be a key lead in solving the murder of André Cools and the dissemination of the Agusta affair.

Unlike in other European countries, Belgian ministers cannot function politically without their ministerial cabinets, although these cabinets are rarely mentioned in state law. This institution consists of personal co-workers of the minister at hand and is very influential – it can best be described as a parallel administration (Alen 1995: 210).

Ministerial cabinets are a form of 'brain trust' or support for the minister. They help to guide and coordinate political problems. They also act as innovators, deal with public relations and handle the contacts of the minister (Dewachter 1995: 242). As a result, these cabinets have political power since they act as a private council for the minister. The people who work there are loyal soldiers or 'brothers-in-arms' that support their minister by using their expertise, networks and flexibility. These co-workers are well aware of the short period of time of their appointment which is steeped with political power. Functioning in the shadows of a delicate charter is not without difficulties. However, these conditions are compensated since they can operate like spiders in a web of power and obtain the power to change things (Suetens and Walgrave 1999: 499–528). Ministerial cabinets function as instruments that can execute political and economic negotiations outside parliamentary control and the pressures inside political parties.

It was Van der Biest, who later committed suicide before standing trial, who gave orders to murder Cools through hired assassins. White-collar crime or more specifically political corruption was the motive of this homicide. Alain Van der Biest, whose political weakness and (public) drunkenness were known to everyone, appointed – deliberately or not – several members in his ministerial cabinet with strong ties to Italian and Albanese criminal groups in Liège. These people were the former police officer from Grâce-Hologne, private secretary Richard Taxquet, and former prison officer from Lantin, driver Pino di Mauro. André Cools discovered Alain Van der Biest used criminal money for his election campaign. Both di Mauro and Taxquet succeeded in professionally isolating Van der Biest from his other cabinet employees. As a result, their power was omnipresent (Carrozzo et al. 1996: 35–61). The criminal underworld successfully infiltrated to the level of ministerial cabinets, and enabled the recruitment of assassins.

The judicial completion

The homicide of André Cools was dealt with in the Criminal Court at Liège. Attorney general Marianne Lejeune opened her requisition with the famous Latin words 'Tu quoque, fili mi'.[8] Alain Van der Biest committed suicide before the trial started. The attorney general quoted these words because Van der Biest was publicly seen as César's guilty son Brutus. Van der Biest was seen as the one who ordered the homicide of André Cools. Several politicians of the Socialist Party witnessed this trial in silence, as did the senators in Rome.

On 7 January 2004, private secretary Richard Taxquet and driver Pino di Mauro were sentenced to prison for 20 years. Di Mauro had delivered the murder weapon to two Tunisian assassins.

During the Criminal Court proceedings, several other key players from the Liège Italian criminal mafia were sentenced (Coeck and Willems 1994: 181). They were all involved in recruiting Cools' assassins.

In addition to the judicial investigation into the homicide of André Cools, the corruption case was brought to court. Attorney general at the Belgian Supreme Court,[9] Jacques Velu, was authorized to investigate criminal acts committed by ministers in their function. He notified the Chamber of Representatives. A special commission of the Chamber of Representatives was gathered. They questioned the former Minister of Defence Guy Coëme and the former Minister of Economy Willy Claes. This special commission concluded that both politicians should be the objects of further judicial investigation. The Chamber of Representatives decided on 19 October 1994 that Willy Claes should be referred and committed to trial. One day after this decision, he resigned as secretary general of NATO (Bats 1995: 104–122). The Belgian Supreme Court decided on 23 December 1998 that Willy Claes, Guy Coëme and the former president of the French-speaking Socialist Party Guy Spitaels were conditionally sentenced to prison for a period of two to three years and barred from any public function for at least five years. Other members of the Socialist Party were also sentenced. The former chamberlain of the Dutch-speaking Socialist Party Etienne Mangé was conditionally sentenced to prison for one year. Assistant secretary Luc Wallyn and a co-worker of the former chief of cabinet Willy Claes, Johan Delanghe, were conditionally sentenced to prison for two years. Other persons who were involved, such as André Bastien and Jean-Louis Mazy, who were both political coworkers of Guy Coëme, received a conditional prison sentence of six months. Several members of the French-speaking Socialist Party were also sentenced. Auguste Merry Hermanus and François Pirot were conditionally sentenced to prison for one year and three months.

The symbiotic relation between the Agusta affair and the homicide of André Cools is a fact, even if the cases were investigated and completed separately due to judicial differences.

Conclusion

The aforementioned definition by Dutch criminologist Gerard Hoefnagels regarding white-collar crime can be applied to this Belgian case study. The criminal misdemeanours can be found in what appear to be political crimes and the illegal stock exchange. Socialist politicians and government authorities, such as co-workers of ministerial cabinets, committed these crimes. Also, business people of the Agusta company with a high social status participated.

The Agusta case aimed at increasing political power for the French-speaking socialists in Wallonia and the Dutch-speaking socialists in Flanders. In their struggle for power they ensured ministerial decisions, administrative manipulations, such as favouring Agusta, and financial gains. These gains were acquired through briberies, compensations and economic investments. The homicide of André Cools was the tip of the iceberg of a complex criminal case. From a criminological viewpoint, the Agusta affair is white-collar crime.

This general and phenomenological conclusion can further be specified. First, it cannot be denied that André Cools abused his political, his economic and his social power. He exercised these privileges through self-obtained channels which were not always transparent. At that time, it seemed to be normal practice for some political parties and mandatories to commit corruption for political gain. As a second conclusion is the hidden character of white-collar crime aspect. The homicide of André Cools that was related to the corruption affair created the appearance of a traditional crime and distracted attention away from the white-collar crime aspect. Third in this case we see some connections with organized crime: the conspiracy of the several participants in the case and the aspect of extreme violence: the ministerial cabinet of Alain Van der Biest in particular underlines this statement. There are indeed traces of a symbiotic collusion (Nelen 1997: 131).

The illegal stock exchange, the white-collar crime, the search and use of assassins require no further explanation. These crimes are criminological phenomena which are interconnected in this case study. Nevertheless, it is apparent that this Belgian casuistry was at the centre of attention amongst journalists. Academic criminologists were less active in evaluating these types of case studies. As a result, only a handful of Belgian criminologists study white-collar crime. This chapter, evaluating the Agusta affair, is an incentive to further elaborate this chapter of Belgian criminology. The functioning of a ministerial cabinet is important for its political power. The so-called Copernicus reformation of the Belgian Federal Government in 2000 abolished ministerial cabinets under the influence of the purple-green[10] administration. They are replaced by a personal cabinet, a policy preparation cell and a personal ministerial cabinet (Van Hooland 2003: 341). Nevertheless, these changes are not far-reaching. In the end, they are nothing more than a semantic exercise (Hondeghem and Depré 2005: 171). Apart from a change of name, they are still invisible bastions of power. This concentration of power can be an incentive for the institutionalization of crime (Hoefnagels 1984: 25).

The Agusta affair and the homicide of André Cools have generated interests in party politics. Apart from a public feeling of defeat (Bats 1995: 13), it was the Flemish nationalist party Vlaams Belang that kept the ongoing debate of this case alive. This political party, situated in the extreme right-winged nationalistic spectrum, never made a secret of their fight against Walloon socialism. They described the homicide of André Cools as symptomatic for Wallonia and its socialistic discourse (Vanhecke and De Man 2007: 11).

To conclude, we wanted to highlight two main issues. First, the intertwinement of white-collar crime and political power that has been described by researchers in state–corporate crime and corruption. However in this case we illustrate the complexity of political power related to political ideology, regional supremacy, the collaboration with the private sector … all coming together in one case. In this light, we can refer to this case as a form of white-collar crime which is embedded in the shadow of political power. Second, case studies offer a tremendous opportunity for scholars to understand the theoretical concept of crime in general. This is also the case for white-collar crime that often operates in a complexity of economic power, state power, political power, interpersonal relations, political ideology. … We support the notion that we cannot fully understand the true nature of white-collar crime without taking into account this complexity.

The Agusta affair and the homicide of André Cools remains a unique case study within Belgian criminological history. In our opinion, several pieces of the puzzle are still missing. Future studies can deliver more criminological insights and considerations. This case study can be seen as an incentive for further research.

Appendix

1 *Geography and languages used in Belgium*

Belgium consists of three communities:

- the Flemish community – Dutch speaking
- the French community – French speaking
- the German-speaking community

Belgium also consists of three regions:

- the Flemish region
- the Walloon region
- the Brussels-Capital region

2 *Political parties involved in the Agusta affair and the homicide of André Cools*

Dutch speaking:

- SP – Socialistische Partij (Socialist Party)

French speaking:

- PSC – Parti Social Chrétien (Christian Social Democratic Party)
- PS – Parti Socialiste (Socialist Party)

3 *List of people involved in the Agusta affair and the homicide of André Cools (alphabetically)*

- Agusta: Italian company that converted an important amount of bribe money for the Belgian Socialist Party.
- Véronique Ancia: magistrate. Led the judicial investigation on the homicide of André Cools. Had relations with Christian Social Democratic Party.

- André Bastien: co-worker of Guy Coëme.
- Guy Binet: colonel of the Belgian army with a socialist background. Approved Agusta's A109 helicopter (political and economic).
- Domenico Castellino: involved in this affair.
- Willy Claes: former Minister of Economy and member of the Dutch-speaking SP. Approved the order of the Agusta helicopters. Denied his role in the Agusta affair.
- Guy Coëme: former Minister of Defence. Decided in favour of Agusta.
- Luigi Contrino: involved in this affair.
- André Cools: member of the French-speaking PS. Former Minister of State. Origin: Liège (Wallonia). Murdered on 18 July 1991.
- Marcel Cools: father of André Cools. Killed by national socialists in Mauthausen-Gusen.
- Solazzo Cosima: friend of Pino di Mauro: provided shelter to the assassins.
- George Cywie: Belgian delegate of Agusta. Tried to discredit Willy Claes.
- Silvio De Benedictis: uncle of Richard Taxquet. Involved in the criminal stock exchange.
- Jean-Marie Dehousse: member of the French-speaking Socialist Party. André Cools accused him of being a conspirator destroying socialism.
- Johan Delanghe: co-worker of Willy Claes. Was arrested during the judicial investigation.
- Pino di Mauro: driver of Alain Van Der Biest. Former prison officer from Lantin (Wallonia). Had ties with Albanese and Italian criminal groups in Liège. Was arrested in 1992 for the sale of stocks stolen by the Turkish and Albanese mafia.
- Mauro De Santis: Involved in the criminal stock exchange.
- Jean Dubois: former army colonel. Liaison of André Cools.
- Armand Fourier: colonel of the Belgian army with a socialist background. Approved Agusta's A109 helicopter (political and economic).
- Carol Gluza: leader of the trade union for metals in Liège (Wallonia). Member of the French-speaking PS. Helped Ancia to reorientate the investigation.
- José Happart: member of the French-speaking Socialist Party. André Cools accused him of being a conspirator destroying socialism.
- Auguste Merry Hermanus: member of the French-speaking PS.
- Alain Jehay: budget expert. Had to explain his actions in court.
- Marie-Hélène Joiret: partner of André Cools. Was severely injured during the attack but survived.
- Etienne Mangé: former chamberlain of the Dutch-speaking SP. Was arrested during the judicial investigation.
- Guy Mathot: former Walloon minister.
- Jean-Louis Mazy: co-worker of Guy Coëme.
- Philippe Moureaux: former minister of justice. Member of the French-speaking PS. Helped Ancia to reorientate the investigation.
- François Pirot: member of the French-speaking PS.
- Zeljka Raznjatovic: involved in the assassination of André Cools.
- Beoît Remiche: co-worker of Melchior Wathelet. Acknowledged the existence of a socialist-driven mafia.
- Corinne Rulmont: press representative. Had to explain her actions in court.
- Guy Spitaels: former president of the French-speaking PS.
- Richard Taxquet: former police officer from Grâce-Hologne. Had ties with Albanese and Italian criminal groups in Liège. He was the private secretary of Alain Van Der Biest. He succeeded to isolate Alain Van Der Biest from his other cabinet employees.
- Mauro Todarello: an acquaintance of Richard Taxquet. Involved in the criminal stock exchange.

- Colagero Todarodie: recruited Cosima in Sicilia.
- Jean-Claude Van Cauwenberghe: member of the French-speaking Socialist Party. André Cools accused him of being a conspirator destroying socialism.
- Jacques Vandenbosch: Chief of Cabinet. Had to explain his actions in court.
- Frank Vandenbroecke: former president of the Dutch-speaking SP. Gave instructions to Etienne Mangé to burn the bribe money from Agusta.
- Alain Van Der Biest: former Walloon minister. Obtained bribe money and compensations (together with Guy Coëme). His ministerial cabinet was a key lead in solving the murder of André Cools and the Agusta affair.
- Jacques Velu: Attorney General at the Belgian Supreme Court. Investigated the criminal acts committed by ministers in their function.
- Lambert Verjus: Chief of Cabinet. Had to explain his actions in court.
- Luc Wallyn: assistant secretary of the Dutch-speaking SP. Was arrested during the judicial investigation.
- Melchior Wathelet: former Minister of Justice. Member of the Christian Social Democratic Party.

Notes

1 Marc Cools is a Professor at the Department of Criminology at the Free University of Brussels (Vrije Universiteit Brussel, Pleinlaan 2, 1050 Brussels, marc.cools@vub.ac.be) and the Department of Criminology, Criminal Law and Social Law at Ghent University (Universiteitsstraat 4, 9000 Gent, marc.cools@ugent.be). Veerle Pashley is a PhD student the Department of Criminology, Criminal Law and Social Law at Ghent University (veerle.pashley@ugent.be).

2 RTT is the abbreviation for Belgische Regie voor Telegraaf en Telefoon or the Belgian group for telegraphs and telephones. In the seventies, one of their employees reported to the press that RTT was guilty of several corruption scandals, such as double tenders and investments (Furnémont 2005).

3 The Ibramco affair was a Belgian political scandal in the seventies, which led to governmental collapse in 1974. The case features the construction of an Iranian oil company in Belgium by Ibramco. This construction was not approved of by the government and mainly served the interests of the Belgian Socialist Party (Furnémont 2005).

4 In the eighties, the Beaulieu group was suspected of a major fraud case where millions of Belgian francs were transferred abroad to avoid taxes (www.detijd.be).

5 The company JC Decaux was accused of corruption in the approval of several advertising contracts (www.detijd.be).

6 In 2002, the party changed its name to Centre Démocratic Humaniste.

7 Alongside the Minister of Defence, the Minister of Economics must also give his approval to order such equipments.

8 Julius Caesar's last words before he died: 'You too, my son'.

9 The highest courtroom in Belgium is the *Cour de Cassation*. This courtroom is not authorized to sentence or judge. However, it can withdraw or cancel sentences or arrests if the judge did not respect the rules of law.

10 The 'purple green' government in 2000 consisted of liberals, socialists and ecologists. Guy Verhofstadt was Prime Minister.

References

Alen, A. (1995) *Handboek van het Belgisch Staatsecht*, Deurne: Kluwer Rechtswetenschappen.
Bats, A. (1995) *Willy-Gate*, Antwerp: Dedalus.
Carrozzo, S., Deghaye, M.-P. and Rogge, G. (1996) *L'Affaire Cools*, Bruxelles: Editions Luc Pire.
Coeck, E. and Willems, J. (1994) *De Walm van de Wetstraat: 20 jaar onfrisse praktijken*, Antwerp: Coda.
Collette, A. and Halleux, P. (1996) *André Cools: Rebelle d'état*, Ottignies: Editions Quorum.

Cools, M. (1999) 'Een criminologische reflectie op corruptie en het bedrijfsleven', in M. Cools and D. Mahieu (eds) *Het verschijnsel corruptie*, St-Eloois-Vijve: Mys & Breesch uitgevers, pp. 15–18.
Cools, M. (2001) 'Integriteit in Europees perspectief', in B. Hoogenboom, R. Kamerling, J. Kuijl, M. Pheijffer and C. Schaap (eds) *Aspecten van integriteit*, The Hague: Koninklijke Vermande, pp. 61–74.
Cools, M. (2009) 'André Cools en Agusta: Een Belgische affaire', *Justitiële Verkenningen*, 3: 59–69.
Dewachter, W. (1995) *Besluitvorming in politiek België*, Leuven: Acco.
Furnémont, J.F. (2005) *Guy Spitaels: Au-delà du pouvoir*, Luik: Editions Luc Pire.
Green, P. and Ward, T. (2004) *State Crime*, London: Pluto Press.
Hoefnagels, G. (1981) *Witte boordencriminaliteit: Opstellen over Misdaad en Macht*, Assen: Van Gorcum.
Hondeghem, A. and Depré, R. (2005) *De Copernicushervorming in perspectief: Veranderingsmanagement in de federale overhead*, Brugge: Vanden Broele.
Kramer, R.C., Michalowski, R.J. and Kauzlarich, D. (2002) 'The origins and development of the concept and theory of state-corporate crime', *Crime & Delinquency*, 48(2): 263–282.
Maraite, L. (2012) *André Cools au fer rouge*, Liège: Editions Luc Pire.
Nelen, H. (1997) 'Hades en Hemel: Een symbiotische relatie onder de loep', in H. de Doelder and A.B. Hoogenboom (eds) *Witteboordencriminaliteit in Nederland*, Deventer: Gouda Quint.
Pearce, F. (1976) *Crimes of the Powerful*, London: Pluto Press.
Sheptycki, J. (2010) 'Edwin Sutherland (1883–1950)', in K. Hayward, S. Maruna and J. Mooney (eds) *Fifty Key Thinkers in Criminology*, London: Routledge, pp. 63–71.
Suetens, M. and Walgrave, S. (1999) 'Leven en werk van de kabinetsleden: Wie zijn de mannen achter de minister en wat doen ze ?', *Res Publica*, 499–528.
Vanhecke, F. and De Man, F. (2007) *L'Etat PS, de maffia aan de macht*, Brussels: Uitgeverij Egmont.
Van Hooland, B. (2003) *Nieuw Publiek Management: Van Bestuurskunde tot Copernicus*, Gent: Academia Press.
Vansevenant, J. (1993) *Maffia aan de Maas: Over Luik, het Agusta-dossier en de moord op André Cools*, Antwerp: Standaard Uitgeverij.
Vansevenant, J. (1994) *De Agusta affaire: Kroniek van een omstreden helikopteraankoop*, Antwerp: Standaard Uitgeverij.
Verhofstadt, G. (1997) *De Belgische ziekte: Diagnose en remedies*, Antwerp: Hadewijch.

22

The Italian Eternit case

Rosalba Altopiedi

Introduction

> In the name of the Italian people, the Court of Turin [...] finds the defendants De Cartier De Marchienne Louis and Schmidheiny Stephan guilty as charged [...] and sentences each to 16 years' jail, as well as to the payment of all the costs of the court proceedings.

Those were the opening words of the ruling read out by the Turin Court on 13 February 2012. The trial was quite impressive in terms of sheer numbers: close to 3000 injured parties (2897 with over 1800 of them deceased), with 6392 *parties civiles* or plaintiffs.[1]

The decision handed down by the Turin Court on 13 February 2012 was a historic indictment of the behaviour of corporate executives. Former executives from the Swiss and Belgian Eternit Groups were found guilty of crimes that led to the asbestos-related deaths of thousands of Italian workers and citizens. The present chapter is part of the tradition of study and research which focuses on the criminal nature of decisions made within organizational contexts with the aim of maximizing profits (Friedrichs 2010; Kramer 1984; 1989; Pearce and Tombs 1990; 1997; 1998; Ruggiero 1998; Slapper and Tombs 1999; Tombs and Whyte 2001; 2007; 2010).

The Turin trial was the biggest and most complex court case involving asbestos disease ever heard in a criminal court in Europe. It represents a judicial turning point in the international jurisprudence cases against asbestos industrialists. It targets the strategic behaviour of multinational asbestos company leaders and their disinformation strategy about the health hazards of asbestos, not only in Italy but beyond. It is the first time that top multinational managers have been indicted for the consequences they have caused in a specific country.

This chapter focuses on the case study of the Italian Eternit factory by tracing the emergence, success, demise and crisis of the largest Italian asbestos plant, as well as by framing this case in the international context in order to better understand the full scale of strategic decisions taken in each country. The Casale Monferrato story is similar to that of other Eternit factory towns (Payerne or Niederurnen in Switzerland, Kapelle-op-den-Bos in Belgium, Aalborg in Denmark, Goor in the Netherlands, etc). It is indeed necessary to take into consideration the European dimension of the phenomenon in order to better understand how the business was managed and clearly identify the perpetrators of the environmental disaster and Eternit disease.

The case study focuses on Casale Monferrato from 2003 to date using a variety of data collection techniques (content analysis of documents; interviews with participants of various groups; participant observation; analysis of the court reports, etc). The qualitative approach allowed us to focus on social mechanisms, processes and relationships through which different groups (workers and workers' relatives, residents, scientists, politician, public officers, etc.) articulated their interests, including the formation of coalitions, as well as on the ways in which the problem emerged.

In analysing the rise and decline of the Casale Monferrato industry, we focus on a grassroots movement (health experts, trade unionists, associations of citizens, etc) that played a major role in fuelling the public debate on the asbestos industry and eventually led to the trial in Turin. The case is an example of direct participation, activism and resistance: the tentative action of a few to turn a series of private tragedies into a powerful collective voice able to vigorously demand 'truth and justice' for all those involved.

The international scenario: actors and strategies

The material known as asbestos cement was invented by the Austrian Hatschek who patented it in 1902 as 'Eternit' from the Latin *aeternitas*. This name was evidently chosen to highlight the strength and lasting properties of the material produced by mixing asbestos fibres and cement with water, a compound which may be used either as panelling or roofing or to produce pipes and other artefacts. A number of companies were established at the time using Hatschek's patent: the first Eternit plant was established in Belgium in 1905, while in the Italian case engineer Adolfo Mazza was the first to produce asbestos cement. Mazza was not only a shrewd businessman but also a pioneer in this regard when he invented and patented machines for the high pressure manufacturing of asbestos cement pipes in 1911, therefore contributing to the global spread of asbestos cement for drinking water systems. Mazza's patent was widely used among foreign manufacturers; Swiss, British and US companies purchased the licence to manufacture pipes.

Evidence of agreements between companies can be found in many documents (Castleman 2005; Tweedale 2000). For example, an agreement with a British company can be found in the UK Government Reports which mention contracts between the UK company Turner & Newall and Eternit Pietra Artificiale signed in November 1929. The latter granted all rights on the patent in the UK in exchange for hefty royalties and also agreed not to manufacture nor sell asbestos cement products in the UK so long as the patent was in force. The success of the Italian manufacturing machines for asbestos went even farther when during World War 2, Eternit Pietra Artificiale SA signed a royalty agreement with the US company Johns Manville which yielded 940,090.47 US dollars.[2]

Four big business families operated in continental Europe in the asbestos cement market: the Austrian Hatscheks, whose founder had patented the asbestos cement mix, the Swiss Schmidheinys, the Belgian Emsens/De Cartiers, and the French Cuveliers. These formed alliances, signed agreements, and developed common interests through cross shareholding and sitting on each other's boards. The early twentieth century was a key moment in the formation of the asbestos cement industry in Europe. Cooperation among producers was formally established and strengthened over time turning itself into a *cartel*. The establishment of formal as well as of personal ties among these European industrialists influenced the trajectory of Italy's asbestos cement.

In 1929 Ernst Schmidheiny, the owner of Eternit Switzerland, and the British Turner & Newall created a new company for technical cooperation among asbestos cement producers in Europe, SAIAC SA (Societé Associé d'Industries Amiantecimint).[3] The company was the formalization of existing agreements and became the basis for alliances destined to last over time.

The Eternit system in Europe

The patent for the production of asbestos cement artefacts spread throughout Europe. As mentioned, the Belgians headed by the Emsens family were first to license the Hatschek patent. In 1905 they started production at Kapelle-op-den-Bos, at a plant which remained operative until the end of the 1990s.[4] Soon other Eternit plants sprang up throughout the continent. The Swiss group was operational in Switzerland where they owned two large plants (in Niederurnen and in Payerne), while the Cuveliers located in France where they owned various factories (in Thiant, Prouvy, Vitry-en-Charollais, Vernouillet, Caronte, Saint-Grégoire and Terssac).

The amazing success of the asbestos cement production created an economic empire which branched out throughout Europe and many other countries of the world. However it also exposed producers to various 'risks': the competition in markets outside Europe, the technological difficulties linked to production in diverse climatic conditions, the need to guarantee a supply of raw material and, above all, the growing body of medical knowledge about the lethality of asbestos. Market sharing and agreements among several producers is confirmed by an important document listed in the Turin trial as 'the Boston Consulting Group'.[5] The document, located in the Johns Manville archives, shows that the production of asbestos and asbestos cement was monopolized by a small number of actors who occupied the international scene. This monopoly enabled these companies to decide not only upon the industrial and commercial policies but also the strategies for concealing information about health risks.

'A miniature League of Nations': the international asbestos cartel

There are several trial records which make it possible to retrace the agreements among and between the asbestos cement industries. In 1929 when Turner & Newall purchased Bell's United Asbestos Company Ltd, Turner & Newall's board of directors informed shareholders of the role of SAIAC SA. This is what they wrote in their financial report of 30 September 1929:

> We have been able to arrange with the principal manufactures of the European countries an International Cartel.

The first aim of the cartel is quite clear: guaranteeing available asbestos supplies at a fixed price.[6] But that is not all; the following were also included: the exchange of technical information; the establishment of a research institute in Switzerland, whose results were to be available to all producers; the establishment of new plants in neutral countries; the coordination of exports, standardization of quality and the reduction of product range; mutual help in guaranteeing supplies. The cartel members wrote about the alliance of the European asbestos cement industry as a 'miniature League of Nations [...] Our object is to give better service and better value to the consuming public, for we recognise that only by so doing can we justify our activities and retain public confidence'.[7]

The picture is very clear: the cartel members were a group of distinct but colluding industrialists who saw the planet as a global market to be shared and ruled.

However, the cartel did not only limit competition and guarantee a monopoly of raw materials: one of their main concerns was to manage the impact of the scientific research on the dangers of asbestos in order to control information on the harmful effects it had on health.

Misrepresenting health risks

By the mid-1950s, as information on the dangers of asbestos started circulating, including among industrialists, gaining control over it became a priority for industry. It is a complex story marked by a number of specific episodes that are detailed in the Turin verdict. They are linked by an underlying theme: how to manage the impact of scientific knowledge by distorting information and how to limit the circulation of such knowledge within the public domain. In practice this strategy took on different forms of implementation: from minimizing risks to actually hiding important information.

We found an illustration of this mechanism in the minutes of French Senate of 20 October 2005. The document shows that already in 1943 a US Turner & Newall subsidiary and other US asbestos companies asked a US laboratory to carry out an experimental study on asbestos-related pathologies. Results were disconcerting: 80 per cent of the mice being tested developed lung cancer in under three years. The circulation of such results could have had a serious impact, which is why industry decided not to disclose them in the report published in 1951. The facts became public in the 1990s when the Chase Manhattan Bank in New York discovered its new world headquarters were riddled with the asbestos supplied by the British company. The bank took Turner & Newall to court suing the company for 180 million dollars. During pre-trial investigation, the Chase Manhattan Bank copied a large portion of Turner & Newall's archive and under American law was able to put the records in the public domain. It is only then that results became public (Tweedale 2000).

Another example is found in an episode in 1954 in which Dr Knox, Turner & Newall's company doctor, commissioned Dr Doll to do an epidemiological mortality study on the effects of asbestos on factory workers. When informed of the conclusions of the study, Knox and a Turner & Newall executive asked Doll not to publish the results. Doll refused to conceal the data and the following year results were published in *The British Journal of Industrial Medicine* (Doll 1955).[8]

These were some of the building blocks that made it possible to reconstruct the criminal design of the asbestos industry. However, in spite of their attempt to conceal scientific evidence, insistent new concerns on the dangers of asbestos were echoed at an international conference held in Johannesburg in 1959. It was a symposium of pneumoconiosis during which a young pathologist named J.C. Wagner gave a paper. The subject was a rare form of cancer called mesothelioma, which was blighting asbestos mining communities in the Northern Cape Province of South Africa. Wagner told a distinguished audience that there might be a serious hazard facing asbestos miners and communities in the area.[9] This was an extremely important statement: not only was mesothelioma being shown to affect the miners, but the victims also included people who merely lived close to contaminating sites (Wagner et al. 1960: 260–265).

Soon after that, in 1964, an international conference was held by the New York Academy of Sciences, organized by Irving Selikoff,[10] an American doctor. In the course of the symposium several studies on mesothelioma in industrialized countries were presented. As Carnevale usefully pointed out:

> 1964 [...] must be considered the anno mirabilis of asbestos [...] when key information on the far reaching and severe effects of asbestos became known to the mainstream scientific community [...] The knowledge available at the time which was officially acknowledged at the famous 1964 New York Conference and then disseminated in 1965 with the publication of the proceedings, were such that they identified the nature and features of mesothelioma beyond doubt.
>
> *(Carnevale 2007: 66)*

The circulation of information on the dangers of asbestos caused problems to industry which reacted by strengthening its international links and fine-tuning strategies. In 1971 the First International Conference of Asbestos Information Bodies was held in London. As the Public Prosecutor mentioned in his final speech at the Turin Court of First Instance, this was a turning point as industries conceived a series of practical actions to defend asbestos and their profits.

There were two kinds of strategy: the proactive actions aiming at highlighting the qualities and advantages of asbestos, and the defensive ones to 'correct' the information being circulated on the relationship between asbestos and health. The latter were summarized by the Turner & Newall representative in the closing speech of the Conference: 'Putting the health situation into perspective wherever it is misrepresented'. However, it was not enough to just react to public criticism and regulatory measures; one had to be ready to act and, in fact, pre-empt 'external' attacks. Once again it was the Turner & Newall representative who called on his colleagues to make immediate preparations for the coming confrontations:

> The maxim 'let sleeping dogs lie' has a good deal in its favour when the time is slow and public and press interest is light. But sleeping dogs wake up suddenly and use their voices and their teeth. And when they are awake they will not sleep again! You must prepare in advance.[11]

Their policy was quite clear: one had to be ready and try to influence regulations and legislation to defend the interests of the industry if governments were going to start introducing more restrictive laws. The global defence of the industry became operational with the establishment of the Asbestos International Association (AIA), an association of all the producers, organized according to tasks and expertise in relation to the goals of the organization.

The analysis of many records disclosed during the trial makes it possible for us to outline the goals of the association.[12] The association had two main aims:

1 concealing health risks, recruiting experts if necessary, and
2 lobbying governments to avoid asbestos being banned or severely regulated.

The attempt to delay the banning of crocidolite (the most dangerous kind of asbestos) was a case in point. Industry used it in pressurized asbestos-cement pipes. The producers worried about a European ban and as a consequence started to influence the future EEC Directive on asbestos. Several documents were made public in the course of the trial disclosing the attempts of industry to gain accreditation with the MEPs and influence the content of the future Directive. The strategy is laid out in a note sent to the AIA members in August 1977:

> It would seem to me that we should press for two main points. First we should make clear that absolute prohibition of crocidolite asbestos would create very considerable problems for manufacturers of A/C pressure pipes, for which the greater part of crocidolite used is intended. Secondly, we should point out the impracticability of restricting the use of asbestos of any kind to the two special and untypical cases which are quoted in the latest draft.[13]

Their attempt failed when the *Guardian* reported on 19 December 1977 that the European Parliament had asked for the use of asbestos to be regulated and had recommended asbestos should be banned where there were safe replacements. Furthermore it recommended that crocidolite should be banned as should the spraying of asbestos.

However, totally discontinuing the use of the fibre at that stage would have been too expensive, leaving market shares to other competitors. Faced with the prospects of major economic losses, companies looked for a way out and came up with the 'controlled-use' approach. The strategy was very simple: asbestos could be used safely if all the necessary precautions were in place. However, the fallacy of the 'controlled-use' approach is proven by several studies that demonstrate that workers exposed to chrysotile fibres (the less dangerous asbestos) also have an increased risk of lung cancer and mesothelioma (LaDou et al. 2010). Furthermore, making plants safe, if it could be done, was a very expensive procedure. As one of the two defendants of the Turin trial, when speaking to his management in 1976, put it, there should be 'maximum protection at minimum cost'.[14] Brinkmanship can be dangerous and the outcome is not always clear-cut especially because in the late 1970s information on the dangers of asbestos was starting to seep out of the 'secret rooms', albeit piecemeal. The trade union movement was experiencing a season of struggles and demands, asking for better working conditions in the workshops, the environmental movement was on the rise, and these conditions would lead many countries to discontinue the use of asbestos, some sooner and some later.

It was a difficult balance which in Italy led to the decision to let the industries go into receivership or bankruptcy, leaving death and illness in their wake, as well as a disastrous environmental situation in the areas close to the plants.

The Italian Eternit's factories

The largest asbestos cement plant in Italy was in Casale Monferrato, a town not far from the so-called *industrial triangle* Genoa–Turin–Milan. The plant opened in March 1907 and production did not even stop during the two world wars. In 1952 the representatives of the largest European asbestos cement groups joined the board, thus putting an end to Mazza's 'family company' management. This was a major shift which changed the future of Eternit in Italy. The importance of this shift is described in the verdict of the Turin trial which retraces in detail how the foreign groups alternated in managing the company.[15] From the time when the company was taken over by the foreign groups it was managed according to the previously mentioned international lines.

In the meantime, Eternit had grown in Italy: in 1939 it purchased the Bagnoli plant (a district of Naples), in 1953 the Saca plant in Cavagnolo (near Turin) and lastly, again in 1953, the Syracuse plant in Sicily. The Rubiera plant, then known as ICAR, was purchased in 1969 directly by the Swiss group that then sold it to Eternit in 1980.

For over 60 years Eternit was Casale Monferrato's largest employer: in the years of the economic boom it employed more than 2000 and between 1906 and 1980 it employed just under 5000 people.

The first crisis was felt in the 1970s: not just the recession, but the shrinking of the asbestos cement market and a cash crisis due to the banks' cutting down on loans. In 1972 the Mazza heirs sold their shares to the Belgian and Swiss groups which became controlling shareholders.

In the late 1970s the company experienced a deeper crisis: strong domestic competition, a drop in exports, the building industry crisis and, last but not least, growing concerns about the dangers of asbestos, which led to a drop in sales. The situation was addressed using drastic measures, such as a downsizing of the workforce resorting to the special Government Redundancy Fund to rationalize production and use up excess stock.

On 16 December 1980, Eternit SpA became a holding and each plant became a separate company 100 per cent owned by Swiss Eternit. The only reason for this change was tax purposes as in fact the management remained unchanged. In spite of the company reorganization due to stagnation in the residential and industrial construction industry and overcapacity in the cement fibre market, on 23 December 1984 Eternit applied to go into receivership which the Genoa Court granted. Two years later, on 4 June 1986, the Genoa Court declared the company bankrupt.

The Turin trial records and the verdict show that the decision to 'let the company go bankrupt' was made in a meeting in Zurich in 1983.[16] The decision was not merely due to the crisis in the asbestos cement market, but was also determined by the Swiss group's decision not to invest in alternative products (that is to say using other fibres to replace asbestos) as it had been doing in other countries such as Germany and Switzerland around the same time. The choice was determined by the conditions of the Italian market, which had many small producers, and to the impossibility of finding an agreement among them.[17]

At that time the rumours about the disastrous effects of exposure to asbestos became stronger and stronger. Witnesses in court spoke about growing concerns as the death notices became increasingly frequent at the factory gates: young people, work mates. Rumours inevitably concerned the top management of the company who were aware of the risks of being 'dragged' to court by those who thought they had been affected.[18] Bankruptcy seemed to be the best option so as to transfer all costs, decontamination included, to the receivers.

The criminalization of the asbestos issue in Italy

The late 1970s and the early 1980s were key moments in the history of the Casale Monferrato factory. At that time, plant workers started developing an opposition fighting the company's lack of health and safety measures and disregard for working conditions. As mentioned, the company was well aware of the risks of working with asbestos. So much so that the wages of those handling raw materials, one of the most risky tasks, had an additional item known as 'danger money', consistent with the idea that health impairment can be compensated by cash.

That was also the time when the risk of environmental asbestos became public; in fact independent researchers were starting to publish and disseminate the results of the first studies on asbestos-related deaths and illnesses. There were not detailed epidemiological studies at this stage, but evidence was sufficient to worry the public and local authorities. In the early 1980s a study carried out at the Casale Monferrato Hospital was published (Capra Marzani et al. 1984): in the 1973–1982 period, 61 mesothelioma cases were diagnosed, only 30 per cent of them Eternit workers, the others were assumed to be related exclusively to environmental exposure. The implications were clear: asbestos was not only a risk for workers, but for the community at large, as in Casale people breathed in a significant number of fibres.

In the scientific community a large body of literature documented a close correlation between exposure to asbestos, even at low levels, and the occurrence of disease. Evidence was substantiated by the report written by two epidemiologists of Turin University: the population of Casale had an abnormal number of lung and pleural cancer deaths. The likelihood of dying of lung and pleural diseases was 6 to 21 times higher than the regional average.

A year after the company filed for bankruptcy the image of an epidemic of deaths became clearer and shook public opinion, the scientific community and the public authorities. In December 1987 Riccardo Coppo, the then mayor of Casale, issued an order, which has since become very well known, banning any form of asbestos throughout the town. Five years later, in compliance with Law 257/1992 the ban was extended to the whole country.

In the meantime the Casale Magistrate's Court (*Pretura di Casale*) began a penal investigation for the deaths and diseases caused by the asbestos exposure at the local Eternit factory. Pre-trial investigations lasted from 1985 to 1990 and ended with the prosecution committing 15 Italian managers to trial. They were accused of multiple manslaughter and bodily harm. On 18 June

1999, eight years after the beginning of the inquiry, the court found four of the 15 defendants guilty and inflicted sentences which ranged from 1 year to three years and four months. The chair of boards and the CEO received the harshest sentences. The Appeal Court in Turin later reduced the sentences inflicted in the Court of First Instance to the chair and the CEO, and the other two managers were acquitted. In other words, the first trial ended with some Italian managers of the group being found guilty.

It took more than ten years before another penal investigation would focus on the top level of the multinational company. In 2004, following a medical report on an Italian citizen who had worked in the Niederurnen Eternit plant in Switzerland, Dr Guariniello, a Turin prosecutor, deemed that the various plants of the Eternit group were in the same framework.

Following a painstakingly long and complex inquiry,[19] the prosecutors in charge of the investigation gathered a substantial amount of evidence that enabled them to identify the links between the Italian and the multinational Eternit which can be summarized as follows: strategies were decided at a central level, and the Italian management had limited authority. The indictment and the framework were validated by the verdict of the Appeal Court which sentenced owner-executive Stephan Schmidheiny to 18 years' imprisonment and to the payment of compensation to plaintiffs, sentencing him for wilful negligence of health and safety measures and wilful disaster.

The Turin trial has often been described as a trial of 'historical importance': for the first time the top tier of a company had been found guilty of the consequences of their criminal behaviour. The defendants' lawyers described as: 'un certo modo di fare industria'. We can translate it as 'one way of industrialists working' or in other words 'ordinary business practices'. This is an inappropriate definition, although the history of industry forcefully entered in the court room showed that, in the asbestos industry at least, Eternit's practices fit a consistent framework of criminal behaviour.

Facts and figures at the trial were quite overwhelming: 2857 aggrieved or injured parties, 1800 of them deceased; and over 6300 *partie civiles* or plaintiffs. Over 60 witnesses and experts for the defendants, plaintiffs and prosecution were heard. When the verdict was read out, there were hundreds of people coming from all over Italy, victims' associations from France, Belgium, Holland, Switzerland, Brazil and the United States.

The national and international media coverage was uninterrupted: not only newspapers and television, but also web blogs and social groups followed the trial throughout.[20] This unprecedented interest in corporate crime mirrored the strong mobilization around the matter. Usually this type of crime doesn't arouse social alarm; it is dealt with as an adverse result of industrial policies. In fact crimes committed by corporations in pursuit of their goals are relatively invisible despite devastating physical, psychological and social effects (Tombs and Whyte 2007).

The rise of the public debate on the Eternit case

The public debate on the Eternit case went hand in hand with the growing public awareness of the dangers of asbestos. The harmfulness of asbestos was long denied, hidden and shrouded by the companies trying to defend their market shares and profits.

However, there came a time when the knowledge of the danger it caused spilled out of the secret boardrooms and spread first among the workers and then into the community at large.

In Casale the history of the mobilization and involvement went through three main stages:

1 *Instrumental milestone*: the 1960s and early 1970s, when bad working conditions were used as an argument to get better pay.[21] The conflict was instrumental and as such negotiable.

2 *Alliance milestone*: the 1970s and early 1980, when the workers and the trade unions began weaving alliances in the local context with doctors, political representatives and so on, with a view to developing a common action and improve working conditions. This phase coincides with the rumours on the increasing number of deaths in the factory, particularly among the workers most exposed to the deadly fibres. At this stage the trade unions which had not yet formed a united front failed to convince the press and public authorities. A major prejudice informed this behaviour: that it was 'culturally acceptable' that workers should fall ill and die through their work, a sort of price to pay for progress in society.
3 *Collective milestone*: the dissemination of the epidemiological results highlighted a statistically significant increase in the number of deaths among members of the community who had never worked in the factory; at this stage the local press and public authorities started listening to the workers' movement.

The alliance between the movement and some members of the scientific community played a key role. The former were doctors from the Casale Hospital and the researchers from the Department of Epidemiology of the University of Turin who took a very firm stand in favour of a complete ban of asbestos.[22]

The turning point in the mobilization history is represented by the Eternit bankruptcy. In 1988, two years after the factory closure, AFLED (Associazione Familiari Lavoratori Eternit Deceduti, the Association of the family members of deceased Eternit workers) was founded. The association was promoted by the local General Confederation of Labour (CGIL) Union branch and specifically by the people who had coordinated the struggles over the years and the demands within the factory. The aim was to become a point of reference for anyone wishing to stand as a plaintiff in the criminal case started by the Casale Courts. As we will see, the criminal case was an opportunity to develop an unusual kind of mobilization against corporate crime.

A year after the AFLED had been created, in March 1989 another association (AEA, Associazione Esposti Amianto) was established thanks to Italo Busto's relations: his brother had died of mesothelioma without ever having worked at Eternit. Unlike AFLED, this association was established by members of the community who had become aware of asbestos-related issues, and right from the beginning it acted as a 'pressure' group on a national and local level with the aim of getting a law to ban asbestos as soon as possible.

The 1989 campaign 'Asbestos kills, I want to live' was one of the first initiatives of the actions the unions and associations organized. The steering committee included the local Lega Ambiente (an environmentalist group), IAC (Italian Alpine Club) and WWF (World Wildlife Fund) chapters. The petition was addressed to the mayor of Casale, the president of the health district, the president of the region Piedmont, the ministers of health, of the environment, of civil protection and industry: it demanded measures that could no longer be delayed such as law banning asbestos, decontamination in the area of Casale, and a strong information campaign to reduce dust-related pollution in the town. The campaign was a great success and between January and April 1989 14,153 people signed it. In February of the same year the CGIL Union organized a big conference in Casale, called 'No all'amianto' (No to asbestos), attended by scientific experts and politicians.

From this moment onwards the demands from the trade union and citizens are knit together into one voice.

At last, in March 1992 asbestos was finally banned in Italy. In the minutes of the parliamentary committees in charge of debating the asbestos issue, the number of bills from Casale was surprisingly high. Particular reference is made to the role of the association aimed at safeguarding and compensation for the damage to the workers and the community.[23]

Currently the association has a membership of over 3000 but it has not only increased in numbers: it is more strongly rooted in the community and it is more visible on a national and international level. The Committee for the Asbestos Dispute (Comitato Vertenza Amianto) which coordinated the various associations, regularly attended international conferences on asbestos, and sent delegations to public initiatives in support of other local associations.

At the local level, the association has become the voice of the whole community, which in turn is now the main player in putting forward demands, bearing the weight of the past and the drive towards change. The growing involvement of young people is another sign of a new phase in the life of the movement: the means to build consensus have also changed, increasingly using the web to inform, and for the 'call to arms'. The ability of the association to network different actors and interests and its public role is acknowledged in the prosecutor's closing speech at the Turin Trial: 'The first trial began thanks to the local trade union, but even more so thanks to the people of Casale, to the men and women affected by a disaster which is still unfolding in their town: they set up associations and demanded justice. In fact the truth is that success in these trials, included this one, has been achieved thanks to the men and women of Casale'.

The grass roots movements and the social construction of victimization

The focus on the victims 'that cannot be seen' is the crucial issue for radical and critical victimology (Croall 2001a; 2001b; 2004; 2007; 2009; Dignan 2005; Whyte 2007). The key questions are 'who has the power to apply the label of victims' and 'what factors are significant in determining whether or not to bestow it'? What is the role of the cultural and economic context? In the case of corporate crime, but also in environmental crime in general, 'the victim status cannot be taken for granted, the conception of the victim and of victimization are optional, discretionary and not innately given' (Whyte 2007: 447). Dealing with such issues is a crucial theoretical challenge and has immediate and obvious criminological relevance, relating to the ways in which oppositional values and interests are presented and represented by different groups of actors involved (state regulators, scientists, industries, communities, workers, general public, etc.) (Brown et al. 2012). Becoming a victim is a social process that starts with a criminal offence but also requires a cognitive decision by the person(s) against whom it is directed to see themselves as, and assume the status of, victims as part of their strategy for coping with it (Dignan 2005: 13–40).

What cognitive strategies did the people involved in this story employ that help them to cope with the damages and the injuries? What was the association's role in mobilizing and involving victims and their families?

In accordance to Vidoni (2000; 2004), I use a model aimed at understanding the causes leading to criminal behaviour (Lemert 1951) in order to have a better understanding of the dynamics of the victimization experience and the impact of such experience on the individual victim(s). The key steps of a 'victimization' career can be outlined as a series of successive stages: from processing the damage, identifying it as a non-accidental event, then the identification of causes, and lastly the recognition of responsibility towards one's self, to finally ascribe culpability to the authors of the crime.

To understand the learning process of the victims it is necessary to focus on two separate moments: a) the first phase is when the social actors who suffered the damage do not display any social or public reaction, do not develop a moral career, nor do they redefine themselves and their identities. This is followed by a second phase b) during which social actors undertake a moral 'career' or follow a moral path redefining their identities, retracing the reasons underlying what happened and making sense of events.

Clearly, just as primary deviance does not lead to a symbolic reorganization of the self and of one's social role, likewise primary victimization only marginally impinges on an individual's psyche. Making sense, that is finding a meaning in what happened, requires rethinking on a personal level and does not affect a person's social identity. On the other hand, secondary victimization, as happens in secondary deviance, implies changing attitude towards one's self and one's social roles, reorganizing one's identity around the events which led to victimization.[24]

What mechanisms lead to the development of a victim's identity? Those underlying role acquisition, the same ones governing specialization and rational orientation present in all forms of social learning.

The acquisition of a role as a victim takes place through collective experiences of direct participation and new citizenry, by establishing relations with others who have comparable experiences (damage). Collective moments make past experience more meaningful and channel one's reaction towards future prospects of action.

In this process, advocates for community members and the community members themselves who have become victims and label themselves as victims can voice their concerns, share their stories. In doing so, they contribute to defining the situation in a different way and enhance democratic participation in that process.

In the case being considered, the association is the point of reference for all the people involved for different reasons, and it supplies the material and cultural bases to process the harm and emancipate one's self from it. The relational context initially consists of a small group of people and is marked by personal relations: this phase plays a key role in orienting the social actors, from the first level victimization (*let's try and forget everything as soon as possible*) to the second level (*let us share our experience*). In this second phase, events are acknowledged as new and abnormal, as criminal behaviour. Anger can also be channelled through it. Channelling of motivations and impulses are a function of the positive or negative (*favourable or unfavourable*) reaction to the damage. Witnesses refer to initial difficulties (*we have been advised more than once to let it go, since we have already paid the price*) which were overcome at a later time thanks to the recognition of the process they had been through. Opposite reactions to 'being there personally' or 'participating' could incline people to withdraw into a totally private sphere: the association used these experiences as key grounds for the learning process of the victims about their role.

The analysis of the reports highlights common approaches: the association is only partly a means to receive material compensation for the damage.. Its hallmark is the assertion of a more transcendent principle, the recognition of an injustice, so that tragedies such as the ones they experienced should never happen again.

The identification of the illegal, unjust, criminal nature of what happened is at the centre of the process to acquire new knowledge, that is to say to develop a different awareness of what was considered normal and now is defined as oppressive. The association is where the trauma acquires a new meaning and is channelled into a vaster struggle. As Whyte pointed out 'the organizations that represent the victims [...] are the key factor in forcing the issue of corporate killing onto the political agenda' (Whyte 2007: 459).

Members of the community become active citizens through the learning process as they acquire the role of victims, and they transform their private (painful) experience into public participation. The association has a double identity (Turnaturi 1991: 86): that of a primary and of a secondary group. It has the identity of a primary group in that it recreates solidarity, close ties among its members and a continuing shared practical experience; life stories are the foundations of a collective identity, and also a resource for the group as a whole. As a secondary group, the association engages with the outside world: organizing actions with the rest of society, behaving as we saw as a pressure group that wants to interface with the establishment, with the representatives of the state. This double nature is what makes these movements so modern and so original: they go beyond the emotional attachment of the primary group and beyond the abstract nature of secondary groups.

Conclusions

The case described in this chapter has important implications related to a number of criminological issues, and particularly how the interests of communities affected by industrial pollution (which caused an extensive toll of deaths and illness) became organically involved in the public sphere and incorporated in legal and policy decisions.

In this analysis, we focus on the role of a victims' group and its connections to local doctors and scientists for the criminalization of the Eternit case. In particular, the alliance between the activists and the scientists was an essential tool of the fight against asbestos, not only in this case but also in general (McCulloch and Tweedale 2008). The asbestos industry long succeeded in imposing a 'scientific' representation of asbestos as an essential material with acceptable and manageable hazards (this strategy is called the 'controlled use' of asbestos). The workers, the victims and their families alone did not have the tools and the capacity to dispute industry or government officials about the science. Through the 'scientization' (Morello-Frosch et al., in Brown et al. 2012) of the protest, activists have succeeded in redefining the situation, leading to the recognition of warnings withheld and harmful acts committed as crimes against individuals and their community.

How was the criminal nature of the Eternit executives and owners revealed? The victims played a key role. The social construction of their victimization generated a mirror that led to a process of criminalization. Looking at it from a theoretical point of view represents a very interesting challenge as it makes it possible to address victimization as a process, by following the path laid out by a constructionist perspective on the acquisition of a deviant identity: it can be thought of as a *moral career* finalized to the redefinition of one's social identity.

The learning process of the victim's role turned into a new type of active citizenry thus contributing to an innovative outcome to the situation. There are clear connections between civil society and the legal system and among the various actors. In the case considered, the behaviour of those who committed the crime underwent a process of social construction, that is effective recognition of criminality which led to a verdict unique (*an unicum*) among corporate crime cases. Thanks to the collective actors (be they associations of relatives, environmental groups, or workers' associations) one can embark on those processes which lead to redefining the situation and can also lead to taking or attributing responsibility for the crimes. Reference to the taking on of responsibility has a definite meaning here as the victims enter the scene as the protagonists building on their own victimization process. However, in the process there are critical moments that can hinder a favourable outcome. There may be cultural or structural obstacles, which develop with variable intensity or range according to the nature of the criminal acts and the personal characteristics of the person(s) who performed such deeds, such as wealth, social standing and so on. The path can be further complicated by the invisibility of the type of crimes being considered in the present chapter: invisibility which is due to the lack of direct relationship between the victim and the perpetrator, where the time elapsing between the actions and their damaging consequences may be decades. One could try to remedy the above by stressing the structural and organizational features of victimization (Pearce and Tombs 1998). The critical points in the process can be traced back to technical and ideological factors. The former include methodological difficulties, as many forms of corporate crime victimizations are not easily assessed especially as victims are often unaware of the cause of the harm (as is the case of harm to consumers, environmental pollution and so on). Or, if they are aware, they are unable to trace responsibility back to the responsible party with adequate evaluation of the available evidence. Other difficulties are due to the fact that these crimes are not generally construed as such. Some argue that workers 'choose' to work in risky jobs (being careful to give only examples where the worker knows about the risks) and that consumers 'choose' to purchase unsafe goods. Ideological reasons are very powerful explanations in (de)constructing the victimization of this type of crime. The relative lack of research on the victimization of these types of crime leads to generalized and unproven assumptions. Some juxtapose victimization following conventional crime (where there is a personal relation between the victim and the perpetrator) to corporate crime victimization (which is impersonal and indirect both in terms of the harmful behaviour and of its consequences). The case analysed in the present essay made it possible to focus on the role of the local mobilization as a mechanism underlying the recognition of the criminal nature of corporate crimes, thus contributing to criminal prosecution and conviction of those in charge.

The identification of the social mechanisms that favoured the mobilization and the surfacing of demands for justice from this specific point of view, through research and analysis, could be a useful tool to raise awareness not just among the victims (be they potential or actual victims) but also in the community as a whole.

Notes

1 On 3 June 2013 the Appeal Court in Turin not only upheld the conviction against Stephan Schmidheiny but increased the prison sentence handed out to the Swiss billionaire from 16 to 18 years. In the meantime, on 21 May 2013, the other defendant, 91-year-old Louis de Cartier de Marchienne died. With his death, the criminal case against him and Etex, the company of which he was owner, was dismissed.

2 The information is to be found in the book of the proceedings of Eternit Board Meetings, specifically the minutes of the 22 February 1949 meeting.

3 The Swiss and the British, Austrian, Spanish, French, Belgian, German, Czech, Dutch, Hungarian and Italian asbestos cement producers also joined. Engineer Mazza, the founder of Italy's Eternit, became the chairman in 1950.

4 The Belgian Emsens and the Swiss Schmidheiny Groups led the European Eternit factories during the 20th century. They shared the international market of asbestos cement artefacts also outside Europe. While the Swiss group progressively ceased asbestos production in the mid 1980s, the Belgians used the deadly fibre until the very last.

5 These are notes referred to a discussion about asbestos supply held on 13 August 1971 in Switzerland at Max Schmidheiny's villa.

6 Asbestos is a constituent of some rocks and soils existing in several locations throughout the world. The term 'asbestos' refers to naturally occurring silicate minerals with long, thin fibrous crystals that can be released by abrasion and other processes in the asbestos mines.

Except for Italy and Corsica there are no major mines in Western Europe. The largest producers were in Russia, Southern Africa and Canada. The primary goal was a constant flow of asbestos supplies at a fixed price.

7 Turner & Newall, Report and Balance Sheet, 30 September 1929, p. 9.

8 Doll's study is considered a milestone in identifying the causal link between exposure to asbestos and the development of cancer.

9 The paper, which was immediately published in *The British Journal of Industrial Medicine*, followed earlier case reports in establishing the link between asbestos and mesothelioma, the most lethal of the asbestos-related diseases, in over 30 cases.

10 Selikoff was the director of the environmental and occupational health at Mount Sinai Hospital in New York. He is considered the leading figure in the battle against the dangers of asbestos from the 1960s until his death in 1992.

11 Proceedings of the International Conference of Asbestos Information Bodies, London, 24 and 25 November 1971.

12 The meetings were held at AIA head office in London. The minutes disclosed relate to the period 1977–1980.

13 In the minutes of the executive committee meeting held on 2 August 1977 can be read that the AIA's general director informed the members of the executive committee of the need to lobby in order that a ban on asbestos be restricted to crocidolite and workings spray.

14 Conference held by Stephan Schmidheiny in Neuss on 28–30 June 1976. The document which was used in the Turin trial was a cornerstone of the prosecution's argument as it made clear that the company management was aware of the danger of asbestos, the number of deaths and that they knowingly decided to continue using it.

15 Initially between 1952 and 1972 the Belgian group was the controlling shareholder; from 1972 until the bankruptcy in 1986, the Swiss group led the Italian plants.

16 This is in one of the trial documents from the so-called Bellodi Files, thus called because of the name of the owner of the PR company which Stephan Schmidheiny had employed to 'manage his image'. In the course of the preliminary investigations in December 2005, following a search of the company offices, a large number of digital and paper documents were seized, reflecting 20 years' work. It was a really surprising discovery which illustrated the defendant's strategies to conceal facts and shun responsibility and liability.

17 As Leo Mittelholzer, the last Eternit Inc. CEO said in the course of his deposition on 5 July 2010 at the Turin trial, the large number of small producers in Italy made it impossible to reach an overall agreement on how and when asbestos fibres should be replaced by other more expensive alternative fibres. Because no agreement had been reached, anyone continuing to use asbestos fibres would have had a competitive advantage.

18 A few years earlier, in 1982, the US giant Johns Manville had gone into receivership. At the time this was widely discussed, as it was the single largest company to apply and have it granted. The reason they gave was the large number of asbestos-related compensation cases (16,500). The Eternit group owned shares in Johns Manville and was therefore well aware of the situation, fearing they might also incur the same troubles.

19 The prosecutors' report for the trial is 230,000 pages long and contains over 5000 documents.

20 The two most updated ones are the 'Processo Eternit' page on Facebook and the 'Asbestos in the Dock' blog.

21 As mentioned in the previous paragraph the workers in the raw material workshop, the area where the sacks of asbestos were opened and dumped into mixing tanks, which was considered to have the most dangerous working conditions received additional payment, a sort of compensation, for the greater risk.

22 An example is the appeal by the doctors in Casale published in the local press called 'All the doctors say "No to the use of asbestos fibres"' (*Tutti i medici ribadiscono 'No all'uso della fibra di amianto'*), *Il Monferrato*, 24 April 1987, p. 5.

23 Documents on the various bills to ban asbestos can be accessed on the House of Deputies' website under 10th Parliament (*Camera dei Deputati, X legislatura, Commissioni riunite Attività produttive (X) e Affari sociali (XII))*, 23 January, 15 May, 14 and 21 November and 18 December 1991.

24 As outlined by Dignan 'victimization is a highly complex process encompassing a number of possible elements. The "primary victimization" comprises whatever interaction may have taken place between offender and "victim" during the commission of the offence, plus any after effects arising from this interaction or from the offence itself. The second element encompasses "the victim's" reaction to the offence, including any change in self-perception that may result from it, plus any formal response that the victim(s) may choose to make to it. The third element consists of any further interactions that may take place between "the victim" and others, including the various criminal justice agencies with whom s/he may come into contact as a result of this response' (2005: 23).

References

Brown, P., Morello-Frosch, R., Zavestoski, S. and The Contested Illness Research Group (eds) (2012) *Contested Illnesses: Citizens, Science and Health Social Movements*, Berkeley: University of California Press.

Capra Marzani, M., Piccolini, E. and Pavesi, M. (1984) 'Il mesotelioma maligno della pleura nell'area di Casale nel decennio 1973–1982', *Gazzettino Medico Italiano*, p. 143.

Carnevale, F. (2007) 'Amianto: Una tragedia di lunga durata. Argomenti utili per una ricostruzione storica dei fatti più rilevanti', *Epidemiologia e Prevenzione*, 31: 53–74.

Castleman, B. (2005) *Asbestos: Medical and Legal Aspects*, 5th edn, New York: Wolters Kluwer Law & Business.
Croall, H. (2001a) *The Victim of White Collar Crime*, Stockholm: The National Council for Crime Prevention.
Croall, H. (2001b) *Understanding White Collar Crime*, Buckingham: Open University Press.
Croall, H. (2004) *Cheated and Poisoned: Exposing the Victims of Economic Crime, Report for Swedish Council of Crime Prevention* (BRA), Stockholm: Swedish Council for Crime Prevention.
Croall, H. (2007) 'Victims of white collar and corporate crime', in P. Davies, P. Francis and C. Greer (eds) *Victims, Crime and Society*, London: Sage, pp. 78–109.
Croall, H. (2009) 'White collar crime, consumers and victimization', *Crime, Law and Social Change*, 51: 127–146.
Dignan J. (2005) *Understanding Victims and Restorative Justice*, Maidenhead: Open University Press.
Doll, R. (1955) 'Mortality from lung cancer in asbestos workers', *British Journal Independent Medicine*, 12: 81–86.
Friedrichs, D.O. (2010) *Trusted Criminals: White Collar Crime in Contemporary Society*, 4th edn, Belmont: Wadsworth Cengage Learning.
Kramer, R.C. (1984) 'Corporate criminality: The development of an idea', in E. Hochstedler (ed.) *Corporations as Criminals*, Beverly Hills, CA: Sage, pp. 13–38.
Kramer, R.C. (1989) 'Criminologists and the social movement against corporate crime', *Social Justice*, 16(2): 146–164.
LaDou, J., Castleman, B., Frank, A., Gochfeld, M., Greenberg, M., Huff, J., Kant, J.T., Landrigan, P.J., Lemen, R., Myers, J., Soffritti, M., Soskolne, C.L., Takahashi, K., Teitelbaum, D., Terracini, B. and Watterson, A. (2010) 'The case for a global ban on asbestos', *Environmental Health Perspectives*, 118(7): 897–901.
Lemert, E.M. (1951) *Social Pathology*, New York: McGraw-Hill.
McCulloch, J. and Tweedale, G. (2008) *Defending the Indefensible: The Global Asbestos Industry and its Fight for Survival*, New York: Oxford University Press.
Pearce, F. and Tombs S. (1990) 'Ideology, hegemony and empiricism: Compliance theories of regulation', *British Journal on Criminology*, 30(4): 423–443.
Pearce, F. and Tombs, S. (1997) 'Hazards, law and class: Contextualising the regulation of corporate crime', *Social & Legal Studies*, 6(1): 79–107.
Pearce, F. and Tombs, S. (1998) *Toxic Capitalism: Corporate Crime in the Chemical Industry*, Aldershot: Ashgate.
Ruggiero V. (1998) 'Review. Maurice Punch, *Dirty Business*', *Theoretical Criminology*, 2(1): 123–125.
Slapper, G. and Tombs, S. (1999) *Corporate Crime*, London: Longman.
Tombs, S. and Whyte, D. (2001) 'Media reporting of crime: Defining corporate crime out of existence?', *Criminal Justice Matters*, 43: 22–3.
Tombs, S. and Whyte, D. (2007) *Safety Crimes*, Portland: Willan Publishing.
Tombs, S. and Whyte, D. (2010) 'Crime, harm and corporate power', in J. Muncie, D. Talbot and R. Walters (eds) *Crime: Local and Global*, Cullompton: Willan Publishing, pp. 137–172.
Turnaturi, G. (1991) *Associati per amore*, Milano: Feltrinelli.
Tweedale, G. (2000) *Magic Mineral to Killer Dust: Turner and Newall and the Asbestos Hazard*, Oxford: Oxford University Press.
Vidoni Guidoni, O. (2000) *Come si diventa non devianti*, Torino: Trauben Edizioni.
Vidoni Guidoni, O. (2004) *La criminalità*, Roma: Carocci.
Wagner, J.C., Sleggs, C.A. and Marchand R. (1960) 'Diffuse pleural mesothelioma and asbestos exposure in the North Western Cape Province', *British Journal Independent Medicine*, 17: 260–271.
Whyte, D. (2007) 'Victims of corporate crime', in S. Walklate (ed.) *Handbook of Victims and Victimology*, Cullompton: Willan Publishing, pp. 446–463.

Part IV

Responses to white-collar crime in Europe

23

Political culture and corporate homicide liability in the UK and Europe

Paul Almond

Introduction

When people die at work, or as a result of illnesses contracted in the course of their work, or as a result of the actions of a corporate body in other contexts (for instance, while using a service as a customer), their deaths constitute something more than just an undoubted tragedy for their families. The individual death of a single worker operating unguarded machinery, and the deaths of numerous workers in a large-scale 'disaster' like an explosion, also pose challenges to the systems of law that govern the safety and welfare of workers. On one level, this challenge arises because a death will usually indicate that something has gone wrong and that the systems and policies that exist to prevent harms arising have failed in some way. The workplace, and many other contexts in which individual citizens interact with business organizations, are perhaps more closely regulated by law now than at any time in the past (Braithwaite 2008), and significant efforts have been made at national, European and international levels to try to ensure that harms associated with the workplace are mitigated (Almond 2013; Gunningham and Johnstone 1999; Hawkins 2002; Hutter 1997; Walters et al. 2011; Wells 2001). In many ways, workplaces are much safer now than they were 50 or 100 years ago. But work-related deaths and injuries do still occur, and when they do, they remind us about the limits of what regulation can achieve, and highlight the risks that we, as workers or members of the public, take in our day-to-day lives (Almond and Colover 2012; Hutter and Lloyd-Bostock 1990). As such, these events are capable of provoking significant public concern.

An additional challenge posed by work-related deaths relates to the issue of legal accountability. One outcome of the scientific, technical and medical developments of the last two centuries is that we are more able to understand the causes of incidents, and less likely to attribute such events to luck, fate or *force majeure* (Green 1997). Once causes are known, it is possible to attribute responsibility to those who create them. This search for accountability has underpinned the development of systems of law to govern risk-creating business activities that lead to injury and death, a process that (in its modern form) dates back to the very start of the nineteenth century (Almond 2013: Ch. 4; Carson 1979; Tombs and Whyte 2007). The earliest forms of industrial safety legislation introduced from 1802 onward in the UK, Europe and elsewhere were highly substantive in nature, imposing specific requirements in relation to particular features of the physical workplace (working hours, the education of child workers, sanitary conditions, machine guarding). This technicality, along with the contested political nature of laws that aimed to curtail the *laissez-faire* creed (Braithwaite 2008; Polanyi 1944) of the new industrial capitalism, led to the categorization of the offences created as something other than criminal in nature, via their content, the enforcement strategies used, and the degree of moral censure attached to them (Carson 1979). The assumptions of the *ordinary* criminal law were not to be applied in this new organizational setting, meaning that the laws created were regarded from the start as functionally and politically distinct.

The twentieth century saw a shift towards a more purposive understanding of regulatory law as a mechanism of social change, granting protective rights to workers as a means of securing social solidarity and freedom from domination (Braithwaite 2008; Prosser 2006; Tucker 1995). Comprehensive structures of legal obligation were created, imposing duties onto employers to manage risks to the safety of their workers. As well as seeking to facilitate *internal* systems to govern health and safety within a workplace, this third wave of regulation also addressed the issue of *external* responsibility, with the establishment of formalized regulatory bureaucracies and proactive inspection and enforcement systems (Tucker 1995: 248). Health and safety offences were created to enforce these obligations, using law coercively to attach a normative value to the obligations imposed. What is clear is that this system of liability still differed markedly from that found elsewhere in the criminal law; the use of enforcement action was more limited and occurred only where less adversarial measures had failed (Carson 1979; Tombs and Whyte 2007; Wells 2001). The result was a two-tier system of law; regulatory law being applied where a legal response was sought following a death or breach of health and safety law (but still a minority of the overall number of deaths or breaches), and the mainstream criminal law of homicide, which did not apply.

The last 25 years have seen a shift towards the extension of criminal law to work-related deaths. England and Wales constitutes a leading jurisdiction in this regard, having introduced an offence of corporate manslaughter in 2007 to allow for the imposition of homicide liability onto corporate bodies whose activities cause death (Gobert 2008; Ormerod and Taylor 2008). This process was prompted by concerns raised about the law's capacity to perform its accountability-securing functions; that the regulatory law lacked the symbolic capacity to appropriately deter and signify the wrongness of gross breaches of health and safety duties, and that the criminal law, when utilized, was ineffective (Almond 2013; Gobert 2008; Tombs and Whyte 2007; Wells 2001). This had been evidenced in a series of high-profile cases of work-related death during the 1980s and 1990s, which also reinforced public concerns about the ever-increasing riskiness of the modern world. The concerns voiced in the British context have also exercised influence elsewhere in Europe, reopening debates about issues of corporate responsibility (Gobert and Pascal 2011; Pieth and Ivory 2011). This chapter will explore the changes which have been introduced in pursuit of the effective control of corporate behaviour, and the reasons why this process has differed across national jurisdictions. It will show that, while legal traditions are important, differences of social and political culture also play a key role in dictating how different national systems respond to the problem of work-related death.

Before proceeding, it is worth reminding ourselves why we should focus on workplace death, which is, after all, just 'one statistically minor dimension of a much more complex problem' (Gobert 2008: 414). Data from Eurostat, the Statistical Office of the European Union, indicates that in 2007 there were 5785 deaths at work across the EU (Eurostat 2010: 347), corresponding to an adjusted rate of fatal accident of 81 per 100,000 workers across the 27 member states. Additionally, a 2007 EU Labour Force Survey found that 8.6 per cent of workers (approximately 20 million people) had suffered some form of work-related ill-health in the preceding 12 months

(Eurostat 2009), while the number of deaths resulting from work-related ill-health within Western Europe is estimated to be as high as 139,519 *per annum* (Hämäläinen et al. 2009: 130). Worldwide, the ILO recorded 18,067 fatal occupational accidents in 2003; the true rate is thought to be as high as 357,948, with a further 1.95 million deaths from work-related ill health (Hämäläinen et al. 2009: 129). Many problems of differential definition and inclusion affect these statistics, but the picture that they paint is sufficiently clear to allow us to conclude that work-related deaths are a significant social problem.

Corporate manslaughter and law reform in England and Wales

The law in England and Wales provides for a two-tier model of legal response to work-related death cases. Comprehensive legal coverage is provided by the terms of the Health and Safety at Work Act 1974 (HSWA), which establishes basic standards of workplace health and safety provision and treats work-related deaths as examples of breaches of these standards (Hawkins 2002; Hutter 1997). Sections 2 and 3 of that Act establish wide-ranging duties to ensure the health, safety and welfare of employees and others affected by business conduct; a work-related death will indicate that this duty has been breached, and so liability may follow, although this will be for the failure to ensure safety, not for the consequence of death (Clarkson 2005: 681). The coverage of these duties is comprehensive, covering deaths to employees, contractors, customers and the wider community. The problem with regulatory control has always been one of implementation; despite the serious failures of safety management found in work-related death cases, prosecutions occur infrequently, and the sanctions that follow are tailored to the underlying breach rather than their fatal consequences, meaning that they often appear insufficient. To illustrate, in 2000–2001, the HSE (the Health and Safety Executive, the UK's primary safety regulator) secured 120 convictions under health and safety law following 436 recorded work-related deaths, resulting in an average fine of £34,369 (Almond 2013: 20). Given that the true number of work-related deaths is likely much higher, and the average penalty is skewed by a tiny number of high-profile cases, regulatory offences do struggle to respond to these cases as matters of serious wrongdoing (Clarkson 2005; Tombs and Whyte 2007).

This perceived problem of under-enforcement led to a shift towards criminalization. Like most other common-law jurisdictions, English law has long recognized the capacity of corporate bodies to bear criminal responsibility, either vicariously via the actions of employees, or directly, but commentators have also recognized the almost complete inability of criminal law to apply to corporate bodies in practice (Carson 1979; Clarkson 2005; Gobert 2008; Norrie 2001; Wells 2001). Since it was established in 1944 that corporations could commit offences of *mens rea*,[1] the problem has always been that responsibility for causing a criminal outcome must be attributed to the corporation via the state of mind of its individual employees. As persons in a legal but not a metaphysical sense, corporations cannot hold a state of mind except through the people who represent them; accordingly, it must be shown that a sufficiently senior person, capable of acting as the corporation for the purposes of the offence in question (a senior manager or director, or person with authority over a particular area of corporate activity), possessed the required *mens rea* on behalf of the corporation. To borrow the famous analogy of one leading English judge, the corporate body is given life by the workers who act as its hands and the managers who act as its brain; we have to locate the intentionality of this brain in order to hold the body responsible for the actions of its hands.[2]

While this appears like a conceptual sleight of hand, designed to subvert the rules of criminal liability, it is a process made necessary by exactly those rules. English criminal law has been historically reluctant to recognize any form of criminal liability that is not purely individualistic in nature (Almond 2013: Ch. 5; Norrie 2001; Wells 2001), at least in relation to organizational offenders (the criminalization of youth gangs is not always so principled: Krebs 2010). Although a relatively recent development in historical terms, the *responsible individual* is a key legitimizing principle of English criminal law, justifying criminalization as a means of apportioning responsibility on the basis of subjective individual moral capacity (Lacey 2001). Criminalization must be presented as a rational, fair process that uses universal criteria which reflect the prevailing norms of a changing society. This necessitated the development of procedures to extend the *responsible individual* model so as to legitimate the application of criminal laws to companies (Almond 2013: Ch. 5). As such, the criminal law has resisted the adoption of holistic models of fault that attach blame to systems and processes, and has attached a lesser status (as regulatory, or quasi-criminal) to offences that apply directly to the body corporate (Carson 1979; Norrie 2001; Wells 2001). The identification doctrine thus conforms to the inflexible logic of the criminal law itself, rather than deviating from it.

The key problem has been the inefficiency of these models of attribution; requiring that a single individual be identified who possesses both a sufficient degree of seniority to represent the corporate body, and a sufficient awareness of the day-to-day operations to provide the advertence to risk required, has proved to be an almost impossible balancing act, particularly in the case of large and more complex corporate bodies (Clarkson 2005; Gobert 2008; Wells 2001). Senior directors tend to be distanced (procedurally and physically) from the shop floor and any breaches of the law that occur there, while supervisors or local managers who are actually implicated in those breaches are insufficiently senior to make the corporation responsible for them. Tying organizational responsibility to an individual is also conceptually false, as most complex system failures have multiple, diverse causes that reside in the policies and processes of the organization, or in the cumulative actions of many individuals (Perrow 1984; Reason 1990; Vaughan 1999); picking one person as the faulty element is thus restrictive and misleading. Despite this procedural difficulty, the criminal law had evolved to the point where it was possible to bring charges under the 'individual' offence of manslaughter.

Case study: *The Herald of Free Enterprise*, 1987

The sinking of the *Herald of Free Enterprise*, a British roll-on, roll-off car ferry, outside Zeebrugge harbour in Belgium, in 1987, is an important case study for four reasons. First, it was one of the most serious cases of loss of life involving corporate activity in British history; 189 people died when the vessel capsized after sailing from port with its bow doors open, allowing the lower car decks to fill with seawater causing a catastrophic loss of stability (it took 90 seconds for the vessel to capsize). Second, it occurred at a moment when debates about the relative power of corporate and regulatory actors were very salient. The Thatcher government of the 1980s had pursued a set of aggressively pro-corporate policies, privatizing state-owned industries, deregulating the economy, reducing the influence of organized labour, and promoting a free-market, entrepreneurial culture (Gamble 1994). Regulators had their powers and resources reduced (Hawkins 2002) and the purposes and goals of regulation were redefined along more facilitative and efficiency-based, and less protective and welfarist lines. The loss of life at Zeebrugge, and in a number of other events, including the fires at the Bradford City football stadium in 1985 (56 fatalities), the King's Cross underground station in 1987 (31), and the Piper Alpha oil rig in 1988 (167), as well as the 1988 Clapham Junction rail crash (35), the 1989 Hillsborough football stadium disaster (96), and the 1989 *Marchioness* sinking (51), thus fitted into a narrative about the profit-first mentality of a political/economic elite which was happy to reap the rewards of risk-taking behaviour while allowing those risks to fall onto other less powerful actors. This led to significant pressure for change (Gobert 2005: 27; 2008; Wells 2001: 120).

Third, the event starkly demonstrated the need to reflect organizational failures through the criminal law. The Sheen Report, outlining the findings of the official public inquiry into the incident, placed the blame at the feet of the operating company, P&O European Ferries (formerly Townsend Thoresen): 'All concerned in management [...] were guilty of fault in that all must be regarded as sharing responsibility for the failure of management. From top to bottom the body corporate was infected with the disease of sloppiness' (Department of Transport 1987: 14.1). It was found that the immediate causes of the incident, including the failure of the assistant bosun to close the bow door because he was asleep (1987: 10.1), and the failures of the chief officer and captain to check the doors were closed, were the outcomes of systemic failures (Wells 2001: 51). The safeguards used by the company were deeply flawed; warning lights were not provided on the bridge to alert the captain that the doors were open, the procedures for closing and checking the doors were imprecise and not monitored, and the safety policies issued to staff were deficient. Crucially, there was an organizational pressure to ensure a quick turnaround of the ship in harbour; to increase profitability, ships had to achieve shorter delays between sailings, and this pressure contributed to the individual oversights listed above (Department of Transport 1987: 10.6; 11.1). Finally, there was a disjunction between safety management at operational and organizational levels. Senior management did not seek out, and were resistant to responding to, information about problems on board ships, thus allowing a number of previous open-door sailings to go unaddressed (Wells 2001: Ch. 6).

Fourthly, the *Herald* case was a seminal moment in the law's development. Although the idea of corporate manslaughter was unfamiliar, the jury sitting in the inquest hearings that followed the disaster were motivated to ignore the coroner's directions that corporate criminal liability could not be found and return verdicts of unlawful killing in relation to those deaths (Wells 2001: 108). This 'mutiny' seemed sufficiently indicative of wider social pressure to prompt the director of public prosecutions to launch a manslaughter prosecution against the operating company, the first of its kind. The trial[3] foundered due to the restrictions imposed by the identification doctrine. Manslaughter was held to require that an identified director must be shown to have acted recklessly with regard to the risk of death present in the case, either by foreseeing it or by not giving any thought to it. This proved to be an insurmountable evidential obstacle and the prosecution collapsed. Crucially, the case highlighted that regulatory forums were unable to provide the evaluation of moral culpability of the offending company desired by the public and the jury in the case (Almond 2013; Gobert 2005; Wells 2001). The search for criminalization would thus go on for almost 20 more years.

Corporate manslaughter and the reform process

Although unsuccessful, the *Herald* prosecution seemingly validated the idea of corporate manslaughter within the UK for the first time. The first successful prosecution came in 1994, when OLL Ltd., a company responsible for a school canoeing trip on which four children died, was convicted of gross negligence manslaughter in relation to those deaths.[4] It was found that a lack of safety equipment, basic precautions (although the trip was in open sea, the coastguard had not been informed), and training for staff had contributed to the outcome, and all were the responsibility of the company, thus establishing a clear duty of care owed to the victims. It proved relatively easy to establish that the sole managing director of the firm, which employed only a handful of people, was directly responsible for day-to-day operations as well as overall management, and so provided the fault element for manslaughter required (by this time, gross negligence) under the identification doctrine to render the company liable. A further five successful prosecutions were brought between 1995 and 2005, all against relatively small companies, and all in situations where the attribution of directorial advertence to the corporate body was straightforward (Almond 2013: 141).

This pattern highlighted two limitations of the law. First, corporate manslaughter prosecutions were only initiated against small companies, creating a two-tier system of liability that applied the most serious offence to the least powerful economic actors on the basis that their senior decision-makers bear direct responsibility for safety. At the same time, large companies could hide behind the corporate veil of complexity (Glasbeek 2002), relying on a lack of direct managerial responsibility for safety as a defence against responsibility. Second, rates of prosecution were very low, suggesting that there was no commitment to the criminalization of egregious safety violations; it happened in a piecemeal, unprincipled fashion, with prosecutions not brought in cases where there appeared to be appalling culpability. So in the case of Simon Jones, a teenage worker decapitated by a crane on his first day of employment in a dockyard, even the presence of a director who had personally supervised serious departures from health and safety law did not lead to a prosecution (Tombs and Whyte 2007: 21–24). At the same time, the prosecution of a railway operator whose systems of safety management were so poor that they led to a crash which killed seven people (the Southall crash, where a passenger train ran a red light on the way into Paddington station and collided with a goods train)[5] failed because responsibility for the crash was shared among management, rather than residing in one person. English law refused to recognize any way in which a corporation could demonstrate criminal culpability apart from via individual subjective responsibility (Almond 2013: 140; Norrie 2001: 104; Wells 2001: 113), and implicitly limited authentically organizational offending to the status of technical, morally neutral breaches of regulatory law rather than fundamental wrongdoing.

The UK's Law Commission, the government body that initiates law reform, issued a consultation paper on involuntary manslaughter (1994) and a subsequent report (1996) which floated the idea of a corporate manslaughter offence in response to the lessons learned from the *Herald* prosecution (1994: paras. 4.20–4.30) and indicted the identification doctrine as a *de facto* barrier to successful prosecution. The commission proposed a new offence, with fault based on the notion of management failure, which would move away from the restrictive directing mind but retain a link to advertent fault. This was subsequently adopted by the Home Office, which issued proposals designed to reform the law in the pursuit of public confidence (2000: 3) and deterrent effect (2005: 7), though the government's support for this measure was perhaps more due to a need to offer a symbolic gesture towards its trade union backers than to any principled commitment to reform (Gobert 2005). This offence was different from the previous law in that it grounded liability in a 'failure to ensure safety in the management or organisation of the corporation's activities' (Law Commission 1996: 8.19), allowing deficiencies in the collective, not just the conduct of an individual, to make a corporation liable for the offence. The 2005 draft bill retained the idea of management failure, but sought to address the uncertainty around that concept by explicitly connecting the management failure test to the actions of a specified class of individuals in a way which had not been done before, requiring that 'the way in which any of the organisation's activities are managed or organised by its senior managers' must cause death and 'amount to a gross breach of a relevant duty of care' (Home Office 2005: draft bill, cl. 1(1)). The failure must be attributable to the senior managers of the firm, the same class of individuals upon whom culpability under the existing law depends (Clarkson 2005; Gobert 2008).

In 2007, the Corporate Manslaughter and Corporate Homicide Act became law. The offence utilizes the model proposed by the Home Office, and although no individual manager need be shown to have breached the duty, and senior management conduct need only be one substantial element contributing to that breach (s.1(3)), the test does 'force the inquiry back onto the issue of identifiable individuals' (Ormerod and Taylor 2008: 604). Is managerial seniority determined according to job title, role performed, or some other criterion? Can the contribution of managers to an operational failure be assessed independent of the actions of other staff (Gobert 2008: 418)? The relevant duties are those enshrined in existing health and safety law, and must be breached in a manner falling far below what is reasonably expected of the organization. The offence can be committed by any qualifying organization, which includes corporations (based in the UK or overseas), as well as partnerships, trade unions, employer associations, police forces and some government departments. A body convicted is liable to an unlimited fine, which the Sentencing Guidelines Council recommended should not ordinarily be less than £500,000, and 'may be measured in millions of pounds' (2010: para. 24). Although this is the same sentence as applied under the old law, the range of sentencing indicated was significantly tougher, with an expectation being communicated that sentencing patterns would become more punitive. There are two ancillary sentences that can also be used; a publicity order which compels the company to publish its conviction in a public media forum, and a remedial order that compels it to rectify breaches identified within a case. Investigative and prosecutorial powers relating to the new offence reside with the police force and Crown Prosecution Service, rather than health and safety regulators, thus connoting the new offence as a matter of mainstream criminal wrongdoing.

Case study: Cotswold Geotechnical Holdings

The first prosecution under the new law came in 2011, when Cotswold Geotechnical Holdings, a small geological surveying company, was convicted following a 2008 incident where a trench dug to allow the collection of soil samples collapsed, burying an employee and causing his death by traumatic asphyxia.[6] The employee had been left alone on site, working in heavy rain in a soil trench that was several metres deep but not supported by timber buttressing; his supervizing manager had left work early, meaning that there was no one on hand to oversee the work or the rescue attempts. The employer was found to have disregarded industry guidance and concerns raised in the past about trench-work, and failed to provide adequate training to employees about the relevant hazards. This was a profoundly unsafe system of work, and the senior manager of the firm (a very small enterprise) was involved in, and aware of, the risks being taken (Dobson 2012). When the case came to trial, the only difficulty related to the absence of the manager in question during the trial due to ill-health; he was unable to give evidence in defence of the company, so the prosecution was required to assume certain burdens of proof in relation to the breach of duty.

The company was convicted of corporate manslaughter and fined £385,000, some way below the level set by the Sentencing Guidelines, but sufficient to put the company out of business. The aims of the offence (deterrence, moral desert) were sufficiently important to ensure that taking account of a defendant company's circumstances did not mean that its future had to be ensured, and so the relatively punitive fine was upheld on appeal (Dobson 2012). The Cotswold decision attracted significant publicity because of its novelty, but although the new offence had been successfully used, the facts of Cotswold were not really sufficiently complex to test the capacity of the new attribution mechanisms. The defendant company was small and the senior manager was heavily involved in day-to-day safety management, so the locating of fault was relatively straightforward (Almond 2013: 33). As such, many key questions about the new offence remained unanswered; would it be easier to attribute fault within a complex organization? Would it be possible to effectively construct fault from across a range of contributions by different elements of management? Cotswold did confirm that defining a breach of duty is not always as straightforward as might have been imagined, and some degree of flexibility was needed to map the new offence onto existing health and safety law (Dobson 2012).

Since the Cotswold case, a further five successful prosecutions have been brought, all of small-scale organizations and all in circumstances where there were direct links between management and operational levels of the company, and several other cases are pending. Of the five cases, two involved deaths on farms,[7] one a death at a leisure resort,[8] one a death from falling through a factory roof,[9] and one a death by crushing during vehicle repairs.[10] The fines levied have ranged from £485,000 in the Lion Steel case to £8,000 in the Mobile Sweepers case, all well below the range set out by the Sentencing Guidelines Council, but each set via reference to the capacities and resources of the company in question. In this last case, for instance, the main punishments of a £183,000 fine and a five-year disqualification from directorship was levied against the individual director/owner as he had dissolved the original company straight after the fatal incident and formed an identical, but separate, company. This does highlight an important point; that none of the cases have been accompanied by successful individual manslaughter charges against the (often sole) directors implicated in the fatalities (often being abandoned during plea bargaining stages: Dobson 2012), thus suggesting that a degree of corporate veiling has occurred in these cases. While prosecutors have been increasingly proactive in mounting prosecutions of this sort, and are developing the expertise needed to do so effectively, the results of reform have been disappointing; six cases in six years does not yet represent a significant step forward from the outcomes achieved under the old law (Almond 2013: 174), and primarily reflects both uncertainty about the new law, the long lag-times for investigation that work-related fatalities bring, as well as an ingrained resistance to corporate liability. Despite that, the trend is towards more aggressive use of the new offence in future, and so it appears that the idea of corporate manslaughter is still coming of age.

Elsewhere in Europe: convergence and change

The countries of mainland Europe have legal traditions that differ from those of the UK, and that are not necessarily straightforwardly compatible with the notion of corporate criminal liability. But the early twenty-first century is the era of mega-corporate capitalism (Braithwaite 2008: 19), and the increasing dominance of multinational corporations leads to pressures for their accountability that transcend national borders (Wells 2001; 2010). Different approaches have been taken across Europe (and the wider world), but one unifying theme is an increasing openness to the idea of corporate manslaughter, even if the implementation of that idea remains limited. As discussed previously, the UK is unique in having a specific offence of corporate manslaughter; the vast majority of countries that impose liability in these situations do so via a process of attribution for an individual offence, similar to the UK prior to law reform. The common-law jurisdictions of the world, including the USA (Beale and Safwat 2004), Canada (Bittle 2012) and Australia (Gunningham and Johnstone 1999), have seen legislative or prosecutorial initiative exercised in order to allow for the pursuit of criminalization to some degree; Canada and Australia have introduced legislation to facilitate liability, while the USA has probably seen the most proactive use of common law homicide offences of any country over the last thirty years.

European jurisdictions have for a long time traditionally resisted the notion of corporate criminal liability, with penal codes drawing rigid distinctions between criminal and administrative law, and conceiving of the former as only applicable to natural persons, in line with Kantian ideals of individualism and moral autonomy (Weigend 2008: 929). On this view, a corporation cannot be said to possess any moral capacity separate from that of the individuals who constitute it, and punishing the corporation is equivalent to punishing a whole class of persons for the actions of a single individual (Orland and Cachera 1995: 112; Weigend 2008: 937). Further, the penal codes of civil law systems do not allow for the kind of piecemeal legal development that has characterized the emergence of corporate liability in common-law jurisdictions. But a range of external pressures, including EU, UN and OECD conventions on bribery and corruption (Wells 2010) requiring that all nations have 'effective, proportionate, and dissuasive non-criminal sanctions' to ensure against corporate wrongdoing and particularly against organized crime gangs,[11] have prompted a degree of convergence. Many European countries now provide for corporate criminal liability that includes involuntary homicide offences, and the issue has achieved a greater profile as a result of a series of major disasters. These include the AZF fertilizer factory explosion in Toulouse, France, in 2001 (29 fatalities), the firework factory explosion in Enschede, Netherlands, in 2000 (23 fatalities), the Viareggio train derailment, Italy, in 2009 (32 fatalities), and the Concorde air crash in Paris, France, in 2000 (113 fatalities).

A thorough review of practices across Europe cannot be undertaken here (see Gobert and Pascal 2011; Pieth and Ivory 2011). Instead, four groupings of countries will be identified, each of which is exemplified by one of the nations of the EU: early adopters of corporate liability (the Netherlands); later adopters (France); indirect adopters (Italy); and non-adopters (Germany). The early adopters are countries where there are relatively longstanding traditions of corporate criminal liability, such as Denmark and the Netherlands, the latter of which has recognized corporate criminal liability for economic offences since 1951, and extended this scope in 1976 via Article 15 of the Dutch Penal Code (Field and Jörg 1991; Keulen and Gritter 2011). Under Art. 15, criminal offences may be committed by a company, including involuntary manslaughter (as evidenced by the conviction of a hospital for negligent homicide in 1987).[12] The Dutch law imposes corporate liability for the acts of employees where it is within the company's power to control whether those acts should occur, and the act is accepted by the corporation as part of business operations[13] (Field and Jörg 1991: 164; Keulen and Gritter 2011: 182). If the company has not exercised due diligence and has fallen below the expected standard in supervising risk-creating activities, then it will be held to have assumed responsibility for the act.[14] This is a pragmatic test that allows safety management systems and the cultural acceptance of risk to be considered in determining liability. Like the UK, the Dutch system primarily handles work-related deaths through a regulatory scheme of offences; manslaughter prosecutions in this context remain something of a rarity, but still signal acceptance of the concept of corporate liability, as well as the policy goals that underpin it.

The later adopters are the countries which have no longstanding traditions of corporate criminal liability, but which have reformed their laws to allow for this during the last 20 years. This category includes the majority of European nations, including Austria, Belgium, Estonia, Finland, Lithuania, Luxembourg, Poland, Portugal, Romania and Slovenia (Gobert and Pascal 2011). Some of these nations have traditions of *societas delinquere potest, sed punier non potest* (corporations could commit offences but not be punished for them), but have recently moved to recognize full criminal liability. Belgium is an example of this, having acknowledged as long ago as 1946 that corporations could be the subjects of criminal statutes, but not allowing that such an entity could be criminally sanctioned for such an offence until 1999 (Faure 1999). France altered its Penal Code in 1994 and again in 2004 so as to allow for corporate criminal liability (Orland and Cachera 1995: 114). Article 221–227 of the Penal Code states that a legal person may incur criminal liability for the offence of manslaughter by 'causing the death of another person by clumsiness, rashness, inattention, negligence, or breach of an obligation of safety or prudence', and may be subject to a fine or other sanction (judicial supervision or publicity order: Article 131–139). Liability is predicated upon the advertent negligence of a high-ranking officer, even if the immediate act causing death is committed by a non-senior employee. In 2008 there were 41 homicide convictions of corporate persons following work-related deaths (*'homicide involontaire par accident du travail'*), leading to an average fine of €21,000 and a maximum of €150,000 (Baux and Timbart 2008; Beauvais 2011: 244). As in the UK, action has arisen in relation to exceptional events such as the 2000 Paris Concorde air crash, which resulted in 113 deaths and led to the conviction in 2010 (subsequently overturned) of Continental Airlines under this causing death by negligence (manslaughter) offence.

The indirect adopters are countries which have introduced modes of corporate criminalization that avoid the direct imposition of liability so as to bypass the doctrinal restrictions of their legal systems. For example, Spain imposes corporate criminal liability indirectly, as a form of accessory liability (termed *ancillary consequences*), on the basis that this does not directly violate the legal norm of *societas delinquere non potest* (Ramkissoon 2011). While Spain does not extend corporate liability to homicide offences, Italy does, having bypassed a constitutional prohibition on corporate criminalization by introducing a quasi-criminal category of offences that operate as *de facto* criminal proceedings while technically falling within the bracket of administrative offences (Gobert and Mugnai 2002). Legislative Decree no. 231/01 (2001) made corporate entities directly responsible for offences committed pursuant to the interests of the company by directors, executives and employees; this was originally limited to financial offending but was extended by Law no. 123 of 2007 to include crimes against the person, including manslaughter committed in violation of safe working practices (de Maglie 2011: 261). Companies can avoid liability if they are not structurally negligent in how they manage safety; this approach arguably comes closer to a corporate culture model than almost any other nation (Gobert and Mugnai 2002: 626).

Lastly, the non-adopting nations retain a strict distinction between the control of corporate behaviour and the criminal law, viewing the latter as purely a matter of individual moral responsibility, tied to a metaphysical conception of normative self-determination as a uniquely human characteristic. *Societas delinquere non potest* is central to the legal culture of countries like Germany; since 1968, German law has applied a class of administrative (non-criminal) offences, known as *Ordnungswidrigkeiten* (OWiG), to corporate bodies, allowing for administrative fines of up to €1 million to be levied against a corporation if it can be shown that a relevant individual committed an offence (Weigend 2008: 130). Corporate liability for an OWiG offence is purely descriptive of factual responsibility and does not imply any normative judgement of fault. These offences, particularly s.30 OWiG, which makes a corporate body liable as an accessory where an individual with organizational control functions commits an offence that breaches an obligation incumbent upon the corporation, can theoretically be used to impose liability in a work-related death scenario, but are rarely, if ever, invoked in relation to negligent homicide. Fining corporate bodies in these circumstances is viewed as at odds with the proper purpose of administrative penalties, given the inherent moral component of a homicide charge (Schneider 2009). Similarly, Sweden (Estrada et al. 2014) and the Czech Republic are wedded to a distinction between administrative and criminal liabilities, and use the former to fulfil EU/OECD requirements for effective legal control over organized crime and corporate wrongdoing. In these nations, established systems of safety regulation govern work-related deaths.

Theorizing corporate homicide: the attractions of the criminal law

From a criminological point of view, the difference between the Anglo-American common law and the European civil law traditions is interesting because it reflects two key conceptual notions in the history of thinking about crime and responsibility. The individual liability-oriented Anglo-American approach can be linked to the pragmatic ends-focused logic of utilitarianism, and the subsequent influential traditions of criminological positivism in those jurisdictions (Cornish and Clarke 1989: 83–91, 93–94; Hart 1994: 244–254). The measure of whether something should be criminalized is, according to this view, whether it will positively shape policy outcomes and the public good. This is a profoundly instrumental view of law's role, and criminalization is thus but one tool of many to be employed in the pursuit of public policy goals, when it is beneficial to do so; this was the logic behind the early criminalization of breaches of the Factory Acts in the UK (Carson 1979) and it also underpins the more contemporary use of Regulatory Impact Assessment tools to measure the instrumental value of enforcement (Almond 2013: 72). The instrumental possibilities of regulatory enforcement have long been debated as factors shaping the use of prosecution (Hawkins 2002; Hutter 1997; Tombs and Whyte 2007), and a desire to use criminalization as a means to an end (that of public protection and reassurance) clearly underpins the introduction of the new offence.

This is consistent with contemporary trends in penal policy within the UK, where a culture of penal populism has seen the expansion of the disciplinary infrastructure of the state and an increasing willingness on the part of policymakers to exploit crime issues for their own ends by introducing new offences that demonstrate that the government of the day is tough on crime (Garland 2001; Lacey 2008; Roberts et al. 2003). As a result, 'punishment policy [is] developed primarily for its anticipated popularity' (Roberts et al. 2003: 65) rather than because it is likely to bring about any positive effect – a form of utilitarianism, but not a particularly principled one. One outcome of this conjunction of instrumentalism and punitiveness is that the criminal law comes to be perceived as fulfilling a problem-solving role, as a tool of wider policy delivery in areas of social welfare, public ordering, the governance of the workplace, and so on (Simon 2007). And this leads to what is sometimes called overcriminalization, the introduction of criminal offences to apply in an ever-wider range of contexts (Husak 2008). In exploring the way that this dynamic maps onto organizational offending, Baldwin (2004) diagnoses a new regulatory punitiveness, which he argues has led to a shift in legislative and regulatory approach so that criminal sanctions and adversarial methods are increasingly widely used (2004: 352). It may be argued that the corporate homicide offence reflects this tendency as it extends the criminal law into the workplace.

The crucial issues for critics of this trend are that offences of this sort are doctrinally unprincipled, allow for the harmful extension of the coercive power of the state (Garland 2001; Simon 2007) and undermine the constructive rationale that underpins systems of regulatory engagement (Baldwin 2004). The counter-argument would be that offences like corporate manslaughter are responding to events that are both harmful and wrongful, but are not currently accounted for by the artificial doctrinal constraints of the criminal law; and that criminalization provides a moral authority which reinforces the legitimacy of systems of regulation by unambiguously illustrating their importance (Almond 2013). Finally, there is another objection which also highlights the limits of this utilitarian model of thought in relation to work-related death; that rates of enforcement are so low that it hardly looks like a coercive culture of regulatory punitiveness in action; six prosecutions in seven years under the new law is unlikely to fundamentally shift the calculation of cost and benefit. Indeed, deterrence sufficient to actually change the utility calculus in relation to health and safety performance has never been tried in practice (Tombs and Whyte 2007). It is also clear that the notion of the public good is disputed in the case of work-related deaths (Almond and Colover 2012), suggesting that claims as to the social utility of criminalization cannot be straightforwardly made, and that when the instrumental calculation of the benefits of criminalization change, the law can change too.

A second idea drawn from criminological history helps to explain why the shift towards criminalization in the UK has not always been mirrored across the rest of Europe. Continental approaches to criminalization have perhaps been more influenced by Kantian notions of morality than by utilitarian conceptions (Gibson and Caldeira 1996; Wieacker and Bodenheimer 1990), and this underpins the historical tendency towards the principle of *societas delinquere non potest* (Weigend 2008); criminal law is a matter of moral responsibility and individual dignity and this is something that is limited to human defendants. As such, corporate criminal liability is often viewed as something of a misnomer, involving the application of concepts to a context in which they make no sense. As such, a distinction between criminal and administrative systems of law emerged which reflected Durkheim's distinction between mechanical and organic societies and forms of law (1893). On this conception, it is in areas of social life characterized by a mechanical solidarity based on similarity and consensus that criminal law has a role, upholding a number of core values and agreed principles through its public sanctioning power. Areas of social life that are characterized by complexity, differentiation and the variability of individual interests and values, however, are better handled via the civil (or private) law of restitution and individual rights and obligations (Prosser 2006). Areas of commercial activity, and the interests of employers and employees as economic actors, are thus properly dealt with via means other than the criminal law, because the rights of individual actors are of central importance. For Durkheim, the shift towards organic solidarity as an outcome of restitutory law is a process of social development towards a higher level of sophistication and so systems of regulation are understood as more advanced, and thus preferable, to the blunter tool of the criminal law (1893: 63).

What Durkheim's model provides us is a means of understanding the reticence to criminalize corporate offending that has existed (and still exists) in some continental European jurisdictions. Regulation, as a form of law that is more individualized, pluralized and more reflexive in situations of complexity (Braithwaite 2008; Hutter 1997; Prosser 2006), is better suited to dealing with these areas of individual liberty, and better at reflecting the collective complexity of corporate bodies. But Durkheim's approach famously recognizes the solidarity-building purpose of crime and punishment, and intimates that there is a consciousness-reinforcing role for offences like those that govern corporate manslaughter. Criminal proceedings restate the wrongness of particular forms of conduct, and of the fundamental values that that conduct offends against. Criminalization via something like the corporate manslaughter offence is intended to provide a more compelling public account of the reasons for regulating the field of occupational health and safety, highlighting its connection to deeper social values (Almond 2013: 171–172). It can do this because it is a normative system of law which involves making judgements about the accountability of the defendant for that wrong. By stating that abuses of health and safety are wrongful, and offend against individuals' citizenship rights to non-exploitation, the manslaughter offence is part of a movement towards a more democratically constituted regulatory system. It may be argued that this is the real appeal of criminalization, rather than deterrence, which is too empirically difficult to measure to rely on.

So why are there countries where criminalization in this context is not regarded as necessary? Germany, Sweden and the Czech Republic are complex, modern, technologically advanced societies which do not have the benefit of criminal laws to fulfil this solidarity-building function in relation to corporate wrongdoing (Gobert and Pascal 2011). The answer perhaps lies in the political and social context within which regulation occurs in those countries. It will be noted that the countries of the world where criminalization is most long-established and widely used are also among the nations that are the most free-market-oriented, economically liberal and resistant to coordinated state intervention in the economic sphere (Almond 2013: Ch. 7; Harvey 2005; Lacey 2008). Within Europe, the tendency is the same; the countries that have most enthusiastically embraced criminalization also display higher levels of income inequality and financial flexibility, and lower levels of employment protection and state intervention, than other, more coordinated, European economies (Hall and Soskice 2001: 19–33; Lacey 2008: 58–60, 111). Within this context, regulation is viewed as a form of interference with individual freedoms which runs counter to the interests of society, which are best served via the maintenance of free markets; the role of regulation is to correct inefficiencies in, and establish the rules of, the market (Braithwaite 2008). This emphasis on freedoms also explains why certain countries that appear more welfarist in nature have also proved to be enthusiastic criminalizers (such as the Netherlands); they perhaps subscribe to a version of political progressivism which emphasizes individual liberty and freedom, rather than social justice, as the goal of social democracy (Gibson and Caldeira 1996: 65–70; Mascini and Houtman 2011). As we have seen, criminalization in these jurisdictions has occurred as an outcome of a reliance on the criminal law as a means of expressing shared values; the corporate manslaughter offence is the small, hard core of control around which a liberal regulatory system coalesces. As an individualistic, freedom-reinforcing system of rules, criminal law is archetypally neo-liberal in form, and entirely consistent with the logic of that political culture (Garland 2001; Harvey 2005; Lacey 2008; Tombs and Whyte 2007).

In nations where criminalization is resisted, however, we tend to see a more cohesively social-democratic form of government which emphasizes a more welfare-oriented, representative and protectionist political culture, where levels of employment protection are more developed, average working hours are lower (Hall and Soskice 2001: 22; Lacey 2008), there is a greater rights culture of worker entitlement to welfare protection, and a greater level of public support for health and safety as a cooperative process. Because the prevailing social and political culture in Sweden and Germany is more aligned with the core rationale behind a welfarist and interventionist regulatory system, there is less need to employ the mechanical solidarity-creating capacity of the criminal law to buttress support for regulation in this sphere. Organic social ordering, via procedural non-penal regulatory law, can be employed within the context of complex and differentiated market systems; this also conforms to a prevailing business orientation within those societies (Boers 2012). A solidaristic regulatory system is here already embedded within a social context that supports it (Polanyi 1944; Prosser 2006), and so does not require the symbolic support of criminal law enforcement to provide a message about the wrongfulness of breaching the regulatory law. That is not to say that criminalization might not be of some instrumental value, but rather that the key benefit offered by criminalization, the moral reinforcement of the idea of regulation, may not be needed in these jurisdictions to the same extent.

Notes

1 *DPP v Kent and Sussex Contractors* [1944] KB 146; *R v ICR Haulage* [1944] KB 551; *Moore v Bresler* [1944] 2 All ER 515.
2 Lord Denning, *H.L. Bolton (Engineering) Co. Ltd. v. T.J. Graham & Sons Ltd.* [1957] 1 QB 159, 172.
3 *R v P&O European Ferries (Dover) Ltd.* [1991] 93 Cr. App. R 72.
4 *R v OLL Ltd.* (1994). Unreported, *The Independent*, 09/12/1994.
5 *R v Great Western Trains* (1999) Central Criminal Court 30/06/1999, case ref. C7800570; *Attorney-General's Reference (No. 2 of 1999)* [2000] 3 All ER 182.
6 *R v Cotswold Geotechnical (Holdings) Ltd.* [2011] EWCA Crim 1337; [2011] All ER (D) 100 (May).
7 *R v JMW Farms* [2012] Belfast Crown Court, NICC 17, unreported (http://www.courtsni.gov.uk/en-GB/Judicial%20Decisions/PublishedByYear/Documents/2012/%5B2012%5D%20NICC%2017/j_j_2012NICC17Final.htm, accessed 27 November 2014); *R v J Murray and Sons* [2013] Belfast Crown Court, NICC 15, unreported (http://www.courtsni.gov.uk/en-GB/Judicial%20Decisions/PublishedByYear/Documents/2013/%5B2013%5D%20NICC%2015/j_j_WEI9007Final.htm, accessed 27 November 2014).

8 *R v Princes Sporting Club* [2013] Westminster Crown Court, 22/11/2013, unreported.
9 *R v Lion Steel Equipment Ltd.* (2012), Manchester Crown Court, 20/07/2012, unreported (https://www.judiciary.gov.uk/judgments/r-v-steel-equip-ltd-sentencing-remarks, accessed 27 November 2014).
10 *R v Mobile Sweepers (Reading)* [2014] Winchester Crown Court, 26/2/2014, unreported.
11 1997 OECD Convention on Combating Bribery of Foreign Public Officials, Art. 2; 1988 Council of Europe Committee of Ministers, Recommendation R (88) 18 (*Concerning Liability of Enterprises Having Legal Personality for Offences Committed in the Exercise of Their Activities*).
12 *Hospital Case*, Rechtbank Leeuwarden, 23/12/1987 (N.J. 1988, 981).
13 *Ijzerdraad Case*, Hoge Raad, 23/02/1954 (N.J. 1954, 378).
14 *Kabeljauw Case*, Hoge Raad, 01/07/1981 (N.J. 1982, 80).

References

Almond, P. (2013) *Corporate Manslaughter and Regulatory Reform*, Basingstoke: Palgrave MacMillan.

Almond, P. and Colover, S. (2012) 'Communication and social regulation: The criminalization of work-related death', *British Journal of Criminology*, 52(5): 997–1016.

Baldwin, R. (2004) 'The new punitive regulation', *Modern Law Review*, 67(3): 351–383.

Baux, D. and Timbart, O. (2008) *Les Condamnations de Personnes Morales en 2005: Infostat Justice Bulletin d'Information Statistique 108*, Paris: Ministère de la Justice. Online. Available HTTP: <http://www.justice.gouv.fr/art_pix/1_stat_infostat103_20081013.pdf> (accessed 30 June 2014).

Beale, S.S. and Safwat, A.G. (2004) 'What developments in Western Europe tell us about American critiques of corporate criminal liability', *Buffalo Criminal Law Review*, 8: 89–163.

Beauvais, P. (2011) 'Country report: France', in J. Gobert and A. Pascal (eds) *European Developments in Corporate Criminal Liability*, Abingdon: Routledge.

Bittle, S. (2012) *Still Dying for a Living: Corporate Criminal Liability after the Westray Mine Disaster*, Vancouver: UBC Press.

Boers, K. (2012) 'Wirtschaftskriminalität und die Privatisierung der DDR-Betriebe', *Bibliothek des Eigentums*, 9: 147–183.

Braithwaite, J. (2008) *Regulatory Capitalism: How it Works, Ideas for Making it Work Better*, Cheltenham: Edward Elgar.

Carson, W.G. (1979) 'The conventionalization of early factory crime', *International Journal of the Sociology of Law*, 7: 37–60.

Clarkson, C. (2005) 'Corporate manslaughter: Yet more government proposals', *Criminal Law Review*, 677–689.

Cornish, W.R. and Clarke, G. de N. (1989) *Law and Society in England 1750–1950*, London: Sweet and Maxwell.

Department of Transport (1987) *MV Herald of Free Enterprise: Report of the Court No. 8047 (The Sheen Report)*, London: HMSO.

Dobson, A. (2012) 'Shifting sands: Multiple counts in prosecutions for corporate manslaughter', *Criminal Law Review*, 3: 200 –.9.

Durkheim, E. (1893) *The Division of Labour in Society*, New York: Free Press.

Estrada, F., Flyghed, J., Nilsson, A. and Bäckman, K. (2014) 'Why are occupational safety crimes increasing?', *Journal of Scandinavian Studies in Criminology and Crime Prevention*, 15: 3–18.

Eurostat (2009) *Statistics in Focus: 63/2009: 8.6% of Workers in the EU Experienced Work-related Health Problems*, Luxembourg: European Commission.

Eurostat (2010) *The Social Situation in the European Union 2009*, Luxembourg: Publications Office of the European Union.

Faure, M. (1999) 'Criminal responsibilities of legal and collective entities: Developments in Belgium', in A. Eser, G. Heine and B. Huber (eds) *Criminal Responsibility of Legal and Collective Entities*, Berlin: Edition Iuscrim.

Field, S. and Jörg, N. (1991) 'Corporate liability and manslaughter: Should we be going Dutch?', *Criminal Law Review*, 156–171.

Gamble, A. (1994) *The Free Economy and the Strong State: The Politics of Thatcherism*, 2nd edn, London: Macmillan.

Garland, D. (2001) *The Culture of Control: Crime and Social Order in Contemporary Society*, Oxford: Oxford University Press.

Gibson, J.L. and Caldeira, G.A. (1996) 'The legal cultures of Europe', *Law & Society Review*, 30(1): 55–86.

Glasbeek, H. (2002) *Wealth by Stealth: Corporate Crime, Corporate Law, and the Perversion of Democracy*, Toronto: Between the Lines.

Gobert, J. (2005) 'The politics of corporate manslaughter: The British experience', *Flinders Journal of Law Reform*, 8(1): 1–38.

Gobert, J. (2008) 'The Corporate Manslaughter and Corporate Homicide Act 2007: Thirteen years in the making but was it worth the wait?', *Modern Law Review*, 71(3): 413–463.
Gobert, J. and Mugnai, E. (2002) 'Coping with corporate crime: Some lessons from Italy', *Criminal Law Review*, 619–629.
Gobert, J. and Pascal, A. (2011) *European Developments in Corporate Criminal Liability*, Abingdon: Routledge.
Green, J. (1997) *Risk and Misfortune: The Social Construction of Accidents*, London: UCL Press.
Gunningham, N. and Johnstone, R. (1999) *Regulating Workplace Safety: Systems and Sanctions*, Oxford: Oxford University Press.
Hall, P. and Soskice, D. (2001) *Varieties of Capitalism: The Institutional Foundations of Comparative Advantage*, Oxford: Oxford University Press.
Hämäläinen, P., Saarela, K.L. and Takala, J. (2009) 'Global trends according to estimated number of occupational accidents and fatal work-related diseases at region and country level', *Journal of Safety Research*, 40: 125–139.
Hart, H.L.A. (1994) *The Concept of Law*, 2nd edn, Oxford: Clarendon Press.
Harvey, D. (2005) *A Brief History of Neoliberalism*, Oxford: Oxford University Press.
Hawkins, K. (2002) *Law as Last Resort: Prosecution Decision-Making in a Regulatory Agency*, Oxford: Oxford University Press.
Home Office (2000) *Reforming the Law of Involuntary Manslaughter: The Government's Proposals*, London: Home Office.
Home Office (2005) *Corporate Manslaughter: The Government's Draft Bill for Reform*, London: The Stationery Office.
Husak, D. (2008) *Overcriminalization: The Limits of the Criminal Law*, New York: Oxford University Press.
Hutter, B. (1997) *Compliance: Regulation and Environment*, Oxford: Clarendon Press.
Hutter, B. and Lloyd-Bostock, S. (1990) 'The power of accidents: The social and psychological impact of accidents and the enforcement of safety regulations', *British Journal of Criminology*, 30(4): 409–422.
Keulen, B.F. and Gritter, E. (2011) 'Corporate criminal liability in the Netherlands', in M. Pieth and R. Ivory (eds) *Corporate Criminal Liability: Emergence, Convergence, and Risk*, New York: Springer, 177–191.
Krebs, B. (2010) 'Joint criminal enterprise', *Modern Law Review*, 73(4): 578–604.
Lacey, N. (2001) 'In search of the responsible subject: History, philosophy and social sciences in criminal law theory', *Modern Law Review*, 64: 350–371.
Lacey, N. (2008) *The Prisoners' Dilemma: Political Economy and Punishment in Contemporary Democracies*, Cambridge: Cambridge University Press.
Law Commission (1994) *Consultation Paper 135: Involuntary Manslaughter*, London: HMSO.
Law Commission (1996) *Report 237: Legislating the Criminal Code: Involuntary Manslaughter*, London: HMSO.
Maglie, C. de (2011) 'Italy', in J. Gobert and A. Pascal (eds) *European Developments in Corporate Criminal Liability*, Abingdon: Routledge.
Mascini, P. and Houtman, D. (2011) 'Resisting administrative tolerance in the Netherlands: A Rightist backlash?', *British Journal of Criminology*, 51(4): 690–706.
Norrie, A. (2001) *Crime, Reason, and History*, 2nd edn, Cambridge: University Press.
Orland, L. and Cachera, C. (1995) 'Corporate crime and punishment in France: Criminal responsibility of legal entities (Personnes Morales) under the new French criminal code (Nouveau Code Penal)', *Connecticut Journal of International Law*, 11: 111–168.
Ormerod, D. and Taylor, R. (2008) 'The corporate manslaughter and Corporate Homicide Act 2007', *Criminal Law Review*, 589–611.
Perrow, C. (1984) *Normal Accidents: Living with High-Risk Technologies*, London: HarperCollins.
Pieth, M. and Ivory, R. (2011) *Corporate Criminal Liability: Emergence, Convergence, and Risk*, New York: Springer.
Polanyi, K. (1944) *The Great Transformation: The Political and Economic Origins of our Time*, Boston: Beacon Hill.
Prosser, T. (2006) 'Regulation and social solidarity', *Journal of Law and Society*, 33(3): 364–387.
Ramkissoon, M. (2011) 'Spain', in J. Gobert and A. Pascal (eds) *European Developments in Corporate Criminal Liability*, Abingdon: Routledge, 310–314.
Reason, J. (1990) *Human Error*, Cambridge: Cambridge University Press.
Roberts, J.V., Stalans, L.J., Indermaur, D. and Hough, M. (2003) *Penal Populism and Public Opinion: Lessons from Five Countries*, Oxford: Oxford University Press.
Schneider, A. (2009) 'Corporate liability for manslaughter: A comparison between English and German Law', *Zeitschrift für Internationale Strafrechtsdogmatik*, 1: 22–43.
Sentencing Guidelines Council (2010) *Corporate Manslaughter & Health and Safety Offences Causing Death: Definitive Guideline*, London: Crown.

Simon, J. (2007) *Governing Through Crime: How the War on Crime Transformed American Democracy and Created a Culture of Fear*, Oxford: Oxford University Press.
Tombs, S. and Whyte, D. (2007) *Safety Crimes*, Cullompton: Willan.
Tucker, E. (1995) 'And defeat goes on: An assessment of third-wave health and safety regulation', in F. Pearce, and L. Snider (eds) *Corporate Crime: Contemporary Debates*, Toronto: University of Toronto Press.
Vaughan, D. (1999) 'The dark side of organizations: Mistake, misconduct, and disaster', *Annual Review of Sociology*, 25: 271–305.
Walters, D., Johnstone, R., Frick, K., Quinlan, M., Baril-Gingras, G. and Thébaud-Mony, A. (2011) *Regulating Workplace Risks: A Comparative Study of Inspection Regimes in Times of Change*, Cheltenham: Edward Elgar.
Weigend, T. (2008) 'Societas delinquere non potest?: A German perspective', *Journal of International Criminal Justice*, 6(5): 927–945.
Wells, C. (2001) *Corporations, Crime and Accountability*, 2nd edn, Oxford: Oxford University Press.
Wells, C. (2010) 'Corporate crime: Opening the eyes of the sentry', *Legal Studies*, 30(3): 370–390.
Wieacker, F. and Bodenheimer, E. (1990) 'Foundations of European legal culture', *The American Journal of Comparative Law*, 38(1): 1–29.

24

Management of tax transgressions in France

A Foucauldian perspective

Anthony Amicelle

Introduction

> The apparatus that resulted in the creation of financial intelligence units under the auspices of the FATF [Financial Action Task Force] has always shown efficiency and flexibility. While this apparatus was initially designed for the fight against the financing of drug trafficking, it has been progressively extended to combat all forms of illicit financial flows as well as terrorist financing. The economic and financial crisis of the past several years has led to new reflections on the need to reinforce regulation instruments in the financial domain and it is likely that these reflections will lead to increasing the role of the original structures, whose surveillance function for financial flows has become an essential corollary of financial liberalization.
>
> *(Jean-Baptiste Carpentier, director of the French financial intelligence unit, Tracfin (Tracfin 2012: 3))*

Financial intelligence units and international norms against money laundering were created in the 1990s largely to deal with drug traffickers and to track the proceeds from drug trafficking. Such apparatus of financial policing is now, however, being presented as a way to monitor and regulate all forms of 'financial crime' as the quote above demonstrates.[1] In France, the recent determination that tax evasion can be considered a predicate offence for money laundering has reinforced this position.

Laundering of gains from all crimes or offences, unreported employment, illicit work, breach of trust, abuse of company assets, fraud, gang fraud, illegal banking practices, fraudulent abuse of a person's weakness, tax offences (evasion, non-disclosure or false disclosure, organizing fraudulent insolvency), possession of stolen property, embezzlement, forgery and the use of forged documents, procuring, bankruptcy, theft, drug offences, corruption, customs offences, counterfeiting of consumer goods, bribery of foreign public officials, influence trading, theft committed by an organized gang, terrorist financing, criminal association, illicit gambling, extortion, misappropriation or improper use of money by a person exercising a public function. Although this list looks like a Prévert-style inventory, it actually covers all the predicate offences that officers of the French financial intelligence unit (Tracfin) have recently investigated in relation to suspicion of money laundering (Tracfin 2012). The list covers a wide spectrum, from property crimes and theft to subtle social games involving the gaps in tax rules.

The fight against 'dirty money' can thus be seen to target such disparate acts as attempts to disguise the illegal origin of financial proceeds, terrorist financing, and actions to conceal the existence or nature of income that is legally earned but is illegally subtracted from taxable income. 'The Union is at the forefront of international efforts to combat the laundering of the proceeds of crime. Flows of dirty money can damage the stability and reputation of the financial sector, while terrorism shakes the very foundations of our society' (European Commission 2013: 1). 'The offence of money laundering is committed when the proceeds of "criminal activity" are laundered. [...] The new FATF standards include "tax crimes (related to direct and indirect taxes)" as a predicate offence' (European Commission 2012: 4). Tax evasion becomes a predicate offence for money laundering and it becomes synonymous with 'dirty money'. Indeed, laundering practices are criminal rituals designed to cleanse the money, which implicitly means that money is dirty in the first place (Peebles 2012).

While it can seem far removed from the rigour attributed to legal language, the notion of dirty money nevertheless explicitly appears in official texts and statements (see, for example, European Union 2005). The content of this poorly delimited notion is not obvious, objective and fixed to the extent that it depends on 'an ongoing process of social boundary construction by interested parties' (Peebles 2012: 1249). In dealing with crimes from terrorism to tax evasion, the scope of transgressions handled by the financial policing apparatus is unprecedented and Tracfin's director has argued that financial intelligence units are at the heart of a 'fight against all forms of illicit financial flows' in the midst of a financial and economic crisis (Tracfin 2012: 3).

While the anti-money-laundering apparatus initially targeted a single category of offender (drug traffickers and money-launderers of profits from drug trafficking), it is now promoted as a way to deal with all natural and legal persons involved in activities that generate 'dirty money'. According to official statements, such as the quote from Tracfin's director given above, the de-compartmentalization of the fight against illicit financial flows means that anti-money-laundering regulations can be used to monitor and punish transgressions related to any kind of trafficking, whether they involve an illegal activity or a legitimate enterprise. Qualifying tax crime as a predicate offence for money laundering is presented as constituting the end of selective tolerance for specific situations and transgressions committed by persons of 'respectability and high social status', such as tax-related white-collar crime.

This chapter examines this assertion and the management of tax transgressions in France in relation to the broader policing of 'financial crime'. To what extent do tax controls (re)produce inequalities in the treatment of citizens? How is the recent qualification of tax evasion as a predicate offence of money laundering enforced in practice? To what extent does this major change in financial policing contribute to reinforcing law enforcement investigations against white-collar-related crime? To answer these questions, I start by presenting the concept of *illegalisms* invented by Michel Foucault.[2] I then consider the heuristic value of this concept for studying the management of white-collar crime and tax transgressions by the fiscal bureaucracy as well as by frontline actors dealing with money laundering. Finally, I look at two high-profile cases of money laundering in relation to tax issues.

Michel Foucault and the concept of illegalisms

The economy of illegalisms

In developing the concept of *illegalisms*, Foucault aimed to analyse the relations between social games (bypassing, diversion or explicit violation) related to norms and activities of differentiation, categorization, prioritization, and management of these social games defined as transgressive behaviour and undisciplined conduct (Foucault 1975; Lascoumes 1996). He was attempting to determine a way to define relational features surrounding transgressive practices, the social position of their perpetrators, and the forms of social reaction they provoke (Spire 2013). The concept of illegalisms and the expression 'economy of illegalisms' were especially used in his 1975 book *Discipline and Punish* as part of his analysis of the normative situation of the *Ancien Régime* in France (sixteenth to eighteenth centuries).

Foucault argues that the *Ancien Régime* involved a number of illegalisms and 'margins of tolerated illegalisms' that concerned the entire society (Foucault 1975: 98). Each segment of the population made use of illegalisms, while their margins of impunity took different forms depending on social status. The nobility, clergy and large landowners benefitted from 'privileged illegalisms' to the extent that they escaped the law through statutory privileges, tolerance, regular exemptions and exceptions (Foucault 1975; 2013). Tolerated bypass strategies involving custom and commercial rules constituted the main 'bourgeois illegalisms'. Weaker social groups had to conquer spaces of tolerance 'by force or obstinacy' on a daily basis in order to survive (Foucault 1975: 98). Popular illegalisms, such as 'smuggling, over-grazing and firewood collection on the King's lands, though threatened with terrible punishments, hardly ever resulted in prosecution' (Foucault 2001a: 1596). These margins of impunity were permitted through silent consent, while others were unintentionally allowed due to the impossibility of effectively enforcing the law and punishing offenders. At the time, social reaction was erratic and mainly symbolic, involving spectacular occasional punishments rather than systematic and pragmatic prosecution.

According to Foucault, tolerance for non-compliance with certain rules and customary laws was a key condition of the exercise of power in the *Ancien Régime*. In practice, the economy of illegalisms in the *Ancien Régime* was based on a very relative law enforcement rather than a systematic enforcement of royal and feudal regulations. 'For instance, the most traditional form of tax fraud, but also the most apparent smuggling, were part of the economic life of the kingdom. In other words, there was a perpetual negotiation between legality and illegality that was a condition of the functioning of power at the time' (Foucault 2001b: 1584). Margins of tolerated illegalisms were not accidental but were part of the functioning of the social, political and economic order and were anchored in the lifestyle of the population (Fischer and Spire 2009). Moreover, Foucault presented illegalisms as an essential element of economic and political life rather than a social pathology or a disruptive factor in the society. The normative situation of the *Ancien Régime* was deeply related to the complex coexistence – from rivalry to complicity – of a multitude of illegalisms that concerned every segment of the population. Social groups were keen to defend their margins of impunity and there were many acts of resistance, especially against tax levies. Tax revolts sometimes resulted in complicity between heterogeneous segments of the population to protest feudal rights that were seen as unfair (Foucault 1975). In the same way, the circumvention of commercial regulations regularly depended on arrangement between merchants and craftsmen (Gros 2010). A wide range of tax transgressions, commercial arrangements and smuggling practices were useful both for the survival of the poor and the economic development of the bourgeoisie.

With regard to this social configuration, bourgeoisie and weaker social groups were in a situation of interdependence as occasional allies against a common adversary, i.e. the feudal taxation in all its forms. On the one hand, most of the popular illegalisms were generally not undertaken to oppose merchants, bourgeois profit or their material property but in order to resist feudal taxes. In other words, this was not theft or damage to property (illegalisms of goods) but anti-feudal fraud (illegalisms of rights). On the other hand, members of the bourgeoisie adopted a flexible position according to their interests. '[The bourgeoisie] supported [popular] anti-legal fights to the extent that they helped it and abandoned them when they became ordinary crime or related to political forms of mobilization. [The bourgeoisie] accepted smuggling and refused banditry; accepted refusal to pay taxes but rejected stagecoach robbery' (Foucault 2013: 147).

The *Ancien Régime*'s economy of illegalisms was thus framed by a form of *modus vivendi* between bourgeois illegalisms and popular illegalisms, which, as Foucault describes, was challenged towards the end of the eighteenth century (2001c). With the end of the *Ancien Régime*, the resulting political and industrial revolutions were associated with a change in social balances in society and in the management of illegalisms. The 'state of relative adjustment' between popular illegalisms and bourgeois illegalisms disappeared. Popular illegalisms were no longer tolerated by the ruling class and became the main target of the new repressive system.

The differential management of illegalisms

'The economy of illegalisms was restructured with the development of capitalist society' (Foucault 1975: 103). Modern state building, the rise of industrial capitalism, and the new status of private property led to a crisis in popular illegalisms. While popular illegalisms had been tolerated and sometimes encouraged by the bourgeoisie, they became intolerable in connection with the bourgeoisie access to hegemonic positions in economy and partly in politics. Foucault discusses this normative reconfiguration in relation to both urban and rural areas.

With regard to rural areas, 'the strengthening of property ties, or rather the new status of private property and its utilization, turned many accepted illegalisms into offences' (Foucault 2001c: 1335). A significant part of landownership was divided and transferred to the bourgeoisie at the end of the *Ancien Régime* with the abolition of feudal rights and the progressive disappearance of communal lands. With increasing land revenues, the new landowners became interested in land investment and more intensive agriculture. Moreover, they were freed from feudal duties to the extent that they benefitted from a newly individualized and almost absolute right to private property. As a consequence, they wanted to maximize land use and no longer tolerated a wide range of peasant customs and previously overlooked irregularities such as grazing rights, firewood collection and so on, especially given the increasing population pressure on the land (Foucault 1975). Non-compliance with former royal rules (illegalisms of rights) became unacceptable violations of landowners' private property (illegalisms of goods). These illegalisms were often vital for poor people's survival and their new systematic repression resulted in 'a series of chain reactions, increasingly illegal or, if you will, increasingly criminal: broken fences, cattle rustling or slaughter of cattle, fires, murders' (Foucault 1975: 101). Spaces of tolerance for popular illegalisms disappeared with the transformations in the rural economy and private property. In this context, popular illegalisms became mostly limited in practice to theft and damage to property ('illegalisms of goods'), which were systematically redefined and punished as penal offences.

The translation of a wide range of tolerated irregularities into clear-cut penal offences also took place in relation to industrial and commercial property in urban areas. Bourgeoisie wealth, based on the industrialization process and capitalist production methods, increasingly involved daily contact between productive forces (the working class) and the assets of the dominant class (raw materials, costly machines and manufactured objects) (Foucault 1975: 101; Gros 2010). Many workers left the craft system for salaried status in big factories and large maritime ports. They no longer owned and managed the objects and materials they worked with and produced. Without the ownership and access to productive assets, they no longer dealt personally with commercial regulations and therefore lost the opportunity and capacity to play with the margins of regulations through illegalisms of rights (fraud). While workers were stripped of property, they literally held bourgeoisie wealth and investment in their hands. From this perspective, their only opportunity for illegalisms was by tackling industrial bourgeois fortunes through depredation in factories and maritime ports (illegalisms of goods). 'Thus, with the development of the capitalist economy, working people were de facto displaced from crafting status to salaried status and were obliged at the same time to move from fraud to theft' (Foucault 2013: 151). While profits increasingly depended on daily contact between workers and goods, the bourgeoisie feared from an increasing number of thefts and attacks in connection with the new scales of industrial production. The rising industrial economy and new mode of production were accompanied by a systematic intolerance for traditional seizure of property, small robberies and other transgressive practices that were now recoded as crimes. Furthermore, the bourgeoisie's fear was not limited to the protection of the material accumulation of capital from the worker. The 'danger' was simultaneously related to infra-legal illegalisms in relation to the worker's body himself as productive force. In other words, the worker had to be disciplined to avoid immorality, laziness, alcoholism, wrongness and indelicacy in order to secure the profit condition (Foucault 2013: 176–178). The crisis in the *Ancien Régime*'s economy of illegalisms was also related to political requirements and popular conduct was carefully categorized and managed to prevent outbreaks that might challenge the new economic, social and political balances (Foucault 2013: 176–178).

Consequently, there was a recoding of popular illegalisms in urban and rural areas in order to monitor and punish them more systematically than before. The emergence of a new wealth associated with industrial capitalism and the proliferation of rural private properties were associated with the development of specific social controls. While members of the bourgeoisie avoided feudal predation through the French Revolution, they began to systematically target popular transgressions. Dominated social groups were no longer able to play with the blurred boundary of legitimate customs and illegitimate abuse of rights. Popular illegalisms became largely synonymous with damage to property and individuals rather than transgressions of regulations and were widely redefined as penal offences. In other words, the former margins of impunity and possibilities of playing with the rules disappeared for poorer people with the penalization of their illegalisms. The end of the *Ancien Régime*'s normative situation resulted in the general redistribution of illegalisms between 'illegalisms of goods' and 'illegalisms of rights'. Dominated social groups were restricted mainly to illegalisms of goods such as theft and attacks on property, i.e. illegalisms perpetrated by someone who works with materials that he or she does not own (Foucault 2013). The dominant class reserved the domain of illegalisms of rights, such as fraud, commercial irregularities, tax evasion and other practices that gamed the rules, i.e. illegalisms committed by someone whose wealth is related to law and offers the possibility of playing with the law (Foucault 2013).

The perpetrators of illegalisms of rights – such as tax illegalisms – have continued to benefit from margins of interpretation regarding the applicable rules. They have retained the possibility of playing with the boundary of legality and, to a certain extent, with the margins of legislation. To put it bluntly, white-collar tax payers can try to manipulate the blurred boundaries of deviant (tax evasion) and lawful (tax avoidance) activities 'to both try to escape tax and stay on the legal side of the boundary' (McBarnet 1991: 83). While the distinction between legal (tax optimization) and illegal (tax fraud) strategies for avoiding taxes is apparently clearly established in law, the reality is much more complicated, given the complexity of tax measures and the constant games of interpretation, diversion and circumvention (Chavagneux et al. 2010). Many scholars are sceptical about the feasibility of drawing a clear analytical boundary between tax avoidance strategies, suggesting instead that it is necessary to recognize 'the existence of a continuum between the optimization tolerated by the texts and that practiced in breaking the rules' (Chavagneux et al. 2010; Spire 2011: 59). As a form of illegalisms of rights, 'tax illegalisms' constitute of many different ways of gaming the rules, some of which take place 'in gaps in the law – gaps that were foreseen by its silences or opened up by de facto tolerance' (Foucault 1975: 103).

Foucault points out that the social redistribution of illegalisms of goods and illegalisms of rights was part of a massive reform of the juridical framework and a re-composition of positive law that reflects a 'differential management of illegalisms' according to the situation and person involved (Foucault 2001d). 'I think that the justice system – and mainly the general system of surveillance that was developed at the end of the 18th century, the beginning of the 19th century, in all European countries – is the confirmation of this new fact: the old popular illegalisms that were tolerated in certain forms under the Ancien Régime became literally impossible' (Foucault 2001d: 1304). Illegalisms of goods (thefts, damage to property, and so on) began to be carefully monitored and increasingly publicly punished as dramatized forms of crime. In other words, illegalisms of goods are handled by police forces, criminal courts and jail, while illegalisms of rights (commercial irregularities, frauds and gaming the rules) are not necessarily part of the criminal justice system but are dealt with mainly by other state administrations that survived the *Ancien Régime*, technical commissions and internal rituals of truth such as commercial courts, and punishment other than imprisonment, such as settlements, negotiated regularization and attenuated fines (Foucault 1975).

The structural divide between the two generic forms of illegalisms involves class opposition (illegalisms of goods/working class vs illegalisms of rights/ruling class) as well as differential categorization (clear-cut penal sanctions vs multi-form and not exclusively penal sanctions) and differential treatment (penal trial/prison/social visibility vs administrative and commercial trial/negotiations/social discretion) (Foucault 1975; Lascoumes 1996). Thus, Foucault's analysis focused on law reform as an indicator of the change in relation to the exercise of power. The juridical dimension of power reflects social domination that is exercised not through attempts to enforce the law but through differentiated management of illegalisms (Gros 2007).

Foucault argued that the judicial system is not designed and implemented to repress or eradicate every form of illegalism but instead attempts their differential management. In other words, the judicial system organizes illegalisms, differentiating them to make it possible 'to order them in a hierarchy' (Foucault 2009: 19) as a way 'of laying down the limits of tolerance, of giving free reign to some, of putting pressure on others, of excluding a particular section, of making another useful, of neutralizing certain individuals and of profiting from others' (Foucault 1975: 277). The law is thus not strictly enforced to the extent that it is seen as a management instrument for dealing with the margins of legality (Harcourt 2013). Social domination is subtler than a simple opposition between presence and absence of control and punishment. Domination refers to the social distribution of illegalisms and the existence of play spaces between the written norm and the practised norm as well as the differential social reaction according to the situation and person involved. Foucault's reflection on this moment of historical transformation and social domination has been put into a couple of other perspectives in relation to other research objects such as business crime.

Using the concept of illegalisms to study white-collar crime and tax controls

The strategic tension between illegalisms and crime

Pierre Lascoumes has extended the Foucauldian research programme concerning the differential management of illegalisms, insisting on the heuristic value of the concept of illegalisms in challenging two traditional assumptions. First, he reminds us that Foucault invented this concept to break with 'the false neutrality of legal categories [such as offence] that present "order" and "disorder" as stable and universal historical facts, as objective facts free from any value judgements'

(Lascoumes 1996: 79). Second, Foucault also contested 'the alleged naturalness of criminological categories [such as delinquency] that assigns the origin of acts of social transgressions to internal individual determinants. The use of interpretative medical concepts hid the political and social basis of transgressions and their repression in the 19th century' (Lascoumes 1996: 80). Lascoumes studies the social reaction to 'business crime' that undermines economic and political rules in France (Lascoumes 1986; 1997; 2011).

To do so, he focuses his analysis on the strategic tension between illegalisms and crime rather than the legal opposition between legality and illegality. He moves away from what Gilles Deleuze called the 'crude opposition of law and illegality' to substitute a 'subtle correlation made between illegalisms and laws' (Deleuze 2004: 37). The classic boundary between legality and illegality implicitly sustains the idea or the ideal of a clear-cut and automatic distribution of cases on the two sides of the boundary. The sociological and criminological use of this binary juridical opposition means that scholars often fail to undertake careful study of economic and political elites' active effort to manipulate it. Instead, the focus on the law–illegalisms correlation and the illegalisms–crime tension (re)introduces uncertainty regarding application of the law, leading to analysis of the subtle phenomena of 'legal avoidance' that take advantage of the margins and gaps in the law. On its own initiative, the law never imposes itself on social facts, meaning that ongoing games continue to overwhelm, displace and challenge the boundaries of legality. According to Doreen McBarnet, 'we need to focus research not just on crime but on the subtler phenomenon of legal avoidance, not just in tax but generally. We need to explore how economic elites actively use the institutions, ideologies, and methods of law to secure immunity from legal control' (1991: 342). Such an epistemological position would encourage the study of a continuum of practices. This analytical continuum covers conducts that are condemned, 'astute manipulations', 'creative' uses of law and conducts that are 'illegal in theory but overlooked in practice because of difficulty in detecting them and control agencies' lack of initiative' (Lascoumes 1997: 239). This position calls to break down the walls of criminological approaches that cannot provide an overview of business illegalisms to the extent that the study is limited to criminal acts that are detected and processed at the judicial level. It is also a way to reject the idea that legitimate research objects in criminology should be limited to acts covered by penal law.

Lascoumes emphasizes the strategic tension between illegalisms and crime to show how the practices of certain commercial or financial companies transgress legal norms without being automatically qualified as business crime. His research method is close to Edwin Sutherland's famous study of white-collar crime in that he not only studies cases that end in criminal conviction but also carefully examines legal processes that orientate the categorization, the management and the settlement of cases. Thus, he also analyses administrative and civil prosecution and cases in which charges were dismissed or dropped in order to understand how various forms of business illegalisms are sorted and managed by the judicial institution (Armand and Lascoumes 1977; Lascoumes 1986; Sutherland 1949). For instance, he contributes to understanding how transgressions are eventually prosecuted in the civil court although they can be heard in a criminal court. The objective is not restricted to denunciation that would be of limited use at the theoretical level with the risk to secure legitimacy for repressive practices that are criticized for their disciplinary effects. Lascoumes systematically analyses criminal law as a component of positive law that includes other normative systems (civil, administrative, commercial and so on). Thus, positive law is understood as a space of complex relations between different systems of formal regulation. These complex relations must be examined to grasp how a particular transgression is not managed by criminal law although criminal law was a possible code of interpretation of this situation.

While illegalisms of goods mainly refer to one system of regulation (criminal procedure), many illegalisms of rights and business illegalisms can be related to several regulation systems at the same time (criminal, civil, commercial or administrative). Consequently, the choice of the regulation system and the juridical qualification is a key issue at stake in relation to business transgressions. This is why there is a 'differential system of regulation for business illegalisms and crime' (Lascoumes 1986: 84). The juridical dimension of power operates throughout the social interaction that aims at categorizing situations always peculiar. According to Lascoumes, the true privilege of business illegalisms is this variety of management modalities that very often leads to the avoidance of the most repressive ones. He emphasizes the difficulty of applying a simple criminal qualification (when it exists) to these multiple games with the legal rules. He argues that

> business illegalisms are those gaming practices that have rules and professional principles that are treated with respect, even to the extent of being overused, and involve abuse or avoidance. At certain times in a company's history (for instance in order to get through a financial crisis or a labor dispute) or in relation to certain business activities (access to foreign markets, management of dangerous competitors), companies – including the most prosperous and significant ones – take actions that transgress legal norms. This does not mean that we can automatically talk about "business crime". The law is a coding system that distinguishes conflicts over values as well as conflicts of interest in order to categorize them so that they can be regulated. We consider actions to be criminal when a criminal sanction is successfully applied to the situation. Activities are considered illegalisms when the practice concerned resists or escapes enforcement under the legal code, either because the practice is not socially visible or because no social actor (whether victim or control agency) is able to enforce the legal code because of the resistance of the perpetrator.
>
> *(Lascoumes 1997: 232–233)*

Finally, Lascoumes agrees with Foucault's historical hypothesis about the differential management of illegalisms.

> Admittedly, there has not been, as we often think, hyper-control on the one hand [regarding popular illegalisms], and complete overlooking on the other [bourgeois-business illegalisms]. While there was a general attempt in the 19th century to make all illegalisms visible, this process was done differentially and heterogeneously. There is a major difference in the way illegalisms were made visible, related to the form of instruments of regulation used. There is 'sunlight' and 'night light', and various positions between shade and light. Making illegalisms visible has been done differentially and varies in relation to issues of person and situation.
>
> *(Lascoumes 1986: 8–9)*

While penal reform made the dominated classes' illegalisms of goods and punishment widely visible, it contributed to maintaining socially hidden the illegalisms of rights of the dominant class. The choice of different instruments of regulation was the key element in maintaining this distinction: from 'sunlight' (mainly arrest, ordinary courts, and prison) to 'night light' (mainly arbitration mechanisms, special courts, and negotiations) (Lascoumes and Moreau-Capdevielle 1984). Lascoumes insists that the perceptions of legal authorities and public opinion have changed regarding white-collar crime and elite illegalisms, which have been increasingly seen as faults that should be penalized rather than the simple errors they had been considered for decades (1997). The transformation of judicial corps and its relations with other social actors (journalists and so on) have also contributed to prosecute business illegalisms in the 1990s (Roussel 2002). However, Lascoumes' quote still appears to be relevant in France in relation to recent initiatives regarding the management of economic activities (Godefroy 2010).

At least, illegalisms of rights are no longer the quasi-monopoly of the dominant social groups due to the transformation of state interventionism in Western countries (Fischer and Spire 2009). The same instruments of regulation (such as those concerning money laundering) also tend to be applied both to illegalisms of rights and illegalisms of goods. Despite this, the contemporary changes do not mean the end of differential management of illegalisms according to situation and person.

The differential management between tax illegalisms

There is currently renewed interest in France in the concept of illegalisms and several French sociologists have used the Foucauldian concept to discuss the transformation of state interventionism in western countries since the 1980s.

> Here, our aim is to return to the notion of 'differential management of illegalisms,' not as a form of privilege of one class over the other but as a mode of domination used by state agents, particularly when they face illicit practices that target the transgression of laws or regulations rather than goods or persons. [...] In contemporary times, 'illegalisms of rights' are no longer the preserve of the dominant class but, more generally, concern all categories of individuals dealing with the state (foreigners without legal right of residence, detainees, taxpayers, or social benefit recipients). The issue of regulating these illegalisms is no longer thought of only in contrast to 'illegalisms of goods' but it is considered in a context in which all social categories of the society are likely to be represented.
>
> *(Fischer and Spire 2009: 11)*

French sociologists also call for a change of analytical perspective in studying the management of illegalisms. With regard to business crime, Pierre Lascoumes has mainly tried to question 'systems of ideological and repressive power on which criminal justice is based', with a specific focus on the judicial sphere as a key component of social reaction (Armand and Lascoumes 1977: 166). From the judicial sphere to the bureaucratic universe, recent studies deal instead with the social conditions related to the implementation of legal norms by 'street level bureaucrats'. They analyse the management of illegalisms in terms of the connections between transgressions and control practices, carefully examining power relationships between state officers and the particular part of the public they are involved with, such as tax officers dealing with tax payer strategies for tax avoidance, border guards dealing with human mobility, custom officers dealing with flows of goods, smuggling, counterfeit and so on (Aguilera 2012; Chantraine and Salle 2009; Chauvin 2009; Fischer 2009; Heyman 2009; Moreau de Bellaing 2009; Spire 2009; 2011; 2012).

Although these studies show that, to a certain extent, illegalisms of rights are no longer limited to any one social group, they do not lead to the conclusion that there is no longer differential management of illegalisms according to issues of person and situation. Alexis Spire's study of tax control in France constitutes a particularly striking example of the way management of illegalisms results in inequality of treatment for the wealthiest tax payers and those in modest households.

Until the 1950s, tax control affected only the wealthiest citizens in France, with only 15 per cent of households considered taxable (direct tax) (Spire 2012). The situation has since changed. On the one hand, various policy measures mean that half of French households have become taxable. On the other hand, reforms of welfare policies have, paradoxically, put non-taxable households in contact with tax administration as they now need a certificate of non-taxation, based on their socio-economic status, in order to receive welfare payments. For the last 15 years, as the result of several reforms, tax officers have both collected taxes and participated in the redistribution of social benefits to non-taxable households who were previously not on the tax administration radar (Spire 2012). As a consequence, the tax bureaucracy has assumed a central position in the control apparatus for social benefit recipients (Spire 2012).

Any social group that deals with the tax bureaucracy is de facto in a situation that can lead to commission of illegalisms of rights in relation to tax rules. Although in principle all citizens are treated equally by the tax administration, Alexis Spire shows that the reality is different and highlights inequalities of treatment produced in relation to the social conditions under which tax rules are implemented (Spire 2009; 2011; 2012). To study tax controls in France, Spire interviewed tax officers and observed face-to-face interactions between tax officers and those suspected of tax transgressions or tax payers challenging the calculation of their tax. He aims to understand how a public institution – with officers very concerned about the public interest and the common good – can (re)produce inequalities. Indeed, he shows that these face-to-face interactions reflect a differential management of transgressions that depends on the categories of both taxes and tax payers and points to inequalities of treatment that have their source in the evolution of control practices and the implementation of official instructions.

With respect to the evolution of tax controls, one of the elements that has exacerbated the differential management of tax illegalisms since the 1990s is computerization. Computerization has increased the ease with which specific taxes and tax payers who earn easily verified incomes, such as salaries, retirement pensions, or social benefits, can be monitored. Tax officers can see on their computer screen whether there is any discrepancy between a tax return and the amount of money officially paid by the agencies involved such as employees' companies, pension funds and so on and so forth (Spire 2012). Computerization is, however, much less efficient in checking and detecting tax transgressions by enterprises, liberal professions and self-employed workers as well as wealthy tax payers. Companies, liberal professions and self-employed workers can adjust their income and business expenses while the French solidarity tax on wealth is based on a self-declaration mechanism that cannot be automatically cross-checked with any paying agencies' documents.[3] Instead, tax officers are heavily reliant on information provided by the tax payer who has wider possibilities for concealment or underestimation of the value of his or her goods and assets (Spire 2012). While lack of correspondence between reported and taxable incomes is fairly easily to detect in some situations, discrepancies in relation to other taxes such as the solidarity tax on wealth are much more difficult to locate, offering greater opportunities to play with the margins of tax rules and thus to abuse the tax system.

As well, political attention directed toward 'social fraud' has contributed to increased computerized surveillance of non-taxable and modest social groups. Increased interconnectability between data systems as well as the widening exchange of information between tax administrations, the medical benefits fund, the family allowance fund and employment centres has allowed systematization of the practices of 'dataveillance' and increased control of benefit frauds. Individuals subject to the solidarity tax on wealth have, however, not been monitored through any similar initiatives, such as the interconnection of files regarding income tax payers, land registration, land tax, property tax, and so on. Moreover, although the amount of companies-related tax illegalisms far exceeds social benefit frauds, the construction of 'social fraud' as a public problem has also contributed to depict persons who abuse social welfare as the main fraudsters (Spire 2012).

With regard to the implementation of official instruction, tax officers are increasingly expected to follow orders and internal guidelines that promote conciliation mechanisms in regularizing the situation of tax payers (Spire 2012). Here, the differential management of illegalisms is obvious to the extent that tax inspectors have an incentive to favour features of negotiation and regularization rather than pure sanction in the name of pragmatism. Wealthy tax payers very often benefit from these negotiation mechanisms as they can call upon the skills and technical support of their own tax advisers and tax accountants in dealing with those concerned with tax controls. In contrast, modest and middle-class households lack access to expensive expert knowledge and are less familiar with the subtle aspects of tax rules. They depend on tax officers rather than tax advisers for help. While tax officers assist modest tax payers to formulate their requests, they are also the ones who ultimately assess these requests. Spire points out inequalities between tax payers in their ability to challenge tax calculations or to justify the way their tax return was calculated in order to avoid, or at least minimize, potential sanctions. As well, the wealthiest tax payers are in the best position to manage face-to-face tax negotiations. Ultimately, they are in the best position to both 'try to escape tax *and* stay on the legal side' of the blurred boundary between tax avoidance and tax offence.

As a result of elements such as computerization, modes of control, high technicality, conciliation mechanisms, new legislations, internal guidelines and the way they are interpreted and adapted in practice by street level bureaucrats, there are increased disparities in treatment regarding tax controls. Any social group may be associated with illegalisms of rights in relation to taxation but a social distinction has been reintroduced within this form of illegalisms. Dominant groups' tax illegalisms mainly consist of using the gaps in law and showing 'good faith' while popular tax illegalisms mainly refer to an explicit violation of legal norms. On the one hand, popular illegalisms are carefully monitored and do not really benefit from margins of interpretation and gaps in tax rules. On the other hand, dominant illegalisms are less constrained by bureaucratic computerized controls and those involved are much better at playing with tax regulations. There is thus a differential management of tax illegalisms according to issues of situation and person. Such a 'complex regime of derogations and differential treatment' regarding taxes challenges the republican principle of equality (Spire 2009: 164). 'As with the case of school, the strength of this mechanism [of social domination and reproduction of inequality] is that it is mainly achieved unbeknownst to the agents who enforce it' (Spire 2012: 13).

While the difference being discussed here is *between* tax illegalisms, there is also another form of differential management that occurs primarily between tax illegalisms and the other illegalisms of rights (and goods) covered by the anti-money-laundering apparatus. In France, tax evasion has been categorized as a predicate offence of money laundering since 2009. Since then, for the first time, the same regulation instrument is now officially used to counter 'all forms of illicit financial flows', regardless of issues of person and situation. However, the social conditions of implementation of the law reproduce a differential management *of* tax illegalisms.

Tax transgressions and the fight against dirty money

Tax fraud as a predicate offence of money laundering

As a dependent offence, money laundering presupposes that a prior – or 'predicate' – crime has been committed, the profits of which are being concealed or at least 'recycled' as 'dirty money'. 'The illegalism punished as money laundering is constructed relative to another illegalism corresponding to the source of the assets laundered' (Cassani 2009: 17). In other words, the laundering of dirty money necessarily results from other transgressive behaviours.

The requirement of a predicate offence aligns money laundering with a type of financial and economic illegalisms that may be described as 'secondary' – not, certainly, in terms of the actors' ultimate aim, which generally remains profit, but in a chronological sense as occurring later. While money laundering is a form of secondary illegalism, the definition of the primary illegalism on the basis of which financial surveillance and intelligence is implemented merits our attention (Amicelle 2011; Amicelle and Favarel-Garrigues 2012). In the course of the first years of international mobilization against money laundering, a frontier was negotiated and drawn between what was potentially a matter of dirty money – which thus, in the absence of further details, fell under the purview of anti-money-laundering legislation – and what was not, including 'tax issues'. 'In what concerns its field of activity, while the laundering of drug money will remain a principal focus for the FATF, its work will continue to cover money laundering of the proceeds of serious crimes and/or offences which generate significant funds. However, as in the past, the FATF will not deal with tax issues' (FATF 1994: 6).

Many academics saw this as more than simply bracketing a form of transgression and as evidence of selective tolerance for acts of white-collar crime. The initial focus of the mobilization against dirty money tended to reduce the previous unprecedented powers to investigate and expose bank secrecy regarding some forms of illegalisms associated with drug traffickers and '(transnational) organized crime' while leaving other business illegalisms – generally those associated with socially more legitimate actors – untouched (Favarel-Garrigues 2005; Strange 1998). However, the situation has recently changed. 'The list of predicate offences for money laundering has been expanded to include serious tax crimes. This will bring the proceeds of tax crimes within the scope of the powers and authorities used to investigate money laundering' (FATF 2012a: 2; 2012b). As a result, the offence of money laundering now tends to cover both illegalisms of rights such as tax transgressions and illegalisms of goods such as armed robbery. Although this major change is very new in international norms, it has been implemented in France since 2009 as a side effect of the third anti-money-laundering directive of the European Union (European Union 2005).

In preparing their third anti-money-laundering directive, European actors drew upon the FATF recommendations and, in particular, embraced the so-called 'threshold method'. In concrete terms this meant that, in addition to providing a list of predicate offences (first illegalisms), the 2005 directive covered all offences punishable by a sentence of more than one year in prison (the threshold for classification as a serious offence). For some European Union member states, including France, tax evasion fully or partly corresponded to the new definitional criteria of 'serious offence' as determined on the threshold method. In these cases, such an offence theoretically fell within the range of predicate offences and could thus be approached and investigated in the same way as the other first illegalisms of laundering. For professionals subject to anti-money-laundering regulation, the direct consequence of this inclusion was apparently straightforward: in the case of suspected tax evasion, they were to discharge their due diligence and reporting obligations under threat of sanction. In other words, the distinction between what was and was not a matter of money laundering was redrawn, with tax illegalisms tending to fall under the category of dirty money.

In France, the application of the third directive set in motion a number of interacting forces, including intense negotiations concerning taxes. The representatives of the institutions covered by the European text – and, in particular, banking establishments – condemned the prospect of indiscriminately including tax fraud in the fight against money laundering.

> In contrast to most European countries, in France [the reporting field of the third directive] will apply to all economic and financial crimes and in particular to all tax fraud, at least if national legislation is not adapted. Failing to distinguish between organized criminality and a form of fiscal incivility, this measure threatens to paralyse Tracfin due to the large number of suspicious transaction reports that will likely flow from it. What's more, there is a risk that this will result in the creation of files for thousands of people. The FBF [French Banking Federation] asks the authorities for a pragmatic solution so that banks can continue to effectively fight money laundering in a clarified legal framework.
>
> *(FBF 2007: 39)*

According to this thinly veiled attempt to reconfigure the situation, all tax fraud is merely a form of incivility, that is, a simple error that contrasts with the misdeeds associated with the dramatized notion of organized criminality.

Numerous discussions took place during the consultations, held under the aegis of the Ministry of Finance, concerning the draft ordinance that would transpose the directive into French law. Among the handful of initiatives considered, serious discussion was given to an approach that would have bisected the existing definition of tax fraud (Amicelle 2013; Favarel-Garrigues et al. 2009). In particular, a solution was considered that would have distinguished between 'aggravated tax fraud' and 'simple tax fraud', with the phenomena covered by the latter expression located outside the scope of the anti-money-laundering directive. This option was supported by the sectors covered by the directive. The proposal thus consisted of reworking a pre-existing legal category: introducing a new degree of differentiation would, it was hoped, help sharpen the qualification/disqualification boundary for certain fiscal illegalisms.

The ordinance ultimately signed by the president of the Republic on 30 January 2009 and ratified by parliament on 12 May 2009 did not opt for revision of the crime of tax fraud, which continues to be punishable by a sentence of up to several years of prison (President of the French Republic 2009). While the executive authorities clearly did not want to run the risk of trivializing a portion of tax fraud by having it fall under the critical threshold of one year of prison, the text was not 'silent' on the subject.

The differential management of tax illegalisms

In contrast to all other predicate money-laundering offences, suspicion of tax fraud, however well-substantiated, is not sufficient grounds for sending a report to Tracfin. In addition to knowing, suspecting, or having good reasons to suspect that a sum or transaction is the result of tax fraud, at least one of 16 criteria for tax fraud laundering set out in a specific decree published under the aegis of the prime minister six months after the original ordinance must also be met (Prime Minister of the French Republic 2009). Introduction of these criteria was justified by reference to the complexity of tax fraud and was intended to supply professionals with indicators that could help them identify cases of fraud. However praiseworthy this last intention may be, it does nothing to conceal the principal effect of this regulatory Act. It has contributed to compensate for the impossibility of formally excluding tax fraud from the category of money laundering. That does limit the volume of information transmitted to Tracfin.

Ultimately, this change in practical management was fully consistent with the differentiation between two types of tax illegalisms in terms of seriousness. While the distinction remains implicit in the 16 criteria, in practice it is explicit. A source of ambiguity and uncertainty, the list of criteria is subject to interpretation by the parties involved in implementation. This involves clarifying the fuzzy limit between, on the one hand, tax illegalisms that are to be reported by banks and, on the other, those that fall outside the scope of the anti-money-laundering apparatus. This process of interpretation focuses on the notion of 'serious and organized tax fraud' to give meaning to the ordinance, although this notion appears neither in the decree nor in other official documents and has no legal value in France. Nevertheless it has become established as an unwritten norm and a shared point of reference relative to which a given tax situation can be described and a decision taken as to whether it should be denounced (Amicelle 2013) and has been adopted not only by the vast majority of banking actors but also by Tracfin agents, who repeat endlessly that 'in regards to the present issue of the notion of tax fraud encountered by professionals, Tracfin insists on the notion of "serious and organized" tax fraud'.[4] Thus in France, all tax fraud is theoretically covered by anti-money-laundering legislation and the associated sanctions. In practical terms, however, a portion of such fraud is protected by selective oversight in accordance with official regulations and the manner in which they are interpreted. This differential management is structured around the notion of 'serious and organized tax fraud' that resulted from the appropriation of the law by the actors involved in its implementation.

By establishing a new explicit differentiation in practice, Tracfin and its 'informers' gave official status to the fact that the anti-money-laundering directive is not to be applied to 'ordinary' tax fraud. The conservation of a space of tolerance for these 'ordinary' tax illegalisms reassured banking actors, who were eager to limit their anti-money-laundering obligations. In addition to acknowledging the organizational routines and representations that have led anti-money-laundering activities to be associated with the repression of organized criminality, this margin of tolerated illegalisms also took Tracfin, which must give pragmatic imperatives priority over legalism, into account. Concern that the service would be deluged by an influx of reports that would be impossible to handle played a decisive role, as did the desire to remain focused on organized crime (understood as the pursuit of major trafficking) and to avoid compromising the relations of trust that had been established with financial circles.

Given this new variation on the notion of tax illegalisms, precisely where 'ordinary' tax fraud stops and 'serious and organized' tax fraud begins remained to be seen. A priori, the response to this question is to consult the official 16 criteria. However, these provide only a collection of distinctive signs; they reduce but do not eliminate the imprecision that characterizes the notion of serious and organized tax fraud (Amicelle 2013). The product of a negotiated adjustment, this notion is not yet a defined legal category in French law, a fact that somewhat increases the margin of manoeuvre of the actors responsible for categorizing the operations they encounter. Adding to the difficulties of detection that characterize most acts of money laundering in general, and tax fraud laundering in particular, the imprecise status and content of this category reveals the relativity of the new anti-money-laundering norm as applied to tax illegalisms. Evaluating the extent to which dominant illegalisms, business illegalisms and therefore white-collar crime are affected by reports of suspicious transactions and the possibility of legal action would require a systematic analysis of practices – and perhaps an ethnographic study – of Tracfin and the regulated actors. Nonetheless, two recent high-profile cases offer some insights into the management of money laundering in relation to tax evasion and the relation between tax issues and the blurred notion of dirty money.

Money laundering in relation to tax transgressions: high-profile cases

The Cahuzac scandal

On 2 April 2013, former budget minister Jérôme Cahuzac admitted that he had had an undeclared bank account in Switzerland and then in Singapore for more than 20 years (Laurent 2013). According to Cahuzac and his lawyer, the bank account contained 600,000 euros derived mainly from his professional activity as a surgeon and his advocacy activities in connection with pharmaceutical companies. Here, the situation is consistent with Sutherland's definition of white-collar crime as 'a crime committed by a person of respectability and high social status in the course of his occupation' (1949: 9). While Cahuzac is a medical professional and worked for the Health Ministry between 1988 and 1991, he was suspected of conflict of interest in relation to his advocacy activities. Cahuzac was eventually prosecuted for money laundering in relation to tax evasion and money laundering in relation to receipt, by a member of a medical profession, of benefits from a company whose services or products are supported by social security (Piel 2013). His prosecution created a major political scandal for the then fairly new government after the presidential election in 2012. His eventual confession ended four months of denial regarding the existence of his secret bank account (Laurent 2013) and created contradictory public reactions.

The Cahuzac case originated in disclosure by a journalist for Mediapart on 4 December 2012 (Arfi 2012), which provoked public disapprobation of Cahuzac. However, the media disclosure was almost immediately transformed into an affair rather than a scandal to the extent that the reaction against the budget minister was not unanimous.[5] In other words, the public space was divided largely into two audible camps. On the one hand, there was the camp of Cahuzac's accusers. On the other hand, there was the camp of the accusers of Cahuzac's accusers, who criticized the whistleblower (Mediapart) for not providing serious evidence against the budget minister (Cazi and Chemin 2013). At first glance, there was a radical division and a clear-cut opposition between journalists, politicians, citizens, and so on to whether Cahuzac should be designated as the guilty party or as a victim in the Cahuzac–Mediapart affair.

Eventually, further evidence and the minister's confession increased the number of those against him and re-transformed the affair into an unanimous scandal. Cahuzac no longer had any public defenders, not even, to a certain extent, himself. Although this chapter is not a sociological study of this controversy, one significant element must be mentioned: social reaction to this case was not initiated by 'street-level bureaucrats' and financial professionals involved in the national, European and international policing of illicit financial flows. Anti-money regulations have been used to prosecute Jérôme Cahuzac but they were not used to detect his financial assets and operations. As is often the case in France, a private disclosure to the press was the main starting point, with whistleblowers acting as law enforcement forces for white-collar crime (Lascoumes 2013).

Another high-profile case of money laundering in relation to tax evasion was recently revealed through anti-money-laundering investigation by law enforcement agencies.

Cleaner than dirty money?

Florence Lamblin, then deputy mayor of Paris's 13th arrondissement, and other individuals, such as a Parisian entrepreneur, commodity expert, lawyer, and art dealer, were prosecuted for money laundering in October 2012 (AFP 2012a). This case is particularly interesting in that it closes the anti-money-laundering loop. In other words, it links France's oldest predicate offence for money laundering (drug trafficking) with its newest predicate offence for money laundering (tax evasion) (AFP 2012b). Eight months before the prosecution began, French policemen in the Central Office against Illicit Drug Trafficking (Office Central pour la Répression du Trafic Illicite des Stupéfiants – OCRTIS) had followed and wiretapped individuals who were importing cannabis from Morocco to Paris (Bordenave 2013; Mallevoüe 2012; Mansour 2012). OCRTIS officers then launched a joint operation – 'Virus' – that involved their colleagues in the Central Office against Major Financial Crime (Office Central pour la Répression de la Grande Délinquance Financière – OCRGDF) in monitoring the laundering of the proceeds from this drug money (Mansour 2012). They discovered a clearing system operating between France and Switzerland that involved drug traffickers and 'white-collar individuals' such as Florence Lamblin.[6]

According to press reports and police declarations, the cannabis traffickers were attempting to recycle the proceeds of their crime and disguise the illegal origin of their money in order to avoid confiscation of assets and punishment. Most of their assets were circulated to intermediaries and then to a Paris-based bagman who participated in a clearing system to avoid any financial traceability (Baudet 2012; Bordenave 2012a). This system involved the chief executive officer of an asset management company (GPF SA) in Geneva as well as an employee of HSBC private bank (Favre 2012; Mansour 2012). The French 'white-collar' individuals involved had undeclared bank accounts in Switzerland and wanted to recover their assets secretly, without suspicious wire transfers or risky transport of cash in suitcases from Geneva to Paris, in order to avoid sanctions (Favre 2012). To do this they used the clearing mechanism offered by the chief executive officer of GPF SA (Mansour 2013).

Lamblin had 350,000 euros in Switzerland. She went to the chief executive officer of GPF SA, whose partner in Paris, the central bagman, arranged for 350,000 euros in cash to be given to Lamblin in Paris without any cross-border transfer and without any direct connection with her Swiss bank account (Mansour 2013; Mallevoüe 2012). Lamblin then received this cash that was already based in Paris and that supposedly belonged to cannabis traffickers under investigation. In other words, she has been indicted for the reception of money that supposedly came from trafficking in cannabis (Bordenave 2012b). Her undeclared bank account was then charged in order to transfer – through financial vehicle corporations – the same amount of money to foreign bank accounts believed to be connected to cannabis traffickers (Bordenave 2012b; Frammery 2012; Mansour 2013). The managers of the clearing system took a commission of several per cent for this operation (Bordenave 2012b).

The case thus includes prosecutable money-laundering practices in relation to tax evasion that were discovered by law enforcement agencies. Contrary to the Cahuzac scandal, Lamblin and other 'white-collar individuals' were prosecuted as a direct result of police investigation that involved anti-money-laundering regulations. Nevertheless, the detection of tax evasion by these white-collar individuals was only a side-effect of an investigation focused primarily on drug trafficking. Although the clearing system had existed for several years to help French tax evaders benefit from secret cash transfers, it was located and targeted only because it involved drug money (Bordenave 2013). According to one of the chief investigators,

> the role of the central bagman was intriguing because he delivered money in plastic bags or suitcases, between 100 000 and 400 000 euros to individuals who were not in the radar of drug-enforcement officers. [...] Several hundred hours of surveillance and wiretapping were necessary to understand 'this circus' and uncover this sophisticated mechanism of financial engineering. [...] The clients certainly did not want to know the origin of the money that they obtained with a snap of the fingers and that they received with a wealth of precautions.
>
> *(Frammery 2012)*

The tax evasion scheme was discovered as an unintended consequence of police operations intended to monitor drug traffickers and their practices in laundering drug money, not as part of an operation to deal with tax transgressions in relation to 'white-collar individuals'.

Lamblin's defence narrative has consisted of drawing a line between illegalisms that should be seen as errors (i.e. tax evasion) and illegalisms that should be dramatized and condemned as major faults (i.e. money laundering by drug traffickers).[7] She and her lawyer have claimed that she was the unfortunate victim of an involuntary connection with a criminal operation to the extent that she did not know the origin of the money she received. According to her lawyer, Lamblin wanted to repatriate 350,000 euros from a family legacy that has been in a Swiss bank account since 1920, on the suggestion of her bank.

> She was advised by a trusted person who put her in contact with a person who deals with this kind of transaction. She was fooled, thinking that the received assets were hers and not drug trafficking-related money. Did she know of the contact person's money laundering activities? Clearly not.
>
> (Le Parisien *2012)*

Her lawyer used a euphemistic strategy to draw a subtle line between tax evasion as an error, a misstep, or a 'naivety' and money laundering (in relation to drug trafficking) as a real fault, a crime. According to her lawyer, 'if one should blame her for anything, it would be at most for not having declared 350 000 euros to the tax authority' (*Le Monde* 2012a). 'Like many French citizens, she committed what I call a lightweight error' (*Le Monde* 2012b).

In an attempt to 'manage stigma' for his client by minimizing her transgression, the lawyer tried to reintroduce the normative boundary that was historically negotiated between tax evasion and the blurred notion of dirty money (Amicelle 2013).[8] Contrary to Doreen McBarnet's famous study about 'tax, fraud insurance, and the management of stigma', Lamblin's lawyer has not attempted to play with the boundaries of deviant and lawful activities to ensure that his client escapes tax and stays on the legal side of boundary. Actually, he has not been able to play with these boundaries to the extent that his client has admitted that she had an undeclared bank account and that she tried to transfer her assets secretly (Bordenave 2012b). Instead, the lawyer has moved from the boundary of legality and illegality to play with the boundary between illegalisms and crime; i.e. between grey money and 'dirty money' to avoid the social stigma and penal qualifications related to money laundering. He has aimed at avoiding a penal form of intervention to the extent that tax illegalisms can be managed by various resolution methods in relation to several normative systems (penal sanctions, administrative regularization, fines, and so on). 'Talking about a differential regulation of disputes consists of emphasizing on the different strategies of regulation implementation: Which mode of regulation will be used by whom and for whom?' (Lascoumes 1986: 204) Lamblin could not appear 'whiter than white collar crime' (McBarnet 1991), but her lawyer wanted her money to appear at least cleaner than dirty money. Although tax evasion is now categorized in law as a predicate offence of money laundering, the narrative defence still aims at resisting the established correspondence between tax fraud and 'dirty money'.

Conclusion

The French situation reflects continued sensitivity in relation to tax issues. It also highlights the current forms of differential management of tax illegalisms regardless of official statements about equal treatment of citizens by the tax bureaucracy or regarding anti-money-laundering apparatus as a 'fight against all forms of illicit financial flows'. On the one hand, there is a differential management *between* tax illegalisms according to issues of person and situation. In this first situation, the same generic sort of illegalisms (i.e. tax illegalisms) are committed, but are handled differently dependent on tax cases and the social situation of those involved. Although the tax administration should, in principle, deal with every citizen in a consistent and equal manner, the normative situation is different in practice. The implementation of tax rules and tax controls produces inequalities in treatment to the extent that control practices are much more efficient against modest social groups than against wealthy tax payers.

On the other hand, there is a differential management *of* tax illegalisms. In this second situation, the generic forms of first illegalisms themselves are different (tax transgressions, drug trafficking, theft and so on and so forth). In France, 'tax issues' are no longer excluded from anti-money-laundering regulations. The relative absence of differentiation in these regulations has led those involved in financial surveillance and intelligence in France to substitute differential management of tax illegalisms in practice. The categorization of tax fraud as a 'predicate offence' does not mean an end to anti-money-laundering regulations as a way to achieve differential management of illegalisms but has instead brought about a transformation in the way illegalisms are handled and a shift of tension between crime and illegalisms. The legal norms include tax transgressions a priori in the category of dirty money. In practice, however, this inclusion remains piecemeal and depends upon expected behaviours among groups of frontline actors in the fight against money laundering. This shift from differential management of illegalisms from 'above' (in the legal norms) to differential management from 'below' (in the practical norms) now extends beyond the somewhat particular framework of France. The recent inclusion of tax issues in supranational norms does not automatically presuppose that they will be fully and completely integrated into the shared norms of the actors responsible for fighting against dirty money on a daily basis.

'In every regime, all social groups, all classes, all castes have their own illegalisms' (Foucault 2001a: 1303). Further research is needed to get a clear picture of the way financial crimes are managed and how the current 'economy of illegalisms' is related to financial capitalism. In contrast to the advent of industrial capitalism described by Michel Foucault (1975) and its specific economy of illegalisms, profits now depend less on 'the worker's hand to hand fight with the merchandise' (Gros 2010: 14) than on the smooth circulation of capital flows, particularly in accordance with fiscal opportunities.

Notes

1 The criminological notion of financial crime is used by the European Commission to deal with both money laundering and terrorist financing: http://ec.europa.eu/internal_market/company/financial-crime/index_en.htm (accessed 2 December 2014).
2 Although the Foucauldian concept of 'illégalismes' has been frequently translated as 'illegalities', I prefer the term 'illegalisms' as it retains the key distinction in French between 'illégalisme' and 'illégalité' (both of which are translated as 'illegality').
3 Tax payers are subject to the wealth tax if their total net wealth exceeds a specific amount of money as of January 1 (e.g. 720,000 euros as of 1 January 2003; 790,000 euros as of 1 January 2010; 1,300,000 euros as of 1 January 2013).
4 Remarks of Jean-Pierre Gautier (Tracfin) during a speech entitled 'The new context of declarative obligations for financial bodies' ('Le nouveau contexte d'obligations déclaratives pour les organismes financiers') at the 9th Annual Anti-Money Laundering and Financial Crime Conference, 24–25 June 2010. An overview of the conference is available at this link: http://grasco.perso.sfr.fr/documents/lutte_anti_blanchiment_lutte_contre_la_criminalite_financiere_9_conference_internationale_paris2c_24_26_25_06_2010.pdf (accessed 2 December 2014).
5 For further information about the sociological use of the notions of 'affair' and 'scandal', see De Blic and Lemieux 2005.
6 The expression 'white-collar individuals' (i.e. '*cols blancs*' in French) has been widely used by journalists in this case.
7 For further information about 'defence narratives' and 'euphemism strategies' in relation to white-collar crime and political corruption, see Black 2007; Lascoumes 2013.
8 For further information about the expression of 'management of stigma' in relation to white-collar crime, see McBarnet 1991.

References

AFP (October 2012a) 'Blanchiment d'argent de la drogue: Une élue parisienne EELV parmi les 17 interpellés', *AFP*.
AFP (October 2012b) 'Blanchiment: un système parfaitement rodé, des "cols blancs" peu scrupuleux', *AFP*.
Aguilera, T. (2012) 'Gouverner les illégalismes: Les politiques urbaines face aux squats à Paris', *Gouvernement et action publique*, 3(3): 101–124.
Amicelle, A. (2011) 'Towards a "new" political anatomy of financial surveillance', *Security Dialogue*, 42/2: 161–78.
Amicelle, A. (2013) 'Gestion différentielle des illégalismes économiques et financiers', *Champ pénal/Penal Field*, 10: 1–24.
Amicelle, A. and Favarel-Garrigues, F. (2012) 'Financial surveillance: Who cares?', *Journal of Cultural Economy*, 5(1): 105–124.

Arfi, F. (December 2012) 'Le compte en Suisse du ministre du budget', *Mediapart*.
Armand, M.F. and Lascoumes P. (1977) 'Malaise et occultation: Perceptions et pratiques du contrôle social de la délinquance d'affaires', *Déviance et société*, 1/2: 135–169.
Baudet, P. (October 2012) 'Blanchiment: Par où passe l'argent de la drogue', *Ouest France*.
Black, W.K. (2007) 'Corruption kills', in H.N. Pontell and G. Geis (eds) *International Handbook of White-Collar and Corporate Crime*, New York: Springer, pp. 439–455.
Bordenave, Y. (October 2012a) 'Sept notables, trois frères et l'argent de la drogue', *Le Monde*.
Bordenave, Y. (October 2012b) 'Florence Lamblin n'as pas "pensé que c'était de l'argent sale"', *Le Monde*.
Bordenave, Y. (January 2013) 'Blanchiment: Le chaînon manquant entre financiers et trafiquants arrêté', *Le Monde*.
Cassani, U. (2009) 'Le puzzle des infractions préalables au blanchiment: Hasard ou système?', in B. Perrin (ed.) *La lutte contre le blanchiment d'argent: Pistes d'action entre prévention et répression*, Paris: L'Harmattan.
Cazi, E. and Chemin, A. (March 2013) 'Et Mediapart passa des critiques aux louanges', *Le Monde*.
Chantraine, G. and Salle, G. (2009) 'Le droit emprisonné? Sociologie des usages sociaux du droit en prison', *Politix*, 3/87: 93–107.
Chauvin, S. (2009) 'En attendant les papiers: L'affiliation bridée des migrants irréguliers aux États-Unis?' *Politix*, 3/87: 47–69.
Chavagneux, C., Murphy, R. and Palan, R. (2010) *Tax Havens: How Globalization Really Works*, London: Cornell University Press.
De Blic, D. and Lemieux, C. (2005) 'Le scandale come épreuve: Éléments de sociologie pragmatique', *Politix*, 3/71: 9–38.
Deleuze, G. (2004) *Foucault*, new edition, Paris: Editions de Minuit.
European Commission (2012) *Rapport de la Commission européenne au Parlement européen et au Conseil concernant l'application de la directive 2005/60/CE du Parlement européen et du Conseil relative à la prévention de l'utilisation du système financier aux fins du blanchiment de capitaux et du financement du terrorisme*, Brussels: Public report.
European Commision (2013) 'Anti-money laundering: Stronger rules to respond to new threats', Brussels. Press release.
European Union (2005) *Directive 2005/60/EC of the European Parliament and of the Council of 26 October 2005 on the Prevention of the Use of the Financial System for the Purpose of Money Laundering and Terrorist Financing*, Brussels.
FATF (1994) *Annual Report V*, Paris.
FATF (2012a) *FATF Recommendations: Information for the Media*, Paris.
FATF (2012b) *Financial Action Group Mandate (2012–2020)*, Paris.
Favarel-Garrigues, G. (2005) 'Domestic reformulation of the moral issues at stake in the drive against money laundering: The case of Russia', *International Social Science Journal*, 57/185: 529–541.
Favarel-Garrigues, G., Godefroy, T. and Lascoumes, P. (2009) *Les sentinelles de l'argent sale: les banques aux prises avec l'anti-blanchiment*, Paris: La Découverte.
Favre, A. (October 2012) 'Blanchiment: La place financière surprise et préoccupée', *Le Temps*.
FBF (French Banking Federation) (2007) *Activity Report*, Paris.
Fischer, N. (2009) 'Une frontière "négociée": L'assistance juridique associative aux étrangers placés en rétention administrative', *Politix*, 3/87: 71–92.
Fischer, N. and Spire, A. (2009) 'L'État face aux "illégalismes"', *Politix*, 3/87: 7–20.
Foucault, M. (1975) *Surveiller et punir: Naissance de la prison*, Paris: Gallimard.
Foucault, M. (2001a) 'La prison vue par un philosophe français', in *Dits et écrits I. 1954–1975*, Paris: Gallimard, pp. 1593–1599.
Foucault, M. (2001b) 'Des supplices aux cellules', in *Dits et écrits I. 1954–1975*, Paris: Gallimard, pp. 1584–1588.
Foucault, M. (2001c) 'La société punitive', in *Dits et écrits I. 1954–1975*, Paris: Gallimard, pp. 1324–1338.
Foucault, M. (2001d) 'À propos de l'enfermement pénitentiaire', in *Dits et écrits I. 1954–1975*, Paris: Gallimard, pp. 1303–1313.
Foucault, M. (2009) 'Alternatives to the prison: Dissemination or decline of social control?', *Theory, Culture & Society*, 26/6: 12–24.
Foucault, M. (2013) *La société punitive: Cours au Collège de France, 1972–1973*, Paris: Seuil/Gallimard.
Frammery, C. (October 2012) 'Une affaire de blanchiment très française et très suisse', *Le Temps*.
Godefroy, T. (2010) 'La délinquance économique et financière serait-elle en voie de disparition?', *CESDIP*.
Gros, F. (2007) *Michel Foucault*, Paris: Presses universitaires de France.
Gros, F. (2010) 'Foucault et la société punitive', *Pouvoirs*, 135: 5–14.

Harcourt, B. (2013) 'Situation du cours', in M. Foucault, *La société punitive: Cours au Collège de France, 1972–1973*, Paris: Seuil/Gallimard, pp. 272–314.
Heyman, J. (2009) 'Risque et confiance dans le contrôle des frontières américaines', *Politix*, 3/87: 21–46.
Lascoumes, P. (1986) *Les affaires ou l'art de l'ombre: Les délinquances économiques et financières et leur contrôle*, Paris: Centurion.
Lascoumes, P. (1996) 'L'illégalisme, outil d'analyse', *Sociétés & Représentations*, 3: 78–84.
Lascoumes, P. (1997) *Élites irrégulières: Essai sur la délinquance d'affaires*, Paris: Gallimard.
Lascoumes, P. (2011) *Une démocratie corruptible*, Paris: Seuil.
Lascoumes, P. (2013) 'Élites délinquantes et résistance au stigmate', *Champ pénal/Penal Field*, 10: 1–18.
Lascoumes, P. and Moreau-Capdevielle, G. (1984) 'Des finesses de citadins à la délinquance des societies commerciales: Place de la justice pénale dans le contrôle de la délinquance des affaires', *Revue de science criminelle et de droit pénal comparé*, 4: 707–722.
Laurent, S. (April 2013) 'Si vous n'avez rien suivi de l'affaire Cahuzac', *Le Monde*.
Le Monde (October 2012a) 'Blanchiment d'argent de la drogue: L'élue EELV se défend', *Le Monde*.
Le Monde (October 2012b) 'Florence Lamblin, élue écologiste de Paris mise en examen, a démissionné', *Le Monde*.
Le Parisien (October 2012) 'Blanchiment: L'embarrassante fortune de l'élue écologiste parisienne', *Le Parisien*.
Mallevoüe, F. (October 2012) 'Blanchiment d'argent: Ce qu'on reproche à l'élue', *Le Figaro*.
Mansour, F. (October 2012) 'La chute brutale de deux financiers genevois', *Le Temps*.
Mansour, F. (January 2013) 'Des blanchisseurs au sort presque scellé', *Le Temps*.
McBarnet, D. (1991) 'Whiter than white collar crime: Tax, fraud insurance and the management of stigma', *The British Journal of Sociology*, 42/3: 323–344.
Moreau de Bellaing, C. (2009) 'Violences illégitimes et publicité de l'action policière', *Politix*, 3/87: 119–141.
Peebles, G. (2012) 'Filth and lucre: The dirty money complex as a taxation regime', *Anthropological Quarterly*, 85/4: 1229–1256.
Piel, S. (April 2013) 'Jérôme Cahuzac encourt cinq ans de prison', *Le Monde*.
President of the French Republic (2009) 'Ordonnance n° 2009–104 du 30 janvier 2009 relative à la prévention de l'utilisation du système financier aux fins de blanchiment de capitaux et de financement du terrorisme', *Journal officiel de la République française*, Paris.
Prime Minister of the French Republic (2009) Décret n° 2009–874 du 16 juillet 2009 pris pour application de l'article L. 561–15-II du code monétaire et financier, *Journal officiel de la République française*, Paris.
Roussel, V. (2002) *Affaires de juges: Les magistrats dans les scandales politiques en France*, Paris: Éditions La Découverte.
Spire, A. (2009) 'Échapper à l'impôt? La gestion différentielle des illégalismes fiscaux', *Politix*, 3/87: 143–165.
Spire, A. (2011) 'La domestication de l'impôt par les classes dominantes', *Actes de la recherche en sciences sociales*, 190: 58–71.
Spire, A. (2012) *Faibles et puissants face à l'impôt*, Paris: Editions Raisons d'agir.
Spire, A. (2013) 'Pour une approche sociologique de la délinquance en col blanc', *Champ pénal/Penal Field*, 10: 1–17.
Strange, S. (1998) *Mad Money*, Manchester: Manchester University Press.
Sutherland, E. (1949) *White Collar Crime*, Westport: Greenwood Press.
Tracfin (2012) *Rapport annuel 2011*, Paris.

25

The prosecution of white-collar crime in a developing economy

A case study of Ireland in the twentieth century

Joe McGrath

Introduction

Criminologists like Sutherland complained that, in other countries, corporate misbehaviours were often defined as civil wrongs, not crimes, despite having all the characteristics of crimes (1949). This debate was often moot in Ireland. Though not thought to be morally reprehensible, corporate wrongdoing was extensively criminalized (McGrath 2010; 2011). There were, for example, 280 separate and distinct criminal offences in the Companies Acts 1963–1990 (McGahon 1991). Nevertheless, despite addressing corporate wrongdoing with its strongest form of censure, the law was rarely enforced. Already in 1958, the Company Law Reform Committee (Cox 1958: 53) concluded that some Irish companies exhibit 'a complete disregard of the requirements of the Companies Acts'. It stated that there 'is undoubtedly a tendency, especially in the case of private companies, to disregard or to be careless about the obligations which the law imposes as to the making of annual returns or even as to the books of account'. It noted (20) that such breaches were not taken as seriously as they should have been because 'in most cases in which prosecutions for offences under the Companies Acts are brought, there is a tendency to regard the offences as being trivial or technical'. Forty years after the publication of the Cox Report, the Working Group on Company Law Compliance and Enforcement (McDowell 1998: para. 1.2) was established due to the emergence of strong indications of abuses of company law. The group echoed the Cox Report, albeit in a sterner and firmer tone. It stated (paras. 2.4–2.5) that Ireland was 'characterised by a culture of non-compliance [...] Those who are tempted to make serious breaches of company law have little reason to fear detection or prosecution. As far as enforcement is concerned, the sound of the enforcers' footsteps on the beat is never heard'. It concluded that 'the great majority of the hundreds of summary offences have never been the subject of any criminal proceedings, and there have only been a handful of occasions on which the indictable offences have been prosecuted'.

The question naturally arises, therefore, as to why white-collar crime was so rarely addressed by the criminal courts in Ireland. In the paragraphs below, the activities of various bodies responsible for the detection and prosecution of white-collar crimes are analysed in order to explore why the under-policing of the corporate sector persisted for so long. Though critically descriptive rather than archival, a large amount of information is analysed and this is broken down and addressed under three sub-headings for the ease of the reader. The first part of this chapter illustrates that corporate deviancy was often addressed by the same machinery of enforcement that tackled ordinary crimes, even though it was ill-suited to this purpose. It progresses by analysing the extent to which specialized agencies were employed to assist in the detection and prosecution of corporate wrongdoing. Finally, the chapter concludes by integrating the failure to enforce company law into the wider social, political, and economic conditions which prevailed in Ireland for most of the twentieth century. It is hypothesized that these conditions created a context where there was little cultural recognition of the dangers posed by corporate harm.

By necessity, capturing a century of legal, social and economic history involves some generalization and some omissions. Some limitations have been inevitable. Though white-collar crime is a broad area of inquiry, including health and safety law, banking law, and environmental law, among others (Tombs 2005), this submission is restricted to an analysis of criminal offences in the Companies Acts. It is also temporally limited to the period between 1922 (the foundation of the Irish State) and 1998. As such, it concludes at a point when the landscape of corporate enforcement was on the cusp of significant transformation brought on by considerable economic and cultural change, developments which are outside the scope of this submission which documents Ireland's historical architecture of enforcement. Therefore, contemporary developments are merely noted in a brief way in the conclusion to this submission. In addition, the usual difficulties of interpreting crime statistics are exacerbated by the poverty of official data on corporate enforcement (O'Donnell et al. 2005; McCullagh 1995), necessitating significant reliance in places on newspapers and governmental reports, an unfortunately common feature in discussions on white-collar crime (Nelken 2007: 734). Moreover, the emphasis is on broad structural patterns rather than detailed legislative provisions or technical rules of evidence underpinning prosecutorial procedure. This 'big-picture' approach may be subject to the criticism that it lends itself to excessive simplification but it is necessary in order to reveal broad structural patterns of enforcement. It assists in teasing out the interaction of social and legal forces, interpenetrating fields that inform each other in ways that are rarely acknowledged, let alone articulated.

Conventional criminal law machinery

The Irish Police Force (An Garda Síochána or 'Gardaí') and the Office of the Director of Public Prosecutions (DPP), formerly the Attorney General, were primarily responsible for the prosecution of all crime in Ireland, including corporate and white-collar crimes like fraudulent trading and offences relating to insolvency (McDowell 1998). The DPP exercised the exclusive right to prosecute indictable crime (tried before a judge and jury) though it concurrently shared the ability to prosecute summary company law offences (tried before a judge without a jury), discussed separately below. However, the composition, education and training of the Gardaí suggest that they were not ideally placed to detect and investigate sophisticated forms of corporate wrongdoing. In the early days of the state, An Garda Síochána was composed mainly from a military or a farming background. Almost two-thirds of all Garda recruits between 1922 and 1952 had been in the Irish Republican Army (IRA) and approximately half of the recruits in this period were either farmers or labourers (McNiffe 1997: 47, 39). Most recruits had received only primary school education (McNiffe 1997: 51) which was supplemented by some very basic legal training on admission to the force. One recruit from this period recalls being told that the law was based on the ten commandments of Christ and that if he could remember this then he would not go far wrong (Ua Maoileoin 1989: 96).

The primary duties of the Gardaí in this period were the enforcement of licensing laws, detecting illicit distillation, detecting agrarian crime, and detecting ordinary crimes against person and property, particularly larceny (Interdepartmental Inquiry 1951). A study conducted in 1950s suggested that the Gardaí outside Dublin spent approximately 40 per cent per cent of their time performing administrative duties, including the collection of agricultural statistics, the distribution of old age pension books, and the enforcement of legislation ensuring that children attended primary school (Interdepartmental Inquiry 1951). It would seem that policing the corporate sector was not a significant priority for the force. The Gardaí also lived among the people they policed and their presence was an on-going reminder both of the existence of the law and the willingness to enforce it. Their presence in the community meant that they were usually aware of the potential opportunities for criminality in their district and as a result of their knowledge were often able to identify trouble-makers. The immediacy of the law was heightened when the Gardaí walked the beat or visited those perceived to be more prone to breaking the law. Information on Garda activity in this period is minimal because the Gardaí did not start publishing reports on its activities until 1950 (Kilcommins et al. 2004: 66). However, it seems likely that this model of policing was not suited to the corporate context because soldiers and farmers, rather than accountants and lawyers, were investigating technical breaches of the Companies Acts.

A specialist subgroup, the Garda Fraud Squad, was subsequently established to police less conventional, more complicated forms of crime. An examination of newspapers from this period suggests that the Fraud Squad was mainly concerned with cheque fraud, embezzlement, and conmen absconding with funds for bogus investments (*Irish Times* 1 November 1973: 17; 7 August 1976: 12; 4 June 1986: 6; 7 October 1987: 8; 19 December 1987: 10). However, the Fraud Squad did not seem to have any specific remit or area of specialization so it seemed to be called upon in any situation outside the expertise of the average Garda member. It investigated substandard deliveries to building sites, planning irregularities, the substitution of disposable napkins for prescription incontinence sheets (a Government minister promised prosecutions), video piracy, the refusal to renew membership with a local GAA sports club, the theft of ransom money for the racing horse 'Shergar', and the leaking of state examination papers (*Irish Times* 11 July 1980: 1; 16 April 1981: 1; 3 May 1982: 6; 31 May 1982: 21; 15 October 1982: 1; 11 November 1983: 1; 26 June 1985: 1). The Fraud Squad also investigated various forms of social welfare fraud, raising the question of whether the state was more concerned with punishing the poor rather than elite wrongdoers (*Irish Times* 18 February 1983: 6; 6 August 1984: 6; 25 March 1988: 10; 12 September 1986: 8; 16 September 1986: 8).

The squad was also severely under-resourced. In 1971, the nationwide force consisted of 17 men. By 1990, the squad was operating with fewer than 30 officers working a shift system that left as few as five officers on duty at any given time (*Irish Times* 25 September 1990: 13). In addition to poor staffing levels, the Garda policy on promotion undermined the effectiveness of the squad. Garda policy dictated that promoted officers were moved out of the branch in which they were working. So when squad officers were promoted, they were moved into non-fraud roles, divesting the squad of acquired expertise. Conversely, when Gardaí were promoted to senior roles in the Fraud Squad, they came from non-fraud backgrounds and lacked the required skills to investigate white-collar crimes. This policy demoralized the squad because members were reassigned if they were too good at their job and because promotion to senior posts in the squad was rarely from within their own ranks (*Irish Times* 25 September 1990: 13). Furthermore, as more Irish people began to avail of higher education, Garda recruits with university degrees in business and accounting felt little desire to specialize in fraud because they could build careers with more ease elsewhere in the force (*Irish Times* 23 February 1990: 9). This also contributed to the failure to develop expertise in the squad. In addition, the Minister for Justice acknowledged that the squad did not retain any full-time accountancy or legal staff to help them analyse and interpret company accounts and papers (Burke Dáil Debates 5 February 1991 col 1480). It was later also suggested that the squad was reluctant to consult outside accountants and auditors for help, feeling it unprofessional to ask civilians to aid them in law enforcement (*Irish Times* 11 April 1995: 13). If this was the case, and considering their general lack of resources, it is questionable to what extent the Gardaí were capable of doing their job, especially when it is considered that economic crimes are generally far more complicated than street crimes, involve intricate accounting practices, double books, enormous amounts of paperwork, and that prosecutors often need to have specialized skills to interpret data and must dedicate large amounts of time to the entire process (Braithwaite 1984: 324; Wilson and Matz 1977: 651).

In addition, the effectiveness of the squad was limited by its operational approach to investigations. It investigated cases only when it received complaints. One officer acknowledged that companies tended not to report frauds from within their own ranks so it may be that most cases were never even investigated (Gallagher 1999: 263). Furthermore, Carney observed that the squad seemed to take a deferential approach to suspects accused of fraud because it 'sees its suspects by appointment rather than dawn raid and it may be that if he or she doesn't confess in remorse at this genteel confrontation which the suspect has prepared for, they have not got the resources to go further and build a case through documents' (*Irish Times* 31 August 1990: 10). He pointed out that this approach, when combined with the lack of forensic accountancy skills, effectively rendered successful prosecution impossible because the 'capacity to build a case through documents without a suspect's co-operation should be a fraud squad's basic skill. The courts have not seen any evidence that such a skill exists in Ireland'.

In part, the failure of the Gardaí to address significant issues of corporate wrongdoing persisted because they were simply unaware that the law had been breached. While lawyers and accountants presumably would have advised their clients to comply with the law, the state did not rely on them as a source of crime detection. Lawyers, accountants and auditors were not under any obligation to report the suspected commission of indictable offences to the authorities. Consequently, the state failed to capitalize on those closest to the potential wrongdoing and it was rarely even aware that a criminal offence had been committed. Company officers that sought professional advice would also have been advised that if they broke the law, they would probably go unpunished (Appleby 2005: 267). Furthermore, professional bodies were not required to report that a disciplinary tribunal had determined that one of their members had not maintained accurate records of a liquidation or receivership, nor were they required to report that they suspected one of their members had committed an indictable offence (McDowell 1998).

By contrast, liquidators were obliged in cases of compulsory liquidations, in accordance with section 299 of the Companies Act 1963, to report their suspicions that a company officer had committed a criminal offence, and to assist with any prosecution arising from this report. In theory, this was an effective way of ensuring that corporate wrongdoing, most of which is often only discovered when the company is wound up, is reported to the authorities. In reality, however, this provision was traditionally of little effect. Most companies in Ireland were not wound up when they ceased to trade (McDowell 1998: para. 2.5). Therefore, most wrongdoing was not discovered or reported. Furthermore, even when companies were wound up and offences were reported to the Office of the DPP, it simply passed on the report to the Garda Fraud Squad for investigation, a body that had neither the resources nor the skills to conduct an effective investigation into complicated company law provisions (McDowell 1998: para. 2.14). In addition, if the liquidator had provided a damning report of the activities of the company and its directors, this would not of itself have provided any admissible evidence for the prosecution (McDowell 1998: para. 2.11).

All of this suggests that the DPP and the Gardaí were often unaware that white-collar crimes were committed. However, it must also be pointed out that even when high-profile cases of corporate wrongdoing were discovered, prosecutions rarely followed. In the case of *Re Aluminium Fabricators* ([1984] ILRM 399), the directors of the company were not prosecuted when they kept double books to divert company funds into their own private bank accounts in the Isle of Man. In *Re Contract Packaging Ltd* (16 January 1992, unreported, High Court), the directors were not prosecuted when they siphoned off in excess of £384,000 of company money for their personal use and defrauded the revenue commissioners. In *Re Kelly's Carpetdrome Ltd* (1 July 1983, unreported, High Court), the directors were not prosecuted when they defrauded the revenue commissioners of €2 million. In an effort to withhold evidence from the liquidator, they burned down the business premises which stored company files, put out other files for waste collection by the local authority, and threatened the bookkeeper with a gun so that he would not give evidence at the trial. The liquidator concluded that company assets had been illegally transferred to another company to defraud the revenue commissioners but the directors were civilly sanctioned, not criminally prosecuted, for this misconduct. In *Re Hunting Lodges* ([1985] ILRM 75), the directors sold the main asset of the company, a pub called 'Durty Nelly's', but the company did not receive the full sale price. The directors had transferred £160,000 of the proceeds to bank accounts with false names to deprive the Revenue Commissioners of stamp duty on the full consideration of the sale price. Though these cases unearthed instances of deliberate corporate fraud, liquidators took civil proceedings under section 297(1) of the Companies Act 1963, even though the directors could have been criminally prosecuted for fraudulent trading under section 297(3) of the same Act.

Arguably, one of the most significant corporate frauds in the Irish State in the twentieth century involved Merchant Banking, a company in the Gallagher Group which failed in the early 1980s owing in excess of £30 million. The liquidator's investigation concluded that Merchant Banking had seriously breached at least five different pieces of legislation including the Companies Acts, the Central Bank Acts and the Larceny Acts. The bank had failed to hold annual general meetings, had falsely recorded transactions, made false returns to the Central Bank and obtained and managed its assets fraudulently (*Irish Times* 23 February 1990: 9; 15 May 1984: 1). These transgressions were facilitated by a weak and ineffective Central Bank. The Central Bank had expressed concerns about the running of Merchant Banking since 1973 but did not send in inspectors to investigate it (*Irish Times* 1 March 1990: 8; 15 March 1990: 5). Though the Gardaí subsequently investigated, they lacked the resources and skills to deal effectively with cases of white-collar crime. It took several fraud squad officers working full-time on the case six years to complete their investigation and for a report to be sent to the Director of Public Prosecutions (*Irish Times* 7 December 1989: 14). Even then, the police had not been able to compile sufficient evidence to ground a successful prosecution so the state decided not to prosecute the case (*Irish Times* 25 May 1990: 1). By contrast, the British authorities dealt much more decisively with Merchant Banking's activities in Northern Ireland. The British conducted a two-year investigation that provided sufficient evidence to prompt Patrick Gallagher, the chairman of the Gallagher Group, to plead guilty to five offences. He was not treated deferentially. He was arrested and initially denied bail (*Irish Times* 31 March 1988, 1; 2 April 1988: 6). He was subsequently sentenced to two years' imprisonment, despite the payment of significant compensation on his behalf (*Irish Times* 2 October 1992: 13). Even though Merchant Banking had a significantly smaller operation in Northern Ireland than in the Republic, the investigation was taken more seriously in the United Kingdom and Patrick Gallagher was serving time there while all that happened in Ireland was that the liquidator considered a civil suit.

The evidence detailed in this chapter certainly suggests that the Garda Fraud Squad was hampered by the absence of an obligation to report offences to it, but perhaps even more so by a lack of resources and expertise to deal with wrongdoing once discovered. Though it is difficult to know precisely how many cases were processed by the Fraud Squad in this period, it is known that it was investigating 39 cases in 1991 (Burke Dáil Debates 5 February 1991 col 1480). Due to inadequate records, it is not clear how many of these cases were referred to the DPP for prosecution, how many were actually prosecuted, or how many resulted in a conviction. However, Carney has suggested that 'major allegations of fraud [...] seem to have gone no farther than the submission of a file to the office of the Director of Public Prosecutions' (*Irish Times* 31 August 1990: 10). Unsurprisingly then, the McDowell Group (1998: para. 2.5) reported that 'enforcement of non-registration type offences is very rare and wholly unpredictable. Most statutory offences have never been the subject of prosecutions, and those which have been prosecuted have resulted in only a handful of convictions'.

Specialized corporate enforcement machinery

The Companies Registration Office (CRO) and the Minister for Industry and Commerce (as it was once known, hereinafter the Minister) were charged with some responsibility for enforcing the Companies Acts. The CRO was mostly concerned with administrative matters. Its main function was to process the registration of companies, maintain records of statutorily required information, and enforce these filing obligations. To this end, it was empowered to prosecute 34 filing offences by in the Companies Acts 1963–1990 (McDowell 1998: Appendix 3). It was specifically empowered under section 125 of the Companies Act 1963 to prosecute a company and its officers for defaults in failing to file annual returns. The Minister was expected to perform a more active role in enforcing the Companies Acts. The Minister was empowered under section 385 of the Companies Act 1963 to prosecute all summary offences. In assuming this responsibility, the Minister (Lynch Dáil Debates 14 November 1962 col 1190) recognized 'there would of course be little point in imposing obligations on companies and their officers unless suitable provisions were made for the prosecution of offenders [...] To the extent that our resources permit, steps will be taken to ensure that the requirements of the law will be complied with and that offenders are punished'.

Though record-keeping on the prosecution of company offences is poor, the annual Companies Reports prepared by the Minister provide some insight into the practice of corporate enforcement in this period. Despite the tough-talking rhetoric of the Minister, they show that corporate wrongdoing was not a significant priority. The Companies Report 1963 (1964: 9) stated that 'during 1963, the institution of legal proceedings was necessary to secure submission of a number of legal returns. To secure compliance with other sections of the Act, proceedings were necessary in a few cases'. It did not identify the number of prosecutions or convictions secured by the state. Although the subsequent Companies Reports continued not to present information in a detailed or consistent manner, the paragraphs below will attempt to specify a number of trends which capture the Irish approach to corporate wrongdoing in the twentieth century.

In 1964, one case was prosecuted for the improper use of the word 'limited'. The case was unsuccessful and was dismissed (1965: 9). In 1965, 60 cases were instituted for the failure to file annual returns and ten were initiated for failing to file notice of situation of registered office and/or the particulars of directors and secretaries. Only two cases were heard that year and the Probation Act, which allows offenders to escape criminal records, was applied in both cases (1966: 9). Between 1966 and 1971, the state prosecuted: the failure to file notice of situation of registered office and/or the particulars of directors and secretaries; the failure to file notice of change of registered office; and the failure to file annual returns. Data on the enforcement of these offences is compiled in Table 25.1. This shows that though 708 cases were reported or 'on hands' for prosecution in 1966, only 361 of these resulted in the imposition of a fine. In addition, the Probation Act was applied 49 times. Though the number of cases fluctuated over the next five years, fines continued to be rarely imposed: only 29 per cent of cases in 1967 (47 out of 162 cases), 28 per cent in 1968 (41 out of 146 cases), 25 per cent in 1969 (20 out of 79 cases), 15 per cent in 1970 (22 out of 148 cases), and 18 per cent in 1971 (47 out of 262 cases). The Probation Act also continued to be applied. In 1971, the Probation Act was applied 19 times when only 47 cases resulted in a fine. This suggests that even when companies did break the law, and were convicted, they were rarely fined and often left the court without a criminal record.

The Companies Reports do not record many details on the enforcement of the Companies Acts between 1972 and 1980. No data is recorded on the number of convictions, the application of the Probation Act, the number of cases withdrawn, etc. However, as depicted in Table 25.2, it is shown that 236 prosecutions were taken for the failure to provide annual returns in 1972, resulting in total fines of £2445 (1973: 11), before rising to 781 prosecutions in 1980, with fines imposed totalling £2482 (1981: 11). There was a significant increase in the number of prosecutions, and therefore presumably convictions also, but the total value of the fines remained relatively constant which suggests that the average fine imposed was reduced.

Table 25.1 Prosecutions under the Companies Act (1966–1971)

Year	*Number of cases on hands since previous year and reported this year*	*Number in which fines imposed*	*Probation Act imposed*
1966	708	361	49
1967	162	47	8
1968	146	41	6
1969	79	20	1
1970	148	22	0
1971	262	47	19

Sources: Companies Reports. Dublin: Stationery Office (1967–1972)

Table 25.2 Failure to provide annual returns (1972–1980)

	Prosecutions	*Fines imposed (£)*
1972	236	2445
1973	103	1373
1974	295	3441
1975	301	6979
1976	176	1983
1977	237	5252
1978	528	2269
1979	633	3145
1980	781	2482

Sources: Companies Reports. Dublin: Stationery Office (1972–1981)

Table 25.3 Failure to provide annual returns (1981–1983)

	Referred for prosecution	*Prosecutions*	*Fines imposed (£)*
1981	897	262	9500
1982	920	192	7420
1983	932	224	15,730

Sources: Companies Reports. Dublin: Stationery Office (1982–1984)

Table 25.4 Prosecutions, convictions and fines for breaching the Companies Acts (1984–1985)

Year	*Convictions*	*Fines imposed (£)*
1984	293	50,845
1985	8	2025

Sources: Companies Reports. Dublin: Stationery Office (1985–1986)

For example, the total amount of fines on foot of 236 prosecutions in 1972 was £2445, which means that the average fine per prosecution in this period was £10.36. By 1980, the average fine per prosecution was £3.18. Small fines became smaller. The reports do not indicate why this occurred.

Slightly more detailed information is provided on the prosecutions for failure to file annual returns for the next three years, as shown in Table 25.3. In 1981, 897 cases were referred for prosecution. These resulted in 262 prosecutions. The total value of the fines imposed was £9500 (1982: 11). In 1982, 192 of the 920 cases referred for prosecution were prosecuted and the value of the fines imposed that year totalled £7420 (1983: 11). In 1983, 224 of the 932 cases referred for prosecution were prosecuted and the value of the fines imposed that year totalled £15,730 (1984: 11). If any trend can be revealed from this information, it is that only a fraction of the cases which could potentially have been prosecuted were actually prosecuted. Of the cases that were prosecuted, low fines were imposed.

In 1984, the Minister ceased to provide information in the same manner as presented in 1983. The reports do not record: the total number of offences prosecuted, the specific offences prosecuted, the number of prosecutions per offence, the number of convictions per offence, details on the application of the Probation Act, and number of cases withdrawn. Two figures were, however, provided: the total number of convictions and the total amount of the fines imposed. From these figures, it is known that in 1984, fines totalling £50,845 were imposed on foot of 293 convictions that year (1985: 11). In 1985, £2025 was imposed on foot of eight convictions (1986: 10).

The Companies Reports in the late 1980s did not record details on convictions or fines. Instead, they provided details on the total number of prosecutions for breaches of the Companies Acts. From this data, collated in Table 25.5, it is known that no prosecutions were initiated in 1986 and 1987, and that only eight prosecutions were taken in 1988 (1993: 11). However, the number of prosecutions did jump in 1989 to 334, peaking in 1990 with 960 prosecutions taken that year, before falling to 29 prosecutions in 1991.

Table 25.5 Prosecutions for breaching the Companies Acts (1986–1991)

Year	*Prosecutions*
1986	0
1987	0
1988	8
1989	334
1990	960
1991	29

Sources: Companies Reports. Dublin: Stationery Office (1987–1992)

It is difficult to explain this sharp peak and fall with certainty. No clues are provided in the Companies Reports for the extraordinary rise and sharp fall in prosecutions in this period. However, the rise in prosecutions did follow the EC Fourth Directive which required the annual accounts of public and private accounts be annexed to the annual returns to the CRO. Prior to this, private companies had not been required to supply this information. The directive was implemented by the Companies Act 1986, though small and medium-sized private companies were exempted from this obligation. A prominent Irish businessman, Fergal Quinn, complained that his largest corporate competitors were forming smaller subsidiaries and exploiting legal loopholes to allow them not to file full annual accounts. He decided to publish his accounts in full to shame his competitors to do the same (*Irish Times* 1 February 1989: 17). The resulting declaration by the Minister that it would prosecute all companies who failed to file full annual accounts was greeted with scepticism by the *Irish Times* (16 February 1989: 11) because 'this is not the first time the Department has said this; and information is as sparse as ever. [...] The old secretness still prevails'. This in turn provoked a letter to the editor by a registration agent for the CRO who stated that greater calls for enforcement failed to consider that the office is so 'seriously understaffed and underequipped' that it is not 'available to check and file the bundles of documents stacked on the floor' (*Irish Times* 23 February 1989: 11). This significant media attention on this issue may correlate with the spike in prosecutions at that time.

The decline in prosecutions was met by a temporary resurgence in subsequent years. Though the data was reported across an 18-month period instead of the usual 12 months, thereby frustrating direct year-on-year tabulated comparisons, the Minister reported that 1963 companies were prosecuted for the failure to file returns between the 1 January 1992 and the 30 June 1993, 'a ten year high' (1993: 8, 23). The maximum penalty for failure to file returns under the Acts at this point was £1000 and the amount of fines imposed totalled £0.501 million, a staggering sum compared with past levels of fines: £2445 in 1972, £1983 in 1976, £2482 in 1980, £2025 in 1985 (1973: 11; 1977: 11; 1981: 11; 1973: 10). Prosecutions subsequently continued but there was a marked preference for prosecuting companies rather than company officers during this period, as shown in Table 25.6. In 1994, 1979 companies were prosecuted, as compared with 103 prosecutions against company directors (1995: 29). Similarly, in 1995, 626 companies were prosecuted but only 116 prosecutions were taken against company directors (1996: 17). Company directors were not prosecuted for failing to file annual returns in 1996 but 18 directors were convicted of that offence in respect of cases carried over from 1995. It also seems that the state had a much

Table 25.6 Prosecutions for failure to provide returns (1994–1998)

	Prosecutions against companies for failure to provide returns			*Prosecutions against directors for failure to provide returns*		
Year	*Number of prosecutions*	*Number of convictions*	*Fines imposed*	*Number of prosecutions*	*Number of convictions*	*Fines imposed*
1994	1979	1418	2,024,550	103	43	11,700
1995	626	546	684,950	116	55	37,675
1996	43	26	16,475	0	18	8630
1997	0	0	0	107	30	52,460
1998	0	0	0	0	0	0

Sources: Companies Reports. Dublin: Stationery Office (1995–1999)

Table 25.7 Compliance rates for filing annual returns (1991–1997)

Year due	*Returns due*	*Returns filed*	*Compliance rate (%)*
1991	78,508	53,845	69
1992	93,102	55,816	60
1993	107,652	55,435	51
1994	121,600	51,062	42
1995	127,279	42,662	34
1996	112,668	38,632	34
1997	136,245	49,242	36

Sources: Companies Reports. Dublin: Stationery Office (1992–1998)

better chance of securing convictions against companies than their officers, perhaps because the state had the burden of proving that officers in default had acted knowingly and wilfully as a precondition to criminal liability, as specified in section 383 of the Companies Act 1963. This 'created a very high evidential burden for the prosecution that necessitated proof of a defendant's subjective state of mind' (Courtney 2012: 1768). This high evidential hurdle was not required to secure convictions against companies. The reports show that while 87 per cent of cases (546 out of 626) against companies resulted in convictions in 1995, only 45 per cent of cases (55 out of 116) in 1995 were successful against company directors, and only 28 per cent of cases against directors (30 out of 107) resulted in convictions in 1997 (1996: 17; 1998: 16).

Nevertheless, even as enforcement increased in the early and mid-1990s, compliance with the obligation to file annual returns under the Companies Acts declined, as shown in Table 25.7. Though 69 per cent of companies eventually complied with their obligation to file annual returns in 1991, this fell to 42 per cent in 1994, and declined further to 36 per cent in 1997. The number of companies filing 'on time' was even lower. The number of 'live' or active companies that filed on time dropped from 16 per cent in 1994 to 13 per cent in 1997 (1998: 16). The Minister admitted that 'the overall compliance rate cannot be regarded as satisfactory' (1995: 13). The emphasis on a more active sanctioning approach had failed to secure better corporate compliance with the law. The number of prosecutions against both companies and company directors subsequently ceased entirely. No companies or company directors were prosecuted in 1998 (1999: 45).

The McDowell Report explained that the Minister had difficulties enforcing the law because his department was inadequately resourced. It determined that the Minister allocated the equivalent of only eight full-time staff members of the department to its Company Law Administration Section, two members of which were concerned with the regulation of credit unions and other societies (1998: para 2.18). The remaining six members were fully absorbed with civil company investigations and performing the wide range of administrative tasks allocated to the Minister. The group concluded (1998: paras. 2.21–2.22):

> As regards Departmental resources for the investigation and prosecution of breaches of the Companies Acts the Group was satisfied the other commitments of the Department left the manpower equivalent of about one half of one full time staff member of the Department to discharge this vital function. In the UK, such functions are discharged by many hundreds of full time public servants. Put shortly, demands on manpower meant that there are currently no Departmental resources allocated for the enforcement of the law. In these circumstances, the Group came to the conclusion that the day to day investigation and prosecution of breaches of company law (other than the Companies Registration Offences) is close to non-existent and that there is no realistic prospect that the Department's function of enforcement as envisaged by the Acts, will be discharged.

Considering that the Minister was charged with a significant role in enforcing company law, but that it had not allocated the equivalent of even one full-time staff member to discharge this function, it is unsurprising that compliance with the Companies Acts was traditionally so low. Similarly, the internal allocation of the CRO, which operated under the aegis of the Minister, also suggests that the detection of white-collar crimes was a low priority. The CRO employed 112 staff in 1998 but only eight of these were allocated to the enforcement of company law, an increase from four members of staff in 1997 (para. 2.39). The remaining members of staff were allocated to performing the CRO's administrative duties.

In summation of this section, a number of broad conclusions relating both to the architecture of enforcement and the practice of enforcement may be drawn from the material discussed above. In the first regard, while specialist agencies have undoubtedly played a role in regulating particular parts of the corporate and financial sector, they played a limited role in enforcing the law in practice. The CRO could prosecute particular filing offences and the Minister possessed the power to prosecute all summary offences in the Companies Acts. However, only a handful of offences of the hundreds of offences in the Acts have ever been prosecuted and only the failure to file annual returns has been prosecuted with any regularity. As observed by Bannon (2006: 6), 'while there were a number of different agencies with some responsibility for the enforcement of company law, it was a priority for none. Moreover, within those agencies, there was an insufficiency of resources assigned to the task'. Low levels of prosecutions were matched by lower levels of convictions and even lower levels of fines. Unsurprisingly, it has been observed that 'the experience of the Department and of the CRO is that it has been the practice of the courts to impose low fines for company law offences' (CLRG 2001: 151). O'Malley (2006: 415–416) has observed that while legislators may set high maximum fines for a number of reasons, and while many considerations may come into play, generally the courts impose penalties proportionate to the perceived gravity of the wrongdoing committed. While the offences prosecuted might be considered relatively minor crimes, filing annual returns is a vital means for people dealing with companies to access information on their financial health. Nevertheless, the low penalties suggest breaches of the Companies Acts, like failing to file annual returns, were viewed as trivial or merely technical breaches of the law, rather than fundamental requirements that must be observed to avail of the privilege of corporate personality. Finally, it would also appear from the data, to the extent that such data is available, that the Probation Act was often applied in favour of corporate defendants. Though the data in the reports is often inconsistent and vague, itself illustrative of the ambivalent attitude to corporate enforcement, the evidence shows that the enforcement of company law, which was underpinned by hundreds of criminal sanctions, was almost non-existent. The next section of this submission attempts to locate this culture of non-compliance and non-enforcement in its political, social and economic context.

Enforcement in context: protectionism, procrastination and inertia in corporate affairs

Writing prior to the economic boom in the 1990s, the so-called 'Celtic Tiger', Lee (1989: 521) suggested 'it is difficult to avoid the conclusion that Irish economic performance has been the least impressive in Western Europe, perhaps in all Europe, in the 20th century'. Though the country possessed relatively little natural resources (particularly coal and iron), it was in an ideal geographical location with easy access to the British market and it suffered comparatively little damage following the world wars (Ferriter 2005: 61, 32; Lee 1989: 527). So why did the Irish economy perform so poorly for so long? In the early decades of the Irish state, protectionism was advanced to ensure that British investors would not gain control of Irish industry and subvert national interests for their own gain (Lee 1989: 187). The Irish parliament enacted the Control of Manufactures Acts 1932 and 1934 which shielded Irish companies from tariffs and strict quotas that foreign companies were required to observe (OECD 2001: 18). They also required that Irish people had to own in excess of half of the equity in Irish firms, thereby ensuring that Irish companies were owned by Irish people (Daly 1984). If companies did not meet this requirement they had to receive a special licence from the Minister to operate in Ireland.

The Acts sheltered Irish companies from foreign competition which gave them a distinct advantage in the home market. However, it also meant that they had difficulties engaging effectively in the export market. The Acts also created other difficulties. Foreign corporate involvement was discouraged so Irish companies may have been denied the opportunity to learn useful skills from large, successful and efficient firms. In addition, the legislation stunted the growth and development of licensed businesses because the Acts 'required that most licensed companies supply the majority of their capital from their own resources and this tended to exert a bias in favour of smaller companies' (Daly 1984: 259). Major investments in enterprise were state affairs not private initiatives, as evinced by the establishment of state companies in banking, food processing and transport sectors. As observed by the OECD (2001: 19), 'from the 1930s on a series of State owned companies were engaged in commercial exercises that were not being undertaken by the private sector or which were felt to be outside the expertise of existing firms'. Though protectionism was designed to assist Irish industry, it seems that it may also have stifled it. Moreover, the Irish people were also afraid to take the financial gambles that were central to developing businesses. Lee (1989: 390–393) writes that the Irish people desired the security of managing the family farm and that even in family businesses, the gifted child was encouraged to join a profession or trade, rather than engage in commercial dealing.

The agricultural sector was Ireland's primary source of income (OECD 2001: 18). In this context, 'national development was synonymous with agricultural development' so 'the idea of promoting industrialisation through a mixture of import substitution and monetary experiment was rejected, the main focus instead being on the cultivation of a robust agricultural sector' (Ferriter 2005: 313). Ireland was a 'peasant economy' (Lee 1989: 284), epitomized by the simple economic plan regularly espoused by successive Ministers for Agriculture from the 1920 to the 1950s: 'one more cow, one more sow, and one more acre under the plough' (O'Brien 1936: 368; Dillion Dáil

Debates 2 December 1954 col 1520). Agriculture was supported by programmes to help tillage in the 1930s, through schemes to improve housing conditions for agricultural labourers, the 1938 Trade Agreement with Britain which ended the Economic War and which removed certain restrictions on Irish agricultural exports to Britain, the Anglo Irish Trade agreement in 1948 involving British subsidization of the Irish cattle industry, but to mention a few. When Ireland did receive some foreign investment in the form of Marshall Aid, a significant portion was invested in agricultural projects like afforestation, land reclamation and bog land development (Ferriter 2005: 468). Such investments, it was suggested, 'brutally exposed the continuing inability of Irish governments to devise a coherent long term programme of public expenditure' (Lee 1989: 305).

Notwithstanding its shortcomings, President DeValera romanticized rural Ireland as poor but happy, stating that

> the Ireland we have dreamed of would be the home of a people who valued material wealth only as a basis of right living, of a people who were satisfied with frugal comfort and devoted their leisure to things of the spirit; a land whose countryside would be bright with cosy homesteads, whose fields and villages would be joyous with the sounds of industry.
>
> *(Moynihan 1980: 466)*

Additionally, any attempts to promote corporate development and increase prosperity may also have been stifled by an 'anti-business Catholic ethos' (Ferriter 2005: 61). It had been suggested that the Irish Roman Catholic Church had opposed modernization through industrialization as part of its general opposition to 'materialism, consumerism and individualism' (Inglis 1998: 250). The Church in Ireland 'was committed ideologically to a rural fundamentalism which was suspicious and fearful of the industrial city and it glorified the family farm and the little village as the pillars of social and economic life' (Fahey 1992: 262). The interconnecting ideas about rural Ireland and the role of religion therein is neatly encapsulated by the views of Canon Hayes who suggested that 'rural Ireland is real Ireland and rural Ireland is Ireland true to Christ' (Ferriter 2005: 376).

Nevertheless, notwithstanding the views of rural Ireland held by bombastic politicians and clergy, Ireland was a 'wasting society', with high emigration levels reflecting the inadequacy of existing government policy and dissatisfaction with rural life (Lee 1989: 334). Mass emigration was so pronounced that the Irish were considered to be 'vanishing' (O'Brien 1954); four out of every five children born in Ireland between 1931 and 1941 emigrated in the 1950s (Tobin 1984: 156). As a result of flawed economic policies, corporate development was visibly stunted. The number of public companies incorporated in Ireland remained relatively static, rising from just 363 in 1925 to 372 in 1956, though the number of private companies (often small and family owned) did increase from 1088 to 7385 in the same period (Cox 1958: 15), relatively modest numbers compared with the 138,215 private companies and 1103 public companies in Ireland by 2005 (CLRG 2006: 16). All of this suggests that the combination of concerns relating to the sovereignty of the new Irish state, poor economic policies relating to protectionism, political deference to the agricultural sector, and the influence of an anti-materialist Roman Catholic Church, reduced Ireland to a state with low levels of corporate activity. In this context, Ireland was more concerned with self-sufficiency than attracting investment and promoting enterprise or regulating business. It could be posited that corporate deviancy was not a significant issue to be pursued vigorously in a state with low levels of corporate activity.

As a result, company law review and reform were far more irregular in Ireland than in England. In England,

> by the end of the nineteenth century the Board of Trade had established the practice of appointing at intervals of about 20 years a Department committee to review company law,

> implementing its recommendations by an amending Act which was then repealed and replaced by a consolidation of all company legislation in a Company Act.
>
> *(Gower 1997: 48)*

In Ireland, by contrast, the UK Companies Consolidation Act 1908 remained the bedrock of Irish company law for more than 50 years 'due in part to the lesser role played by industry and business in a predominantly Irish agricultural economy' (Keane 1985: 15). The Cox Report (1958) acknowledged that Irish company law lacked transparency, joined-up thinking, and contained inadequate protections for various stakeholders. The legislature enacted the Companies Act 1959 and 1963 to implement the report and consolidate the law. The increased interest in regulatory governance and the enactment of these new Companies Acts in quick succession suggests some departure from the inertia and hegemony of before. However, the content of the legislation suggested a continued lack of interest in matters of corporate governance. The 1959 and 1963 Acts borrowed heavily from the Companies Act 1948 in the UK. While creating a shared company law framework with England may have made sense, given Ireland's reliance on the UK as a trading partner, it adopted rules and policies from England and Wales that were already defeated there (Delaney 1959: 305). This culture of imitation may have reflected the lack of expertise on corporate regulation in the state and a lack of reflection on the propriety of using English law in an Irish context.

Moreover, members of parliament explicitly detailed their disinterest in corporate issues. Deputy Norton, for example, stated that the legislation was of the kind that 'restless minds did not read with much avidity. It was as dry as dust. Many sections could not be less interesting than they were' (Dáil Debates 5 November 1963 col 821). He seemed happy enough for company law to sit on the legislative shelf without further attention for some time, stating, 'the last Companies Bill was passed, I think in 1908, well over fifty five years ago. It will probably be another fifty years before we pass another one' (Dáil Debates 5 November 1963 col 821). Though the 1963 Act was amended in mostly minor ways over the next four decades, it continued to be the foundational framework for Irish company law in the twentieth century and is still referred to as the 'Primary Act'. The Companies Act 1990 was its most substantial amendment and it was heavily influenced by legislation in the UK, specifically the Companies Act 1985, the Insolvency Act 1986 and the Company Directors Disqualification Act 1986 (Appleby 2005). Ireland continued to imitate the UK, perhaps reflecting a continued lack of original thinking in addressing corporate reform, and the same continued inertia in corporate affairs. Another committee, the Company Law Review Group, would not report on reforming Irish company law until 1994, 36 years after the Cox report, and regular company law reform would not be statutorily required until the twenty-first century.

Nevertheless, despite the expressions of apathy in commercial affairs evident in the commercial regulatory affairs, the corporate nature of Irish society changed significantly. It is submitted that a number of matters coincided to stimulate this change. The release of the Cox Report coincided with the publication of the report *Economic Development* (Whitaker 1958). In this report, Whitaker argued that the state should abandon protectionism, embrace competition and free trade, and develop indigenous industry so that it could compete in export markets. In addition, he suggested that the state needed laws to protect investments, encourage profits, and attract foreign enterprises. These reports also coincided with a change in political leadership which was pro-competition, pro-industry, and pro-European integration (Murphy 2005). Ireland liberalized its trading rules initiating 'a radical turnaround in policy focused on the attraction of foreign-owned export orientated manufacturing industries with the objective of fast-tracking economic development' (Forfas 2002: 34). It repealed the Control of Manufactures Acts in 1964 and joined the internal common market created by the EEC in 1973. The National Economic Plan (1982: 7) recognized that 'national income depends on our ability to produce and sell goods and services which are competitive in price and quality with those of other nations'.

Ireland actively marketed itself as an attractive place for business. It lowered corporation tax from 50 per cent to 12.5 per cent (MacSharry and White 2000; Reddan 2008), making it substantially lower than that of the USA (35 per cent) or those of its European neighbours, like the UK (30 per cent), France (33.33 per cent) or Germany (26.38 per cent) (Industrial Development Authority 2004: 8). The government also negotiated agreements with employers and trade unions in the 1980s to keep wages low in exchange for low taxes, a process known as social partnership. The idea was to make Ireland more attractive to business by ensuring an inexpensive supply of labour, fewer 'lost' days and relative stability through fewer industrial actions and strikes (Hardiman 2002; O'Donnell and O'Reardon 2000). In an effort to develop Ireland into a more commercially driven society, with a new emphasis on professionalism, the state also reduced class sizes at primary schools to improve teacher–student ratios, built more secondary schools and regional third-level colleges, and provided free education and more generous scholarships for those of modest means. Six times as many students attended third level in 1994 than in 1964 (Smith 2005: 4). When debating the Primary Act, the Minister for Industry and Commerce acknowledged: 'it would be most unwise to impose on our companies more onerous obligations [...] than those which prevail in neighbouring countries, since this would place them at a competitive disadvantage' (Lynch Dáil Debates 14 November 1962 col 1176–1177). In 1990, the Minister for Finance stated that commerce would be regulated 'with commendable flexibility and without detailed rule books' (Reddan 2008: 71). In advertisements posted internationally in papers such as the *New York Times*, it emphasized its reputation as a state 'noted for its favourable government attitudes towards business' (MacSharry and White 2000: 257–258). However, evidence in support of Ireland's increasingly flexible regulatory regime is not merely anecdotal. The OECD (2001: 7) reported that 'by the end of 1997, Ireland was one of the less regulated OECD countries in terms of barriers to entry and entrepreneurship, market openness, and labour markets'.

All of this suggests that Ireland moved from a closed, protected, agrarian state to one that embraced free trade and favoured export-focused industrial development. The natural question arises, therefore, as to why white-collar crimes were so rarely prosecuted throughout this period. Why are white-collar crimes not considered threats or risks which the state had to address? Mary Douglas (1992) explains that the ability to perceive risk is culturally contingent. The risks we identify, and do not identify, reveal as much about society at a given time as they do about hazards in our environment. The socio-economic context in Ireland in the decades following independence was one which had idealized rural living, frugality and isolationism, which had resisted foreign investment and industrialization as an assertion of sovereignty. Understandably, in this context, white-collar criminality did not animate a state that was largely agrarian in orientation and had low levels of corporate activity. Subsequently, when the state advanced policies which were pro-competition, pro-industry, and pro-European integration, increased corporate activity was associated with purely positive concepts such as wealth creation, employment, and as a way to escape economic depression. Getting tough on white-collar crimes was clearly not a strategic governance issue when the state was actively courting foreign investment on the basis of its light-touch regulatory regime. Instead, increased employment and increased prosperity were the chief concerns. Indeed, in an examination of opinion polls run by Irish newspapers leading up to general elections in the 1980s and early 1990s, Kilcommins et al. (2004: 136) found that 'the problem of crime was a low priority for voters. The over-riding concern was unemployment, usually followed closely by anxiety about how to get by in difficult economic circumstances'. As such, the public was more concerned that jobs were created, not whether and how corporate wrongdoing was being addressed. This way of thinking may have supported the routine marginalization of corporate accountability within the legal system. Friedman (1975: 108) stated, 'a law which goes against the grain, culturally speaking, will be hard to enforce and probably ineffective'. The criminalization of the commercial community, bringing jobs and prosperity, went 'against the grain' and had little social or political support in practice. Consequently, corporate enforcement was not resourced or supported and Ireland over-looked the prosecution of corporate criminal offences in a way it would never have done with more conventional crime. Ireland exhibited a classic characteristic in the breakdown of the rule of law, identified by Fuller (1964: 39), 'a failure of congruence between the rules as announced and their actual administration'.

This context started to change when Ireland experienced a significant economic boom in the 1990s, the so-called 'Celtic Tiger'. Unemployment fell, immigration replaced emigration, and living standards were boosted considerably (OECD 2001). Ireland became 'the fourth largest European funds centre; the eighth largest global banking centre; the fourth largest reinsurance centre; and the leading European cross-border centre for life insurance' (Reddan 2008: 7). It has also enticed other major players like Pfizer, GSK, Intel and General Electric from the pharmaceutical and electronic industries, among others. Summarizing the composition of the work force in 2005, McWilliams noted, 'manufacturing is on the way out. Only 16% of us make anything anymore. Less than one in 20 works the land. One in ten works in construction [...] The rest of us, which is just under three in every five, toil away at the water cooler in office jobs [...] We are all white-collar'. However, as more workers became white-collar in the 1990s, more opportunities to commit white-collar crimes emerged and 'a series of scandals shook confidence in sectors of the business world' (Keogh 2005: 390). Some of Ireland's most prominent companies and financial institutions were implicated, like Goodmans and National Irish Bank (McCullagh 2002). A series of public tribunals of inquiry, including the Hamilton 'Beef' Tribunal; the McCracken Tribunal, the Moriarty Tribunal and the Flood/Mahon Tribunal, also chronicled the corporate corruption of politics at the highest levels (Byrne 2012). They revealed 'an atmosphere of insider intimacy in which cronyism thrived continued to hang over boomtime Ireland' (O'Toole 2009). Ireland was also implicated in high-profile international scandals involving Enron, Parmalat and AIG because these companies operated, in part, through subsidiaries based in Ireland (Reddan 2008: 228). Ireland had competed internationally to attract some of the biggest players in the global financial markets, flaunting its lax regulatory regime but now this had come back to haunt it, particularly when the *New York Times* dubbed the Irish financial services sector the 'wild west of European finance' (*New York Times* 1 April 2005: C1).

In order to protect Ireland's reputation as an attractive place in which to do business, the state created specialist regulatory agencies with significant powers of investigation and prosecution, like the Office of the Director of Corporate Enforcement (ODCE). It also enhanced the arsenal of available sanctions, including civil and administrative sanctions, to secure corporate accountability. The state was acting to reassure market players operating within the law that they were safe from the deviant behaviour of other operators acting outside it. Existing sentiments requiring increased corporate responsibility then crystallized further in 2008 when it was revealed that regulators had failed to address serious irresponsibility in the Irish banking sector (Honohan 2010; Regling and Watson 2010). The state guaranteed the debts of the Irish banks so that they could continue to borrow capital from the foreign markets, transforming private liabilities into sovereign debt. However, these debts were overwhelmingly greater than anticipated. The national economy declined and unemployment rose from 4.9 per cent in 2007 to 18.1 per cent by 2012

(Central Statistics Office 2013: 31). It was understood that white-collar crimes had the potential to damage the economic security of the state and could be at least as serious as conventional crimes. When the state assumed the debts of Anglo Irish Bank caused by the allegedly criminal activities of its senior management, hundreds of people took to the streets in protest (*Irish Times* 19 May 2010: 7). One particularly irate protestor immobilized a concrete mixing truck at the entrance to the Irish parliament. The vehicle had the words 'Toxic Bank Anglo' painted on it (*Irish Times* 30 September 2010: 9).

Politicians now urge that the prosecution of white-collar crimes must take place and condemn these crimes in the strongest of language. The Minister for Justice in 2009, Dermot Ahern, emphasized that the law would 'bring to justice those who may have played hard and fast with the financial security of this country. We operate the rule of law. [...] whether you have a balaclava, a sawn-off shotgun or a white collar and designer suit, the same rules apply' (*Irish Times* 25 February 2009: 1). Minster Noel Dempsey accused the bankers of 'economic treason', pledging that they would 'pay a price' (*Irish Times* 24 February 2009: 1). Not to be outdone, an opposition spokesman, Leo Varadkar, thundered that bankers did more damage to the state than the IRA and should be treated like subversives (*Irish Times* 29 October 2010: 10). If, in the past, the Irish public allowed the state to pick up the tab for corporate wrongdoing with a sort of quiet indifference (Kilcommins et al. 2004: 131), this was no longer the case. The state successfully prosecuted two former executives at Anglo Irish Bank for providing financial assistance to purchase the shares of the bank, contrary to the Companies Acts. This is considered the most complex criminal trial in the history of the state and criminal investigations into other alleged offences at the bank are on-going. The deference to financial elites is dissipating.

Conclusion

As was acknowledged in the introduction to this chapter, the goal of this chapter was to gather together broad structural patterns concerning the enforcement of the Irish Companies Acts in the twentieth century only. It was also noted that it is difficult to capture all threads in a momentum behind a century of legal and socio-economic history. Difficulties of generalization and omission naturally arise when trends are pigeonholed into one period in a particular timescale. By necessity, the discontinuities which were not considered to accurately reflect broader patterns were not analysed. Instead, the emphasis was on excavating assumptions, discourses, political interests and cultural understandings to reveal a broad 'logic of action' which characterized this space and time. This approach was necessary to construct an institutional analysis of the practice of corporate enforcement in Ireland and locate it in its socio-economic context. It was shown that Ireland had an agrarian economy which stagnated for much of the twentieth century. It employed inward-looking economic policies which did not sufficiently promote Ireland as an attractive place in which to do business. The state was concerned with self-sufficiency, was politically deferential to the agricultural sector, romanticized rural Ireland, and may have been influenced by an anti-business church which tied Catholicism to rural life and anti-materialism. The combination of these factors caused Ireland's economic health to suffer, high levels of emigration, and, crucially, low levels of corporate activity to persist. Consequently, the state was not concerned with issues of corporate crime or corporate accountability. This is demonstrated by the chronic failure to review company law with any regularity, the continued culture of policy imitation with the UK, the explicit statements in parliament detailing the disinterest in corporate affairs, and the willingness to embrace light-touch regulation as part of a package to court foreign enterprise.

It is in this context that company law was so rarely enforced. While caution is necessary to avoid confusing causation with correlation, it may be the case that addressing corporate wrongdoing was not a significant priority in a state which experienced low levels of incorporation, and which subsequently viewed increased corporate activity as a positive force which could stimulate prosperity. Institutional responses to corporate enforcement also mirrored the apathy shown by the political establishment and society more generally. Corporate non-compliance with the law was widespread, yet prosecutions rarely took place and convictions were rarely achieved. Even when corporate offenders were successfully convicted, they were usually subject to very low levels of sanctions reflecting once again the sentiment that corporate crime was not sufficiently serious to demand severe penalties. A culture of corporate non-compliance and non-enforcement reigned. This culture stands in stark contrast to the contemporary approach which is starting to emerge. White-collar crime has become politicized. Specialist regulators with enhanced powers are now more likely to address wrongdoing. In addition, the state has successfully prosecuted some of the most senior former bankers in the state, though it may be too early to tell whether these prosecutions are merely symbolic scapegoating and whether the residual resistance to regularly prosecute white-collar offenders has entirely subsided.

References

Appleby, P. (2005) 'Corporate regulation in Ireland', in J. O'Brien (ed.) *Governing the Corporation: Regulation and Corporate Governance in an Age of Scandal and Global Markets*, Chichester: John Wiley & Sons, pp. 255–272.

Bannon, A. (2006) *Company Law Offences: Corporate Crime Elective in Professional Practice Course Part 2*, Dublin: Law Society of Ireland.

Braithwaite, J. (1984) *Corporate Crime in the Pharmaceutical Industry*, London: Routledge & Kegan Paul.

Byrne, E. (2012) *Political Corruption in Ireland 1922–2010: A Crooked Harp?*, Manchester: Manchester University Press.

Central Statistics Office (2013) *Statistical Yearbook on Ireland*, Dublin: Stationery Office.

CLRG (2001) *First Report*, Dublin: Stationery Office.

Courtney, T.B. (2012) *The Law of Private Companies*, 3rd edn, Dublin: Bloomsbury Professional.

Cox, A. (1958) *Report of the Company Law Reform Committee*, Dublin: Stationery Office.

Daly, M.E. (1984) 'An Irish-Ireland for Irish business?: The Control of Manufactures Acts, 1932 and 1934', *Irish Historical Studies*, 24: 246–272.

Delaney, V.T.H. (1959) 'Company law reform in Ireland', *The Modern Law Review*, 22: 304–308.

Douglas, M. (1992) *Risk and Blame: Essays in Cultural Theory*, London: Routledge.

Fahey, T. (1992) 'Catholicism and industrial society in Ireland', in J. Goldthorpe and C. Whelan (eds) *The Development of Industrial Society in Ireland*, Oxford: Oxford University Press, pp. 241–263.

Ferriter, D. (2005) *The Transformation of Ireland 1900–2000*, Dublin: Profile Books.

Forfas (2002) *International Trade and Investment Report 2001*, Dublin: Forfas.

Friedman, L.M. (1975) *The Legal System: A Social Science Perspective*, New York: Russel Sage.

Fuller, L. (1964) *The Morality of Law*, New Haven: Yale University Press.

Gallagher, E. (1999) '"Collaring" the white collar criminal', *Commercial Law Practitioner*, 6: 263–266.

Gower, L.C.B. (1997) *Principles of Modern Company Law*, London: Sweet and Maxwell.

Hardiman, N. (2002) 'The political economy of growth', in W. Crotty and D. Schmitt (eds) *Ireland on the World Stage*, Harlow: Longman, pp. 168–188.

Honohan, P. (2010) *The Irish Banking Crisis Regulatory and Financial Stability Policy 2003–2008*, Dublin: Central Bank.

Industrial Development Authority (2004) *Ireland Annual Report*, Dublin.

Inglis, T. (1998) *Moral Monopoly*, 2nd edn, Dublin: University College Dublin Press.

Interdepartmental Inquiry 1950 (1951) Dublin: Stationery Office.

Keane, R. (1985) *Company Law in the Republic of Ireland*, London: Butterworths.

Keogh, D. (2005) *Twentieth Century Ireland*, Dublin: Gill and Macmillan.

Kilcommins, S., O'Donnell, I., O'Sullivan, E. and Vaughan, B. (2004) *Crime Punishment and the Search for Law and Order in Ireland*, Dublin: IPA.

Lee, J. (1989) *Ireland 1912–1985; Politics and Society*, Cambridge: Cambridge University Press.

MacSharry, R. and White, P. (2000) *The Making of the Celtic Tiger: The Inside Story of Ireland's Boom Economy*, Cork: Mercier Press.

McCullagh, C. (1995) 'Getting the criminals we want: The social production of the criminal population', in P. Clancy (ed.) *Irish Society: Sociological Perspectives*, Dublin: Sociological Association of Ireland, pp. 410–431.
McCullagh, C. (2002) 'How dirty is the white-collar? Analysing white-collar crime', in P. O'Mahony (ed.) *Criminal Justice in Ireland*, Dublin: Institute of Public Administration, pp. 155–175.
McDowell, M. (1998) *Report of the Working Group in Company Law Compliance and Enforcement*, Dublin: Stationery Office.
McGahon, D. (1991) *Irish Company Law Index*, Dublin: Gill and MacMillan.
McGrath, J. (2010) 'The traditional court of crime approach to the definition of a crime', in S. Kilcommins and U. Kilkelly (eds) *Regulatory Crime in Ireland*, Dublin: Lonsdale, pp. 29–61.
McGrath, J. (2010/2011) 'Confronting our continuing failure to prosecute respectable wrongdoers', *First Law Criminal Law*, December/January: 112–114.
McNiffe, L. (1997) *A History of the Garda Síochána*, Dublin: Wolfhound Press.
McWilliams, D. (2005) *The Pope's Children: Ireland's New Elite*, London: Gill and Macmillan.
Moynihan, M. (1980) *Speeches and Statements by Eamon DeValera 1917–73*, Dublin: Gill and Macmillan.
Murphy, G. (2005) 'From economic nationalism to European Union', in B. Girvin and G. Murphy (eds) *The Lemass Era: Politics and Society in the Ireland of Sean Lemass*, Dublin: University College Dublin Press, pp. 28–48.
Nelken, D. (2007) 'White collar and corporate crime', in M. Maguire (eds) *The Oxford Handbook of Criminology*, 4th edn, Oxford: Oxford University Press, pp. 733–770.
O'Brien, A. (1954) *The Vanishing Irish: The Enigma of the Modern World*, London: Allen.
O'Brien, G. (1936) 'Patrick Hogan: Minister for Agriculture 1922–1932', *Studies: An Irish Quarterly Review*, 25: 353–368.
O'Donnell, I., O'Sullivan, E. and Healy, D. (2005) *Crime and Punishment in Ireland 1922 to 2003: A Statistical Sourcebook*, Dublin: Institute of Public Administration.
O'Donnell, R. and O'Reardon, C. (2000) 'Social partnership in Ireland's economic transformation', in G. Fajertag and P. Pochet (eds) *Social Pacts in Europe*, Brussels: European Trade Union Institute, pp. 237–256.
OECD (2001) *Regulatory Reform in Ireland*, Paris: OECD.
O'Malley, T. (2006) *Sentencing Law and Practice*, 2nd edn, Dublin: Thomson Round Hall.
O'Toole, F. (2009) *Ship of Fools: How Stupidity and Corruption Sank the Celtic Tiger*, London: Faber and Faber.
Reddan, F. (2008) *Ireland's IFSC: A Story of Global Financial Success*, Dublin: Mercier Press.
Regling, K. and Watson, M. (2010) *A Preliminary Report on the Sources of Ireland's Banking Crisis*, Dublin: Stationery Office.
Smith, N.J. (2005), *Showcasing Globalisation: The Political Economy of the Irish Republic*, Manchester: Manchester University Press.
Sutherland, E. (1949) *White Collar Crime*, New York: Dryden Press.
Tobin, F. (1984) *The Best of Decades: Ireland in the 1960s*, Dublin: Gill and Macmillan.
Tombs, S. (2005) 'Corporate crime', in C. Hale, K. Hayward, A. Wahidin and E. Wincup (eds) *Criminology*, Oxford: Oxford University Press, pp. 267–288.
Ua Maoileoin, P. (1989) *De Reir Uimhreacha*, Baile Atha Cliath: Sairseal – O Marcaigh.
Various (Various Years) *Companies Report*, Dublin: Stationery Office.
Whitaker, T.K. (1958) *Economic Development*, Dublin: Stationery Office.
Wilson, S.V. and Matz, A.H. (1977) 'Obtaining evidence for federal economic prosecutions: An overview and analysis of investigative methods', *American Criminal Law Review*, 14: 651–716.

26

Whistleblowing in Europe

Regulatory frameworks and empirical research

Ralf Kölbel

Terminology and differentiation

Whistleblowing is defined as the act of disclosing the misconduct of organizations, authorities, etc. by organization members (Friedrichs 2010: 20–25). In scientific literature, the term usually refers to the disclosure by organization members (former or current) of illegal, immoral or illegitimate practices under the control of their employers, to persons or organizations that may be able to effect action (cf. Miceli et al. 2008: 6; Miceli et al. 2012: 925). It refers, therefore, to the conduct of informers, which exposes hidden organization-related or inner-organizational shortcomings to outsiders. In the context of white-collar crime these revelations mostly concern actions that allow the organization unlawful advantages (corporate crime) or, alternatively, refer to crimes committed by individual employees at the expense of the organization (occupational crime).

Whistleblowing typically involves persons that are or were directly connected to the organization concerned – i.e. generally people who still are or at one time were employees of that organization. However, they can also have obtained a special insight into irregular actions through other ways, e.g. as a customer or a business partner (cf. Hansson's study 2012). The reasons why insiders divulge their knowledge of illegal practices is irrelevant for the classification. If we only referred to whistleblowing as morally motivated reporting, the question would arise what to do with disclosures which are prompted by personal gain or for questionable purposes. Moreover, this would wrongly narrow the analytical field down to ethical resisters (cf. also Callahan and Dworkin 1992: 318–319).

Equally characteristic for whistleblowing are the receivers of the disclosed information. If normally the employee informs his immediate next in line, the whistleblower will avoid the regular official channels. Instead, he will either bypass his immediate superior and contact company management or the available special contact points within the organization (internal revision, audit committee, helpline, ombudsman, etc.), or he will pass his information on to authorities, law enforcement institutions, media or interest groups. In the first place it concerns internal, and in the second external whistleblowing (on this not always clearly applicable distinction cf. King 1999: 316; Miceli et al. 2008: 7–8).

This chapter describes and analyses both types of (institutionalized) whistleblowing and their contradictory functions. Additionally, it compares whistleblowing regulations in European countries and (with) the USA. In presenting empirical findings, moreover, the chapter shows the need to relativize the criminal-political potential of said systems.

Comparison of legal frameworks

Whistleblowing, particularly in connection with the social control of economic crime, has been institutionalized in some legal systems, especially in the Anglo-American countries (Miceli et al. 2008). However, over the past 20 years we have seen a similar, albeit often more hesitant, development in Europe. But there is, for instance, no uniformity in the legal positions among European states (for an overview of non-European industrial nations, cf. Vandekerckhove 2006). This becomes all the more clear in view of the entirely different legal treatment of the informers.

It is generally assumed that informers are very often afraid of retaliation and are, in fact, confronted with it frequently. Both have been empirically documented (cf. summarized Gobert and Punch 2000; Miceli et al. 2008; also Pemberton et al. 2012: 269–270; for Scandinavia cf. case histories from Bjørkelo et al. 2008; Hedin and Mänsson 2012).[1] The main legal question is, therefore, if whistleblowers should be protected through labour legislation or guaranteed anonymity.[2] The European legal systems, however, are relatively inconsistent in this respect.[3] Strictly speaking, even the conditions under which whistleblowing is permitted at all vary (especially regarding the external variation).[4] And yet, on a national legal level, we find several different types which, as a rule, must be clearly distinguished from the situation in the US.

Activating and protecting forms of regulation

In the United States whistleblowing is legally largely accepted ('activating type of regulation'). Internal corporate whistleblowing systems are very often prescribed by law, in which case companies must provide their employees with concrete contact points and reporting channels for whistleblowing and must guarantee that the employees will face no disadvantages (cf. e.g. Sec. 301 of the Sarbanes–Oxley Act – SOA). Apart from such explicit obligations there is at least an indirect legal pressure of implementation, as each organization that disposes of a whistleblowing system will obtain a penalty bonus in case a corporate crime occurs (cf. § 8 B 2.1. (b)(5)(C) of the US Sentencing Guidelines). At the same time individual whistleblowers are legally protected in many social sectors. In the US the government guarantees this by means of special measures for organizations that have entered into a commercial relationship with the government (FAR – Federal Acquisition Regulation Part 3.9). In the Federal Administration, the Whistleblower Protection Act (WPA) prohibits any discrimination towards employees who disclose illegal events, mismanagement or abuse of power. Apart from the SOA (Sec. 806), multiple similar laws exist both on federal and state level. These warranties often equally apply (as in the FAR) to disclosures to government authorities. In various cases hotlines are offered to this end[5] and external disclosures are financially stimulated (e.g. through the False Claims Act (FCA) and the Dodd Frank Act).

In Great Britain a protectionist type of regulation has been implemented. Here too, listed companies are obliged to install internal whistleblowing systems (Combined Code on Corporate Governance C.3.4). This is, however, on a comply or explain basis, which allows organizations to deviate from regulations in case of related disclosures and explanatory statements. Apart from this, the 1999 Public Interest Disclosure Act (PIDA) is significant (see related Standard PAS 1998: 2000). According to section 47 B, whistleblowers in any area of society – the only exceptions being the self-employed or those working for security – shall suffer no detriment (if they report in *the public interest*). Concerning the accuracy of the allegation, it is no more assumed that the whistleblower acts in good faith.[6] Nevertheless, external whistleblowing is obviously regarded as objectionable. Contrary to internal whistleblowing behaviour, it is allowed only under additional requirements and is considered a less-than-ideal solution. In case the whistleblower yields publicity and was driven by self-interest, it is possible to sanction him by means of the Employment Law (section 43 G I (c) – cf. Gobert and Punch 2000; also Schmidt 2005: 154–155).

The ambivalent situation in continental Europe

Whereas both the activating and protectionist types of regulation clearly or implicitly state that whistleblowing is principally or under certain conditions allowed, so far no such national parallel regulation has been implemented in, for example, Germany (ambivalent type of regulation). The government is, indeed, currently working on the implementation of corporate compliance programmes (e.g. through §§ 25a, 25c KWG, 33 Ch. 1 Nr. 1 WpHG), however without specifically involving whistleblowing systems. Internal whistleblower contact points need therefore not be established. However, their implementation (voluntarily or in order to fulfil obligations in foreign states) is lawful if proceeded in accordance with certain data protection requirements (Maschmann 2013: 99–100: possibly confidential treatment of identity instead of anonymity for the whistleblower).[7] The individual internal reports by employees are allowed anyway. In contrast, the legality of external information is regulated very restrictively. Since this can harm legally protected company secrecy interests, the whistleblower might even incur a penalty (§ 17 UWG), if he had other means at his disposal or if he had dishonourable reasons (cf. Engländer and Zimmermann 2012). Moreover, labour law penalties are only prohibited in case of honourable intentions and even then only if the information proves to be correct (or if the whistleblower acted in good faith) and there were no other options than to notify the authorities, the media, etc. (for the relevant legislation of the Federal Labour Court and the European Court of Human Rights cf. Maschmann 2013: 100). So far, the initiatives to implement an overall statutory authorization for whistleblowing have shown no results, nor can this be expected in the near future. In certain special cases (health and safety, corruption) and for certain professional categories (civil servants) the obligation of secrecy was lifted (§ 17 II ArbSchG; § 37 II Nr. 3 BeamtStG). In all other cases, external whistleblowing remains legally risky in Germany.

The situation in Italy resembles that of Germany (Guyer and Peterson 2013: 17) and the same goes for Austria, Poland and those European countries where there is no or only a marginal regulation concerning whistleblowing.[8] A number of other states have chosen a further type of regulation, i.e. a restricted protectionist type of regulation, which can be situated in between the other two European variants. From a legal point of view, this type basically ensures a fundamental protection to bona fide whistleblowers. However, this protection is partly only fragmentary and confined to the public service and/or specific reports on corruption. This is, for instance, the case for France (cf. Art. L 1161-1 French Labour Code; also Sankowicz and Henry 2012), but also for Belgium and the Netherlands, Romania and Ireland (see Hassink et al. 2007: 27; in more detail Vandekerckhove 2010a), as well as for Norway and Sweden (Skivenes and Trygstad 2010: 1073; Hansson 2012: 4). In these countries the respective legal situations show major differences in the details and are in some instances closer to the British type of regulation and in others to the ambivalent type.

The contradictory instrumentalization of whistleblowing

Whistleblowing is fundamentally different from traditional forms of reporting offences or in-company reporting. Today's whistleblowing is not only an individual phenomenon, but also a subject and result of a certain control strategy. The more the state tries to stimulate company insiders to report wrongdoings, the more whistleblowing becomes an 'element of a regulatory strategy' (Pemberton et al. 2012: 265). That's why the meaning and significance of whistleblowing can be better understood, if we analyse it in the context of general regulatory structures, which should enable the enforcement of economic law and economic penal law.

One approach in this regard aims at improving the state tools of enforcing criminal law. The other approach tries to strengthen self-control mechanisms within the organizations. Especially in the first case, detecting corporate crime obviously goes along with considerable difficulties (Shover and Hochstetler 2006) and a limited rate of success (Dyck et al. 2007). Corporate self-control, however, basically faces the same problem (Bussmann 2007). Therefore, both programmes try to raise the information retrieval rate by reinforcing the recruitment of informers. Whistleblowing, which originally only occurred sporadically and was considered purely an issue of conscience – more precisely an exceptional form of behaviour of individuals motivated by moral courage[9] – is now stimulated systematically. Thus it is to become commonplace behaviour with as many company insiders as possible blowing the whistle on malpractices. Naturally, this process of normalization, of institutionalization and instrumentalization, occurs in different ways.

External whistleblowing as part of public corporate control

The state traditionally relies on the steering effect of conventional mechanisms of sovereign law enforcement to guarantee compliance in the economy. The beginning of the 21st century, in particular, has seen a tentative rediscovery of the use of penal law (Snyder 2007) as a reaction to serious corporate crime and the crises at the financial markets (Snyder 2007) – although Europe has been more reluctant in doing so than countries overseas (cf. also Shover and Grabosky 2010). Along with this development, we have seen a growing cooperation between the public and private institutions as far as crime control is concerned. Such public–private partnerships primarily aim at acquiring information about fraudulent actions which is needed for their prosecution, and for the acquisition of which the public relies on the service of civilians. This is exactly where the growing relevance of external whistleblowing procedures becomes apparent. Public investigative authorities no longer only draw on information obtained by official control mechanisms or reported sporadically by individual informers of their own accord. On the contrary, they aim at enlarging the number of whistleblowers and witnesses by setting up reporting systems, thus facilitating public prosecution of, above all, corporate crimes (cf. Dugan and Gibbs 2009: 121; Miethe and Rothschild 1994: 328, 341).

At the point where potential informers are strategically encouraged to report wrongdoings, it becomes a real system. Easy acceptance when it comes to the receipt of disclosures, protection measures and financial incentives are the means by which a whistleblowing-system works.[10] The state does, in fact, partly rely on financial stimuli, although this is only relatively common in the US, where the informant can get a share of the fine (respectively the recovery) imposed on the enterprise (e.g. 42 U.S.C. § 1395b-5 or Security Exchange Act Sec. 21F as well as Brink et al. 2013: 96; Callahan and Dworkin 1992: 280; Ebersole 2011: 135–144; Miceli et al. 2008: 164; Pope and Lee 2013: 598–602).[11] In Europe, this hasn't been implemented yet (Guyer and Peterson 2013: 18). Although an award scheme has been under discussion,[12] Europe does not yet go beyond offering special and easily accessible channels for reporting irregularities, protecting whistleblowers, in some cases, by guaranteeing anonymity and/or by providing other forms of protection. This concept is already being rudimentarily implemented in places where the police or other authorities offer easy to use ways of refunding penal charges online (so-called *Internetwachen*, German online police stations). Generally, irregularities can also be reported anonymously (cf. thereto in the healthcare system the printed papers of the German Federal Parliament BT-print. 17/13588). Other online reporting processes go even further in that they technically guarantee full anonymity (also as far as the computer identification is concerned), while public investigators can nonetheless steadily communicate with the whistleblowers. In Germany, this occurs using the so-called Business Keeper Monitoring System (Linssen and Pfeiffer 2009), regardless of the legal ambiguity of thus encouraged whistleblowing.

An even more radical form of instrumentalization of whistleblowers is private law enforcement. Here, corporate insiders are not only motivated to support law enforcement by disclosing information, but to take this over completely in lieu of the state. So-called civil penalties play a key role, which can be claimed by competitors, injured parties or individuals accordingly against organizations acting illegally. As this is also supposed to have a deterring steering effect, public crime prosecution becomes superfluous. This is based on the *punitive damages* and in particular the *multiple damages* which are prescribed by law in the US (e.g. in the part on civil law of the so-called RICO Acts 18 U.S.C. § 1964(c)). In case of infringements of competition law, for example, injured parties should be encouraged, animated by the prospect of receiving an overcompensating proportion of any recovered damages, to systematically file private actions, on the basis of their insider knowledge, thus virtually substituting public law enforcement (cf. Jones 1999).

European antitrust law has not adopted this model yet, albeit approximation can be observed (Basedow 2007). The form of private crime prosecution which comes closest to individual whistleblowing is, in fact, the so-called *qui tam* action under the False Claims Act. If employees have reasonable grounds for believing that their organization is defrauding public authorities, they can, in accordance with this option, file actions on behalf of the state under *treble damages* and a civil penalty. Prevailing plaintiffs receive a relator's share, the amount of which (15–30 per cent of the sum) depends on whether a state has joined the lawsuit; primarily, however, it varies according to the quality of the information and the evidence merits of the insider (in detail Kölbel 2008; cf. also the instructive trial reports on several FCA trials in Bucy 2004). In Europe where, so far, there has not been an equivalent of said US institution, adopting it is only under discussion (Home Office 2007; Riley 2003).

Whistleblowing as an element of corporate self-control

Yet again following the example of the US, European states have furthermore proceeded to urge organizations to guarantee their own compliance by way of internal self-control. Legal obligations or the prospect of milder punishment in case of a crime encourage organizations to set up their own compliance programmes in order to prevent corporate and occupational crime These programmes triggered by the state, however, also show a reactive element. They include a set of tools allowing organizations to deal with violations that have already been committed – not only damages caused to the organization but also non-compliances within the company which affect the outside world. For this purpose, companies either create their own in-house units or call upon external professional service providers (lawyers and consulting companies) for investigation (Williams 2005). Internal whistleblowing systems are regularly connected with structures of this kind. As such, they serve as information channels offering employees (and to a certain extent also customers, subcontractors, etc.) easily accessible, risk-free disclosure channels by means of which detection units should increasingly be provided with reports on wrongdoings, necessary for initiating internal detection and handling processes (Berry 2004: 1–2; Miceli et al. 2008; Miethe and Rothschild 1994: 328; 1999: 126). In its quest to promote self-regulating structures, the state at all times intends corporate compliance programmes to include said means of information disclosure (Pemberton et al. 2012: 264).

Hence, the establishment of a compliance programme usually involves the creation of a whistleblower disclosure procedure which guarantees anonymity, e.g. a contact point, a telephone hotline or an online portal. This has become commonplace in larger European organizations (Bussmann and Matschke 2008),[13] albeit to a lesser extent than in the US (latest findings on the nationwide existence: cf. Kaptein 2010; Weber and Wasielewski 2013). Even in Germany, where there are no according regulations, more than one-third of the organizations have introduced an in-house whistleblowing system (PricewaterhouseCoopers 2010: 31; 2011: 70).[14] Business codes of the organizations often specifically demand that employees make use of this system (Hassink et al. 2007: 34, 36). Moreover, organizations generally guarantee that violations may be disclosed on a confidential basis. In addition, various financial stimuli to encourage the disclosure of wrongdoings are being considered (Wrase and Fabritius 2011).

Structural incompatibilities of public and private whistleblowing systems

In Europe, as in most countries of the Western world, both law enforcement strategies are pursued, i.e. efforts to take legal action more effectively as well as stronger self-monitoring. Therefore internal and external whistleblowing systems are often found side by side. Sometimes both information channels are even initiated in parallel by the legal systems, though this rarely happens as clearly as it does in the United States. Over there, in the case of an offence, the said FCA sees to it that in many branches employees are financially motivated to report externally and their employers even have a duty to inform them about this. At the same time, companies are legally and by order of the Sentencing Guidelines obliged to install internal whistleblowing systems (cf. Carson et al. 2008: 367). In Europe both systems seldom appear parallel in such a pronounced form. However, in principle the whistleblower's actions, whether within the company or externally, are at the same time activated – though not necessarily in the framework of an intentional political programme, but definitely supported by objective structures. This duality, finally, is not particularly reasonable.

That is due to the fact that the compliance programmes and with them the internal reporting systems develop their own logic in the day-to-day corporate reality, which is very different from what the government expects to achieve by implementing whistleblowing regulation and from what initially legitimized it. From the point of view of the organizations these compliance measures give rise to several instruments of liability avoidance. From their point of view, the things that are most important from the perspective of regulation – i.e. the steering effect (in the sense of better compliance) – are of secondary importance whereas the handling of penal and other liability risks in the economic interest of the organization is predominant.

This is especially noticeable in the reactive elements of the compliance programme. As far as the regulatory aims are concerned, these measurements should guarantee that violations within organizations are exposed and a public judicial process can be initiated (as this will most likely eliminate criminogenic organizational structure and implement prevention measures). But for a company, government involvement constitutes just one of several options: reactive compliance measures can only be of need to a company if they manage to process the criminal offence with as little damage as possible and if they manage to reduce the economic disruption. For this reason, internal investigations are solely aligned with this logic of economic concerns and not with disclosure or prosecution interests of the public, victims or any third parties involved. In practice this generally results in damage management, which is entirely focused on the interests of the organization involved (minimization of sanction and liability costs; reputation; avoidance of damage in business relationships; avoidance of irritations in personnel issues, etc.)[15]

When serious irregularities are internally exposed, the authorities are generally not consulted. The state is, therefore, only consulted on a highly selective and in a purely instrumental way, i.e. only in those rare cases where it would exceptionally bring about tactical advantages to the economic aims of the organization.[16] In other cases, the official procedure, which is ruled by non-economic criteria and on which organizations barely have an influence, brings about too many disadvantages (fines, damage of image, administrative requirements, etc.). For this reason, companies tend to adhere to the *culture of secrecy* (Zedner 2006: 272) and deal with violations committed within the company in common interest discreetly as an internal matter (Williams 2005; Ziegleder 2007: 254–255).

Thus, it is also imperative to try to prevent external whistleblowing as much as possible. Indeed, if an employee blows the whistle on internal wrongdoing outside the organization, this will entail the very official procedures which organizations seek to avoid because of secondary and collateral damage. External whistleblowing represents a threat to corporate business interests (Barnett 1992; Miceli et al. 2009; Schmidt 2005: 150 f.; Williams 2005: 328) owing to its harmful economic effects organizations concerned are frequently confronted with (to this now the findings of Bowen et al. 2010). That is why companies need a technique that channels the potential willingness of the employee to impart with information from the outset within the boundaries of the companies' interests. This is precisely the possibility an internal reporting system offers, since it systematically turns any potential external whistleblowing into internal information (Berry 2004: 1, 10–11; Callahan and Dworkin 1992: 334–335; Hassink et al. 2007: 30; Miceli et al. 2009: 381, 385–386; Miceli and Near 1994: 66–67; 1996: 509; Schmidt 2005: 162). Because of this, businesses install these systems and it is exactly why they urgently recommend their employees in (most of) their codes of conduct to only report any kind of malpractice internally (Hassink et al. 2007: 35, 37; Ziegleder 2007: 250–251). What is more, some British companies (primarily belonging to the National Health Service) even offer a reward for employees who keep silent instead of reporting misbehaviour to the outside world (so-called gag orders, cf. Guyer and Peterson 2013: 18).[17]

It appears, therefore, that internal whistleblowing is not serving its intended purpose as an early warning system to ensure *corporate hygiene* (Callahan and Dworkin 1992: 334). In contrast, it is actually functioning as a means of preventing captious internal corporate behaviour from being exposed and of handling corporate malpractice in the organization's interest solely within the organization. If internal corporate whistleblowing systems from a regulatory perspective aim at enforcing law, then this objective is partly undermined by corporate logic as the concerning systems are more likely to control information and steer the consequences of malpractices in accordance with the organization's interests. More so: this is at the same time in stark contrast with the functions of external whistleblowing, of which the efficiency decreases as internal whistleblowing (i.a. by the government) is accelerated and becoming more important.

Internal whistleblowing systems prevent what police and public whistleblowing facilities are institutionalized for: they prevent external reporting from which public corporate crime prosecution stands to benefit. They block the influx of insider knowledge of wrong-doings for which public prosecution bodies and companies compete against each other. So, whereas the economic operators lose control over the handling of wrongdoings in case of external whistleblowing, the public sector loses power of control when information remains inside the organization. In other words, when the government decidedly encourages and requires internal whistleblowing systems, it undermines at the same time its own power of enforcement (Kölbel and Herold 2010). To say that internal whistleblowing systems constitute a win–win situation for prevention, as is often stated (for example Miceli and Near 1988: 278), and provide a higher level of corporate norm compliance (cf. only Miceli et al. 2009: 380) completely rules out the possibility of a contra-indicated use of information from a regulatory point of view.

State-of-the-art empirical research

Analysing the operational conflicts alone cannot provide the full picture of the actual effects. What the real consequences are when two functionally incompatible whistleblowing systems – a public system and a corporate one – expand and enter into downright competition with each other to obtain information from company insiders, can only be determined through empirical observation. This first of all requires information on the effectiveness of both systems. Secondly, the decision criteria that influence a whistleblower to internally or externally impart with his information need to be reconstructed.

The decisions of (potential) whistleblowers

Variants of action

The first question to arise is what brings certain people to talk where others keep silent. Existing survey data show that most people tend to show solidarity with the organization. Internal disclosures are clearly preferred and external whistleblowing is often only used as a last resort (cf. Callahan and Collins 1992: 942; Callahan and Dworkin 1994: 176; ERC 2012b: 2; Larmer 1992: 127). Most external whistleblowing is, moreover, often preceded by failed internal attempts (for empirical evidence see e.g. Brink et al. 2013: 95; ERC 2012b: 2; Miceli and Near 2010: 77–78; Miceli et al. 2008: 9–10; in a European context: Bjørkelo et al. 2011; Hedin and Mänsson 2012).[18] Admittedly, the extent and rigidity of company loyalty differ in different cultures. It is, for instance, stronger in Asia than it is in the USA (cf. Brody et al. 1999; Martens and Kelleher 2005; cf. also Hassink et al. 2007: 29; Miceli et al. 2009: 381). Considering the conception of company loyalty in those countries, one can assume that more extensive reservations towards external whistleblowing also exist in Europe and due to the historical denunciation experiences especially in Germany (cf. amongst others Pittroff 2011: 12–13). Research to date (for a summary of cross-national research: cf. Vandekerckhove 2010b) has shown that this assumption is plausible (cf. specifically on France Katz and Lenglet 2010). It has not, however, been able to empirically confirm it (rather indications to the contrary by Jackson and Calafell Artola 1997: 1170–1171).

Apart from this question, many company employees who observe misconduct or wrongdoing keep this information to themselves anyway. According to the obviously heavily fluctuating available survey data approximately 50 per cent, if not more, of the employees with knowledge about any wrongdoing are so-called silent observers (summary Miceli et al. 2008: 22–23; Miceli and Near 2010: 80; Rothschild 2000: 421).[19] For a criminological analysis it is, therefore, important to know which factors persuade someone to take this double-contraindicative decision: to start acting in the first place and, more than that, to report to an external channel.

Factors affecting whistleblowing behaviour

Research papers about managerial, organizational and behavioural science to date have shown that the complex decision-making process (for a relevant model, see Miceli and Near 1992: 48) is mostly affected by personal, situational and company-specific circumstances (cf. Barnett 1992:

949; Hassink et al. 2007: 29; King 1999: 316–317; Miceli and Near 1996: 511; Miethe and Rothschild 1994: 325; Sims and Keenan 1998: 411). Bearing in mind that so far there is no proof for the fact that its findings can be applied to the situation in Europe, research conducted predominantly in the US has drawn the attention to the following specific correlations:[20]

a Most studies primarily looked at personal characteristics of whistleblowers which influenced the decision in relation to if and why they reported any wrongdoing. This, however, did not provide explicitly consistent findings. Age, a feeling of solidarity and the position in the organization could partly be qualified as relevant factors. Internal whistleblowers appear to be more often long-time, high-ranking and higher-educated employees, whereas external whistleblowers tend to be older (> 40) and better paid (cf. for Europe Bjørkelo et al. 2011: 216–217; for the USA Miceli and Near 1988: 268–269, 276–277; 1996: 511–512; Miceli et al. 1991: 123; partly different findings Dworkin and Baucus 1998: 1290; Miethe and Rothschild 1999: 113). Concerning the influence of gender, there are different observations (greater willingness to testify by women in Mazerolle and Cassematis 2010: 134; for different results Miceli and Near 1988; 1996). Religious orientation and/or social values also play a certain role (on weaker and inconsistent links: Mesmer-Magnus and Viswesvaran 2005: 290; Miethe and Rothschild 1999: 119; Sims and Keenan 1998: 416–417). On the whole, however, the differences in character between internal and external informants as well as silent observers are small (Miceli and Near 2010: 82; Miethe and Rothschild 1999: 113). This can hardly be surprising since most external whistleblowing only happens after internal whistleblowing has failed.
b The situational context influences the decision, as the risks and benefits of disclosure differ depending on the individual case. Thus, qualitative and quantitative characteristics of any specific inner-organizational wrongdoing influence insiders' decisions. From the subjective point of view the persons who decide to take action interpret the grievance as more serious than the silent observers (cf. Miceli et al. 2008: 10). If the matter concerns issues of health and safety and if the person judges he possesses sufficient insight and proof, he is more likely to proceed to external whistleblowing (Brink et al. 2013: 96; Callahan and Dworkin 1994: 173; Dworkin and Baucus 1998: 1281–1282, 1296; Miceli et al. 2012: 939; Zipparo 1999: 284). Wrongdoing by higher-ranked staff members is less often disclosed than wrongdoing by lower- or equally ranked colleagues (Mazerolle and Cassematis 2010: 135; Skivenes and Trygstad 2010: 1083). Financial motivation can at least partially explain external whistleblowing (cf. Callahan and Dworkin 1992: 283–284; Carson et al. 2008: 361, 372; Dyck et al. 2007: 31; Pope and Lee 2013: 605) – especially if one considers the promised reward as a gratification for the result of the triggered enquiry (in depth Callahan and Dworkin 1992: 278–279, 283). To what extent external whistleblowing is hindered by a real or imagined fear of retaliation (whether by employer or informally) is largely unknown. Though many external whistleblowers indicate that they have barely been influenced by conceivable disadvantages or retaliation measures (Miceli et al. 2009: 380) – at least once they had decided to act (cf. the meta-analysis by Mesmer-Magnus and Viswesvaran 2005: 290) – silent observers are of course not included in these studies. Experimental studies with neutral test persons revealed (with inconsistent results) that the danger of dismissal generally did play a role at the beginning of the decision-making stage (cf. Callahan and Collins 1992: 945; Zipparo 1999: 284). On the other hand, the willingness to talk does not automatically increase when anonymity is guaranteed (Pope and Lee 2013: 605).
c Lastly, organizational conditions constitute external factors which affect decisions and the scale of whistleblower behaviour, by either facilitating or hampering one of the two

whistleblowing variants. Indeed, the complexity and lavishness of communication channels often increase with the size of an organization, so that established whistleblowing channels are difficult to use or are even totally unknown (cf. Barnett 1992: 956; King 1999: 324; Miceli and Near 1996: 511; Miceli et al. 2009: 387; Zipparo 1999: 282–283). Internal communication channels are equally constrained in a bureaucratic, strongly authoritarian and hierarchic organizational structure (cf. Barnett 1992: 949–950; King 1999: 317; Miceli and Near 1996: 517). Companies where the unions are well represented generally have a higher level of willingness to proceed to external reporting, whereby it is not certain if the respective industry is a deciding factor (Barnett 1992: 956; Rothschild and Miethe 1999: 177). In contrast, internal whistleblowing is facilitated by means of well-directed support measures (easily accessible contact points) and encouragement from superiors, as well as an ethical business climate and/or one that is open to criticism (cf. Hassink et al. 2007: 30; Kaptein 2011; Miceli and Near 1992: 150; Miceli et al. 2009; Sims and Keenan 1998: 418; Zipparo 1999: 275). Appropriate specifications in the profession or business code, however, do not increase the willingness to report (Beets and Killough 1990).

The results of whistleblowing systems

Reporting procedures are not beyond critique. That whistleblowing borders on denunciation and is therefore morally and ethically questionable (to this discussion for example Carson et al. 2008) is a valid objection, which should be further elaborated in a different disciplinarian context. In contrast, the functionality of whistleblowing is definitely a criminological issue. It is, for instance, doubtful whether whistleblowing leads to the expected effects of disclosure and detection which compensate for its downside, i.e. the resource expenditure and the disruption of the interaction within the organization. The nature of whistleblowing institutions inevitably entails a potentially explosive possibility of abuse (cf. Gobert and Punch 2000: 44–45, 49–50; Schmidt 2005: 158–159). Many informants might be less concerned with bringing wrongdoing out into the open than with discrediting certain persons, departments or companies (out of vengeance/competition) or with acquiring the advantages of the whistleblower status (i.e. the financial bonus, immunity under labour legislation, etc.). Under these circumstances the creditability of disclosures is highly questionable.

To judge the validity of this criticism, a systematic evaluation of whistleblowing institutions would be required. The focus would have to lie on the volume and the substance, the reliability and the usability of the acquired information. Companies, however, are reluctant to release evaluations of their internal systems, so that information in this respect is very limited. Miceli et al. (2008: 21) report parenthetically on revisions, which proved that an important part (though the number could not be established exactly) of internal disclosures could not be confirmed (likewise PricewaterhouseCoopers 2010: 34–35). Although data is sometimes collected on internal investigations which are triggered by internal whistleblowing (e.g. Bussmann and Werle 2006: 1134–1135: 4 per cent; PricewaterhouseCoopers 2011: 70: 10 per cent), it remains unknown how much information would have been disclosed if there hadn't been a suitable contact point (by means of an official communication or as a chance discovery). A more recent German study has revealed that company systems are of almost no importance as far as the exposure of malpractice is concerned; in fact, it turned out they are used for denunciations and general complaints (Boemke et al. 2012: 88; more positive results however from Hülsberg and Engels 2011: 15, 18). Recent surveys have also shown that compliance rates of the organizations benefit only marginally if at all from whistleblowing structures (Parker and Nielsen 2009; Simpson et al. 2013). On top of that, the limited amount of research available on this topic leads to the assumption that internal disclosures only rarely lead to the required inner-organizational changes (summarized Skivenes and Trygstad 2010: 1085 with further references).

As far as governmental whistleblowing institutions are concerned, research data is also sporadic. This means that in this field the empirical base must be considered to be rather weak. However, in the following two examples it becomes apparent that the aforementioned criticism is not unfounded. First indications can be obtained from practical experiences in the US with the FCA and the *qui tam* trials (in more detail: Kölbel 2008). Here, the available findings (US DOJ 2012) make it clear that a financial incentive can to a certain extent act as motivation. As it happens, a mentionable rise in the number of private claims from whistleblowers, which had already been allowed for a long time, only occurred when the obtainable relator's shares were raised to an attractive level, thereby offering the informer an attractive prospect of gain. In this respect, the stimulus generates without doubt a surplus of internal disclosures.[21] The number of people who decide to make a report and to file a complaint is nonetheless so small (still 400 to 650 per annum) that only a marginal amount of wrongdoing is unveiled. It seems that the circle of insiders is only partially activated by the rewards of the FCA. Moreover, the information supplied is often irrelevant, unusable or unsubstantiated, since in only 20 per cent to 25 per cent of the cases the government joins the private action or the actions are successful.

Another example which especially elucidates the aspect of guaranteed anonymity is provided by the experience of the police force of the Business Keeper Monitoring System in the German State of Lower Saxony. Out of 1239 reports received there between the end of 2003 and 2007, 724 pre-investigations were started (mostly related to economic offences). However, initial suspicion that allows a formal criminal investigation was found in only 350 cases. An exorbitant 82.6 per cent of these investigations ended in a suspension because of insufficient evidence. Apart from the eight procedures which were still pending by the end of 2008, there were only 39 convictions (Linssen and Pfeiffer 2009: 174–175). Hence, although the system yields a significant increase of private complaints registered by the police, these generated only a minor result. This had already been illustrated in an earlier evaluation study (four convictions/sentences until December 2004 as opposed to more than 90 per cent dismissals for insufficient evidence) (cf. Backes and Lindemann 2006). A qualitative analysis of internal disclosures that was carried out there showed that there was a significant though not specified proportion of evidence which pointed at problematic motives like jealousy, revenge or frustration (cf. Backes and Lindemann 2006: 100–101).

Taking stock and legal outlook

There is reason to believe that empirical research data available so far is only of limited use. The information gathered on cultural, organizational, situational and personal reasons potential whistleblowers have for disclosing any wrongdoing, albeit ample in quantity, is, for now, only preliminary. This is especially the case as there is no information yet on the interdependency and interaction of the different reasons. Nor can findings obtained in the US be readily applied to Europe. One general finding, however, becomes apparent: institutionalized incentives to encourage whistleblowing behaviour, which aim at increasing the number of reports on violations, are currently only addressing a minority of potential whistleblowers. Moreover, the people it does mobilize and who report via its information channels disclose information which only too often is of little use as these informers evidently represent the wrong target group (i.e. they are not real insiders with authentic knowledge of inner-organizational misbehaviour). At any rate, law enforcement authorities currently bring about only a moderate increase in the detection rate through their whistleblowing systems. And although it still needs to be fully determined whether the situation is significantly different for internal whistleblowing systems, this is hardly likely to be the case (Pemberton et al. 2012: 271).

On the whole, therefore, the efficiency of the entire institution is, at present, often surprisingly weak. The expectations criminal policy has towards whistleblowing are barely fulfilled. Its actual relevancy – especially in Europe – remains disproportionate to the scope and intensity of the scientific debate on it. This is arguably the reason why even when internal and external whistleblowing are made use of side by side, their inconsistency and competition have, to date, hardly become noticeable. The picture would be different if the willingness to report were to rise. Recent observations in Europe have shown that this does not depend on further technical improvement of hotlines and internet platforms or even on making report channels even more readily accessible and less prone to reprisal.

A large Norwegian survey (Skivenes and Trygstad 2010) showed that there was an exceptionally high proportion of employees in the public sector that reported observed wrongdoing internally or externally (76 per cent). Thirty-six per cent of the employees took several internal attempts and 7 per cent reported outside the organization. Despite the fact that the risk of suffering from any disadvantages increased with the intensity of the reporting behaviour, only a very small number of informers (17 per cent) faced any form of reprisal. Inversely, a great number of them (64 per cent) observed intra-organizational changes as a result of their blowing the whistle (both were confirmed by the findings of Bjørkelo et al. 2011: 219–220). The authors of the survey see the reason for their remarkable findings in the employment market structures of northern European welfare states, in which employees feel more inclined to fight wrongdoings acting from the secure job positions they have in these countries. They especially highlight the largely institutionalized corporate management culture in Scandinavian countries, which is co-operative, informal and dialogic and thus enables employees to take an influence. Communicative and open corporate cultures of this kind facilitate internal whistleblowing and enable the appropriate handling of whistleblowing reports. Said interpretation is clearly supported by some of the above mentioned findings as well as, and especially by research which has shown that internal compliance programmes generally only have a preventive effect where they are integrated in a democratic, conformity- and value-oriented corporate culture (cf. e.g. Parker and Nielsen 2009).

Under these conditions, it might become more apparent that potential informers generally tend to be loyal to the organization. When they have the choice, insiders will ever more noticeably choose to disclose their knowledge of malpractice internally, and will only go outside the organization under certain circumstances: i.e. in case of inaccessibility and inefficacy of internal information channels (or when, in view of a specific case, internal remedy has to be discarded from the beginning). Hence, in the competition of internal and external systems, it would come, under these circumstances, to a (further) shift towards internal alternatives (cf. also the corresponding indications in manager surveys Barnett et al. 1993). The amount of information disclosed to the police and to company investigators would increase even further at the expense of the authorities. Consequently, the existence of external channels would, if at all, only be required in single cases (i.e. when self-regulation fails), albeit not necessarily anonymously.

In the light of American and European findings, it becomes clear that the ideal Norwegian conditions described above are exceptional. To date, corporate compliance and whistleblowing systems rarely function as described by Skivenes and Trygstad (2010). As far as the aspect of regulations is concerned, it is, therefore, still preferable not to leave action against wrongdoing solely in the hands of the non-juridical economic calculus of the companies. Instead, it is in the interest of the public to direct insider information on wrongdoing to public recipients. However, the number of competing internal information channels, though originally triggered by the state, is meanwhile growing steadily. This development cannot be stopped any more.

Attempts at countering it by installing anonymous external hotlines would presumably show little result. Apart from the fact that such systems are ineffective and inferior, they also bear the risk of denunciation and abuse. For this reason, there have been calls in Europe to disregard these problematic whistleblowing channels, and to stick to the traditional public reporting channels (cf. e.g. Backes and Lindemann 2006).

Convincing decisions in this political question require an even closer look into the factors that influence whistleblower behaviour. Hence a clear need for further research is marked. But if we differentiate between whistleblowing systems and individual behaviour within these systems, and if we look closely at the latter, the main problem here – i.e. whether whistleblowers need protection – is an issue which can be addressed immediately. Fully apart from the drawbacks which institutionalized systems of whistleblowing have shown, there is no justification for the fact that some legal systems reject clear legal safeguards even in case of commendable disclosure of real wrongdoing. A well-shaped external right to report is as appropriate as a differentiated set of instruments for protecting whistleblowers from reprisal. Therefore, there is a need for the development of a binding homogenous minimum standard in Europe, offering whistleblowing a firm basis whenever it occurs altruistically or at least without artificial triggers.

Notes

1 For, compared therewith, a relatively small percentage of retaliation in case of internal whistleblowing – 27 per cent when reported to management, 40 per cent when reported to a company hotline – however: cf. ERC 2012a: 6.

2 Leniency programmes provide not only whistleblower protection, but also exemption from punishment for criminally involved informants. Due to its particular moral and judicial issues this special kind of regulation is disregarded here.

3 In fact, the Scandinavian studies quoted in the text indicate that whistleblowers, although legally protected, may suffer serious personal consequences. Against soft punishments by the social surroundings (isolation, stigmatization, etc.) the possibilities of legal safeguards must be small. In the end, long-term cultural transformation processes are required, in which whistleblowing is reinterpreted as a positive action.

4 The fact that employees of an organization are explicitly bound to report serious irregularities is absolutely unusual – apart from the situation of EU civil servants (cf. Art. 22a, 22b EU Regulations for Civil Servants as well as the Guidelines on Whistleblowing from 6/12/2012 – SEC(2012) 679 final). Mostly, the legal issue is whether whistleblowing is facilitated and if typical barriers are eliminated.

5 Cf. for an arbitrary example: http://www.epa.gov/oig/hotline.html (accessed 7 April 7 2014).

6 This is the state of the Enterprise and Regulatory Reform Act 2013. For the former situation cf. Bowers 2012.

7 These are ultimately requirements of the EU Data Protection Law. Cf. also the reservations of the French data protection authorities (http://cnil.fr/fileadmin/documents/en/CNIL-recommandations-whistleblowing-VA.pdf, accessed 7 April 2014) as well as the contemplations of the so-called Art.-29-Data Protection Group (WP 117, 00195/06/EU). For implementations in Belgium, Portugal and Spain, cf. http://ec.europa.eu/justice/data-protection/document/national-policy/whistleblowing/index_en.htm, accessed 7 April 2014. Models that enable anonymous disclosing without explicitly encouraging it, however, are, e.g. in Germany, not criticized in practice.

8 Cf. compilation of Vandekerckhove (2010a); also, specifically for Eastern Europe, the report on the legal position in that area: http://www.whistleblowing-cee.org/summing-study (accessed 7 April 2014).

9 The intermediate results of a study which I am currently conducting with N. Herold and which is mainly based on qualitative interviews with whistleblowers, however, have already shown that ethical motives for reporting are by no means the rule and are, moreover, always intertwined with other motives (mostly downright practical ones and even with self-interest in mind) (cf. also Miceli and Near 2010: 77).

10 Obligations to report (underpinned by sanctions) are a further technique of motivation. It can get a practical relevance in companies (3.2) due to Labour Law and corresponding requirements in the codes of conduct (thereto cf. Vandekerckhove and Tsahuridu 2010).

11 See e.g. the case of the Swiss Bank UBS (http://articles.washingtonpost.com/2012-09-11/business/35494823_1_ubs-whistleblower-bradley-birkenfeld-report-tax-fraud, accessed 7 April 2014).
12 Cf. the draft of a market abuse regulation of the EU from 20/10/2011 (KOM (2011) 651 final), notably art 29 II, which provides a reward for whistleblowers, issued by the Member States.
13 Despite limitations due to data protection regulations (above note 7).
14 According to the survey by Pittroff (2011), however, the organization and extent of the systems varies amongst the 30 largest companies listed on the stock exchange in the Federal Republic of Germany.
15 It may sometimes also be a case of more neatly hiding a profitable but legally borderline action in future (cf. Miceli and Near 1995: 695; Schmidt 2005: 148–149).
16 E.g. if exposure to the public cannot be avoided anyway; if the impression of solidarity must be avoided by means of clear dissociation; if severe sanctions against the company can be avoided through cooperation – or if responsibility can be shifted to the employees by an official complaint (specifically on that point: Laufer 1999: 1343).
17 See for an exemplary case: www.telegraph.co.uk/health/healthnews/9869579/NHS-whistleblower-faces-ruin-after-speaking-out-about-patient-safety.html (accessed 7 April 2014).
18 These findings are confirmed by my own interview study (note 9).
19 These numbers are higher (53 to 65 per cent since 2000) if we include situations whereby the conventional disclosure to a superior constitutes a realistic and workable option (cf. ERC 2012b: 1).
20 For most studies it consisted of standardized (e-mail) interviews of the most diverse groups of people in the US (different categories of employees, students, etc.). The behaviour is frequently measured with case vignettes and scenarios and interpreted as an indication of the willingness to proceed to whistleblowing. The validity and generalization of the findings are therefore limited (also the assessments by Dworkin and Baucus 1998: 1296; Hassink et al. 2007: 42; Miceli and Near 1988: 279).
21 Cf. also Dyck et al. (2007: 5), according to whom three times as many corporate crimes were uncovered through whistleblowing within the jurisdiction of the FCA compared with the rest of the economic systems.

References

Backes, O. and Lindemann, M. (2006) *Staatliche organisierte Anonymität als Ermittlungsmethode bei Korruptions- und Wirtschaftsdelikten*, Heidelberg: C.F. Müller.

Barnett, T. (1992) 'A preliminary investigation of the relationship between selected organizational characteristics and external whistleblowing by employees', *Journal of Business Ethics*, 11(12): 949–959.

Barnett, T., Cochran, S.D. and Taylor, G.S. (1993) 'The internal disclosure policies of private-sector employers', *Journal of Business Ethics*, 12(2): 127–136.

Basedow, J. (ed.) (2007) *Private Enforcement of EC Competition Law*, Alphen a.d.R.: Kluwer Law International.

Beets, S. and Killough, L. (1990) 'The effectiveness of a compliant-based ethics enforcement system', *Journal of Business Ethics*, 9(2): 115–126.

Berry, B. (2004) 'Organizational culture: A framework and strategies for facilitating employee whistleblowing', *Employee Responsibility and Rights Journal*, 16(1): 1–11.

Bjørkelo, B., Einarsen, S., Nielsen, M. and Matthiesen, S. (2011) 'Silence is golden? Characteristics and experiences of self-reported whistleblowers', *European Journal of Work and Organizational Psychology*, 20(2): 206–238.

Bjørkelo, B., Ryberg, W., Matthiesen, S. and Einarsen, S. (2008) 'When you talk and talk and nobody listens', *International Journal of Organisational Behaviour*, 13(2): 18–40.

Boemke, B., Grau, K., Kißling, K. and Schneider, H. (2012) 'Evidenzbasierte Kriminalprävention im Unternehmen', *Denkströme*, 9: 79–94.

Bowen, R., Call, A. and Rajgopal, S. (2010) 'Whistle-blowing: Target firm characteristics and economic consequences', *The Accounting Review*, 85(4): 1239–1271.

Bowers, J. (2012) *Whistleblowing: Law and Practice*, Oxford: Oxford University Press.

Brink, A., Lowe, J. and Victoravich, L. (2013) 'The effect of evidence strength and internal rewards on intentions to report fraud in the Dodd-Frank regulatory environment', *Auditing*, 32(3): 87–104.

Brody, R.G., Coulter, J.M. and Suming, L. (1999) 'The effect of national culture on whistle-blowing perceptions', *Teaching Business Ethics*, 3(4): 385–400.

Bucy, P. (2004) 'Games and stories: Game theory and the Civil False Claims Act', *Florida State University Law Review*, 31(3): 603–676.

Bussmann, K. (2007) 'The control paradox and the impact of business ethics: A comparison of US and German companies', *Monatsschrift für Kriminologie und Strafrechtsreform*, 90(2–3): 260–276.

Bussmann, K. and Matschke, S. (2008) 'The impact of the US legislation on company measures of control and prevention', *Criminal Law & Social Change*, 49(5): 349–364.

Bussmann, K. and Werle, M. (2006) 'Addressing crime in companies', *British Journal of Criminology*, 46(6): 1128–1144.

Callahan, E.S. and Collins, J.W. (1992) 'Employee attitudes toward whistleblowing', *Journal of Business Ethics*, 11(12): 939–948.

Callahan, E.S. and Dworkin, T.M. (1992) 'Do good and get rich', *Villanova Law Review*, 37: 273–336.

Callahan, E.S. and Dworkin, T.M. (1994) 'Who blows the whistle to the media, and why', *American Business Law Journal*, 32(2): 151–184.

Carson, T.L., Verdu, M.E. and Wokutch, R.E. (2008) 'Whistle-blowing for profit', *Journal of Business Ethics*, 77(3): 361–376.

Dugan, L. and Gibbs, C. (2009) 'The role of organizational structure in the control of corporate crime and terrorism', in S. Simpson and D. Weisburd (eds) *The Criminology of White-Collar Crime*, New York: Springer.

Dworkin, T.M. and Baucus, M.S. (1998) 'Internal vs. external whistleblowing', *Journal of Business Ethics*, 17(12): 1281–1298.

Dyck, A., Morse, A. and Zingales, L. (2007) 'Who blows the whistle on corporate fraud?', *NBER Working Paper Series*: 1–66.

Ebersole, D. (2011) 'Blowing the whistle on the Dodd-Frank whistleblower provisions', *Ohio State Entrepreneurial Business Law Journal*, 6(1): 123–174.

Engländer, A. and Zimmermann, T. (2012) 'Whistleblowing als strafbarer Verrat von Geschäfts- und Betriebsgeheimnissen', *Neue Zeitschrift für Wirtschaftsstrafrecht*, 328–332.

ERC (2012a) *Retaliation: When Whistleblowers Become Victims*, Washington: Ethics Resource Center.

ERC (2012b) *Inside the Mind of a Whistleblower*, Washington: Ethics Resource Center.

Friedrichs, D. (2010) *Trusted Criminals*, Belmont, CA: Thomson Higher.

Gobert, J. and Punch, M. (2000) 'Whistleblowers, the public interest, and the Public Interest Disclosure Act 1998', *The Modern Law Review*, 63(1): 25–54.

Guyer, T. and Peterson, N. (2013) *The Current State of Whistleblowing Law in Europe*, Government Accountability Project.

Hansson, L. (2012) 'The private whistleblower: Defining a new role in the public procurement system', *Business and Politics*, 14(2): 1–28.

Hassink, H., de Vries, M. and Bollen, L. (2007) 'A content analysis of whistleblowing policies of leading European companies', *Journal of Business Ethics*, 25–44.

Hedin, U. and Mänsson, S. (2012) 'Whistleblowing processes in Swedish public organisations: Complaints and consequences', *European Journal of Social Work*, 15(2): 151–167.

Home Office (2007) *Asset Recovery Action Plan. A Consultation Document.* Online. Available HTTP: <http://www.lccsa.org.uk/assets/documents/consultation/asset-recovery-consultation.pdf> (accessed 7 April 2014).

Hülsberg, F. and Engels, O. (2011) 'Wirtschaftskriminalität und Compliance', *Zeitschrift für Wirtschaftsstrafrecht und Haftung im Unternehmen*, 1: 14–18.

Jackson, T. and Artola, M.C. (1997) 'Ethical beliefs and management behaviour: A cross-cultural comparison', *Journal of Business Ethics*, 16(11): 116–1173.

Jones, C.A. (1999) *Private Enforcement of Antitrust Law in the EU, UK and USA*, Oxford: Oxford University Press.

Kaptein, M. (2010) 'The ethics of organizations', *Journal of Business Ethics*, 92(4): 601–618.

Kaptein, M. (2011) 'From inaction to external whistleblowing', *Journal of Business Ethics*, 98(3): 513–530.

Katz, G. and Lenglet, M. (2010) 'Whistleblowing in French corporations. Anatomy of a national taboo', *Philosophy of Management*, 9(1): 103–122.

King III, G. (1999) 'The implications of an organization's structure on whistleblowing', *Journal of Business Ethics*, 20(4): 315–326.

Kölbel, R. (2008) 'Zur wirtschaftsstrafrechtlichen Institutionalisierung des Whistleblowing', *Juristenzeitung*, 63(23): 1134–1141.

Kölbel, R. and Herold, N. (2010) 'Whistleblowing: Eine kriminologische Analyse aus Anlass der aktuellen kriminalpolitischen Debatte', *Monatsschrift für Kriminologie und Strafrechtsreform*, 93(6): 425–441.

Larmer, R.A. (1992) 'Whistleblowing and employee loyalty', *Journal of Business Ethics*, 11(2): 125–8.

Laufer, W. (1999) 'Corporate liability, risk shifting, and the paradox of compliance', *Vanderbilt Law Review*, 52: 1343–1420.

Linssen, R. and Pfeiffer, H. (2009) 'Strategien zur Korruptionsbekämpfung als Sicherheitsfaktor für Organisationen', in S.M. Litzcke and H. Müller-Enbergs (eds) *Sicherheit in Organisationen*, Frankfurt am Main: Verlag für Polizeiwissenschaften.

Martens, L.T. and Kelleher, A. (2005) 'A global perspective on whistleblowing', *International Business Ethics Review*, 7(2): 445–450.

Maschmann, F. (2013) 'Compliance und Mitarbeiterrechte', in L. Kuhlen, H. Kudlich and I. Ortiz der Urbina (eds) *Compliance und Strafrecht*, Heidelberg u.a.: C.F. Müller.

Mazerolle, P. and Cassematis, P. (2010) 'Whistle while you work', in D. Lewis (ed.) *A Global Approach to Public Interest Disclosure*, Cheltenham/Northampton, MA: Edward Elgar Publishing.

Mesmer-Magnus, J.R. and Viswesvaran, C. (2005) 'Whistleblowing in organizations', *Journal of Business Ethics*, 62(3): 277–297.

Miceli, M.P. and Near, J.P. (1988) 'Individual and situational correlates of whistle-blowing', *Personnel Psychology*, 41(2): 267–281.

Miceli, M.P. and Near, J.P. (1992) *Blowing the Whistle. The Organizational and Legal Implications for Companies and Employees*, New York/Toronto: Lexington Books.

Miceli, M.P. and Near, J.P. (1994) 'Whistleblowing: Reaping the benefits', *Academy of Management Executive*, 8(3): 65–72.

Miceli, M.P. and Near, J.P. (1995) 'Effective whistle-blowing', *Academy of Management Review*, 20(3): 679–708.

Miceli, M.P. and Near, J.P. (1996) 'Whistle-blowing: Myth and reality', *Journal of Management*, 22(3): 507–526.

Miceli, M.P. and Near, J.P. (2010) 'When do observers of organizational wrongdoing step up?', in D. Lewis (ed.) *A Global Approach to Public Interest Disclosure*, Cheltenham/Northampton, MA: Edward Elgar Publishing.

Miceli, M.P., Near, J.P. and Dworkin, T.M. (2008) *Whistle-blowing in Organizations*, New York: Routledge.

Miceli, M.P., Near, J.P. and Dworkin, T.M. (2009) 'A word to the wise', *Journal of Business Ethics*, 86(3): 379–396.

Miceli, M.P., Near, J., Rehg, M. and van Scotter, J. (2012) 'Predicting employee reactions to perceived organizational wrongdoing: Demoralization, justice, proactive personality, and whistle-blowing', *Human Relations*, 65: 923–954.

Miceli, M.P., Near, J.P. and Schwenk, C.R. (1991) 'Who blows the whistle and why', *Industrial and Labor Relations Review*, 45(1): 113–130.

Miethe, T.D. and Rothschild, J. (1994) 'Whistleblowing and the control of organizational misconduct', *Sociological Inquiry*, 64(3): 322–347.

Miethe, T.D. and Rothschild, J. (1999) 'Whistle-blower disclosure and management retaliation', *Work and Occupations*, 26(1): 107–128.

Parker, C. and Nielsen, V. (2009) 'Corporate compliance systems: Could they make any difference?', *Administration & Society*, 41(1): 3–37.

Pemberton, S., Tombs, S., Chan, M. and Seal, L. (2012) 'Whistleblowing, organisational harm and the self-regulating organisation', *Policy & Politics*, 40(2): 263–279.

Pittroff, E. (2011) *Whistle-Blowing-Systeme in deutschen Unternehmen: Eine Untersuchung zur Wahrnehmung und Implementierung*, Wiesbaden: Gabler Verlag.

Pope, K.R. and Lee, C. (2013) 'Could the Dodd–Frank Wall Street reform and Consumer Protection Act of 2010 be helpful in reforming corporate America?', *Journal of Business Ethics*, 112(4): 597–607.

PricewaterhouseCoopers (2010) *Compliance und Unternehmenskultur*, Frankfurt am Main: Kohlhammer und Wallishauser GmbH.

PricewaterhouseCoopers (2011) *Wirtschaftskriminalität*, Frankfurt am Main: Kohlhammer und Wallishauser.

Riley, A. (2003) *The Civil False Claims Act: Using Lincoln's Law to Protect the European Community Budget*, CEPS Policy Briefs, Brussels: Centre for European Policy Studies.

Rothschild, J. (2000) 'Whistleblowing', in C. Bryant (ed.) *Encyclopedia of Criminology and Deviant Behavior*, Volume I, Philadelphia: Taylor & Francis Publisher.

Sankowicz, D. and Henry, S. (March 2012) 'Update on whistleblowing in France', *International Bar Association on Legal Practice Division*. Online. Available HTTP: <http://www.paulhastings.com/assets/pdfs/whistleblowing_article.pdf> (accesssed 3 December 2014).

Schmidt, M. (2005) '"Whistle blowing" regulation and accounting standards enforcement in Germany and Europe', *International Review of Law and Economics*, 25(2): 143–168.
Shover, N. and Hochstetler, A. (2006) *Choosing White-Collar Crime*, Cambridge: Cambridge University Press.
Shover, N. and Grabosky, P. (eds) (2010) 'Special Issue: The global economy, economic crisis, and white-collar crime', *Criminology & Public Policy*, 9(3): 429–654.
Simpson, S., Gibbs, C., Rorie, M., Slocum, L., Cohen, M. and Vandenbergh, M. (2013) 'An empirical assessment of corporate environmental crime-control strategies', *Journal of Criminal Law and Criminology*, 103(1): 231–278.
Sims, R.L. and Keenan, J.P. (1998) 'Predictors of external whistleblowing', *Journal of Business Ethics*, 17(4): 411–421.
Skivenes, M. and Trygstad, S. (2010) 'When whistle-blowing works: The Norwegian case', *Human Relations*, 63(7): 1071–1097.
Snyder, L. (2007) '"This time we really mean it!": Cracking down on stock market fraud', in H. Pontell and G. Geis (eds) *International Handbook of White-Collar and Corporate Crime*, New York: Springer.
US Department of Justice (2012) *Fraud Statistics – Overview*, 1 October 1987 – 30 September 2012. Online. Available HTTP: <http://www.taf.org/DoJ-FCA-statistics-2012.pdf> (accessed 7 April 2014).
Vandekerckhove, W. (2006) *Whistleblowing and Organizational Social Responsibility*, Farnham: Ashgate.
Vandekerckhove, W. (2010a) 'European whistleblower protection: Tiers or tears?', in D. Lewis (ed.) *A Global Approach to Public Interest Disclosure*, Cheltenham/Northampton, MA: Edward Elgar Publishing.
Vandekerckhove, W. (2010b) 'Perception of whistleblowing worldwide', in M. Arszulowicz and W. Gasparski (eds) *Whistleblowing: In Defense of Proper Action*, New Brunswick/London: Transaction Publishers.
Vandekerckhove, W. and Tsahuridu, E. (2010) 'Risky rescues and the duty to blow the whistle', *Journal of Business Ethics*, 97(3): 365–380.
Weber, J. and Wasielewski, D. (2013) 'Corporate ethics and compliance programs: Report, analysis and critique', *Journal of Business Ethics*, 112(4): 609–626.
Williams, J.W. (2005) 'Reflections on the private versus public policing of economic crime', *The British Journal of Criminology*, 45(3): 316–339.
Wrase, S. and Fabritius, C. (2011) 'Prämien für Hinweisgeber bei Kartellverstößen?', *Corporate Compliance Zeitschrift*, 2: 69–73.
Zedner, L. (2006) 'Liquid security', *Criminology & Criminal Justice*, 6(3): 267–288.
Ziegleder, D. (2007) 'Corporate governance of security: The regulation and control of economic crime in the business world', *Monatsschrift für Kriminologie und Strafrechtsreform*, 90(2–3): 245–59.
Zipparo, L. (1999) 'Factors which deter public officials from reporting corruption', *Crime, Law & Social Change*, 30(3): 273–287.

27

The impact of personality and company culture on company anti-corruption programmes

Kai Bussmann

Introduction

Companies are paying increasing attention to the prevention of white-collar crime under the rubric of compliance. In fact, however, this concept refers to something that should be self-evident: companies have to comply particularly with criminal laws and prevent their staff and managers from violating them. However, this has not always been the practice in every company up to now. Economic crimes such as corruption or cartel law infringements were frequently simply a normal part of everyday business. By introducing compliance programmes, companies are now trying to introduce an effective way of preventing occupational and corporate crime. Nonetheless, the legal departments that have been assigned responsibility for this up to now prove to be completely inadequate, because they fail to implement any future-oriented prevention that needs to include such preventive measures as ethical guidelines, schoolings, whistle-blower systems, a compliance officer, an ombudsman, or internal sanctions.

At this point, however, it becomes necessary to ask whether companies are in any way seriously interested in introducing and applying such programmes or whether they are merely 'window dressing'. Any answer to this question requires an understanding of the parameters of programme development. This leads to the question of whether companies are in any way capable of building up effective prevention measures to counter occupational and corporate crime when these offences have, until now, always been a part of everyday business. Hence, the second section in this chapter will examine factors that could hinder or promote effective compliance such as the personality of managers, their socialization in organizations, the company culture, and the existing values both in business and within a particular region.

The development of compliance and anti-corruption programmes

The law and business as driving forces

The topic of crime prevention in companies has been attracting increasing attention under the collective term of compliance taken from Anglo-Saxon business law. This can be seen in both the growing number of compliance officers in companies and the countless conferences and handbooks on the topic. In purely quantitative terms, the change is impressive. In the German study by PwC and the author in the summer of 2011, a total of 52 per cent of large companies reported having a compliance programme that generally also contained measures to fight corruption (PwC and Bussmann 2011). Only two years later, the proportion of companies with a compliance programme had grown to 72 per cent (PwC and Bussmann 2013).

Both growing legal demands worldwide and stock exchanges have been pressurizing companies to act. In particular, strict US regulations such as the Sarbanes–Oxley Act, Foreign Corrupt Practices Act (FCPA), and the US Federal Sentencing Guidelines have further increased the pressure on all companies by calling for the introduction of various measures such as compliance programmes, business ethics, training courses, whistle-blowing systems and compliance reviewing. The stricter US legal requirements are playing a particularly leading role in promoting global advances in the prevention of economic crime (Bussmann and Matschke 2008). It is above all stock-exchange-listed companies that are orienting themselves towards these worldwide standards. More than any other group of companies, they are subject to the intensive scrutiny of rating agencies, auditors, the media, regulatory bodies, and supervisory bodies, and this encourages transparency and increases the demands to implement legal regulations.

Moreover, the indirect side effects such as damage to their reputation contribute decisively to disciplining a broader range of companies. The market exploits every weakness; one can soon become a candidate for a takeover; and directors' chairs swiftly change occupants. This alone has started to worry both managers and shareholders. At the end of the day, it is individuals who head companies, and they are exposed personally to the risk of criminal proceedings, pre-trial detention, liability under private law and public disgrace. For many, this may mean losing their management post.

This explains the popularity of the cynical phrase 'if you think compliance is expensive, try non-compliance' cited so frequently at conferences and in the compliance literature. Over the next few years, it will be above all the larger companies that will need to successfully get their compliance problems under permanent control. It is becoming just too simple for them to view themselves only as the beneficiaries of criminal business models. They are increasingly becoming victims themselves. A very close look even reveals signs for the formation of deterrent mechanisms, because non-compliance is leading increasingly to competitive disadvantages.

The beneficiaries and the effects of the control paradox

In addition, there are also beneficiaries within the economic system who make a living from the newly acknowledged crime risks. Business is in no way a monolithic block when it comes to pursuing its interests. Professional conference companies offer their services to managers in need of information. Company representatives report on their compliance practices. Major law firms and accountants fish for lucrative mandates by reporting on the highly dynamic changes in the law at conferences. They are cultivating a sense of right and wrong within what is to some extent a very murky legal sphere that, unlike the classical criminal norms on robbery, theft or fraud, lacks a clear consensus on what is right and wrong.

In Germany, the Federal Criminal Police Office (Bundeskriminalamt 2012) is also contributing to awareness of the problem in its annual legal reports on economic crime in general and corruption in particular. And it has also found partners that supply the general public with data on crime trends and prevention measures. Studies on economic crime by accounting firms such as PwC, KPMG and Ernst & Young are busy feeding the discussion with empirical data. As a result of these many observers, consultants, and campaigners, the compliance discourse spiral is spinning ever faster. Even politicians are unable to evade this development. The legislative machinery is being geared up in the field of penal law for business offences, and the legal system is being obliged to enforce it increasingly rigorously.

This development is also leading to the formation of a 'white-collar' or 'economic criminology'. Criminologists are entering the discourse on best practice with their critical analyses, and this is only just the beginning. Although this perspective was already processed criminologically at a very early stage (Braithwaite and Fisse 1983), it is not just criminology but also penal law for business offences that is increasingly seeing companies as major actors in crime prevention. The growing interest in the topic of compliance in companies has now also set off a broad expansion of research in criminology and in criminal law that is closely examining not only the numerous causes of economic crime but also the effects of prevention measures. For example, both the US-American FCPA and the British Bribery Act in force since 2011 require all companies within their jurisdiction to implement numerous compliance measures to effectively fight corruption.

Moreover, one should not overlook the paradoxes in this development. Companies themselves are now becoming the driving forces in this movement. An examination of the processes on the micro-level reveals that the more companies introduce control and prevention measures to fight, for example, corruption, the more they increase the monitoring of economic crime. A social fact always first becomes visible through perception and communication. One could expect that increased controls, like more prevention, would lead to less crime. However, an inspection of the individual phases reveals that this is not the case. A better control environment leads to more offences being detected, and hence an increase in the amount of crime visible without any immediate crime-sinking effect on the dark figure. From a criminological perspective, this is a *control paradox* (Bussmann 2007). Nowadays, more economic crime offences are uncovered than ever before simply because of the greater awareness and the improved control environment. This also explains why prevention measures such as business ethics or training courses also lead to an increase in detection, because they also heighten awareness of the problem. Companies more frequently detect various forms of economic crime in this way – an impression that has long been apparent merely through perusing media reports, especially those on corruption and cartel law infringements.

The future of compliance

This outlines the framework for the increasing international expansion of compliance programmes. This process has already developed its own momentum despite the setbacks to be expected in single companies and also the fact that it will certainly take many more years in the growth markets and developing countries. Nonetheless, no international company will be able to avoid such programmes in the near future. Globally, development is proceeding in a top-down way from the mostly large stock-exchange-listed major companies, to medium-sized businesses, and so on. Major companies are beginning to pass on the 'compliance pressure' to their business partners in order to avoid negative exposure by association with criminal partners. A comparison of the features of companies with versus without a compliance programme reveals that the former are, on average, markedly larger, more international, and more frequently stock-exchange-listed (Bussmann and Matschke 2008; PwC and Bussmann 2011). In other words, these global players are simultaneously drivers of this change.

Although economic crime is worldwide a widespread threat particularly in the emerging markets, it is notable that globalization is not an opponent but a proponent of compliance development. In developing countries as well, it is advantageous to be known as a company possessing integrity. The emerging middle class in these countries has a strong interest in freeing itself from old corrupt structures. Compliance is now also beginning to develop an economic value for companies. A concept that they originally considered to be alien to their systems is now mutating into a business, into part of their marketing strategy. Although, as corporate actors, companies do not possess a conscience, the market is beginning to take over this important immunization function to counter the temptations of the market economy. Hence the significant motors in the current trend towards an increasing spread of compliance management systems are as follows:

- Legal liability risks, particularly through the United States with FCPA and SEC
- A stock exchange listing, legal requirements as in the United States, but also the expectations of the financial market
- International expansion of companies through numerous foreign offices
- Business consultancies through consulting services and studies on economic crime
- Increasing detection of economic crimes such as corruption through internal company compliance measures
- Publicity, non-governmental organizations such as Transparency International, the mass media, and spectacular single cases
- Science and criminology.

Factors promoting effective compliance management systems

Despite the aforementioned developments, there are numerous claims (Hefendehl 2006; McBarnet 2006) that companies are not really implementing the compliance efforts demanded by societies, but, due to the dominance of economic rationality, are engaging only in window-dressing (Di Lorenzo 2007). In many cases, this may well have been true during the initial phase of compliance development, but from a long-term perspective, companies face structural pressures from both the market and law enforcement to implement effective measures. Hence, the long-term question is not whether companies introduce such compliance programmes and strive seriously to ensure they are effective. It is far more whether they can actually succeed in doing this. This question on the impact of compliance programmes and, specifically, anti-corruption programmes will be examined on the following five levels:

1 The personalities of managers and economic criminals
2 Socialization in the company
3 Values in business
4 Values in society
5 The role of company culture in compliance.

The personalities of managers and economic criminals

Unlike classical criminal offenders, economic criminals are difficult for criminological research to explain. Deficits in primary and secondary socialization are of little help, because it is highly apparent that this is a group that has enjoyed what would seem to be an ideal socialization from the primary and secondary socialization agencies of the family, school and friends. They are well integrated in society and there are no signs of any socialization deficits. Sutherland (1949) already pointed to these differences compared with offenders in other fields with his original definition of the white-collar criminal. An analysis of who these offenders are generally reveals a middle-aged male with an above-average education who has already been working in his company for several years and holds a position in senior or top management (Bussmann and Werle 2006). Moreover, these persons have successful careers and often lead respectable private lives. The majority of traditional so-called 'deficit crime theories', which explain crime particularly through deficits of all kinds such as social inequality, delinquent subcultures or deviant value systems, do not fit them at all.

However, one difference compared with classical offenders that should not be underestimated is the company framework: in many cases, economic criminals commit their offences within their company or proceeding from their company. This suggests that the specific company culture also needs to be considered when analysing the personalities of managers. Even today, it is not known how far a specific company culture may shape managers psychologically, and, in addition, there may well be selection effects that lead to certain personality traits being found more frequently in this group.

Hence, it is necessary to differentiate: when company representatives fix prices or actively engage in bribing, they are trying – from the micro-perspective – to establish or maintain favourable market structures for themselves or to ensure that certain orders or sales will go ahead. For them, the accompanying legal infringement is only a collateral damage (Sutherland 1949: 260). One cannot even accuse them of naked greed, because optimizing profit margins is a major guiding principle in business (Huisman and Vande Walle 2010: 150–157). In these cases, it is necessary to pay more attention to the company culture rather than to the personality traits of managers (see below). All managers will engage in economic crimes such as corruption if it is in the company's interest or is even demanded by the company, regardless of their personality traits.

Studies comparing managers with the rest of the population in terms of the Big Five personality model (Costa and McCrae 1992: 5–13) have shown that it is particularly *conscientiousness* – reflecting self-discipline, persistence and dependability – that influences the success of managers' careers (Specht et al. 2011). The author's own analyses based on data from the German Socio-Economic Panel have shown that top and middle management are, on average, more extraverted, conscientious and markedly more open to experience than the general population. This is not surprising, because *openness to experience* relates to intelligence and, above all, to education (McCrae and Costa 2011: 67). Likewise, they are less neurotic and only slightly less agreeable – reflecting friendliness, cooperativeness and a warm-hearted approach to others – than the general population (Specht et al. 2011).

Drawing on the state of research on the personality traits of economic criminals, Blickle et al. (2006) reported that incarcerated economic criminals also show a stronger tendency to be conscientious. They interpreted this as being due particularly to the fact that many of the incarcerated respondents had acted in the interest of their company – in the sense of blind obedience. This indicates that conscientiousness may well also be a risk factor when certain managers engage in economic crime for their company. Other studies, in contrast, show that the personality of economic criminals is characterized by lower rather than higher conscientiousness (Ragatz and Fremouw 2010: 389) and by lower agreeableness (Schön et al. 2011: 15). Economic criminals also reveal a lower acceptance of social norms and a greater willingness to take risks, a lower sense of responsibility, less trust in others, more anxiety and lower self-control (Collins and Schmidt 1993: 307–308; Ragatz et al. 2012: 991). Connelly and Ones (2008: 373) studied the relation between personality and corruption on an international level. In a study covering 54 countries, they found that respondents from countries with a higher level of corruption had lower average scores on openness to experience and higher scores on neuroticism.

Due to the selective personnel recruitment of managers, one could conceive that personality characteristics of managers in the USA differ from those in European nations. However, there is a paucity of research on this. Although cross-cultural psychology has confirmed relations between, for example, the collectivistic orientation of a nation and the personality factors agreeableness, openness to experience, and conscientiousness (Helfrich 2013: 139–145), there is a lack of psychological cross-country research (Simpson 2013: 325) confirming their effects on economic crime.

Moreover, given the present state of knowledge, it cannot be ruled out that at least some companies will reveal an accumulation of problematic personality traits. This has led to an increasing emphasis in research on constructs such as psychopathy and organizational cynicism. Findings on the relation between psychopathic traits and occupational success have come particularly from the English-speaking world. Various studies suggest that persons with high psychopathy scores, whose behaviour is characterized by a lack of conscience, cold-heartedness and the manipulation of others, advance more rapidly in their careers and are more likely to be found in higher positions. Litzcke et al. (2012: 19–20) have also concluded that persons with high psychopathy scores have a greater tolerance of corrupt activities.

The concept of organizational cynicism is used to describe employees' negative outlook on their organization in terms of three dimensions: belief that the organization lacks integrity, negative emotional reactions towards the organization, and the tendency to engage in disparaging behaviour (Litzcke et al. 2012: 20–21). In general, this construct has been studied as an indicator for a job change or for an attitude that rejects organizational changes (Albrecht 2002: 320–343). However, there are indications that organizational cynicism is also a risk factor for corruption and deviant behaviour (Hartl and Jonas 2009: 153). Litzcke et al. (2012: 119–122) concluded that persons who have a cynical attitude towards their organization tend to appraise corruption as being normal. However, it may well be that this is more a company culture phenomenon than an individual psychological one. A company culture that is not oriented towards integrity may well encourage organizational cynicism in managers with the corresponding negative behavioural reactions.

Whatever ways a company culture exerts a decisive impact on the construct of organizational cynicism, the general problem facing research is that economic crimes such as corruption are frequently part of a company's business model, so that offences are carried out regardless of its managers' personality traits. It is only when managers act primarily to their own personal advantage without considering the benefits for their company that they come closer to the classical individual offender. Only then would it seem theoretically more meaningful to ask about their personality traits. However, many studies give the impression that neither this aspect nor company culture have been controlled sufficiently.

In summary, the state of research shows that attempts to detect potential offenders with a 'criminogenic character' should not blind research to systemic causes such as company culture, normal practice in that branch of industry, or the normality of economic crimes. One should not make the classic mistake of concluding that somebody is bad because they have done something wrong. A lapse in behaviour does not have to be due to a 'fault' in the offender; the 'fault' may also lie in the company and the company's environment. When trying to understand the motives and incentives of offenders, it is more adequate to look at economic crime not only from the perspective of penal law but also from the perspective of business practice. Most companies and persons see themselves as acting in a morally impeccable way even though they are quite aware that they are breaking the law. This is because strict compliance with criminal law does not belong to the norms that count in their occupational world. In this context, it should not be overlooked that training in economics promotes a basically critical attitude towards the law, because it is seen as more of a hindrance of a free market economy than a necessary regulatory economic framework. 'Economic' crime is also not a topic to be found in the literature used to teach economics (Burkatzki 2011).

Socialization in the company

This leads to the question regarding how far the socialization efforts of compliance departments can in any way be effective in a company. Can they achieve a comparably formative socialization to that produced in the family, school, peers, and the community during childhood and adolescence? The reason for this question is that criminology assigns a major importance to the socialization of offenders. Primary socialization takes place in the family; secondary socialization, among friends, at school and at work. In this chapter, it is argued that the socialization that takes place in a company acquires a far from negligible significance in the prevention of economic crime. This is reinforced by the findings on the age of economic criminals and how long they have belonged to their company – in Germany, an average of ten years. Accordingly, they are not at the start of their careers; it is far more the case that they have 'grown up' in the company, and the company has socialized them for their careers (Bussmann and Werle 2006).

Essentially, the question is whether purposefully changing company culture can achieve a long-lasting occupational socialization or, to use a different terminology, whether it can succeed in internalizing the relatively recent prohibitions to be found particularly in business penal law that regulate against corruption in the private sector, cartel law infringements, money laundering, insider trading, and so forth. It is clear that the socialization within the family in no way succeeds in addressing these prohibitions. A socialization that makes people feel guilty specifically when engaging in corrupt activities, price fixing or insider trading does not take place in either the family or at school. A comparable primary and secondary socialization to that condemning classical criminality does not take place for economic crime. At best, there may be an effective familial socialization against fraud. Bribing officials provides a good example of the differentiated and fragmentary ways in which values are imparted and their corresponding socialization. At least in Central European cultures, the unacceptability of bribing officials has received a relatively robust socialization. In contrast, the unacceptability of the comparable crime of corruption is still far from receiving such a far-reaching socialization in the business world – as confirmed by a comparative study of the level of corruption in administrative bodies and companies (PwC and Bussmann 2010a).

It has to be remembered that in the domain of classical crime, criminal law finds it relatively easy (nowadays) to assume that a stable sense of wrongdoing has generally been acquired at an early age. However, the primary and secondary socialization in the family and school or among peers offers hardly any guidance when it comes to succeeding in a market economy and competing with rival companies. Many offenders must be aware that their activities may well be punishable. However, for many offences, they see no need to fall back to the same extent on the protective justification mechanisms and neutralization techniques to excuse themselves morally. From their perspective, the offences are simply petty.

One reason for this is that economic crimes are in no ways self-evident offences. At least from a present-day perspective, the injustice of many classical offences seems completely unquestionable and the underlying values such as the right of property, protection of life and limb, sexual self-determination, and freedom are defended energetically. However, in past centuries, these were not anchored as self-evidently as they are taken to be today. This already creates hope for the very recent canon of economic crimes: there is no reason why a socialization, that is, an internalization of these norms, should be fundamentally impossible.

However, achieving a normative socialization represents a major challenge for many economic crimes such as corruption, insider trading or cartel law infringements, because the damage they cause is mostly not self-evident. The negative effects of these economic crimes do not stand out in the same way as the effects of classical crimes such as assault, sexual abuse, fraud, theft and embezzlement. Hence, the primary victim in cases of corruption is society or also the market economy when corruption undermines it. Therefore it is quite correct to talk about indirect damages or even 'victim-less' offences today. The victims are almost impossible to individualize, and in contrast to, for example, robbery or fraud, the damages are in no way so visible.

Our analysis of the initial situation shows that there are hardly any socialization agencies that can help to promote business penal law: it has to start from a precarious position. In the business world, it is not easy for either a moral conscience to develop through the support of primary and secondary socialization, or for a feeling of empathy for the damages suffered by victims to emerge. The damages caused by economic crime are scarcely understandable for most actors in the business world. This will change only if society succeeds in developing or heightening their sensitivity for this. This shows the need for additional socialization agencies. The necessary socialization work will have to be carried out at the location in which these forms of behaviour are actually acquired as rational alternatives: in the company, in the business world.

Values in business

However, it is necessary to ask whether there is even any possibility of achieving a 'law-abiding' socialization in the independent functional system of the business world, even when individual companies honestly seek it. One could hypothesize that the modern economic society itself has created those values that are partly responsible for an increase in property crime. Therefore, criminological research explains the crimes of business elites precisely in terms of their failure to accept the given norms and values (Coleman 1998; Frehsee 1991; Karstedt 1999; Simon and Hagan 1999).

A representative study of property crime by private individuals revealed the following major explanatory factors: lack of moral commitment to the law, criminal networks, victimizations and neutralizations (Bussmann et al. 2004). Hence, criminal motivation does not increase in line with economic 'hardship', but may well develop alongside growing prosperity when the framing conditions are favourable – as expressed so aptly in the phrase 'crime from greed rather than from need'. This fits in well with Daniel Bell's (1953) classic article with its significant title 'Crime as an American way of life', in which he pointed to the emergence of a culture of rigid competition in which values such as solidarity and considerateness have become alien and are replaced by social Darwinism. More recent criminological theories point to the particular lure and opportunity structures of the market economy (Shover and Hochstetler 2006).

This suggests the hypothesis that in the expressly competitively oriented US-American economy, the barriers to imparting values that promote integrity will be higher than in Europe in which welfare-state institutions are much more firmly entrenched. In principle, however, economic crime occurs in all national economies. Nonetheless, recent social anthropological research does indicate that egoistic behaviour depends on the society in which it is embedded (Schröder 2011). Persons are much more willing to share when they are used to having to cooperate in their society. This would suggest that in a social market economy, it is easier to impart market economy rules that may be disadvantageous for the actors in the short term. The author's study confirmed a similar effect: fairness in the market economy – towards customers, suppliers and competitors – has a high preventive impact on crime (Bussmann et al. 2004). 'Consumers do not riot today, but neither are they inclined to dismiss unfair practices in the marketplace as a mere inconvenience … they react with strong intentions to … hit back whenever the opportunity arises' (Karstedt and Farrall 2006: 1029). This indicates that the way in which business is practised is always a decisive factor for a culture of integrity. However, social responsibility and fairness are experienced not only in business relations but also in the relation between the state and its citizens. In societies with a stronger welfare state orientation, these values should be more strongly anchored in society in general and therefore in companies as well. One could therefore speculate that a sound socialization of the penal law of business offences could succeed more easily in states that feel obligated to the welfare ideal.

In principle, however, it is no simple task for companies to convey to their employees that they should forgo advantages in order to promote the long-term benefits of an unimpeded competitive market economy in every type of economic society – including welfare-state ones. This is also because – as mentioned above – damages are hard to perceive and socialization within the family provides little preparation for such an approach. All these factors indicate that economic crime is a particularly difficult field in which to assert the virtue of integrity. This renders the starting conditions for this comparatively young penal law particularly *precarious*. From a criminological perspective, it is still in an anomic phase (Huisman and Vande Walle 2010: 146–147; Karstedt and Farrall 2006), because the validity of its norms currently finds little acceptance, and the actors on the market have little trust in them.

Nonetheless, the 'compliance movement' has introduced a structural change to the functional system of business that is leading to the development of more trust. The short-sighted outlook that continues to dominate in many companies can change. The pursuit of short-term advantages can be abandoned when the long-term disadvantages are taken into account without the company having to abandon its rational choice perspective. The wide-ranging research on game theory nowadays reveals scarcely any support for a simple rational choice concept and supports our thesis. The human being as *homo oeconomicus* or, as Armatya K. Sen says (1977), as a 'rational fool' who always does everything for personal gain is now taken to be a myth in both criminology and game theory. The long dominant assumption of self-interest has been relativized to show that the preferences of rationally acting egoists are also open to choice. They may continue to act rationally, but no longer necessarily in their own (short-term) self-interest (Ockenfels and Raub 2011: 128). Even for egoists, it may be clever to compete fairly, to orient themselves toward the common good, and to waive short-term advantages (Esser 2011: 47). People can respond to situations with varying rationalities.

Hence, only insight is required in order to see the advantages of deciding in favour of public goods such as a functioning market economy or social integration. Even in commerce, rationally acting egoists can still have a strong interest in social integration and can decide in favour of long-term advantages (Kirchgässner 1999: 124–125). Why should they not favour market regulations as well when the benefits are made clear to them? Hence, it is not impossible for economists to take ethical aspects into account when formulating rational choice decision-making models (Pies 2008; Suchanek 2001). However, studies on corporate crime show impressively how much the lack of or the loosening of moral ties encourages simple cost–benefit decisions in favour of economic crime (Paternoster and Simpson 1996: 586). Nonetheless, as business ethicists point out, companies are not always the beneficiaries of economic crime. They may well even become the natural allies of citizens in the fight against extortionate corruption when, for example, the company making the bribe is itself the primary victim (e.g. when having to pay 'speed money'; Pies 2005: 63–64). Hence, there is a host of ways in which companies can be made to see the benefits of penal law for business offences.

Moreover, market participants have to be able to assume that others will also decide generally in favour of the public good, in this case, for the rules of a competitive market economy. In other words, there has to be trust. However, this is what is so broadly lacking. This deficit is particularly conspicuous in cases of corruption and price fixing. The growing practice of integrity agreements between companies when, for example, working together on major building projects highlights precisely this need (Solmssen 2011: 12).

Norm compliance based on insight becomes difficult when behaving morally leads to excessively high costs and severe economic disadvantages. However, the compliance policy in stock-exchange-listed companies may well lead to changes over the mid-term. Although criminal sanctions generally have a relatively low deterrent effect, over the long term, they help to increase awareness of the norms and of injustice. They are an aid in conveying values and, together with publicity in the mass media, they create incentives to establish compliance programmes as pointed out above. Within this process, criminal law provides only the stimuli to implement this internal company socialization – and naturally, as in classic crime, it permanently confirms the validity of the norms. Without effective criminal law and exacting legislation, this entire process would never get started nor could it continue.

Nowadays, however, such negative stimuli are also being joined by positive ones. For example, 31 per cent of the companies in the PwC 2009 study reported planning to introduce a target agreement to attain their compliance goals in sensitive domains (trainings for all staff, revision of contracts, etc.) that could also be integrated into employee bonus schemes (PwC and Bussmann 2010b: 24–25). Moreover, the market can also take over the rewards to be gained from social recognition. Some companies have even started to view integrity as a competitive advantage; they advertise themselves through their integrity and strive to gain certifications that confirm it. As interest in compliance increases, companies are learning to implement integrity as a production factor. Compliance is beginning to pay off.

Values in society

The values of a company are not just embedded in either an expressly competitive or a more welfare-state-oriented society, but also in the social culture as a whole. Comprehensive national cultural research by, among others, Hofstede (2001) has shown that national cultures shape not only the people in a nation but also its companies. Indeed, the influence of the specific national culture can explain approximately one-quarter of the variance in organizational culture (Gerhart 2009: 253).

Moreover, studies also point to the significance of the social structure and the value orientations in a society for the example of corruption (cf. Barr and Serra 2010; Husted 1999; Karstedt 2003; Uslaner 2005). These indicate that corruption takes advantage of institutional and sociostructural as well as cultural factors. Corruption is more widespread in nations with strongly hierarchic and elitist social structures and cultures than in countries organized along more egalitarian lines. In hierarchic and elitist societies, corruption offers the only route to upward social mobility because elites seal themselves off from the rest of society. And because the elites themselves are in a position to fend off any control from below within their exclusive networks, their corruption goes unchecked and flourishes. ‘Power corrupts and absolute power corrupts absolutely’ (Karstedt 2003: 408).

Alongside social structure, cultural value orientations make their own independent contribution. Somewhat surprisingly perhaps, individualistic value orientations in no way encourage corruption. Even in European nations that have more extensive welfare-state components than, for example, the USA, citizens are far more individualistically oriented than those in most of the developing nations. Indeed, it is not a greater degree of individualistic orientations that leads to corruption, but collectivistic values that promote forms of structural corruption in social networks. Members of societies sharing these values first consider the benefits for their relatives, friends, or even clans. Under such conditions, it is individualistic values that oppose particularly dangerous networks of corruption. Corruption justifies itself in such networks through the idea of caring for one’s peers.

Moreover, cross-national comparisons show that hierarchic and elitist values promote corruption to a major extent. Societies with predominantly authoritarian values reveal major uncertainties when interacting with those who are higher in the hierarchy in politics, business and administration. Administrative decisions threaten to be arbitrary. In addition, collectivistic and authoritarian values impede the development of a generalized trust in state institutions, because every trust in others that goes beyond the borders of one's own in-group is fragile (Karstedt 2003: 394–397). In such societies, corruption serves to compensate for uncertainty, particularly when there is a strong lack of constitutional procedures as well.

Hence, it is also necessary to differentiate between European nations, and one cannot simply distinguish between the competitive US economy and nations with more of a welfare state.

The role of company culture in compliance

This leads finally to the question of the significance of the specific company culture. Can integrity simply be commanded or does it require a company culture that promotes it? This question is hard to answer, because there are hardly any studies on the effectiveness of compliance programmes (for an overview, see Pape 2009). The few studies in English-speaking countries have concentrated mainly on questions of corporate compliance and specifically on norms to protect employees and consumers (McKendall et al. 2002). But even here, results have been inconsistent. Although Parker and Nielsen's (2009) study on compliance regarding crimes against competition and consumer offences found a positive effect, this was based on only one survey of companies ($N = 999$). Of particular interest, in contrast is Trevino et al.'s (1999) study that asked more than 10,000 employees from six companies about offences such as kick-back transactions, doctoring balance sheets, theft and environmental damage. Results showed that the formal implementation of a compliance programme had no effect in itself; it had to be embedded within a company culture that promoted it.

It is easy to imagine that the effectiveness of any compliance measure depends on how willing top management is to implement it. However, the latest research indicates that this may well be not only a question of the willingness to implement a programme but also of the company culture. Steßl (2012: 161–175) asked 357 employees in an internationally operating German company about illegal activities in their work. Taking an institutional economic approach, she concluded that the quality of relations between the employees and their management, to direct superiors, and to business partners exerts a decisive influence on the effectiveness of compliance management. In addition, effectiveness is also influenced by the perceived company culture, commitment and informal social controls backed up by internal normative company directives.

Hence, the company culture can share responsibility not only for the occurrence of criminal acts but also for the success or failure of compliance measures. It can be defined as a set of shared basic premises that a group has learned to use in order to handle the problems it has with fitting into its external environment and with integrating itself in its internal one (Schein 2004). This set is considered to be tried and tested – and thereby also to be binding – and it is passed on to new company members as a valid system of internal values (Eigenstetter et al. 2007).

Employees continuously have to ask themselves what they need to do whenever they have to apply the normative obligations of their company in their business activities. They perceive their company's behavioural norms and factor these into their decisions. This leads to the emergence of institutionalized norms that are known to all members of a company. As a result, every company possesses its own characteristic ethical climate, and this can be assessed systematically as an all-pervading feature. Studies confirm the postulated relations between the perceived moral norms in companies and the attitudes and behaviours of their employees (Eigenstetter et al. 2007). Research on justice in organizational sociology and social psychology (Liebig 2002; Tyler 1990) also confirms that perceived fairness and justice have a clear effect on variables such as work performance, job satisfaction and commitment (Lind 1994; Viswesvaran and Ones 2002). A relationship can also be found between a lack of justification for wage cuts and an increase in the theft rate (Greenberg 1990; Marcus 2000: 107–108). In contrast, strong commitment is accompanied by an attitude rejecting illegal activities. In addition, it exerts a positive influence on the attitude of employees towards economic crime and particularly towards corruption.

However, a strong level of commitment can also lead to blind obedience and esprit de corps. It can encourage the concealment and tacit approval of unethical acts because these are still considered to be correct within the company framework (Felfe 2008: 12–13; Ones et al. 1993). In such cases, compliance programmes will be ineffective as long as they run counter to a company's prevailing norms. Hence, a strong corporate identity is no guarantee for corporate integrity (for a discussion of this term, see Paine 1994: 106–107). Therefore, it is probable that compliance programmes will not develop their preventive impact in each and every company culture (Bussmann 2007: 274; Bussmann and Salvenmoser 2008). They require a supportive company culture and an ethical company climate.

In a research project, the authors have carried out a web-based survey of 4207 managers working in 12 major German companies in various industries, like Deutsche Bahn AG, Fraport AG, Daimler AG, Metro AG. The goal of the survey was to ascertain which conditions a company culture has to meet if anti-corruption programmes are to function optimally. In addition, it is assessing the personality traits of managers and their commitment to their company. The dependent variables are corrupt behaviour, acceptance of the anti-corruption programme, and the informal social control over compliance violations.

In their jobs, these persons face a particularly strong risk of being confronted with corrupt business practices. Alongside various scales assessing attitudes and perceptions, the core of the survey instrument is a set of scenarios addressing corruption-specific dilemmas. Respondents should report how frequently they have found themselves in a comparable situation, how their company deals with it, and how they judge these situations personally.

There are three elements in a company culture:

- The company culture of success ('career culture')
- The tone from the top
- Ethical leadership from superiors.

The company culture of success is being assessed by asking respondents to characterize successful colleagues in their company on a specially constructed scale. We are not interested in an 'official value ideal', as published occasionally in ethical guidelines and other internal brochures of companies, but a value reality within which company employees can also pursue their careers successfully. However, the success of a compliance programme depends decisively on whether the company's culture of success serves its integrity. Theoretically, this links up with research questions posed by a range of authors studying company culture, ethical organizational climate and illegal activities within organizations (Daumenlang et al. 2004: 103–127; Eigenstetter et al. 2007; Steßl 2012: 161–169). By assessing which behaviours help employees to succeed and advance their careers in a company, this scale delivers an indirect description of the company culture. The approach is based on the assumption that business activities that lead to success in a company are supported by the company and its culture. This culture scale is divided into four subscales, each reflecting particular aspects of a company's culture of success:

- Individualism
- Communication

- Rule compliance
- Transparency.

Our 'culture of success' scale is made up, in turn, of four elements that can either impede or promote integrity. The dimension 'individualism' describes how far acting independently and asserting one's own authority are considered to be normal for the staff in a company and are therefore understood as part of the company culture. The second element is the need for an 'open communication culture' that promotes a frank discussion of problems and hence also of rule infringements. The third significant element is how binding the staff perceives the existing company guidelines to be and whether they also address infringements of the rules by colleagues ('conformity with the rules'). Finally, there needs to be an honest and transparent approach to colleagues and business partners ('transparency'). Transparent management decisions promote a company culture in which dishonest behaviour is harder to conceal.

Alongside the interest in implementing programmes on the side of top management, how far employees accept them depends decisively on how they perceive the behaviour of their top management and immediate superiors. This involves aspects such as how credibly and consistently the company implements internal company guidelines, compliance measures, and integrity measures.

The company culture of immediate superiors and top management covers two aspects:

- Ethical leadership
- Tone from the top.

The author's study understands the so-called 'tone from the top' as how top management functions as a role model for dealing with bribery and corruption. Respondents should report how they think their top management deals with corruption and how obligatory they perceive the internal company regulations to be in light of the time pressure and the pressure to achieve they face in their daily work. The construct is derived from Steßl's (2012) scale assessing illegal actions. Brown et al.'s (2005: 125) Ethical Leadership Scale (ELS) is being used to describe the behaviour of immediate superiors by adapting it to refer directly to corruption and corruption prevention. The assumption is that the more positive the perception of immediate superiors and top management, the more they will be able to exert a positive influence on employees (Brown et al. 2005: 119–120) and the stronger the acceptance of the programme in the company as a whole (Weaver et al. 1999: 50–53).

As previous research has already shown (see the section 'The personalities of managers and economic criminals'), it would be wrong to ignore the influence of person-specific factors on the disposition to act corruptly. The individual attitude towards corruption is what is important here, because this determines the concrete intention that will lead to a corrupt act (Rabl 2011: 371–372). To explain the direction of effects along with the effect sizes for the influence of person-specific factors, this research project is assessing the respondents' personality (in terms of the Big Five personality model, Rammstedt and John 2007: 211), their risk tolerance (adaptation of the F-DUPN, Müller 2001: 247–250) and their affective commitment to the company (Felfe et al. 2004).

The personality of respondents covers three aspects:

- The Big Five
- Risk tolerance
- Commitment to the company.

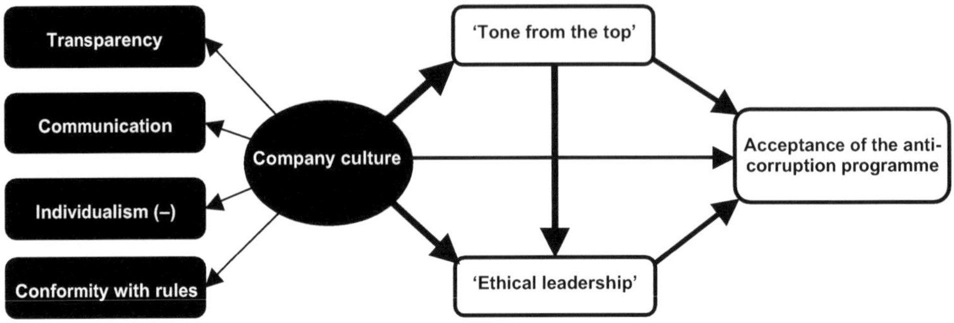

Figure 27.1 Model of the structure of the relation between company culture and the internal leadership style on all company levels

The affective commitment to a company is characterized by a strong acceptance and identification with its values and goals, a willingness to make a special effort for it, and the desire to remain a member of it. This form of commitment depends on how far features of the company satisfy individual needs (Collier and Esteban 2007: 23). As other studies have already shown, emotional attachment to a company relates closely to perceived leadership behaviour and to the framing conditions of company culture (Westphal and Gmür 2009: 220). Moreover, it can be assumed that employees who are attached to their company will exploit the freedoms available to them less for personal gain but more strongly for the benefit of their company (van Dick 2004: 8). Finally, it is anticipated that the commitment to the company will contribute to the avoidance of behaviour that may cause it harm.

The findings of the author's study show that the culture of success plays a central role, whereas the impact of personality traits was not provable. The more that this culture of success is perceived to be oriented towards integrity, the more readily measures and guidelines such as anti-corruption programmes are accepted by a company's employees. Hence, what is decisive is a culture of transparency, conformity with the rules, open communication, and a low level of individualism. These have a direct effect. The significance of a culture of success can also be seen in the fact that it is perceived by the staff as influencing not only the top management ('tone from the top') but also the immediate superior ('ethical leadership'). The culture of success functions like a pair of glasses through which staff view their superiors and company management: it either supports or relativizes the 'official integrity talk'.

Although the 'tone from the top' impacts directly on the acceptance of the anti-corruption programme, the analysis also shows that this message is conveyed in the daily business of the company by the ethical leadership of the immediate superior. Hence, integrity cannot be simply ordained in a 'top-down' way; it is something that concerns everybody and that the majority of superiors also need to possess.

There is much to suggest that the way top management functions as a role model and the culture it practises can well be used to influence the attitudes of employees and bring them into line with a company's goals. This study also shows already that the acceptance of informal social control, which has a strong preventive impact, also depends on aspects of company culture.

Conclusion

Studies confirm the existence of an integrity-promoting company culture that can be assessed on various dimensions. The acceptance of an anti-corruption programme is influenced strongly by various aspects of a company culture and the internal company leadership style. A company culture that is perceived positively influences how far staff accept the application and implementation of anti-corruption programmes in their daily business work. A positive company culture is characterized by a high level of transparency, conformity with rules, open communication, and a low level of individualism in the staff. A company culture with these characteristics can be considered to have an integrity-promoting impact. However, surveys suggest that in the expressly competitively oriented US-American economy, the barriers to imparting values that promote integrity will be higher than in Europe in which welfare-state institutions are much more firmly entrenched.

The utopian outlook is for future managers to not even think about maximizing or achieving profits through economic crimes such as corruption or price fixing simply because they are personally embedded within a company culture that considers corruption to be wrong. In such an environment, mechanisms of intrinsic control and social control will have a preventive effect. Companies are able to learn, and business values do not stand in the way of effective crime prevention. With the growing implementation of compliance management systems, there is an increasing chance of sustained change even in the minds of rationally acting egoists.

Nonetheless, anyone familiar with classical crime is aware of the fact that even with the positive trend to be seen here, expectations should not be too exaggerated. Companies also consist essentially of human beings. There can be no doubt that the ongoing process of implementing compliance programmes will eventually lead to a normative socialization of managers that will certainly seem utopian by today's standards. This process will take generations to unfold and will spread only gradually throughout the world. However, a start has been made; the expansion of compliance programmes in companies is irreversible, and company culture plays a decisive role in launching the process of an autonomous and effective crime prevention.

References

Albrecht, S.L. (2002) 'Perception of integrity, competence and trust in senior management as determinants of cynicism towards change', *Public Administration & Management: An Interactive Journal*, 7/4: 320–343.

Barr, A. and Serra, D. (2010) 'Corruption and culture: An experimental analysis', *Journal of Public Economics*, 94: 862–869.

Bell, D. (1953) 'Crime as an American way of life', *The Antioch Review*, 13/2: 131–154.

Blickle, G., Schlegel, A., Fassbender, P. and Klein, U. (2006) 'Some personality correlates of business white-collar crime', *Applied Psychology*, 55/2: 220–233.

Braithwaite, J. and Fisse, B. (1983) *The Impact of Publicity on Corporate Offenders*, Albany: State University of New York Press.

Bribery Act (2011) Online. Available HTTP: <http://www.legislation.gov.uk/ukpga/2010/23/contents> (accessed 1 August 2013).

Brown, M.E., Trevino, L.K. and Harrison, D.A. (2005) 'Ethical leadership: A social learning perspective for construct development and testing', *Organizational Behavior and Human Decision Processes*, 97/2: 117–134.

Bundeskriminalamt (2012) *Korruption, Bundeslagebild 2011*, Wiesbaden. Online. Available HTTP: <http://www.bka.de/nn_193376/DE/Publikationen/JahresberichteUndLagebilder/Korruption/korruption__node.html?__nnn=true> (accessed 1 July 2014).

Burkatzki, E. (2011) 'Legalität und Legitimität im Marktkontext Institutionentheoretische Überlegungen zu den Entstehungsbedingungen wirtschaftskriminellen Handelns', *Zeitschrift für Internationale Strafrechtsdogmatik*, 6/3: 160–171.

Bussmann, K. (2007) 'The control paradox and the impact of business ethics: A comparison of US and German companies', *Monatsschrift für Kriminologie und Strafrechtsreform*, 90/2–3: 260–276.

Bussmann, K. and Matschke, S. (2008) 'The impact of the US legislation on company measures of control and prevention', *Crime, Law and Social Change*, 49/5: 349–364.

Bussmann, K. and Salvenmoser, S. (2008) 'Der Wert von Compliance und Unternehmenskultur', *Corporate Compliance Zeitschrift*, 5: 192–196.

Bussmann, K. and Werle, M.M. (2006) 'Addressing crime in companies: First findings from a global survey of economic crime', *British Journal of Criminology*, 46/6: 1128–1144.
Bussmann, K., England, P. and Hienzsch, A. (2004) 'Risikofaktor Wirtschaft? Forschungsergebnisse zur Bereicherungs-und Wirtschaftskriminalität', *Monatsschrift für Kriminologie und Strafrechtsreform*, 87/3–4: 244–260.
Coleman, J.W. (1998) *The Criminal Elite: Understanding White-Collar Crime*, New York: St. Martin's Press.
Collier, J. and Esteban, R. (2007) 'Corporate social responsibility and employee commitment', *Business Ethics: A European Review*, 16/1: 19–33.
Collins, J.M. and Schmidt, F.L. (1993) 'Personality, integrity, and white collar crime: A construct validity study', *Personnel Psychology*, 46/2: 295–311.
Connelly, B.S. and Ones, D.S. (2008) 'The personality of corruption: A national-level analysis', *Cross-Cultural Research*, 42/4: 353–385.
Costa, P.T. and McCrae, R.R. (1992) 'Normal personality assessment in clinical practice: The NEO Personality Inventory', *Psychological Assessment*, 4/1: 5–13.
Daumenlang, K., Müskens, W. and Harder, U. (2004) *FEO: Fragebogen zur Erfassung des Organisationsklimas*, Göttingen: Hogrefe.
Di Lorenzo, V. (2007) 'Business ethics: Law as a determinant of business conduct', *Journal of Business Ethics*, 71/3: 275–299.
Eigenstetter, M., Dobiasch, S. and Trimpop, R. (2007) 'Commitment and counterproductive work behavior as correlates of ethical climate in organizations', *Monatsschrift für Kriminologie und Strafrechtsreform*, 90/2–3: 224–244.
Esser, H. (2011) 'Das Modell der Frame-Selektion: Eine Allgemeine Handlungstheorie für die Sozialwissenschaften?', *Kölner Zeitschrift für Soziologie und Sozialpsychologie. Sonderheft*, 50: 45–62.
FCPA (1977) Online. Available HTTP: <http://www.justice.gov/criminal/fraud/fcpa/docs/fcpa-english.pdf> (accessed 1 August 2013).
Felfe, J. (2008) *Mitarbeiterbindung: Wirtschaftspsychologie*, Göttingen: Hogrefe.
Felfe, J., Six, B., Schmook, R. and Knorz, C. (2004) 'Fragebogen zur Erfassung von Affektivem, Kalkulatorischem und Normativem Commitment gegenüber der Organisation, dem Beruf/der Tätigkeit und der Beschäftigungsform (COBB)', in A. Glöckner-Rist (ed.) *Informationssystem: Elektronisches Handbuch sozialwissenschaftlicher Erhebungsinstrumente*, ZIS Version, 8, Mannheim: ZUMA.
Frehsee, D. (1991) 'Zur Abweichung der Angepassten', *Kriminologisches Journal*, 23/1: 25–45.
Gerhart, B. (2009) 'How much does national culture constrain organizational culture?', *Management and Organization Review*, 5(2): 241–259.
Greenberg, J. (1990) 'Employee theft as a reaction to underpayment inequity: The hidden cost of pay cuts', *Journal of Applied Psychology*, 75/5: 561–568.
Hartl, A. and Jonas, E. (2009) 'Organisationaler Wandel und Extra-Rollenverhalten', in C. Korunka, E. Kirchler and H. Ulfterst (eds) *Entscheidungen und Veränderungen in Arbeit, Organisation und Wirtschaft. 6. Tagung der Fachgruppe Arbeits- und Organisationspsychologie der Deutschen Gesellschaft für Psychologie*, Wien: Facultas.wuv.
Hefendehl, R. (2006) 'Corporate governance und business ethics: Scheinbetrug oder Alternativen bei der Bekämpfung der Wirtschaftskriminalität', *Juristenzeitung*, 61/3: 119–125.
Helfrich, H. (2013) *Kulturvergleichende Psychologie*, Wiesbaden: Springer.
Hofstede, G. (2001) *Culture's Consequences: Comparing Values, Behaviors, Institutions, and Organisations across Nations*, 2nd edn, Thousand Oaks: Sage Publications.
Huisman, W. and Vande Walle, G. (2010) 'The criminology of corruption', in G. De Graaf, P. von Maravic and P. Wagenaar (eds) *The Good Cause: Theoretical Perspectives on Corruption*, Opladen: Budrich Publishing, pp. 132–169.
Husted, B.W. (1999) 'Wealth, culture, and corruption', *Journal of International Business Studies*, 30/2: 339–360.
Karstedt, S. (1999) 'Globalisierung und transnationale Kriminalität: Zum Erfolg "archaischer" Strukturen in der illegalen globalen Ökonomie', in G. Schmidt and R. Trinczek (eds) *Soziale Welt, Globalisierung: Ökonomische und Soziale Herausforderungen am Ende des Zwanzigsten Jahrhunderts. Sonderband, 1*, Baden-Baden: Nomos, pp. 259–272.
Karstedt, S. (2003) 'Macht, Ungleichheit und Korruption: Strukturelle und kulturelle Determinanten im internationalen Vergleich' G, *Soziologie der Kriminalität, Sonderheft der KZfSS*, 43: 384–412.
Karstedt, S. and Farrall, S. (2006) 'The moral economy of everyday crime markets, consumers and citizens', *British Journal of Criminology*, 46/6: 1011–1036.

Kirchgässner, G. (1999) 'Soziale Integration Rationaler Egoisten? Zur Erklärung Sozialer Integration auf der Basis des Ökonomischen Handlungsmodells', *Kölner Zeitschrift für Soziologie und Sozialpsychologie. Sonderheft*, 39: 115–131.

Liebig, S. (2002) 'Gerechtigkeit in Organisationen: Theoretische Überlegungen und Empirische Ergebnisse zu einer Theorie Korporativer Gerechtigkeit', *Organisationssoziologie: Kölner Zeitschrift für Soziologie und Sozialpsychologie, Sonderband*, 42: 151–187.

Lind, E.A. (1994) 'Procedural justice and culture: Evidence for ubiquitous process concerns', *Zeitschrift für Rechtssoziologie*, 15: 24–36.

Litzcke, S., Linssen, R., Maffenbeier, S. and Schilling, J. (2012) *Korruption: Risikofaktor Mensch: Wahrnehmung – Rechtfertigung – Meldeverhalten*, Wiesbaden: Springer Fachmedien.

Marcus, B. (2000) *Kontraproduktives Verhalten im Betrieb: Eine individuumsbezogene Perspektive*, Göttingen: Verl. für Angewandte Psychologie.

McBarnet, D. (2006) 'After Enron will "whiter than white collar crime" still wash?', *British Journal of Criminology*, 46/6: 1091–1109.

McCrae, R.R. and Costa, P.T. (2011) 'The Five-Factor Theory of Personality', in O.P. John, R.W. Robins and L.A. Pervin (eds) *Handbook of Personality: Theory and Research*, New York: Guilford, pp. 159–181.

McKendall, M., DeMarr, B. and Jones-Rikkers, C. (2002) 'Ethical compliance programs and corporate illegality: Testing the assumptions of the corporate sentencing guidelines', *Journal of Business Ethics*, 37/4: 367–383.

Müller, G.F. (2001) 'F-DUP. Fragebogen zur Diagnose unternehmerischer Potentiale', in H. Wottawa and W. Sarges (eds) *Handbuch wirtschaftspsychologischer Testverfahren*, Lengerich: Pabst Science Publishers, pp. 247–250.

Ockenfels, A. and Raub, W. (2011) 'Rational und fair', *Kölner Zeitschrift für Soziologie und Sozialpsychologie: Sonderheft*, 50: 119–136.

Ones, D.S., Viswesvaran, C. and Schmidt, F.L. (1993) 'Comprehensive meta-analysis of integrity test validities: Findings and implications for personnel selection and theories of job performance', *Journal of Applied Psychology*, 78/4: 679–703.

Paine, L.S. (1994) 'Managing for organizational integrity', *Harvard Business Review*, 72: 106–117.

Pape, J. (2009) 'Zur Wirksamkeit von Corporate Compliance', *Corporate Compliance Zeitschrift*, 2/6: 233–236.

Parker, C. and Nielsen, V.L. (2009) 'Corporate compliance systems: Could they make any difference?', *Administration & Society*, 41/1: 3–37.

Paternoster, R. and Simpson, S. (1996) 'Sanction threats and appeals to morality: Testing a rational choice model of corporate crime', *Law and Society Review*, 30/3: 549–583.

Pies, I. (2005) 'Korruption: Diagnose und Therapie aus wirtschaftsethischer Sicht', in S.A. Jansen and B.P. Priddat (eds) *ZU – Schriften der Zeppelin University zwischen Wirtschaft, Kultur und Politik: Korruption. Unaufgeklärter Kapitalismus – multidisziplinäre Perspektiven zu Funktionen und Folgen der Korruption*, Wiesbaden: VS, Verl. für Sozialwiss, pp. 63–84.

Pies, I. (2008) 'Markt und Organisation: Programmatische Überlegungen zur Wirtschafts- und Unternehmensethik', in F. Ahlmann, W. Kersting and C. Langbehn (eds) *Moral und Kapital: Grundfragen der Wirtschafts- und Unternehmensethik*, Paderborn: Mentis, pp. 27–59.

PricewaterhouseCoopers (PwC) and Bussmann, K. (2010a) *Kriminalität im öffentlichen Sektor: Auf der Spur von Korruption und Co*, Halle-Wittenberg: Martin-Luther-Universität.

PricewaterhouseCoopers (PwC) and Bussmann, K. (2010b) *Compliance und Unternehmenskultur: Zur aktuellen Situation in deutschen Großunternehmen*, Halle-Wittenberg: Martin-Luther-Universität.

PricewaterhouseCoopers (PwC) and Bussmann, K. (2011) *Wirtschaftskriminalität 2011: Sicherheitslage in deutschen Großunternehmen*.

PricewaterhouseCoopers (PwC) and Bussmann, K. (2013) *Wirtschaftskriminalität und Unternehmenskultur 2013*.

Rabl, T. (2011) 'Wie Korruption entsteht – Eine Analyse der Entscheidungsprozesse korrupter Akteure', in T. Kliche and S. Thiel (eds) *Korruption. Forschungsstand, Prävention, Probleme*, Lengerich: Pabst Science Publishers, pp. 361–381.

Ragatz, L. and Fremouw, W. (2010) 'A critical examination of research on the psychological profiles of white-collar criminals', *Journal of Forensic Psychology Practice*, 10/5: 373–402.

Ragatz, L., Fremouw, W. and Baker, E. (2012) 'The psychological profile of white-collar offenders: Demographics, criminal thinking, psychopathic traits, and psychopathology', *Criminal Justice and Behavior*, 39/7: 978–997.

Rammstedt, B. and John, O.P. (2007) 'Measuring personality in one minute or less: A 10-item short version of the Big Five Inventory in English and German', *Journal of Research in Personality*, 41/1: 203–212.

Schein, E.H. (2004) *Organizational Culture and Leadership*, San Francisco: Jossey-Bass.

Schön, F., Litzcke, S., Linssen, R. and Schilling, J. (2011) *Korruption und Gewissenhaftigkeit*, Hannover.

Schröder, M. (2011) 'Vom Experiment zur Praxis: Wie moralische Argumente wirtschaftliche Selbstinteressen beeinflussen', *Kölner Zeitschrift für Soziologie und Sozialpsychologie*, 63/1: 61–81.

Sen, A. (1977) 'Rational fools: A critique of the behavioural foundations of economic theory', *Philosophy and Public Affairs*, 6: 317–344.

Shover, N. and Hochstetler, A. (2006) *Choosing White-Collar Crime: Cambridge Studies in Criminology*, Cambridge, New York: Cambridge University Press.

Simon, D.R. and Hagan, F.E. (1999) *White-Collar Deviance*, Boston: Allyn & Bacon.

Simpson, S.S. (2013) 'White-collar crime: A review of recent developments and promising directions for future research', *Annual Review of Sociology*, 39: 309–331.

Solmssen, P.Y. (2011, 27 January) 'Es geht auch ohne Korruption in Indien', *Frankfurter Allgemeine Zeitung*, 22, 12. Online available HTTP: <http://www.faz.net/themenarchiv/2.1159/standpunkt-peter-y-solmssen-es-geht-auch-ohne-korruption-in-indien-1582369.html> (accessed 5 March 2013).

Specht, J., Egloff, B. and Schmukle, S.C. (2011) 'Stability and change of personality across the life course: The impact of age and major life events on mean-level and rank-order stability of the Big Five', *Journal of Personality and Social Psychology*, 101/4: 862–882.

Steßl, A. (2012) *Effektives Compliance Management*, Wiesbaden: Springer Fachmedien.

Suchanek, A. (2001) *Ökonomische Ethik*, UTB für Wissenschaft Wirtschaftswissenschaften, Tübingen: Mohr Siebeck.

Sutherland, E. (1949) *White Collar Crime*, New York: Dryden Press.

Trevino, L.K., Gibson, D.G., Weaver, G.R. and Toffler, B.L. (1999) 'Managing ethics and legal compliance: What works and what hurts', *California Management Review*, 41/2: 131–151.

Tyler, T.R. (1990) *Why People Obey the Law*, New Haven: Yale University Press.

Uslaner, E.M. (2005) 'Trust and corruption', in J.G. Lambsdorff, M. Taube and M. Schramm (eds) *The New Institutional Economics of Corruption*, London: Routledge, pp. 76–92.

van Dick, R. (2004) *Commitment und Identifikation mit Organisationen: Praxis der Personalpsychologie 5. Praxis der Personalpsychologie*, Göttingen: Hogrefe.

Viswesvaran, C. and Ones, D.S. (2002) 'Examining the construct of organizational justice: A meta-analytic evaluation of relations with work attitudes and behaviors', *Journal of Business Ethics*, 38/3: 193–203.

Weaver, G.R., Trevino, L. Klebe and Cochran, P.L. (1999) 'Corporate ethics programs as control systems: Influences of executive commitment and environmental factors', *Academy of Management Journal*, 42/1: 41–57.

Westphal, A. and Gmür, M. (2009) 'Organisationales commitment und seine Einflussfaktoren: Eine qualitative Metaanalyse', *Journal für Betriebswirtschaft*, 59/4: 201–229.

28

The comparative political economy of financial crimes and their enforcement

The case of insider trading

Csaba Győry

Introduction: an American crime

When the then new District Attorney in the Southern District of New York, Preet Bharara, was invited to give a speech under the title 'The future of white collar enforcement: A prosecutor's view' (2010) before the New York City Bar Association in October 2010, observers were expecting a policy speech about the focus on white-collar enforcement following the financial crisis.[1] And that is what they got, only that it was about a topic which had not much to do with the financial turmoil that started in 2008: insider trading. A series of widely publicized investigations and trials duly followed. Two years later, *Time* magazine published a long story on post-crisis enforcement (featuring Mr. Bharara looking icily into the camera under the title 'This man is busting Wall Street'[2]) that was entirely about insider trading investigations, and without even vaguely reflecting on the fact that insider trading actually had nothing to do with the crisis.

America seems to be obsessed with insider trading. Insider trading scandals are widely covered by the press. The legal treatises, handbooks and journal articles written on it could fill libraries. Meanwhile, in most of the European countries, insider trading remains one of those exotic crimes which are far too rarely prosecuted to attract the interest of legal scholars, let alone criminologists. It occupies a dusty corner of the realm of white-collar crimes.

One of the major reasons for this is apparent: in most of the European countries, notwithstanding their political economy, insider trading *had not even been prohibited* until the end of the twentieth century, and even after the introduction of the insider trading prohibition, it appears to be *less intensively enforced*.[3]

How can it be that such differences can exist? How come that a financial crime can attain such enormous significance in one country and be not prohibited in another?

This chapter argues that the reason for this lies in the political economy of a financial system and financial regulation. It further contends that political economy can be a valuable tool for a criminologist in the comparative analysis of national and regional differences in the regulation and enforcement of a wide range of regulatory offences.

In this sense, this chapter is also a case study of a theoretical and methodological approach: it analyses economic criminal law and corporate crime in light of their economic, legal and political settings. It puts forward the argument that the political economy of an economic system is a crucial factor in determining how financial crimes are defined by law, which crimes are most likely to be more intensively enforced but also which financial crimes are most likely to be committed.

It argues that financial crimes and their enforcement only 'make sense' in a particular economic, legal and political setting. It further argues that this is not only true of the overall economic systems, that is, whether it is based on a socialist or a capitalist logic, where the economic institutions protected by criminal law are fundamentally different, but also of different forms of capitalism.

Capitalism namely has no 'perfect' form, but many varieties. The success of a particular form of capitalism depends not on the question of whether its economic and legal institutions comply with theoretical ideals but on whether the functional division of the institutions (including criminal law) that constitute it is stable and effective (Hall and Soskice 2001).

To prove this point, the chapter will compare the prohibition and enforcement of insider trading in two countries with radically different political economies: the United States, where the prohibition originates, and Germany, the biggest economy in Europe, where insider trading had not been prohibited until the mid-nineties. In this comparison, Germany represents a system that is in many ways radically different from US-style capitalism, but resembles many other European economies.[4]

After a brief primer on insider trading and the rationale of its prohibition, the chapter will outline the argument in detail, and will proceed to provide a comparative analysis of the political economy of the US and German financial systems, financial regulation and corporate governance. This will be followed by the analysis of the political economy of the regulation and enforcement of the insider trading prohibition in the second part. The latter will also attempt to answer the question of why insider trading, while considered to be the cornerstone for securities regulation in the US, had not been prohibited in Germany for decades, and why there still remain differences in enforcement intensity.

Why insider trading?

The prohibition and enforcement of insider trading is particularly suitable for comparative analysis, for several reasons. First, while considerable differences exist in the definition and the scope of the criminal prohibition of, for example, embezzlement, corruption or theft across legal systems, most of them have for long had criminal offences in place which functionally speaking prohibits the same kind of activity. Insider trading, however, while having attained enormous significance in one major capitalist economy, the USA, for a long time, had not even been prohibited in most of the other main ones like Germany, Great Britain or France.

But even in the USA, insider trading is a highly contested concept: the necessity, the rationale and the scope of the prohibition are constantly called into question. Thus, insider trading also clearly exemplifies the economic, moral and legal ambiguities that mar many white-collar offences.

However there is one further reason why insider trading is worthy of a more thorough comparative investigation. By delineating legitimate and illegitimate forms of information asymmetry on financial markets, it touches upon the very fundamentals of the capitalist economy, and also positively defines market behaviour. It belongs to the group of white-collar offences (along with those defined by competition law, for example) which not only prohibit economic activity damaging to others, but define basic and general rules for how markets should operate (Riles 2011).

What is insider trading and why is it (should it be) prohibited?

Insider trading, at its core, means using inside information (any sort of non-public information capable of moving[5] the share price of a listed company, either upward or downward) for trading in corporate securities (stocks, stock options or bonds).

The economic rationale behind the prohibition could be manifold. Within mainstream economics it is widely accepted that insider trading is *detrimental to the efficient operation of capital markets*. There are differing views, however, as to why insider trading is harmful.

One theory suggests that insider trading raises the cost of capital by widening the bid–ask spread (Bhattacharya and Daouk 2002).[6] A second theory puts forward the argument that persistent information asymmetry between insider and outsiders will distort prices. This is the same reasoning as the expectation that used cars have some hidden faults distorts prices in the used-car market. (Klock 1994). This approach also suggest that widespread insider trading also raises the cost of capital by reducing liquidity: if investors expect that they will be outsiders in a market they might decide to invest elsewhere, which again raises the cost of capital (Bhattacharya and Daouk 2002).

There is a minority view, though, associated with the Chicago School of Economics and mostly voiced by libertarians, which calls the rationale of the prohibition into question. The most important dissenting voice is Henry Manne, who views insider trading as a mode of compensation for corporate managers: the possibility of insider trading is a reward and incentive for corporate managers to innovate (Manne 1966).[7] A more plausible argument points out that insider trading contributes to the efficient allocation of capital. It helps to move market prices towards the proper price of a security – because other securities professionals would detect insider trading patterns and will react accordingly (Bainbridge 2001).

A radically different approach is taken by those who view the prohibition in light of property rights. In this view the prohibition of insider trading has the very same rationale as the ban on patent infringement or stealing of trade secrets (Bainbridge 2001). Trading on inside information by the corporate insider is thus akin to the infringement on the property rights of the corporation.

Economic arguments, however, concern the question of whether insider trading should be prohibited or not, and do not address the issue of whether insider trading should be criminalized or should only entail civil and/or administrative sanctions.

Scholarship on the criminalization of insider trading mostly concentrates on the issue whether it – along with many other white-collar offences – can be regarded as amoral.[8] There are powerful voices in both the common law (Kadish 1963) and the German legal tradition (Hassemer 2010) which argue for the decriminalization of regulatory offences on the ground that they only constitute *mala prohibita*, conduct prohibited only by virtue of the economic and regulatory context, as opposed to *mala per se*, offences with a strong moral frame of reference (Haines and Beaton-Wells 2009: 221). Others object to the description of insider trading (and other business offences) as morally neutral: Green (2006), for example, sees the rationale of its criminalization in its deeply amoral character involving cheating on the company whose securities are involved and lying to the other party to the transaction (2006: 123–145).

Both the economic and moral considerations about the prohibition and criminalization of insider trading could be explored empirically. The latter involves empirical investigation into the perception of insider trading among laypersons, financial industry professionals, or regulators, law enforcement officials and judges.[9]

This chapter, however, deals only with the former, and concentrates on the empirical context of the economic (and corresponding political and policy) rationale of the insider trading prohibition.

The political economy of finance, financial regulation and corporate governance

This chapter is inspired by three distinct theoretical traditions. One of these is *varieties of capitalism*, which holds that national economies can have radically different arrangements of economic and legal institutions, which are the result of long-term historical developments (Dore et al. 1999). Provided they are established and functioning effectively, they can maintain the integrity of their respective institutional arrangements despite external pressures for change (such as forces of globalization). The equilibrium of these arrangements can also prove to be highly resistant to internal efforts to change them, for example via regulatory reform (Hall and Soskice 2001). Their historical development is to a great extent path-dependent (Deeg 2001). Accordingly, financial markets in the US and Germany are two distinct sets of institutional constellations which differ due to the discrete historical processes that have shaped them.

The other two sources of inspiration are recent studies in economic sociology and social anthropology which study the financial markets in their embeddedness of social and cultural institutions (Granovetter 1985; Polányi 2001). The difference between American and German capitalism, namely, not only refer to dissimilarities in the macro-level structure and functioning of the US and German financial markets, and to the role they play in their respective national economies. There can also be differences in the way notions about corporate efficiency (Fligstein 1990; 2001), as well as about the ideal form and state of the financial markets, are constructed (Dobbin and Zorn 2005; Zorn et al. 2004). Likewise, cultural representations about shareholding and investment such as the 'shareholder nation'[10] in the United States shape everyday saving and borrowing practices of households, and with that, a range of other characteristics of the US economy, such as the allocation of capital (Langley 2008).

Finally, this chapter is also inspired by an emerging field in social anthropology (Abolafia 2001; Ho 2011; Zaloom 2006), which sets out to describe financial markets as distinct micro-level social practices, cultural norms, networks of social actors. 'Wall Street', in this sense, denotes a particular set of cultural practices, institutional and interpersonal networks and values (Abolafia 2001: 8; Ho 2011: 4). The same applies to Frankfurt as a financial centre.

To provide background for the case study, the following two sections will outline the political economy of the US and German financial system and corporate governance.

Shareholder nation: financial system and corporate governance in the US

The US financial system usually serves as the prime example of a market-based financial system (Hall and Soskice 2001). The most important characteristics of the US financial system are the well-developed, large and liquid capital markets.

The major source of capital for American firms are equities: stocks and bonds. American stock markets are by far the largest in the world. The market capitalization of listed companies stood at 119 per cent of the US GDP in 2012 and the number of companies listed at stock exchanges was 4102 in the same year.[11]

US households have traditionally been more willing to invest their savings in the capital markets. In 1989, stocks, mutual fund investments and retirement accounts accounted for 48.4 per cent of the savings of an American household, while the proportion of direct bank deposits remained at 28.3 per cent (Kennickel and Surette 2000). Up until the late 1970s securities investments were usually realized through individual brokerage accounts. From the early 1980s, mutual funds became the major form of non-pension-related securities investment for the American public (Toporowksi 2000).

The constant influx of household savings to the capital markets is further ensured by the US pension system, which – though a state-run pay-as-you-go system also exists – is dominated by private pension plans or employer-financed pension funds with individual accounts. Payments to the latter two are also invested in the capital markets (Holden et al. 2005).

The foundations for the US federal securities regulation were laid after the Great Crash of 1929 as the part of the New Deal: the Securities Act of 1933, which regulates the primary securities markets (the issuance of securities), and the Securities Exchange Act of 1934,[12] regulating the secondary markets (the buying and selling of existing securities). The latter also created the Securities and Exchange Commission, the federal securities regulatory agency, which was authorized by the 1934 Act with promulgating rules for the secondary markets. The third most important regulation is the Investment Company Act of 1940, which regulates mutual funds, and the Investment Advisers Act of 1940, which regulates investment advisers.

The priority of these new regulations was to address the information asymmetry that exists between issuers and buyers on the primary markets, and actors on the secondary markets. On the primary markets, the new laws regulated the minimum content for prospectuses, and imposed mandatory registration of every new issuance with the SEC. On the secondary markets, they introduced strict disclosure requirements for publicly traded companies, and strengthened the rights of minority shareholders. All in all, the main aim of the US securities regulation is to ensure that the financial markets are a fair, level playing field for all potential investors. Accordingly, a large part of the regulation was intended to protect the less informed retail investors. For the very same reasons, the laws also contain robust anti-fraud provisions, both for the primary and the secondary markets to prevent various forms of stock fraud, market abuse and insider trading.

The US system of corporate governance regime is complementary to the market-dominated financial system and disclosure-based securities regulation (Cioffi 2007). It knows only one level of control at the firm: the board of directors, which is legally separated from the management, but executive managers have great influence on the selection and election of board members, and usually also serve as members of the board. The weaknesses of shareholder representation is theoretically counter-balanced by the fiduciary duty of corporate directors, but it hardly worked in practice, mostly because the large and liquid financial markets also enable investors to react to management problems with the liquidation of their holdings rather than actively engaging in actual control (Cioffi 2007). This control problem programmed into the system was more exacerbated by the absence of concentrated ownership.

This was, however, beginning to change in the late 1980s, which saw a rapid rise of private investments in the capital markets. While in 1989, 48.4 per cent of the US household assets were kept in stocks mutual funds, and retirement accounts, and 29.3 per cent in deposits, just nine years later, in 1998, these numbers were 71.3 per cent and 19.7 per cent respectively. Yet these investments were different than in the previous decades: instead of direct investment via a brokerage account, they were mostly made through retirement plans and mutual funds (Kennickel and Surette 2000). This, in turn, made institutional investors like mutual funds and pension funds the largest owners of corporate stock and major players on the capital markets.

This rise of institutional investors altered the dynamics of US corporate governance. As their main goal was increasing the returns for their investors, they began to demand more aggressively that the interest of shareholders should come first, and that the major goal for corporate management should be to increase the profit of shareholders. This approach came to be known as the shareholder value approach.

Deutschland AG: the political economy of German finance and corporate governance

The post-war German economic model, alternatively coined as 'Rheinland capitalism'[13] or 'Deutschland AG' ('Germany, Inc.'), is usually regarded as the prime example of a 'coordinated market economy' (Hall and Soskice 2001).

Germany's financial system is traditionally bank-centred. As opposed to the market-based system of the United States and the UK, the major source of capital for companies is long-term bank loans (Vitols 2001).This applies to both the (in Germany) traditionally strong small and middle enterprises (SME),[14] which are usually private companies, and the big industrial and manufacturing corporations, the other traditional tier of the German economy, which are typically public corporations.

Most companies have established long-term ties with a single bank (called 'Hausbank', or 'bank of the house'). In the case of the SME sector this bank is usually the local public savings bank or cooperative bank, and in the case of large manufacturing and industrial companies one of the big universal banks.

As the German banking system was large enough to provide enough capital to sustain the post-war economic development, securities markets remained illiquid and underdeveloped. The market capitalization of listed companies in Germany barely hit the mark of 60 per cent of the GDP right before the 2008 financial crisis, and in 2012 it stood at 43.5 per cent.[15] The total value of stocks traded in Germany was 36 per cent in relation to the GDP in 2012, while in the US it was 136.6 per cent.[16] The number of listed companies fluctuated at around 600.[17]

Tax system incentives also pushed the companies towards bank loans instead of equity financing. Long-term loans from banks which were often also shareholders, fitted well the profile of Germany's economy, which has for long been dominated by capital-intensive, incrementally innovating manufacturing. Banks provided 'patient capital' with a focus on long-term growth.

Two further characteristics of German capitalism also contribute to the weakness of equity markets in Germany: household saving behaviour and the pension system. German households are traditionally risk-averse, and hold the majority of their savings in bank deposits and insurance policies (Bundesbank 2012). As the latest survey of the Bundesbank finds:

> the most widespread assets are current accounts along with savings deposits (78 per cent). Endowment life insurance policies come a distant second with a share of 40 per cent, followed by savings and loan contracts (36 per cent). The predominant type of investment securities is mutual fund shares (22 per cent). By comparison, shares (11 per cent), bonds (5 per cent) and certificates (2 per cent) were only directly held by a small proportion of households.
>
> *(Bundesbank 2012)*

While in the US, private pension plans and company pension schemes provide a constant influx of capital for the equities markets, the major pillar of the German pension system is the mandatory state pension, which is a pay-as-you-go system. Company pension schemes are usually funded by cash reserves (Vitols 2001).

As a result, unlike in the US, equities investments have not been part of the everyday culture for the German middle classes: investment securities are more typical among wealthy and high-income households (Bundesbank 2012).

The existing securities markets were dominated by the large banks, which were involved both in underwriting and trading. Banks were also the largest shareholders of publicly traded companies, especially of the ones with which they have ties as commercial banks. Up to the early

1990s, German securities law remained state law, and the major stock exchanges implemented their own regulatory regimes independently. With the banks being not only the biggest lenders and shareholders of public companies, but also acting as leading underwriters and brokerages, stock markets basically became 'cartels of large banks' (Lütz 2000).

As a result of the bank-centred financial system and underdeveloped financial markets, corporate ownership remained concentrated. Large banks and other financial services firms (such as the insurance giant Allianz) owned considerable stakes in big industrial companies, but also in each other. This led to the existence of dense cross-shareholding networks. The cross-ownership also manifested in overlapping supervisory and management board memberships of a closed corporate elite (Beyer 2002; Heinze 2001), also dubbed 'Deutschland AG' ('Germany, Inc.').

Until the late 1990s, disclosure rules were not stronger for public than for private companies (Becht and Böhmer 1999; Vitols 2004). As a result, company finances remained opaque, which discouraged foreign investors and the larger number of retail investors from entering the equities markets (Heinze 2001).

Under German company law, public corporations have a two-tier board structure: the supervisory board (*Aufsichtsrat*) is separated from the management board (*Vorstand*). The management board is responsible for the day-to-day operation of the company. The supervisory board, which decides upon major corporate policies and strategy, consists of an even number or employees' and shareholders' representatives.[18] The supervisory board members representing them are elected by the shareholders at the annual general meeting (AGM). AGMs were usually dominated by large banks and other financial institutions. The voting power of banks was further increased by the legal possibility of them as brokerages voting on behalf of their clients who deposited shares with them.[19] Based on their dominance, banks could elect their representatives to supervisory boards with relative ease. The protection of minority shareholders was also weak.[20]

In this corporate governance model, the external control of shareholders is internalized (as opposed to external control by market participants) and institutionalized in the form of their representation on supervisory boards. Shareholder representatives on the supervisory boards, however, could have more influence and control over the management than they were granted by law. The combined effects of weak capital markets, concentrated ownership, banking regulation which allowed lenders to become major shareholders, and dense network of cross-ownership led to an 'insider system' of control by a close corporate elite with overlapping management and supervisory board ownerships (Deeg 2001; Lane 2004).

This system started to show the first cracks in the late 1980s. By the mid-1990s, radical changes were already underway both in German finance and corporate governance. This was partly induced by economic developments and partly by regulatory reforms. In the globalizing finance markets of the early 1990s, Germany appeared secluded and insular. Large German corporations, such as Daimler, Siemens and Mannesmann, however, saw in globalization a chance of expansion and transformation into global conglomerates. They also hoped to tap into foreign capital markets, partly in order to finance their expansion, but also to diversify the sources of their capital.

This interest met the interests of the large private banks. Due to excessive competition in commercial lending and increasing market saturation large banks were facing diminishing profits from the early 1980s (Deeg 2001). Yet, due to regulatory constraints they remained, though in terms of assets among the largest financial institutions of the world, mostly minor players in the global financial markets. From financial modernization they hoped for the introduction of more sophisticated financial services, which would boost their profits, which in turn they could use to finance a global acquisition strategy which would elevate them to the group of leading global financial institutions.

This shift in business strategies in both large financial institutions and industrial companies led to the gradual winding down of the cross-ownership system (Ziegler 2000). Especially Deutsche Bank led the charge as it gradually withdrew from supervisory boards (Lane 2004). This also heralded a different approach to share ownership, one that is more shareholder-value-oriented, and more interested in short-term profits.

The German political elite also realized that Germany was heading towards a structural crisis and that it needed financial reforms. This happened in the context of the EU-wide push towards financial liberalization and a more market-based financial system. German financial regulation was reshaped to a considerable extent as a result, and was moved closer to the US/British model.

One of the most important changes was the adoption of federal securities regulation and the establishment of a federal financial supervisory authority (Bundesaufsichtsamt für den Wertpapierhandel, BaWh, later united with the insurance supervisor and renamed Bundesanstalt für Finanzdienstleistungsaufsicht, BaFin). The new federal securities regulation contained many elements of the American model: it brought more robust rights for minority shareholders and strengthened disclosure requirements for public companies, and introduced the insider trading prohibition into German law. The reforms also re-regulated the stock exchanges, ending their regional diffusion and created the Deutsche Börse in Frankfurt as the major German stock exchange. They also introduced a spinoff of the Frankfurt Stock Exchange for tech companies based on the NASDAQ model, the Neue Markt, which was intended to attract more venture capital for new IT and technology companies.

Measures were also taken to encourage the public to engage in equity investment. The pension system was also reformed: a new tier, a private pension scheme was introduced, along with tax incentives that aimed to encourage middle- and high-income individuals to move parts of their savings into individual pension plans (and to the capital markets).

Despite these reforms, German capitalism never really became so market-driven as its American counterpart. The market capitalization of listed companies never really took off following the reform.[21] In the United States, this was 119 per cent, in the UK 124 per cent in the same year. The number of listed companies also has not changed considerably, and remained around 600 (in 2012 there were 675 companies listed on stock exchanges, compared with 4102 in the United States, 2179 in the UK). The Neue Markt, intended to become the stock exchange for new technology and IT firms, did not survive the burst of the tech bubble and was actually closed down in 2003.

The result of the reform can be described more as the evolution of a hybrid model with elements of both the market-based and the coordinated system. The SME sector was left largely untouched by the changes (Hausch 2004), and so was the public savings bank and cooperative bank sector. Many of the large corporations, such as Siemens, Deutsche Telekom, Volkswagen and Daimler, on the other hand, underwent radical strategic and organisational adjustments towards a more market- and shareholder-oriented model (Lane 2004). This also applies to the large private universal banks (and also to other financial service companies, such as the insurance giant Allianz). Partly with the help of acquisitions in the US and the UK, the leading private universal banks transformed themselves into global investment banks and major players in global finance. Despite efforts to encourage German middle-class households to invest their savings in the equities markets, savings behaviour also has not changed considerably (Bundesbank 2012).

The political economy of the insider trading prohibition and its enforcement: a German–US comparison

Insider trading is an American crime: it originates in the United States, where it has been prohibited since the early twentieth century, and has been increasingly intensively enforced in the post-war decades. Meanwhile, insider trading was not prohibited in most European countries for most of the same period, and where it was, it was certainly much less intensively enforced than in the United States (Beny 2002). Now, having explained the dissimilarities in the political economy of German and US finance, let us return to our original question: what can explain these differences, and what role does political economy play in them?

Defending the retail investor: insider trading prohibition in the United States

In the United States, the prohibition of insider trading first evolved in state corporate law in the early twentieth century (Bainbridge 2001: 9). At the time, the prohibition of insider trading was applied only to corporate directors buying shares of their own corporations while hiding facts, which, were they to become public, would increase the share price (Bainbidge 2001: 5). As it was seen as the breach of fiduciary duty of directors towards shareholders, the prohibition only applied to face-to-face dealings, and not to transactions executed at stock exchanges.

The cornerstone of the federal securities regulation, the Securities Exchange Act of 1934, did not explicitly forbid insider trading. Instead, it contained a general definition of fraud committed in connection with securities in section 10(b),[22] which also gave the newly founded securities regulator, the SEC, authority to promulgate rules that prohibit specific types of fraud. It was only in 1942, eight years after the Exchange Act came into force, when the SEC adopted Rule 10(b)-5, which now forms the base of the modern insider trading prohibition in most legal systems:

> It shall be unlawful for any person, directly or indirectly, by the use of any means or instrumentality of interstate commerce, or of the mails or of any facility of any national securities exchange,
>
> (a) To employ any device, scheme, or artifice to defraud,
> (b) To make any untrue statement of a material fact or to omit to state a material fact necessary in order to make the statements made, in the light of the circumstances under which they were made, not misleading, or
> (c) To engage in any act, practice, or course of business which operates or would operate as a fraud or deceit upon any person, in connection with the purchase or sale of any security.

At the beginning, however, in line with earlier state law, the SEC did not interpret the prohibition as one that applies to impersonal transactions of stock exchanges. This changed only with two now classic cases in the early 1960s,[23] which involved stock market transactions. It was in these cases where another important element of the modern insider trading prohibition was born: the requirement for corporate insiders to disclose the material non-public information they possess before trading ('disclose or abstain rule'). These cases moved the insider trading prohibition from the narrow confines of the director–shareholder relationship of corporate law to a wider setting of securities markets. Though the prohibition has not departed from the basic concept of the breach of fiduciary duty, the SEC constantly and seemingly strategically tried to extend its scope, and apply it to fiduciary relationships beyond the corporate insider–shareholder relation.

While the SEC regularly pursued insider trading cases during the 1970s, the next step in the development of the prohibition arrived in the 1980s, during the years of large corporate mergers and acquisitions. These could lead to unprecedented rises in the share price of takeover targets in a matter of days, making insider trading a much more profitable activity than ever before. It is not a coincidence that most major corporate scandals of the time, such as that of Ivan Boesky and Michael Milken, involved insider dealings.[24]

The merger-mania of the 1980s also dramatically extended the group of people who could possess inside information: these now included, apart from the 'traditional' corporate insiders, investment bankers,[25] attorneys,[26] journalists[27] and even workers in print presses that produced disclosure materials.[28] The narrative of SEC enforcement about equal access remained the same, yet it was increasingly difficult to squeeze these people, none of whom were corporate insiders, into any sort of fiduciary relationship. This was accomplished only by the courts extending the scope of the insider trading prohibition to every relationship based on trust which involves the handling of material non-public information: the investment bankers, lawyers and the like were now found to owe a fiduciary duty to their own employers. The theoretical foundation of this extension is provided by the 'misappropriation theory' which holds that those who misappropriate, and then trade on, confidential information in violation of a duty of trust or confidence owed to the source of the information can be liable for insider trading.

This trend of extending the scope did not stop when merger mania subsided. In the first decade of the twenty-first century notable cases that further tried to extend the prohibition included professional criminals who bribed employees of a print press which printed an influential business newspaper[29] and a hacker who traded on embargoed information he found after hacking into the system of a news service.[30]

When analysed from a strictly legal point of view, the extension of the scope of transactions prohibited under insider trading rules while keeping them within the original fiduciary-duty-centred framework required increasingly complex legal acrobatics on the side of the SEC and the courts. Yet from the political economy perspective, it made perfect sense.

The leading narrative of the enforcement agencies in most of the cases (presented in court filings and other documents, as well as in public statements) was that the insider trading prohibition was meant to ensure that all investors have equal access to information on the capital markets. In this respect, trading while in possession of non-public information that would affect the share price without the counterparty knowing (or having a chance to know) the same information is akin to cheating, is inherently unfair, and creates inequalities between investors. And if investors think that capital markets are unfair and that insiders have an unfair advantage over outsiders, then these outsiders might decide to invest elsewhere.

And in the context of the political economy of US securities markets this theoretical hypothesis made sense: as most US corporations are financed from the capital markets, the constant influx of fresh capital is vital to the US economy. This explains the US political discourse on 'shareholder nation', as well as its many policy implications from tax incentives to regulation of pension plans.

This also makes the prohibition of insider trading (along with other forms of fraud on the secondary markets, such as boiler room fraud) one of the central tenets of the disclosure-centred US securities regulation. And as a considerable part of this capital comes from household savings, it is also crucial to maintain the confidence of these 'everyday investors' in the integrity of the capital markets (Langevoort 2009).

The argument had also been made that the strongly transparent enforcement and wide-ranging disclosure rules make also the American capital markets more attractive to both foreign investors and issuers (Coffee 2001).

This mindset deeply influences the self-concept and priorities of US securities enforcement (Seligman 2003). However, the quest to reduce the imbalances of economic power between 'Main Street and Wall Street' also has political appeal, which could at least partly explain why insider trading enforcement features so prominently in self-representations of US enforcement agencies.

As discussed in the previous section, the number of US households investing on the capital markets continually rose since the late 1970s; at the same time, however, direct retail investment declined: most households invest via intermediaries – which means that the large institutional investors that reshaped US finance in the last couple of decades now invest, to a large part, American household savings on the behalf of the latter. In the light of these changes, many argued, the 'Main Street vs. Wall Street' divide would not make any sense any more (Langevoort 2009). Calls were made to the SEC to abandon its concentration on the protection of the retail investor and reorient its focus on the marketplace now dominated by institutional investors (Langevoort 2009).

An especially controversial issue was the growing practice of corporations sharing inside information with analysts and a select group of major shareholders. This selective disclosure presented ample opportunity for insider trading, potentially harming the retail investors directly invested on the securities markets. Proponents argued, however, that this could shift the balance of power in corporate governance from the management towards shareholders, making shareholder control more effective. The SEC, however, decided to strengthen the disclosure regulation by adopting 'Regulation Fair Disclosure' (Reg FD), which made selective disclosure illegal.[31] These developments, however, do not necessarily weaken, at least in terms of political appeal, the fairness of the market argument, as the large number of households which invested in securities still might feel that they 'have a stake' in capital markets and still make them receptive to the 'even playing field for every investor' argument.

Insider deals in Deutschland AG: Germany's hesitant prohibition

German securities laws were not disclosure-oriented as in the American system (Ziegler 2000), and the protection of minority rights were weak (Höpfner 2001). In the German political economy, however, this was not necessarily a problem, as ownership was concentrated and the large majority of shareholders were also lenders and had long-term vested interest in the corporation.

Insider trading in this 'insider system' (Höpfner 2001; Lane 2004) of corporate ownership and control was, of course, also possible, yet it did not pose the same theoretical dangers as in the US system. The need for capital provided by 'outsider' investors was low. Illiquid capital markets did not pose the risk of increasing the cost of capital, and the risk of eroding investor confidence was not considerable. The proxy-voting system which enabled large universal banks to vote on behalf of their brokerage customers aligned the interest of the small number of minority shareholders with that of the majority.

This could explain why German securities law completely lacked an insider trading prohibition for the most part of the post-war decades.

A voluntary Insider Trading Guideline was adopted, though, in 1970, which was later revised and amended in 1976 and 1988. The guidelines were binding only for those who submitted themselves voluntarily by virtue of a contract, which was usually a contract of employment. The guidelines defined insider trading only in relation to employees towards the corporation (as in the earliest version of the American prohibition). The only sanction the guidelines foresaw was a disgorgements of profits, and, in the case of refusal, a civil action for breach of contract (Standen 1995). The guidelines, thus, effectively delegated the decision to pursue their own managers and supervisory board members to the corporation, to which, of course, there was little incentive.

It is not a surprise in this light that, even though the majority of German corporations adopted the guidelines, investigations remained scarce – 32 cases altogether between the adoption of the guidelines and the introduction of the legal prohibition (Magnus 1994). Even though newspapers frequently uncovered suspected insider transactions, these rarely had any legal consequences (Magnus 1994).[32]

There are strong indications, however, that the small number of cases does not mean that insider trading was rare. Insider trading, due to the nature of corporate ownership and control, combined with the weak regulation, continued to flourish, and this fact was well-known among foreign investors, who only tended to invest when they were insiders (Pfeil 1996). Insider dealing within the German corporate elite who held overlapping supervisory and management board memberships was widespread and commonly tolerated (Magnus 1994).[33] Due to their presence on supervisory boards, it was not uncommon that even trade union officials were suspected of insider trading.[34]

It was only in the early 1990s that regulatory reform introduced insider trading prohibition into German law. The prohibition largely followed the 1989 EC Directive on Insider Trading[35] (which Germany implemented with a considerable delay). The German prohibition (and the EC directive) does not apply the fiduciary duty-based definition of the American model, just simply distinguishes between primary insiders, that is, anyone who has acquired inside knowledge in his or her official function (be it a corporate executive, a simple employee, an accountant, lawyer or banker), and secondary insiders, who simply come into the possession of inside information (for example by chance). All trade by corporate insiders must be reported to the company and to the regulatory authority. The prohibition was supplemented by provisions about ad hoc publicity which required issuers to publish all potentially market-moving information to the investing public by way of electronic media defined in the statute.

The prohibition of insider trading was seen as a necessary prerequisite for attracting foreign investors, and for the increasing willingness of German households to invest their savings in the capital markets. The introduction of the prohibition was intended to convey the message that the traditional view of the German securities markets as an 'insider system' was now over (Cioffi 2007).

Yet the German regulatory authority did not seem to view the enforcement of the prohibition among its priorities. In the first year of the prohibition, eight cases were pursued (BaFin 1995). This number slowly rose over the following years and now fluctuates between 25 and 40 cases each year. Insider trading cases, though from time to time reported in the financial media, rarely receive the frantic publicity that surrounds other corporate scandals.

One of the reasons for this might be that – contrary to the intention of the regulatory reforms in the mid-1990s – the changes to the political economy of German securities markets were, arguably, not substantial. The market capitalization of listed companies has not risen considerably; neither did the number of companies listed. The investment behaviour of German households also has not changed dramatically: capital market investments, though risen, still have a minor share of total German household savings, and this still remains mostly confined to high-income households.

Many cases of insider trading occurred during the German dot-com bubble at the specialized stock exchange 'Neue Markt'.[36] This, paradoxically, might have led to decreasing the confidence in capital markets, instead of increasing it.

As opposed to the insider trading related scandals of the 1970s and 1980s, however, cases now rarely involve prominent members of the corporate elite in leadership positions of large financial and industrial corporations.[37] This might be explained by the gradual dismantling of cross-ownership networks, which reduced the opportunities of gaining inside knowledge. But this might also indicate the success of the increased transparency and more stringent disclosure requirements the reforms brought about in larger corporations.

All in all, though increasingly pursued, the intensity of the enforcement of the insider trading prohibition in Germany still does not reach that of the US. The political economy of their respective financial systems can offer some tentative conclusions about why these differences persist. In Germany, banks are still the centre of the financial system, and securities markets remained underdeveloped for most of the post-war decades. The ownership structure and corporate governance this system entailed, though the opportunistic insider trading appeared to be widespread among the corporate elite, did not pose dangers to the integrity of the financial markets and thus to the economy. Retail investors played almost no role in the financial markets. Despite the regulatory reforms and concerted governmental efforts to change them, the latter two characteristics of the German political economy have not changed in the last decades. Insider trading, therefore, though it became prohibited, could not attain the same significance as in the US.

Conclusion: towards the comparative political economy of financial crimes and their enforcement

One of the biggest problems European scholars (and lecturers) of corporate crime are facing is that most of the classic case studies, such as the Enron saga, are US cases. They happened not only in a radically different regulatory setting, but also in the unique environment of American capitalism.

This handbook, as the editors detail in their introduction, intends to change this, and provide a foundation for the coordinated research of *European* white-collar and corporate crime. To achieve this goal, it not only contains theoretical reflections, but also several case studies from European countries.

Yet the attention of European white-collar crime scholars cannot move entirely away from the political economy of the US financial system and regulatory environment, and comparative studies that contrast US and European regulation can deliver novel and useful insights, for several reasons. One is that with the US capital markets remaining the largest and the most liquid in the world, they will exert considerable influence on capital market regulation in several other countries for the foreseeable future. International corporations with access to US capital or multinationals that invest in US securities have to adhere to several US regulations, ranging from accounting to disclosure rules. For compliance professionals, be they in Germany, the Netherlands or Spain, US financial regulation is everyday practice.

This also means that corporate crimes are increasingly international in nature. The investigation into the European corporate scandals of the day at the time of the writing of this chapter (autumn 2013), the scandals concerning the alleged rigging of the LIBOR rates,[38] is also partly driven by the American authorities. The banks involved are facing parallel investigations and indictments in the US[39] and in Europe.

The LIBOR rate-rigging scandal also exemplifies how (abusive) local practices and interpersonal and inter-institutional relationships at a global financial centre affect global capital markets. The manipulation of the LIBOR rate was perpetrated by a small group of bankers and traders who knew each other well. The mechanism of setting the LIBOR rate was not based on international regulation or economic modelling, but on a practice that developed in the same gentlemanly, clubby atmosphere[40] of the pre-globalized City in London in the 1950s (where insider trading was also a fact of life[41]). Later, the markets changed and with them, the incentives of the banks involved in rigging the rate, yet the practice remained the same enabling the fraud to take place with staggering global implications.

The internationalization, of course, applies not only to the US–European comparison. Comparative studies of white-collar and corporate crime *within Europe* could also gain new insights if informed by political economy. Financial markets and corporate governance still radically differ in European countries, and so does corporate crime.

It is customarily assumed, for example, that the differences between corporate governance in the US and in Europe, especially the two-tiered board structure compulsory above a certain size in most European company laws, have prevented accounting scandals of the magnitude of Enron from happening, or at least from going on so long in Europe (e.g. Coffee 2005).

Yet while Enron-type cases arguably never happened in Germany,[42] they did occur (such as the Dutch Ahold scandal, or the Parmalat case) in other European countries where a two-tiered board is also compulsory. In exploring what other factors contributed to these differences, the comparative analysis of political economy and corporate governance could also play a role. It is possible, for example, that Germany could be considered different not simply because it applies a two-tier structure, but due to the fact organized labour and representatives of the biggest lenders sit on supervisory boards – a fact that is rooted in the unique German political economy.

Another possible field of research is the how differences in the political economies of Eastern European and Western European countries affect white-collar and corporate crime. How and in what respect is corporate and white-collar crime different in a nascent capitalism from in an established one?

One of the most important repercussions of globalization is that the conflicts between political economies described in this chapter now might play out *within firms*. This intra-firm conflict of political economies can create compliance problems and distinct opportunities for corporate crime. The alleged rigging of the LIBOR rates can again serve as a good example.

In the course of the 1980s and 1990s traditional European financial institutions, such as Deutsche Bank or the Dutch cooperative bank Rabobank, decided to expand into global finance. To reach that goal, they founded subsidiaries in American and Asian financial centres, or used their financial might to buy up financial institutions operating there. Yet this move not only created a range of compliance issues, but also greatly affected their business practices and institutional cultures. Whether the long list of corporate scandals that mar Deutsche Bank can be attributed to its transformation[43] from a traditional German bank into a Wall Street giant and global financial institution – as it is widely discussed in the German financial media[44] – might deserve a proper scholarly investigation.

Whether the now indicted Rabobank employees responsible for submitting the LIBOR rates[45] (sitting in Utrecht in the Netherlands) could be regarded, in terms of market and institutional culture, as Dutch or London city bankers, is another facet of the LIBOR scandal which might be interesting for criminologists to explore, and where the political economy of a particular marketplace might also come to play a role.

Another possible field of research which can benefit from the political economy perspective is the study of cross-border corporate crime. International tax evasion and tax fraud, for example, is a crime which by nature capitalizes on differences in regulatory frameworks and political economies. Offshore finance, for instance, and its role in financial crimes, cannot really be understood without considering the political economy of offshore financial centres.

The political economy framework could, thus, contribute to our understanding of why and where European corporate and white-collar crime is different.

Notes

1 The Federal District Attorney's office in the Southern District of New York, which has jurisdiction over Manhattan, is probably the single most important law enforcement office in the US in white-collar and financial crimes. http://www.nycbar.org/44th-street-blog/2010/10/21/preet-bharara-on-the-future-of-white-collar-enforcement-a-prosecutors-view/ (accessed 15 September 2013).

2 Calabresi and Saporito 2012.

3 Enforcement intensity is hard to measure. In this chapter, when talking about enforcement intensity, I do not only refer to quantitative, 'hard' (number of investigations; indictments and judgments annually), but also qualitative 'soft' indicators (such as the self-representations of enforcement agencies towards the public, in budgetary negotiations, parliamentary oversight bodies, etc.). For more on these methodological considerations see Győry 2014.
4 It is important to note that the widely cited division between Anglo-Saxon and social market (continental) capitalism (Albert 1993; Hall and Soskice 2001) does not apply here: Great Britain was just as inert to introduce (and then enforce) an insider trading prohibition as the other European countries (Barnes 2011; Nelken 2007: 758). Our hypothesis, elaborated below, is that the main reason for the ascent of the insider trading prohibition in the United States is to a great extent due to one of the few characteristics British and American capitalism do not have in common: the large base of retail investors.
5 This capability of moving the price of a security is called the 'materiality' of the information. The question as to what counts as material information is one of the most notoriously vague points of the regulation.
6 The bid–ask spread is the spread between the price at which a market maker buys and at which it sells a particular security. It is the bid–ask spread via which a market maker makes its profit. It was found that in the case of suspected insider trading this bid–ask spread is wider, increasing the cost of capital (Bhattacharya and Daouk 2002).
7 This argument, however, obviously falls short in light of the fact that insiders can make money not only on good news, but also on bad news.
8 Even though an economic argument could be made for the more powerful deterrent effect of criminal sanctions, this has not been done to my knowledge in the context of insider trading.
9 For the empirical study on laypersons' perception of insider trading, see Green and Kugler 2012. For a qualitative study of attitudes among regulators and law enforcement officials and prosecutors, see Győry 2014.
10 That is, that it is almost a civic duty to invest household savings in the capital markets.
11 http://data.worldbank.org/indicator/CM.MKT.LCAP.GD.ZS/countries/1W-DE-US-XC-NL?display=default (accessed 15 September 2013).
12 The 1934 Act only regulated stock exchanges in its original form. This was later amended so that it applied to over-the-counter (OTC, meaning: not on stock exchanges) sale of stocks. In 1963, the law was amended again and now it applies to the sale of any securities (irrespective whether they are listed or not).
13 The term was coined by the French political economist Michel Albert (Albert 1993).
14 German SMEs (*Mittelstand*) are usually export-oriented, highly specialized, capital-intensive engineering or industrial companies, manufacturing complex products for global niche markets on which they are usually dominant players or even enjoy monopolies. SMEs are responsible for almost 40 per cent of the German GDP (Günterberg 2012).
15 http://data.worldbank.org/indicator/CM.MKT.LCAP.GD.ZS/countries/1W-DE-US-XC-NL?display=default (accessed 15 September 2013).
16 http://data.worldbank.org/indicator/CM.MKT.TRAD.GD.ZS/countries/1W-DE-US-XC-NL?display=default (accessed 15 September 2013).
17 http://data.worldbank.org/indicator/CM.MKT.LDOM.NO/countries/DE-US?display=default (accessed 15 September 2013).
18 In the case of companies employing 2000 individuals and upward. The balance was, though, lightly tilted towards the shareholders as they have the right to elect the president who has two votes in case of an even vote.
19 This is proxy voting system was called the *Depotstimmrecht*.
20 Though their rights were formally relatively strong, courts tended to side with the larger shareholders (Heinze 2001).
21 See note 11.
22 15. USC. § 78J. This reads: '10. It shall be unlawful for any person, directly or indirectly, by the use of any means or instrumentality of interstate commerce or of the mails, or of any facility of any national securities exchange [...] (b) To use or employ, in connection with the purchase or sale of any security registered on a national securities exchange or any security not so registered [...] any manipulative or deceptive device or contrivance in contravention of such rules and regulations as the Commission may prescribe as necessary or appropriate in the public interest or for the protection of investors.'
23 *In Re Cady, Roberts & Co.* 40. SEC. 907 (1961) and *SEC v. Texas Gulf Sulphur Co.* 401. F.2d 833 (2d. Cir. 1968).

24 The latter insider trading case also inspired one of the most prominent cultural representations of Wall Street greed: the arbitrageur Gordon Gekko, who makes his money on insider trading in Oliver Stone's movie *Wall Street*.
25 *United States v. Newman* 664 F.2d 12 (2d. Cir. 1981).
26 *United States v. O'Hagan* 521 U.S. 642, 655 (1997).
27 *Carpenter v. United States*, 484 U.S. 19 (1987).
28 *Chiarella vs. United States* 445 U.S. 222 (1980).
29 *SEC v. Anticevic et al.* 05 Civ. 6991 (KMW) (S.D.N.Y.).
30 *SEC v. Dorozkho* 574 F.3d 42 (2d Cir. 2009).
31 http://www.sec.gov/rules/final/33-7881.htm (accessed 15 September 2013). The arguments clearly follow the 'integrity of the market' rhetoric.
32 Magnus compiled a list, which also includes references to the press articles that uncovered them. The compilation reads like the who's who of the German economy: managers of supervisory board members of Daimler Benz, RWE, Bayer, Audi, Neckermann, AEG and Springer were all suspected of insider trading transactions in this period.
33 This very much resembles the situation in the City of London (Britain was also hesitant in incorporating the insider trading prohibition into its law), where insider trading was considered to be one of the perks of being a trader (Cole 1990: 162).
34 The then-head of IG Metall, the largest German labour union, Franz Steinkühler, was forced to resign in 1993 after he used his inside knowledge as the member of the supervisory board of Daimler AG to tip members of his family off about an impending share swap.
35 EC Directive 89/592, 1989 O.J. (L334) 30.
36 Insider scandals concerned some of the most celebrated companies of the era, such as the IT companies Biodata AG, IXOS AG and Heyde AG, as well as media businesses such as Viva Media, Brainpool and Kinowelt.
37 Own compilation of data based on BaFin annual reports and case files.
38 LIBOR (London Interbank Offered Rate) is an average interest rate at which major banks borrow from each other in London. The rate is calculated every day from submissions from a select number of banks, which report the rates they are borrowing, or expect to borrow, from other banks. Many interest payments around the world (such as mortgages, student loans, etc.) are pegged to LIBOR.
39 The US jurisdiction is based on the fact that the interest payments of several types of loans and mortgages are based on the LIBOR.
40 'The rotten heart of finance: A scandal over interest rates is about to go global', *Economist*, print edition, 7 July 7 2012. http://www.economist.com/node/21558281.
41 See note 37.
42 At least in magnitude – there were some notorious cases in Germany during the 1980s and the 1990s with similar characteristics to the Enron case (such as the scandal involving the companies IBH Holding and Balsam AG), but these concerned relatively small SMEs with unitary/family ownership where predatory pricing or aggressive acquisitions were conducted without proper strategy and funding, and false accounting was used to cover up the losses caused by them. But the financial loss caused was negligible compared with Enron, and the practices were relatively quickly uncovered.
43 A fact that is acknowledged by a curious CEO duopoly: the former New York and London investment banker Anshu Jain (who does not speak German but used to run one of the most profitable operations in Deutsche Bank in London and New York) represents the Anglo-Saxon-style investment banking arm, while Jürgen Fitschen, a German banker, runs the traditional core businesses (such as corporate lending). For the political and economic context of this transformation, see the section on the political economy of German finance in this chapter.
44 These scandals include investigations into fraud connected to trading in emission certificates, cooking the books to avoid government bailout, and large-scale tax evasion. Deutsche Bank also featured in many crisis-related cases due to its involvement in the US mortgage market, and is (as of autumn 2013) also under investigation for rigging the LIBOR and EURIBOR rates. http://www.spiegel.de/international/business/deutsche-bank-reputation-at-stake-amid-a-multitude-of-scandals-a-873544.html (accessed 15 September 2013).
45 http://dealbook.nytimes.com/2014/01/13/three-former-rabobank-traders-charged-in-libor-case/?_php=true&_type=blogs&_r=0 (accessed 15 September 2013).

References

Abolafia, M. (2001) *Making Markets: Opportunism and Restraint on Wall Street*, Cambridge: Harvard University Press.

Albert, M. (1993) *Capitalism Against Capitalism*, London: Whurr.

BaFin (1995) *Jahresbericht des Bundesaufsichtsamtes für den Wertpapierhandel*. http://www.bafin.de/SharedDocs/Downloads/DE/Jahresbericht/dl_jb_1995_bawe.html?nn=281858 (accessed 15 September 2013).

Bainbridge, S. (2001) *Insider Trading: An Overview*. http://ssrn.com/abstract=132529 (accessed 15 September 2013).

Barnes, P. (2011) 'Insider dealing and market abuse: The UK's record of enforcement', *International Journal of Law, Crime and Justice*, 39: 174–189.

Becht, M. and Böhmer, E. (1999) 'Transparency of ownership and control in Germany', Working Paper No. 69, Humboldt University.

Beny, L. (2002) 'The political economy of insider trading legislation and enforcement: International evidence', The Harvard John M. Olin Discussion Paper Series Discussion Paper No. 348 01/2002.

Beyer, J. (2002) 'Deutschland AG a.D.: Deutsche Bank, Allianz und das Verflechtungszentrum großer deutscher Unternehmen', MPIfG Working Paper 02/4.

Bharara, P. (2010) 'The future of white collar enforcement: A prosecutor's view'. Speech at the New York City Bar Association. http://www.nycbar.org/44th-street-blog/2010/10/21/preet-bharara-on-the-future-of-white-collar-enforcement-a-prosecutors-view/ (accessed 15 September 2013).

Bhattacharya, U. and Daouk, H. (2002) *The World Price of Insider Trading*. http://ssrn.com/abstract=249708 (accessed 15 September 2013).

Bundesbank (2012) *Die wirtschaftliche Lage private Haushalte*, Frankfurt a.M.

Calabresi, M. and Saporito, B. (2012) 'The street fighter', *Time Magazine*, Monday, Feb. 13, 2012. http://content.time.com/time/magazine/article/0,9171,2105971,00.html (accessed 15 September 2013).

Cioffi, J. (2007) 'Corporate governance reform, regulatory politics, and the foundations of finance capitalism in the United States and Germany', *German Law Journal*, 7: 533–562.

Coffee, J.C. (2001) 'Law and the market: The impact of enforcement', Columbia Law and Economics Working Paper No. 304.

Coffee, J.C. (2005) 'A theory of corporate scandals: Why the U.S. and Europe differ', Columbia Law and Economics Working Paper No. 274. http://papers.ssrn.com/sol3/papers.cfm?abstract_id=694581.

Cole, Margaret (Mar. 17, 2007) *Insider Dealing in the City*. Speech by the Director of Enforcement, Financial Services Authority, London School of Economics. Transcript available at http://www.fsa.gov.uk/library/communication/speeches/2007/0317_mc.shtml (accessed September 13, 2013).

Deeg, R. (2001) 'Institutional change and the uses and limits of path dependency: The case of German finance', Max Planck Institute for the Study of Societies Discussion Paper 01/6.

Dobbin, F. and Zorn, D. (2005) 'Corporate malfeasance and the myth of shareholder value', *Political Power and Social Theory*, 17: 179–198.

Dore, R., Lazonick, W. and O'Sullivan, M. (1999) 'Varieties of capitalism in the twentieth century', *Oxford Review of Economic Policy*, 15(4): 102–120.

Fligstein, N. (1990) *The Transformation of Corporate Control*, Cambridge: Harvard University Press.

Fligstein, N. (2001) *The Architecture of Markets: An Economic Sociology of Capitalist Societies*, Princeton: Princeton University Press.

Granovetter, M. (1985) 'Economic action and social structure: The problem of embeddedness', *American Journal of Sociology*, 91: 481–510.

Green, S.P. (2006) *Lying, Cheating, and Stealing: A Moral Theory of White Collar Crime*, Oxford: Oxford University Press

Green, S.P. and Kugler, M. (2012) 'When is it wrong to trade stocks on the basis of non-public information? Public views of the morality of insider trading', *Fordham Urban Law Journal*, 44: 445–472.

Günterberg, B. (2012) *Unternehmensgrößenstatistik – Unternehmen, Umsatz und sozialversicherungspflichtig Beschäftigte 2004 bis 2009 in Deutschland, Ergebnisse des Unternehmensregisters*, Institut für Mittelstandsforschung Bonn: Daten und Fakten Nr. 2. Bonn.

Györy, C. (2014) 'The political economy of the insider trading prohibition: A German-American comparison'. PhD Dissertation, University of Freiburg.

Haines, F. and Beaton-Wells, C. (2009) 'Making cartel conduct criminal: A case study of ambiguity in controlling business conduct', *Australia and New Zealand Journal of Criminology*, 42(2): 218.

Hall, P. and Soskice, D. (2001) *Varieties of Capitalism: The Institutional Foundations of Comparative Advantage*, Oxford: Oxford University Press.

Hassemer, W. (2010) 'Der Basis des Wirtschafsstrafrechts', in E. Kempf, K. Lüderssen and K. Volk (eds) *Die Handlungsfreiheit des Unternehmens: Wirtschaftliche Perspektiven, strafrechtliche und ethische Schranken*, Berlin: DeGruyter.
Hausch, K. (2004) *Corporate Governance im deutschen Mittelstand: Veränderung externer Rahmenbedingungen und interner Elemente*, Wiesbaden: Deutscher Universitätsverlag.
Heinze, T. (2001) 'Transformation des deutschen Unternehmenskontroll-Systems? Eine empirische Analyse zum Stellenwert der feindlichen Übernahme der Mannesmann-AG für die Unternehmenskontroll-Debatte', *Kölner Zeitschrift für Soziologie und Sozialpsychologie*, 53: 641–674.
Ho, K. (2011) *Liquidated: An Ethnography of Wall Street*, Durham: Duke University Press.
Holden, S., Ireland, K., Leonard-Chambers, V. and Bogda, M. (2005) 'The individual retirement account at age 30: A retrospective', *Investment Company Institute Perspective*, 11: 1–24.
Höpfner, M. (2001) 'Corporate governance in transition: Ten empirical findings on shareholder value and industrial relations in Germany', Max Planck Institute for the Study of Societies Discussion Paper 01/5.
Kadish, S.H. (1963) 'Some observations on the use of criminal sanctions in enforcing economic regulations', *University of Chicago Law Review*, 30: 423–449.
Kennickel, S.-M. and Surette, J. (2000) 'Recent changes in U.S. family finances: Results from the 1998 Survey of Consumer Finances', *Federal Reserve Bulletin*, 86: 1–29.
Klock, M. (1994) 'Mainstream economics and the case for prohibiting insider trading', *Georgia State University Law Review*, 10: 297–335.
Lane, C. (2004) 'Changes in corporate governance of German corporations: Convergence to the Anglo-American model?', ESRC Centre for Business Research, University of Cambridge Working Paper No. 259.
Langevoort, D. (2009) 'The SEC, retail investors, and the institutionalization of the securities markets', *Virginia Law Review*, 95: 1025–1083.
Langley, P. (2008) *The Everyday Life of Global Finance: Saving and Borrowing in Anglo-America*, Oxford: Oxford University Press.
Lütz, S. (2000) 'From managed to market capitalism? German finance in transition', MPIfG Working Paper 02/4.
Magnus, M. (1994) 'Insidergeschäfte und Regelungsbedarf aus ökonomischer Sicht', *Zeitschrift für das Gesamte Kreditwesen*, 11: 531–563.
Manne, H. (1966) *Insider Trading and the Stock Market*, New York: The Free Press.
Nelken, D. (2007) 'White-collar and corporate crime', in *The Oxford Handbook of Criminology*, Oxford: Oxford University Press, pp. 733–770.
Pfeil, U. (1996) 'Finanzplatz Deutschland: Germany enacts insider trading legislation', *American University International Law Review*, 11: 137–193.
Polányi, K. (2001) *The Great Transformation: The Political and Economic Origins of Our Time*, Boston: Beacon Press.
Riles, A. (2011) *Collateral Knowledge: Legal Reasoning in the Global Financial Markets*, Chicago: Chicago University Press.
Seligman, J. (2003) *The Transformation of Wall Street: A History of the Securities and Exchange Comission and Modern Corporate Finance*, New York: Aspen.
Standen, J.(1995) 'Insider trading reforms sweep across Germany: Bracing for the cold winds of change', *Harvard International Law Journal*, 36: 195–201.
Toporowski, J. (2000) *The End of Finance: Capital Market Inflation, Financial Derivatives and Pension Fund Capitalism*, London: Routledge
Vitols, S. (2001) 'The origins of bank-based and market-based financial systems: Germany, Japan, and the United States', Wissenschaftszentrum Berlin Discussion Paper FS I 01–302.
Vitols, S. (2004) *Changes in Germany's Bank-Based Financial System: A Varieties of Capitalism Perspective*, Wissenschaftszentrum Berlin Discussion Paper SP II 2004–3.
Zaloom, C. (2006) *Out of the Pits: Traders and Technology from Chicago to London*, Chicago: University of Chicago Press.
Ziegler, N. (2000) 'Corporate governance and the politics of property rights in Germany', *Politics and Society*, 28(4): 195–221.
Zorn, D., Dobbin, F., Dierkes, J. and Kwok, M. (2004) 'Managing investors: How financial markets reshaped the American firm', in K. Knorr-Cetina and A. Preda (eds) *The Sociology of Financial Markets*, London: Oxford University Press, pp. 269–289.

29

Global governance = global compliance?

The uneven playing field in anti-money laundering

Antoinette Verhage

Introduction

On 6–8 September 2013, a dialogue on anti-money laundering was launched between the public and private sector professionals of the G8 and Eastern and Southern Africa. This dialogue was expected to be an impetus for the professionalization of AML (anti-money laundering) in sub-Saharan Africa, as part of the global battle against money laundering.[1] African states are developing states, which, apart from growing economic opportunities (seven out of ten fastest-growing economies in the world today are African), also implies a growing vulnerability for financial crime. The G8 summit wanted to raise awareness and emphasize the importance of this vulnerability. They stress the need for robust and effective measures in the field of AML. After all, as they state, anti-money laundering will only work when all potential anti-money-laundering partners start the same battles and fight with equal arms.[2] But although it is understandable that the AML hymn (or as van Duyne calls it, the financial integrity hymn (van Duyne 2009: 1)) is also sung in African regions, even within the borders of Europe, where AML has found solid ground, the fight against money laundering is not always fought with equal arms. This in spite of the fact that one might assume, after more than 22 years since the formal battle against AML in Europe began, that AML theoretically might have reached some stage of maturity.

In this chapter, the aim is to demonstrate that although a level playing field is crucial in the fight against money laundering, it is not a reality today within Europe. While it may seem that the approach to AML is a global battle, with countries united in the fight against money laundering, in reality, coherence and uniformity are still lacking gravely (Pieth and Aiolfi 2005: 30). National systems – especially within the EU – are all based on the same European directives, building upon the same AML principles. Every state receives the same building blocks and building instructions. Still, each country decides on how to place them, resulting in a diversity of block towers, some with high towers and deep moats (with intrinsic AML defences), some with lots of colours but low-level buildings (seemingly having implemented AML legislation on the outside, but very little enforcement once you take a closer look), and others with strong foundations but weak lines of defence (with strict rules and regulations, but very little controls).

These different block towers are in themselves not surprising, as European regulation leaves enough room for member states to place their own emphasis (Pieth and Aiolfi 2005: 30) on the basis of the risk-based approach. This implies that within the EU, although theoretically a level playing field exists, different emphases can be noticed, different oversight systems and diverse monitoring processes, leading to an uneven playing field in practice. This uneven playing field implies a number of serious problems: unfair competition between countries, reduced legal certainty, fragmentation of the AML approach and gaps in compliance. These impacts will be discussed more in detail in the next paragraphs.

The battle against money laundering: an overview

Money laundering has been formally criminalized since the late 1980s, and an issue for European member states ever since (Verhage 2012). Money laundering has links with white-collar, organized and corporate crime. Some state that money laundering is mostly white-collar crime (Unger 2006). Money laundering indeed can be seen as a type of white-collar crime, as money laundering is often inherently linked to the crime itself (Levi and Reuter 2006). Levi and Reuter exemplify this by referring to the Enron case where shell corporations were used as shelter mechanisms and money-laundering systems at the same time. In this case, the perpetrators are also the ones that launder the money (as the skills that are needed for both crimes are similar) (Levi and Reuter 2006). This is not (necessarily) the case when you look at money laundering as a method used by organized crime, where professional money-laundering agents may be hired for this aim. In those cases where banks or other intermediary institutions are engaged in the money-laundering scheme, money laundering can be referred to as a type of corporate crime.

All over Europe, the fight against money laundering can be typified by a dual approach: a preventive and a repressive pillar (Reuter and Truman 2005: 45), including both public and private partners. Between the 1990s and now, three European directives have governed the way in which money laundering should be tackled.[3] These European directives have had several results. First of all, the directives made clear that a preventive approach was necessary to combat money laundering. The repressive approach, characterized by criminal investigations in which *following the money* became central, was not sufficient in the battle against money laundering.

Second, the instalment of a preventive system on AML is founded on the detection and reporting of suspicious transactions. It implies the engagement of a large number of public and private (in Belgium alone comprising over 58,000[4]) actors – of a large diversity, such as lawyers, notaries, exchange offices, guarding companies and financial institutions. These actors (both individuals and organizations) are obliged to report each potentially suspicious transaction or client to a central unit, the Financial Intelligence Unit (or FIU). The establishment of an FIU was inserted in the Financial Action Task Force (FATF) recommendations since 2003 (IMF 2004).

The reporting duty on the first level of the chain requires a thorough insight into clients and transactions (Verhage 2012). It implies that organizations are able to distinguish suspicious transactions from non-suspicious transactions. It also entails that organizations need to invest in the battle against money laundering, in order to develop skills, instruments and competences that should allow them to detect potential money launderers and people related to terrorist activities.

The FIU subsequently investigates (a selection of) these reports and decides whether or not they should be sent to the national Public Prosecutor. The FIU's main objective is gathering information and analysing this information in view of the battle against money laundering. They are bound by a strict professional secrecy which makes information exchange with other actors very limited. This chain of events and actors is what we have called the anti-money laundering (AML) chain (Verhage 2009c: 14).

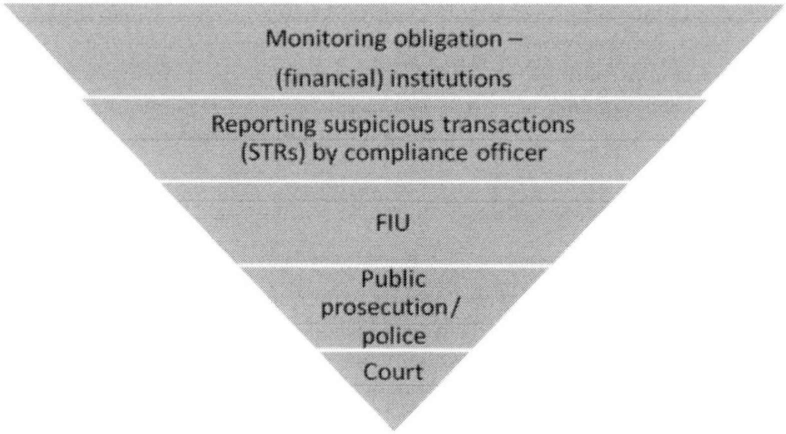

Figure 29.1 The AML chain

Source: Verhage 2009c: 14

Financial (but also non-financial) organizations, also triggered by a number of other impetuses (such as the need to protect their reputation), have been given a specific place in this amalgam of reporting actors. The financial sector is crucial in its control of the entrance into the world of the formal economy but is also very vulnerable (reputation wise) for abuses of their systems. This is why financial and non-financial institutions have invested largely – not solely voluntarily as regulators have also forced them to (Favarel-Garrigues et al. 2011: 180; Harvey and Lau 2009: 59–60; Levi 2002: 191–192; Verhage 2011: 36–38) – in AML compliance (Harvey 2007: 3; Verhage 2009b: 119–120). Costs of AML are hence not to be underestimated (Zimiles 2004: 29). A report by the EU, in which private reporting units were consulted on the implementation of the 3rd European Directive,[5] stated that costs for reporting institutions of screening and monitoring transactions add up to more than 400 million dollars[6] (European Commission 2011: 4).

This AML chain functions within a broader context, the *AML complex* (Verhage 2009c: 10). This complex consists of the activities of private and public actors, carrying out regulatory, monitoring, reporting, investigatory and judicial tasks. The objectives of the AML complex are prevention, crime fighting and law enforcement, and its foundations are legislation and regulation. The AML complex is a heterogeneous complex, consisting of a multiplicity of actors, surrounding, supporting or actively engaged in the battle against money laundering. One of the targets of this complex is focusing on the development of a level playing field in AML. This level playing field could be reached through the development of similar trajectories for AML. After all, differences in AML systems may result in a different level of AML protection in each country. In itself, this can result in a number of challenges for a European-wide anti-money-laundering system, inviting money launderers to look for the way of least resistance.

However, the fight against money laundering is based on a *risk-based approach* (FATF 2007: 1–2). Instead of focusing on mere rule abidance or the application of objective indicators, the legislator installed a system that provided room for interpretation and discretion (Verhage 2009a: 212). The focus of this system is on the investigation of transactions and clients that represent a higher risk of money laundering. The system is based on intelligent reporting (as opposed to automatic reporting on the basis of specific objective criteria): reporting entities are therefore given room for discretion with regard to reporting transactions to the FIU, potentially resulting in a more efficient functioning of the system. On the other hand, this discretion also has downsides: it implies that the position of the actors within the AML chain is inherently linked to many dilemmas and choices. Second, it also implies that, because of the room for manoeuvre that is granted to actors, different approaches to AML have developed through the years. This could have an impact on the level playing field with regard to AML and compliance.

Striving for a level playing field?

In European regions, a number of institutions have tried to work towards a level playing field with regard to AML. A key player here is the EU, which has issued regulations on the fight against money laundering. This has, as stated, led to the implementation of (up until now) three money-laundering directives. The 4th Directive is on the way as this article is being written.[7]

The first three AML directives have tried to implement a common scheme to fight money laundering. They do leave some discretionary room for member states: art. 5 of the 3rd Directive allows member states to lay down measures that go beyond the obligations in the directive (Tavares et al. 2010: 13). Still, the key to success in combating money laundering is to make sure that there are as few loopholes as possible and that every player plays by the same rules. The regime is also built around the assumption that it is to become a global system (Levi and Reuter 2006: 291). This global aspiration also implies that more lenient countries should be monitored – as these will be the attraction pools for money launderers, who are supposedly looking for the ways of least resistance. This can subsequently impact the reliability and trustworthiness of these countries and hence affect their financial systems.

Furthermore, strict states which are tough on money laundering can, on the other hand, encounter financial losses as a result of unfair competition. A famous illustration is the adherence to banking secrecy, for example in Switzerland and Luxembourg, which leads to unfair competition with regard to other countries that have stricter regulations. The level of banking secrecy (and enforcement thereof) of course impacts the starting points with regard to the implementation of AML and the amount of mobile capital that flows to financial centres (Christensen 2012: 327–328). Levelling the playing field is therefore important if the anti-money-laundering battle wants to be effective.

Of course, apart from the EU, other organizations have striven for harmonization of regulation and approach of anti-money laundering as well. The IMF and the World Bank have both played an active role in spreading the AML agenda (Levi and Reuter 2006: 291). The FATF, installed in 1989, issued 40 Recommendations with the goal to support states in implementing AML policies and providing transparency in AML. The FATF Recommendations are currently applied by more than 180 countries, and can be seen as an evaluative method and as a minimal standard for AML.[8] The FATF also assesses the level of compliance by its members and beyond (Pieth and Aiolfi 2005: 6) by listing countries and territories that are non-cooperative. We will look further into this in the next paragraphs.

The Basel Committee on Banking Supervision also strives for uniformization. The committee consists of Central Banks (currently representing 27 countries), supports international cooperation and functions as a forum for banking oversight worldwide. In that last role, the committee has issued a statement on the prevention of the use of the banking system for the purpose of money laundering (BCBS 1988), including a number of ethical rules for banks. The Basel Committee has also published recommendations on client investigations and identification striving for a harmonization of the AML approach.[9]

The Egmont Group is an international forum for cooperation on the level of the FIUs. The Egmont Group is another international player and acts as an international meeting point for FIUs and aims to share information, experiences and expertise between FIUs. This forum can also serve as a forum for coordination. Members of the Egmont Group meet a number of criteria for processing reports from the reporting entities. Finally, the Wolfsberg Group unites 11 global banks, who, as key players in the fight against money laundering are very well positioned in the AML chain. The Wolfsberg Group aims to develop standards for AML for the entire financial services industry, the Wolfsberg Principles.[10]

More global forces also play a role in the harmonization attempt. The pressure of the US (after all the founding father of the AML regime) on other countries is striking. Levi and Reuter illustrate this by the financial pressure and the process for imposing economic sanctions on countries that 'do not play their part, by slowing down their international transactions and making it almost impossible for their banks to clear funds through other countries' (Levi and Reuter 2006: 291). 9/11 has also served as an important impetus for the expansion of the regime, both horizontally (expanding to other businesses and professions, widening the scope of the definition of money laundering) (Gelemerova 2011: 69–70; Gouvin 2003: 970–971) and vertically (more intrusive methods and demands). Levi and Reuter (2006: 291) rightly asked themselves where this will end. Still, the effect of this pressure is mainly that the AML regime has expanded, which does not necessarily mean that it also harmonizes.

How uneven is the playing field?

In spite of several efforts towards harmonization, a number of studies and evaluations have shown that AML efforts are not implemented universally and that levels of compliance may differ depending on which country is studied (European Commission 2013a: 22; Levi and Reuter 2006: 304; Maurer 2008: 164; Pieth and Aiolfi 2005: 7). As stated, a level playing field is nevertheless important, not only with a view to efficacy and efficiency, but also for those involved: competition between financial centres can be impacted highly by the imposition of AML costs. When countries are reluctant to meet international criteria, they have a competitive advantage over the complying countries. As a result, 'those who win the race of implementing the internationally agreed standards lose out on the business side' (Pieth and Aiolfi 2005: 4). Or, in the words of Levi and Reuter, 'nations with tougher AML regimes might lose financial business to those with lax rules' (Levi and Reuter 2006: 307). A global type of governance is hence necessary if we want to aim for a level playing field in the domain of anti-money laundering and avoid the creation of loopholes in the system. In practice, this global approach is not entirely realized.

By means of illustration of the diversity, the calculations made by Walker (cited in Unger 2006) are discussed shortly. Walker assumed that the more tolerant a country is towards money laundering, the higher the attractiveness for money laundering of the country in question is. He developed a model to calculate attractiveness, in which banking secrecy is an important factor (next to government's attitude and the level of corruption (Unger 2006: 51)). Unger (Unger 2006: 52) has adapted this model[11] and made an attempt to calculate the different levels of attractiveness. In her calculation, she finds that Luxembourg, Bermuda and Switzerland form the top three most attractive countries for money laundering. It also becomes clear that there are differences between several EU member states with regard to this score. The differences in scores show that, even though countries are subjected to the same rules and regulations, they do implement these in a different manner.

Although one might argue that these attractiveness scores are unreliable as indicators of actual money laundering they give at least some insight into how different approaches are with regard to financial activities. They also illustrate that in spite of global governance with regard to AML, countries choose their own approach or at least place their own emphasis, which results in differences

Table 29.1 Attractiveness for money laundering

	Score
Luxembourg	55.4
Bermuda	26.4
Switzerland	25.7
Cayman Islands, Norway, Hong Kong, Austria, Liechtenstein	21–20
Belgium, Aruba, Jersey	19–18
Iceland, Canada, Ireland, Singapore, Australia, Isle of Man, Vatican City	17–15
France, San Marino, Guernsey/Alderney/Sark, Germany, Netherlands	15–13

Score source: Unger 2006: 53

in standards and in attraction or deterrence of money-laundering activities. Not exactly a level playing field, in other words.

The upcoming 4th Directive is aware of this uneven playing field, and states that when measures are only taken on a national level, and when there is a lack of coordination between member states, this might have a negative impact on the financial market in the EU and result in fragmentation. One of the focal points of the 4th Directive is therefore to aim for a level playing field. The directive also strives for a consistent model of obligations with regard to AML and anti-terrorist financing.[12] In preparation of this directive, a study was ordered by the European Commission. This study was carried out by Deloitte, and published in 2011. In this study, Deloitte contacted stakeholders, through European associations, the local Deloitte offices[13] and asked them to complete a questionnaire.

The Deloitte study reveals that all member states have implemented the AML directives, but not to the same extent. The directives provide member states with minimum requirements in view of harmonization, but allow them to implement stricter measures. Member states can therefore decide to issue stricter measures, following the principle of subsidiarity (Tavares et al. 2010: 13).

Most member states indeed report having implemented stricter measures than is required by the directive.[14] However, from the Deloitte study it is not clear what member states mean by stricter and which measures they refer to. As cross-border comparison is very difficult due to language issues and diverging legal systems, international differences are very hard to assess (Deloitte 2011: 27). Differences are found in relation to the definition of money laundering (which elements are included in the definition),[15] the list of entities subject to AML legislation (for example, Belgium also includes security companies, while in Bulgaria also political parties and sports organizations are included, and Spain extended the list to dealers in antiques or art and other professions), or the definition of PEPs[16] (and who falls within the scope of their immediate family members), to name a few. This is in line with earlier research that has shown that AML regimes can differ in these respects, stating that, in general, AML systems seem to be more similar at the front end (where clients are taken in, identification is carried out, or accounts are started) than at the back end (when to report suspicious transactions, which types of predicate crimes should be reported, how to deal with them, how reports are dealt with) (Levi and Reuter 2006).

The Deloitte report also mentions that reporting obligations are interpreted differently; Austria for example, also requires reporting entities to report suspicions of violations of the duty to disclose fiduciary relationship (instead of the suspicion of money laundering or terrorist financing). In France, entities are expected to report any transaction in which the identity of one of the parties remains doubtful, while in Lithuania every report should be submitted within three working hours and Latvia also requires reporting of unusual transactions (Deloitte 2011: 39). Furthermore, the report notices the insufficient amount of guidance on the use of the risk-based approach.

Stakeholders commented in the Deloitte study that the application of more stringent rules results in higher compliance costs and impacts on cross-border competition. After all, organizations are in some cases asked to report more types of transactions – resulting in higher compliance investments – or will be expected to monitor for a wider array of criminal activities, also resulting in higher compliance costs. On the other hand, some stakeholders also were convinced of the fact that having stricter measures helps them prevent money laundering or even leads to displacement of money-laundering flows (Deloitte 2011: 44). Some stakeholders are also of the opinion that it helps raise awareness of the seriousness of money laundering.

Eurostat attempted to make a comparison of statistics on money laundering in all member states.[17] It has presented the results of this comparison in 2010, but with great caution. The report continuously emphasizes the fact that the definition of the concepts that are used in the statistics may differ fundamentally.[18] Eurostat states that each member state has made strategic choices in AML, resulting in different routes, which makes it difficult to compare AML data across countries (Tavares et al. 2010: 5). Counting rules can also be different throughout several countries. One example is the fact that the Netherlands also includes unusual transactions reports in the total number of suspicious activity reports/suspicious transactions reports (Tavares et al. 2010: 13). Another example is the way in which FIUs count cases (cases can be reports, or files, or transactions). In a very recent report, Eurostat underlines these differences, summarizing them in three explanations for diversity: legal reasons, operational reasons and statistical reasons (Eurostat 2013).

Keeping these differences in mind, and also keeping in mind that the statistics gathered should actually be seen within the entire context of the member state (financial context, size of financial markets and so on), there are however some figures that can be presented as a result of the Eurostat report. First, member states were asked to communicate the number of suspicious transaction reports (STRs).

As is clear from Figure 29.2, representing the number of reports in 2010 a number of countries report an extremely high number of suspicious transaction reports.[19] The statistics that are presented represent the countries for which information was available (also depending on the type of reports that are made: here only STRs are presented[20]). Important to note here is that the structure of the AML chain may have an important impact on the figures here (for example the structure of the FIU – administrative or police-based can be of large importance). When compared with the number of cases that are brought to prosecution (originating from STRs, CTRs[21] and independent law enforcement investigation), the picture changes (Figure 29.3), but the differences remain remarkable. Please note that in Figure 29.3 the total number of prosecutions are presented (not only those stemming from STRs).

Following this study, the impact assessment preceding the proposal for the 4th Directive, the European Commission underlines the divergence and diversity in application of EU rules and warns of the reduced legal certainty that may be the result (European Commission 2013a: 21). In this impact assessment, the diversity in implementation is discussed as Problem Driver 2, and refers to inconsistent implementation. The effect of this on organizations (especially cross-border organizations, such as international banking groups) in view of uncertainties in international implementation and the impact on the effectiveness on the AML system is stressed (European Commission 2013a: 22).

The European Commission summarizes the main differences in approach of AML, one of which focuses on the inconsistency of statistical data on STRs, resulting in a very limited

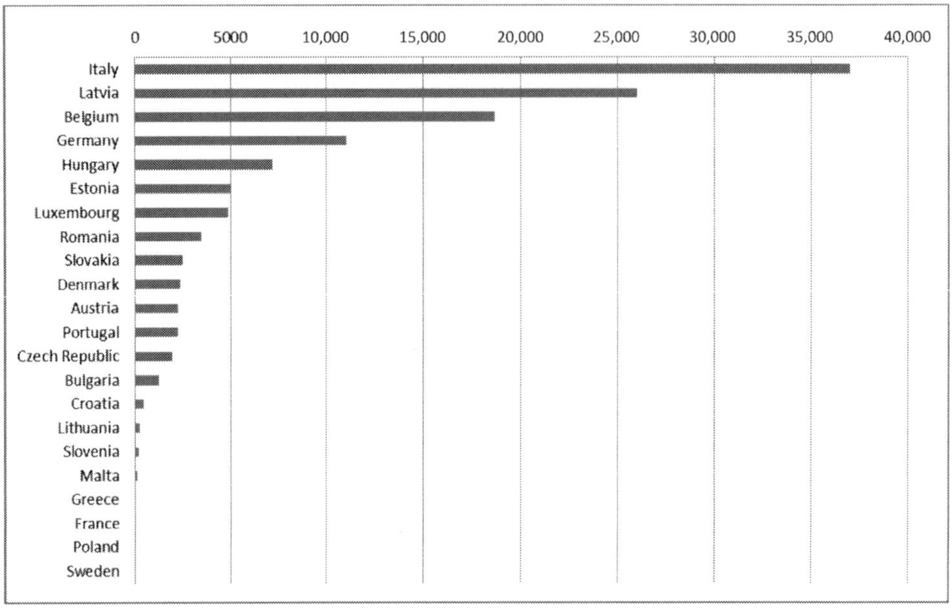

Figure 29.2 Total number of suspicious transaction reports, 2010

Source: Eurostat 2013 (graph by the author)

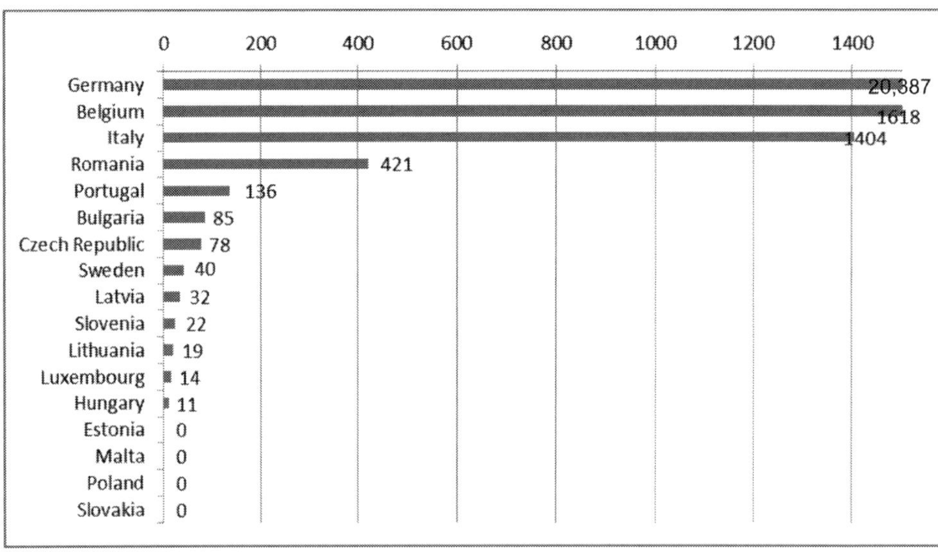

Figure 29.3 Total number of cases brought to prosecution, 2010 (originating from STRs, CTRs or law enforcement)

Source: Eurostat 2013 (graph by the author)

comparability of data. Another focus is on the supervision on AML, that can also vary between member states, resulting in gaps in compliance and legal uncertainty (European Commission 2013a: 24). The divergent interpretations of the provisions in the directive lead to different levels of compliance within the EU, which makes cross-border compliance even more challenging. The European Commission gives a number of examples, e.g. the different thresholds for cash transactions (ranging from 3000 to 15,000 euros), different organizational natures of European FIUs leading to difficulties in communication and information exchange between them, etc. (European Commission 2013a: 25–26). This challenge was also noted by a number of players in the AML field, namely the European payment institutions. They pointed out in a position paper that the (soon) 28 different regimes on AML within the EU lead to problems in the field of market competition (different levels of investment in AML, different levels of protection for customers with regard to AML/CTF[22] across countries). They illustrate this by referring to the threshold for customer identification in case of money remittances, which can vary from 0 to 1000 euros.[23] This example is only one among many to illustrate that establishing a global policy on AML is a major challenge for international or global organizations. According to a KPMG study in 2011,[24] half of all respondents that had a global AML policy in place had to make local adaptations following the national legislation. The exception to this rule were the banks, who were able to take a more global approach to AML (85 per cent had a global policy), but even then, the majority of those banks also made specific local procedures (KPMG 2011: 9).

Looking at the genesis of the AML system, as a top-down international enforcement regime, the differences in implementation between countries in a uniform regulatory environment like the EU are striking. There are, however, a number of elements that can explain these differences. First of all, every implementation in national law requires a transplantation of regulation into an existing national legal framework. It therefore has to take into account the national legal culture, traditions and rules. This also applies for the establishment of new institutions, like the FIU. The Belgian FIU, for example, is an administrative institution, functioning as a barrier between law enforcement and private organizations. This was installed in this manner because of the fear that banks would not be inclined to report direct to law enforcement agencies. This sensitivity is different in every country, resulting in different pictures everywhere (e.g. other FIUs as part of the police services, or as part of the judiciary – naturally also resulting in different powers for the FIU in question). Furthermore, the place of the actors that are involved in the AML complex and their powers in terms of influencing decision making (or in hampering policy), also differ in each country, resulting in different complexes in each country, with different rules.

In short, apart from the benefits that a flexible system may offer: efficiency, for example, and the opportunity to make a tailor-made approach on AML in each country, the diversity in implementation of more strict measures also has several negative implications. It may – as the authors of the Deloitte study note – have an impact on cross-border compliance (Deloitte 2011: 5). It may hinder effective AML efforts, not only between countries, but may also make things very complex for group organizations (banks, for example) to implement AML regulations in their organizations. It also hinders (cross-border) comparative research into the effects of the AML system.

Towards a level playing field: blacklisting and predicate crimes

Within and beyond Europe, this unlevelled playing field is acknowledged by the FATF, which, in its review of global AML standards, exposes countries that are insufficiently improving their AML/compliance regime. At the moment of writing this chapter, countries such as Angola, Nepal and Zimbabwe are named on the FATF website as countries that will be monitored closely in the next few years.[25] This monitoring system and the continuous reviewing of AML procedures and systems can be considered as an attempt to harmonize AML systems, or at least a first step towards a global level playing field. Within Europe, a similar process takes place through the mutual evaluations of the FATF, in which peer reviews are made of the level of implementation of FATF recommendations. We should also mention the evaluations that are carried out by the Council of Europe's Moneyval, which assesses compliance with all relevant international standards of countries that are not FATF members.[26] The evaluations are carried out on the basis of the FATF procedures and regulations. The Moneyval evaluations will not be a subject of discussion in this chapter as we here focus on the FATF evaluations.

Blacklisting

In the past, the FATF made use of naming and shaming through the publication of blacklists. Blacklists can be seen as instruments to reduce the risk of developing tax havens or money-laundering havens (Masciandaro 2004: 3). In these blacklists the FATF evaluated countries' compliance with their 40 + 9 Recommendations against money laundering and criminal financial activity (Maurer 2008: 168). The FATF was not the first to do this: the first blacklist was published by the IMF (International Monetary Fund), in 1999 (Unger and Ferwerda 2008: 3). After this first blacklist of tax havens, the IMF delegated the blacklisting to the FATF. They named countries with poor anti-money-laundering records and designated them as non-cooperative countries (Unger and Ferwerda 2008: 3). This naming and shaming policy probably had some effect on the level of compliance in the books, as peer pressure helped states to implement AML measures: no member state wants to be the one at the bottom of the class. Sharman also notes that several countries indeed changed their policy out of fear for reputational damage (Sharman 2009: 574). Research has indeed shown that financial institutions assume that it is best to be situated somewhere around the compliance benchmark (not too much, not too little compliance) (Verhage 2011: 82–83).

There are some positive effects of blacklisting that should be mentioned. Tax havens' jurisdictions assumedly did implement a number of measures (they installed new financial services commissions; they have put Know Your Customer and due diligence procedures in place) (Unger and Ferwerda 2008: 15). The FATF also concluded that the fact that no country was left on the money-laundering blacklist at some point in time is a positive outcome: all countries had adjusted and improved their regulatory framework to combat money laundering (Unger and Ferwerda 2008: 26) – at least to a minimal extent.

However, the consequences of blacklisting or reasons for de-listing are unclear (Gelemerova 2011). Did countries feel pressured at the time to comply with laws and regulations? Did their financial flows change? (Gelemerova 2011: 232). Were they de-listed because money-laundering opportunities diminished or simply because they followed the procedures (in the books, that is)? Furthermore, blacklisting could also have the opposite effect: it might signal countries in their role of tax havens, and push them even more into the role of money-laundering instruments (Masciandaro 2004: 18). Blacklisting has indeed punished some of the countries, but has benefitted others (Unger 2013: 24). Hence, it may very well be the case that blacklisting does not reduce money laundering and crime, it simply reshuffles it.

Money-laundering blacklisting has assumedly failed, because in October 2006 the last country on the list was erased (Myanmar – Burma) leaving the list empty. As from then, the list seemed no longer to be kept (Gelemerova 2011: 53). Today, in September 2014, the FATF mentions a number of non-cooperative countries, being Algeria, Ecuador, Indonesia and Myanmar. In 2014, the FATF also mentions jurisdictions that are 'subject to a FATF call on its members and other jurisdictions to apply counter-measures to protect the international financial system from the on-going and substantial money laundering and terrorist financing (ML/TF) risks emanating from the jurisdictions', a list which almost traditionally contains Iran and the Democratic People's Republic of Korea (DPRK).[27]

Tax haven listing still prevails and a list is being produced by the OECD. By 2008, the list contained only three countries and lacked legitimacy (Unger and Ferwerda 2008), and in 2013, no jurisdiction was listed as an un-cooperative tax haven.[28] Masciandaro furthermore notes that only naming and shaming is not enough; the risk of being placed in a financial quarantine (Masciandaro 2004: 19) by other countries might however serve as an important stick, in combination with the blacklisting practice.

Predicate crimes: the case of tax crime

With regard to levelling the playing field, the 4th Directive also proposes the inclusion of tax crimes as predicate crimes.[29] In a number of countries, tax crimes are a predicate crime for money laundering (OECD 2012: 72), but not all countries follow this viewpoint, sometimes based on the view that tax is still an inherently national competence (Rawlings 2007: 56). Levi points out that 'getting international consensus is easier for dealing with drug trafficking than with corruption, environmental crime, tax evasion or – at least prior to the carnage of 11 September 2001 – terrorism' (Levi 2002: 182). To add tax crime to the list of predicate crimes, is in many countries still a very sensitive topic and reason for political debate (European Commission 2013a).

Tax evasion does not qualify as a predicate crime for the US and the EU did not directly include tax evasion in the money-laundering definition in its first three directives – although the 3rd Directive tried to synchronize the approach to predicate crimes and legal definitions (Unger 2013: 4). This in spite of the assumption that tax evasion might be the largest part of the shadow economy (Levi and Reuter 2006: 329–330; Unger and den Hertog 2012: 291).

The first official steps towards inclusion of tax crime as a predicate crime on a global level[30] were made by the FATF in 2010, in an attempt to qualify tax crime as a predicate offence, aiming for a harmonization between countries (Unger 2013: 4). The FATF organized a public consultation on a number of proposed revisions of its recommendations. In its report of 2012, it summarizes the concerns of the private sector to include tax crimes and state that the majority of the representative bodies have concerns about or even reject the proposal altogether (FATF 2012: 3). Concerns of the respondents relate to the level of expertise that is needed for detecting tax crimes, the broad scope of tax crime and the need for a level playing field. Based on these concerns, the FATF proposes to include only *serious* tax crime and to grant some flexibility to countries on the decision on which offences will be included in the scope (FATF 2012: 2). After extensive consultation, in February 2012 the FATF revised its standards. One major revision was to formalize tax-related offences as part of money laundering. Through this, in the FATF Recommendations, tax evasion became a predicate offence for money laundering (FATF 2013: 2).

The inclusion of tax crimes as predicate crime was also underlined by the European Parliament in its report on organized crime, corruption and money laundering[31] and part of the current proposal for the 4th Directive. These initiatives form a next step on the way to harmonization, although it is not clear how the inclusion of tax crimes should be operationalized. This is not explained in the FATF Recommendations. Further explanation is therefore needed if we want to aim for harmonization in practice also.

To conclude: harmonization or divergence?

The introduction of the fight against money laundering has led to an unstoppable flow of obligations, regulations, procedures, monitoring systems, new functions and much more. The effects of AML are ubiquitous and felt on many levels of society (public institutions, private organizations but also on the level of the private life of the individual). All the more reason to plead for a measurable system, that can be made accountable, and of which the effects are countable (or at least visible). The current framework, with its diversity in implementations and interpretations, makes international comparison very difficult, if not impossible. Leaving the diversity aside, even if all member states do provide statistics on money laundering, for a correct interpretation of those statistics, what is needed is an overall view on the context of those statistics: the practical functioning of their AML chain. After all, simply having the figures is uninformative without context of those figures (as reporting thresholds may differ, registration counting rules are diverse). Today, this context is lacking; even more, it is almost impossible to follow a specific money-laundering file through the AML chain (Tavares et al. 2010: 15). Comparative research – almost non-existent today in this domain – then becomes a very challenging adventure.

In our view, the first step towards a higher degree of harmonization of the AML approach is in mapping the diversity. The Deloitte report suggests that a central database of all stricter measures should be set up (Deloitte 2011: 286). Indeed, making an inventory of how diverse the approaches are, making them transparent, taking into account how difficult this may be considering different legal systems and different AML chains, is a necessary part of the route towards uniformity. Only then can statistics tell us how (and if) AML works in a specific country, and only then can comparative research provide us with necessary insights in the functioning of a global system. This is a starting point for a more global approach. After all, when we need to play the game, it should be in the framework of an AML approach that builds on similar fundaments and plays by the same rules. An unlevelled playing field opens up opportunities for those who are looking for the ways with the least resistance or the loopholes. This implies that not only a sound and transparent legal framework should be in place, but that this framework is put in practice on a consistent manner, providing the necessary guidance and support, assisted by high-quality tools and instruments.

Notes

1 UK Government website: Gov.uk <https://www.gov.uk/government/news/g8-public-private-sector-dialogue-on-anti-money-laundering-and-countering-terrorist-finance> (accessed 4 July 2014).
2 <http://www.fatf-gafi.org/documents/documents/ppsdsept13.html> (accessed 4 July 2014).
3 Directive 2005/60/EC of the European Parliament and of the Council of 26 October 2005 on the prevention of the use of the financial system for the purpose of money laundering and terrorist financing; Directive 2001/97/EC of the European Parliament and Council of 4 December 2001 amending Council Directive 91/308/EEC on prevention of the use of the financial system for the purpose of money laundering; and Directive 91/308/EEC of the Council of 10 June 1991 on prevention of the use of the financial system for the purpose of money laundering. The 4th Directive was adopted by the Commission in February 2013. Its implementation is expected in 2015/16.
4 Information provided by the Belgian FIU, 4 March 2011.
5 Directive 2005/60/EC of the European Parliament and of the Council of 26 October 2005 on the prevention of the use of the financial system for the purpose of money laundering and terrorist financing.
6 This report however also estimates that 99 per cent of all alerts are false positives.
7 September 2013; for recent information and updates, please consult <http://ec.europa.eu/internal_market/company/financial-crime/index_en.htm> (accessed 4 July 2014).
8 FATF-GAFI, 2012. URL: <http://www.fatf-gafi.org/media/fatf/documents/Press%20handout%20FATF%20Recommendations%202012.pdf> (accessed 19 September 2013).

9 <http://www.bis.org/bcbs/> (accessed 4 July 2014).
10 <http://www.wolfsberg-principles.com/> (accessed 4 July 2014).
11 Unger added 'financial deposits' and 'member of the Egmont Group or not', to the formula (Unger 2006: 52).
12 One of the elements of this 4th Directive is the inclusion of *tax crimes* as a predicate crime in AML legislation for all member states. European Commission, Proposal for a Directive of The European Parliament and of The Council on the prevention of the use of the financial system for the purpose of money laundering and terrorist financing, 5 February 2013.
13 Telephone contact with Deloitte researcher of the report on 20 January 2014. Information was gathered using a survey and a number of interviews. Response of these stakeholders was very diverse: lawyers for example, and financial institutions were very interested, while other sectors (trusts, notaries, etc.) responded considerably less. A number of interviews were also carried out.
14 *Final Report from the Commission to the European Parliament and the Council on the Application of Directive 2005/60/Ec on the Prevention of the Use of the Financial System for the Purpose of Money Laundering and Terrorist Financing*, Brussels, 11/4/2012 COM(2012): 168.
15 For example, in Estonia, Hungary, Ireland and in the United Kingdom, a stricter definition of money laundering is used.
16 Politically exposed persons.
17 In the framework of the EU Action Plan 2006–2010, a working group was established, aiming to gather basic data on money laundering with the goal of being able to monitor the implementation of legislation and support the prevention and combat of money laundering by both policymakers and practitioners (European Commission, Call for comments from the Financial Crime Subgroup on the draft guidelines for the Money Laundering Pilot Project. 7 April 2009). The Financial Crime Subgroup, organized in the framework of the EU Action Plan Criminal Statistics 2006–2010, was composed of experts in the field of money laundering and was set up to advise the European Commission on the set of indicators on ML. The subgroup established (not surprisingly) that basic data may be available on a national level, but these are often diverse, which hinders international comparisons. The subgroup therefore aimed to introduce 'efficiency indicators' that would allow the assessment of AML policy. Based on 24 provisional indicators, Eurostat gathered information (by sending out requests to Member States in May 2008 – Tavares et al. 2010: 7) and made a first analysis in November 2008.
18 The report repeatedly refers to 'significant definitional and systemic differences (e.g. different notions of what constitutes a "report", different processing of reports, different approaches towards prosecution of cases)' (European Commission 2013b: 22) and states that 'these figures should be used with caution and with reference to the associated metadata and the comments on the interpretation of data' (Tavares et al. 2010: 26).
19 To be clear: this figure only represents statistics on STRs, not on countries that make use of other types of reports, such as unusual transaction reports, or suspicious activity reports.
20 Not all countries make use of these, for example in the Netherlands, unusual transaction reports were counted, which is why these are not presented in the figure. The UK, Cyprus and Finland use suspicious activity reports, and Ireland and France were not able to provide data (Tavares et al. 2010: 26–28).
21 CTRs are cash transaction reports, implying that parties are obliged to report on the basis of a cash threshold.
22 CTF = counter terrorist financing.
23 EPIF (European Payment Institutions Federation) (2013), *EPIF's Position Paper on the European Commission's Proposal for the 4th Anti-Money Laundering Directive*, 30 May 2013, <http://www.paymentinstitutions.eu/documents/download/18/attachement/epif-position-paper-on-the-proposed-4th-amld.pdf> (accessed 19 September 2013).
24 With regard to methodology, the report states 'KPMG International commissioned RS Consulting, an independent research agency based in the United Kingdom, to conduct a telephone survey of banks across the major sectors (retail banking, corporate and business banking, private banking, investment banking and wholesale banking) during late 2010. These banks were drawn from the top 1000 global banks according to the July 2010 edition of *The Banker Magazine*' (KPMG 2011: 8).
25 FATF, *Improving Global AML/CFT Compliance: On-going Process*, 16 February 2012, <http://www.fatf-gafi.org/topics/high-riskandnon-cooperativejurisdictions/documents/improvingglobalamlcftcomplianceon-goingprocess-16february2012.html> (accessed 5 September 2013).
26 For a list of non-members, please see <http://www.fatf-gafi.org/fr/pages/conseildeleuropemoneyval.html#note> (accessed 25 September 2013).

27 http://www.fatf-gafi.org/topics/high-riskandnon-cooperativejurisdictions/documents/public-statement-june-2013.html> (accessed 25 September 2013).

28 OECD, <http://www.oecd.org/countries/monaco/listofunco-operativetaxhavens.htm> (accessed 4 July 2014).

29 Predicate crimes are those crimes that underlie and precede the crime of money laundering (for example drug crimes, human trafficking, or, in Belgium, serious and organized fiscal fraud). Reporting entities are only supposed to report those cases of money laundering where they suspect that a listed type of predicate crime has occurred.

30 There have been national initiatives in this field, such as the draft law by Van der Maelen in Belgium, in 2007 (Wetsvoorstel tot wijziging van de wet van 11 januari 1993 tot wijziging van het gebruik van het financiële stelsel voor het witwassen van geld en de financiering van terrorisme voor wat betreft de gelden en activa die als illegaal worden beschouwd – ingediend door de heer Dirk Van der Maelen. DOC 0549/001 Belgische Kamer van Volksvertegenwoordigers, 12 December 2007 [Draft law to change the Law of 11 January 1993 for the prevention of the use of the financial system for money laundering and terrorism financing with regard to funds and assets that are considered illegal – submitted by Mr. Dirk Van der Maelen, DOC 0549/011 Belgian Chamber of Representatives, 12 December 2007]).

31 Special Committee on Organised Crime, Corruption and Money Laundering, *Report on Organised Crime, Corruption, and Money Laundering: Recommendations on Action and Initiatives to be Taken* (interim report) (2012/2117(INI))PE 506.051v02-00, A7-0175/2013, 17 May 2013.

References

BCBS (1988) *Prevention of Criminal Use of the Banking System for the Purpose of Money-Laundering*. Online. Available HTTP: <http://www.bis.org/publ/bcbsc137.pdf> (accessed 4 July 2014).

Christensen, J. (2012) 'The hidden trillions: Secrecy, corruption, and the offshore interface', *Crime, Law and Social Change*, 57(3): 325–343.

Deloitte (2011) *Final Study on the Application of the Anti-Money Laundering Directive*. Online. Available HTTP: <http://ec.europa.eu/internal_market/company/docs/financial-crime/20110124_study_amld_en.pdf> (accessed 4 July 2014).

European Commission (2011) *Meeting with EU Private Stakeholders on Anti-Money Laundering and Counter Terrorist Financing Policy on 1st February 2011*, Brussels. Online. Available HTTP: <http://ec.europa.eu/internal_market/company/docs/financial-crime/20110218-report_en.pdf> (accessed 4 July 2014).

European Commission (2013a) *Proposal for a Directive of the European Parliament and of the Council on the Prevention of the Use of the Financial System for the Purpose of Money Laundering, Including Terrorist Financing*. Online. Available HTTP: <http://eur-lex.europa.eu/legal-content/EN/TXT/?uri=CELEX:52013PC0045> (accessed 3 July 2014).

European Commission (2013b) *Proposal for a Regulation of the European Parliament and of the Council on Information Accompanying Transfers of Funds*. Online. Available HTTP: <http://eur-lex.europa.eu/legal-content/EN/TXT/?uri=CELEX:52013PC0044> (accessed 4 July 2014).

Eurostat (2013) Eurostat Statistical Working Papers, Luxembourg: Publications Office of the European Union. Online. Available HTTP: <http://epp.eurostat.ec.europa.eu/cache/ITY_OFFPUB/KS-TC-13-007/EN/KS-TC-13-007-EN.PDF> (accessed 4 July 2014).

FATF (2007) *Guidance on the Risk-Based Approach to Combating Money Laundering and Terrorist Financing: High Level Principles and Procedures*. Online. Available HTTP: <http://www.fatf-gafi.org/documents/riskbasedapproach/fatfguidanceontherisk-basedapproachtocombatingmoneylaunderingandterroristfinancing-highlevelprinciplesandprocedures.html> (accessed 4 July 2014).

FATF (2012) *FATF's Response to the Public Consultation on the Revision of the FATF Recommendations*. Online. Available HTTP: <http://www.fatf-gafi.org/topics/fatfrecommendations/documents/fatfsresponsetothepublicconsultationontherevisionofthefatfrecommendation.html> (accessed 4 July 2014).

FATF (2013) *FATF Recommendations: Media Narrative*. Online. Available HTTP: <http://www.fatf-gafi.org/media/fatf/documents/Press%20handout%20FATF%20Recommendations%202012.pdf> (accessed 4 July 2014).

Favarel-Garrigues, G., Godefroy, T. and Lascoumes, P. (2011) 'Reluctant partners?', *Security Dialogue*, 42(2): 179–96.

Gelemerova, L. (2011) *The Anti-Money Laundering System in the Context of Globalisation: A Panopticon Built on Quicksand?*, Tilburg: Wolf Legal Publishers.

Gouvin, D. (2003) 'Bringing out the big guns: The USA Patriot Act, money laundering, and the war on terrorism', *Baylor Law Review*, 55(101): 955–990.

Harvey, J. (2004) 'Compliance and reporting issues arising for financial institutions from money laundering regulations: A preliminary cost benefit study', *Journal of Money Laundering Control*, 7(4): 1–14.

Harvey, J. (2007) 'Just how effective is money laundering legislation?', *Security Journal*, 21: 189–211.

Harvey, J. and Lau, S. (2009) 'Crime-money, reputation and reporting', *Crime, Law and Social Change*, 52(1): 57–72.

International Monetary Fund (2004) *The IMF and the Fight Against Money Laundering and the Financing of Terrorism: A Fact Sheet*. Online. Available HTTP: <Http://Www.Imf.Org/External/Np/Exr/Facts/Aml.Htm> (accessed 4 July 2014).

KPMG (2011) *Global Anti-Money Laundering Survey 2011: How Banks Are Facing Up to the Challenge*. Online. Available HTTP: <http://www.kpmg.com/cn/en/issuesandinsights/articlespublications/pages/global-anti-money-laundering-survey-o-201109.aspx> (accessed 4 July 2014).

Levi, M. (2002) 'Money laundering and its regulation', *The Annals of the American Academy of Political and Social Science*, 582(1): 181–194.

Levi, M. and Reuter, P. (2006) *Money Laundering*, Chicago: University of Chicago Press.

Masciandaro, D. (2004) 'Combating black money: Money laundering and terrorism finance, international cooperation and the G8 role', paper presented at the 'Security, Prosperity and Freedom: Why America Needs the G8' conference at Indiana University, Bloomington. Online. Available HTTP: <http://papers.ssrn.com/sol3/papers.cfm?abstract_id=561183> (accessed 4 July 2014).

Maurer, B. (2008) 'Re-regulating offshore finance?', *Geography Compass*, 2(1): 155–175.

OECD (2012) *OECD's Current Tax Agenda*. Online. Available HTTP: <http://www.oecd.org/tax/OECDCurrentTaxAgenda2012.pdf> (accessed 4 July 2014).

Pieth, M. and Aiolfi, G. (2005) *Anti-Money Laundering: Leveling the Playing Field*. Basel: Basel Institute on Governance. Online. Available HTTP: <http://www.baselgovernance.org/fileadmin/docs/publications/working_papers/01_Levelling_the_Playing_Field.pdf> (accessed 4 July 2014).

Rawlings, G. (2007) 'Taxes and transnational treaties: Responsive regulation and the reassertion of offshore sovereignty', *Law and Policy*, 29(1): 51–66.

Reuter, P. and Truman, E. (2005) *Chasing Dirty Money: The Fight Against Money Laundering*, Washington DC: Peterson Institute for International Economics.

Sharman, J.C. (2009) 'The bark is the bite: International organizations and blacklisting', *Review of International Political Economy*, 16(4): 573–596.

Tavares, C., Thomas, G. and Roudaut, M. (2010) *Money Laundering in Europe: Report of Work Carried Out by Eurostat and DG Home Affairs*. Online. Available HTTP: <http://epp.eurostat.ec.europa.eu/cache/ITY_OFFPUB/KS-RA-10-003/EN/KS-RA-10-003-EN.PDF> (accessed 4 July 2014).

Unger, B. (2006) *The Amounts and the Effects of Money Laundering: Report for the Ministry of Finance*, The Hague. Online. Available HTTP: <http://www.rijksoverheid.nl/documenten-en-publicaties/rapporten/2006/02/16/onderzoeksrapport-the-amounts-and-the-effects-of-money-laundering.html> (accessed 4 July 2014).

Unger, B. (2013) 'Can money laundering decrease?', *Public Finance Review*, 31(5): 658—676.

Unger, B. and Ferwerda, J. (2008) *Regulating Money Laundering and Tax Havens: The Role of Blacklisting*. Online. Available HTTP: <http://ideas.repec.org/p/use/tkiwps/0812.html> (accessed 4 July 2014).

Unger, B. and den Hertog, J. (2012) 'Water always finds its way: Identifying new forms of money laundering', *Crime, Law and Social Change*, 57(3): 287–304.

Van Duyne, P. (2009) 'Serving the integrity of the Mammon and the Compulsive Excessive Regulatory Disorder', *Crime, Law and Social Change*, 52(1): 1–8.

Verhage, A. (2009a) 'The beauty of grey? AML as a risk factor for compliance officers', in P. Van Duyne, S. Donati, J. Harvey, A. Maljevic and K. Von Lampe (eds) *Crime, Money and Criminal Mobility in Europe*, Nijmegen: Wolf Legal Publishers, pp. 205–242.

Verhage, A. (2009b) 'Compliance and AML in Belgium: A booming sector with growing pains', *Journal of Money Laundering Control*, 12(2): 113–133.

Verhage, A. (2009c) 'Between the hammer and the anvil? The anti-money laundering complex and its interactions with the compliance industry', *Crime, Law and Social Change*, 52(1): 9–32.

Verhage, A. (2011) *The Anti Money Laundering Complex and the Compliance Industry*, London: Routledge.

Verhage, A. (2012) 'The social analysis of the anti money laundering complex and the compliance industry', in P. Ponsaers (ed) *Social Analysis of Security*, Boom, het Groene Gras, Den Haag, pp. 57–82.

Zimiles, E. (2004) 'KPMG survey: Banks accept more costly money laundering laws, expect heightened cooperation with regulators', *The Journal of Investment Compliance*, 5(3): 26–30.

30

The perception of Seveso regulation and inspection in chemical corporations

Marieke Kluin

Introduction

Law enforcement agencies are dealing with corporate crime in various European countries. The enforcement of law and the 'controlling' of corporate activity is an important aspect of the work of law enforcement agencies. In Europe they focus on a specific branch of the criminal law and most of these violations can be placed in the field of white-collar crime, for example violations of health and safety regulation at work or violations of the environmental criminal law as mentioned in this book (Ponsaers, this volume). In 1982 the European Union issued chemical industrial safety regulations in response to chemical disasters in England (Flixborough 1974) and Italy (Seveso 1976). The resultant Seveso directive now applies to approximately 10,000 industrial establishments in the European Union where dangerous substances are produced, used and stored. The main purpose of the Seveso directive is two-fold. First, it aims to prevent major accident hazards involving dangerous substances. Second, since accidents do unfortunately continue to occur, the directive is aimed at limiting the consequences of such accidents not only for humans (health and safety) but also for the environment (environmental and external aspects). It requires that the operators of major hazard facilities show the regulator that they have identified, assessed and controlled the hazards present in their facilities. The normality of law breaking within the chemical industry was investigated by Pearce and Tombs (1998) in a study that focused on chemical corporations and the exploration of the Bhopal disaster. Their view is that accidents arise because of criminogenic organizational structures. They are not therefore solely attributable to human error or to technologically complex processes. Accidents can be organizationally or systematically created and could be viewed as crimes from the point of view of criminology. Research into corporations and regulatory enforcement has been performed in the Netherlands, but more in other industrial sectors (than chemical) and on the basis of different research approaches (Huisman 2001; Mascini and van Wijk 2008; Van Wingerde 2012) or, alternatively, the studies were conducted rather a long time ago (Koolhaas 1990; Versluis 2003). In contrast to many studies on European Union regulations, this chapter will describe the way in which chemical corporation employees perceive enforcement practice in the Netherlands.

This chapter reports on the results of a questionnaire that forms part of a broader research project within the framework of interaction between field-level inspectors and regulatees and it has its focus on the enforcement of regulations by field-level inspectors drawn from three different inspectorates: the Regional Environmental Protection Agency (EPA), the Occupational Safety and Health Inspection Agency (OSHA) and the Fire Department. Seveso inspectors (or field-level inspectors) play a crucial part in occupational, safety, health and environmental policy but the relevant studies are limited, dated or devote only minimal attention to how the interaction between inspectors and regulatees is performed (Hawkins 1984; Lipsky 2010; Mascini and van Wijk 2009b; May and Burby 1998; May and Winter 2000; May and Wood 2003; Pautz 2009a; 2009b; 2010). Inspectors and those who are regulated endeavour, on a daily basis, to put Seveso regulations into practice. The chemical corporation employees who are the subject of the questionnaire are the individuals at various Seveso corporations who are responsible for ensuring that their corporation is complying with the regulations or is at least implementing those regulations on a daily basis. It is therefore important to explore how chemical corporation employees perceive Seveso regulations, Seveso inspectors and the inspections. The results of the questionnaire describe the perception that chemical corporation employees have of the inspector's behaviour, how the corporation reacts to the inspector's visit and the respondent's general views concerning the rules and regulations attached to the Seveso II directive.

This research was conducted in the most densely populated area of the Netherlands; an area known as Rotterdam – Rijnmond. It is a heavily industrialized area with large chemical plants, refineries, waste disposal corporations and residential areas and it has the largest concentration of Seveso corporations (140) in the Netherlands. The 15 international chemical corporations involved in this research are based in the Netherlands, but they produce, store and transport dangerous goods throughout Europe and to the rest of the world. The age and size of the corporations involved in this research varied. In terms of their age, seven of the corporations were less than 30 years old but eight corporations were more than 30 years old. The corporations ranged in size from fewer than 50 employees (3), fewer than 250 employees (5) and more than 250 employees (7). These corporations automatically fall under the Seveso II directive when the amounts of permitted quantities of hazardous substances rise above a certain level. There are two thresholds known as the lower- and upper-tier thresholds and for each threshold there is a limiting amount of dangerous substances as defined in Annex 1 of the Seveso directive. The lower-tier corporations have to define their major accident prevention policy and adhere to a safety management system while the upper-tier corporations also need to produce a safety report. Upper-tier corporations need to be inspected at least once a year in line with stipulations laid down in the Dutch Major Accident Hazards Decree of 1999. Four of the 15 corporations are obliged to have a major accident prevention policy and an active safety management system as stipulated in the Seveso II directive since they are lower-tier corporations. All the other corporations incorporated in this study (11) fell under the upper-tier ruling.

The structure of this chapter is as follows. In the following section a brief introduction is given to the evolution of industrial risk regulations and to the implementation of the Seveso directive in the Netherlands. After that I go on to review the relevant literature on enforcement style, on keeping risk as low as is reasonably achievable, deterrence and the compliance incentives of corporations. These four main topics will be integrated into the questionnaire and will either relate to regulatory literature debates or pertain to Seveso rules and regulations. The questionnaire will then be presented and the results will be analysed and discussed. I shall conclude by discussing the results and implications for future research.

The implementation of the Seveso II directive in the Netherlands

The Member States of the European Union have complete control when it comes to enforcing EU legislation and it is up to each country to decide how to execute the enforcement of such legislation. Although the regulating of major hazards in the Netherlands dates back to 1810 (Ale

2002), major disasters in the 1970s (Flixborough, Seveso and Bhopal) were not only of growing concern in Dutch circles but also at European Union level. Indeed, that was to culminate in the introduction of the legislation under discussion here. The Directive on Major Hazards [European Union Directives 82/5OIIEEG (Pb EG 1982, L 230) and 87/2I6IEEG (Pb EG 1987, L 85)] obliged all members of the European Union to explicitly take into account the hazards linked to industrial activities, to assemble information and to subsequently report to the European Union.

At that time the Netherlands had some experience with dealing with external safety issues, for example with quantitative risk assessment (COVO 1990). The Seveso directive I requirements were first implemented in the Netherlands in 1989. Already before that safety measures were an obligation for all the corporations involved, since they were obliged to have a permit in line with the Dutch Environmental Management Act. The above-mentioned experience with qualitative risk assessment turned out to be an advantage for Dutch corporations since the implementation of the Seveso directive made it obligatory to submit a report on external safety (part of which consists of quantitative risk analysis) and an internal safety report (occupational safety) (Ale 2002; Bottelberghs 2000). The Environmental Management Act lays down broad demands for corporations that apply for a licence. Corporations that fall under the auspices of the Seveso directive are obliged to have a major accident prevention policy, an implemented safety management system and a safety report (in the case of an upper-tier establishment) that has to be submitted together with the licence application. If it is an upper-tier corporation, the safety report includes safety measures and forms an integral part of the licence (Major Accident Hazards Decree 1988).

The European Commission and the European Parliament decided to completely revise the directive after the occurrence of new accidents and to focus more on general management systems. Porter and Wettig stated that this was 'due to the recognition that approximately 85 per cent of over 300 accidents reported under Seveso I have shown some deficiencies in the management system' (1999: 3). The Seveso directive II still concerns the control of major accident hazards involving dangerous substances. As stated in Article 1 the 'directive is aimed at the prevention of major accidents which involve dangerous substances, and the limitation of their consequences for man and the environment, with a view to ensuring high levels of protection throughout' the European Union (Article 1 Seveso directive). It contains several different elements in comparison to the first Seveso directive:

- The emphasis is on entire corporations rather than on installations.
- The corporations are assessed on the basis of modified qualifying criteria in which the emphasis is on the harmful properties of chemicals, and, in addition, a limited list of named substances.
- There is a major accident prevention policy and a safety management system.
- The inspection system falls under the control of the authorities.
- There is land use planning around Seveso corporations (Bottelberghs 2000).

The new Seveso directive took two years to be phased in because amendments needed to be made to several Dutch Acts and to the Major Accident Hazards Decree as well (1999). Land-use planning and safety distances are applicable to the situation around an establishment. All of this is based on generic risk modelling in relation to the type of installation, in combination with risk acceptability criteria. The risk parameters for large Dutch chemical corporations are specifically calculated because the complexity of such plants does not make it possible to determine a generic safety distance. It is on the bases of these calculated risks that the licensing and planning around the corporations then takes place. Here it is important to bear in mind that risk acceptance and judgement concerning hazardous activities always remain a contextual exercise and depend on the country, time, activity, risks and benefits (Ale 2002; Piers and Ale 2000). In any research into external safety and risk parameters comparisons are made between various European countries. It turned out that the Netherlands is less strict than other European countries when it comes to the risk parameters of its Seveso corporations (DHV 2002) as could be predicted from the size of the country and the density of the population (Ale 2005). This means that we can argue that Dutch regulatory norms accept higher levels of risk than other European countries in the case of land-use planning in relation to Seveso corporations.

The questionnaire has been divided into four main parts, the details of which can be found in the section 'Questionnaire'. The four main topics either relate to debates in the regulatory literature or they can be viewed in the context of the Seveso rules and regulations. They are: the enforcement style, keeping risk as low as is reasonably achievable, deterrence and the compliance incentives of corporations. The next section will provide insight into these topics.

Enforcement style

According to various scholars, differences in enforcement styles do exist. Enforcement style is defined here as 'the interactions of inspectors and regulated entities' (May and Winter 2011: 223). The focus of this study is on what May and Winter call the day-to-day interaction of inspectors with regulated entities (1999; 2000; 2011), and not the choices made by regulatory agencies (enforcement strategy). Even in the same regulatory settings different authors stated that variations in enforcement style could be detected (Gormley 1998; Hawkins 1984; Hutter 1989; Nielsen 2006; Winter and May 2001). Scholars studying regulatory actors have suggested that enforcement can be arranged along a continuum. The style at one end of the spectrum is labelled 'accommodative' (Hutter 1988; 1989; Shover et al. 1984) or 'compliance'-oriented style (Hawkins 1984; Reis 1984). Inspectors in this category are viewed as helpful, prepared to offer advice and responsive. The other end of the continuum is characterized more as a 'deterring' (Reis 1984) or 'sanctioning' style (Bardach and Kagan 1982; Hawkins 1984). Inspectors who apply this style go strictly by the book and use more punitive measures to achieve compliance. These two enforcement styles represent extremes and, according to Gunningham, hypothetical constructs which are unlikely to be found in a pure form (2011: 201). May and Winter (2000) suggest that the degree of formality or coercion applied by inspectors need not go hand in hand. Empirical research has demonstrated that inspectors use both styles in varying combinations depending on the given situations, settings, personal variables and the bureaucratic and political context (Braithwaite et al. 1987; Gormley 1998; Hutter 1988; 1989; May and Winter 2000; Pautz and Wamsley 2012; Van Rooij 2006). Research into corporations and regulatory enforcement has been performed in the Netherlands, but more in other industrial sectors, according to different research approaches (Huisman 2001; Mascini and van Wijk 2008) or otherwise a long time ago (Koolhaas 1990; Versluis 2003). How, then, do Seveso inspectors apply the rules? Do they attempt to explain them as though they are consultants or do they behave more like police officers? This subject: the enforcement style of Seveso inspectors, is therefore also part of the questionnaire, the results of which are also described in this chapter.

Keeping risk as low as is reasonably achievable (ALARA)

OSHA, EPA and Fire Department inspectors jointly perform Seveso inspections in the Netherlands. Inspectors affiliated to Seveso corporations make assessments and evaluations of hazardous activities and technologies themselves and judge how chemical corporation employees are practising their jobs. The chemical corporations need to demonstrate that major accident hazards have been identified and that the necessary measures have been taken to prevent such accidents and to limit their consequences for humans and the environment (Article 9 of the Seveso directive II). The respondents involved in this study make decisions relating to risk and safety in the course of their daily work. The available safety science literature indicates that employee attitudes and perceptions are positively related to safety behaviour (Cox and Flin 1998; Zohar 1980). Risk perception is seen as a critical social and psychological phenomenon that should drive different kinds of decision making. Slovic (1987: 280) defines risk perception as: 'Studies of risk perception examine the judgments people make when they are asked to characterize and evaluate hazardous activities and technologies'. Further to this one could add the summary given by Mearns and Flin (1995: 299): 'risk perception is the study of people's beliefs, attitudes, judgements and feelings about hazards, danger and risk-taking within the wider context of social and cultural values'. This is important for regulators as well, since they need to understand how people think about and respond to risk. Ale (2009: 105) stated that the acceptability of risk is never an isolated issue. It is the result of a decision about an activity with more aspects attached to it than probability and consequence alone. When safety becomes an issue we are interested in the probability that a person or group of people could be harmed. 'Individual risk is the probability that an individual will come to harm' (Ale 2009: 108). Another issue is the 'group or societal risk which is the probability or frequency that a group of a certain size will be harmed by the same event or accident' (Ale 2009: 109). Individual risk is location-dependent in terms of geographic position and may not be viewed as characteristic for any person outside a given establishment. The group or societal risk aspect is not location-dependent but rather attributable to a combination of the hazardous activities and the (populated) surroundings of an establishment. The ALARA and the precautionary principle were developed to limit possible side-effects. The ALARA principle means: As Low As Reasonably Achievable which basically means that all measures have to be taken to reduce risk as long as these measures are not unreasonable and what is not furthermore explicitly approved is prohibited unless it can be justified. This principle is applicable to hazardous activities. Ale concluded that simply combining this principle with the obligation of the hazard producer to demonstrate that he has done what is reasonable and practicable can be a powerful risk-reducing policy (2009: 111) in itself. In the Netherlands this means that in practice it is considered unreasonable if the costs exceed the benefits since costs are detrimental to a corporation. In addition to this, the overall question in relationship to safety always remains: how safe is safe enough? The other principle is the following: 'The precautionary principle is that an activity should not be embarked on if there are risks' (Ale 2009: 111). Again this principle has a negative side to it: there is no reason to assume that the new risks will be worse than the existing ones and that they will not prove to be worth the benefits (Jongejan et al. 2006). Entrepreneurs and users of technology have the power to influence what is culturally defined as an acceptable risk (Vaughan 2011: 293). Acceptable risk is not only an important issue in the matter of external safety or in determining risk parameters outside corporations; it is also an important issue within the organizations where the respondents to this questionnaire are employed. An excellent example of how insight into decision-making with high risks can be provided is given in the work of Vaughan on the *Challenger* launch decision (1996).

Vaughan determined in her research into the *Challenger* launch decision that NASA had developed an acceptable risk category. In reconstructing the history of decision-making she found out that technical deviations were first identified as signals of potential danger only to be redefined as acceptable risk after engineering analysis. She demonstrated that every decision and organizational procedure conformed to NASA rules and concluded that the accident was a mistake and not linked to misconduct (1996; 2004; 2011). NASA created a decision sequence and after each incident the technical deviations were normalized. This was what Vaughan termed the production of culture: the normalization of deviance that emerged as a key concept, explaining how

NASA gradually came to accept more and more technical deviations. The contributing factors were the competitive environment, structural secrecy, organizational culture and the structure of safety regulations. It is especially the last factor, safety regulation, that is of importance here. She describes it as follows: 'External safety regulators had the advantage of independence but were handicapped by infrequent visits and dependence upon NASA for information. Unless NASA engineers defined something as a serious problem they did not bring it to regulators' attention' (Vaughan forthcoming: 25). Already in 1978 Turner showed that disasters were preceded by a long incubation period during which early warning signals were ignored. A possible explanation for this could be the normalization of deviance. Other categories of organizational deviance alongside the mistake category developed by Vaughan are: misconduct and disaster (see Vaughan 1999: 283–297). She determined via various studies that mistakes and misconduct are often traceable to the prehistory of accidents and disasters. Vaughan's conclusion in relation to 'the normalization of deviance' explained how and why signals of potential danger tend to be misinterpreted. She determined that technical anomalies deviated from design aspects and expectations so that they were not interpreted as warning signs but instead became acceptable and routine aspects (1996). She therefore demonstrated that not all corporate misbehaviour involves acts of misconduct (or intentional acts). The regulatory environment has an influence on acceptable risk as well since they have a power-dependence relationship with their regulatees which could undermine the effective monitoring, investigating and sanctioning of producers and users (Vaughan 1999: 293). Especially in the chemical industry, a potential risk in relation to mistakes, misconduct or disasters is the type of normalization of deviance mentioned by Vaughan. If inspection agencies are not informed or are kept in the dark about serious problems then it is very difficult for outsiders to judge the assessments that chemical corporation employees make concerning acceptable risk. Simpson argues that the organizations that prepare best for these kinds of situations are the ones that are most susceptible to this problem (2002: 157). Statements relating to risk and safety were posed in this questionnaire and the results can be seen in the section 'Attitude towards safety and regulations'. Another form of risk perception is the risk of getting caught, better known as deterrence, which is explained in more detail in the next section.

Deterrence and corporations

The concept of deterrence may be defined as 'the omission of a criminal act because of the fear of sanctions or punishment' (Paternoster 2010: 766). Deterrence is an important pillar of the criminal justice system. Not only has the perspective of deterrence existed for a very long time (Beccaria 1764), it has come into being a complete field of research so it is impossible to fully outline it here, especially since the questionnaire involves other subjects as well. The relevant findings are therefore summarized below and, where necessary, reference is made to more extensive reviews. Objective and perceptual models of deterrent processes have been developed (Paternoster 1987) and, according to Simpson et al. (2007), perceptual models dictate the following: 'Perceptual deterrence assumes that the true impact of criminal sanctions on offending depends on an individual's assessment of his/her own risks of getting caught and punished' (Simpson et al. 2007: 2). Elements of deterrence are celerity, certainty and severity (Simpson and Koper 1992). We can divide deterrence into general and specific facets. General deterrence assumes that if people who have violated the law are punished such sanctions will prevent others from offending. Specific deterrence refers to offenders who have violated the law, received sanctions and will not re-offend in the future as a result of their punishment. Alternatively it can refer, in this chapter, to the effect that an inspection or enforcement activity has on a particular corporation and its performance in relation to Seveso rules and regulations. Simpson and Koper

(1992) found little evidence of specific deterrence within previously sanctioned groups that have violated anti-trust regulations in basic manufacturing industries. They noted that recidivism on the part of the corporations was generally not affected by prior criminal or civil sanctions. Regulatory interventions had a negative (but also irrelevant) correlation to recidivism. The empirical studies on corporate crime are meagre and, according to Simpson, when corporate deterrence is studied, the individual or organization may be the unit of analysis whilst the research outcomes remain inconsistent and inconclusive (Simpson 2002). A classic explanation for non-compliance on the part of corporations is that they decide to violate the rules because they rationally calculate the costs and benefits (Huisman 2001: 137). Recent studies on deterrence were performed in a rational choice model to predict corporate misconduct, but produced mixed results (Braithwaite and Makkai 1991; Grasmick and Bursik 1990; Nagin and Paternoster 1993; Paternoster and Simpson 1996). Braithwaite and Makkai (1991) ascertained in their research conducted at nursing homes that only the manager's perception of the probability of detection provided evidence for a deterrence effect and thus declared it to be a 'stark failure'. Paternoster and Simpson (1996) found stronger perceptual deterrent effects in their testing of rational choice theory. They stated that managers appear to take both their own risks and those of the corporation into account when considering illegal behaviour (p. 579). As Simpson (2002) clearly points out, there are many issues inherent to corporations and deterrence and so it is possible that the effects of deterrence will result in failure because of the way in which criminal law is constructed and the way in which corporations respond to sanctions. Some examples of the problems arising in conjunction with corporate deterrence are: organizational complexities, reincarnation and problems with corporate rationality (see Simpson 2002: 45–60). Two interesting cross-sectional studies have recently been performed. One longitudinal study focused on (EPA) violations and sanctions (Simpson et al. 2007) and they found 'little evidence of a deterrent effect' concerning any kind of sanction on recidivism (p. 2). The other study showed through a panel analysis on OSHA data (Simpson and Schell 2009) a negative relationship between past and current offending although when cross-sectional analysis techniques were applied, a positive relationship was found to exist between past and current offending (pp. 72–73). Several studies showed that rule violations were less frequent within corporations that had been recently inspected (Gray and Scholz 1991; Gray and Shadbegian 2005; Mendeloff and Gray 2005). How do the visits of Seveso inspectors affect corporations? Are they less eager to deal with problems that go unnoticed by inspectors or are corporations more likely to violate rules when the corporation can profit from this? Of course it is possible to clean up the entire corporation very thoroughly in advance on multiple levels since inspections are announced beforehand and the inspection areas are usually made known as well. How do Seveso corporations in the Netherlands perceive the probability of violation detection; what do they think about the severity of the sanctions? This can be seen in the sections 'Deterrence' and 'Impact of visits'.

Compliance incentives for corporations

Not only a corporation's perception of the probability of detection of violation seems to be reason enough for a corporation to comply (or at least a deterrent), but there are other motives as well. Research on compliance motives is extensive, varied and diversified, and only the most relevant literature is summarized below. For a more extended overview see for example Parker and Nielsen (2011); Nielsen and Parker (2012). Literature on regulation suggests that there are three general compliance categories which may be classified as follows: calculated (for example Becker 1968; Ehrlich 1972), normative (for example Tyler 2006; Winter and May 2001) and social motivations for compliance (for example Grasmick and Bursik 1990; Winter and May 2001).

When a corporation has calculated or economic motives for compliance, this means that it has estimated that the benefits of compliance exceed the costs of compliance. Theoretically is assumed that an economically driven corporation can be affected by the likelihood of detection (frequency of inspection) and by speed, certainty and sanction size. Empirical research showed a mixed set of conclusions. The perceived risk of detection is more important than the likelihood and severity of sanctions (Burby and Paterson 1993; Gray and Scholz 1991). As mentioned in the section 'Deterrence and corporations', Braithwaite and Makkai's study on nursing homes found little evidence to support the notion that inspections or sanctions serve as deterrents. Gray and Scholz (1993) on the other hand did find significant specific deterring effects resulting from inspections that impose sanctions and which thus result in changes in injury patterns at sanctioned corporations.

The second incentive to comply involves a sense of moral duty in combination with agreement on the importance of a specific regulation (Parker and Nielsen 2011; Winter and May 2001). An individual or corporation might believe that a law is just and that obeying it fits in with internalized moral or ideological values and so the regulatory agencies that administer the law will be trusted (Tyler 2006). Acceptance of rules and their features (such as the reasonableness of the rules, the fairness of the authorities and the enactment of the rules) plays an important and significant role in the case of this particular motive since matters are difficult to disentangle because of the sense of duty that affects the evaluation of the specific regulation (Winter and May 2001).

The third motive, that of complying with rules and regulations, is 'the extent to which the firm is committed to earning the approval and respect of significant people with whom an actor interacts' (Grasmick and Bursik 1990; Parker and Nielsen 2011: 11). Since regulatory enforcement is seen in this study (and in other research as well) as an interactive framework, expectations between inspectors and regulatees as to what constitutes an acceptable level of compliance might exist (Hawkins 1984). Motivations for compliance are important if one thinks that an economically driven corporation could be influenced by having a large fine imposed and therefore motivated to comply, while a small fine would be equally effective if a corporation is socially motivated Parker and Nielsen (2011); Nielsen and Parker (2012). According to regulatory theory the range of relevant incentives is extensive and they may be seen to interact with each other. Etienne (2013) observed that regulators and regulatees have multiple motives, and that their respective behaviour cannot only be seen as self-interested calculation, but that it also entails a more complex and dynamic understanding of compliance motivations. The results of this research set out to shed more light on this interactive and complex framework of enforcement regulation between Seveso inspectors and chemical corporations. Companies' reasons for complying with Seveso rules and regulations are explored in the questionnaire and the results are noted down in the sections 'Ability and capability to comply' and 'Impact of visits'. The questionnaire will be briefly introduced in the following section before elaborating on the results.

Questionnaire

Participant observations of 19 inspections[1] and trend analysis in all the chemical corporations was carried out in the course of the broader research project (Kluin 2013; Kluin and Jagtman 2014). The trend analysis provided insight into all registered violations of occupational health and safety and environmental regulations between 1999 and 2011 in each of the respective chemical corporations. Both research methods provided insight into the interaction between field-level inspectors and regulatees but a more objective approach was adopted. The fieldwork consisted of participant observation in chemical corporations while employees underwent inspection and it included observations of inspectors as they went about their daily activities. The trend analysis showed the sanctioning practice of the Occupational Safety and Health Agency and the Environmental Protection Agency. The results of this questionnaire give a more subjective view of the perceptions that chemical corporation employees have of inspectors' behaviour, the reaction of corporations to inspectors' visits and the general views of respondents concerning the rules and regulations attached to the Seveso II directive. The main focus of this study is on inspection agencies and on the daily activities of inspectors in relation to Seveso inspections. Participant observation and trend analysis therefore focused primarily on inspectors or on the inspection agency's databases. The questionnaire was designed to examine the 15 chemical corporations and their perceptions of Seveso inspections and regulations. The questionnaire research method was chosen because the inspections were already time-consuming enough for the employees in question at the various chemical corporations. It proved to be a successful approach and to provide good insight into the perceptions that corporations have of inspections and regulation (Mascini and van Wijk 2008; 2009a; 2009b). Information and results were gathered from the 2007 and 2011 questionnaires distributed to Dutch chemical corporations in conjunction with the Dutch national approach to monitoring Seveso corporations (LATrb 2008; 2012). Just two questions from that particular survey were of interest in the context of the present study and they are considered in the sections 'Perceptions concerning the presence of inspection agencies' and 'Attitude towards safety and regulations'. Other questions related more to the key performance indicators of the inspection agencies themselves, for example concerning the content of the inspection schedule and the quality of the inspection report.

The Seveso survey included six blocks of questions preceded by an introduction outlining the purpose of the questionnaire. Table 30.1 shows the main questions per block or topic area. It is the

Table 30.1 Layout of the Seveso questionnaire

1. Working details	* Name of corporation * Age * Years employed at corporation * Involvement of Seveso inspections * Presence of Seveso inspectors * Prior experience of Seveso inspectors
2. Perceived attitude of inspectors / Enforcement style as perceived	* Attitude of OSHA inspector (6 statements) * Attitude of environmental inspector (6 statements) * Statements on the perceived attitude of inspectors (6) * Attitude of Seveso inspectors (3 statements) * Attitude of OSHA inspector to enforcement actions > *comment field available* * Attitude of environmental inspector (enforcement actions) > *comment field available*
3. Rules and enforcement action	* Motivation for compliance (3 statements) * Deterrence (4 statements)
4. Compliance	* Ability and capacity to comply (3 statements) * Safety and legislation (3 statements) * Views on regulations (7 statements)
5. Impact of visit	* Impact of regulations (3 statements) * Effective use of regulations (4 statements) * Deterrence (5 statements)
6. Comments	Open question for any other concerns or suggestions > *comment field available*

Mascini and van Wijk questionnaire (2008; 2009a; 2009b) that has been taken as the template. Each question had several answer categories. In the following blocks (topics 2 to 5), respondents were asked to what extent they agree (ranging from strongly disagree to very much agree) with each statement on a 5-point Likert scale per subtopic. The 5-point Likert scale was similar to that of the Mascini and van Wijk (2009a) questionnaire. A total of 18 statements, which were not relevant to this industrial sector, were not asked. Two extra questions were asked that related to the perceived attitude of inspectors during the enforcement procedure and three additional statements had to do with the relationship between sanctioning and safety. All the topics in the questionnaire relate to several debates on corporations' responses to regulation (May and Winter 2000; Mendeloff and Gray 2005).

Response

The survey was administered online after the yearly Seveso inspections of 15 chemical corporations in the Netherlands had taken place. The inspections were also observed within the context of the broader study. Respondents were approached directly by means of a personalized email message relating to the relevant inspection. Forty-eight chemical corporation employees responded to the survey out of the 75 respondents that were approached. Two environmental advisors at two different corporations did not want me to directly contact their colleagues. One of them did, however, send my message to other employees within the same corporation. The environmental advisor at the other corporation did not pass on the request to other employees; although I did send him the complete questionnaire at his request in a different file so he could show it to his superior for approval. This means that in some cases just one respondent from a corporation filled in the questionnaire. Middle-management and site managers constituted two-thirds of the survey respondents (65 per cent). The other respondents were, for example, engineers, safety and health engineers or operators (33 per cent). One respondent did not provide information on his current position. Forty-eight per cent of the respondents were between 46 and 55 years of age. Twenty-one respondents (44 per cent) had worked for 21 years or longer at their corporation. Most of them had previous experience (four inspections or more) of Seveso inspections (65 per cent). This was sometimes experience of Seveso inspections in current jobs or in previous jobs as well. It was an indication that this particular group of employees has plentiful Seveso inspection experience. It is thus conceivable that such interdependence has bred strong ties between the regulator and the regulated (Braithwaite 1984; May and Wood 2003; McCaffrey et al. 2007). It is important to bear in mind that the respondents in this research are not lay people; most of them are technical experts familiar with assessing risk and safety on a daily basis. However, according to Slovic (1987: 281) experts appear to be prone to many of the same biases as the general public when it comes to matters of risk perception.

The views of the regulated

Perceptions concerning the presence of inspection agencies

In the questionnaire, multiple questions were asked to establish how chemical corporation employees perceived the attitudes and enforcement styles of inspectors. The questionnaire started by asking which inspectors, according to the respondents, were present during the inspection because not all inspection agencies were always present.

The perceived presence of inspection agencies does not correspond with the observations I made or with the inspection reports on inspections. Inspectors from the Environmental Protection Agency and the Fire Department were always present during the inspections I observed. The

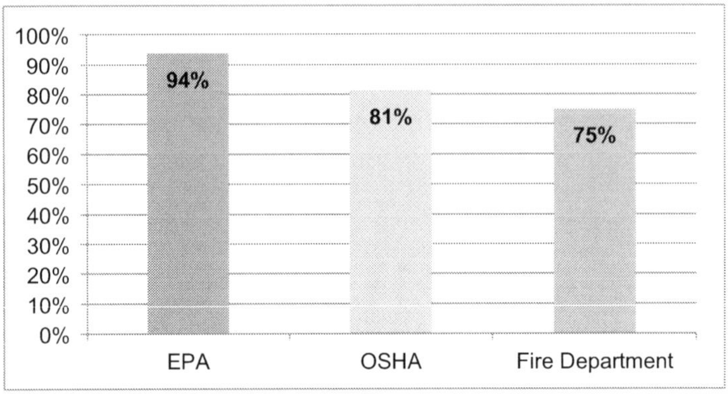

Figure 30.1 Presence of inspection agencies (*N* = 48)

results provided by the respondents are not therefore consistent with the actual presence of inspectors during these inspections. This could be explained by the fact that not all respondents were present throughout the entire inspection and at some times inspectors did split up into different teams. The questionnaire on 143 corporations in 2011 (LATrb 2012) showed that corporations perceived the same lower attendance of OSHA inspectors (78 per cent), but higher attendance in the case of Fire Department inspectors (97 per cent). A decrease is seen in the presence of OSHA inspectors if the results of the same questionnaire are compared with the 2007 (LATrb 2008) statistics. Of the 19 Seveso inspections I observed, Occupational Health and Safety Agency inspectors were not present on seven occasions. The organizational resources available to an inspection agency have an influence on enforcement practices (Hutter 1989). Availability and capacity in the case of occupational health and safety inspectors is what explains the non-attendance in the case of the above-mentioned seven inspections. This clearly reminds one of the statements made by Van der Heijden and De Jong (2009: 1040) to the effect that enforcement agencies have limited capacity, therefore it is not possible to monitor all corporation activities and some rule breaking is easier to detect than other bending of the rules. The resources available to an inspection agency determine how frequently any one inspector can visit corporations. When more frequent inspections are carried out, increased corporation perception of violation detection probability becomes apparent (Gray and Scholz 1991; May and Winter 2000; 2011).

Perceived attitude of inspectors

The questionnaire continued by asking the respondents: *According to you, how did the inspector behave during the last inspection?*

The response classifications used in this question can be traced to the different enforcement styles seen in various empirical research on law enforcement officials. The reason for posing the question here was to determine how the regulatees perceived the inspector's enforcement style (Bardach and Kagan 1982; Hawkins 1984; Hutter 1988; 1989; Mascini and van Wijk 2009a; 2009b; May and Burby 1998; May and Wood 2003; Reiss 1984; Shover et al. 1984). The first three statements (behaving like an advisor, being prepared to cooperate and to compromise) are operationalizations relating to the accommodative or compliance-oriented style whilst the last three propositions (acting like a police officer, being impersonal and unreasonable) relate to the deterrence or sanctioning style. Both the inspectors followed in this study were generally perceived more as advisors than as police officers. Further analysis of these statements revealed that an EPA

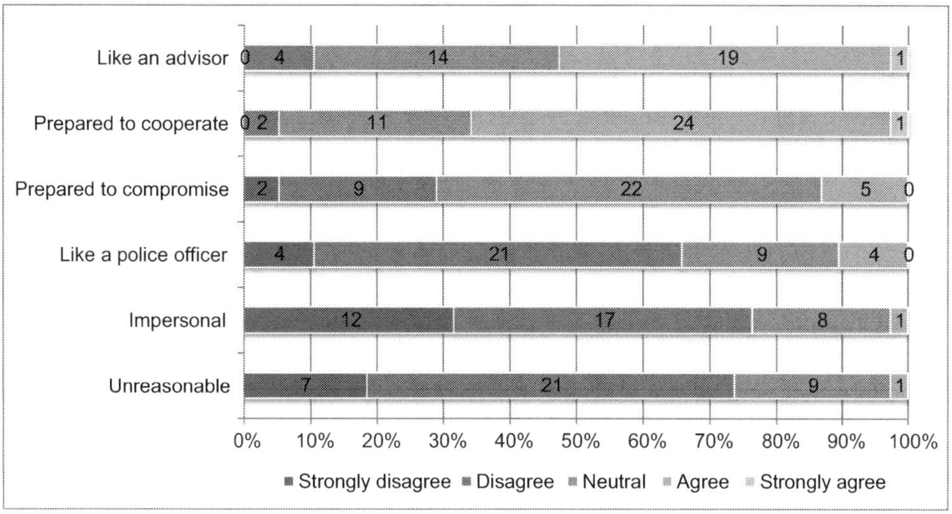

Figure 30.2 Attitude of Occupational Safety and Health Agency inspector (*N* = 38)

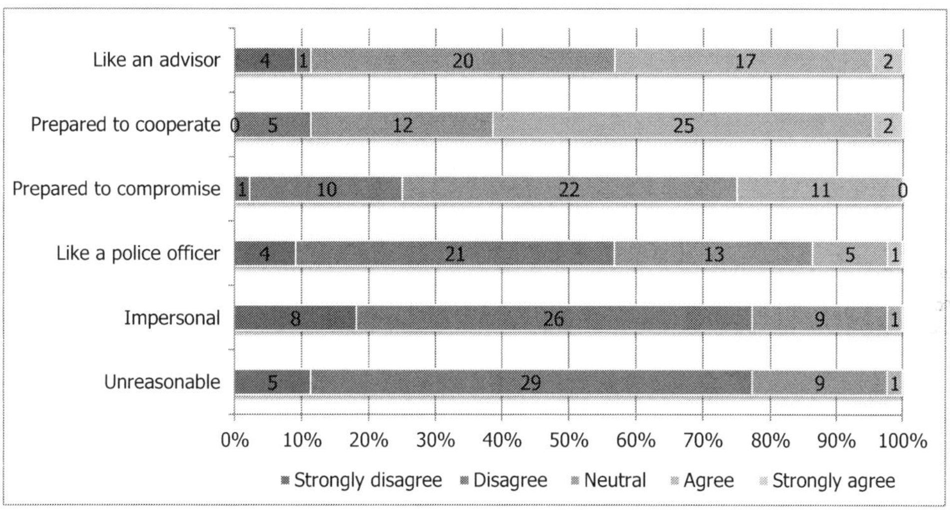

Figure 30.3 Attitude of Environmental Protection Agency inspector (*N* = 44)

inspector is significantly more prepared to compromise than an OSHA inspector (t (36) = 2.253, p = .030). The two-tailed test result showed that OSHA inspectors were even less prepared to compromise than EPA inspectors. This was an unexpected but important finding. Although the number of respondents was not high, it was a substantial result. All other categories showed no significant difference based on these data. Koolhaas's (1990) research on the same EPA inspection agency showed a different view of EPA inspectors. He concluded that they were more distant, had less of an advisory role and acted less as mediators. This contradicted the perception of the current respondents. One explanation could be that his research dates back nearly three decades and the enforcement style, policy and personnel management have changed since then. Most of the respondents were of the opinion that both inspectors were reasonable and personal (average of 75 per cent). The perceived attitude of inspectors in general is consistent with results derived from other research on field-level inspectors (Hawkins 1984; Hutter 1988; 1989; May and Winter 2000; May and Wood 2003; Pautz and Wamsley 2012) that can be categorized as fitting into the compliance oriented or accommodative approach. Securing compliance with this approach was sought through cooperative or more conciliatory means (Hawkins 1984; Hutter 1988; 1989; Pautz and Wamsley 2012). However, when necessary, a more deterring or sanctioning approach (Hawkins 1984) was adopted by inspectors as observed during the inspections. When presenting these results to inspectors at both inspection agencies, they did not deny the views of respondents concerning roles and enforcement styles.

Perceived enforcement style

Figure 30.4 shows that chemical corporation employees again mostly agreed that inspectors had an advisory role because they help corporations to rectify their mistakes (67 per cent). According to the respondents, Seveso inspectors also gave the impression that in working together with them, compliance could be ensured (57 per cent). Just one respondent agreed with the statement that 'he was treated as a crook'. A possible explanation for why this person tended to agree with this statement was because inspectors discovered a high number of violations during that particular inspection. Other respondents from the same corporation did not, however, agree with this statement. According to 67 per cent of the respondents, inspectors were willing to maintain dialogue. The overall view corresponds with the previous results and with the next question that was: *How did you judge Seveso inspectors during the inspection*? ($N = 45$). The majority (63 per cent) maintained that they tended to confer, the second category thought they were more inclined to consult (53 per cent) and only six respondents thought they were punitive (13 per cent). The work situations surrounding regulatory compliance are complex and a mixture of methods was used to achieve compliance. Regulators cannot simply be divided into 'hard' or 'soft' enforcement styles; both were used even within the same inspection session as observed during the inspections reported on here. This perception again returns in Figure 30.5 where the proposition *'Inspectors took the ideas on compliance seriously'* is presented. The majority of the respondents, 56 per cent, agreed with this statement and only 5 per cent disagreed with it.

Deterrence

The questionnaire continued by providing more insight into how chemical corporation employees perceive the sanctioning practice of the Seveso rules and regulations executed by the two different inspection agencies (EPA and OSHA). The majority (70 per cent) disagree with the proposition that the chance of getting caught is very small. This question was relevant in the context of crime deterrence. Deterrence assumes that the rule violator will stop himself from committing a crime because he assesses the risk of being caught and punished to be high. Perceptions surrounding the risk of being caught could also result from prior offending. On the other hand in this questionnaire, the perceived attitude to risk perception could also result from giving socially desirable answers.

The three remaining propositions relating to the sanctioning practice were answered mostly neutrally:

- OSHA has severe sanctions for violations (67 per cent neutral).
- EPA has severe sanctions for violations (58 per cent neutral).
- There is little time between enforcement action and the execution of punishment (56 per cent neutral).

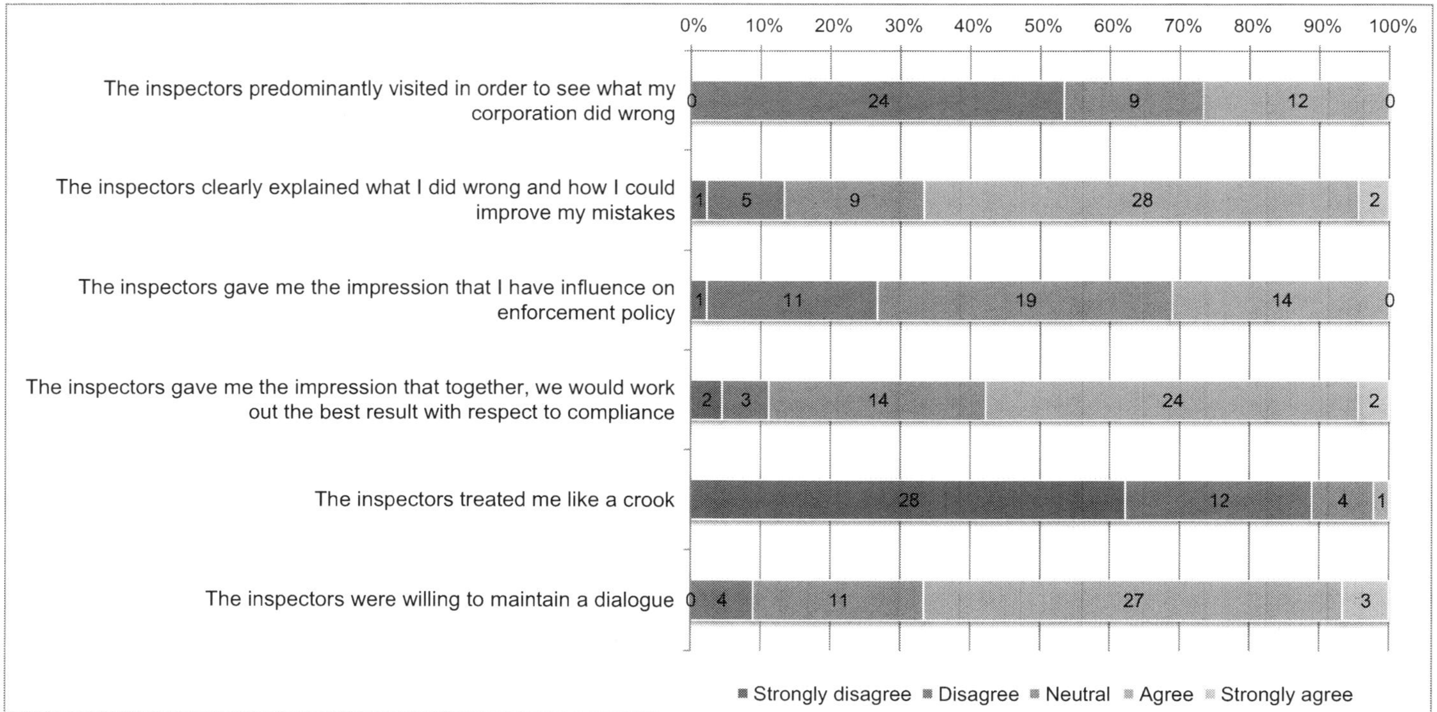

Figure 30.4 Enforcement style as perceived ($N = 45$)

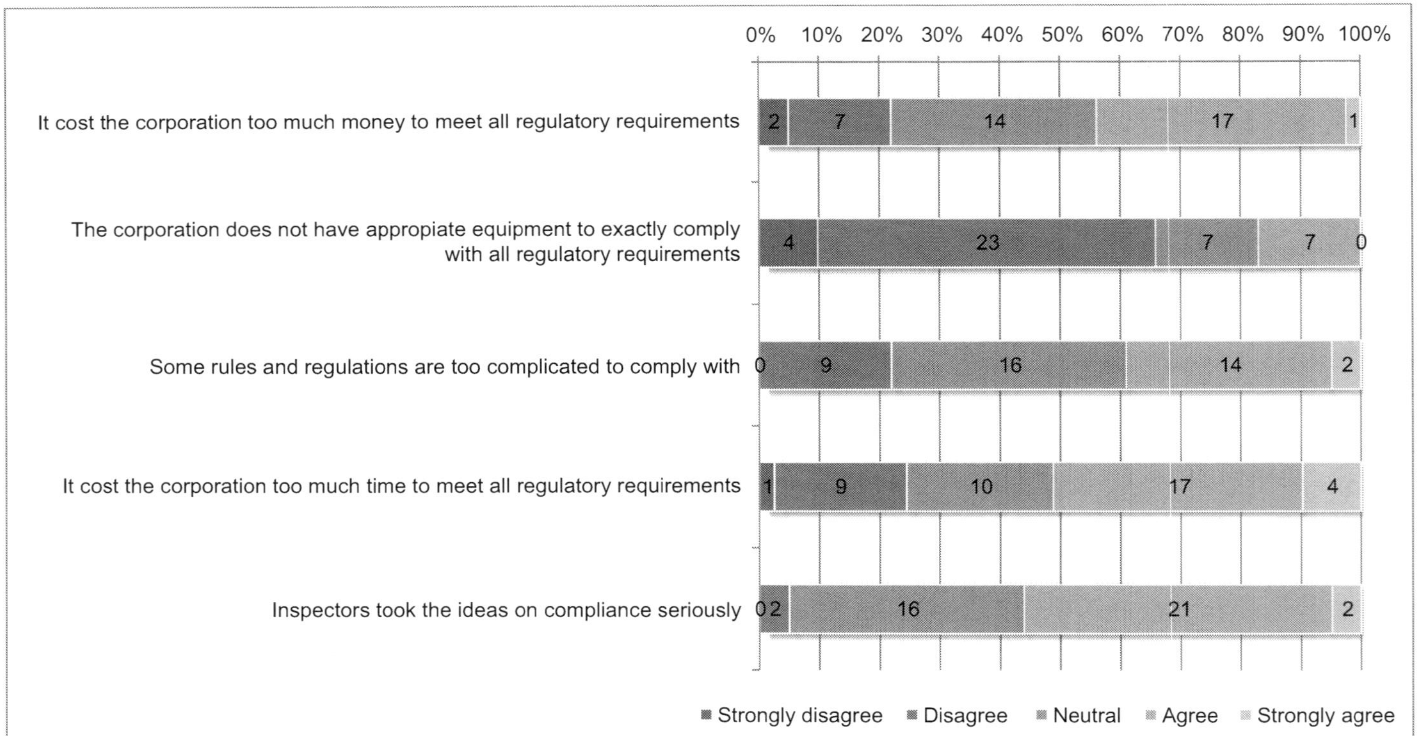

Figure 30.5 Ability and capability to comply ($N = 41$)

Another reason why the respondents answered these statements mostly neutrally could be because the propositions addressed in these issues were sensitive or too sensitive. The results of this questionnaire were in line with the perceptual deterrence studies because Simpson (2002) stresses: 'how subjective judgements of punishment risk and consequence influence the criminality of individuals (perceptual deterrence)' (p. 27).

Ability and capability to comply

The following propositions provided more insight into the extent to which corporations were able to meet all the requirements linked to Seveso rules and regulations.

Under Seveso rules and regulations corporations can be requested to change in order to meet regulatory requirements, for example they might be asked to implement a safety management system which could lead to high costs for the corporation since it would probably need to rearrange its internal procedures and the relevant work instructions. Forty-three per cent of the respondents agreed with the proposition that it cost the corporation too much money to meet all the requirements and only 23 per cent did not agree with this (see Figure 30.5). The cost of compliance is an important issue in regulatory compliance (Hutter 1989; Kagan 1989: 104) for many reasons. The temptation to display non-compliance behaviour is higher within corporations when regulations have to be endured that are expensive to implement if the regulatory demands are to be met (Leone 1986). Other aspects are the economic viability of the regulated corporation, economic resilience (Gunningham 1987) and what inspectors have to bear in mind in relation to extreme costs that could force a corporation to go bankrupt. Regulators often make cost–benefit analyses in these kinds of situations. They need to assess the economic situation of the corporation, the costs of stopping noncompliance operations and, of course, the seriousness of the risks involved. Some 51 per cent of the chemical corporation employees agreed that it takes the corporation too much time to comply. The equipment used in Seveso corporations varies from fire extinguishers, level indicators, sensors and pipes to internal and external procedures. When starting to work in or manage a chemical corporation one would expect the employers and employees to have the appropriate equipment to do their job. Recent experience of regulators within chemical corporations in the Netherlands (other than in the sample) turned out to be different. Van de Bunt (1992) determined that the rationality of corporations is limited and that many violations arise due to organizational failure. Corporations should not only want to comply, but they should need to be able to comply as well (Huisman 2001: 171). The majority of the respondents to the proposition *'The corporation does not have appropriate equipment to exactly comply with all regulatory requirements'* did not agree with this, only 17 per cent ($N = 7$) did. The ability and capacity to comply are motivations that were studied by May and Winter (May and Wood 2003; 2011; Nielsen and Parker 2009; Winter and May 2001). Not only appropriate equipment forms part of that, but also knowledge of the rules and that came into the following statement made in the questionnaire. Awareness of what regulation requires is also central to compliance. If the regulation in question is too complicated, too new or too vague, then precisely what is required may well be misunderstood. Thirty-nine per cent of the respondents agreed with the proposition that some rules and regulations are too complicated to comply with which is probably related to the fact that Seveso regulations stipulate the performance objectives and not the specific required actions. Hutter (1988: 42–43) surmised that this is a factor that reduces the probability of prosecution because such broad standards need to be interpreted and inspectors determine what may be defined as an offence (or discretion is used).

Attitude towards safety and regulations

Attitude towards safety has been found to be connected to risk perception as well as to risk behaviour (Rundmo 1997; 2000). This works the other way around as well since the cause–effects relationships are not clear either. Risk perception can be a causal behaviour factor in line with safety attitudes. Rundmo determined the following in his 2000 research conducted within a sample of 731 respondents in relation to the violations of rules: *'Acceptability of rule violations is seen as the most important predictor of behaviour, probably because acceptability also affected how often the respondents took chances and broke safety rules'* (p. 47). Now, we shall take a closer look at how the respondents in this research regarded safety and regulations. Some 61 per cent of the respondents did not agree with the first proposition regarding safety and regulatory compliance and 83 per cent agreed that legislation is important in the chemical industry if unsafe situations are to be prevented. This is in line with the opinion that 88 per cent of the respondents agreed that Seveso inspectors and their inspections are necessary if companies want to avoid unsafe situations. It also corresponded with the questionnaire distributed to 143 Dutch chemical corporations in 2011 where 63 per cent proved to be of the opinion that a Seveso inspection does have added value. Corporations indicated that the critical view of outside experts ensures that the corporations remain vigilant (LATrb 2012). However 64 per cent of the respondents involved in this questionnaire agreed with the proposition that they are pleased that Seveso inspectors do inspect once a year. May and Winter (2011: 226) stated that more inspections are likely to increase the risk that corporations will perceive their violations as being detected. These results reflect a positive attitude, but 26 per cent of the respondents agreed that there could be more freedom in dealing with all the requirements. In addition to this, if we combine the categories disagree and neutral then 61 per cent of the chemical corporation employees will at least doubt whether their corporation functions better when it complies with all the rules and regulations. Dutch chemical corporation employees were sometimes frustrated by the many rules and regulations they need to abide by, as observed during the inspections. Nevertheless, the majority of the respondents (71 per cent) agreed with the proposition that the rules they have to comply to are significant.

Impact of visits

The next statements relate to the results of inspections and visits made by inspectors. Respondents were asked a variety of propositions about the impact of the inspectors' visits. This was not only relevant in terms of deterrence, but also in relation to how they perceived the inspectors and the existing system of inspections, what kind of conclusions are drawn by the corporation afterwards and what kind of action they will take prior to future inspections.

As a result of the visit of the inspectors

Statements marked with > in Figure 30.7 relate to the unintended consequences of inspection (Mascini and van Wijk 2009a; 2009b). The results of this research cannot be interpreted in the same way as the research done by Mascini and van Wijk. This study involved fewer respondents and inspectors were not interviewed on the matter of the enforcement style of inspectors before the inspection. Most of the time the respondents answered the propositions marked with > negatively or neutrally. Since this study does not focus exclusively on compliance with occupational and environmental health regulations, statements relating to safety were also added. Several studies have shown that attitudes among employees predisposing them to accept rule violations is the strongest predictor of risk behaviour (Mearns et al. 2001; Rundmo and Hale 2003). This

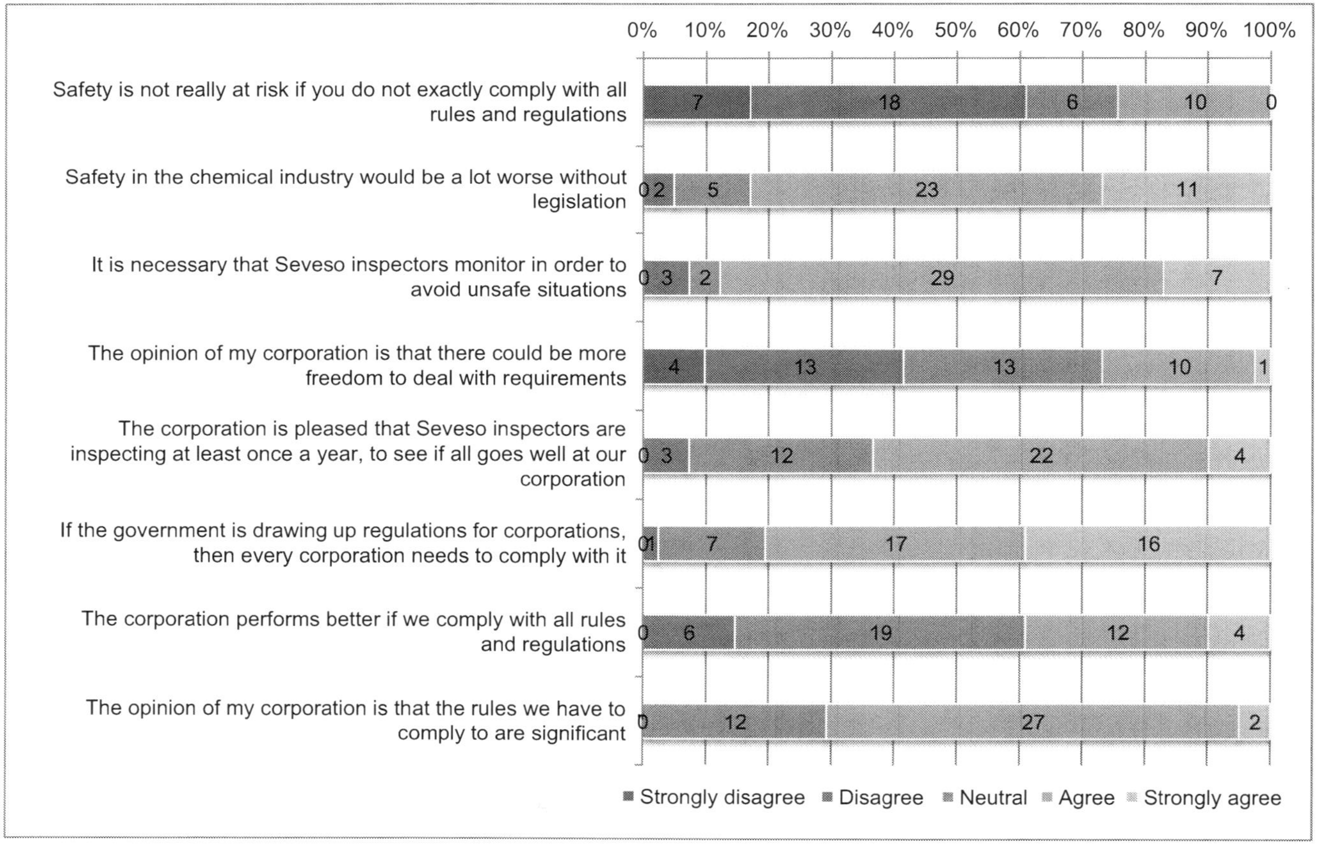

Figure 30.6 Perception of safety and regulations ($N = 41$)

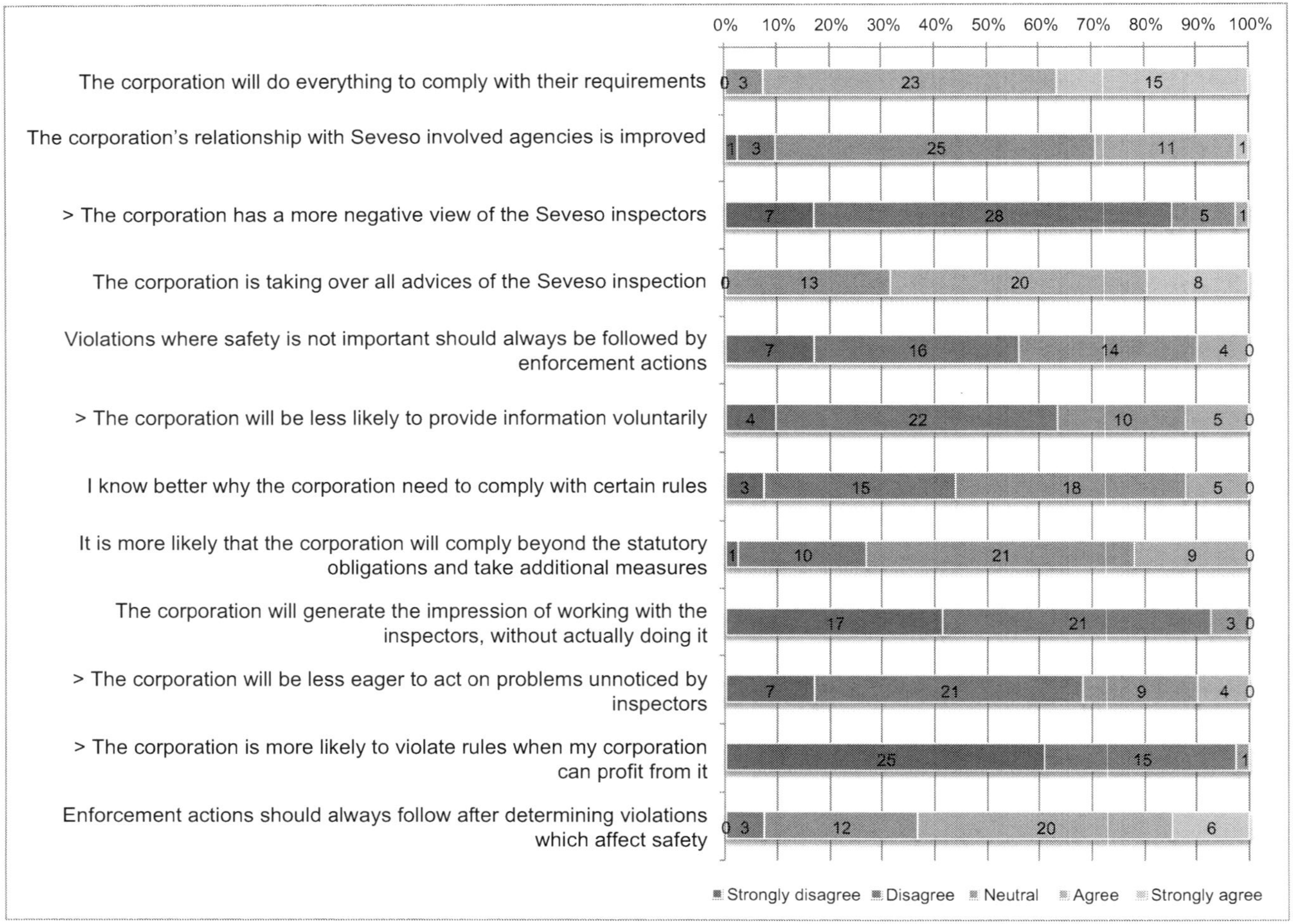

Figure 30.7 Impact of visits ($N = 41$)

questionnaire did not explicitly ask the respondents about their acceptance of violations, but it did ask if violations not related to safety are important enough for enforcement action to be taken. A small majority, 56 per cent, did not agree; only 10 per cent of the respondents agreed that violations not relating to safety should be enforced. The questionnaire also put this proposition the other way around. There 64 per cent of the respondents agreed or strongly agreed that when violations relate to safety, enforcement action should be taken. Only 7 per cent of the respondents disagreed maintaining that all safety-related violations should be enforced. Chemical corporation employees are concerned about enforcement activities, especially when the violation relates to safety. Only 64 per cent of the respondents agreed with the statement mentioned earlier to the effect that enforcement actions should always follow the determining of violations which affect safety. If they had given socially acceptable answers then the percentage of respondents agreeing with the statement would probably have been higher. The results relating to two other propositions are worth mentioning here since they are indications of noncompliance. Twelve per cent of the respondents agreed with the statement that as a result of the visit of the inspectors they would be less likely to provide information voluntarily and 10 per cent of the chemical corporation employees agreed that they will be less eager to deal with problems that go unnoticed by the inspectors. The Seveso inspections gave rise to more negative views on compliance among these respondents and possibly created a negative mindset or created opportunities for breaking the rules. Of course the statement that the corporation is more likely to violate rules when it can profit from this, is important as well in this context. In this case 98 per cent of the respondents disagreed with this statement but, as mentioned before, socially acceptable response could be of influence here.

Attitude of inspectors during sanctioning

Mascini and van Wijk (2009b) ascertained that inspectors behave inconsistently. This research did not interview inspectors on the topic of their enforcement styles before inspections. Instead the questionnaire asked the respondents how inspectors behaved during the enforcement follow-up or sanctioning and whether this was different or the same as during the inspection. The questionnaire asked the following question: *According to you, how did the occupational health and safety inspector behave during the enforcement follow-up?* Here 58 per cent thought that the OSHA inspector behaved the same as during the inspection. However, 42 per cent were of the opinion that it was different. Half of the respondents who answered the explanation said that they did not have any experience with enforcement actions, since the OSHA inspector did not impose sanctions. Examples of explanations were: suspicious at first, more compromising, very strict with no room for manoeuvre and very formal. Of course the questionnaire asked the respondent: *According to you, how did the environmental inspector behave during the enforcement follow-up?* Of the respondents 72 per cent thought that the environmental inspector behaved the same as during the inspection whereas 29 per cent were of the opinion that the behaviour was different. Half of the respondents said that they did not have any experience with enforcement actions, since the environmental inspector did not demand sanctioning. Some examples of the explanations given are these: more compromising, more consulting and more understanding. We note here that the comments concerning OSHA enforcement practice are substantially more numerous and have a more negative slant than the opinions concerning EPA enforcement practice. One explanation for the difference in behaviour could be that the sanctioning part was handled by a different inspector. That is not really a very wise strategy. Furthermore, a new inspector does not have thorough knowledge of what happened during the actual inspection when violations were detected. Another explanation for the difference in behaviour could be that EPA inspectors are perceived to be more compromising than OSHA inspectors during inspections. It is possible that during enforcement EPA inspectors are stricter and that OSHA inspectors have an approach that is more consistent with the inspection period. The results of this questionnaire do not provide a definitive answer to this question.

Discussion and conclusion

This chapter aims to provide insight into the perception that chemical corporation employees have of Seveso regulations and inspections. Both organizational resources and organizational contexts have an influence on inspection agencies (Hutter 1989; Mascini and van Wijk 2009b; May and Wood 2003). The presence of inspectors as perceived by chemical corporation employees revealed that Occupational Safety and Health Agency and Fire Department inspectors were less commonly seen than EPA inspectors. As argued in this chapter, these results were not in line with the observations I made or with the inspection reports of those inspections, but the respondents noted a different result. One important aspect of the actual inspection days is deterrence which relates to the probability of violation detection. The visible presence of inspectors assessing installations in great detail showed enforcement in action to the chemical corporation employees concerned. When frequent inspection and enforcement action is absent, corporations still invest in improvements or even go beyond compliance as can sometimes be seen during observations and in other empirical research as well (Braithwaite 1989: 349; Gibbs 2012; Kagan et al. 2011: 41).

The questionnaire asked respondents in various ways how inspectors behaved during the most recent inspection. OSHA and EPA inspectors are generally perceived more as advisors than as police officers. Further analysis of these statements revealed that an EPA inspector is significantly more prepared to compromise than an OSHA inspector. The perceived attitude and enforcement style of Fire Department inspectors was not examined in this questionnaire. Koolhaas's research (1990) on the same EPA inspection agency showed a different perception of EPA inspectors. Inspectors' attitudes and enforcement styles do change over time as can be seen in other research as well (for example: Lo et al. 2009) since this could be affected by enforcement strategy and policy changes and probably by other influences as well. Respondents to this questionnaire tended to agree with the proposition that inspectors have an advisory role and serve to inform corporations on how to rectify their mistakes. As in many studies on deterrence, the questionnaire did not explicitly investigate deterrence itself. Instead the more general focus was on compliance and the regulatory measures of inspection agencies. The questionnaire did ask how chemical corporation employees perceive sanctioning practice. The majority disagreed with the proposition that the chance of getting caught is very small. Since an inspection schedule with inspection topics is sent beforehand and the inspections are announced I doubt that the chance of violation detection is really that small. Unfortunately the results of this questionnaire did not deliver more insight into this matter because the other statements on the same topic were answered mostly neutrally, although 25 per cent of the respondents agreed with the statement that the EPA has severe sanctions for violations which was slightly higher than their opinions concerning OSHA sanctions (19 per cent).

Corporations should not only want to comply, but they need to be able to as well (Huisman 2001: 171). The ability and capability to comply are reasons for regulatory compliance (May and Winter 2011; Nielsen and Parker 2009; Winter and May 2001) as well and were also subjects integrated into this questionnaire. Cost of compliance is a significant topic for regulators and regulatees as this questionnaire proved since 43 per cent of the respondents agreed that the costs of compliance are too high. Regulators assess costs as well in the context of the reasonable and acceptable risk surrounding the investments that a corporation needs to take to comply. Knowledge of the rules and regulations is something that is vital to regulatory compliance and apparently 4 out of 10 Dutch chemical corporation employees find that the Seveso rules and regulations are too complicated (39 per cent). This is a remarkable result from the point of view that these corporations need to comply with the rules for a long periods of time and the respondents had been working at these Seveso corporations for 21 years or even longer. In addition to this, in the Netherlands Seveso corporations are considered to be the corporations with the highest risk potential. They work with dangerous substances on a daily basis and should be familiar with these standards.

What is important to bear in mind is the fact that an acceptance of rule violations seems to be the most important predictor of behaviour, probably because acceptability also affects how often the respondents take chances and break safety rules (Rundmo 2000). The questionnaire showed that the majority of the respondents agreed with the statements to the effect that legislation is important in the chemical industry if unsafe situations (83 per cent) are to be prevented and that Seveso inspectors and their inspections are necessary if unsafe situations (88 per cent) are to be avoided. The questionnaire did not explicitly ask the respondents about their acceptance of violations, but did ask whether when violations relate to safety, enforcement action should be taken and 64 per cent agreed with this statement. On the other hand, 26 per cent of the respondents agreed that there could be more freedom in dealing with all the requirements. In addition to this, if we combine disagree and neutral, at least 61 per cent of the chemical corporation employees doubt whether their corporation functions better if it complies with all the rules and regulations. Future research should ideally focus on the acceptability of rule violations in the chemical industry since that may help to advance theoretical discussions on the relationship between incidents and compliance.

The enforcement styles of inspectors during the sanctioning part of the Seveso inspections differed from inspectors' attitudes during the inspections, according to the respondents. Forty-two per cent of the respondents stated that the OSHA inspector behaved differently during the enforcement follow-up, but half of them noted that they did not have any experience of enforcement. A lower percentage perceived a difference in the enforcement style of the EPA inspector (29 per cent). Explanations for the difference in experience could be attributable to another inspector having handled the sanctioning part and it was furthermore so that EPA inspectors were perceived to be more compromising during the inspections. The perceived attitude of inspectors in general is consistent with results derived from other research conducted on street-level bureaucrats (Hawkins 1984; Hutter 1988; 1989; May and Winter 2000; May and Wood 2003; Pautz and Wamsley 2012; Winter and May 2001) which can be categorized as fitting into the compliance-oriented or accommodative approach. When necessary a more deterrent-oriented or sanctioning approach was used by inspectors as was observed during the inspections. Future research should focus on the motivation underlying non-compliance behaviour within corporations since this questionnaire did not provide more insight into the matter and the theoretical value is high.

The results of the questionnaire indicate that respondents believe that they can influence the monitoring and regulatory compliance of Seveso rules and regulations. The trend analysis of all registered violations of occupational health and safety and environmental regulations during the 1999 to 2011 period for each chemical corporation showed a different picture. Rule violations increased, decreased and fluctuated between 1999 and 2011. In addition to this, all registered violations showed huge differences between corporations in terms of the number of violations as well as the enforcement actions (Kluin 2013; Kluin and Jagtman 2014). The responses of certain respondents to two propositions relating to the impact of the visits made by the inspectors showed that the inspections resulted in more negative views on compliance. More research is imperative if we are to understand to what degree indications of non-compliance behaviour influence the decision-making processes of chemical corporation employees and encourage them to violate rules. Learning more about the day-to-day perceptions of employees at corporations may provide more insight into the 'flip-side' of traditional regulatory studies. We learned from the results emanating from this study that the perceptions that chemical corporation employees have of Seveso inspections and its rules and regulations go much further than simply being positive or negative and are much more complex.

Acknowledgements

I am grateful to all the respondents who took the time to complete the questionnaire and provide additional feedback. I thank Ben Ale, Wim Huisman and Ellen Jagtman for their valuable comments on a previous version of this chapter.

Note

1 The participant observations were carried out between November 2009 and December 2012. Multiple Seveso inspections were observed in three chemical corporations. A follow-up inspection was observed at one corporation. All other chemical corporations (12 in total) were observed once during their annual Seveso inspections.

References

Ale, B.J.M. (2002) 'Risk assessment practices in the Netherlands', *Safety Science*, 40: 105–126.
Ale, B.J.M. (2005) 'Tolerable or acceptable: A comparison of risk regulation in the United Kingdom and in the Netherlands', *Risk Analysis*, 25: 231–241.
Ale, B.J.M. (2009) *Risk: An Introduction – The Concepts of Risk, Danger and Change*, London/New York: Routledge.
Bardach, E. and Kagan, R.A. (1982) *Going by the Book: The Problem of Regulatory Unreasonableness*, Philadelphia: Temple University Press.
Beccaria, C. (1764 (1982)) *On Crimes and Punishments* [Over misdaad en straffen. Ingeleid, van aantekeningen voorzien en vertaald door J.M. Michiels], Antwerpen/Zwolle: Kluwer/Tjeenk Willink.
Becker, G.S. (1968) 'Crime and punishment: An economic approach', *Journal of Political Economy*, 76(2): 169–217.
Bottelberghs, P.H. (2000) 'Risk analysis and safety policy developments in the Netherlands', *Journal of Hazardous Materials*, 71: 59–84.
Braithwaite, J. (1984) *Corporate Crime in the Pharmaceutical Industry*, London: Routledge and Kegan Paul.
Braithwaite, J. (1989) 'Criminological theory and organizational crime', *Justice Quarterly*, 6: 333–358.
Braithwaite, J. and Makkai, T. (1991) 'Testing an Expected Utility Model of Corporate Deterrence', *Law & Society Review*, 25: 7–40.
Braithwaite, J., Walker, J. and Grabosky, P. (1987) 'An enforcement taxonomy of regulatory agencies', *Law & Policy*, 9: 323–351.
Bunt, H.G. van de (1992) *Organisatiecriminaliteit*, Arnhem: Gouda Quint.
Burby, R.J. and Paterson, R.G. (1993) 'Improving compliance with state environmental regulations', *Journal of Policy Analysis and Management*, 12: 753–772.
COVO (1990) *Report on the COVO Study to the Rijnmond Authority*, Reidel.
Cox, S. and Flin, R. (1998) 'Safety culture: Philosopher's stone or man of straw?', *Work & Stress*, 12(3): 189–201.
DHV (2002) *Internationale Vergelijking EV Beleid* (No. S0772–69.002), Den Haag: Ministerie van Economische Zaken.
Ehrlich, I. (1972) 'The deterrent effect of criminal law enforcement', *The Journal of Legal Studies*, 1: 259–276.
Etienne, J. (2013) 'Ambiguity and relational signals in regulator–regulatee relationships', *Regulation & Governance*, 7: 30–47.

Gibbs, C. (2012) 'Corporate citizenship and corporate environmental performance', *Crime, Law and Social Change*, 57: 345–372.
Gormley, W.T. (1998) 'Regulatory enforcement styles', *Political Research Quarterly*, 51(2): 363–383.
Grasmick, H.G. and Bursik Jr, R.J. (1990) 'Conscience, significant others, and rational choice: Extending the deterrence model', *Law and Society Review*, 24: 837–861.
Gray, W.B. and Scholz, J.T. (1991) 'Analyzing the equity and efficiency of OSHA Enforcement', *Law & Policy*, 13(3): 185–214.
Gray, W.B. and Scholz, J.T. (1993) 'Does regulatory enforcement work?: A panel analysis of OSHA enforcement', *Law & Society Review*, 27(1): 177–213.
Gray, W.B. and Shadbegian, R.J. (2005) 'When and why do plants comply? Paper mills in the 1980s', *Law & Policy*, 27(2): 238–261.
Gunningham, N. (1987) Negotiated non-compliance: A case study of regulatory failure', *Law & Policy*, 9(1): 69–95.
Gunningham, N. (2011) 'Strategizing compliance and enforcement: Responsive regulation and beyond', in C. Parker and V.L. Nielsen (eds) *Explaining Compliance: Business Responses to Regulation*, Cheltenham/Northampton: Edward Elgar Publishing, pp. 199–221.
Hawkins, K. (1984) *Environment and Enforcement: Regulation and the Social Definition of Pollution*, Oxford: Clarendon Press.
Heijden, J. van der and Jong, J. de (2009) 'Towards a better understanding of building regulation', *Environment and Planning*, 36(6): 1038–1052.
Huisman, W. (2001) *Tussen winst en moraal: Achtergronden van regelnaleving en regelovertreding door ondernemingen*, The Hague: Boom Juridische uitgevers.
Hutter, B.M. (1988) *The Reasonable Arm of the Law*, Oxford/New York: Clarendon Press.
Hutter, B.M. (1989) 'Variations in regulatory enforcement styles', *Law & Policy*, 11(2): 153–174.
Jongejan, R., Ale, B. and Vrijling, J. (2006) 'FN-criteria for risk regulation and probabilistic design.' Paper presented at the 8th International Conference on Probabilistic Safety Assessment and Management (PSAM-0275), New Orleans, May.
Kagan, R.A. (1989) 'Editor's introduction: Understanding regulatory enforcement', *Law & Policy*, 11(2): 89–119.
Kagan, R.A., Gunningham, N. and Thornton, D. (2011) 'Fear, duty, and regulatory compliance: Lessons from three research projects', in C. Parker and V.L. Nielsen (eds) *Explaining Compliance: Business Responses to Regulation*, Cheltenham/Northampton: Edward Elgar Publishing, pp. 37–58.
Kluin, M.H.A. (2013) 'Environmental regulation in chemical corporations: Preliminary results of a case study research', in R. Walters, D. Westerhuis and T. Wyatt (eds) *Emerging Issues in Green Criminology: Exploring Power, Justice and Harm*, Houndmills: Palgrave Macmillan.
Kluin, M.H.A. and Jagtman, H.M. (2014) 'A decade of violations of the Dutch chemical industry', in M.H.A. Kluin, T. Spapens and R. White (eds) *Environmental Crime and its Victims*, Farnham: Ashgate.
Koolhaas, E. (1990) 'Milieu, handhavingsstrategieën en beleid', *Justitiële Verkenningen*, 16(3): 92–109.
LATrb (2008) *Resultaten BTO BelanghebbendenTevredenheidsOnderzoek inspectiejaar 2007*: LAT Risicobeheersing bedrijven. Retrieved from: http://www.latrb.nl/lat/publicaties/ (accessed 1 September 2013).
LATrb (2012) *Resultaten BTO BelanghebbendenTevredenheidsOnderzoek BRZO inspectiejaar 2011*: Lat Risicobeheersing bedrijven. Retrieved from: http://www.latrb.nl/lat/publicaties/ (accessed 1 September 2013).
Leone, R.A. (1986) *Who Profits: Winners, Losers, and Government Regulation*, New York: Basic Books.
Lipsky, M. (2010) *Street-level Bureaucracy*, New York: Russell Sage Foundation.
Lo, C.W.-H., Fryxell, G.E. and Van Rooij, B. (2009) 'Changes in enforcement styles among environmental enforcement officials in China', *Environment and Planning*, A, 41(11), 2706.
Mascini, P. and Wijk, E. van (2008) 'Vis ruikt nou eenmaal zo: Responsive regulation door de Voedsel en Waren Autoriteit', *Tijdschrift voor Criminologie*, 50(2): 114–129.
Mascini, P. and Wijk, E. van (2009a) *Responsive regulation bij de Voedsel en Waren Autoriteit*, The Hague: Boom Juridische uitgevers.
Mascini, P. and Wijk, E. van (2009b) 'Responsive regulation at the Dutch Food and Consumer Product Safety Authority: An empirical assessment of assumptions underlying the theory', *Regulation & Governance*, 3(1): 27–47.
May, P.J. and Burby, R. (1998) 'Making sense out of regulatory enforcement', *Law & Policy*, 20(2): 157–182.
May, P.J. and Winter, S.C. (1999) 'Regulatory enforcement and compliance: Examining Danish agro-environmental policy', *Journal of Policy Analysis and Management*, 18(4): 625–651.
May, P.J. and Winter, S.C. (2000) 'Reconsidering styles of regulatory enforcement: Patterns in Danish agro-environmental inspection', *Law & Policy*, 22(2): 143–173.

May, P.J. and Winter, S.C. (2011) 'Regulatory enforcement styles and compliance', in C. Parker and V.L. Nielsen (eds) *Explaining Regulatory Compliance: Business Responses to Regulation*, Cheltenham/Northampton: Edward Elgar Publishing, pp. 222–244.
May, P.J. and Wood, R.S. (2003) 'At the regulatory front lines: Inspectors' enforcement styles and regulatory compliance', *Journal of Public Administration Research and Theory*, 13(2): 117–139.
McCaffrey, D.P., Smith, A.E. and Martinez-Moyano, I.J. (2007) '"Then let's have a dialogue": Interdependence and negotiation in a cohesive regulatory system', *Journal of Public Administration Research and Theory*, 17(2): 307–334.
Mearns, K. and Flin, R. (1995) 'Risk perception and attitudes to safety by personnel in the offshore oil and gas industry: A review', *Journal of Loss Prevention in the Process Industries*, 8(5): 299–305.
Mearns, K., Flin, R., Gordon, R. and Fleming, M. (2001) 'Human and organizational factors in offshore safety', *Work & Stress*, 15(2): 144–160.
Mendeloff, J. and Gray, W.B. (2005) 'Inside the black box: How do OSHA inspections lead to reductions in workplace injuries?', *Law & Policy*, 27(2): 219–237.
Nagin, D.S. and Paternoster, R. (1993) 'Enduring individual differences and rational choice theories of crime', *Law & Society Review*, 27(3): 467–496.
Nielsen, V.L. (2006) 'Are regulators responsive?', *Law & Policy*, 28(3): 395–416.
Nielsen, V.L. and Parker, C. (2009) 'Testing responsive regulation in regulatory enforcement', *Regulation & Governance*, 3(4): 376–399.
Nielsen, V.L. and Parker, C. (2012) 'Mixed motives: Economic, social, and normative motivations in business compliance', *Law & Policy*, 34(4): 428–462.
Parker, C. and Nielsen, V.L. (2011) *Explaining Regulatory Compliance: Business Responses to Regulation*, Cheltenham/Northampton: Edward Elgar Publishing.
Paternoster, R. (1987) 'The deterrent effect of the perceived certainty and severity of punishment: A review of the evidence and issues', *Justice Quarterly*, 4(2): 173–217.
Paternoster, R. (2010) 'How much do we really know about criminal deterrence?', *Journal of Criminal Law & Criminology*, 100: 765.
Paternoster, R. and Simpson, S. (1996) 'Sanction threats and appeals to morality: Testing a rational choice model of corporate crime', *Law & Society Review*, 30(3): 549–583.
Pautz, M.C. (2009a) 'Trust between regulators and the regulated: A case study of environmental inspectors and facility personnel in Virginia', *Politics & Policy*, 37(5): 1047–1072.
Pautz, M.C. (2009b) 'Perceptions of the regulated community in environmental policy: The view from below', *Review of Policy Research*, 26(5): 533–550.
Pautz, M.C. (2010) 'Front-line regulators and their approach to environmental regulation in Southwest Ohio', *Review of Policy Research*, 27(6): 761–780.
Pautz, M.C. and Wamsley, C.S. (2012) 'Pursuing trust in environmental regulatory interactions: The significance of inspectors' interactions with the regulated community', *Administration & Society*, 44(7): 853–884.
Pearce, F. and Tombs, S. (1998) *Toxic Capitalism: Corporate Crime and the Chemical Industry*, Dartmouth: Ashgate.
Piers, M.A. and Ale, B.J.M. (2000) *Policy options for managing societal risk around Schiphol*, NLR-CR-2000-084/RIVM 610066011, 24 February 2000.
Porter, S. and Wettig, J. (1999) 'Policy issues on the control of major accident hazards and the new Seveso II directive', *Journal of Hazardous Materials*, 65: 1–14.
Reiss, A.J. (1984) 'Selecting strategies of social control over organizational life', in K. Hawkins and J.M. Thomas (eds) *Enforcing Regulation*, Boston: Kluwer-Nijhoff, pp. 23–35.
Rooij, B. van (2006) *Regulating Land and Pollution in China: Lawmaking, Compliance, and Enforcement: Theory and Cases*, Amsterdam: Amsterdam University Press.
Rundmo, T. (1997) 'Associations between risk perception and safety', *Safety Science*, 24(3): 197–209.
Rundmo, T. (2000) 'Safety climate, attitudes and risk perception in Norsk Hydro', *Safety Science*, 34: 47–59.
Rundmo, T. and Hale, A.R. (2003) 'Managers' attitudes towards safety and accident prevention', *Safety Science*, 41(7): 557–574.
Shover, N., Lynxwiler, J., Groce, S. and Clelland, D. (1984) 'Regional variation in regulatory law enforcement: The surface mining control and reclamation act of 1977', in K. Hawkins and J.M. Thomas (eds) *Enforcing Regulation*, Boston: Kluwer–Nijhoff Publishing, pp. 121–145.
Simpson, S.S. (2002) *Corporate Crime, Law, and Social Control*, Cambridge: Cambridge University Press.
Simpson, S.S., Garner, J. and Gibbs, C. (2007) *Why do Corporations Obey Environmental Law? Assessing Punitive and Cooperative Strategies of Corporate Crime Control*, Washington: U.S. Department of Justice.
Simpson, S.S. and Koper, C.S. (1992) 'Deterring corporate crime', *Criminology*, 30(3): 347–376.

Simpson, S.S. and Rorie, M. (2011) 'Motivating compliance: Economic and material motives for compliance', in C. Parker and V.L. Nielsen (eds) *Explaining Compliance: Business Responses to Regulation*, Cheltenham/Northampton: Edward Elgar Publishing, pp. 59–77.

Simpson, S. and Schell, N. (2009) 'Persistent heterogeneity or state dependence? An analysis of occupational safety and health act violations', in S. Simpson and D. Weisburd (eds) *The Criminology of White-collar Crime*, New York: Springer, pp. 63–78.

Simpson, S.S., Smith, N.C. and Huang, C.-Y. (2007) 'Why managers fail to do the right thing: An empirical study of unethical and illegal conduct', *Business Ethics Quarterly*, 17: 633–667.

Slovic, P. (1987) 'Perception of risk', *Science*, 236(4799): 280–285.

Tyler, T.R. (2006) *Why People Obey the Law*, Princeton: Princeton University Press.

Van Wingerde, C.G. (2012) De afschrikking voorbij. Beyond deterrence. (Dissertation). Nijmegen: Wolf Legal Publishers.

Vaughan, D. (1996) *The Challenger Launch Decision*, Chicago: University of Chicago Press.

Vaughan, D. (1999) 'The dark side of organizations: Mistake, misconduct, and disaster', *Annual Review of Sociology*, 25: 271–305.

Vaughan, D. (2004) 'Theorizing disaster: Analogy, historical ethnography, and the Challenger accident', *Ethnography*, 5(3): 315–347.

Vaughan, D. (2011) 'Theorizing the dark side', *Organizational Studies* (Special issue on The Dark Side of Organizations).

Versluis, E. (2003) *Enforcement Matters: Enforcement and Compliance of European Directives in Four Member States*, Delft: Uitgeverij Eburon.

Winter, S.C. and May, P.J. (2001) 'Motivation for compliance with environmental regulations', *Journal of Policy Analysis and Management*, 20(4): 675–698.

Zohar, D. (1980) 'Safety climate in industrial organizations: theoretical and applied implications', *Journal of Applied Psychology*, 65(1): 96–102.

31

How does law enforcement respond to entrepreneurial white-collar crime?

Some insights from Portugal

José N. Cruz, Rita Faria, André Lamas Leite and Pedro Sousa

Introduction

In November 2007, one of the Portuguese police forces (*Polícia Judiciária* (PJ)) put into action operation *Império das Sucatas* (Scrap-Iron Empire) and, in November 2008, authorities were able to recover 105 million euros from corporations of the scrap-iron sector that were convicted via this operation. Fifty-six persons were formally accused of money laundering and tax fraud. In fact, for more than a decade, the large, medium-sized and small corporations of this sector had jointly built a complex crime scheme that combined true and forged economic activities and involved a large number of entrepreneurs in order to lower their payments of income corporation tax and with the aim of obtaining VAT tax credits from the state for transactions with other EU countries. The innovation of this scheme resided in the establishment of three circuits of movements (commercial, documental and financial): in concomitance with licit transactions, many forged operations and forged commercial documentation were set up with enough accuracy to ensure that every forged document would have the corresponding payment registered in bank accounts[1] (accounting expertise was a crucial competence involved in this fraud). The opportunity element lay in the fact that enterprises and individuals that sold scrap-iron to small scrap dealers were not required to register these sales. Then the organized network of intermediate and large scrap dealers could make advantageous agreements with small ones (not part of the network) for launching a false documental circuit. What should be noted in this case is the care, precision and competence with which these crimes were set up. Only when a team of specialists in various areas tackled this problem using the most sophisticated means was it possible to prove the criminal nature of the behaviour.

Innovation, recognizing opportunities and risk taking are prominent features not only of entrepreneurship, but also of many types of white-collar crime (WCC). The perception of a parallelism between entrepreneurship and WCC led us to think that it would be interesting to understand how law enforcement responds to entrepreneurial WCC. Therefore, the scope of this study was to analyse whether the criminal justice system (CJS) is able to deal with offences committed by powerful people with special skills, training and expertise.

In the first section of this chapter, the similarities between entrepreneurship and WCC, and the potential difficulties of the CJS in dealing with it, are discussed. Some examples from Portugal are presented. In section two, some current hermeneutical legal difficulties are provided, especially concerning the rigid nature of penal law principles. In section three, official data on the reaction of the Portuguese CJS to WCC and the results of interviews with eight CJS key actors are provided. The interviews sought to identify the persisting difficulties that limit the effectiveness of the Portuguese CJS, as well as to determine whether some improvements should be introduced into the CJS to respond to the entrepreneurial attitude of WCC offenders. Finally, some conclusions are highlighted. Overall, this empirical research underscored the major difficulties of the Portuguese CJS when dealing with the entrepreneurial talent of WCC offenders.

White-collar crime and entrepreneurship

According to Friedrichs (2010), the concept of WCC has been the object of much discussion, and there are several competing definitions in the literature, almost all of which have in common the fact that they associate this phenomenon to occupation, profession or owning a business. For example, Edelhertz (1970, cited in Geis 1991: 16) practically established a direct link between WCC and entrepreneurship when he defined WCC as:

> '[a]n illegal act or series of illegal acts committed by nonphysical means and by concealment or guile, to obtain money or property, to avoid the payment or loss of money or property, or to obtain business or personal advantage'.

This author divided WCC into four categories, to include diverse forms of WCC, two of which are highly related to entrepreneurship:

> (3) crimes incidental to and in furtherance of business operations, but not the central purpose of such business operations; and (4) white-collar crime as a business, or as the central activity of the business.
>
> *(Edelhertz 1970, cited in Geis 1991: 16)*

However, many sociologists criticized this definition, rejecting the expansion of the term WCC to such variety of behaviours. Finally, in 1996, a group of criminologists who met specifically to establish the definition of WCC proposed the following:

> White collar crimes are illegal and unethical acts that violate fiduciary responsibility of public trust committed by an individual or organization, usually during the course of legitimate occupational activity, by person of high or respectable social status for personal or organizational gain.
>
> *(Helmkamp et al. 1996: 351, cited in Friedrichs 2010: 6)*[2]

This definition does not exclude entrepreneurial behaviour. In fact, the link between WCC and professional status is an important element. In addition, Benson and Simpson (2009) enhance two additional elements involved in WCC: *opportunity* and *risk taking*.

In this study, we argue that one can find some parallelism between these elements of WCC and entrepreneurship. However, it should be noted that not every WCC offender is an entrepreneur and, similarly, not all WCC is destructive entrepreneurship. Nevertheless, professional skills, the recognition of opportunities and risk taking are associated with both entrepreneurship and many types of WCC. Another crucial element that is deeply related to entrepreneurial action is innovation (Schumpeter 1934). This is not also uncommon in WCC, because most WCCs are intelligently prepared, use complex knowledge and innovate in relation to what had been done previously. For example, on 2 November 2008, Portugal was surprised by the announcement of the nationalization of the *Banco Português de Negócios* (Business Portuguese Bank – BPN). The executive board of this bank had built a Ponzi scheme, involving dozens of offshores where huge losses had been hidden using complex financial circuits, and leading clients to believe that they were not incurring in high levels of risk. The scheme was so well-shaped that until now authorities have not been able to recover 700 million euros still in offshores. Bailing out BPN represented a loss for taxpayers of about 7 billion euros.[3]

As one can see, the concealing of the offence demands entrepreneurial skills.[4] To prove this, we engaged in a brief exercise that consisted in selecting some well-known definitions of entrepreneurship and replacing the word entrepreneur (or entrepreneurship) with white-collar crime offender (or white-collar criminality). The concepts continued to make sense. For example, in the definition of Shane and Venkataraman (2000):[5] 'The field of entrepreneurship [*white-collar criminality*] involves the study of sources of opportunities; the processes of discovery, evaluation, and exploitation of opportunities; and the set of individuals who discover, evaluate, and exploit them'.

Another example, using Von Mises' definition of entrepreneurship (1949):[6] '[t]he entrepreneur [*white-collar crime offender*] is always a speculator. He deals with the uncertain conditions of the future. His success or failure depends on the correctness of his anticipation of uncertain events. If he fails in his understanding of things to come he is doomed'.

A third example might be found in the definition of entrepreneurship by Ireland, Hitt and Sirmon (2003):[7] '[e]ntrepreneurship [*white-collar crime criminality*] is a context dependent social process through which individuals and teams create wealth by bringing together unique packages of resources to exploit marketplace opportunities'. Gottschalk and Smith (2011: 301) provided support to the extension of this definition to criminal entrepreneurship:

> The criminal entrepreneurs' task is similar but they have to discover and exploit opportunities, situations in which there [is] a profit to be made in criminal activity. [...] Opportunity discovery relates to the generation of value, where the entrepreneur determines or influences the set of resource choices required to create value. Thus, the criminal entrepreneur faces the same challenges as the legal entrepreneur.

Many other examples could be added, and it is also possible to find some research supporting the similarities between WCC and entrepreneurship. According to Baumol (1990), individuals (and organizations) choose between productive and unproductive entrepreneurship (in which WCC and organized crime may be included) according to the expected net return on the use of their skills.[8] Weitzel et al. (2010) found a significant positive correlation between entrepreneurship and selfish behaviour.[9] For Smith (2009: 259):

> [e]ntrepreneurial behaviour becomes visible in the planning and organizing of the crime, and in the aftermath when covering their tracks and disposing of the proceeds – manifested as trading, arbitrage and wheeling and dealing.

Along the same lines, Gottschalk and Smith (2011: 300) pointed out that:

> A legal entrepreneur is a person who operates a new enterprise or venture and assumes some accountability for the inherent risk. Similarly, the criminal entrepreneur's task is to discover and exploit opportunities.

Arnulf and Gottschalk (2012: 3) also recognized this similitude:

> Different theories of white-collar crime focus on different mechanisms driving criminal behaviour. Central to these theories are concepts such as opportunity, trust and (core) competence. These are central concepts of doing business in organizations.

Arnulf and Gottschalk (2012), based on the principal-agent theory, proposed a classification of the role of WCC offenders in terms of the interactions with their victims. They defined six categories of WCC offenders, one of which was the entrepreneur criminal. In an empirical analysis of WCC in Norway, those authors concluded that 'the most typical role of a white-collar criminal by far is the entrepreneur criminal' (Arnulf and Gottschalk 2012: 12).

Yet, probably only some types of WCC include the elements that allow them to be classified as destructive entrepreneurship. Gottschalk and Smith (2011: 303) present some prevailing categorizations of WCC; however, none of them allows the identification of the types of WCC that can be classified as destructive entrepreneurship, and the types that do not fulfil the requirements of entrepreneurial behaviour. Thus, one of the purposes of this work was to draw attention to the need for a conceptualization of WCC that enables the separation between entrepreneurial WCC and non-entrepreneurial WCC. This does not imply the annulment of existing classifications, because, for instance, entrepreneurial behaviour might take the form of occupational or corporate crime, which implies that it is still relevant to distinguish the two phenomena. Another complexity is the fact that destructive entrepreneurial behaviour does not involve WCC exclusively; rather, there is entrepreneurial criminal behaviour that falls outside the notion of WCC, as is the case of offences committed by criminal organizations, terrorists and even burglars who have to be innovative.

An additional problem regarding the notion of entrepreneurial WCC comes from the institutional choices when defining which acts should be labelled as illicit. These choices vary across countries and societies. Although there is no doubt that destructive entrepreneurship should cover illicit behaviour, for Passas (2005) it should also include offences that do not break the law, such as 'practices that are within the letter of the law and yet have multiple adverse social consequences' (Passas 2005: 771) or, using the terminology of economics, practices with negative externalities to society (Passas and Goodwin 2004). McBarnet (1991) exemplifies this using tax avoidance, where the boundaries of deviant and lawful activities are manipulated to ensure that the taxpayers 'escape tax *and* stay on the legal side of the boundary' (McBarnet 1991: 323). In fact, the complex schemes of tax avoidance without breaking the law push a vast amount of capitals away to offshore accounts established in tax havens that allow multinational corporations and wealthy individuals to lower their tax burden, thus distorting tax systems against the poor and the middle class. Passas (2005) points out that globalization raised the possibility that these crimes without law breaking pose increased difficulties to CJSs.

It is precisely the incorporation of entrepreneurial talent into WCC that is making it very difficult for judicial authorities to react to the phenomenon. Normally, WC offences are hidden under the guise of legality, or combine legitimate with illegitimate elements on complex structures (McBarnet 1991: 331).[10] For example, the determination of whether an innovative tax-planning scheme – using tax havens or several subsidiary corporations without violating any rule of law directly – gives rise to a situation of tax avoidance or fraud is not straightforward. One example was the case of Espírito Santo Activos Financeiros Premium (ESAF) that was integrated in the Espírito Santo Group, financed by Banco Espírito Santo (BES). This company participated in a cascade of seven entities established in several tax havens to transact real estate with two kinds of benefits: paying low tax rates and withholding the identities of the holders. In 2006, ESAF was issued with a fine of 1.25 million euros by the Portuguese Securities Market Commission for 'violating the duty of diligence, and professionalism, jeopardizing the transparency and credibility in the market' (Pena 2014: 87).

In fact, in the last two decades, the world has undergone several transformations in economic and financial interactions that were not accomplished by changes in legal systems. The liberalization of capital flows, globalization and the application of new information and communication technologies to economic relations enabled the emergence of new and sophisticated opportunities for economic and financial crime. In a few seconds, anyone sited in his or her office can place orders for transactions in several parts of the world. The use of tax havens (also called secrecy jurisdictions) facilitated the possibility of hiding capital flows and property transactions from judicial authorities (Christensen 2012). In Portugal, on 10 September 2013, the public prosecutor gave a prison sentence or a bail of 10 million euros to the former CEO of the Banco Comercial Português (Portuguese Commercial Bank – BCP). In this trial, this individual and several other managers were accused of manipulating the market and of document forgery in crimes committed between 1999 and 2007. According to the public prosecutor, they used 17 offshore societies headquartered in tax havens and established by BCP to influence the market value of the bank's shares and the rates of the securities of BCP. They were also accused of having falsified the bank's accounting to hide losses. However, some jurisdictions did not cooperate in sending the information required by judicial investigators on time, which led to the time-barred benefit of the offence. Therefore, the application of entrepreneurial talent and knowledge to the design of innovative WCCs with an international dimension has proliferated in this globalized world, and WCC offenders tend to evade the regulatory power of legal systems and judicial institutions. Cunha Rodrigues, who is a former Attorney General, said about WCC: 'It is no longer a by-product of business to be a business in itself. It is no stranger to the economy: it operates according to its rules, organizing them and shaping them' (Rodrigues 1999: 7). In fact, the opinion of many prestigious jurists in Portugal is that the legal system is not prepared to face WCC. Bravo (2011: 158) refers to the 'almost inevitable necessity of "refounding the legal system" [...] with the attribution of more creative, flexible and regulatory competences to the interpreter and law enforcer, rather than using solutions encompassed in traditional frames of strict normativity'.

Assuming that it is true that the incorporation of entrepreneurial talent into WCC allows WCC offenders to circumvent the limitations of the judicial system by exploring grey areas or clear-cut omissions of law, and profiting from the deficiencies and inefficiencies of the law system, how can law enforcement respond to entrepreneurial WCC? Considering that a large number of WCC lawsuits lapse in Portugal for procedural reasons, does the legal system have enough flexibility to adapt to non-foreseeable criminal innovations? Should the CJS react to entrepreneurial WCC via the implementation of new solutions in terms of enacting laws, law interpretation, conducting police investigations or considering evidence?

Penal law, WCC and entrepreneurship

As far as penal law is concerned, it is almost a truism to say that criminals are always at least one step ahead of the legal provisions and their crystallization in any form of written statute. Innovation and refined ways to conceal the unlawful results of a human behaviour are part of a white-collar criminal's general features.

From the Portuguese context, let us briefly go through some examples.

One of the best representations of this is the offence of *illicit enrichment*, which was recently proposed by the Portuguese government to the Parliament; this entity approved it, and the President of the Republic sent it to constitutional control by the competent Court.[11] In February

2012, the Constitutional Court ruled that the law was unconstitutional because it did not identify a clear legal protected interest and it affected the principle of the defendant's presumption of innocence, as it prescribed an inversion of the burden of proof. Not only were criminal behaviours not described in a manner that they could be foreseeable by citizens, but also the law demands suspects to prove that assets are legally acquired.

This is a case of the disjunction of means between the criminal legal system and the perpetrators of offences: the latter do not have to obey any kind of principle in the course of their actions, contrary to penal law which is embedded in the rule of law. Another difficulty is common to civil law-tradition countries such as Portugal: the use of *ius aequum* (undetermined) concepts in offences. For example, legal expressions such as *acts contrary to the agents' duties* demand jurisprudence concretization. This technique has advantages in terms of avoiding the impossibility of prosecuting facts not covered by written statute, but, at the same time, it can be an instrument of criminals' entrepreneurial abilities. In fact, legal hermeneutics entails the use of discursive and rhetoric capacities that require innovation, particularly in civil law states, where the determination of the legally protected interest (*Rechtsgut*) and the skills required to have a full-range overview of the elements of the offence's concept (legal determination – *nullum crimen* ... – , illicit character of the conduct, blame or culpability and possibility of punishment[12]) are quite demanding.

For example, in the case of money laundering (article 368-A of the Penal Code), predicate offences are bound to a rigid list of crimes, according to binding international regulations for Portugal. However, the determination of the moment of the perpetration of the offence (*tempus delicti*) has striking consequences, as the provision was added to the Penal Code only in 2004.[13] Before that, it was part of a law that included fewer predicate offences. Corruption in the public sector has always been envisaged as one of the most serious forms of WCC in Portugal. The legislative history is one of continuous punitivity and of criminalizing new behaviours. It has also been the centre of strong parliamentary debate, as in the 2010 amendments. The current framework distinguishes active from passive corruption[14] according to whether the public servant is led to the unlawful action by the agent or if he/she himself/herself asks for any kind of bribery, respectively. The latter is punished more harshly. Other unlawful income or advantage that a public servant may ask for is also sanctioned.[15] This offence is not easy to ascertain, as mentioned previously. Urban-planning rule violation has also been made an offence since 2010,[16] using definitions such as National or Agricultural Ecological Reserve and properties in the public domain, which are true blank criminal statutes[17] that are necessary to apprehend all the social reality, but lacking the determinability that could be an instrument against entrepreneur WCC behaviour.

The always fragile equilibrium between obtaining the procedural truth and the defendant's rights and guarantees is particularly clear in WCC, in which the sophistication of the means used to perpetrate the offences can be seriously questionable, e.g. in terms of the use of wiretap recording in lawsuits other than those for which this evidence-collecting method. André, vê se concordas was authorized judicially, or of the proceedings of tapping the President of the Republic, the Prime Minister (PM) or the President of the Parliament. This has been a sensitive subject in the judicial or political context, as when the former PM José Sócrates was tapped speaking on the phone with a suspect of WCC, which led to the suspicion that the PM might have committed a crime of attempt against the rule of law state. The determination of whether the competence to authorize and to decide on the recordings belonged to the President of the Supreme Court or to the judge of the court that firstly gave permission for the wiretapping remains a subject of vivid discussion.[18]

Finally, it is a popular subject to highlight that prosecutors and the police are not fully capable of gathering much expert evidence in a reasonable amount of time, as they lack professional and economic resources[19] (Barreiros 2014).

Empirical evidence of WCC: quantitative meet qualitative data

Methodological preliminaries

The purpose of this section is to present data that allow the understanding of how the Portuguese CJS deals with entrepreneurial WCC. An empirical research was designed to provide a comprehensive view of the phenomenon, by combining quantitative data retrieved from the Portuguese official crime statistics with qualitative data obtained through interviews with key actors of the CJS.

It is common to state that the standard caution that is needed when analysing statistical data in criminology (e.g. Aebi 2000) is intensified when focusing on WCC.[20] In the case of Portugal, official crime records, as supplied by *Estatísticas da Justiça*, must be read with care for several reasons: in addition to the potentially high rates of dark figures, which is common to that observed in other countries, data are categorized according to the definitions of the penal law, which underwent serious changes in 1995, 1998 and 2007; and the collecting and recording mechanisms have been subject to changes. This partially restricts international comparisons and does not allow exploring exhaustively all the dimensions considered in the WCC definition used in this chapter (offenders' profession, organizational context and the amount of profit intended from the practice of the offence).

Nonetheless, crime statistics allow a first glance at the workings of the CJS. For this purpose, the analysis that is described here has to be understood in light of the following methodological choices: (1) the period considered in the analysis was 1993–2011; (2) the grouping of crimes (against patrimony, against society, against the public sector, and offences prescribed by separate regulation) was performed by the statistical department of the Ministry of Justice considering the structure of the Portuguese Penal Law Code; (3) several offences, WC and non-WC, were ascribed to each of these main groups; and (4) in the present chapter, the analysis was conducted by excluding from those groups offences that were considered to be non-WC,[21] so that the list of WCCs retrieved from the official statistics and analysed here is that presented in the Appendix.

Quantitative data limitations provide additional utility to qualitative methods. Statistical data were complemented by data obtained through interviews, conducted with eight key actors of the Portuguese CJS: one agent from the judiciary police, two judges and five public prosecutors,[22] who are considered to have special knowledge and know-how in investigating, prosecuting and sentencing WCCs and related offenders. The sample consisted of three males and five females with varying ages and different professional paths. As the Portuguese system of public prosecutors and judges implies a nomadic trend (professionals change locations and areas of expertise from time to time), we were able to find persons who could compare their experience in investigating and judging WCCs with that of other types of offences.[23]

A qualitative approach was also undertaken to understand how law enforcement reacts to entrepreneurial WCC. How effective is the Portuguese CJS against the innovative and complex techniques used by WCC offenders? And how does it react to WCC at various levels: criminal investigation and collection of evidence, application and interpretation of the law during trial and, finally, sentencing? What are the limitations perceived by its actors?

The qualitative data gathered allowed us not only to understand the main limitations of the Portuguese CJS, but also to obtain a sketch of the delinquent system. The data also lead us to understand why it is so difficult to fight innovative and highly prepared WCC offenders. It also allowed us to learn about the role played by the media on public opinion about WCC. Finally, it calls for a more creative law enforcement toward these crimes. The following section will present the results.

Numbers and words: lessons on WCC and entrepreneurship

From 1993 to 2011, as for all recorded crimes, the number of recorded WCC offences increased. The average proportion of WCCs among all recorded offences was 5.1 per cent (minimum 3.2 per cent in 1993; maximum 7 per cent in 2011). Considering smaller periods,[24] the average proportion was 4.9 per cent in 1998–2007 and 6.7 per cent in 2008–2011. The same level of increase was found in the number of reported victims, accused defendants, concluded lawsuits and convictions.

In the period of 2008–2011, the average proportions of recorded offences related to WCCs was significantly higher in terms of accused offenders (12.8 per cent), concluded lawsuits (10.1 per cent) and convictions (12.2 per cent) compared with detentions (5.1 per cent). Because WCCs are usually known as victimless crimes, it is not surprising that, when focusing on recorded victims, we found that only 3.7 per cent of all recorded victims were WCCs.

Looking at the official statistics and after doing some calculations for the 2008–2011 period, concluded WCC lawsuits represented an average of 34.8 per cent of the recorded WCCs, which was approximately 11.7 percentage points higher than that observed in the all recorded crimes group. Considering the large time period (1993–2011), the evidence was similar: concluded lawsuits represented 38.8 per cent of the recorded WCCs, which was 13.4 percentage points higher than that observed for all recorded crimes. The comparison between accused and convicted offenders revealed that WCC was not very different from the all recorded crimes larger group: in the 1993–2011 period, for each group of 100 WCC-accused offenders, there was an average of 57 convictions (two more than in the all recorded crimes group). In the 2008–2011 period, for each group of 100 WCC-accused offenders, there was an average of 60 convictions (against 62 in the all recorded crimes group). However, once the analysis goes backwards in the process and considers average rates for the 1993–2011 period, it is clear that for each 100 WCC suspects in the phase of investigation, on average, there were 69 accused offenders, among whom 39 were convicted (but not necessarily imprisoned[25]). It will be shown, as assessed by the qualitative analysis performed here, that interviewees perceived that much of the work toward investigating crimes is lost along the process, that few defendants ever proceed to trial and that even fewer among those are found guilty and convicted.

As mentioned above, the statistical data about WCCs were obtained by considering different offences aggregated into four groups (see Appendix). From 1993 to 2011, the most prevalent WCC group consisted of offences against patrimony, in spite of lost relevance over the last years; concomitantly, the proportion of offences prescribed by separate regulation increased steadily (Figure 31.1). This trend can be interpreted better by considering that criminalization and the enactment of separate regulation have grown, and by considering the statements of some of the interviewees: that strategic choices made in the investigation phase led them to investigate tax crimes preferably, which are prescribed by separate regulation. Therefore, higher rates of success are guaranteed for more complex cases. Moreover, tax crimes are easier to investigate and to prove during trial. Thus, it seems that the CJS has found ways to adapt and react more effectively in the fight against WCC.

The same trend was observed when focusing on the number of accused defendants: there was a strong decrease in the proportion of accused defendants in offences against patrimony

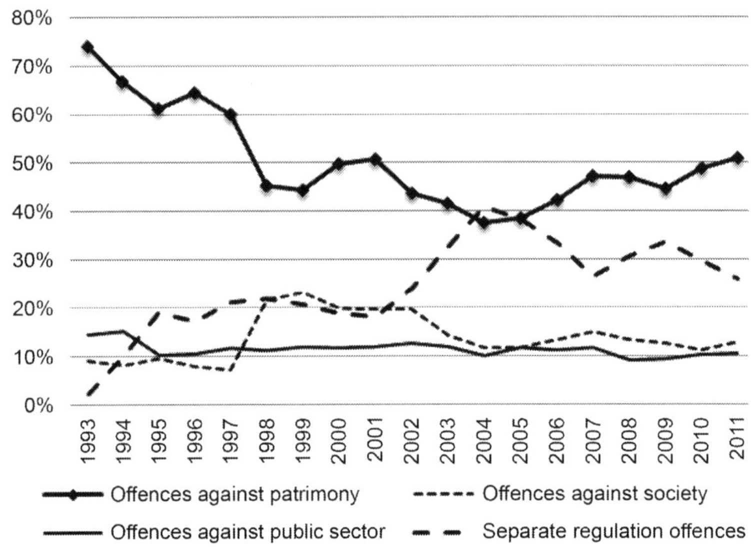

Figure 31.1 WCC categories (1993–2011)

Source: Data from *Estatísticas da Justiça* (Portuguese Ministry of Justice 2012). Adapted by the authors

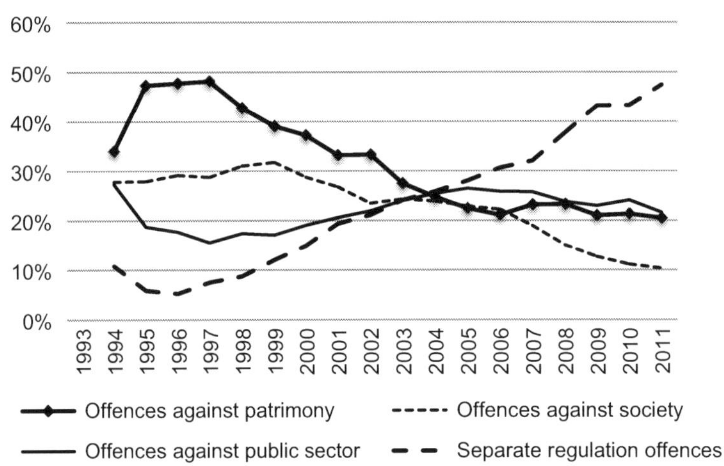

Figure 31.2 Defendants accused of WCCs (1994–2011)

Source: Data from *Estatísticas da Justiça* (Portuguese Ministry of Justice 2012). Adapted by the authors

(from 34 per cent in 1994 to 21 per cent in 2011) and an increase in the proportion of accused defendants in offences prescribed by separate regulation (from 11 per cent in 1994 to 47 per cent in 2011) (Figure 31.2), which was perhaps due to the increase of the enactment of statutes belonging to the latter group.

An identical trend was found in the case of convictions – a strong increase in the proportion of the perpetrators of offences prescribed by separate regulation (from 8 per cent in 1994 to 51 per

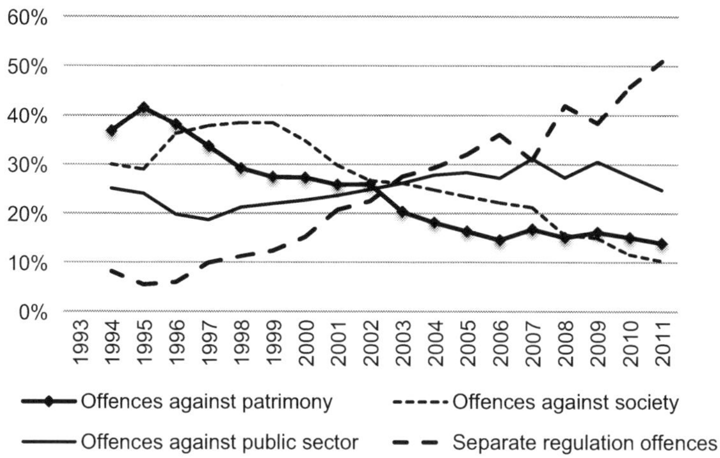

Figure 31.3 WCC convictions (1994–2011)

Source: Data from *Estatísticas da Justiça* (Portuguese Ministry of Justice 2012). Adapted by the authors

cent in 2011) and a decrease in the proportion of convictions of perpetrators of offences against patrimony (from 37 per cent in 1994 to 21 per cent in 2011) (Figure 31.3).

As a summary of the information provided by the quantitative data, the weight of WCCs among total crimes increased sustainably; a higher proportion of WCCs was detected when looking at accused offenders, concluded lawsuits and convictions, whereas a lower proportion was observed when considering victims. In conclusion, for each 100 suspects, 69 were accused on average, resulting in 39 convictions (but not necessarily in imprisonment). Taking into account the specific crimes that constitute WCCs, throughout the 1993–2011 period, a strong decrease was observed in the proportion of offences against patrimony; simultaneously, a strong increase in the proportion of WCCs prescribed by separate regulation was found, largely because of a growing move toward criminalization and a readjustment of the CJS, which now prosecutes these offences with a seemingly guaranteed higher level of success.

This was also true when looking at the data obtained through the interviews. Interviewees mentioned more frequently having to deal with tax crimes[26] (mentioned by all interviewees); corruption, embezzlement and money laundering were some of the other offences mentioned. Moreover, and because of some procedural concerns, embezzlement, public sector authority abuse and influence trafficking were also reported.

The words of the interviewees provided a description of the defendants and enabled sketching an image of the delinquent system (beyond the individual offender):

> it is a broad and yet narrow circuit. It is broad because there are lots of people involved and it is organized; it is narrow because they have a code, a pact, as if it was a mafia (A2).

The Portuguese CJS has to deal with complex interactions of actors, mechanisms and structures that are put in place for the perpetration of WCCs: a delinquent system with groups of individuals who weave relationships among themselves, many of whom exhibit typical elements of entrepreneurs: using professional skills, profiting from opportunity recognition, being innovative in finding new solutions at the boundaries of the law and using complex knowledge in schemes prepared intelligently, in a legitimate business or combined with some hidden illicit choices. They are influential, socially respected people who have money, power and status. They make decisions surrounded by experts and advisors in law, accounting, economics and business, who help overcome constraints and build up a legal (albeit only formally) path of action. Interviewees considered the defendants of WCCs to be moved by ambition, greed and profit and to be reinforced by a sense of impunity, built through the work of specialized lawyers during trial and by the sentencing to which they are (not) subjected. Contrary to ordinary offenders, who know that *sooner or later things might go wrong* (A5), these individuals are considered to reiterate deliberately behaviours that harm both the state and its citizens. Interviewees also considered them to benefit from the support of the public opinion and a broader culture that tolerates corruption and fraud.[27]

As mentioned previously, not all WCC offenders have an entrepreneur profile; some get caught and are found guilty. Usually, they engage in some business but are ill-prepared, cannot afford good lawyers and do not have enough money – they are *poor devils* (A1) who confess their deeds and augment the numbers of successful cases reported in official statistics.

Let us now turn to the criminal process. At this point, the judiciary police and public prosecutors have to work closely together to produce an investigative strategy and collect evidence that allows formal charges. The interviews conducted stressed the difficulty caused by the invisibility or immateriality of WCC. Because they are crimes harder to perceive, to see, even more so when the police are trained to investigate traditional crimes[28] and are, therefore, not prepared to be proactive in overseeing business and political practices. Moreover, public complaints[29] tend to fail in providing specific evidence that can serve as a basis for the police work; human and economic resources are spent investigating cases that are several years old, a situation which strongly influences the rate of dismissals; and there are hardly any whistle-blowers or infiltrated police agents in the *underworld of business* (C1).

Therefore, what kind of investigative strategy is put into place? When the CJS actors are pursuing a case that has happened recently, they usually order wiretapping, searches and seizures to secure information and control communications. When the case under investigation is several years old (three, five or more), there is an exhaustive collection of documents that must be properly interpreted with the help of experts and advisors on administrative law, accountancy, economics and so on. Moreover, much of the evidence is gathered by forced cooperation with the financial system – although Portugal has ceased to have bank secrecy, banks are very resistant to, and uncooperative regarding, disclosing accounts and actively helping investigations: *they are extra cautious* (A3) in providing information and resist cooperation.[30] Nevertheless, the money obtained illegally and transferred to national and foreign financial entities should become the visible element of these crimes: if *the money is the dead body* (C1), the police and prosecutors should strongly try to find any evidence of money laundering and prosecute on those grounds.

Interviewees also mentioned that the media produce some entropy over the criminal investigation. Journalists anticipate police searches and leak information to the public and to offenders. Moreover, the media tend to interpret any complex offence as corruption, causing people to get confused and distrust the Portuguese CJS.[31] As stated by one of the interviewees, there is an excess of media visibility *which does not match with judiciary visibility* (C1), i.e. with the success or failure of the investigation and prosecution by the CJS. Nonetheless, media accounts influence public opinion strongly and, indirectly, may increase or reduce the number of complaints received by the CJS.

The difficulties do not end here. On one hand, witnesses are considered not to be trustworthy, which demands a change in the *evidence paradigm* (B1) that guides the investigation of traditional offences. On the other hand, the CJS actors strongly perceive their lack of training and lack of financial and human resources in researching WCC,[32] be it because they lack a proper integrated system of information and communication, or because they were trained in investigating traditional crimes and are not *routinized* (A5) in the specific features of WCC. In the end, and although some efforts have been made over the last years, the investigation phase requires the specialization of the CJS actors and the constitution of adequate and multidisciplinary long-term teams.

Based on the evidence produced, prosecutors will then build up narratives of the offences via formal charges. These have to be properly grounded on the evidence collected:

> an accusation is a story that does not end with the facts [...] there has to be a proper storytelling [...] in the simplest language possible. We [prosecutors] have to tell the story in a way the judge may understand.
>
> *(A1c)*

Nonetheless, interviewees considered that the rate of dismissal is high (Figure 31.4). Moreover, although some of the prosecutors interviewed unburdened the personal frustration felt in these situations, others considered dismissal as important as formal charges, because it allowed them to learn from previous mistakes, thus building a database and know-how that could prove useful in future cases.

When asked about suggestions on how to improve the rates of success, the interviewees recommended criminalizing *illicit enrichment* (A5) and did not consider the inversion of the burden of proof to be an obstacle, because it was already in place in drug crimes (A1b); others considered that the police should react to WCC the same way they react to terrorism: via *modern means of fighting crime* (C1).

When cases do go to trial, judges will validate in court the evidence gathered and the narrative provided by previous actors, and they will interpret and apply the law. Most of the interviewees considered Portuguese law, in abstract, to be satisfactory, although the international framework in which the country is included may have led to some inaccuracies, namely when the Portuguese legal system simply translates and introduces acritically new international directives. Probing a bit more, some of the key actors considered that some changes lacked a clear criminal-policy strategy, for legal reforms were made *under pressure* and *inconsistently* (B2). The major difficulties mentioned were bound to a perceived excess of defendants' guarantees, difficulty in proving authorship and guilt by organizations,[33] general clauses that are difficult to apply to specific cases, lack of a clear description of the offence (unlike traditional crimes, with clear-cut descriptions) and legal omissions.

The completion of trials may take years and powerful defendants will surround themselves with highly skilled lawyers who, by using delaying tactics and constant appeals and by raising obstacles, will do almost everything to let time elapse. All of this is done under the set of *guarantees for defendants that they invoke all the time and, thus, have the right to do almost anything* (A1). Moreover, the elapsing of time may have serious consequences regarding the chosen sanction. When asked if legally prescribed sentences were (in abstraction) adequate, most of the interviewees considered them to be sufficient, eventually a bit harsher than they actually are, but never more than those enacted for crimes against life.[34] However, when considering specific cases, the CJS actors criticized the sentences that are usually found in jurisprudence. First, the elapsing of time during trial *dilutes the punitive function of the state* (A1) and hinders considerations

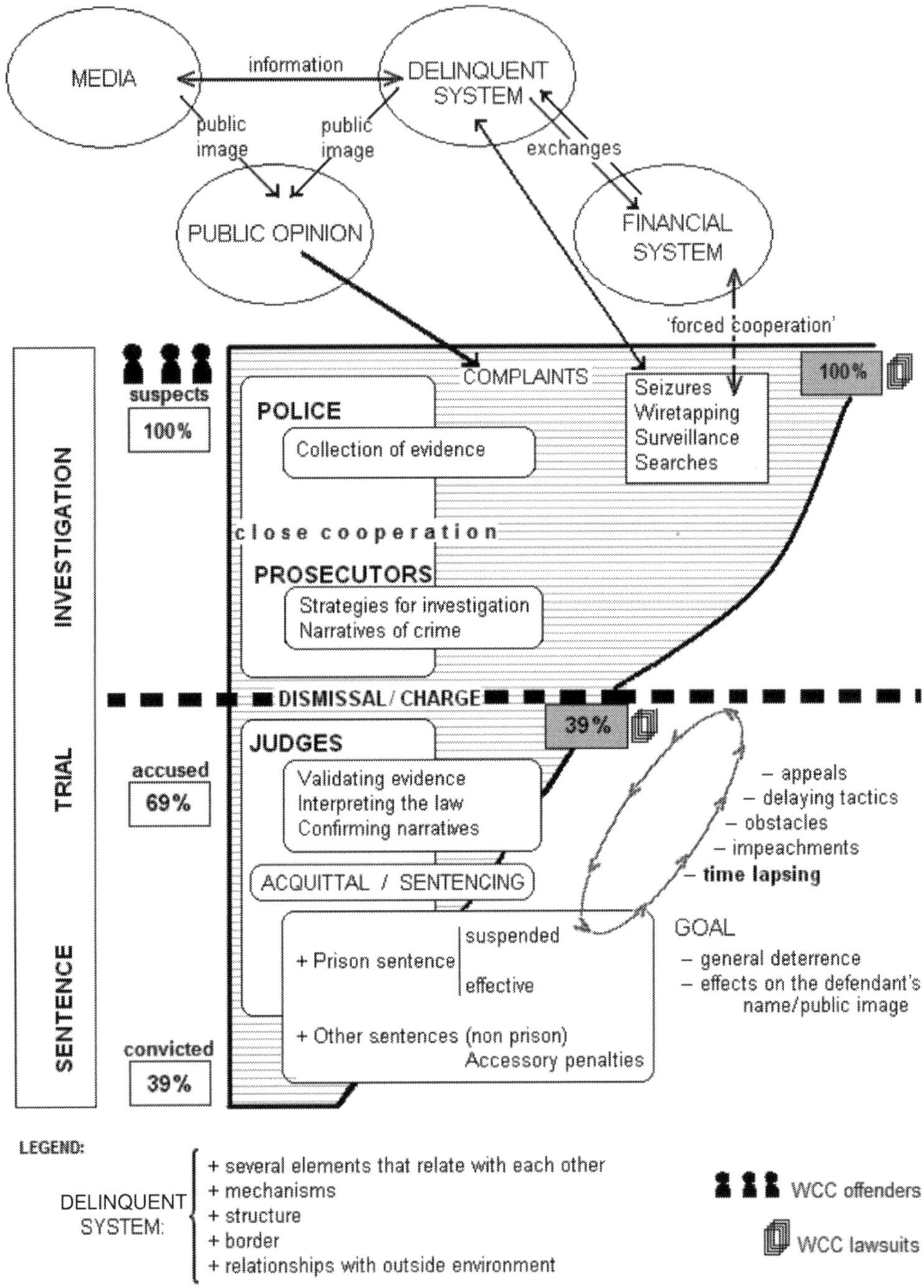

Figure 31.4 Overview of the CJS reaction to WCC entrepreneurship

Source: Data from interviews and from the *Estatísticas da Justiça* (Portuguese Ministry of Justice 2012). Period: 1993–2011. Computations and diagram by the authors

of specific deterrence. Second, some of the interviewees considered that judges would *condone defendants when specifying the* quantum *of the sentence* (A5), when, in fact, they should demand a *special respect in complying with the social contract* (B1). Although most of the individuals interviewed considered that the mere threat of a sentence has null effects on WCC offenders, some deemed a conviction with any kind of sentence (as long as it exceeded the profit made by the crime) to be sufficient and others stated the need for an effective prison sentence, considering that it would damage the offender's public image and have general deterrent effects, thus being used as an example for the public.

A description of the difficulties of the Portuguese CJS has been provided, namely, its main features along the processes of investigating and prosecuting WCC. Let us now synthesize, by addressing several analytical axes, on how well equipped and prepared the Portuguese CJS is to fight entrepreneurial WCC. These data have been collected through the interviews mentioned above.

Regarding the mastery of the law, offenders are very much aware of how to explore the existing gaps in the law, or how to fulfil formal requirements so that legal demands are fulfilled.[35] Conversely, the CJS actors are equally aware of the law, its requirements and gaps, and thus master it rather well. It is not the use and interpretation of the law that hinder the reaction to WCC.

When asked if offenders were intelligent and risk taking, interviewees considered them to be clever plan-makers who cover their tracks and act cautiously when aware of being investigated.[36] It is obvious that the CJS actors are also intelligent, as they were recruited from academic law elites and all clearly stated the need to respect the legal boundaries of investigation, even when considering, for instance, that the defendant's guarantees are inflated.

However, the main difficulties of the CJS in dealing with entrepreneurial WCC seemed to be felt when considering a proactive approach to crime, allocation of resources, exchange of information and public image of trust. Interviewees assigned the ability to recognize opportunities for committing crimes to WCC offenders, and clearly admitted the inability of the CJS to be proactive and fast and proceed simultaneously with the criminal events. Because of their academic skills or expertise, offenders are trained in the *modus operandi* of some complex WCCs, unlike the CJS. In fact, improved training and economic resources that allow hiring teams of experts seem to be, for those interviewed, one of the main weapons in preventing and fighting WCC. Offenders have access to computers, cell phones and top-of-the-line information systems, whereas the Portuguese CJS struggles with out-dated resources and incipient systems for exchanging information. Interviewees also mentioned the general lack of a clear strategy against WCC, which causes disorientation and unsystematic investigations.

Finally, the social status and economic and political power of the CJS actors seem to be rather low in the Portuguese climate. Interviewees mentioned a *culture of corruption*[37] (A2) that exists in Portugal and the distrust that people feel about the working of the justice system. In contrast, WCC offenders are able to build images of public trust[38] and to amass political and economic power, be it from their legitimate professions or from their illegitimate activities.

Conclusions

Some reports in the literature argue that many WCC offenders have entrepreneurial talent and use it to commit WCCs and escape conviction (destructive entrepreneurship). In fact, it is possible to find in many WCC offenders a profile that is similar to that of entrepreneurs, namely, the presence of professional skills, an ability for opportunity recognition, creativity for finding new solutions on the boundaries of the law, expertise to launch a business and some propensity for risk taking. However, it should be noted that not every WCC offender is an entrepreneur.

The last financial crisis, which affected Portugal deeply, brought to light the high frequency and adverse nature of destructive entrepreneurship. Currently, the feeling persists that the CJS is unable to deal with influential, socially respected people with money, power and status in the Portuguese society. They take decisions surrounded by experts and advisors in law, accounting, economics, business, etc., who help them to settle on how to overcome constraints and build a legal path of action.

To understand how law enforcement responds to entrepreneurial WCC in Portugal specifically, we intersected official crime statistics with data obtained through interviews of key actors from the justice setting.

According to official data, among all recorded crimes, the weight of WCC increased sustainably throughout the 1993–2011 period. Furthermore, an even higher weight is found for WCC when attention is focused on data about offenders, concluded lawsuits and convictions. Contrarily to this evidence, victims of this type of offences represent a very small proportion among all crime victims.

Taking into account the specific crimes that constitute WCC, a strong decrease in the proportion of offences against patrimony and, simultaneously, a strong increase in the proportion of WCC prescribed by separate regulation were observed. Perhaps this was due to the increase of the enactment of statutes belonging to the latter group. As a matter of fact, in that period, there was growing criminalization and enacting of separate regulations against WCC in Portugal. This expansion might be interpreted as some reaction on the CJS side, translated into dynamics of the law. In fact, the increase in the proportion of WCC prescribed by these new statutes is a sign of some success of the CJS regarding the improved management of the growing complexity and innovation of many WC offences. Nonetheless, it is normal that the law, and especially the penal law, is one step behind human creativity and the entrepreneurial ability of criminals. In what concerns countries with a civil-law tradition, such as Portugal, where legal concepts require exquisite hermeneutics and have to deal with definitions coming from other branches of the law, one can picture a low dynamism in criminal statutes. When the lawmaker tries to enhance this issue, legal doubts are raised, particularly in what concerns new criminalization. In fact, in the interviews, some of the key actors considered that some legal changes were emptied of a clear criminal-policy strategy, as if legal reforms were achieved *under pressure* and *inconsistently*.

Another conclusion that emanates from the data is a strong attrition rate in the reaction of the CJS to WCC. Interviewees perceived that much of the work dedicated to investigating WCC is lost along the process: few accused ever proceed to trial, and fewer are convicted and seldom serve a prison sentence. One of the major difficulties mentioned was a perceived excess of defendants' guarantees. Other obstacles encountered by the CJS actors were the invisibility of the offences, the limited resources of the Portuguese CJS and the special features of the WCC offenders, namely their entrepreneurial talent to escape conviction.

In summary, it seems clear that, in Portugal – similarly to what happens around the world – entrepreneurial behaviour is present in WCC. This sheds light on the current difficulties (in the criminal-investigation, trial and conviction phases) felt by the actors in their efforts to fight WCC.

Appendix

White-collar crimes in Portuguese penal law

1. Offences against patrimony	
1.1	Against property (e.g. breach of trust)
1.2	Against patrimony in general (e.g. fraud in banking)
1.3	Against patrimonial rights (e.g. intentional or negligent bankruptcy)
1.4	Other offences against patrimony
2. Offences against society	
2.1	Forgery crimes
2.2	General danger crimes against society (e.g. pollution)
3. Offences against the public sector	
3.1	Influence trafficking
3.2	Offences against rule-of-law enforcement
3.3	Crimes against public authority (e.g. usurpation of public office)
3.4	Crimes against justice application (e.g. laundering of benefits of illicit origin*)
3.5	Crimes against the public economic sector (e.g. corruption)
3.6	Other crimes against the public sector
4. Offences prescribed by separate regulation	
4.1	Crimes at the stock market (e.g. insider trading)
4.2	Crimes against industrial property
4.3	Ordinary tributary crimes (e.g. tributary fraud)
4.4	Customs' crimes (e.g. fraud in customs regulations)
4.5	Tax fraud
4.6	Offences against social security
4.7	Offences against national economy (e.g. market speculation)
4.8	Frauds in informatics
4.9	Money laundering*

* Money laundering was criminalized in 1993 and was limited to benefits obtained in drug crimes. In 2002, it was extended to cover benefits obtained by tax fraud and a general clause was introduced in order for it to be applied to all crimes sentenced to imprisonment for more than five years. Finally, in 2004, money laundering was introduced in the Penal Code.

Notes

1 For further details on the *scrap-iron case*, see Trogano (2011).
2 This is the WCC definition assumed throughout our study.
3 See the report of journalistic investigation http://sicnoticias.sapo.pt/programas/afraude (accessed 9 May 2014).
4 Typically, in the case of WCC, the goal of the offender is not to conceal himself/herself, like a common criminal, but to conceal the offence itself.
5 Cited in Ahmad and Seymour (2008: 7).
6 Ibid.
7 Ibid.
8 According to Baumol (1990), productive entrepreneurship leads to the creation of social value in the economy. Unproductive entrepreneurship includes rent-seeking (such as the discovery of a legal loophole that allows pioneers to capture rents, as in the case of abusive tax-avoidance schemes) and destructive activities that are profitable for those who exploit them, despite the decrease in

social value. Also see Desai and Acs (2007) for a more complete definition of these types of entrepreneurship.

9 The authors tested the hypothesis of selfish profit-seeking entrepreneurs, i.e. the extent to which entrepreneurs would be willing to harm others to increase their profits. The results indicate that the notion of a selfish entrepreneur cannot be ruled out.

10 The complexity of these schemes is well illustrated by McBarnet (1991: 331): 'Avoidance schemes are rarely simple and they usually involve a number of stages or separate transactions with a total view being necessary to recognise the sum of the parts as avoidance'.

11 The Parliament's decree proposed the addition of a new offence (*illicit enrichment*) to the Penal Code (article 335-A), with the following text: '1 Whoever, by himself/herself or using another natural or legal person, acquires, possesses or detains patrimony, without licit determined origin, which is incompatible with its incomes and legitimate assets, is punished with imprisonment up to three years, provided no harsher penalty is applicable to the case. 2- For the purpose of the previous number, patrimony is defined as all the patrimonial assets existing inland or abroad, including real estate properties, any kind of shares in companies, rights over ships, boats, aircrafts or cars, securities portfolio, bank accounts, equivalent financial applications and credit rights, as well as the expenses to acquire goods or services or related to liberalities inland or abroad. 3- For the purpose of no. 1, incomes and legitimate goods are all gross income that are declared to tax administration or that should have been declared to, as well as other incomes and goods with determined licit origins. 4- If the incompatibility's value referred in no. 1 does not exceed 100 minimum wages [now 48,500 euros] the conduct is not punishable. 5- If the incompatibility's value referred in no. 1 exceeds 350 minimum wages [now 169,750 euros] the agent is punished with imprisonment from one to five years'.

12 An example can be found in the proposed article 335-A, 4, of the Penal Code, as described in the previous footnote.

13 Law no. 11/2004, 27 March 27. See footnote in the Appendix.

14 Articles 374 and 373 of the Penal Code, respectively.

15 Article 372 of the Penal Code.

16 Article 278-A of the Penal Code, which was enforced 1 March 2011.

17 These are statutes using concepts that stem from different branches of the law (e.g. civil, administrative, tax or labour law), thus posing the question of whether they should be interpreted in penal law with the same exact meaning as that of the proceeding branch, or with a different one, probably more appropriate to the goals of penal law. Furthermore, defendants tend to argue any kind of misrepresentation of those concepts (legal error, *ignorantia legis* or *iuris*) and, given its technical characteristics, they tend to change considerably over time, this being another area where 'innovative' interpretation that is favourable to defendants may be applicable.

18 See Andrade (2010) and Leite (2008).

19 This was clear when Public Prosecutor Maria José Morgado, a notorious magistrate in fighting WCC, complained of the lack of human and technical resources within the police (see *Diário de Notícias*, 2010/03/31).

20 For an extensive review, please see other chapters in this book.

21 Please see the WCC definition provided earlier (Helmkamp et al. 1996, cited in Friedrichs 2010).

22 Quotations of interviewees are numbered and categorized: 'A' identifies prosecutors, 'B' judges and 'C' judiciary police.

23 These key actors were contacted using a snow-ball technique. Interviews lasted from 20 minutes to 1 hour and 45 minutes. Biased results may be present because of preponderance of female interviewees and of public prosecutors compared with other professionals, and also because of the geographical proximity of some of them, which might have undermined the variety of answers.

24 In the definition of these time periods, we considered the moments at which Portuguese penal law was subjected to the most relevant reforms.

25 Official crime statistics fail to present the criminal sanction applied in each case. As described in the section 'Penal law, WCC and entrepreneurship', penal law allows choosing from a range of sanctions, including fines, imprisonment and accessory penalties. This calculus is performed by the judge taking into consideration prescribed criteria (first-time offender, recidivism, etc.).

26 Prescribed by separate regulation and which have been reported more frequently, as shown by official statistics.

27 In Portugal, 18.5 per cent of respondents to an inquiry think that bribing is unproblematic and 65 per cent have a negative image of whistleblowers. When reporting corruption to the police, people are

motivated by feelings of envy, but situations of small or petty corruption tend to be condoned (Ferreira and Baptista 1992, cited in Faria et al. 2013). Portuguese people tend to have harsher feelings regarding bribery, peculation and practices of nepotism, due to feelings of relative deprivation, and are not very critical regarding civil servants that accept bribes while benefitting the community (Sousa and Triães 2008, cited in Faria et al. 2013). Apparently, perceptions of corrupt practices are statistically correlated to dissatisfaction with the functioning of the Portuguese democratic model (Jalali 2008, cited in Faria et al. 2013).

28 'In a murder case what do you have? You have a dead body. And then we go back. In white-collar crime we have to move forward [...]. Our police are prepared for immediate results: there's a dead body and in two days you figure out who the killer was [...]' (C1).

29 Complaints depend on public opinion, which, in turn, is influenced by media accounts of offences and defendants. The fact is that defendants work toward building a public image anchored in '*candour*' (A2) and transparency – when done properly, in a culture that is tolerant to corruption and fraud, the probability of complaint falls abruptly. Moreover, there is no opportunity principle in Portugal that allows investigators to choose the cases they want to investigate.

30 This resistance may be due to the exchanges of information and money with the delinquent system.

31 For media coverage on corruption news, see Grilo (2005) and Maia (2008), cited in Faria et al. (2013).

32 Because of the economic crisis, budgetary cuts and worsening of working and retirement conditions for public officers in the tax administration and other public institutions (which are supposed to supervise risk transactions), interviewees worried about the cost of hiring experts, the dismissal of human resources in public administration and the downgrading of computers and other types of resources.

33 It is obvious that behind the behaviour of the organization there may be an individual or group of individuals, namely entrepreneurs, who decide on its course of action.

34 The hierarchy of the sentences provided by the Penal Code relates to the perceived seriousness of the offence: life and human integrity are considered the most important legally protected interests.

35 One of the interviewees commented on a case where a mayor who, when deciding on the attribution of a public office for a relative, left the room and the jurors at the time of voting, as required by law. The fulfilment of the legal requirement did not prevent his influence to be felt by all other jurors who decided positively regarding the attribution of the post.

36 Curiously, this seems to be contrary to the risk-taking feature. It might be that WCC offenders are prone to risk taking when they decide to go against the law and, once they decide on it, they are sufficiently cautious to avoid being caught.

37 Please recall note 29 about tolerance to corruption found in other empirical studies and also previous notes on the framing of public images about corruption and corrupts by the media account. Apparently, this sense of an existing 'culture of corruption' as mentioned by interviewees has more to do with the citizens' views on the banality of the phenomenon, and not so much as a tolerance coming from the CJS itself.

38 It is well known and has become almost anecdotal that mayors charged with and judged on WCC still ran in local elections – and some of them were actually elected again.

References

Aebi, M. (2000) 'Les indicateurs de la criminalité: Leurs limitations, leur complémentarité et leur influence sur les théories criminologiques', *Revue Internationale de Criminologie et de Police Technique et Scientifique*, 53(2): 131–156.

Ahmad, N. and Seymour, R.G. (2008) 'Defining entrepreneurial activity: Definitions supporting frameworks for data collection', *OECD Statistics Working Paper*, 24/01/2008. Online. Available HTTP: <http://papers.ssrn.com/sol3/papers.cfm?abstract_id=1090372> (accessed 2 July 2014).

Andrade, M.d.C. (2010) 'Escutas telefónicas, conhecimentos fortuitos e Primeiro Ministro', *Revista de Legislação e de Jurisprudência*, 3962(139): 269–289.

Arnulf, J. and Gottschalk, P. (2012) 'Principals, agents and entrepreneurs in white-collar crime: An empirical typology of white-collar criminals in a national sample', *Journal of Strategic-Management Education*, 8(3): 1–22.

Barreiros, J.A. (2014) 'Prova pericial: Uma oportunidade perdida', in A.L. Leite (org.) *As alterações de 2013 aos Códigos Penal e de Processo Penal: Uma reforma 'cirúrgica'?*, Coimbra: Coimbra Editora.

Baumol, W. (1990) 'Entrepreneurship: Productive; unproductive; and destructive', *Journal of Business Venturing*, 11(1): 3–22.
Benson M.L. and Simpson, S. (2009) *White-Collar Crime: An Opportunity Perspective*, New York: Routledge.
Bravo, J.d.R. (2011) 'Criminalidade económico-financeira e organizada: Um desafio sem resposta? Para um conceito estratégico de prevenção e combate à criminalidade económico-financeira e organizada', *Revista do Centro de Estudos Judiciários*, 2nd semester, 16: 151–201.
Christensen, J. (2012) 'The hidden trillions: Secrecy, corruption, and the offshore interface', *Crime, Law and Social Change*, 57(3): 325–343.
Desai, S. and Acs, Z. (2007) 'A theory of destructive entrepreneurship', *Jena Economic Research Papers*, no. 2007, 0085. Online. Available HTTP: <http://www.econstor.eu/bitstream/10419/25657/1/553834517.PDF> (accessed 2 July 2014).
Faria, R., Cruz, J., Leite, A.L. and Sousa, P. (2013) 'Economic and financial criminality in Portugal', in S. Will, S. Handelman and D.C. Brotherton (eds) *How They Got Away with It: White Collar Criminals and the Financial Meltdown*, New York: Columbia University Press.
Friedrichs, D. (2010) *Trusted Criminals: White Collar Crime in Contemporary Society*, 4th edn, Belmont: Wadsworth Cengage Learning.
Geis, G. (1991) 'White-collar crime: What is it?', *Current Issues in Criminal Justice*, 3(1): 9–24.
Gottschalk, P. and Smith, R. (2011) 'Criminal entrepreneurship, white-collar criminality, and neutralization theory', *Journal of Enterprising Communities: People and Places in the Global Economy*, 5(4): 300–308.
Leite, A.L. (2008) 'Entre Péricles e Sísifo: O novo regime legal das escutas telefónicas', *Revista Portuguesa de Ciência Criminal*, 17(4): 613–669.
McBarnet, D. (1991) 'Whiter than white collar crime: Tax, fraud insurance and the management of stigma', *The British Journal of Sociology*, 42(3): 323–344.
Passas, N. (2005) 'Lawful but awful: "Legal corporate crimes"', *The Journal of Socio-Economics*, 34(6): 771–786.
Passas, N. and Goodwin, N. (2004) 'Introduction', in N. Passas and N. Goodwin (ed). *It's Legal, but It Ain't Right: Harmful Social Consequences of Legal Industries, Ann Arbor*: University of Michigan Press.
Pena, P. (2014) *Jogos de Poder*, Lisboa: A Esfera dos Livros.
Portuguese Ministry of Justice (2012) *Estatísticas da Justiça*. Online. Available HTTP: <http://www.siej.dgpj.mj.pt> (accessed 20 November 2012).
Rodrigues, C. (1999) 'Os senhores do crime', *Revista Portuguesa de Ciência Criminal*, 9(1): 7–30.
Schumpeter, J.A. (1934) *The Theory of Economic Development*, Cambridge, MA: Harvard University Press (original work published 1911).
Smith, R. (2009) 'Understanding entrepreneurial behaviour in organized criminals', *Journal of Enterprising Communities: People and Places in the Global Economy*, 3(3): 256–268.
Trogano, A. (2011) 'A investigação da criminalidade tributária organizada: Relato de uma experiência', in M.F. Palma, A.S. Dias and P.S. Mendes (eds) *2.ºCongresso de Investigação Criminal*, Coimbra: Almedina.
Weitzel, U., Urbig, D., Desai, S., Sanders, M. and Acs, Z. (2010) 'The good, the bad, and the talented: Entrepreneurial talent and selfish behaviour', *Journal of Economic Behaviour & Organization*, 76(1): 64–81.

Part V

Anglo-American reflections on white-collar crime in Europe

32

White-collar crime in Europe

Afterword

Hazel Croall

Introductory remarks

The first task of this epilogue must be to congratulate the editors for initiating the project and compiling such a timely and thought-provoking collection of chapters reflecting the considerable volume of research and scholarship on many different dimensions of white-collar and corporate crime across Europe. From the Nordic countries to the Mediterranean, from the Celtic Fringe to the Balkans, from old Europe to countries in transition, these provide a fascinating snapshot of major European cases and European dimensions of global crimes such as environmental crimes, money laundering, tax frauds, and many different forms of corruption. It will provide an invaluable source for scholars, researchers and students, not only in Europe but across the globe. The present author, who is very pleased to have been asked to contribute, would most certainly have welcomed such a volume when researching, teaching and writing about the subject – having, like many other British and English-speaking scholars, been somewhat reluctantly reliant on US scholarship and research, albeit of such high quality.

As many authors in this volume and elsewhere have pointed out, white-collar crime has been relatively neglected within criminology, and has been very much dominated by what is sometimes known as Anglo-American, or more precisely, Anglo-American-Australasian work, and more particularly by work from the United States. Britain was no exception to the general underrepresentation of the subject within criminology, with one noted commentator having, less than 20 years ago, described British white-collar crime scholars as 'lone rangers' (Punch 1996). Others cited the relative neglect of white-collar, corporate and other 'crimes of the powerful' citing their underrepresentation in texts, academic criminology journals and conferences (Croall 2001; Tombs and Whyte 2003). This author well remembers this situation when attending annual British criminology conferences which typically had one or no workshops on the subject. Punch's 1996 book *Dirty Business*, which did make reference to Europe, included details of major cases, the majority of which were based in the US with one British, one Italian and one Dutch case.

This is not to indicate that the activities widely recognized as white-collar crime were absent from Britain or Europe – indeed as will be seen below, fraud, financial scandals and other white-collar crimes have existed throughout European and indeed world history, and scholars had discussed issues of law, regulation and individual cases. As is so often the case, however, many were not regarded as crimes but as scandals, affairs, tragedies or accidents, and were not seen as part of the subject matter of criminology. As Korsell (2001) pointed out, while an interest in the subject developed in Sweden during the 1970s, previous affairs, including the Kreuger crash mentioned by Sutherland (1949) were not dealt with in the context of white-collar crime, and many such scandals were not known outside their individual countries. While it remains the case that much of what scholars, particularly critical scholars, define as white-collar crime is not widely perceived as a criminal issue, the latter part of the twentieth century saw a greater willingness to explore the possibilities of rendering companies found to be responsible for accidents or disasters criminally liable. Also, as seen in this volume and elsewhere, many forms of white-collar crime, such as those dealing with the environment, food, corporate tax evasion, banking and financial frauds, particularly in the wake of the global financial crisis, are now subject, in Europe as elsewhere, to discussions of criminalization and control.

The predominance of so-called Anglo-American scholarship and US cases undoubtedly has many causes – as Friedrichs in his afterword to this volume argues, the size of the US is significant in terms of crime and criminology, as is the greater volume of work published in the English language. Therefore, to scholars in Britain and other English-speaking countries, and to Europeans familiar with English, work from English-speaking countries was more readily accessible and much of it referred to broadly similar legal systems and traditions. Europe on the other hand presented would-be researchers with an array of different languages, legal systems, socioeconomic and political systems and cultural traditions. These hampered communication between scholars, particularly in the days before cheap flights and the ability to communicate via email and the internet, let alone the opportunities presented by instant, if limited, packages such as Google Translate. A further barrier to collaborative or comparative research was and continues to be the differing legal and criminological categorizations of white-collar and corporate crime across European countries, and, as seen in this collection, the variety of terms used to define it. In Sweden and other Nordic countries, for example, the term white-collar crime is rarely used, with a clear preference for the term *economic crime*. Activities generally assumed to belong in the category such as insider dealing, corruption and the formation of cartels are differently defined and criminalized in different countries.

Some groups did pursue an interest in European issues, particularly around individual offences, and there were seminars on aspects of white-collar crime, such as a Scandinavian symposium attended by the author, including British, American and Scandinavian scholars (Lindgren 2001). From 1973, the European Group, formerly the European Group for the Study of Deviance and Social Control,[1] has been a forum for critical criminological scholarship across Europe, has included state and corporate crime and led to publications challenging conventional definitions of crime (see, for example, Hillyard et al. 2004). The development of the European Society for Criminology, which, while dominated by the concerns of mainstream criminology with so-called conventional crimes, provided a meeting point for scholars across Europe, including those from former state socialist countries culminating in the creation of the special interest group on organizational crime, linked to this volume.

It is nonetheless difficult to identify, as the author was invited to do for this chapter, any distinctively European dimensions to white-collar crime let alone to compare this with Anglo-American crime or criminology. Both of these widely used general terms are extremely problematic and laden with political baggage. Writing from Scotland, which in 2014 faced a referendum on independence from the UK, the author is all too aware of the contentious issues surrounding terms such as Anglo, British or European which feature regularly in political debates. The UK itself incorporates the separate legal jurisdictions of England and Wales, Northern Ireland and Scotland, with different approaches to crime and criminal justice in general (Croall 2012; McAra 2008) and corporate crime in particular (Ross and Croall 2010) and other countries across the continent also incorporate variations – as Cools and Pashley (this volume) indicate, Belgium encompasses very different languages, cultures and legal traditions. The American in Anglo-American is generally assumed to refer to North (as opposed to South) America which in itself contains Canada and the United States, both with significant local variations and traditions, and different laws in respect of white-collar crime. Much seminal work in relation to white-collar crime has emerged from Australia, in itself a federal jurisdiction with variations between states, and New Zealand. Moreover as Friedrichs, in his concluding reflections, points out, in all of these countries there are variations between mainstream criminological approaches and more critical traditions.

Generalizing about Anglo-American is therefore difficult enough, without entering into the politically laden issue of whether Britain, for example, should be considered to be European. While it lies beyond the scope of this chapter and the expertise of this author to discuss the many meanings of the term European, it is evident that few generalizations can be made given the heterogeneity of the continent and divisions implied in commonly used comparisons between old or new or northern and southern Europe, which incorporate assumptions about socioeconomic and political differences, as did former references to East and West Europe. These divisions are important when considering the two related areas of organized and white-collar crime, as citizens of less affluent European countries may be victimized by exploitation by those in more affluent countries through, for example, environmental crimes, human trafficking and the exploitation of migrant labour and money laundered across borders.

This signals the importance of the increasingly transnational or global nature of white-collar crime, in the face of which it is increasingly difficult to identify local, regional or national differences. To what extent for example can any form of white-collar crime be said to be particularly distinctive of any one country? Corporations across the globe, which increasingly base themselves offshore, commit crimes on a global scale, and residents and those responsible for businesses in all countries evade taxes, neglect safety, health or environmental regulations and commit occupational crime. Citizens of any region or jurisdiction suffer from the many harms engendered by global and forms of white-collar crime. Nonetheless, and this may well be a task for future research, specific socioeconomic, geopolitical, legal and cultural factors affect the likelihood of different forms of crime and victimization and the economic characteristics of any area will have an influence on what kinds of economic or white-collar crime are likely to be more prevalent.

This begs the question of the extent to which Europe is any more than a continent which is the site of universal or global forms of white-collar crime. While acknowledging the difficulties of addressing such a question, particularly given the limited expertise of this author, and taking a very broad brush, it can nonetheless be argued that there are some significant, if not unique, European dimensions to aspects of white-collar crime and its regulation. These are related to European history and traditions and to European institutions which provide an important tier of legislation and regulation along with space for forms of euro crime. Also significant and distinctively European are the experiences of so-called countries in transition. At the same time, however, the contributions to this book, drawn as they are from so many different countries, underline many of the key themes familiar to scholars of white-collar crime across the globe, albeit played out differently across jurisdictions.

White-collar crime: European dimensions

Historical aspects

European thought and grand theorists such as Marx, Weber and Durkheim have had a profound influence on analyses of crime, deviance and social structure and culture and on theoretical and sociological criminology. As Friedrichs (this volume) reminds us, Engels used the term 'murder' to refer to the harmful activities of capitalists who exploited workers and Hebberecht (this volume) points to the significance of Bonger's (1916) work on the relationship between crime in the bourgeoisie and the motivating ideologies of capitalism. Even earlier, the British social commentator Daniel Defoe regarded stockbrokers with disdain and commented on the 'little visible difference between the lawful applications of industry and business and the unlawful desires after exorbitant wealth' (Ruggiero 1997). All of this preceded Sutherland's (1949) work although as Friedrichs (this volume) points out, he can nonetheless be described justifiably as the founding father of white-collar crime as he established it as a criminological concept and was followed by a rich criminological tradition in the United States.

Albeit not defined as such, examples of white-collar and corporate crime can be found throughout European history. A few extremely selective examples include the variety of harms associated with commercial activities dating back to pre-biblical times. Scarce commodities such as food have been subject to crimes, documented in the Roman Empire, of hoarding and price fixing, and practices of forestalling, regrating and engrossing featured in the works of writers such as Bunyan and Dante. In ancient Greece, the architect of the Parthenon had to flee Athens to escape charges of embezzlement (Geis 1988). In Britain, the use of false weights and measures or the adulteration of food (one of the oldest forms of fraud) was subject to harsh penalties such as excommunication, fines, the pillory or banishment (O'Keefe 1966). Stockbrokers, as early as 1697, unlawfully combined to fix the value of bank stock and bills and in both Britain and the United States, the railway mania and the early days of capitalism were characterized by many forms of investment frauds (Robb 1992). Historical and European scholars would undoubtedly add more examples including activities associated with and included within white-collar crime such as the exploitation of labour across states, slavery from Roman times to contemporary forms of *new slavery* (Croall 2013) and the many crimes, whether involving trade, commerce, finance or exploitation, associated with the development of European trading corporations and European colonialism.

Europe was the site of some of the most horrific crimes of the twentieth century, including the Holocaust, and this book includes a contribution (Van Baar) adding to the body of research pointing to the considerable involvement of European companies in these crimes (Friedrichs 1992; Huisman and Van Baar 2010) – through, for example, the employment of slave labour, the aryanization of companies, conducting medical experiments and the development of technology related to mass extermination and disposal. To Van Baar this represents corporate-facilitated state crime. Europe was also the site of ethnic cleansing in, for example, Bosnia where approximately 200,000 Muslim residents were victims of executions, massacres or forced resettlements on the part of Serb and Croat forces (Rothe 2009).

As regards regulation, the development of modern forms of capitalism in Europe led to, as Ponsaers (this volume) illustrates, the development of the special forms of regulation of economic activity, emerging from diverse sources such as the guilds, absolute monarchies, the Napoleonic code or the Industrial Revolution in Britain. These form the forerunners of the thousands of regulatory agencies tasked with protecting consumers, workers or the public from the harmful activities of economic enterprises. These in turn influenced the new world and contributed to the now well documented forms of regulation, so often compared to crime control (Croall 2004), used in respect of many forms of white-collar and corporate crime.

The second half of the twentieth century saw the emergence of the European Union with its massive array of organizations, regulatory conventions and directives many of which are relevant to white-collar, corporate crime and human rights, adding a new, and potentially powerful, layer of legislation and regulation. These are now of considerable relevance to all forms of regulatory crime – with regulations covering, for example, the environment, consumer law, food quality, safety and labelling and other issues of health and safety. Many directives and agencies also deal with financial and corporate crime, well described in different contributions, particularly Verhage's (this volume) account of money-laundering controls.

Also uniquely European and highly significant for students of white-collar crime has been the emergence of capitalism in the former state socialist countries which has seen great changes in the nature of crime in these societies with, in particular, the emergence of many forms of white-collar crime and corruption. A particular strength of EUROC and this collection is the inclusion of scholarship and papers from many of these countries.

'White-collar euro crime'?

The development of the European Union and its many regulations has itself been associated with the development of specifically European forms of crime, and a range of studies focused on the massive losses to the European Union of *euro fraud*, notoriously difficult to measure (Passas and Nelken 1993). By 1995 estimates suggested that somewhere between 2 and 10 per cent of the EU budget was subject to fraud (Clarke 1994). The Common Agricultural Policy (CAP) which dealt with intervention in relation to farming subsidies and surplus produce was particularly criminogenic and subsidies frauds involved wine, olive oil, beef and cereals (Clarke 1994), forms of fraud which continue today (Croall 2013). European fishing quotas continue to be a source of controversy and have been associated, in, for example, Spain, Scotland and Norway, with illegal fishing and *black fishing*, the practice of catching fish not officially declared (Croall 2007). These could involve partnerships between white-collar and organized crime (Ruggiero 1996), and some also required the collusion of government officials – related, argued Passas and Nelken (1993), to the political and fraud cultures typical in different countries.

Global economic crime has been associated with utilizing the spaces between laws (Michalowski and Kramer 1987) and within Europe, different regulations and tax regimes also create spaces within which crimes can flourish. Van Duyne's (2003) work on cigarette smuggling well illustrates one considerable trade. While often associated with small networks, large tobacco companies have been found to be complicit in illegal trades – in one case Imperial Tobacco was said to have exported large numbers of cigarettes to European countries such as Latvia where demand was low, enabling them to be smuggled back into the UK. While not uniquely a European problem, many food frauds, a particular interest of this author (Croall 2013), operate across European borders. In one case of food laundering for example, Dutch food companies imported cheap frozen chicken from Thailand and Brazil, some of it salted to avoid EU tariffs on fresh meat. The meat was then defrosted, injected with water and additives, processed and refrozen with much ending up in take-away food (Lawrence 2004). In the recent European horsemeat scandal of 2013, tests revealed up to 100 per cent horsemeat in frozen lasagne and spaghetti bolognese sold by major names in Britain such as Tesco, Aldi and Findus. Subsequent inquiries revealed a European-wide complex network of food suppliers with one giant firm, ABP, at the centre (Lawrence 2013).

Tax evasion and money laundering are also assisted by the existence, within Europe, of a host of tax havens. While there have been many attempts to plug many of these loopholes, including controls on banking in Switzerland, a speedy Google search reveals at least one 2013 guide to European tax havens for those who 'have no problem with dicey business practices'[2] which include financial centres such as London along with Luxembourg, Cyprus, the Channel Islands and the Isle of Man. The failure to provide a level playing field in respect of regulation is well described by Verhage (this volume) and creates gaps in compliance and unfair competition between different countries – as seen for example in the banking laws of Switzerland and Luxembourg.

Inequalities between countries within Europe and between Europe and the third world have also produced crimes associated with migrant labour – as those from poorer countries within or without Europe seek to escape poverty or political persecution by entering *Fortress Europe*. This has led to the growth of people trafficking, smuggling, and what is often described as *new slavery*, some of which has involved the exploitation of citizens of different European countries, particularly those from former Eastern Europe. These activities are often associated with forms of organized crime, but as with other examples, legitimate organizations are also involved whether by knowingly recruiting exploited labour or by turning a blind eye to the conditions under which food, for example, is produced (Ruggiero 1996). The situation of migrant labour involved in picking Spanish salad crops, forced to live without sanitation or access to drinking water and paid less than half the minimum wage, has been described by Anti-Slavery International as the 'de facto state sanctioning of slavery in the 21st century' (Lawrence 2011). And as Van Wingerde's contribution to this volume on the *Probo Koala* case also reminds us, the disposal of toxic waste is also a problem across Europe and between Europe and the third world (White 2011).

Twentieth-century Europe also saw the emergence of countries in transition from state socialism to capitalism. Many contributions to this volume illustrate the many issues associated with this transition, which involved, as in Germany (Boers et al., this volume) large-scale privatization and the development of new companies with only minimal regulation. This was associated with the emergence of a range of illegitimate opportunity structures for white-collar and corporate crimes including those involving procurement, bankruptcy, banking, customs, traffic, pharmaceuticals and education – all assisted by the corruption of those in legitimate occupations. As well as being affected by national cultural traditions as seen in Hungary, in many cases, post-socialist changes failed to live up to expectations, producing many forms of crime (Inzelt, this volume).

Global themes, local differences

A striking feature of this collection is that despite the enormous range of political regimes, laws, cultures and regulatory arrangements across Europe, themes familiar to students of white-collar crime emerge, albeit played out differently in specific locales. However defined, the activities generally assumed to fall under the ambit of white-collar crime remain difficult to categorize, pin down in law, measure, regulate and sanction. Taken together with the wide variety of different cases, activities and regulations, this signals the considerable potential of collaborative and comparative work – much of which is reflected or suggested in individual contributions.

Defining white-collar crime?

Many contributions illustrate the ambiguities and terminological problems so long associated with the concept of white-collar crime itself (Croall 2001; Nelken 2007). What should it include? How is it described? Is it really crime? As outlined above, terminology across Europe varies, and terms such as economic crime, unethical behaviour and illegalisms associated with the bourgeoisie (Amicelle, this volume) are used. In his contribution Friedrichs discusses definitional issues at length, and, while having some sympathy with a view that less time should be spent on these rather tedious debates, his call for agreement over some basic concepts and terminology is valid. Furthermore there are good arguments to retain the term white-collar crime, as it carries a certain resonance – Friedrichs argues that it distinguishes a group of crimes from crimes of the underclass in a way that economic crime does not, and Braithwaite (1985) has argued that it is more widely understood and more meaningful than any of the alternatives. We should however be aware of its many varieties and elsewhere I have argued for an inclusive definition (Croall 2001) incorporating activities not covered by criminal law – thus rendering a discussion of what is or what is not criminalized possible, and reflecting the often very blurred boundaries between legal and illegal behaviour typified in the distinction (common to many regimes) between tax evasion and avoidance. This is also important for comparative work which may involve countries with different levels of tolerance or criminalization. Also attracting general agreement has been the distinction between occupational, or individual white-collar crime, carried out for personal gain, and organizational or corporate crime, and this author would agree that the concept of white-collar crime should also incorporate discussions of what can be described as political and state crime as well as various forms of state–corporate and global crime – including instances in which state agencies, particularly the police and regulatory agencies, are involved as actors or facilitators (Croall 2014).

Criminalizing white-collar crime

Another major issue reflected in many contributions is the problematic criminal status of white-collar crime, however defined, and in many countries there are ongoing debates about how best to control many of these harmful activities, with the criminal law universally being regarded as only one among many tools which include non-criminal forms of law and self-regulation, with pro-business lobbies tending to resist criminalization (Croall 2004). Moreover, irrespective of the many different legal traditions – between, for example, common law countries and others – white-collar crime, and particularly corporate crime, presents legislators and regulators with a range of problems. This constitutes an area well worth cross-jurisdictional analysis. A good example of this, familiar to the author, is the complex issue of corporate responsibility.

The twentieth century saw many examples, across the globe, of mass deaths, often regarded as accidents or disasters, subsequently, after successive and often lengthy inquiries, found to have been attributable to some form of management fault (Punch 2000; Tombs and Whyte 2007). These included high-profile cases such as, in the US, the Ford Pinto car, associated with around 500 burn deaths (Dowie 1977), the Westray coal mining disaster in Canada which killed 26 (Glasbeek 2002), the world's worst offshore oil disaster in which an explosion killed 167 workers on the oil production platform *Piper Alpha* off the Scottish coast (Ross and Croall 2010), the sinking of the ferry *Herald of Free Enterprise* outside the port of Zeebrugge killing 192 passengers and the spate of rail disasters in England, responsible for multiple deaths (Tombs and Whyte 2007). These are only a small sample, and, as Altopiedi's contribution reminds us, the thousands of deaths attributable to the use of asbestos after its dangers were known could well be added. They are significant cases in that they raised crucial questions about the difficulties of establishing blame and, in many jurisdictions, of criminally prosecuting either guilty individuals or corporations and led to successive law reviews in relation to corporate homicide or killing. These also reflected a greater willingness to perceive corporations as criminal (Wells 1993), and within criminology, to define such crimes as corporate or organizational violence.

While many reviews took place in respect of Anglo-American and Australian jurisdictions, including Canada (Glasbeek 2002), Australia (Sarre 2007), England and Wales (Gobert 2008) and Scotland, a review in which the current author was involved (Scottish Executive 2005), they also took place across Europe, in France (Gilbert and Russell 2002), and the Netherlands (Field and Jorg 1991) and contrasts and comparisons were made across different jurisdictions and legal traditions. Thus some countries such as Belgium, Germany, Sweden, Spain and Switzerland held notions of corporate responsibility which could be contrasted with, for example, the Netherlands, where companies could be found guilty of any criminal offence as if they were individuals (Gobert and Punch 2003). This is but one example of how similar issues can be approached in very different ways and where much can be learnt from comparing the different approaches of different jurisdictions.

Counting white-collar crime

Many contributions, in particular those by Korsell and Lord and Levi, refer to the widely documented problems of counting white-collar and corporate crime and the way in which it can be rendered relatively invisible by low rates of reporting and recording. These issues require little reiteration here. Few jurisdictions have clear-cut categories of white-collar crime in general, let alone specific offences, and its potential extent has to be deduced from reading across a wide variety of sources, all of which have limitations. The activities in question are not, as seen above, universally regarded as criminal or even illegal and there are many variations in the extent to which victims are aware of any harm or are likely to enforce it. Not only does this limit our ability, as Lord and Levi point out, to address the question of what works in relation, for example to corruption, as we have no accurate estimate of the extent of the activities, but it also seriously inhibits comparative research.

Accounting for white-collar crime?

As Friedrichs comments, Europe, with its very different cultural traditions and political and economic systems, raises the possibility of addressing important questions about variations in the nature and extent of different kinds of white-collar offending. Do these vary for example, between Europe and Anglo-American countries? Between countries in transition and other European countries? Between the Nordic countries with their stronger welfarist traditions and those which are more market oriented? Are any offences particular to any one jurisdiction? Do similar criminogenic factors account for offending across radically different cultures and traditions? Undoubtedly definitional, legal and measurement difficulties inhibit research on these questions, but some important criminogenic factors do emerge from the contributions in this volume, which echo those identified in white-collar crime scholarship.

Scholars of white-collar crime have long recognized the significance of culture as it affects different levels of tolerance of activities and as providing space in which the commission of crimes can be justified (Croall 2001). Many contributions refer to and reflect on cultural influences. Case studies, such as the Belgian Agusta case (Cools and Pashley, this volume), illustrate the importance of locating particular crimes in their specific cultural and political context, and in some countries there are different perceptions of whether white-collar crime is a problem – in Ireland for example there was, during the twentieth century, little awareness of any problem (McGrath, this volume), whereas it has been seen as a Belgian disease. Attitudes to corruption have been found to vary enormously across Europe which affects those forms of cross-border crime that depend on the willingness of public officials to be involved in corrupt exchanges (Passas and Nelken 1993) and

Cruz et al. (this volume) talk of a Portuguese culture of corruption. Inzelt (this volume) locates forms of corruption in the tradition of baksheesh prevalent in Hungary during the period of Turkish domination and refers to what is described as a national game of tax fraud. Hungary is not alone in this respect as others, such as Amicelle from France, also talk of the widespread tolerance of tax evasion and in Britain beating the tax man has long been culturally tolerated (Cook 1989) and indeed has been characterized as an everyday crime (Karstedt and Farrall 2006). On the other hand, tax offences may be less likely to be tolerated and subject to harsher penalties in more welfarist societies such as Sweden (Alalehto and Larsson; Korsell, this volume).

Corporate cultures have been widely recognized as a significant element in the generation of offending, and some contributions have related these broad cultural differences to organizational cultures. Bussman for example, argues that there may be differences between corporate cultures in welfarist and free market economies, and Kölbel suggests a greater propensity to whistleblowing among public servants in Norway, whose positions are secure, and further characterizes Scandinavian corporate culture as more democratic and value oriented. So significant is corporate culture that it has found its way into legislation as a factor in corporate responsibility (Gobert and Punch 2003).

Case studies of many cases of corporate violence such as those outlined above confirm the significance of cultural influences. In the Zeebrugge case for example, the shipping company P&O was described in a subsequent inquiry as having been 'infected with the disease of sloppiness' (Sheen Report 1987: 14–16). Deviance can become normalized within corporate cultures as vividly illustrated in Vaughan's (1998) account of the *Challenger* Space Shuttle disaster in which risk taking became acceptable and Punch (2000) discusses how ethical values are suspended in a process of corporate group think. This can be illustrated by the common use of euphemistic phrases for forms of deviance, such as, in the Ford Pinto case, justifying the decision not to recall the car on the basis of cost–benefit analysis (Dowie 1977). In the Siemens case described in this volume, Klinkhammer refers to the euphemistic way in which corrupt payments were described – illustrating how deeply rooted they are within the corporation. As Klinkhammer goes on to point out, such a deeply ingrained culture can be resistant to formal measures and legislation and internal corporate policies, and Bussman (this volume), in a detailed German study looking at corruption and compliance, argues that compliance cannot be commanded but has to be embedded with a corporate culture.

White-collar crime scholarship has identified a wide range of other criminogenic factors within organizations and their environment – too many to detail here. These are reflected in some contributions. In a fascinating account of the port of Antwerp, for example, Bisschop (this volume) describes some of the criminogenic features of ports which, while each has its own characteristics, include the anonymity of containers, difficulties of communication and the pressures of a large volume of goods being handled in a short time frame. To Georgoulas and Voulvouli, the creation of research units which are virtually private companies contributes to what they describe as a criminogenic university corporation in Greece, and this may be the case in many other countries with the enhanced significance of research funding for universities (see for example, Tombs and Whyte 2003). Indeed as the contributions from countries in transition suggest, the privatization of previously public industries in itself can be seen as criminogenic (Boers et al., this volume), a factor also linked to corruption in the public service in Britain following the introduction of elements of privatization, which has also been linked with safety crimes in relation to the rail industry (Croall 2001; Tombs and Whyte 2007).

In Antwerp, the form of regulation in itself was a factor in generating offences, and regulation may affect patterns of crime in different ways. In general terms an absence of strong regulation is itself criminogenic – indeed the state's failure to strongly enforce laws against white-collar crime can be seen as form of state–corporate crime. A further illustration of how regulation affects crime is provided in McGrath's account of Ireland, where light regulation was a deliberate tactic to encourage inward investment – and indeed analyses of global crime clearly indicate the way in which companies use gaps and variations in regulation to avoid a range of legislation. Other instances of weak regulation contributing to crime are found in countries in transition such as Serbia, Hungary and East Germany, where rules and enforcement were slow to follow the rapid development of companies and privatization.

This of course begs the question of the extent to which capitalism, with its values condoning the single-minded pursuit of profit, can itself be seen as criminogenic, although as Friedrichs (this volume) and others (Nelken 2007) have pointed out, it was far from absent, albeit denied, in former state socialist countries. Many however point to the relationship between key values of capitalism and neoliberalism and crime. The characteristics of entrepreneurs, long associated with innovation and risk taking and often described as *mavericks* (Ruggiero 1996), are referred to in Cruz et al.'s contribution from Portugal. Capitalism and more recently neoliberalism have been associated with placing a high value on greed, with aspects such as the financialization of the new economy (Tillman and Indergaard 2006) and payment systems and the bonus culture of senior executives (Friedrichs 2009) all having been associated with financial crimes. The capitalist drive to continually exploit the environment and the earth's natural resources (White 2008), and the corporate colonization of nature (South 2007) have been associated with environmental crime. Broad explanatory factors used to account for other forms of regulatory crime are the prioritization of profits over safety, health, environmental and consumer considerations; criminogenic markets characterized by the dominance in many sectors of global corporate giants (Croall 2013); and the strong resistance, amongst businesses, to any further regulation on the ideological grounds that anything which hampers the pursuit of profit is bad (Croall 2001).

Victims of white-collar crime

An often invisible feature of white-collar crime, which the current author has sought to address, is the nature and extent of victimization (Croall 2009; 2010; forthcoming 2015). A major part of this invisibility is the unawareness of victims and the apparently victimless nature of offences. Many lack immediately identifiable bleeding victims and offences such as money laundering, insider trading, corruption and other financial crimes, many discussed in this collection, involve largely secondary or tertiary victims (Croall 2010). Indeed the invisibility of victims is in itself part of the cultural justification for crimes such as tax evasion and avoidance – seen as merely harming the government. Nonetheless, white-collar crime scholars have pointed to the many, albeit indirect, harms associated with these crimes – corruption, particularly where it deals with public procurement, can lead to wasteful overpayments and possibly dangerous public buildings being constructed or environmentally damaging practices being overlooked (Croall 2001). Tax evasion and avoidance deprive governments of income which could be used to enhance spending on welfare – thus most adversely affecting the poorest who would receive these benefits, and these and other financial crimes may involve the delegitimation of financial institutions and public agencies (Shover et al. 1994). The financial crisis of 2008, so often not associated with crime or criminal victimization, could be characterized as victimization on a grand scale (MacGurrin and Friedrichs 2010), with huge human consequences across the globe including loss of earnings, employment, housing – all of which can have adverse effects on self-confidence and family life and, in some cases, lead to illness and suicide (Shover et al. 1994).

Some contributions, notably those concerning the *Probo Koala* (Van Wingerde, this volume) and asbestos (Altopiedi, this volume) cases do point to real and direct harms and to the considerable victimization with which they were associated and the many forms of corporate violence referred to above also involve direct physical harms. Consumer, and in particular, food crimes also have adverse physical effects (Croall 2009; 2013). In 2011, 49 consumers died from *E. coli* in France and Germany as a result of contaminated Egyptian fenugreek seeds – illustrating the potential international spread of harm (Goetz 2011). Across Europe therefore these forms of crime cause considerable physical and economic harm, and it has been argued that, while all citizens suffer from white-collar and corporate crime, the least disadvantaged suffer more, and more severely, particularly as they lack the means to protect themselves or seek redress (Croall 2010; forthcoming 2015). It is interesting, as Altopiedi (this volume) illustrates, that it was victims, who, having defined themselves as victims, became active citizens and played a major role in exposing the crimes and contributed to the eventual Italian prosecution in the Eternit case. Victim groups also played an important role in the successive campaigns leading to the eventual British law reforms in relation to corporate manslaughter and homicide (Tombs and Whyte 2007).

Controlling white-collar crime

Many contributions to this book deal with regulation, and the vast array of regulatory arrangements, including national, EU and international, public and self-regulation, which operate across Europe are illustrated in relation, for example, to corruption, money laundering and tax evasion (Amicelle; Lord and Levi, this volume). Despite the many differences in regimes, the all too familiar story of laws, even stringent ones, being weakly and partially enforced (Croall 2004) emerges and while some regulations apply across the European Union, different countries have different levels of enforcement (Verhage, this volume). Whether in Ireland, whose low rate of regulation could be related to the mindset of traditional Ireland (McGrath, this volume), Portugal or Antwerp, whether dealing with financial or environmental crimes such as the *Probo Koala* case, a lack of expertise and resources hampers regulatory efforts.

It would appear that across Europe, as elsewhere, relatively few white-collar offences reach the courts, and when they do, all too often receive sentences widely criticized for being too lenient, either because they are insufficiently deterrent or because they appear unjust in terms of wealthy or powerful offenders receiving favourable treatment. A consistent theme for example is the extent to which the treatment of offenders represents a class advantage – Amicelle (this volume) points to how the differential treatment of wealthy offenders in respect of tax evasion in France challenges republican notions of inequality. Offenders, particularly corporate offenders, rarely receive anything other than monetary penalties, which, even when considerable, may be very small in relation to corporate turnover. To Van Wingerde (this volume) the sanctions in the *Probo Koala* case illustrate the limits of even strengthened EU-based regulation in the face of large corporations whose turnover may exceed that of individual nations. While alternative sanctions have long been discussed in the literature on white-collar and corporate crime, and indeed, some heavier sentences have been provided in some jurisdictions (Croall 2005), there still appear to be gross inequities, and problems about sanctioning particularly corporate offenders.

Concluding comments: challenges and opportunities

The diversity of Europe undoubtedly presents both challenges and opportunities for scholars and researchers and it is to be hoped that the kind of research contained in this volume, and the volume itself, taken together with the development of EUROC, signal important milestones in the development of more collaborative and comparative research, both within Europe and between Europe and elsewhere. This should include not only Anglo-American jurisdictions but, as Friedrichs rightly points out, Asia, and one could add South America and Africa, both continents which have for long been the site of victimization from some of the most serious forms of corporate, environmental and state corporate crime. Enhanced communication between scholars across jurisdictions can vastly increase our knowledge and understanding of some of the many factors underlying white-collar crime and some of the alternative means of controlling it which form a key part of any research agenda. Before approaching such questions, however, there has to be, as Friedrichs suggests in his contribution, some progress on the vexed issues of categorization and measurement – difficult, but not by any means impossible, with the development of greater communication across jurisdictional boundaries.

Some of the most interesting questions to be asked when looking at differences within Europe or between Europe and other parts of the globe have been outlined above. How do different criminogenic factors manifest themselves within specific countries? To what extent does a particular mix of natural resources, industrial and geopolitical factors affect the overall profile of white-collar crime in particular regions and countries? How are these affected by broader cultural and political factors? To what extent are contemporary capitalism and its associated features such as privatization criminogenic? To what extent do countries with a stronger welfare orientation vary from others in respect of rates of offending, levels of tolerance and regulation?

Definition and measurement difficulties aside, these are not easy questions to research, as many factors are in practice interrelated. A major question emerging from some contributions, and one for which European research is particularly appropriate, concerns variations between countries with a stronger welfare ideology and others. While not looking specifically at white-collar crime, the current author has been involved in research on different approaches to penal policy within the UK, and Scotland being widely perceived to have a stronger welfarist approach than England, albeit that this could be somewhat mythological (Croall 2012; McAra 2008; Munro et al. 2010). Following devolution, however, which coincided with a period of popular punitivism in England, Scotland's penal policy became detartanized and closer to that of England and Wales rather than, as might have been predicted, more welfarist. A variety of factors were involved: a government of the same political persuasion as the British government, the greater direct involvement of a local parliament and local politicians in criminal justice, and a strongly felt perception on the part of key policy makers and politicians that some measures, such as anti-social behaviour orders, were more democratic and in tune with constituents' concerns (Mooney et al. forthcoming 2015). In practice therefore, it is extremely difficult to disentangle the respective effects of actual or perceived cultural predispositions such as welfarism and other local factors.

Identifying the factors underlying white-collar crime is of course vital when considering policies for its control and in this respect comparative work has enormous potential significance. How do the widely recognized criminogenic factors operate in different legal and cultural settings? How can they be tackled using different approaches? Even if asking a 'what works question' is hampered by measurement and evidential difficulties, exploring alternative forms of law, different levels of state and self-regulation, compliance policies and different forms of sanction through comparative work and case studies is of great importance. In the era of globalization, international collaboration within Europe and between Europe and other countries is also vital as so many offences make use of the gaps and spaces between laws in different jurisdictions. Here European countries can, as seen in some contributions, play a vital role in the international arena. This is likely to be of greater importance given the increased political salience of many forms of white-collar crime both locally and globally.

Notes

1 http://www.europeangroup.org (accessed 24 April 2014).
2 http://www.dw.de/the-whos-who-of-european-tax-havens/a-16753202 (accessed 24 April 2014).

References

Bonger, W.A. (1916) *Criminality and Economic Conditions*, Boston: Little, Brown and Company.

Braithwaite, J. (1985) 'White collar crime', *Annual Review of Sociology*, 11: 1–25.

Clarke, M. (1994) 'EC fraud, issues in sociology and social policy', occasional paper no. 4, Department of Sociology, Social Policy and Social Work Studies, University of Liverpool.

Cook, D. (1989) *Rich Law, Poor Law: Different Responses to Tax and Supplementary Benefit Fraud*, Milton Keynes: Open University Press.

Croall, H. (2001) *Understanding White Collar Crime*, Buckingham: Open University Press.

Croall, H. (2004) 'Combatting financial crime: Regulatory versus crime control approaches', *Journal of Financial Crime*, 11(1): 45.

Croall, H. (2005) *Penalties for Corporate Homicide: Annex to Scottish Executive Expert Group on Corporate Homicide*. Online. Available HTTP: <http://www.scotland.gov.uk/Publications/2005/11/14133559/36003> (accessed 2 July 2014).

Croall, H. (2007) 'Food crime', in P. Beirne and N. South (eds) *Issues in Green Criminology: Confronting Harms Against Environments, Humanity and Other Animals*, Cullompton: Willan, pp. 206–229.

Croall, H. (2009) 'White collar crime, consumers and victimization', *Crime, Law and Social Change*, 51: 127–146.

Croall, H. (2010) 'Economic crime and victimology: A critical appraisal', *International Journal of Victimology*, 8(2). Online. Available HTTP: http://www.jidv.com/njidv/images/pdf/JIDV23/6_jidv23_word_pdf_croal.pdf (accessed 2 July 2014).

Croall, H. (2012) 'Criminal justice, social inequalities and social justice', in G. Mooney and G. Scott (eds) *Social Justice and Social Policy in Scotland*, Bristol: Policy Press, pp. 179–202.

Croall, H. (2013) 'Food crime: A green criminology perspective', in N. South and A. Brisman (eds) *International Handbook of Green Criminology*, London: Routledge, pp. 167–183.

Croall, H. (forthcoming 2015) 'Criminal victimisation by the powerful', in P. Davies, P. Francis and C. Greer (eds) *Victims, Crime and Society*, 2nd edn, London: Sage.

Dowie, M. (1977) 'Pinto madness', in S. Hills (ed.) (1987) *Corporate Violence; Injury and Death for Profit*, Totowa, NJ: Rowman & Littlefield, pp. 13–29.

Field, S. and Jorg, N. (1991) 'Corporate liability and manslaughter: Should we be going Dutch?', *Criminal Law Review*, 191: 156.

Friedrichs, D.O. (1992) 'State crime or governmental crime: Making sense of the conceptual confusion', in J. Ross (ed.) *Controlling State Crime*, New York: Garland, pp. 53–79.

Friedrichs, D.O. (2009) 'Exorbitant CEO compensation: Just reward or grand theft?', *Crime, Law and Social Change*, 51(1): 45–72.

Geis, G. (1988) 'From Deuteronomy to deniability: A historical perlustration on white-collar crime', *Justice Quarterly*, 5(1):7–23.

Gilbert, M.J. and Russell, S. (2002) 'Globalization of criminal justice in the corporate context', *Crime, Law and Social Change*, 38(3): 211–238.

Glasbeek, H. (2002) *Wealth by Stealth: Corporate Crime, Corporate Law, and the Perversion of Democracy*, Toronto: Between the Lines.

Gobert, J. (2008) 'The evolving test of corporate liability', in J. Minkes and L. Minkes (eds) *Corporate and White Collar Crime*, London: Sage, pp. 61–81.

Gobert, J. and Punch, M. (2003) *Rethinking Corporate Crime*, London: Butterworths/LexisNexis.

Goetz, G. (2011) *Germany's E. coli Outbreak: A Global Lesson*, Food Safety News. Online. Available HTTP: <http://www.foodsafetynews.com/2011/06/germanys-e-coli-outbreak-a-global-lesson/#.U7PTovl_tng> (accessed 2 July 2014).

Hillyard, P., Pantazis, C., Tombs, S. and Gordon, D. (eds) (2004) *Beyond Criminology: Taking Harm Seriously*, London: Pluto Press.

Huisman, W. and van Baar, A. (2010) 'The oven-builders of the Holocaust', *Tijdschrift voor Criminologie*, 52(1): 3–18.

Karstedt, S. and Farrall, S. (2006) 'The moral economy of everyday crime: Markets, consumers and citizens', *British Journal of Criminology*, 46(6): 1011–1036.

Korsell, L. (2001) 'Three decades of researching and combating economic crime: The Swedish case', in Lindgren, S. (ed.) *White-Collar Crime Research: Old Views and Future Potentials. Lectures and Papers from a Scandinavian Seminar*, Sweden: The Swedish National Council for Crime Prevention (Brottsförebyggande rådet).
Lawrence, F. (2004) *Not on the Label! What Really Goes into the Food on Your Plate*, London: Penguin Books.
Lawrence, F. (2011) 'The global food crisis: ABCD of food – how the multinationals dominate trade', *The Guardian*, 2/6/11. Online. Available HTTP: <http://www.guardian.co.uk/global-development/poverty-matters/2011/jun/02/abcd-food-giants-dominate-trade?INTCMP=SRCH> (accessed 2 July 2014).
Lawrence, F. (2013) 'Horsemeat scandal: The essential guide', *The Guardian*, 15/02/13. Online. Available HTTP: <www.theguardian.com/uk/2013/feb/15/horsemeat-scandal-the-essential-guide> (accessed 2 July 2014).
Lindgren, S. (ed.) (2001) *White-Collar Crime Research: Old Views and Future Potentials. Lectures and Papers from a Scandinavian Seminar*, Sweden: The Swedish National Council for Crime Prevention (Brottsförebyggande rådet).
McAra, L. (2008) 'Crime, criminology and criminal justice in Scotland', *European Journal of Criminology*, 5(4): 481–504.
MacGurrin, D. and Friedrichs, D.O. (2010) 'Victims of economic crime – on a grand scale', *International Journal of Victimology*, 8(2): 147–157.
Michalowski, R. and Kramer, R. (1987) 'The space between laws: The problem of corporate crime in a transnational context', *Social Problems*, 34(1): 113–121.
Mooney, G., Croall, H., Munro, M. and Scott, G. (forthcoming 2015) 'Scottish criminal justice: Devolution, divergence and distinctiveness', *Criminology and Criminology Justice*. Online First 2014. Available HTTP: <http://oro.open.ac.uk/40334/> (accessed 2 July 2014).
Munro, M., Mooney, G. and Croall, H. (2010) 'Criminal justice in Scotland: Overview and prospects', in H. Croall, G. Mooney and M. Munro (eds) *Criminal Justice in Scotland*, Cullompton: Willan, pp. 261–278.
Nelken, D. (2007) 'White collar and corporate crime', in M. Maguire, R. Morgan and R. Reiner (eds) *The Oxford Handbook of Criminology*, 4th edn, Oxford: Oxford University Press, pp. 733–770.
O'Keefe, J. (1966) *Law of Weights and Measures*, London: Butterworths.
Passas, N. and Nelken, D. (1993) 'The thin line between legitimate and criminal enterprises: Subsidy frauds in the European Union', *Crime, Law and Social Change*, 19(3): 223–243.
Punch, M. (1996) *Dirty Business: Exploring Corporate Misconduct*, London: Sage.
Punch, M. (2000) 'Suite violence: Why managers murder and corporations kill', *Crime Law and Social Change*, 33(3): 243–280.
Robb, G. (1992) *White Collar Crime in Modern England: Financial Fraud and Business Morality 1845–1929*, Cambridge: Cambridge University Press.
Ross, J. and Croall, H. (2010) 'Corporate crime in Scotland', in H. Croall, G. Mooney and M. Munro (eds) *Criminal Justice in Scotland*, Cullompton: Willan, pp. 132–151.
Rothe, D. (2009) *State Criminality: The Crime of All Crimes*, Lanham, MD: Lexington Books.
Ruggiero, V. (1996) *Organized and Corporate Crime in Europe: Offers That Can't Be Refused*, Aldershot: Dartmouth.
Ruggiero, V. (1997) 'Daniel Defoe and business crime', *Social and Legal Studies,* 6(3): 323–342.
Sarre, R. (2007) 'White-collar crime and prosecution for "industrial manslaughter" as a means to reduce workplace deaths', in H. Pontell and G. Geis (eds) *International Handbook of White-Collar and Corporate Crime*, New York: Springer, pp. 648–662.
Scottish Executive (2005) *Corporate Homicide. Expert Group Report*, Edinburgh: Scottish Executive. Online. Available HTTP: <http://www.nm.stir.ac.uk/documents/expert-group-report.pdf> (accessed on 2 July 2014).
Sheen Report (1987) *M.V. Herald of Free Enterprise: Report of the Court No. 8074, Formal Investigation*, Department of Transport, London: HMSO. Online. Available HTTP: <http://www.maib.gov.uk/cms_resources.cfm?file=/HofFEfinal.pdf> (accessed 2 July 2014).
Shover, N., Fox, G.R. and Mills, M. (1994) 'Consequences of victimization by white-collar crime', *Justice Quarterly*, 11: 75–98.
South, N. (2007) 'The "corporate colonization of nature": Bio-prospecting, bio-piracy and the development of green criminology', in P. Beirne and N. South (eds) *Issues in Green Criminology*, Cullompton: Willan, pp. 230–247.
Sutherland, E. (1949) *White Collar Crime*, New York: Holt, Rinehart and Winston.
Tillman, R. and Indergaard, M. (2006) 'Corporate corruption in the new economy', in H. Pontell and G. Geis (eds) *International Handbook of White-Collar and Corporate Crime*, New York: Springer, pp. 474–489.

Tombs, S. and Whyte, D. (2003) 'Scrutinizing the powerful: Crime, contemporary political economy, and critical social research', in S. Tombs and D. Whyte (eds) *Unmasking the Crimes of the Powerful*, New York: Lang, pp. 3–48.
Tombs, S. and Whyte, D. (2007) *Safety Crime*, Cullompton: Willan.
Van Duyne, P.C. (2003) 'Organizing cigarette smuggling and policy making, ending up in smoke', *Crime, Law and Social Change*, 39(3): 285–317.
Vaughan, D. (1998) 'Rational choice, situated action, and the social control of organizations', *Law and Society Review*, 32(1): 1–44.
Wells, C. (1993) *Corporations and Criminal Responsibility*, Oxford: Clarendon.
White, R. (2008) *Crimes Against Nature: Environmental Criminology and Ecological Justice*, Cullompton: Willan.
White, R. (2011) *Transnational Environmental Crime: Toward an Eco-global Criminology*, London: Routledge.

33

White-collar crime in Europe

American reflections

David O. Friedrichs

Opening observations: American reflections?

My assignment here is to offer some *American reflections* on an emerging European criminology of white-collar crime, which is so thoroughly represented in this handbook. As a native-born, lifelong American citizen, and as someone who has been thoroughly engaged with the criminology of white-collar crime over a long period of time – and especially over the past 25 years or so – I should be up to this challenge. But I would also note that my parents were refugees from Nazi Germany in the 1930s and I grew up in a home with a German-born father, a French-born mother, and an English-born grandmother: i.e. in a home suffused with a European sensibility. I first visited Europe as a young child in 1952 – when some of the bomb damage of World War II was still very visible – and I have visited Europe many times in the intervening years. In recent years I have especially enjoyed participating in stimulating criminological symposia in Prato, Maastricht, London, Onati and Utrecht. Most recently, in May–June 2013, I did a brief visiting professor stint at Stockholm University, addressed the Finnish Economic Crime Investigators during their annual educational cruise, and made a presentation at the University of Iceland. So I am certainly an American, but one with a completely European ancestry and family heritage and multiple ties to a European world. Before proceeding further, however, one could note that both *American* and *European* are obviously somewhat problematic terms in relation to any notion of a unified or homogeneous perspective. As Hazel Croall correctly notes, in her Afterword, the term 'American' itself is problematic in terms of whether it refers to North American only, as is the norm, or all the Americas (i.e. Central and South America as well). And of course the term is commonly applied, as is the case here, even more restrictively, to the United States. Altogether, American white-collar crime scholars adopt quite diverse approaches. In my case, I identify primarily with a humanistic (as opposed to positivistic) and critical (as opposed to mainstream) approach. And to the extent that there are somewhat different (although increasingly eroding) regional cultural differences within the United States, I am a product of a Northeastern (specifically metropolitan New York City) background. Needless to say, European white-collar crime scholars come to the topic with even more pronounced country-specific experiences – e.g. from Albanian to Norwegian, and everything in between – in addition to the whole range of other differences in orientation, with generational cohort differences applying as well for both Americans and Europeans. In sum, these reflections are very much those of one American white-collar crime scholar on the work of a diverse – and sometimes sharply divided – group of European white-collar crime scholars.

I was flattered to be invited to contribute to this handbook, and was pleased to accept the invitation. In particular, I am much heartened by the dramatic upsurge of scholarly activity relating to white-collar crime in Europe that is so richly represented in this handbook. As the editors observe, the criminology of white-collar crime has to date been a predominantly Anglo-American enterprise (with a substantial Australian/New Zealand and Canadian presence), but this dominance is now increasingly challenged, not only by European criminologists but in other parts of the world, such as Asia. Indeed, American dominance of criminology itself appears to be increasingly less pronounced, especially in terms of theoretical initiatives and empirical research, than was true for the mid- to latter half of the twentieth century. But what explains the historical conspicuousness of Americans in the criminology of white-collar crime? In part, there is the central role of an American criminologist, Edwin H. Sutherland: for some, the single most important criminologist of the twentieth century. Sutherland famously introduced the concept of white-collar crime in his presidential address to the American Sociological Society in 1939, and ten years later – shortly before his death in 1950 – published his landmark book, *White Collar Crime* (1949). Of course it needs to be noted that Sutherland did not produce the concept of white-collar crime out of whole cloth. Many earlier scholars – European and American in particular – had recognized in some context that rich and powerful members of society commit crimes with profoundly harmful consequences for ordinary members of society. I have noted, in my book, the obvious role of Marx and Engels in this regard, with their characterization of the law as serving to protect the interests of the ownership class and the activities of this class as intrinsically a form of crime on a monumental scale against workers, and the powerless. Engels (1845/1958), in *The Condition of the Working Class of England*, specifically invokes the notion of murder for the actions of factory owners whose establishment of fundamentally unsafe conditions for workers is certain to produce premature deaths. But in a chapter published in 1980 I noted that the American Edward Livingston – scion of a prominent family and himself the holder of a number of important political offices – wrote in the preliminary report of his model penal code (1822/1968: 45) that: 'Everywhere, with but few exceptions, the interest of the many has, from the earliest ages, been sacrificed to the power of the few. Everywhere penal laws have been framed to support this power.' Karl Marx was four years old when these lines were published. Then some 80 years later we find Clarence Darrow (1904), the most celebrated American lawyer of his time, observing that the privileged classes – for example, the owners of gas and coal companies – set exploitative prices that can be regarded as criminal acts against ordinary citizens. During the same period – and in the decades leading up to 1939 – we find other Americans writing about *white-collar bandits*, *robber barons*, *criminaloids*, *corporate crime* and *industrial crime* (Schoepfer and Tibbets 2012). Patrick Hebberecht, in his contribution to this handbook, calls for recognition of the Dutch criminologist Willem Bonger as 'the unrecognized European pioneer of the study of white collar crime'. Bonger certainly made a significant contribution in addressing the crimes of capitalism, and the influence of capitalism on conventional crime. He recognized the significance of *great criminals* in the privileged capitalist classes, including stock manipulators. But it seems to me that neither Bonger nor any of the other European and American scholars and writers specifically succeeded in establishing white-collar crime per se as a legitimate and significant focus of criminological attention, as Sutherland did. In this sense I believe it remains fair and essentially accurate to characterize Sutherland as the *founding father* of the criminology of white-collar crime.

Sutherland (unlike myself) was thoroughly American in all respects – his great-grandparents immigrated to America from Scotland – and a product of the American heartland, growing up in Nebraska and Kansas and spending his entire life in the American Midwest (Gaylord and Galliher 1988; Geis 2007). Furthermore, Sutherland was anything but a cosmopolitan, in the sense of someone well-travelled and thoroughly attuned to a world beyond his own country's borders. Aside from a brief trip to England to study its prison system, I am not aware of any other direct experience of Sutherland's with Europe, much less any other part of the world. Several of his articles were published, between 1929 and 1937, in the *Monatsschrift für Kriminalpsychologie und Strafrechsreform* and he made one contribution to a French publication in 1935, but I think it is fair to say that Sutherland's focus during the course of his career was almost wholly on crime and criminal justice within the United States. Furthermore, Sutherland's interest in white-collar crime was at least partly driven by his response to the 1929 crash of the American stock market, and the subsequent onset of the Great Depression in the United States.

While acknowledging the immense value of Sutherland's contribution in bringing attention to the hitherto neglected realm of white-collar crime, some limitations of Sutherland's contribution are also worth noting. First, by offering up several different (and somewhat incomplete) definitions of white-collar crime, Sutherland contributed to the definitional confusion that plagues the field to this day. Second, Sutherland's (1949) *White Collar Crime* book, which addresses the corporate form of white-collar crime, only attends to corporate crime with financial consequences, and wholly disregards corporate violence (i.e. corporate physical harm to citizens, consumers and workers). And third, Sutherland almost wholly disregards governmental forms of white-collar crime, and crimes of states. So if Sutherland commendably chastised criminologists for not attending to the crimes of corporations and businessmen, he himself paid no attention to hugely consequential forms of crime, namely that carried out by political officials for their own benefit and that carried out by government leaders and officials on behalf of states. It is especially striking that Sutherland's book was written during the course of the 1940s, a decade during which the monumental crimes of the Nazis were both perpetrated and – through the Nuremberg trials – adjudicated. Sutherland's book includes a chapter on *war crimes*, but this chapter is devoted principally to profiteering and tax evasion by American businesses during the war, not to crimes carried out on behalf of states.

The American criminology of white-collar crime after Sutherland

Over the course of several decades after Sutherland introduced the concept of white-collar crime only a few isolated criminological studies of such crime – by Donald Cressey, Marshall Clinard and Gilbert Geis, among others – were produced. The bulk of the scholarship of the criminology of white-collar crime has been produced over the past several decades. There are now well over one hundred members – principally Americans – of the White Collar Crime Research Consortium, a growing number of textbooks, and a wealth of monographs, journal articles and book chapters emanating out of a criminology of white-collar crime. But some 75 years after Sutherland's landmark white-collar crime presidential address, white-collar crime remains a relatively small specialty within criminology and criminal justice, with the great majority of criminology and criminal justice scholars focused upon conventional forms of crime and their control, as well as more recently emerging interests – e.g. international and domestic terrorism. It has been thoroughly documented that white-collar crime continues to be dramatically underrepresented in leading American criminology and criminal justice journals, introductory textbooks, and in Ph.D. programmes through the first decade of the new century (McGurrin et al. 2013). And it probably remains true that a young person embarking on an academic career in criminology or criminal justice can achieve professional success most efficiently by focusing on conventional crime and crime control topics via mainstream orientations: professional, public and student interests continue to be heavily weighted in this direction; research funding is more readily available; and both the explanation of as well as the adjudication of conventional offending and offenders is more straightforward and less complex than for white-collar crime offending and offenders (Simpson 2013). From my vantage point, it would be interesting to know whether the representation of criminologists in European countries who have a specialized interest in white-collar crime and its control is proportionately greater, equivalent to, or smaller than that of American criminologists, relative to the conventional crime and its control focus. There is a long-standing impression that European criminologists are relatively more focused upon abuses of power – broadly conceived – and are more likely to be aligned with critical criminological perspectives than is true of American criminologists, although perhaps this impression needs to be subjected to empirical inquiry. Either way, a handbook such as this one has the potential to contribute measurably to the legitimation of white-collar and corporate crime as criminological topics and ideally to encourage graduate students and young scholars to undertake a specialized focus in this realm.

The dominant American role in white-collar crime scholarship

To the extent that American criminologists have produced a disproportionately large part of this scholarship, several factors can be mentioned. First, there is simply the large size of the American criminological enterprise, to the best of my knowledge significantly larger than that to be found in any other country. Second, there is the inevitable *criminological cohort* effect: i.e. at least some American criminologists, directly exposed to Sutherland and then those who were his students or were inspired by this work, themselves developed an interest in white-collar crime, which in turn inspired that of at least some of their students, and so on (Savelsberg and Flood 2004). Third, the huge visibility and size of the American corporate, financial and business – and professional – sectors, has meant that crimes in these sectors tend to be both immensely consequential and widely publicized, with the potent and widely diffused American media playing a role here. Fourth, there is simply the much broader reach of a criminology of white-collar crime produced in the English language – as the editors of this handbook note – than in one of the numerous European (to say nothing of Asian or African) languages in which a significant proportion of country-specific white-collar crime scholarship is published.

On this last point: it is obviously a plus that this handbook is published in English, since it will then surely reach a larger interested audience than if it were published in any other language. Indeed, by some measures, English has for some time been the principal language of global scholarly discourse, and may be en route to becoming a universal language (in an increasingly globalized world), more broadly. Speaking personally, I am always impressed by the remarkable English fluency of European criminologists whose native language is something other than English, and indeed in so many cases the multi-lingual fluency of such a large number of European criminologists. I am abashed (and somewhat frustrated) by the fact that I am myself fluent in English only. But I think it is less a matter of Anglo-American chauvinism (even if that is not entirely absent) and more a matter of practical realities, that in an increasingly interconnected world the adoption of a single language for scholarly work is hugely beneficial.

Finally, there is another dimension of the notion of an American perspective on white-collar crime, alluded to earlier but in need of some elaboration. If Sutherland was a product of the American Heartland, and someone whose education and professional socialization in the early part of the twentieth century led him to regard himself as a social scientist, he was also influenced by a progressive American populism that was deeply resentful of crimes committed by economic elites on Wall Street and elsewhere that had such devastating consequences for ordinary Americans through the famous 1929 Stock Market Crash and the Great Depression that followed. Accordingly, both contemporary American criminologists who address white-collar crime and who identify essentially with a positivist mainstream approach and those who identify with some strain of critical criminological perspective can look to Sutherland as an important source of inspiration. The Yale project of the 1970s and 1980s – which produced a series of books on such topics as white-collar crime sentencing, defending those accused of white-collar crimes, and crimes of the middle class – exemplifies a mainstream criminological approach to white-collar crime. Sally Simpson, Michael Benson and Nicole Leeper Piquero are just three examples of prominent white-collar crime scholars today associated with this approach. On the other hand, there is also a long-standing critical criminological tradition, exemplified by Jeffrey Reiman and Paul Leighton's (2012) *The Rich Get Richer and the Poor Get Prison* and David Simon's (2012) *Elite Deviance*. Raymond Michalowski and Ronald Kramer (2006) – especially associated with the concept of *state–corporate crime* – are part of this tradition. While my own ideological orientation is very much in this camp – progressive being my favoured term for this leftist critique – I quite consciously attempted to produce a book, *Trusted Criminals*, that would both draw upon and be useful to those in the mainstream and the critical camps (and it has been gratifying to me that there is evidence of this having occurred). My own view is that it is most productive to be mutually respectful, wherever possible, and to view our work in many – although not all – respects as complementary rather than competitive. For the 2012 Annual Meeting of the American Society of Criminology I organized an Authors Meet Critics session featuring books on the financial crisis as white-collar crime, one (*Who Are the Criminals?*) by John Hagan (2010) – principally associated with a criminological mainstream – and one (*Theft of a Nation*) by Gregg Barak (2012) – who has been a mainstay of critical criminology over a period of several decades. This session resulted in a Symposium Review in *Contemporary Sociology* in August 2013. I believe this session reflected the complementary value of different approaches to the criminology of white-collar crime. But my broader point in the present context is to acknowledge that the existence of quite distinct approaches to conceptualizing and studying white-collar crime is still another way in which the notion of an American perspective has to be qualified.

White-collar, corporate – and economic – crime: the terminological conundrum

The concept of white-collar crime is and always has been famously contentious, and as has been noted earlier this circumstance can at least partially be blamed on Sutherland himself. The late, legendary Gil Geis (1974: 283) once characterized the definitional issues as 'a mess'. I have elsewhere addressed the definitional issues at some length (e.g. Friedrichs 1992; 1996; 2010; 2014), and will not attempt to expend significant space here on a detailed reconsideration of these issues. And I am thoroughly aware of a view held by many that we should not get bogged down in interminable and tedious definitional disputes, but need to get on with the work of addressing white-collar crime and its control substantively (Simpson 2013; Tombs 2012). Nevertheless, the stark reality here is that the failure to resolve the definitional issues perpetrates endless confusion within the substantive white-collar crime literature itself, and in particular renders the increasingly larger enterprise of cross-cultural comparisons on such crime immensely problematic. My own view – elaborated on in my *Trusted Criminals* text (Friedrichs 2010) – is that we should treat white-collar crime as a broad umbrella term for a class of crimes fundamentally distinct from conventional crimes, and disproportionately involving middle- and upper-class individuals and organizations. Corporate crime – crime committed on behalf of corporate interests – and occupational crime – crime committed within the context of a legitimate occupation for personal advantage – are the two principal forms of white-collar crime. In my book, I also address what I characterize as cognate, hybrid and marginal types of white-collar crime, including: governmental crime; state–corporate crime; crimes of globalization; finance crime; enterprise crime; contrepreneurial crime; technocrime; and avocational crime. In effect, my argument is that we can begin with a broad differentiation of white-collar crime from conventional forms of crime, but then need to specify as clearly as possible which type of white-collar crime we are addressing. The late editor of the *Encyclopedia of White-Collar and Corporate Crime* (Salinger 2013) and the editors of the *International Handbook of White-Collar and Corporate Crime* (Pontell and Geis 2007), also the late Gil Geis (2007) in his Masters Series in Criminology volume – chose to differentiate between white-collar crime generally and arguably its most consequential form, corporate crime. The editors of this handbook have also made this choice. My own preference would have been to go with 'white-collar crime' only, leaving corporate crime out of the title. In my view, it minimizes confusion to invoke white-collar crime as a broad, umbrella term, even while acknowledging the special dimensions and hugely harmful consequences of corporate crime. In their titles by far the most contributors to this handbook go with white-collar crime (or offenders) – at least seventeen, far more than with any other term. Three of the chapters invoke the term *corporate crime* specifically, while some go with related terms: corporate wrongdoing, violations; deviance; and homicide. The term organizational crime – or misbehaviour – is also invoked. In this context some mention needs to be made of organized – as opposed to organizational – crime. Here, too, we have a long history of conceptual confusion. There is now a large literature on transnational organized crime in Europe and elsewhere. It might be argued, however, that it has become increasingly difficult to disentangle where organized crime ends and white-collar crime begins. Students of white-collar crime need to be mindful of these conceptual issues as well as the complex interrelations between different forms of crime.

Other terms that surface in titles include: economic crime – more on this follows – financial crime, corruption and fraud. Some contributors avoid invoking any one of these terms but rather opt to focus on specific types of offences, offenders or responders: i.e. Nazi crime, health care fraud, insider trading, illegal flows or whistleblowing. And some contributors go with very specific cases: e.g. the *Probo Koala* case or the Eternit case. These kinds of choices in this volume, incidentally, parallel choices in American, British, Canadian and Australian/New Zealand anthologies in this realm, as far as I can determine. This conceptual diversity has some potential for generating confusion, in relation to comparative analysis across cases, different types of activities, different countries and different regions. Ideally, then, it seems to me that a useful purpose is served to the extent that a global consensus on core terminology is realized, and when any work of scholarship in this realm situates the specific focus of its book, article or chapter within a typological framework for white-collar crime.

In Europe, of course, the term *economic crime* has been widely adopted in relation to activities encompassed by the American-originated term white-collar crime. As was noted above, several (three) of the contributors to this handbook invoke the term economic crime instead of white-collar crime. My own preference for white-collar crime as opposed to economic crime, as an umbrella term in this realm, is based upon several considerations. First, due to Sutherland, the former term was established earlier and I believe is even today the more universally recognized and adopted term. Second, the term white-collar crime – despite all of its limitations – does signal quite unambiguously that much highly significant crime is committed by people other than the traditional criminal *underclass*, the poor and lower class members of society. The term economic crime – at least as understood by an American – does not really signal this. Third, even if the term white-collar crime originally referred to crimes wholly limited to financial consequences, the term itself does not necessarily suggest this in the way that *economic* crime does. With all due recognition of the obvious limitations of the term white-collar crime, and with sensitivity to understandable undercurrents of resistance in many quarters to yet again adopting a conceptual framework of American as opposed to European origin, I persist in my view that the field as a whole will benefit if all interested parties move toward the adoption of a common conceptual framework and related definitions.

There is, of course, still another highly problematic concept or term that arises in this context: corruption. Several of the chapters or abstracts in this handbook invoke this term. Here again there is a very large literature on the definitional disputes in relation to this term (Mikkelsen 2013; Piquero and Albanese 2011). It is surely most readily associated with wrong-doing in the political realm, and would seem to be most widely invoked in relation to bribery, broadly defined. In some countries – China and Russia would seem to be notable examples – the term corruption appears to be the favoured term for a broad range of wrong-doing that occurs across the public and private sector. In both countries – and especially so in the case of China – the state and business sectors are so intertwined that corruption is at the centre of much if not all wrong-doing in this realm (Cheng and Friedrichs 2014). In my own text I have characterized the classic form of corruption – taking of bribes by public officials in return for political favours to private sector organizations and individuals – as political white-collar crime. But corruption, broadly defined, is deeply embedded in the American political economy, exemplified by the disproportionate influence of Wall Street and major corporations – *big money* – in government policy-making (Lessig 2011). The concept of state–corporate crime – introduced in 1990 by Michalowski and Kramer (2006) – captures one important dimension of this systemic corruption, namely harm and wrong-doing that arises out of cooperative state and corporate activity. The role of major corporations in relation to the Holocaust is a classic manifestation of state–corporate crime (Matthews 2006; Van Baar and Huisman 2012), as exemplified by the cases of IG Farben and Topf and Sohne. Steve Tombs (2012) has offered a critique of the term state–corporate crime, with its focus on state and corporate actors rather than on the systemic and symbiotic nature of such crime. Dawn Rothe and I (Friedrichs and Rothe in press) have addressed the almost total neglect of certain kinds of institutions – i.e. major financial institutions, international financial institutions and government-sponsored enterprises – in the existing state–corporate crime literature. But all of these forms of analysis recognize the pervasiveness of corruption, broadly defined, in advanced developed nations. Within the context of this handbook: can systemic corruption be compared and measured, between the United States and Europe on the one hand, and between European countries on the other? Disentangling the different dimensions of corruption in relation to white-collar crime, and state entities, is a complex challenge.

In what follows I propose to outline some further challenges in relation to American and European approaches to white-collar crime, in effect to identify an agenda for further work. It would be presumptuous to suggest that there are easy answers to the questions posed here.

Explaining white-collar crime: American and European approaches

Students of white-collar crime quite uniformly embrace the proposition that such crime is more complex than conventional (or street) crime. Claims made to the contrary – for example, by Gottfredson and Hirschi in relation to their general theory of crime – can I believe be potently refuted (Friedrichs 2014; Friedrichs and Schwartz 2008). If one accepts the complexity claim it follows from this that explaining white-collar crime incorporates some special challenges relative to explaining conventional forms of crime (Friedrichs 2010; Simpson 2013). Beyond the factors that would apply across different countries there are bound to be some factors within specific countries that are especially pronounced and must be taken into account. In terms of conventional criminal homicide, for example, it is widely accepted that the pervasive availability of guns in the United States – and laws that facilitate gun ownership – is a significant factor accounting for the dramatically higher homicide rate found in the United States in comparison with European countries (Webster and Vernick 2013). Homicide rates – for all kinds of reasons – lend themselves to more accurate measurement than virtually any forms of white-collar crimes.

In relation to conventional crime, there is another dimension to consider. It is also well-understood that responses to such crime in the United States over the past 40 years or so have been harshly punitive, and of course it is well-known that the per capita incarceration rate (overwhelming for conventional offences) in the United States vastly exceeds that of European countries. In a world of finite justice system resources, how do relative allocations of such resources differ between the United States and European countries, specifically proportional allocations to address conventional crime and white-collar crime? Since 9/11 in the United States in particular a high proportion of resources were directed toward the war on terrorism, with at least some of these resources specifically shifted away from investigations of white-collar crime.

James W. Coleman (1987) and John Braithwaite (1988) engaged in a well-known debate on the centrality of a capitalist system to the generation of white-collar crime, with Coleman highlighting this centrality and Braithwaite countering with performance pressures in socialist systems generating parallel pressures for engaging in white-collar crime. If the United States has been characterized by an especially robust (but hardly pure) capitalist political economy with an attendant culture, the European countries have diverse histories in this regard. So ideally the propositions set forth by Coleman and Braithwaite can over time be more thoroughly explored, although no one should have illusions about the daunting methodological challenges in doing so.

Altogether, if so much of the scholarly literature on white-collar crime is American, the question of American exceptionalism arises: to what extent are conditions in the United States unique and not easily comparable to that of other countries? Are there cultural dimensions in the American context that are more pronounced (e.g. hyper-individualism and materialism) that can be correlated with higher levels of engagement in white-collar crime? Can such moral orientations as commitment to integrity on the one hand and the privileging of loyalty to an organization on the other hand be shown to differ measurably between the United States and European countries? Is the structure of opportunity within the American political economy demonstrably more conducive to white-collar crime? And is the justice system and regulatory apparatus in the United States more or less effective in constraining – and in responding effectively to – white-collar crime than is the case in European countries?

A systematic review of the kinds of explanations and theories favoured by Americans and by Europeans in accounting for white-collar crime, and then between Europeans – especially those based in formerly communist/socialist countries and those not in such countries – would be a worthwhile project.

Core themes of a European criminology of white-collar crime

There are some differences between the 50 states that compose the United States, and many comparisons have been made between different states in relation to crime rates, criminal justice policies and the like. But of course the differences between European states – including those that make up the European Union – are in many cases significantly more pronounced. And differences between European countries that have had relatively stable political economies and those that have undergone a basic transition from one type of system to another are especially dramatic. In the case of white-collar crime the effects of such transitions, to the extent that they can be assessed, are of special interest. If many forms of corruption were intrinsic to the socialistic regimes of the East, the process of privatization led to white-collar crimes on a grand scale, with the collective wealth of a country's people being stolen outright. Altogether, there would appear to be many opportunities for exploring the transformation of perceptions of white-collar crime, patterns of behaviour involving white-collar crime, and public policy responses to such crime within the context of European countries that have undergone fundamental transitions, some of which are on-going.

In an American criminology of white-collar crime some types of such crime are accorded much attention and other types relatively little. Overall, corporate crime has received more attention than occupational crime; some subtypes of corporate and occupational crime have received more attention than others. Inevitably, one can make a case that some types of corporate and occupational crime are almost wholly disregarded. And I have made a case for recognizing cognate, hybrid and marginal types of white-collar crime, which are accorded variable amounts of criminological attention. It is a core thesis of the *Crimes of Globalization* book that I have co-authored with Dawn Rothe that the crimes of international financial institutions (the World Bank and the International Monetary Fund) have been almost wholly neglected by students of white-collar crime (Rothe and Friedrichs 2015). Within the occupational (and individual) category I have argued that the white-collar crimes of academics have received less attention than those of some other professionals (e.g. doctors). It would be interesting to know – presumably through some form of content analysis – whether there are measurable differences in the types of white-collar crime addressed by American and European criminologists, and then between different European countries. And to the extent that there are in fact measurable differences, to what can this be attributed? It has also been long argued – indeed, it is a core claim of victimology – that victims of crime have been neglected relative to the degree of attention accorded offenders and criminal justice personnel. If this has also been true in the realm of white-collar crime, is proportionally more or less attention accorded victims of such crime within the European as opposed to the American white-collar crime literature? I have the impression that it is more, but of course this impression would need to be empirically verified.

What types of harmful activities call for criminalization, and when does criminalizing some type of allegedly harmful activity cause more harm than it prevents? This is, of course, an enduring question within the realm of law and public policy. In relation to conventional or street crime – broadly defined – obviously public order crime or so-called crimes without victims have been most fully debated in this respect. But the issues of over-criminalization versus under-criminalization have always been especially intense in relation to white-collar crime, with the corporate and business world in particularly fiercely resistant to regulating, much less criminalizing, activities that generate profits. How does this historical and on-going debate differ in the European context – and again, arguably between European countries – in comparison with in the American context? And then to the extent that criminalization in relation to corporate, business, professional and legitimate occupational activities occurs, how specifically does the policing, prosecution and adjudication of such activities differ between the United States and European countries? What is the proportional difference between public and private policing of such crime?

Altogether, then, we presently have a rather rich body of information now on white-collar crime and its control in the United States, and this handbook testifies to the significant recent expansion of such an information base within European countries. It seems to me that this allows for the further application of a comparative approach in this realm that at least potentially could produce highly interesting and useful knowledge.

On white-collar crime and crimes of states

For Sutherland, and for many white-collar crime scholars who have followed in his wake, white-collar crime is a private sector phenomenon. However, criminological attention to crime committed within the public sector has increased lately, and more specifically recognition of crimes of states has been one of the significant developments within the recent history of criminology (Chambliss 1989; Green and Ward 2004; Smeulers and Haveman 2008; Rothe 2009). My own long-standing impression is one of a proportionately higher European criminological interest in crimes of states than is true of American criminologists, for whom it remains a marginalized endeavour. Susanne Karstedt (2013: 148) is surely correct in observing that Europeans have suffered greatly from state violence but have also taken a lead in addressing it. European nations were hugely complicit in the monumental crimes committed in the name of imperialism and colonialism. Reference was made earlier to the cooperative and complicit nature of public and private sector entities. But both the differences and the similarities between harmful activities that are primarily concentrated in the public sector, or within the state, and primarily concentrated in the private sector, or within corporations and businesses, needs more attention from students of white-collar crime. Since there is far more diversity between European states in terms of the histories of political economies and specifically the forms of governance within states as well as the kind of economic systems adopted than is true of American states, it seems to me that European white-collar crime scholars are especially well-situated to engage in the type of comparative study called for here.

The global emergence of a criminology of white-collar crime

Globalization is one of the core themes of the current era, and the expansion of globalization as a force in the world has received much attention over the past quarter of a century in particular. Crime, criminal justice and the criminological enterprise itself are all affected by this development. Historically, there is an on-going evolution of crime and criminal justice from largely local, to state (in the American sense), to federal, to regional (in the European Union sense) to global. The establishment of the European Union is quite recent, of course, in relation to the establishment of the United States of America. In terms of white-collar crime and its control it is commonly noted that in the United States both its manifestation and its control are proportionately much more likely to be a federal phenomenon than is true of conventional crime, which is disproportionately a local phenomenon. Within the European Union we need to disentangle the dimensions of white-collar crime that are now best understood as European, as opposed to specific to states and localities within states. Altogether, white-collar crime must increasingly be thought of in comparative, transnational, international and global terms (Friedrichs 2011). Henry Pontell and Gilbert Geis's (2007) *International Handbook of White-Collar and Corporate Crime* was a seminal contribution to recognition of these developments. An emerging European criminology of white-collar crime is certain to be one dimension of an evolving global understanding of white-collar crime and the challenges involved in controlling it. I was pleased to recently co-author a chapter on 'White-collar and corporate crime in China' (Cheng and Friedrichs 2014) for *The Routledge Handbook of Chinese Criminology*, because it is clear that white-collar crime (often conflated with corruption) is a huge issue in China, although a criminology of such crime in China is still pretty much in its infancy. But going forward in the twenty-first century China (and Asia, more broadly) will play a major role in global developments, so much is at stake in understanding white-collar crime and addressing it effectively in this country. And of course parallel concerns arise with regard to other regions of the world – e.g. Latin America and Africa – although to date, for various reasons, a criminology of white-collar crime in both of these regions is a limited enterprise.

Future directions

Traditionally, both within the United States and within European countries, conventional crime has overwhelming been the focus of societal concern and attention, relative to white-collar crime. And in both the United States and in European countries this pattern is reflected in the concerns of criminologists. A highly regarded American criminologist, John Hagan (2010), in *Who Are the Criminals?*, has provided a masterful account of fundamental shifts in the perception of and response to crime in the United States, from the 'Age of Roosevelt' to the 'Age of Reagan'. He calls for a fundamental realignment, both on the level of public policy and within criminology as an academic endeavour, to move away from the catastrophic policies addressing conventional crime and to attend far more fully to the catastrophic crimes committed by the powerful.

The decline in conventional crime – not only in the United States but in many developed countries – has been one of the most striking criminological developments of the recent era. This decline, at least in the United States, has occurred in conjunction with a recent decline in the prison population. This is not the place to explore possible reasons for the decline. But my own view is that going forward conventional crime will become increasingly limited and more successfully controlled. Ideally, this occurs as a consequence of favourable transformations in the political economy, in the cultural value system, and in educational and treatment programmes. But pervasive surveillance and massive information-gathering, on the other side of this, render many forms of conventional crime less and less feasible. Of course one can envision some future developments that might lead to upward spikes in at least some forms of conventional crime, but the overall trajectory would appear to be downward. In the far more complex and often sophisticated realm of white-collar crime, broadly defined, it is less clear that it will decline and will be more successfully controlled, and for all kinds of reasons it could conceivably increase and expand. If these projections are correct then it seems likely that the work of criminologists and students of criminal justice will increasingly have to shift to a focus on white-collar crime, and its control. This handbook should provide one significant basis, within the European context in particular, for meeting the challenges ahead.

An agenda for an emerging global criminology of white-collar crime – of which a criminology of white-collar crime in Europe constitutes a significant aspect – would include the following: moving toward great uniformity in terminology, concepts and the language of white-collar crime itself; the development of effective templates in relation to the formidable measurement problems confronting students of white-collar crime; the development of a fully fledged comparative criminology of white-collar crime; the disentanglement of theoretical approaches that can be applied to the understanding of white-collar crime across borders, and theoretical dimensions that apply with special force within particular countries. This handbook should provide a core foundation for further explorations of white-collar crime and its control within Europe; it should prove immensely useful to non-European white-collar crime criminologists – including Americans – in both enriching their understanding of white-collar crime outside their own country but also for comparative purposes; and it should make a key contribution to the evolving project of establishing a global criminology of white-collar crime.

References

Barak, G. (2012) *Theft of a Nation*, Lanham, MD: Rowman & Littlefield Publishers.
Braithwaite, J. (1988) 'White-collar crime, competition, and capitalism: Comment on Coleman', *American Journal of Sociology*, 94: 627–632.
Chambliss, W.J. (1989) 'State-organized crime', *Criminology*, 27: 183–208.

Cheng, H. and Friedrichs, D.O. (2014) 'White-collar and corporate crime in China', in L. Cao, I.Y. Sun and B. Hebenton (eds) *The Routledge Handbook of Chinese Criminology*, London: Routledge.

Coleman, J.W. (1987) 'Toward an integrated theory of white-collar crime', *American Journal of Sociology*, 93: 406–439.

Darrow, C. (1904; 2nd edn 1979) 'Address to the prisoners of the Cook County jail', in J.J. Bonsignore, E. Katsh, P. d'Errico, R.M. Pipkin, S. Arons and J. Rifkin (eds) *Before the Law: An Introduction to the Legal Process*, Boston: Houghton Mifflin.

Engels, F. (1845/1958) *The Condition of the Working Class in England*, trans. W.O. Henderson and W.H. Chaldner, Stanford, CA: Stanford University Press.

Friedrichs, D.O. (1992) 'White collar crime and the definitional quagmire: A provisional solution', *Journal of Human Justice*, 3: 5–21.

Friedrichs, D.O. (1996) 'Governmental crime, Hitler, and white collar crime: A problematic relationship', *Caribbean Journal of Criminology and Social Psychology*, 1: 44–63.

Friedrichs, D.O. (2010) *Trusted Criminals: White Collar Crime in Contemporary Society*, 4th edn, Belmont, CA: Cengage Learning/Wadsworth.

Friedrichs, D.O. (2011) 'Comparative criminology and global criminology as complementary projects', in D. Nelken (ed.) *Comparative Criminal Justice and Globalization*, London: Routledge.

Friedrichs, D.O. (2014) 'Transcending the conventional definition of crime: Toward a twenty-first century criminology', 2013 Presidential Panel Papers: American Society of Criminology website. Online. Available HTTP: <https://asc41.com/Annual_Meeting/2013/Presidential%20Papers/Friedrichs,%20David.pdf> (accessed 4 July 2014).

Friedrichs, D.O. and Rothe, D.L. (2014) 'State-corporate crime and major financial institutions: Interrogating an absence', *State Crime*, 3(2): 146–162.

Friedrichs, D.O. and Schwartz, M.D. (2008) 'Low self-control and high organizational control: The paradoxes of white collar crime', in E. Goode (ed.) *Out of Control: Assessing the General Theory of Crime*, Stanford, CA: Stanford Social Sciences.

Gaylord, M.S. and Galliher, J.F. (1988) *The Criminology of Edwin Sutherland*, New Brunswick, NJ: Transaction Books.

Geis, G. (1974) 'Avocational crime', in D. Glaser (ed.) *Handbook of Criminology*, New York: Rand McNally.

Geis, G. (2007) *White-Collar and Corporate Crime*, Upper Saddle River, NJ: Pearson.

Green, P. and Ward, T. (2004) *State Crime: Governments, Violence and Corruption*, London: Pluto Press.

Hagan, J. (2010) *Who Are the Criminals? The Politics of Crime Policy from the Age of Roosevelt to the Age of Reagan*, Princeton: Princeton University Press.

Karstedt, S. (2013) 'State crime: The European experience', in S. Body-Gendrot, M. Hough, K. Kerezsi, R. Levy and S. Snacken (eds) *The Routledge Handbook of European Criminology*, London: Routledge.

Lessig, L. (2011) *Republic, Lost*, New York: Twelve Books.

Livingston, E. (1822/1968) *The Complete Works: On Criminal Jurisprudence*, Montclair, NJ: Patterson Smith.

Matthews, R.A. (2006) 'Ordinary business in Nazi Germany', in R.J. Michalowski and R.C. Kramer (eds) *State-Corporate Crime*, New Brunswick, NJ: Rutgers University Press.

McGurrin, D., Jarrell, M., Jahn, A. and Cochrane, B. (2013) 'White collar crime representation in the criminological literature revisited, 2001– 2010', *Western Criminology Review*, 14: 3–19.

Michalowski, R.J. and Kramer, R.C. (eds) (2006) *State-Corporate Crime*, New Brunswick, NJ: Rutgers University Press.

Mikkelsen, K.S. (2013) 'In murky waters: A disentangling of corruption and related concepts', *Crime, Law and Social Change*, 60: 357–374.

Piquero, N.L. and Albanese, J.S. (2011) 'The relationship between corruption and financial crime', in A. Graycar and R.G. Smith (eds) *Handbook of Global Research and Practice in Corruption*, Cheltenham: Edward Elgar.

Pontell, H.N. and Geis, G. (2007) *International Handbook of White-Collar and Corporate Crime*, New York: Springer.

Reiman, J. and Leighton, P. (2012) *The Rich Get Richer and the Poor Get Prison*, 10th edn, Boston: Allyn & Bacon.

Rothe, D.L. (2009) *State Criminality*, Lanham, MD: Lexington Books.

Rothe, D.L. and Friedrichs, D.O. (2015) *Crimes of Globalization*, London: Routledge.

Salinger, L. (ed.) (2013) *The Encyclopedia of White-Collar and Corporate Crime*, 2nd edn, Los Angeles: Sage.

Savelsberg, J.J. and Flood, S.M. (2004) 'Criminological knowledge: Period and cohort effects in scholarship', *Criminology*, 42: 1009–1041.

Schoepfer, A. and Tibbetts, S. (2012) 'From early white-collar bandits and robber barons to modern-day white-collar criminals', in D. Shichor, L. Gaines and A. Schoepfer (eds) *Reflecting on White-Collar and Corporate Crime*, Long Grove, IL: Waveland Press.
Simon, D.R. (2012) *Elite Deviance*, 10th edn, Boston: Pearson.
Simpson, S.S. (2013) 'White-collar crime: A review of recent developments and promising directions for future research', *Annual Review of Sociology*, 39: 309–331.
Smeulers, A. and Haveman, R. (eds) (2008) *Supranational Criminology: Towards a Criminology of International Crimes*, Antwerp: Intersentia.
Sutherland, E.H. (1949) *White Collar Crime*, New York: Holt, Rinehart and Winston.
Tombs, S. (2012) 'State-corporate symbiosis in the production of crime and harm', *State Crime*, 1: 170–195.
Van Baar, A. and Huisman, W. (2012) 'The oven builders of the Holocaust: A case study of corporate complicity in international crimes', *British Journal of Criminology*, 52: 1033–1050.
Webster, D.W. and Vernick, J.S. (eds) (2013) *Reducing Gun Violence in America*. Baltimore, MD: John Hopkins University Press.

Index

Note: Page numbers in *italics* represent tables
Page numbers in **bold** represent figures
Page numbers followed by 'n' refer to notes

FSC
www.fsc.org
MIX
Papier | Fördert gute Waldnutzung
FSC® C083411

Kolibri 360 GmbH
Ferdinand-Jühlke-Straße 7
99095 Erfurt, Deutschland
produktsicherheit@kolibri360.de